Algrove Publishing Limited
1090 Morrison Drive
Ottawa, Ontario
Canada K2H 1C2

Cover Credit: The model on the cover was made by Marc Guilhemjouan as an example of how
he builds timber-frame homes using the French scribe system. The model is $41^{1}/2''$w $\times$ 12$''$d
$\times$ 29$''$h. The cover is a close-up of one corner to show the fine details of this traditional form of
timber framing.

National Library of Canada Cataloguing in Publication Data

Main entry under title:

   Wood handbook : wood as an engineering material / Forest Products Laboratory, Forest
Service, U.S. Dept. of Agriculture.

Includes index.
Reprint. Originally published: Madison, WI : United States Department of Agriculture Forest
   Service, Forest Products Laboratory, 1999.
ISBN 1-894572-54-8

   1. Wood--Handbooks, manuals, etc. I. Forest Products Laboratory (U.S.)

TA419.W65 2002   620.1'2   C2002-901461-1

Printed in Canada
#10402

Publisher's Note

The *Wood Handbook* is one of the best-kept secrets in woodworking literature. The USDA Forest Products Laboratory has brought together in this volume more useful information about wood than one can find in any other single volume in print today. The range of information is both remarkable and detailed. It is a credit to the Forest Service of the USDA and a godsend to woodworkers everywhere.

All the information in the original 1999 USDA version of the Handbook is included here with one change; we used sequential pagination in preference to pagination by chapter as was the style of the original. To ease communication between users of different editions, we include an equivalency table on page 464.

Leonard G. Lee
Ottawa
April, 2002

Wood Handbook

Wood as an Engineering Material

Forest Products Laboratory
USDA Forest Service
Madison, Wisconsin

Abstract

Summarizes information on wood as an engineering material. Presents properties of wood and wood-based products of particular concern to the architect and engineer. Includes discussion of designing with wood and wood-based products along with some pertinent uses.

Keywords: wood structure, physical properties (wood), mechanical properties (wood), lumber, wood-based composites, plywood, panel products, design, fastenings, wood moisture, drying, gluing, fire resistance, finishing, decay, sandwich construction, preservation, and wood-based products

March 1999

Forest Products Laboratory. 1999. Wood handbook—Wood as an engineering material. Gen. Tech. Rep. FPL–GTR–113. Madison, WI: U.S. Department of Agriculture, Forest Service, Forest Products Laboratory. 463 p.

The Forest Products Laboratory is maintained in cooperation with the University of Wisconsin.

Pesticide Precautionary Statement

This publication reports research involving pesticides. It does not contain recommendations for their use, nor does it imply that the uses discussed here have been registered. All uses of pesticides must be registered by appropriate State and/or Federal agencies before they can be recommended.

Caution: Pesticides can be injurious to humans, domestic animals, desirable plants, and fish or other wildlife, if they are not handled or applied properly. Use all pesticides selectively and carefully. Follow recommended practices for the disposal of surplus pesticides and pesticide containers.

Contents

Preface

Efficient use of our nation's timber resource is a vital concern. Because a major use of wood in the United States is in construction, particularly housing construction, good practice in this endeavor can have a profound impact on the resource. This handbook is intended as an aid to more efficient use of wood as a construction material. It provides engineers, architects, and others with a source of information on the physical and mechanical properties of wood and how these properties are affected by variations in the wood itself. Continuing research and evaluation techniques hold promise for wider and more efficient utilization of wood and for more advanced industrial, structural, and decorative uses.

This handbook was prepared by the Forest Products Laboratory (FPL), a unit of the research organization of the Forest Service, U.S. Department of Agriculture. The Laboratory, established in 1910, is maintained at Madison, Wisconsin, in cooperation with the University of Wisconsin. It was the first institution in the world to conduct general research on wood and its utilization. The accumulation of information that has resulted from its engineering and allied investigations of wood and wood products over nine decades—along with knowledge of everyday construction practices and problems—is the chief basis for this handbook.

The *Wood Handbook* was first issued in 1935, and slightly revised in 1939, as an unnumbered publication. Further revisions in 1955, 1974, and 1987 were published by the U.S. Department of Agriculture as Agriculture Handbook No. 72. This current work is a complete revision of the 1987 edition. This revision was necessary to reflect more recent research accomplishments and technological changes.

The audience for the *Wood Handbook* is fairly broad. Therefore, the coverage of each chapter is aimed at providing a general discussion of the topic, with references included for additional information. Past versions of the *Wood Handbook* tended to report only the findings and applications of FPL research. Although the handbook is not intended to be a state-of-the-art review, this approach would now leave significant gaps in some important areas. The current edition has broadened the sources of information to provide better coverage of important topics.

The organization of this version of the *Wood Handbook* is similar to previous ones, with some modifications:

- Plywood (chapter 11 in the previous version), insulation board, hardboard, medium-density fiberboard (part of chapter 21 in the previous version), and wood-based particle panel materials (chapter 22 in the previous version) are now included in a new chapter on wood-based composites and panel products.

- Structural sandwich construction (chapter 12 in the previous version) is now included in the chapter on glued structural members.

- Moisture movement and thermal insulation in light-frame structures (chapter 20 in the previous version) are now part of a new chapter on use of wood in buildings and bridges.

- Bent wood members (chapter 13 in the previous version), modified woods, and paper-based laminates (chapter 23 in the previous version) are now included in a chapter on specialty treatments.

Consistent with movement by many U.S. standards agencies and industry associations toward use of metric units and near-universal implementation of metric usage in the international community, units of measurement in this version of the handbook are provided primarily in metric units, with customary inch–pound equivalents as secondary units. All conversions in this handbook to metric units, including conversions of empirically derived equations, are direct (or soft) conversions from previously derived inch–pound values. At some future time, metric expressions may need to be derived from a reevaluation of original research.

Acknowledgments

We gratefully acknowledge the extraordinary effort of the following individuals in their review of the final draft of this entire volume. Their effort has substantially enhanced the clarity, consistency, and coverage of the *Wood Handbook*.

Donald Bender
Wood Materials & Engineering Laboratory
Washington State University
Pullman, Washington

Arthur Brauner
Forest Products Society
Madison, Wisconsin

Bradford Douglas
American Forest & Paper Association
Washington, DC

David Green
USDA Forest Service, Forest Products Laboratory
Madison, Wisconsin

Michael Hunt
Department of Forestry and Natural Resources
Purdue University
West Lafayette, Indiana

Thomas McLain
Department of Forest Products
Oregon State University
Corvallis, Oregon

Russell Moody
Madison, Wisconsin

Michael O'Halloran
APA—The Engineered Wood Association
Tacoma, Washington

Erwin Schaffer
Sun City West, Arizona

Contributors to the *Wood Handbook* are indebted to the following individuals and organizations for their early technical review of chapter manuscripts.

Terry Amburgey
Forest Products Laboratory
Mississippi State University
Mississippi State, Mississippi

Jon Arno
Troy, Minnesota

B. Alan Bendtsen
Madison, Wisconsin

A. William Boehner
Trus Joist MacMillan
Boise, Idaho

R. Michael Caldwell
American Institute of Timber Construction
Englewood, Colorado

Donald Carr
NAHB—National Research Center
Upper Marlboro, Maryland

Richard Caster
Weyerhaeuser Company
Tacoma, Washington

Kevin Cheung
Western Wood Products Association
Portland, Oregon

Stephen Clark
Northeastern Lumber Manufacturers Association
Cumberland Center, Maine

Richard Cook
National Casein Company
Santa Ana, California

William Crossman
Atlanta Wood Industries
Savannah, Georgia

Thomas Daniels
Energy Products of Idaho
Coeur D'Alene, Idaho

Donald DeVisser
West Coast Lumber Inspection Bureau
Portland, Oregon

Bradford Douglas
American Forest and Paper Association
Washington, DC

Stan Elberg
National Oak Flooring Manufacturers Association
Memphis, Tennessee

Paul Foehlich
Southern Cypress Manufacturers Association
Pittsburgh, Pennsylvania

Barry Goodell
Forest Products Laboratory
University of Maine
Orono, Maine

Kevin Haile
HP&VA
Reston, Virginia

Daniel Hare
The Composite Panel Association
Gaithersburg, Maryland

R. Bruce Hoadley
Forestry Department
University of Massachusetts
Amherst, Massachusetts

David Hon
Department of Forest Resources
Clemson University
Clemson, South Carolina

Robert Hunt
Western Wood Products Association
Portland, Oregon

Lisa Johnson
Southern Pine Inspection Bureau
Pensacola, Florida

Tom Jones
Southern Pine Inspection Bureau
Pensacola, Florida

Charles Jourdain
California Redwood Association
Novato, California

John Kressbach
Gillette, New Jersey

Robert Kundrot
Nestle Resins Corporation
Springfield, Oregon

Steven Lawser
Wood Component Manufacturers Association
Marietta, Georgia

Phillip Line
American Forest & Paper Association
Washington, DC

Joseph Loferski
Brooks Forest Products Center
Blacksburg, Virginia

Maple Flooring Manufacturers Association
Northbrook, Illinois

Thomas McLain
Department of Forest Products
Oregon State University
Corvallis, Oregon

David McLean
Civil Engineering Department
Washington State University
Pullman, Washington

Rodney McPhee
Canadian Wood Council
Ottawa, Ontario, Canada

Michael Milota
Oregon State University
Corvallis, Oregon

Jeffrey Morrell
Department of Forest Products
Oregon State University
Corvallis, Oregon

National Hardwood Lumber Association
Memphis, Tennessee

Darrel Nicholas
Forest Products Laboratory
Mississippi State University
Mississippi State, Mississippi

Michael O'Halloran
APA—The Engineered Wood Association
Tacoma, Washington

Perry Peralta
Department of Wood and Paper Science
North Carolina State University
Raleigh, North Carolina

David Plackett
Forintek Canada Corporation
Vancouver, British Columbia, Canada

David Pollock
Civil Engineering Department
Washington State University
Pullman, Washington

Redwood Inspection Service
Mill Valley, California

Alan Ross
Kop–Coat Inc.
Pittsburgh, Pennsylvania

Thomas Searles
American Lumber Standards Committee
Germantown, Maryland

James Shaw
Weyerhaeuser Company
Tacoma, Washington

Bradley Shelley
West Coast Lumber Inspection Bureau
Portland, Oregon

Ramsey Smith
Louisiana Forest Products Laboratory
Baton Rouge, Louisiana

William Smith
SUNY–ESF
Wood Products Engineering
Syracuse, New York

Edward Starostovic
PFS/TECO Corporations
Madison, Wisconsin

Louis Wagner
American Hardwood Association
Palatine, Illinois

Eugene Wengert
Department of Forestry
University of Wisconsin
Madison, Wisconsin

Michael Westfall
Red Cedar Shingle & Handsplit Shake Bureau
Bellevue, Washington

Borjen Yeh
APA—The Engineered Wood Association
Tacoma, Washington

Contributors

The following staff of the Forest Products Laboratory contributed to the writing, revision, and compilation of information contained in the *Wood Handbook*.

Mark A. Dietenberger
Research General Engineer

David W. Green
Supervisory Research General Engineer

David E. Kretschmann
Research General Engineer

Roland Hernandez
Research General Engineer

Terry L. Highley
Supervisory Research Plant Pathologist (retired)

Rebecca E. Ibach
Chemist

Jen Y. Liu
Research General Engineer

Kent A. McDonald
Research Forest Products Technologist (retired)

Regis B. Miller
Botanist

Russell C. Moody
Supervisory Research General Engineer (retired)

Roger M. Rowell
Supervisory Research Chemist

William T. Simpson
Research Forest Products Technologist

Lawrence A. Soltis
Research General Engineer

Anton TenWolde
Research Physicist

Ronald W. Wolfe
Research General Engineer

Charles B. Vick
Research Forest Products Technologist

Robert H. White
Supervisory Wood Scientist

R. Sam Williams
Supervisory Research Chemist

Jerrold E. Winandy
Research Forest Products Technologist

John A. Youngquist
Supervisory Research General Engineer

Chapter 1

Characteristics and Availability of Commercially Important Woods

Regis B. Miller

Contents

Throughout history, the unique characteristics and comparative abundance of wood have made it a natural material for homes and other structures, furniture, tools, vehicles, and decorative objects. Today, for the same reasons, wood is prized for a multitude of uses.

All wood is composed of cellulose, lignin, hemicelluloses, and minor amounts (5% to 10%) of extraneous materials contained in a cellular structure. Variations in the characteristics and volume of these components and differences in cellular structure make woods heavy or light, stiff or flexible, and hard or soft. The properties of a single species are relatively constant within limits; therefore, selection of wood by species alone may sometimes be adequate. However, to use wood to its best advantage and most effectively in engineering applications, specific characteristics or physical properties must be considered.

Historically, some species filled many purposes, while other less available or less desirable species served only one or two needs. For example, because white oak is tough, strong, and durable, it was highly prized for shipbuilding, bridges, cooperage, barn timbers, farm implements, railroad crossties, fence posts, and flooring. Woods such as black walnut and cherry were used primarily for furniture and cabinets. Hickory was manufactured into tough, hard, and resilient striking-tool handles, and black locust was prized for barn timbers. What the early builder or craftsman learned by trial and error became the basis for deciding which species were appropriate for a given use in terms of their characteristics. It was commonly accepted that wood from trees grown in certain locations under certain conditions was stronger, more durable, more easily worked with tools, or finer grained than wood from trees in other locations. Modern research on wood has substantiated that location and growth conditions do significantly affect wood properties.

The gradual reductions in use of old-growth forests in the United States has reduced the supply of large clear logs for lumber and veneer. However, the importance of high-quality logs has diminished as new concepts of wood use have been introduced. Second-growth wood, the remaining old-growth forests, and imports continue to fill the needs for wood in the quality required. Wood is as valuable an engineering material as ever, and in many cases, technological advances have made it even more useful.

The inherent factors that keep wood in the forefront of raw materials are many and varied, but a chief attribute is its availability in many species, sizes, shapes, and conditions to suit almost every demand. Wood has a high ratio of strength to weight and a remarkable record for durability and performance as a structural material. Dry wood has good insulating properties against heat, sound, and electricity. It tends to absorb and dissipate vibrations under some conditions of use, and yet it is an incomparable material for such musical instruments as the violin. The grain patterns and colors of wood make it an esthetically pleasing material, and its appearance may be easily enhanced by stains, varnishes, lacquers, and other finishes. It is easily shaped with tools and fastened with adhesives, nails, screws, bolts, and dowels. Damaged wood is easily repaired, and wood structures are easily remodeled or altered. In addition, wood resists oxidation, acid, saltwater, and other corrosive agents, has high salvage value, has good shock resistance, can be treated with preservatives and fire retardants, and can be combined with almost any other material for both functional and esthetic uses.

Timber Resources and Uses

In the United States, more than 100 wood species are available to the prospective user, but all are unlikely to be available in any one locality. About 60 native woods are of major commercial importance. Another 30 species are commonly imported in the form of logs, cants, lumber, and veneer for industrial uses, the building trade, and crafts.

A continuing program of timber inventory is in effect in the United States through the cooperation of Federal and State agencies, and new information on wood resources is published in State and Federal reports. Two of the most valuable sourcebooks are *An Analysis of the Timber Situation in the United States 1989–2040* (USDA 1990) and *The 1993 RPA Timber Assessment Update* (Haynes and others 1995).

Current information on wood consumption, production, imports, and supply and demand is published periodically by the Forest Products Laboratory (Howard 1997) and is available from the Superintendent of Documents, U.S. Government Printing Office, Washington, DC.

Hardwoods and Softwoods

Trees are divided into two broad classes, usually referred to as hardwoods and softwoods. These names can be confusing since some softwoods are actually harder than some hardwoods, and conversely some hardwoods are softer than some softwoods. For example, softwoods such as longleaf pine and Douglas-fir are typically harder than the hardwoods basswood and aspen. Botanically, hardwoods are Angiosperms; the seeds are enclosed in the ovary of the flower. Anatomically, hardwoods are porous; that is, they contain vessel elements. A vessel element is a wood cell with open ends; when vessel elements are set one above another, they form a continuous tube (vessel), which serves as a conduit for transporting water

or sap in the tree. Typically, hardwoods are plants with broad leaves that, with few exceptions in the temperate region, lose their leaves in autumn or winter. Most imported tropical woods are hardwoods. Botanically, softwoods are Gymnosperms or conifers; the seeds are naked (not enclosed in the ovary of the flower). Anatomically, softwoods are nonporous and do not contain vessels. Softwoods are usually cone-bearing plants with needle- or scale-like evergreen leaves. Some softwoods, such as larches and baldcypress, lose their needles during autumn or winter.

Major resources of softwood species are spread across the United States, except for the Great Plains where only small areas are forested. Softwood species are often loosely grouped in three general regions, as shown in Table 1–1. Hardwoods also occur in all parts of the United States, although most grow east of the Great Plains. Hardwood species are shown by region in Table 1–2.

Commercial Sources of Wood Products

Softwoods are available directly from the sawmill, wholesale and retail yards, or lumber brokers. Softwood lumber and plywood are used in construction for forms, scaffolding, framing, sheathing, flooring, moulding, paneling, cabinets, poles and piles, and many other building components. Softwoods may also appear in the form of shingles, sashes, doors, and other millwork, in addition to some rough products such as timber and round posts.

Hardwoods are used in construction for flooring, architectural woodwork, interior woodwork, and paneling. These items are usually available from lumberyards and building supply dealers. Most hardwood lumber and dimension stock are remanufactured into furniture, flooring, pallets, containers, dunnage, and blocking. Hardwood lumber and dimension

Table 1–1. Major resources of U.S. softwoods according to region

Western	Northern	Southern
Incense-cedar	Northern white-cedar	Atlantic white-cedar
Port-Orford-cedar	Balsam fir	Baldcypress
Douglas-fir	Eastern hemlock	Fraser fir
White firs	Fraser fir	Southern Pine
Western hemlock	Jack pine	Eastern redcedar
Western larch	Red pine	
Lodgepole pine	Eastern white pine	
Ponderosa pine	Eastern redcedar	
Sugar pine	Eastern spruces	
Western white pine	Tamarack	
Western redcedar		
Redwood		
Engelmann spruce		
Sitka spruce		
Yellow-cedar		

Table 1–2. Major resources of U.S. hardwoods according to region

Southern	Northern and Appalachia	Western
Ash	Ash	Red alder
Basswood	Aspen	Oregon ash
American beech	Basswood	Aspen
Butternut	Buckeye	Black cottonwood
Cottonwood	Butternut	California black oak
Elm	American beech	Oregon white oak
Hackberry	Birch	Bigleaf maple
Pecan hickory	Black cherry	Paper birch
True hickory	American chestnut[a]	Tanoak
Honeylocust	Cottonwood	
Black locust	Elm	
Magnolia	Hackberry	
Soft maple	True hickory	
Red oaks	Honeylocust	
White oaks	Black locust	
Sassafras	Hard maple	
Sweetgum	Soft maple	
American sycamore	Red oaks	
Tupelo	White oaks	
Black walnut	American sycamore	
Black willow	Black walnut	
Yellow-poplar	Yellow-poplar	

[a]American chestnut is no longer harvested, but chestnut lumber from salvaged timbers can still be found on the market.

stock are available directly from the manufacturer, through wholesalers and brokers, and from some retail yards.

Both softwood and hardwood products are distributed throughout the United States. Local preferences and the availability of certain species may influence choice, but a wide selection of woods is generally available for building construction, industrial uses, remanufacturing, and home use.

Use Classes and Trends

The production and consumption levels of some of the many use-classifications for wood are increasing with the overall national economy, and others are holding about the same. The most vigorously growing wood-based industries are those that convert wood to thin slices (veneer), particles (chips, flakes), or fiber pulps and reassemble the elements to produce various types of engineered panels such as plywood, particleboard, strandboard, veneer lumber, paper, paperboard, and fiberboard products. Another growing wood industry is the production of laminated wood. For a number of years, the lumber industry has produced almost the same volume of wood per year. Modest increases have occurred in the production of railroad crossties, cooperage, shingles, and shakes.

Species Descriptions

In this chapter, each species or group of species is described in terms of its principal location, characteristics, and uses. More detailed information on the properties of these and other species is given in various tables throughout this handbook. Information on historical and traditional uses is provided for some species. Common and botanical names follow the *Checklist of United States Trees* (Little 1979).

U.S. Wood Species

Hardwoods

Alder, Red

Red alder (*Alnus rubra*) grows along the Pacific coast between Alaska and California. It is the principal hardwood for commercial manufacture of wood products in Oregon and Washington and the most abundant commercial hardwood species in these two states.

The wood of red alder varies from almost white to pale pinkish brown, and there is no visible boundary between heartwood and sapwood. Red alder is moderately light in weight and intermediate in most strength properties but low in shock resistance. It has relatively low shrinkage.

The principal use of red alder is for furniture, but it is also used for sash and door panel stock and other millwork.

Ash (White Ash Group)

Important species of the white ash group are American white ash (*Fraxinus americana*), green ash (*F. pennsylvanica*), blue ash (*F. quadrangulata*), and Oregon ash (*F. latifolia*). The first three species grow in the eastern half of the United States. Oregon ash grows along the Pacific Coast.

The heartwood of the white ash group is brown, and the sapwood is light-colored or nearly white. Second-growth trees are particularly sought after because of the inherent qualities of the wood from these trees: it is heavy, strong, hard, and stiff, and it has high resistance to shock. Oregon ash has somewhat lower strength properties than American white ash, but it is used for similar purposes on the West Coast.

American white ash is used principally for nonstriking tool handles, oars, baseball bats, and other sporting and athletic goods. For handles of the best grade, some handle specifications call for not less than 2 nor more than 7 growth rings per centimeter (not less than 5 nor more than 17 growth rings per inch). The additional weight requirement of 690 kg/m^3 (43 lb/ft^3) or more at 12% moisture content ensures high quality material. Principal uses for the white ash group are decorative veneer, cabinets, furniture, flooring, millwork, and crates.

Ash (Black Ash Group)

The black ash group includes black ash (*F. nigra)* and pumpkin ash (*F. profunda*). Black ash grows in the Northeast and Midwest, and pumpkin ash in the South.

The heartwood of black ash is a darker brown than that of American white ash; the sapwood is light-colored or nearly white. The wood of the black ash group is lighter in weight (basic specific gravity of 0.45 to 0.48) than that of the white ash group (>0.50). Pumpkin ash, American white ash, and green ash that grow in southern river bottoms, especially in areas frequently flooded for long periods, produce buttresses that contain relatively lightweight and brash wood.

Principal uses for the black ash group are decorative veneer, cabinets, millwork, furniture, cooperage, and crates.

Aspen

Aspen is a generally recognized name that is applied to bigtooth (*Populus grandidentata*) and quaking (*P. tremuloides*) aspen. Aspen does not include balsam poplar (*P. balsamifera)* and the other species of *Populus* that are included in the cottonwoods. In lumber statistics of the U.S. Bureau of the Census, however, the term cottonwood includes all the preceding species. Also, the lumber of aspen and cottonwood may be mixed in trade and sold as either popple or cottonwood. The name popple should not be confused with yellow-poplar (*Liriodendron tulipifera*), also known in the trade as poplar. Aspen lumber is produced principally in the Northeastern and Lake States, with some production in the Rocky Mountain States.

The heartwood of aspen is grayish white to light grayish brown. The sapwood is lighter colored and generally merges gradually into the heartwood without being clearly marked. Aspen wood is usually straight grained with a fine, uniform texture. It is easily worked. Well-dried aspen lumber does not impart odor or flavor to foodstuffs. The wood of aspen is lightweight and soft. It is low in strength, moderately stiff, and moderately low in resistance to shock and has moderately high shrinkage.

Aspen is cut for lumber, pallets, boxes and crating, pulpwood, particleboard, strand panels, excelsior, matches, veneer, and miscellaneous turned articles. Today, aspen is one of the preferred species for use in oriented strandboard, a panel product that is increasingly being used as sheathing.

Basswood

American basswood (*Tilia americana*) is the most important of the native basswood species; next in importance is white basswood (*T. heterophylla*), and no attempt is made to distinguish between these species in lumber form. In commercial usage, "white basswood" is used to specify the white wood or sapwood of either species. Basswood grows in the eastern half of the United States from the Canadian provinces southward. Most basswood lumber comes from the Lake, Middle Atlantic, and Central States.

The heartwood of basswood is pale yellowish brown with occasional darker streaks. Basswood has wide, creamy white or pale brown sapwood that merges gradually into heartwood. When dry, the wood is without odor or taste. It is soft and light in weight, has fine, even texture, and is straight grained and easy to work with tools. Shrinkage in width and thickness during drying is rated as high; however, basswood seldom warps in use.

Basswood lumber is used mainly in venetian blinds, sashes and door frames, moulding, apiary supplies, wooden ware, and boxes. Some basswood is cut for veneer, cooperage, excelsior, and pulpwood, and it is a favorite of wood carvers.

Beech, American

Only one species of beech, American beech (*Fagus grandifolia*), is native to the United States. It grows in the eastern one-third of the United States and adjacent Canadian provinces. The greatest production of beech lumber is in the Central and Middle Atlantic States.

In some beech trees, color varies from nearly white sapwood to reddish-brown heartwood. Sometimes there is no clear line of demarcation between heartwood and sapwood. Sapwood may be roughly 7 to 13 cm (3 to 5 in.) wide. The wood has little figure and is of close, uniform texture. It has no characteristic taste or odor. The wood of beech is classed as heavy, hard, strong, high in resistance to shock, and highly suitable for steam bending. Beech shrinks substantially and therefore requires careful drying. It machines smoothly, is an excellent wood for turning, wears well, and is rather easily treated with preservatives.

Most beech is used for flooring, furniture, brush blocks, handles, veneer, woodenware, containers, and cooperage. When treated with preservative, beech is suitable for railway ties.

Birch

The three most important species are yellow birch (*Betula alleghaniensis*), sweet birch (*B. lenta*), and paper birch (*B. papyrifera*). These three species are the source of most birch lumber and veneer. Other birch species of some commercial importance are river birch (*B. nigra*), gray birch (*B. populifolia*), and western paper birch (*B. papyrifera* var. *commutata*). Yellow, sweet, and paper birch grow principally in the Northeast and the Lake States; yellow and sweet birch also grow along the Appalachian Mountains to northern Georgia.

Yellow birch has white sapwood and light reddish-brown heartwood. Sweet birch has light-colored sapwood and dark brown heartwood tinged with red. For both yellow and sweet birch, the wood is heavy, hard, and strong, and it has good shock-resisting ability. The wood is fine and uniform in texture. Paper birch is lower in weight, softer, and lower in strength than yellow and sweet birch. Birch shrinks considerably during drying.

Yellow and sweet birch lumber is used primarily for the manufacture of furniture, boxes, baskets, crates, wooden ware, cooperage, interior woodwork, and doors; veneer plywood is used for flush doors, furniture, paneling, cabinets, aircraft, and other specialty uses. Paper birch is used for toothpicks, tongue depressors, ice cream sticks, and turned products, including spools, bobbins, small handles, and toys.

Buckeye

Buckeye consists of two species, yellow buckeye (*Aesculus octandra*) and Ohio buckeye (*A. glabra*). These species range from the Appalachians of Pennsylvania, Virginia, and North Carolina westward to Kansas, Oklahoma, and Texas. Buckeye is not customarily separated from other species when manufactured into lumber and can be used for the same purposes as aspen (*Populus*), basswood (*Tilia*), and sapwood of yellow-poplar (*Liriodendron tulipifera*).

The white sapwood of buckeye merges gradually into the creamy or yellowish white heartwood. The wood is uniform in texture, generally straight grained, light in weight, weak when used as a beam, soft, and low in shock resistance. It is rated low on machinability such as shaping, mortising, boring, and turning.

Buckeye is suitable for pulping for paper; in lumber form, it has been used principally for furniture, boxes and crates, food containers, wooden ware, novelties, and planing mill products.

Butternut

Also called white walnut, butternut (*Juglans cinerea*) grows from southern New Brunswick and Maine west to Minnesota. Its southern range extends into northeastern Arkansas and eastward to western North Carolina.

The narrow sapwood is nearly white and heartwood is light brown, frequently modified by pinkish tones or darker brown streaks. The wood is moderately light in weight (about the same as eastern white pine), rather coarse textured, moderately weak in bending and endwise compression, relatively low in stiffness, moderately soft, and moderately high in shock resistance. Butternut machines easily and finishes well. In many ways, butternut resembles black walnut especially when stained, but it does not have the same strength or hardness.

Principal uses are for lumber and veneer, which are further manufactured into furniture, cabinets, paneling, interior woodwork, and miscellaneous rough items.

Cherry, Black

Black cherry (*Prunus serotina*) is sometimes known as cherry, wild black cherry, and wild cherry. It is the only native species of the genus *Prunus* of commercial importance for lumber production. Black cherry is found from southeastern Canada throughout the eastern half of the United States. Production is centered chiefly in the Middle Atlantic States.

The heartwood of black cherry varies from light to dark reddish brown and has a distinctive luster. The nearly white sapwood is narrow in old-growth trees and wider in second-growth trees. The wood has a fairly uniform texture and very good machining properties. It is moderately heavy, strong, stiff, and moderately hard; it has high shock resistance and moderately high shrinkage. Black cherry is very dimensionally stable after drying.

Black cherry is used principally for furniture, fine veneer panels, and architectural woodwork. Other uses include burial caskets, wooden ware, novelties, patterns, and paneling.

Chestnut, American

American chestnut (*Castanea dentata*) is also known as sweet chestnut. Before this species was attacked by a blight in the 1920s, it grew in commercial quantities from New England to northern Georgia. Practically all standing chestnut has been killed by blight, and most supplies of the lumber come from salvaged timbers. Because of the species' natural resistance to decay, standing dead trees in the Appalachian Mountains continued to provide substantial quantities of lumber for several decades after the blight, but this source is now exhausted.

The heartwood of chestnut is grayish brown or brown and darkens with age. The sapwood is very narrow and almost white. The wood is coarse in texture; growth rings are made conspicuous by several rows of large, distinct pores at the beginning of each year's growth. Chestnut wood is moderately light in weight, moderately hard, moderately low in strength, moderately low in resistance to shock, and low in stiffness. It dries well and is easy to work with tools.

Chestnut was once used for poles, railroad crossties, furniture, caskets, boxes, shingles, crates, and corestock for veneer panels. At present, it appears most frequently as wormy chestnut for paneling, interior woodwork, and picture frames.

Cottonwood

Cottonwood includes several species of the genus *Populus*. Most important are eastern cottonwood (*P. deltoides* and varieties), also known as Carolina poplar and whitewood; swamp cottonwood (*P. heterophylla*), also known as cottonwood, river cottonwood, and swamp poplar; black cottonwood (*P. trichocarpa*); and balsam poplar (*P. balsamifera*). Eastern and swamp cottonwood grow throughout the eastern half of the United States. Greatest production of lumber is in the Southern and Central States. Black cottonwood grows on the West Coast and in western Montana, northern Idaho, and western Nevada. Balsam poplar grows from Alaska across Canada and in the northern Great Lakes States.

The heartwood of cottonwood is grayish white to light brown. The sapwood is whitish and merges gradually with the heartwood. The wood is comparatively uniform in texture and generally straight grained. It is odorless when well dried. Eastern cottonwood is moderately low in bending and compressive strength, moderately stiff, moderately soft, and moderately low in ability to resist shock. Most strength properties of black cottonwood are slightly lower than those of eastern cottonwood. Both eastern and black cottonwood have moderately high shrinkage. Some cottonwood is difficult to work with tools because of its fuzzy surface, which is mainly the result of tension wood (see discussion of Reaction Wood in Ch. 4).

Cottonwood is used principally for lumber, veneer, pulpwood, excelsior, and fuel. Lumber and veneer are used primarily for boxes, crates, baskets, and pallets.

Elm

Six species of elm grow in the eastern United States: American (*Ulmus americana*), slippery (*U. rubra*), rock (*U. thomasii*), winged (*U. alata*), cedar (*U. crassifolia*), and September (*U. serotina*) elm. American elm is also known as white, water, and gray elm; slippery elm as red elm; rock elm as cork and hickory elm; winged elm as wahoo; cedar elm as red and basket elm; and September elm as red elm. American elm is threatened by two diseases, Dutch Elm disease and phloem necrosis, which have killed hundreds of thousands of trees.

Sapwood of elm is nearly white and heartwood light brown, often tinged with red. Elm may be divided into two general classes, soft and hard, based on the weight and strength of the wood. Soft elm includes American and slippery elm. It is moderately heavy, has high shock resistance, and is moderately hard and stiff. Hard elm includes rock, winged, cedar, and September elm. These species are somewhat heavier than soft elm. Elm has excellent bending qualities.

Historically, elm lumber was used for boxes, baskets, crates, and slack cooperage; furniture; agricultural supplies and implements; caskets and burial boxes; and wood components in vehicles. Today, elm lumber and veneer are used mostly for furniture and decorative panels. Hard elm is preferred for uses that require strength.

Hackberry

Hackberry (*Celtis occidentalis*) and sugarberry (*C. laevigata*) supply the lumber known in the trade as hackberry. Hackberry grows east of the Great Plains from Alabama, Georgia, Arkansas, and Oklahoma northward, except along the Canadian boundary. Sugarberry overlaps the southern part of the hackberry range and grows throughout the Southern and South Atlantic States.

Sapwood of both species varies from pale yellow to greenish or grayish yellow. The heartwood is commonly darker. The wood resembles elm in structure. Hackberry lumber is moderately heavy. It is moderately strong in bending, moderately weak in compression parallel to grain, moderately hard to very hard, and high in shock resistance, but low in stiffness. Hackberry has high shrinkage but keeps its shape well during drying.

Most hackberry is cut into lumber; small amounts are used for furniture parts, dimension stock, and veneer.

Hickory (Pecan Group)

Species of the pecan hickory group include bitternut hickory (*Carya cordiformis*), pecan (*C. illinoensis*), water hickory (*C. aquatica*), and nutmeg hickory (*C. myristiciformis*). Bitternut hickory grows throughout the eastern half of the United States; pecan hickory, from central Texas and Louisiana to Missouri and Indiana; water hickory, from Texas to South Carolina; and nutmeg hickory, in Texas and Louisiana.

The sapwood of this group is white or nearly white and relatively wide. The heartwood is somewhat darker. The wood is heavy and sometimes has very high shrinkage.

Heavy pecan hickory is used for tool and implement handles and flooring. The lower grades are used for pallets. Many higher grade logs are sliced to provide veneer for furniture and decorative paneling.

Hickory (True Group)

True hickories are found throughout the eastern half of the United States. The species most important commercially are shagbark (*Carya ovata*), pignut (*C. glabra*), shellbark (*C. laciniosa*), and mockernut (*C. tomentosa*). The greatest commercial production of the true hickories for all uses is in the Middle Atlantic and Central States, with the Southern and South Atlantic States rapidly expanding to handle nearly half of all hickory lumber.

The sapwood of the true hickory group is white and usually quite wide, except in old, slow-growing trees. The heartwood is reddish. The wood is exceptionally tough, heavy, hard, and strong, and shrinks considerably in drying. For some purposes, both rings per centimeter (or inch) and weight are limiting factors where strength is important.

The major use for high quality hickory is for tool handles, which require high shock resistance. It is also used for ladder rungs, athletic goods, agricultural implements, dowels, gymnasium apparatuses, poles, and furniture. Lower grade hickory is not suitable for the special uses of high quality hickory because of knottiness or other growth features and low density. However, the lower grade is useful for pallets and similar items. Hickory sawdust, chips, and some solid wood are used to flavor meat by smoking.

Honeylocust

The wood of honeylocust (*Gleditsia triacanthos*) has many desirable qualities, such as attractive figure and color, hardness, and strength, but it is little used because of its scarcity. Although the natural range of honeylocust has been extended by planting, this species is found most commonly in the eastern United States, except for New England and the South Atlantic and Gulf Coastal Plains.

Sapwood is generally wide and yellowish, in contrast to the light red to reddish-brown heartwood. The wood is very heavy, very hard, strong in bending, stiff, resistant to shock, and durable when in contact with the ground.

When available, honeylocust is primarily used locally for fence posts and general construction. It is occasionally used with other species in lumber for pallets and crating.

Locust, Black

Black locust (*Robinia pseudoacacia*) is sometimes called yellow or post locust. This species grows from Pennsylvania along the Appalachian Mountains to northern Georgia and Alabama. It is also native to western Arkansas and southern Missouri. The greatest production of black locust timber is in Tennessee, Kentucky, West Virginia, and Virginia.

Locust has narrow, creamy white sapwood. The heartwood, when freshly cut, varies from greenish yellow to dark brown. Black locust is very heavy, very hard, very resistant to shock, and very strong and stiff. It has moderately low shrinkage. The heartwood has high decay resistance.

Black locust is used for round, hewed, or split mine timbers as well as fence posts, poles, railroad crossties, stakes, and fuel. Other uses are for rough construction, crating, and mine equipment. Historically, black locust was important for the manufacture of insulator pins and wooden pegs used in the construction of ships, for which the wood was well adapted because of its strength, decay resistance, and moderate shrinkage and swelling.

Magnolia

Commercial magnolia consists of three species: southern magnolia (*Magnolia grandiflora*), sweetbay (*M. virginiana*), and cucumbertree (*M. acuminata*). Other names for southern magnolia are evergreen magnolia, big laurel, bull bay, and laurel bay. Sweetbay is sometimes called swamp magnolia. The lumber produced by all three species is simply called magnolia. The natural range of sweetbay extends along the Atlantic and Gulf Coasts from Long Island to Texas, and that of southern magnolia extends from North Carolina to Texas. Cucumbertree grows from the Appalachians to the Ozarks northward to Ohio. Louisiana leads in the production of magnolia lumber.

Sapwood of southern magnolia is yellowish white, and heartwood is light to dark brown with a tinge of yellow or green. The wood, which has close, uniform texture and is generally straight grained, closely resembles yellow-poplar (*Liriodendron tulipifera*). It is moderately heavy, moderately low in shrinkage, moderately low in bending and compressive strength, moderately hard and stiff, and moderately high in shock resistance. Sweetbay is much like southern magnolia. The wood of cucumbertree is similar to that of yellow-poplar (*L. tulipifera*); cucumbertree that grows in the yellow-poplar range is not separated from that species on the market.

Magnolia lumber is used principally in the manufacture of furniture, boxes, pallets, venetian blinds, sashes, doors, veneer, and millwork.

Maple, Hard

Hard maple includes sugar maple (*Acer saccharum*) and black maple (*A. nigrum*). Sugar maple is also known as hard and rock maple, and black maple as black sugar maple. Maple lumber is manufactured principally in the Middle Atlantic and Great Lake States, which together account for about two-thirds of production.

The heartwood is usually light reddish brown but sometimes considerably darker. The sapwood is commonly white with a slight reddish-brown tinge. It is roughly 7 to 13 cm or more (3 to 5 in. or more) wide. Hard maple has a fine, uniform texture. It is heavy, strong, stiff, hard, and resistant to shock and has high shrinkage. The grain of sugar maple is generally straight, but birdseye, curly, or fiddleback grain is often selected for furniture or novelty items.

Hard maple is used principally for lumber and veneer. A large proportion is manufactured into flooring, furniture, cabinets, cutting boards and blocks, pianos, billiard cues, handles, novelties, bowling alleys, dance and gymnasium floors, spools, and bobbins.

Maple, Soft

Soft maple includes silver maple (*Acer saccharinum*), red maple (*A. rubrum*), boxelder (*A. negundo*), and bigleaf maple (*A. macrophyllum*). Silver maple is also known as white, river, water, and swamp maple; red maple as soft, water, scarlet, white, and swamp maple; boxelder as ash-leaved, three-leaved, and cut-leaved maple; and bigleaf maple as Oregon maple. Soft maple is found in the eastern United States except for bigleaf maple, which comes from the Pacific Coast.

Heartwood and sapwood are similar in appearance to hard maple: heartwood of soft maple is somewhat lighter in color and the sapwood, somewhat wider. The wood of soft maple, primarily silver and red maple, resembles that of hard maple but is not as heavy, hard, and strong.

Soft maple is used for railroad crossties, boxes, pallets, crates, furniture, veneer, wooden ware, and novelties.

Oak (Red Oak Group)

Most red oak comes from the Eastern States. The principal species are northern red (*Quercus rubra*), scarlet (*Q. coccinea*), Shumard (*Q. shumardii*), pin (*Q. palustris*), Nuttall (*Q. nuttallii*), black (*Q. velutina*), southern red (*Q. falcata*), cherrybark (*Q. falcata* var. *pagodaefolia*), water (*Q. nigra*), laurel (*Q. laurifolia*), and willow (*Q. phellos*) oak.

The sapwood is nearly white and roughly 2 to 5 cm (1 to 2 in.) wide. The heartwood is brown with a tinge of red. Sawn lumber of the red oak group cannot be separated by species on the basis of wood characteristics alone.

Red oak lumber can be separated from white oak by the size and arrangement of pores in latewood and because it generally lacks tyloses in the pores. The open pores of red oak make this species group unsuitable for tight cooperage, unless the barrels are lined with sealer or plastic. Quartersawn lumber of the oaks is distinguished by the broad and conspicuous rays. Wood of the red oaks is heavy. Rapidly grown second-growth wood is generally harder and tougher than finer textured old-growth wood. The red oaks have fairly high shrinkage in drying.

The red oaks are primarily cut into lumber, railroad crossties, mine timbers, fence posts, veneer, pulpwood, and fuelwood. Ties, mine timbers, and fence posts require preservative treatment for satisfactory service. Red oak lumber is remanufactured into flooring, furniture, general millwork, boxes, pallets and crates, agricultural implements, caskets, wooden ware, and handles. It is also used in railroad cars and boats.

Oak (White Oak Group)

White oak lumber comes chiefly from the South, South Atlantic, and Central States, including the southern Appalachian area. Principal species are white (*Quercus alba*), chestnut (*Q. prinus*), post (*Q. stellata*), overcup (*Q. lyrata*), swamp chestnut (*Q. michauxii*), bur (*Q. macrocarpa*), chinkapin (*Q. muehlenbergii*), swamp white (*Q. bicolor*), and live (*Q. virginiana*) oak.

The sapwood of the white oaks is nearly white and roughly 2 to 5 cm or more (1 to 2 in. or more) wide. The heartwood is generally grayish brown. Heartwood pores are usually plugged with tyloses, which tend to make the wood impenetrable by liquids. Consequently, most white oaks are suitable for tight cooperage. Many heartwood pores of chestnut oak lack tyloses. The wood of white oak is heavy, averaging somewhat greater in weight than red oak wood. The heartwood has good decay resistance.

White oaks are usually cut into lumber, railroad crossties, cooperage, mine timbers, fence posts, veneer, fuelwood, and many other products. High-quality white oak is especially sought for tight cooperage. Live oak is considerably heavier and stronger than the other oaks, and it was formerly used extensively for ship timbers. An important use of white oak is for planking and bent parts of ships and boats; heartwood is often specified because of its decay resistance. White oak is also used for furniture, flooring, pallets, agricultural implements, railroad cars, truck floors, furniture, doors, and millwork.

Sassafras

Sassafras (*Sassafras albidum*) ranges through most of the eastern half of the United States, from southeastern Iowa and eastern Texas eastward.

Sassafras is easily confused with black ash, which it resembles in color, grain, and texture. Sapwood is light yellow, and heartwood varies from dull grayish brown to dark brown, sometimes with a reddish tinge. Freshly cut surfaces have the characteristic odor of sassafras. The wood is moderately heavy, moderately hard, moderately weak in bending and endwise compression, quite high in shock resistance, and resistant to decay.

Sassafras was highly prized by the Indians for dugout canoes, and some sassafras lumber is still used for small boats. Locally, sassafras is used for fence posts and rails and for general millwork.

Sweetgum

Sweetgum (*Liquidambar styraciflua*) grows from southwestern Connecticut westward into Missouri and southward to the Gulf Coast. Almost all lumber is produced in the Southern and South Atlantic States.

The lumber from sweetgum is usually marked as sap gum (the light-colored sapwood) or redgum (the reddish-brown heartwood). Sweetgum often has a form of cross grain called interlocked grain, and it must be dried slowly. When quartersawn, interlocked grain produces a ribbon-type stripe that is desirable for interior woodwork and furniture. The wood is moderately heavy and hard. It is moderately strong, moderately stiff, and moderately high in shock resistance.

Sweetgum is used principally for lumber, veneer, plywood, slack cooperage, railroad crossties, fuel, pulpwood, boxes and crates, furniture, interior moulding, and millwork.

Sycamore, American

American sycamore (*Platanus occidentalis*) is known as sycamore and sometimes as buttonwood, buttonball-tree, and in the United Kingdom, planetree. Sycamore grows from Maine to Nebraska, southward to Texas, and eastward to Florida.

The heartwood of sycamore is reddish brown; the sapwood is lighter in color and from 4 to 8 cm (1-1/2 to 3 in.) wide. The wood has a fine texture and interlocked grain. It has high shrinkage in drying; is moderately heavy, moderately hard, moderately stiff, and moderately strong; and has good resistance to shock.

Sycamore is used principally for lumber, veneer, railroad crossties, slack cooperage, fence posts, and fuel. The lumber is used for furniture, boxes (particularly small food containers), pallets, flooring, handles, and butcher blocks. Veneer is used for fruit and vegetable baskets and some decorative panels and door skins.

Tanoak

Tanoak (*Lithocarpus densiflorus*) has recently gained some commercial value, primarily in California and Oregon. It is also known as tanbark–oak because high-grade tannin was once obtained from the bark in commercial quantities. This species is found in southwestern Oregon and south to Southern California, mostly near the coast but also in the Sierra Nevada.

Sapwood of tanoak is light reddish brown when first cut and turns darker with age to become almost indistinguishable from heartwood, which also ages to dark reddish brown. The wood is heavy and hard; except for compression perpendicular to grain, the wood has roughly the same strength properties as those of eastern white oak. Tanoak has higher shrinkage during drying than does white oak, and it has a tendency to collapse during drying. Tanoak is quite susceptible to decay, but the sapwood takes preservatives easily. Tanoak has straight grain, machines and glues well, and takes stains readily.

Because of its hardness and abrasion resistance, tanoak is excellent for flooring in homes or commercial buildings. It is also suitable for industrial applications such as truck flooring. Tanoak treated with preservative has been used for railroad crossties. The wood has been manufactured into baseball bats with good results, and it is also suitable for veneer, both decorative and industrial, and for high quality furniture.

Tupelo

The tupelo group includes water (*Nyssa aquatica*), black (*N. sylvatica*), swamp (*N. sylvatica* var. *biflora*), and Ogeechee (*N. ogeche*) tupelo. Water tupelo is also known as tupelo gum, swamp tupelo, and sourgum; black tupelo, as blackgum and sourgum; swamp tupelo, as swamp blackgum, blackgum, and sourgum; and Ogeechee tupelo, as sour tupelo, gopher plum, and Ogeechee plum. All except black tupelo grow principally in the southeastern United States. Black tupelo grows in the eastern United States from Maine to Texas and Missouri. About two-thirds of the production of tupelo lumber is from Southern States.

Wood of the different tupelo species is quite similar in appearance and properties. The heartwood is light brownish gray and merges gradually into the lighter-colored sapwood, which is generally many centimeters wide. The wood has fine, uniform texture and interlocked grain. Tupelo wood is moderately heavy, moderately strong, moderately hard and stiff, and moderately high in shock resistance. Buttresses of trees growing in swamps or flooded areas contain wood that is much lighter in weight than that from upper portions of the same trees. Because of interlocked grain, tupelo lumber requires care in drying.

Tupelo is cut principally for lumber, veneer, pulpwood, and some railroad crossties and slack cooperage. Lumber goes into boxes, pallets, crates, baskets, and furniture.

Walnut, Black

Black walnut (*Juglans nigra*), also known as American black walnut, ranges from Vermont to the Great Plains and southward into Louisiana and Texas. About three-quarters of walnut wood is grown in the Central States.

The heartwood of black walnut varies from light to dark brown; the sapwood is nearly white and up to 8 cm (3 in.) wide in open-grown trees. Black walnut is normally straight grained, easily worked with tools, and stable in use. It is heavy, hard, strong, and stiff, and has good resistance to shock. Black walnut is well suited for natural finishes.

Because of its good properties and interesting grain pattern, black walnut is much valued for furniture, architectural woodwork, and decorative panels. Other important uses are gunstocks, cabinets, and interior woodwork.

Willow, Black

Black willow (*Salix nigra*) is the most important of the many willows that grow in the United States. It is the only willow marketed under its own name. Most black willow comes from the Mississippi Valley, from Louisiana to southern Missouri and Illinois.

The heartwood of black willow is grayish brown or light reddish brown and frequently contains darker streaks. The sapwood is whitish to creamy yellow. The wood is uniform in texture, with somewhat interlocked grain, and light in weight. It has exceedingly low strength as a beam or post, is moderately soft, and is moderately high in shock resistance. It has moderately high shrinkage.

Black willow is principally cut into lumber. Small amounts are used for slack cooperage, veneer, excelsior, charcoal, pulpwood, artificial limbs, and fence posts. The lumber is remanufactured principally into boxes, pallets, crates, caskets, and furniture.

Yellow-Poplar

Yellow-poplar (*Liriodendron tulipifera*) is also known as poplar, tulip-poplar, and tulipwood. Sapwood from yellow-poplar is sometimes called white poplar or whitewood. Yellow-poplar grows from Connecticut and New York southward to Florida and westward to Missouri. The greatest commercial production of yellow-poplar lumber is in the South and Southeast.

Yellow-poplar sapwood is white and frequently several centimeters wide. The heartwood is yellowish brown, sometimes streaked with purple, green, black, blue, or red. These colorations do not affect the physical properties of the wood. The wood is generally straight grained and comparatively uniform in texture. Slow-grown wood is moderately light in weight and moderately low in bending strength, moderately soft, and moderately low in shock resistance. The wood has moderately high shrinkage when dried from a green condition, but it is not difficult to dry and is stable after drying. Much of the second-growth wood is heavier, harder, and stronger than that of older trees that have grown more slowly.

The lumber is used primarily for furniture, interior moulding, siding, cabinets, musical instruments, and structural components. Boxes, pallets, and crates are made from lower-grade stock. Yellow-poplar is also made into plywood for paneling, furniture, piano cases, and various other special products.

Figure 1–1. Cypress-tupelo swamp near New Orleans, LA. Species include baldcypress (*Taxodium distichum*)), tupelo (*Nyssa*), ash (*Fraxinus*), willow (*Salix*), and elm (*Ulmus*). Swollen buttresses and "knees" are typically present in cypress.

Softwoods

Baldcypress

Baldcypress or cypress (*Taxodium distichum*) is also known as southern-cypress, red-cypress, yellow-cypress, and white-cypress. Commercially, the terms tidewater red-cypress, gulf-cypress, red-cypress (coast type), and yellow-cypress (inland type) are frequently used. About half of the cypress lumber comes from the Southern States and about a fourth from the South Atlantic States (Fig. 1–1). Old-growth baldcypress is no longer readily available, but second-growth wood is available.

Sapwood of baldcypress is narrow and nearly white. The color of heartwood varies widely, ranging from light yellowish brown to dark brownish red, brown, or chocolate. The wood is moderately heavy, moderately strong, and moderately hard. The heartwood of old-growth baldcypress is one of the most decay resistant of U.S. species, but second-growth wood is only moderately resistant to decay. Shrinkage is moderately low but somewhat higher than that of the cedars and lower than that of Southern Pine. The wood of certain baldcypress trees frequently contains pockets or localized areas that have been attacked by a fungus. Such wood is known as pecky cypress. The decay caused by this fungus is stopped when the wood is cut into lumber and dried. Pecky cypress is therefore durable and useful where water tightness is unnecessary, appearance is not important, or a novel effect is desired.

When old-growth wood was available, baldcypress was used principally for building construction, especially where resistance to decay was required. It was also used for caskets, sashes, doors, blinds, tanks, vats, ship and boat building,

and cooling towers. Second-growth wood is used for siding and millwork, including interior woodwork and paneling. Pecky cypress is used for paneling in restaurants, stores, and other buildings.

Douglas-Fir

Douglas-fir (*Pseudotsuga menziesii*) is also known locally as red-fir, Douglas-spruce, and yellow-fir. Its range extends from the Rocky Mountains to the Pacific Coast and from Mexico to central British Columbia.

Sapwood of Douglas-fir is narrow in old-growth trees but may be as much as 7 cm (3 in.) wide in second-growth trees of commercial size. Young trees of moderate to rapid growth have reddish heartwood and are called red-fir. Very narrow-ringed heartwood of old-growth trees may be yellowish brown and is known on the market as yellow-fir. The wood of Douglas-fir varies widely in weight and strength. When lumber of high strength is needed for structural uses, selection can be improved by selecting wood with higher density.

Douglas-fir is used mostly for building and construction purposes in the form of lumber, marine fendering (Fig. 1–2), piles, and plywood. Considerable quantities are used for railroad crossties, cooperage stock, mine timbers, poles, and fencing. Douglas-fir lumber is used in the manufacture of various products, including sashes, doors, laminated beams, general millwork, railroad-car construction, boxes, pallets, and crates. Small amounts are used for flooring, furniture, ship and boat construction, and tanks. Douglas-fir plywood has found application in construction, furniture, cabinets, marine use, and other products.

Firs, True (Eastern Species)

Balsam fir (*Abies balsamea*) grows principally in New England, New York, Pennsylvania, and the Great Lake States. Fraser fir (*A. fraseri*) grows in the Appalachian Mountains of Virginia, North Carolina, and Tennessee.

The wood of the eastern true firs, as well as the western true firs, is creamy white to pale brown. The heartwood and sapwood are generally indistinguishable. The similarity of wood structure in the true firs makes it impossible to distinguish the species by examination of the wood alone. Balsam and Fraser firs are lightweight, have low bending and compressive strength, are moderately low in stiffness, are soft, and have low resistance to shock.

The eastern firs are used mainly for pulpwood, although some lumber is produced for structural products, especially in New England and the Great Lake States.

Firs, True (Western Species)

Six commercial species make up the western true firs: subalpine fir (*Abies lasiocarpa*), California red fir (*A. magnifica*), grand fir (*A. grandis*), noble fir (*A. procera*), Pacific silver fir (*A. amabilis*), and white fir (*A. concolor*). The western true firs are cut for lumber primarily in Washington, Oregon, California, western Montana, and northern Idaho, and they are marketed as white fir throughout the United States.

Figure 1–2. Wood is favored for waterfront structures, particularly fendering, because of its shock-absorbing qualities. The fendering on this dock in Key West, FL, is made of creosote-treated Douglas-fir (*Pseudotsuga menziesii*). Some tropical species are resistant to attack by decay fungi and marine borers and are used for marine construction without preservative treatment.

The wood of the western true firs is similar to that of the eastern true firs, which makes it impossible to distinguish the true fir species by examination of the wood alone. Western true firs are light in weight but, with the exception of subalpine fir, have somewhat higher strength properties than does balsam fir. Shrinkage of the wood is low to moderately high.

Lumber of the western true firs is primarily used for building construction, boxes and crates, planing-mill products, sashes, doors, and general millwork. In house construction, the lumber is used for framing, subflooring, and sheathing. Some western true fir lumber is manufactured into boxes and crates. High-grade lumber from noble fir is used mainly for interior woodwork, moulding, siding, and sash and door stock. Some of the highest quality material is suitable for aircraft construction. Other special uses of noble fir are venetian blinds and ladder rails.

Hemlock, Eastern

Eastern hemlock (*Tsuga canadensis*) grows from New England to northern Alabama and Georgia, and in the Great Lake States. Other names are Canadian hemlock and hemlock–spruce. The production of hemlock lumber is divided fairly evenly among the New England States, Middle Atlantic States, and Great Lake States.

The heartwood of eastern hemlock is pale brown with a reddish hue. The sapwood is not distinctly separated from the heartwood but may be lighter in color. The wood is coarse and uneven in texture (old trees tend to have considerable shake); it is moderately lightweight, moderately hard, moderately low in strength, moderately stiff, and moderately low in shock resistance.

Eastern hemlock is used principally for lumber and pulpwood. The lumber is used primarily in building construction (framing, sheathing, subflooring, and roof boards) and in the manufacture of boxes, pallets, and crates.

Hemlock, Western and Mountain

Western hemlock (*Tsuga heterophylla*) is also known as West Coast hemlock, Pacific hemlock, British Columbia hemlock, hemlock–spruce, and western hemlock–fir. It grows along the Pacific coast of Oregon and Washington and in the northern Rocky Mountains north to Canada and Alaska. A relative of western hemlock, mountain hemlock (*T. mertensiana*) grows in mountainous country from central California to Alaska. It is treated as a separate species in assigning lumber properties.

The heartwood and sapwood of western hemlock are almost white with a purplish tinge. The sapwood, which is sometimes lighter in color than the heartwood, is generally not more than 2.5 cm (1 in.) wide. The wood often contains small, sound, black knots that are usually tight and dimensionally stable. Dark streaks are often found in the lumber; these are caused by hemlock bark maggots and generally do not reduce strength. Western hemlock is moderately light in weight and moderate in strength. It is also moderate in hardness, stiffness, and shock resistance. Shrinkage of western hemlock is moderately high, about the same as that of Douglas-fir (*Pseudotsuga menziesii*). Green hemlock lumber contains considerably more water than does Douglas-fir and requires longer kiln-drying time. Mountain hemlock has approximately the same density as that of western hemlock but is somewhat lower in bending strength and stiffness.

Western hemlock and mountain hemlock are used principally for pulpwood, lumber, and plywood. The lumber is used primarily for building material, such as sheathing, siding, subflooring, joists, studding, planking, and rafters, as well as in the manufacture of boxes, pallets, crates, flooring, furniture, and ladders.

Incense-Cedar

Incense-cedar (*Calocedrus decurrens* (synonym *Libocedrus decurrens*)) grows in California, southwestern Oregon, and extreme western Nevada. Most incense-cedar lumber comes from the northern half of California.

Sapwood of incense-cedar is white or cream colored, and heartwood is light brown, often tinged with red. The wood has a fine, uniform texture and a spicy odor. Incense-cedar is light in weight, moderately low in strength, soft, low in shock resistance, and low in stiffness. It has low shrinkage and is easy to dry, with little checking or warping.

Incense-cedar is used principally for lumber and fence posts. Nearly all the high-grade lumber is used for pencils and venetian blinds; some is used for chests and toys. Much incense-cedar wood is more or less pecky; that is, it contains pockets or areas of disintegrated wood caused by advanced stages of localized decay in the living tree. There is no further development of decay once the lumber is dried. This low-quality lumber is used locally for rough construction where low cost and decay resistance are important. Because of its resistance to decay, incense-cedar is well suited for fence posts. Other uses are railroad crossties, poles, and split shingles.

Larch, Western

Western larch (*Larix occidentalis*) grows in western Montana, northern Idaho, northeastern Oregon, and on the eastern slope of the Cascade Mountains in Washington. About two-thirds of the lumber of this species is produced in Idaho and Montana and one-third in Oregon and Washington.

The heartwood of western larch is yellowish brown and the sapwood, yellowish white. The sapwood is generally not more than 2.5 cm (1 in.) wide. The wood is stiff, moderately strong and hard, moderately high in shock resistance, and moderately heavy. It has moderately high shrinkage. The wood is usually straight grained, splits easily, and is subject to ring shake. Knots are common but generally small and tight.

Western larch is used mainly for rough dimension wood in building construction, small timbers, planks and boards, and railroad crossties and mine timbers. It is used also for piles, poles, and posts. Some high-grade material is manufactured into interior woodwork, flooring, sashes, and doors. The properties of western larch are similar to those of Douglas-fir (*Pseudotsuga menziesii*), and these species are sometimes sold mixed.

Pine, Eastern White

Eastern white pine (*Pinus strobus*) grows from Maine to northern Georgia and in the Great Lake States. It is also known as white pine, northern white pine, Weymouth pine, and soft pine. About one-half the production of eastern white pine lumber occurs in New England, about one-third in the Great Lake States, and most of the remainder in the Middle Atlantic and South Atlantic States.

The heartwood of eastern white pine is light brown, often with a reddish tinge. It turns darker on exposure to air. The wood has comparatively uniform texture and is straight grained. It is easily kiln dried, has low shrinkage, and ranks high in stability. It is also easy to work and can be readily glued. Eastern white pine is lightweight, moderately soft, moderately low in strength, low in shock resistance, and low in stiffness.

Practically all eastern white pine is converted into lumber, which is used in a great variety of ways. A large proportion, mostly second-growth knotty wood or lower grades, is used for structural lumber. High-grade lumber is used for patterns for castings. Other important uses are sashes, doors, furniture, interior woodwork, knotty paneling, caskets, shade and map rollers, and toys.

Pine, Jack

Jack pine (*Pinus banksiana*), sometimes known as scrub, gray, and black pine in the United States, grows naturally in the Great Lake States and in a few scattered areas in New England and northern New York. Jack pine lumber is sometimes not separated from the other pines with which it grows, including red pine (*Pinus resinosa*) and eastern white pine (*Pinus strobus*).

Sapwood of jack pine is nearly white; heartwood is light brown to orange. Sapwood may constitute one-half or more of the volume of a tree. The wood has a rather coarse texture and is somewhat resinous. It is moderately lightweight, moderately low in bending strength and compressive strength, moderately low in shock resistance, and low in stiffness. It also has moderately low shrinkage. Lumber from jack pine is generally knotty.

Jack pine is used for pulpwood, box lumber, and pallets. Less important uses include railroad crossties, mine timber, slack cooperage, poles, posts, and fuel.

Pine, Jeffrey (see Pine, Ponderosa)

Pine, Lodgepole

Lodgepole pine (*Pinus contorta*), also known as knotty, black, and spruce pine, grows in the Rocky Mountain and Pacific Coast regions as far northward as Alaska. Wood for lumber and other products is produced primarily in the central Rocky Mountain States; other producing regions are Idaho, Montana, Oregon, and Washington.

The heartwood of lodgepole pine varies from light yellow to light yellow-brown. The sapwood is yellow or nearly white. The wood is generally straight grained with narrow growth rings. The wood is moderately lightweight, is fairly easy to work, and has moderately high shrinkage. It is moderately low in strength, moderately soft, moderately stiff, and moderately low in shock resistance.

Lodgepole pine is used for lumber, mine timbers, railroad crossties, and poles. Less important uses include posts and fuel. Lodgepole pine is being used increasingly for framing, siding, millwork, flooring, and cabin logs.

Pine, Pitch

Pitch pine (*Pinus rigida*) grows from Maine along the mountains to eastern Tennessee and northern Georgia.

The heartwood is brownish red and resinous; the sapwood is wide and light yellow. The wood of pitch pine is moderately heavy to heavy, moderately strong, stiff, and hard, and moderately high in shock resistance. Shrinkage ranges from moderately low to moderately high.

Pitch pine is used for lumber, fuel, and pulpwood. The lumber is classified as a minor species in grading rules for the Southern Pine species group.

Pine, Pond

Pond pine (*Pinus serotina*) grows in the coastal region from New Jersey to Florida. It occurs in small groups or singly, mixed with other pines on low flats.

Sapwood of pond pine is wide and pale yellow; heartwood is dark orange. The wood is heavy, coarse grained, and resinous. Shrinkage is moderately high. The wood is moderately strong, stiff, moderately hard, and moderately high in shock resistance.

Figure 1–3. Ponderosa pine (*Pinus ponderosa*) growing in an open or park-like habitat.

Pond pine is used for general construction, railway crossties, posts, and poles. The lumber of this species is also graded as a minor species in grading rules for the Southern Pine species group.

Pine, Ponderosa

Ponderosa pine (*Pinus ponderosa*) is also known as ponderosa, western soft, western yellow, bull, and blackjack pine. Jeffrey pine (*P. jeffreyi*), which grows in close association with ponderosa pine in California and Oregon, is usually marketed with ponderosa pine and sold under that name. Major ponderosa pine producing areas are in Oregon, Washington, and California (Fig. 1–3). Other important producing areas are in Idaho and Montana; lesser amounts come from the southern Rocky Mountain region, the Black Hills of South Dakota, and Wyoming.

The heartwood of ponderosa pine is light reddish brown, and the wide sapwood is nearly white to pale yellow. The wood of the outer portions of ponderosa pine of sawtimber size is generally moderately light in weight, moderately low in strength, moderately soft, moderately stiff, and moderately low in shock resistance. It is generally straight grained and has moderately low shrinkage. It is quite uniform in texture and has little tendency to warp and twist.

Ponderosa pine is used mainly for lumber and to a lesser extent for piles, poles, posts, mine timbers, veneer, and railroad crossties. The clear wood is used for sashes, doors, blinds, moulding, paneling, interior woodwork, and built-in cases and cabinets. Low-grade lumber is used for boxes and crates. Much intermediate- or low-grade lumber is used for sheathing, subflooring, and roof boards. Knotty ponderosa pine is used for interior woodwork.

Pine, Red

Red pine (*Pinus resinosa*) is frequently called Norway pine and occasionally known as hard pine and pitch pine. This species grows in New England, New York, Pennsylvania, and the Great Lake States.

The heartwood of red pine varies from pale red to reddish brown. The sapwood is nearly white with a yellowish tinge and is generally from 5 to 10 cm (2 to 4 in.) wide. The wood resembles the lighter weight wood of the Southern Pine species group. Latewood is distinct in the growth rings. Red pine is moderately heavy, moderately strong and stiff, moderately soft, and moderately high in shock resistance. It is generally straight grained, not as uniform in texture as eastern white pine (*Pinus strobus*), and somewhat resinous. The wood has moderately high shrinkage, but it is not difficult to dry and is dimensionally stable when dried.

Red pine is used principally for lumber, cabin logs, and pulpwood, and to a lesser extent for piles, poles, posts, and fuel. The lumber is used for many of the same purposes as for eastern white pine (*Pinus strobus*). Red pine lumber is used primarily for building construction, including treated lumber for decking, siding, flooring, sashes, doors, general mill-work, and boxes, pallets, and crates.

Pine, Southern

A number of species are included in the group marketed as Southern Pine lumber. The four major Southern Pine species and their growth ranges are as follows: (a) longleaf pine (*Pinus palustris*), eastern North Carolina southward into Florida and westward into eastern Texas; (b) shortleaf pine (*P. echinata*), southeastern New York and New Jersey southward to northern Florida and westward into eastern Texas and Oklahoma; (c) loblolly pine (*P. taeda*), Maryland southward through the Atlantic Coastal Plain and Piedmont Plateau into Florida and westward into eastern Texas; (d) slash pine (*P. elliottii*), Florida and southern South Carolina, Georgia, Alabama, Mississippi, and Louisiana east of the Mississippi River. Lumber from these four species is classified as Southern Pine by the grading standards of the industry. These standards also classify lumber produced from the longleaf and slash pine species as longleaf pine if the lumber conforms to the growth-ring and latewood require-ments of such standards. Southern Pine lumber is produced principally in the Southern and South Atlantic States. Geor-gia, Alabama, North Carolina, Arkansas, and Louisiana lead in Southern Pine lumber production.

The wood of these southern pines is quite similar in appear-ance. Sapwood is yellowish white and heartwood, reddish brown. The sapwood is usually wide in second-growth stands. The heartwood begins to form when the tree is about 20 years old. In old, slow-growth trees, sapwood may be only 2 to 5 cm (1 to 2 in.) wide.

Longleaf and slash pine are classified as heavy, strong, stiff, hard, and moderately high in shock resistance. Shortleaf and loblolly pine are usually somewhat lighter in weight than is longleaf. All the southern pines have moderately high shrinkage but are dimensionally stable when properly dried. To obtain heavy, strong wood of the southern pines for structural purposes, a density rule has been written that specifies a certain percentage of latewood and growth rates for structural timbers.

The denser and higher strength southern pines are exten-sively used in the form of stringers in construction of facto-ries, warehouses, bridges, trestles, and docks, and also for roof trusses, beams, posts, joists, and piles. Lumber of lower density and strength is also used for building material, such as interior woodwork, sheathing, and subflooring, as well as boxes, pallets, and crates. Southern Pine is used also for tight and slack cooperage. When used for railroad crossties, piles, poles, mine timbers, and exterior decking, it is usually treated with preservatives. The manufacture of structural-grade plywood from Southern Pine is a major wood-using industry, as is the production of preservative-treated lumber.

Pine, Spruce

Spruce pine (*Pinus glabra*), also known as cedar, poor, Walter, and bottom white pine, is classified as a minor species in the Southern Pine species group. Spruce pine grows most commonly on low moist lands of the coastal regions of southeastern South Carolina, Georgia, Alabama, Mississippi, and Louisiana, and northern and northwestern Florida.

The heartwood of spruce pine is light brown, and the wide sapwood is nearly white. Spruce pine wood is lower in most strength values than the wood of the major Southern Pine species group. Spruce pine compares favorably with the western true firs in important bending properties, crushing strength (perpendicular and parallel to grain), and hardness. It is similar to denser species such as coast Douglas-fir (*Pseudotsuga menziesii*) and loblolly pine (*Pinus taeda*) in shear parallel to grain.

In the past, spruce pine was principally used locally for lumber, pulpwood, and fuelwood. The lumber reportedly was used for sashes, doors, and interior woodwork because of its low specific gravity and similarity of earlywood and latewood. In recent years, spruce pine has been used for plywood.

Pine, Sugar

Sugar pine (*Pinus lambertiana*), the world's largest species of pine, is sometimes called California sugar pine. Most sugar pine lumber grows in California and southwestern Oregon.

The heartwood of sugar pine is buff or light brown, some-times tinged with red. The sapwood is creamy white. The wood is straight grained, fairly uniform in texture, and easy to work with tools. It has very low shrinkage, is readily dried without warping or checking, and is dimensionally stable. Sugar pine is lightweight, moderately low in strength, moderately soft, low in shock resistance, and low in stiffness.

Sugar pine is used almost exclusively for lumber products. The largest volume is used for boxes and crates, sashes, doors, frames, blinds, general millwork, building construction, and foundry patterns. Like eastern white pine (*Pinus strobus*), sugar pine is suitable for use in nearly every part of a house because of the ease with which it can be cut, its dimensional stability, and its good nailing properties.

Pine, Virginia

Virginia pine (*Pinus virginiana*), also known as Jersey and scrub pine, grows from New Jersey and Virginia throughout the Appalachian region to Georgia and the Ohio Valley. It is classified as a minor species in the grading rules for the Southern Pine species group.

The heartwood is orange, and the sapwood is nearly white and relatively wide. The wood is moderately heavy, moderately strong, moderately hard, and moderately stiff and has moderately high shrinkage and high shock resistance.

Virginia pine is used for lumber, railroad crossties, mine timbers, and pulpwood.

Pine, Western White

Western white pine (*Pinus monticola*) is also known as Idaho white pine or white pine. About four-fifths of the wood for lumber from this species is from Idaho and Washington; small amounts are cut in Montana and Oregon.

The heartwood of western white pine is cream colored to light reddish brown and darkens on exposure to air. The sapwood is yellowish white and generally from 2 to 8 cm (1 to 3 in.) wide. The wood is straight grained, easy to work, easily kiln-dried, and stable after drying. This species is moderately lightweight, moderately low in strength, moderately soft, moderately stiff, and moderately low in shock resistance and has moderately high shrinkage.

Practically all western white pine is sawn into lumber, which is used mainly for building construction, matches, boxes, patterns, and millwork products, such as sashes and door frames. In building construction, lower-grade boards are used for sheathing, knotty paneling, and subflooring. High-grade material is made into siding of various kinds, exterior and interior woodwork, and millwork. Western white pine has practically the same uses as eastern white pine (*Pinus strobus*) and sugar pine (*Pinus lambertiana*).

Port-Orford-Cedar

Port-Orford-cedar (*Chamaecyparis lawsoniana*) is sometimes known as Lawson-cypress, Oregon-cedar, and white-cedar. It grows along the Pacific Coast from Coos Bay, Oregon, southward to California. It does not extend more than 64 km (40 mi) inland.

The heartwood of Port-Orford-cedar is light yellow to pale brown. The sapwood is narrow and hard to distinguish from the heartwood. The wood has fine texture, generally straight grain, and a pleasant spicy odor. It is moderately light-

weight, stiff, moderately strong and hard, and moderately resistant to shock. Port-Orford-cedar heartwood is highly resistant to decay. The wood shrinks moderately, has little tendency to warp, and is stable after drying.

Some high-grade Port-Orford-cedar was once used in the manufacture of storage battery separators, matchsticks, and specialty millwork. Today, other uses are archery supplies, sash and door construction, stadium seats, flooring, interior woodwork, furniture, and boats.

Redcedar, Eastern

Eastern redcedar (*Juniperus virginiana*) grows throughout the eastern half of the United States, except in Maine, Florida, and a narrow strip along the Gulf Coast, and at the higher elevations in the Appalachian Mountain Range. Commercial production is principally in the southern Appalachian and Cumberland Mountain regions. Another species, southern redcedar (*J. silicicola*), grows over a limited area in the South Atlantic and Gulf Coastal Plains.

The heartwood of redcedar is bright or dull red, and the narrow sapwood is nearly white. The wood is moderately heavy, moderately low in strength, hard, and high in shock resistance, but low in stiffness. It has very low shrinkage and is dimensionally stable after drying. The texture is fine and uniform, and the wood commonly has numerous small knots. Eastern redcedar heartwood is very resistant to decay.

The greatest quantity of eastern redcedar is used for fence posts. Lumber is manufactured into chests, wardrobes, and closet lining. Other uses include flooring, novelties, pencils, scientific instruments, and small boats. Southern redcedar is used for the same purposes. Eastern redcedar is reputed to repel moths, but this claim has not been supported by research.

Redcedar, Western

Western redcedar (*Thuja plicata*) grows in the Pacific Northwest and along the Pacific Coast to Alaska. It is also called canoe-cedar, giant arborvitae, shinglewood, and Pacific redcedar. Western redcedar lumber is produced principally in Washington, followed by Oregon, Idaho, and Montana.

The heartwood of western redcedar is reddish or pinkish brown to dull brown, and the sapwood is nearly white. The sapwood is narrow, often not more than 2.5 cm (1 in.) wide. The wood is generally straight grained and has a uniform but rather coarse texture. It has very low shrinkage. This species is lightweight, moderately soft, low in strength when used as a beam or posts, and low in shock resistance. The heartwood is very resistant to decay.

Western redcedar is used principally for shingles, lumber, poles, posts, and piles. The lumber is used for exterior siding, decking, interior woodwork, greenhouse construction, ship and boat building, boxes and crates, sashes, and doors.

Redwood

Redwood (*Sequoia sempervirens*) grows on the coast of California and some trees are among the tallest in the world. A closely related species, giant sequoia (*Sequoiadendron giganteum*), is volumetrically larger and grows in a limited area in the Sierra Nevadas of California, but its wood is used in very limited quantities. Other names for redwood are coast redwood, California redwood, and sequoia. Production of redwood lumber is limited to California, but the market is nationwide.

The heartwood of redwood varies from light "cherry" red to dark mahogany. The narrow sapwood is almost white. Typical old-growth redwood is moderately lightweight, moderately strong and stiff, and moderately hard. The wood is easy to work, generally straight grained, and shrinks and swells comparatively little. The heartwood from old-growth trees has high decay resistance; heartwood from second-growth trees generally has low to moderate decay resistance.

Most redwood lumber is used for building. It is remanufactured extensively into siding, sashes, doors, blinds, millwork, casket stock, and containers. Because of its durability, redwood is useful for cooling towers, decking, tanks, silos, wood-stave pipe, and outdoor furniture. It is used in agriculture for buildings and equipment. Its use as timbers and large dimension in bridges and trestles is relatively minor. Redwood splits readily and plays an important role in the manufacture of split products, such as posts and fence material. Some redwood veneer is produced for decorative plywood.

Spruce, Eastern

The term eastern spruce includes three species: red (*Picea rubens*), white (*P. glauca*), and black (*P. mariana*). White and black spruce grow principally in the Great Lake States and New England, and red spruce grows in New England and the Appalachian Mountains.

The wood is light in color, and there is little difference between heartwood and sapwood. All three species have about the same properties, and they are not distinguished from each other in commerce. The wood dries easily and is stable after drying, is moderately lightweight and easily worked, has moderate shrinkage, and is moderately strong, stiff, tough, and hard.

The greatest use of eastern spruce is for pulpwood. Eastern spruce lumber is used for framing material, general millwork, boxes and crates, and piano sounding boards.

Spruce, Engelmann

Engelmann spruce (*Picea engelmannii*) grows at high elevations in the Rocky Mountain region of the United States. This species is also known as white spruce, mountain spruce, Arizona spruce, silver spruce, and balsam. About two-thirds of the lumber is produced in the southern Rocky Mountain States and most of the remainder in the northern Rocky Mountain States and Oregon.

The heartwood of Engelmann spruce is nearly white, with a slight tinge of red. The sapwood varies from 2 to 5 cm (3/4 to 2 in.) in width and is often difficult to distinguish from the heartwood. The wood has medium to fine texture and is without characteristic odor. Engelmann spruce is rated as lightweight, and it is low in strength as a beam or post. It is also soft and low in stiffness, shock resistance, and shrinkage. The lumber typically contains many small knots.

Engelmann spruce is used principally for lumber and for mine timbers, railroad crossties, and poles. It is used also in building construction in the form of dimension lumber, flooring, and sheathing. It has excellent properties for pulp and papermaking.

Spruce, Sitka

Sitka spruce (*Picea sitchensis*) is a large tree that grows along the northwestern coast of North America from California to Alaska. It is also known as yellow, tideland, western, silver, and west coast spruce. Much Sitka spruce timber is grown in Alaska, but most logs are sawn into cants for export to Pacific Rim countries. Material for U.S. consumption is produced primarily in Washington and Oregon.

The heartwood of Sitka spruce is a light pinkish brown. The sapwood is creamy white and shades gradually into the heartwood; the sapwood may be 7 to 15 cm (3 to 6 in.) wide or even wider in young trees. The wood has a comparatively fine, uniform texture, generally straight grain, and no distinct taste or odor. It is moderately lightweight, moderately low in bending and compressive strength, moderately stiff, moderately soft, and moderately low in resistance to shock. It has moderately low shrinkage. On the basis of weight, Sitka spruce rates high in strength properties and can be obtained in long, clear, straight-grained pieces.

Sitka spruce is used principally for lumber, pulpwood, and cooperage. Boxes and crates account for a considerable amount of the remanufactured lumber. Other important uses are furniture, planing-mill products, sashes, doors, blinds, millwork, and boats. Sitka spruce has been by far the most important wood for aircraft construction. Other specialty uses are ladder rails and sounding boards for pianos.

Tamarack

Tamarack (*Larix laricina*), also known as eastern larch and locally as hackmatack, is a small to medium tree with a straight, round, slightly tapered trunk. It grows from Maine to Minnesota, with the bulk of the stand in the Great Lake States.

The heartwood of tamarack is yellowish brown to russet brown. The sapwood is whitish, generally less than 2.5 cm (1 in.) wide. The wood is coarse in texture, without odor or taste, and the transition from earlywood to latewood is abrupt. The wood is intermediate in weight and in most mechanical properties.

Tamarack is used principally for pulpwood, lumber, railroad crossties, mine timbers, fuel, fence posts, and poles. Lumber is used for framing material, tank construction, and boxes, pallets, and crates. The production of tamarack lumber has declined in recent years.

White-Cedar, Northern and Atlantic

Two species of white-cedar grow in the eastern part of the United States: northern white-cedar (*Thuja occidentalis*) and Atlantic white-cedar (*Chamaecyparis thyoides*). Northern white-cedar is also known as arborvitae or simply as cedar. Atlantic white-cedar is also known as southern white-cedar, swamp-cedar, and boat-cedar. Northern white-cedar grows from Maine along the Appalachians and westward through the northern part of the Great Lake States. Atlantic white-cedar grows near the Atlantic Coast from Maine to northern Florida and westward along the Gulf Coast to Louisiana. It is strictly a swamp tree. Production of northern white-cedar lumber is greatest in Maine and the Great Lake States. Production of Atlantic white-cedar centers in North Carolina and along the Gulf Coast.

The heartwood of white-cedar is light brown, and the sapwood is white or nearly so. The sapwood is usually narrow. The wood is lightweight, rather soft, and low in strength and shock resistance. It shrinks little in drying. It is easily worked and holds paint well, and the heartwood is highly resistant to decay. Northern and Atlantic white-cedar are used for similar purposes, primarily for poles, cabin logs, railroad crossties, lumber, posts, and decorative fencing. White-cedar lumber is used principally where a high degree of durability is needed, as in tanks and boats, and for wooden ware.

Yellow-Cedar

Yellow-cedar (*Chamaecyparis nootkatensis*) grows in the Pacific Coast region of North America from southeastern Alaska southward through Washington to southern Oregon.

The heartwood of yellow-cedar is bright, clear yellow. The sapwood is narrow, white to yellowish, and hardly distinguishable from the heartwood. The wood is fine textured and generally straight grained. It is moderately heavy, moderately strong and stiff, moderately hard, and moderately high in shock resistance. Yellow-cedar shrinks little in drying and is stable after drying, and the heartwood is very resistant to decay. The wood has a mild, distinctive odor.

Yellow-cedar is used for interior woodwork, furniture, small boats, cabinetwork, and novelties.

Imported Woods

This section does not purport to describe all the woods that have been at one time or another imported into the United States. It includes only those species that at present are considered to be commercially important. The same species may be marketed in the United States under other common names. Because of the variation in common names, many cross-references are included. Text information is necessarily brief, but when used in conjunction with the shrinkage and strength data tables (Ch. 3 and 4), a reasonably good picture may be obtained of a particular wood. The references at the end of this chapter contain information on many species not described in this section.

Hardwoods

Afara (see Limba)

Afrormosia

Afrormosia or kokrodua (*Pericopsis elata*), a large West African tree, is sometimes used as a substitute for teak (*Tectona grandis*).

The heartwood is fine textured, with straight to interlocked grain. The wood is brownish yellow with darker streaks and moderately hard and heavy, weighing about 700 kg/m^3 (43 lb/ft^3) at 15% moisture content. The wood strongly resembles teak in appearance but lacks its oily nature and has a different texture. The wood dries readily with little degrade and has good dimensional stability. It is somewhat heavier and stronger than teak. The heartwood is highly resistant to decay fungi and termite attack and is extremely durable under adverse conditions.

Afrormosia is often used for the same purposes as teak, such as boat construction, joinery, flooring, furniture, interior woodwork, and decorative veneer.

Albarco

Albarco, or jequitiba as it is known in Brazil, is the common name applied to species in the genus *Cariniana*. The 10 species are distributed from eastern Peru and northern Bolivia through central Brazil to Venezuela and Colombia.

The heartwood is reddish or purplish brown and sometimes has dark streaks. It is usually not sharply demarcated from the pale brown sapwood. The texture is medium and the grain straight to interlocked. Albarco can be worked satisfactorily with only slight blunting of tool cutting edges because of the presence of silica. Veneer can be cut without difficulty. The wood is rather strong and moderately heavy, weighing about 560 kg/m^3 (35 lb/ft^3) at 12% moisture content. In general, the wood has about the same strength as that of U.S. oaks (*Quercus* spp.). The heartwood is durable, particularly the deeply colored material. It has good resistance to drywood termite attack.

Albarco is primarily used for general construction and carpentry wood, but it can also be used for furniture components, shipbuilding, flooring, veneer for plywood, and turnery.

Amaranth (see Purpleheart)

Anani (see Manni)

Anaura (see Marishballi)

Andiroba

Because of the widespread distribution of andiroba (*Carapa guianensis*) in tropical America, the wood is known under a variety of names, including cedro macho, carapa, crabwood, and tangare. These names are also applied to the related species *Carapa nicaraguensis*, whose properties are generally inferior to those of *C. guianensis*.

The heartwood varies from medium to dark reddish brown. The texture is like that of true mahogany (*Swietenia macrophylla*), and andiroba is sometimes substituted for true mahogany. The grain is usually interlocked but is rated easy to work, paint, and glue. The wood is rated as durable to very durable with respect to decay and insects. Andiroba is heavier than true mahogany and accordingly is markedly superior in all static bending properties, compression parallel to grain, hardness, shear, and durability.

On the basis of its properties, andiroba appears to be suited for such uses as flooring, frame construction in the tropics, furniture and cabinetwork, millwork, utility and decorative veneer, and plywood.

Angelin (see Sucupira)

Angelique

Angelique (*Dicorynia guianensis*) comes from French Guiana and Suriname.

Because of the variability in heartwood color between different trees, two forms are commonly recognized by producers. The heartwood that is russet-colored when freshly cut and becomes superficially dull brown with a purplish cast is referred to as "gris." The heartwood that is more distinctly reddish and frequently shows wide purplish bands is called "angelique rouge." The texture of the wood is somewhat coarser than that of black walnut (*Juglans nigra*), and the grain is generally straight or slightly interlocked. In strength, angelique is superior to teak (*Tectona grandis*) and white oak (*Quercus alba*), when green or air dry, in all properties except tension perpendicular to grain. Angelique is rated as highly resistant to decay and resistant to marine borer attack. Machining properties vary and may be due to differences in density, moisture content, and silica content. After the wood is thoroughly air or kiln dried, it can be worked effectively only with carbide-tipped tools.

The strength and durability of angelique make it especially suitable for heavy construction, harbor installations, bridges, heavy planking for pier and platform decking, and railroad bridge ties. The wood is also suitable for ship decking, planking, boat frames, industrial flooring, and parquet blocks and strips.

Apa (see Wallaba)

Apamate (see Roble)

Apitong (see Keruing)

Avodire

Avodire (*Turraeanthus africanus*) has a rather extensive range in Africa, from Sierra Leone westward to the Congo region and southward to Zaire and Angola. It is most common in the eastern region of the Ivory Coast and is scattered elsewhere. Avodire is a medium-size tree of the rainforest where it forms fairly dense but localized and discontinuous timber stands.

The wood is cream to pale yellow with high natural luster; it eventually darkens to a golden yellow. The grain is sometimes straight but more often wavy or irregularly interlocked, which produces an unusual and attractive mottled figure when sliced or cut on the quarter. Although avodire weighs less than northern red oak (*Quercus rubra*), it has almost identical strength properties except that it is lower in shock resistance and shear. The wood works fairly easily with hand and machine tools and finishes well in most operations.

Figured material is usually converted into veneer for use in decorative work, and it is this kind of material that is chiefly imported into the United States. Other uses include furniture, fine joinery, cabinetwork, and paneling.

Azobe (Ekki)

Azobe or ekki (*Lophira alata*) is found in West Africa and extends into the Congo basin.

The heartwood is dark red, chocolate-brown, or purple–brown with conspicuous white deposits in the pores (vessels). The texture is coarse, and the grain is usually interlocked. The wood is strong, and its density averages about 1,120 kg/m³ (70 lb/ft³) at 12% moisture content. It is very difficult to work with hand and machine tools, and tools are severely blunted if the wood is machined when dry. Azobe can be dressed to a smooth finish, and gluing properties are usually good. Drying is very difficult without excessive degrade. The heartwood is rated as very durable against decay but only moderately resistant to termite attack. Azobe is very resistant to acid and has good weathering properties. It is also resistant to teredo attack. The heartwood is extremely resistant to preservative treatment.

Azobe is excellent for heavy construction work, harbor construction, heavy-duty flooring, and railroad crossties.

Bagtikan (see Seraya, White)

Balata

Balata or bulletwood (*Manilkara bidentata*) is widely distributed throughout the West Indies, Central America, and northern South America.

The heartwood of balata is light to dark reddish brown and not sharply demarcated from the pale brown sapwood. Texture is fine and uniform, and the grain is straight to occasionally wavy or interlocked. Balata is a strong and very heavy wood; density of air-dried wood is 1,060 kg/m³ (66 lb/ft³). It is generally difficult to air dry, with a tendency to develop severe checking and warp. The wood is moderately easy to work despite its high density, and it is rated good to excellent in all machining operations. Balata is very resistant to attack by decay fungi and highly resistant to subterranean termites but only moderately resistant to dry-wood termites.

Balata is suitable for heavy construction, textile and pulpmill equipment, furniture parts, turnery, tool handles, flooring, boat frames and other bentwork, railroad crossties, violin bows, billiard cues, and other specialty uses.

Balau

Balau, red balau, and selangan batu constitute a group of species that are the heaviest of the 200 *Shorea* species. About 45 species of this group grow from Sri Lanka and southern India through southeast Asia to the Philippines.

The heartwood is light to deep red or purple–brown, and it is fairly distinct from the lighter and yellowish- to reddish- or purplish-brown sapwood. The texture is moderately fine to coarse, and the grain is often interlocked. The wood weighs more than 750 kg/m^3 (47 lb/ft^3) at 12% moisture content. Balau is a heavy, hard, and strong timber that dries slowly with moderate to severe end checks and splits. The heartwood is durable to moderately durable and very resistant to preservative treatments.

Balau is used for heavy construction, frames of boats, decking, flooring, and utility furniture.

Balau, Red (see Balau)

Balsa

Balsa (*Ochroma pyramidale*) is widely distributed throughout tropical America from southern Mexico to southern Brazil and Bolivia, but Ecuador has been the principal source of supply since the wood gained commercial importance. It is usually found at lower elevations, especially on bottomland soils along streams and in clearings and cutover forests. Today, it is often cultivated in plantations.

Several characteristics make balsa suitable for a wide variety of uses. It is the lightest and softest of all woods on the market. The lumber selected for use in the United States weighs, on the average, about 180 kg/m^3 (11 lb/ft^3) when dry and often as little as 100 kg/m^3 (6 lb/ft^3). The wood is readily recognized by its light weight; nearly white or oatmeal color, often with a yellowish or pinkish hue; and unique velvety feel.

Because of its light weight and exceedingly porous composition, balsa is highly efficient in uses where buoyancy, insulation against heat or cold, or low propagation of sound and vibration are important. Principal uses are for life-saving equipment, floats, rafts, corestock, insulation, cushioning, sound modifiers, models, and novelties.

Banak (Cuangare)

Various species of banak (*Virola*) occur in tropical America, from Belize and Guatemala southward to Venezuela, the Guianas, the Amazon region of northern Brazil, and southern Brazil, and on the Pacific Coast to Peru and Bolivia. Most of the wood known as banak is *V. koschnyi* of Central America and *V. surinamensis* and *V. sebifera* of northern South America. Botanically, cuangare (*Dialyanthera*) is closely related to banak, and the woods are so similar that they are

generally mixed in the trade. The main commercial supply of cuangare comes from Colombia and Ecuador. Banak and cuangare are common in swamp and marsh forests and may occur in almost pure stands in some areas.

The heartwood of both banak and cuangare is usually pinkish or grayish brown and is generally not differentiated from the sapwood. The wood is straight grained and is of a medium to coarse texture. The various species are nonresistant to decay and insect attack but can be readily treated with preservatives. Machining properties are very good, but when zones of tension wood are present, machining may result in surface fuzziness. The wood finishes readily and is easily glued. Strength properties of banak and cuangare are similar to those of yellow-poplar (*Liriodendron tulipifera*).

Banak is considered a general utility wood for lumber, veneer, and plywood. It is also used for moulding, millwork, and furniture components.

Benge (Ehie, Bubinga)

Although benge (*Guibourtia arnoldiana*), ehie or ovangkol (*Guibourtia ehie*), and bubinga (*Guibourtia* spp.) belong to the same West African genus, they differ rather markedly in color and somewhat in texture.

The heartwood of benge is pale yellowish brown to medium brown with gray to almost black stripes. Ehie heartwood tends to be more golden brown to dark brown with gray to almost black stripes. Bubinga heartwood is pink, vivid red, or red–brown with purple streaks, and it becomes yellow or medium brown with a reddish tint upon exposure to air. The texture of ehie is moderately coarse, whereas that of benge and bubinga is fine to moderately fine. All three woods are moderately hard and heavy, but they can be worked well with hand and machine tools. They are listed as moderately durable and resistant to preservative treatment. Drying may be difficult, but with care, the wood dries well.

These woods are used in turnery, flooring, furniture components, cabinetwork, and decorative veneers.

Brown Silverballi (see Kaneelhart)

Bubinga (see Benge)

Bulletwood (see Balata)

Carapa (see Andiroba)

Cativo

Cativo (*Prioria copaifera*) is one of the few tropical American species that occur in abundance and often in nearly pure stands. Commercial stands are found in Nicaragua, Costa Rica, Panama, and Colombia.

Sapwood may be very pale pink or distinctly reddish, and it is usually wide. In trees up to 76 cm (30 in.) in diameter, heartwood may be only 18 cm (7 in.) in diameter. The grain is straight and the texture of the wood is uniform, comparable with that of true mahogany (*Swietenia macrophylla*). On flat-sawn surfaces, the figure is rather subdued as a result of exposure of the narrow bands of parenchyma tissue. The wood can be dried rapidly and easily with very little degrade. Dimensional stability is very good—practically equal to that of true mahogany. Cativo is classified as a nondurable wood with respect to decay and insects. It may contain appreciable quantities of gum. In wood that has been properly dried, however, the aromatics in the gum are removed and there is no difficulty in finishing.

Considerable quantities of cativo are used for interior woodwork, and resin-stabilized veneer is an important pattern material. Cativo is widely used for furniture and cabinet parts, lumber core for plywood, picture frames, edge banding for doors, joinery, and millwork.

Cedro (see Spanish-Cedar)

Cedro Macho (see Andiroba)

Cedro-Rana (see Tornillo)

Ceiba

Ceiba (*Ceiba pentandra*) is a large tree, which grows to 66 m (200 ft) in height with a straight cylindrical bole 13 to 20 m (40 to 60 ft) long. Trunk diameters of 2 m (6 ft) or more are common. Ceiba grows in West Africa, from the Ivory Coast and Sierra Leone to Liberia, Nigeria, and the Congo region. A related species is lupuna (*Ceiba samauma*) from South America.

Sapwood and heartwood are not clearly demarcated. The wood is whitish, pale brown, or pinkish brown, often with yellowish or grayish streaks. The texture is coarse, and the grain is interlocked or occasionally irregular. Ceiba is very soft and light; density of air-dried wood is 320 kg/m³ (20 lb/ft³). In strength, the wood is comparable with basswood (*Tilia americana*). Ceiba dries rapidly without marked deterioration. It is difficult to saw cleanly and dress smoothly because of the high percentage of tension wood. It provides good veneer and is easy to nail and glue. Ceiba is very susceptible to attack by decay fungi and insects. It requires rapid harvest and conversion to prevent deterioration. Treatability, however, is rated as good.

Ceiba is available in large sizes, and its low density combined with a rather high degree of dimensional stability make it ideal for pattern and corestock. Other uses include blockboard, boxes and crates, joinery, and furniture components.

Chewstick (see Manni)

Courbaril (Jatoba)

The genus *Hymenaea* consists of about 25 species that occur in the West Indies and from southern Mexico through Central America into the Amazon basin of South America. The best-known and most important species is *H. courbaril*, which occurs throughout the range of the genus. Courbaril is often called jatoba in Brazil.

Sapwood of courbaril is gray–white and usually quite wide. The heartwood, which is sharply differentiated from the sapwood, is salmon red to orange–brown when freshly cut and becomes russet or reddish brown when dried. The heartwood is often marked with dark streaks. The texture is medium to rather coarse, and the grain is mostly interlocked. The wood is hard and heavy (about 800 kg/m³ (50 lb/ft³) at 12% moisture content). The strength properties of courbaril are quite high and very similar to those of shagbark hickory (*Carya ovata*), a species of lower specific gravity. Courbaril is rated as moderately to very resistant to attack by decay fungi and dry-wood termites. The heartwood is not treatable, but the sapwood is treatable with preservatives. Courbaril is moderately difficult to saw and machine because of its high density, but it can be machined to a smooth surface. Turning, gluing, and finishing properties are satisfactory. Planing, however, is somewhat difficult because of the interlocked grain. Courbaril compares favorably with white oak (*Quercus alba*) in steam bending behavior.

Courbaril is used for tool handles and other applications that require good shock resistance. It is also used for steam-bent parts, flooring, turnery, furniture and cabinetwork, veneer and plywood, railroad crossties, and other specialty items.

Crabwood (see Andiroba)

Cristobal (see Macawood)

Cuangare (see Banak)

Degame

Degame or lemonwood (*Calycophyllum candidissimum*) grows in Cuba and ranges from southern Mexico through Central America to Colombia and Venezuela. It may grow in pure stands and is common on shaded hillsides and along waterways.

The heartwood of degame ranges from light brown to oatmeal-colored and is sometimes grayish. The sapwood is lighter in color and merges gradually with the heartwood. The texture is fine and uniform. The grain is usually straight or infrequently shows shallow interlocking, which may produce a narrow and indistinct stripe on quartered faces. In strength, degame is above the average for woods of similar density; density of air-dried wood is 817 kg/m³ (51 lb/ft³). Tests show degame superior to persimmon (*Diospyros virginiana*) in all respects but hardness. Natural durability is low when degame is used under conditions favorable to stain, decay, and insect attack. However, degame is reported to be highly resistant to marine borers. Degame is moderately difficult to machine because of its density and hardness, although it does not dull cutting tools to any extent. Machined surfaces are very smooth.

Degame is little used in the United States, but its characteristics have made it particularly adaptable for shuttles, picker sticks, and other textile industry items that require resilience and strength. Degame was once prized for the manufacture of archery bows and fishing rods. It is also suitable for tool handles and turnery.

Determma

Determa (*Ocotea rubra*) is native to the Guianas, Trinidad, and the lower Amazon region of Brazil.

The heartwood is light reddish brown with a golden sheen and distinct from the dull gray or pale yellowish brown sapwood. The texture is rather coarse, and the grain is interlocked to straight. Determa is a moderately strong and heavy wood (density of air-dried wood is 640 to 720 kg/m^3 (40 to 45 lb/ft^3)); this wood is moderately difficult to air dry. It can be worked readily with hand and machine tools with little dulling effect. It can be glued readily and polished fairly well. The heartwood is durable to very durable in resistance to decay fungi and moderately resistant to dry-wood termites. Weathering characteristics are excellent, and the wood is highly resistant to moisture absorption.

Uses for determa include furniture, general construction, boat planking, tanks and cooperage, heavy marine construction, turnery, and parquet flooring.

Ehie (see Benge)

Ekki (see Azobe)

Ekop

Ekop or gola (*Tetraberlinia tubmaniana*) grows only in Liberia.

The heartwood is light reddish brown and is distinct from the lighter colored sapwood, which may be up to 5 cm (2 in.) wide. The wood is medium to coarse textured, and the grain is interlocked, with a narrow striped pattern on quartered surfaces. The wood weighs about 735 kg/m^3 (46 lb/ft^3) at 12% moisture content. It dries fairly well but with a marked tendency to end and surface checks. Ekop works well with hand and machine tools and is an excellent wood for turnery. It also slices well into veneer and has good gluing properties. The heartwood is only moderately durable and is moderately resistant to impregnation with preservative treatments.

Ekop is a general utility wood that is used for veneer, plywood, and furniture components.

Encino (see Oak)

Gola (see Ekop)

Goncalo Alves

Most imports of goncalo alves (*Astronium graveolens* and *A. fraxinifolium*) have been from Brazil. These species range from southern Mexico through Central America into the Amazon basin.

Freshly cut heartwood is russet brown, orange–brown, or reddish brown to red with narrow to wide, irregular, medium- to very-dark brown stripes. After exposure to air, the heartwood becomes brown, red, or dark reddish brown with nearly black stripes. The sapwood is grayish white and sharply demarcated from the heartwood. The texture is fine to medium and uniform. The grain varies from straight to interlocked and wavy.

Goncalo alves turns readily, finishes very smoothly, and takes a high natural polish. The heartwood is highly resistant to moisture absorption; pigmented areas may present some difficulties in gluing because of their high density. The heartwood is very durable and resistant to both white- and brown-rot organisms. The high density (1,010 kg/m^3 (63 lb/ft^3)) of the air-dried wood is accompanied by equally high strength values, which are considerably higher in most respects than those of any U.S. species. Despite its strength, however, goncalo alves is imported primarily for its beauty.

In the United States, goncalo alves has the greatest value for specialty items such as archery bows, billiard cue butts, brushbacks, and cutlery handles, and in turnery and carving applications.

Greenheart

Greenheart (*Chlorocardium rodiei* [= *Ocotea rodiei*]) is essentially a Guyana tree although small stands also occur in Suriname.

The heartwood varies from light to dark olive green or nearly black. The texture is fine and uniform, and the grain is straight to wavy. Greenheart is stronger and stiffer than white oak (*Quercus alba*) and generally more difficult to work with tools because of its high density; density of air-dried wood is more than 960 kg/m^3 (60 lb/ft^3). The heartwood is rated as very resistant to decay fungi and termites. It is also very resistant to marine borers in temperate waters but much less so in warm tropical waters.

Greenheart is used principally where strength and resistance to wear are required. Uses include ship and dock building, lock gates, wharves, piers, jetties, vats, piling, planking, industrial flooring, bridges, and some specialty items (fishing rods and billiard cue butts).

Guatambu (see Pau Marfim)

Guayacan (see Ipe)

Hura

Hura (*Hura crepitans*) grows throughout the West Indies from Central America to northern Brazil and Bolivia.

It is a large tree, commonly reaching a height of 30 to 43 m (90 to 130 ft), with clear boles of 12 to 23 m (40 to 75 ft). The diameter often reaches 1 to 1.5 m (3 to 5 ft) and occasionally to 3 m (9 ft).

The pale yellowish-brown or pale olive-gray heartwood is indistinct from the yellowish-white sapwood. The texture is fine to medium and the grain straight to interlocked. Hura is a low-strength and low-density wood (density of air-dried wood is 240 to 448 kg/m^3 (15 to 28 lb/ft^3)); the wood is moderately difficult to air dry. Warping is variable and sometimes severe. The wood usually machines easily, but green material is somewhat difficult to work because of tension wood, which results in a fuzzy surface. The wood finishes well and is easy to glue and nail. Hura is variable in resistance to attack by decay fungi, but it is highly susceptible to blue stain and very susceptible to wood termites. However, the wood is easy to treat with preservative.

Hura is often used in general carpentry, boxes and crates, and lower grade furniture. Other important uses are veneer and plywood, fiberboard, and particleboard.

Ilomba

Ilomba (*Pycnanthus angolensis*) is a tree of the rainforest and ranges from Guinea and Sierra Leone through tropical West Africa to Uganda and Angola. Common names include pycnanthus, walele, and otie.

The wood is grayish white to pinkish brown and, in some trees, a uniform light brown. There is generally no distinction between heartwood and sapwood. The texture is medium to coarse, and the grain is generally straight. This species is generally similar to banak (*Virola*) but has a coarser texture. Air-dry density is about 512 kg/m³ (31 lb/ft³), and the wood is about as strong as yellow-poplar (*Liriodendron tulipifera*). Ilomba dries rapidly but is prone to collapse, warp, and splits. It is easily sawn and can be worked well with hand and machine tools. It is excellent for veneer and has good gluing and nailing characteristics. Green wood is subject to insect and fungal attack. Logs require rapid extraction and conversion to avoid degrade. Both sapwood and heartwood are permeable and can be treated with preservatives.

In the United States, this species is used only in the form of plywood for general utility purposes. However, ilomba is definitely suited for furniture components, interior joinery, and general utility purposes.

Ipe

Ipe, the common name for the lapacho group of the genus *Tabebuia*, consists of about 20 species of trees and occurs in practically every Latin America country except Chile. Other commonly used names are guayacan and lapacho.

Sapwood is relatively wide, yellowish gray or gray–brown, and sharply differentiated from heartwood, which is light to dark olive brown. The texture is fine to medium. The grain is straight to very irregular and often narrowly interlocked. The wood is very heavy and averages about 1,025 kg/m³ (64 lb/ft³) at 12% moisture content. Thoroughly air-dried heartwood specimens generally sink in water. Because of its high density and hardness, ipe is moderately difficult to machine, but glassy smooth surfaces can be produced. Ipe is very strong; in the air-dried condition, it is comparable with greenheart (*Chlorocardium rodiei*). Hardness is two to three times that of white oak (*Quercus alba*) or keruing (*Dipterocarpus*). The wood is highly resistant to decay and insects, including both subterranean and dry-wood termites, but susceptible to marine borer attack. The heartwood is impermeable, but the sapwood can be readily treated with preservatives.

Ipe is used almost exclusively for heavy-duty and durable construction. Because of its hardness and good dimensional stability, it is particularly well suited for heavy-duty flooring in trucks and boxcars. It is also used for decks, railroad crossties, turnery, tool handles, decorative veneers, and some specialty items in textile mills.

Ipil (see Merbau)

Iroko

Iroko consists of two species (*Milicia excelsa* [= *Chlorophora excelsa*] and *M. regia* [= *C. regia*]). *Milicia excelsa* grows across the entire width of tropical Africa from the Ivory Coast southward to Angola and eastward to East Africa. *Milicia regia*, however, is limited to extreme West Africa from Gambia to Ghana; it is less resistant to drought than is *M. excelsa*.

The heartwood varies from a pale yellowish brown to dark chocolate brown with light markings occurring most conspicuously on flat-sawn surfaces; the sapwood is yellowish white. The texture is medium to coarse, and the grain is typically interlocked. Iroko can be worked easily with hand or machine tools but with some tearing of interlocked grain. Occasional deposits of calcium carbonate severely damage cutting edges. The wood dries rapidly with little or no degrade. The strength is similar to that of red maple (*Acer rubrum*), and the weight is about 688 kg/m³ (43 lb/ft³) at 12% moisture content. The heartwood is very resistant to decay fungi and resistant to termite and marine borer attack.

Because of its color and durability, iroko has been suggested as a substitute for teak (*Tectona grandis*). Its durability makes it suitable for boat building, piles, other marine work, and railroad crossties. Other uses include joinery, flooring, furniture, veneer, and cabinetwork.

Jacaranda (see Rosewood, Brazilian)

Jarrah

Jarrah (*Eucalyptus marginata*) is native to the coastal belt of southwestern Australia and is one of the principal species for that country's sawmill industry.

The heartwood is a uniform pink to dark red, often turning to deep brownish red with age and exposure to air. The sapwood is pale and usually very narrow in old trees. The texture is even and moderately coarse, and the grain is frequently interlocked or wavy. The wood weighs about 865 kg/m³ (54 lb/ft³) at 12% moisture content. The common defects of jarrah include gum veins or pockets, which in extreme instances, separate the log into concentric shells. Jarrah is a heavy, hard timber possessing correspondingly high strength properties. It is resistant to attack by termites and rated as very durable with respect to decay. The wood is difficult to work with hand and machine tools because of its high density and irregular grain.

Jarrah is used for decking and underframing of piers, jetties, and bridges, as well as piles and fenders for docks and harbors. As flooring, jarrah has high resistance to wear, but it is inclined to splinter under heavy traffic. It is also used for railroad crossties and other heavy construction.

Jatoba (see Courbaril)

Jelutong

Jelutong (*Dyera costulata*) is an important species in Malaysia where it is best known for its latex production in the manufacture of chewing gum rather than for its wood.

The wood is white or straw colored, and there is no differentiation between heartwood and sapwood. The texture is moderately fine and even. The grain is straight, and luster is low. The wood weighs about 465 kg/m³ (28 lb/ft³) at 12% moisture content. The wood is very easy to dry with little tendency to split or warp, but staining may cause trouble. It is easy to work in all operations, finishes well, and glues satisfactorily. The wood is rated as nondurable but readily permeable to preservatives.

Because of its low density and ease of working, jelutong is well suited for sculpture and pattern making, wooden shoes, picture frames, and drawing boards.

Jequitiba (see Albarco)

Kakaralli (see Manbarklak)

Kaneelhart

Kaneelhart or brown silverballi are names applied to the genus *Licaria*. Species of this genus grow mostly in New Guinea and Papau New Guinea and are found in association with greenheart (*Chlorocardium rodiei*) on hilly terrain and wallaba (*Eperua*) in forests.

The orange or brownish yellow heartwood darkens to yellowish or coffee brown on exposure to air. The wood is sometimes tinged with red or violet. The texture is fine to medium, and the grain is straight to slightly interlocked. The wood has a fragrant odor, which is lost in drying. Kaneelhart is a very strong and very heavy wood (density of air-dried wood is 833 to 1,153 kg/m³ (52 to 72 lb/ft³)); the wood is difficult to work. It cuts smoothly and takes an excellent finish but requires care in gluing. Kaneelhart has excellent resistance to both brown- and white-rot fungi and is also rated very high in resistance to dry-wood termites.

Uses of kaneelhart include furniture, turnery, boat building, heavy construction, and parquet flooring.

Kapur

The genus *Dryobalanops* consists of nine species distributed over parts of Malaysia and Indonesia. For the export trade, the species are combined under the name kapur.

The heartwood is reddish brown and clearly demarcated from the pale sapwood. The wood is fairly coarse textured but uniform. In general, the wood resembles keruing (*Dipterocarpus*), but on the whole, kapur is straighter grained and not quite as coarse in texture. Density of the wood averages about 720 to 800 kg/m³ (45 to 50 lb/ft³) at 12% moisture

content. Strength properties are similar to those of keruing at comparable specific gravity. The heartwood is rated resistant to attack by decay fungi; it is reported to be vulnerable to termites. Kapur is extremely resistant to preservative treatment. The wood works with moderate ease in most hand and machine operations, but blunting of cutters may be severe because of silica content, particularly when the dry wood is machined. A good surface can be obtained from various machining operations, but there is a tendency toward raised grain if dull cutters are used. Kapur takes nails and screws satisfactorily. The wood glues well with urea formaldehyde but not with phenolic adhesives.

Kapur provides good and very durable construction wood and is suitable for all purposes for which keruing (*Dipterocarpus*) is used in the United States. In addition, kapur is extensively used in plywood either alone or with species of *Shorea* (lauan–meranti).

Karri

Karri (*Eucalyptus diversicolor*) is a very large tree limited to southwestern Australia.

Karri resembles jarrah (*E. marginata*) in structure and general appearance. It is usually paler in color and, on average, slightly heavier (913 kg/m³ (57 lb/ft³)) at 12% moisture content. Karri is a heavy hardwood with mechanical properties of a correspondingly high order, even somewhat higher than that of jarrah. The heartwood is rated as moderately durable, though less so than that of jarrah. It is extremely difficult to treat with preservatives. The wood is fairly hard to machine and difficult to cut with hand tools. It is generally more resistant to cutting than is jarrah and has a slightly more dulling effect on tool edges.

Karri is inferior to jarrah for underground use and waterworks. However, where flexural strength is required, such as in bridges, floors, rafters, and beams, karri is an excellent wood. Karri is popular in heavy construction because of its strength and availability in large sizes and long lengths that are free of defects.

Kauta (see Marishballi)

Kempas

Kempas (*Koompassia malaccensis*) is distributed throughout the lowland forest in rather swampy areas of Malaysia and Indonesia.

When exposed to air, the freshly cut brick-red heartwood darkens to an orange–red or red–brown with numerous yellow–brown streaks as a result of the soft tissue (axial parenchyma) associated with the pores. The texture is rather coarse, and the grain is typically interlocked. Kempas is a hard, heavy wood (density of air-dried wood is 880 kg/m³ (55 lb/ft³)); the wood is difficult to work with hand and machine tools. The wood dries well, with some tendency to warp and check. The heartwood is resistant to attack by decay fungi but vulnerable to termite activity. However, it treats readily with preservative retention as high as 320 kg/m³ (20 lb/ft³).

Kempas is ideal for heavy construction work, railroad crossties, and flooring.

Keruing (Apitong)

Keruing or apitong (*Dipterocarpus*) is widely scattered throughout the Indo-Malaysian region. Most of the more than 70 species in this genus are marketed under the name keruing. Other important species are marketed as apitong in the Philippine Islands and yang in Thailand.

The heartwood varies from light to dark red–brown or brown to dark brown, sometimes with a purple tint; the heartwood is usually well defined from the gray or buff-colored sapwood. Similar to kapur (*Dryobalanops*), the texture of keruing is moderately coarse and the grain is straight or shallowly interlocked. The wood is strong, hard, and heavy (density of air-dried wood is 720 to 800 kg/m^3 (45 to 50 lb/ft^3)); this wood is characterized by the presence of resin ducts, which occur singly or in short arcs as seen on end-grain surfaces. This resinous condition and the presence of silica can present troublesome problems. Sapwood and heartwood are moderately resistant to preservative treatments. However, the wood should be treated with preservatives when it is used in contact with the ground. Durability varies with species, but the wood is generally classified as moderately durable. Keruing generally takes to sawing and machining, particularly when green, but saws and cutters dull easily as a result of high silica content in the wood. Resin adheres to machinery and tools and may be troublesome. Also, resin may cause gluing and finishing difficulties.

Keruing is used for general construction work, framework for boats, flooring, pallets, chemical processing equipment, veneer and plywood, railroad crossties (if treated), truck floors, and boardwalks.

Khaya (see Mahogany, African)

Kokrodua (see Afrormosia)

Korina (see Limba)

Krabak (see Mersawa)

Kwila (see Merbau)

Lapacho (see Ipe)

Lapuna (see Ceiba)

Lauan (see Meranti Groups)

Lemonwood (see Degame)

Lignumvitae

For many years, the only species of lignumvitae used on a large scale was *Guaiacum officinale*, which is native to the West Indies, northern Venezuela, northern Colombia, and Panama. With the near exhaustion of *G. officinale*, harvesters turned to *G. sanctum*, which is now the principal commercial species. *Guaiacum sanctum* occupies the same range as *G. officinale* but is more extensive and includes the Pacific side of Central America as well as southern Mexico.

Lignumvitae is one of the heaviest and hardest woods on the market. The wood is characterized by its unique green color and oily or waxy feel. The wood has a fine uniform texture and closely interlocked grain. Its resin content may constitute up to one-fourth of the air-dried weight of the heartwood.

Lignumvitae wood is used chiefly for bearing or bushing blocks for ship propeller shafts. The great strength and tenacity of lignumvitae, combined with self-lubricating properties resulting from the high resin content, make it especially adaptable for underwater use. It is also used for such articles as mallets, pulley sheaves, caster wheels, stencil and chisel blocks, and turned products.

Limba

Limba (*Terminalia superba*), also referred to as afara, is widely distributed from Sierra Leone to Angola and Zaire in the rainforest and savanna forest. Limba is also favored as a plantation species in West Africa.

The heartwood varies from gray–white to creamy or yellow brown and may contain dark streaks that are nearly black, producing an attractive figure that is valued for decorative veneer. The light color of the wood is considered an important asset for the manufacture of blond furniture. The wood is generally straight grained and of uniform but coarse texture. The wood is easy to dry and shrinkage is reported to be rather low. Limba is not resistant to decay, insects, or termites. It is easy to work with all types of tools and is made into veneer without difficulty.

Principal uses include plywood, furniture, interior joinery, and sliced decorative veneer.

Macacauba (see Macawood)

Macawood (Trebol)

Macawood and trebol are common names applied to species in the genus *Platymiscium*. Other common names include cristobal and macacauba. This genus is distributed across continental tropical America from southern Mexico to the Brazilian Amazon region and Trinidad.

The bright red to reddish or purplish brown heartwood is more or less striped. Darker specimens look waxy, and the sapwood is sharply demarcated from the heartwood. The texture is medium to fine, and the grain is straight to curly or striped. The wood is not very difficult to work, and it finishes smoothly and takes on a high polish. Generally, macawood air dries slowly with a slight tendency to warp and check. Strength is quite high, and density of air-dried wood ranges from 880 to 1,170 kg/m^3 (55 to 73 lb/ft^3). The heartwood is reported to be highly resistant to attack by decay fungi, insects, and dry-wood termites. Although the sapwood absorbs preservatives well, the heartwood is resistant to treatment.

Macawood is a fine furniture and cabinet wood. It is also used in decorative veneers, musical instruments, turnery, joinery, and specialty items such as violin bows and billiard cues.

Machinmango (see Manbarklak)

Mahogany

The name mahogany is presently applied to several distinct kinds of commercial wood. The original mahogany wood, produced by *Swietenia mahagoni*, came from the American West Indies. This was the premier wood for fine furniture cabinet work and shipbuilding in Europe as early as the 1600s. Because the good reputation associated with the name mahogany is based on this wood, American mahogany is sometimes referred to as true mahogany. A related African wood, of the genus *Khaya*, has long been marketed as "African mahogany" and is used for much the same purposes as American mahogany because of its similar properties and overall appearance. A third kind of wood called mahogany, and the one most commonly encountered in the market, is "Philippine mahogany." This name is applied to a group of Asian woods belonging to the genus *Shorea*. In this chapter, information on the "Philippine mahoganies" is given under lauan and meranti groups.

Mahogany, African—The bulk of "African mahogany" shipped from west–central Africa is *Khaya ivorensis*, the most widely distributed and plentiful species of the genus found in the coastal belt of the so-called high forest. The closely allied species *K. anthotheca* has a more restricted range and is found farther inland in regions of lower rainfall but well within the area now being used for the export trade.

The heartwood varies from pale pink to dark reddish brown. The grain is frequently interlocked, and the texture is medium to coarse, comparable with that of American mahogany (*Swietenia macrophylla*). The wood is easy to dry, but machining properties are rather variable. Nailing and gluing properties are good, and an excellent finish is readily obtained. The wood is easy to slice and peel. In decay resistance, African mahogany is generally rated as moderately durable, which is below the durability rating for American mahogany.

Principal uses for African mahogany include furniture and cabinetwork, interior woodwork, boat construction, and veneer.

Mahogany, American—True, American, or Honduras mahogany (*Swietenia macrophylla*) ranges from southern Mexico through Central America into South America as far south as Bolivia. Plantations have been established within its natural range and elsewhere throughout the tropics.

The heartwood varies from pale pink or salmon colored to dark reddish brown. The grain is generally straighter than that of African mahogany (*Khaya ivorensis*); however, a wide variety of grain patterns are obtained from American mahogany. The texture is rather fine to coarse. American mahogany is easily air or kiln dried without appreciable warp or checks, and it has excellent dimensional stability. It is rated as durable in resistance to decay fungi and moderately resistant to dry-wood termites. Both heartwood and sapwood are resistant to treatment with preservatives. The wood is very easy to work with hand and machine tools, and it slices and rotary cuts into fine veneer without difficulty. It also is easy to finish and takes an excellent polish. The air-dried strength of American mahogany is similar to that of American elm (*Ulmus americana*). Density of air-dried wood varies from 480 to 833 kg/m^3 (30 to 52 lb/ft^3).

The principal uses for mahogany are fine furniture and cabinets, interior woodwork, pattern woodwork, boat construction, fancy veneers, musical instruments, precision instruments, paneling, turnery, carving, and many other uses that call for an attractive and dimensionally stable wood.

Mahogany, Philippine (see Meranti Groups)

Manbarklak

Manbarklak is a common name applied to species in the genus *Eschweilera*. Other names include kakaralli machinmango, and mata–mata. About 80 species of this genus are distributed from eastern Brazil through the Amazon basin, to the Guianas, Trinidad, and Costa Rica.

The heartwood of most species is light, grayish, reddish brown, or brownish buff. The texture is fine and uniform, and the grain is typically straight. Manbarklak is a very hard and heavy wood (density of air-dried wood ranges from 768 to 1,185 kg/m^3 (48 to 74 lb/ft^3)) that is rated as fairly difficult to dry. Most species are difficult to work because of the high density and high silica content. Most species are highly resistant to attack by decay fungi. Also, most species have gained wide recognition for their high degree of resistance to marine borer attack. Resistance to dry-wood termite attack is variable depending on species.

Manbarklak is an ideal wood for marine and other heavy construction uses. It is also used for industrial flooring, mill equipment, railroad crossties, piles, and turnery.

Manni

Manni (*Symphonia globulifera*) is native to the West Indies, Mexico, and Central, North, and South America. It also occurs in tropical West Africa. Other names include ossol (Gabon), anani (Brazil), waika (Africa), and chewstick (Belize), a name acquired because of its use as a primitive toothbrush and flossing tool.

The heartwood is yellowish, grayish, or greenish brown and is distinct from the whitish sapwood. The texture is coarse and the grain straight to irregular. The wood is very easy to work with both hand and machine tools, but surfaces tend to roughen in planing and shaping. Manni air-dries rapidly with only moderate warp and checking. Its strength is similar to that of hickory (*Carya*), and the density of air-dried wood is 704 kg/m^3 (44 lb/ft^3). The heartwood is durable in ground contact but only moderately resistant to dry-wood and subterranean termites. The wood is rated as resistant to treatment with preservatives.

Manni is a general purpose wood that is used for railroad ties, general construction, cooperage, furniture components, flooring, and utility plywood.

Marishballi

Marishballi is the common name applied to species of the genus *Licania*. Other names include kauta and anaura. Species of *Licania* are widely distributed in tropical America but most abundant in the Guianas and the lower Amazon region of Brazil.

The heartwood is generally a yellowish to dark brown, sometimes with a reddish tinge. The texture is fine and close, and the grain is usually straight. Marishballi is strong and very heavy; density of air-dried wood is 833 to 1,153 kg/m^3 (52 to 72 lb/ft^3). The wood is rated as easy to moderately difficult to air dry. Because of its high density and silica content, marishballi is difficult to work. The use of hardened cutters is suggested to obtain smooth surfaces. Durability varies with species, but marishballi is generally considered to have low to moderately low resistance to attack by decay fungi. However, it is known for its high resistance to attack by marine borers. Permeability also varies, but the heartwood is generally moderately responsive to treatment.

Marishballi is ideal for underwater marine construction, heavy construction above ground, and railroad crossties (treated).

Mata–Mata (see Manbarklak)

Mayflower (see Roble)

Melapi (see Meranti Groups)

Meranti Groups

Meranti is a common name applied commercially to four groups of species of *Shorea* from southeast Asia, most commonly Malaysia, Indonesia, and the Philippines. There are thousands of common names for the various species of *Shorea*, but the names Philippine mahogany and lauan are often substituted for meranti. The four groups of meranti are separated on the basis of heartwood color and weight (Table 1–3). About 70 species of *Shorea* belong to the light and dark red meranti groups, 22 species to the white meranti group, and 33 species to the yellow meranti group.

Meranti species as a whole have a coarser texture than that of mahogany (*Swietenia macrophylla*) and do not have dark-colored deposits in pores. The grain is usually interlocked.

All merantis have axial resin ducts aligned in long, continuous, tangential lines as seen on the end surface of the wood. These ducts sometimes contain white deposits that are visible to the naked eye, but the wood is not resinous like some keruing (*Dipterocarpus*) species that resemble meranti. All the meranti groups are machined easily except white meranti, which dulls cutters as a result of high silica content in the wood. The light red and white merantis dry easily without degrade, but dark red and yellow merantis dry more slowly with a tendency to warp. The strength and shrinkage properties of the meranti groups compare favorably with that of northern red oak (*Quercus rubra*). The light red, white, and yellow merantis are not durable in exposed conditions or in ground contact, whereas dark red meranti is moderately durable. Generally, heartwood is extremely resistant to moderately resistant to preservative treatments.

Species of meranti constitute a large percentage of the total hardwood plywood imported into the United States. Other uses include joinery, furniture and cabinetwork, moulding and millwork, flooring, and general construction. Some dark red meranti is used for decking.

Merbau

Merbau (Malaysia), ipil (Philippines), and kwila (New Guinea) are names applied to species of the genus *Intsia*, most commonly *I. bijuga*. *Intsia* is distributed throughout the Indo–Malaysian region, Indonesia, Philippines, and many western Pacific islands, as well as Australia.

Freshly cut yellowish to orange–brown heartwood turns brown or dark red–brown on exposure to air. The texture is rather coarse, and the grain is straight to interlocked or wavy. The strength of air-dried merbau is comparable with that of hickory (*Carya*), but density is somewhat lower (800 kg/m^3 (50 lb/ft^3) at 12% moisture content). The wood dries well with little degrade but stains black in the presence of iron and moisture. Merbau is rather difficult to saw because it sticks to saw teeth and dulls cutting edges. However, the wood dresses smoothly in most operations and finishes well. Merbau has good durability and high resistance to termite attack. The heartwood resists treatment, but the sapwood can be treated with preservatives.

Table 1–3. Woods belonging to *Shorea* and *Parashorea* genera

Name	Color	Density of air-dried wood
Dark red meranti (also called tanguile and dark red seraya)	Dark brown; medium to deep red, sometimes with a purplish tinge	640+ kg/m^3 (40+ lb/ft^3)
Light red meranti (also called red seraya)	Variable—from almost white to pale pink, dark red, pale brown, or deep brown	400 to 640 kg/m^3, averaging 512 kg/m^3 (25 to 40 lb/ft^3, averaging 32 lb/ft^3)
White meranti (also called melapi)	Whitish when freshly cut, becoming light yellow-brown on exposure to air	480 to 870 kg/m^3 (30 to 54 lb/ft^3)
Yellow meranti (also called yellow seraya)	Light yellow or yellow-brown, sometimes with a greenish tinge; darkens on exposure to air	480 to 640 kg/m^3 (30 to 40 lb/ft^3)

Merbau is used in furniture, fine joinery, turnery, cabinets, flooring, musical instruments, and specialty items.

Mersawa

Mersawa is one of the common names applied to the genus *Anisoptera*, which has about 15 species distributed from the Philippine Islands and Malaysia to east Pakistan. Names applied to this wood vary with the source, and three names are generally used in the lumber trade: krabak (Thailand), mersawa (Malaysia), and palosapis (Philippines).

Mersawa wood is light in color and has a moderately coarse texture. Freshly sawn heartwood is pale yellow or yellowish brown and darkens on exposure to air. Some wood may show a pinkish cast or pink streaks, but these eventually disappear on exposure to air. The wood weighs between 544 and 752 kg/m^3 (34 and 47 lb/ft^3) at 12% moisture content and about 945 kg/m^3 (59 lb/ft^3) when green. The sapwood is susceptible to attack by powderpost beetles, and the heartwood is not resistant to termites. The heartwood is rated as moderately resistant to fungal decay and should not be used under conditions that favor decay. The heartwood does not absorb preservative solutions readily. The wood machines easily, but because of the presence of silica, the wood severely dulls the cutting edges of ordinary tools and is very hard on saws.

The major volume of mersawa will probably be used as plywood because conversion in this form presents considerably less difficulty than does the production of lumber.

Mora

Mora (*Mora excelsa* and *M. gonggrijpii*) is widely distributed in the Guianas and also occurs in the Orinoco Delta of Venezuela.

The yellowish red–brown, reddish brown, or dark red heartwood with pale streaks is distinct from the yellowish to pale brown sapwood. The texture is moderately fine to rather coarse, and the grain is straight to interlocked. Mora is a strong and heavy wood (density of air-dried wood is 945 to 1,040 kg/m^3 (59 to 65 lb/ft^3)); this wood is moderately difficult to work but yields smooth surfaces in sawing, planing, turning, and boring. The wood is generally rated as moderately difficult to dry. Mora is rated as durable to very durable in resistance to brown- and white-rot fungi. *Mora gonggrijpii* is rated very resistant to dry-wood termites, but *M. excelsa* is considerably less resistant. The sapwood responds readily to preservative treatments, but the heartwood resists treatment.

Mora is used for industrial flooring, railroad crossties, shipbuilding, and heavy construction.

Oak (Tropical)

The oaks (*Quercus*) are abundantly represented in Mexico and Central America with about 150 species, which are nearly equally divided between the red and white oak groups. More than 100 species occur in Mexico and about 25 in Guatemala; the number diminishes southward to Colombia, which has two species. The usual Spanish name applied to the oaks is encino or roble, and both names are used interchangeably irrespective of species or use of the wood.

In heartwood color, texture, and grain characteristics, tropical oaks are similar to the oaks in the United States, especially live oak (*Quercus virginiana*). In most cases, tropical oaks are heavier (density of air-dried wood is 704 to 993 kg/m^3 (44 to 62 lb/ft^3)) than the U.S. species. Strength data are available for only four species, and the values fall between those of white oak (*Q. alba*) and live oak (*Q. virginiana*) or are equal to those of live oak. Average specific gravity for the tropical oaks is 0.72 based on volume when green and ovendry weight, with an observed maximum average of 0.86 for one species from Guatemala. The heartwood is rated as very resistant to decay fungi and difficult to treat with preservatives.

Utilization of the tropical oaks is very limited at present because of difficulties encountered in the drying of the wood. The major volume is used in the form of charcoal, but the wood is used for flooring, railroad crossties, mine timbers, tight cooperage, boat and ship construction, and decorative veneers.

Obeche

Obeche (*Triplochiton scleroxylon*) trees of west–central Africa reach a height of 50 m (150 ft) or more and a diameter of up to 2 m (5 ft). The trunk is usually free of branches for a considerable height so that clear lumber of considerable size can be obtained.

The wood is creamy white to pale yellow with little or no difference between sapwood and heartwood. The wood is fairly soft, of uniform medium to coarse texture, and the grain is usually interlocked but sometimes straight. Air-dry wood weighs about 385 kg/m^3 (24 lb/ft^3). Obeche dries readily with little degrade. It is not resistant to decay, and green sapwood is subject to blue stain. The wood is easy to work and machine, veneers and glues well, and takes nails and screws without splitting.

The characteristics of obeche make it especially suitable for veneer and corestock. Other uses include furniture, components, millwork, blockboard, boxes and crates, particleboard and fiberboard, patterns, and artificial limbs.

Ofram (see Limba)

Okoume

The natural distribution of okoume (*Aucoumea klaineana*) is rather restricted; the species is found only in west–central Africa and Guinea. However, okoume is extensively planted throughout its natural range.

The heartwood is salmon-pink in color, and the narrow sapwood is whitish or pale gray. The wood has a high luster and uniform texture. The texture is slightly coarser than that of birch (*Betula*). The nondurable heartwood dries readily with little degrade. Sawn lumber is somewhat difficult to machine because of the silica content, but the wood glues, nails, and peels into veneer easily. Okoume offers unusual flexibility in finishing because the color, which is of medium intensity, permits toning to either lighter or darker shades.

In the United States, okoume is generally used for decorative plywood paneling, general utility plywood, and doors. Other uses include furniture components, joinery, and light construction.

Opepe

Opepe (*Nauclea diderrichii*) is widely distributed in Africa from Sierra Leone to the Congo region and eastward to Uganda. It is often found in pure stands.

The orange or golden yellow heartwood darkens on exposure to air and is clearly defined from the whitish or pale yellow sapwood. The texture is rather coarse, and the grain is usually interlocked or irregular. The density of air-dried wood (752 kg/m^3 (47 lb/ft^3)) is about the same as that of true hickory (*Carya*), but strength properties are somewhat lower. Quartersawn stock dries rapidly with little checking or warp, but flat-sawn lumber may develop considerable degrade. The wood works moderately well with hand and machine tools. It also glues and finishes satisfactorily. The heartwood is rated as very resistant to decay and moderately resistant to termite attacks. The sapwood is permeable to preservatives, but the heartwood is moderately resistant to preservative treatment.

Opepe is a general construction wood that is used in dock and marine work, boat building, railroad crossties, flooring, and furniture.

Ossol (see Manni)

Otie (see Ilomba)

Ovangkol (see Benge)

Palosapis (see Mersawa)

Para–Angelim (see Sucupira)

Pau Marfim

The range of pau marfim (*Balfourodendron riedelianum*) is rather limited, extending from the State of Sao Paulo, Brazil, into Paraguay and the provinces of Corrientes and Missiones of northern Argentina. In Brazil, it is generally known as pau marfim and in Argentina and Paraguay, as guatambu.

In color and general appearance, pau marfim wood is very similar to birch (*Betula*) or sugar maple (*Acer saccharum*) sapwood. Although growth rings are present, they do not show as distinctly as those in birch and maple. There is no apparent difference in color between heartwood and sapwood. The wood is straight grained and easy to work and finish, but it is not considered resistant to decay. In Brazil, average specific gravity of pau marfim is about 0.73 based on volume of green wood and ovendry weight. Average density of air-dried wood is about 802 kg/m^3 (50 lb/ft^3). On the basis of

specific gravity, strength values are higher than those of sugar maple, which has an average specific gravity of 0.56.

In its areas of growth, pau marfim is used for much the same purposes as are sugar maple and birch in the United States. Introduced to the U.S. market in the late 1960s, pau marfim has been very well received and is especially esteemed for turnery.

Peroba, White (see Peroba de Campos)

Peroba de Campos

Peroba de campos (*Paratecoma peroba*), also referred to as white peroba, grows in the coastal forests of eastern Brazil, ranging from Bahia to Rio de Janeiro. It is the only species in the genus *Paratecoma*.

The heartwood varies in color but is generally shades of brown with tendencies toward olive and red. The sapwood is a yellowish gray and is clearly defined from the heartwood. The texture is relatively fine and approximates that of birch (*Betula*). The grain is commonly interlocked, with a narrow stripe or wavy figure. The wood machines easily; however, particular care must be taken in planing to prevent excessive grain tearing of quartered surfaces. There is some evidence that the fine dust from machining operations may produce allergic responses in certain individuals. Density of air-dried wood averages about 738 kg/m^3 (46 lb/ft^3). Peroba de campos is heavier than teak (*Tectona grandis*) or white oak (*Quercus alba*), and it is proportionately stronger than either of these species. The heartwood of peroba de campos is rated as very durable with respect to decay and difficult to treat with preservatives.

In Brazil, peroba de campos is used in the manufacture of fine furniture, flooring, and decorative paneling. The principal use in the United States is shipbuilding, where peroba de campos serves as substitute for white oak (*Quercus alba*) for all purposes except bent members.

Peroba Rosa

Peroba rosa is the common name applied to a number of similar species in the genus *Aspidosperma*. These species occur in southeastern Brazil and parts of Argentina.

The heartwood is a distinctive rose-red to yellowish, often variegated or streaked with purple or brown, and becomes brownish yellow to dark brown upon exposure to air; the heartwood is often not demarcated from the yellowish sapwood. The texture is fine and uniform, and the grain is straight to irregular. The wood is moderately heavy; weight of air-dried wood is 752 kg/m^3 (47 lb/ft^3). Strength properties are comparable with those of U.S. oak (*Quercus*). The wood dries with little checking or splitting. It works with moderate ease, and it glues and finishes satisfactorily. The heartwood is resistant to decay fungi but susceptible to dry-wood termite attack. Although the sapwood takes preservative treatment moderately well, the heartwood resists treatment.

Peroba is suited for general construction work and is favored for fine furniture and cabinetwork and decorative veneers. Other uses include flooring, interior woodwork, sashes and doors, and turnery.

Pilon

The two main species of pilon are *Hyeronima alchorneoides* and *H. laxiflora*, also referred to as suradan. These species range from southern Mexico to southern Brazil including the Guianas, Peru, and Colombia. Pilon species are also found throughout the West Indies.

The heartwood is a light reddish brown to chocolate brown or sometimes dark red; the sapwood is pinkish white. The texture is moderately coarse and the grain interlocked. The wood air-dries rapidly with only a moderate amount of warp and checking. It has good working properties in all operations except planing, which is rated poor as a result of the characteristic interlocked grain. The strength of pilon is comparable with that of true hickory (*Carya*), and the density of air-dried wood ranges from 736 to 849 kg/m^3 (46 to 53 lb/ft^3). Pilon is rated moderately to very durable in ground contact and resistant to moderately resistant to subterranean and dry-wood termites. Both heartwood and sapwood are reported to be treatable with preservatives by both open tank and pressure vacuum processes.

Pilon is especially suited for heavy construction, railway crossties, marinework, and flooring. It is also used for furniture, cabinetwork, decorative veneers, turnery, and joinery.

Piquia

Piquia is the common name generally applied to species in the genus *Caryocar*. This genus is distributed from Costa Rica southward into northern Colombia and from the upland forest of the Amazon valley to eastern Brazil and the Guianas.

The yellowish to light grayish brown heartwood is hardly distinguishable from the sapwood. The texture is medium to rather coarse, and the grain is generally interlocked. The wood dries at a slow rate; warping and checking may develop, but only to a minor extent. Piquia is reported to be easy to moderately difficult to saw; cutting edges dull rapidly. The heartwood is very durable and resistant to decay fungi and dry-wood termites but only moderately resistant to marine borers.

Piquia is recommended for general and marine construction, heavy flooring, railway crossties, boat parts, and furniture components. It is especially suitable where hardness and high wear resistance are needed.

Primavera

The natural distribution of primavera (*Tabebuia donnell–smithii* [=*Cybistax donnell-smithii*]) is restricted to southwestern Mexico, the Pacific coast of Guatemala and El Salvador, and north-central Honduras. Primavera is regarded as one of the primary light-colored woods, but its use has been limited because of its rather restricted range and relative scarcity of naturally grown trees. Recent plantations have increased the availability of this species and have provided a more constant source of supply. The quality of the plantation-grown wood is equal in all respects to the wood obtained from naturally grown trees.

The heartwood is whitish to straw-yellow, and in some logs, it may be tinted with pale brown or pinkish streaks. The texture is medium to rather coarse, and the grain is straight to wavy, which produces a wide variety of figure patterns. The wood also has a very high luster. Shrinkage is rather low, and the wood shows a high degree of dimensional stability. Despite considerable grain variation, primavera machines remarkably well. The density of air-dried wood is 465 kg/m^3 (29 lb/ft^3), and the wood is comparable in strength with water tupelo (*Nyssa aquatica*). Resistance to both brown- and white-rot fungi varies. Weathering characteristics are good.

The dimensional stability, ease of working, and pleasing appearance make primavera a suitable choice for solid furniture, paneling, interior woodwork, and special exterior uses.

Purpleheart

Purpleheart, also referred to as amaranth, is the name applied to species in the genus *Peltogyne*. The center of distribution is in the north-central part of the Brazilian Amazon region, but the combined range of all species is from Mexico through Central America and southward to southern Brazil.

Freshly cut heartwood is brown. It turns a deep purple upon exposure to air and eventually dark brown upon exposure to light. The texture is medium to fine, and the grain is usually straight. This strong and heavy wood (density of air-dried wood is 800 to 1,057 kg/m^3 (50 to 66 lb/ft^3)) is rated as easy to moderately difficult to air dry. It is moderately difficult to work with using either hand or machine tools, and it dulls cutters rather quickly. Gummy resin exudes when the wood is heated by dull tools. A slow feed rate and specially hardened cutters are suggested for optimal cutting. The wood turns easily, is easy to glue, and takes finishes well. The heartwood is rated as highly resistant to attack by decay fungi and very resistant to dry-wood termites. It is extremely resistant to treatment with preservatives.

The unusual and unique color of purpleheart makes this wood desirable for turnery, marquetry, cabinets, fine furniture, parquet flooring, and many specialty items, such as billiard cue butts and carvings. Other uses include heavy construction, shipbuilding, and chemical vats.

Pycnanthus (see Ilomba)

Ramin

Ramin (*Gonystylus bancanus*) is native to southeast Asia from the Malaysian Peninsula to Sumatra and Borneo.

Both the heartwood and sapwood are the color of pale straw, yellow, or whitish. The grain is straight or shallowly interlocked. The texture is even, moderately fine, and similar to that of American mahogany (*Swietenia macrophylla*). The wood is without figure or luster. Ramin is moderately hard and heavy, weighing about 672 kg/m³ (42 lb/ft³) in the air-dried condition. The wood is easy to work, finishes well, and glues satisfactorily. Ramin is rated as not resistant to decay but permeable with respect to preservative treatment.

Ramin is used for plywood, interior woodwork, furniture, turnery, joinery, moulding, flooring, dowels, and handles of nonstriking tools (brooms), and as a general utility wood.

Roble

Roble, a species in the roble group of *Tabebuia* (generally *T. rosea*), ranges from southern Mexico through Central America to Venezuela and Ecuador. The name roble comes from the Spanish word for oak (*Quercus*). In addition, *T. rosea* is called roble because the wood superficially resembles U.S. oak. Other names for *T. rosea* are mayflower and apamate.

The sapwood becomes a pale brown upon exposure to air. The heartwood varies from golden brown to dark brown, and it has no distinctive odor or taste. The texture is medium and the grain narrowly interlocked. The wood weighs about 642 kg/m³ (40 lb/ft³) at 12% moisture content. Roble has excellent working properties in all machine operations. It finishes attractively in natural color and takes finishes with good results. It weighs less than the average of U.S. white oaks (*Quercus*) but is comparable with respect to bending and compression parallel to grain. The heartwood of roble is generally rated as moderately to very durable with respect to decay; the darker and heavier wood is regarded as more resistant than the lighter-colored woods.

Roble is used extensively for furniture, interior woodwork, doors, flooring, boat building, ax handles, and general construction. The wood veneers well and produces attractive paneling. For some applications, roble is suggested as a substitute for American white ash (*Fraxinus americana*) and oak (*Quercus*).

Rosewood, Brazilian

Brazilian rosewood (*Dalbergia nigra*), also referred to as jacaranda, occurs in eastern Brazilian forests from the State of Bahia to Rio de Janeiro. Since it was exploited for a long time, Brazilian rosewood is no longer abundant.

The heartwood varies with respect to color, through shades of brown, red, and violet, and it is irregularly and conspicuously streaked with black. It is sharply demarcated from the white sapwood. Many kinds of rosewood are distinguished locally on the basis of prevailing color. The texture is coarse, and the grain is generally straight. The heartwood has an oily or waxy appearance and feel, and its odor is fragrant and distinctive. The wood is hard and heavy (weight of air-dried wood is 752 to 897 kg/m³ (47 to 56 lb/ft³)); thoroughly air-dried wood will barely float in water. Strength properties of Brazilian rosewood are high and are more than adequate for the purposes for which this wood is used.

For example, Brazilian rosewood is harder than any U.S. native hardwood species used for furniture and veneer. The wood machines and veneers well. It can be glued satisfactorily, provided the necessary precautions are taken to ensure good glue bonds, with respect to oily wood. Brazilian rosewood has an excellent reputation for durability with respect to fungal and insect attack, including termites, although the wood is not used for purposes where durability is necessary.

Brazilian rosewood is used primarily in the form of veneer for decorative plywood. Limited quantities are used in the solid form for specialty items such as cutlery handles, brush backs, billiard cue butts, and fancy turnery.

Rosewood, Indian

Indian rosewood (*Dalbergia latifolia*) is native to most provinces of India except in the northwest.

The heartwood varies in color from golden brown to dark purplish brown with denser blackish streaks at the end of growth zones, giving rise to an attractive figure on flat-sawn surfaces. The narrow sapwood is yellowish. The average weight is about 849 kg/m³ (53 lb/ft³) at 12% moisture content. The texture is uniform and moderately coarse. Indian rosewood is quite similar in appearance to Brazilian (*Dalbergia nigra*) and Honduran (*Dalbergia stevensonii*) rosewood. The wood is reported to kiln-dry well though slowly, and the color improves during drying. Indian rosewood is a heavy wood with high strength properties; after drying, it is particularly hard for its weight. The wood is moderately hard to work with hand tools and offers a fair resistance in machine operations. Lumber with calcareous deposits tends to dull tools rapidly. The wood turns well and has high screw-holding properties. If a very smooth surface is required for certain purposes, pores (vessels) may need to be filled.

Indian rosewood is essentially a decorative wood for high-quality furniture and cabinetwork. In the United States, it is used primarily in the form of veneer.

Sande

Practically all commercially available sande (mostly *Brosimum utile*) comes from Pacific Ecuador and Colombia. However, the group of species ranges from the Atlantic Coast in Costa Rica southward to Colombia and Ecuador.

The sapwood and heartwood show no distinction; the wood is uniformly yellowish white to yellowish or light brown. The texture is medium to moderately coarse and even, and the grain can be widely and narrowly interlocked. The density of air-dried wood ranges from 384 to 608 kg/m³ (24 to 38 lb/ft³), and the strength is comparable with that of U.S. oak (*Quercus*). The lumber air dries rapidly with little or no degrade. However, material containing tension wood is subject to warp, and the tension wood may cause fuzzy grain as well as overheating of saws as a result of pinching. The wood is not durable with respect to stain, decay, and insect attack, and care must be exercised to prevent degrade from these agents. The wood stains and finishes easily and presents no gluing problems.

Sande is used for plywood, particleboard, fiberboard, carpentry, light construction, furniture components, and moulding.

Santa Maria

Santa Maria (*Calophyllum brasiliense*) ranges from the West Indies to southern Mexico and southward through Central America into northern South America.

The heartwood is pinkish to brick red or rich reddish brown and marked by fine and slightly darker striping on flat-sawn surfaces. The sapwood is lighter in color and generally distinct from the heartwood. The texture is medium and fairly uniform, and the grain is generally interlocked. The heartwood is rather similar in appearance to dark red meranti (*Shorea*). The wood is moderately easy to work and good surfaces can be obtained when attention is paid to machining operations. The wood averages about 608 kg/m^3 (38 lb/ft^3) at 12% moisture content. Santa Maria is in the density class of sugar maple (*Acer saccharum*), and its strength properties are generally similar; the hardness of sugar maple is superior to that of Santa Maria. The heartwood is generally rated as moderately durable to durable in contact with the ground, but it apparently has no resistance against termites and marine borers.

The inherent natural durability, color, and figure on the quarter-sawn face suggest that Santa Maria could be used as veneer for plywood in boat construction. Other uses are flooring, furniture, cabinetwork, millwork, and decorative plywood.

Sapele

Sapele (*Entandrophragma cylindricum*) is a large African tree that occurs from Sierra Leone to Angola and eastward through the Congo to Uganda.

The heartwood ranges in color from that of American mahogany (*Swietenia macrophylla*) to a dark reddish or purplish brown. The lighter-colored and distinct sapwood may be up to 10 cm (4 in.) wide. The texture is rather fine. The grain is interlocked and produces narrow and uniform striping on quarter-sawn surfaces. The wood averages about 674 kg/m^3 (42 lb/ft^3) at 12% moisture content, and its mechanical properties are in general higher than those of white oak (*Quercus alba*). The wood works fairly easily with machine tools, although the interlocked grain makes it difficult to plane. Sapele finishes and glues well. The heartwood is rated as moderately durable and is resistant to preservative treatment.

As lumber, sapele is used for furniture and cabinetwork, joinery, and flooring. As veneer, it is used for decorative plywood.

Selangan Batu (see Balau)

Sepetir

The name sepetir applies to species in the genus *Sindora* and to *Pseudosindora palustris*. These species are distributed throughout Malaysia, Indochina, and the Philippines.

The heartwood is brown with a pink or golden tinge that darkens on exposure to air. Dark brown or black streaks are sometimes present. The sapwood is light gray, brown, or straw-colored. The texture is moderately fine and even, and the grain is narrowly interlocked. The strength of sepetir is similar to that of shellbark hickory (*Carya laciniosa*), and the density of the air-dried wood is also similar (640 to 720 kg/m^3 (40 to 45 lb/ft^3)). The wood dries well but rather slowly, with a tendency to end-split. The wood is difficult to work with hand tools and has a rather rapid dulling effect on cutters. Gums from the wood tend to accumulate on saw teeth, which causes additional problems. Sepetir is rated as nondurable in ground contact under Malaysian exposure. The heartwood is extremely resistant to preservative treatment; however, the sapwood is only moderately resistant.

Sepetir is a general carpentry wood that is also used for furniture and cabinetwork, joinery, flooring (especially truck flooring), plywood, and decorative veneers.

Seraya, Red and Dark Red (see Meranti Groups)

Seraya, White

White seraya or bagtikan, as it is called in the Philippines, is a name applied to the 14 species of *Parashorea*, which grow in Sabah and the Philippines.

The heartwood is light brown or straw-colored, sometimes with a pinkish tint. The texture is moderately coarse and the grain interlocked. White seraya is very similar in appearance and strength properties to light red meranti, and sometimes the two are mixed in the market. White seraya dries easily with little degrade, and works fairly well with hand and machine tools. The heartwood is not durable to moderately durable in ground contact, and it is extremely resistant to preservative treatments.

White seraya is used for joinery, light construction, moulding and millwork, flooring, plywood, furniture, and cabinet work.

Seraya, Yellow (see Meranti Groups)

Silverballi, Brown (see Kaneelhart)

Spanish-Cedar

Spanish-cedar or cedro consists of a group of about seven species in the genus *Cedrela* that are widely distributed in tropical America from southern Mexico to northern Argentina.

Spanish-cedar is one of only a few tropical species that are ring-porous. The heartwood varies from light to dark reddish brown, and the sapwood is pinkish to white. The texture is rather fine and uniform to coarse and uneven. The grain is not interlocked. The heartwood is characterized by a distinctive odor. The wood dries easily. Although Spanish-cedar is not high in strength, most other properties are similar to those of American mahogany (*Swietenia macrophylla*), except for hardness and compression perpendicular to the grain, where mahogany is definitely superior. Spanish-cedar is considered decay resistant; it works and glues well.

Spanish-cedar is used locally for all purposes that require an easily worked, light but straight grained, and durable wood. In the United States, the wood is favored for millwork, cabinets, fine furniture, boat building, cigar wrappers and boxes, humidores, and decorative and utility plywood.

Sucupira (Angelin, Para-Angelim)

Sucupira, angelin, and para-angelim apply to species in four genera of legumes from South America. Sucupira applies to *Bowdichia nitida* from northern Brazil, *B. virgilioides* from Venezuela, the Guianas, and Brazil, and *Diplotropis purpurea* from the Guianas and southern Brazil. Angelin (*Andira inermis*) is a widespread species that occurs throughout the West Indies and from southern Mexico through Central America to northern South America and Brazil. Para-angelim (*Hymenolobium excelsum*) is generally restricted to Brazil.

The heartwood of sucupira is chocolate-brown, red–brown, or light brown (especially in *Diplotropis purpurea*). Angelin heartwood is yellowish brown to dark reddish brown; para-angelim heartwood turns pale brown upon exposure to air. The sapwood is generally yellowish to whitish and is sharply demarcated from the heartwood. The texture of all three woods is coarse and uneven, and the grain can be interlocked. The density of air-dried wood of these species ranges from 720 to 960 kg/m^3 (45 to 60 lb/ft^3), which makes them generally heavier than true hickory (*Carya*). Their strength properties are also higher than those of true hickory. The heartwood is rated very durable to durable in resistance to decay fungi but only moderately resistant to attack by drywood termites. Angelin is reported to be difficult to treat with preservatives, but para-angelim and sucupira treat adequately. Angelin can be sawn and worked fairly well, except that it is difficult to plane to a smooth surface because of alternating hard (fibers) and soft (parenchyma) tissue. Para-angelim works well in all operations. Sucupira is difficult to moderately difficult to work because of its high density, irregular grain, and coarse texture.

Sucupira, angelin, and para-angelim are ideal for heavy construction, railroad crossties, and other uses that do not require much fabrication. Other suggested uses include flooring, boat building, furniture, turnery, tool handles, and decorative veneer.

Suradan (see Pilon)

Tangare (see Andiroba)

Tanguile (see Lauan–Meranti Groups)

Teak

Teak (*Tectona grandis*) occurs in commercial quantities in India, Burma, Thailand, Laos, Cambodia, North and South Vietnam, and the East Indies. Numerous plantations have been developed within its natural range and in tropical areas of Latin America and Africa, and many of these are now producing teakwood.

The heartwood varies from yellow–brown to dark golden–brown and eventually turns a rich brown upon exposure to air. Teakwood has a coarse uneven texture (ring porous), is usually straight grained, and has a distinctly oily feel. The heartwood has excellent dimensional stability and a very high degree of natural durability. Although teak is not generally used in the United States where strength is of prime importance, its properties are generally on par with those of U.S. oaks (*Quercus*). Teak is generally worked with moderate ease with hand and machine tools. However, the presence of silica often dulls tools. Finishing and gluing are satisfactory, although pretreatment may be necessary to ensure good bonding of finishes and glues.

Teak is one of the most valuable woods, but its use is limited by scarcity and high cost. Because teak does not cause rust or corrosion when in contact with metal, it is extremely useful in the shipbuilding industry, for tanks and vats, and for fixtures that require high acid resistance. Teak is currently used in the construction of boats, furniture, flooring, decorative objects, and decorative veneer.

Tornillo

Tornillo (*Cedrelinga cateniformis*), also referred to as cedrorana, grows in the Loreton Huanuco provinces of Peru and in the humid terra firma of the Brazilian Amazon region. Tornillo can grow up to 52.5 m (160 ft) tall, with trunk diameters of 1.5 to 3 m (5 to 9 ft). Trees in Peru are often smaller in diameter, with merchantable heights of 15 m (45 ft) or more.

The heartwood is pale brown with a golden luster and prominently marked with red vessel lines; the heartwood gradually merges into the lighter-colored sapwood. The texture is coarse. The density of air-dried material collected in Brazil averages 640 kg/m^3 (40 lb/ft^3); for Peruvian stock, average density is about 480 kg/m^3 (30 lb/ft^3). The wood is comparable in strength with American elm (*Ulmus americana*). Tornillo cuts easily and can be finished smoothly, but areas of tension wood may result in woolly surfaces. The heartwood is fairly durable and reported to have good resistance to weathering.

Tornillo is a general construction wood that can be used for furniture components in lower-grade furniture.

Trebol (see Macawood)

Virola (see Banak)

Waika (see Manni)

Walele (see Ilomba)

Wallaba

Wallaba is a common name applied to the species in the genus *Eperua*. Other names include wapa and apa. The center of distribution is in the Guianas, but the species extends into Venezuela and the Amazon region of northern Brazil. Wallaba generally occurs in pure stands or as the dominant tree in the forest.

The heartwood ranges from light to dark red to reddish or purplish brown with characteristically dark, gummy streaks. The texture is rather coarse and the grain typically straight. Wallaba is a hard, heavy wood; density of air-dried wood is 928 kg/m^3 (58 lb/ft^3). Its strength is higher than that of shagbark hickory (*Carya ovata*). The wood dries very slowly with a marked tendency to check, split, and warp. Although the wood has high density, it is easy to work with hand and machine tools. However, the high gum content clogs saw-teeth and cutters. Once the wood has been kiln dried, gum exudates are not a serious problem in machining. The heart-wood is reported to be very durable and resistant to subterra-nean termites and fairly resistant to dry-wood termites.

Wallaba is well suited for heavy construction, railroad crossties, poles, industrial flooring, and tank staves. It is also highly favored for charcoal.

Wapa (see Wallaba)

Yang (see Keruing)

Softwoods

Cypress, Mexican

Native to Mexico and Guatemala, Mexican cypress (*Cupressus lusitanica*) is now widely planted at high elevations throughout the tropical world.

The heartwood is yellowish, pale brown, or pinkish, with occasional streaking or variegation. The texture is fine and uniform, and the grain is usually straight. The wood is fragrantly scented. The density of air-dried wood is 512 kg/m^3 (32 lb/ft^3), and the strength is comparable with that of yellow-cedar (*Chamaecyparis nootkatensis*) or western hemlock (*Tsuga heterophylla*). The wood is easy to work with hand and machine tools, and it nails, stains, and pol-ishes well. Mexican cypress air dries very rapidly with little or no end- or surface-checking. Reports on durability are conflicting. The heartwood is not treatable by the open tank process and seems to have an irregular response to pres-sure–vacuum systems.

Mexican cypress is used mainly for posts and poles, furniture components, and general construction.

Parana Pine

The wood commonly called parana pine (*Araucaria angusti-folia*) is a softwood but not a true pine. It grows in south-eastern Brazil and adjacent areas of Paraguay and Argentina.

Parana pine has many desirable characteristics. It is available in large-size clear boards with uniform texture. The small pinhead knots (leaf traces) that appear on flat-sawn surfaces and the light or reddish-brown heartwood provide a desirable figure for matching in paneling and interior woodwork.

Growth rings are fairly distinct and similar to those of eastern white pine (*Pinus strobus*). The grain is not interlocked, and the wood takes paint well, glues easily, and is free from resin ducts, pitch pockets, and pitch streaks. Density of air-dried wood averages 545 kg/m^3 (34 lb/ft^3). The strength of parana pine compares favorably with that of U.S. softwood species of similar density and, in some cases, approaches that of species with higher density. Parana pine is especially strong in shear strength, hardness, and nail-holding ability, but it is notably deficient in strength in compression across the grain. The tendency of the kiln-dried wood to split and warp is caused by the presence of compression wood, an abnormal type of wood with intrinsically large shrinkage along the grain. Boards containing compression wood should be excluded from exacting uses.

The principal uses of parana pine include framing lumber, interior woodwork, sashes and door stock, furniture case goods, and veneer.

Pine, Caribbean

Caribbean pine (*Pinus caribaea*) occurs along the Caribbean side of Central America from Belize to northeastern Nicaragua. It is also native to the Bahamas and Cuba. This low-elevation tree is widely introduced as a plantation species throughout the world tropics.

The heartwood is golden- to red-brown and distinct from the sapwood, which is light yellow and roughly 2 to 5 cm (1 to 2 in.) wide. This softwood species has a strong resinous odor and a greasy feel. The weight varies considerably and may range from 416 to 817 kg/m^3 (26 to 51 lb/ft^3) at 12% moisture content. Caribbean pine may be appreciably heavier than slash pine (*P. elliottii*), but the mechanical properties of these two species are rather similar. The lumber can be kiln dried satisfactorily. Caribbean pine is easy to work in all machining operations, but its high resin content may cause resin to accumulate on the equipment. Durability and resis-tance to insect attack vary with resin content; in general, the heartwood is rated as moderately durable. The sapwood is highly permeable and is easily treated by open tank or pres-sure–vacuum systems. The heartwood is rated as moderately resistant to preservative treatment, depending on resin content.

Caribbean pine is used for the same purposes as are the southern pines (*Pinus* spp.).

Pine, Ocote

Ocote pine (*Pinus oocarpa*) is a high-elevation species that occurs from northwestern Mexico southward through Guatemala into Nicaragua. The largest and most extensive stands occur in Guatemala, Nicaragua, and Honduras.

The sapwood is a pale yellowish brown and generally up to 7 cm (3 in.) wide. The heartwood is a light reddish brown. The grain is not interlocked. The wood has a resinous odor, and it weighs about 656 kg/m^3 (41 lb/ft^3) at 12% moisture content. The strength properties of ocote pine are comparable in most respects with those of longleaf pine (*P. palustris*).

Decay resistance studies have shown ocote pine heartwood to be very durable with respect to white-rot fungal attack and moderately durable with respect to brown rot.

Ocote pine is comparable with the southern pines (*Pinus*) in workability and machining characteristics. It is a general construction wood suited for the same uses as are the southern pines.

Pine, Radiata

Radiata pine (*Pinus radiata*), also known as Monterey pine, is planted extensively in the southern hemisphere, mainly in Chile, New Zealand, Australia, and South Africa. Plantation-grown trees may reach a height of 26 to 30 m (80 to 90 ft) in 20 years.

The heartwood from plantation-grown trees is light brown to pinkish brown and is distinct from the paler cream-colored sapwood. Growth rings are primarily wide and distinct. False rings may be common. The texture is moderately even and fine, and the grain is not interlocked. Plantation-grown radiata pine averages about 480 kg/m^3 (30 lb/ft^3) at 12% moisture content. Its strength is comparable with that of red pine (*P. resinosa*), although location and growth rate may cause considerable variation in strength properties. The wood air or kiln dries rapidly with little degrade. The wood machines easily although the grain tends to tear around large knots. Radiata pine nails and glues easily, and it takes paint and finishes well. The sapwood is prone to attack by stain fungi and vulnerable to boring insects. However, plantation-grown stock is mostly sapwood, which treats readily with preservatives. The heartwood is rated as durable above ground and is moderately resistant to preservative treatment.

Radiata pine can be used for the same purposes as are the other pines grown in the United States. These uses include veneer, plywood, pulp, fiberboard, construction, boxes, and millwork.

References

Alden, H.A. 1995. Hardwoods of North America. Gen. Tech. Rep. FPL–GTR–83. Madison, WI: U.S. Department of Agriculture, Forest Service, Forest Products Laboratory.

Alden, H.A. 1997. Softwoods of North America. Gen. Tech. Rep. FPL–GTR–102. Madison, WI: U.S. Department of Agriculture, Forest Service, Forest Products Laboratory.

Berni, C.A.; Bolza, E.; Christensen, F.J. 1979. South American timbers—characteristics, properties, and uses of 190 species. Melbourne, Australia: Commonwealth Scientific and Industrial Research Organization, Division of Building Research.

Bolza, E.; Keating, W.G. 1972. African timbers—the properties, uses, and characteristics of 700 species. Melbourne, Australia: Commonwealth Scientific and Industrial Research Organization, Division of Building Research.

Building Research Establishment, Department of Environment. 1977. A handbook of softwoods. London: H. M. Stationery Office.

Building Research Establishment, Princes Risborough Laboratory; Farmer, R.H. 1972. Handbook of hardwoods. Rev., 2d ed. London: H. M. Stationery Office.

Chudnoff, Martin. 1984. Tropical timbers of the world. Agric. Handb. 607. Washington DC: U.S. Department of Agriculture.

Hardwood Market Report: Lumber News Letter. [Current edition]. Memphis, TN.

Haynes, Richard W.; Adams, Darius M.; Mills, John R. 1993. The 1993 RPA timber assessment update. Gen. Tech. Rep. RM–GTR–259. Fort Collins, Colorado: U.S. Department of Agriculture, Forest Service, Rocky Mountain Forest and Range Experiment Station.

Howard, James L. 1997. U.S. timber production, trade, consumption, and price statistics, 1965–1994. Gen. Tech. Rep. FPL–GTR–98. Madison, Wisconsin: U.S. Department of Agriculture, Forest Service, Forest Products Laboratory.

Keating, W.G.; Bolza, E. 1982. Characteristics, properties, and uses of timbers: Vol. 1. Southeast Asia, Northern Australia, and the Pacific. Melbourne, Australia: Inkata Press.

Kukachka, B.F. 1970. Properties of imported tropical woods. Res. Pap. FPL 125. Madison, WI: U.S. Department of Agriculture, Forest Service, Forest Products Laboratory.

Little E.L. 1979. Checklist of United States trees (native and naturalized). Agric. Handb. 541. Washington, DC: U.S. Department of Agriculture.

Markwardt, L.J. 1930. Comparative strength properties of woods grown in the United States. Tech. Bull. 158. Washington, DC: U.S. Department of Agriculture.

Panshin, A.J.; deZeeuw, C. 1980. Textbook of wood technology. 4th ed. New York: McGraw–Hill.

Record, S.J.; Hess, R.W. 1949. Timbers of the new world. New Haven, CT: Yale University Press.

Ulrich, Alice H. 1981. U.S. timber production, trade, consumption, and price statistics, 1950–1980. Misc. Pub. 1408. Washington, DC: U.S. Department of Agriculture.

USDA. 1990. An analysis of the timber situation in the United States: 1989–2040. Gen. Tech. Rep. RM–199. Fort Collins, CO: U.S. Department of Agriculture, Forest Service, Rocky Mountain Forest and Range Experiment Station.

Structure of Wood

Regis B. Miller

Contents

The fibrous nature of wood strongly influences how it is used. Wood is primarily composed of hollow, elongate, spindle-shaped cells that are arranged parallel to each other along the trunk of a tree. When lumber and other products are cut from the tree, the characteristics of these fibrous cells and their arrangement affect such properties as strength and shrinkage as well as the grain pattern of the wood. This chapter briefly describes some elements of wood structure.

Bark, Wood, Branches, and Cambium

A cross section of a tree (Fig. 2–1) shows the following well-defined features (from outside to center): bark, which may be divided into an outer corky dead part (A), whose thickness varies greatly with species and age of trees, and an inner thin living part (B), which carries food from the leaves to growing parts of the tree; wood, which in merchantable trees of most species is clearly differentiated into sapwood (D) and heartwood (E); and pith (F), a small core of tissue located at the center of tree stems, branches, and twigs about which initial wood growth takes place. Sapwood contains both living and dead tissue and carries sap from the roots to the leaves. Heartwood is formed by a gradual change in the sapwood and is inactive. The wood rays (G), horizontally oriented tissue through the radial plane of the tree, vary in size from one cell wide and a few cells high to more than 15 cells wide and several centimeters high. The rays connect various layers from pith to bark for storage and transfer of food. The cambium layer (C), which is inside the inner bark and forms wood and bark cells, can be seen only with a microscope.

As the tree grows in height, branching is initiated by lateral bud development. The lateral branches are intergrown with the wood of the trunk as long as they are alive. After a branch dies, the trunk continues to increase in diameter and surrounds that portion of the branch projecting from the trunk when the branch died. If the dead branches drop from the tree, the dead stubs become overgrown and clear wood is formed.

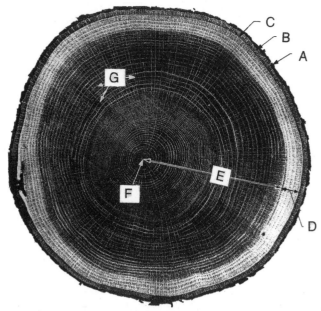

Figure 2–1. Cross section of white oak tree trunk: (A) outer bark (dry dead tissue), (B) inner bark (living tissue), (C) cambium, (D) sapwood, (E) heartwood, (F) pith, and (G) wood rays.

Most growth in thickness of bark and wood is caused by cell division in the cambium (Fig. 2–1C). No growth in diameter takes place in wood outside the cambial zone; new growth is purely the addition and growth of new cells, not the further development of old ones. New wood cells are formed on the inside of the cambium and new bark cells on the outside. Thus, new wood is laid down to the outside of old wood and the diameter of the woody trunk increases.

In most species, the existing bark is pushed outward by the formation of new bark, and the outer bark layers become stretched, cracked, and ridged and are finally sloughed off.

Sapwood and Heartwood

Sapwood is located between the cambium and heartwood (Fig. 2–1D). Sapwood contains both living and dead cells and functions primarily in the storage of food; in the outer layers near the cambium, sapwood handles the transport of water or sap. The sapwood may vary in thickness and number of growth rings. Sapwood commonly ranges from 4 to 6 cm (1-1/2 to 2 in.) in radial thickness. In certain species, such as catalpa and black locust, the sapwood contains few growth rings and usually does not exceed 1 cm (1/2 in.) in thickness. The maples, hickories, ashes, some southern pines, and ponderosa pine of North America and cativo (*Prioria copaifera*), ehie (*Guibourtia ehie*), and courbaril (*Hymenaea courbaril*) of tropical origin may have sapwood 8 to 15 cm (3 to 6 in.) or more in thickness, especially in second-growth trees. As a rule, the more vigorously growing trees have wider sapwood. Many second-growth trees of merchantable size consist mostly of sapwood.

In general, heartwood consists of inactive cells that do not function in either water conduction or food storage. The transition from sapwood to heartwood is accompanied by an increase in extractive content. Frequently, these extractives darken the heartwood and give species such as black walnut and cherry their characteristic color. Lighter colored heartwood occurs in North American species such as the spruces (except Sitka spruce), hemlocks, true firs, basswood, cottonwood, and buckeye, and in tropical species such as ceiba (*Ceiba pentandra*), obeche (*Triplochiton scleroxylon*), and ramin (*Gonystylus bancanus*). In some species, such as black locust, western redcedar, and redwood, heartwood extractives make the wood resistant to fungi or insect attack. All dark-colored heartwood is not resistant to decay, and some nearly colorless heartwood is decay resistant, as in northern white-cedar. However, none of the sapwood of any species is resistant to decay. Heartwood extractives may also affect wood by (a) reducing permeability, making the heartwood slower to dry and more difficult to impregnate with chemical preservatives, (b) increasing stability in changing moisture conditions, and (c) increasing weight (slightly). However, as sapwood changes to heartwood, no cells are added or taken away, nor do any cells change shape. The basic strength of the wood is essentially not affected by the transition from sapwood cells to heartwood cells.

In some species, such as the ashes, hickories, and certain oaks, the pores (vessels) become plugged to a greater or lesser extent with ingrowths known as tyloses. Heartwood in which the pores are tightly plugged by tyloses, as in white oak, is suitable for tight cooperage, because the tyloses prevent the passage of liquid through the pores. Tyloses also make impregnation of the wood with liquid preservatives difficult.

Growth Rings

In most species in temperate climates, the difference between wood that is formed early in a growing season and that formed later is sufficient to produce well-marked annual growth rings (Fig. 2–2). The age of a tree at the stump or the age at any cross section of the trunk may be determined by counting these rings. However, if the growth in diameter is interrupted, by drought or defoliation by insects for example, more than one ring may be formed in the same season. In such an event, the inner rings usually do not have sharply defined boundaries and are termed false rings. Trees that have only very small crowns or that have accidentally lost most of their foliage may form an incomplete growth layer, sometimes called a discontinuous ring.

The inner part of the growth ring formed first in the growing season is called earlywood and the outer part formed later in the growing season, latewood. Actual time of formation of these two parts of a ring may vary with environmental and weather conditions. Earlywood is characterized by cells with relatively large cavities and thin walls. Latewood cells have smaller cavities and thicker walls. The transition from earlywood to latewood may be gradual or abrupt, depending on

Figure 2–2. Cross section of ponderosa pine log showing growth rings. Light bands are earlywood, dark bands latewood. An annual (growth) ring is composed of an inner earlywood zone and outer latewood zone.

the kind of wood and the growing conditions at the time it was formed.

Growth rings are most readily seen in species with sharp contrast between latewood formed in one year and earlywood formed in the following year, such as in the native ring-porous hardwoods ash and oak, and in softwoods like southern pines. In some other species, such as water tupelo, aspen, and sweetgum, differentiation of earlywood and latewood is slight and the annual growth rings are difficult to recognize. In many tropical regions, growth may be practically continuous throughout the year, and no well-defined growth rings are formed.

When growth rings are prominent, as in most softwoods and ring-porous hardwoods, earlywood differs markedly from latewood in physical properties. Earlywood is lighter in weight, softer, and weaker than latewood. Because of the greater density of latewood, the proportion of latewood is sometimes used to judge the strength of the wood. This method is useful with such species as the southern pines, Douglas-fir, and the ring-porous hardwoods (ash, hickory, and oak).

Wood Cells

Wood cells—the structural elements of wood tissue—are of various sizes and shapes and are quite firmly cemented together. Dry wood cells may be empty or partly filled with deposits, such as gums and resins, or with tyloses. The majority of wood cells are considerably elongated and pointed at the ends; these cells are customarily called fibers or tracheids. The length of wood fibers is highly variable

within a tree and among species. Hardwood fibers average about 1 mm (1/25 in.) in length; softwood fibers range from 3 to 8 mm (1/8 to 1/3 in.) in length.

In addition to fibers, hardwoods have cells of relatively large diameter known as vessels or pores. These cells form the main conduits in the movement of sap. Softwoods do not contain vessels for conducting sap longitudinally in the tree; this function is performed by the tracheids.

Both hardwoods and softwoods have cells (usually grouped into structures or tissues) that are oriented horizontally in the direction from pith toward bark. These groups of cells conduct sap radially across the grain and are called rays or wood rays (Fig. 2–1G). The rays are most easily seen on edge-grained or quartersawn surfaces, and they vary greatly in size in different species. In oaks and sycamores, the rays are conspicuous and add to the decorative features of the wood. Rays also represent planes of weakness along which seasoning checks readily develop.

Another type of wood cells, known as longitudinal or axial parenchyma cells, function mainly in the storage of food.

Chemical Composition

Dry wood is primarily composed of cellulose, lignin, hemicelluloses, and minor amounts (5% to 10%) of extraneous materials. Cellulose, the major component, constitutes approximately 50% of wood substance by weight. It is a high-molecular-weight linear polymer consisting of chains of 1 to more than 4 β-linked glucose monomers. During growth of the tree, the cellulose molecules are arranged into ordered strands called fibrils, which in turn are organized into the larger structural elements that make up the cell wall of wood fibers. Most of the cell wall cellulose is crystalline. Delignified wood fibers, which consist mostly of cellulose, have great commercial value when formed into paper. Delignified fibers may also be chemically altered to form textiles, films, lacquers, and explosives.

Lignin constitutes 23% to 33% of the wood substance in softwoods and 16% to 25% in hardwoods. Although lignin occurs in wood throughout the cell wall, it is concentrated toward the outside of the cells and between cells. Lignin is often called the cementing agent that binds individual cells together. Lignin is a three-dimensional phenylpropanol polymer, and its structure and distribution in wood are still not fully understood. On a commercial scale, it is necessary to remove lignin from wood to make high-grade paper or other paper products.

Theoretically, lignin might be converted to a variety of chemical products, but in commercial practice a large percentage of the lignin removed from wood during pulping operations is a troublesome byproduct, which is often burned for heat and recovery of pulping chemicals. One sizable commercial use for lignin is in the formulation of oil-well drilling muds. Lignin is also used in rubber compounding and concrete mixes. Lesser amounts are processed to yield vanillin for flavoring purposes and to produce solvents. Current research is examining the potential of using lignin in the manufacture of wood adhesives.

The hemicelluloses are associated with cellulose and are branched, low-molecular-weight polymers composed of several different kinds of pentose and hexose sugar monomers. The relative amounts of these sugars vary markedly with species. Hemicelluloses play an important role in fiber-to-fiber bonding in the papermaking process. The component sugars of hemicellulose are of potential interest for conversion into chemical products.

Unlike the major constituents of wood, extraneous materials are not structural components. Both organic and inorganic extraneous materials are found in wood. The organic component takes the form of extractives, which contribute to such wood properties as color, odor, taste, decay resistance, density, hygroscopicity, and flammability. Extractives include tannins and other polyphenolics, coloring matter, essential oils, fats, resins, waxes, gum starch, and simple metabolic intermediates. This component is termed extractives because it can be removed from wood by extraction with solvents, such as water, alcohol, acetone, benzene, or ether. Extractives may constitute roughly 5% to 30% of the wood substance, depending on such factors as species, growth conditions, and time of year when the tree is cut.

The inorganic component of extraneous material generally constitutes 0.2% to 1.0% of the wood substance, although greater values are occasionally reported. Calcium, potassium, and magnesium are the more abundant elemental constituents. Trace amounts (<100 parts per million) of phosphorus, sodium, iron, silicon, manganese, copper, zinc, and perhaps a few other elements are usually present.

Valuable nonfibrous products produced from wood include naval stores, pulp byproducts, vanillin, ethyl alcohol, charcoal, extractives, and products made from bark.

Species Identification

Many species of wood have unique physical, mechanical, or chemical properties. Efficient utilization dictates that species should be matched to end-use requirements through an understanding of their properties. This requires identification of the species in wood form, independent of bark, foliage, and other characteristics of the tree.

General wood identification can often be made quickly on the basis of readily visible characteristics such as color, odor, density, presence of pitch, or grain pattern. Where more positive identification is required, a laboratory investigation must be made of the microscopic anatomy of the wood. Identifying characteristics are described in publications such as the *Textbook of Wood Technology* by Panshin and de Zeeuw and *Identifying Wood: Accurate Results With Simple Tools* by R.B. Hoadley.

References

Bratt, L.C. 1965. Trends in the production of silvichemicals in the United States and abroad. Tappi Journal. 48(7): 46A–49A.

Browning, B.L. 1975. The chemistry of wood. Huntington, NY: Robert E. Krieger Publishing Company.

Core, H.A.; Côté, W.A.; Day, A.C. 1979. Wood structure and identification. 7th ed. Syracuse, NY: Syracuse University Press.

Desch, H.E.; revised by Dinwoodie, J.M. 1996. Timber, structure, properties, conversion, and use. 7th ed. London: MacMillan Press, Ltd.

Fengel, D.; Wegener, G. 1984. Wood: Chemistry, ultrastructure, reactions. Berlin and New York: W. deGruyter.

Hamilton, J.K.; Thompson, N.C. 1959. A comparison of the carbohydrates of hardwoods and softwoods. Tappi Journal. 42: 752–760.

Hoadley, R.B. 1980. Identifying wood: Accurate results with simple tools. Newtown, CT: Taunton Press.

Hoadley, R.B. 1990. Understanding wood: A craftsmen's guide to wood technology. Newtown, CT: Taunton Press.

Kribs, D.A. 1968. Commercial woods on the American market. New York: Dover Publications.

Panshin, A.J.; de Zeeuw, C. 1980. Textbook of wood technology. 4th ed. New York: McGraw–Hill.

Rowell, R.M. 1984. The chemistry of solid wood. Advances in Chemistry Series No. 207. Washington, DC: American Chemical Society.

Sarkanen, K.V.; Ludwig, C.H. (eds.). 1971. Lignins: occurrence, formation, structure and reactions. New York: Wiley–Interscience.

Sjöström, E. 1981. Wood chemistry: fundamentals and applications. New York: Academic Press.

Stamm, A.J. 1964. Wood and cellulose science. New York: Ronald Press Company.

Chapter 3

Physical Properties and Moisture Relations of Wood

William Simpson and Anton TenWolde

Contents

 he versatility of wood is demonstrated by a wide variety of products. This variety is a result of a spectrum of desirable physical characteristics or properties among the many species of wood. In many cases, more than one property of wood is important to the end product. For example, to select a wood species for a product, the value of appearance-type properties, such as texture, grain pattern, or color, may be evaluated against the influence of characteristics such as machinability, dimensional stability, or decay resistance.

Wood exchanges moisture with air; the amount and direction of the exchange (gain or loss) depend on the relative humidity and temperature of the air and the current amount of water in the wood. This moisture relationship has an important influence on wood properties and performance. This chapter discusses the physical properties of most interest in the design of wood products.

Some physical properties discussed and tabulated are influenced by species as well as variables like moisture content; other properties tend to be independent of species. The thoroughness of sampling and the degree of variability influence the confidence with which species-dependent properties are known. In this chapter, an effort is made to indicate either the general or specific nature of the properties tabulated.

Appearance

Grain and Texture

The terms grain and texture are commonly used rather loosely in connection with wood. Grain is often used in reference to annual rings, as in fine grain and coarse grain, but it is also used to indicate the direction of fibers, as in straight grain, spiral grain, and curly grain. Grain, as a synonym for fiber direction, is discussed in detail relative to mechanical properties in Chapter 4. Wood finishers refer to wood as open grained and close grained, which are terms reflecting the relative size of the pores, which determines whether the surface needs a filler. Earlywood and latewood within a growth increment usually consist of different kinds and sizes of wood cells. The difference in cells results in difference in appearance of the growth rings, and the resulting appearance is the texture of the wood. Coarse texture can result from wide bands of large vessels, such as in oak.

"Even" texture generally means uniformity in cell dimensions. Fine-textured woods have small, even-textured cells. Woods that have larger even-sized cells are considered medium-textured woods. When the words grain or texture are used in connection with wood, the meaning intended should be made clear (see Glossary).

Plainsawn and Quartersawn

Lumber can be cut from a log in two distinct ways: (a) tangential to the annual rings, producing flatsawn or plainsawn lumber in hardwoods and flatsawn or slash-grained lumber in softwoods, and (b) radially from the pith or parallel to the rays, producing quartersawn lumber in hardwoods and edge-grained or vertical-grained lumber in softwoods (Fig. 3–1). Quartersawn lumber is not usually cut strictly parallel with the rays. In plainsawn boards, the surfaces next to the edges are often far from tangential to the rings. In commercial practice, lumber with rings at angles of 45° to 90° to the wide surface is called quartersawn, and lumber with rings at angles of 0° to 45° to the wide surface is called plainsawn. Hardwood lumber in which annual rings form angles of 30° to 60° to the wide faces is sometimes called bastard sawn.

For many purposes, either plainsawn or quartersawn lumber is satisfactory. Each type has certain advantages that can be important for a particular use. Some advantages of plainsawn and quartersawn lumber are given in Table 3–1.

Decorative Features

The decorative value of wood depends upon its color, figure, and luster, as well as the way in which it bleaches or takes fillers, stains, and transparent finishes. Because of the combinations of color and the multiplicity of shades found in wood, it is impossible to give detailed color descriptions of the various kinds of wood. Sapwood of most species is light in color; in some species, sapwood is practically white.

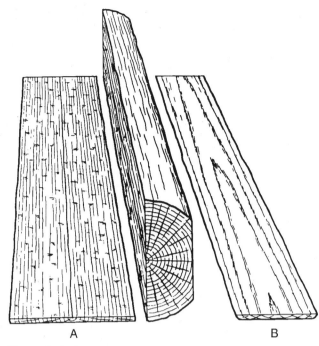

Figure 3–1. Quartersawn (A) and plainsawn (B) boards cut from a log.

White sapwood of certain species, such as maple, may be preferred to the heartwood for specific uses. In most species, heartwood is darker and fairly uniform in color. In some species, such as hemlock, spruce, the true firs, basswood, cottonwood, and beech, there is little or no difference in color between sapwood and heartwood. Table 3–2 describes the color and figure of several common domestic woods.

On the surface of plainsawn boards and rotary-cut veneer, the annual growth rings frequently form elliptic and parabolic patterns that make striking figures, especially when the rings are irregular in width and outline on the cut surface.

Table 3–1. Some advantages of plainsawn and quartersawn lumber

Plainsawn	Quartersawn
Shrinks and swells less in thickness	Shrinks and swells less in width
Surface appearance less affected by round or oval knots compared to effect of spike knots in quartersawn boards; boards with round or oval knots not as weak as boards with spike knots	Cups, surface-checks, and splits less in seasoning and in use
Shakes and pitch pockets, when present, extend through fewer boards	Raised grain caused by separation in annual rings does not become as pronounced
Figure patterns resulting from annual rings and some other types of figure brought out more conspicuously	Figure patterns resulting from pronounced rays, interlocked grain, and wavy grain are brought out more conspicuously
Is less susceptible to collapse in drying	Does not allow liquids to pass through readily in some species
Costs less because it is easy to obtain	Holds paint better in some species
	Sapwood appears in boards at edges and its width is limited by the width of the log

Table 3–2. Color and figure of several common domestic woods

Species	Color of dry heartwood[a]	Type of figure — Plainsawn lumber or rotary-cut veneer	Type of figure — Quartersawn lumber or quarter-sliced veneer
Hardwoods			
Alder, red	Pale pinkish brown	Faint growth ring	Scattered large flakes, sometimes entirely absent
Ash, black	Moderately dark grayish brown	Conspicuous growth ring; occasional burl	Distinct, inconspicuous growth ring stripe; occasional burl
Ash, Oregon	Grayish brown, sometimes with reddish tinge	Conspicuous growth ring; occasional burl	Distinct, inconspicuous growth ring stripe; occasional burl
Ash, white	Grayish brown, sometimes with reddish tinge	Conspicuous growth ring; occasional burl	Distinct, inconspicuous growth ring stripe; occasional burl
Aspen	Light brown	Faint growth ring	None
Basswood	Creamy white to creamy brown, sometimes reddish	Faint growth ring	None
Beech, American	White with reddish to reddish brown tinge	Faint growth ring	Numerous small flakes up to 3.2 mm (1/8 in.) in height
Birch, paper	Light brown	Faint growth ring	None
Birch, sweet	Dark reddish brown	Distinct, inconspicuous growth ring; occasionally wavy	Occasionally wavy
Birch, yellow	Reddish brown	Distinct, inconspicuous growth ring; occasionally wavy	Occasionally wavy
Butternut, light	Chestnut brown with occasional reddish tinge or streaks	Faint growth ring	None
Cherry, black	Light to dark reddish brown	Faint growth ring; occasional burl	Occasional burl
Chestnut, American	Grayish brown	Conspicuous growth ring	Distinct, inconspicuous growth ring stripe
Cottonwood	Grayish white to light grayish brown	Faint growth ring	None
Elm, American & rock	Light grayish brown, usually with reddish tinge	Distinct, inconspicuous grown ring with fine wavy pattern	Faint growth ring stripe
Elm, slippery	Dark brown with shades of red	Conspicuous growth ring with fine pattern	Distinct, inconspicuous growth ring stripe
Hackberry	Light yellowish or greenish gray	Conspicuous growth ring	Distinct, inconspicuous growth ring stripe
Hickory	Reddish brown	Distinct, inconspicuous growth ring	Faint growth ring stripe
Honeylocust	Cherry red	Conspicuous growth ring	Distinct, inconspicuous growth ring stripe
Locust, black	Golden brown, sometimes with tinge of green	Conspicuous growth ring	Distinct, inconspicuous growth ring stripe
Magnolia	Light to dark yellowish brown with greenish or purplish tinge	Faint growth ring	None
Maple: black, bigleaf, red, silver, and sugar	Light reddish brown	Faint growth ring, occasionally birds-eye, curly, and wavy	Occasionally curly and wavy
Oaks, all red oaks	Light brown, usually with pink or red tinge	Conspicuous growth ring	Pronounced flake; distinct, inconspicuous growth ring stripe
Oaks, all white oaks	Light to dark brown, rarely with reddish tinge	Conspicuous growth ring	Pronounced flake; distinct, inconspicuous growth ring stripe
Sweetgum	Reddish brown	Faint growth ring; occasional irregular streaks	Distinct, inconspicuous ribbon; occasional streak
Sycamore	Light to dark or reddish brown	Faint growth ring	Numerous pronounced flakes up to 6.4 mm (1/4 in.) in height
Tupelo, black and water	Pale to moderately dark brownish gray	Faint growth ring	Distinct, not pronounced ribbon
Walnut, black	Chocolate brown, occasionally with darker, sometimes purplish streaks	Distinct, inconspicuous growth ring; occasionally wavy, curly, burl, and other types	Distinct, inconspicuous growth ring stripe; occasionally wavy, curly, burl, crotch, and other types
Yellow-poplar	Light to dark yellowish brown with greenish or purplish tinge	Faint growth ring	None

Table 3–2. Color and figure of several common domestic woods—con.

Species	Color of dry heartwood[a]	Plainsawn lumber or rotary-cut veneer	Quartersawn lumber or quarter-sliced veneer
		Type of figure	
Softwoods			
Baldcypress	Light yellowish to reddish brown	Conspicuous irregular growth ring	Distinct, inconspicuous growth ring stripe
Cedar, Atlantic White	Light brown with reddish tinge	Distinct, inconspicuous growth ring	None
Cedar, Eastern red	Brick red to deep reddish brown	Occasionally streaks of white sapwood alternating with heartwood	Occasionally streaks of white sapwood alternating with heartwood
Cedar, incense	Reddish brown	Faint growth ring	Faint growth ring stripe
Cedar, northern White	Light to dark brown	Faint growth ring	Faint growth ring stripe
Cedar, Port-Orford	Light yellow to pale brown	Faint growth ring	None
Cedar, western red	Reddish brown	Distinct, inconspicuous growth ring	Faint growth ring stripe
Cedar, yellow	Yellow	Faint growth ring	None
Douglas-fir	Orange red to red, sometimes yellow	Conspicuous growth ring	Distinct, inconspicuous growth ring stripe
Fir, balsam	Nearly white	Distinct, inconspicuous growth ring	Faint growth ring stripe
Fir, white	Nearly white to pale reddish brown	Conspicuous growth ring	Distinct, inconspicuous growth ring stripe
Hemlock, eastern	Light reddish brown	Distinct, inconspicuous growth ring	Faint growth ring stripe
Hemlock, western	Light reddish brown	Distinct, inconspicuous growth ring	Faint growth ring stripe
Larch, western	Russet to reddish brown	Conspicuous growth ring	Distinct, inconspicuous growth ring stripe
Pine, eastern white	Cream to light reddish brown	Faint growth ring	None
Pine, lodgepole	Light reddish brown	Distinct, inconspicuous growth ring; faint pocked appearance	None
Pine, ponderosa	Orange to reddish brown	Distinct, inconspicuous growth ring	Faint growth ring
Pine, red	Orange to reddish brown	Distinct, inconspicuous growth ring	Faint growth ring
Pine, Southern: longleaf, loblolly, shortleaf, and slash	Orange to reddish brown	Conspicuous growth ring	Distinct, inconspicuous growth ring stripe
Pine, sugar	Light creamy brown	Faint growth ring	None
Pine, western white	Cream to light reddish brown	Faint growth ring	None
Redwood	Cherry red to deep reddish brown	Distinct, inconspicuous growth ring; occasionally wavy and burl	Faint growth ring stripe; occasionally wavy and burl
Spruce: black, Engelmann, red, and white	Nearly white	Faint growth ring	None
Spruce, Sitka	Light reddish brown	Distinct, inconspicuous growth ring	Faint growth ring stripe
Tamarack	Russet brown	Conspicuous growth ring	Distinct, inconspicuous growth ring stripe

[a]Sapwood of all species is light in color or virtually white unless discolored by fungus or chemical stains.

On quartersawn surfaces, these rings form stripes, which are not especially ornamental unless they are irregular in width and direction. The relatively large rays sometimes appear as flecks that can form a conspicuous figure in quartersawn oak and sycamore. With interlocked grain, which slopes in alternate directions in successive layers from the center of the tree outward, quartersawn surfaces show a ribbon effect, either because of the difference in reflection of light from successive layers when the wood has a natural luster or because cross grain of varying degree absorbs stains unevenly. Much of this type of figure is lost in plainsawn lumber.

In open-grained hardwoods, the appearance of both plainsawn and quartersawn lumber can be varied greatly by the use of fillers of different colors. In softwoods, the annual growth layers can be made to stand out by applying a stain. The visual effect of applying stain to softwood is an overall darkening and a contrast reversal with earlywood of initially lighter color absorbing more stain, thus becoming darker than latewood. The final contrast is often greater than that in unstained softwood and sometimes appears unnatural.

Knots, pin wormholes, bird pecks, decay in isolated pockets, birdseye, mineral streaks, swirls in grain, and ingrown bark are decorative in some species when the wood is carefully selected for a particular architectural treatment.

Moisture Content

Moisture content of wood is defined as the weight of water in wood expressed as a fraction, usually a percentage, of the weight of ovendry wood. Weight, shrinkage, strength, and other properties depend upon the moisture content of wood.

In trees, moisture content can range from about 30% to more than 200% of the weight of wood substance. In softwoods, the moisture content of sapwood is usually greater than that of heartwood. In hardwoods, the difference in moisture content between heartwood and sapwood depends on the species. The average moisture content of heartwood and sapwood of some domestic species is given in Table 3–3. These values are considered typical, but there is considerable variation within and between trees. Variability of moisture content exists even within individual boards cut from the same tree. Additional information on moisture in wood is given in Chapter 12.

Green Wood and Fiber Saturation Point

Moisture can exist in wood as liquid water (free water) or water vapor in cell lumens and cavities and as water held chemically (bound water) within cell walls. Green wood is often defined as freshly sawn wood in which the cell walls are completely saturated with water; however, green wood usually contains additional water in the lumens. The moisture content at which both the cell lumens and cell walls are completely saturated with water is the maximum possible moisture content. Specific gravity is the major determinant of maximum moisture content. Lumen volume decreases as specific gravity increases, so maximum moisture content also decreases as specific gravity increases because there is less room available for free water. Maximum moisture content M_{max} for any specific gravity can be calculated from

$$M_{max} = 100(1.54 - G_b)/1.54G_b \qquad (3-1)$$

where G_b is basic specific gravity (based on ovendry weight and green volume) and 1.54 is specific gravity of wood cell walls. Maximum possible moisture content varies from 267% at specific gravity of 0.30 to 44% at specific gravity 0.90. Maximum possible moisture content is seldom attained in trees. However, green moisture content can be quite high in some species naturally or through waterlogging. The moisture content at which wood will sink in water can be calculated by

$$M_{sink} = 100(1 - G_b)/G_b \qquad (3-2)$$

Conceptually, the moisture content at which only the cell walls are completely saturated (all bound water) but no water exists in cell lumens is called the fiber saturation point. While a useful concept, the term fiber saturation point is not very precise. In concept, it distinguishes between the two ways water is held in wood. In fact, it is possible for all cell lumens to be empty and have partially dried cell walls in one part of a piece of wood, while in another part of the same piece, cell walls may be saturated and lumens partially or completely filled with water. It is even probable that a cell wall will begin to dry before all the water has left the lumen of that same cell. The fiber saturation point of wood averages about 30% moisture content, but in individual species and individual pieces of wood it can vary by several percentage points from that value. The fiber saturation point also is often considered as that moisture content below which the physical and mechanical properties of wood begin to change as a function of moisture content. During drying, the outer parts of a board can be less than fiber saturation while the inner parts are still greater than fiber saturation.

Equilibrium Moisture Content

The moisture content of wood below the fiber saturation point is a function of both relative humidity and temperature of the surrounding air. Equilibrium moisture content (EMC) is defined as that moisture content at which the wood is neither gaining nor losing moisture; an equilibrium condition has been reached. The relationship between EMC, relative humidity, and temperature is shown in Table 3–4. For most practical purposes, the values in Table 3–4 may be applied to wood of any species. Data in Table 3–4 can be approximated by the following:

$$M = \frac{1,800}{W}\left[\frac{Kh}{1-Kh} + \frac{K_1Kh + 2K_1K_2K^2h^2}{1 + K_1Kh + K_1K_2K^2h^2}\right] \qquad (3-3)$$

where h is relative humidity (%/100), and M is moisture content (%).

For temperature T in Celsius,

$$W = 349 + 1.29T + 0.0135T^2$$
$$K = 0.805 + 0.000736T - 0.00000273T^2$$
$$K_1 = 6.27 - 0.00938T - 0.000303T^2$$
$$K_2 = 1.91 + 0.0407T - 0.000293T^2$$

and for temperature in Fahrenheit,

$$W = 330 + 0.452T + 0.00415T^2$$
$$K = 0.791 + 0.000463T - 0.0000000844T^2$$
$$K_1 = 6.34 + 0.000775T - 0.0000935T^2$$
$$K_2 = 1.09 + 0.0284T - 0.0000904T^2$$

Wood in service is exposed to both long-term (seasonal) and short-term (daily) changes in relative humidity and temperature of the surrounding air. Thus, wood is always undergoing at least slight changes in moisture content. These changes usually are gradual, and short-term fluctuations tend to influence only the wood surface. Moisture content changes can be retarded, but not prevented, by protective coatings, such as varnish, lacquer, or paint. The objective of wood drying is to bring the wood close to the moisture content a finished product will have in service (Chs. 12 and 15).

Table 3–3. Average moisture content of green wood, by species

Species	Moisture content[a] (%)		Species	Moisture content[a] (%)	
	Heartwood	Sapwood		Heartwood	Sapwood
Hardwoods			**Softwoods**		
Alder, red	—	97	Baldcypress	121	171
Apple	81	74	Cedar, eastern red	33	—
Ash, black	95	—	Cedar, incense	40	213
Ash, green	—	58	Cedar, Port-Orford	50	98
Ash, white	46	44	Cedar, western red	58	249
Aspen	95	113	Cedar, yellow	32	166
Basswood, American	81	133	Douglas-fir, coast type	37	115
Beech, American	55	72	Fir, balsam	88	173
Birch, paper	89	72	Fir, grand	91	136
Birch, sweet	75	70	Fir, noble	34	115
Birch, yellow	74	72	Fir, Pacific silver	55	164
Cherry, black	58	—	Fir, white	98	160
Chestnut, American	120	—	Hemlock, eastern	97	119
Cottonwood	162	146	Hemlock, western	85	170
Elm, American	95	92	Larch, western	54	119
Elm, cedar	66	61	Pine, loblolly	33	110
Elm, rock	44	57	Pine, lodgepole	41	120
Hackberry	61	65	Pine, longleaf	31	106
Hickory, bitternut	80	54	Pine, ponderosa	40	148
Hickory, mockernut	70	52	Pine, red	32	134
Hickory, pignut	71	49	Pine, shortleaf	32	122
Hickory, red	69	52	Pine, sugar	98	219
Hickory, sand	68	50	Pine, western white	62	148
Hickory, water	97	62	Redwood, old growth	86	210
Magnolia	80	104	Spruce, black	52	113
Maple, silver	58	97	Spruce, Engelmann	51	173
Maple, sugar	65	72	Spruce, Sitka	41	142
Oak, California black	76	75	Tamarack	49	—
Oak, northern red	80	69			
Oak, southern red	83	75			
Oak, water	81	81			
Oak, white	64	78			
Oak, willow	82	74			
Sweetgum	79	137			
Sycamore, American	114	130			
Tupelo, black	87	115			
Tupelo, swamp	101	108			
Tupelo, water	150	116			
Walnut, black	90	73			
Yellow-poplar	83	106			

[a]Based on weight when ovendry.

Table 3–4. Moisture content of wood in equilibrium with stated temperature and relative humidity

Temperature		Moisture content (%) at various relative humidity values																		
(°C)	(°F))	5%	10%	15%	20%	25%	30%	35%	40%	45%	50%	55%	60%	65%	70%	75%	80%	85%	90%	95%
–1.1	(30)	1.4	2.6	3.7	4.6	5.5	6.3	7.1	7.9	8.7	9.5	10.4	11.3	12.4	13.5	14.9	16.5	18.5	21.0	24.3
4.4	(40)	1.4	2.6	3.7	4.6	5.5	6.3	7.1	7.9	8.7	9.5	10.4	11.3	12.3	13.5	14.9	16.5	18.5	21.0	24.3
10.0	(50)	1.4	2.6	3.6	4.6	5.5	6.3	7.1	7.9	8.7	9.5	10.3	11.2	12.3	13.4	14.8	16.4	18.4	20.9	24.3
15.6	(60)	1.3	2.5	3.6	4.6	5.4	6.2	7.0	7.8	8.6	9.4	10.2	11.1	12.1	13.3	14.6	16.2	18.2	20.7	24.1
21.1	(70)	1.3	2.5	3.5	4.5	5.4	6.2	6.9	7.7	8.5	9.2	10.1	11.0	12.0	13.1	14.4	16.0	17.9	20.5	23.9
26.7	(80)	1.3	2.4	3.5	4.4	5.3	6.1	6.8	7.6	8.3	9.1	9.9	10.8	11.7	12.9	14.2	15.7	17.7	20.2	23.6
32.2	(90)	1.2	2.3	3.4	4.3	5.1	5.9	6.7	7.4	8.1	8.9	9.7	10.5	11.5	12.6	13.9	15.4	17.3	19.8	23.3
37.8	(100)	1.2	2.3	3.3	4.2	5.0	5.8	6.5	7.2	7.9	8.7	9.5	10.3	11.2	12.3	13.6	15.1	17.0	19.5	22.9
43.3	(110)	1.1	2.2	3.2	4.0	4.9	5.6	6.3	7.0	7.7	8.4	9.2	10.0	11.0	12.0	13.2	14.7	16.6	19.1	22.4
48.9	(120)	1.1	2.1	3.0	3.9	4.7	5.4	6.1	6.8	7.5	8.2	8.9	9.7	10.6	11.7	12.9	14.4	16.2	18.6	22.0
54.4	(130)	1.0	2.0	2.9	3.7	4.5	5.2	5.9	6.6	7.2	7.9	8.7	9.4	10.3	11.3	12.5	14.0	15.8	18.2	21.5
60.0	(140)	0.9	1.9	2.8	3.6	4.3	5.0	5.7	6.3	7.0	7.7	8.4	9.1	10.0	11.0	12.1	13.6	15.3	17.7	21.0
65.6	(150)	0.9	1.8	2.6	3.4	4.1	4.8	5.5	6.1	6.7	7.4	8.1	8.8	9.7	10.6	11.8	13.1	14.9	17.2	20.4
71.1	(160)	0.8	1.6	2.4	3.2	3.9	4.6	5.2	5.8	6.4	7.1	7.8	8.5	9.3	10.3	11.4	12.7	14.4	16.7	19.9
76.7	(170)	0.7	1.5	2.3	3.0	3.7	4.3	4.9	5.6	6.2	6.8	7.4	8.2	9.0	9.9	11.0	12.3	14.0	16.2	19.3
82.2	(180)	0.7	1.4	2.1	2.8	3.5	4.1	4.7	5.3	5.9	6.5	7.1	7.8	8.6	9.5	10.5	11.8	13.5	15.7	18.7
87.8	(190)	0.6	1.3	1.9	2.6	3.2	3.8	4.4	5.0	5.5	6.1	6.8	7.5	8.2	9.1	10.1	11.4	13.0	15.1	18.1
93.3	(200)	0.5	1.1	1.7	2.4	3.0	3.5	4.1	4.6	5.2	5.8	6.4	7.1	7.8	8.7	9.7	10.9	12.5	14.6	17.5
98.9	(210)	0.5	1.0	1.6	2.1	2.7	3.2	3.8	4.3	4.9	5.4	6.0	6.7	7.4	8.3	9.2	10.4	12.0	14.0	16.9
104.4	(220)	0.4	0.9	1.4	1.9	2.4	2.9	3.4	3.9	4.5	5.0	5.6	6.3	7.0	7.8	8.8	9.9			
110.0	(230)	0.3	0.8	1.2	1.6	2.1	2.6	3.1	3.6	4.2	4.7	5.3	6.0	6.7						
115.6	(240)	0.3	0.6	0.9	1.3	1.7	2.1	2.6	3.1	3.5	4.1	4.6								
121.1	(250)	0.2	0.4	0.7	1.0	1.3	1.7	2.1	2.5	2.9										
126.7	(260)	0.2	0.3	0.5	0.7	0.9	1.1	1.4												
132.2	(270)	0.1	0.1	0.2	0.3	0.4	0.4													

Sorption Hysteresis

The amount of water adsorbed from a dry condition to equilibrium with any relative humidity is always less than the amount retained in the process of drying from a wetter condition to equilibrium with that same relative humidity. The ratio of adsorption EMC to desorption EMC is constant at about 0.85. Furthermore, EMC in the initial desorption (that is, from the original green condition of the tree) is always greater than in any subsequent desorptions. Data in Table 3–4 were derived primarily under conditions described as oscillating desorption (Stamm and Loughborough 1935), which is thought to represent a condition midway between adsorption and desorption and a suitable and practical compromise for use when the direction of sorption is not always known. Hysteresis is shown in Figure 3–2.

Shrinkage

Wood is dimensionally stable when the moisture content is greater than the fiber saturation point. Wood changes dimension as it gains or loses moisture below that point. It shrinks when losing moisture from the cell walls and swells when gaining moisture in the cell walls. This shrinking and swelling can result in warping, checking, splitting, and loosening of tool handles, gaps in strip flooring, or performance problems that detract from the usefulness of the wood product. Therefore, it is important that these phenomena be understood and considered when they can affect a product in which wood is used.

With respect to shrinkage characteristics, wood is an anisotropic material. It shrinks most in the direction of the annual growth rings (tangentially), about half as much across the rings (radially), and only slightly along the grain (longitudinally). The combined effects of radial and tangential shrinkage can distort the shape of wood pieces because of the difference in shrinkage and the curvature of annual rings. The major types of distortion as a result of these effects are illustrated in Figure 3–3.

Transverse and Volumetric

Data have been collected to represent the average radial, tangential, and volumetric shrinkage of numerous domestic species by methods described in American Society for Testing and Materials (ASTM) D143—Standard Method of Testing Small Clear Specimens of Timber (ASTM 1997). Shrinkage values, expressed as a percentage of the green dimension, are listed in Table 3–5. Shrinkage values

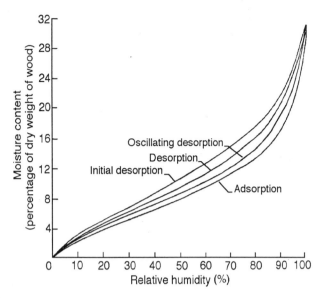

Figure 3–2. Moisture content–relative humidity relationship for wood under adsorption and various desorption conditions.

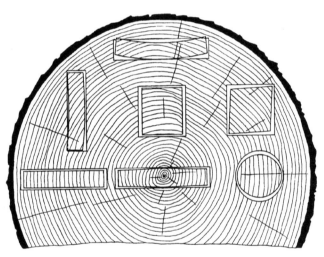

Figure 3–3. Characteristic shrinkage and distortion of flat, square, and round pieces as affected by direction of growth rings. Tangential shrinkage is about twice as great as radial.

collected from the world literature for selected imported species are listed in Table 3–6.

The shrinkage of wood is affected by a number of variables. In general, greater shrinkage is associated with greater density. The size and shape of a piece of wood can affect shrinkage, and the rate of drying for some species can affect shrinkage. Transverse and volumetric shrinkage variability can be expressed by a coefficient of variation of approximately 15%.

Longitudinal

Longitudinal shrinkage of wood (shrinkage parallel to the grain) is generally quite small. Average values for shrinkage from green to ovendry are between 0.1% and 0.2% for most species of wood. However, certain types of wood exhibit excessive longitudinal shrinkage, and these should be avoided in uses where longitudinal stability is important. Reaction wood, whether compression wood in softwoods or tension wood in hardwoods, tends to shrink excessively parallel to the grain. Wood from near the center of trees (juvenile wood) of some species also shrinks excessively lengthwise. Reaction wood and juvenile wood can shrink 2% from green to ovendry. Wood with cross grain exhibits increased shrinkage along the longitudinal axis of the piece.

Reaction wood exhibiting excessive longitudinal shrinkage can occur in the same board with normal wood. The presence of this type of wood, as well as cross grain, can cause serious warping, such as bow, crook, or twist, and cross breaks can develop in the zones of high shrinkage.

Moisture–Shrinkage Relationship

The shrinkage of a small piece of wood normally begins at about the fiber saturation point and continues in a fairly linear manner until the wood is completely dry. However, in the normal drying of lumber or other large pieces, the surface of the wood dries first. When the surface gets below the fiber saturation point, it begins to shrink. Meanwhile, the interior can still be quite wet and not shrink. The result is that shrinkage of lumber can begin before the average moisture content of the entire piece is below the fiber saturation point, and the moisture content–shrinkage curve can actually look like the one in Figure 3–4. The exact form of the curve depends on several variables, principally size and shape of the piece, species of wood, and drying conditions used.

Considerable variation in shrinkage occurs for any species. Shrinkage data for Douglas-fir boards, 22.2 by 139.7 mm (7/8 by 5-1/2 in.) in cross section, are given in Figure 3–5. The material was grown in one locality and dried under mild conditions from green to near equilibrium at 18°C (65°F) and 30% relative humidity. The figure shows that it is impossible to accurately predict the shrinkage of an individual piece of wood; the average shrinkage of a quantity of pieces is more predictable.

If the shrinkage–moisture content relationship is not known for a particular product and drying condition, data in Tables 3–5 and 3–6 can be used to estimate shrinkage from the green condition to any moisture content using

$$S_{\mathrm{m}} = S_0 \left(\frac{30 - M}{30} \right) \qquad (3\text{–}4)$$

where S_{m} is shrinkage (%) from the green condition to moisture content M (<30%), and S_0 is total shrinkage (radial, tangential, or volumetric (%)) from Table 3–5 or 3–6.

Table 3–5. Shrinkage values of domestic woods

Species	Shrinkage[a] (%) from green to ovendry moisture content			Species	Shrinkage[a] (%) from green to ovendry moisture content		
	Radial	Tangential	Volumetric		Radial	Tangential	Volumetric
Hardwoods				Oak, white—con.			
Alder, red	4.4	7.3	12.6	Chestnut			
Ash				Live	6.6	9.5	14.7
Black	5.0	7.8	15.2	Overcup	5.3	12.7	16.0
Blue	3.9	6.5	11.7	Post	5.4	9.8	16.2
Green	4.6	7.1	12.5	Swamp, chestnut	5.2	10.8	16.4
Oregon	4.1	8.1	13.2	White	5.6	10.5	16.3
Pumpkin	3.7	6.3	12.0	Persimmon, common	7.9	11.2	19.1
White	4.9	7.8	13.3	Sassafras	4.0	6.2	10.3
Aspen				Sweetgum	5.3	10.2	15.8
Bigtooth	3.3	7.9	11.8	Sycamore, American	5.0	8.4	14.1
Quaking	3.5	6.7	11.5	Tanoak	4.9	11.7	17.3
Basswood, American	6.6	9.3	15.8	Tupelo			
Beech, American	5.5	11.9	17.2	Black	5.1	8.7	14.4
Birch				Water	4.2	7.6	12.5
Alaska paper	6.5	9.9	16.7	Walnut, black	5.5	7.8	12.8
Gray	5.2	—	14.7	Willow, black	3.3	8.7	13.9
Paper	6.3	8.6	16.2	Yellow-poplar	4.6	8.2	12.7
River	4.7	9.2	13.5	**Softwoods**			
Sweet	6.5	9.0	15.6	Cedar			
Yellow	7.3	9.5	16.8	Yellow	2.8	6.0	9.2
Buckeye, yellow	3.6	8.1	12.5	Atlantic white	2.9	5.4	8.8
Butternut	3.4	6.4	10.6	Eastern redcedar	3.1	4.7	7.8
Cherry, black	3.7	7.1	11.5	Incense	3.3	5.2	7.7
Chestnut, American	3.4	6.7	11.6	Northern white	2.2	4.9	7.2
Cottonwood				Port-Orford	4.6	6.9	10.1
Balsam poplar	3.0	7.1	10.5	Western redcedar	2.4	5.0	6.8
Black	3.6	8.6	12.4	Douglas-fir,			
Eastern	3.9	9.2	13.9	Coast[b]	4.8	7.6	12.4
Elm				Interior north[b]	3.8	6.9	10.7
American	4.2	9.5	14.6	Interior west[b]	4.8	7.5	11.8
Cedar	4.7	10.2	15.4	Fir			
Rock	4.8	8.1	14.9	Balsam	2.9	6.9	11.2
Slippery	4.9	8.9	13.8	California red	4.5	7.9	11.4
Winged	5.3	11.6	17.7	Grand	3.4	7.5	11.0
Hackberry	4.8	8.9	13.8	Noble	4.3	8.3	12.4
Hickory, pecan	4.9	8.9	13.6	Pacific silver	4.4	9.2	13.0
Hickory, true				Subalpine	2.6	7.4	9.4
Mockernut	7.7	11.0	17.8	White	3.3	7.0	9.8
Pignut	7.2	11.5	17.9	Hemlock			
Shagbark	7.0	10.5	16.7	Eastern	3.0	6.8	9.7
Shellbark	7.6	12.6	19.2	Mountain	4.4	7.1	11.1
Holly, American	4.8	9.9	16.9	Western	4.2	7.8	12.4
Honeylocust	4.2	6.6	10.8	Larch, western	4.5	9.1	14.0
Locust, black	4.6	7.2	10.2	Pine			
Madrone, Pacific	5.6	12.4	18.1	Eastern white	2.1	6.1	8.2
Magnolia				Jack	3.7	6.6	10.3
Cucumbertree	5.2	8.8	13.6	Loblolly	4.8	7.4	12.3
Southern	5.4	6.6	12.3	Lodgepole	4.3	6.7	11.1
Sweetbay	4.7	8.3	12.9	Longleaf	5.1	7.5	12.2
Maple				Pitch	4.0	7.1	10.9
Bigleaf	3.7	7.1	11.6	Pond	5.1	7.1	11.2
Black	4.8	9.3	14.0	Ponderosa	3.9	6.2	9.7
Red	4.0	8.2	12.6	Red	3.8	7.2	11.3
Silver	3.0	7.2	12.0	Shortleaf	4.6	7.7	12.3
Striped	3.2	8.6	12.3	Slash	5.4	7.6	12.1
Sugar	4.8	9.9	14.7	Sugar	2.9	5.6	7.9
Oak, red				Virginia	4.2	7.2	11.9
Black	4.4	11.1	15.1	Western white	4.1	7.4	11.8
Laurel	4.0	9.9	19.0	Redwood			
Northern red	4.0	8.6	13.7	Old growth	2.6	4.4	6.8
Pin	4.3	9.5	14.5	Young growth	2.2	4.9	7.0
Scarlet	4.4	10.8	14.7	Spruce			
Southern red	4.7	11.3	16.1	Black	4.1	6.8	11.3
Water	4.4	9.8	16.1	Engelmann	3.8	7.1	11.0
Willow	5.0	9.6	18.9	Red	3.8	7.8	11.8
Oak, white	4.4	8.8	12.7	Sitka	4.3	7.5	11.5
Bur	5.3	10.8	16.4	Tamarack	3.7	7.4	13.6

[a]Expressed as a percentage of the green dimension.
[b]Coast type Douglas-fir is defined as Douglas-fir growing in the States of Oregon and Washington west of the summit of the Cascade Mountains. Interior West includes the State of California and all counties in Oregon and Washington east of but adjacent to the Cascade summit. Interior North includes the remainder of Oregon and Washington and the States of Idaho, Montana, and Wyoming.

Table 3–6. Shrinkage for some woods imported into the United States[a]

Species	Shrinkage[b] from green to ovendry moisture content (%)				Species	Shrinkage[b] from green to ovendry moisture content (%)			
	Radial	Tan-gential	Volu-metric	Loca-tion[c]		Radial	Tan-gential	Volu-metric	Loca-tion[c]
Afrormosia (*Pericopsis elata*)	3.0	6.4	10.7	AF	Lauan, white (*Pentacme contorta*)	4.0	7.7	11.7	AS
Albarco (*Cariniana* spp.)	2.8	5.4	9.0	AM	Limba (*Terminalia superba*)	4.5	6.2	10.8	AF
Andiroba (*Carapa guianensis*)	3.1	7.6	10.4	AM	Macawood (*Platymiscium* spp.)	2.7	3.5	6.5	AM
Angelin (*Andira inermis*)	4.6	9.8	12.5	AM	Mahogany, African (*Khaya* spp.)	2.5	4.5	8.8	AF
Angelique (*Dicorynia guianensis*)	5.2	8.8	14.0	AM	Mahogany, true (*Swietenia macrophylla*)	3.0	4.1	7.8	AM
Apitong (*Dipterocarpus* spp.)	5.2	10.9	16.1	AS	Manbarklak (*Eschweilera* spp.)	5.8	10.3	15.9	AM
Avodire (*Turreanthus africanus*)	4.6	6.7	12.0	AF	Manni (*Symphonia globulifera*)	5.7	9.7	15.6	AM
Azobe (*Lophira alata*)	8.4	11.0	17.0	AM	Marishballi (*Licania* spp.)	7.5	11.7	17.2	AM
Balata (*Manilkara bidentata*)	6.3	9.4	16.9	AM	Meranti, white (*Shorea* spp.)	3.0	6.6	7.7	AS
Balsa (*Ochroma pyramidale*)	3.0	7.6	10.8	AM	Meranti, yellow (*Shorea* spp.)	3.4	8.0	10.4	AS
Banak (*Virola* spp.)	4.6	8.8	13.7	AM	Merbau (*Intsia bijuga* and *I. palembanica*)	2.7	4.6	7.8	AS
Benge (*Guibourtia arnoldiana*)	5.2	8.6	13.8	AF	Mersawa (*Anisoptera* spp.)	4.0	9.0	14.6	AS
Bubinga (*Guibourtia* spp.)	5.8	8.4	14.2	AF	Mora (*Mora* spp.)	6.9	9.8	18.8	AM
Bulletwood (*Manilkara bidentata*)	6.3	9.4	16.9	AM	Obeche (*Triplochiton scleroxylon*)	3.0	5.4	9.2	AF
Caribbean pine (*Pinus caribaea*)	6.3	7.8	12.9	AM	Ocota pine (*Pinus oocarpa*)	4.6	7.5	12.3	AM
Cativo (*Prioria copaifera*)	2.4	5.3	8.9	AM	Okoume (*Aucoumea klaineana*)	4.1	6.1	11.3	AF
Ceiba (*Ceiba pentandra*)	2.1	4.1	10.4	AM	Opepe (*Nauclea* spp.)	4.5	8.4	12.6	AF
Cocobolo (*Dalbergia retusa*)	2.7	4.3	7.0	AM	Ovangkol (*Guibourta ehie*)	4.5	8.2	12	AF
Courbaril (*Hymenaea courbaril*)	4.5	8.5	12.7	AM	Para-angelium (*Hymenolobium excelsum*)	4.4	7.1	10.2	AM
Cuangare (*Dialyanthera* spp.)	4.2	9.4	12.0	AM	Parana pine (*Araucaria angustifolia*)	4.0	7.9	11.6	AS
Degame (*Calycophyllum cand idissimum*)	4.8	8.6	13.2	AM	Pau Marfim (*Balfourodendron riedelianum*)	4.6	8.8	13.4	AM
Determa (*Ocotea rubra*)	3.7	7.6	10.4	AM	Peroba de campos (*Paratecoma peroba*)	3.8	6.6	10.5	AM
Ebony, East Indian (*Diospyros* spp.)	5.4	8.8	14.2	AS	Peroba Rosa (*Aspidosperma* spp.)	3.8	6.4	11.6	AM
Ebony, African (*Diospyros* spp.)	9.2	10.8	20.0	AF	Piquia (*Caryocar* spp.)	5.0	8.0	13.0	AM
Ekop (*Tetraberlinia tubmaniana*)	5.6	10.2	15.8	AF	Pilon (*Hyeronima* spp.)	5.4	11.7	17.0	AM
Gmelina (*Gmelina arborea*)	2.4	4.9	8.8	AS	Primavera (*Cybistax donnell-smithii*)	3.1	5.1	9.1	AM
Goncalo alves (*Astronium graveolens*)	4.0	7.6	10.0	AM	Purpleheart (*Peltogyne* spp.)	3.2	6.1	9.9	AM
Greenheart (*Ocotea rodiaei*)	8.8	9.6	17.1	AM	Ramin (*Gonystylus* spp.)	4.3	8.7	13.4	AS
Hura (*Hura crepitans*)	2.7	4.5	7.3	AM	Roble (*Quercus* spp.)	6.4	11.7	18.5	AM
Ilomba (*Pycnanthus angolensis*)	4.6	8.4	12.8	AF	Roble (*Tabebuia* spp. Roble group)	3.6	6.1	9.5	AM
Imbuia (*Phoebe porosa*)	2.7	6.0	9.0	AM	Rosewood, Brazilian (*Dalbergia nigra*)	2.9	4.6	8.5	AM
Ipe (*Tabebuia* spp.)	6.6	8.0	13.2	AM	Rosewood, Indian (*Dalbergia latifolia*)	2.7	5.8	8.5	AS
Iroko (*Chlorophora excelsa* and *C. regia*)	2.8	3.8	8.8	AF	Rubberwood (*Hevea brasiliensis*)	2.3	5.1	7.4	AM
Jarrah (*Eucalyptus marginata*)	7.7	11.0	18.7	AS	Sande (*Brosimum* spp. Utile group)	4.6	8.0	13.6	AM
Jelutong (*Dyera costulata*)	2.3	5.5	7.8	AS	Sapele (*Entandrophragma cylindricum*)	4.6	7.4	14.0	AF
Kaneelhart (*Licaria* spp.)	5.4	7.9	12.5	AM	Sepetir (*Pseudosindora* spp. and *Sindora* spp.)	3.7	7.0	10.5	AS
Kapur (*Dryobalanops* spp.)	4.6	10.2	14.8	AS	Spanish-cedar (*Cedrela* spp.)	4.2	6.3	10.3	AM
Karri (*Eucalyptus diversicolor*)	7.8	12.4	20.2	AS	Sucupira (*Diplotropis purpurea*)	4.6	7.0	11.8	AM
Kempas (*Koompassia malaccensis*)	6.0	7.4	14.5	AS	Teak (*Tectona grandis*)	2.5	5.8	7.0	AS
Keruing (*Dipterocarpus* spp.)	5.2	10.9	16.1	AS	Wallaba (*Eperua* spp.)	3.6	6.9	10.0	AM
Lauan, light red and red (*Shorea* spp.)	4.6	8.5	14.3	AS					
Lauan, dark red (*Shorea* spp.)	3.8	7.9	13.1	AS					

[a]Shrinkage values were obtained from world literature and may not represent a true species average.
[b]Expressed as a percentage of the green dimension.
[c]AF is Africa; AM is Tropical America; AS is Asia and Oceania.

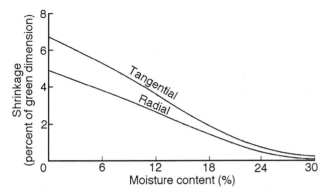

Figure 3–4. Typical moisture content–shrinkage curves.

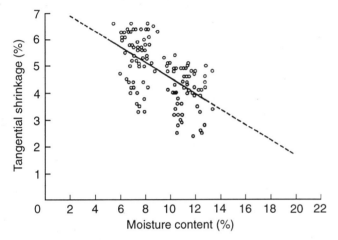

Figure 3–5. Variation in individual tangential shrinkage values of several Douglas-fir boards from one locality, dried from green condition.

If the moisture content at which shrinkage from the green condition begins is known to be other than 30% for a species, the shrinkage estimate can be improved by replacing the value of 30 in Equation (3–4) with the appropriate moisture content value.

Tangential values for S_0 should be used for estimating width shrinkage of flatsawn material and radial values for quarter-sawn material. For mixed or unknown ring orientations, tangential values are suggested. Shrinkage values for individual pieces will vary from predicted shrinkage values. As noted previously, shrinkage variability is characterized by a coefficient of variation of approximately 15%. This applies to pure tangential or radial ring orientation and is probably somewhat greater in commercial lumber, where ring orientation is seldom aligned perfectly parallel or perpendicular to board faces. Chapter 12 contains additional discussion of shrinkage–moisture content relationships, including a method to estimate shrinkage for the relatively small moisture content changes of wood in service. Shrinkage assumptions for commercial lumber, which typically is not perfectly plainsawn or quartersawn, are discussed in Chapter 6.

Weight, Density, and Specific Gravity

Two primary factors affect the weight of wood products: density of the basic wood structure and moisture content. A third factor, minerals and extractable substances, has a marked effect only on a limited number of species.

The density of wood, exclusive of water, varies greatly both within and between species. Although the density of most species falls between about 320 and 720 kg/m^3 (20 and 45 lb/ft^3), the range of density actually extends from about 160 kg/m^3 (10 lb/ft^3) for balsa to more than 1,040 kg/m^3 (65 lb/ft^3) for some other imported woods. A coefficient of variation of about 10% is considered suitable for describing the variability of density within common domestic species.

Wood is used in a wide range of conditions and has a wide range of moisture content values in use. Moisture makes up part of the weight of each product in use; therefore, the density must reflect this fact. This has resulted in the density of wood often being determined and reported on the basis of moisture content in use.

The calculated density of wood, including the water contained in the wood, is usually based on average species characteristics. This value should always be considered an approximation because of the natural variation in anatomy, moisture content, and ratio of heartwood to sapwood that occurs. Nevertheless, this determination of density usually is sufficiently accurate to permit proper utilization of wood products where weight is important. Such applications range from the estimation of structural loads to the calculation of approximate shipping weights.

To standardize comparisons of species or products and estimations of product weight, specific gravity is used as a standard reference basis, rather than density. The traditional definition of specific gravity is the ratio of the density of the wood to the density of water at a specified reference temperature (often 4.4°C (40°F)) where the density of water is 1.0000 g/cm^3). To reduce confusion introduced by the variable of moisture content, the specific gravity of wood usually is based on the ovendry weight and the volume at some specified moisture content.

Commonly used bases for determining specific gravity are ovendry weight and volume at (a) green, (b) ovendry, and (c) 12% moisture content. Ovendry weight and green volume are often used in databases to characterize specific gravity of species, which is referred to as basic specific gravity. Some specific gravity data are reported in Tables 4–3, 4–4, and 4–5 (Ch. 4) on both the 12% and green volume basis. A coefficient of variation of about 10% describes the variability inherent in many common domestic species.

Design specifications for wood, such as contained in the *National Design Specification for Wood Construction*, are based on ovendry weight and ovendry volume.

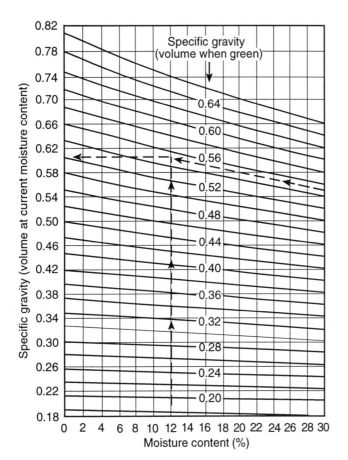

Figure 3–6. Relationship of specific gravity and moisture content.

If the specific gravity of wood is known, based on ovendry weight and volume at a specified moisture content, the specific gravity at any other moisture content between 0 and 30% can be approximated from Figure 3–6. This figure adjusts for average shrinkage and swelling that occurs below 30% moisture content and affects the volume of wood. The specific gravity of wood based on ovendry weight does not change at moisture content values above approximately 30% (the approximate fiber saturation point) because the volume does not change. To use Figure 3–6, locate the inclined line corresponding to the known specific gravity (volume when green). From this point, move left parallel to the inclined lines until vertically above the target moisture content. Then, read the new specific gravity corresponding to this point at the left-hand side of the graph.

For example, to estimate the density of white ash at 12% moisture content, consult Table 4–3a in Chapter 4. The average green (basic) specific gravity G_b for this species is 0.55. Using Figure 3–6, the 0.55 green specific gravity curve is found to intersect with the vertical 12% moisture content line at a point corresponding to a specific gravity of 0.605 based on ovendry weight and volume at 12% moisture content, G_m (see dashed lines in Fig. 3–6). The density of wood including water at this moisture content can then be obtained from Table 3–7, which converts the specific gravity of 0.605 to a density of 675 kg/m³ (42 lb/ft³). An alternative to

usage of Figure 3–6 is direct calculation of G_m using the following:

$$G_m = G_b /(1 - 0.265aG_b) \qquad (3–5)$$

where G_m is specific gravity based on volume at moisture content M, G_b is basic specific gravity (based on green volume), and $a = (30 - M)/30$, where $M < 30$.

Alternatively, the density values in Table 3–7 can be calculated by

$$\rho = 1,000\, G_m(1 + M/100) \quad (kg/m^3) \qquad (3–6a)$$

$$\rho = 62.4\, G_m(1 + M/100) \quad (lb/ft^3) \qquad (3–6b)$$

It is often useful to know the weight of lumber on a volumetric basis. We can make these estimates using Table 3–7 or with equations only. These results assume an average shrinkage–specific gravity relationship and provide a good estimate. Both methods are illustrated. For weights based on the actual shrinkage of individual species, refer to the *Dry Kiln Operator's Manual* (Simpson 1991).

Method 1—Use of Table 3–7

Determine the weight per actual unit volume (cubic meter or 1,000 board feet) of sugar maple at 20% moisture content and at 50% moisture content. From Table 4–3a, the specific gravity G_b (ovendry weight–green volume) is 0.56. Because the specific gravity in Table 3–7 is based on volume at tabulated moisture content G_m, we must convert G_b to G_m by either Figure 3–6 or Equation (3–5):

At 20%,

$$G_m = 0.56/\{1 - 0.265[(30 - 20)/30]0.56\} = 0.59$$

Determine the density from Table 3–7 at $G_m = 0.59$ and 20% moisture content. The result is approximately 708 kg/m³ (44.1 lb/ft³) (by interpolation).

At 50%,

$$G_m = G_b = 0.56$$

Determine the density from Table 3–7 at $G_m = 0.56$ and 50% moisture content. The result is 840 kg/m³ (52.4 lb/ft³).

Method 2—Use of equations only

At 20%, G_m is calculated as 0.589 as in Method 1. Density is then calculated from Equation (3–6) as

$$\rho = 1,000\, G_m(1+M/100)$$
$$= 1,000\, (0.58\, (1+20/100) = 707\ kg/m^3$$

$$\rho = 62.4\, G_m(1+M/100)$$
$$= 62.4(0.589)\, (1+20/100) = 44.1\ lb/ft^3$$

At 50%,

$$\rho = 1,000\, (0.56)(1+50/100) = 840\ kg/m^3$$

$$\rho = 62.4(0.56)(1+50/100) = 52.4\ lb/ft^3$$

Table 3–7a. Density of wood as a function of specific gravity and moisture content (metric)

Moisture content of wood (%)	Density (kg/m³) when the specific gravity G_m is																				
	0.30	0.32	0.34	0.36	0.38	0.40	0.42	0.44	0.46	0.48	0.50	0.52	0.54	0.56	0.58	0.60	0.62	0.64	0.66	0.68	0.70
0	300	320	340	360	380	400	420	440	460	480	500	520	540	560	580	600	620	640	660	680	700
4	312	333	354	374	395	416	437	458	478	499	520	541	562	582	603	624	645	666	686	707	728
8	324	346	367	389	410	432	454	475	497	518	540	562	583	605	626	648	670	691	713	734	756
12	336	358	381	403	426	448	470	493	515	538	560	582	605	627	650	672	694	717	739	762	784
16	348	371	394	418	441	464	487	510	534	557	580	603	626	650	673	696	719	742	766	789	812
20	360	384	408	432	456	480	504	528	552	576	600	624	648	672	696	720	744	768	792	816	840
24	372	397	422	446	471	496	521	546	570	595	620	645	670	694	719	744	769	794	818	843	868
28	384	410	435	461	486	512	538	563	589	614	640	666	691	717	742	768	794	819	845	870	896
32	396	422	449	475	502	528	554	581	607	634	660	686	713	739	766	792	818	845	871	898	924
36	408	435	462	490	517	544	571	598	626	653	680	707	734	762	789	816	843	870	898	925	952
40	420	448	476	504	532	560	588	616	644	672	700	728	756	784	812	840	868	896	924	952	980
44	432	461	490	518	547	576	605	634	662	691	720	749	778	806	835	864	893	922	950	979	1,008
48	444	474	503	533	562	592	622	651	681	710	740	770	799	829	858	888	918	947	977	1,006	1,036
52	456	486	517	547	578	608	638	669	699	730	760	790	821	851	882	912	942	973	1,003	1,034	1,064
56	468	499	530	562	593	624	655	686	718	749	780	811	842	874	905	936	967	998	1,030	1,061	1,092
60	480	512	544	576	608	640	672	704	736	768	800	832	864	896	928	960	992	1,024	1,056	1,088	1,120
64	492	525	558	590	623	656	689	722	754	787	820	853	886	918	951	984	1,017	1,050	1,082	1,115	1,148
68	504	538	571	605	638	672	706	739	773	806	840	874	907	941	974	1,008	1,042	1,075	1,109	1,142	1,176
72	516	550	585	619	854	688	722	757	791	826	860	894	929	963	998	1,032	1,066	1,101	1,135	1,170	1,204
76	528	563	598	634	669	704	739	774	810	845	8B0	915	950	986	1,021	1,056	1,091	1,126	1,162	1,197	
80	540	576	612	648	684	720	756	792	828	864	900	936	972	1,008	1,044	1,080	1,116	1,152	1,188		
84	552	589	626	662	699	736	773	810	846	883	920	957	994	1030	1,067	1,104	1,141	1,178			
88	564	602	639	677	714	752	790	827	865	902	940	978	1,015	1,053	1,090	1,128	1,166				
92	576	614	653	691	730	768	806	845	883	922	960	998	1,037	1,075	1,114	1,152	1,190				
96	588	627	666	706	745	784	823	862	902	941	980	1,019	1,058	1,098	1,137	1,176					
100	600	640	680	720	760	800	840	880	920	960	1,000	1,040	1,080	1,120	1,160	1,200					
110	630	672	714	756	798	840	832	924	966	1,008	1,050	1,092	1,134	1,176	1,218						
120	660	704	748	792	836	880	924	968	1,012	1,056	1,100	1,144	1,188	1,232							
130	690	736	782	828	874	920	966	1,012	1,058	1,104	1,150	1,196	1,242	1,288							
140	720	768	816	864	912	960	1,008	1,056	1,104	1,152	1,200	1,248	1,296								
150	750	800	850	900	950	1,000	1,050	1,100	1,150	1,200	1,250	1,300	1,350								

Table 3–7b. Density of wood as a function of specific gravity and moisture content (inch–pound)

Moisture content of wood (%)	Density (lb/ft^3) when the specific gravity G_m is																				
	0.30	0.32	0.34	0.36	0.38	0.40	0.42	0.44	0.46	0.48	0.50	0.52	0.54	0.56	0.58	0.60	0.62	0.64	0.66	0.68	0.70
0	18.7	20.0	21.2	22.5	23.7	25.0	26.2	27.5	28.7	30.0	31.2	32.4	33.7	34.9	36.2	37.4	38.7	39.9	41.2	42.4	43.7
4	19.5	20.8	22.1	23.4	24.7	26.0	27.2	28.6	29.8	31.2	32.4	33.7	35.0	36.6	37.6	38.9	40.2	41.5	42.8	44.1	45.4
8	20.2	21.6	22.9	24.3	25.6	27.0	28.3	29.6	31.0	32.3	33.7	35.0	36.4	37.7	39.1	40.4	41.8	43.1	44.5	45.8	47.2
12	21.0	22.4	23.8	25.2	26.6	28.0	29.4	30.8	32.2	33.5	34.9	36.3	37.7	39.1	40.5	41.9	43.3	44.7	46.1	47.5	48.9
16	21.7	23.2	24.6	26.0	27.5	29.0	30.4	31.8	33.3	34.7	36.2	37.6	39.1	40.5	42.0	43.4	44.9	46.3	47.8	49.2	50.7
20	22.5	24.0	25.5	27.0	28.4	30.0	31.4	32.9	34.4	35.9	37.4	38.9	40.4	41.9	43.4	44.9	46.4	47.9	49.4	50.9	52.4
24	23.2	24.8	26.3	27.8	29.4	31.0	32.5	34.0	35.6	37.1	38.7	40.2	41.8	43.3	44.9	46.4	48.0	49.5	51.1	52.6	54.2
28	24.0	25.6	27.2	28.8	30.4	31.9	33.5	35.1	36.7	38.3	39.9	41.5	43.1	44.7	46.3	47.9	49.5	51.1	52.7	54.3	55.9
32	24.7	26.4	28.0	29.7	31.3	32.9	34.6	36.2	37.9	39.5	41.2	42.8	44.5	46.1	47.8	49.4	51.1	52.7	54.4	56.0	57.7
36	25.5	27.2	28.9	30.6	32.2	33.9	35.6	37.3	39.0	40.7	42.4	44.1	45.8	47.5	49.2	50.9	52.6	54.3	56.0	57.7	59.4
40	26.2	28.0	29.7	31.4	33.2	34.9	36.7	38.4	40.2	41.9	43.7	45.4	47.2	48.9	50.7	52.4	54.2	55.9	57.7	59.4	61.2
44	27.0	28.8	30.6	32.3	34.1	35.9	37.7	39.5	41.3	43.1	44.9	46.7	48.5	50.3	52.1	53.9	55.7	57.5	59.3	61.1	62.9
48	27.7	29.6	31.4	33.2	35.1	36.9	38.8	40.6	42.5	44.3	46.2	48.0	49.9	51.7	53.6	55.4	57.3	59.1	61.0	62.8	64.6
52	28.5	30.4	32.2	34.1	36.0	37.9	39.8	41.7	43.6	45.5	47.4	49.3	51.2	53.1	55.0	56.9	58.8	60.7	62.6	64.5	66.4
56	29.2	31.2	33.1	35.0	37.0	38.9	40.9	42.8	44.8	46.7	48.7	50.6	52.6	54.5	56.5	58.4	60.4	62.3	64.2	66.2	68.1
60	30.0	31.9	33.9	35.9	37.9	39.9	41.9	43.9	45.9	47.9	49.9	51.9	53.9	55.9	57.9	59.9	61.9	63.9	65.9	67.9	69.9
64	30.7	32.7	34.8	36.8	38.9	40.9	43.0	45.0	47.1	49.1	51.2	53.2	55.3	57.3	59.4	61.4	63.4	65.5	67.5	69.6	71.6
68	31.4	33.5	35.6	37.7	39.8	41.9	44.0	46.1	48.2	50.3	52.4	54.5	56.6	58.7	60.8	62.9	65.0	67.1	69.2	71.3	73.4
72	32.2	34.3	36.5	38.6	40.8	42.9	45.1	47.2	49.4	51.5	53.7	55.8	58.0	60.1	62.3	64.4	66.5	68.7	70.8	73.0	75.1
76	32.9	35.1	37.3	39.5	41.7	43.9	46.1	48.3	50.5	52.7	54.9	57.1	59.3	61.5	63.7	65.9	68.1	70.3	72.5		
80	33.7	35.9	38.2	40.4	42.7	44.9	47.2	49.4	51.7	53.9	56.2	58.4	60.7	62.9	65.1	67.4	69.6	71.9	74.1		
84	34.4	36.7	39.0	41.3	43.6	45.9	48.2	50.5	52.8	55.1	57.4	59.7	62.0	64.3	66.6	68.9	71.2	73.5			
88	35.2	37.5	39.9	42.2	44.6	46.9	49.3	51.6	54.0	56.3	58.7	61.0	63.3	65.7	68.0	70.4	72.7				
92	35.9	38.3	40.7	43.1	45.5	47.9	50.3	52.7	55.1	57.5	59.9	62.3	64.7	67.1	69.5	71.9	74.3				
96	36.7	39.1	41.6	44.0	46.5	48.9	51.4	53.8	56.3	58.7	61.2	63.6	66.0	68.5	70.9	73.4					
100	37.4	39.9	42.4	44.9	47.4	49.9	52.4	54.9	57.4	59.9	62.4	64.9	67.4	69.9	72.4	74.9					
110	39.3	41.9	44.6	47.2	49.8	52.4	55.0	57.7	60.3	62.9	65.5	68.1	70.8	73.4	76.0						
120	41.2	43.9	46.7	49.4	52.2	54.9	57.7	60.4	63.1	65.9	68.6	71.4	74.1	76.9							
130	43.1	45.9	48.8	51.7	54.5	57.4	60.3	63.1	66.0	68.9	71.8	74.6	77.5	80.4							
140	44.9	47.9	50.9	53.9	56.9	59.9	62.9	65.9	68.9	71.9	74.9	77.9	80.9								
150	46.8	49.9	53.0	56.2	59.3	62.4	65.5	68.6	71.8	74.9	78.0	81.1	84.2								

Working Qualities

The ease of working wood with hand tools generally varies directly with the specific gravity of the wood. The lower the specific gravity, the easier it is to cut the wood with a sharp tool. Tables 4–3 and 4–5 (Ch. 4) list the specific gravity values for various native and imported species. These specific gravity values can be used as a general guide to the ease of working with hand tools.

A wood species that is easy to cut does not necessarily develop a smooth surface when it is machined. Consequently, tests have been made with many U.S. hardwoods to evaluate them for machining properties. Results of these evaluations are given in Table 3–8.

Machining evaluations are not available for many imported woods. However, three major factors other than density can affect production of smooth surfaces during wood machining: interlocked and variable grain, hard mineral deposits, and reaction wood, particularly tension wood in hardwoods. Interlocked grain is characteristic of a few domestic species and many tropical species, and it presents difficulty in planing quartersawn boards unless attention is paid to feed rate, cutting angles, and sharpness of knives. Hard deposits in the cells, such as calcium carbonate and silica, can have a pronounced dulling effect on all cutting edges. This dulling effect becomes more pronounced as the wood is dried to the usual in-service requirements. Tension wood can cause fibrous and fuzzy surfaces. It can be very troublesome in species of lower density. Reaction wood can also be responsible for the pinching effect on saws as a result of stress relief. The pinching can result in burning and dulling of the saw teeth. Table 3–9 lists some imported species that have irregular grain, hard deposits, or tension wood.

Decay Resistance

Wood kept constantly dry does not decay. In addition, if wood is kept continuously submerged in water, even for long periods of time, it does not decay significantly by the common decay fungi regardless of the wood species or the presence of sapwood. Bacteria and certain soft-rot fungi can attack submerged wood, but the resulting deterioration is very slow. A large proportion of wood in use is kept so dry at all times that it lasts indefinitely.

Moisture and temperature, which vary greatly with local conditions, are the principal factors that affect rate of decay. Wood deteriorates more rapidly in warm, humid areas than in cool or dry areas. High altitudes, as a rule, are less favorable to decay than are low altitudes because the average temperatures at higher altitudes are lower and the growing season for fungi, which cause decay, is shorter. The heartwood of common native species of wood has varying degrees of natural decay resistance. Untreated sapwood of substantially all species has low resistance to decay and usually has a short service life under decay-producing conditions. The decay resistance of heartwood is greatly affected by differences in the preservative qualities of the wood extractives, the attacking fungus, and the conditions of exposure.

Considerable difference in service life can be obtained from pieces of wood cut from the same species, even from the same tree, and used under apparently similar conditions. There are further complications because, in a few species, such as the spruces and the true firs (not Douglas-fir), heartwood and sapwood are so similar in color that they cannot be easily distinguished.

Marketable sizes of some species, such as the southern and eastern pines and baldcypress, are becoming primarily second growth and contain a high percentage of sapwood. Consequently, substantial quantities of heartwood lumber of these species are not available.

Precise ratings of decay resistance of heartwood of different species are not possible because of differences within species and the variety of service conditions to which wood is exposed. However, broad groupings of many native species, based on service records, laboratory tests, and general experience, are helpful in choosing heartwood for use under conditions favorable to decay. Table 3–10 lists such groupings for some domestic and imported woods, according to their average heartwood decay resistance. The extent of variations in decay resistance of individual trees or wood samples of a species is much greater for most of the more resistant species than for the slightly or nonresistant species.

Where decay hazards exist, heartwood of species in the resistant or very resistant category generally gives satisfactory service, but heartwood of species in the other two categories will usually require some form of preservative treatment. For mild decay conditions, a simple preservative treatment—such as a short soak in preservative after all cutting and boring operations are complete—will be adequate for wood low in decay resistance. For more severe decay hazards, pressure treatment is often required. Even the very decay-resistant species may require preservative treatment for important structural uses or other uses where failure would endanger life or require expensive repairs. Preservative treatments and methods for wood are discussed in Chapter 14.

Thermal Properties

Four important thermal properties of wood are thermal conductivity, heat capacity, thermal diffusivity, and coefficient of thermal expansion.

Conductivity

Thermal conductivity is a measure of the rate of heat flow through one unit thickness of a material subjected to a temperature gradient. The thermal conductivity of common structural woods is much less than the conductivity of metals with which wood often is mated in construction. It is about two to four times that of common insulating material. For example, the conductivity of structural softwood lumber at 12% moisture content is in the range of 0.1 to 1.4 W/(m·K) (0.7 to 1.0 Btu·in/(h·ft^2·°F)) compared with 216 (1,500) for aluminum, 45 (310) for steel, 0.9 (6) for concrete, 1 (7) for glass, 0.7 (5) for plaster, and 0.036 (0.25) for mineral wool.

Table 3–8. Some machining and related properties of selected domestic hardwoods

Kind of wood[a]	Planing: perfect pieces (%)	Shaping: good to excellent pieces (%)	Turning: fair to excellent pieces (%)	Boring: good to excellent pieces (%)	Mortising: fair to excellent pieces (%)	Sanding: good to excellent pieces (%)	Steam bending: unbroken pieces (%)	Nail splitting: pieces free from complete splits (%)	Screw splitting: pieces free from complete splits (%)
Alder, red	61	20	88	64	52	—	—	—	—
Ash	75	55	79	94	58	75	67	65	71
Aspen	26	7	65	78	60	—	—	—	—
Basswood	64	10	68	76	51	17	2	79	68
Beech	83	24	90	99	92	49	75	42	58
Birch	63	57	80	97	97	34	72	32	48
Birch, paper	47	22	—	—	—	—	—	—	—
Cherry, black	80	80	88	100	100	—	—	—	—
Chestnut	74	28	87	91	70	64	56	66	60
Cottonwood[b]	21	3	70	70	52	19	44	82	78
Elm, soft[b]	33	13	65	94	75	66	74	80	74
Hackberry	74	10	77	99	72	—	94	63	63
Hickory	76	20	84	100	98	80	76	35	63
Magnolia	65	27	79	71	32	37	85	73	76
Maple, bigleaf	52	56	80	100	80	—	—	—	—
Maple, hard	54	72	82	99	95	38	57	27	52
Maple, soft	41	25	76	80	34	37	59	58	61
Oak, red	91	28	84	99	95	81	86	66	78
Oak, white	87	35	85	95	99	83	91	69	74
Pecan	88	40	89	100	98	—	78	47	69
Sweetgum[b]	51	28	86	92	58	23	67	69	69
Sycamore[b]	22	12	85	98	96	21	29	79	74
Tanoak	80	39	81	100	100	—	—	—	—
Tupelo, water[b]	55	52	79	62	33	34	46	64	63
Tupelo, black[b]	48	32	75	82	24	21	42	65	63
Walnut, black	62	34	91	100	98	—	78	50	59
Willow	52	5	58	71	24	24	73	89	62
Yellow-poplar	70	13	81	87	63	19	58	77	67

[a]Commercial lumber nomenclature.
[b]Interlocked grain present.

Table 3–9. Some characteristics of imported woods that may affect machining

Irregular and interlocked grain	Hard mineral deposits (silica or calcium carbonate)	Reaction wood (tension wood)
Avodire	Angelique	Andiroba
Courbaril	Iroko	Banak
Ekop	Kapur	Cativo
Goncalo alves	Keruing (Apitong)	Ceiba
Ipe	Manbarklak	Hura
Iroko	Marishballi	Mahogany, African
Jarrah	Mersawa	Mahogany, American
Kapur	Okoume	Sande
Karri	Rosewood, Indian	Spanish-cedar
Keruing (Apitong)	Teak	
Kokrodua		
Lauan/meranti		
Lignumvitae		
Limba		
Mahogany, African		
Merasawa		
Obeche		
Okoume		
Rosewood, Indian		
Santa Maria		
Sapele		

The thermal conductivity of wood is affected by a number of basic factors: density, moisture content, extractive content, grain direction, structural irregularities such as checks and knots, fibril angle, and temperature. Thermal conductivity increases as density, moisture content, temperature, or extractive content of the wood increases. Thermal conductivity is nearly the same in the radial and tangential directions with respect to the growth rings. Conductivity along the grain has been reported as 1.5 to 2.8 times greater than conductivity across the grain, with an average of about 1.8, but reported values vary widely.

For moisture content levels below 25%, approximate thermal conductivity k across the grain can be calculated with a linear equation of the form

$$k = G(B + CM) + A \qquad (3–7)$$

where G is specific gravity based on ovendry weight and volume at a given moisture content M (%) and A, B, and C are constants. For specific gravity >0.3, temperatures around 24°C (75°F), and moisture content values <25%, $A = 0.01864$, $B = 0.1941$, and $C = 0.004064$ (with k in W/(m·K)) (or $A = 0.129$, $B = 1.34$, and $C = 0.028$ with k in Btu·in/(h·ft²·°F)). Equation (3–7) was derived from measurements made by several researchers on a variety of species. Table 3–11 provides average approximate conductivity values for selected wood species, based on Equation (3–7). However, actual conductivity may vary as much as 20% from the tabulated values.

Although thermal conductivity measurements have been made at moisture content values >25%, measurements have been few in number and generally lacking in accuracy.

Therefore, we do not provide values for moisture content values >25%.

The effect of temperature on thermal conductivity is relatively minor: conductivity increases about 2% to 3% per 10°C (1% to 2% per 10°F).

Heat Capacity

Heat capacity is defined as the amount of energy needed to increase one unit of mass (kg or lb) one unit in temperature (K or °F). The heat capacity of wood depends on the temperature and moisture content of the wood but is practically independent of density or species. Heat capacity of dry wood c_{p0} (kJ/kg·K, Btu/lb·°F) is approximately related to temperature t (K, °F) by

$$c_{p0} = 0.1031 + 0.003867t \qquad \text{(metric)} \qquad (3–8a)$$

$$c_{p0} = 0.2605 + 0.0005132t \qquad \text{(inch–pound)} \qquad (3–8b)$$

The heat capacity of wood that contains water is greater than that of dry wood. Below fiber saturation, it is the sum of the heat capacity of the dry wood and that of water (c_{pw}) and an additional adjustment factor A_c that accounts for the additional energy in the wood–water bond:

$$c_p = (c_{p0} + 0.01Mc_{pw})/(1 + 0.01M) + A_c \qquad (3–9)$$

where M is moisture content (%). The heat capacity of water is about 4.19 kJ/kg·K (1 Btu/lb·°F). The adjustment factor can be derived from

$$A_c = M(b_1 + b_2t + b_3M) \qquad (3–10)$$

with $b_1 = -0.06191$, $b_2 = 2.36 \times 10^{-4}$, and $b_3 = -1.33 \times 10^{-4}$ with temperature in kelvins ($b_1 = -4.23 \times 10^{-4}$, $b_2 = 3.12 \times 10^{-5}$, and $b_3 = -3.17 \times 10^{-5}$ with temperature in °F). These formulas are valid for wood below fiber saturation at temperatures between 7°C (45°F) and 147°C (297°F). Representative values for heat capacity can be found in Table 3–12. The moisture above fiber saturation contributes to specific heat according to the simple rule of mixtures.

Thermal Diffusivity

Thermal diffusivity is a measure of how quickly a material can absorb heat from its surroundings; it is the ratio of thermal conductivity to the product of density and heat capacity. Diffusivity is defined as the ratio of conductivity to the product of heat capacity and density; therefore, conclusions regarding its variation with temperature and density are often based on calculating the effect of these variables on heat capacity and conductivity. Because of the low thermal conductivity and moderate density and heat capacity of wood, the thermal diffusivity of wood is much lower than that of other structural materials, such as metal, brick, and stone. A typical value for wood is 0.161×10^{-6} m²/s (0.00025 in²/s) compared with 12.9×10^{-6} m²/s (0.02 in²/s) for steel and 0.645×10^{-6} m²/s (0.001 in²/s) for mineral wool. For this reason, wood does not feel extremely hot or cold to the touch as do some other materials.

Table 3–10. Grouping of some domestic and imported woods according to average heartwood decay resistance

Resistant or very resistant	Moderately resistant	Slightly or nonresistant
Domestic		
Baldcypress, old growth	Baldcypress, young growth	Alder, red
Catalpa	Douglas-fir	Ashes
Cedar	Larch, western	Aspens
Atlantic white	Pine, longleaf, old growth	Beech
Eastern redcedar	Pine, slash, old growth	Birches
Incense	Redwood, young growth	Buckeye
Northern white	Tamarack	Butternut
Port-Orford		Cottonwood
Western redcedar		Elms
Yellow	Pine, eastern white, old growth	Basswood
Cherry, black		Firs, true
Chestnut		Hackberry
Cypress, Arizona		Hemlocks
Junipers		Hickories
Locust,		Magnolia
Black[a]		Maples
Honeylocust		Pines (other than those listed)[b]
Mesquite		Spruces
Mulberry, red[a]		Sweetgum
Oaks, white[b]		Sycamore
Osage orange[a]		Tanoak
Redwood, old growth		Willows
Sassafras		Yellow-poplar
Walnut, black		
Yew, Pacific[a]		
Imported		
Aftotmosia (Kokrodua)	Andiroba	Balsa
Angelique[a]	Avodire	Banak
Apamate (Roble)	Benge	Cativo
Azobe[a]	Bubinga	Ceiba
Balata[a]	Ehie	Hura
Balau[b]	Ekop	Jelutong
Courbaril	Keruing[b]	Limba
Determa	Mahogany, African	Meranti, light red[b]
Goncalo alves[a]	Meranti, dark red[b]	Meranti, yellow[b]
Greenheart[a]	Mersawa[b]	Meranti, white[b]
Ipe (lapacho)[a]	Sapele	Obeche
Iroko	Teak , young growth	Okoume
Jarrah[a]	Tornillo	Parana pine
Kapur		Ramin
Karri		Sande
Kempas		Sepitir
Lignumvitae[a]		Seraya, white
Mahogany, American		
Manni		
Purpleheart[a]		
Spanish-cedar		
Sucupira		
Teak, old growth[a]		
Wallaba		

[a]Exceptionally high decay resistance.
[b]More than one species included, some of which may vary in resistance from that indicated.

Table 3–11. Thermal conductivity of selected hardwoods and softwoods[a]

Species	Specific gravity	Conductivity (W/m·K (Btu·in/h·ft²·°F))		Resistivity (K·m/W (h·ft²·°F/Btu·in))	
		Ovendry	12% MC	Ovendry	12% MC
Hardwoods					
Ash					
Black	0.53	0.12 (0.84)	0.15 (1.0)	8.2 (1.2)	6.8 (0.98)
White	0.63	0.14 (0.98)	0.17 (1.2)	7.1 (1.0)	5.8 (0.84)
Aspen					
Big tooth	0.41	0.10 (0.68)	0.12 (0.82)	10 (1.5)	8.5 (1.2)
Quaking	0.40	0.10 (0.67)	0.12 (0.80)	10 (1.5)	8.6 (1.2)
Basswood, American	0.38	0.092 (0.64)	0.11 (0.77)	11 (1.6)	9.0 (1.3)
Beech, American	0.68	0.15 (1.0)	0.18 (1.3)	6.6 (0.96)	5.4 (0.78)
Birch					
Sweet	0.71	0.16 (1.1)	0.19 (1.3)	6.4 (0.92)	5.2 (0.76)
Yellow	0.66	0.15 (1.0)	0.18 (1.2)	6.8 (0.98)	5.6 (0.81)
Cherry, black	0.53	0.12 (0.84)	0.15 (1.0)	8.2 (1.2)	6.8 (0.98)
Chestnut, American	0.45	0.11 (0.73)	0.13 (0.89)	9.4 (1.4)	7.8 (1.1)
Cottonwood					
Black	0.35	0.087 (0.60)	0.10 (0.72)	12 (1.7)	9.6 (1.4)
Eastern	0.43	0.10 (0.71)	0.12 (0.85)	9.8 (1.4)	8.1 (1.2)
Elm					
American	0.54	0.12 (0.86)	0.15 (1.0)	8.1 (1.2)	6.7 (0.96)
Rock	0.67	0.15 (1.0)	0.18 (1.3)	6.7 (0.97)	5.5 (0.80)
Slippery	0.56	0.13 (0.88)	0.15 (1.1)	7.9 (1.1)	6.5 (0.93)
Hackberry	0.57	0.13 (0.90)	0.16 (1.1)	7.7 (1.1)	6.4 (0.92)
Hickory, pecan	0.69	0.15 (1.1)	0.19 (1.3)	6.6 (0.95)	5.4 (0.77)
Hickory, true					
Mockernut	0.78	0.17 (1.2)	0.21 (1.4)	5.9 (0.85)	4.8 (0.69)
Shagbark	0.77	0.17 (1.2)	0.21 (1.4)	5.9 (0.86)	4.9 (0.70)
Magnolia, southern	0.52	0.12 (0.83)	0.14 (1.0)	8.4 (1.2)	6.9 (1.0)
Maple					
Black	0.60	0.14 (0.94)	0.16 (1.1)	7.4 (1.1)	6.1 (0.88)
Red	0.56	0.13 (0.88)	0.15 (1.1)	7.9 (1.1)	6.5 (0.93)
Silver	0.50	0.12 (0.80)	0.14 (0.97)	8.6 (1.2)	7.1 (1.0)
Sugar	0.66	0.15 (1.0)	0.18 (1.2)	6.8 (0.98)	5.6 (0.81)
Oak, red					
Black	0.66	0.15 (1.0)	0.18 (1.2)	6.8 (0.98)	5.6 (0.81)
Northern red	0.65	0.14 (1.0)	0.18 (1.2)	6.9 (1.0)	5.7 (0.82)
Southern red	0.62	0.14 (0.96)	0.17 (1.2)	7.2 (1.0)	5.9 (0.85)
Oak, white					
Bur	0.66	0.15 (1.0)	0.18 (1.2)	6.8 (0.98)	5.6 (0.81)
White	0.72	0.16 (1.1)	0.19 (1.3)	6.3 (0.91)	5.2 (0.75)
Sweetgum	0.55	0.13 (0.87	0.15 (1.1)	8.0 (1.2)	6.6 (0.95)
Sycamore, American	0.54	0.12 (0.86)	0.15 (1.0)	8.1 (1.2)	6.7 (0.96)
Tupelo					
Black	0.54	0.12 (0.86)	0.15 (1.0)	8.1 (1.2)	6.7 (0.96)
Water	0.53	0.12 (0.84)	0.15 (1.0)	8.2 (1.2)	6.8 (0.98)
Yellow-poplar	0.46	0.11 (0.75)	0.13 (0.90)	9.3 (1.3)	7.7 (1.1)

Table 3–11. Thermal conductivity of selected hardwoods and softwoods[a]—con.

Species	Specific gravity	Conductivity (W/m·K (Btu·in/h·ft²·°F))		Resistivity (W/m·K (h·ft²·°F/Btu·in))	
		Ovendry	12% MC	Ovendry	12% MC
Softwoods					
Baldcypress	0.47	0.11 (0.76)	0.13 (0.92)	9.1 (1.3)	7.5 (1.1)
Cedar					
Atlantic white	0.34	0.085 (0.59)	0.10 (0.70)	12 (1.7)	9.9 (1.4)
Eastern red	0.48	0.11 (0.77)	0.14 (0.94)	8.9 (1.3)	7.4 (1.1)
Northern white	0.31	0.079 (0.55)	0.094 (0.65)	13 (1.8)	11 (1.5)
Port-Orford	0.43	0.10 (0.71)	0.12 (0.85)	9.8 (1.4)	8.1 (1.2)
Western red	0.33	0.083 (0.57)	0.10 (0.68)	12 (1.7)	10 (1.5)
Yellow	0.46	0.11 (0.75)	0.13 (0.90)	9.3 (1.3)	7.7 (1.1)
Douglas-fir					
Coast	0.51	0.12 (0.82)	0.14 (0.99)	8.5 (1.2)	7.0 (1.0)
Interior north	0.50	0.12 (0.80)	0.14 (0.97)	8.6 (1.2)	7.1 (1.0)
Interior west	0.52	0.12 (0.83)	0.14 (1.0)	8.4 (1.2)	6.9 1.0)
Fir					
Balsam	0.37	0.090 (0.63)	0.11 (0.75)	11 (1.6)	9.2 (1.3)
White	0.41	0.10 (0.68)	0.12 (0.82)	10 (1.5)	8.5 (1.2)
Hemlock					
Eastern	0.42	0.10 (0.69)	0.12 (0.84)	10 (1.4)	8.3 (1.2)
Western	0.48	0.11 (0.77)	0.14 (0.94)	8.9 (1.3)	7.4 (1.1)
Larch, western	0.56	0.13 (0.88)	0.15 (1.1)	7.9 (1.1)	6.5 (0.93)
Pine					
Eastern white	0.37	0.090 (0.63)	0.11 (0.75)	11 (1.6)	9.2 (1.3)
Jack	0.45	0.11 (0.73)	0.13 (0.89)	9.4 (1.4)	7.8 (1.1)
Loblolly	0.54	0.12 (0.86)	0.15 (1.0)	8.1 (1.2)	6.7 (0.96)
Lodgepole	0.43	0.10 (0.71)	0.12 (0.85)	9.8 (1.4)	8.1 (1.2)
Longleaf	0.62	0.14 (0.96)	0.17 (1.2)	7.2 (1.0)	5.9 (0.85)
Pitch	0.53	0.12 (0.84)	0.15 (1.0)	8.2 (1.2)	6.8 (0.98)
Ponderosa	0.42	0.10 (0.69)	0.12 (0.84)	10 (1.4)	8.3 (1.2)
Red	0.46	0.11 (0.75)	0.13 (0.90)	9.3 (1.3)	7.7 (1.1)
Shortleaf	0.54	0.12 (0.86)	0.15 (1.0)	8.1 (1.2)	6.7 (0.96)
Slash	0.61	0.14 (0.95)	0.17 (1.2)	7.3 (1.1)	6.0 (0.86)
Sugar	0.37	0.090 (0.63)	0.11 (0.75)	11 (1.6)	9.2 (1.3)
Western white	0.40	0.10 (0.67)	0.12 (0.80)	10 (1.5)	8.6 (1.2)
Redwood					
Old growth	0.41	0.10 (0.68)	0.12 (0.82)	10 (1.5)	8.5 (1.2)
Young growth	0.37	0.090 (0.63)	0.11 (0.75)	11 (1.6)	9.2 (1.3)
Spruce					
Black	0.43	0.10 (0.71)	0.12 (0.85)	9.8 (1.4)	8.1 (1.2)
Engelmann	0.37	0.090 (0.63)	0.11 (0.75)	11 (1.6)	9.2 (1.3)
Red	0.42	0.10 (0.69)	0.12 (0.84)	10 (1.4)	8.3 (1.2)
Sitka	0.42	0.10 (0.69)	0.12 (0.84)	10 (1.4)	8.3 (1.2)
White	0.37	0.090 (0.63)	0.11 (0.75)	11 (1.6)	9.2 (1.3)

[a]Values in this table are approximate and should be used with caution; actual conductivities may vary by as much as 20%. The specific gravities also do not represent species averages.

Table 3–12. Heat capacity of solid wood at selected temperatures and moisture contents

Temperature			Specific heat (kJ/kg·K (Btu/lb·°F))			
(K)	(°C	(°F))	Ovendry	5% MC	12% MC	20% MC
280	7	(45)	1.2 (0.28)	1.3 (0.32)	1.5 (0.37)	1.7 (0.41)
290	17	(75)	1.2 (0.29)	1.4 (0.33)	1.6 (0.38)	1.8 (0.43)
300	27	(80)	1.3 (0.30)	1.4 (0.34)	1.7 (0.40)	1.9 (0.45)
320	47	(116)	1.3 (0.32)	1.5 (0.37)	1.8 (0.43)	2.0 (0.49)
340	67	(152)	1.4 (0.34)	1.6 (0.39)	1.9 (0.46)	2.2 (0.52)
360	87	(188)	1.5 (0.36)	1.7 (0.41)	2.0 (0.49)	2.3 (0.56)

Thermal Expansion Coefficient

The coefficient of thermal expansion is a measure of the change of dimension caused by temperature change. The thermal expansion coefficients of completely dry wood are positive in all directions; that is, wood expands on heating and contracts on cooling. Limited research has been carried out to explore the influence of wood property variability on thermal expansion. The thermal expansion coefficient of ovendry wood parallel to the grain appears to be independent of specific gravity and species. In tests of both hardwoods and softwoods, the parallel-to-grain values have ranged from about 0.000031 to 0.0000045 per K (0.0000017 to 0.0000025 per °F).

The thermal expansion coefficients across the grain (radial and tangential) are proportional to wood specific gravity. These coefficients range from about 5 to more than 10 times greater than the parallel-to-grain coefficients and are of more practical interest. The radial and tangential thermal expansion coefficients for ovendry wood, α_r and α_t, can be approximated by the following equations, over an ovendry specific gravity range of about 0.1 to 0.8:

$$\alpha_r = (32.4G + 9.9)10^{-6} \text{ per K} \qquad (3\text{–}11a)$$

$$\alpha_r = (18G + 5.5)10^{-6} \text{ per °F} \qquad (3\text{–}11b)$$

$$\alpha_t = (32.4G + 18.4)10^{-6} \text{ per K} \qquad (3\text{–}12a)$$

$$\alpha_t = (18G + 10.2)10^{-6} \text{ per °F} \qquad (3\text{–}12b)$$

Thermal expansion coefficients can be considered independent of temperature over the temperature range of –51.1°C to 54.4°C (–60°F to 130°F).

Wood that contains moisture reacts differently to varying temperature than does dry wood. When moist wood is heated, it tends to expand because of normal thermal expansion and to shrink because of loss in moisture content. Unless the wood is very dry initially (perhaps 3% or 4% moisture content or less), shrinkage caused by moisture loss on heating will be greater than thermal expansion, so the net dimensional change on heating will be negative. Wood at intermediate moisture levels (about 8% to 20%) will expand when first heated, then gradually shrink to a volume smaller than the initial volume as the wood gradually loses water while in the heated condition.

Even in the longitudinal (grain) direction, where dimensional change caused by moisture change is very small, such changes will still predominate over corresponding dimensional changes as a result of thermal expansion unless the wood is very dry initially. For wood at usual moisture levels, net dimensional changes will generally be negative after prolonged heating.

Electrical Properties

The most important electrical properties of wood are conductivity, dielectric constant, and dielectric power factor. The conductivity of a material determines the electric current that will flow when the material is placed under a given voltage gradient. The dielectric constant of a nonconducting material determines the amount of potential electric energy, in the form of induced polarization, that is stored in a given volume of the material when that material is placed in an electric field. The power factor of a nonconducting material determines the fraction of stored energy that is dissipated as heat when the material experiences a complete polarize–depolarize cycle.

Examples of industrial wood processes and applications in which electrical properties of wood are important include crossarms and poles for high voltage powerlines, utility worker's tools, and the heat-curing of adhesives in wood products by high frequency electric fields. Moisture meters for wood utilize the relationship between electrical properties and moisture content to estimate the moisture content.

Conductivity

The electrical conductivity of wood varies slightly with applied voltage and approximately doubles for each temperature increase of 10°C (18°F). The electrical conductivity of wood (or its reciprocal, resistivity) varies greatly with moisture content, especially below the fiber saturation point. As the moisture content of wood increases from near zero to fiber saturation, electrical conductivity increases (resistivity decreases) by 10^{10} to 10^{13} times. Resistivity is about 10^{14} to 10^{16} Ω·m for ovendry wood and 10^{3} to 10^{4} Ω·m for wood at fiber saturation. As the moisture content increases from fiber saturation to complete saturation of the wood structure, the

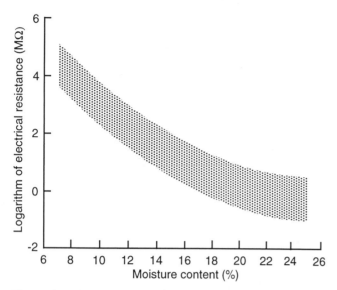

Figure 3–7. Change in electrical resistance of wood with varying moisture content levels for many U.S. species; 90% of test values are represented by the shaded area.

further increase in conductivity is smaller and erratic, generally amounting to less than a hundredfold.

Figure 3–7 illustrates the change in resistance along the grain with moisture content, based on tests of many domestic species. Variability between test specimens is illustrated by the shaded area. Ninety percent of the experimental data points fall within this area. The resistance values were obtained using a standard moisture meter electrode at 27°C (80°F). Conductivity is greater along the grain than across the grain and slightly greater in the radial direction than in the tangential direction. Relative conductivity values in the longitudinal, radial, and tangential directions are related by the approximate ratio of 1.0:0.55:0.50.

When wood contains abnormal quantities of water-soluble salts or other electrolytic substances, such as preservative or fire-retardant treatment, or is in prolonged contact with seawater, electrical conductivity can be substantially increased. The increase is small when the moisture content of the wood is less than about 8% but quickly increases as the moisture content exceeds 10% to 12%.

Dielectric Constant

The dielectric constant is the ratio of the dielectric permittivity of the material to that of free space; it is essentially a measure of the potential energy per unit volume stored in the material in the form of electric polarization when the material is in a given electric field. As measured by practical tests, the dielectric constant of a material is the ratio of the capacitance of a capacitor using the material as the dielectric to the capacitance of the same capacitor using free space as the dielectric.

The dielectric constant of ovendry wood ranges from about 2 to 5 at room temperature and decreases slowly but steadily with increasing frequency of the applied electric field. It increases as either temperature or moisture content increases, with a moderate positive interaction between temperature and moisture. There is an intense negative interaction between moisture and frequency. At 20 Hz, the dielectric constant may range from about 4 for dry wood to near 1,000,000 for wet wood; at 1 kHz, from about 4 when dry to about 5,000 when wet; and at 1 MHz, from about 3 when dry to about 100 when wet. The dielectric constant is larger for polarization parallel to the grain than across the grain.

Dielectric Power Factor

When a nonconductor is placed in an electric field, it absorbs and stores potential energy. The amount of energy stored per unit volume depends upon the dielectric constant and the magnitude of the applied field. An ideal dielectric releases all this energy to the external electric circuit when the field is removed, but practical dielectrics dissipate some of the energy as heat. The power factor is a measure of that portion of the stored energy converted to heat. Power factor values always fall between zero and unity. When the power factor does not exceed about 0.1, the fraction of the stored energy that is lost in one charge–discharge cycle is approximately equal to 2π times the power factor of the dielectric; for larger power factors, this fraction is approximated simply by the power factor itself.

The power factor of wood is large compared with that of inert plastic insulating materials, but some materials, for example some formulations of rubber, have equally large power factors. The power factor of wood varies from about 0.01 for dry, low density woods to as large as 0.95 for dense woods at high moisture levels. The power factor is usually, but not always, greater for electric fields along the grain than across the grain.

The power factor of wood is affected by several factors, including frequency, moisture content, and temperature. These factors interact in complex ways to cause the power factor to have maximum and minimum values at various combinations of these factors.

Coefficient of Friction

The coefficient of friction depends on the moisture content of the wood and the roughness of the surface. It varies little with species except for those species, such as lignumvitae, that contain abundant oily or waxy extractives.

On most materials, the coefficients of friction for wood increase continuously as the moisture content of the wood increases from ovendry to fiber saturation, then remain about constant as the moisture content increases further until considerable free water is present. When the surface is flooded with water, the coefficient of friction decreases.

Static coefficients of friction are generally greater than sliding coefficients, and the latter depend somewhat on the speed of sliding. Sliding coefficients of friction vary only slightly with speed when the wood moisture content is less than about 20%; at high moisture content, the coefficient of friction decreases substantially as the speed increases.

Coefficients of sliding friction for smooth, dry wood against hard, smooth surfaces commonly range from 0.3 to 0.5; at intermediate moisture content, 0.5 to 0.7; and near fiber saturation, 0.7 to 0.9.

Nuclear Radiation

Radiation passing through matter is reduced in intensity according to the relationship

$$I = I_0 \exp(-\mu x) \tag{3–13}$$

where I is the reduced intensity of the beam at depth x in the material, I_0 is the incident intensity of a beam of radiation, and μ, the linear absorption coefficient of the material, is the fraction of energy removed from the beam per unit depth traversed. When density is a factor of interest in energy absorption, the linear absorption coefficient is divided by the density of the material to derive the mass absorption coefficient. The absorption coefficient of a material varies with the type and energy of radiation.

The linear absorption coefficient of wood for γ radiation is known to vary directly with moisture content and density and inversely with the γ ray energy. As an example, the irradiation of ovendry yellow-poplar with 0.047-MeV γ rays yields linear absorption coefficients ranging from about 0.065 to about 0.11 cm^{-1} over the ovendry specific gravity range of about 0.33 to 0.62. An increase in the linear absorption coefficient of about 0.01 cm^{-1} occurs with an increase in moisture content from ovendry to fiber saturation. Absorption of γ rays in wood is of practical interest, in part for measuring the density of wood.

The interaction of wood with β radiation is similar in character to that with γ radiation, except that the absorption coefficients are larger. The linear absorption coefficient of wood with a specific gravity of 0.5 for a 0.5-MeV β ray is about 3.0 cm^{-1}. The result of the larger coefficient is that even very thin wood products are virtually opaque to β rays.

The interaction of neutrons with wood is of interest because wood and the water it contains are compounds of hydrogen, and hydrogen has a relatively large probability of interaction with neutrons. Higher energy neutrons lose energy much more quickly through interaction with hydrogen than with other elements found in wood. Lower energy neutrons that result from this interaction are thus a measure of the hydrogen density of the specimen. Measurement of the lower energy level neutrons can be related to the moisture content of the wood.

When neutrons interact with wood, an additional result is the production of radioactive isotopes of the elements present in the wood. The radioisotopes produced can be identified by the type, energy, and half-life of their emissions, and the specific activity of each indicates the amount of isotope present. This procedure, called neutron activation analysis, provides a sensitive nondestructive method of analysis for trace elements.

In the previous discussions, moderate radiation levels that leave the wood physically unchanged have been assumed. Very large doses of γ rays or neutrons can cause substantial degradation of wood. The effect of large radiation doses on the mechanical properties of wood is discussed in Chapter 4.

References

ASHRAE. 1981. American Society of Heating, Refrigeration, and Air-Conditioning Engineers handbook, 1981 fundamentals. Atlanta, GA: American Society of Heating, Refrigeration, and Air-Conditioning Engineers.

ASTM. 1997. Standard methods for testing small clear specimens of timber. ASTM D143. West Conshohocken, PA: American Society for Testing and Materials.

Beall, F.C. 1968. Specific heat of wood—further research required to obtain meaningful data. Res. Note FPL–RN–0184. Madison, WI: U.S. Department of Agriculture, Forest Service, Forest Products Laboratory.

James, W.L. 1975. Electric moisture meters for wood. Gen. Tech. Rep. FPL–GTR–6. Madison WI: U.S. Department of Agriculture, Forest Service, Forest Products Laboratory.

Kleuters, W. 1964. Determining local density of wood by beta ray method. Forest Products Journal. 14(9): 414.

Kollman, F.F.P.; Côté, W.A., Jr. 1968. Principles of wood science and technology I—solid wood. New York, Springer–Verlag New York, Inc.

Kubler, H.; Liang, L.; Chang, L.S. 1973. Thermal expansion of moist wood. Wood and Fiber. 5(3): 257–267.

Kukachka, B.F. 1970. Properties of imported tropical woods. Res. Pap. FPL–RP–125. Madison, WI: U.S. Department of Agriculture, Forest Service, Forest Products Laboratory.

Lin, R.T. 1967. Review of dielectric properties of wood and cellulose. Forest Products Journal. 17(7): 61.

McKenzie, W.M.; Karpovich, H. 1968. Frictional behavior of wood. Munich: Wood Science and Technology. 2(2): 138.

Murase, Y. 1980. Frictional properties of wood at high sliding speed. Journal of the Japanese Wood Research Society. 26(2): 61–65.

Panshin, A.J.; deZeeuw, C. 1980. Textbook of wood technology. New York: McGraw–Hill. Vol. 1, 4th ed.

Simpson, W.T., ed. 1991. Dry kiln operator's manual. Agric. Handb. 188. Washington, DC: U.S. Department of Agriculture, Forest Service.

Simpson, W.T. 1993. Specific gravity, moisture content, and density relationships for wood. U.S. Department of Agriculture Gen. Tech. Rep. FPL–GTR–76. Madison, WI: U.S. Department of Agriculture, Forest Service, Forest Products Laboratory.

Skaar, C. 1988. Wood–water relations. New York: Springer–Verlag. New York, Inc.

Stamm, A.J.; Loughborough, W.K. 1935. Thermodynamics of the swelling of wood. Journal of Physical Chemistry. 39(1): 121.

Steinhagen, H.P. 1977. Thermal conductive properties of wood, green or dry, from −40° to +100°C: a literature review. Gen. Tech. Rep. FPL–GTR–9. Madison, WI: U.S. Department of Agriculture, Forest Service, Forest Products Laboratory.

TenWolde, A., McNatt, J.D., Krahn, L. 1988. Thermal properties of wood panel products for use in buildings. ORNL/Sub/87–21697/1. Oak Ridge, TN: Oak Ridge National Laboratory.

Weatherwax, R.C.; Stamm, A.J. 1947. The coefficients of thermal expansion of wood and wood products. Transactions of American Society of Mechanical Engineers. 69(44): 421–432.

Chapter 4

Mechanical Properties of Wood

David W. Green, Jerrold E. Winandy, and David E. Kretschmann

Contents

T he mechanical properties presented in this chapter were obtained from tests of small pieces of wood termed "clear" and "straight grained" because they did not contain characteristics such as knots, cross grain, checks, and splits. These test pieces did have anatomical characteristics such as growth rings that occurred in consistent patterns within each piece. Clear wood specimens are usually considered "homogeneous" in wood mechanics.

Many of the mechanical properties of wood tabulated in this chapter were derived from extensive sampling and analysis procedures. These properties are represented as the average mechanical properties of the species. Some properties, such as tension parallel to the grain, and all properties for some imported species are based on a more limited number of specimens that were not subjected to the same sampling and analysis procedures. The appropriateness of these latter properties to represent the average properties of a species is uncertain; nevertheless, the properties represent the best information available.

Variability, or variation in properties, is common to all materials. Because wood is a natural material and the tree is subject to many constantly changing influences (such as moisture, soil conditions, and growing space), wood properties vary considerably, even in clear material. This chapter provides information, where possible, on the nature and magnitude of variability in properties.

This chapter also includes a discussion of the effect of growth features, such as knots and slope of grain, on clear wood properties. The effects of manufacturing and service environments on mechanical properties are discussed, and their effects on clear wood and material containing growth features are compared. Chapter 6 discusses how these research results have been implemented in engineering standards.

Orthotropic Nature of Wood

Wood may be described as an orthotropic material; that is, it has unique and independent mechanical properties in the directions of three mutually perpendicular axes: longitudinal, radial, and tangential. The longitudinal axis L is parallel to the fiber (grain); the radial axis R is normal to the growth rings (perpendicular to the grain in the radial direction); and

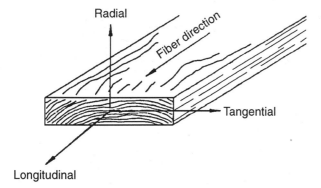

Radial

Fiber direction

Tangential

Longitudinal

Figure 4–1. Three principal axes of wood with respect to grain direction and growth rings.

Table 4–1. Elastic ratios for various species at approximately 12% moisture content[a]

Species	E_T/E_L	E_R/E_L	G_{LR}/E_L	G_{LT}/E_L	G_{RT}/E_L
Hardwoods					
Ash, white	0.080	0.125	0.109	0.077	—
Balsa	0.015	0.046	0.054	0.037	0.005
Basswood	0.027	0.066	0.056	0.046	—
Birch, yellow	0.050	0.078	0.074	0.068	0.017
Cherry, black	0.086	0.197	0.147	0.097	—
Cottonwood, eastern	0.047	0.083	0.076	0.052	—
Mahogany, African	0.050	0.111	0.088	0.059	0.021
Mahogany, Honduras	0.064	0.107	0.066	0.086	0.028
Maple, sugar	0.065	0.132	0.111	0.063	—
Maple, red	0.067	0.140	0.133	0.074	—
Oak, red	0.082	0.154	0.089	0.081	—
Oak, white	0.072	0.163	0.086	—	—
Sweet gum	0.050	0.115	0.089	0.061	0.021
Walnut, black	0.056	0.106	0.085	0.062	0.021
Yellow-poplar	0.043	0.092	0.075	0.069	0.011
Softwoods					
Baldcypress	0.039	0.084	0.063	0.054	0.007
Cedar, northern white	0.081	0.183	0.210	0.187	0.015
Cedar, western red	0.055	0.081	0.087	0.086	0.005
Douglas-fir	0.050	0.068	0.064	0.078	0.007
Fir, subalpine	0.039	0.102	0.070	0.058	0.006
Hemlock, western	0.031	0.058	0.038	0.032	0.003
Larch, western	0.065	0.079	0.063	0.069	0.007
Pine					
Loblolly	0.078	0.113	0.082	0.081	0.013
Lodgepole	0.068	0.102	0.049	0.046	0.005
Longleaf	0.055	0.102	0.071	0.060	0.012
Pond	0.041	0.071	0.050	0.045	0.009
Ponderosa	0.083	0.122	0.138	0.115	0.017
Red	0.044	0.088	0.096	0.081	0.011
Slash	0.045	0.074	0.055	0.053	0.010
Sugar	0.087	0.131	0.124	0.113	0.019
Western white	0.038	0.078	0.052	0.048	0.005
Redwood	0.089	0.087	0.066	0.077	0.011
Spruce, Sitka	0.043	0.078	0.064	0.061	0.003
Spruce, Engelmann	0.059	0.128	0.124	0.120	0.010

[a]E_L may be approximated by increasing modulus of elasticity values in Table 4–3 by 10%.

the tangential axis T is perpendicular to the grain but tangent to the growth rings. These axes are shown in Figure 4–1.

Elastic Properties

Twelve constants (nine are independent) are needed to describe the elastic behavior of wood: three moduli of elasticity E, three moduli of rigidity G, and six Poisson's ratios μ. The moduli of elasticity and Poisson's ratios are related by expressions of the form

$$\frac{\mu_{ij}}{E_i} = \frac{\mu_{ji}}{E_j}, \quad i \neq j \quad i,j = L,R,T \quad (4–1)$$

General relations between stress and strain for a homogeneous orthotropic material can be found in texts on anisotropic elasticity.

Modulus of Elasticity

Elasticity implies that deformations produced by low stress are completely recoverable after loads are removed. When loaded to higher stress levels, plastic deformation or failure occurs. The three moduli of elasticity, which are denoted by E_L, E_R, and E_T, respectively, are the elastic moduli along the longitudinal, radial, and tangential axes of wood. These moduli are usually obtained from compression tests; however, data for E_R and E_T are not extensive. Average values of E_R and E_T for samples from a few species are presented in Table 4–1 as ratios with E_L; the Poisson's ratios are shown in Table 4–2. The elastic ratios, as well as the elastic constants themselves, vary within and between species and with moisture content and specific gravity.

The modulus of elasticity determined from bending, E_L, rather than from an axial test, may be the only modulus of elasticity available for a species. Average E_L values obtained from bending tests are given in Tables 4–3 to 4–5. Representative coefficients of variation of E_L determined with bending tests for clear wood are reported in Table 4–6. As tabulated, E_L includes an effect of shear deflection; E_L from bending can be increased by 10% to remove this effect approximately.

This adjusted bending E_L can be used to determine E_R and E_T based on the ratios in Table 4–1.

Poisson's Ratio

When a member is loaded axially, the deformation perpendicular to the direction of the load is proportional to the deformation parallel to the direction of the load. The ratio of the transverse to axial strain is called Poisson's ratio. The Poisson's ratios are denoted by μ_{LR}, μ_{RL}, μ_{LT}, μ_{TL}, μ_{RT}, and μ_{TR}. The first letter of the subscript refers to direction of applied stress and the second letter to direction of lateral deformation. For example, μ_{LR} is the Poisson's ratio for deformation along the radial axis caused by stress along the longitudinal axis. Average values of Poisson's ratios for samples of a few species are given in Table 4–2. Values for μ_{RL} and μ_{TL} are less precisely determined than are those for the other Poisson's ratios. Poisson's ratios vary within and between species and are affected by moisture content and specific gravity.

Table 4–2. Poisson's ratios for various species at approximately 12% moisture content

Species	μ_{LR}	μ_{LT}	μ_{RT}	μ_{TR}	μ_{RL}	μ_{TL}
Hardwoods						
Ash, white	0.371	0.440	0.684	0.360	0.059	0.051
Aspen, quaking	0.489	0.374	—	0.496	0.054	0.022
Balsa	0.229	0.488	0.665	0.231	0.018	0.009
Basswood	0.364	0.406	0.912	0.346	0.034	0.022
Birch, yellow	0.426	0.451	0.697	0.426	0.043	0.024
Cherry, black	0.392	0.428	0.695	0.282	0.086	0.048
Cottonwood, eastern	0.344	0.420	0.875	0.292	0.043	0.018
Mahogany, African	0.297	0.641	0.604	0.264	0.033	0.032
Mahogany, Honduras	0.314	0.533	0.600	0.326	0.033	0.034
Maple, sugar	0.424	0.476	0.774	0.349	0.065	0.037
Maple, red	0.434	0.509	0.762	0.354	0.063	0.044
Oak, red	0.350	0.448	0.560	0.292	0.064	0.033
Oak, white	0.369	0.428	0.618	0.300	0.074	0.036
Sweet gum	0.325	0.403	0.682	0.309	0.044	0.023
Walnut, black	0.495	0.632	0.718	0.378	0.052	0.035
Yellow-poplar	0.318	0.392	0.703	0.329	0.030	0.019
Softwoods						
Baldcypress	0.338	0.326	0.411	0.356	—	—
Cedar, northern white	0.337	0.340	0.458	0.345	—	—
Cedar, western red	0.378	0.296	0.484	0.403	—	—
Douglas-fir	0.292	0.449	0.390	0.374	0.036	0.029
Fir, subalpine	0.341	0.332	0.437	0.336	—	—
Hemlock, western	0.485	0.423	0.442	0.382	—	—
Larch, western	0.355	0.276	0.389	0.352	—	—
Pine						
Loblolly	0.328	0.292	0.382	0.362	—	—
Lodgepole	0.316	0.347	0.469	0.381	—	—
Longleaf	0.332	0.365	0.384	0.342	—	—
Pond	0.280	0.364	0.389	0.320	—	—
Ponderosa	0.337	0.400	0.426	0.359	—	—
Red	0.347	0.315	0.408	0.308	—	—
Slash	0.392	0.444	0.447	0.387	—	—
Sugar	0.356	0.349	0.428	0.358	—	—
Western white	0.329	0.344	0.410	0.334	—	—
Redwood	0.360	0.346	0.373	0.400	—	—
Spruce, Sitka	0.372	0.467	0.435	0.245	0.040	0.025
Spruce, Engelmann	0.422	0.462	0.530	0.255	0.083	0.058

Modulus of Rigidity

The modulus of rigidity, also called shear modulus, indicates the resistance to deflection of a member caused by shear stresses. The three moduli of rigidity denoted by G_{LR}, G_{LT}, and G_{RT} are the elastic constants in the LR, LT, and RT planes, respectively. For example, G_{LR} is the modulus of rigidity based on shear strain in the LR plane and shear stresses in the LT and RT planes. Average values of shear moduli for samples of a few species expressed as ratios with E_L are given in Table 4–1. As with moduli of elasticity, the moduli of rigidity vary within and between species and with moisture content and specific gravity.

Strength Properties
Common Properties

Mechanical properties most commonly measured and represented as "strength properties" for design include modulus of rupture in bending, maximum stress in compression parallel to grain, compressive stress perpendicular to grain, and shear strength parallel to grain. Additional measurements are often

made to evaluate work to maximum load in bending, impact bending strength, tensile strength perpendicular to grain, and hardness. These properties, grouped according to the broad forest tree categories of hardwood and softwood (not correlated with hardness or softness), are given in Tables 4–3 to 4–5 for many of the commercially important species. Average coefficients of variation for these properties from a limited sampling of specimens are reported in Table 4–6.

Modulus of rupture—Reflects the maximum load-carrying capacity of a member in bending and is proportional to maximum moment borne by the specimen. Modulus of rupture is an accepted criterion of strength, although it is not a true stress because the formula by which it is computed is valid only to the elastic limit.

Work to maximum load in bending—Ability to absorb shock with some permanent deformation and more or less injury to a specimen. Work to maximum load is a measure of the combined strength and toughness of wood under bending stresses.

Compressive strength parallel to grain—Maximum stress sustained by a compression parallel-to-grain specimen having a ratio of length to least dimension of less than 11.

Compressive stress perpendicular to grain—Reported as stress at proportional limit. There is no clearly defined ultimate stress for this property.

Shear strength parallel to grain—Ability to resist internal slipping of one part upon another along the grain. Values presented are average strength in radial and tangential shear planes.

Impact bending—In the impact bending test, a hammer of given weight is dropped upon a beam from successively increased heights until rupture occurs or the beam deflects 152 mm (6 in.) or more. The height of the maximum drop, or the drop that causes failure, is a comparative value that represents the ability of wood to absorb shocks that cause stresses beyond the proportional limit.

Tensile strength perpendicular to grain—Resistance of wood to forces acting across the grain that tend to split a member. Values presented are the average of radial and tangential observations.

Hardness—Generally defined as resistance to indentation using a modified Janka hardness test, measured by the load required to embed a 11.28-mm (0.444-in.) ball to one-half its diameter. Values presented are the average of radial and tangential penetrations.

Tensile strength parallel to grain—Maximum tensile stress sustained in direction parallel to grain. Relatively few data are available on the tensile strength of various species of clear wood parallel to grain. Table 4–7 lists average tensile strength values for a limited number of specimens of a few species. In the absence of sufficient tension test data, modulus of rupture values are sometimes substituted for tensile strength of small, clear, straight-grained pieces of wood. The modulus of rupture is considered to be a low or conservative estimate of tensile strength for clear specimens (this is not true for lumber).

Table 4–3a. Strength properties of some commercially important woods grown in the United States (metric)[a]

Common species names	Moisture content	Specific gravity[b]	Static bending — Modulus of rupture (kPa)	Static bending — Modulus of elasticity[c] (MPa)	Static bending — Work to maximum load (kJ/m³)	Impact bending (mm)	Compression parallel to grain (kPa)	Compression perpendicular to grain (kPa)	Shear parallel to grain (kPa)	Tension perpendicular to grain (kPa)	Side hardness (N)
						Hardwoods					
Alder, red	Green	0.37	45,000	8,100	55	560	20,400	1,700	5,300	2,700	2,000
	12%	0.41	68,000	9,500	58	510	40,100	3,000	7,400	2,900	2,600
Ash											
Black	Green	0.45	41,000	7,200	83	840	15,900	2,400	5,900	3,400	2,300
	12%	0.49	87,000	11,000	103	890	41,200	5,200	10,800	4,800	3,800
Blue	Green	0.53	66,000	8,500	101	—	24,800	5,600	10,600	—	—
	12%	0.58	95,000	9,700	99	—	48,100	9,800	14,000	—	—
Green	Green	0.53	66,000	9,700	81	890	29,000	5,000	8,700	4,100	3,900
	12%	0.56	97,000	11,400	92	810	48,800	9,000	13,200	4,800	5,300
Oregon	Green	0.50	52,000	7,800	84	990	24,200	3,700	8,200	4,100	3,500
	12%	0.55	88,000	9,400	99	840	41,600	8,600	12,300	5,000	5,200
White	Green	0.55	66,000	9,900	108	970	27,500	4,600	9,300	4,100	4,300
	12%	0.60	103,000	12,000	115	1,090	51,100	8,000	13,200	6,500	5,900
Aspen											
Bigtooth	Green	0.36	37,000	7,700	39	—	17,200	1,400	5,000	—	—
	12%	0.39	63,000	9,900	53	—	36,500	3,100	7,400	—	—
Quaking	Green	0.35	35,000	5,900	44	560	14,800	1,200	4,600	1,600	1,300
	12%	0.38	58,000	8,100	52	530	29,300	2,600	5,900	1,800	1,600
Basswood, American	Green	0.32	34,000	7,200	37	410	15,300	1,200	4,100	1,900	1,100
	12%	0.37	60,000	10,100	50	410	32,600	2,600	6,800	2,400	1,800
Beech, American	Green	0.56	59,000	9,500	82	1,090	24,500	3,700	8,900	5,000	3,800
	12%	0.64	103,000	11,900	104	1,040	50,300	7,000	13,900	7,000	5,800
Birch											
Paper	Green	0.48	44,000	8,100	112	1,240	16,300	1,900	5,800	2,600	2,500
	12%	0.55	85,000	11,000	110	860	39,200	4,100	8,300	—	4,000
Sweet	Green	0.60	65,000	11,400	108	1,220	25,800	3,200	8,500	3,000	4,300
	12%	0.65	117,000	15,000	124	1,190	58,900	7,400	15,400	6,600	6,500
Yellow	Green	0.55	57,000	10,300	111	1,220	23,300	3,000	7,700	3,000	3,600
	12%	0.62	114,000	13,900	143	1,400	56,300	6,700	13,000	6,300	5,600
Butternut	Green	0.36	37,000	6,700	57	610	16,700	1,500	5,200	3,000	1,700
	12%	0.38	56,000	8,100	57	610	36,200	3,200	8,100	3,000	2,200
Cherry, black	Green	0.47	55,000	9,000	88	840	24,400	2,500	7,800	3,900	2,900
	12%	0.50	85,000	10,300	79	740	49,000	4,800	11,700	3,900	4,200
Chestnut, American	Green	0.40	39,000	6,400	48	610	17,000	2,100	5,500	3,000	1,900
	12%	0.43	59,000	8,500	45	480	36,700	4,300	7,400	3,200	2,400
Cottonwood											
Balsam poplar	Green	0.31	27,000	5,200	29	—	11,700	1,000	3,400	—	—
	12%	0.34	47,000	7,600	34	—	27,700	2,100	5,400	—	—
Black	Green	0.31	34,000	7,400	34	510	15,200	1,100	4,200	1,900	1,100
	12%	0.35	59,000	8,800	46	560	31,000	2,100	7,200	2,300	1,600
Eastern	Green	0.37	37,000	7,000	50	530	15,700	1,400	4,700	2,800	1,500
	12%	0.40	59,000	9,400	51	510	33,900	2,600	6,400	4,000	1,900
Elm											
American	Green	0.46	50,000	7,700	81	970	20,100	2,500	6,900	4,100	2,800
	12%	0.50	81,000	9,200	90	990	38,100	4,800	10,400	4,600	3,700
Rock	Green	0.57	66,000	8,200	137	1,370	26,100	4,200	8,800	—	—
	12%	0.63	102,000	10,600	132	1,420	48,600	8,500	13,200	—	—
Slippery	Green	0.48	55,000	8,500	106	1,190	22,900	2,900	7,700	4,400	2,900
	12%	0.53	90,000	10,300	117	1,140	43,900	5,700	11,200	3,700	3,800
Hackberry	Green	0.49	45,000	6,600	100	1,220	18,300	2,800	7,400	4,300	3,100
	12%	0.53	76,000	8,200	88	1,090	37,500	6,100	11,000	4,000	3,900

Common species names	Moisture content	Specific gravity[b]	Static bending			Impact bending (mm)	Compression parallel to grain (kPa)	Compression perpendicular to grain (kPa)	Shear parallel to grain (kPa)	Tension perpendicular to grain (kPa)	Side hardness (N)
			Modulus of rupture (kPa)	Modulus of elasticity[c] (MPa)	Work to maximum load (kJ/m³)						
Hickory, pecan											
Bitternut	Green	0.60	71,000	9,700	138	1,680	31,500	5,500	8,500	—	—
	12%	0.66	118,000	12,300	125	1,680	62,300	11,600	—	—	—
Nutmeg	Green	0.56	63,000	8,900	157	1,370	27,400	5,200	7,100	—	—
	12%	0.60	114,000	11,700	173	—	47,600	10,800	—	—	—
Pecan	Green	0.60	68,000	9,400	101	1,350	27,500	5,400	10,200	4,700	5,800
	12%	0.66	94,000	11,900	95	1,120	54,100	11,900	14,300	—	8,100
Water	Green	0.61	74,000	10,800	130	1,420	32,100	6,100	9,900	—	—
	12%	0.62	123,000	13,900	133	1,350	59,300	10,700	—	—	—
Hickory, true											
Mockernut	Green	0.64	77,000	10,800	180	2,240	30,900	5,600	8,800	—	—
	12%	0.72	132,000	15,300	156	1,960	61,600	11,900	12,000	—	—
Pignut	Green	0.66	81,000	11,400	219	2,260	33,200	6,300	9,400	—	—
	12%	0.75	139,000	15,600	210	1,880	63,400	13,700	14,800	—	—
Shagbark	Green	0.64	76,000	10,800	163	1,880	31,600	5,800	10,500	—	—
	12%	0.72	139,000	14,900	178	1,700	63,500	12,100	16,800	—	—
Shellbark	Green	0.62	72,000	9,200	206	2,640	27,000	5,600	8,200	—	—
	12%	0.69	125,000	13,000	163	2,240	55,200	12,400	14,500	—	—
Honeylocust	Green	0.60	70,000	8,900	87	1,190	30,500	7,900	11,400	6,400	6,200
	12%	—	101,000	11,200	92	1,190	51,700	12,700	15,500	6,200	7,000
Locust, black	Green	0.66	95,000	12,800	106	1,120	46,900	8,000	12,100	5,300	7,000
	12%	0.69	134,000	14,100	127	1,450	70,200	12,600	17,100	4,400	7,600
Magnolia											
Cucumber tree	Green	0.44	51,000	10,800	69	760	21,600	2,300	6,800	3,000	2,300
	12%	0.48	85,000	12,500	84	890	43,500	3,900	9,200	4,600	3,100
Southern	Green	0.46	47,000	7,700	106	1,370	18,600	3,200	7,200	4,200	3,300
	12%	0.50	77,000	9,700	88	740	37,600	5,900	10,500	5,100	4,500
Maple											
Bigleaf	Green	0.44	51,000	7,600	60	580	22,300	3,100	7,700	4,100	2,800
	12%	0.48	74,000	10,000	54	710	41,000	5,200	11,900	3,700	3,800
Black	Green	0.52	54,000	9,200	88	1,220	22,500	4,100	7,800	5,000	3,700
	12%	0.57	92,000	11,200	86	1,020	46,100	7,000	12,500	4,600	5,200
Red	Green	0.49	53,000	9,600	79	810	22,600	2,800	7,900	—	3,100
	12%	0.54	92,000	11,300	86	810	45,100	6,900	12,800	—	4,200
Silver	Green	0.44	40,000	6,500	76	740	17,200	2,600	7,200	3,900	2,600
	12%	0.47	61,000	7,900	57	640	36,000	5,100	10,200	3,400	3,100
Sugar	Green	0.56	65,000	10,700	92	1,020	27,700	4,400	10,100	—	4,300
	12%	0.63	109,000	12,600	114	990	54,000	10,100	16,100	—	6,400
Oak, red											
Black	Green	0.56	57,000	8,100	84	1,020	23,900	4,900	8,400	—	4,700
	12%	0.61	96,000	11,300	94	1,040	45,000	6,400	13,200	—	5,400
Cherrybark	Green	0.61	74,000	12,300	101	1,370	31,900	5,200	9,100	5,500	5,500
	12%	0.68	125,000	15,700	126	1,240	60,300	8,600	13,800	5,800	6,600
Laurel	Green	0.56	54,000	9,600	77	990	21,900	3,900	8,100	5,300	4,400
	12%	0.63	87,000	11,700	81	990	48,100	7,300	12,600	5,400	5,400
Northern red	Green	0.56	57,000	9,300	91	1,120	23,700	4,200	8,300	5,200	4,400
	12%	0.63	99,000	12,500	100	1,090	46,600	7,000	12,300	5,500	5,700
Pin	Green	0.58	57,000	9,100	97	1,220	25,400	5,000	8,900	5,500	4,800
	12%	0.63	97,000	11,900	102	1,140	47,000	7,000	14,300	7,200	6,700
Scarlet	Green	0.60	72,000	10,200	103	1,370	28,200	5,700	9,700	4,800	5,300
	12%	0.67	120,000	13,200	141	1,350	57,400	7,700	13,000	6,000	6,200
Southern red	Green	0.52	48,000	7,900	55	740	20,900	3,800	6,400	3,300	3,800
	12%	0.59	75,000	10,300	65	660	42,000	6,000	9,600	3,500	4,700
Water	Green	0.56	61,000	10,700	77	990	25,800	4,300	8,500	5,700	4,500
	12%	0.63	106,000	13,900	148	1,120	46,700	7,000	13,900	6,300	5,300

67

Table 4–3a. Strength properties of some commercially important woods grown in the United States (metric)[a]—con.

Common species names	Moisture content	Specific gravity[b]	Static bending Modulus of rupture (kPa)	Static bending Modulus of elasticity[c] (MPa)	Static bending Work to maximum load (kJ/m³)	Impact bending (mm)	Compression parallel to grain (kPa)	Compression perpendicular to grain (kPa)	Shear parallel to grain (kPa)	Tension perpendicular to grain (kPa)	Side hardness (N)
Oak, red—con.											
Willow	Green	0.56	51,000	8,900	61	890	20,700	4,200	8,100	5,200	4,400
	12%	0.69	100,000	13,100	101	1,070	48,500	7,800	11,400	—	6,500
Oak, white											
Bur	Green	0.58	50,000	6,100	74	1,120	22,700	4,700	9,300	5,500	4,900
	12%	0.64	71,000	7,100	68	740	41,800	8,300	12,500	4,700	6,100
Chestnut	Green	0.57	55,000	9,400	65	890	24,300	3,700	8,300	4,800	4,000
	12%	0.66	92,000	11,000	76	1,020	47,100	5,800	10,300	—	5,000
Live	Green	0.80	82,000	10,900	85	—	37,400	14,100	15,200	—	—
	12%	0.88	127,000	13,700	130	—	61,400	19,600	18,300	—	—
Overcup	Green	0.57	55,000	7,900	87	1,120	23,200	3,700	9,100	5,000	4,300
	12%	0.63	87,000	9,800	108	970	42,700	5,600	13,800	6,500	5,300
Post	Green	0.60	56,000	7,500	76	1,120	24,000	5,900	8,800	5,400	5,000
	12%	0.67	91,000	10,400	91	1,170	45,300	9,900	12,700	5,400	6,000
Swamp chestnut	Green	0.60	59,000	9,300	88	1,140	24,400	3,900	8,700	4,600	4,900
	12%	0.67	96,000	12,200	83	1,040	50,100	7,700	13,700	4,800	5,500
Swamp white	Green	0.64	68,000	11,000	100	1,270	30,100	5,200	9,000	5,900	5,200
	12%	0.72	122,000	14,100	132	1,240	59,300	8,200	13,800	5,700	7,200
White	Green	0.60	57,000	8,600	80	1,070	24,500	4,600	8,600	5,300	4,700
	12%	0.68	105,000	12,300	102	940	51,300	7,400	13,800	5,500	6,000
Sassafras	Green	0.42	41,000	6,300	49	—	18,800	2,600	6,600	—	—
	12%	0.46	62,000	7,700	60	—	32,800	5,900	8,500	—	—
Sweetgum	Green	0.46	49,000	8,300	70	910	21,000	2,600	6,800	3,700	2,700
	12%	0.52	86,000	11,300	82	810	43,600	4,300	11,000	5,200	3,800
Sycamore, American	Green	0.46	45,000	7,300	52	660	20,100	2,500	6,900	4,300	2,700
	12%	0.49	69,000	9,800	59	660	37,100	4,800	10,100	5,000	3,400
Tanoak	Green	0.58	72,000	10,700	92	—	32,100	—	—	—	—
	12%	—	—	—	—	—	—	—	—	—	—
Tupelo											
Black	Green	0.46	48,000	7,100	55	760	21,000	3,300	7,600	3,900	2,800
	12%	0.50	66,000	8,300	43	560	38,100	6,400	9,200	3,400	3,600
Water	Green	0.46	50,000	7,200	57	760	23,200	3,300	8,200	4,100	3,200
	12%	0.50	66,000	8,700	48	580	40,800	6,000	11,000	4,800	3,900
Walnut, black	Green	0.51	66,000	9,800	101	940	29,600	3,400	8,400	3,900	4,000
	12%	0.55	101,000	11,600	74	860	52,300	7,000	9,400	4,800	4,500
Willow, black	Green	0.36	33,000	5,400	76	—	14,100	1,200	4,700	—	—
	12%	0.39	54,000	7,000	61	—	28,300	3,000	8,600	—	—
Yellow-poplar	Green	0.40	41,000	8,400	52	660	18,300	1,900	5,400	3,500	2,000
	12%	0.42	70,000	10,900	61	610	38,200	3,400	8,200	3,700	2,400
Softwoods											
Baldcypress	Green	0.42	46,000	8,100	46	640	24,700	2,800	5,600	2,100	1,700
	12%	0.46	73,000	9,900	57	610	43,900	5,000	6,900	1,900	2,300
Cedar											
Atlantic white	Green	0.31	32,000	5,200	41	460	16,500	1,700	4,800	1,200	1,300
	12%	0.32	47,000	6,400	28	330	32,400	2,800	5,500	1,500	1,600
Eastern redcedar	Green	0.44	48,000	4,500	103	890	24,600	4,800	7,000	2,300	2,900
	12%	0.47	61,000	6,100	57	560	41,500	6,300	—	—	4,000
Incense	Green	0.35	43,000	5,800	44	430	21,700	2,600	5,700	1,900	1,700
	12%	0.37	55,000	7,200	37	430	35,900	4,100	6,100	1,900	2,100
Northern white	Green	0.29	29,000	4,400	39	380	13,700	1,600	4,300	1,700	1,000
	12%	0.31	45,000	5,500	33	300	27,300	2,100	5,900	1,700	1,400

Table 4–3a. Strength properties of some commercially important woods grown in the United States (metric)[a]—con.

| Common species names | Moisture content | Specific gravity[b] | Static bending | | | Impact bending (mm) | Compression parallel to grain (kPa) | Compression perpendicular to grain (kPa) | Shear parallel to grain (kPa) | Tension perpendicular to grain (kPa) | Side hardness (N) |
			Modulus of rupture (kPa)	Modulus of elasticity[c] (MPa)	Work to maximum load (kJ/m³)						
Cedar—con.											
Port-Orford	Green	0.39	45,000	9,000	51	530	21,600	2,100	5,800	1,200	1,700
	12%	0.43	88,000	11,700	63	710	43,100	5,000	9,400	2,800	2,800
Western redcedar	Green	0.31	35,900	6,500	34	430	19,100	1,700	5,300	1,600	1,200
	12%	0.32	51,700	7,700	40	430	31,400	3,200	6,800	1,500	1,600
Yellow	Green	0.42	44,000	7,900	63	690	21,000	2,400	5,800	2,300	2,000
	12%	0.44	77,000	9,800	72	740	43,500	4,300	7,800	2,500	2,600
Douglas-fir[d]											
Coast	Green	0.45	53,000	10,800	52	660	26,100	2,600	6,200	2,100	2,200
	12%	0.48	85,000	13,400	68	790	49,900	5,500	7,800	2,300	3,200
Interior West	Green	0.46	53,000	10,400	50	660	26,700	2,900	6,500	2,000	2,300
	12%	0.50	87,000	12,600	73	810	51,200	5,200	8,900	2,400	2,900
Interior North	Green	0.45	51,000	9,700	56	560	23,900	2,500	6,600	2,300	1,900
	12%	0.48	90,000	12,300	72	660	47,600	5,300	9,700	2,700	2,700
Interior South	Green	0.43	47,000	8,000	55	380	21,400	2,300	6,600	1,700	1,600
	12%	0.46	82,000	10,300	62	510	43,000	5,100	10,400	2,300	2,300
Fir											
Balsam	Green	0.33	38,000	8,600	32	410	18,100	1,300	4,600	1,200	1,300
	12%	0.35	63,000	10,000	35	510	36,400	2,800	6,500	1,200	1,800
California red	Green	0.36	40,000	8,100	44	530	19,000	2,300	5,300	2,600	1,600
	12%	0.38	72,400	10,300	61	610	37,600	4,200	7,200	2,700	2,200
Grand	Green	0.35	40,000	8,600	39	560	20,300	1,900	5,100	1,700	1,600
	12%	0.37	61,400	10,800	52	710	36,500	3,400	6,200	1,700	2,200
Noble	Green	0.37	43,000	9,500	41	480	20,800	1,900	5,500	1,600	1,300
	12%	0.39	74,000	11,900	61	580	42,100	3,600	7,200	1,500	1,800
Pacific silver	Green	0.40	44,000	9,800	41	530	21,600	1,500	5,200	1,700	1,400
	12%	0.43	75,800	12,100	64	610	44,200	3,100	8,400	—	1,900
Subalpine	Green	0.31	34,000	7,200	—	—	15,900	1,300	4,800	—	1,200
	12%	0.32	59,000	8,900	—	—	33,500	2,700	7,400	—	1,600
White	Green	0.37	41,000	8,000	39	560	20,000	1,900	5,200	2,100	1,500
	12%	0.39	68,000	10,300	50	510	40,000	3,700	7,600	2,100	2,100
Hemlock											
Eastern	Green	0.38	44,000	7,400	46	530	21,200	2,500	5,900	1,600	1,800
	12%	0.40	61,000	8,300	47	530	37,300	4,500	7,300	—	2,200
Mountain	Green	0.42	43,000	7,200	76	810	19,900	2,600	6,400	2,300	2,100
	12%	0.45	79,000	9,200	72	810	44,400	5,900	10,600	—	3,000
Western	Green	0.42	46,000	9,000	48	560	23,200	1,900	5,900	2,000	1,800
	12%	0.45	78,000	11,300	57	580	49,000	3,800	8,600	2,300	2,400
Larch, western	Green	0.48	53,000	10,100	71	740	25,900	2,800	6,000	2,300	2,300
	12%	0.52	90,000	12,900	87	890	52,500	6,400	9,400	3,000	3,700
Pine											
Eastern white	Green	0.34	34,000	6,800	36	430	16,800	1,500	4,700	1,700	1,300
	12%	0.35	59,000	8,500	47	460	33,100	3,000	6,200	2,100	1,700
Jack	Green	0.40	41,000	7,400	50	660	20,300	2,100	5,200	2,500	1,800
	12%	0.43	68,000	9,300	57	690	39,000	4,000	8,100	2,900	2,500
Loblolly	Green	0.47	50,000	9,700	57	760	24,200	2,700	5,900	1,800	2,000
	12%	0.51	88,000	12,300	72	760	49,200	5,400	9,600	3,200	3,100
Lodgepole	Green	0.38	38,000	7,400	39	510	18,000	1,700	4,700	1,500	1,500
	12%	0.41	65,000	9,200	47	510	37,000	4,200	6,100	2,000	2,100
Longleaf	Green	0.54	59,000	11,000	61	890	29,800	3,300	7,200	2,300	2,600
	12%	0.59	100,000	13,700	81	860	58,400	6,600	10,400	3,200	3,900
Pitch	Green	0.47	47,000	8,300	63	—	20,300	2,500	5,900	—	—
	12%	0.52	74,000	9,900	63	—	41,000	5,600	9,400	—	—

Table 4–3a. Strength properties of some commercially important woods grown in the United States (metric)[a]—con.

Common species names	Moisture content	Specific gravity[b]	Static bending			Impact bending (mm)	Compression parallel to grain (kPa)	Compression perpendicular to grain (kPa)	Shear parallel to grain (kPa)	Tension perpendicular to grain (kPa)	Side hardness (N)
			Modulus of rupture (kPa)	Modulus of elasticity[c] (MPa)	Work to maximum load (kJ/m³)						
Pine—con.											
Pond	Green	0.51	51,000	8,800	52	—	25,200	3,000	6,500	—	—
	12%	0.56	80,000	12,100	59	—	52,000	6,300	9,500	—	—
Ponderosa	Green	0.38	35,000	6,900	36	530	16,900	1,900	4,800	2,100	1,400
	12%	0.40	65,000	8,900	49	480	36,700	4,000	7,800	2,900	2,000
Red	Green	0.41	40,000	8,800	42	660	18,800	1,800	4,800	2,100	1,500
	12%	0.46	76,000	11,200	68	660	41,900	4,100	8,400	3,200	2,500
Sand	Green	0.46	52,000	7,000	66	—	23,700	3,100	7,900	—	—
	12%	0.48	80,000	9,700	66	—	47,700	5,800	—	—	—
Shortleaf	Green	0.47	51,000	9,600	57	760	24,300	2,400	6,300	2,200	2,000
	12%	0.51	90,000	12,100	76	840	50,100	5,700	9,600	3,200	3,100
Slash	Green	0.54	60,000	10,500	66	—	26,300	3,700	6,600	—	—
	12%	0.59	112,000	13,700	91	—	56,100	7,000	11,600	—	—
Spruce	Green	0.41	41,000	6,900	—	—	19,600	1,900	6,200	—	2,000
	12%	0.44	72,000	8,500	—	—	39,000	5,000	10,300	—	2,900
Sugar	Green	0.34	34,000	7,100	37	430	17,000	1,400	5,000	1,900	1,200
	12%	0.36	57,000	8,200	38	460	30,800	3,400	7,800	2,400	1,700
Virginia	Green	0.45	50,000	8,400	75	860	23,600	2,700	6,100	2,800	2,400
	12%	0.48	90,000	10,500	94	810	46,300	6,300	9,300	2,600	3,300
Western white	Green	0.36	32,000	8,200	34	480	16,800	1,300	4,700	1,800	1,200
	12%	0.38	67,000	10,100	61	580	34,700	3,200	7,200	—	1,900
Redwood											
Old-growth	Green	0.38	52,000	8,100	51	530	29,000	2,900	5,500	1,800	1,800
	12%	0.40	69,000	9,200	48	480	42,400	4,800	6,500	1,700	2,100
Young-growth	Green	0.34	41,000	6,600	39	410	21,400	1,900	6,100	2,100	1,600
	12%	0.35	54,000	7,600	36	380	36,000	3,600	7,600	1,700	1,900
Spruce											
Black	Green	0.38	42,000	9,500	51	610	19,600	1,700	5,100	700	1,600
	12%	0.46	74,000	11,100	72	580	41,100	3,800	8,500	—	2,300
Engelmann	Green	0.33	32,000	7,100	35	410	15,000	1,400	4,400	1,700	1,150
	12%	0.35	64,000	8,900	44	460	30,900	2,800	8,300	2,400	1,750
Red	Green	0.37	41,000	9,200	48	460	18,800	1,800	5,200	1,500	1,600
	12%	0.40	74,000	11,100	58	640	38,200	3,800	8,900	2,400	2,200
Sitka	Green	0.33	34,000	7,900	43	610	16,200	1,400	4,400	1,700	1,600
	12%	0.36	65,000	9,900	65	640	35,700	3,000	6,700	2,600	2,300
White	Green	0.37	39,000	7,400	41	560	17,700	1,700	4,800	1,500	1,400
	12%	0.40	68,000	9,200	53	510	37,700	3,200	7,400	2,500	2,100
Tamarack	Green	0.49	50,000	8,500	50	710	24,000	2,700	5,900	1,800	1,700
	12%	0.53	80,000	11,300	49	580	49,400	5,500	8,800	2,800	2,600

[a]Results of tests on small clear specimens in the green and air-dried conditions, converted to metric units directly from Table 4–3b. Definition of properties: impact bending is height of drop that causes complete failure, using 0.71-kg (50-lb) hammer; compression parallel to grain is also called maximum crushing strength; compression perpendicular to grain is fiber stress at proportional limit; shear is maximum shearing strength; tension is maximum tensile strength; and side hardness is hardness measured when load is perpendicular to grain.

[b]Specific gravity is based on weight when ovendry and volume when green or at 12% moisture content.

[c]Modulus of elasticity measured from a simply supported, center-loaded beam, on a span depth ratio of 14/1. To correct for shear deflection, the modulus can be increased by 10%.

[d]Coast Douglas-fir is defined as Douglas-fir growing in Oregon and Washington State west of the Cascade Mountains summit. Interior West includes California and all counties in Oregon and Washington east of, but adjacent to, the Cascade summit; Interior North, the remainder of Oregon and Washington plus Idaho, Montana, and Wyoming; and Interior South, Utah, Colorado, Arizona, and New Mexico.

Table 4–3b. Strength properties of some commercially important woods grown in the United States (inch–pound)[a]

Common species names	Moisture content	Specific gravity[b]	Static bending — Modulus of rupture (lbf/in²)	Static bending — Modulus of elasticity[c] (×10⁶ lbf/in²)	Static bending — Work to maximum load (in-lbf/in³)	Impact bending (in.)	Compression parallel to grain (lbf/in²)	Compression perpendicular to grain (lbf/in²)	Shear parallel to grain (lbf/in²)	Tension perpendicular to grain (lbf/in²)	Side hardness (lbf)
Hardwoods											
Alder, red	Green	0.37	6,500	1.17	8.0	22	2,960	250	770	390	440
	12%	0.41	9,800	1.38	8.4	20	5,820	440	1,080	420	590
Ash											
Black	Green	0.45	6,000	1.04	12.1	33	2,300	350	860	490	520
	12%	0.49	12,600	1.60	14.9	35	5,970	760	1,570	700	850
Blue	Green	0.53	9,600	1.24	14.7	—	4,180	810	1,540	—	—
	12%	0.58	13,800	1.40	14.4	—	6,980	1,420	2,030	—	—
Green	Green	0.53	9,500	1.40	11.8	35	4,200	730	1,260	590	870
	12%	0.56	14,100	1.66	13.4	32	7,080	1,310	1,910	700	1,200
Oregon	Green	0.50	7,600	1.13	12.2	39	3,510	530	1,190	590	790
	12%	0.55	12,700	1.36	14.4	33	6,040	1,250	1,790	720	1,160
White	Green	0.55	9,500	1.44	15.7	38	3,990	670	1,350	590	960
	12%	0.60	15,000	1.74	16.6	43	7,410	1,160	1,910	940	1,320
Aspen											
Bigtooth	Green	0.36	5,400	1.12	5.7	—	2,500	210	730	—	—
	12%	0.39	9,100	1.43	7.7	—	5,300	450	1,080	—	—
Quaking	Green	0.35	5,100	0.86	6.4	22	2,140	180	660	230	300
	12%	0.38	8,400	1.18	7.6	21	4,250	370	850	260	350
Basswood, American	Green	0.32	5,000	1.04	5.3	16	2,220	170	600	280	250
	12%	0.37	8,700	1.46	7.2	16	4,730	370	990	350	410
Beech, American	Green	0.56	8,600	1.38	11.9	43	3,550	540	1,290	720	850
	12%	0.64	14,900	1.72	15.1	41	7,300	1,010	2,010	1,010	1,300
Birch											
Paper	Green	0.48	6,400	1.17	16.2	49	2,360	270	840	380	560
	12%	0.55	12,300	1.59	16.0	34	5,690	600	1,210	—	910
Sweet	Green	0.60	9,400	1.65	15.7	48	3,740	470	1,240	430	970
	12%	0.65	16,900	2.17	18.0	47	8,540	1,080	2,240	950	1,470
Yellow	Green	0.55	8,300	1.50	16.1	48	3,380	430	1,110	430	780
	12%	0.62	16,600	2.01	20.8	55	8,170	970	1,880	920	1,260
Butternut	Green	0.36	5,400	0.97	8.2	24	2,420	220	760	430	390
	12%	0.38	8,100	1.18	8.2	24	5,110	460	1,170	440	490
Cherry, black	Green	0.47	8,000	1.31	12.8	33	3,540	360	1,130	570	660
	12%	0.50	12,300	1.49	11.4	29	7,110	690	1,700	560	950
Chestnut, American	Green	0.40	5,600	0.93	7.0	24	2,470	310	800	440	420
	12%	0.43	8,600	1.23	6.5	19	5,320	620	1,080	460	540
Cottonwood											
Balsam, poplar	Green	0.31	3,900	0.75	4.2	—	1,690	140	500	—	—
	12%	0.34	6,800	1.10	5.0	—	4,020	300	790	—	—
Black	Green	0.31	4,900	1.08	5.0	20	2,200	160	610	270	250
	12%	0.35	8,500	1.27	6.7	22	4,500	300	1,040	330	350
Eastern	Green	0.37	5,300	1.01	7.3	21	2,280	200	680	410	340
	12%	0.40	8,500	1.37	7.4	20	4,910	380	930	580	430
Elm											
American	Green	0.46	7,200	1.11	11.8	38	2,910	360	1,000	590	620
	12%	0.50	11,800	1.34	13.0	39	5,520	690	1,510	660	830
Rock	Green	0.57	9,500	1.19	19.8	54	3,780	610	1,270	—	940
	12%	0.63	14,800	1.54	19.2	56	7,050	1,230	1,920	—	1,320
Slippery	Green	0.48	8,000	1.23	15.4	47	3,320	420	1,110	640	660
	12%	0.53	13,000	1.49	16.9	45	6,360	820	1,630	530	860
Hackberry	Green	0.49	6,500	0.95	14.5	48	2,650	400	1,070	630	700
	12%	0.53	11,000	1.19	12.8	43	5,440	890	1,590	580	880

71

Table 4–3b. Strength properties of some commercially important woods grown in the United States (inch–pound)[a]—con.

Common species names	Moisture content	Specific gravity[b]	Static bending — Modulus of rupture (lbf/in^2)	Static bending — Modulus of elasticity[c] ($\times 10^6$ lbf/in^2)	Static bending — Work to maximum load (in-lbf/in^3)	Impact bending (in.)	Compression parallel to grain (lbf/in^2)	Compression perpendicular to grain (lbf/in^2)	Shear parallel to grain (lbf/in^2)	Tension perpendicular to grain (lbf/in^2)	Side hardness (lbf)
Hickory, pecan											
Bitternut	Green	0.60	10,300	1.40	20.0	66	4,570	800	1,240	—	—
	12%	0.66	17,100	1.79	18.2	66	9,040	1,680	—	—	—
Nutmeg	Green	0.56	9,100	1.29	22.8	54	3,980	760	1,030	—	—
	12%	0.60	16,600	1.70	25.1	—	6,910	1,570	—	—	—
Pecan	Green	0.60	9,800	1.37	14.6	53	3,990	780	1,480	680	1,310
	12%	0.66	13,700	1.73	13.8	44	7,850	1,720	2,080	—	1,820
Water	Green	0.61	10,700	1.56	18.8	56	4,660	880	1,440	—	—
	12%	0.62	17,800	2.02	19.3	53	8,600	1,550	—	—	—
Hickory, true											
Mockernut	Green	0.64	11,100	1.57	26.1	88	4,480	810	1,280	—	—
	12%	0.72	19,200	2.22	22.6	77	8,940	1,730	1,740	—	—
Pignut	Green	0.66	11,700	1.65	31.7	89	4,810	920	1,370	—	—
	12%	0.75	20,100	2.26	30.4	74	9,190	1,980	2,150	—	—
Shagbark	Green	0.64	11,000	1.57	23.7	74	4,580	840	1,520	—	—
	12%	0.72	20,200	2.16	25.8	67	9,210	1,760	2,430	—	—
Shellbark	Green	0.62	10,500	1.34	29.9	104	3,920	810	1,190	—	—
	12%	0.69	18,100	1.89	23.6	88	8,000	1,800	2,110	—	—
Honeylocust	Green	0.60	10,200	1.29	12.6	47	4,420	1,150	1,660	930	1,390
	12%	—	14,700	1.63	13.3	47	7,500	1,840	2,250	900	1,580
Locust, black	Green	0.66	13,800	1.85	15.4	44	6,800	1,160	1,760	770	1,570
	12%	0.69	19,400	2.05	18.4	57	10,180	1,830	2,480	640	1,700
Magnolia											
Cucumbertree	Green	0.44	7,400	1.56	10.0	30	3,140	330	990	440	520
	12%	0.48	12,300	1.82	12.2	35	6,310	570	1,340	660	700
Southern	Green	0.46	6,800	1.11	15.4	54	2,700	460	1,040	610	740
	12%	0.50	11,200	1.40	12.8	29	5,460	860	1,530	740	1,020
Maple											
Bigleaf	Green	0.44	7,400	1.10	8.7	23	3,240	450	1,110	600	620
	12%	0.48	10,700	1.45	7.8	28	5,950	750	1,730	540	850
Black	Green	0.52	7,900	1.33	12.8	48	3,270	600	1,130	720	840
	12%	0.57	13,300	1.62	12.5	40	6,680	1,020	1,820	670	1,180
Red	Green	0.49	7,700	1.39	11.4	32	3,280	400	1,150	—	700
	12%	0.54	13,400	1.64	12.5	32	6,540	1,000	1,850	—	950
Silver	Green	0.44	5,800	0.94	11.0	29	2,490	370	1,050	560	590
	12%	0.47	8,900	1.14	8.3	25	5,220	740	1,480	500	700
Sugar	Green	0.56	9,400	1.55	13.3	40	4,020	640	1,460	—	970
	12%	0.63	15,800	1.83	16.5	39	7,830	1,470	2,330	—	1,450
Oak, red											
Black	Green	0.56	8,200	1.18	12.2	40	3,470	710	1,220	—	1,060
	12%	0.61	13,900	1.64	13.7	41	6,520	930	1,910	—	1,210
Cherrybark	Green	0.61	10,800	1.79	14.7	54	4,620	760	1,320	800	1,240
	12%	0.68	18,100	2.28	18.3	49	8,740	1,250	2,000	840	1,480
Laurel	Green	0.56	7900	1.39	11.2	39	3,170	570	1,180	770	1,000
	12%	0.63	12,600	1.69	11.8	39	6,980	1,060	1,830	790	1,210
Northern red	Green	0.56	8300	1.35	13.2	44	3,440	610	1,210	750	1,000
	12%	0.63	14,300	1.82	14.5	43	6,760	1,010	1,780	800	1,290
Pin	Green	0.58	8300	1.32	14.0	48	3,680	720	1,290	800	1,070
	12%	0.63	14000	1.73	14.8	45	6,820	1,020	2,080	1,050	1,510
Scarlet	Green	0.60	10,400	1.48	15.0	54	4,090	830	1,410	700	1,200
	12%	0.67	17400	1.91	20.5	53	8,330	1,120	1,890	870	1,400
Southern red	Green	0.52	6,900	1.14	8.0	29	3,030	550	930	480	860
	12%	0.59	10,900	1.49	9.4	26	6,090	870	1,390	510	1,060

Table 4–3b. Strength properties of some commercially important woods grown in the United States (inch–pound)[a]—con.

Common species names	Moisture content	Specific gravity[b]	Static bending Modulus of rupture (lbf/in²)	Static bending Modulus of elasticity[c] (×10⁶ lbf/in²)	Static bending Work to maximum load (in-lbf/in³)	Impact bending (in.)	Compression parallel to grain (lbf/in²)	Compression perpendicular to grain (lbf/in²)	Shear parallel to grain (lbf/in²)	Tension perpendicular to grain (lbf/in²)	Side hardness (lbf)
Oak, red—con.											
Water	Green	0.56	8,900	1.55	11.1	39	3,740	620	1,240	820	1,010
	12%	0.63	15,400	2.02	21.5	44	6,770	1,020	2,020	920	1,190
Willow	Green	0.56	7400	1.29	8.8	35	3,000	610	1,180	760	980
	12%	0.69	14,500	1.90	14.6	42	7,040	1,130	1,650	—	1,460
Oak, white											
Bur	Green	0.58	7,200	0.88	10.7	44	3,290	680	1,350	800	1,110
	12%	0.64	10,300	1.03	9.8	29	6,060	1,200	1,820	680	1,370
Chestnut	Green	0.57	8,000	1.37	9.4	35	3,520	530	1,210	690	890
	12%	0.66	13,300	1.59	11.0	40	6,830	840	1,490	—	1,130
Live	Green	0.80	11,900	1.58	12.3	—	5,430	2,040	2,210	—	—
	12%	0.88	18,400	1.98	18.9	—	8,900	2,840	2,660	—	—
Overcup	Green	0.57	8,000	1.15	12.6	44	3,370	540	1,320	730	960
	12%	0.63	12,600	1.42	15.7	38	6,200	810	2,000	940	1,190
Post	Green	0.60	8,100	1.09	11.0	44	3,480	860	1,280	790	1,130
	12%	0.67	13,200	1.51	13.2	46	6,600	1,430	1,840	780	1,360
Swamp chestnut	Green	0.60	8,500	1.35	12.8	45	3,540	570	1,260	670	1,110
	12%	0.67	13,900	1.77	12.0	41	7,270	1,110	1,990	690	1,240
Swamp white	Green	0.64	9,900	1.59	14.5	50	4,360	760	1,300	860	1,160
	12%	0.72	17,700	2.05	19.2	49	8,600	1,190	2,000	830	1,620
White	Green	0.60	8,300	1.25	11.6	42	3,560	670	1,250	770	1,060
	12%	0.68	15,200	1.78	14.8	37	7,440	1,070	2,000	800	1,360
Sassafras	Green	0.42	6,000	0.91	7.1	—	2,730	370	950	—	—
	12%	0.46	9,000	1.12	8.7	—	4,760	850	1,240	—	—
Sweetgum	Green	0.46	7,100	1.20	10.1	36	3,040	370	990	540	600
	12%	0.52	12,500	1.64	11.9	32	6,320	620	1,600	760	850
Sycamore, American	Green	0.46	6,500	1.06	7.5	26	2,920	360	1,000	630	610
	12%	0.49	10,000	1.42	8.5	26	5,380	700	1,470	720	770
Tanoak	Green	0.58	10,500	1.55	13.4	—	4,650	—	—	—	—
	12%	—	—	—	—	—	—	—	—	—	—
Tupelo											
Black	Green	0.46	7,000	1.03	8.0	30	3,040	480	1,100	570	640
	12%	0.50	9,600	1.20	6.2	22	5,520	930	1,340	500	810
Water	Green	0.46	7,300	1.05	8.3	30	3,370	480	1,190	600	710
	12%	0.50	9,600	1.26	6.9	23	5,920	870	1,590	700	880
Walnut, Black	Green	0.51	9,500	1.42	14.6	37	4,300	490	1,220	570	900
	12%	0.55	14,600	1.68	10.7	34	7,580	1,010	1,370	690	1,010
Willow, Black	Green	0.36	4,800	0.79	11.0	—	2,040	180	680	—	—
	12%	0.39	7,800	1.01	8.8	—	4,100	430	1,250	—	—
Yellow-poplar	Green	0.40	6,000	1.22	7.5	26	2,660	270	790	510	440
	12%	0.42	10,100	1.58	8.8	24	5,540	500	1,190	540	540
Softwoods											
Baldcypress	Green	0.42	6,600	1.18	6.6	25	3,580	400	810	300	390
	12%	0.46	10,600	1.44	8.2	24	6,360	730	1,000	270	510
Cedar											
Atlantic white	Green	0.31	4,700	0.75	5.9	18	2,390	240	690	180	290
	12%	0.32	6,800	0.93	4.1	13	4,700	410	800	220	350
Eastern redcedar	Green	0.44	7,000	0.65	15.0	35	3,570	700	1,010	330	650
	12%	0.47	8,800	0.88	8.3	22	6,020	920	—	—	—
Incense	Green	0.35	6,200	0.84	6.4	17	3,150	370	830	280	390
	12%	0.37	8,000	1.04	5.4	17	5,200	590	880	270	470
Northern White	Green	0.29	4,200	0.64	5.7	15	1,990	230	620	240	230
	12%	0.31	6,500	0.80	4.8	12	3,960	310	850	240	320

| Common species names | Moisture content | Specific gravity[b] | Static bending | | | Impact bending (in.) | Compression parallel to grain (lbf/in^2) | Compression perpendicular to grain (lbf/in^2) | Shear parallel to grain (lbf/in^2) | Tension perpendicular to grain (lbf/in^2) | Side hardness (lbf) |
			Modulus of rupture (lbf/in^2)	Modulus of elasticity[c] ($\times 10^6$ lbf/in^2)	Work to maximum load (in-lbf/in^3)						
Cedar—con.											
Port-Orford	Green	0.39	6,600	1.30	7.4	21	3,140	300	840	180	380
	12%	0.43	12,700	1.70	9.1	28	6,250	720	1,370	400	630
Western redcedar	Green	0.31	5,200	0.94	5.0	17	2,770	240	770	230	260
	12%	0.32	7,500	1.11	5.8	17	4,560	460	990	220	350
Yellow	Green	0.42	6,400	1.14	9.2	27	3,050	350	840	330	440
	12%	0.44	11,100	1.42	10.4	29	6,310	620	1,130	360	580
Douglas-fir[d]											
Coast	Green	0.45	7,700	1.56	7.6	26	3,780	380	900	300	500
	12%	0.48	12,400	1.95	9.9	31	7,230	800	1,130	340	710
Interior West	Green	0.46	7,700	1.51	7.2	26	3,870	420	940	290	510
	12%	0.50	12,600	1.83	10.6	32	7,430	760	1,290	350	660
Interior North	Green	0.45	7,400	1.41	8.1	22	3,470	360	950	340	420
	12%	0.48	13,100	1.79	10.5	26	6,900	770	1,400	390	600
Interior South	Green	0.43	6,800	1.16	8.0	15	3,110	340	950	250	360
	12%	0.46	11,900	1.49	9.0	20	6,230	740	1,510	330	510
Fir											
Balsam	Green	0.33	5,500	1.25	4.7	16	2,630	190	662	180	290
	12%	0.35	9,200	1.45	5.1	20	5,280	404	944	180	400
California red	Green	0.36	5,800	1.17	6.4	21	2,760	330	770	380	360
	12%	0.38	10,500	1.50	8.9	24	5,460	610	1,040	390	500
Grand	Green	0.35	5,800	1.25	5.6	22	2,940	270	740	240	360
	12%	0.37	8,900	1.57	7.5	28	5,290	500	900	240	490
Noble	Green	0.37	6,200	1.38	6.0	19	3,010	270	800	230	290
	12%	0.39	10,700	1.72	8.8	23	6,100	520	1,050	220	410
Pacific silver	Green	0.40	6,400	1.42	6.0	21	3,140	220	750	240	310
	12%	0.43	11,000	1.76	9.3	24	6,410	450	1,220	—	430
Subalpine	Green	0.31	4,900	1.05	—	—	2,300	190	700	—	260
	12%	0.32	8,600	1.29	—	—	4,860	390	1,070	—	350
White	Green	0.37	5,900	1.16	5.6	22	2,900	280	760	300	340
	12%	0.39	9,800	1.50	7.2	20	5,800	530	1,100	300	480
Hemlock											
Eastern	Green	0.38	6,400	1.07	6.7	21	3,080	360	850	230	400
	12%	0.40	8,900	1.20	6.8	21	5,410	650	1,060	—	500
Mountain	Green	0.42	6,300	1.04	11.0	32	2,880	370	930	330	470
	12%	0.45	11,500	1.33	10.4	32	6,440	860	1,540	—	680
Western	Green	0.42	6,600	1.31	6.9	22	3,360	280	860	290	410
	12%	0.45	11,300	1.63	8.3	23	7,200	550	1,290	340	540
Larch, western	Green	0.48	7,700	1.46	10.3	29	3,760	400	870	330	510
	12%	0.52	13,000	1.87	12.6	35	7,620	930	1,360	430	830
Pine											
Eastern white	Green	0.34	4,900	0.99	5.2	17	2,440	220	680	250	290
	12%	0.35	8,600	1.24	6.8	18	4,800	440	900	310	380
Jack	Green	0.40	6,000	1.07	7.2	26	2,950	300	750	360	400
	12%	0.43	9,900	1.35	8.3	27	5,660	580	1,170	420	570
Loblolly	Green	0.47	7,300	1.40	8.2	30	3,510	390	860	260	450
	12%	0.51	12,800	1.79	10.4	30	7,130	790	1,390	470	690
Lodgepole	Green	0.38	5,500	1.08	5.6	20	2,610	250	680	220	330
	12%	0.41	9,400	1.34	6.8	20	5,370	610	880	290	480
Longleaf	Green	0.554	8,500	1.59	8.9	35	4,320	480	1,040	330	590
	12%	0.59	14,500	1.98	11.8	34	8,470	960	1,510	470	870
Pitch	Green	0.47	6,800	1.20	9.2	—	2,950	360	860	—	—
	12%	0.52	10,800	1.43	9.2	—	5,940	820	1,360	—	—

Table 4–3b. Strength properties of some commercially important woods grown in the United States (inch–pound)[a]—con.

Common species names	Moisture content	Specific gravity[b]	Modulus of rupture (lbf/in²)	Modulus of elasticity[c] (×10⁶ lbf/in²)	Work to maximum load (in-lbf/in³)	Impact bending (in.)	Compression parallel to grain (lbf/in²)	Compression perpendicular to grain (lbf/in²)	Shear parallel to grain (lbf/in²)	Tension perpendicular to grain (lbf/in²)	Side hardness (lbf)
Pine—con.											
Pond	Green	0.51	7,400	1.28	7.5	—	3,660	440	940	—	—
	12%	0.56	11,600	1.75	8.6	—	7,540	910	1,380	—	—
Ponderosa	Green	0.38	5,100	1.00	5.2	21	2,450	280	700	310	320
	12%	0.40	9,400	1.29	7.1	19	5,320	580	1,130	420	460
Red	Green	0.41	5,800	1.28	6.1	26	2,730	260	690	300	340
	12%	0.46	11,000	1.63	9.9	26	6,070	600	1,210	460	560
Sand	Green	0.46	7,500	1.02	9.6	—	3,440	450	1,140	—	—
	12%	0.48	11,600	1.41	9.6	—	6,920	836	—	—	—
Shortleaf	Green	0.47	7,400	1.39	8.2	30	3,530	350	910	320	440
	12%	0.51	13,100	1.75	11.0	33	7,270	820	1,390	470	690
Slash	Green	0.54	8,700	1.53	9.6	—	3,820	530	960	—	—
	12%	0.59	16,300	1.98	13.2	—	8,140	1020	1,680	—	—
Spruce	Green	0.41	6,000	1.00	—	—	2,840	280	900	—	450
	12%	0.44	10,400	1.23	—	—	5,650	730	1,490	—	660
Sugar	Green	0.34	4,900	1.03	5.4	17	2,460	210	720	270	270
	12%	0.36	8,200	1.19	5.5	18	4,460	500	1,130	350	380
Virginia	Green	0.45	7,300	1.22	10.9	34	3,420	390	890	400	540
	12%	0.48	13,000	1.52	13.7	32	6,710	910	1,350	380	740
Western white	Green	0.35	4,700	1.19	5.0	19	2,430	190	680	260	260
	12%	0.38	9,700	1.46	8.8	23	5,040	470	1,040	—	420
Redwood											
Old-growth	Green	0.38	7,500	1.18	7.4	21	4,200	420	800	260	410
	12%	0.40	10,000	1.34	6.9	19	6,150	700	940	240	480
Young-growth	Green	0.34	5,900	0.96	5.7	16	3,110	270	890	300	350
	12%	0.35	7,900	1.10	5.2	15	5,220	520	1,110	250	420
Spruce											
Black	Green	0.38	6,100	1.38	7.4	24	2,840	240	739	100	370
	12%	0.42	10,800	1.61	10.5	23	5,960	550	1,230	—	520
Engelmann	Green	0.33	4,700	1.03	5.1	16	2,180	200	640	240	260
	12%	0.35	9,300	1.30	6.4	18	4,480	410	1,200	350	390
Red	Green	0.37	6,000	1.33	6.9	18	2,720	260	750	220	350
	12%	0.40	10,800	1.61	8.4	25	5,540	550	1,290	350	490
Sitka	Green	0.37	5,700	1.23	6.3	24	2,670	280	760	250	350
	12%	0.40	10,200	1.57	9.4	25	5,610	580	1,150	370	510
White	Green	0.33	5,000	1.14	6.0	22	2,350	210	640	220	320
	12%	0.36	9,400	1.43	7.7	20	5,180	430	970	360	480
Tamarack	Green	0.49	7,200	1.24	7.2	28	3,480	390	860	260	380
	12%	0.53	11,600	1.64	7.1	23	7,160	800	1,280	400	590

[a]Results of tests on small clear specimens in the green and air-dried conditions. Definition of properties: impact bending is height of drop that causes complete failure, using 0.71-kg (50-lb) hammer; compression parallel to grain is also called maximum crushing strength; compression perpendicular to grain is fiber stress at proportional limit; shear is maximum shearing strength; tension is maximum tensile strength; and side hardness is hardness measured when load is perpendicular to grain.
[b]Specific gravity is based on weight when ovendry and volume when green or at 12% moisture content.
[c]Modulus of elasticity measured from a simply supported, center-loaded beam, on a span depth ratio of 14/1. To correct for shear deflection, the modulus can be increased by 10%.
[d]Coast Douglas-fir is defined as Douglas-fir growing in Oregon and Washington State west of the Cascade Mountains summit. Interior West includes California and all counties in Oregon and Washington east of, but adjacent to, the Cascade summit; Interior North, the remainder of Oregon and Washington plus Idaho, Montana, and Wyoming; and Interior South, Utah, Colorado, Arizona, and New Mexico.

Table 4–4a. Mechanical properties of some commercially important woods grown in Canada and imported into the United States (metric)[a]

Common species names	Moisture content	Specific gravity	Static bending		Compression parallel to grain (kPa)	Compression perpendicular to grain (kPa)	Shear parallel to grain (kPa)
			Modulus of rupture (kPa)	Modulus of elasticity (MPa)			
Hardwoods							
Aspen							
Quaking	Green	0.37	38,000	9,000	16,200	1,400	5,000
	12%		68,000	11,200	36,300	3,500	6,800
Big-toothed	Green	0.39	36,000	7,400	16,500	1,400	5,400
	12%		66,000	8,700	32,800	3,200	7,600
Cottonwood							
Black	Green	0.30	28,000	6,700	12,800	700	3,900
	12%		49,000	8,800	27,700	1,800	5,900
Eastern	Green	0.35	32,000	6,000	13,600	1,400	5,300
	12%		52,000	7,800	26,500	3,200	8,000
Balsam, poplar	Green	0.37	34,000	7,900	14,600	1,200	4,600
	12%		70,000	11,500	34,600	2,900	6,100
Softwoods							
Cedar							
Northern white	Green	0.30	27,000	3,600	13,000	1,400	4,600
	12%		42,000	4,300	24,800	2,700	6,900
Western redcedar	Green	0.31	36,000	7,200	19,200	1,900	4,800
	12%		54,000	8,200	29,600	3,400	5,600
Yellow	Green	0.42	46,000	9,200	22,300	2,400	6,100
	12%		80,000	11,000	45,800	4,800	9,200
Douglas-fir	Green	0.45	52,000	11,100	24,900	3,200	6,300
	12%		88,000	13,600	50,000	6,000	9,500
Fir							
Subalpine	Green	0.33	36,000	8,700	17,200	1,800	4,700
	12%		56,000	10,200	36,400	3,700	6,800
Pacific silver	Green	0.36	38,000	9,300	19,100	1,600	4,900
	12%		69,000	11,300	40,900	3,600	7,500
Balsam	Green	0.34	36,000	7,800	16,800	1,600	4,700
	12%		59,000	9,600	34,300	3,200	6,300
Hemlock							
Eastern	Green	0.40	47,000	8,800	23,600	2,800	6,300
	12%		67,000	9,700	41,200	4,300	8,700
Western	Green	0.41	48,000	10,200	24,700	2,600	5,200
	12%		81,000	12,300	46,700	4,600	6,500
Larch, western	Green	0.55	60,000	11,400	30,500	3,600	6,300
	12%		107,000	14,300	61,000	7,300	9,200
Pine							
Eastern white	Green	0.36	35,000	8,100	17,900	1,600	4,400
	12%		66,000	9,400	36,000	3,400	6,100
Jack	Green	0.42	43,000	8,100	20,300	2,300	5,600
	12%		78,000	10,200	40,500	5,700	8,200
Lodgepole	Green	0.40	39,000	8,800	19,700	1,900	5,000
	12%		76,000	10,900	43,200	3,600	8,500
Ponderosa	Green	0.44	39,000	7,800	19,600	2,400	5,000
	12%		73,000	9,500	42,300	5,200	7,000
Red	Green	0.39	34,000	7,400	16,300	1,900	4,900
	12%		70,000	9,500	37,900	5,200	7,500
Western white	Green	0.36	33,000	8,200	17,400	1,600	4,500
	12%		64,100	10,100	36,100	3,200	6,300
Spruce							
Black	Green	0.41	41,000	9,100	19,000	2,100	5,500
	12%		79,000	10,500	41,600	4,300	8,600
Engelmann	Green	0.38	39,000	8,600	19,400	1,900	4,800
	12%		70,000	10,700	42,400	3,700	7,600
Red	Green	0.38	41,000	9,100	19,400	1,900	5,600
	12%		71,000	11,000	38,500	3,800	9,200
Sitka	Green	0.35	37,000	9,400	17,600	2,000	4,300
	12%		70,000	11,200	37,800	4,100	6,800
White	Green	0.35	35,000	7,900	17,000	1,600	4,600
	12%		63,000	10,000	37,000	3,400	6,800
Tamarack	Green	0.48	47,000	8,600	21,600	2,800	6,300
	12%		76,000	9,400	44,900	6,200	9,000

[a]Results of tests on small, clear, straight-grained specimens. Property values based on ASTM Standard D2555–88. Information on additional properties can be obtained from Department of Forestry, Canada, Publication No. 1104. For each species, values in the first line are from tests of green material; those in the second line are adjusted from the green condition to 12% moisture content using dry to green clear wood property ratios as reported in ASTM D2555–88. Specific gravity is based on weight when ovendry and volume when green.

Table 4–4b. Mechanical properties of some commercially important woods grown in Canada and imported into the United States (inch–pound)[a]

| Common species names | Moisture content | Specific gravity | Static bending | | Compression parallel to grain (lbf/in^2) | Compression perpendicular to grain (lbf/in^2) | Shear parallel to grain (lbf/in^2) |
			Modulus of rupture (lbf/in^2)	Modulus of elasticity ($\times 10^6$ lbf/in^2)			
Hardwoods							
Aspen							
Quaking	Green	0.37	5,500	1.31	2,350	200	720
	12%		9,800	1.63	5,260	510	980
Bigtooth	Green	0.39	5,300	1.08	2,390	210	790
	12%		9,500	1.26	4,760	470	1,100
Cottonwood							
Balsam, poplar	Green	0.37	5,000	1.15	2,110	180	670
	12%		10,100	1.67	5,020	420	890
Black	Green	0.30	4,100	0.97	1,860	100	560
	12%		7,100	1.28	4,020	260	860
Eastern	Green	0.35	4,700	0.87	1,970	210	770
	12%		7,500	1.13	3,840	470	1,160
Softwoods							
Cedar							
Northern white	Green	0.30	3,900	0.52	1,890	200	660
	12%		6,100	0.63	3,590	390	1,000
Western redcedar	Green	0.31	5,300	1.05	2,780	280	700
	12%		7,800	1.19	4,290	500	810
Yellow	Green	0.42	6,600	1.34	3,240	350	880
	12%		11,600	1.59	6,640	690	1,340
Douglas-fir	Green	0.45	7,500	1.61	3,610	460	920
	12%		12,800	1.97	7,260	870	1,380
Fir							
Balsam	Green	0.34	5,300	1.13	2,440	240	680
	12%		8,500	1.40	4,980	460	910
Pacific silver	Green	0.36	5,500	1.35	2,770	230	710
	12%		10,000	1.64	5,930	520	1,190
Subalpine	Green	0.33	5,200	1.26	2,500	260	680
	12%		8,200	1.48	5,280	540	980
Hemlock							
Eastern	Green	0.40	6,800	1.27	3,430	400	910
	12%		9,700	1.41	5,970	630	1,260
Western	Green	0.41	7,000	1.48	3,580	370	750
	12%		11,800	1.79	6,770	660	940
Larch, western	Green	0.55	8,700	1.65	4,420	520	920
	12%		15,500	2.08	8,840	1,060	1,340
Pine							
Eastern white	Green	0.36	5,100	1.18	2,590	240	640
	12%		9,500	1.36	5,230	490	880
Jack	Green	0.42	6,300	1.17	2,950	340	820
	12%		11,300	1.48	5,870	830	1,190
Lodgepole	Green	0.40	5,600	1.27	2,860	280	720
	12%		11,000	1.58	6,260	530	1,240
Ponderosa	Green	0.44	5,700	1.13	2,840	350	720
	12%		10,600	1.38	6,130	760	1,020
Red	Green	0.39	5,000	1.07	2,370	280	710
	12%		10,100	1.38	5,500	720	1,090
Western white	Green	0.36	4,800	1.19	2,520	240	650
	12%		9,300	1.46	5,240	470	920
Spruce							
Black	Green	0.41	5,900	1.32	2,760	300	800
	12%		11,400	1.52	6,040	620	1,250
Engelmann	Green	0.38	5,700	1.25	2,810	270	700
	12%		10,100	1.55	6,150	540	1,100
Red	Green	0.38	5,900	1.32	2,810	270	810
	12%		10,300	1.60	5,590	550	1,330
Sitka	Green	0.35	5,400	1.37	2,560	290	630
	12%		10,100	1.63	5,480	590	980
White	Green	0.35	5,100	1.15	2,470	240	670
	12%		9,100	1.45	5,360	500	980
Tamarack	Green	0.48	6,800	1.24	3,130	410	920
	12%		11,000	1.36	6,510	900	1,300

[a]Results of tests on small, clear, straight-grained specimens. Property values based on ASTM Standard D2555–88. Information on additional properties can be obtained from Department of Forestry, Canada, Publication No. 1104. For each species, values in the first line are from tests of green material; those in the second line are adjusted from the green condition to 12% moisture content using dry to green clear wood property ratios as reported in ASTM D2555–88. Specific gravity is based on weight when ovendry and volume when green.

Table 4–5a. Mechanical properties of some woods imported into the United States other than Canadian imports (metric)[a]

| Common and botanical names of species | Moisture content | Specific gravity | Static bending | | | Compression parallel to grain (kPa) | Shear parallel to grain (kPa) | Side hardness (N) | Sample origin[b] |
			Modulus of rupture (kPa)	Modulus of elasticity (MPa)	Work to maximum load (kJ/m³)				
Afrormosia (*Pericopsis elata*)	Green	0.61	102,000	12,200	135	51,600	11,500	7,100	AF
	12%		126,900	13,400	127	68,500	14,400	6,900	
Albarco (*Cariniana* spp.)	Green	0.48	—	—	—	—	—	—	AM
	12%		100,000	10,300	95	47,000	15,900	4,500	
Andiroba (*Carapa guianensis*)	Green	0.54	71,000	11,700	68	33,000	8,400	3,900	AM
	12%	—	106,900	13,800	97	56,000	10,400	5,000	
Angelin (*Andira inermis*)	Green	0.65	—	—	—	—	—	—	AF
	12%		124,100	17,200	—	63,400	12,700	7,800	
Angelique (*Dicorynia guianensis*)	Green	0.6	78,600	12,700	83	38,500	9,200	4,900	AM
	12%	—	120,000	15,100	105	60,500	11,400	5,700	
Avodire (*Turraeanthus africanus*)	Green	0.48	—	—	—	—	—	—	AF
	12%		87,600	10,300	65	49,300	14,000	4,800	
Azobe (*Lophira alata*)	Green	0.87	116,500	14,900	83	65,600	14,100	12,900	AF
	12%		168,900	17,000	—	86,900	20,400	14,900	
Balsa (*Ochroma pyramidale*)	Green	0.16	—	—	—	—	—	—	AM
	12%		21,600	3,400	14	14,900	2,100	—	
Banak (*Virola* spp.)	Green	0.42	38,600	11,300	28	16,500	5,000	1,400	AM
	12%	—	75,200	14,100	69	35,400	6,800	2,300	
Benge (*Guibourtia arnoldiana*)	Green	0.65	—	—	—	—	—	—	AF
	12%		147,500	14,100	—	78,600	14,400	7,800	
Bubinga (*Guibourtia* spp.)	Green	0.71	—	—	—	—	—	—	AF
	12%		155,800	17,100	—	72,400	21,400	12,000	
Bulletwood (*Manilkara bidentata*)	Green	0.85	119,300	18,600	94	59,900	13,100	9,900	AM
	12%		188,200	23,800	197	80,300	17,200	14,200	
Cativo (*Prioria copaifera*)	Green	0.4	40,700	6,500	37	17,000	5,900	2,000	AM
	12%	—	59,300	7,700	50	29,600	7,300	2,800	
Ceiba (*Ceiba pentandra*)	Green	0.25	15,200	2,800	8	7,300	2,400	1,000	AM
	12%		29,600	3,700	19	16,400	3,800	1,100	
Courbaril (*Hymenaea courbaril*)	Green	0.71	88,900	12,700	101	40,000	12,200	8,800	AM
	12%	—	133,800	14,900	121	65,600	17,000	10,500	
Cuangare (*Dialyanthera* spp.)	Green	0.31	27,600	7,000	—	14,300	4,100	1,000	AM
	12%		50,300	10,500	—	32,800	5,700	1,700	
Cypress, Mexican (*Cupressus lustianica*)	Green	0.93	42,700	6,300	—	19,900	6,600	1,500	AF
	12%		71,000	7,000	—	37,100	10,900	2,000	
Degame (*Calycophyllum candidissimum*)	Green	0.67	98,600	13,300	128	42,700	11,400	7,300	AM
	12%		153,800	15,700	186	66,700	14,600	8,600	
Determa (*Ocotea rubra*)	Green	0.52	53,800	10,100	33	25,900	5,900	2,300	AM
	12%		72,400	12,500	44	40,000	6,800	2,900	
Ekop (*Tetraberlinia tubmaniana*)	Green	0.6	—	—	—	—	—	—	AF
	12%		115,100	15,200	—	62,100	—	—	
Goncalo alves (*Astronium graveolens*)	Green	0.84	83,400	13,400	46	45,400	12,100	8,500	AM
	12%	—	114,500	15,400	72	71,200	13,500	9,600	
Greenheart (*Chlorocardium rodiei*)	Green	0.8	133,100	17,000	72	64,700	13,300	8,400	AM
	12%		171,700	22,400	175	86,300	18,100	10,500	
Hura (*Hura crepitans*)	Green	0.38	43,400	7,200	41	19,200	5,700	2,000	AM
	12%		60,000	8,100	46	33,100	7,400	2,400	

Table 4–5a. Mechanical properties of some woods imported into the United States other than Canadian imports (metric)[a]—con.

Common and botanical names of species	Moisture content	Specific gravity	Static bending			Compression parallel to grain (kPa)	Shear parallel to grain (kPa)	Side hardness (N)	Sample origin[b]
			Modulus of rupture (kPa)	Modulus of elasticity (MPa)	Work to maximum load (kJ/m³)				
Ilomba (*Pycnanthus angolensis*)	Geen	0.4	37,900	7,900	—	20,000	5,800	2,100	AF
	12%		68,300	11,000	—	38,300	8,900	2,700	
Ipe (*Tabebuia* spp., lapacho group)	Green	0.92	155,800	20,100	190	71,400	14,600	13,600	AM
	12%		175,100	21,600	152	89,700	14,200	16,400	
Iroko (*Chlorophora* spp.)	Green	0.54	70,300	8,900	72	33,900	9,000	4,800	AF
	12%		85,500	10,100	62	52,300	12,400	5,600	
Jarrah (*Eucalyptus marginata*)	Green	0.67	68,300	10,200	—	35,800	9,100	5,700	AS
	12%	—	111,700	13,000	—	61,200	14,700	8,500	
Jelutong (*Dyera costulata*)	Green	0.36	38,600	8,000	39	21,000	5,200	1,500	AS
	15%		50,300	8,100	44	27,000	5,800	1,700	
Kaneelhart (*Licaria* spp.)	Green	0.96	153,800	26,300	94	92,300	11,600	9,800	AM
	12%		206,200	28,000	121	120,000	13,600	12,900	
Kapur (*Dryobalanops* spp.)	Green	0.64	88,300	11,000	108	42,900	8,100	4,400	AS
	12%		126,200	13,000	130	69,600	13,700	5,500	
Karri (*Eucalyptus diversicolor*)	Green	0.82	77,200	13,400	80	37,600	10,400	6,000	AS
	12%		139,000	17,900	175	74,500	16,700	9,100	
Kempas (*Koompassia malaccensis*)	Green	0.71	100,000	16,600	84	54,700	10,100	6,600	AS
	12%		122,000	18,500	106	65,600	12,300	7,600	
Keruing (*Dipterocarpus* spp.)	Green	0.69	82,000	11,800	96	39,200	8,100	4,700	AS
	12%		137,200	14,300	162	72,400	14,300	5,600	
Lignumvitae (*Guaiacum* spp.)	Green	1.05	—	—	—	—	—	—	AM
	12%	—	—	—	—	78,600	—	20,000	
Limba (*Terminalia superba*)	Green	0.38	41,400	5,300	53	19,200	600	1,800	AF
	12%		60,700	7,000	61	32,600	9,700	2,200	
Macawood (*Platymiscium* spp.)	Green	0.94	153,800	20,800	—	72,700	12,700	14,800	AM
	12%		190,300	22,100	—	111,000	17,500	14000	
Mahogany, African (*Khaya* spp.)	Green	0.42	51,000	7,900	49	25,700	6,400	2,800	AF
	12%		73,800	9,700	57	44,500	10,300	3,700	
Mahogany, true (*Swietenia macrophylla*)	Green	0.45	62,100	9,200	63	29,900	8,500	3,300	AM
	12%	—	79,300	10,300	52	46,700	8,500	3,600	
Manbarklak (*Eschweilera* spp.)	Green	0.87	117,900	18,600	120	50,600	11,200	10,100	AM
	12%		182,700	21,600	230	77,300	14,300	15,500	
Manni (*Symphonia globulifera*)	Green	0.58	77,200	13,500	77	35,600	7,900	4,200	AM
	12%		116,500	17,000	114	60,800	9,800	5,000	
Marishballi (*Lincania* spp.)	Green	0.88	117,900	20,200	92	52,300	11,200	10,000	AM
	12%		191,000	23,000	98	92,300	12,100	15,900	
Merbau (*Intsia* spp.)	Green	0.64	88,900	13,900	88	46,700	10,800	6,100	AS
	15%	—	115,800	15,400	102	58,200	12,500	6,700	
Mersawa (*Anisoptera* spp.)	Green	0.52	55,200	12,200	—	27,300	5,100	3,900	AS
	12%		95,100	15,700	—	50,800	6,100	5,700	
Mora (*Mora* spp.)	Green	0.78	86,900	16,100	93	44,100	9,700	6,400	AM
	12%		152,400	20,400	128	81,600	13,100	10,200	
Oak (*Quercus* spp.)	Green	0.76	—	—	—	—	—	—	AM
	12%		158,600	20,800	114	—	—	11,100	
Obeche (*Triplochiton scleroxylon*)	Green	0.3	35,200	5,000	43	17,700	4,600	1,900	AF
	12%		51,000	5,900	48	27,100	6,800	1,900	

Table 4–5a. Mechanical properties of some woods imported into the United States other than Canadian imports (metric)[a]—con.

Common and botanical names of species	Moisture content	Specific gravity	Static bending Modulus of rupture (kPa)	Static bending Modulus of elasticity (MPa)	Static bending Work to maximum load (kJ/m³)	Compression parallel to grain (kPa)	Shear parallel to grain (kPa)	Side hardness (N)	Sample origin[b]
Okoume (*Aucoumea klaineana*)	Green	0.33	—	—	—	—	—	—	AF
	12%		51,000	7,900	—	27,400	6,700	1,700	
Opepe (*Nauclea diderrichii*)	Green	0.63	93,800	11,900	84	51,600	13,100	6,800	AF
	12%		120,000	13,400	99	71,700	17,100	7,300	
Ovangkol (*Guibourtia ehie*)	Green	0.67	—	—	—	—	—	—	AF
	12%		116,500	17,700	—	57,200	—	—	
Para-angelim (*Hymenolobium excelsum*)	Green	0.63	100,700	13,400	88	51,400	11,000	7,700	AM
	12%		121,300	14,100	110	62,000	13,900	7,700	
Parana-pine (*Araucaria augustifolia*)	Green	0.46	49,600	9,300	67	27,600	6,700	2,500	AM
	12%	—	93,100	11,100	84	52,800	11,900	3,500	
Pau marfim (*Balfourodendron riedelianum*)	Green	0.73	99,300	11,400	—	41,900	—	—	AM
	15%		130,300	—	—	56,500	—	—	
Peroba de campos (*Paratecoma peroba*)	Green	0.62	—	—	—	—	—	—	AM
	12%		106,200	12,200	70	61,200	14,700	7,100	
Peroba rosa (*Aspidosperma* spp., peroba group)	Green	0.66	75,200	8,900	72	38,200	13,000	7,000	AM
	12%		83,400	10,500	63	54,600	17,200	7,700	
Pilon (*Hyeronima* spp.)	Green	0.65	73,800	13,000	57	34,200	8,300	5,400	AM
	12%		125,500	15,700	83	66,300	11,900	7,600	
Pine, Caribbean (*Pinus caribaea*)	Green	0.68	77,200	13,000	74	33,800	8,100	4,400	AM
	12%	—	115,100	15,400	119	58,900	14,400	5,500	
Pine, ocote (*Pinus oocarpa*)	Green	0.55	55,200	12,000	48	25,400	7,200	2,600	AM
	12%	—	102,700	15,500	75	53,000	11,900	4,000	
Pine, radiata (*Pinus radiata*)	Green	0.42	42,100	8,100	—	19,200	5,200	2,100	AS
	12%	—	80,700	10,200	—	41,900	11,000	3,300	
Piquia (*Caryocar* spp.)	Green	0.72	85,500	12,500	58	43,400	11,300	7,700	AM
	12%		117,200	14,900	109	58,000	13,700	7,700	
Primavera (*Tabebuia donnell–smithii*)	Green	0.4	49,600	6,800	50	24,200	7,100	3,100	AM
	12%		65,500	7,200	44	38,600	9,600	2,900	
Purpleheart (*Peltogyne* spp.)	Green	0.67	9,400	13,800	102	48,400	11,300	8,100	AM
	12%		132,400	15,700	121	71,200	15,300	8,300	
Ramin (*Gonystylus bancanus*)	Green	0.52	67,600	10,800	62	37,200	6,800	2,800	AS
	12%	—	127,600	15,000	117	69,500	10,500	5,800	
Robe (*Tabebuia* spp., roble group)	Green	0.52	74,500	10,000	81	33,900	8,600	4,000	AM
	12%		95,100	11,000	86	50,600	10,000	4,300	
Rosewood, Brazilian (*Dalbergia nigra*)	Green	0.8	97,200	12,700	91	38,000	16,300	10,900	AM
	12%	—	131,000	13,000	—	66,200	14,500	12,100	
Rosewood, Indian (*Dalbergia latifolia*)	Green	0.75	63,400	8,200	80	31,200	9,700	6,900	AS
	12%		116,500	12,300	90	63,600	14,400	14,100	
Sande (*Brosimum* spp., utile group)	Green	0.49	58,600	13,400	—	31,000	7,200	2,700	AM
	12%		98,600	16,500	—	56,700	8,900	4,000	
Santa Maria (*Calophyllum brasiliense*)	Green	0.52	72,400	11,000	88	31,400	8,700	4,000	AM
	12%	—	100,700	12,600	111	47,600	14,300	5,100	
Sapele (*Entandrophragma cylindricum*)	Green	0.55	70,300	10,300	72	34,500	8,600	4,500	AF
	12%	—	105,500	12,500	108	56,300	15,600	6,700	
Sepetir (*Pseudosindora palustris*)	Green	0.56	77,200	10,800	92	37,600	9,000	4,200	AS
	12%		118,600	13,600	92	61,200	14,000	6,300	

Table 4–5a. Mechanical properties of some woods imported into the United States other than Canadian imports (metric)[a]—con.

Common and botanical names of species	Moisture content	Specific gravity	Static bending			Compression parallel to grain (kPa)	Shear parallel to grain (kPa)	Side hardness (N)	Sample origin[b]
			Modulus of rupture (kPa)	Modulus of elasticity (MPa)	Work to maximum load (kJ/m^3)				
Shorea (*Shorea* spp., baulau group)	Green	0.68	80,700	14,500	—	37,100	9,900	6,000	AS
	12%		129,600	18,000	—	70,200	15,100	7,900	
Shorea, lauan–meranti group									
Dark red meranti	Green	0.46	64,800	10,300	59	32,500	7,700	3,100	AS
	12%		87,600	12,200	95	50,700	10,000	3,500	
Light red meranti	Green	0.34	45,500	7,200	43	23,000	4,900	2,000	AS
	12%		65,500	8,500	59	40,800	6,700	2,000	
White meranti	Green	0.55	67,600	9,000	57	37,900	9,100	4,400	AS
	15%		85,500	10,300	79	43,800	10,600	5,100	
Yellow meranti	Green	0.46	55,200	9,000	56	26,800	7,100	3,300	AS
	12%		78,600	10,700	70	40,700	10,500	3,400	
Spanish-cedar (*Cedrela* spp.)	Green	0.41	51,700	9,000	49	23,200	6,800	2,400	AM
	12%	—	79,300	9,900	65	42,800	7,600	2,700	
Sucupira (*Bowdichia* spp.)	Green	0.74	118,600	15,700	—	67,100	—	—	AM
	15%		133,800	—	—	76,500	—	—	
Sucupira (*Diplotropis purpurea*)	Green	0.78	120,000	18,500	90	55,300	12,400	8,800	AM
	12%		142,000	19,800	102	83,700	13,500	9,500	
Teak (*Tectona grandis*)	Green	0.55	80,000	9,400	92	41,100	8,900	4,100	AS
	12%		100,700	10,700	83	58,000	13,000	4,400	
Tornillo (*Cedrelinga cateniformis*)	Green	0.45	57,900	—	—	28,300	8,100	3,900	AM
	12%	—	—	—	—	—	—	—	
Wallaba (*Eperua* spp.)	Green	0.78	98,600	16,100	—	55,400	—	6,900	AM
	12%	—	131,700	15,700	—	74,200	—	9,100	

[a]Results of tests on small, clear, straight-grained specimens. Property values were taken from world literature (not obtained from experiments conducted at the Forest Products Laboratory). Other species may be reported in the world literature, as well as additional data on many of these species. Some property values have been adjusted to 12% moisture content.

[b]AF is Africa; AM, America; AS, Asia.

Table 4–5b. Mechanical properties of some woods imported into the United States other than Canadian imports (inch–pound)[a]

Common and botanical names of species	Moisture content	Specific gravity	Static bending — Modulus of rupture (lbf/in^2)	Static bending — Modulus of elasticity ($\times 10^6$ lbf/in^2)	Static bending — Work to maximum load (in-lbf/in^3)	Compression parallel to grain (lbf/in^2)	Shear parallel to grain (lbf/in^2)	Side hardness (lbf)	Sample origin[b]
Afrormosia (*Pericopsis elata*)	Green	0.61	14,800	1.77	19.5	7,490	1,670	1,600	AF
	12%		18,400	1.94	18.4	9,940	2,090	1,560	
Albarco (*Cariniana* spp.)	Green	0.48	—	—	—	—	—	—	AM
	12%		14,500	1.5	13.8	6,820	2,310	1,020	
Andiroba (*Carapa guianensis*)	Green	0.54	10,300	1.69	9.8	4,780	1,220	880	AM
	12%	—	15,500	2	14	8,120	1,510	1,130	
Angelin (*Andira inermis*)	Green	0.65	—	—	—	—	—	—	AF
	12%		18,000	2.49	—	9,200	1,840	1,750	
Angelique (*Dicorynia guianensis*)	Green	0.6	11,400	1.84	12	5,590	1,340	1,100	AM
	12%	—	17,400	2.19	15.2	8,770	1,660	1,290	
Avodire (*Turraeanthus africanus*)	Green	0.48	—	—	—	—	—	—	AF
	12%		12,700	1.49	9.4	7,150	2,030	1,080	
Azobe (*Lophira alata*)	Green	0.87	16,900	2.16	12	9,520	2,040	2,890	AF
	12%		24,500	2.47	—	12,600	2,960	3,350	
Balsa (*Ochroma pyramidale*)	Green	0.16	—	—	—	—	—	—	AM
	12%		3,140	0.49	2.1	2,160	300	—	
Banak (*Virola* spp.)	Green	0.42	5,600	1.64	4.1	2,390	720	320	AM
	12%	—	10,900	2.04	10	5,140	980	510	
Benge (*Guibourtia arnoldiana*)	Green	0.65	—	—	—	—	—	—	AF
	12%		21,400	2.04	—	11,400	2,090	1,750	
Bubinga (*Guibourtia* spp.)	Green	0.71	—	—	—	—	—	—	AF
	12%		22,600	2.48	—	10,500	3,110	2,690	
Bulletwood (*Manilkara bidentata*)	Green	0.85	17,300	2.7	13.6	8,690	1,900	2,230	AM
	12%		27,300	3.45	28.5	11,640	2,500	3,190	
Cativo (*Prioria copaifera*)	Green	0.4	5,900	0.94	5.4	2,460	860	440	AM
	12%	—	8,600	1.11	7.2	4,290	1,060	630	
Ceiba (*Ceiba pentandra*)	Green	0.25	2,200	0.41	1.2	1,060	350	220	AM
	12%		4,300	0.54	2.8	2,380	550	240	
Courbaril (*Hymenaea courbaril*)	Green	0.71	12,900	1.84	14.6	5,800	1,770	1,970	AM
	12%	—	19,400	2.16	17.6	9,510	2,470	2,350	
Cuangare (*Dialyanthera* spp.)	Green	0.31	4,000	1.01	—	2,080	590	230	AM
	12%		7,300	1.52	—	4,760	830	380	
Cypress, Mexican (*Cupressus lustianica*)	Green	0.93	6,200	0.92	—	2,880	950	340	AF
	12%		10,300	1.02	—	5,380	1,580	460	
Degame (*Calycophyllum candidissimum*)	Green	0.67	14,300	1.93	18.6	6,200	1,660	1,630	AM
	12%		22,300	2.27	27	9,670	2,120	1,940	
Determa (*Ocotea rubra*)	Green	0.52	7,800	1.46	4.8	3,760	860	520	AM
	12%		10,500	1.82	6.4	5,800	980	660	
Ekop (*Tetraberlinia tubmaniana*)	Green	0.6	—	—	—	—	—	—	AF
	12%		16,700	2.21	—	9,010	—	—	
Goncalo alves (*Astronium graveolens*)	Green	0.84	12,100	1.94	6.7	6,580	1,760	1,910	AM
	12%	—	16,600	2.23	10.4	10,320	1,960	2,160	
Greenheart (*Chlorocardium rodiei*)	Green	0.8	19,300	2.47	10.5	9,380	1,930	1,880	AM
	12%		24,900	3.25	25.3	12,510	2,620	2,350	
Hura (*Hura crepitans*)	Green	0.38	6,300	1.04	5.9	2,790	830	440	AM
	12%		8,700	1.17	6.7	4,800	1,080	550	

Table 4–5b. Mechanical properties of some woods imported into the United States other than Canadian imports (inch–pound)[a]—con.

Common and botanical names of species	Moisture content	Specific gravity	Static bending Modulus of rupture (lbf/in²)	Static bending Modulus of elasticity (×10⁶ lbf/in²)	Static bending Work to maximum load (in-lbf/in³)	Compression parallel to grain (lbf/in²)	Shear parallel to grain (lbf/in²)	Side hardness (lbf)	Sample origin[b]
Ilomba (*Pycnanthus angolensis*)	Geen	0.4	5,500	1.14	—	2,900	840	470	AF
	12%		9,900	1.59	—	5,550	1,290	610	
Ipe (*Tabebuia* spp., lapacho group)	Green	0.92	22,600	2.92	27.6	10,350	2,120	3,060	AM
	12%		25,400	3.14	22	13,010	2,060	3,680	
Iroko (*Chlorophora* spp.)	Green	0.54	10,200	1.29	10.5	4,910	1,310	1,080	AF
	12%		12,400	1.46	9	7,590	1,800	1,260	
Jarrah (*Eucalyptus marginata*)	Green	0.67	9,900	1.48	—	5,190	1,320	1,290	AS
	12%	—	16,200	1.88	—	8,870	2,130	1,910	
Jelutong (*Dyera costulata*)	Green	0.36	5,600	1.16	5.6	3,050	760	330	AS
	15%		7,300	1.18	6.4	3,920	840	390	
Kaneelhart (*Licaria* spp.)	Green	0.96	22,300	3.82	13.6	13,390	1,680	2,210	AM
	12%		29,900	4.06	17.5	17,400	1,970	2,900	
Kapur (*Dryobalanops* spp.)	Green	0.64	12,800	1.6	15.7	6,220	1,170	980	AS
	12%		18,300	1.88	18.8	10,090	1,990	1,230	
Karri (*Eucalyptus diversicolor*)	Green	0.82	11,200	1.94	11.6	5,450	1,510	1,360	AS
	12%		20,160	2.6	25.4	10,800	2,420	2,040	
Kempas (*Koompassia malaccensis*)	Green	0.71	14,500	2.41	12.2	7,930	1,460	1,480	AS
	12%		17,700	2.69	15.3	9,520	1,790	1,710	
Keruing (*Dipterocarpus* spp.)	Green	0.69	11,900	1.71	13.9	5,680	1,170	1,060	AS
	12%		19,900	2.07	23.5	10,500	2,070	1,270	
Lignumvitae (*Guaiacum* spp.)	Green	1.05	—	—	—	—	—	—	AM
	12%	—	—	—	—	11,400	—	4,500	
Limba (*Terminalia superba*)	Green	0.38	6,000	0.77	7.7	2,780	88	400	AF
	12%		8,800	1.01	8.9	4,730	1,410	490	
Macawood (*Platymiscium* spp.)	Green	0.94	22,300	3.02	—	10,540	1,840	3,320	AM
	12%		27,600	3.2	—	16,100	2,540	3,150	
Mahogany, African (*Khaya* spp.)	Green	0.42	7,400	1.15	7.1	3,730	931	640	AF
	12%		10,700	1.4	8.3	6,460	1,500	830	
Mahogany, true (*Swietenia macrophylla*)	Green	0.45	9,000	1.34	9.1	4,340	1,240	740	AM
	12%	—	11,500	1.5	7.5	6,780	1,230	800	
Manbarklak (*Eschweilera* spp.)	Green	0.87	17,100	2.7	17.4	7,340	1,630	2,280	AM
	12%		26,500	3.14	33.3	11,210	2,070	3,480	
Manni (*Symphonia globulifera*)	Green	0.58	11,200	1.96	11.2	5,160	1,140	940	AM
	12%		16,900	2.46	16.5	8,820	1,420	1,120	
Marishballi (*Lincania* spp.)	Green	0.88	17,100	2.93	13.4	7,580	1,620	2,250	AM
	12%		27,700	3.34	14.2	13,390	1,750	3,570	
Merbau (*Intsia* spp.)	Green	0.64	12,900	2.02	12.8	6,770	1,560	1,380	AS
	15%	—	16,800	2.23	14.8	8,440	1,810	1,500	
Mersawa (*Anisoptera* spp.)	Green	0.52	8,000	1.77	—	3,960	740	880	AS
	12%		13,800	2.28	—	7,370	890	1,290	
Mora (*Mora* spp.)	Green	0.78	12,600	2.33	13.5	6,400	1,400	1,450	AM
	12%		22,100	2.96	18.5	11,840	1,900	2,300	
Oak (*Quercus* spp.)	Green	0.76	—	—	—	—	—	—	AM
	12%		23,000	3.02	16.5	—	—	2,500	
Obeche (*Triplochiton scleroxylon*)	Green	0.3	5,100	0.72	6.2	2,570	660	420	AF
	12%		7,400	0.86	6.9	3,930	990	430	

83

Table 4–5b. Mechanical properties of some woods imported into the United States other than Canadian imports (inch–pound)[a]—con.

| Common and botanical names of species | Moisture content | Specific gravity | Static bending | | | Compression para to grain llel (lbf/in^2) | Shear parallel to grain (lbf/in^2) | Side hardness (lbf) | Sample origin[b] |
			Modulus of rupture (lbf/in^2)	Modulus of elasticity ($\times 10^6$ lbf/in^2)	Work to maximum load (in-lbf/in^3)				
Okoume (*Aucoumea klaineana*)	Green	0.33	—	—	—	—	—	—	AF
	12%		7,400	1.14	—	3,970	970	380	
Opepe (*Nauclea diderrichii*)	Green	0.63	13,600	1.73	12.2	7,480	1,900	1,520	AF
	12%		17,400	1.94	14.4	10,400	2,480	1,630	
Ovangkol (*Guibourtia ehie*)	Green	0.67	—	—	—	—	—	—	AF
	12%		16,900	2.56	—	8,300	—	—	
Para-angelim (*Hymenolobium excelsum*)	Green	0.63	14,600	1.95	12.8	7,460	1,600	1,720	AM
	12%		17,600	2.05	15.9	8,990	2,010	1,720	
Parana-pine (*Araucaria augustifolia*)	Green	0.46	7,200	1.35	9.7	4,010	970	560	AM
	12%	—	13,500	1.61	12.2	7,660	1,730	780	
Pau marfim (*Balfourodendron riedelianum*)	Green	0.73	14,400	1.66	—	6,070	—	—	AM
	15%		18,900	—	—	8,190	—	—	
Peroba de campos (*Paratecoma peroba*)	Green	0.62	—	—	—	—	—	—	AM
	12%		15,400	1.77	10.1	8,880	2,130	1,600	
Peroba rosa (*Aspidosperma* spp., peroba group)	Green	0.66	10,900	1.29	10.5	5,540	1,880	1,580	AM
	12%		12,100	1.53	9.2	7,920	2,490	1,730	
Pilon (*Hyeronima* spp.)	Green	0.65	10,700	1.88	8.3	4,960	1,200	1,220	AM
	12%		18,200	2.27	12.1	9,620	1,720	1,700	
Pine, Caribbean (*Pinus caribaea*)	Green	0.68	11,200	1.88	10.7	4,900	1,170	980	AM
	12%	—	16,700	2.24	17.3	8,540	2,090	1,240	
Pine, ocote (*Pinus oocarpa*)	Green	0.55	8,000	1.74	6.9	3,690	1,040	580	AM
	12%	—	14,900	2.25	10.9	7,680	1,720	910	
Pine, radiata (*Pinus radiata*)	Green	0.42	6,100	1.18	—	2,790	750	480	AS
	12%	—	11,700	1.48	—	6,080	1,600	750	
Piquia (*Caryocar* spp.)	Green	0.72	12,400	1.82	8.4	6,290	1,640	1,720	AM
	12%		17,000	2.16	15.8	8,410	1,990	1,720	
Primavera (*Tabebuia donnell–smithii*)	Green	0.4	7,200	0.99	7.2	3,510	1,030	700	AM
	12%		9,500	1.04	6.4	5,600	1,390	660	
Purpleheart (*Peltogyne* spp.)	Green	0.67	1,370	2	14.8	7,020	1,640	1,810	AM
	12%		19,200	2.27	17.6	10,320	2,220	1,860	
Ramin (*Gonystylus bancanus*)	Green	0.52	9,800	1.57	9	5,390	990	640	AS
	12%	—	18,500	2.17	17	10,080	1,520	1,300	
Robe (*Tabebuia* spp., roble group)	Green	0.52	10,800	1.45	11.7	4,910	1,250	910	AM
	12%		13,800	1.6	12.5	7,340	1,450	960	
Rosewood, Brazilian (*Dalbergia nigra*)	Green	0.8	14,100	1.84	13.2	5,510	2,360	2,440	AM
	12%	—	19,000	1.88	—	9,600	2,110	2,720	
Rosewood, Indian (*Dalbergia latifolia*)	Green	0.75	9,200	1.19	11.6	4,530	1,400	1,560	AS
	12%		16,900	1.78	13.1	9,220	2,090	3,170	
Sande (*Brosimum* spp., utile group)	Green	0.49	8,500	1.94	—	4,490	1,040	600	AM
	12%		14,300	2.39	—	8,220	1,290	900	
Santa Maria (*Calophyllum brasiliense*)	Green	0.52	10,500	1.59	12.7	4,560	1,260	890	AM
	12%	—	14,600	1.83	16.1	6,910	2,080	1,150	
Sapele (*Entandrophragma cylindricum*)	Green	0.55	10,200	1.49	10.5	5,010	1,250	1,020	AF
	12%	—	15,300	1.82	15.7	8,160	2,260	1,510	
Sepetir (*Pseudosindora palustris*)	Green	0.56	11,200	1.57	13.3	5,460	1,310	950	AS
	12%		17,200	1.97	13.3	8,880	2,030	1,410	

Table 4–5b. Mechanical properties of some woods imported into the United States other than Canadian imports (inch–pound)[a]—con.

Common and botanical names of species	Moisture content	Specific gravity	Static bending Modulus of rupture (lbf/in²)	Static bending Modulus of elasticity (×10⁶ lbf/in²)	Static bending Work to maximum load (in-lbf/in³)	Compression parallel to grain (lbf/in²)	Shear parallel to grain (lbf/in²)	Side hardness (lbf)	Sample origin[b]
Shorea (Shorea spp., bullau group)	Green	0.68	11,700	2.1	—	5,380	1,440	1,350	AS
	12%		18,800	2.61	—	10,180	2,190	1,780	
Shorea, lauan–meranti group									
Dark red meranti	Green	0.46	9,400	1.5	8.6	4,720	1,110	700	AS
	12%		12,700	1.77	13.8	7,360	1,450	780	
Light red meranti	Green	0.34	6,600	1.04	6.2	3,330	710	440	AS
	12%		9,500	1.23	8.6	5,920	970	460	
White meranti	Green	0.55	9,800	1.3	8.3	5,490	1,320	1,000	AS
	15%		12,400	1.49	11.4	6,350	1,540	1,140	
Yellow meranti	Green	0.46	8,000	1.3	8.1	3,880	1,030	750	AS
	12%		11,400	1.55	10.1	5,900	1,520	770	
Spanish-cedar (*Cedrela* spp.)	Green	0.41	7,500	1.31	7.1	3,370	990	550	AM
	12%	—	11,500	1.44	9.4	6,210	1,100	600	
Sucupira (*Bowdichia* spp.)	Green	0.74	17,200	2.27	—	9,730	—	—	AM
	15%		19,400	—	—	11,100	—	—	
Sucupira (*Diplotropis purpurea*)	Green	0.78	17,400	2.68	13	8,020	1,800	1,980	AM
	12%		20,600	2.87	14.8	12,140	1,960	2,140	
Teak (*Tectona grandis*)	Green	0.55	11,600	1.37	13.4	5,960	1,290	930	AS
	12%		14,600	1.55	12	8,410	1,890	1,000	
Tornillo (*Cedrelinga cateniformis*)	Green	0.45	8,400	—	—	4,100	1,170	870	AM
	12%	—	—	—	—	—	—	—	
Wallaba (*Eperua* spp.)	Green	0.78	14,300	2.33	—	8,040	—	1,540	AM
	12%	—	19,100	2.28	—	10,760	—	2,040	

[a]Results of tests on small, clear, straight-grained specimens. Property values were taken from world literature (not obtained from experiments conducted at the Forest Products Laboratory). Other species may be reported in the world literature, as well as additional data on many of these species. Some property values have been adjusted to 12% moisture content.
[b]AF is Africa; AM, America; AS, Asia.

Table 4–6. Average coefficients of variation for some mechanical properties of clear wood

Property	Coefficient of variation[a] (%)
Static bending	
Modulus of rupture	16
Modulus of elasticity	22
Work to maximum load	34
Impact bending	25
Compression parallel to grain	18
Compression perpendicular to grain	28
Shear parallel to grain, maximum shearing strength	14
Tension parallel to grain	25
Side hardness	20
Toughness	34
Specific gravity	10

[a]Values based on results of tests of green wood from approximately 50 species. Values for wood adjusted to 12% moisture content may be assumed to be approximately of the same magnitude.

Table 4–7. Average parallel-to-grain tensile strength of some wood species[a]

Species	Tensile strength (kPa (lb/in²))	
Hardwoods		
Beech, American	86,200	(12,500)
Elm, cedar	120,700	(17,500)
Maple, sugar	108,200	(15,700)
Oak		
Overcup	77,900	(11,300)
Pin	112,400	(16,300)
Poplar, balsam	51,000	(7,400)
Sweetgum	93,800	(13,600)
Willow, black	73,100	(10,600)
Yellow-poplar	109,600	(15,900)
Softwoods		
Baldcypress	58,600	(8,500)
Cedar		
Port-Orford	78,600	(11,400)
Western redcedar	45,500	(6,600)
Douglas-fir, interior north	107,600	(15,600)
Fir		
California red	77,900	(11,300)
Pacific silver	95,100	(13,800)
Hemlock, western	89,600	(13,000)
Larch, western	111,700	(16,200)
Pine		
Eastern white	73,100	(10,600)
Loblolly	80,000	(11,600)
Ponderosa	57,900	(8,400)
Virginia	94,500	(13,700)
Redwood		
Virgin	64,800	(9,400)
Young growth	62,700	(9,100)
Spruce		
Engelmann	84,800	(12,300)
Sitka	59,300	(8,600)

[a]Results of tests on small, clear, straight-grained specimens tested green. For hardwood species, strength of specimens tested at 12% moisture content averages about 32% higher; for softwoods, about 13% higher.

Table 4–8. Average toughness values for a few hardwood species[a]

Species	Moisture content	Specific gravity	Toughness	
			Radial (J (in-lbf))	Tangential (J (in-lbf))
Birch, yellow	12%	0.65	8,100 (500)	10,100 (620)
Hickory (mocker-nut, pignut, sand)	Green	0.64	11,400 (700)	11,700 (720)
	12%	0.71	10,100 (620)	10,700 (660)
Maple, sugar	14%	0.64	6,000 (370)	5,900 (360)
Oak, red				
Pin	12%	0.64	7,000 (430)	7,000 (430)
Scarlet	11%	0.66	8,300 (510)	7,200 (440)
Oak, white				
Overcup	Green	0.56	11,900 (730)	11,100 (680)
	13%	0.62	5,500 (340)	5,000 (310)
Sweetgum	Green	0.48	5,500 (340)	5,400 (330)
	13%	0.51	4,200 (260)	4,200 (260)
Willow, black	Green	0.38	5,000 (310)	5,900 (360)
	11%	0.4	3,400 (210)	3,700 (230)
Yellow-poplar	Green	0.43	5,200 (320)	4,900 (300)
	12%	0.45	3,600 (220)	3,400 (210)

Less Common Properties

Strength properties less commonly measured in clear wood include torsion, toughness, rolling shear, and fracture toughness. Other properties involving time under load include creep, creep rupture or duration of load, and fatigue strength.

Torsion strength—Resistance to twisting about a longitudinal axis. For solid wood members, torsional shear strength may be taken as shear strength parallel to grain. Two-thirds of the value for torsional shear strength may be used as an estimate of the torsional shear stress at the proportional limit.

Toughness—Energy required to cause rapid complete failure in a centrally loaded bending specimen. Tables 4–8 and 4–9 give average toughness values for samples of a few hardwood and softwood species. Average coefficients of variation for toughness as determined from approximately 50 species are shown in Table 4–6.

Creep and duration of load—Time-dependent deformation of wood under load. If the load is sufficiently high and the duration of load is long, failure (creep–rupture) will eventually occur. The time required to reach rupture is commonly called duration of load. Duration of load is an important factor in setting design values for wood. Creep and duration of load are described in later sections of this chapter.

Fatigue—Resistance to failure under specific combinations of cyclic loading conditions: frequency and number of cycles, maximum stress, ratio of maximum to minimum stress, and other less-important factors. The main factors affecting fatigue in wood are discussed later in this chapter. The discussion also includes interpretation of fatigue data and information on fatigue as a function of the service environment.

Rolling shear strength—Shear strength of wood where shearing force is in a longitudinal plane and is acting perpendicular to the grain. Few test values of rolling shear in solid wood have been reported. In limited tests, rolling shear strength averaged 18% to 28% of parallel-to-grain shear values. Rolling shear strength is about the same in the longitudinal–radial and longitudinal–tangential planes.

Fracture toughness—Ability of wood to withstand flaws that initiate failure. Measurement of fracture toughness helps identify the length of critical flaws that initiate failure in materials.

To date there is no standard test method for determining fracture toughness in wood. Three types of stress fields, and associated stress intensity factors, can be defined at a crack tip: opening mode (I), forward shear mode (II), and transverse shear mode (III) (Fig. 4–2a). A crack may lie in one of these

Table 4–9. Average toughness values for a few softwood species[a]

Species	Moisture content	Specific gravity	Toughness Radial (J (in-lbf))		Toughness Tangential (J (in-lbf))	
Cedar						
Western red	9%	0.33	1,500	(90)	2,100	(130)
Yellow	10%	0.48	3,400	(210)	3,700	(230)
Douglas-fir						
Coast	Green	0.44	3,400	(210)	5,900	(360)
	12%	0.47	3,300	(200)	5,900	(360)
Interior west	Green	0.48	3,300	(200)	4,900	(300)
	13%	0.51	3,400	(210)	5,500	(340)
Interior north	Green	0.43	2,800	(170)	3,900	(240)
	14%	0.46	2,600	(160)	4,100	(250)
Interior south	Green	0.38	2,100	(130)	2,900	(180)
	14%	0.4	2,000	(120)	2,900	(180)
Fir						
California red	Green	0.36	2,100	(130)	2,900	(180)
	12%	0.39	2,000	(120)	2,800	(170)
Noble	Green	0.36	—	—	3,900	(240)
	12%	0.39	—	—	3,600	(220)
Pacific silver	Green	0.37	2,400	(150)	3,700	(230)
	13%	0.4	2,800	(170)	4,200	(260)
White	Green	0.36	2,300	(140)	3,600	(220)
	13%	0.38	2,100	(130)	3,300	(200)
Hemlock						
Mountain	Green	0.41	4,100	(250)	4,600	(280)
	14%	0.44	2,300	(140)	2,800	(170)
Western	Green	0.38	2,400	(150)	2,800	(170)
	12%	0.41	2,300	(140)	3,400	(210)
Larch, western	Green	0.51	4,400	(270)	6,500	(400)
	12%	0.55	3,400	(210)	5,500	(340)
Pine						
Eastern white	Green	0.33	2,000	(120)	2,600	(160)
	12%	0.34	1,800	(110)	2,000	(120)
Jack	Green	0.41	3,300	(200)	6,200	(380)
	12%	0.42	2,300	(140)	3,900	(240)
Loblolly	Green	0.48	5,000	(310)	6,200	(380)
	12%	0.51	2,600	(160)	4,200	(260)
Lodgepole	Green	0.38	2,600	(160)	3,400	(210)
Ponderosa	Green	0.38	3,100	(190)	4,400	(270)
	11%	0.43	2,400	(150)	3,100	(190)
Red	Green	0.4	3,400	(210)	5,700	(350)
	12%	0.43	2,600	(160)	4,700	(290)
Shortleaf	Green	0.47	4,700	(290)	6,500	(400)
	13%	0.5	2,400	(150)	3,700	(230)
Slash	Green	0.55	5,700	(350)	7,300	(450)
	12%	0.59	3,400	(210)	5,200	(320)
Virginia	Green	0.45	5,500	(340)	7,600	(470)
	12%	0.49	2,800	(170)	4,100	(250)
Redwood						
Old-growth	Green	0.39	1,800	(110)	3,300	(200)
	11%	0.39	1,500	(90)	2,300	(140)
Young-growth	Green	0.33	1,800	(110)	2,300	(140)
	12%	0.34	1,500	(90)	1,800	(110)
Spruce,	Green	0.34	2,400	(150)	3,100	(190)
Engelmann	12%	0.35	1,800	(110)	2,900	(180)

[a]Results of tests on small, clear, straight-grained specimens.

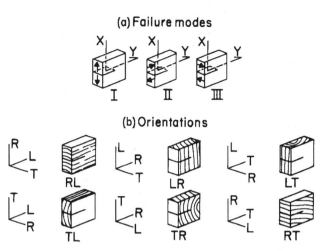

Figure 4–2. Possible crack propagation systems for wood.

three planes and may propagate in one of two directions in each plane. This gives rise to six crack-propagation systems (*RL*, *TL*, *LR*, *TR*, *LT*, and *RT*) (Fig. 4–2b). Of these crack-propagation systems, four systems are of practical importance: *RL*, *TL*, *TR*, and *RT*. Each of these four systems allow for propagation of a crack along the lower strength path parallel to the grain. The *RL* and *TL* orientations in wood (where *R* or *T* is perpendicular to the crack plane and *L* is the direction in which the crack propagates) will predominate as a result of the low strength and stiffness of wood perpendicular to the grain. It is therefore one of these two orientations that is most often tested. Values for Mode I fracture toughness range from 220 to 550 kPa$\sqrt{m}$ (200 to 500 lbf / in^2$\sqrt{in}$.) and for Mode II range from 1,650 to 2,400 kPa$\sqrt{m}$ (1,500 to 2,200 lbf / in^2$\sqrt{in}$.). Table 4–10 summarizes selected mode I and mode II test results at 10% to 12% moisture content available in the literature. The limited information available on moisture content effects on fracture toughness suggests that fracture toughness is either insensitive to moisture content or increases as the material dries, reaching a maximum between 6% and 15% moisture content; fracture toughness then decreases with further drying.

Vibration Properties

The vibration properties of primary interest in structural materials are speed of sound and internal friction (damping capacity).

Speed of Sound

The speed of sound in a structural material is a function of the modulus of elasticity and density. In wood, the speed of sound also varies with grain direction because the transverse modulus of elasticity is much less than the longitudinal value (as little as 1/20); the speed of sound across the grain is about one-fifth to one-third of the longitudinal value. For example, a piece of wood with a longitudinal modulus of elasticity of 12.4 GPa (1.8 × 10^6 lbf/in^2) and density of

Table 4–10. Summary of selected fracture toughness results

| Species | Fracture toughness ($kPa\sqrt{m}$ ($lbf/in^2\sqrt{in.}$)) | | | |
| | Mode I | | Mode II | |
	TL	RL	TL	RL
Douglas-fir	320 (290)	360 (330)		2,230 (2,030)
Western hemlock	375 (340)		2,240 (2,040)	
Pine				
Western white	250 (225)	260 (240)		
Scots	440 (400)	500 (455)	2,050 (1,860)	
Southern	375 (340)		2,070 (1,880)	
Ponderosa	290 (265)			
Red spruce	420 (380)		2,190 (1,990)	1,665 (1,510)
Northern red oak	410 (370)			
Sugar maple	480 (430)			
Yellow-poplar	517 (470)			

480 kg/m³ (30 lb/ft³) would have a speed of sound in the longitudinal direction of about 3,800 m/s (12,500 ft/s). In the transverse direction, modulus of elasticity would be about 690 MPa (100×10^3 lbf/in²) and the speed of sound approximately 890 m/s (2,900 ft/s).

The speed of sound decreases with increasing temperature or moisture content in proportion to the influence of these variables on modulus of elasticity and density. The speed of sound decreases slightly with increasing frequency and amplitude of vibration, although for most common applications this effect is too small to be significant. There is no recognized independent effect of species on the speed of sound. Variability in the speed of sound in wood is directly related to the variability of modulus of elasticity and density.

Internal Friction

When solid material is strained, some mechanical energy is dissipated as heat. Internal friction is the term used to denote the mechanism that causes this energy dissipation. The internal friction mechanism in wood is a complex function of temperature and moisture content. In general, there is a value of moisture content at which internal friction is minimum. On either side of this minimum, internal friction increases as moisture content varies down to zero or up to the fiber saturation point. The moisture content at which minimum internal friction occurs varies with temperature. At room temperature (23°C (73°F)), the minimum occurs at about 6% moisture content; at −20°C (−4°F), it occurs at about 14% moisture content, and at 70°C (158°F), at about 4%. At 90°C (194°F), the minimum is not well defined and occurs near zero moisture content.

Similarly, there are temperatures at which internal friction is minimum, and the temperatures of minimum internal friction vary with moisture content. The temperatures of minimum internal friction are higher as the moisture content is decreased. For temperatures above 0°C (32°F) and moisture content greater than about 10%, internal friction increases strongly as temperature increases, with a strong positive interaction with moisture content. For very dry wood, there is a general tendency for internal friction to decrease as the temperature increases.

The value of internal friction, expressed by logarithmic decrement, ranges from about 0.1 for hot, moist wood to less than 0.02 for hot, dry wood. Cool wood, regardless of moisture content, would have an intermediate value.

Mechanical Properties of Clear Straight-Grained Wood

The mechanical properties listed in Table 4–1 through Table 4–9 are based on a variety of sampling methods. Generally, the most extensive sampling is represented in Tables 4–3 and 4–4. The values in Table 4–3 are averages derived for a number of species grown in the United States. The tabulated value is an estimate of the average clear wood property of the species. Many values were obtained from test specimens taken at a height of 2.4 to 5 m (8 to 16 ft) above the stump of the tree. Values reported in Table 4–4 represent estimates of the average clear wood properties of species grown in Canada and commonly imported into the United States.

Methods of data collection and analysis changed over the years during which the data in Tables 4–3 and 4–4 were collected. In addition, the character of some forests has changed with time. Because not all the species were reevaluated to reflect these changes, the appropriateness of the data should be reviewed when used for critical applications such as stress grades of lumber.

Values reported in Table 4–5 were collected from the world literature; thus, the appropriateness of these properties to represent a species is not known. The properties reported in Tables 4–1, 4–2, 4–5, 4–7, 4–8, 4–9 and 4–10 may not necessarily represent average species characteristics because of inadequate sampling; however, they do suggest the relative influence of species and other specimen parameters on the mechanical behavior recorded.

Variability in properties can be important in both production and consumption of wood products. The fact that a piece may be stronger, harder, or stiffer than the average is often of less concern to the user than if the piece is weaker; however, this may not be true if lightweight material is selected for a specific purpose or if harder or tougher material is difficult to work. Some indication of the spread of property values is therefore desirable. Average coefficients of variation for many mechanical properties are presented in Table 4–6.

The mechanical properties reported in the tables are significantly affected by specimen moisture content at time of test. Some tables include properties that were evaluated at differing moisture levels; these moisture levels are reported. As indicated in the tables, many of the dry test data were adjusted to a common moisture content base of 12%.

Specific gravity is reported in many tables because this property is used as an index of clear wood mechanical properties. The specific gravity values given in Tables 4–3 and 4–4 represent the estimated average clear wood specific gravity of the species. In the other tables, the specific gravity values represent only the specimens tested. The variability of specific gravity, represented by the coefficient of variation derived from tests on 50 species, is included in Table 4–6.

Mechanical and physical properties as measured and reported often reflect not only the characteristics of the wood but also the influence of the shape and size of the test specimen and the test mode. The test methods used to establish properties in Tables 4–3, 4–4, 4–7, 4–8 and 4–9 are based on standard procedures (ASTM D143). The test methods for properties presented in other tables are referenced in the selected bibliography at the end of this chapter.

Common names of species listed in the tables conform to standard nomenclature of the U.S. Department of Agriculture, Forest Service. Other names may be used locally for a species. Also, one common name may be applied to groups of species for marketing.

Natural Characteristics Affecting Mechanical Properties

Clear straight-grained wood is used for determining fundamental mechanical properties; however, because of natural growth characteristics of trees, wood products vary in specific gravity, may contain cross grain, or may have knots and localized slope of grain. Natural defects such as pitch pockets may occur as a result of biological or climatic elements influencing the living tree. These wood characteristics must be taken into account in assessing actual properties or estimating the actual performance of wood products.

Specific Gravity

The substance of which wood is composed is actually heavier than water; its specific gravity is about 1.5 regardless of wood species. In spite of this, the dry wood of most species floats in water, and it is thus evident that part of the volume of a piece of wood is occupied by cell cavities and pores. Variations in the size of these openings and in the thickness of the cell walls cause some species to have more wood substance per unit volume than other species and therefore higher specific gravity. Thus, specific gravity is an excellent index of the amount of wood substance contained in a piece of wood; it is a good index of mechanical properties as long as the wood is clear, straight grained, and free from defects. However, specific gravity values also reflect the presence of

gums, resins, and extractives, which contribute little to mechanical properties.

Approximate relationships between various mechanical properties and specific gravity for clear straight-grained wood of hardwoods and softwoods are given in Table 4–11 as power functions. Those relationships are based on average values for the 43 softwood and 66 hardwood species presented in Table 4–3. The average data vary around the relationships, so that the relationships do not accurately predict individual average species values or an individual specimen value. In fact, mechanical properties within a species tend to be linearly, rather than curvilinearly, related to specific gravity; where data are available for individual species, linear analysis is suggested.

Knots

A knot is that portion of a branch that has become incorporated in the bole of a tree. The influence of a knot on the mechanical properties of a wood member is due to the interruption of continuity and change in the direction of wood fibers associated with the knot. The influence of knots depends on their size, location, shape, and soundness; attendant local slope of grain; and type of stress to which the wood member is subjected.

The shape (form) of a knot on a sawn surface depends upon the direction of the exposing cut. A nearly round knot is produced when lumber is sawn from a log and a branch is sawn through at right angles to its length (as in a flatsawn board). An oval knot is produced if the saw cut is diagonal to the branch length (as in a bastard-sawn board) and a "spiked" knot when the cut is lengthwise to the branch (as in a quartersawn board).

Knots are further classified as intergrown or encased (Fig. 4–3). As long as a limb remains alive, there is continuous growth at the junction of the limb and the bole of the tree, and the resulting knot is called intergrown. After the branch has died, additional growth on the trunk encloses the dead limb, resulting in an encased knot; bole fibers are not continuous with the fibers of the encased knot. Encased knots and knotholes tend to be accompanied by less cross-grain than are intergrown knots and are therefore generally less problematic with regard to most mechanical properties.

Most mechanical properties are lower in sections containing knots than in clear straight-grained wood because (a) the clear wood is displaced by the knot, (b) the fibers around the knot are distorted, resulting in cross grain, (c) the discontinuity of wood fiber leads to stress concentrations, and (d) checking often occurs around the knots during drying. Hardness and strength in compression perpendicular to the grain are exceptions, where knots may be objectionable only in that they cause nonuniform wear or nonuniform stress distributions at contact surfaces.

Knots have a much greater effect on strength in axial tension than in axial short-column compression, and the effects on bending are somewhat less than those in axial tension.

Table 4–11a. Functions relating mechanical properties to specific gravity of clear, straight-grained wood (metric)

| | Specific gravity–strength relationship | | | |
| | Green wood | | Wood at 12% moisture content | |
Property[a]	Softwoods	Hardwoods	Softwoods	Hardwoods
Static bending				
MOR (kPa)	$109{,}600\,G^{1.01}$	$118{,}700\,G^{1.16}$	$170{,}700\,G^{1.01}$	$171{,}300\,G^{0.13}$
MOE (MPa)	$16{,}100\,G^{0.76}$	$13{,}900\,G^{0.72}$	$20{,}500\,G^{0.84}$	$16{,}500\,G^{0.7}$
WML (kJ/m^3)	$147\,G^{1.21}$	$229\,G^{1.52}$	$179\,G^{1.34}$	$219\,G^{1.54}$
Impact bending (N)	$353\,G^{1.35}$	$422\,G^{1.39}$	$346\,G^{1.39}$	$423\,G^{1.65}$
Compression parallel (kPa)	$49{,}700\,G^{0.94}$	$49{,}000\,G^{1.11}$	$93{,}700\,G^{0.97}$	$76{,}000\,G^{0.89}$
Compression perpendicular (kPa)	$8{,}800\,G^{1.53}$	$18{,}500\,G^{2.48}$	$16{,}500\,G^{1.57}$	$21{,}600\,G^{2.09}$
Shear parallel (kPa)	$11{,}000\,G^{0.73}$	$17{,}800\,G^{1.24}$	$16{,}600\,G^{0.85}$	$21{,}900\,G^{1.13}$
Tension perpendicular (kPa)	$3{,}800\,G^{0.78}$	$10{,}500\,G^{1.37}$	$6{,}000\,G^{1.11}$	$10{,}100\,G^{1.3}$
Side hardness (N)	$6{,}230\,G^{1.41}$	$16{,}550\,G^{2.31}$	$85{,}900\,G^{1.5}$	$15{,}300\,G^{2.09}$

[a]Compression parallel to grain is maximum crushing strength; compression perpendicular to grain is fiber stress at proportional limit. MOR is modulus of rupture; MOE, modulus of elasticity; and WML, work to maximum load. For green wood, use specific gravity based on ovendry weight and green volume; for dry wood, use specific gravity based on ovendry weight and volume at 12% moisture content.

Table 4–11b. Functions relating mechanical properties to specific gravity of clear, straight-grained wood (inch–pound)

| | Specific gravity–strength relationship | | | |
| | Green wood | | Wood at 12% moisture content | |
Property[a]	Softwoods	Hardwoods	Softwoods	Hardwoods
Static bending				
MOR (lb/in^2)	$15{,}890\,G^{1.01}$	$17{,}210\,G^{1.16}$	$24{,}760\,G^{1.01}$	$24{,}850\,G^{0.13}$
MOE ($\times 10^6$ lb/in^2)	$2.33\,G^{0.76}$	$2.02\,G^{0.72}$	$2.97\,G^{0.84}$	$2.39\,G^{0.7}$
WML (in-lbf/in^3)	$21.33\,G^{1.21}$	$33.2\,G^{1.52}$	$25.9\,G^{1.34}$	$31.8\,G^{1.54}$
Impact bending (lbf)	$79.28\,G^{1.35}$	$94.9\,G^{1.39}$	$77.7\,G^{1.39}$	$95.1\,G^{1.65}$
Compression parallel (lb/in^2)	$7{,}210\,G^{0.94}$	$7{,}110\,G^{1.11}$	$13{,}590\,G^{0.97}$	$11{,}030\,G^{0.89}$
Compression perpendicular (lb/in^2)	$1{,}270\,G^{1.53}$	$2{,}680\,G^{2.48}$	$2{,}390\,G^{1.57}$	$3{,}130\,G^{2.09}$
Shear parallel (lb/in^2)	$1{,}590\,G^{0.73}$	$2{,}580\,G^{1.24}$	$2{,}410\,G^{0.85}$	$3{,}170\,G^{1.13}$
Tension perpendicular (lb/in^2)	$550\,G^{0.78}$	$1{,}520\,G^{1.37}$	$870\,G^{1.11}$	$1{,}460\,G^{1.3}$
Side hardness (lbf)	$1{,}400\,G^{1.41}$	$3{,}720\,G^{2.31}$	$1{,}930\,G^{1.5}$	$3{,}440\,G^{2.09}$

[a]Compression parallel to grain is maximum crushing strength; compression perpendicular to grain is fiber stress at proportional limit. MOR is modulus of rupture; MOE, modulus of elasticity; and WML, work to maximum load. For green wood, use specific gravity based on ovendry weight and green volume; for dry wood, use specific gravity based on ovendry weight and volume at 12% moisture content.

For this reason, in a simply supported beam, a knot on the lower side (subjected to tensile stresses) has a greater effect on the load the beam will support than does a knot on the upper side (subjected to compressive stresses).

In long columns, knots are important because they affect stiffness. In short or intermediate columns, the reduction in strength caused by knots is approximately proportional to their size; however, large knots have a somewhat greater relative effect than do small knots.

Knots in round timbers, such as poles and piles, have less effect on strength than do knots in sawn timbers. Although the grain is irregular around knots in both forms of timber, the angle of the grain to the surface is smaller in naturally round timber than in sawn timber. Furthermore, in round timbers there is no discontinuity in wood fibers, which results from sawing through both local and general slope of grain.

The effects of knots in structural lumber are discussed in Chapter 6.

Slope of Grain

In some wood product applications, the directions of important stresses may not coincide with the natural axes of fiber orientation in the wood. This may occur by choice in design, from the way the wood was removed from the log, or because of grain irregularities that occurred while the tree was growing.

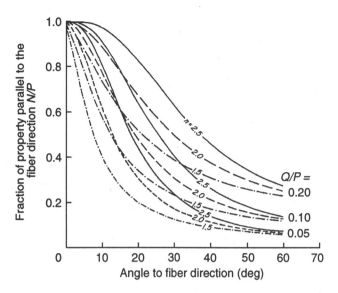

Figure 4–4. Effect of grain angle on mechanical property of clear wood according to Hankinson-type formula. Q/P is ratio of mechanical property across the grain (Q) to that parallel to the grain (P); n is an empirically determined constant.

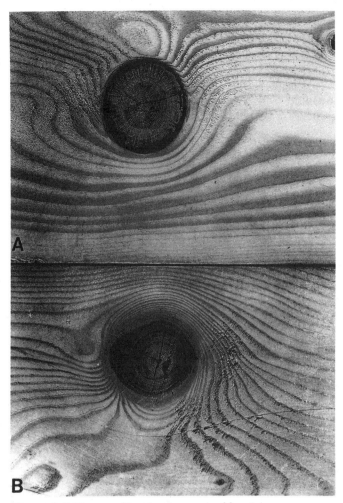

Figure 4–3. Types of knots. A, encased knot; B, intergrown.

Elastic properties in directions other than along the natural axes can be obtained from elastic theory. Strength properties in directions ranging from parallel to perpendicular to the fibers can be approximated using a Hankinson-type formula (Bodig and Jayne 1982):

$$N = \frac{PQ}{P\sin^n \theta + Q\cos^n \theta} \qquad (4\text{–}2)$$

where N is strength at angle θ from fiber direction, Q strength perpendicular to grain, P strength parallel to grain, and n an empirically determined constant.

This formula has been used for modulus of elasticity as well as strength properties. Values of n and associated ratios of Q/P tabulated from available literature are as follows:

Property	n	Q/P
Tensile strength	1.5–2	0.04–0.07
Compression strength	2–2.5	0.03–0.40
Bending strength	1.5–2	0.04–0.10
Modulus of elasticity	2	0.04–0.12
Toughness	1.5–2	0.06–0.10

The Hankinson-type formula can be graphically depicted as a function of Q/P and n. Figure 4–4 shows the strength in any direction expressed as a fraction of the strength parallel to fiber direction, plotted against angle to the fiber direction θ. The plot is for a range of values of Q/P and n.

The term slope of grain relates the fiber direction to the edges of a piece. Slope of grain is usually expressed by the ratio between 25 mm (1 in.) of the grain from the edge or long axis of the piece and the distance in millimeters (inches) within which this deviation occurs (tan θ). The effect of grain slope on some properties of wood, as determined from tests, is shown in Table 4–12. The values for modulus of rupture fall very close to the curve in Figure 4–4 for $Q/P = 0.1$ and $n = 1.5$. Similarly, the impact bending values fall close to the curve for $Q/P = 0.05$ and $n = 1.5$, and the compression values for the curve for $Q/P = 0.1$, $n = 2.5$.

The term cross grain indicates the condition measured by slope of grain. Two important forms of cross grain are spiral and diagonal (Fig. 4–5). Other types are wavy, dipped, interlocked, and curly.

Spiral grain is caused by winding or spiral growth of wood fibers about the bole of the tree instead of vertical growth. In sawn products, spiral grain can be defined as fibers lying in the tangential plane of the growth rings, rather than parallel to the longitudinal axis of the product (see Fig. 4–5 for a simple case). Spiral grain in sawn products often goes undetected by ordinary visual inspection. The best test for spiral grain is to split a sample section from the piece in the radial direction. A visual method of determining the presence of spiral grain is to note the alignment of pores, rays, and resin ducts on a flatsawn face. Drying checks on a flatsawn surface follow the fibers and indicate the slope of the fiber. Relative

91

Table 4–12. Strength of wood members with various grain slopes compared with strength of a straight-grained member[a]

Maximum slope of grain in member	Modulus of rupture (%)	Impact bending (%)	Compression parallel to grain (%)
Straight-grained	100	100	100
1 in 25	96	95	100
1 in 20	93	90	100
1 in 15	89	81	100
1 in 10	81	62	99
1 in 5	55	36	93

[a]Impact bending is height of drop causing complete failure (0.71-kg (50-lb) hammer); compression parallel to grain is maximum crushing strength.

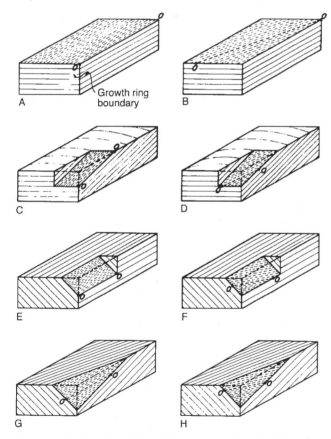

Figure 4–5. Relationship of fiber orientation (O-O) to axes, as shown by schematic of wood specimens containing straight grain and cross grain. Specimens A through D have radial and tangential surfaces; E through H do not. Specimens A and E contain no cross grain; B, D, F, and H have spiral grain; C, D, G, and H have diagonal grain.

change in electrical capacitance is an effective technique for measuring slope of grain.

Diagonal grain is cross grain caused by growth rings that are not parallel to one or both surfaces of the sawn piece. Diagonal grain is produced by sawing a log with pronounced taper parallel to the axis (pith) of the tree. Diagonal grain also occurs in lumber sawn from crooked logs or logs with butt swell.

Cross grain can be quite localized as a result of the disturbance of a growth pattern by a branch. This condition, termed local slope of grain, may be present even though the branch (knot) may have been removed by sawing. The degree of local cross grain may often be difficult to determine. Any form of cross grain can have a deleterious effect on mechanical properties or machining characteristics.

Spiral and diagonal grain can combine to produce a more complex cross grain. To determine net cross grain, regardless of origin, fiber slopes on the contiguous surface of a piece must be measured and combined. The combined slope of grain is determined by taking the square root of the sum of the squares of the two slopes. For example, assume that the spiral grain slope on the flat-grained surface of Figure 4–5D is 1 in 12 and the diagonal-grain slope is 1 in 18. The combined slope is

$$\sqrt{(1/18)^2 + (1/12)^2} = 1/10$$

or a slope of 1 in 10.

A regular reversal of right and left spiraling of grain in a tree stem produces the condition known as interlocked grain. Interlocked grain occurs in some hardwood species (Ch. 3, Table 3–9) and markedly increases resistance to splitting in the radial plane. Interlocked grain decreases both the static bending strength and stiffness of clear wood specimens. The data from tests of domestic hardwoods shown in Table 4–3 do not include pieces that exhibited interlocked grain. Some mechanical property values in Table 4–5 are based on specimens with interlocked grain because that is a characteristic of some species. The presence of interlocked grain alters the relationship between bending strength and compressive strength of lumber cut from tropical hardwoods.

Annual Ring Orientation

Stresses perpendicular to the fiber (grain) direction may be at any angle from 0° (T) to 90° (R) to the growth rings (Fig. 4–6). Perpendicular-to-grain properties depend somewhat upon orientation of annual rings with respect to the direction of stress. The compression perpendicular-to-grain values in Table 4–3 were derived from tests in which the load was applied parallel to the growth rings (T direction); shear parallel-to-grain and tension perpendicular-to-grain values are averages of equal numbers of specimens with 0° and 90° growth ring orientations. In some species, there is no difference in 0° and 90° orientation properties. Other species exhibit slightly higher shear parallel or tension perpendicular-to-grain properties for the 0° orientation than for

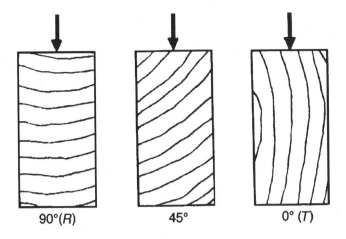

Figure 4–6. Direction of load in relation to direction of annual growth rings: 90° or perpendicular (R), 45°, 0° or parallel (T).

Figure 4–7. Projecting tension wood fibers on sawn surface of mahogany board.

the 90° orientation; the converse is true for about an equal number of species.

The effects of intermediate annual ring orientations have been studied in a limited way. Modulus of elasticity, compressive perpendicular-to-grain stress at the proportional limit, and tensile strength perpendicular to the grain tend to be about the same at 45° and 0°, but for some species these values are 40% to 60% lower at the 45° orientation. For those species with lower properties at 45° ring orientation, properties tend to be about equal at 0° and 90° orientations. For species with about equal properties at 0° and 45° orientations, properties tend to be higher at the 90° orientation.

Reaction Wood

Abnormal woody tissue is frequently associated with leaning boles and crooked limbs of both conifers and hardwoods. It is generally believed that such wood is formed as a natural response of the tree to return its limbs or bole to a more normal position, hence the term reaction wood. In softwoods, the abnormal tissue is called compression wood; it is common to all softwood species and is found on the lower side of the limb or inclined bole. In hardwoods, the abnormal tissue is known as tension wood; it is located on the upper side of the inclined member, although in some instances it is distributed irregularly around the cross section. Reaction wood is more prevalent in some species than in others.

Many of the anatomical, chemical, physical, and mechanical properties of reaction wood differ distinctly from those of normal wood. Perhaps most evident is the increase in density compared with that of normal wood. The specific gravity of compression wood is commonly 30% to 40% greater than that of normal wood; the specific gravity of tension wood commonly ranges between 5% and 10% greater than that of normal wood, but it may be as much as 30% greater.

Compression wood is usually somewhat darker than normal wood because of the greater proportion of latewood, and it frequently has a relatively lifeless appearance, especially in woods in which the transition from earlywood to latewood is abrupt. Because compression wood is more opaque than normal wood, intermediate stages of compression wood can be detected by transmitting light through thin cross sections; however, borderline forms of compression wood that merge with normal wood can commonly be detected only by microscopic examination.

Tension wood is more difficult to detect than is compression wood. However, eccentric growth as seen on the transverse section suggests its presence. Also, because it is difficult to cleanly cut the tough tension wood fibers, the surfaces of sawn boards are "woolly," especially when the boards are sawn in the green condition (Fig. 4–7). In some species, tension wood may be evident on a smooth surface as areas of contrasting colors. Examples of this are the silvery appearance of tension wood in sugar maple and the darker color of tension wood in mahogany.

Reaction wood, particularly compression wood in the green condition, may be stronger than normal wood. However, compared with normal wood with similar specific gravity, reaction wood is definitely weaker. Possible exceptions to this are compression parallel-to-grain properties of compression wood and impact bending properties of tension wood.

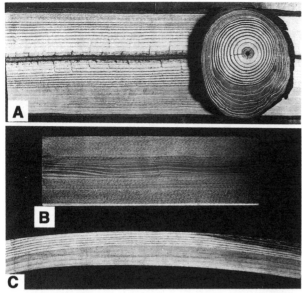

Figure 4–8. Effects of compression wood. A, eccentric growth about pith in cross section containing compression wood—dark area in lower third of cross section is compression wood; B, axial tension break caused by excessive longitudinal shrinkage of compression wood; C, warp caused by excessive longitudinal shrinkage.

Because of the abnormal properties of reaction wood, it may be desirable to eliminate this wood from raw material. In logs, compression wood is characterized by eccentric growth about the pith and the large proportion of latewood at the point of greatest eccentricity (Fig. 4–8A). Fortunately, pronounced compression wood in lumber can generally be detected by ordinary visual examination.

Compression and tension wood undergo extensive longitudinal shrinkage when subjected to moisture loss below the fiber saturation point. Longitudinal shrinkage in compression wood may be up to 10 times that in normal wood and in tension wood, perhaps up to 5 times that in normal wood. When reaction wood and normal wood are present in the same board, unequal longitudinal shrinkage causes internal stresses that result in warping. In extreme cases, unequal longitudinal shrinkage results in axial tension failure over a portion of the cross section of the lumber (Fig. 4–8B). Warp sometimes occurs in rough lumber but more often in planed, ripped, or resawn lumber (Fig. 4–8C).

Juvenile Wood

Juvenile wood is the wood produced near the pith of the tree; for softwoods, it is usually defined as the material 5 to 20 rings from the pith depending on species. Juvenile wood has considerably different physical and anatomical properties than that of mature wood (Fig. 4–9). In clear wood, the properties that have been found to influence mechanical behavior include fibril angle, cell length, and specific gravity, the latter a composite of percentage of latewood, cell wall thickness, and lumen diameter. Juvenile wood has a high fibril angle (angle between longitudinal axis of wood cell

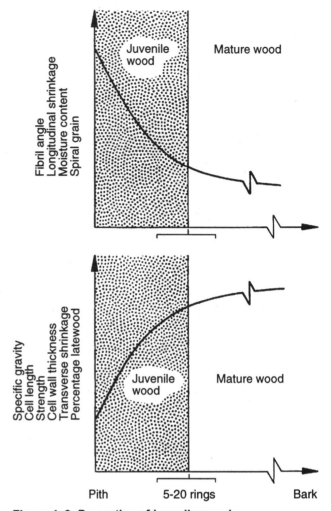

Figure 4–9. Properties of juvenile wood.

and cellulose fibrils), which causes longitudinal shrinkage that may be more than 10 times that of mature wood. Compression wood and spiral grain are also more prevalent in juvenile wood than in mature wood and contribute to longitudinal shrinkage. In structural lumber, the ratio of modulus of rupture, ultimate tensile stress, and modulus of elasticity for juvenile to mature wood ranges from 0.5 to 0.9, 0.5 to 0.95, and 0.45 to 0.75, respectively. Changes in shear strength resulting from increases in juvenile wood content can be adequately predicted by monitoring changes in density alone for all annual ring orientations. The same is true for perpendicular-to-grain compressive strength when the load is applied in the tangential direction. Compressive strength perpendicular-to-grain for loads applied in the radial direction, however, is more sensitive to changes in juvenile wood content and may be up to eight times less than that suggested by changes in density alone. The juvenile wood to mature wood ratio is lower for higher grades of lumber than for lower grades, which indicates that juvenile wood has greater influence in reducing the mechanical properties of high-grade structural lumber. Only a limited amount of research has been done on juvenile wood in hardwood species.

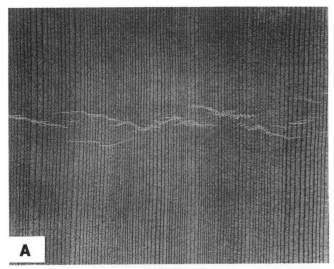

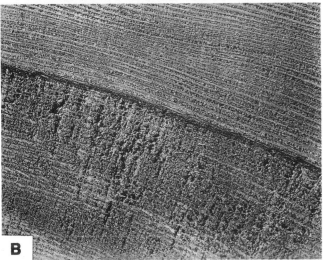

Figure 4–10. Compression failures. A, compression failure shown by irregular lines across grain; B, fiber breakage in end-grain surfaces of spruce lumber caused by compression failures below dark line.

Compression Failures

Excessive compressive stresses along the grain that produce minute compression failures can be caused by excessive bending of standing trees from wind or snow; felling of trees across boulders, logs, or irregularities in the ground; or rough handling of logs or lumber. Compression failures should not be confused with compression wood. In some instances, compression failures are visible on the surface of a board as minute lines or zones formed by crumpling or buckling of cells (Fig. 4–10A), although the failures usually appear as white lines or may even be invisible to the naked eye. The presence of compression failures may be indicated by fiber breakage on end grain (Fig. 4–10B). Since compression failures are often difficult to detect with the unaided eye, special efforts, including optimum lighting, may be required for detection. The most difficult cases are detected only by microscopic examination.

Products containing visible compression failures have low strength properties, especially in tensile strength and shock resistance. The tensile strength of wood containing compression failures may be as low as one-third the strength of matched clear wood. Even slight compression failures, visible only under a microscope, may seriously reduce strength and cause brittle fracture. Because of the low strength associated with compression failures, many safety codes require certain structural members, such as ladder rails and scaffold planks, to be entirely free of such failures.

Pitch Pockets

A pitch pocket is a well-defined opening that contains free resin. The pocket extends parallel to the annual rings; it is almost flat on the pith side and curved on the bark side. Pitch pockets are confined to such species as the pines, spruces, Douglas-fir, tamarack, and western larch.

The effect of pitch pockets on strength depends upon their number, size, and location in the piece. A large number of pitch pockets indicates a lack of bond between annual growth layers, and a piece with pitch pockets should be inspected for shake or separation along the grain.

Bird Peck

Maple, hickory, white ash, and a number of other species are often damaged by small holes made by woodpeckers. These bird pecks often occur in horizontal rows, sometimes encircling the tree, and a brown or black discoloration known as a mineral streak originates from each hole. Holes for tapping maple trees are also a source of mineral streaks. The streaks are caused by oxidation and other chemical changes in the wood. Bird pecks and mineral streaks are not generally important in regard to strength of structural lumber, although they do impair the appearance of the wood.

Extractives

Many wood species contain removable extraneous materials or extractives that do not degrade the cellulose–lignin structure of the wood. These extractives are especially abundant in species such as larch, redwood, western redcedar, and black locust.

A small decrease in modulus of rupture and strength in compression parallel to grain has been measured for some species after the extractives have been removed. The extent to which extractives influence strength is apparently a function of the amount of extractives, the moisture content of the piece, and the mechanical property under consideration.

Properties of Timber From Dead Trees

Timber from trees killed by insects, blight, wind, or fire may be as good for any structural purpose as that from live trees, provided further insect attack, staining, decay, or drying degrade has not occurred. In a living tree, the heartwood is entirely dead and only a comparatively few sapwood cells are alive. Therefore, most wood is dead when cut, regardless of whether the tree itself is living or not. However, if a tree stands on the stump too long after its death, the sapwood is likely to decay or to be attacked severely by wood-boring insects, and eventually the heartwood will be similarly affected. Such deterioration also occurs in logs that have been cut from live trees and improperly cared for afterwards. Because of variations in climatic and other factors that affect deterioration, the time that dead timber may stand or lie in the forest without serious deterioration varies.

Tests on wood from trees that had stood as long as 15 years after being killed by fire demonstrated that this wood was as sound and strong as wood from live trees. Also, the heartwood of logs of some more durable species has been found to be thoroughly sound after lying in the forest for many years.

On the other hand, in nonresistant species, decay may cause great loss of strength within a very brief time, both in trees standing dead on the stump and in logs cut from live trees and allowed to lie on the ground. The important consideration is not whether the trees from which wood products are cut are alive or dead, but whether the products themselves are free from decay or other degrading factors that would render them unsuitable for use.

Effects of Manufacturing and Service Environments

Moisture Content

Many mechanical properties are affected by changes in moisture content below the fiber saturation point. Most properties reported in Tables 4–3, 4–4, and 4–5 increase with decrease in moisture content. The relationship that describes these changes in clear wood property at about 21°C (70°F) is

$$P = P_{12}\left(\frac{P_{12}}{P_g}\right)^{\left(\frac{12-M}{M_p-12}\right)} \qquad (4\text{--}3)$$

where P is the property at moisture content M (%), P_{12} the same property at 12% MC, P_g the same property for green wood, and M_p moisture content at the intersection of a horizontal line representing the strength of green wood and an inclined line representing the logarithm of the strength–moisture content relationship for dry wood. This assumed linear relationship results in an M_p value that is slightly less than the fiber saturation point. Table 4–13 gives values of M_p for a few species; for other species, $M_p = 25$ may be assumed.

Average property values of P_{12} and P_g are given for many species in Tables 4–3 to 4–5. The formula for moisture content adjustment is not recommended for work to maximum load, impact bending, and tension perpendicular to grain. These properties are known to be erratic in their response to moisture content change.

The formula can be used to estimate a property at any moisture content below M_p from the species data given. For

Table 4–13. Intersection moisture content values for selected species[a]

Species	M_p (%)
Ash, white	24
Birch, yellow	27
Chestnut, American	24
Douglas-fir	24
Hemlock, western	28
Larch, western	28
Pine, loblolly	21
Pine, longleaf	21
Pine, red	24
Redwood	21
Spruce, red	27
Spruce, Sitka	27
Tamarack	24

[a]Intersection moisture content is point at which mechanical properties begin to change when wood is dried from the green condition.

example, suppose you want to find the modulus of rupture of white ash at 8% moisture content. Using information from Tables 4–3a and 4–13,

$$P_8 = 103,000\left[\frac{103,000}{66,000}\right]^{4/12} = 119,500 \text{ kPa}$$

Care should be exercised when adjusting properties below 12% moisture. Although most properties will continue to increase while wood is dried to very low moisture content levels, for most species some properties may reach a maximum value and then decrease with further drying (Fig. 4–11). For clear Southern Pine, the moisture content at which a maximum property has been observed is given in Table 4–14.

This increase in mechanical properties with drying assumes small, clear specimens in a drying process in which no deterioration of the product (degrade) occurs. For 51-mm-(2-in.-) thick lumber containing knots, the increase in property with decreasing moisture content is dependent upon lumber quality. Clear, straight-grained lumber may show increases in properties with decreasing moisture content that approximate those of small, clear specimens. However, as the frequency and size of knots increase, the reduction in strength resulting from the knots begins to negate the increase in property in the clear wood portion of the lumber. Very low quality lumber, which has many large knots, may be insensitive to changes in moisture content. Figures 4–12 and 4–13 illustrate the effect of moisture content on the properties of lumber as a function of initial lumber strength (Green and others 1989). Application of these results in adjusting allowable properties of lumber is discussed in Chapter 6.

Additional information on influences of moisture content on dimensional stability is included in Chapter 12.

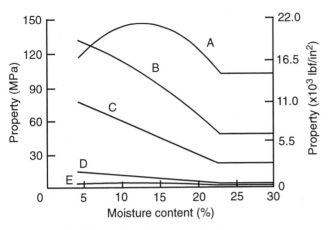

Figure 4–11. Effect of moisture content on wood strength properties. A, tension parallel to grain; B, bending; C, compression parallel to grain; D, compression perpendicular to grain; and E, tension perpendicular to grain.

Table 4–14. Moisture content for maximum property value in drying clear Southern Pine from green to 4% moisture content

Property	Moisture content at which peak property occurs (%)
Ultimate tensile stress parallel to grain	12.6
Ultimate tensile stress perpendicular to grain	10.2
MOE tension perpendicular to grain	4.3
MOE compression parallel to grain	4.3
Modulus of rigidity, G_{RT}	10.0

Temperature

Reversible Effects

In general, the mechanical properties of wood decrease when heated and increase when cooled. At a constant moisture content and below approximately 150°C (302°F), mechanical properties are approximately linearly related to temperature. The change in properties that occurs when wood is quickly heated or cooled and then tested at that condition is termed an immediate effect. At temperatures below 100°C (212°F), the immediate effect is essentially reversible; that is, the property will return to the value at the original temperature if the temperature change is rapid.

Figure 4–14 illustrates the immediate effect of temperature on modulus of elasticity parallel to grain, modulus of rupture, and compression parallel to grain, 20°C (68°F), based on a composite of results for clear, defect-free wood. This figure represents an interpretation of data from several investigators.

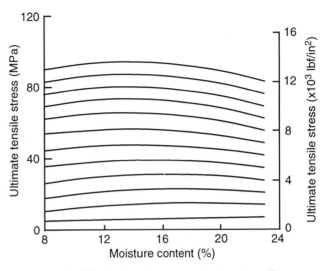

Figure 4–12. Effect of moisture content on tensile strength of lumber parallel to grain.

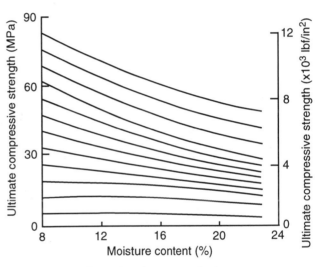

Figure 4–13. Effect of moisture content on compressive strength of lumber parallel to grain.

The width of the bands illustrates variability between and within reported trends.

Table 4–15 lists changes in clear wood properties at –50°C (–58°F) and 50°C (122°F) relative to those at 20°C (68°F) for a number of moisture conditions. The large changes at –50°C (–58°F) for green wood (at fiber saturation point or wetter) reflect the presence of ice in the wood cell cavities.

The strength of dry lumber, at about 12% moisture content, may change little as temperature increases from –29°C (–20°F) to 38°C (100°F). For green lumber, strength generally decreases with increasing temperature. However, for temperatures between about 7°C (45°F) and 38°C (100°F), the changes may not differ significantly from those at room temperature. Table 4–16 provides equations that have been

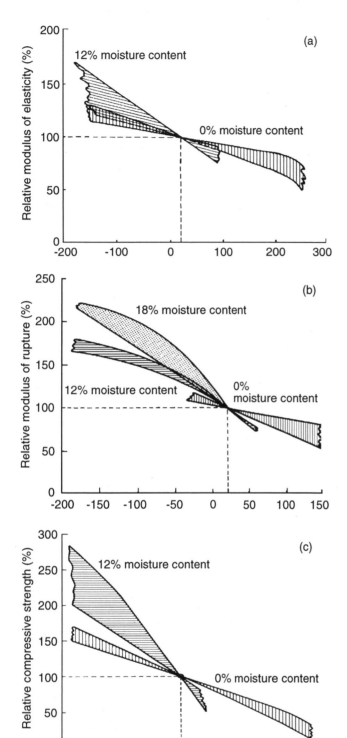

Figure 4–14. Immediate effect of temperature at two moisture content levels relative to value at 20°C (68°F) for clear, defect-free wood: (a) modulus of elasticity parallel to grain, (b) modulus of rupture in bending, (c) compressive strength parallel to grain. The plot is a composite of results from several studies. Variability in reported trends is illustrated by width of bands.

Table 4–15. Approximate middle-trend effects of temperature on mechanical properties of clear wood at various moisture conditions

Property	Moisture condition[a] (%)	Relative change in mechanical property from 20°C (68°F) at	
		−50°C (−58°F) (%)	+50°C (+122°F) (%)
MOE parallel to grain	0	+11	−6
	12	+17	−7
	>FSP	+50	—
MOE perpendicular to grain	6	—	−20
	12	—	−35
	≥20	—	−38
Shear modulus	>FSP	—	−25
Bending strength	≤4	+18	−10
	11–15	+35	−20
	18–20	+60	−25
	>FSP	+110	−25
Tensile strength parallel to grain	0–12	—	−4
Compressive strength parallel to grain	0	+20	−10
	12–45	+50	−25
Shear strength parallel to grain	>FSP	—	−25
Tensile strength perpendicular to grain	4–6	—	−10
	11–16	—	−20
	≥18	—	−30
Compressive strength perpendicular to grain at proportional limit	0–6	—	−20
	≥10	—	−35

[a]FSP indicates moisture content greater than fiber saturation point.

used to adjust some lumber properties for the reversible effects of temperature.

Irreversible Effects

In addition to the reversible effect of temperature on wood, there is an irreversible effect at elevated temperature. This permanent effect is one of degradation of wood substance, which results in loss of weight and strength. The loss depends on factors that include moisture content, heating medium, temperature, exposure period, and to some extent, species and size of piece involved.

The permanent decrease of modulus of rupture caused by heating in steam and water is shown as a function of temperature and heating time in Figure 4–15, based on tests of clear pieces of Douglas-fir and Sitka spruce. In the same studies, heating in water affected work to maximum load more than modulus of rupture (Fig. 4–16). The effect of heating dry wood (0% moisture content) on modulus of rupture and modulus of elasticity is shown in Figures 4–17 and 4–18, respectively, as derived from tests on four softwoods and two hardwoods.

Table 4–16. Percentage change in bending properties of lumber with change in temperature[a]

| Property | Lumber grade[b] | Moisture content | ((P–P₇₀) / P₇₀)100 = A + BT + CT² | | | Temperature range | |
			A	B	C	T_{min}	T_{max}
MOE	All	Green	22.0350	–0.4578	0	0	32
		Green	13.1215	–0.1793	0	32	150
		12%	7.8553	–0.1108	0	–15	150
MOR	SS	Green	34.13	–0.937	0.0043	–20	46
		Green	0	0	0	46	100
		12%	0	0	0	–20	100
	No. 2 or less	Green	56.89	–1.562	0.0072	–20	46
		Green	0	0	0	46	100
		Dry	0	0	0	–20	100

[a]For equation, P is property at temperature T in °F; P_{70}, property at 21°C (70°F).
[b]SS is Select Structural.

Figure 4–19 illustrates the permanent loss in bending strength of Spruce–Pine–Fir standard 38- by 89-mm (nominal 2- by 4-in.) lumber heated at 66°C (150°F) and about 12% moisture content. During this same period, modulus of elasticity barely changed. Most in-service exposures at 66°C (150°F) would be expected to result in much lower moisture content levels. Additional results for other lumber products and exposure conditions will be reported as Forest Products Laboratory studies progress.

The permanent property losses discussed here are based on tests conducted after the specimens were cooled to room temperature and conditioned to a range of 7% to 12% moisture content. If specimens are tested hot, the percentage of strength reduction resulting from permanent effects is based on values already reduced by the immediate effects. Repeated exposure to elevated temperature has a cumulative effect on wood properties. For example, at a given temperature the property loss will be about the same after six 1-month exposure as it would be after a single 6-month exposure.

The shape and size of wood pieces are important in analyzing the influence of temperature. If exposure is for only a short time, so that the inner parts of a large piece do not reach the temperature of the surrounding medium, the immediate effect on strength of the inner parts will be less than that for the outer parts. However, the type of loading must be considered. If the member is to be stressed in bending, the outer fibers of a piece will be subjected to the greatest stress and will ordinarily govern the ultimate strength of the piece; hence, under this loading condition, the fact that the inner part is at a lower temperature may be of little significance.

For extended noncyclic exposures, it can be assumed that the entire piece reaches the temperature of the heating medium and will therefore be subject to permanent strength losses throughout the volume of the piece, regardless of size and mode of stress application. However, in ordinary construction wood often will not reach the daily temperature extremes of the air around it; thus, long-term effects should be based on the accumulated temperature experience of critical structural parts.

Time Under Load

Rate of Loading

Mechanical property values, as given in Tables 4–3, 4–4, and 4–5, are usually referred to as static strength values. Static strength tests are typically conducted at a rate of loading or rate of deformation to attain maximum load in about 5 min. Higher values of strength are obtained for wood loaded at a more rapid rate and lower values are obtained at slower rates. For example, the load required to produce failure in a wood member in 1 s is approximately 10% higher than that obtained in a standard static strength test. Over several orders of magnitude of rate of loading, strength is approximately an exponential function of rate. See Chapter 6 for application to treated woods.

Figure 4–20 illustrates how strength decreases with time to maximum load. The variability in the trend shown is based on results from several studies pertaining to bending, compression, and shear.

Creep and Relaxation

When initially loaded, a wood member deforms elastically. If the load is maintained, additional time-dependent deformation occurs. This is called creep. Creep occurs at even very low stresses, and it will continue over a period of years. For sufficiently high stresses, failure eventually occurs. This failure phenomenon, called duration of load (or creep rupture), is discussed in the next section.

At typical design levels and use environments, after several years the additional deformation caused by creep may approximately equal the initial, instantaneous elastic deformation. For illustration, a creep curve based on creep as a function of initial deflection (relative creep) at several stress levels is shown in Figure 4–21; creep is greater under higher stresses than under lower ones.

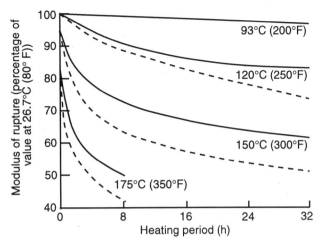

Figure 4–15. Permanent effect of heating in water (solid line) and steam (dashed line) on modulus of rupture of clear, defect-free wood. All data based on tests of Douglas-fir and Sitka spruce at room temperature.

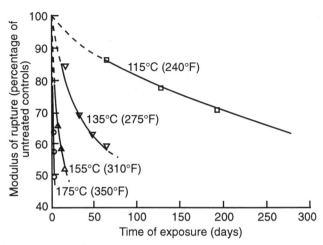

Figure 4–17. Permanent effect of oven heating at four temperatures on modulus of rupture, based on clear pieces of four softwood and two hardwood species. All tests conducted at room temperature.

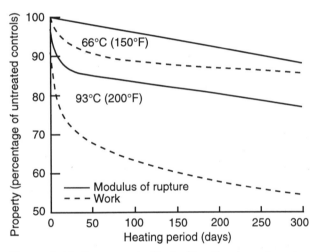

Figure 4–16. Permanent effect of heating in water on work to maximum load and modulus of rupture of clear, defect-free wood. All data based on tests of Douglas-fir and Sitka spruce at room temperature.

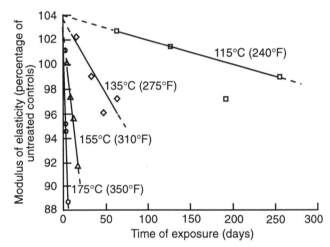

Figure 4–18. Permanent effect of oven heating at four temperatures on modulus of elasticity, based on clear pieces of four softwood and two hardwood species. All tests conducted at room temperature.

Ordinary climatic variations in temperature and humidity will cause creep to increase. An increase of about 28°C (50°F) in temperature can cause a two- to threefold increase in creep. Green wood may creep four to six times the initial deformation as it dries under load.

Unloading a member results in immediate and complete recovery of the original elastic deformation and after time, a recovery of approximately one-half the creep at deformation as well. Fluctuations in temperature and humidity increase the magnitude of the recovered deformation.

Relative creep at low stress levels is similar in bending, tension, or compression parallel to grain, although it may be somewhat less in tension than in bending or compression under varying moisture conditions. Relative creep across the grain is qualitatively similar to, but likely to be greater than, creep parallel to the grain. The creep behavior of all species studied is approximately the same.

If instead of controlling load or stress, a constant deformation is imposed and maintained on a wood member, the initial stress relaxes at a decreasing rate to about 60% to 70% of its original value within a few months. This reduction of stress with time is commonly called relaxation.

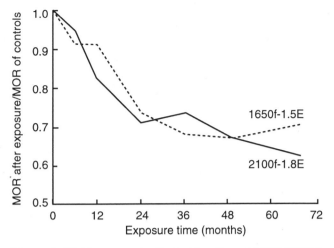

Figure 4–19. Permanent effect of heating at 66°C (150°F) on modulus of rupture for two grades of machine-stress-rated Spruce–Pine–Fir lumber at 12% moisture content. All tests conducted at room temperature.

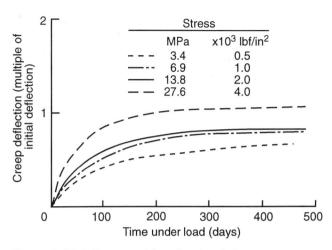

Figure 4–21. Influence of four levels of stress on creep (Kingston 1962).

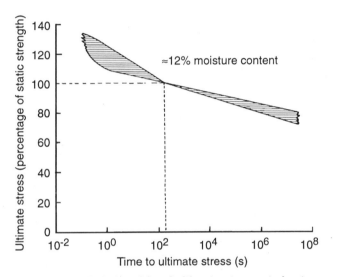

Figure 4–20. Relationship of ultimate stress at short-time loading to that at 5-min loading, based on composite of results from rate-of-load studies on bending, compression, and shear parallel to grain. Variability in reported trends is indicated by width of band.

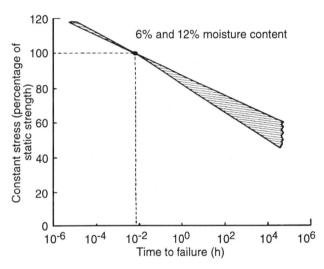

Figure 4–22. Relationship between stress due to constant load and time to failure for small clear wood specimens, based on 28 s at 100% stress. The figure is a composite of trends from several studies; most studies involved bending but some involved compression parallel to grain and bending perpendicular to grain. Variability in reported trends is indicated by width of band.

In limited bending tests carried out between approximately 18°C (64°F) and 49°C (120°F) over 2 to 3 months, the curve of stress as a function of time that expresses relaxation is approximately the mirror image of the creep curve (deformation as a function of time). These tests were carried out at initial stresses up to about 50% of the bending strength of the wood. As with creep, relaxation is markedly affected by fluctuations in temperature and humidity.

Duration of Load

The duration of load, or the time during which a load acts on a wood member either continuously or intermittently, is an important factor in determining the load that the member can safely carry. The duration of load may be affected by changes in temperature and relative humidity.

The constant stress that a wood member can sustain is approximately an exponential function of time to failure, as illustrated in Figure 4–22. This relationship is a composite of results of studies on small, clear wood specimens, conducted at constant temperature and relative humidity.

For a member that continuously carries a load for a long period, the load required to produce failure is much less than that determined from the strength properties in Tables 4–3 to 4–5. Based on Figure 4–22, a wood member under the continuous action of bending stress for 10 years may carry only 60% (or perhaps less) of the load required to produce failure in the same specimen loaded in a standard bending strength test of only a few minutes duration. Conversely, if the duration of load is very short, the load-carrying capacity may be higher than that determined from strength properties given in the tables.

Time under intermittent loading has a cumulative effect. In tests where a constant load was periodically placed on a beam and then removed, the cumulative time the load was actually applied to the beam before failure was essentially equal to the time to failure for a similar beam under the same load applied continuously.

The time to failure under continuous or intermittent loading is looked upon as a creep–rupture process; a member has to undergo substantial deformation before failure. Deformation at failure is approximately the same for duration of load tests as for standard strength tests.

Changes in climatic conditions increase the rate of creep and shorten the duration during which a member can support a given load. This effect can be substantial for very small wood specimens under large cyclic changes in temperature and relative humidity. Fortunately, changes in temperature and relative humidity are moderate for wood in the typical service environment.

Fatigue

In engineering, the term fatigue is defined as the progressive damage that occurs in a material subjected to cyclic loading. This loading may be repeated (stresses of the same sign; that is, always compression or always tension) or reversed (stresses of alternating compression and tension). When sufficiently high and repetitious, cyclic loading stresses can result in fatigue failure.

Fatigue life is a term used to define the number of cycles that are sustained before failure. Fatigue strength, the maximum stress attained in the stress cycle used to determine fatigue life, is approximately exponentially related to fatigue life; that is, fatigue strength decreases approximately linearly as the logarithm of number of cycles increases. Fatigue strength and fatigue life also depend on several other factors: frequency of cycling; repetition or reversal of loading; range factor (ratio of minimum to maximum stress per cycle); and other factors such as temperature, moisture content, and specimen size. Negative range factors imply repeated reversing loads, whereas positive range factors imply nonreversing loads.

Results from several fatigue studies on wood are given in Table 4–17. Most of these results are for repeated loading with a range ratio of 0.1, meaning that the minimum stress per cycle is 10% of the maximum stress. The maximum stress per cycle, expressed as a percentage of estimated static

Table 4–17. Summary of reported results on cyclic fatigue[a]

Property	Range ratio	Cyclic frequency (Hz)	Maximum stress per cycle[b] (%)	Approximate fatigue life ($\times 10^6$ cycles)
Bending, clear, straight grain				
Cantilever	0.45	30	45	30
Cantilever	0	30	40	30
Cantilever	−1.0	30	30	30
Center-point	−1.0	40	30	4
Rotational	−1.0	—	28	30
Third-point	0.1	8-1/3	60	2
Bending, third-point				
Small knots	0.1	8-1/3	50	2
Clear, 1:12 slope of grain	0.1	8-1/3	50	2
Small knots, 1:12 slope of grain	0.1	8-1/3	40	2
Tension parallel to grain				
Clear, straight grain	0.1	15	50	30
Clear, straight grain	0	40	60	3.5
Scarf joint	0.1	15	50	30
Finger joint	0.1	15	40	30
Compression parallel to grain				
Clear, straight grain	0.1	40	75	3.5
Shear parallel to grain				
Glue-laminated	0.1	15	45	30

[a]Initial moisture content about 12% to 15%.
[b]Percentage of estimated static strength.

strength, is associated with the fatigue life given in millions of cycles. The first three lines of data, which list the same cyclic frequency (30 Hz), demonstrate the effect of range ratio on fatigue strength (maximum fatigue stress that can be maintained for a given fatigue life); fatigue bending strength decreases as range ratio decreases. Third-point bending results show the effect of small knots or slope of grain on fatigue strength at a range ratio of 0.1 and frequency of 8.33 Hz. Fatigue strength is lower for wood containing small knots or a 1-in-12 slope of grain than for clear straight-grained wood and even lower for wood containing a combination of small knots and a 1-in-12 slope of grain. Fatigue strength is the same for a scarf joint in tension as for tension parallel to the grain, but a little lower for a finger joint in tension. Fatigue strength is slightly lower in shear than in tension parallel to the grain. Other comparisons do not have much meaning because range ratios or cyclic frequency differ; however, fatigue strength is high in compression parallel to the grain compared with other properties. Little is known about other factors that may affect fatigue strength in wood.

Creep, temperature rise, and loss of moisture content occur in tests of wood for fatigue strength. At stresses that cause failure in about 106 cycles at 40 Hz, a temperature rise of

15°C (27°F) has been reported for parallel-to-grain compression fatigue (range ratio slightly greater than zero), parallel-to-grain tension fatigue (range ratio = 0), and reversed bending fatigue (range ratio = −1). The rate of temperature rise is high initially but then diminishes to moderate; a moderate rate of temperature rise remains more or less constant during a large percentage of fatigue life. During the latter stages of fatigue life, the rate of temperature rise increases until failure occurs. Smaller rises in temperature would be expected for slower cyclic loading or lower stresses. Decreases in moisture content are probably related to temperature rise.

Aging

In relatively dry and moderate temperature conditions where wood is protected from deteriorating influences such as decay, the mechanical properties of wood show little change with time. Test results for very old timbers suggest that significant losses in clear wood strength occur only after several centuries of normal aging conditions. The soundness of centuries-old wood in some standing trees (redwood, for example) also attests to the durability of wood.

Exposure to Chemicals

The effect of chemical solutions on mechanical properties depends on the specific type of chemical. Nonswelling liquids, such as petroleum oils and creosote, have no appreciable effect on properties. Properties are lowered in the presence of water, alcohol, or other wood-swelling organic liquids even though these liquids do not chemically degrade the wood substance. The loss in properties depends largely on the amount of swelling, and this loss is regained upon removal of the swelling liquid. Anhydrous ammonia markedly reduces the strength and stiffness of wood, but these properties are regained to a great extent when the ammonia is removed. Heartwood generally is less affected than sapwood because it is more impermeable. Accordingly, wood treatments that retard liquid penetration usually enhance natural resistance to chemicals.

Chemical solutions that decompose wood substance (by hydrolysis or oxidation) have a permanent effect on strength. The following generalizations summarize the effect of chemicals:

- Some species are quite resistant to attack by dilute mineral and organic acids.

- Oxidizing acids such as nitric acid degrade wood more than do nonoxidizing acids.

- Alkaline solutions are more destructive than are acidic solutions.

- Hardwoods are more susceptible to attack by both acids and alkalis than are softwoods.

- Heartwood is less susceptible to attack by both acids and alkalis than is sapwood.

Because both species and application are extremely important, reference to industrial sources with a specific history of use is recommended where possible. For example, large cypress tanks have survived long continuous use where exposure conditions involved mixed acids at the boiling point. Wood is also used extensively in cooling towers because of its superior resistance to mild acids and solutions of acidic salts.

Chemical Treatment

Wood is often treated with chemicals to enhance its fire performance or decay resistance in service. Each set of treatment chemicals and processes has a unique effect on the mechanical properties of the treated wood.

Fire-retardant treatments and treatment methods distinctly reduce the mechanical properties of wood. Some fire-retardant-treated products have experienced significant in-service degradation on exposure to elevated temperatures when used as plywood roof sheathing or roof-truss lumber. New performance requirements within standards set by the American Standards for Testing and Materials (ASTM) and American Wood Preservers' Association (AWPA) preclude commercialization of inadequately performing fire-retardant-treated products.

Although preservative treatments and treatment methods generally reduce the mechanical properties of wood, any initial loss in strength from treatment must be balanced against the progressive loss of strength from decay when untreated wood is placed in wet conditions. The effects of preservative treatments on mechanical properties are directly related to wood quality, size, and various pretreatment, treatment, and post-treatment processing factors. The key factors include preservative chemistry or chemical type, preservative retention, initial kiln-drying temperature, post-treatment drying temperature, and pretreatment incising (if required). North American design guidelines address the effects of incising on mechanical properties of refractory wood species and the short-term duration-of-load adjustments for all treated lumber. These guidelines are described in Chapter 6.

Oil-Type Preservatives

Oil-type preservatives cause no appreciable strength loss because they do not chemically react with wood cell wall components. However, treatment with oil-type preservatives can adversely affect strength if extreme in-retort seasoning parameters are used (for example, Boultonizing, steaming, or vapor drying conditions) or if excessive temperatures or pressures are used during the treating process. To preclude strength loss, the user should follow specific treatment processing requirements as described in the treatment standards.

Waterborne Preservatives

Waterborne preservative treatments can reduce the mechanical properties of wood. Treatment standards include specific processing requirements intended to prevent or limit strength reductions resulting from the chemicals and the waterborne preservative treatment process. The effects of waterborne preservative treatment on mechanical properties are related to species, mechanical properties, preservative chemistry or type, preservative retention, post-treatment drying temperature, size and grade of material, product type, initial kiln-drying temperature, incising, and both temperature and moisture in service.

Species—The magnitude of the effect of various waterborne preservatives on mechanical properties does not appear to vary greatly between different species.

Mechanical property—Waterborne preservatives affect each mechanical property differently. If treated according to AWPA standards, the effects are as follows: modulus of elasticity (MOE), compressive strength parallel to grain, and compressive stress perpendicular to grain are unaffected or slightly increased; modulus of rupture (MOR) and tensile strength parallel to grain are reduced from 0% to 20%, depending on chemical retention and severity of redrying temperature; and energy-related properties (for example, work to maximum load and impact strength) are reduced from 10% to 50%.

Preservative chemistry or type—Waterborne preservative chemical systems differ in regard to their effect on strength, but the magnitude of these differences is slight compared with the effects of treatment processing factors. Chemistry-related differences seem to be related to the reactivity of the waterborne preservative and the temperature during the fixation/precipitation reaction with wood.

Retention—Waterborne preservative retention levels of ≤16 kg/m^3 (≤1.0 lb/ft^3) have no effect on MOE or compressive strength parallel to grain and a slight negative effect (−5% to −10%) on tensile or bending strength. However, energy-related properties are often reduced from 15% to 30%. At a retention level of 40 kg/m^3 (2.5 lb/ft^3), MOR and energy-related properties are further reduced.

Post-treatment drying temperature—Air drying after treatment causes no significant reduction in the static strength of wood treated with waterborne preservative at a retention level of 16 kg/m^3 (1.0 lb/ft^3). However, energy-related properties are reduced. The post-treatment redrying temperature used for material treated with waterborne preservative has been found to be critical when temperatures exceed 75 °C (167 °F). Redrying limitations in treatment standards have precluded the need for an across-the-board design adjustment factor for waterborne-preservative-treated lumber in engineering design standards. The limitation on post-treatment kiln-drying temperature is set at 74°C (165°F).

Size of material—Generally, larger material, specifically thicker, appears to undergo less reduction in strength than does smaller material. Recalling that preservative treatments usually penetrate the treated material to a depth of only 6 to 51 mm (0.25 to 2.0 in.), depending on species and other factors, the difference in size effect appears to be a function of the product's surface-to-volume ratio, which affects the relative ratio of treatment-induced weight gain to original wood weight.

Grade of material—The effect of waterborne preservative treatment is a quality-dependent phenomenon. Higher grades of wood are more affected than lower grades. When viewed over a range of quality levels, higher quality lumber is reduced in strength to a proportionately greater extent than is lower quality lumber.

Product type—The magnitude of the treatment effect on strength for laminated veneer lumber conforms closely to effects noted for higher grades of solid-sawn lumber. The effects of waterborne preservative treatment on plywood seem comparable to that on lumber. Fiber-based composite products may be reduced in strength to a greater extent than is lumber. This additional effect on fiber-based composites may be more a function of internal bond damage caused by waterborne-treatment-induced swelling rather than actual chemical hydrolysis.

Initial kiln-drying temperature—Although initial kiln drying of some lumber species at 100°C to 116°C (212°F to 240°F) for short durations has little effect on structural properties, such drying results in more hydrolytic degradation of the cell wall than does drying at lower temperature kiln schedules. Subsequent preservative treatment and redrying of material initially dried at high temperatures causes additional hydrolytic degradation. When the material is subsequently treated, initial kiln drying at 113°C (235°F) has been shown to result in greater reductions over the entire bending and tensile strength distributions than does initial kiln drying at 91°C (196°F). Because Southern Pine lumber, the most widely treated product, is most often initially kiln dried at dry-bulb temperatures near or above 113°C (235°F), treatment standards have imposed a maximum redrying temperature limit of 74°C (165°F) to preclude the cumulative effect of thermal processing.

Incising—Incising, a pretreatment mechanical process in which small slits (incisions) are punched in the surface of the wood product, is used to improve preservative penetration and distribution in difficult-to-treat species. Incising may reduce strength; however, because the increase in treatability provides a substantial increase in biological performance, this strength loss must be balanced against the progressive loss in strength of untreated wood from the incidence of decay. Most incising patterns induce some strength loss, and the magnitude of this effect is related to the size of material being incised and the incision depth and density (that is, number of incisions per unit area). In less than 50 mm (2 in.) thick, dry lumber, incising and preservative treatment induces losses in MOE of 5% to 15% and in static strength properties of 20% to 30%. Incising and treating timbers or tie stock at an incision density of ≤1,500 incisions/m^2 (≤140 incisions/ft^2) and to a depth of 19 mm (0.75 in.) reduces strength by 5% to 10%.

In-service temperature—Both fire-retardant and preservative treatments accelerate the thermal degradation of bending strength of lumber when exposed to temperatures above 54°C (130°F).

In-service moisture content—Current design values apply to material dried to ≤19% maximum (15% average) moisture content or to green material. No differences in strength have been found between treated and untreated material when tested green or at moisture contents above 12%. When very dry treated lumber of high grade was tested at 10% moisture content, its bending strength was reduced compared with that of matched dry untreated lumber.

Duration of load—When subjected to impact loads, wood treated with chromated copper arsenate (CCA) does not exhibit the same increase in strength as that exhibited by untreated wood. However, when loaded over a long period, treated and untreated wood behave similarly.

Polymerization

Wood is also sometimes impregnated with monomers, such as methyl methacrylate, which are subsequently polymerized. Many of the mechanical properties of the resultant wood–plastic composite are higher than those of the original wood, generally as a result of filling the void spaces in the wood structure with plastic. The polymerization process and both the chemical nature and quantity of monomers influence composite properties.

Nuclear Radiation

Wood is occasionally subjected to nuclear radiation. Examples are wooden structures closely associated with nuclear reactors, the polymerization of wood with plastic using nuclear radiation, and nondestructive estimation of wood density and moisture content. Very large doses of gamma rays or neutrons can cause substantial degradation of wood. In general, irradiation with gamma rays in doses up to about 1 megarad has little effect on the strength properties of wood. As dosage exceeds 1 megarad, tensile strength parallel to grain and toughness decrease. At a dosage of 300 megarads, tensile strength is reduced about 90%. Gamma rays also affect compressive strength parallel to grain at a dosage above 1 megarad, but higher dosage has a greater effect on tensile strength than on compressive strength; only approximately one-third of compressive strength is lost when the total dose is 300 megarads. Effects of gamma rays on bending and shear strength are intermediate between the effects on tensile and compressive strength.

Mold and Stain Fungi

Mold and stain fungi do not seriously affect most mechanical properties of wood because such fungi feed on substances within the cell cavity or attached to the cell wall rather than on the structural wall itself. The duration of infection and the species of fungi involved are important factors in determining the extent of degradation.

Although low levels of biological stain cause little loss in strength, heavy staining may reduce specific gravity by 1% to 2%, surface hardness by 2% to 10%, bending and crushing strength by 1% to 5%, and toughness or shock resistance by 15% to 30%. Although molds and stains usually do not have a major effect on strength, conditions that favor these organisms also promote the development of wood-destroying (decay) fungi and soft-rot fungi (Ch. 13). Pieces with mold and stain should be examined closely for decay if they are used for structural purposes.

Decay

Unlike mold and stain fungi, wood-destroying (decay) fungi seriously reduce strength by metabolizing the cellulose fraction of wood that gives wood its strength.

Early stages of decay are virtually impossible to detect. For example, brown-rot fungi may reduce mechanical properties in excess of 10% before a measurable weight loss is observed and before decay is visible. When weight loss reaches 5% to 10%, mechanical properties are reduced from 20% to 80%. Decay has the greatest effect on toughness, impact bending, and work to maximum load in bending, the least effect on shear and hardness, and an intermediate effect on other properties. Thus, when strength is important, adequate measures should be taken to (a) prevent decay before it occurs, (b) control incipient decay by remedial measures (Ch. 13), or (c) replace any wood member in which decay is evident or believed to exist in a critical section. Decay can be prevented from starting or progressing if wood is kept dry (below 20% moisture content).

No method is known for estimating the amount of reduction in strength from the appearance of decayed wood. Therefore, when strength is an important consideration, the safe procedure is to discard every piece that contains even a small amount of decay. An exception may be pieces in which decay occurs in a knot but does not extend into the surrounding wood.

Insect Damage

Insect damage may occur in standing trees, logs, and undried (unseasoned) or dried (seasoned) lumber. Although damage is difficult to control in the standing tree, insect damage can be eliminated to a great extent by proper control methods. Insect holes are generally classified as pinholes, grub holes, and powderpost holes. Because of their irregular burrows, powderpost larvae may destroy most of a piece's interior while only small holes appear on the surface, and the strength of the piece may be reduced virtually to zero. No method is known for estimating the reduction in strength from the appearance of insect-damaged wood. When strength is an important consideration, the safe procedure is to eliminate pieces containing insect holes.

References

ASTM. [Current edition]. Standard methods for testing small clear specimens of timber. ASTM D143-94. West Conshohocken, PA: American Society for Testing and Materials.

Bendtsen, B.A. 1976. Rolling shear characteristics of nine structural softwoods. Forest Products Journal. 26(11): 51–56.

Bendtsen, B.A.; Freese, F.; Ethington, R.L. 1970. Methods for sampling clear, straight-grained wood from the forest. Forest Products Journal. 20(11): 38–47.

Bodig, J.; Goodman, J.R. 1973. Prediction of elastic parameters for wood. Wood Science. 5(4): 249–264.

Bodig, J.; Jayne, B.A. 1982. Mechanics of wood and wood composites. New York: Van Nostrand Reinhold Company.

Boller, K.H. 1954. Wood at low temperatures. Modern Packaging. 28(1): 153–157.

Chudnoff, M. 1987. Tropical timbers of the world. Agric. Handb. 607. Washington DC: U.S. Department of Agriculture.

Coffey, D.J. 1962. Effects of knots and holes on the fatigue strength of quarter-scale timber bridge stringers. Madison, WI: University of Wisconsin, Department of Civil Engineering. M.S. Thesis.

Gerhards, C.C. 1968. Effects of type of testing equipment and specimen size on toughness of wood. Res. Pap. FPL–RP–97. Madison, WI: U.S. Department of Agriculture, Forest Service, Forest Products Laboratory.

Gerhards, C.C. 1977. Effect of duration and rate of loading on strength of wood and wood based materials. Res. Pap. FPL–RP–283. Madison, WI: U.S. Department of Agriculture, Forest Service, Forest Products Laboratory.

Gerhards, C.C. 1979. Effect of high-temperature drying on tensile strength of Douglas-fir 2 by 4's. Forest Products Journal. 29(3): 39–46.

Gerhards, C.C. 1982. Effect of moisture content and temperature on the mechanical properties of wood: an analysis of immediate effects. Wood and Fiber. 14(1): 4–36.

Green, D.W.; Evans, J.W. 1994. Effect of ambient temperatures on the flexural properties of lumber. In: PTEC 94 Timber shaping the future: Proceedings, Pacific timber engineering conference; 1994 July 11–15; Gold Coast, Australia. Fortitude Valley MAC, Queensland, Australia: Timber Research Development and Advisory Council: 190–197. Vol. 2.

Green, D.W.; Rosales, A. 1996. Property relationships for tropical hardwoods. In: Proceedings, international wood engineering conference ; 1996 October 21–31; New Orleans, LA. Madison, WI: Forest Products Society: 3-516–3-521.

Green, D.W.; Shelley, B.E.; Vokey, H.P. (eds). 1989. In-grade testing of structural lumber. Proceedings 47363. Madison, WI: Forest Products Society.

Hearmon, R.F.S. 1948. The elasticity of wood and plywood. Special Rep. 7. London, England: Department of Scientific and Industrial Research, Forest Products Research.

Hearmon, R.F.S. 1961. An introduction to applied anisotropic elasticity. London, England: Oxford University Press.

Kingston, R.S.T. 1962. Creep, relaxation, and failure of wood. Research Applied in Industry. 15(4).

Kollmann, F.F.P.; Cote, W.A., Jr. 1968. Principles of wood science and technology. New York: Springer Verlag.

Koslik, C.J. 1967. Effect of kiln conditions on the strength of Douglas-fir and western hemlock. Rep. D–9. Corvallis, OR: Oregon State University, School of Forestry, Forestry Research Laboratory.

Little, E.L., Jr. 1979. Checklist of United States trees (native and naturalized). Agric. Handb. 541. Washington, DC: U.S. Department of Agriculture.

Kretschmann, D.E.; Bendtsen, B.A. 1992. Ultimate tensile stress and modulus of elasticity of fast-grown plantation loblolly pine lumber. Wood and Fiber Science. 24(2): 189–203.

Kretschmann, D.E.; Green, D.W. 1996. Modeling moisture content–mechanical property relationships for clear Southern Pine. Wood and Fiber Science. 28(3): 320–337.

Kretschmann, D.E.; Green, D.W.; Malinauskas, V. 1991. Effect of moisture content on stress intensity factors in Southern Pine. In: Proceedings, 1991 international timber engineering conference; 1991 September 2–5; London. London: TRADA: 3.391–3.398. Vol. 3.

LeVan, S.L.; Winandy, J.E. 1990. Effects of fire-retardant treatments on wood strength: a review. Wood and Fiber Science. 22(1): 113–131.

MacLean, J.D. 1953. Effect of steaming on the strength of wood. American Wood-Preservers' Association. 49: 88–112.

MacLean, J.D. 1954. Effect of heating in water on the strength properties of wood. American Wood-Preservers' Association. 50: 253–281.

Mallory, M.P.; Cramer S. 1987. Fracture mechanics: a tool for predicting wood component strength. Forest Products Journal. 37(7/8): 39–47.

Mark, R.E.; Adams, S.F.; Tang, R.C. 1970. Moduli of rigidity of Virginia pine and tulip poplar related to moisture content. Wood Science. 2(4): 203–211.

McDonald, K.A.; Bendtsen, B.A. 1986. Measuring localized slope of grain by electrical capacitance. Forest Products Journal. 36(10): 75–78.

McDonald, K.A.; Hennon, P.E.; Stevens, J.H.; Green, D.W. 1997. Mechanical properties of salvaged yellow-cedar in southeastern Alaska—Phase I. Res. Pap. FPL–RP–565. Madison, WI: U.S. Department of Agriculture, Forest Service, Forest Products Laboratory.

Millett, M.A.; Gerhards, C.C. 1972. Accelerated aging: residual weight and flexural properties of wood heated in air at 115°C to 175°C. Wood Science. 4(4): 193–201.

Nicholas, D.D. 1973. Wood deterioration and its prevention by preservative treatments. Vol. I. Degradation and protection of Wood. Syracuse, NY: Syracuse University Press.

Pillow, M.Y. 1949. Studies of compression failures and their detection in ladder rails. Rep. D 1733. Madison, WI: U.S. Department of Agriculture, Forest Service, Forest Products Laboratory.

Sliker, A.; Yu, Y. 1993. Elastic constants for hardwoods measured from plate and tension tests. Wood and Fiber Science. 25(1): 8–22.

Sliker, A.; Yu, Y.; Weigel, T.; Zhang, W. 1994. Orthotropic elastic constants for eastern hardwood species. Wood and Fiber Science. 26(1): 107–121.

Soltis, L.A.; Winandy J.E. 1989. Long-term strength of CCA-treated lumber. Forest Products Journal. 39(5): 64–68.

Timell, T.E. 1986. Compression wood in gymnosperms. Vol. I–III. Berlin: Springer–Verlag.

U. S. Department of Defense. 1951. Design of wood aircraft structures. ANC–18 Bull. Subcommittee on Air Force–Navy Civil Aircraft, Design Criteria Aircraft Commission. 2d ed. Munitions Board Aircraft Committee.

Wangaard, F.F. 1966. Resistance of wood to chemical degradation. Forest Products Journal. 16(2): 53–64.

Wilcox, W.W. 1978. Review of literature on the effects of early stages of decay on wood strength. Wood and Fiber. 9(4): 252–257.

Wilson, T.R.C. 1921. The effect of spiral grain on the strength of wood. Journal of Forestry. 19(7): 740–747.

Wilson, T.R.C. 1932. Strength-moisture relations for wood. Tech. Bull. 282. Washington, DC: U.S. Department of Agriculture.

Winandy, J.E. 1995a. Effects of waterborne preservative treatment on mechanical properties: A review. In: Proceedings, 91st annual meeting of American Wood Preservers' Association; 1995, May 21–24; New York, NY. Woodstock, MD: American Wood Preservers' Association. 91: 17–33.

Winandy, J.E. 1995b. The Influence of time-to-failure on the strength of CCA-treated lumber. Forest Products Journal. 45(2): 82–85.

Winandy, J.E. 1995c. Effects of moisture content on strength of CCA-treated lumber. Wood and Fiber Science. 27(2): 168–177.

Winandy, J.E. 1994. Effects of long-term elevated temperature on CCA-treated Southern Pine lumber. Forest Products Journal. 44(6): 49–55.

Winandy, J.E.; Morrell, J.J. 1993. Relationship between incipient decay, strength, and chemical composition of Douglas-fir heartwood. Wood and Fiber Science. 25(3): 278–288.

Woodfin, R.O.; Estep, E.M. (eds). 1978. In: The dead timber resource. Proceedings, 1978 May 22–24, Spokane, WA. Pullman, WA: Engineering Extension Service, Washington State University.

Chapter 5

Commercial Lumber

Kent A. McDonald and David E. Kretschmann

Contents

In a broad sense, commercial lumber is any lumber that is bought or sold in the normal channels of commerce. Commercial lumber may be found in a variety of forms, species, and types, and in various commercial establishments, both wholesale and retail. Most commercial lumber is graded by standardized rules that make purchasing more or less uniform throughout the country.

When sawn, a log yields lumber of varying quality. To enable users to buy the quality that best suits their purposes, lumber is graded into use categories, each having an appropriate range in quality.

Generally, the grade of a piece of lumber is based on the number, character, and location of features that may lower the strength, durability, or utility value of the lumber. Among the more common visual features are knots, checks, pitch pockets, shake, and stain, some of which are a natural part of the tree. Some grades are free or practically free from these features. Other grades, which constitute the great bulk of lumber, contain fairly numerous knots and other features. With proper grading, lumber containing these features is entirely satisfactory for many uses.

The grading operation for most lumber takes place at the sawmill. Establishment of grading procedures is largely the responsibility of manufacturers' associations. Because of the wide variety of wood species, industrial practices, and customer needs, different lumber grading practices coexist. The grading practices of most interest are considered in the sections that follow, under the major categories of hardwood lumber and softwood lumber.

Hardwood Lumber

The principal use of hardwood lumber is for remanufacture into furniture, cabinetwork, and pallets, or direct use as flooring, paneling, moulding, and millwork. Hardwood lumber is graded and marketed in three main categories: Factory lumber, dimension parts, and finished market products. Several hardwood species are graded under the American Softwood Lumber Standard and sold as structural lumber (Ch. 6). Also, specially graded hardwood lumber can be used for structural glued-laminated lumber.

Prior to 1898, hardwoods were graded by individual mills for local markets. In 1898, manufacturers and users formed the National Hardwood Lumber Association to standardize grading for hardwood lumber. Between 1898 and 1932, grading was based on the number and size of visual features. In 1932, the basis for grading was changed to standard clear-cutting sizes.

Both Factory lumber and dimension parts are intended to serve the industrial customer. The important difference is that for Factory lumber, the grades reflect the proportion of a piece that can be cut into useful smaller pieces, whereas the grades for dimension parts are based on use of the entire piece. Finished market products are graded for their unique end-use with little or no remanufacture. Examples of finished products include moulding, stair treads, and hardwood flooring.

Factory Lumber

Grades

The rules adopted by the National Hardwood Lumber Association are considered standard in grading hardwood lumber intended for cutting into smaller pieces to make furniture or other fabricated products. In these rules, the grade of a piece of hardwood lumber is determined by the proportion of a piece that can be cut into a certain number of smaller pieces of material, commonly called cuttings, which are generally clear on one side, have the reverse face sound, and are not smaller than a specified size.

The best grade in the Factory lumber category is termed FAS. The second grade is F1F. The third grade is Selects, which is followed by No. 1 Common, No. 2A Common, No. 2B Common, Sound Wormy, No. 3A Common, and No. 3B Common. Except for F1F and Selects, the poorer side of a piece is inspected for grade assignment. Standard hardwood lumber grades are described in Table 5–1. This table illustrates, for example, that FAS includes pieces that will allow at least 83-1/3% of their surface measure to be cut into clear face material. Except for Sound Wormy, the minimum acceptable length, width, surface measure, and percentage of piece that must work into a cutting decrease with decreasing grade. Figure 5–1 is an example of grading for cuttings.

This brief summary of grades for Factory lumber should not be regarded as a complete set of grading rules because many details, exceptions, and special rules for certain species are not included. The complete official rules of the National Hardwood Lumber Association (NHLA) should be followed as the only full description of existing grades (see Table 5–2 for addresses of NHLA and other U.S. hardwood grading associations). Table 5–3 lists names of commercial domestic hardwood species that are graded by NHLA rules.

Standard Dimensions

Standard lengths of hardwood lumber are in 300-mm (1-ft) increments from 1.2 to 4.8 m (4 to 16 ft). Standard thickness values for hardwood lumber, rough and surfaced on two sides (S2S), are given in Table 5–4. The thickness of S1S lumber is subject to contract agreement. Abbreviations commonly used in contracts and other documents for the purchase and sale of lumber are listed at the end of this chapter.

Hardwood lumber is usually manufactured to random width. The hardwood lumber grades do not specify standard widths; however, the grades do specify minimum width for each grade as follows:

Grade	Minimum width (mm (in.))
FAS	150 (6)
F1F	150 (6)
Selects	100 (4)
No. 1, 2A, 2B, 3A, 3B Common	80 (3)

If the width is specified by purchase agreement, S1E or S2E lumber is 10 mm (3/8 in.) scant of nominal size in lumber less than 200 mm (8 in.) wide and 13 mm (1/2 in.) scant in lumber ≥200 mm (≥8 in.) wide.

Dimension and Component Parts

The term "dimension parts" for hardwoods signifies stock that is processed in specific thickness, width, and length, or multiples thereof and ranges from semi-machined to completely machined component products. This stock is sometimes referred to as "hardwood dimension stock" or "hardwood lumber for dimension parts." This stock should not be confused with "dimension lumber," a term used in the structural lumber market to mean lumber standard 38 mm to less than 114 mm thick (nominal 2 in. to less than 5 in. thick).

Dimension component parts are normally kiln dried and generally graded under the rules of the Wood Components Manufacturers Association (WCMA). These rules encompass three classes of material, each of which is classified into various grades:

Hardwood dimension parts (flat stock)	Solid kiln-dried squares (rough)	Solid kiln-dried squares (surfaced)
Clear two faces	Clear	Clear
Clear one face	Select	Select
Paint	Sound	Paint
Core		Second
Sound		

Each class may be further defined as semifabricated (rough or surfaced) or completely fabricated, including edge-glued panels. The rough wood component parts are blank-sawn and ripped to size. Surfaced semifabricated parts have been through one or more manufacturing stages. Completely fabricated parts have been completely processed for their end use.

Table 5–1. Standard hardwood lumber grades[a,b]

Grade and allowable lengths	Allowable width (in.)	Allowable surface measure of pieces (ft²)	Minimum amount of piece in clearface cuttings (%)	Allowable cuttings	
				Maximum no.	Minimum size
FAS[c]	6+	4 to 9	83-1/3	1	4 in. by 5 ft, or 3 in. by 7 ft
		10 to 14		2	
		15+		3	
F1F[c]	6+	4 to 7	83-1/3	1	4 in. by 5 ft, or 3 in. by 7 ft
		6 and 7	91-2/3	2	
		8 to 11	83-1/3	2	
		8 to 11	91-2/3	3	
		12 to 15	83-1/2	3	
		12 to 15	91-2/3	4	
		16+	83-1/3	4	
Selects 6 to 16 ft (will admit 30% of 6 to 11 ft)	4+	2 and 3	91-2/3	1	4 in. by 5 ft, or 3 in. by 7 ft
		4+	—[d]		
No. 1 Common 4 to 16 ft (will admit 10% of 4 to 7 ft, 1/2 of which may be 4 and 5 ft)	3+	1	100	0	4 in. by 2 ft, or 3 in. by 3 ft
		2	75	1	
		3 and 4	66-2/3	1	
		3 and 4	75	2	
		5 to 7	66-2/3	2	
		5 to 7	75	3	
		8 to 10	66-2/3	3	
		11 to 13	66-2/3	4	
		14+	66-2/3	5	
No. 2 Common 4 to 16 ft (will admit 30% of 4 to 7 ft, 1/3 of which may be 4 and 5 ft)	3+	1	66-2/3	1	3 in. by 2 ft
		2 and 3	50	1	
		2 and 3	66-2/3	2	
		4 and 5	50	2	
		4 and 5	66-2/3	3	
		6 and 7	50	3	
		6 and 7	66-2/3	4	
		8 and 9	50	4	
		10 and 11	50	5	
		12 and 13	50	6	
		14+	50	7	
Sound Wormy[e] No. 3A Common 4 to 16 ft (will admit 50% of 4 to 7 ft, 1/2 of which may be 4 and 5 ft)	3+	1+	33-1/3[f]	—[g]	3 in. by 2 ft
Sound Wormy[e] No. 3B Common 4 to 16 ft (will admit 50% of 4 to 7 ft, 1/2 of which may be 4 and 5 ft)	3+	1+	25[h]	—[g]	1-1/2 in. by 2 ft

[a]Current grading rules are written only in the inch–pound system of measurement.
[b]Inspection made on poorer side of piece, except in Selects grade.
[c]FAS is a grade that designates Firsts and Seconds. F1F is a grade that designates FAS one face.
[d]Same as F1F, with reverse side of board not below No. 1 Common or reverse side of sound cuttings.
[e]Same requirements as those for No. 1 Common and better except that wormholes and limited sound knots and other imperfections are allowed in cuttings.
[f]Also admits pieces that grade not below No. 2 Common on the good face and reverse side of sound cuttings.
[g]Unlimited.
[h]Cuttings must be sound; clear face not required.

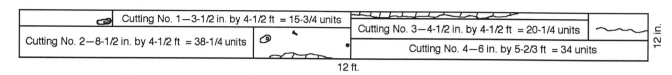

| | Cutting No. 1—3-1/2 in. by 4-1/2 ft = 15-3/4 units | | Cutting No. 3—4-1/2 in. by 4-1/2 ft = 20-1/4 units | |
| Cutting No. 2—8-1/2 in. by 4-1/2 ft = 38-1/4 units | | | Cutting No. 4—6 in. by 5-2/3 ft = 34 units | 12 in. |

12 ft.

1. Determine Surface Measure (S.M.) using lumber scale stick or from formula:

$$\frac{\text{Width in inches} \times \text{length in feet}}{12} = \frac{12 \text{ in.} \times 12 \text{ ft}}{12}$$

$$= 12 \text{ ft}^2 \text{ S.M.}$$

2. No. 1 Common is assumed grade of board. Percent of clear-cutting area required for No. 1 Common—66⅔% or ⁸⁄₁₂.

3. Determine maximum number of cuttings permitted.

   For No. 1 Common grade (S.M. + 1) ÷ 3

   $$= \frac{(12 + 1)}{3} = \frac{13}{3} = 4 \text{ cuttings.}$$

4. Determine minimum size of cuttings.
   For No. 1 Common grade 4 in. × 2 ft or 3 in. × 3 ft.

5. Determine clear-face cutting units needed.

   For No. 1 Common grade S.M. × 8 = 12 × 8 = 96 units

6. Determine total area of permitted clear-face cutting in units.

   Width in inches and fractions of inches × length in feet and fractions of feet

   Cutting #1—3½ in. × 4½ ft = 15¾ units
   Cutting #2—8½ in. × 4½ ft = 38   units
   Cutting #3—4½ in. × 4½ ft = 20¼ units
   Cutting #4—6 in.   × 5⅔ ft = 34   units

   Total Units   108

   Units required for No. 1 Common—96.

7. Conclusion: Board meets requirements for No. 1 Common grade.

Figure 5–1. Example of hardwood grading for cuttings using No. 1 Common lumber grade. Current grading rules are written only in the inch–pound system of measurement.

Table 5–2. Hardwood grading associations in United States[a]

Name and address	Species covered by grading rules (products)
National Hardwood Lumber Association P.O. Box 34518 Memphis, TN 38184–0518	All hardwood species (furniture cuttings, construction lumber, siding, panels)
Wood Components Manufacturers Association 1000 Johnson Ferry Rd., Suite A-130 Marietta, GA 30068	All hardwood species (hardwood furniture dimension, squares, laminated stock, interior trim, stair treads and risers)
Maple Flooring Manufacturers Association 60 Revere Dr., Suite 500 Northbrook, IL 60062	Maple, beech, birch (flooring)
National Oak Flooring Manufacturers Association P.O. Box 3009 Memphis, TN 38173–0009 www.nofma.org	Oak, ash, pecan, hickory, pecan, beech, birch, hard maple (flooring, including prefinished)

[a]Grading associations that include hardwood species in structural grades are listed in Table 5–5.

Table 5–3. Nomenclature of commercial hardwood lumber

Commercial name for lumber	Common tree name	Botanical name	Commercial name for lumber	Common tree name	Botanical name
Alder, Red	Red alder	*Alnus rubra*	Maple, Oregon	Big leaf maple	*Acer macrophyllum*
Ash, Black	Black ash	*Fraxinus nigra*	Maple, Soft	Red maple	*Acer rubrum*
Ash, Oregon	Oregon ash	*Fraxinus latifolia*		Silver maple	*Acer saccharinum*
Ash, White	Blue ash	*Fraxinus quadrangulata*	Oak, Red	Black oak	*Quercus velutina*
	Green ash	*Fraxinus pennsylvanica*		Blackjack oak	*Quercus marilandica*
	White ash	*Fraxinus americana*		California black oak	*Quercus kelloggi*
Aspen (popple)	Bigtooth aspen	*Populus grandidentata*		Cherrybark oak	*Quercus falcata* var. *pagodaefolia*
	Quaking aspen	*Populus tremuloides*		Laurel oak	*Quercus laurifolia*
Basswood	American basswood	*Tilia americana*		Northern pin oak	*Quercus ellipsoidalis*
	White basswood	*Tilia heterophylla*		Northern red oak	*Quercus rubra*
Beech	American beech	*Fagus grandifolia*		Nuttall oak	*Quercus nuttallii*
Birch	Gray birch	*Betula populifolia*		Pin oak	*Quercus palustris*
	Paper birch	*Betula papyrifera*		Scarlet oak	*Quercus coccinea*
	River birch	*Betula nigra*		Shumard oak	*Quercus shumardii*
	Sweet birch	*Betula lenta*		Southern red oak	*Quercus falcata*
	Yellow birch	*Betula alleghaniensis*		Turkey oak	*Quercus laevis*
Box Elder	Boxelder	*Acer negundo*		Willow oak	*Quercus phellos*
Buckeye	Ohio buckeye	*Aesculus glabra*	Oak, White	Arizona white oak	*Quercus arizonica*
	Yellow buckeye	*Aesculus octandra*		Blue oak	*Quercus douglasii*
Butternut	Butternut	*Juglans cinerea*		Bur oak	*Quercus macrocarpa*
Cherry	Black cherry	*Prunus serotina*		Valley oak	*Quercus lobata*
Chestnut	American chestnut	*Castanea dentata*		Chestnut oak	*Quercus prinus*
Cottonwood	Balsam poplar	*Populus balsamifera*		Chinkapin oak	*Quercus muehlenbergii*
	Eastern cottonwood	*Populus deltoides*		Emory oak	*Quercus emoryi*
	Black cottonwood	*Populus trichocarpa*		Gambel oak	*Quercus gambelii*
Cucumber	Cucumbertree	*Magnolia acuminata*		Mexican blue oak	*Quercus oblongifolia*
Dogwood	Flowering dogwood	*Cornus florida*		Live oak	*Quercus virginiana*
	Pacific dogwood	*Cornus nuttallii*		Oregon white oak	*Quercus garryana*
Elm, Rock	Cedar elm	*Ulmus crassifolia*		Overcup oak	*Quercus lyrata*
	Rock elm	*Ulmus thomasii*		Post oak	*Quercus stellata*
	September elm	*Ulmus serotina*		Swamp chestnut oak	*Quercus michauxii*
	Winged elm	*Ulmus alata*		Swamp white oak	*Quercus bicolor*
Elm, Soft	American elm	*Ulmus americana*		White oak	*Quercus alba*
	Slippery elm	*Ulmus rubra*	Oregon Myrtle	California-laurel	*Umbellularia californica*
Gum	Sweetgum	*Liquidambar styraciflua*	Osage Orange	Osage-orange	*Maclura pomifera*
Hackberry	Hackberry	*Celtis occidentalis*	Pecan	Bitternut hickory	*Carya cordiformis*
	Sugarberry	*Celtis laevigata*		Nutmeg hickory	*Carya myristiciformis*
Hickory	Mockernut hickory	*Carya tomentosa*		Water hickory	*Carya aquatica*
	Pignut hickory	*Carya glabra*		Pecan	*Carya illinoensis*
	Shagbark hickory	*Carya ovata*	Persimmon	Common persimmon	*Diospyros virginiana*
	Shellbark hickory	*Carya lacinosa*	Poplar	Yellow-poplar	*Liriodendron tulipifera*
Holly	American holly	*Ilex opaca*	Sassafras	Sassafras	*Sassafras albidum*
Ironwood	Eastern hophornbeam	*Ostrya virginiana*	Sycamore	Sycamore	*Platanus occidentalis*
Locust	Black locust	*Robinia pseudoacacia*	Tanoak	Tanoak	*Lithocarpus densiflorus*
	Honeylocust	*Gleditsia triacanthos*	Tupelo	Black tupelo, blackgum	*Nyssa sylvatica*
Madrone	Pacific madrone	*Arbutus menziesii*		Ogeechee tupelo	*Nyssa ogeche*
Magnolia	Southern magnolia	*Magnolia grandiflora*		Water tupelo	*Nyssa aquatica*
	Sweetbay	*Magnolia virginiana*	Walnut	Black walnut	*Juglans nigra*
Maple, Hard	Black maple	*Acer nigrum*	Willow	Black willow	*Salix nigra*
	Sugar maple	*Acer saccharum*		Peachleaf willow	*Salix amygdaloides*

Table 5–4. Standard thickness values for rough and surfaced (S2S) hardwood lumber

Rough		Surfaced	
(mm	(in.))	(mm	(in.))
9.5	(3/8)	4.8	(3/16)
12.7	(1/2)	7.9	(5/16)
15.9	(5/8)	9.4	(7/16)
19.0	(3/4)	14.3	(9/16)
25.4	(1)	20.6	(13/16)
31.8	(1-1/4)	27.0	(1-1/16)
38.1	(1-1/2)	33.3	(1-5/16)
44.4	(1-3/4)	38.1	(1-1/2)
50.8	(2)	44.4	(1-3/4)
63.5	(2-1/2)	57.2	(2-1/4)
76.2	(3)	69.8	(2-3/4)
88.9	(3-1/2)	82.6	(3-1/4)
101.6	(4)	95.2	(3-3/4)
114.3	(4-1/2)	—[a]	—[a]
127.0	(5)	—[a]	—[a]
139.7	(5-1/2)	—[a]	—[a]
152.4	(6)	—[a]	—[a]

[a]Finished size not specified in rules. Thickness subject to special contract.

Finished Market Products

Some hardwood lumber products are graded in relatively finished form, with little or no further processing anticipated. Flooring is probably the finished market product with the highest volume. Other examples are lath, siding, ties, planks, carstock, construction boards, timbers, trim, moulding, stair treads, and risers. Grading rules promulgated for flooring anticipate final consumer use and are summarized in this section. Details on grades of other finished products are found in appropriate association grading rules.

Hardwood flooring generally is graded under the rules of the Maple Flooring Manufacturers Association (MFMA) or the National Oak Flooring Manufacturers Association (NOFMA). Tongued-and-grooved, end-matched hardwood flooring is commonly furnished. Square-edge, square-end-strip flooring is also available as well as parquet flooring suitable for laying with mastic.

The grading rules of the Maple Flooring Manufacturers Association cover flooring that is manufactured from hard maple, beech, and birch. Each species is graded into four categories:

- First grade—one face practically free of all imperfections; variations in natural color of wood allowed

- Second grade—tight, sound knots (except on edges or ends) and other slight imperfections allowed; must be possible to lay flooring without waste

- Third grade—may contain all visual features common to hard maple, beech, and birch; will not admit voids on edges or ends, or holes over 9.5-mm (3/8-in.) in diameter; must permit proper laying of floor and provide a serviceable floor; few restrictions on imperfections; must be possible to lay flooring properly

- Fourth grade—may contain all visual features, but must be possible to lay a serviceable floor, with some cutting

Combination grades of "Second and Better" and "Third and Better" are sometimes specified. There are also special grades based on color and species.

The standard thickness of MFMA hard maple, beech, and birch flooring is 19.8 mm (25/32 in.). Face widths are 38, 51, 57, and 83 mm (1-1/2, 2, 2-1/4, and 3-1/4 in.). Standard lengths are 610 mm (2 ft) and longer in First- and Second-grade flooring and 381 mm (1-1/4 ft) and longer in Third-grade flooring.

The Official Flooring Grading Rules of NOFMA cover oak (unfinished and prefinished), beech, birch, hard maple, ash, and hickory/pecan. Flooring grades are determined by the appearance of the face surface.

Oak is separated as red oak and white oak and by grain direction: plain sawn (all cuts), quartersawn (50% quartered character), rift sawn (75% rift character), and quarter/rift sawn (a combination). Oak flooring has four main grade separations—Clear, Select, No. 1 Common, and No. 2 Common. Clear is mostly heartwood and accepts a 10-mm (3/8-in.) strip of bright sapwood or an equivalent amount not more than 25 mm (1 in.) wide along the edge and a minimum number of character marks and discoloration, allowing for all natural heartwood color variations. Select allows all color variations of natural heartwood and sapwood along with characters such as small knots, pinworm holes, and brown streaks. No. 1 Common contains prominent variations in coloration, which include heavy streaks, sticker stains, open checks, knots, and small knot holes that fill. No. 2 Common contains sound natural variation of the forest product and manufacturing imperfections to provide a serviceable floor.

Average lengths for unfinished oak grades are as follows:

Grade	Standard packaging		Shorter packaging	
Clear	1.14 m	(3-3/4 ft)	1.07 m	(3-1/2 ft)
Select	0.99 m	(3-1/4 ft)	0.91 m	(3 ft)
No. 1 Common	0.84 m	(2-3/4 ft)	0.76 m	(2-/1/2 ft)
No. 2 Common	0.69 m	(2-1/4 ft)	0.61 m	(2 ft)

andard packaging refers to nominal 2.4-m (8-ft) pallets or
sted bundles. Shorter packaging refers to nominal 2.13-m
-ft) and shorter pallets or nested bundles.

andard and special NOFMA grades for species other than
k are as follows:

ecies	Grade
	Standard grades
ech, birch, d hard maple	First, Second, Third, Second & Better, Third & Better
ckory and pecan	First, Second, Third, Second & Better, Third & Better
sh	Clear, Select, No. 1 Common, No. 2 Common
	Special grades
ech and birch	First Grade Red
ard maple	First Grade White
ckory and pecan	First Grade White, First Grade Red, Second Grade Red

andard thickness values for NOFMA tongue and groove
ooring are 19, 12, 9.5 (3/4, 1/2, 3/8 in.), with 19.8, and
6.2 mm (25/32 and 33/32 in.) for maple flooring. Standard
ace widths are 38, 51, 57, and 83 mm (1-1/2, 2, 2-1/4, and
-1/4 in.). Strips are random length from minimum 0.23 m
 maximum 2.59 m (9 to 102 in.).

Lumber Species

he names used by the trade to describe commercial lumber
 the United States are not always the same as the names of
ees adopted as official by the USDA Forest Service.
able 5–3 shows the common trade name, the USDA Forest
ervice tree name, and the botanical name. United States
gencies and associations that prepare rules for and supervise
rading of hardwoods are given in Table 5–2.

Softwood Lumber

or many years, softwood lumber has demonstrated the
ersatility of wood by serving as a primary raw material for
onstruction and manufacture. In this role, softwood lumber
as been produced in a wide variety of products from many
ifferent species. The first industry-sponsored grading rules
product descriptions) for softwoods, which were established
efore 1900, were comparatively simple because sawmills
narketed their lumber locally and grades had only local
ignificance. As new timber sources were developed and
umber was transported to distant points, each producing
egion continued to establish its own grading rules; thus,
umber from various regions differed in size, grade name, and
llowable grade characteristics. When different species were
raded under different rules and competed in the same con-
uming areas, confusion and dissatisfaction were inevitable.

To minimize unnecessary differences in the grading rules of
softwood lumber and to improve and simplify these rules, a
number of conferences were organized by the U.S. Department of Commerce from 1919 to 1925. These meetings were
attended by representatives of lumber manufacturers, distributors, wholesalers, retailers, engineers, architects, and contractors. The result was a relative standardization of sizes,
definitions, and procedures for deriving allowable design
properties, formulated as a voluntary American Lumber
Standard. This standard has been modified several times,
including addition of hardwood species to the standard
beginning in 1970. The current edition is the American
Softwood Lumber Standard PS–20. Lumber cannot be
graded as American Standard lumber unless the grade rules
have been approved by the American Lumber Standard
Committee (ALSC), Inc., Board of Review.

Softwood lumber is classified for market use by form of
manufacture, species, and grade. For many products, the
American Softwood Lumber Standard and the grading rules
certified through it serve as a basic reference. For specific
information on other products, reference must be made to
grade rules, industry marketing aids, and trade journals.

Lumber Grades

Softwood lumber grades can be classified into three major
categories of use: (a) yard lumber, (b) structural lumber, and
(c) Factory and Shop lumber. Yard lumber and structural
lumber relate principally to lumber expected to function as
graded and sized after primary processing (sawing and planing). Factory and Shop refer to lumber that will undergo a
number of further manufacturing steps and reach the consumer
in a significantly different form.

Yard Lumber

The grading requirements of yard lumber are specifically
related to the construction uses intended, and little or no
further grading occurs once the piece leaves the sawmill.
Yard lumber can be placed into two basic classifications,
Select and Common. Select and Common lumber, as
categorized here, encompass those lumber products in which
appearance is of primary importance; structural integrity,
while sometimes important, is a secondary feature.

Select Lumber—Select lumber is generally non-stress-
graded, but it forms a separate category because of the distinct importance of appearance in the grading process. Select
lumber is intended for natural and paint finishes. This category of lumber includes lumber that has been machined to a
pattern and S4S lumber. Secondary manufacture of these
items is usually restricted to on-site fitting such as cutting to
length and mitering. The Select category includes trim,
siding, flooring, ceiling, paneling, casing, base, stepping,
and finish boards.

Most Select lumber grades are generally described by letters
and combinations of letters (B&BTR, C&BTR, D) or
names (Superior, Prime) depending upon the species and the
grading rules under which the lumber is graded. (See list of

commonly used lumber abbreviations at the end of this chapter.) The specifications FG (flat grain), VG (vertical grain), and MG (mixed grain) are offered as a purchase option for some Select lumber products.

In cedar and redwood, there is a pronounced difference in color between heartwood and sapwood. Heartwood also has high natural resistance to decay, so some grades are denoted as "heart." Because Select lumber grades emphasize the quality of one face, the reverse side may be lower in quality. Select lumber grades are not uniform across species and products, so certified grade rules for the species must be used for detailed reference.

Common Lumber—Common lumber is normally a non-stress-graded product. The grades of Common lumber are suitable for construction and utility purposes. Common lumber is generally separated into three to five different grades depending upon the species and grading rules involved. Grades may be described by number (No. 1, No. 2, No. 1 Common, No. 2 Common) or descriptive term (Select Merchantable, Construction, Standard).

Because there are differences in the inherent properties of various species and their corresponding names, the grades for different species are not always interchangeable. The top-grade boards (No. 1, No. 1 Common, Select Merchantable) are usually graded for serviceability, but appearance is also considered. These grades are used for such purposes as siding, cornice, shelving, and paneling. Features such as knots and knotholes are permitted to be larger and more frequent as the grade level becomes lower. Intermediate-grade boards are often used for such purposes as subfloors, roof and wall sheathing, and rough concrete work. The lower grade boards are selected for adequate strength, not appearance. They are used for roof and wall sheathing, subfloor, and rough concrete form work (Fig. 5–2).

Grading provisions for other non-stress-graded products vary by species, product, and applicable grading rules. For detailed descriptions, consult the appropriate grade rule for these products (see Table 5–5 for softwood grading organizations).

Structural Lumber—Almost all softwood lumber standard 38 to 89 mm thick (nominal 2 to 4 in. thick, actual 1-1/2 to 3-1/2 in. thick) is produced as dimension lumber. Dimension lumber is stress graded and assigned allowable properties under the National Grading Rule, a part of the American Softwood Lumber Standard. For dimension lumber, a single set of grade names and descriptions is used throughout the United States, although the allowable properties vary with species. Timbers (lumber standard 114 mm (nominal 5 in.) or more in least dimension) are also structurally graded under ALSC procedures. Unlike grade descriptions for dimension lumber, grade descriptions for structural timbers are not standardized across species. For most species, timber grades are classified according to intended use. Beams and stringers are members standard 114 mm (nominal 5 in.) or more in thickness with a width more than 51 mm (2 in.) greater than

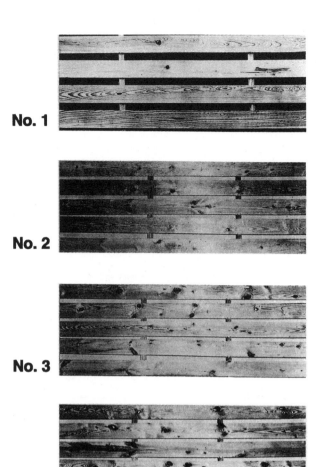

No. 1

No. 2

No. 3

No. 4

Figure 5–2. Typical examples of softwood boards in the lower grades.

the thickness. Beams and stringers are primarily used to resist bending stresses, and the grade description for the middle third of the length of the beam is more stringent than that for the outer two-thirds. Posts and timbers are members standard 114 by 114 mm (nominal 5 by 5 in.) and larger, where the width is not more than 51 mm (2 in.) greater than the thickness. Post and timbers are primarily used to resist axial stresses. Structural timbers of Southern Pine are graded without regard to anticipated use, as with dimension lumber. Other stress-graded products include decking and some boards. Stress-graded lumber may be graded visually or mechanically. Stress grades and the National Grading Rule are discussed in Chapter 6.

Structural Laminations—Structural laminating grades describe the characteristics used to segregate lumber to be used in structural glued-laminated (glulam) timbers. Generally, allowable properties are not assigned separately to laminating grades; rather, the rules for laminating grades are based on the expected effect of that grade of lamination on the combined glulam timber.

Table 5–5. Organizations promulgating softwood grades

Name and address	Species covered by grading rules
Cedar Shingle & Shake Bureau 515 116th Avenue NE, Suite 275 Bellevue, WA 98004–5294	Western redcedar (shingles and shakes)
National Hardwood Lumber Association P.O. Box 34518 Memphis, TN 38184–0518	Baldcypress, eastern redcedar
National Lumber Grades Authority[a] 406 First Capital Place 960 Quamside Drive New Westminister, BC, Canada V3M6G2	Northern white cedar, western red cedar, yellow cedar, alpine fir, amabilis fir, balsam fir, Douglas-fir, grand fir, eastern hemlock, western hemlock, western larch, eastern white pine, jack pine, lodgepole pine, ponderosa pine, red pine, western white pine, black spruce, sitka spruce, red spruce, Engelmann spruce, white spruce, tamarack, aspen, black cottonwood, balsam poplar, red alder, white birch
Northeastern Lumber Manufacturers Association, Inc. 272 Tuttle Road, P.O. Box 87A Cumberland Center, ME 04021	Balsam fir, eastern white pine, red pine, eastern hemlock, black spruce, white spruce, red spruce, pitch pine, tamarack, jack pine, northern white cedar, aspen, red maple, mixed maple, beech, birch, hickory, mixed oaks, red oak, northern red oak, white oak, yellow poplar
Northern Softwood Lumber Bureau[a] 272 Tuttle Road, P.O. Box 87A Cumberland Center, ME 04021	Eastern white pine, jack pine, red pine, pitch pine, eastern spruce (red, white, and black), balsam fir, eastern hemlock, tamarack, eastern cottonwood, aspen (bigtooth and quaking), yellow poplar
Redwood Inspection Service 405 Enfrente Drive, Suite 200 Novato, CA 94949	Redwood
Southern Cypress Manufacturers Association 400 Penn Center Boulevard Suite 530 Pittsburgh, PA 15235	Baldcypress
Southern Pine Inspection Bureau[a] 4709 Scenic Highway Pensacola, FL 32504	Longleaf pine, slash pine, shortleaf pine, loblolly pine, Virginia pine, pond pine, pitch pine
West Coast Lumber Inspection Bureau[a] Box 23145 6980 SW. Varns Road Portland, OR 97223	Douglas-fir, western hemlock, western redcedar, incense-cedar, Port-Orford-cedar, yellow-cedar, western true firs, mountain hemlock, Sitka spruce, western larch
Western Wood Products Association[a] Yeon Building, 522 SW Fifth Avenue Portland, OR 97204–2122	Ponderosa pine, western white pine, Douglas-fir, sugar pine, western true firs, western larch, Engelmann spruce, incense-cedar, western hemlock, lodgepole pine, western redcedar, mountain hemlock, red alder, aspen, alpine fir, Idaho white pine

[a]Publishes grading rules certified by the Board of Review of the American Lumber Standard Committee as conforming to the American Softwood Lumber Standard PS–20.

There are two kinds of graded material: visually graded and E-rated. Visually graded material is graded according to one of three sets of grading rules: (1) the first set is based on the grading rules certified as meeting the requirements of the American Softwood Lumber Standard with additional requirements for laminating; (2) the second set involves laminating grades typically used for visually graded western species and includes three basic categories (L1, L2, L3); and (3) the third set includes special requirements for tension members and outer tension laminations on bending members. The visual grades have provisions for dense, close-grain, medium-grain, or coarsegrain lumber.

The E-rated grades are categorized by a combination of visual grading criteria and lumber stiffness. These grades are expressed in terms of the size of maximum edge characteristic permitted (as a fraction of the width) along with a specified long-span modulus of elasticity (for example, 1/6–2.2E).

Factory and Shop Lumber

A wide variety of species, grades, and sizes of softwood lumber is supplied to industrial accounts for cutting to specific smaller sizes, which become integral parts of other products. In the secondary manufacturing process, grade descriptions, sizes, and often the entire appearance of the wood piece are changed. Thus, for Factory and Shop lumber, the role of the grading process is to reflect as accurately as possible the yield to be obtained in the subsequent cutting operation. Typical of lumber for secondary manufacture are the factory grades, industrial clears, box lumber, moulding stock, and ladder stock. The variety of species available for these purposes has led to a variety of grade names and grade definitions. The following sections briefly outline some of the more common classifications. For details, reference must be made to industry sources, such as certified grading rules. Availability and grade designation often vary by region and species.

Factory (Shop) Grades—Traditionally, softwood lumber used for cuttings has been called Factory or Shop. This lumber forms the basic raw material for many secondary manufacturing operations. Some grading rules refer to these grades as Factory, while others refer to them as Shop. All impose a somewhat similar nomenclature in the grade structure. Shop lumber is graded on the basis of characteristics that affect its use for general cut-up purposes or on the basis of size of cutting, such as for sash and doors. Factory Select and Select Shop are typical high grades, followed by No. 1 Shop, No. 2 Shop, and No. 3 Shop.

Grade characteristics of boards are influenced by the width, length, and thickness of the basic piece and are based on the amount of high-quality material that can be removed by cutting. Typically, Factory Select and Select Shop lumber would be required to contain 70% of cuttings of specified size, clear on both sides. No. 1 Shop would be required to have 50% cuttings and No. 2 Shop, 33-1/3%. Because of different characteristics assigned to grades with similar nomenclature, the grades of Factory and Shop lumber must be referenced to the appropriate certified grading rules.

Industrial Clears—These grades are used for trim, cabinet stock, garage door stock, and other product components where excellent appearance, mechanical and physical properties, and finishing characteristics are important. The principal grades are B&BTR, C, and D Industrial. Grading is primarily based on the best face, although the influence of edge characteristics is important and varies depending upon piece width and thickness. In redwood, the Industrial Clear All Heart grade includes an "all heart" requirement for decay resistance in the manufacture of cooling towers, tanks, pipe, and similar products.

Moulding, Ladder, Pole, Tank, and Pencil Stock— Within producing regions, grading rules delineate the requirements for a variety of lumber classes oriented to specific consumer products. Custom and the characteristics of the wood supply have led to different grade descriptions and terminology. For example, in West Coast species, the ladder industry can choose from one "ladder and pole stock" grade plus two ladder rail grades and one ladder rail stock grade. In Southern Pine, ladder stock is available as Select and Industrial. Moulding stock, tank stock, pole stock, stave stock, stadium seat stock, box lumber, and pencil stock are other typical classes oriented to the final product. Some product classes have only one grade level; a few offer two or three levels. Special features of these grades may include a restriction on sapwood related to desired decay resistance, specific requirements for slope of grain and growth ring orientation for high-stress use such as ladders, and particular cutting requirements as in pencil stock. All references to these grades should be made directly to current certified grading rules.

Lumber Manufacture

Size

Lumber length is recorded in actual dimensions, whereas width and thickness are traditionally recorded in "nominal" dimensions—actual dimensions are somewhat less.

Softwood lumber is manufactured in length multiples of 300 mm (1 ft) as specified in various grading rules. In practice, 600-mm (2-ft) multiples (in even numbers) are common for most construction lumber. Width of softwood lumber varies, commonly from standard 38 to 387 mm (nominal 2 to 16 in.). The thickness of lumber can be generally categorized as follows:

- Boards—lumber less than standard 38 mm (nominal 2 in.) in thickness

- Dimension—lumber from standard 38 mm (nominal 2 in.) to, but not including, 114 mm (5 in.) in thickness

- Timbers—lumber standard 114 mm (nominal 5 in.) or more in thickness in least dimension

To standardize and clarify nominal to actual sizes, the American Softwood Lumber Standard PS–20 specifies the actual thickness and width for lumber that falls under the standard. The standard sizes for yard and structural lumber are given in Table 5–6. Timbers are usually surfaced while "green" (unseasoned); therefore, only green sizes are given.

Because dimension lumber and boards may be surfaced green or dry at the prerogative of the manufacturer, both green and dry standard sizes are given. The sizes are such that a piece of green lumber, surfaced to the standard green size, will shrink to approximately the standard dry size as it dries to about 15% moisture content. The definition of dry is lumber that has been seasoned or dried to a maximum moisture content of 19%. Lumber may also be designated as kiln dried (KD), meaning the lumber has been seasoned in a chamber to a predetermined moisture content by applying heat.

Table 5–6. American Standard Lumber sizes for yard and structural lumber for construction

Item	Thickness Nominal (in.)	Thickness Minimum dressed Dry (mm	(in.))	Thickness Minimum dressed Green (mm	(in.))	Face width Nominal (in.)	Face width Minimum dressed Dry (mm	(in.))	Face width Minimum dressed Green (mm	(in.))
Boards	1	19	(3/4)	20	(25/32)	2	38	(1-1/2)	40	(1-9/16)
	1-1/4	25	(1)	26	(1-1/32)	3	64	(2-1/2)	65	(2-9/16)
	1-1/2	32	(1-1/4)	33	(1-9/32)	4	89	(3-1/2)	90	(3-9/16)
						5	114	(4-1/2)	117	(4-5/8)
						6	140	(5-1/2)	143	(5-5/8)
						7	165	(6-1/2)	168	(6-5/8)
						8	184	(7-1/4)	190	(7-1/2)
						9	210	(8-1/4)	216	(8-1/2)
						10	235	(9-1/4)	241	(9-1/2)
						11	260	(10-1/4)	267	(10-1/2)
						12	286	(11-1/4)	292	(11-1/2)
						14	337	(13-1/4)	343	(13-1/2)
						16	387	(15-1/4)	394	(15-1/2)
Dimension	2	38	(1-1/2)	40	(1-9/16)	2	38	(1-1/2)	40	(1-9/16)
	2-1/2	51	(2)	52	(2-1/16)	3	64	(2-1/2)	65	(2-9/16)
	3	64	(2-1/2)	65	(2-9/16)	4	89	(3-1/2)	90	(3-9/16)
	3-1/2	76	(3)	78	(3-1/16)	5	114	(4-1/2)	117	(4-5/8)
	4	89	(3-1/2)	90	(3-9/16)	6	140	(5-1/2)	143	(5-5/8)
	4-1/2	102	(4)	103	(4-1/16)	8	184	(7-1/4)	190	(7-1/2)
						10	235	(9-1/4)	241	(9-1/2)
						12	286	(11-1/4)	292	(11-1/2)
						14	337	(13-1/4)	343	(13-1/2)
						16	387	(15-1/4)	394	(15-1/2)
Timbers	≥5	13 mm off	(1/2 in. off)	13 mm off	(1/2 in. off)	≥5	13 mm off	(1/2 in. off)	13 mm off	(1/2 in. off)

Factory and Shop lumber for remanufacture is offered in specified sizes to fit end-product requirements. Factory (Shop) grades for general cuttings are offered in thickness from standard 19 to 89 mm (nominal 1 to 4 in.). Thicknesses of door cuttings start at 35 mm (nominal 1-3/8 in.). Cuttings are of various lengths and widths. Laminating stock is sometimes offered oversize, compared with standard dimension sizes, to permit resurfacing prior to laminating. Industrial Clears can be offered rough or surfaced in a variety of sizes, starting from standard 38 mm (nominal 2 in.) and thinner and as narrow as standard 64 mm (nominal 3 in.). Sizes for special product grades such as moulding stock and ladder stock are specified in appropriate grading rules or handled by purchase agreements.

Surfacing

Lumber can be produced either rough or surfaced (dressed). Rough lumber has surface imperfections caused by the primary sawing operations. It may be greater than target size by variable amounts in both thickness and width, depending upon the type of sawmill equipment. Rough lumber serves as a raw material for further manufacture and also for some decorative purposes. A roughsawn surface is common in post and timber products. Because of surface roughness, grading of rough lumber is generally more difficult.

Surfaced lumber has been surfaced by a machine on one side (S1S), two sides (S2S), one edge (S1E), two edges (S2E), or combinations of sides and edges (S1S1E, S2S1E, S1S2, S4S). Lumber is surfaced to attain smoothness and uniformity of size.

Imperfections or blemishes defined in the grading rules and caused by machining are classified as "manufacturing imperfections." For example, chipped and torn grain are surface irregularities in which surface fibers have been torn out by the surfacing operation. Chipped grain is a "barely perceptible" characteristic, while torn grain is classified by depth. Raised grain, skip, machine burn and gouge, chip marks, and wavy surfacing are other manufacturing imperfections. Manufacturing imperfections are defined in the American Softwood

Lumber Standard and further detailed in the grading rules. Classifications of manufacturing imperfections (combinations of imperfections allowed) are established in the rules as Standard A, Standard B, and so on. For example, Standard A admits very light torn grain, occasional slight chip marks, and very slight knife marks. These classifications are used as part of the grade rule description of some lumber products to specify the allowable surface quality.

Patterns

Lumber that has been matched, shiplapped, or otherwise patterned, in addition to being surfaced, is often classified as "worked lumber." Figure 5–3 shows typical patterns.

Softwood Lumber Species

The names of lumber species adopted by the trade as standard may vary from the names of trees adopted as official by the USDA Forest Service. Table 5–7 shows the American Softwood Lumber Standard commercial names for lumber, the USDA Forest Service tree names, and the botanical names. Some softwood species are marketed primarily in combinations. Designations such as Southern Pine and Hem–Fir represent typical combinations. Grading rule agencies (Table 5–5) should be contacted for questions regarding combination names and species not listed in Table 5–7. Species groups are discussed further in Chapter 6.

Softwood Lumber Grading

Most lumber is graded under the supervision of inspection bureaus and grading agencies. These organizations supervise lumber mill grading and provide re-inspection services to resolve disputes concerning lumber shipments. Some of these agencies also write grading rules that reflect the species and products in the geographic regions they represent. These grading rules follow the American Softwood Lumber Standard (PS–20). This is important because it provides for recognized uniform grading procedures. Names and addresses of rules-writing organizations in the United States and the species with which they are concerned are listed in Table 5–5. Canadian softwood lumber imported into the United States and graded by inspection agencies in Canada also follows the PS–20 standard. Names and addresses of accredited Canadian grading agencies may be obtained from the American Lumber Standard Committee, P.O. Box 210, Germantown, Maryland 20874.

Purchase of Lumber

After primary manufacture, most lumber products are marketed through wholesalers to remanufacturing plants or retail outlets. Because of the extremely wide variety of lumber products, wholesaling is very specialized—some organizations deal with only a limited number of species or products. Where the primary manufacturer can readily identify the customers, direct sales may be made. Primary manufacturers often sell directly to large retail-chain contractors, manufacturers of mobile and modular housing, and truss fabricators.

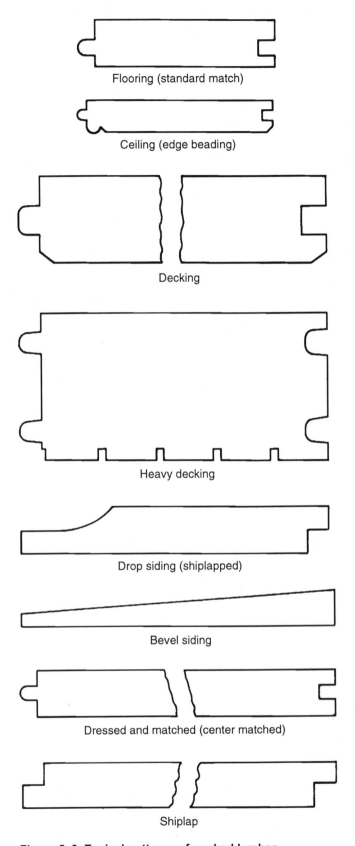

Flooring (standard match)

Ceiling (edge beading)

Decking

Heavy decking

Drop siding (shiplapped)

Bevel siding

Dressed and matched (center matched)

Shiplap

Figure 5–3. Typical patterns of worked lumber.

Table 5–7. Nomenclature of commercial softwood lumber

Commercial species or species group names under American Softwood Lumber Standard	Tree name used in this handbook	Botanical name
Cedar		
Alaska	yellow-cedar	*Chamaecyparis nootkatensis*
Eastern Red	eastern redcedar	*Juniperus virginiana*
Incense	incense-cedar	*Libocedrus decurrens*
Northern White	northern white-cedar	*Thuja occidentalis*
Port Orford	Port-Orford-cedar	*Chamaecyparis lawsoniana*
Southern White	Atlantic white-cedar	*Chamaecyparis thyoides*
Western Red	western redcedar	*Thuja plicata*
Cypress		
Baldcypress	baldcypress	*Taxodium distichum*
Pond cypress	pond cypress	*Taxodium distichum* var. *nutans*
Fir		
Alpine	subalpine fir (alpine fir)	*Abies lasiocarpa*
Balsam	balsam fir	*Abies balsamea*
California Red	California red fir	*Abies magnifica*
Douglas Fir	Douglas-fir	*Pseudotsuga menziesii*
Fraser	Fraser fir	*Abies fraseri*
Grand	grand fir	*Abies grandis*
Noble Fir	noble fir	*Abies procera*
Pacific Grand	Pacific silver fir	*Abies amabilis*
White	white fir	*Abies concolor*
Hemlock		
Carolina	Carolina hemlock	*Tsuga caroliniana*
Eastern	eastern hemlock	*Tsuga canadensis*
Mountain	mountain hemlock	*Tsuga mertensiana*
Western	western hemlock	*Tsuga heterophylla*
Juniper		
Western	alligator juniper	*Juniperus deppeana*
	Rocky Mountain juniper	*Juniperus scopulorum*
	Utah juniper	*Juniperus osteosperma*
	western juniper	*Juniperus occidentalis*
Larch		
Western	western larch	*Larix occidentalis*
Pine		
Bishop	bishop pine	*Pinus muricata*
Coulter	Coulter pine	*Pinus coulteri*
Digger	Digger pine	*Pinus sabibiana*
Knobcone	knobcone pine	*Pinus attenuata*
Idaho White	western white pine	*Pinus monticola*
Jack	jack pine	*Pinus banksiana*
Jeffrey	Jeffrey pine	*Pinus jeffreyi*
Limber	limber pine	*Pinus flexilis*
Lodgepole	lodgepole pine	*Pinus contorta*
Longleaf	longleaf pine	*Pinus palustris*
	slash pine	*Pinus elliottii*
Northern White	eastern white pine	*Pinus strobus*
Norway	red pine	*Pinus resinosa*
Pitch	pitch pine	*Pinus rigida*
Ponderosa	ponderosa pine	*Pinus ponderosa*
Southern Pine Major	loblolly pine	*Pinus taeda*
	longleaf pine	*Pinus palustris*
	shortleaf pine	*Pinus echinata*
	slash pine	*Pinus elliottii*
Southern Pine Minor	pond pine	*Pinus serotina*
	sand pine	*Pinus clausa*
	spruce pine	*Pinus glabra*
	Virginia pine	*Pinus virginiana*
Southern Pine Mixed	loblolly pine	*Pinus taeda*
	longleaf pine	*Pinus palustris*
	pond pine	*Pinus serotina*
	shortleaf pine	*Pinus echinata*
	slash pine	*Pinus elliottii*
	Virginia pine	*Pinus virginiana*
Radiata/Monterey Pine	Monterey pine	*Pinus radiata*

Table 5–7. Nomenclature of commercial softwood lumber—con.

Commercial species or species group names under American Softwood Lumber Standard	Tree name used in this handbook	Botanical name
Pine—con.		
Sugar	sugar pine	*Pinus lambertiana*
Whitebark	whitebark pine	*Pinus albicaulis*
Redwood		
Redwood	redwood	*Sequoia sempervirens*
Spruce		
Blue	blue spruce	*Picea pungens*
Eastern	black spruce	*Picea mariana*
	red spruce	*Picea rubens*
	white spruce	*Picea glauca*
Engelmann	Engelmann spruce	*Picea engelmannii*
Sitka	Sitka spruce	*Picea sitchensis*
Tamarack		
Tamarack	tamarack	*Larix larcinia*
Yew		
Pacific	Pacific yew	*Taxus brevifolia*
Coast Species	Douglas-fir	*Pseudotsuga menziesii*
	western larch	*Larix occidentalis*
Eastern Softwoods	black spruce	*Picea mariana*
	red spruce	*Picea rubens*
	white spruce	*Picea glauca*
	balsam fir	*Abies balsamea*
	eastern white pine	*Pinus strobus*
	jack pine	*Pinus banksiana*
	pitch pine	*Pinus rigida*
	red pine	*Pinus resinosa*
	eastern hemlock	*Tsuga canadensis*
	tamarack	*Larix occidentalis*
Hem–Fir	western hemlock	*Tsuga heterophylla*
	California red fir	*Abies magnifica*
	grand fir	*Abies grandis*
	noble fir	*Abies procera*
	Pacific silver fir	*Abies amabilis*
	white fir	*Abies concolor*
Hem–Fir (North)	western hemlock	*Tsuga heterophylla*
	Pacific silver fir	*Abies amabilis*
Northern Pine	jack pine	*Pinus banksiana*
	pitch pine	*Pinus rigida*
	red pine	*Pinus resinosa*
North Species	northern white cedar	*Thuja occidentalis*
	western redcedar	*Thuja plicanta*
	yellow-cedar	*Chamaecyparis nootkatensis*
	eastern hemlock	*Tsuga canadensis*
	western hemlock	*Tsuga heterophylla*
	Douglas-fir	*Pseudotsuga menziesii*
	balsam fir	*Abies balsamea*
	grand fir	*Abies grandis*
	Pacific silver fir	*Abies amabilis*
	subalpine (alpine) fir	*Abies lasiocarpa*
	western larch	*Larix occidentalis*
	tamarack	*Larix laricina*
	eastern white pine	*Pinus strobus*
	jack pine	*Pinus banksiana*
	lodgepole pine	*Pinus contorta*
	ponderosa pine	*Pinus ponderosa*
	red pine	*Pinus resinosa*
	western white pine	*Pinus monticola*
	whitebark pine	*Pinus albicaulis*
	black spruce	*Picea mariana*
	Engelmann spruce	*Picea engelmannii*
	red spruce	*Picea rubens*
	Sitka spruce	*Picea sitchensis*

Table 5–7. Nomenclature of commercial softwood lumber—con.

Commercial species or species group names under American Softwood Lumber Standard	Tree name used in this handbook	Botanical name
North Species—con.	white spruce	*Picea glauca*
	bigtooth aspen	*Populus grandidentata*
	quaking aspen	*Populus tremuloides*
	black cottonwood	*Populus trichocarpa*
	balsam poplar	*Populus balsamifera*
Southern Pine	loblolly pine	*Pinus taeda*
	longleaf pine	*Pinus palustris*
	shortleaf pine	*Pinus echinata*
	slash pine	*Pinus elliottii*
Spruce–Pine–Fir	black spruce	*Picea mariana*
	Engelmann spruce	*Picea engelmannii*
	red spruce	*Picea rubens*
	balsam fir	*Abies balsamea*
	subalpine (alpine) fir	*Abies lasiocarpa*
	jack pine	*Pinus banksiana*
	lodgepole pine	*Pinus contorta*
Spruce–Pine–Fir (South)	black spruce	*Picea mariana*
	Engelmann spruce	*Picea engelmannii*
	red spruce	*Picea rubens*
	Sitka spruce	*Picea sitchensis*
	white spruce	*Picea glauca*
	balsam fir	*Abies balsamea*
	jack pine	*Pinus banksiana*
	lodgepole pine	*Pinus contorta*
	red pine	*Pinus resinosa*
Western Cedars	incense cedar	*Libocedrus decurrens*
	western redcedar	*Thuja plicata*
	Port-Orford-cedar	*Chamaecyparis lawsoniana*
	yellow-cedar	*Chamaecyparis nootkatensis*
Western Cedar (North)	western redcedar	*Thuja plicata*
	yellow-cedar	*Chamaecyparis nootkatensis*
Western Woods	Douglas-fir	*Pseudotsuga menziesii*
	California red fir	*Abies magnifica*
	grand fir	*Abies grandis*
	noble fir	*Abies procera*
	Pacific silver fir	*Abies amabilis*
	subalpine fir	*Abies lasiocarpa*
	white fir	*Abies concolor*
Hemlock	mountain	*Tsuga mertensiana*
	western hemlock	*Tsuga heterophylla*
	western larch	*Larix occidentalis*
	Engelmann spruce	*Picea engelmannii*
	Sitka spruce	*Picea sitchensis*
	lodgepole pine	*Pinus contorta*
	ponderosa pine	*Pinus ponderosa*
	sugar pine	*Pinus lambertiana*
	western white pine	*Pinus monticola*
White Woods	California red fir	*Abies magnifica*
	grand fir	*Abies grandis*
	noble fir	*Abies procera*
	Pacific silver fir	*Abies amabilis*
	subalpine fir	*Abies lasiocarpa*
	white fir	*Abies concolor*
	mountain hemlock	*Tsuga mertensiana*
	western hemlock	*Tsuga heterophylla*
	Engelmann spruce	*Picea engelmannii*
	Sitka spruce	*Picea sitchensis*
	lodgepole pine	*Pinus contorta*
	ponderosa pine	*Pinus ponderosa*
	sugar pine	*Pinus lambertiana*
	western white pine	*Pinus monticola*

Some primary manufacturers and wholesalers set up distribution yards in lumber-consuming areas to distribute both hardwood and softwood products more effectively. Retail yards draw inventory from distribution yards and, in wood-producing areas, from local lumber producers. The wide range of grades and species covered in the grade rules may not be readily available in most retail outlets.

Transportation is a vital factor in lumber distribution. Often, the lumber shipped by water is green because weight is not a major factor in this type of shipping. On the other hand, lumber reaching the East Coast from the Pacific Coast by rail is usually kiln-dried because rail shipping rates are based on weight. A shorter rail haul places southern and northeastern species in a favorable economic position in regard to shipping costs in this market.

Changing transportation costs have influenced shifts in market distribution of species and products. Trucks have become a major factor in lumber transport for regional remanufacture plants, for retail supply from distribution yards, and for much construction lumber distribution.

The increased production capacity of foreign hardwood and softwood manufacturing and the availability of water transport has brought foreign lumber products to the U.S. market, particularly in coastal areas.

Retail Yard Inventory

The small retail yards throughout the United States carry softwoods for construction purposes and often carry small stocks of one or two hardwoods in grades suitable for finishing or cabinetwork. Special orders must be made for other hardwoods. Trim items such as moulding in either softwood or hardwood are available cut to standard size and pattern. Millwork plants usually make ready-for-installation cabinets, and retail yards carry or catalog many common styles and sizes. Hardwood flooring is available to the buyer only in standard patterns. Most retail yards carry stress grades of lumber.

The assortment of species in general construction items carried by retail yards depends to a great extent upon geographic location, and both transportation costs and tradition are important factors. Retail yards within, or close to, a major lumber-producing region commonly emphasize local timber. For example, a local retail yard on the Pacific Northwest Coast may stock only green Douglas Fir and cedar in dimension grades, dry pine and hemlock in boards and moulding, and assorted special items such as redwood posts, cedar shingles and shakes, and rough cedar siding. The only hardwoods may be walnut and "Philippine mahogany" (the common market name encompassing many species, including tanguile, red meranti, and white lauan). Retail yards located farther from a major softwood supply, such as in the Midwest, may draw from several growing areas and may stock spruce and Southern Pine, for example. Because they are located in a major hardwood production

area, these yards may stock, or have available to them, a different and wider variety of hardwoods.

Geography has less influence where consumer demands are more specific. For example, where long construction lumber (6 to 8 m (20 to 26 ft)) is required, West Coast species are often marketed because the height of the trees in several species makes long lengths a practical market item. Ease of preservative treatability makes treated Southern Pine construction lumber available in a wide geographic area.

Structural Lumber for Construction

Dimension lumber is the principal stress-graded lumber available in a retail yard. It is primarily framing lumber for joists, rafters, and studs. Strength, stiffness, and uniformity of size are essential requirements. Dimension lumber is stocked in almost all yards, frequently in only one or two of the general purpose construction woods such as pine, fir, hemlock, or spruce. Standard 38- by 89-mm (nominal 2- by 4-in.) and wider dimension lumber is found in Select Structural, No. 1, No. 2, and No. 3 grades. Standard 38- by 89-mm (nominal 2- by 4-in.) dimension lumber may also be available as Construction, Standard, Utility, and STUD grades. STUD grade is also available in wider widths.

Dimension lumber is often found in standard 38-, 89-, 140-, 184-, 235-, and 286-mm (nominal 2-, 4-, 6-, 8-, 10-, and 12-in.) widths and 2.4- to 5.4-m (8- to 18-ft) lengths in multiples of 0.6 m (2 ft). Dimension lumber formed by structural end-jointing procedures may be available. Dimension lumber thicker than standard 38 mm (nominal 2 in.) and longer than 5.4 m (18 ft) is not commonly available in many retail yards.

Other stress-graded products generally available are posts and timbers; some beams and stringers may also be in stock. Typical grades in these products are Select Structural, No. 1, and No. 2.

Yard Lumber for Construction

Boards are the most common non-stress-graded general purpose construction lumber in the retail yard. Boards are stocked in one or more species, usually in standard 19 mm (nominal 1 in.) thickness. Common widths are standard 38, 64, 89, 140, 184, 235, and 286 mm (nominal 2, 3, 4, 6, 8, 10, and 12 in.). Grades generally available in retail yards are No. 1 Common, No. 2 Common, and No. 3 Common (Construction, Standard, No. 1, No. 2, etc.). Boards are sold square edged, dressed (surfaced) and matched (tongued and grooved), or with a shiplapped joint. Boards formed by end-jointing of shorter sections may constitute an appreciable portion of the inventory.

Select Lumber

Completion of a construction project usually depends on the availability of lumber items in finished or semi-finished form. The following items often may be stocked in only a few species, finishes, or sizes depending on the lumber yard.

Finish—Finish boards usually are available in a local yard in one or two species, principally in grade C&BTR. Cedar and redwood have different grade designations: grades such as Clear Heart, A, or B are used in cedar; Clear All Heart, Clear, and B grade are typical in redwood. Finish boards are usually standard 19 mm (nominal 1 in.) thick, surfaced on two sides to 19 mm (3/4 in.); 38- to 286-mm (2- to 12-in.) widths are usually stocked, in even increments.

Siding—Siding is specifically intended to cover exterior walls. Beveled siding is ordinarily stocked only in white pine, ponderosa pine, western redcedar, cypress, or redwood. Drop siding, also known as rustic or barn siding, is usually stocked in the same species as is beveled siding. Siding may be stocked as B&BTR or C&BTR except in cedar, where Clear, A, and B grades may be available, and redwood, where Clear All Heart, Clear, and B grades may be found. Vertical grain (VG) is sometimes part of the grade designation. Drop siding is also sometimes stocked in sound knotted C and D grades of Southern Pine, Douglas Fir, and hemlock. Drop siding may be surfaced and matched, or shiplapped. Knotty grades of cedar (Select Tight Knot (STK)) and redwood (Rustic) are commonly available.

Flooring—Flooring is made chiefly from hardwoods, such as oak and maple, and the harder softwood species, such as Douglas-fir, western larch, and Southern Pine. Often, at least one softwood and one hardwood are stocked. Flooring is usually 19 mm (3/4 in.) thick. Thicker flooring is available for heavy-duty floors. Thinner flooring is available, especially for re-covering old floors. Vertical- and flat-grained (also called quartersawn and plainsawn) flooring is manufactured from both softwoods and hardwoods. Vertical-grained flooring shrinks and swells less than flat-grained flooring, is more uniform in texture, and wears more uniformly, and the edge joints have less tendency to open.

Softwood flooring is usually available in B&BTR, C Select, or D Select grades. In maple, the chief grades are Clear, No. 1, and No. 2. The grades in quartersawn oak are Clear and Select, and in plainsawn, Clear, Select, and No. 1 Common. Quartersawn hardwood flooring has the same advantages as does vertical-grained softwood flooring. In addition, the silver or flaked grain of quartersawn flooring is frequently preferred to the figure of plainsawn flooring.

Casing and Base—Casing and base are standard items in the more important softwoods and are stocked in most yards in at least one species. The chief grade, B&BTR, is designed to meet the requirements of interior trim for dwellings. Many casing and base patterns are surfaced to 17.5 by 57 mm (11/16 by 2-1/4 in.); other sizes include 14.3 mm (9/16 in.) by 76 mm (3 in.), by 83 mm (3-1/4 in.), and by 89 mm (3-1/2 in.). Hardwoods for the same purposes, such as oak and birch, may be carried in stock in the retail yard or obtained on special order.

Shingles and Shakes—Commonly available shingles are sawn from western redcedar and northern white-cedar. For western redcedar, the shingle grades are No. 1, No. 2, and No. 3; for northern white-cedar, Extra, Clear, 2nd Clear, Clearwall, and Utility.

Shingles that contain only heartwood are more resistant to decay than are shingles that contain sapwood. Edge-grained shingles are less likely to warp and split than flat-grained shingles, thick-butted shingles less likely than thin-butted shingles, and narrow shingles less likely than wide shingles. The standard thickness values of thin-butted shingles are described as 4/2, 5/2-1/4, and 5/2 (four shingles to 51 mm (2 in.) of butt thickness, five shingles to 57 mm (2-1/4 in.) of butt thickness, and five shingles to 51 mm (2 in.) of butt thickness). Lengths may be 406, 457, or 610 mm (16, 18, or 24 in.). Random widths and specified ("dimension" shingle) widths are available in western redcedar, redwood, and cypress.

Shingles are usually packed four bundles to a square. A square of shingles will cover roughly 9 m^2 (100 ft^2) of roof area when the shingles are applied at standard weather exposures.

Shakes are hand split or hand split and resawn from western redcedar. Shakes are of a single grade and must be 100% clear. In the case of hand split and resawn material, shakes are graded from the split face. Hand-split shakes are graded from the best face. Shakes must be 100% heartwood. The standard thickness of shakes ranges from 9.5 to 32 mm (3/8 to 1-1/4 in.). Lengths are 457 and 610 mm (18 and 24 in.), with a special "Starter–Finish Course" length of 381 mm (15 in.).

Important Purchase Considerations

Some points to consider when ordering lumber or timbers are the following:

1. Quantity—Lineal measure, board measure, surface measure, number of pieces of definite size and length. Consider that the board measure depends on the thickness and width nomenclature used and that the interpretation of these must be clearly delineated. In other words, such features as nominal or actual dimensions and pattern size must be considered.

2. Size—Thickness in millimeters or inches—nominal or actual if surfaced on faces; width in millimeters or inches—nominal or actual if surfaced on edges; length in meters or feet—may be nominal average length, limiting length, or a single uniform length. Often a trade designation, "random" length, is used to denote a nonspecified assortment of lengths. Such an assortment should contain critical lengths as well as a range. The limits allowed in making the assortment random can be established at the time of purchase.

3. Grade—As indicated in grading rules of lumber manufacturing associations. In softwoods that are in compliance with the American Softwood Lumber Standard, each piece of lumber may be grade stamped with its official grade species identification, a name or number identifying

the producing mill, the dryness at the time of surfacing, and a symbol identifying the inspection agency supervising the grading inspection. The grade designation stamped on a piece indicates the quality at the time the piece was graded. Subsequent exposure to unfavorable storage conditions, improper drying, or careless handling may cause the material to fall below its original grade.

Working or recutting a graded product to a pattern may change or invalidate the original grade. The purchase specification should be clear in regard to regrading or acceptance of worked lumber. In softwood lumber, grades for dry lumber generally are determined after kiln drying and surfacing. However, this practice is not general for hardwood Factory lumber, where the grade is generally based on quality and size prior to kiln drying. To be certain the product grade is correct, refer to the grading rule by number and paragraph.

4. Species or species group of wood—Such as Douglas Fir, Southern Pine, Hem–Fir. Some species have been grouped for marketing convenience; others are sold under a variety of names. Be sure the species or species group is correctly and clearly described on the purchase specification.

5. Product—Such as flooring, siding, timbers, boards. Nomenclature varies by species, region, and grading association. To be certain the nomenclature is correct for the product, refer to the grading rule by number and paragraph.

6. Condition of seasoning—Such as air dry, kiln dry. Softwood lumber less than 114 mm (nominal 5 in.) in thickness dried to 19% moisture content or less is defined as dry by the American Softwood Lumber Standard. Kiln-dried lumber is lumber that has been seasoned in a chamber to a predetermined moisture content by applying heat. Green lumber is lumber less than 114 mm (nominal 5 in.) in thickness, which has a moisture content in excess of 19%. If the moisture requirement is critical, the level of moisture content and the method by which it will be achieved must be specified.

7. Surfacing and working—Rough (unplaned), surfaced (dressed, planed), or patterned stock. Specify condition. If surfaced, indicate code (S4S, S1S1E). If patterned, list pattern number with reference to appropriate grade rules.

8. Grading rules—Official grading agency name and name of official rules under which product is graded, product identification, paragraph and page number of rules, and date of rules or official rule edition may be specified by the buyer.

9. Manufacturer—Name of manufacturer or trade name of specific product or both. Most lumber products are sold without reference to a specific manufacturer. If proprietary names or quality features of a manufacturer are required, this must be stipulated clearly on the purchase agreement.

10. Reinspection—Procedures for resolution of purchase disputes. The American Softwood Lumber Standard provides for procedures to be followed in resolution of manufacturer–wholesaler–consumer conflicts over quality or quantity of ALS lumber grades. The dispute may be resolved by reinspecting the shipment. Time limits, liability, costs, and complaint procedures are outlined in the grade rules of both softwood and hardwood agencies under which the disputed shipment was graded and purchased.

Commonly Used Lumber Abbreviations

The following standard lumber abbreviations are commonly used in contracts and other documents for purchase and sale of lumber.

AAR	Association of American Railroads
AD	air dried
ADF	after deducting freight
AF	alpine fir
ALS	American Lumber Standard
AST	antistain treated; at ship tackle (western softwoods)
AV or avg	average
AW&L	all widths and lengths
B1S	see EB1S, CB1S, and E&CB1S
B2S	see EB2S, CB2S, and E&CB2S
B&B, B&BTR	B and Better
B&S	beams and stringers
BD	board
BD FT	board feet
BDL	bundle
BEV	bevel or beveled
BH	boxed heart
B/L, BL	bill of lading
BM	board measure
BSND	bright sapwood, no defect
BTR	better
CB	center beaded
CB1S	center bead on one side
CB2S	center bead on two sides
CC	cubical content
cft or cu. ft.	cubic foot or feet
CF	cost and freight
CIF	cost, insurance, and freight
CIFE	cost, insurance, freight, and exchange
CG2E	center groove on two edges
C/L	carload
CLG	ceiling
CLR	clear

CM	center matched
Com	Common
CONST	construction
CS	caulking seam
CSG	casing
CV	center V
CV1S	center V on one side
CV2S	center V on two sides
DB Clg	double-beaded ceiling (E&CB1S)
DB Part	double-beaded partition (E&CB2S)
DET	double end-trimmed
DF	Douglas-fir
DF–L	Douglas-fir plus larch
DIM	dimension
DKG	decking
D/S, DS, D/Sdg	drop siding
D1S, D2S	see S1S and S2S
D&M	dressed and matched
D&CM	dressed and center matched
D&SM	dressed and standard matched
D2S&CM	dressed two sides and center matched
D2S&SM	dressed two sides and standard matched
E	edge
EB1S	edge bead one side
EB2S, SB2S	edge bead on two sides
EE	eased edges
EG	edge (vertical or rift) grain
EM	end matched
EV1S, SV1S	edge V one side
EV2S, SV2S	edge V two sides
E&CB1S	edge and center bead one side
E&CB2S, DB2S, BC&2S	edge and center bead two sides
E&CV1S, DV1S,V&CV1S	edge and center V one side
E&CV2S, DV2S, V&CV2S	edge and center V two sides
ES	Engelmann spruce
F_b, F_t, F_c, F_v, F_{cx}	allowable stress (MPa (lb/in^2)) in bending; tension, compression and shear parallel to grain; and in compression perpendicular to grain, respectively
FA	facial area
Fac	factory
FAS	free alongside (vessel)
FAS	Firsts and Seconds
FAS1F	Firsts and Seconds one face
FBM, Ft. BM	feet board measure
FG	flat or slash grain
FJ	finger joint; end-jointed lumber using finger-joint configuration

FLG, Flg	flooring
FOB	free on board (named point)
FOHC	free of heart center
FOK	free of knots
FRT, Frt	freight
FT, ft	foot, feet
FT. SM	feet surface measure
G	girth
GM	grade marked
G/R	grooved roofing
HB, H.B.	hollow back
HEM	hemlock
H-F	mixed hemlock and fir (Hem–Fir)
Hrt	heart
H&M	hit and miss
H or M	hit or miss
IC	incense cedar
IN, in.	inch, inches
Ind	industrial
IWP	Idaho white pine
J&P	joists and planks
JTD	jointed
KD	kiln dried
KDAT	kiln-dried after treatment
L	western larch
LBR, Lbr	lumber
LCL	less than carload
LGR	longer
LGTH	length
Lft, Lf	lineal foot, feet
LIN, Lin	lineal
LL	longleaf
LNG, Lng	lining
LP	lodgepole pine
M	thousand
MBM, MBF, M.BM	thousand (feet) board measure
MC, M.C.	moisture content
MERCH, Merch	merchantable
MFMA	Maple Flooring Manufacturers Association
MG	medium grain or mixed grain
MH	mountain hemlock
MLDG, Mldg	moulding
Mft	thousand feet
M-S	mixed species
MSR	machine stress rated
N	nosed
NBM	net board measure
NOFMA	National Oak Flooring Manufacturers Association
No.	number

N1E or N2E	nosed one or two edges		S&E	side and edge (surfaced on)
Ord	order		S1E	surfaced one edge
PAD	partially air-dried		S2E	surfaced two edges
PAR, Par	paragraph		S1S	surfaced one side
PART, Part	partition		S2S	surfaced two sides
PAT, Pat	pattern		S4S	surfaced four sides
Pcs.	pieces		S1S&CM	surfaced one side and center matched
PE	plain end		S2S&CM	surfaced two sides and center matched
PET	precision end-trimmed		S4S&CS	surfaced four sides and caulking seam
PP	ponderosa pine		S1S1E	surfaced one side, one edge
P&T	posts and timbers		S1S2E	surfaced one side, two edges
P1S, P2S	see S1S and S2S		S2S1E	surfaced two sides, one edge
RDM	random		S2S&SL	surfaced two sides and shiplapped
REG, Reg	regular		S2S&SM	surfaced two sides and standard matched
Rfg.	roofing		TBR	timber
RGH, Rgh	rough		T&G	tongued and grooved
R/L, RL	random lengths		TSO	treating service only (nonconforming to standard)
R/W, RW	random widths		UTIL	utility
RES	resawn		VG	vertical (edge) grain
SB1S	single bead one side		V1S	see EV1S, CV1S, and E&CV1S
SDG, Sdg	siding		V2S	see EV2S, CV2S, and E&CV2S
S-DRY	surfaced dry; lumber ≤ 19% moisture content per ALS for softwood		WC	western cedar
			WCH	West Coast hemlock
SE	square edge		WCW	West Coast woods
SEL, Sel	Select or Select grade		WDR, wdr	wider
SE&S	square edge and sound		WF	white fir
SG	slash or flat grain		WHAD	worm holes (defect)
S-GRN	surfaced green; lumber unseasoned, >19% moisture content per ALS for softwood		WHND	worm holes (no defect)
			WT	weight
SGSSND	sapwood, gum spots and streaks, no defect		WTH	width
SIT. SPR	Sitka spruce		WRC	western redcedar
S/L, SL, S/Lap	shiplap		WW	white woods (Engelmann spruce, any true firs, any hemlocks, any pines)
SM	surface measure			
Specs	specifications			
SP	sugar pine			
SQ	square			
SQRS	squares			
SRB	stress-rated board			
STD, Std	standard			
Std. lgths.	standard lengths			
STD. M	standard matched			
SS	Sitka spruce			
SSE	sound square edge			
SSND	sap stain, no defect (stained)			
STK	Select tight knot			
STK	stock			
STPG	stepping			
STR, STRUCT	structural			
SYP	Southern Pine			

Reference

USDC. [Current edition]. American softwood lumber standard. Prod. Stand. PS–20–94. Washington, DC: U.S. Department of Commerce.

Chapter 6

Lumber Stress Grades and Design Properties

David E. Kretschmann and David W. Green

Contents

umber sawn from a log, regardless of species and size, is quite variable in mechanical properties. Pieces may differ in strength by several hundred percent. For simplicity and economy in use, pieces of lumber of similar mechanical properties are placed in categories called stress grades, which are characterized by (a) one or more sorting criteria, (b) a set of properties for engineering design, and (c) a unique grade name.

This chapter briefly discusses the U.S. Department of Commerce American Softwood Lumber Standard PS20 (1994) sorting criteria for two stress-grading methods, and the philosophy of how properties for engineering design are derived. The derived properties are then used in one of two design formats: (a) the load and resistance factor design (LRFD), which is based on a reference strength at the 5th percentile 5-min bending stress (AF&PA 1996), or (b) the allowable stress design (ASD), which is based on a design stress at the lower 5th percentile 10-year bending stress. The properties depend on the particular sorting criteria and on additional factors that are independent of the sorting criteria. Design properties are lower than the average properties of clear, straight-grained wood tabulated in Chapter 4.

From one to six design properties are associated with a stress grade: bending modulus of elasticity for an edgewise loading orientation and stress in tension and compression parallel to the grain, stress in compression perpendicular to the grain, stress in shear parallel to the grain, and extreme fiber stress in bending. As is true of the properties of any structural material, the allowable engineering design properties must be either inferred or measured nondestructively. In wood, the properties are inferred through visual grading criteria, nondestructive measurement such as flatwise bending stiffness or density, or a combination of these properties. These nondestructive tests provide both a sorting criterion and a means of calculating appropriate mechanical properties.

The philosophies contained in this chapter are used by a number of organizations to develop visual and machine stress grades. References are made to exact procedures and the resulting design stresses, but these are not presented in detail.

Responsibilities and Standards for Stress Grading

An orderly, voluntary, but circuitous system of responsibilities has evolved in the United States for the development, manufacture, and merchandising of most stress-graded lumber. The system is shown schematically in Figure 6–1. Stress-grading principles are developed from research findings and engineering concepts, often within committees and subcommittees of the American Society for Testing and Materials.

American Lumber Standard Committee

Voluntary product standards are developed under procedures published by the U.S. Department of Commerce. The Department of Commerce National Institute of Standards and Technology (NIST), working with rules-writing agencies, lumber inspection agencies, lumber producers, distributors and wholesalers, retailers, end users, and members of Federal agencies, work through the American Lumber Standard Committee (ALSC) to maintain a voluntary consensus softwood standard, called the American Softwood Lumber Standard (PS 20–94). The PS 20–94 Standard prescribes the ways in which stress-grading principles can be used to formulate grading rules designated as conforming to the

American Lumber Standard. Under the auspices of the ALSC is the National Grading Rule, which specifies grading characteristics for different grade specifications.

Organizations that write and publish grading rule books containing stress-grade descriptions are called rules-writing agencies. Grading rules that specify American Softwood Lumber Standard PS 20–94 must be certified by the ALSC Board of Review for conformance with this standard. Organizations that write grading rules, as well as independent agencies, can be accredited by the ALSC Board of Review to provide grading and grade-marking supervision and reinspection services to individual lumber manufacturers. Accredited rules-writing and independent agencies are listed in Table 6–1. The continued accreditation of these organizations is under the scrutiny of the ALSC Board of Review.

Most commercial softwood species manufactured in the United States are stress graded under American Lumber Standard practice. Distinctive grade marks for each species or species grouping are provided by accredited agencies. The principles of stress grading are also applied to several hardwood species under provisions of the American Softwood Lumber Standard. Lumber found in the marketplace may be stress graded under grading rules developed in accordance

Table 6–1. Sawn lumber grading agencies[a]

Rules-writing agencies
  Northeastern Lumber Manufacturers Association (NELMA)
  Northern Softwood Lumber Bureau (NSLB)
  Redwood Inspection Service (RIS)
  Southern Pine Inspection Bureau (SPIB)
  West Coast Lumber Inspection Bureau (WCLIB)
  Western Wood Products Association (WWPA)
  National Lumber Grades Authority (NLGA)

Independent agencies
  California Lumber Inspection Service
  Pacific Lumber Inspection Bureau, Inc.
  Renewable Resource Associates, Inc.
  Timber Products Inspection
  Alberta Forest Products Association
  Canadian Lumbermen's Association
  Canadian Mill Services Association
  Canadian Softwood Inspection Agency, Inc.
  Cariboo Lumber Manufacturers Association
  Central Forest Products Association
  Coniferous Lumber Inspection Bureau
  Council of Forest Industries of British Columbia
  Interior Lumber Manufacturers Association
  MacDonald Inspection
  Maritime Lumber Bureau
  Newfoundland Lumber Producers Association
  Northern Forest Products Association
  Ontario Lumber Manufacturers Association
  Pacific Lumber Inspection Bureau
  Quebec Lumber Manufacturers Association

[a]For updated information, contact American Lumber Standard Committee, P.O. Box 210, Germantown, MD 20874.

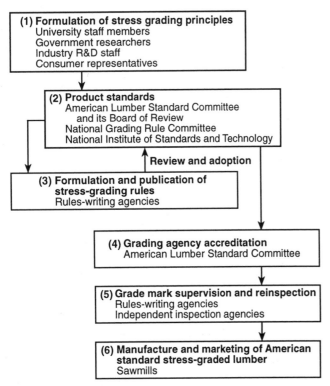

Figure 6–1. Voluntary system of responsibilities for stress grading under the American Softwood Lumber Standard.

with methods approved by the ALSC or by some other stress-grading rule, or it may not be stress graded. Only those stress grades that meet the requirements of the voluntary American Softwood Lumber Standard system are discussed in this chapter.

National Grading Rule

Stress grading under the auspices of the ALSC is applied to many sizes and several patterns of lumber that meet the American Softwood Lumber Standard provision. However, most stress-graded lumber is dimension lumber (standard 38 to 89 mm (nominal 2 to 4 in.) thick) and is governed by uniform specifications under the National Grading Rule. The National Grading Rule provides guidelines for writing grading rules for lumber in this thickness range and specifies grading characteristics for different grade specifications. American Softwood Lumber Standard dimension lumber in this thickness range is required to conform to the National Grading Rule, except for special products such as scaffold planks. Grade rules for other sizes, such as nominal 5-in. (standard 114-mm) or larger structural timbers may vary between rules-writing agencies or species.

The National Grading Rule establishes the lumber classifications and grade names for visually stress-graded dimension lumber (Table 6–2) and also provides for the grading of dimension lumber by a combination of machine and visual methods. Visual requirements for this type of lumber are developed by the respective rules-writing agencies for particular species grades.

Table 6–2. Visual grades described in National Grading Rule

Lumber classification[a]	Grade name	Bending strength ratio (%)
Light framing[b]	Construction	34
	Standard	19
	Utility	9
Structural light framing[b]	Select Structural	67
	1	55
	2	45
	3	26
Stud[c]	Stud	26
Structural joists and planks[d]	Select Structural	65
	1	55
	2	45
	3	26

[a]Contact rules-writing agencies for additional information.
[b]Standard 38 to 89 mm (nominal 2 to 4 in.) thick and wide. Widths narrower than 89 mm (4 in.) may have different strength ratio than shown.
[c]Standard 38 to 89 mm (nominal 2 to 4 in.) thick, ≥38 mm (≥4 in.) wide.
[d]Standard 38 to 89 mm (nominal 2 to 4 in.) thick, ≥140 mm (≥6 in.) wide.

Standards

Table 6–2 also shows associated minimum bending strength ratios to provide a comparative index of quality. The strength ratio is the hypothetical ratio of the strength of a piece of lumber with visible strength-reducing growth characteristics to its strength if those characteristics were absent. Formulas for calculating strength ratios are given in American Society of Testing and Materials (ASTM) standard D245. The corresponding visual description of the dimension lumber grades can be found in the grading rule books of the rules-writing agencies listed in Table 6–1. Design properties will vary by species. The design properties for each species and grade are published in the appropriate rule books and in the *National Design Specification for Wood Construction* (AF&PA 1997).

Grouping of Species

Most species are grouped together and the lumber from them treated as equivalent. Species are usually grouped when they have about the same mechanical properties, when the wood of two or more species is very similar in appearance, or for marketing convenience. For visual stress grades, ASTM D2555 contains procedures for calculating clear wood properties for groups of species to be used with ASTM D245. ASTM D1990 contains procedures for calculating design properties for groups of species tested as full-sized members. The properties assigned to a group by such procedures will often be different from those of any species that make up the group. The group will have a unique identity, with nomenclature approved by the Board of Review of the ALSC. The identities, properties, and characteristics of individual species of the group are found in the grade rules for any particular species or species grouping. In the case of machine stress grading, the inspection agency that supervises the grading certifies by testing that the design properties in that grade are appropriate for the species or species grouping and the grading process.

Foreign species

Currently, the importation of structural lumber is governed by two ALSC guidelines that describe the application of the American Lumber Standard and ASTM D1990 procedures to foreign species. The approval process is outlined in Table 6–3.

Visually Graded Structural Lumber

Visual Sorting Criteria

Visual grading is the original method for stress grading. It is based on the premise that mechanical properties of lumber differ from mechanical properties of clear wood because many growth characteristics affect properties and these characteristics can be seen and judged by eye. Growth characteristics are used to sort lumber into stress grades. The typical visual sorting criteria discussed here are knots, slope of grain,

Table 6–3. Approval process for acceptance of design values for foreign species

1	Rules-writing agency seeks approval to include species in grade-rule book.
2	Agency develops sampling and testing plan, following American Lumber Standard Committee (ALSC) foreign importation guidelines, which must then be approved by ALSC Board of Review.
3	Lumber is sampled and tested in accordance with approved sampling and testing plan.
4	Agency analyzes data by ALSC Board of Review and ASTM D1990 procedures and other appropriate criteria (if needed).
5	Agency submits proposed design values to ALSC Board of Review.
6	Submission is reviewed by ALSC Board of Review and USDA Forest Service, Forest Products Laboratory.
7	Submission is available for comment by other agencies and interested parties.
8	ALSC Board of Review approves (or disapproves) design values, with modification (if needed) based on all available information.
9	Agency publishes new design values for species.

checks and splits, shake, density, decay, heartwood and sapwood, pitch pockets, and wane.

Knots

Knots cause localized cross grain with steep slopes. A very damaging aspect of knots in sawn lumber is that the continuity of the grain around the knot is interrupted by the sawing process.

In general, knots have a greater effect on strength in tension than compression; in bending, the effect depends on whether a knot is in the tension or compression side of a beam (knots along the centerline have little or no effect). Intergrown (or live) knots resist (or transmit) some kinds of stress, but encased knots (unless very tight) or knotholes resist (or transmit) little or no stress. On the other hand, distortion of grain is greater around an intergrown knot than around an encased (or dead) knot of equivalent size. As a result, overall strength effects are roughly equalized, and often no distinction is made in stress grading between intergrown knots, dead knots, and knotholes.

The zone of distorted grain (cross grain) around a knot has less "parallel to piece" stiffness than does straight-grained wood; thus, localized areas of low stiffness are often associated with knots. However, such zones generally constitute only a minor part of the total volume of a piece of lumber. Because overall stiffness of a piece reflects the character of all parts, stiffness is not greatly influenced by knots.

The presence of a knot has a greater effect on most strength properties than on stiffness. The effect on strength depends approximately on the proportion of the cross section of the piece of lumber occupied by the knot, knot location, and distribution of stress in the piece. Limits on knot sizes are therefore made in relation to the width of the face and location on the face in which the knot appears. Compression members are stressed about equally throughout, and no limitation related to location of knots is imposed. In tension, knots along the edge of a member cause an eccentricity that induces bending stresses, and they should therefore be more

restricted than knots away from the edge. In simply supported structural members subjected to bending, stresses are greater in the middle of the length and at the top and bottom edges than at midheight. These facts are recognized in some grades by differing limitations on the sizes of knots in different locations.

Knots in glued-laminated structural members are not continuous as in sawn structural lumber, and different methods are used for evaluating their effect on strength (Ch. 11).

Slope of Grain

Slope of grain (cross grain) reduces the mechanical properties of lumber because the fibers are not parallel to the edges. Severely cross-grained pieces are also undesirable because they tend to warp with changes in moisture content. Stresses caused by shrinkage during drying are greater in structural lumber than in small, clear straight-grained specimens and are increased in zones of sloping or distorted grain. To provide a margin of safety, the reduction in design properties resulting from cross grain in visually graded structural lumber is considerably greater than that observed in small, clear specimens that contain similar cross grain.

Checks and Splits

Checks are separations of the wood that normally occur across or through the annual rings, usually as a result of seasoning. Splits are a separation of the wood through the piece to the opposite surface or to an adjoining surface caused by tearing apart of the wood cells. As opposed to shakes, checks and splits are rated by only the area of actual opening. An end-split is considered equal to an end-check that extends through the full thickness of the piece. The effects of checks and splits on strength and the principles of their limitation are the same as those for shake.

Shake

Shake is a separation or a weakness of fiber bond, between or through the annual rings, that is presumed to extend lengthwise without limit. Because shake reduces resistance to shear in members subjected to bending, grading rules therefore restrict shake most closely in those parts of a bending member where shear stresses are highest. In members with limited cross grain, which are subjected only to tension or compression, shake does not affect strength greatly. Shake may be limited in a grade because of appearance and because it permits entrance of moisture, which results in decay.

Density

Strength is related to the mass per unit volume (density) of clear wood. Properties assigned to lumber are sometimes modified by using the rate of growth and percentage of latewood as measures of density. Typically, selection for density requires that the rings per unit length and the percentage of latewood be within a specified range. It is possible to eliminate some very low-strength pieces from a grade by excluding those that are exceptionally low in density.

Decay

Decay in most forms should be prohibited or severely restricted in stress grades because the extent of decay is difficult to determine and its effect on strength is often greater than visual observation would indicate. Decay of the pocket type (for example, *Fomes pini*) can be permitted to some extent in stress grades, as can decay that occurs in knots but does not extend into the surrounding wood.

Heartwood and Sapwood

Heartwood does not need to be taken into account in stress grading because heartwood and sapwood have been assumed to have equal mechanical properties. However, heartwood is sometimes specified in a visual grade because the heartwood of some species is more resistant to decay than is the sapwood; heartwood may be required if untreated wood will be exposed to a decay hazard. On the other hand, sapwood takes preservative treatment more readily than heartwood and it is preferable for lumber that will be treated with preservatives.

Pitch Pockets

Pitch pockets ordinarily have so little effect on structural lumber that they can be disregarded in stress grading if they are small and limited in number. The presence of a large number of pitch pockets, however, may indicate shake or weakness of bond between annual rings.

Wane

Wane refers to bark or lack of wood on the edge or corner of a piece of lumber, regardless of cause (except eased edges). Requirements of appearance, fabrication, or ample bearing or nailing surfaces generally impose stricter limitations on wane than does strength. Wane is therefore limited in structural lumber on those bases.

Procedures for Deriving Design Properties

The mechanical properties of visually graded lumber may be established by (a) tests of a representative sample of full-size members (ASTM D1990 in-grade testing procedure) or (b) appropriate modification of test results conducted on small clear specimens (ASTM D245 procedure for small clear wood). Design properties for the major commercial softwood dimension lumber species given in current design specification and codes in the United States have been derived from full-size member test results. However, design properties for most hardwood dimension and structural timbers (larger than standard 89-mm- (nominal 4-in.-, actual 3-1/2-in.-) thick "timbers") of all species are still derived using results of tests on small clear samples.

Procedure for Small Clear Wood

The derivation of mechanical properties of visually graded lumber was historically based on clear wood properties with appropriate modifications for the lumber characteristics allowed by visual sorting criteria. Sorting criteria that influence mechanical properties are handled with "strength ratios" for the strength properties and with "quality factors" for the modulus of elasticity.

From piece to piece, there is variation in both the clear wood properties and the occurrence of growth characteristics. The influence of this variability on lumber properties is handled differently for strength properties than for modulus of elasticity.

Strength Properties—Each strength property of a piece of lumber is derived from the product of the clear wood strength for the species and the limiting strength ratio. The strength ratio is the hypothetical ratio of the strength of a piece of lumber with visible strength-reducing growth characteristics to its strength if those characteristics were absent. The true strength ratio of a piece of lumber is never known and must be estimated. Therefore, the strength ratio assigned to a growth characteristic serves as a predictor of lumber strength. Strength ratio is expressed as a percentage, ranging from 0 to 100.

Estimated strength ratios for cross grain and density have been obtained empirically; strength ratios for other growth characteristics have been derived theoretically. For example, to account for the weakening effect of knots, the assumption is made that the knot is effectively a hole through the piece, reducing the cross section, as shown in Figure 6–2. For a beam containing an edge knot, the bending strength ratio can be idealized as the ratio of the bending moment that can be resisted by a beam with a reduced cross section to that of a beam with a full cross section:

$$SR = 1 - \left(k/h\right)^2$$

where SR is strength ratio, k knot size, and h width of face containing the knot. This is the basic expression for the effect of a knot at the edge of the vertical face of a beam that is deflected vertically. Figure 6–3 shows how strength ratio changes with knot size according to the formula.

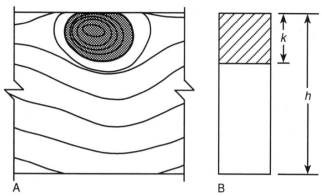

Figure 6–2. Effect of edge knot: A, edge knot in lumber and B, assumed loss of cross section (cross-hatched area).

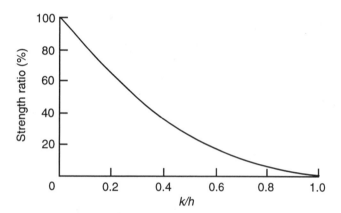

Figure 6–3. Relation between bending strength ratio and size of edge knot expressed as fraction of face width. *k* is knot size; *h*, width of face containing the knot.

Strength ratios for all knots, shakes, checks, and splits are derived using similar concepts. Strength ratio formulas are given in ASTM D245. The same reference contains guidelines for measuring various growth characteristics.

An individual piece of lumber will often have several characteristics that can affect any particular strength property. Only the characteristic that gives the lowest strength ratio is used to derive the estimated strength of the piece. In theory, a visual stress grade contains lumber ranging from pieces with the minimum strength ratio permitted in the grade up to pieces with the strength ratio just below the next higher grade. In practice, there are often pieces in a grade with strength ratios of a higher grade. This is a result of grade reduction for appearance factors such as wane that do not affect strength.

The range of strength ratios in a grade and the natural variation in clear wood strength give rise to variation in strength between pieces in the grade. To account for this variation and to ensure safety in design, it is intended that the actual strength of at least 95% of the pieces in a grade exceed the design properties (before reduction for duration of load and

safety) assigned to that grade. In visual grading, according to ASTM D245, this is handled by using a near-minimum clear wood strength as a base value and multiplying it by the minimum strength ratio permitted in the grade to obtain the grade strength property. The near-minimum value is called the 5% exclusion limit. ASTM D2555 provides clear wood strength data and gives a method for estimating the 5% exclusion limit.

For example, suppose a 5% exclusion limit for the clear wood bending strength of a species in the green condition is 48 MPa (7,000 lb/in^2). Suppose also that among the characteristics allowed in a grade of lumber, one characteristic (a knot, for example) provides the lowest strength ratio in bending—assumed in this example as 40%. Using the numbers, the bending strength for the grade is estimated by multiplying the strength ratio (0.40) by 48 MPa (7,000 lb/in^2), equaling 19 MPa (2,800 lb/in^2) (Fig. 6–4). The bending strength in the green condition of 95% of the pieces in this species in a grade that has a strength ratio of 40% is expected to be ≥19 MPa (≥2,800 lb/in^2). Similar procedures are followed for other strength properties, using the appropriate clear wood property value and strength ratio. Additional multiplying factors are then applied to produce properties for design, as summarized later in this chapter.

Modulus of Elasticity—Modulus of elasticity E is a measure of the ability of a beam to resist deflection or of a column to resist buckling. The assigned E is an estimate of the average modulus, adjusted for shear deflection, of the lumber grade when tested in static bending. The average modulus of elasticity for clear wood of the species, as recorded in ASTM D2555, is used as a base. The clear wood average is multiplied by empirically derived "quality factors" to represent the reduction in modulus of elasticity that occurs by lumber grade for pieces tested in an edgewise orientation. This procedure is outlined in ASTM D245.

For example, assume a clear wood average modulus of elasticity of 12.4 GPa (1.8 × 10^6 lb/in^2) for the example shown earlier. The limiting bending strength ratio was 40%. ASTM D245 assigns a quality multiplying factor of 0.80 for lumber with this bending strength ratio. The modulus of elasticity for that grade would be the product of the clear wood modulus and the quality factor; that is, 12.4 × 0.8 = 9.9 GPa (1.8 × 0.8 = 1.44 × 10^6 lb/in^2).

Actual modulus of elasticity of individual pieces of a grade varies from the average assumed for design (Fig. 6–5). Small individual lots of lumber can be expected to deviate from the distribution shown by this histogram. The additional multiplying factors used to derive final design values of modulus of elasticity are discussed later in this chapter.

In-Grade Procedure

To establish the mechanical properties of specified grades of lumber from tests of full-size specimens, a representative sample of the lumber population is obtained following procedures in ASTM D2915 and D1990. The specimens are tested using appropriate procedures given in ASTM D198

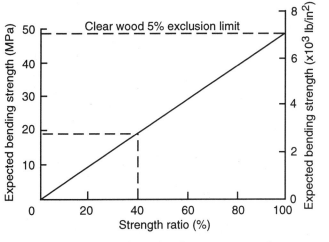

Figure 6–4. Example of relation between strength and strength ratio.

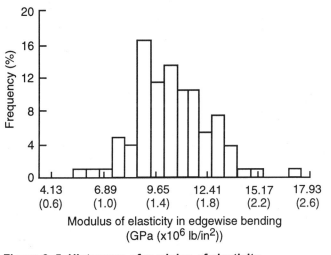

Figure 6–5. Histogram of modulus of elasticity observed in a single visual grade, from pieces selected over a broad geographical range.

or D4761. Because the range of quality with any one specific grade may be large, it is necessary to assess the grade quality index (GQI) of the sampled material in relation to the assumed GQI. In the North American In-Grade Program, GQI was the strength ratio calculated according to formulas in ASTM D245. The sample GQI and the assumed GQI are compared to see if adjustment to the test data is necessary. An average value for the edgewise modulus of elasticity or a near-minimum estimate of strength properties is obtained using ASTM D1990 procedures. The grade GQI is also used as a scaling perimeter that allows for modeling of strength and modulus of elasticity with respect to grade. These properties are further modified for design use by consideration of service moisture content, duration of load, and safety.

Machine-Graded Structural Lumber

Machine-graded lumber is lumber evaluated by a machine using a nondestructive test followed by visual grading to evaluate certain characteristics that the machine cannot or may not properly evaluate. Machine-stress-rated (MSR), machine-evaluated-lumber (MEL), and *E*-rated lumber are three types of machine-graded lumber. Machine-graded lumber allows for better sorting of material for specific applications in engineered structures. The basic components of a machine-grading system are as follows:

1. sorting and prediction of strength through machine-measured nondestructive determination of properties coupled with visual assessment of growth characteristics,

2. assignment of design properties based on strength prediction, and

3. quality control to ensure that assigned properties are being obtained. The quality control procedures ensure

   a. proper operation of the machine used to make the nondestructive measurements,

   b. appropriateness of the predictive parameter–bending strength relationship, and

   c. appropriateness of properties assigned for tension and compression.

The MSR and MEL systems differ in grade names, quality control, and coefficient of variation (COV) for *E* values. Grade names for MSR lumber are a combination of the design bending stress and average modulus of elasticity, whereas grade names for MEL lumber start with an M designation. For quality control, MSR requires pieces to be tested daily for at least one strength property and bending modulus of elasticity in an edgewise orientation, whereas MEL requires daily tension quality control and edgewise bending strength and stiffness testing. Finally, MSR grades are assigned a COV = 11% on *E*, whereas MEL grades are assigned a COV ≤ 15% on *E*. Grade names for a wide range of machine-graded lumber commonly available across North America are given in Table 6–4. Not all grades are available in all sizes or species.

Machine Sorting Criteria

The most common method of sorting machine-graded lumber is modulus of elasticity *E*. When used as a sorting criterion for mechanical properties of lumber, *E* can be measured in a variety of ways. Usually, the apparent *E*, or deflection related to stiffness, is actually measured. Because lumber is heterogeneous, the apparent *E* depends on span, orientation (edge- or flatwise in bending), load speed of test (static or dynamic), and method of loading (tension, bending, concentrated, or uniform). Any of the apparent *E* values can be used, as long as the grading machine is properly calibrated, to

Table 6–4. Common grades for machine-graded lumber[a]

Grade name	F_b (MPa (lb/in^2))		E (GPa ($\times 10^6$ lb/in^2))		F_t (MPa (lb/in^2))		$F_{c\parallel}$ (MPa (lb/in^2))	
MSR								
1350f–1.3E	9.3	(1,350)	9.0	(1.3)	5.2	(750)	11.0	(1,600)
1450f–1.3E	10.0	(1,450)	9.0	(1.3)	5.5	(800)	11.2	(1,625)
1650f–1.5E	11.4	(1,650)	10.3	(1.5)	7.0	(1,020)	11.7	(1,700)
1800f–1.6E	12.4	(1,800)	11.0	(1.6)	8.1	(1,175)	12.1	(1,750)
1950f–1.7E	13.4	(1,950)	11.7	(1.7)	9.5	(1,375)	12.4	(1,800)
2100f–1.8E	14.5	(2,100)	12.4	(1.8)	10.9	(1,575)	12.9	(1,875)
2250f–1.9E	15.5	(2,250)	13.1	(1.9)	12.1	(1,750)	13.3	(1,925)
2400f–2.0E	16.5	(2,400)	13.8	(2.0)	13.3	(1,925)	13.6	(1,975)
2550f–2.1E	17.6	(2,550)	14.5	(2.1)	14.1	(2,050)	14.0	(2,025)
2700F–2.2E	18.6	(2,700)	15.2	(2.2)	14.8	(2,150)	14.4	(2,100)
2850f–2.3E	19.7	(2,850)	15.9	(2.3)	15.9	(2,300)	14.8	(2,150)
MEL								
M–10	9.7	(1,400)	8.3	(1.2)	5.5	(800)	11.0	(1,600)
M–11	10.7	(1,550)	10.3	(1.5)	5.9	(850)	11.5	(1,675)
M–14	12.4	(1,800)	11.7	(1.7)	6.9	(1,000)	12.1	(1,750)
M–19	13.8	(2,000)	11.0	(1.6)	9.0	(1,300)	12.6	(1,825)
M–21	15.9	(2,300)	13.1	(1.9)	9.7	(1,400)	13.4	(1,950)
M–23	16.5	(2,400)	12.4	(1.8)	13.1	(1,900)	13.6	(1,975)
M–24	18.6	(2,700)	13.1	(1.9)	12.4	(1,800)	14.5	(2,100)

[a]Forest Products Society 1997. Other grades are available and permitted.
F_b is allowable 10-year load duration bending stress parallel to grain.
E is modulus of elasticity.
F_t is allowable 10-year load duration tensile stress parallel to grain.
$F_{c\parallel}$ is allowable 10-year load duration compressive stress parallel to grain.

assign the graded piece to a "not to exceed" grade category. Most grading machines in the United States are designed to detect the lowest flatwise bending E that occurs in any approximately 1.2-m (4-ft) span and the average flatwise E for the entire length of the piece.

Another method of sorting machine-graded lumber is using density measurements to estimate knot sizes and frequency. X-ray sources in conjunction with a series of detectors are used to determine density information. Density information is then used to assign the graded piece to a "not to exceed" grade category.

In the United States and Canada, MSR and MEL lumber are also subjected to a visual override because the size of edge knots in combination with E is a better predictor of strength than is E alone. Maximum edge knots are limited to a specified proportion of the cross section, depending on grade level. Other visual restrictions, which are primarily appearance rather than strength criteria, are placed on checks, shake, skips (portions of board "skipped" by the planer), splits, wane, and warp.

Procedures for Deriving Design Properties

Allowable Stress for Bending

A stress grade derived for machine-graded lumber relates design strength to a nondestructive parameter. For this example, it will be considered to be E. Because E is an imperfect predictor of strength, lumber sorted solely by average E falls into one of four categories, one of which is sorted correctly and three incorrectly (Fig. 6–6).

Consider, for example, the most simple case (sometimes referred to as "go" or "no go") where lumber is sorted into two groups: one with sufficient strength and stiffness for a specific application, the other without. In Figure 6–6a, a regression line relating E and strength is used as the prediction model. The "accept–reject" groups identified by the regression sort can be classified into four categories:

- Category 1—Material that has been accepted correctly, that is, pieces have sufficient strength and stiffness as defined

- Category 2—Material that has been accepted incorrectly, that is, pieces do not have sufficient strength

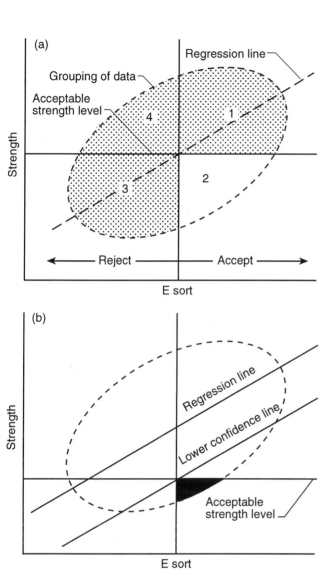

(a)

Strength

Regression line

Grouping of data

Acceptable strength level

4   1

3   2

← Reject ——— Accept →

E sort

(b)

Strength

Regression line

Lower confidence line

Acceptable strength level

E sort

Figure 6–6. Schematic _E_ sort: (a) using a regression line as the predictor showing four categories: 1—accepted correctly; 2—accepted incorrectly; 3—rejected correctly; and 4—rejected correctly; (b) using a lower confidence line as the predictor and showing the relatively low proportion of material in the accepted incorrectly category (lower right).

- Category 3—Material that has been rejected correctly because it does not have sufficient strength

- Category 4—Material that has been rejected correctly because it does not have sufficient stiffness

Thus, the sort shown in Figure 6–6a has worked correctly for categories 1, 3, and 4 but incorrectly for category 2. Pieces in category 2 present a problem. These pieces are accepted as having sufficient strength but in reality they do not, and they are mixed with the accepted pieces of category 1. The number of problem pieces that fall in category 2 depends on the variability in the prediction model.

To minimize the material that falls into category 2, adjustments are made to the property assignment claims made about the sorted material. An appropriate model is one that minimizes the material in category 2 or at least reduces it to a lower risk level. Additional grading criteria (edge-knot limitations, for example) are also added to improve the efficiency of the sorting system relative to the resource and the claimed properties.

Commonly, a lower confidence line is used as the prediction model (Fig. 6–6b). The number of pieces that fall into category 2 is now low compared with the regression line model. Furthermore, the probability of a piece (and thus the number of pieces) falling into category 2 is controlled by the confidence line selected.

In actual MSR systems, the lumber is sorted (graded) into _E_ classes. In the United States and Canada, the number of grades has increased as specific market needs have developed for MSR lumber. Today, individual grading agencies list as many as 13 _E_ classifications and more than 20 different grades. The grades are designated by the recommended extreme fiber stress in bending F_b and edgewise modulus of elasticity _E_. For example, "2100F–1.8E" designates an MSR grade with a design stress F_b = 14 MPa (2,100 lb/in^2) and _E_ = 12.4 GPa (1.8 × 10^6 lb/in^2).

In theory, any _F–E_ combination can be marketed that can be supported by test data. In practice, a mill will usually produce only a few of the possible existing _F–E_ classifications depending on the potential of the timber being harvested, mill production capabilities, and product or market demand. When a mill has determined the grades it would like to produce (based on their lumber resource and marketing issues), grade boundary machine settings are used to separate the lumber into _F–E_ classifications. A qualification sample of lumber is tested by a grading agency for strength and stiffness, to verify that the proper machine settings are being used. After initial qualification, additional quality control tests are performed during production.

Figure 6–7 illustrates how F_b–_E_ classifications have been developed historically for species groups. Data for a particular species group are collected, the relationship of _E_ and MOR is evaluated, and a lower confidence line is established for the species, as illustrated in Figure 6–6b. Using the lower confidence line of this relationship, an MOR value corresponding to the "minimum _E_" assigned to the grade is determined. The "minimum _E_" assigned to the grade represents the 5th percentile of the _E_ distribution. The 5th percentile value is expected to be exceeded by 95% of the pieces in a grade or class. In this example, for a grade with an assigned _E_ of 13.8 GPa (2.0 × 10^6 lb/in^2), the "minimum _E_" is 11.3 GPa (1.64 × 10^6 lb/in^2). The corresponding MOR value from the lower confidence line prediction model, approximately a 5th percentile MOR value, is 34.8 MPa (5.04 × 10^3 lb/in^2). This value is then adjusted by a factor (2.1) for assumed 10-year duration of load and safety to obtain F_b. This factor applied to an estimated 5th percentile

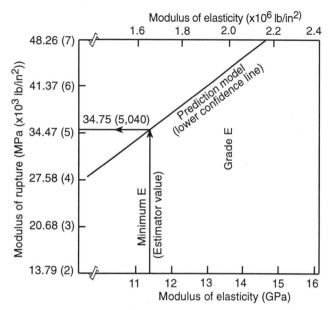

Figure 6–7. Typical assignment of F_b–E values for MSR lumber in United States (solid lines are minimum E for the F_b–E classification and bending strengths predicted by minimum E values).

MOR value of 34.8 MPa (5.04×10^3 lb/in²) yields an F_b of 16.5 MPa (2.40×10^3 lb/in²) for the 2.0E grade; in other words, a 2400f –2.0E MSR grade.

Design Stresses for Other Properties

Properties in tension and compression are commonly developed from relationships with bending rather than estimated directly by the nondestructive parameter E. In Canada and the United States, the relationships between the 5th percentile 10-year bending stress and those in tension and compression are based upon limited lumber testing for the three properties but supported by years of successful experience in construction with visual stress grades of lumber. For tension, it is assumed that the ratio of design bending stress F_b to design tensile stress F_c is between 0.5 and 0.8, depending on the grade, whereas the relationship between F_b and fiber stress in design compressive stress F_c is assumed to be

$$F_c = [0.338 \, (2.1F_b) + 2060.7]/1.9$$

Strength in shear parallel to the grain and in compression perpendicular to the grain is poorly related to modulus of elasticity. Therefore, in machine stress grading these properties are assumed to be grade-independent and are assigned the same values as those for visual lumber grades, except when predicted from specific gravity on a mill-by-mill basis. It is permissible to assign higher allowable stress for shear parallel to grain and compression perpendicular to grain to specific grades based on additional specific gravity research.

Quality Control

Quality control procedures are necessary to ensure that stresses assigned by a machine-grading system reflect the actual properties of the lumber graded. These procedures must check for correct machine operation. Verification of the relationships between bending and other properties may also be required by the rules-writing agency, particularly for fiber stress in tension F_t.

Daily or even more frequent calibration of machine operation may be necessary. Depending upon machine principle, calibration may involve operating the machine on a calibration bar of known stiffness, comparing grading machine E values to those obtained on the same pieces of lumber by calibrated laboratory test equipment, determining if machine-predicted density matches a calibration sample density, or in some instances, using two or more procedures. Machine operation should be certified for all sizes of lumber being produced. Machine settings may need to be adjusted to produce the same grade material from different widths.

Quality control procedures of the MSR prediction model (E–bending strength relationship) have been adopted in Canada and the United States. Daily, or more frequently, lumber production is representatively sampled and proof-loaded, usually in bending, with supplementary testing in tension. The pieces are proof-loaded to at least twice the design stress (F_b or F_t) for the assigned F_b –E classification. In bending, the pieces are loaded on a random edge with the maximum-edge defect within the maximum moment area (middle one-third span in third-point loading) or as near to that point as possible. In tension, the pieces are tested with a 2.4-m (8-ft) gauge length.

If the number of pieces in the sample failing the proof-test load indicates a high probability that the population from which the pieces came does not meet the minimum grade criteria, a second sampling and proof test are conducted immediately. If the second sample confirms the results of the first sample, the MSR grading system is declared "out of control" and the operation is shut down to isolate and correct the problem. The lumber that was incorrectly labeled is then correctly labeled.

Cumulative machine calibration records are useful for detecting trends or gradual change in machine operation that might coincide with use and wear of machine parts. The proof-test results are also accumulated. Standard statistical quality control procedures (such as control charts) are used to monitor the production process so that it can be modified as needed in response to change in the timber resource, and to make the output fit the assumed model.

Too many failures in one, or even consecutive, samples do not necessarily indicate that the system is out of control. If the prediction line is based on 95% confidence, it can be expected by chance alone that 1 sample in 20 will not meet the proof-load requirements. One or more out-of-control samples may also represent a temporary aberration in material properties (E–strength relationship). In any event, this situation would call for inspection of the cumulative quality control records for trends to determine if machine adjustment might be needed. A "clean" record (a period when the system does not go out of control) rectifies the evaluation of a system thought to be out of control.

Adjustment of Properties for Design Use

The mechanical properties associated with lumber quality are adjusted to give design unit stresses and a modulus of elasticity suitable for engineering uses. First, a lower confidence level is determined for the material, and this value is then adjusted for shrinkage, size, duration of load, and in ASD, an additional factor of safety. These adjustment factors are discussed in the following text (specific adjustments are given in ASTM designations D245 and D1990).

Shrinkage

As described in Chapter 3, lumber shrinks and swells with changes in moisture content. The amount of dimensional change depends on a number of factors, such as species and ring angle. The American Softwood Lumber Standard, PS 20, lists specific shrinkage factors from green to 15% moisture content that were used historically to set green lumber dimensions for most species (2.35% for thickness and 2.80% for width). The standard does not provide a means of adjusting lumber dimensions to any other moisture content. The standard also does not provide specific shrinkage factors for species such as redwood and the cedars, which shrink less than most species. Using the PS 20 recommendations and an assumed green moisture content M_g, we derive equations that can be used with most species to calculate the shrinkage of lumber as a function of percentage of moisture content M. The equation is applicable to lumber of all annual ring orientations. For dimension lumber, the dimensions at different moisture contents can be estimated with the following equation:

$$d_2 = d_1 \frac{1-(a-bM_2)/100}{1-(a-bM_1)/100}$$

where d_1 is dimension (mm, in.) at moisture content M_1, d_2 dimension (mm, in.) at moisture content M_2, M_1 moisture content (%) at d_1, M_2 moisture content (%) at d_2, and a and b are variables from Table 6–5.

Size Factor

In general, a size effect causes small members to have a greater unit strength than that of large members. There are two procedures for calculating size-adjustment factors, small clear and In-grade.

Table 6–5. Coefficients for equations to determine dimensional changes with moisture content change in dimension lumber

Species	Width		Thickness		
	a	b	a	b	M_g[a]
Redwood, western red-cedar, and northern white cedar	3.454	0.157	2.816	0.128	22
Other species	6.031	0.215	5.062	0.181	28

[a]M_g is assumed green moisture content.

Table 6–6. Exponents for adjustment of dimension lumber mechanical properties with change in size[a]

Exponent	MOR	UTS	UCS
w	0.29	0.29	0.13
l	0.14	0.14	0

[a]MOR is modulus of rupture; UTS, ultimate tensile stress; and UCS, ultimate compressive stress.

Small Clear Procedure

ASTM D245 provides only a formula for adjusting bending strength. The bending strength for lumber is adjusted to a new depth F_n other than 2 in. (51 mm) using the formula

$$F_n = \left(\frac{d_o}{d_n}\right)^{\frac{1}{9}} F_o$$

where d_o is original depth (51 mm, 2 in.), d_n new depth, and F_o original bending strength.

This formula is based on an assumed center load and a span-to-depth ratio of 14. A depth effect formula for two equal concentrated loads applied symmetrical to the midspan points is given in Chapter 8.

In–Grade Test Procedures

ASTM D1990 provides a formula for adjusting bending, tension, and compression parallel to grain. No size adjustments are made to modulus of elasticity or for thickness effects in bending, tension, and compression. The size adjustments to dimension lumber are based on volume using the formula

$$P_1 = P_2 \left(\frac{W_1}{W_2}\right)^w \left(\frac{L_1}{L_2}\right)^l$$

where P_1 is property value (MPa, lb/in^2) at volume 1, P_2 property value (MPa, lb/in^2) at volume 2, W_1 width (mm, in.) at P_1, W_2 width (mm, in.) at P_2, L_1 length (mm, in.) at P_1, and L_2 length (mm, in.) at P_2. Exponents are defined in Table 6–6.

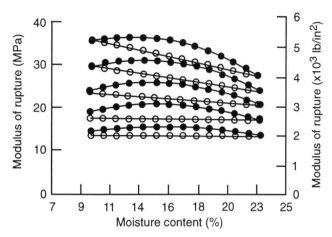

Figure 6–8. Modulus of rupture as a function of moisture content for dimension lumber. Open dots represent the ASTM D1990 model, and solid dots represent the more precise quadratic surface model on which the ASTM D1990 model was based.

Moisture Adjustments

For lumber ≤102 mm (≤4 in.) thick that has been dried, strength properties have been shown to be related quadratically to moisture content. Two relationships for modulus of rupture at any moisture content are shown in Figure 6–8. Both models start with the modulus of elasticity of green lumber. The curves with solid dots represent a precise quadratic model fit to experimental results. In typical practice, adjustments are made to correspond to average moisture contents of 15% and 12% with expected maximum moisture contents of 19% and 15%, respectively, using simplified expressions represented by the open dot curves. Below about 8% moisture content, some properties may decrease with decreasing moisture content values, and care should be exercised in these situations. Equations applicable to adjusting properties to other moisture levels between green and 10% moisture content are as follows:

For MOR, ultimate tensile stress (UTS), and ultimate compressive stress (UCS), the following ASTM D1990 equations apply:

$$\text{For MOR} \leq 16.7 \text{ MPa } (2{,}415 \text{ lb/in}^2)$$
$$\text{UTS} \leq 21.7 \text{ MPa } (3{,}150 \text{ lb/in}^2)$$
$$\text{UCS} \leq 9.7 \text{ MPa } (1{,}400 \text{ lb/in}^2)$$
$$P_1 = P_2$$

Thus, there is no adjustment for stresses below these levels.

$$\text{For MOR} > 16.6 \text{ MPa } (2{,}415 \text{ lb/in}^2)$$
$$\text{UTS} > 21.7 \text{ MPa } (3{,}150 \text{ lb/in}^2)$$
$$\text{UCS} > 9.7 \text{ MPa } (1{,}400 \text{ lb/in}^2)$$

Table 6–7. Coefficients for moisture adjustment of dimension lumber mechanical properties with change in moisture content[a]

Coefficients	Property (MPa (lb/in²))		
	MOR	UTS	UCS
B_1	16.6 (2,415)	21.7 (3,150)	9.6 (1,400)
B_2	0.276 (40)	0.552 (80)	0.234 (34)

[a]MOR is modulus of rupture; UTS, ultimate tensile stress; and UCS, ultimate compressive stress.

$$P_2 = P_1 + \left(\frac{P_1 - B_1}{B_2 - M_1}\right)(M_1 - M_2)$$

where M_1 is moisture content 1 (%), M_2 is moisture content 2 (%), and B_1, B_2 are constants from Table 6–7.

For E, the following equation applies:

$$E_1 = E_2 \left(\frac{1.857 - (0.0237 M_2)}{1.857 - (0.0237 M_1)}\right)$$

where E_1 is property (MPa, lb/in²) at moisture content 1 and E_2 is property (MPa, lb/in²) at moisture content 2.

For lumber thicker than 102 mm (4 in.), often no adjustment for moisture content is made because properties are assigned on the basis of wood in the green condition. This lumber is usually put in place without drying, and it is assumed that drying degrade offsets the increase in strength normally associated with loss in moisture.

Duration of Load

Design may be based on either design stresses and a duration of load factor or on ultimate limit state design stresses and a time effects factor. Both the duration of load and time effects factor describe the same phenomenon. In allowable stress design, design stresses are based on an assumed 10-year loading period (called normal loading). If duration of loading, either continuously or cumulatively, is expected to exceed 10 years, design stresses are reduced 10%. If the expected duration of loading is for shorter periods, published design stresses can be increased using Figure 6–9. Ultimate limit-state design stresses are based on a 5-min loading period. If the duration of loading is expected to exceed 5 min, limit-state design stresses are reduced by applying the time effects factor. Intermittent loading causes cumulative effects on strength and should be treated as continuous load of equivalent duration. The effects of cyclic loads of short duration must also be considered in design (see discussion of fatigue in Ch. 4). These duration of load modifications are not applicable to modulus of elasticity.

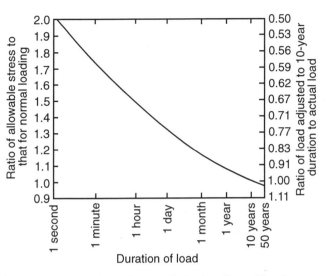

Figure 6–9. Relation of strength to duration of load.

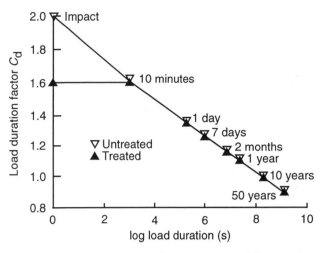

Figure 6–10. Load duration factor for material treated with waterborne preservative.

In many design circumstances there are several loads on the structure, some acting simultaneously and each with a different duration. When loads of different time duration are applied, the load duration factor corresponding to the shortest time duration is used. Each increment of time during which the total load is constant should be treated separately, and the most severe condition governs the design. Either the design stress or the total design load (but not both) can be adjusted using Figure 6–9.

For example, suppose a structure is expected to support a load of 4.8 kPa (100 lb/ft²) on and off for a cumulative duration of 1 year. Also, it is expected to support its own dead load of 0.96 kPa (20 lb/ft²) for the anticipated 50-year life of the structure. The adjustments to be made to arrive at an equivalent 10-year design load are listed in Table 6–8.

The more severe design load is 5.36 kPa (112 lb/ft²), and this load and the design stress for lumber would be used to select members of suitable size. In this case, it was convenient to adjust the loads on the structure, although the same result can be obtained by adjusting the design stress.

Treatment Effects

Treatments have been shown to affect the final strength of wood (Ch. 4 for detailed discussion). There is a 5% reduction in E and a 15% reduction in strength properties of incised and treated dimension lumber for both dry- and wet-use conditions in the United States. In Canada, a 10% reduction in E and a 30% reduction in all strength properties from incising is applied to dry-use conditions whereas 5% and 15% reductions are used for wet-use conditions. The wet-use factors are applied in addition to the traditional wet-use service factor. Reductions in energy-related properties are about 1.5 to 2 times those reported for static strength properties. There is no difference in long-term duration of load behavior between treated and untreated material (Fig. 6–10). Current design standards prohibit increases in design stresses beyond the 1.6 factor for short-term duration of load when considering impact-type loading for material treated with waterborne preservative.

Table 6–8. Example of duration of load adjustments

Time (year)	Total load (kPa (lb/ft²))	Load adjustment[a]	Equivalent 10-year design load (kPa (lb/ft²))
1	4.8 (100) + 0.96 (20) = 5.7 (120)	0.93	5.36 (112)
50	0.96 (20)	1.04	1.0 (21)

[a]Figure 6–9.

Table 6–9. Property adjustment factors for in-service temperature exposures

Design values	In-service moisture content	Factor		
		$T \leq 37°C$ ($T \leq 100°F$)	$37°C < T \leq 52°C$ ($100°F < T \leq 125°F$)	$52°C < T \leq 65°C$ ($125°F < T \leq 150°F$)
F_t, E	Wet or dry	1.0	0.9	0.9
F_b, F_v, F_c, $F_{c\perp}$	Dry	1.0	0.8	0.7
	Wet	1.0	0.7	0.5

Temperature Effects

As wood is cooled below normal temperatures, its properties increase. When heated, its properties decrease. The magnitude of the change depends upon moisture content. Up to 65°C (150°F), the effect of temperature is assumed by design codes to be reversible. For structural members that will be exposed to temperatures up to 65°C (150°F), design values are multiplied by the factors given in Table 6–9 (AF&PA 1997). Prolonged exposure to heat can lead to a permanent loss in strength (see Ch. 4).

References

AF&PA. 1997. Washington, DC: American Forest & Paper Association.

National design specification for wood construction.

Design values for wood construction—a supplement to the national design specification for wood construction.

AF&PA. 1996. Load and resistance factor design manual for engineered wood construction. Washington, DC: American Forest & Paper Association.

ASTM. 1998. West Conshohocken, PA: American Society for Testing and Materials.

ASTM D198–97. Standard methods of static tests of timbers in structural sizes.

ASTM D245–93. Standard methods for establishing structural grades for visually graded lumber.

ASTM D1990–97. Standard methods for establishing allowable properties for visually-graded dimension lumber from In-grade tests of full-size specimens.

ASTM D2555–96. Standard methods for establishing clear wood strength values.

ASTM D2915–94. Standard method for evaluating properties for stress grades of structural lumber.

ASTM D4761–96. Standard methods for mechanical properties of lumber and wood-base structural materials.

Forest Products Society. 1997. Machine-graded lumber. Madison, WI: Forest Products Society. Wood Design Focus. 8(2): 1–24.

Galligan, W.L.; Green, D.W.; Gromala, D.S.; Haskell, J.H. 1980. Evaluation of lumber properties in the United States and their application to structural research. Forest Products Journal. 30(10): 45–51.

Gerhards, C.C. 1977. Effect of duration and rate of loading on strength of wood and wood based materials. Res. Pap. FPL–RP–283. Madison, WI: U.S. Department of Agriculture, Forest Service, Forest Products Laboratory.

Green, D.W. 1989. Moisture content and the shrinkage of lumber. Res. Pap. FPL–RP–489. Madison, WI: U.S. Department of Agriculture, Forest Service, Forest Products Laboratory.

Green, D.W.; Evans, J.W. 1987. Mechanical properties of visually graded dimension lumber. Vol. 1–Vol. 7. Springfield VA: National Technical Information Service. PB–88–159–371.

Green, D.W.; Kretschmann, D.E. 1992. Properties and grading of Southern Pine timbers. Forest Products Journal. 47(9): 78–85.

Green, D.W.; Shelley, B.E. 1992. Guidelines for assigning allowable properties to visually grade foreign species based on test data from full sized specimens. Germantown, MD: American Lumber Standards Committee.

Green, D.W.; Shelley, B.E. 1993. Guidelines for assigning allowable properties to mechanically graded foreign species. Germantown, MD: American Lumber Standards Committee.

Green, D.W.; Shelley, B.E.; and Vokey, H.P. 1989. In-grade testing of structural lumber. In: Proceedings of workshop sponsored by In-grade Testing Committee and Forest Products Society. Proceedings 47363. Madison, WI: Forest Products Society.

Kretschmann, D.E.; Green D.W. 1996. Modeling moisture content–mechanical property relationships for clear Southern Pine. Wood and Fiber Science. 28(3): 320–337.

U.S. Department of Commerce. 1994. American softwood lumber standard. Prod. Stand. PS20–94. Washington, DC: U.S. Department of Commerce.

Winandy, J.E. 1995. The influence of time–to–failure on the strength of CCA-treated lumber. Forest Products Journal. 45(2): 82–85.

Fastenings

Lawrence A. Soltis

Contents

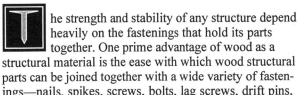

The strength and stability of any structure depend heavily on the fastenings that hold its parts together. One prime advantage of wood as a structural material is the ease with which wood structural parts can be joined together with a wide variety of fastenings—nails, spikes, screws, bolts, lag screws, drift pins, staples, and metal connectors of various types. For utmost rigidity, strength, and service, each type of fastening requires joint designs adapted to the strength properties of wood along and across the grain and to dimensional changes that may occur with changes in moisture content.

Maximum lateral resistance and safe design load values for small-diameter (nails, spikes, and wood screws) and large-diameter dowel-type fasteners (bolts, lag screws, and drift pins) were based on an empirical method prior to 1991. Research conducted during the 1980s resulted in lateral resistance values that are currently based on a yield model theory. This theoretical method was adapted for the 1991 edition of the *National Design Specification for Wood Construction* (NDS). Because literature and design procedures exist that are related to both the empirical and theoretical methods, we refer to the empirical method as pre-1991 and the theoretical method as post-1991 throughout this chapter. Withdrawal resistance methods have not changed, so the pre- and post-1991 refer only to lateral resistance.

The information in this chapter represents primarily Forest Products Laboratory research results. A more comprehensive discussion of fastenings is given in the American Society of Civil Engineers Manuals and Reports on Engineering Practice No. 84, *Mechanical Connections in Wood Structures*. The research results of this chapter are often modified for structural safety, based on judgment or experience, and thus information presented in design documents may differ from information presented in this chapter. Additionally, research by others serves as a basis for some current design criteria. Allowable stress design criteria are presented in the *National Design Specification for Wood Construction* published by the American Forest and Paper Association; limit states design criteria are presented in the *Standard for Load and Resistance Factor Design (LRFD) for Engineered Wood Construction* published by the American Society of Civil Engineers.

Nails

Nails are the most common mechanical fastenings used in wood construction. There are many types, sizes, and forms of nails (Fig. 7–1). The load equations presented in this chapter apply for bright, smooth, common steel wire nails driven into wood when there is no visible splitting. For nails other than common wire nails, the loads can be adjusted by factors given later in the chapter.

Nails in use resist withdrawal loads, lateral loads, or a combination of the two. Both withdrawal and lateral resistance are affected by the wood, the nail, and the condition of use. In general, however, any variation in these factors has a more pronounced effect on withdrawal resistance than on lateral resistance. The serviceability of joints with nails laterally loaded does not depend greatly on withdrawal resistance unless large joint distortion is tolerable.

The diameters of various penny or gauge sizes of bright common nails are given in Table 7–1. The penny size designation should be used cautiously. International nail producers sometimes do not adhere to the dimensions of Table 7–1. Thus penny sizes, although still widely used, are obsolete. Specifying nail sizes by length and diameter dimensions is recommended. Bright box nails are generally of the same length but slightly smaller diameter (Table 7–2), while cement-coated nails such as coolers, sinkers, and coated box nails are slightly shorter (3.2 mm (1/8 in.)) and of smaller diameter than common nails of the same penny size. Helically and annularly threaded nails generally have smaller diameters than common nails for the same penny size (Table 7–3).

Withdrawal Resistance

The resistance of a nail shank to direct withdrawal from a piece of wood depends on the density of the wood, the diameter of the nail, and the depth of penetration. The surface condition of the nail at the time of driving also influences the initial withdrawal resistance.

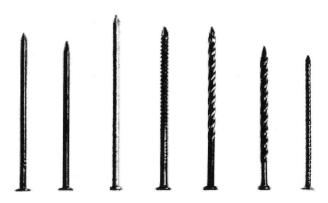

Figure 7–1. Various types of nails: (left to right) bright smooth wire nail, cement coated, zinc-coated, annularly threaded, helically threaded, helically threaded and barbed, and barbed.

Table 7–1. Sizes of bright common wire nails

Size	Gauge	Length (mm (in.))		Diameter (mm (in.))	
6d	11-1/2	50.8	(2)	2.87	(0.113)
8d	10-1/4	63.5	(2-1/2)	3.33	(0.131)
10d	9	76.2	(3)	3.76	(0.148)
12d	9	82.6	(3-1/4)	3.76	(0.148)
16d	8	88.9	(3-1/2)	4.11	(0.162)
20d	6	101.6	(4)	4.88	(0.192)
30d	5	114.3	(4-1/2)	5.26	(0.207)
40d	4	127.0	(5)	5.72	(0.225)
50d	3	139.7	(5-1/2)	6.20	(0.244)
60d	2	152.4	(6)	6.65	(0.262)

Table 7–2. Sizes of smooth box nails

Size	Gauge	Length (mm (in.))		Diameter (mm (in.))	
3d	14-1/2	31.8	(1-1/4)	1.93	(0.076)
4d	14	38.1	(1-1/2)	2.03	(0.080)
5d	14	44.5	(1-3/4)	2.03	(0.080)
6d	12-1/2	50.8	(2)	2.49	(0.098)
7d	12-1/2	57.2	(2-1/4)	2.49	(0.098)
8d	11-1/2	63.5	(2-1/2)	2.87	(0.113)
10d	10-1/2	76.2	(3)	3.25	(0.128)
16d	10	88.9	(3-1/2)	3.43	(0.135)
20d	9	101.6	(4)	3.76	(0.148)

Table 7–3. Sizes of helically and annularly threaded nails

Size	Length (mm (in.))		Diameter (mm (in.))	
6d	50.8	(2)	3.05	(0.120)
8d	63.5	(2-1/2)	3.05	(0.120)
10d	76.2	(3)	3.43	(0.135)
12d	82.6	(3-1/4)	3.43	(0.135)
16d	88.9	(3-1/2)	3.76	(0.148)
20d	101.6	(4)	4.50	(0.177)
30d	114.3	(4-1/2)	4.50	(0.177)
40d	127.0	(5)	4.50	(0.177)
50d	139.7	(5-1/2)	4.50	(0.177)
60d	152.4	(6)	4.50	(0.177)
70d	177.8	(7)	5.26	(0.207)
80d	203.2	(8)	5.26	(0.207)
90d	228.6	(9)	5.26	(0.207)

For bright common wire nails driven into the side grain of seasoned wood or unseasoned wood that remains wet, the results of many tests have shown that the maximum withdrawal load is given by the empirical equation

$$p = 54.12G^{5/2}DL \qquad \text{(metric)} \qquad (7\text{--}1a)$$

$$p = 7,850G^{5/2}DL \qquad \text{(inch--pound)} \qquad (7\text{--}1b)$$

where p is maximum load (N, lb), L depth (mm, in.) of penetration of the nail in the member holding the nail point, G specific gravity of the wood based on ovendry weight and volume at 12% moisture content (see Ch. 4, Tables 4–2 to 4–5), and D diameter of the nail (mm, in.). (The NDS and LRFD use ovendry weight and volume as a basis.)

The loads expressed by Equation (7–1) represent average data. Certain wood species give test values that are some-what greater or less than the equation values. A typical load–displacement curve for nail withdrawal (Fig. 7–2) shows that maximum load occurs at relatively small values of displacement.

Although the equation for nail-withdrawal resistance indicates that the dense, heavy woods offer greater resistance to nail withdrawal than do the lower density ones, lighter species should not be disqualified for uses requiring high resistance to withdrawal. As a rule, the less dense species do not split as readily as the denser ones, thus offering an opportunity for increasing the diameter, length, and number of the nails to compensate for the wood's lower resistance to nail withdrawal.

The withdrawal resistance of nail shanks is greatly affected by such factors as type of nail point, type of shank, time the nail remains in the wood, surface coatings, and moisture content changes in the wood.

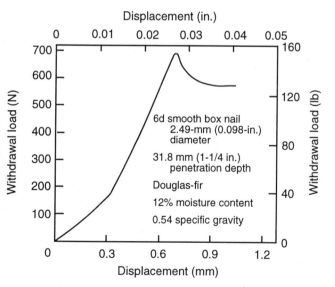

Figure 7–2. Typical load–displacement curve for direct withdrawal of a nail.

Effect of Seasoning

With practically all species, nails driven into green wood and pulled before any seasoning takes place offer about the same withdrawal resistance as nails driven into seasoned wood and pulled soon after driving. However, if common smooth-shank nails are driven into green wood that is al-lowed to season, or into seasoned wood that is subjected to cycles of wetting and drying before the nails are pulled, they lose a major part of their initial withdrawal resistance. The withdrawal resistance for nails driven into wood that is subjected to changes in moisture content may be as low as 25% of the values for nails tested soon after driving. On the other hand, if the wood fibers deteriorate or the nail corrodes under some conditions of moisture variation and time, with-drawal resistance is erratic; resistance may be regained or even increased over the immediate withdrawal resistance. However, such sustained performance should not be relied on in the design of a nailed joint.

In seasoned wood that is not subjected to appreciable mois-ture content changes, the withdrawal resistance of nails may also diminish due to relaxation of the wood fibers with time. Under all these conditions of use, the withdrawal resistance of nails differs among species and shows variation within individual species.

Effect of Nail Form

The surface condition of nails is frequently modified during the manufacturing process to improve withdrawal resistance. Such modification is usually done by surface coating, surface roughening, or mechanical deformation of the shank. Other factors that affect the surface condition of the nail are the oil film remaining on the shank after manufacture or corrosion resulting from storage under adverse conditions; but these factors are so variable that their influence on withdrawal resistance cannot be adequately evaluated.

Surface Modifications—A common surface treatment for nails is the so-called cement coating. Cement coatings, contrary to what the name implies, do not include cement as an ingredient; they generally are a composition of resin applied to the nail to increase the resistance to withdrawal by increasing the friction between the nail and the wood. If properly applied, they increase the resistance of nails to withdrawal immediately after the nails are driven into the softer woods. However, in the denser woods (such as hard maple, birch, or oak), cement-coated nails have practically no advantage over plain nails, because most of the coating is removed in driving. Some of the coating may also be re-moved in the side member before the nail penetrates the main member.

Good-quality cement coatings are uniform, not sticky to the touch, and cannot be rubbed off easily. Different techniques of applying the cement coating and variations in its ingredients may cause large differences in the relative resistance to with-drawal of different lots of cement-coated nails. Some nails may show only a slight initial advantage over plain nails. In the softer woods, the increase in withdrawal resistance of cement-coated nails is not permanent but drops off significantly after a month or so. Cement-coated nails are used primarily in construction of boxes, crates, and other containers usually built for rough handling and relatively short service.

Nails that have galvanized coatings, such as zinc, are intended primarily for uses where corrosion and staining resistance are important factors in permanence and appearance. If the zinc coating is evenly applied, withdrawal resistance may be increased, but extreme irregularities of the coating may actually reduce it. The advantage that uniformly coated galvanized nails may have over nongalvanized nails in resistance to initial withdrawal is usually reduced by repeated cycles of wetting and drying.

Nails have also been made with plastic coatings. The usefulness and characteristics of these coatings are influenced by the quality and type of coating, the effectiveness of the bond between the coating and base fastener, and the effectiveness of the bond between the coating and wood fibers. Some plastic coatings appear to resist corrosion or improve resistance to withdrawal, while others offer little improvement.

Fasteners with properly applied nylon coating tend to retain their initial resistance to withdrawal compared with other coatings, which exhibit a marked decrease in withdrawal resistance within the first month after driving.

A chemically etched nail has somewhat greater withdrawal resistance than some coated nails, as the minutely pitted surface is an integral part of the nail shank. Under impact loading, however, the withdrawal resistance of etched nails is little different from that of plain or cement-coated nails under various moisture conditions.

Sand-blasted nails perform in much the same manner as chemically etched nails.

Shape Modifications—Nail shanks may be varied from a smooth, circular form to give an increase in surface area without an increase in nail weight. Special nails with barbed, helically or annularly threaded, and other irregular shanks (Fig. 7–1) are commercially available.

The form and magnitude of the deformations along the shank influence the performance of the nails in various wood species. In wood remaining at a uniform moisture content, the withdrawal resistance of these nails is generally somewhat greater than that of common wire nails of the same diameter. For instance, annular-shank nails have about 40% greater resistance to withdrawal than common nails. However, under conditions involving changes in moisture content of the wood, some special nail forms provide considerably greater withdrawal resistance than the common wire nail—about four times greater for annularly and helically threaded nails of the same diameter. This is especially true of nails driven into green wood that subsequently dries. In general, annularly threaded nails sustain larger withdrawal loads, and helically threaded nails sustain greater impact withdrawal work values than do the other nail forms.

Nails with deformed shanks are sometimes hardened by heat treatments for use where driving conditions are difficult or to obtain improved performance, such as in pallet assembly. Hardened nails are brittle and care should be exercised to avoid injuries from fragments of nails broken during driving.

Nail Point—A smooth, round shank nail with a long, sharp point will usually have a greater withdrawal resistance, particularly in the softer woods, than the common wire nail (which usually has a diamond point). However, sharp points accentuate splitting in certain species, which may reduce withdrawal resistance. A blunt or flat point without taper reduces splitting, but its destruction of the wood fibers when driven reduces withdrawal resistance to less than that of the common wire nail. A nail tapered at the end and terminating in a blunt point will cause less splitting. In heavier woods, such a tapered, blunt-pointed nail will provide about the same withdrawal resistance, but in less dense woods, its resistance to withdrawal is less than that of the common nail.

Nail Head—Nail head classifications include flat, oval, countersunk, deep-countersunk, and brad. Nails with all types of heads, except the deep-countersunk, brad, and some of the thin flathead nails, are sufficiently strong to withstand the force required to pull them from most woods in direct withdrawal. The deep-countersunk and brad nails are usually driven below the wood surface and are not intended to carry large withdrawal loads. In general, the thickness and diameter of the heads of the common wire nails increase as the size of the nail increases.

The development of some pneumatically operated portable nailers has introduced nails with specially configured heads, such as T-nails and nails with a segment of the head cut off.

Corrosion and Staining

In the presence of moisture, metals used for nails may corrode when in contact with wood treated with certain preservative or fire-retardant salts (Chs. 14 and 17). Use of certain metals or metal alloys will reduce the amount of corrosion. Nails of copper, silicon bronze, and 304 and 316 stainless steel have performed well in wood treated with ammoniacal copper arsenate and chromated copper arsenate. The choice of metals for use with fire-retardant-treated woods depends upon the particular fire-retardant chemical.

Staining caused by the reaction of certain wood extractives (Ch. 3) and steel in the presence of moisture is a problem if appearance is important, such as with naturally finished siding. Use of stainless steel, aluminum, or hot-dipped galvanized nails can alleviate staining.

In general, the withdrawal resistance of copper and other alloy nails is comparable with that of common steel wire nails when pulled soon after driving.

Driving

The resistance of nails to withdrawal is generally greatest when they are driven perpendicular to the grain of the wood. When the nail is driven parallel to the wood fibers (that is, into the end of the piece) withdrawal resistance in the softer woods drops to 75% or even 50% of the resistance obtained when the nail is driven perpendicular to the grain. The difference between side- and end-grain withdrawal loads is less for dense woods than for softer woods. With most species, the ratio between the end- and side-grain withdrawal loads of nails pulled after a time interval, or after moisture content changes have occurred, is usually somewhat greater than that of nails pulled immediately after driving.

Toe nailing, a common method of joining wood framework, involves slant driving a nail or group of nails through the end or edge of an attached member and into a main member. Toe nailing requires greater skill in assembly than does ordinary end nailing but provides joints of greater strength and stability. Tests show that the maximum strength of toenailed joints under lateral and uplift loads is obtained by (a) using the largest nail that will not cause excessive splitting, (b) allowing an end distance (distance from the end of the attached member to the point of initial nail entry) of approximately one-third the length of the nail, (c) driving the nail at a slope of 30° with the attached member, and (d) burying the full shank of the nail but avoiding excessive mutilation of the wood from hammer blows.

The results of withdrawal tests with multiple nail joints in which the piece attached is pulled directly away from the main member show that slant driving is usually superior to straight driving when nails are driven into drywood and pulled immediately, and decidedly superior when nails are driven into green or partially dry wood that is allowed to season for a month or more. However, the loss in depth of penetration due to slant driving may, in some types of joints, offset the advantages of slant nailing. Cross slant driving of groups of nails through the side grain is usually somewhat more effective than parallel slant driving through the end grain.

Nails driven into lead holes with a diameter slightly smaller (approximately 90%) than the nail shank have somewhat greater withdrawal resistance than nails driven without lead holes. Lead holes also prevent or reduce splitting of the wood, particularly for dense species.

Clinching

The withdrawal resistance of smooth-shank, clinched nails is considerably greater than that of unclinched nails. The point of a clinched nail is bent over where the nail protrudes through the side member. The ratio between the loads for clinched and unclinched nails varies enormously, depending upon the moisture content of the wood when the nail is driven and withdrawn, the species of wood, the size of nail, and the direction of clinch with respect to the grain of the wood.

In dry or green wood, a clinched nail provides 45% to 170% more withdrawal resistance than an unclinched nail when withdrawn soon after driving. In green wood that seasons after a nail is driven, a clinched nail gives 250% to 460% greater withdrawal resistance than an unclinched nail.

However, this improved strength of a clinched-nail joint does not justify the use of green lumber, because the joints may loosen as the lumber seasons. Furthermore, laboratory tests were made with single nails, and the effects of drying, such as warping, twisting, and splitting, may reduce the efficiency of a joint that has more than one nail. Clinching of nails is generally confined to such construction as boxes and crates and other container applications.

Nails clinched across the grain have approximately 20% more resistance to withdrawal than nails clinched along the grain.

Fastening of Plywood

The nailing characteristics of plywood are not greatly different from those of solid wood except for plywood's greater resistance to splitting when nails are driven near an edge. The nail withdrawal resistance of plywood is 15% to 30% less than that of solid wood of the same thickness. The reason is that fiber distortion is less uniform in plywood than in solid wood. For plywood less than 12.5 mm (1/2-in.) thick, the greater splitting resistance tends to offset the lower withdrawal resistance compared with solid wood. The withdrawal resistance per unit length of penetration decreases as the number of plies per unit length increases. The direction of the grain of the face ply has little influence on the withdrawal resistance from the face near the end or edge of a piece of plywood. The direction of the grain of the face ply may influence the pull-through resistance of staples or nails with severely modified heads, such as T-heads. Fastener design information for plywood is available from APA–The Engineered Wood Association.

Allowable Loads

The preceding discussion dealt with maximum withdrawal loads obtained in short-time test conditions. For design, these loads must be reduced to account for variability, duration-of-load effects, and safety. A value of one-sixth the average maximum load has usually been accepted as the allowable load for long-time loading conditions. For normal duration of load, this value may be increased by 10%. Normal duration of load is defined as a load of 10-year duration.

Lateral Resistance

Pre-1991

Test loads at joint slips of 0.38 mm (0.015 in.) (approximate proportional limit load) for bright common wire nails in lateral resistance driven into the side grain (perpendicular to the wood fibers) of seasoned wood are expressed by the empirical equation

$$p = KD^{3/2} \tag{7–2}$$

where p is lateral load per nail, K a coefficient, and D diameter of the nail. Values of coefficient K are listed in Table 7–4 for ranges of specific gravity of hardwoods and softwoods. The loads given by the equation apply only where the side member and the member holding the nail point are of

Table 7–4. Coefficients for computing test loads for fasteners in seasoned wood[a] (pre-1991)

Specific gravity range[b]	Lateral load coefficient K (metric (inch–pound))					
	Nails[c]		Screws		Lag screws	
Hardwoods						
0.33–0.47	50.04	(1,440)	23.17	(3,360)	26.34	(3,820)
0.48–0.56	69.50	(2,000)	31.99	(4,640)	29.51	(4,280)
0.57–0.74	94.52	(2,720)	44.13	(6,400)	34.13	(4,950)
Softwoods						
0.29–0.42	50.04	(1,440)	23.17	(3,360)	23.30	(3,380)
0.43–0.47	62.55	(1,800)	29.79	(4,320)	26.34	(3,820)
0.48–0.52	76.45	(2,200)	36.40	(5,280)	29.51	(4,280)

[a]Wood with a moisture content of 15%.
[b]Specific gravity based on ovendry weight and volume at 12% moisture content.
[c]Coefficients based on load at joint slip of 0.38 mm (0.015 in.)

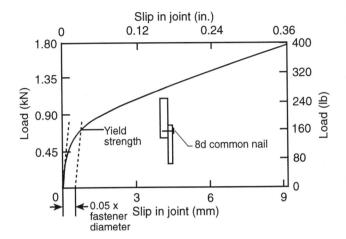

Figure 7–3. Typical relation between lateral load and slip in the joint and 5% offset definition.

approximately the same density. The thickness of the side member should be about one-half the depth of penetration of the nail in the member holding the point.

The ultimate lateral nail loads for softwoods may approach 3.5 times the loads expressed by the equation, and for hardwoods they may be 7 times as great. The joint slip at maximum load, however, is more than 20 times 0.38 mm (0.015 in.). This is demonstrated by the typical load–slip curve shown in Figure 7–3. To maintain a sufficient ratio between ultimate load and the load at 0.38 mm (0.015 in.), the nail should penetrate into the member holding the point by not less than 10 times the nail diameter for dense woods (specific gravity greater than 0.61) and 14 times the diameter for low density woods (specific gravity less than 0.42). For species having densities between these two ranges, the penetration may be found by straight line interpolation.

Post-1991

The yield model theory selects the worst case of yield modes based on different possibilities of wood bearing and nail bending. It does not account for nail head effects. A description of the various combinations is given in Figure 7–4. Mode I is a wood bearing failure in either the main or side member; mode II is a rotation of the fastener in the joint without bending; modes III and IV are a combination of wood bearing failure and one or more plastic hinge yield formations in the fastener. Modes I_m and II have not been observed in nail and spike connections. The yield model theory is applicable to all types of dowel fasteners (nails, screws, bolts, lag screws), and thus the wood bearing capacity is described by a material property called the dowel bearing strength.

The yield mode equations (Table 7–5) are entered with the dowel bearing strength and dimensions of the wood members and the bending yield strength and diameter of the fastener.

The dowel bearing strength of the wood is experimentally determined by compressing a dowel into a wood member. The strength basis is the load representing a 5% diameter offset on the load–deformation curve (Fig. 7–3). Dowel bearing strength F_e (Pa, lb/in^2) is empirically related to specific gravity G by

$$F_e = 114.5G^{1.84} \qquad \text{(metric)} \qquad (7\text{–}3a)$$

$$F_e = 16{,}600G^{1.84} \qquad \text{(inch–pound)} \qquad (7\text{–}3b)$$

where specific gravity is based on ovendry weight and volume.

Spacing

End distance, edge distance, and spacing of nails should be such as to prevent unusual splitting. As a general rule, nails should be driven no closer to the edge of the side member than one-half its thickness and no closer to the end than the thickness of the piece. Smaller nails can be driven closer to the edges or ends than larger ones because they are less likely to split the wood.

Grain Direction Effects

The lateral load for side-grain nailing applies whether the load is in a direction parallel to the grain of the pieces joined or at right angles to it. When nails are driven into the end grain (parallel with the wood fibers), limited data on softwood species indicate that their maximum resistance to lateral displacement is about two-thirds that for nails driven into the side grain. Although the average proportional limit loads appear to be about the same for end- and side-grain nailing, the individual results are more erratic for end-grain nailing, and the minimum loads approach only 75% of corresponding values for side-grain nailing.

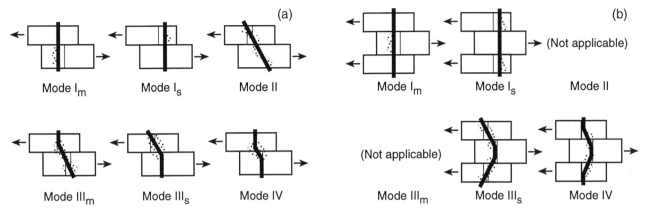

Figure 7–4. Various combinations of wood-bearing and fastener-bending yields for (a) two-member connections and (b) three-member connections.

Moisture Content Effects

Nails driven into the side grain of unseasoned wood give maximum lateral resistance loads approximately equal to those obtained in seasoned wood, but the lateral resistance loads at 0.38 mm (0.015 in.) joint slip are somewhat less. To prevent excessive deformation, lateral loads obtained for seasoned wood should be reduced by 25% for unseasoned wood that will remain wet or be loaded before seasoning takes place.

When nails are driven into green wood, their lateral proportional limit loads after the wood has seasoned are also less than when they are driven into seasoned wood and loaded. The erratic behavior of a nailed joint that has undergone one or more moisture content changes makes it difficult to establish a lateral load for a nailed joint under these conditions. Structural joints should be inspected at intervals, and if it is apparent that the joint has loosened during drying, the joint should be reinforced with additional nails.

Deformed-Shank Nails

Deformed-shank nails carry somewhat higher maximum lateral loads than do the same pennyweight common wire nails, but both perform similarly at small distortions in the joint. It should be noted that the same pennyweight deformed-shank nail has a different diameter than that of the common wire nail. These nails often have higher bending yield strength than common wire nails, resulting in higher lateral strength in modes III and IV.

Lateral Load–Slip Models

A considerable amount of work has been done to describe, by mathematical models, the lateral load–slip curve of nails. These models have become important because of their need as input parameters for advanced methods of structural analysis.

One theoretical model, which considers the nail to be a beam supported on an elastic foundation (the wood), describes the initial slope of the curve:

$$\delta = P\left[2(L_1 + L_2) - \frac{(J_1 - J_2)^2}{(K_1 + K_2)} \right] \qquad (7\text{–}4)$$

where P is the lateral load and δ is the joint slip. The factors L_1, L_2, J_1, J_2, K_1, and K_2 (Table 7–6) are combinations of hyperbolic and trigonometric functions of the quantities $\lambda_1 a$ and $\lambda_2 b$ in which a and b are the depth of penetration of the nail in members 1 and 2, respectively. For smooth round nails,

$$\lambda = 2\sqrt[4]{\frac{k_0}{\pi ED^3}} \qquad (7\text{–}5)$$

where k_0 is elastic bearing constant, D nail diameter, and E modulus of elasticity of the nail. For seasoned wood, the elastic bearing constant k_0 (N/mm^3, lb/in^3) has been shown to be related to average species specific gravity G if no lead hole is used by

$$k_0 = 582G \qquad \text{(metric)} \qquad (7\text{–}6a)$$

$$k_0 = 2,144,000G \qquad \text{(inch–pound} \qquad (7\text{–}6b)$$

If a prebored lead hole equal to 90% of the nail diameter is used,

$$k_0 = 869G \qquad \text{(metric)} \qquad (7\text{–}7a)$$

$$k_0 = 3,200,000G \qquad \text{(inch–pound)} \qquad (7\text{–}7b)$$

Other empirically derived models attempt to describe the entire load–slip curve. One such expression is

$$P = A \log_{10}(1 + B\delta) \qquad (7\text{–}8)$$

where the parameters A and B are empirically fitted.

Table 7–5. The 5% offset lateral yield strength (Z) for nails and screws for a two-member joint

Mode	Z value for nails	Z value for screws
I_s	Dt_sF_{es}	Dt_sF_{es}
III_m	$\dfrac{k_1DpF_{em}}{1+2R_e}$	—
III_s	$\dfrac{k_2Dt_sF_{em}}{2+R_e}$	$\dfrac{k_3Dt_sF_{em}}{2+R_e}$
IV	$D^2\sqrt{\dfrac{2F_{em}F_{yb}}{3(1+R_e)}}$	$D^2\sqrt{\dfrac{1.75F_{em}F_{yb}}{3(1+R_e)}}$

Definitions

D nail, spike, or screw diameter, mm (in.) (for annularly threaded nails, D is thread-root diameter; for screws, D is either the shank diameter or the root diameter if the threaded portion of the screw is in the shear plane)

F_{em} dowel bearing stress of main member (member holding point), kPa (lb/in^2)

F_{es} dowel bearing stress of side member, kPa (lb/in^2)

F_{yb} bending yield stress of nail, spike, or screw, kPa (lb/in^2)

p penetration of nail or spike in main member, mm (in.)

t_s thickness of side member, mm (in.)

Z offset lateral yield strength

R_e $= F_{em}/F_{es}$

$$k_1 = -1 + \sqrt{2(1+R_e) + \frac{2F_{yb}(1+2R_e)D^2}{3\,F_{em}\,p^2}}$$

$$k_2 = -1 + \sqrt{\frac{2(1+R_e)}{R_e} + \frac{2F_{yb}(2+R_e)D^2}{3\,F_{em}\,t_s^2}}$$

$$k_3 = -1 + \sqrt{\frac{2(1+R_e)}{R_e} + \frac{F_{yb}(2+R_e)D^2}{2\,F_{em}\,t_s^2}}$$

Spikes

Common wire spikes are manufactured in the same manner as common wire nails. They have either a chisel point or a diamond point and are made in lengths of 76 to 305 mm (3 to 12 in.). For corresponding lengths in the range of 76 to 152 (3 to 6 in.), they have larger diameters (Table 7–7) than common wire nails, and beyond the 60d size they are usually designated by diameter.

Table 7–6. Expressions for factors in Equation (7–4)

Factor	Expression[a]
L_1	$\dfrac{\lambda_1}{k_1}\dfrac{\sinh\lambda_1a\,\cosh\lambda_1a-\sin\lambda_1a\,\cos\lambda_1a}{\sinh^2\lambda_1a-\sin^2\lambda_1a}$
L_2	$\dfrac{\lambda_2}{k_2}\dfrac{\sinh\lambda_2b\,\cosh\lambda_2b-\sin\lambda_2b\,\cos\lambda_2b}{\sinh^2\lambda_2b-\sin^2\lambda_2b}$
J_1	$\dfrac{\lambda_1^2}{k_1}\dfrac{\sinh^2\lambda_1a+\sin^2\lambda_1a}{\sinh^2\lambda_1a-\sin^2\lambda_1a}$
J_2	$\dfrac{\lambda_2^2}{k_2}\dfrac{\sinh^2\lambda_2b+\sin^2\lambda_2b}{\sinh^2\lambda_2b-\sin^2\lambda_2b}$
K_1	$\dfrac{\lambda_1^3}{k_1}\dfrac{\sinh\lambda_1a\,\cosh\lambda_1a+\sin\lambda_1a\,\cos\lambda_1a}{\sinh^2\lambda_1a-\sin^2\lambda_1a}$
K_2	$\dfrac{\lambda_2^3}{k_2}\dfrac{\sinh\lambda_2b\,\cosh\lambda_2b+\sin\lambda_2b\,\cos\lambda_2b}{\sinh^2\lambda_2b-\sin^2\lambda_2b}$

[a]$k_1 = k_{01}d$ and $k_2 = k_{02}d$, where k_1 and k_2 are the foundation moduli of members 1 and 2, respectively.

The withdrawal and lateral resistance equations and limitations given for common wire nails are also applicable to spikes, except that in calculating the withdrawal load for spikes, the depth of penetration is taken as the length of the spike in the member receiving the point, minus two-thirds the length of the point.

Staples

Different types of staples have been developed with various modifications in points, shank treatment and coatings, gauge, crown width, and length. These fasteners are available in clips or magazines for use in pneumatically operated portable staplers. Most factors that affect the withdrawal and lateral loads of nails similarly affect the loads on staples. The withdrawal resistance, for example, varies almost directly with the circumference and depth of penetration when the type of point and shank are similar to nails. Thus, Equation (7–1) has been used to predict the withdrawal load for one leg of a staple, but no verification tests have been done.

The load in lateral resistance varies approximately as the 3/2 power of the diameter when other factors, such as quality of metal, type of shank, and depth of penetration, are similar to nails. The diameter of each leg of a two-legged staple must therefore be about two-thirds the diameter of a nail to provide a comparable load. Equation (7–2) has been used to predict the lateral resistance of staples. However, yield model theory equations have not yet been experimentally verified for staples.

Table 7–7. Sizes of common wire spikes

Size	Length (mm (in.))	Diameter (mm (in.))
10d	76.2 (3)	4.88 (0.192)
12d	82.6 (3-1/4)	4.88 (0.192)
16d	88.9 (3-1/2)	5.26 (0.207)
20d	101.6 (4)	5.72 (0.225)
30d	114.3 (4-1/2)	6.20 (0.244)
40d	127.0 (5)	6.68 (0.263)
50d	139.7 (5-1/2)	7.19 (0.283)
60d	152.4 (6)	7.19 (0.283)
5/16 in.	177.8 (7)	7.92 (0.312)
3/8 in.	215.9 (8-1/2)	9.53 (0.375)

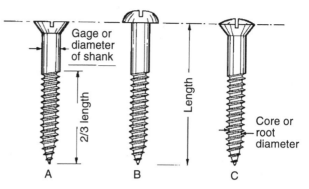

Figure 7–5. Common types of wood screws: A, flathead; B, roundhead; and C, ovalhead.

In addition to the immediate performance capability of staples and nails as determined by test, factors such as corrosion, sustained performance under service conditions, and durability in various uses should be considered in evaluating the relative usefulness of a stapled connection.

Drift Bolts

A drift bolt (or drift pin) is a long pin of iron or steel, with or without head or point. It is driven into a bored hole through one timber and into an adjacent one, to prevent the separation of the timbers connected and to transmit lateral load. The hole in the second member is drilled sufficiently deep to prevent the pin from hitting the bottom.

The ultimate withdrawal load of a round drift bolt or pin from the side grain of seasoned wood is given by

$$p = 45.51G^2DL \quad \text{(metric)} \quad (7\text{–}9a)$$

$$p = 6,600G^2DL \quad \text{(inch–pound)} \quad (7\text{–}9b)$$

where p is the ultimate withdrawal load (N, lb), G specific gravity based on the ovendry weight and volume at 12% moisture content of the wood, D diameter of the drift bolt (mm, in.), and L length of penetration of the bolt (mm, in.). (The NDS and LRFD use ovendry weight and volume as a basis.)

This equation provides an average relationship for all species, and the withdrawal load for some species may be above or below the equation values. It also presumes that the bolts are driven into prebored holes having a diameter 3.2 mm (1/8 in.) less than the bolt diameter.

Data are not available on lateral resistance of drift bolts. The yield model should provide lateral strength prediction, but the model has not been experimentally verified for drift bolts. Designers have used bolt data and design methods based on experience. This suggests that the load for a drift bolt driven into the side grain of wood should not exceed, and ordinarily should be taken as less than, that for a bolt of the same diameter. Bolt design values are based on the thickness of the main member in a joint. Thus the depth of penetration of the drift bolt must be greater than or equal to the main-member thickness on which the bolt design value is based. However, the drift bolt should not fully penetrate its joint.

Wood Screws

The common types of wood screws have flat, oval, or round heads. The flathead screw is most commonly used if a flush surface is desired. Ovalhead and roundhead screws are used for appearance, and roundhead screws are used when countersinking is objectionable. The principal parts of a screw are the head, shank, thread, and core (Fig. 7–5). The root diameter for most sizes of screws averages about two-thirds the shank diameter. Wood screws are usually made of steel, brass, other metals, or alloys, and may have specific finishes such as nickel, blued, chromium, or cadmium. They are classified according to material, type, finish, shape of head, and diameter or gauge of the shank.

Current trends in fastenings for wood also include tapping screws. Tapping screws have threads the full length of the shank and may have some advantage for certain specific uses.

Withdrawal Resistance

Experimental Loads

The resistance of wood screw shanks to withdrawal from the side grain of seasoned wood varies directly with the square of the specific gravity of the wood. Within limits, the withdrawal load varies directly with the depth of penetration of the threaded portion and the diameter of the screw, provided the screw does not fail in tension. The screw will fail in tension when its strength is exceeded by the withdrawal strength from the wood. The limiting length to cause a tension failure decreases as the density of the wood increases since the withdrawal strength of the wood increases with density. The longer lengths of standard screws are therefore superfluous in dense hardwoods.

The withdrawal resistance of type A tapping screws, commonly called sheet metal screws, is in general about 10% greater than that for wood screws of comparable diameter and length of threaded portion. The ratio between the withdrawal resistance of tapping screws and wood screws varies from 1.16 in denser woods, such as oak, to 1.05 in lighter woods, such as redwood.

Ultimate test values for withdrawal loads of wood screws inserted into the side grain of seasoned wood may be expressed as

$$p = 108.25G^2DL \quad \text{(metric)} \quad (7\text{--}10a)$$

$$p = 15,700G^2DL \quad \text{(inch--pound)} \quad (7\text{--}10b)$$

where p is maximum withdrawal load (N, lb), G specific gravity based on ovendry weight and volume at 12% moisture content, D shank diameter of the screw (mm, in.), and L length of penetration of the threaded part of the screw (mm, in.). (The NDS and LRFD use ovendry weight and volume as a basis.) These values are based on reaching ultimate load in 5- to 10-min.

This equation is applicable when screw lead holes have a diameter of about 70% of the root diameter of the threads in softwoods, and about 90% in hardwoods.

The equation values are applicable to the screw sizes listed in Table 7–8. (Shank diameters are related to screw gauges.)

For lengths and gauges outside these limits, the actual values are likely to be less than the equation values.

The withdrawal loads of screws inserted in the end grain of wood are somewhat erratic, but when splitting is avoided, they should average 75% of the load sustained by screws inserted in the side grain.

Lubricating the surface of a screw with soap or similar lubricant is recommended to facilitate insertion, especially in dense woods, and it will have little effect on ultimate withdrawal resistance.

Fastening of Particleboard

Tapping screws are commonly used in particleboard where withdrawal strength is important. Care must be taken when tightening screws in particleboard to avoid stripping the threads. The maximum amount of torque that can be applied to a screw before the threads in the particleboard are stripped is given by

$$T = 3.16 + 0.0096X \quad \text{(metric)} \quad (7\text{--}11a)$$

$$T = 27.98 + 1.36X \quad \text{(inch--pound)} \quad (7\text{--}11b)$$

where T is torque (N–m, in–lb) and X is density of the particleboard (kg/m^3, lb/ft^3). Equation (7–11) is for 8-gauge screws with a depth of penetration of 15.9 mm (5/8 in.). The maximum torque is fairly constant for lead holes of 0 to 90% of the root diameter of the screw.

Ultimate withdrawal loads P (N, lb) of screws from particleboard can be predicted by

$$P = KD^{1/2}(L - D/3)^{5/4}G^2 \quad (7\text{--}12)$$

where D is shank diameter of the screw (mm, in.), L depth of embedment of the threaded portion of the screw (mm, in.), and G specific gravity of the board based on ovendry weight and volume at current moisture content. For metric measurements, $K = 41.1$ for withdrawal from the face of the board and $K = 31.8$ for withdrawal from the edge; for inch–pound measurements, $K = 2,655$ for withdrawal from the face and $K = 2,055$ for withdrawal from the edge. Equation (7–12) applies when the setting torque is between 60% to 90% of T (Eq. (7–11)).

Withdrawal resistance of screws from particleboard is not significantly different for lead holes of 50% to 90% of the root diameter. A higher setting torque will produce a somewhat higher withdrawal load, but there is only a slight difference (3%) in values between 60% to 90% setting torques (Eq. (7–11)). A modest tightening of screws in many cases provides an effective compromise between optimizing withdrawal resistance and stripping threads.

Equation (7–12) can also predict the withdrawal of screws from fiberboard with $K = 57.3$ (metric) or 3,700 (inch–pound) for the face and $K = 44.3$ (metric) or 2,860 (inch–pound) for the edge of the board.

Lateral Resistance

Pre-1991

The proportional limit loads obtained in tests of lateral resistance for wood screws in the side grain of seasoned wood are given by the empirical equation

$$p = KD^2 \quad (7\text{--}13)$$

where p is lateral load, D diameter of the screw shank, and K a coefficient depending on the inherent characteristics of the wood species. Values of screw shank diameters for various screw gauges are listed in Table 7–9.

Table 7–8. Screw sizes appropriate for Equation (7–10)

Screw length (mm (in.))	Gauge limits
12.7 (1/2)	1 to 6
19.0 (3/4)	2 to 11
25.4 (1)	3 to 12
38.1 (1-1/2)	5 to 14
50.8 (2)	7 to 16
63.5 (2-1/2)	9 to 18
76.2 (3)	12 to 20

Table 7–9. Screw shank diameters for various screw gauges

Screw number or gauge	Diameter (mm (in.))
4	2.84 (0.112)
5	3.18 (0.125)
6	3.51 (0.138)
7	3.84 (0.151)
8	4.17 (0.164)
9	4.50 (0.177)
10	4.83 (0.190)
11	5.16 (0.203)
12	5.49 (0.216)
14	6.15 (0.242)
16	6.81 (0.268)
18	7.47 (0.294)
20	8.13 (0.320)
24	9.45 (0.372)

Values of K are based on ranges of specific gravity of hardwoods and softwoods and are given in Table 7–4. They apply to wood at about 15% moisture content. Loads computed by substituting these constants in the equation are expected to have a slip of 0.18 to 0.25 mm (0.007 to 0.010 in.), depending somewhat on the species and density of the wood.

Equation (7–13) applies when the depth of penetration of the screw into the block receiving the point is not less than seven times the shank diameter and when the side member and the main member are approximately of the same density. The thickness of the side member should be about one-half the depth of penetration of the screw in the member holding the point. The end distance should be no less than the side member thickness, and the edge distances no less than one-half the side member thickness.

This depth of penetration (seven times shank diameter) gives an ultimate load of about four times the load obtained by the equation. For a depth of penetration of less than seven times the shank diameter, the ultimate load is reduced about in proportion to the reduction in penetration, and the load at the proportional limit is reduced somewhat less rapidly. When the depth of penetration of the screw in the holding block is four times the shank diameter, the maximum load will be less than three times the load expressed by the equation, and the proportional limit load will be approximately equal to that given by the equation. When the screw holds metal to wood, the load can be increased by about 25%.

For these lateral loads, the part of the lead hole receiving the shank should be the same diameter as the shank or slightly smaller; that part receiving the threaded portion should be the same diameter as the root of the thread in dense species or slightly smaller than the root in low-density species.

Screws should always be turned in. They should never be started or driven with a hammer because this practice tears the wood fibers and injures the screw threads, seriously reducing the load carrying capacity of the screw.

Post-1991

Screw lateral strength is determined by the yield model theory (Table 7–5). Modes I, III, and IV failures may occur (Fig. 7–4). The dowel bearing strength values are based on the same specific gravity equation used to establish values for nails (Eq. (7–3)). Further discussion of screw lateral strength is found in ASCE Manual No. 84, *Mechanical Connections in Wood Structures*.

Lag Screws

Lag screws are commonly used because of their convenience, particularly where it would be difficult to fasten a bolt or where a nut on the surface would be objectionable. Commonly available lag screws range from about 5.1 to 25.4 mm (0.2 to 1 in.) in diameter and from 25.4 to 406 mm (1 to 16 in.) in length. The length of the threaded part varies with the length of the screw and ranges from 19.0 mm (3/4 in.) with the 25.4- and 31.8-mm (1- and 1-1/4-in.) screws to half the length for all lengths greater than 254 mm (10 in.). Lag screws have a hexagonal-shaped head and are tightened by a wrench (as opposed to wood screws, which have a slotted head and are tightened by a screw driver). The following equations for withdrawal and lateral loads are based on lag screws having a base metal average tensile yield strength of about 310.3 MPa (45,000 lb/in^2) and an average ultimate tensile strength of 530.9 MPa (77,000 lb/in^2).

Withdrawal Resistance

The results of withdrawal tests have shown that the maximum direct withdrawal load of lag screws from the side grain of seasoned wood may be computed as

$$p = 125.4G^{3/2}D^{3/4}L \qquad \text{(metric)} \qquad (7\text{–}14a)$$

$$p = 8{,}100G^{3/2}D^{3/4}L \qquad \text{(inch–pound)} \qquad (7\text{–}14b)$$

where p is maximum withdrawal load (N, lb), D shank diameter (mm, in.), G specific gravity of the wood based on ovendry weight and volume at 12% moisture content, and L length (mm, in.) of penetration of the threaded part. (The NDS and LRFD use ovendry weight and volume as a basis.) Equation (7–14) was developed independently of Equation (7–10) but gives approximately the same results.

Lag screws, like wood screws, require prebored holes of the proper size (Fig. 7–6). The lead hole for the shank should be the same diameter as the shank. The diameter of the lead hole for the threaded part varies with the density of the wood: For low-density softwoods, such as the cedars and white pines, 40% to 70% of the shank diameter; for Douglas-fir and Southern Pine, 60% to 75%; and for dense hardwoods, such as oaks, 65% to 85%. The smaller percentage in each range applies to lag screws of the smaller diameters and the larger

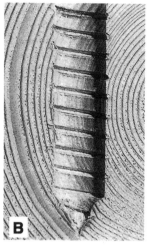

Figure 7–6. A, Clean-cut, deep penetration of thread made by lag screw turned into a lead hole of proper size, and B, rough, shallow penetration of thread made by lag screw turned into oversized lead hole.

Table 7–10. Multiplication factors for loads computed from Equation (7–15)

Ratio of thickness of side member to shank diameter of lag screw	Factor
2	0.62
2.5	0.77
3	0.93
3.5	1.00
4	1.07
4.5	1.13
5	1.18
5.5	1.21
6	1.22
6.5	1.22

Table 7–11. Multiplication factors for loads applied perpendicular to grain computed from Equation (7–15) with lag screw in side grain of wood

Shank diameter of lag screw (mm (in.))	Factor
4.8 (3/16)	1.00
6.4 (1/4)	0.97
7.9 (5/16)	0.85
9.5 (3/8)	0.76
11.1 (7/16)	0.70
12.7 (1/2)	0.65
15.9 (5/8)	0.60
19.0 (3/4)	0.55
22.2 (7/8)	0.52
25.4 (1)	0.50

percentage to lag screws of larger diameters. Soap or similar lubricants should be used on the screw to facilitate turning, and lead holes slightly larger than those recommended for maximum efficiency should be used with long screws.

In determining the withdrawal resistance, the allowable tensile strength of the lag screw at the net (root) section should not be exceeded. Penetration of the threaded part to a distance about seven times the shank diameter in the denser species (specific gravity greater than 0.61) and 10 to 12 times the shank diameter in the less dense species (specific gravity less than 0.42) will develop approximately the ultimate tensile strength of the lag screw. Penetrations at intermediate densities may be found by straight-line interpolation.

The resistance to withdrawal of a lag screw from the end-grain surface of a piece of wood is about three-fourths as great as its resistance to withdrawal from the side-grain surface of the same piece.

Lateral Resistance

Pre-1991

The experimentally determined lateral loads for lag screws inserted in the side grain and loaded parallel to the grain of a piece of seasoned wood can be computed as

$$p = KD^2 \qquad (7\text{–}15)$$

where p is proportional limit lateral load (N, lb) parallel to the grain, K a coefficient depending on the species specific gravity, and D shank diameter of the lag screw (mm, in.). Values of K for a number of specific gravity ranges can be found in Table 7–4. These coefficients are based on average results for several ranges of specific gravity for hardwoods and softwoods. The loads given by this equation apply when the thickness of the side member is 3.5 times the shank diameter of the lag screw, and the depth of penetration in the main

member is seven times the diameter in the harder woods and 11 times the diameter in the softer woods. For other thicknesses, the computed loads should be multiplied by the factors listed in Table 7–10.

The thickness of a solid wood side member should be about one-half the depth of penetration in the main member.

When the lag screw is inserted in the side grain of wood and the load is applied perpendicular to the grain, the load given by the lateral resistance equation should be multiplied by the factors listed in Table 7–11.

For other angles of loading, the loads may be computed from the parallel and perpendicular values by the use of the Scholten nomograph for determining the bearing strength of wood at various angles to the grain (Fig. 7–7).

154

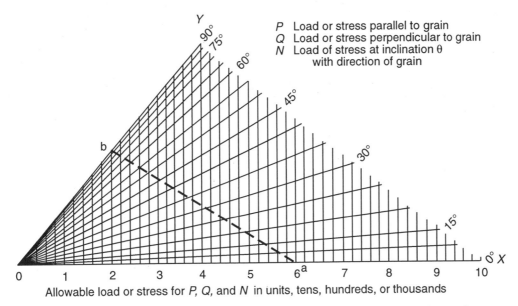

P   Load or stress parallel to grain
Q   Load or stress perpendicular to grain
N   Load of stress at inclination θ
     with direction of grain

Figure 7–7. Scholten nomograph for determining the bearing stress of wood at various angles to the grain. The dashed line *ab* refers to the example given in the text.

The nomograph provides values as given by the Hankinson equation,

$$N = \frac{PQ}{P\sin^2\theta + Q\cos^2\theta} \qquad (7\text{–}16)$$

where P is load or stress parallel to the grain, Q load or stress perpendicular to the grain, and N load or stress at an inclination θ with the direction of the grain.

Example: P, the load parallel to grain, is 6,000 lb, and Q, the load perpendicular to the grain, is 2,000 lb. The load at an angle of 40° to grain, N, is found as follows: Connect with a straight line 6,000 lb (a) on line OX of the nomograph with the intersection (b) on line OY of a vertical line through 2,000 lb. The point where line ab intersects the line representing the given angle 40° is directly above the load, 3,300 lb.

Values for lateral resistance as computed by the preceding methods are based on complete penetration of the unthreaded shank into the side member but not into the main member. When the shank penetrates the main member, the permitted increases in loads are given in Table 7–12.

When lag screws are used with metal plates, the lateral loads parallel to the grain may be increased 25%, provided the plate thickness is sufficient so that the bearing capacity of the steel is not exceeded. No increase should be made when the applied load is perpendicular to the grain.

Lag screws should not be used in end grain, because splitting may develop under lateral load. If lag screws are so used, however, the loads should be taken as two-thirds those for lateral resistance when lag screws are inserted into side grain and the loads act perpendicular to the grain.

The spacings, end and edge distances, and net section for lag screw joints should be the same as those for joints with bolts (discussed later) of a diameter equal to the shank diameter of the lag screw.

Lag screws should always be inserted by turning with a wrench, not by driving with a hammer. Soap, beeswax, or other lubricants applied to the screw, particularly with the denser wood species, will facilitate insertion and prevent damage to the threads but will not affect performance of the lag screw.

Post-1991

Lag screw lateral strength is determined by the yield model theory table similar to the procedure for bolts. Modes I, III, and IV yield may occur (Fig. 7–4). The dowel bearing

Table 7–12. Permitted increases in loads when lag screw unthreaded shank penetrates foundation member

Ratio of penetration of shank into foundation member to shank diameter	Increase in load (%)
1	8
2	17
3	26
4	33
5	36
6	38
7	39

155

strength values are based on the same parallel- and perpendicular-to-grain specific gravity equations used to establish values for bolts.

Bolts

Bearing Stress of Wood Under Bolts

The bearing stress under a bolt is computed by dividing the load on a bolt by the product LD, where L is the length of a bolt in the main member and D is the bolt diameter. Basic parallel-to-grain and perpendicular-to-grain bearing stresses have been obtained from tests of three-member wood joints where each side member is half the thickness of the main member. The side members were loaded parallel to grain for both parallel- and perpendicular-to-grain tests. Prior to 1991, bearing stress was based on test results at the proportional limit; since 1991, bearing stress is based on test results at a yield limit state, which is defined as the 5% diameter offset on the load–deformation curve (similar to Fig. 7–3).

The bearing stress at proportional limit load is largest when the bolt does not bend, that is, for joints with small L/D values. The curves of Figures 7–8 and 7–9 show the reduction in proportional limit bolt-bearing stress as L/D increases. The bearing stress at maximum load does not decrease as L/D increases, but remains fairly constant, which means that the ratio of maximum load to proportional limit load increases as L/D increases. To maintain a fairly constant ratio between maximum load and design load for bolts, the relations between bearing stress and L/D ratio have been adjusted as indicated in Figures 7–8 and 7–9.

The proportional limit bolt-bearing stress parallel to grain for small L/D ratios is approximately 50% of the small clear crushing strength for softwoods and approximately 60% for hardwoods. For bearing stress perpendicular to the grain, the ratio between bearing stress at proportional limit load and the small clear proportional limit stress in compression perpendicular to grain depends upon bolt diameter (Fig. 7–10) for small L/D ratios.

Species compressive strength also affects the L/D ratio relationship, as indicated in Figure 7–9. Relatively higher bolt proportional-limit stress perpendicular to grain is obtained with wood low in strength (proportional limit stress of 3,930 kPa (570 lb/in²)) than with material of high strength (proportional limit stress of 7,860 kPa (1,140 lb/in²)). This effect also occurs for bolt-bearing stress parallel to grain, but not to the same extent as for perpendicular-to-grain loading.

The proportional limit bolt load for a three-member joint with side members half the thickness of the main member may be estimated by the following procedures.

For parallel-to-grain loading, (a) multiply the species small clear compressive parallel strength (Tables 4–3, 4–4, or 4–5) by 0.50 for softwoods or 0.60 for hardwoods, (b) multiply this product by the appropriate factor from Figure 7–8 for the L/D ratio of the bolt, and (c) multiply this product by LD.

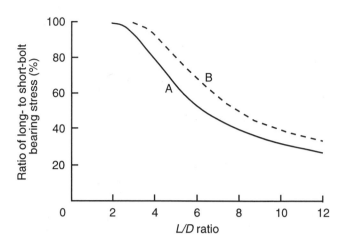

Figure 7–8. Variation in bolt-bearing stress at the proportional limit parallel to grain with L/D ratio. Curve A, relation obtained from experimental evaluation; curve B, modified relation used for establishing design loads.

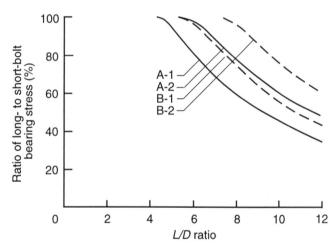

Figure 7–9. Variation in bolt-bearing stress at the proportional limit perpendicular to grain with L/D ratio. Relations obtained from experimental evaluation for materials with average compression perpendicular stress of 7,860 kPa (1,140 lb/in²) (curve A–1) and 3,930 kPa (570 lb/in²) (curve A–2). Curves B–1 and B–2, modified relations used for establishing design loads.

For perpendicular-to-grain loading, (a) multiply the species compression perpendicular-to-grain proportional limit stress (Tables 4–3, 4–4, or 4–5) by the appropriate factor from Figure 7–10, (b) multiply this product by the appropriate factor from Figure 7–9, and (c) multiply this product by LD.

Loads at an Angle to the Grain

For loads applied at an angle intermediate between those parallel to the grain and perpendicular to the grain, the bolt-bearing stress may be obtained from the nomograph in Figure 7–7.

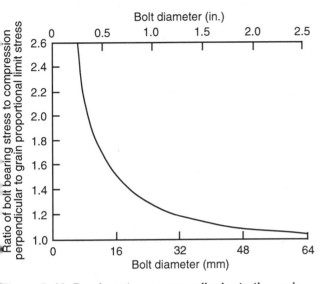

Figure 7–10. Bearing stress perpendicular to the grain as affected by bolt diameter.

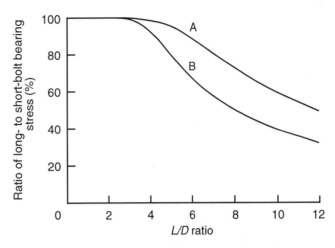

Figure 7–11. Variation in the proportional limit bolt-bearing stress parallel to grain with *L/D* ratio. Curve A, bolts with yield stress of 861.84 MPa (125,000 lb/in²); curve B, bolts with yield stress of 310.26 MPa (45,000 lb/in²).

Steel Side Plates

When steel side plates are used, the bolt-bearing stress parallel to grain at joint proportional limit is approximately 25% greater than that for wood side plates. The joint deformation at proportional limit is much smaller with steel side plates. If loads at equivalent joint deformation are compared, the load for joints with steel side plates is approximately 75% greater than that for wood side plates. Pre-1991 design criteria included increases in connection strength with steel side plates; post-1991 design criteria include steel side plate behavior in the yield model equations.

For perpendicular-to-grain loading, the same loads are obtained for wood and steel side plates.

Bolt Quality

Both the properties of the wood and the quality of the bolt are factors in determining the strength of a bolted joint. The percentages given in Figures 7–8 and 7–9 for calculating bearing stress apply to steel machine bolts with a yield stress of 310 MPa (45,000 lb/in²). Figure 7–11 indicates the increase in bearing stress parallel to grain for bolts with a yield stress of 862 MPa (125,00 lb/in²).

Effect of Member Thickness

The proportional limit load is affected by the ratio of the side member thickness to the main member thickness (Fig. 7–12).

Pre-1991 design values for bolts are based on joints with the side member half the thickness of the main member. The usual practice in design of bolted joints is to take no increase in design load when the side members are greater than half the thickness of the main member. When the side members are less than half the thickness of the main member, a design

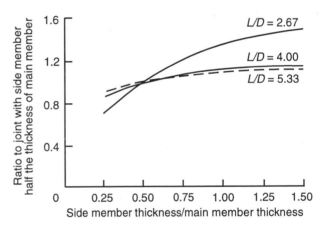

Figure 7–12. Proportional limit load related to side member thickness for three-member joints. Center member thickness was 50.8 mm (2 in.).

load for a main member that is twice the thickness of the side member is used. Post-1991 design values include member thickness directly in the yield model equations.

Two-Member, Multiple-Member Joints

In pre-1991 design, the proportional limit load was taken as half the load for a three-member joint with a main member the same thickness as the thinnest member for two-member joints.

For four or more members in a joint, the proportional limit load was taken as the sum of the loads for the individual shear planes by treating each shear plane as an equivalent two-member joint.

Post-1991 design for joints with four or more members also results in values per shear plane. Connection strength for any number of members is conservatively found by multiplying the value for the weakest shear plane by the number of shear planes.

Spacing, Edge, and End Distance

The center-to-center distance along the grain should be at least four times the bolt diameter for parallel-to-grain loading. The minimum center-to-center spacing of bolts in the across-the-grain direction for loads acting through metal side plates and parallel to the grain need only be sufficient to permit the tightening of the nuts. For wood side plates, the spacing is controlled by the rules applying to loads acting parallel to grain if the design load approaches the bolt-bearing capacity of the side plates. When the design load is less than the bolt-bearing capacity of the side plates, the spacing may be reduced below that required to develop their maximum capacity.

When a joint is in tension, the bolt nearest the end of a timber should be at a distance from the end of at least seven times the bolt diameter for softwoods and five times for hardwoods. When the joint is in compression, the end margin may be four times the bolt diameter for both softwoods and hardwoods. Any decrease in these spacings and margins will decrease the load in about the same ratio.

For bolts bearing parallel to the grain, the distance from the edge of a timber to the center of a bolt should be at least 1.5 times the bolt diameter. This margin, however, will usually be controlled by (a) the common practice of having an edge margin equal to one-half the distance between bolt rows and (b) the area requirements at the critical section. (The critical section is that section of the member taken at right angles to the direction of load, which gives the maximum stress in the member based on the net area remaining after reductions are made for bolt holes at that section.) For parallel-to-grain loading in softwoods, the net area remaining at the critical section should be at least 80% of the total area in bearing under all the bolts in the particular joint under consideration; in hardwoods it should be 100%.

For bolts bearing perpendicular to the grain, the margin between the edge toward which the bolt pressure is acting and the center of the bolt or bolts nearest this edge should be at least four times the bolt diameter. The margin at the opposite edge is relatively unimportant.

Effect of Bolt Holes

The bearing strength of wood under bolts is affected considerably by the size and type of bolt holes into which the bolts are inserted. A bolt hole that is too large causes nonuniform bearing of the bolt; if the bolt hole is too small, the wood will split when the bolt is driven. Normally, bolts should fit so that they can be inserted by tapping lightly with a wood mallet. In general, the smoother the hole, the higher the bearing values will be (Fig. 7–13). Deformations

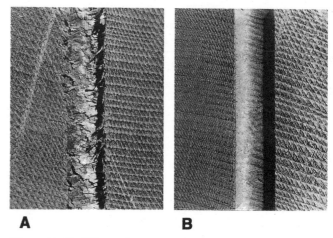

A   **B**

Figure 7–13. Effect of rate of feed and drill speed on the surface condition of bolt holes drilled in Sitka spruce. A, hole was bored with a twist drill rotating at a peripheral speed of 7.62 m/min (300 in/min); feed rate was 1.52 m/min (60 in/min). B, hole was bored with the same drill at a peripheral speed of 31.75 m/min (1,250 in/min); feed rate was 50.8 mm/min (2 in/min).

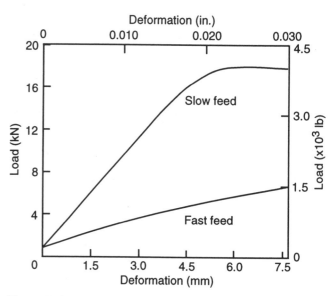

Figure 7–14. Typical load–deformation curves showing the effect of surface condition of bolt holes, resulting from a slow feed rate and a fast feed rate, on the deformation in a joint when subjected to loading under bolts. The surface conditions of the bolt holes were similar to those illustrated in Figure 7–13.

accompanying the load are also less with a smoother bolt-hole surface (Fig. 7–14).

Rough holes are caused by using dull bits and improper rates of feed and drill speed. A twist drill operated at a peripheral speed of approximately 38 m/min (1,500 in/min) produces uniformly smooth holes at moderate feed rates. The rate of feed depends upon the diameter of the drill and the speed of rotation but should enable the drill to cut rather than tear the wood. The drill should produce shavings, not chips.

Proportional limit loads for joints with bolt holes the same diameter as the bolt will be slightly higher than for joints with a 1.6-mm (1/16-in.) oversized hole. However, if drying takes place after assembly of the joint, the proportional limit load for snug-fitting bolts will be considerably less due to the effects of shrinkage.

Pre-1991 Allowable Loads

The following procedures are used to calculate allowable bolt loads for joints with wood side members, each half the thickness of the main member.

Parallel to Grain—The starting point for parallel-to-grain bolt values is the maximum green crushing strength for the species or group of species. Procedures outlined in ASTM D2555 are used to establish a 5% exclusion value. The exclusion value is divided by a factor of 1.9 to adjust to a 10-year normal duration of load and provide a factor of safety. This value is multiplied by 1.20 to adjust to a seasoned strength. The resulting value is called the basic bolt-bearing stress parallel to grain.

The basic bolt-bearing stress is then adjusted for the effects of L/D ratio. Table 7–13 gives the percentage of basic stress for three classes of species. The particular class for the species is determined from the basic bolt-bearing stress as indicated in Table 7–14. The adjusted bearing stress is further multiplied

Table 7–13. Percentage of basic bolt-bearing stress used for calculating allowable bolt loads

Ratio of bolt length to diameter (L/D)	L/D adjustment factor by class[a]						
	Parallel to grain			Perpendicular to grain			
	1	2	3	1	2	3	4
1	100.0	100.0	100.0	100.0	100.0	100.0	100.0
2	100.0	100.0	100.0	100.0	100.0	100.0	100.0
3	100.0	100.0	99.0	100.0	100.0	100.0	100.0
4	99.5	97.4	92.5	100.0	100.0	100.0	100.0
5	95.4	88.3	80.0	100.0	100.0	100.0	100.0
6	85.6	75.8	67.2	100.0	100.0	100.0	96.3
7	73.4	65.0	57.6	100.0	100.0	97.3	86.9
8	64.2	56.9	50.4	100.0	96.1	88.1	75.0
9	57.1	50.6	44.8	94.6	86.3	76.7	64.6
10	51.4	45.5	40.3	85.0	76.2	67.2	55.4
11	46.7	41.4	36.6	76.1	67.6	59.3	48.4
12	42.8	37.9	33.6	68.6	61.0	52.0	42.5
13	39.5	35.0	31.0	62.2	55.3	45.9	37.5

[a]Class determined from basic bolt-bearing stress according to Table 7–14.

Table 7–14. L/D adjustment class associated with basic bolt-bearing stress

Loading direction	Basic bolt-bearing stress for species group (MPa (lb/in²))		L/D adjustment (Table 7–13)
	Softwoods	Hardwoods	
Parallel	<7.93 (<1,150)	<7.33 (<1,063)	1
	7.93–10.37 (1,150–1,504)	7.33–9.58 (1,063–1,389)	2
	>10.37 (>1,504)	>9.58 (>1,389)	3
Perpendicular	<1.31 (<190)	<1.44 (<209)	1
	1.31–2.00 (190–290)	1.44–2.20 (209–319)	2
	2.00–2.59 (291–375)	2.21–2.84 (320–412)	3
	>2.59 (>375)	>2.84 (>412)	4

by a factor of 0.80 to adjust to wood side plates. The allowable bolt load in pounds is then determined by multiplying by the projected bolt area, *LD*.

Perpendicular to Grain—The starting point for perpendicular-to-grain bolt values is the average green proportional limit stress in compression perpendicular to grain. Procedures in ASTM D2555 are used to establish compression perpendicular values for groups of species. The average proportional limit stress is divided by 1.5 for ring position (growth rings neither parallel nor perpendicular to load during test) and a factor of safety. This value is then multiplied by 1.20 to adjust to a seasoned strength and by 1.10 to adjust to a normal duration of load. The resulting value is called the basic bolt-bearing stress perpendicular to grain.

The basic bolt-bearing stress is then adjusted for the effects of bolt diameter (Table 7–15) and *L/D* ratio (Table 7–13). The allowable bolt load is then determined by multiplying the adjusted basic bolt-bearing stress by the projected bolt area, *LD*.

Post-1991 Yield Model

The empirical design approach used prior to 1991 was based on a tabular value for a single bolt in a wood-to-wood, three-member connection where the side members are each a minimum of one-half the thickness of the main member. The single-bolt value must then be modified for any variation from these reference conditions. The theoretical approach, after 1991, is more general and is not limited to these reference conditions.

The theoretical approach is based on work done in Europe (Johansen 1949) and is referred to as the European Yield Model (EYM). The EYM describes a number of possible yield modes that can occur in a dowel-type connection (Fig. 7–4). The yield strength of these different modes is determined from a static analysis that assumes the wood and the bolt are both perfectly plastic. The yield mode that results in the lowest yield load for a given geometry is the theoretical connection yield load.

Equations corresponding to the yield modes for a three-member joint are given in Table 7–16. (Equations for two-member allowable values are given in the AF&PA *National Design Specification for Wood Construction*) The nominal single-bolt value is dependent on the joint geometry (thickness of main and side members), bolt diameter and bending yield strength, dowel bearing strength, and direction of load to the grain. The equations are equally valid for wood or steel side members, which is taken into account by thickness and dowel bearing strength parameters. The equations are also valid for various load-to-grain directions, which are taken into account by the K_θ and F_e parameter.

The dowel bearing strength is a material property not generally familiar to structural designers. The dowel bearing strength of the wood members is determined from tests that relate species specific gravity and dowel diameter to bearing strength. Empirical equations for these relationships are as follows:

Parallel to grain

$$F_e = 77.2G \qquad \text{(metric)} \qquad (7\text{–}17a)$$

$$F_e = 11,200\,G \qquad \text{(inch–pound)} \qquad (7\text{–}17b)$$

Perpendicular to grain

$$F_e = 212.0G^{1.45}D^{-0.5} \qquad \text{(metric)} \qquad (7\text{–}18a)$$

$$F_e = 6,100G^{1.45}D^{-0.5} \qquad \text{(inch–pound)} \qquad (7\text{–}18b)$$

where F_e is dowel bearing strength (MPa, lb/in^2), G specific gravity based on ovendry weight and volume, and D bolt diameter (mm, in.).

Connector Joints

Several types of connectors have been devised that increase joint bearing and shear areas by utilizing rings or plates around bolts holding joint members together. The primary load-carrying portions of these joints are the connectors; the bolts usually serve to prevent transverse separation of the members but do contribute some load-carrying capacity.

The strength of the connector joint depends on the type and size of the connector, the species of wood, the thickness and width of the member, the distance of the connector from the end of the member, the spacing of the connectors, the direction of application of the load with respect to the direction of the grain of the wood, and other factors. Loads for wood joints with steel connectors—split ring (Fig. 7–15) and shear plate (Fig. 7–16)—are discussed in this section. These connectors require closely fitting machined grooves in the wood members.

Parallel-to-Grain Loading

Tests have demonstrated that the density of the wood is a controlling factor in the strength of connector joints. For split-ring connectors, both maximum load and proportional limit load parallel to grain vary linearly with specific gravity (Figs. 7–17 and 7–18). For shear plates, the maximum load and proportional limit load vary linearly with specific gravity for the less dense species (Figs. 7–19 and 7–20). In the higher density species, the shear strength of the bolts becomes the controlling factor. These relations were obtained for seasoned members, approximately 12% moisture content.

Perpendicular-to-Grain Loading

Loads for perpendicular-to-grain loading have been established using three-member joints with the side members loaded parallel to grain. Specific gravity is a good indicator of perpendicular-to-grain strength of timber connector joints. For split-ring connectors, the proportional limit loads perpendicular to grain are 58% of the parallel-to-grain proportional limit loads. The joint deformation at proportional limit is 30% to 50% more than for parallel-to-grain loading.

Table 7–15. Factors for adjusting basic bolt-bearing stress perpendicular to grain for bolt diameter when calculating allowable bolt loads

Bolt diameter (mm (in.))		Adjustment factor
6.35	(1/4)	2.50
9.53	(3/8)	1.95
12.70	(1/2)	1.68
15.88	(5/8)	1.52
19.05	(3/4)	1.41
22.23	(7/8)	1.33
25.40	(1)	1.27
31.75	(1-1/4)	1.19
38.10	(1-1/2)	1.14
44.45	(1-3/4)	1.10
50.80	(2)	1.07
63.50	(2-1/2)	1.03
>76.20	(>3 or over)	1.00

Table 7–16. The 5% offset yield lateral strength (Z) for three-member bolted joints

Mode	Z value for three-member bolted joint
Mode I$_m$	$\dfrac{Dt_m F_{em}}{K_\theta}$
Mode I$_s$	$\dfrac{2Dt_s F_{es}}{K_\theta}$
Mode III$_s$	$\dfrac{2k_4 Dt_s F_{em}}{(2+R_e)K_\theta}$
Mode IV	$\dfrac{2D^2}{K_\theta}\sqrt{\dfrac{2F_{em}F_{yb}}{3(1+R_e)}}$

Definitions

D nominal bolt diameter, mm (in.)
F_{em} dowel bearing strength of main (center) member, kPa (lb/in^2)
F_{es} dowel bearing strength of side members, kPa (lb/in^2)
F_{yb} bending yield strength of bolt, kPa (lb/in^2)
K_θ $1 + \theta/360$
t_m thickness of main (center) member, mm (in.)
t_s thickness of side member, mm (in.)
Z nominal single bolt design value
θ angle of load to grain (degrees)
R_e $= F_{em}/F_{es}$

$$k_4 = -1 + \sqrt{\frac{2(1+R_e)}{R_e} + \frac{2F_{yb}(2+R_e)D^2}{3F_{em}t_s^2}}$$

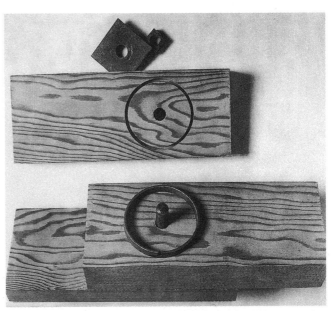

Figure 7–15. Joint with split-ring connector showing connector, precut groove, bolt, washer, and nut.

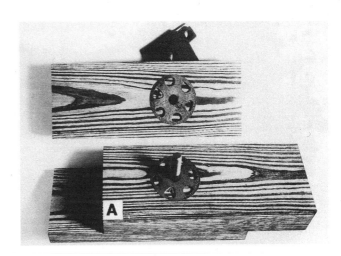

Figure 7–16. Joints with shear-plate connectors with (A) wood side plates and (B) steel side plates.

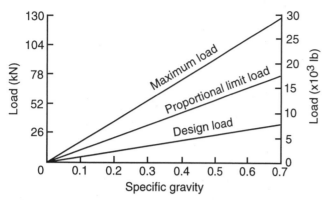

Figure 7–17. Relation between load bearing parallel to grain and specific gravity (ovendry weight, volume at test) for two 63.5-mm (2-1/2-in.) split rings with a single 12.7-mm (1/2-in.) bolt in air-dry material. Center member was thickness 101.6 mm (4 in.) and side member thickness was 50.8 mm (2 in.).

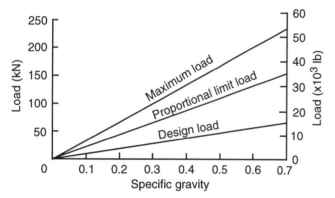

Figure 7–18. Relation between load bearing parallel to grain and specific gravity (ovendry weight, volume at test) for two 101.6-mm (4-in.) split rings and a single 19.1-mm- (3/4-in.-) diameter bolt in air-dry material. Center member thickness was 127.0 mm (5 in.) and side member thickness was 63.5 mm (2-1/2 in.).

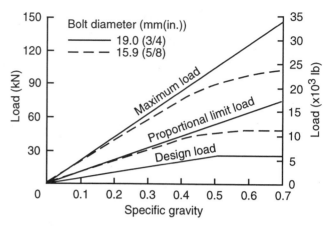

Figure 7–19. Relation between load bearing parallel to grain and specific gravity (ovendry weight, volume at test) for two 66.7-mm (2-5/8-in.) shear plates in air-dry material with steel side plates. Center member thickness was 76.2 mm (3 in.).

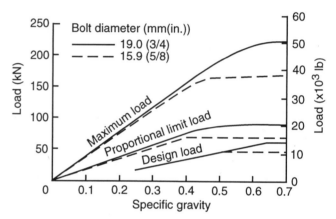

Figure 7–20. Relation between load bearing parallel to grain and specific gravity (ovendry weight, volume at test) for two 101.6-mm (4-in.) shear plates in air-dry material with steel side plates. Center member thickness was 88.9 mm (3-1/2 in.).

For shear-plate connectors, the proportional limit and maximum loads vary linearly with specific gravity (Figs. 7–21 and 7–22). The wood strength controls the joint strength for all species.

Design Loads

Design loads for parallel-to-grain loading have been established by dividing ultimate test loads by an average factor of 4. This gives values that do not exceed five-eighths of the proportional limit loads. The reduction accounts for variability in material, a reduction to long-time loading, and a factor of safety. Design loads for normal duration of load are 10% higher.

For perpendicular-to-grain loading, ultimate load is given less consideration and greater dependence placed on load at

proportional limit. For split rings, the proportional limit load is reduced by approximately half. For shear plates, the design loads are approximately five-eighths of the proportional limit test loads. These reductions again account for material variability, a reduction to long-time loading, and a factor of safety.

Design loads are presented in Figures 7–17 to 7–22. In practice, four wood species groups have been established, based primarily on specific gravity, and design loads assigned for each group. Species groupings for connectors are presented in Table 7–17. The corresponding design loads (for long-continued load) are given in Table 7–18. The *National Design Specification for Wood Construction* gives design values for normal-duration load for these and additional species.

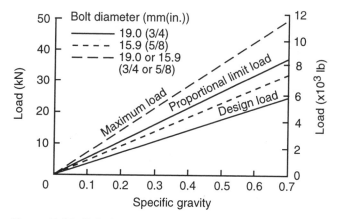

Figure 7–21. Relation between load bearing perpendicular to grain and specific gravity (ovendry weight, volume at test) for two 66.7-mm (2-5/8-in.) shear plates in air-dry material with steel side plates. Center member thickness was 76.2 mm (3 in.).

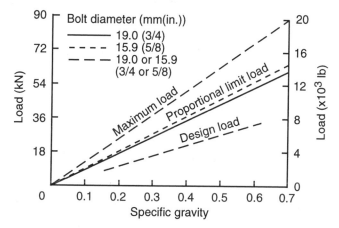

Figure 7–22. Relation between load bearing perpendicular to grain and specific gravity (ovendry weight, volume at test) for two 101.6-mm (4-in.) shear plates in air-dry material with steel side plates. Center member thickness was 88.9 mm (3-1/2 in.).

Modifications

Some factors that affect the loads of connectors were taken into account in deriving the tabular values. Other varied and extreme conditions require modification of the values.

Steel Side Plates

Steel side plates are often used with shear-plate connectors. The loads parallel to grain have been found to be approximately 10% higher than those with wood side plates. The perpendicular-to-grain loads are unchanged.

Exposure and Moisture Condition of Wood

The loads listed in Table 7–18 apply to seasoned members used where they will remain dry. If the wood will be more or less continuously damp or wet in use, two-thirds of the

Table 7–17. Species groupings for connector loads[a]

Connector	Species or species group		
Group 1	Aspen	Basswood	Cottonwood
	Western redcedar	Balsam fir	White fir
	Eastern hemlock	Eastern white pine	Ponderosa pine
	Sugar pine	Western white pine	Engelmann spruce
Group 2	Chestnut	Yellow-poplar	Baldcypress
	Yellow-cedar	Port-Orford-cedar	Western hemlock
	Red pine	Redwood	Red spruce
	Sitka spruce	White spruce	
Group 3	Elm, American	Elm, slippery	Maple, soft
	Sweetgum	Sycamore	Tupelo
	Douglas-fir	Larch, western	Southern Pine
Group 4	Ash, white	Beech	Birch
	Elm, rock	Hickory	Maple, hard
	Oak		

[a]Group 1 woods provide the weakest connector joints; group 4 woods, the strongest.

tabulated values should be used. The amount by which the loads should be reduced to adapt them to other conditions of use depends upon the extent to which the exposure favors decay, the required life of the structure or part, the frequency and thoroughness of inspection, the original cost and the cost of replacements, the proportion of sapwood and durability of the heartwood of the species (if untreated), and the character and efficiency of any treatment. These factors should be evaluated for each individual design. Industry recommendations for the use of connectors when the condition of the lumber is other than continuously wet or continuously dry are given in the *National Design Specification for Wood Construction.*

Ordinarily, before fabrication of connector joints, members should be seasoned to a moisture content corresponding as nearly as practical to that which they will attain in service. This is particularly desirable for lumber for roof trusses and other structural units used in dry locations and in which shrinkage is an important factor. Urgent construction needs sometimes result in the erection of structures and structural units employing green or inadequately seasoned lumber with connectors. Because such lumber subsequently dries out in most buildings, causing shrinkage and opening the joints, adequate maintenance measures must be adopted. The maintenance for connector joints in green lumber should include inspection of the structural units and tightening of all bolts as needed during the time the units are coming to moisture equilibrium, which is normally during the first year.

Table 7–18. Design loads for one connector in a joint[a]

	Minimum thickness of wood member (mm (in.))		Minimum width all members (mm (in.))	Load (N (lb))							
				Group 1 woods		Group 2 woods		Group 3 woods		Group 4 woods	
Connector	With one connector only	With two connectors in opposite faces, one bolt[b]		At 0° angle to grain	At 90° angle to grain	At 0° angle to grain	At 90° angle to grain	At 0° angle to grain	At 90° angle to grain	At 0° angle to grain	At 90° angle to grain
Split ring											
63.5-mm (2-1/2-in.) diameter, 19.0 mm (3/4 in.) wide, with 12.7-mm (1/2-in.) bolt	25 (1)	51 (2)	89 (3-1/2)	7,940 (1,785)	4,693 (1,055)	9,274 (2,085)	5,471 (1,230)	11,032 (2,480)	6,561 (1,475)	12,789 (2,875)	7,673 (1,725)
101.6-mm (4-in.) diameter, 25.4 mm (1 in.) wide, with 19.0-mm (3/4-in.) bolt	38 (1-1/2)	76 (3)	140 (5-1/2)	15,324 (3,445)	8,874 (1,995)	17,726 (3,985)	10,275 (2,310)	21,262 (4,780)	12,344 (2,775)	24,821 (5,580)	14,390 (3,235)
Shear plate											
66.7-mm (2-5/8-in.) diameter, 10.7 mm (0.42 in.) wide, with 19.0-mm (3/4-in.) bolt	38 (1-1/2)	67 (2-5/8)	89 (3-1/2)	8,407 (1,890)	4,871 (1,095)	9,742 (2,190)	5,649 (1,270)	11,699 (2,630)	6,784 (1,525)	11,854 (2,665)	7,918 (1,780)
101.6-mm (4-in.) diameter,16.2 mm (0.64 in.) wide, with 19.0-mm or 22.2-mm (3/4- or 7/8-in.) bolt	44 (1-3/4)	92 (3-518)	140 (5-1/2)	12,677 (2,850)	7,362 (1,655)	14,701 (3,305)	8,518 (1,915)	17,637 (3,965)	10,231 (2,300)	20,573 (4,625)	11,943 (2,685)

[a]The loads apply to seasoned timbers in dry, inside locations for a long-continued load. It is also assumed that the joints are properly designed with respect to such features as centering of connectors, adequate end distance, and suitable spacing. Group 1 woods provide the weakest connector joints, group 4 woods the strongest. Species groupings are given in Table 7–17.
[b]A three-member assembly with two connectors takes double the loads indicated.

Grade and Quality of Lumber

The lumber for which the loads for connectors are applicable should conform to the general requirements in regard to quality of structural lumber given in the grading rule books of lumber manufacturers' associations for various commercial species.

The loads for connectors were obtained from tests of joints whose members were clear and free from checks, shakes, and splits. Cross grain at the joint should not be steeper than 1 in 10, and knots in the connector area should be accounted for as explained under Net Section.

Loads at Angle with Grain

The loads for the split-ring and shear-plate connectors for angles of 0° to 90° between direction of load and grain may be obtained by the Hankinson equation (Eq. (7–16)) or by the nomograph in Figure 7–7.

Thickness of Member

The relationship between the loads for the different thicknesses of lumber is based on test results for connector joints. The least thickness of member given in Table 7–18 for the various sizes of connectors is the minimum to obtain optimum load. The loads listed for each type and size of connector are the maximum loads to be used for all thicker lumber. The loads for wood members of thicknesses less than those listed can be obtained by the percentage reductions indicated in Figure 7–23. Thicknesses below those indicated by the curves should not be used.

When one member contains a connector in only one face, loads for thicknesses less than those listed in Table 7–18 can be obtained by the percentage reductions indicated in Figure 7–23 using an assumed thickness equal to twice the actual member thickness.

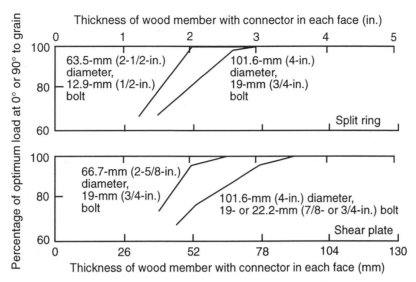

Figure 7–23. Effect of thickness of wood member on the optimum load capacity of a timber connector.

Width of Member

The width of member listed for each type and size of connector is the minimum that should be used. When the connectors are bearing parallel to the grain, no increase in load occurs with an increase in width. When they are bearing perpendicular to the grain, the load increases about 10% for each 25-mm (1-in.) increase in width of member over the minimum widths required for each type and size of connector, up to twice the diameter of the connectors. When the connector is placed off center and the load is applied continuously in one direction only, the proper load can be determined by considering the width of member as equal to twice the edge distance (the distance between the center of the connector and the edge of the member toward which the load is acting). The distance between the center of the connector and the opposite edge should not, however, be less than half the permissible minimum width of the member.

Net Section

The net section is the area remaining at the critical section after subtracting the projected area of the connectors and bolt from the full cross-sectional area of the member. For sawn timbers, the stress in the net area (whether in tension or compression) should not exceed the stress for clear wood in compression parallel to the grain. In using this stress, it is assumed that knots do not occur within a length of half the diameter of the connector from the net section. If knots are present in the longitudinal projection of the net section within a length from the critical section of one-half the diameter of the connector, the area of the knots should be subtracted from the area of the critical section.

In laminated timbers, knots may occur in the inner laminations at the connector location without being apparent from the outside of the member. It is impractical to assure that

there are no knots at or near the connector. In laminated construction, therefore, the stress at the net section is limited to the compressive stress for the member, accounting for the effect of knots.

End Distance and Spacing

The load values in Table 7–18 apply when the distance of the connector from the end of the member (end distance e) and the spacing s between connectors in multiple joints are not factors affecting the strength of the joint (Fig. 7–24A). When the end distance or spacing for connectors bearing parallel to the grain is less than that required to develop the full load, the proper reduced load may be obtained by multiplying the loads in Table 7–18 by the appropriate strength ratio given in Table 7–19. For example, the load for a 102-mm (4-in.) split-ring connector bearing parallel to the grain, when placed 178 mm or more (7 in. or more) from the end of a Douglas-fir tension member that is 38 mm (1-1/2 in.) thick is 21.3 kN (4,780 lb). When the end distance is only 133 mm (5-1/4 in.), the strength ratio obtained by direct interpolation between 178 and 89 mm (7 and 3-1/2 in.) in Table 7–19 is 0.81, and the load equals 0.81 times 21.3 (4,780) or 17.2 kN (3,870 lb).

Placement of Multiple Connectors

Preliminary investigations of the placement of connectors in a multiple-connector joint, together with the observed behavior of single-connector joints tested with variables that simulate those in a multiple-connector joint, are the basis for some suggested design practices.

When two or more connectors in the same face of a member are in a line at right angles to the grain of the member and

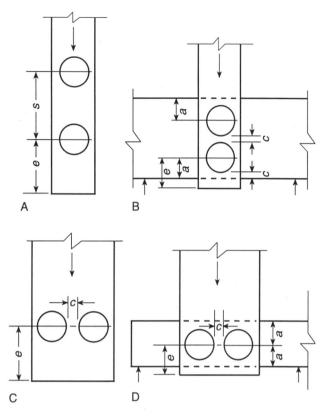

Figure 7–24. Types of multiple-connector joints: A, joint strength depends on end distance e and connector spacing s; B, joint strength depends on e, clear c, and edge a distances; C, joint strength depends on end e and clear c distances; D, joint strength depends on end e, clear c, and edge a distances.

are bearing parallel to the grain (Fig. 7–24C), the clear distance c between the connectors should not be less than 12.7 mm (1/2 in.). When two or more connectors are acting perpendicular to the grain and are spaced on a line at right angles to the length of the member (Fig. 7–24B), the rules for the width of member and edge distances used with one connector are applicable to the edge distances for multiple connectors. The clear distance c between the connectors should be equal to the clear distance from the edge of the member toward which the load is acting to the connector nearest this edge.

In a joint with two or more connectors spaced on a line parallel to the grain and with the load acting perpendicular to the grain (Fig. 7–24D), the available data indicate that the load for multiple connectors is not equal to the sum of the loads for individual connectors. Somewhat more favorable results can be obtained if the connectors are staggered so that they do not act along the same line with respect to the grain of the transverse member. Industry recommendations for various angle-to-grain loadings and spacings are given in the *National Design Specification for Wood Construction.*

Cross Bolts

Cross bolts or stitch bolts placed at or near the end of members joined with connectors or at points between connectors will provide additional safety. They may also be used to reinforce members that have, through change in moisture content in service, developed splits to an undesirable degree.

Multiple-Fastener Joints

When fasteners are used in rows parallel to the direction of loading, total joint load is unequally distributed among fasteners in the row. Simplified methods of analysis have been developed to predict the load distribution among the fasteners in a row. These analyses indicate that the load distribution is a function of (a) the extensional stiffness EA of the joint members, where E is modulus of elasticity and A is gross cross-sectional area, (b) the fastener spacing, (c) the number of fasteners, and (d) the single-fastener load-deformation characteristics.

Theoretically, the two end fasteners carry a majority of the load. For example, in a row of six bolts, the two end bolts will carry more than 50% of the total joint load. Adding bolts to a row tends to reduce the load on the less heavily loaded interior bolts. The most even distribution of bolt loads occurs in a joint where the extensional stiffness of the main member is equal to that of both splice plates. Increasing the fastener spacing tends to put more of the joint load on the end fasteners. Load distribution tends to be worse for stiffer fasteners.

The actual load distribution in field-fabricated joints is difficult to predict. Small misalignment of fasteners, variations in spacing between side and main members, and variations in single-fastener load–deformation characteristics can cause the load distribution to be different than predicted by the theoretical analyses.

For design purposes, modification factors for application to a row of bolts, lag screws, or timber connectors have been developed based on the theoretical analyses. Tables are given in the *National Design Specification for Wood Construction.*

A design equation was developed to replace the double entry required in the *National Design Specification for Wood Construction* tables. This equation was obtained by algebraic simplification of the Lantos analysis that these tables are based on

$$C_g = \left[\frac{m(1 - m^{2n})}{n\left[(1 + R_{EA}m^n)(1+m) - 1 + m^{2n}\right]} \right] \left(\frac{1 + R_{EA}}{1 - m} \right) \quad (7\text{--}19)$$

where C_g is modification factor, n number of fasteners in a row, R_{EA} the lesser of $(E_sA_s)/(E_mA_m)$ or $(E_mA_m)/(E_sA_s)$, E_m

Table 7–19. Strength ratio for connectors for various longitudinal spacings and end distances[a]

Connector diameter (mm (in.))	Spacing[c] (mm (in.))	Spacing strength ratio	End distance[b] (mm (in.))		End distance strength ratio
			Tension member	Compression member	
Split-ring					
63.5 (2-1/2)	171.4+ (6-3/4+)	100	139.7+ (5-1/2+)	101.6+ (4+)	100
63.5 (2-1/2)	85.7 (3-3/8)	50	69.8 (2-3/4)	63.5 (2-1/2)	62
101.6 (4)	228.6+ (9+)	100	177.8+ (7+)	139.7+ (5-1/2+)	100
101.6 (4)	123.8 (4-7/8)	50	88.9 (3-1/2)	82.6 (3-1/4)	62
Shear-plate					
66.7 (2-5/8)	171.4+ (6-3/4+)	100	139.7+(5-1/2+)	101.6+ (4+)	100
66.7 (2-5/8)	85.7 (3-3/8)	50	69.8 (2-3/4)	63.5 (2-1/2)	62
101.6 (4)	228.6+ (9+)	100	177.8+ (7+)	139.7+ (5-1/2+)	100
101.6 (4)	114.3 (4-1/2)	50	88.9 (3-1/2)	82.6 (3-1/4)	62

[a]Strength ratio for spacings and end distances intermediate to those listed may be obtained by interpolation and multiplied by the loads in Table 7–18 to obtain design load. The strength ratio applies only to those connector units affected by the respective spacings or end distances. The spacings and end distances should not be less than the minimum shown.
[b]End distance is distance from center of connector to end of member (Fig. 7–24A).
[c]Spacing is distance from center to center of connectors (Fig. 7–24A).

modulus of elasticity of main member, E_s modulus of elasticity of side members, A_m gross cross-sectional area of main member, A_s sum of gross cross-sectional areas of side members, $m = u - \sqrt{u^2 - 1}$, $u = 1 + \gamma(s/2)(1/E_m A_m + 1/E_s A_s)$, s center-to-center spacing between adjacent fasteners in a row, and γ load/slip modulus for a single fastener connection. For 102-mm (4-in.) split-ring or shear-plate connectors,

$$\gamma = 87,560 \text{ kN/m} \quad (500,000 \text{ lb/in})$$

For 64-mm (2-1/2-in.) split ring or 67-mm (2-5/8-in.) split ring or shear plate connectors,

$$\gamma = 70,050 \text{ kN/m} \quad (400,000 \text{ lb/in})$$

For bolts or lag screws in wood-to-wood connections,

$$\gamma = 246.25 \, D^{1.5} \quad \text{(metric)}$$
$$= 180,000 \, D^{1.5} \quad \text{(inch–pound)}$$

For bolts or lag screws in wood-to-metal connections,

$$\gamma = 369.37 \, D^{1.5} \quad \text{(metric)}$$
$$= 270,000 \, D^{1.5} \quad \text{(inch–pound)}$$

where D is diameter of bolt or lag screw.

Metal Plate Connectors

Metal plate connectors, commonly called truss plates, have become a popular means of joining, especially in trussed rafters and joists. These connectors transmit loads by means of teeth, plugs, or nails, which vary from manufacturer to manufacturer. Examples of such plates are shown in Figure 7–25. Plates are usually made of light-gauge galvanized steel and have an area and shape necessary to transmit the forces on the joint. Installation of plates usually requires a hydraulic press or other heavy equipment, although some plates can be installed by hand.

Basic strength values for plate connectors are determined from load–slip curves from tension tests of two butted wood members joined with two plates. Some typical curves are shown in Figure 7–26. Design values are expressed as load per tooth, nail, plug, or unit area of plate. The smallest value as determined by two different means is the design load for normal duration of load: (1) the average load of at least five specimens at 0.38-mm (0.015-in.) slip from plate to wood member or 0.76-mm (0.030-in.) slip from member to member is divided by 1.6; (2) the average ultimate load of at least five specimens is divided by 3.0.

The strength of a metal plate joint may also be controlled by the tensile or shear strength of the plate.

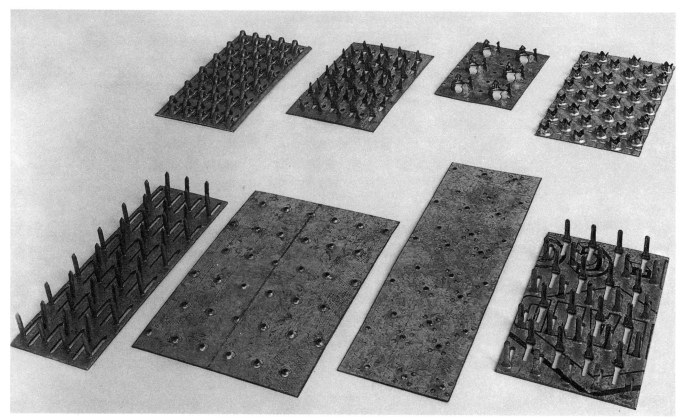

Figure 7–25. Some typical metal plate connectors.

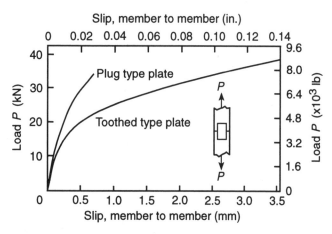

Figure 7–26. Typical load–slip curves for two types of metal plate connectors loaded in tension.

Fastener Head Embedment

The bearing strength of wood under fastener heads is important in such applications as the anchorage of building framework to foundation structures. When pressure tends to pull the framing member away from the foundation, the fastening loads could cause tensile failure of the fastenings, withdrawal of the fastenings from the framing member, or embedment of the fastener heads in the member. The fastener head could even be pulled completely through.

The maximum load for fastener head embedment is related to the fastener head perimeter, while loads at low embedments (1.27 mm (0.05 in.)) are related to the fastener head bearing area. These relations for several species at 10% moisture content are shown in Figures 7–27 and 7–28.

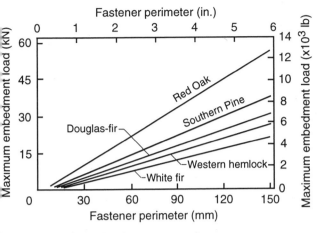

Figure 7–27. Relation between maximum embedment load and fastener perimeter for several species of wood.

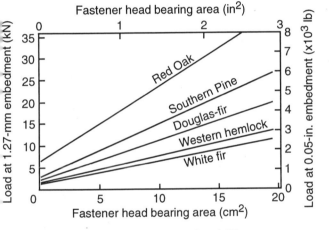

Figure 7–28. Relation between load at 1.27-mm (0.05-in.) embedment and fastener bearing area for several species.

References

AF&PA. 1997. National design specification for wood construction. Washington, DC: American Forest & Paper Association.

ASCE. 1995. Standard for load and resistance factor design (LRFD) for engineered wood construction. Washington, DC: American Society of Civil Engineers.

ASCE. 1996. Mechanical connections in wood structures. Washington, DC: American Society of Civil Engineers.

ASTM. (current edition). Philadelphia, PA: American Society for Testing and Materials.

ASTM F1667. Specification for driven fasteners: nails, spiker, staples.

ASTM D2555–96. Standard methods for establishing clear wood strength values.

ASTM F547. Standard terminology of nails for use with wood and wood-base materials.

ASTM D5652–95. Standard test methods for bolted connections in wood and wood-base products.

ASTM D1761–88. Standard test methods for mechanical fasteners in wood.

Anderson, L.O. 1959. Nailing better wood boxes and crates. Agric. Handb. 160. Washington, DC: U.S. Department of Agriculture.

Anderson, L.O. 1970. Wood-frame house construction. Agric. Handb. 73 (rev.). Washington, DC: U.S. Department of Agriculture.

Cramer, C.O. 1968. Load distribution in multiple-bolt tension joints. Proc. Pap. 5939. Journal of Structural Division, American Society of Civil Engineers. 94(ST5): 11011117.

Doyle, D.V.; Scholten, J.A. 1963. Performance of bolted joints in Douglas-fir. Res. Pap. FPL 2. Madison, WI: U.S. Department of Agriculture, Forest Service, Forest Products Laboratory.

Eckelman, C.A. 1975. Screw holding performance in hardwoods and particleboard. Forest Products Journal. 25(6): 30–35.

Fairchild, I.J. 1926. Holding power of wood screws. Technol. Pap. 319. Washington, DC: U.S. National Bureau of Standards.

Forest Products Laboratory. 1962. General observations on the nailing of wood. FPL Tech. Note 243. Madison, WI: U.S. Department of Agriculture, Forest Service, Forest Products Laboratory.

Forest Products Laboratory. 1964. Nailing dense hardwoods. Res. Note FPL–037. Madison, WI: U.S. Department of Agriculture, Forest Service, Forest Products Laboratory.

Forest Products Laboratory. 1965. Nail withdrawal resistance of American woods. Res. Note FPL–RN–033. Madison, WI: U.S. Department of Agriculture, Forest Service, Forest Products Laboratory.

Goodell, H.R.; Philipps, R.S. 1944. Bolt-bearing strength of wood and modified wood: effect of different methods of drilling bolt holes in wood and plywood. FPL Rep. 1523. Madison, WI: U.S. Department of Agriculture, Forest Service, Forest Products Laboratory.

Johansen, K.W. 1949. Theory of timber connections. Zurich, Switzerland: Publications of International Association for Bridge and Structural Engineering. 9: 249–262.

Jordan, C.A. 1963. Response of timber joints with metal fasteners to lateral impact loads. FPL Rep. 2263. Madison, WI: U.S. Department Agriculture, Forest Service, Forest Products Laboratory.

Kuenzi, E.W. 1951. Theoretical design of a nailed or bolted joint under lateral load. FPL Rep. 1951. Madison, WI: U.S. Department of Agriculture, Forest Service, Forest Products Laboratory.

Kurtenacker, R.S. 1965. Performance of container fasteners subjected to static and dynamic withdrawal. Res. Pap. FPL 29. Madison, WI: U.S. Department of Agriculture, Forest Service, Forest Products Laboratory.

Lantos, G. 1969. Load distribution in a row of fasteners subjected to lateral load. Madison, WI: Wood Science. 1(3): 129–136.

Markwardt, L.J. 1952. How surface condition of nails affects their holding power in wood. FPL Rep. D1927. Madison, WI: U.S. Department of Agriculture, Forest Service, Forest Products Laboratory.

Markwardt, L.J.; Gahagan, J.M. 1930. Effect of nail points on resistance to withdrawal. FPL Rep. 1226. Madison, WI: U.S. Department of Agriculture, Forest Service, Forest Products Laboratory.

Markwardt, L.J.; Gahagan, J.M. 1952. Slant driving of nails. Does it pay? Packing and Shipping. 56(10): 7–9,23,25.

McLain, T.E. 1975. Curvilinear load-slip relations in laterally-loaded nailed joints. Fort Collins, CO: Department of Forestry and Wood Science, Colorado State University. Thesis.

NPA. 1968. Screw holding of particleboard. Tech. Bull. 3. Washington, DC: National Particleboard Association.

Newlin, J.A.; Gahagan, J.M. 1938. Lag screw joints: their behavior and design. Tech. Bull. 597. Washington, DC: U.S. Department of Agriculture.

Perkins, N.S.; Landsem, P.; Trayer, G.W. 1933. Modern connectors for timber construction. Washington, DC: U.S. Department of Commerce, National Committee on Wood Utilization, and U.S. Department of Agriculture, Forest Service.

Scholten, J.A. 1944. Timber-connector joints, their strength and design. Tech. Bull. 865. Washington, DC: U.S. Department of Agriculture.

Scholten, J.A. 1946. Strength of bolted timber joints. FPL Rep. R1202. Madison, WI: U.S. Department of Agriculture, Forest Service, Forest Products Laboratory.

Scholten, J.A. 1950. Nail-holding properties of southern hardwoods. Southern Lumberman. 181(2273): 208–210.

Scholten, J.A.; Molander, E. G. 1950. Strength of nailed joints in frame walls. Agricultural Engineering. 31(11): 551–555.

Soltis, L.A.; Wilkinson, T.L. 1987. Bolted connection design. Gen. Tech. Rep. FPL–GTR–54. Madison, WI: U.S. Department of Agriculture, Forest Service, Forest Products Laboratory.

Stern, E.G. 1940. A study of lumber and plywood joints with metal split-ring connectors. Bull. 53. State College, PA: Pennsylvania Engineering Experiment Station.

Stern, E.G. 1950. Nails in end-grain lumber. Timber News and Machine Woodworker. 58(2138): 490–492.

Trayer, G.W. 1932. Bearing strength of wood under bolts. Tech. Bull. 332. Washington, DC: U.S. Department of Agriculture.

Truss Plate Institute. [n.d.] Design specification for metal plate connected wood trusses. TPI–78. Madison, WI: Truss Plate Institute.

Wilkinson, T.L. 1971. Bearing strength of wood under embedment loading of fasteners. Res. Pap. FPL 163. Madison, WI: U.S. Department of Agriculture, Forest Service, Forest Products Laboratory.

Wilkinson, T.L. 1971. Theoretical lateral resistance of nailed joints. Proceedings of American Society of Civil Engineering. Journal of Structural Division. ST5(97): (Pap. 8121): 1381–1398.

Wilkinson, T.L. 1978. Strength of bolted wood joints with various ratios of member thicknesses. Res. Pap. FPL 314. Madison, WI: U.S. Department of Agriculture, Forest Service, Forest Products Laboratory.

Wilkinson, T.L. 1980. Assessment of modification factors for a row of bolts or timber connectors. Res. Pap. FPL 376. Madison, WI: U.S. Department of Agriculture, Forest Service, Forest Products Laboratory.

Wilkinson, T.L. 1991. Dowel bearing strength. Res. Paper FPL–RP–505. Madison, WI: U.S. Department of Agriculture, Forest Service, Forest Products Laboratory.

Wilkinson, T.L. 1991. Bolted connection allowable loads based on the European yield model. Madison, WI: U.S. Department of Agriculture, Forest Service, Forest Products Laboratory.

Wilkinson, T.L.; Laatsch, T.R. 1970. Lateral and withdrawal resistance of tapping screws in three densities of wood. Forest Products Journal. 20(7): 34–41.

Zahn, J.J. 1991. Design equation for multiple-fastener wood connections. New York, NY: Journal of Structural Engineering, American Society of Civil Engineers. Vol. 117(11): 3477–3485. Nov.

Chapter 8

Structural Analysis Equations

Lawrence A. Soltis

Contents

Equations for deformation and stress, which are the basis for tension members and beam and column design, are discussed in this chapter. The first two sections cover tapered members, straight members, and special considerations such as notches, slits, and size effect. A third section presents stability criteria for members subject to buckling and for members subject to special conditions. The equations are based on mechanics principles and are not given in the design code format found in Allowable Stress Design or Load and Resistance Factor Design specifications.

Deformation Equations

Equations for deformation of wood members are presented as functions of applied loads, moduli of elasticity and rigidity, and member dimensions. They may be solved to determine minimum required cross-sectional dimensions to meet deformation limitations imposed in design. Average moduli of elasticity and rigidity are given in Chapter 4. Consideration must be given to variability in material properties and uncertainties in applied loads to control reliability of the design.

Axial Load

The deformation of an axially loaded member is not usually an important design consideration. More important considerations will be presented in later sections dealing with combined loads or stability. Axial load produces a change of length given by

$$\delta = \frac{PL}{AE} \tag{8–1}$$

where δ is change of length, L length, A cross-sectional area, E modulus of elasticity (E_L when grain runs parallel to member axis), and P axial force parallel to grain.

Bending

Straight Beam Deflection

The deflection of straight beams that are elastically stressed and have a constant cross section throughout their length is given by

$$\delta = \frac{k_b W L^3}{EI} + \frac{k_s W L}{GA'} \qquad (8\text{--}2)$$

where δ is deflection, W total beam load acting perpendicular to beam neutral axis, L beam span, k_b and k_s constants dependent upon beam loading, support conditions, and location of point whose deflection is to be calculated, I beam moment of inertia, A' modified beam area, E beam modulus of elasticity (for beams having grain direction parallel to their axis, $E = E_L$), and G beam shear modulus (for beams with flat-grained vertical faces, $G = G_{LT}$, and for beams with edge-grained vertical faces, $G = G_{LR}$). Elastic property values are given in Tables 4–1 and 4–2 (Ch. 4).

The first term on the right side of Equation (8–2) gives the bending deflection and the second term the shear deflection. Values of k_b and k_s for several cases of loading and support are given in Table 8–1.

The moment of inertia I of the beams is given by

$$I = \frac{bh^3}{12} \quad \text{for beam of rectangular cross section}$$

$$= \frac{\pi d^4}{64} \quad \text{for beam of circular cross section} \qquad (8\text{--}3)$$

where b is beam width, h beam depth, and d beam diameter. The modified area A' is given by

$$A' = \frac{5}{6} bh \quad \text{for beam of rectangular cross section}$$

$$= \frac{9}{40} \pi d^2 \quad \text{for beam of circular cross section} \qquad (8\text{--}4)$$

If the beam has initial deformations such as bow (lateral bend) or twist, these deformations will be increased by the bending loads. It may be necessary to provide lateral or torsional restraints to hold such members in line. (See Interaction of Buckling Modes section.)

Tapered Beam Deflection

Figures 8–1 and 8–2 are useful in the design of tapered beams. The ordinates are based on design criteria such as span, loading, difference in beam height $(h_c - h_0)$ as required by roof slope or architectural effect, and maximum allowable deflection, together with material properties. From this, the value of the abscissa can be determined and the smallest beam depth h_0 can be calculated for comparison with that given by the design criteria. Conversely, the deflection of a beam can be calculated if the value of the abscissa is known. Tapered beams deflect as a result of shear deflection in addition to bending deflections (Figs. 8–1 and 8–2), and this shear deflection Δ_s can be closely approximated by

$$\Delta_s = \frac{3WL}{20Gbh_0} \quad \text{for uniformly distributed load}$$

$$\qquad (8\text{--}5)$$

$$= \frac{3PL}{10Gbh_0} \quad \text{for midspan-concentrated load}$$

The final beam design should consider the total deflection as the sum of the shear and bending deflection, and it may be necessary to iterate to arrive at final beam dimensions. Equations (8–5) are applicable to either single-tapered or double-tapered beams. As with straight beams, lateral or torsional restraint may be necessary.

Effect of Notches and Holes

The deflection of beams is increased if reductions in cross-section dimensions occur, such as by holes or notches. The deflection of such beams can be determined by considering them of variable cross section along their length and appropriately solving the general differential equations of the elastic curves, $EI(d^2y/dx^2) = M$, to obtain deflection expressions or by the application of Castigliano's theorem. (These procedures are given in most texts on strength of materials.)

Table 8–1. Values of k_b and k_s for several beam loadings

Loading	Beam ends	Deflection at	k_b	k_s
Uniformly distributed	Both simply supported	Midspan	5/384	1/8
	Both clamped	Midspan	1/384	1/8
Concentrated at midspan	Both simply supported	Midspan	1/48	1/4
	Both clamped	Midspan	1/192	1/4
Concentrated at outer quarter span points	Both simply supported	Midspan	11/768	1/8
	Both simply supported	Load point	1/96	1/8
Uniformly distributed	Cantilever, one free, one clamped	Free end	1/8	1/2
Concentrated at free end	Cantilever, one free, one clamped	Free end	1/3	1

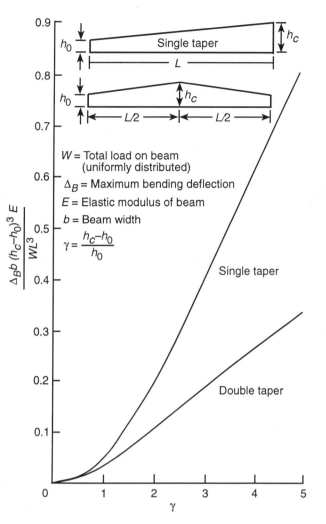

Figure 8–1. Graph for determining tapered beam size based on deflection under uniformly distributed load.

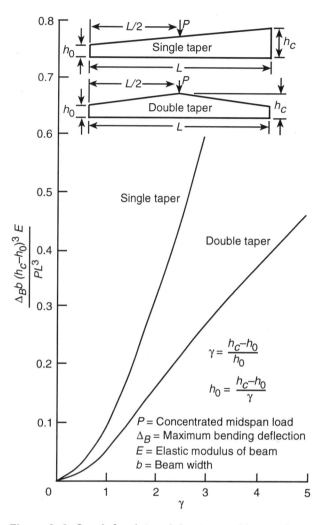

Figure 8–2. Graph for determining tapered beam size on deflection under concentrated midspan load.

Effect of Time: Creep Deflections

In addition to the elastic deflections previously discussed, wood beams usually sag in time; that is, the deflection increases beyond what it was immediately after the load was first applied. (See the discussion of creep in Time Under Load in Ch. 4.)

Green timbers, in particular, will sag if allowed to dry under load, although partially dried material will also sag to some extent. In thoroughly dried beams, small changes in deflection occur with changes in moisture content but with little permanent increase in deflection. If deflection under longtime load with initially green timber is to be limited, it has been customary to design for an initial deflection of about half the value permitted for longtime deflection. If deflection under longtime load with initially dry timber is to be limited, it has been customary to design for an initial deflection of about two-thirds the value permitted for longtime deflection.

Water Ponding

Ponding of water on roofs already deflected by other loads can cause large increases in deflection. The total deflection Δ due to design load plus ponded water can be closely estimated by

$$\Delta = \frac{\Delta_0}{1 - S/S_{cr}} \tag{8–6}$$

where Δ_0 is deflection due to design load alone, S beam spacing, and S_{cr} critical beam spacing (Eq. (8–31)).

Combined Bending and Axial Load

Concentric Load

Addition of a concentric axial load to a beam under loads acting perpendicular to the beam neutral axis causes increase in bending deflection for added axial compression and decrease in bending deflection for added axial tension.

173

The deflection under combined loading at midspan for pin-ended members can be estimated closely by

$$\Delta = \frac{\Delta_0}{1 \pm P/P_{cr}} \tag{8-7}$$

where the plus sign is chosen if the axial load is tension and the minus sign if the axial load is compression, Δ is midspan deflection under combined loading, Δ_0 beam midspan deflection without axial load, P axial load, and P_{cr} a constant equal to the buckling load of the beam under axial compressive load only (see Axial Compression in Stability Equations section.) based on flexural rigidity about the neutral axis perpendicular to the direction of bending loads. This constant appears regardless of whether P is tension or compression. If P is compression, it must be less than P_{cr} to avoid collapse. When the axial load is tension, it is conservative to ignore the P/P_{cr} term. (If the beam is not supported against lateral deflection, its buckling load should be checked using Eq. (8–35).)

Eccentric Load

If an axial load is eccentrically applied to a pin-ended member, it will induce bending deflections and change in length given by Equation (8–1). Equation (8–7) can be applied to find the bending deflection by writing the equation in the form

$$\delta_b + \varepsilon_0 = \frac{\varepsilon_0}{1 \pm P/P_{cr}} \tag{8-8}$$

where δ_b is the induced bending deflection at midspan and ε_0 the eccentricity of P from the centroid of the cross section.

Torsion

The angle of twist of wood members about the longitudinal axis can be computed by

$$\theta = \frac{TL}{GK} \tag{8-9}$$

where θ is angle of twist in radians, T applied torque, L member length, G shear modulus (use $\sqrt{G_{LR}G_{LT}}$, or approximate G by $E_L/16$ if measured G is not available), and K a cross-section shape factor. For a circular cross section, K is the polar moment of inertia:

$$K = \frac{\pi D^4}{32} \tag{8-10}$$

where D is diameter. For a rectangular cross section,

$$K = \frac{hb^3}{\phi} \tag{8-11}$$

where h is larger cross-section dimension, b is smaller cross-section dimension, and ϕ is given in Figure 8–3.

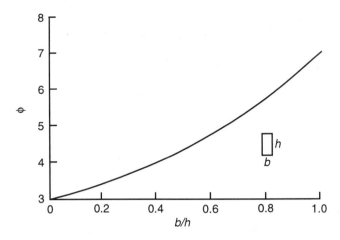

Figure 8–3. Coefficient ϕ for determining torsional rigidity of rectangular member (Eq. (8 –11)).

Stress Equations

The equations presented here are limited by the assumption that stress and strain are directly proportional (Hooke's law) and by the fact that local stresses in the vicinity of points of support or points of load application are correct only to the extent of being statically equivalent to the true stress distribution (St. Venant's principle). Local stress concentrations must be separately accounted for if they are to be limited in design.

Axial Load

Tensile Stress

Concentric axial load (along the line joining the centroids of the cross sections) produces a uniform stress:

$$f_t = \frac{P}{A} \tag{8-12}$$

where f_t is tensile stress, P axial load, and A cross-sectional area.

Short-Block Compressive Stress

Equation (8–12) can also be used in compression if the member is short enough to fail by simple crushing without deflecting laterally. Such fiber crushing produces a local "wrinkle" caused by microstructural instability. The member as a whole remains structurally stable and able to bear load.

Bending

The strength of beams is determined by flexural stresses caused by bending moment, shear stresses caused by shear load, and compression across the grain at the end bearings and load points.

Straight Beam Stresses

The stress due to bending moment for a simply supported pin-ended beam is a maximum at the top and bottom edges. The concave edge is compressed, and the convex edge is under tension. The maximum stress is given by

$$f_b = \frac{M}{Z} \qquad (8\text{–}13)$$

where f_b is bending stress, M bending moment, and Z beam section modulus (for a rectangular cross section, $Z = bh^2/6$; for a circular cross section, $Z = \pi D^3/32$).

This equation is also used beyond the limits of Hooke's law with M as the ultimate moment at failure. The resulting pseudo-stress is called the "modulus of rupture," values of which are tabulated in Chapter 4. The modulus of rupture has been found to decrease with increasing size of member. (See Size Effect section.)

The shear stress due to bending is a maximum at the centroidal axis of the beam, where the bending stress happens to be zero. (This statement is not true if the beam is tapered—see following section.) In wood beams this shear stress may produce a failure crack near mid-depth running along the axis of the member. Unless the beam is sufficiently short and deep, it will fail in bending before shear failure can develop; but wood beams are relatively weak in shear, and shear strength can sometimes govern a design. The maximum shear stress is

$$f_s = k\frac{V}{A} \qquad (8\text{–}14)$$

where f_s is shear stress, V vertical shear force on cross section, A cross-sectional area, and $k = 3/2$ for a rectangular cross section or $k = 4/3$ for a circular cross section.

Tapered Beam Stresses

For beams of constant width that taper in depth at a slope less than 25°, the bending stress can be obtained from Equation (8–13) with an error of less than 5%. The shear stress, however, differs markedly from that found in uniform beams. It can be determined from the basic theory presented by Maki and Kuenzi (1965). The shear stress at the tapered edge can reach a maximum value as great as that at the neutral axis at a reaction.

Consider the example shown in Figure 8–4, in which concentrated loads farther to the right have produced a support reaction V at the left end. In this case the maximum stresses occur at the cross section that is double the depth of the beam at the reaction. For other loadings, the location of the cross section with maximum shear stress at the tapered edge will be different.

For the beam depicted in Figure 8–4, the bending stress is also a maximum at the same cross section where the shear stress is maximum at the tapered edge. This stress situation also causes a stress in the direction perpendicular to the neutral axis that is maximum at the tapered edge. The effect of combined stresses at a point can be approximately accounted for by an interaction equation based on the Henky–von Mises theory of energy due to the change of shape. This theory applied by Norris (1950) to wood results in

$$\frac{f_x^2}{F_x^2} + \frac{f_{xy}^2}{F_{xy}^2} + \frac{f_y^2}{F_y^2} = 1 \qquad (8\text{–}15)$$

where f_x is bending stress, f_y stress perpendicular to the neutral axis, and f_{xy} shear stress. Values of F_x, F_y, and F_{xy} are corresponding stresses chosen at design values or maximum values in accordance with allowable or maximum values being determined for the tapered beam. Maximum stresses in

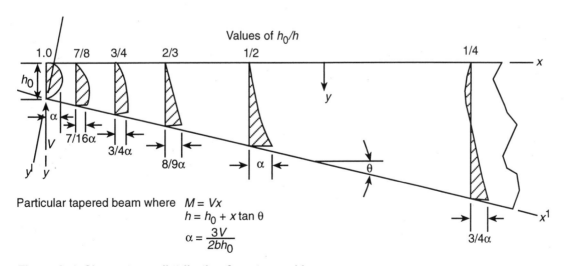

Particular tapered beam where $M = Vx$
$$h = h_0 + x\tan\theta$$
$$\alpha = \frac{3V}{2bh_0}$$

Figure 8–4. Shear stress distribution for a tapered beam.

the beam depicted in Figure 8–4 are given by

$$f_x = \frac{3M}{2bh_0^2}$$

$$f_{xy} = f_x \tan \theta \qquad (8\text{–}16)$$

$$f_y = f_x \tan^2 \theta$$

Substitution of these equations into the interaction Equation (8–15) will result in an expression for the moment capacity M of the beam. If the taper is on the beam tension edge, the values of f_x and f_y are tensile stresses.

Example: Determine the moment capacity (newton-meters) of a tapered beam of width b = 100 mm, depth h_0 = 200 mm, and taper $\tan \theta$ = 1/10. Substituting these dimensions into Equation (8–16) (with stresses in pascals) results in

$$f_x = 375M$$

$$f_{xy} = 37.5M$$

$$f_y = 3.75M$$

Substituting these into Equation (8–15) and solving for M results in

$$M = \frac{1}{3.75\left[10^4/F_x^2 + 10^2/F_{xy}^2 + 1/F_y^2\right]^{1/2}}$$

where appropriate allowable or maximum values of the F stresses (pascals) are chosen.

Size Effect

The modulus of rupture (maximum bending stress) of wood beams depends on beam size and method of loading, and the strength of clear, straight-grained beams decreases as size increases. These effects were found to be describable by statistical strength theory involving "weakest link" hypotheses and can be summarized as follows: For two beams under two equal concentrated loads applied symmetrical to the midspan points, the ratio of the modulus of rupture of beam 1 to the modulus of rupture of beam 2 is given by

$$\frac{R_1}{R_2} = \left[\frac{h_2 L_2(1+ma_2/L_2)}{h_1 L_1(1+ma_1/L_1)}\right]^{1/m} \qquad (8\text{–}17)$$

where subscripts 1 and 2 refer to beam 1 and beam 2, R is modulus of rupture, h beam depth, L beam span, a distance between loads placed $a/2$ each side of midspan, and m a constant. For clear, straight-grained Douglas-fir beams, m = 18. If Equation (8–17) is used for beam 2 size (Ch. 4) loaded at midspan, then h_2 = 5.08 mm (2 in.), L_2 = 71.112 mm (28 in.), and a_2 = 0 and Equation (8–17) becomes

$$\frac{R_1}{R_2} = \left[\frac{361.29}{h_1 L_1(1+ma_1/L_1)}\right]^{1/m} \quad \text{(metric)} \quad (8\text{–}18a)$$

$$\frac{R_1}{R_2} = \left[\frac{56}{h_1 L_1(1+ma_1/L_1)}\right]^{1/m} \quad \text{(inch–pound)} \quad (8\text{–}18b)$$

Example: Determine modulus of rupture for a beam 10 in. deep, spanning 18 ft, and loaded at one-third span points compared with a beam 2 in. deep, spanning 28 in., and loaded at midspan that had a modulus of rupture of 10,000 lb/in². Assume m = 18. Substituting the dimensions into Equation (8–18) produces

$$R_1 = 10{,}000\left[\frac{56}{2{,}160(1+6)}\right]^{1/18}$$

$$= 7{,}330 \text{ lb/in}^2$$

Application of the statistical strength theory to beams under uniformly distributed load resulted in the following relationship between modulus of rupture of beams under uniformly distributed load and modulus of rupture of beams under concentrated loads:

$$\frac{R_u}{R_c} = \left[\frac{\left(1+18a_c/L_c\right)h_c L_c}{3.876 h_u L_u}\right]^{1/18} \qquad (8\text{–}19)$$

where subscripts u and c refer to beams under uniformly distributed and concentrated loads, respectively, and other terms are as previously defined.

Shear strength for non-split, non-checked, solid-sawn, and glulam beams also decreases as beam size increases. A relationship between beam shear τ and ASTM shear block strength τ_{ASTM}, including a stress concentration factor for the re-entrant corner of the shear block, C_f, and the shear area A, is

$$\tau = \frac{1.9 C_f \tau_{ASTM}}{A^{1/5}} \qquad \text{(metric)} \qquad (8\text{–}20a)$$

$$\tau = \frac{1.3 C_f \tau_{ASTM}}{A^{1/5}} \qquad \text{(inch–pound)} \qquad (8\text{–}20b)$$

where τ is beam shear (MPa, lb/in²), C_f stress concentration factor, τ_{ASTM} ASTM shear block strength (MPa, lb/in²), and A shear area (cm², in²).

This relationship was determined by empirical fit to test data. The shear block re-entrant corner concentration factor is approximately 2; the shear area is defined as beam width multiplied by the length of beam subjected to shear force.

Effect of Notches, Slits, and Holes

In beams having notches, slits, or holes with sharp interior corners, large stress concentrations exist at the corners. The local stresses include shear parallel to grain and tension

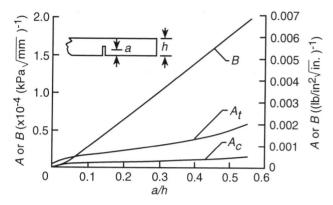

Figure 8–5. Coefficients *A* and *B* for crack-initiation criterion (Eq. (8–21)).

perpendicular to grain. As a result, even moderately low loads can cause a crack to initiate at the sharp corner and propagate along the grain. An estimate of the crack-initiation load can be obtained by the fracture mechanics analysis of Murphy (1979) for a beam with a slit, but it is generally more economical to avoid sharp notches entirely in wood beams, especially large wood beams, since there is a size effect: sharp notches cause greater reductions in strength for larger beams. A conservative criterion for crack initiation for a beam with a slit is

$$\sqrt{h}\left[A\left(\frac{6M}{bh^2}\right) + B\left(\frac{3V}{2bh}\right)\right] = 1 \qquad (8\text{–}21)$$

where h is beam depth, b beam width, M bending moment, and V vertical shear force, and coefficients A and B are presented in Figure 8–5 as functions of a/h, where a is slit depth. The value of A depends on whether the slit is on the tension edge or the compression edge. Therefore, use either A_t or A_c as appropriate. The values of A and B are dependent upon species; however, the values given in Figure 8–5 are conservative for most softwood species.

Effects of Time: Creep Rupture, Fatigue, and Aging

See Chapter 4 for a discussion of fatigue and aging. Creep rupture is accounted for by duration-of-load adjustment in the setting of allowable stresses, as discussed in Chapters 4 and 6.

Water Ponding

Ponding of water on roofs can cause increases in bending stresses that can be computed by the same amplification factor (Eq. (8–6)) used with deflection. (See Water Ponding in the Deformation Equations section.)

Combined Bending and Axial Load

Concentric Load

Equation (8–7) gives the effect on deflection of adding an end load to a simply supported pin-ended beam already bent by transverse loads. The bending stress in the member is modified by the same factor as the deflection:

$$f_b = \frac{f_{b0}}{1 \pm P/P_{cr}} \qquad (8\text{–}22)$$

where the plus sign is chosen if the axial load is tension and the minus sign is chosen if the axial load is compression, f_b is net bending stress from combined bending and axial load, f_{b0} bending stress without axial load, P axial load, and P_{cr} the buckling load of the beam under axial compressive load only (see Axial Compression in the Stability Equations section), based on flexural rigidity about the neutral axis perpendicular to the direction of the bending loads. This P_{cr} is not necessarily the minimum buckling load of the member. If P is compressive, the possibility of buckling under combined loading must be checked. (See Interaction of Buckling Modes.)

The total stress under combined bending and axial load is obtained by superposition of the stresses given by Equations (8–12) and (8–22).

Example: Suppose transverse loads produce a bending stress f_{b0} tensile on the convex edge and compressive on the concave edge of the beam. Then the addition of a tensile axial force P at the centroids of the end sections will produce a maximum tensile stress on the convex edge of

$$f_{t\,max} = \frac{f_{b0}}{1 + P/P_{cr}} + \frac{P}{A}$$

and a maximum compressive stress on the concave edge of

$$f_{c\,max} = \frac{f_{b0}}{1 + P/P_{cr}} - \frac{P}{A}$$

where a negative result would indicate that the stress was in fact tensile.

Eccentric Load

If the axial load is eccentrically applied, then the bending stress f_{b0} should be augmented by $\pm P\varepsilon_0/Z$, where ε_0 is eccentricity of the axial load.

Example: In the preceding example, let the axial load be eccentric toward the concave edge of the beam. Then the maximum stresses become

$$f_{t\,max} = \frac{f_{b0} - P\varepsilon_0/Z}{1 + P/P_{cr}} + \frac{P}{A}$$

$$f_{c\,max} = \frac{f_{b0} - P\varepsilon_0/Z}{1 + P/P_{cr}} - \frac{P}{A}$$

Torsion

For a circular cross section, the shear stress induced by torsion is

$$f_s = \frac{16T}{\pi D^3} \qquad (8\text{–}23)$$

where T is applied torque and D diameter. For a rectangular cross section,

$$f_s = \frac{T}{\beta h b^2} \qquad (8\text{–}24)$$

where T is applied torque, h larger cross-section dimension, and b smaller cross-section dimension, and β is presented in Figure 8–6.

Stability Equations

Axial Compression

For slender members under axial compression, stability is the principal design criterion. The following equations are for concentrically loaded members. For eccentrically loaded columns, see Interaction of Buckling Modes section.

Long Columns

A column long enough to buckle before the compressive stress P/A exceeds the proportional limit stress is called a "long column." The critical stress at buckling is calculated by Euler's formula:

$$f_{cr} = \frac{\pi^2 E_L}{(L/r)^2} \qquad (8\text{–}25)$$

where E_L is elastic modulus parallel to the axis of the member, L unbraced length, and r least radius of gyration (for a rectangular cross section with b as its least dimension, $r = b/\sqrt{12}$, and for a circular cross section, $r = d/4$). Equation (8–25) is based on a pinned-end condition but may be used conservatively for square ends as well.

Short Columns

Columns that buckle at a compressive stress P/A beyond the proportional limit stress are called "short columns." Usually the short column range is explored empirically, and appropriate design equations are proposed. Material of this nature is presented in *USDA Technical Bulletin 167* (Newlin and Gahagan 1930). The final equation is a fourth-power parabolic function that can be written as

$$f_{cr} = F_c \left[1 - \frac{4}{27\pi^4} \left(\frac{L}{r} \sqrt{\frac{F_c}{E_L}} \right)^4 \right] \qquad (8\text{–}26)$$

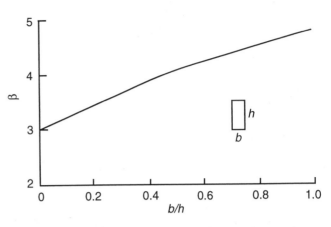

Figure 8–6. Coefficient β for computing maximum shear stress in torsion of rectangular member (Eq. (8 –24)).

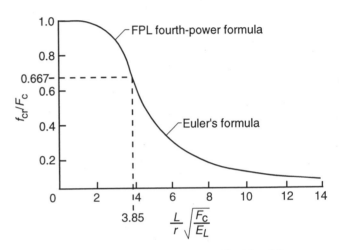

Figure 8–7. Graph for determining critical buckling stress of wood columns.

where F_c is compressive strength and remaining terms are defined as in Equation (8–25). Figure 8–7 is a graphical representation of Equations (8–25) and (8–26).

Short columns can be analyzed by fitting a nonlinear function to compressive stress–strain data and using it in place of Hooke's law. One such nonlinear function proposed by Ylinen (1956) is

$$\varepsilon = \frac{F_c}{E_L} \left[c \frac{f}{F_c} - (1-c) \log_e \left(1 - \frac{f}{F_c} \right) \right] \qquad (8\text{–}27)$$

where ε is compressive strain, f compressive stress, c a constant between 0 and 1, and E_L and F_c are as previously defined. Using the slope of Equation (8–27) in place of E_L in Euler's formula (Eq. (8–25)) leads to Ylinen's buckling equation

$$f_{cr} = \frac{F_c + f_e}{2c} - \sqrt{\left(\frac{F_c + f_e}{2c} \right)^2 - \frac{F_c f_e}{c}} \qquad (8\text{–}28)$$

where F_c is compressive strength and f_e buckling stress given by Euler's formula (Eq. (8–25)). Equation (8–28) can be made to agree closely with Figure 8–7 by choosing $c = 0.957$.

Comparing the fourth-power parabolic function Equation (8–26) to experimental data indicates the function is nonconservative for intermediate L/r range columns. Using Ylinen's buckling equation with $c = 0.8$ results in a better approximation of the solid-sawn and glued-laminated data.

Built-Up and Spaced Columns

Built-up columns of nearly square cross section with the lumber nailed or bolted together will not support loads as great as if the lumber were glued together. The reason is that shear distortions can occur in the mechanical joints.

If built-up columns are adequately connected and the axial load is near the geometric center of the cross section, Equation (8–28) is reduced with a factor that depends on the type of mechanical connection. The built-up column capacity is

$$f_{cr} = K_f \left[\frac{F_c + f_e}{2c} - \sqrt{\left(\frac{F_c + f_e}{2c} \right)^2 - \frac{F_c f_e}{c}} \right] \qquad (8–29)$$

where F_c, f_e, and c are as defined for Equation (8–28). K_f is the built-up stability factor, which accounts for the efficiency of the connection; for bolts, $K_f = 0.75$, and for nails, $K_f = 0.6$, provided bolt and nail spacing requirements meet design specification approval.

If the built-up column is of several spaced pieces, the spacer blocks should be placed close enough together, lengthwise in the column, so that the unsupported portion of the spaced member will not buckle at the same or lower stress than that of the complete member. "Spaced columns" are designed with previously presented column equations, considering each compression member as an unsupported simple column; the sum of column loads for all the members is taken as the column load for the spaced column.

Columns With Flanges

Columns with thin, outstanding flanges can fail by elastic instability of the outstanding flange, causing wrinkling of the flange and twisting of the column at stresses less than those for general column instability as given by Equations (8–25) and (8–26). For outstanding flanges of cross sections such as I, H, +, and L, the flange instability stress can be estimated by

$$f_{cr} = 0.044 E \frac{t^2}{b^2} \qquad (8–30)$$

where E is column modulus of elasticity, t thickness of the outstanding flange, and b width of the outstanding flange. If the joints between the column members are glued and reinforced with glued fillets, the instability stress increases to as much as 1.6 times that given by Equation (8–30).

Bending

Beams are subject to two kinds of instability: lateral–torsional buckling and progressive deflection under water ponding, both of which are determined by member stiffness.

Water Ponding

Roof beams that are insufficiently stiff or spaced too far apart for their given stiffness can fail by progressive deflection under the weight of water from steady rain or another continuous source. The critical beam spacing S_{cr} is given by

$$S_{cr} = \frac{m\pi^4 EI}{\rho L^4} \qquad (8–31)$$

where E is beam modulus of elasticity, I beam moment of inertia, ρ density of water (1,000 kg/m^3, 0.0361 lb/in^3), L beam length, and $m = 1$ for simple support or $m = 16/3$ for fixed-end condition. To prevent ponding, the beam spacing must be less than S_{cr}.

Lateral–Torsional Buckling

Since beams are compressed on the concave edge when bent under load, they can buckle by a combination of lateral deflection and twist. Because most wood beams are rectangular in cross section, the equations presented here are for rectangular members only. Beams of I, H, or other built-up cross section exhibit a more complex resistance to twisting and are more stable than the following equations would predict.

Long Beams—Long slender beams that are restrained against axial rotation at their points of support but are otherwise free to twist and to deflect laterally will buckle when the maximum bending stress f_b equals or exceeds the following critical value:

$$f_{bcr} = \frac{\pi^2 E_L}{\alpha^2} \qquad (8–32)$$

where α is the slenderness factor given by

$$\alpha = \sqrt{2\pi} \ \sqrt[4]{\frac{EI_y}{GK}} \ \frac{\sqrt{L_e h}}{b} \qquad (8–33)$$

where EI_y is lateral flexural rigidity equal to $E_L hb^3/12$, h is beam depth, b beam width, GK torsional rigidity defined in Equation (8–9), and L_e effective length determined by type of loading and support as given in Table 8–2. Equation (8–32) is valid for bending stresses below the proportional limit.

Short Beams—Short beams can buckle at stresses beyond the proportional limit. In view of the similarity of Equation (8–32) to Euler's formula (Eq. (8–25)) for column buckling, it is recommended that short-beam buckling be analyzed by using the column buckling criterion in Figure 8–7 applied with α in place of L/r on the abscissa

Table 8–2. Effective length for checking lateral–torsional stability of beams[a]

Support	Load	Effective length L_e
Simple support	Equal end moments	L
	Concentrated force at center	$\dfrac{0.742L}{1-2\,h/L}$
	Uniformly distributed force	$\dfrac{0.887L}{1-2\,h/L}$
Cantilever	Concentrated force at end	$\dfrac{0.783L}{1-2\,h/L}$
	Uniformly distributed force	$\dfrac{0.489L}{1-2\,h/L}$

[a]These values are conservative for beams with a width-to-depth ratio of less than 0.4. The load is assumed to act at the top edge of the beam.

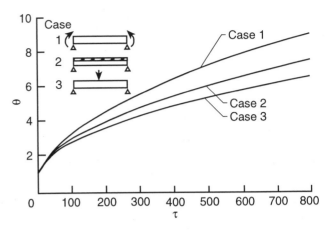

Figure 8–8. Increase in buckling stress resulting from attached deck; simply supported beams. To apply this graph, divide the effective length by θ.

and f_{bcr}/F_b in place of f_{cr}/F_c on the ordinate. Here F_b is beam modulus of rupture.

Effect of Deck Support—The most common form of support against lateral deflection is a deck continuously attached to the top edge of the beam. If this deck is rigid against shear in the plane of the deck and is attached to the compression edge of the beam, the beam cannot buckle. In regions where the deck is attached to the tension edge of the beam, as where a beam is continuous over a support, the deck cannot be counted on to prevent buckling and restraint against axial rotation should be provided at the support point.

If the deck is not very rigid against in-plane shear, as for example standard 38-mm (nominal 2-in.) wood decking, Equation (8–32) and Figure 8–7 can still be used to check stability except that now the effective length is modified by dividing by θ, as given in Figure 8–8. The abscissa of this figure is a deck shear stiffness parameter τ given by

$$\tau = \frac{SG_D L^2}{EI_y} \qquad (8\text{–}34)$$

where EI_y is lateral flexural rigidity as in Equation (8–33), S beam spacing, G_D in-plane shear rigidity of deck (ratio of shear force per unit length of edge to shear strain), and L actual beam length. This figure applies only to simply supported beams. Cantilevers with the deck on top have their tension edge supported and do not derive much support from the deck.

Interaction of Buckling Modes

When two or more loads are acting and each of them has a critical value associated with a mode of buckling, the combination can produce buckling even though each load is less than its own critical value.

The general case of a beam of unbraced length l_e includes a primary (edgewise) moment M_1, a lateral (flatwise) moment M_2, and axial load P. The axial load creates a secondary moment on both edgewise and flatwise moments due to the deflection under combined loading given by Equation (8–7). In addition, the edgewise moment has an effect like the secondary moment effect on the flatwise moment.

The following equation contains two moment modification factors, one on the edgewise bending stress and one on the flatwise bending stress that includes the interaction of biaxial bending. The equation also contains a squared term for axial load to better predict experimental data:

$$\left(\frac{f_c}{F_c}\right)^2 + \frac{f_{b1} + 6(e_1/d_1)f_c(1.234 - 0.234\theta_{c1})}{\theta_{c1}F'_{b1}}$$
$$+ \frac{f_{b2} + 6(e_2/d_2)f_c(1.234 - 0.234\theta_{c2})}{\theta_{c2}F'_{b2}} \le 1.0 \qquad (8\text{–}35)$$

where f is actual stress in compression, edgewise bending, or flatwise bending (subscripts c, b1, or b2, respectively), F buckling strength in compression or bending (a single prime denotes the strength is reduced for slenderness), e/d ratio of eccentricity of the axial compression to member depth ratio for edgewise or flatwise bending (subscripts 1 or 2, respectively), and θ_c moment magnification factors for edgewise and flatwise bending, given by

$$\theta_{c1} = 1 - \left(\frac{f_c}{F_{c1}''} + \frac{S}{S_{cr}} \right) \qquad (8\text{--}36)$$

$$\theta_{c2} = 1 - \left(\frac{f_c}{F_{c2}''} + \frac{f_{b1} + 6(e_1/d_1)f_c}{F_{b1}''} \right) \qquad (8\text{--}37)$$

$$F_{c1}'' = \frac{0.822E}{(l_{e1}/d_1)^2} \qquad (8\text{--}38)$$

$$F_{c2}'' = \frac{0.822E}{(l_{e2}/d_2)^2} \qquad (8\text{--}39)$$

$$F_{b1}'' = \frac{1.44E}{l_e} \frac{d_2}{d_1} \qquad (8\text{--}40)$$

where l_e is effective length of member and S and S_{cr} are previously defined ponding beam spacing.

References

ASTM. [current edition]. Standard methods for testing clear specimens of timber. ASTM D143–94. West Conshohocken, PA: American Society for Testing and Materials.

Bohannan, B. 1966. Effect of size on bending strength of wood members. Res. Pap. FPL–RP–56. Madison, WI: U.S. Department of Agriculture, Forest Service, Forest Products Laboratory.

Gerhardt, T.D.; Liu, J.Y. 1983. Orthotropic beams under normal and shear loading. Journal of Engineering Mechanics, ASCE. 109(2): 394–410.

Kuenzi, E.W.; Bohannan, B. 1964. Increases in deflection and stress caused by ponding of water on roofs. Forest Products Journal. 14(9): 421–424.

Liu, J.Y. 1980. Shear strength of wood beams: A Weibull analysis. Journal of Structural Division, ASCE. 106(ST10): 2035– 2052.

Liu, J.Y. 1981. Shear strength of tapered wood beams. Journal of Structural Division, ASCE. 107(ST5): 719–731.

Liu, J.Y. 1982. A Weibull analysis of wood member bending strength. Transactions, American Society of Mechanical Engineers. Journal of Mechanical Design. 104: 572–579.

Liu, J.Y. 1984. Evaluation of the tensor polynomial strength theory for wood. Journal of Composite Materials. 18(3): 216–226. (May).

Liu, J.Y.; Cheng, S. 1979. Analysis of orthotropic beams. Res. Pap. FPL–RP–343. Madison, WI: U.S. Department of Agriculture, Forest Service, Forest Products Laboratory.

Maki, A C.; Kuenzi, E.W. 1965. Deflection and stresses of tapered wood beams. Res. Pap. FPL–RP–34. Madison, WI: U.S. Department of Agriculture, Forest Service, Forest Products Laboratory.

Malhorta, S.K.; Sukumar, A.P. 1989. A simplied procedure for built-up wood compression members. St. Johns,

New Foundland: Annual conference, Canadian Society for Civil Engineering: 1–18 (June).

Murphy, J.F. 1979. Using fracture mechanics to predict failure of notched wood beams. In: Proceedings of first international conference on wood fracture; 1978, Aug. 14–16; Banff, AB. Vancouver, BC: Forintek Canada Corporation: 159: 161–173.

Newlin, J.A.; Gahagan, J.M. 1930. Tests of large timber columns and presentation of the Forest Products Laboratory column formula. Tech. Bull. 167. Madison, WI: U.S. Department of Agriculture, Forest Service, Forest Products Laboratory.

Newlin, J.A.; Trayer, G.W. 1924. Deflection of beams with special reference to shear deformations. Rep. 180. Washington, DC: U.S. National Advisory Committee on Aeronautics.

Norris, C.B. 1950. Strength of orthotropic materials subjected to combined stresses. Rep. 1816. Madison, WI: U.S. Department of Agriculture, Forest Service, Forest Products Laboratory.

Rammer, D.R.; Soltis, L.A. 1994. Experimental shear strength of glued-laminated beams. Res. Rep. FPL–RP–527. Madison, WI, U.S. Department of Agriculture, Forest Service, Forest Products Laboratory.

Rammer, D.R.; Soltis, L.A.; Lebow, P.K. 1996. Experimental shear strength of unchecked solid sawn Douglas-fir. Res. Pap. FPL–RP–553. Madison, WI: U.S. Department of Agriculture, Forest Service, Forest Products Laboratory.

Soltis, L.A., Rammer, D.R. 1997. Bending to shear ratio approach to beam design. Forest Products Journal. 47(1): 104–108.

Trayer, G.W. 1930. The torsion of members having sections common in aircraft construction. Rep. 334. Washington, DC: U.S. National Advisory Committee on Aeronautics.

Trayer, G.W.; March, H.W. 1931. Elastic instability of members having sections common in aircraft construction. Rep. 382. Washington, DC: U.S. National Advisory Committee on Aeronautics.

Ylinen, A. 1956. A method of determining the buckling stress and the required cross-sectional area for centrally loaded straight columns in elastic and inelastic range. Publication of the International Association for Bridge and Structural Engineering. Zurich. Vol. 16.

Zahn, J.J. 1973. Lateral stability of wood beam-and-deck systems. Journal of the Structural Division, ASCE. 99(ST7): 1391–1408.

Zahn, J.J. 1986. Design of wood members under combined loads. Journal of Structural Engineering, ASCE. 112(ST9): 2109–2126.

Zahn, J.J. 1988. Combined-load stability criterion for wood beam-columns. Journal of Structural Engineering, ASCE. 114(ST11): 2612–2628.

Chapter 9

Adhesive Bonding of Wood Materials

Charles B. Vick

Contents

Adhesive bonding of wood components has played an essential role in the development and growth of the forest products industry and has been a key factor in the efficient utilization of our timber resource. The largest use of adhesives is in the construction industry. By far, the largest amounts of adhesives are used to manufacture building materials, such as plywood, structural flakeboards, particleboards, fiberboards, structural framing and timbers, architectural doors, windows and frames, factory-laminated wood products, and glass fiber insulation. Adhesives are used in smaller amounts to assemble building materials in residential and industrial construction, particularly in panelized floor and wall systems. Significant amounts are also used in nonstructural applications, such as floor coverings, countertops, ceiling and wall tile, trim, and accessories.

Adhesives can effectively transfer and distribute stresses, thereby increasing the strength and stiffness of the composite. Effective transfer of stress from one member to another depends on the strength of the links in an imaginary chain of an adhesive-bonded joint. Thus, performance of the bonded joint depends on how well we understand and control the complexity of factors that constitute the individual links—wood, adhesive, and the interphasing regions between—which ultimately determine the strength of the chain.

Adhesion to Wood

The American Society for Testing and Materials (ASTM) defines an adhesive as a substance capable of holding materials together by surface attachment. An adherend is a substrate held to another substrate by an adhesive. Adhesion is the state in which two surfaces are held together by interfacial forces, which may be valence forces, interlocking action, or both. Valence forces are forces of attraction produced by the interactions of atoms, ions, and molecules that exist within and at the surfaces of both adhesive and adherend. Interlocking action, also called mechanical bonding, means surfaces are held together by an adhesive that has penetrated the porous surface while it is liquid, then anchored itself during solidification. The extent to which valence forces and interlocking action develop between adhesive polymers and wood adherends is uncertain, but both are generally acknowledged as essential for the most effective bonding. Bonding to porous surfaces, such as wood, paper, and textiles, was thought to be primarily mechanical, but now there is evidence supporting bonding by primary valence forces. In contrast, bonding to hard metal surfaces was believed to involve only valence forces, but this is no longer the accepted view. Metal surfaces roughened by chemical etching or made microscopically porous with a layer of oxide are capable of mechanical interlocking with an adhesive to produce exceptionally strong and durable bonds.

Mechanical interlocking is probably the primary mechanism by which adhesives adhere to porous structures, such as wood. Effective mechanical interlocking takes place when adhesives penetrate beyond the surface debris and damaged fibers into sound wood two to six cells deep. Deeper penetration into the fine microstructure increases the surface area of contact between adhesive and wood for more effective mechanical interlocking. The most durable structural bonds to wood are believed to develop not only when an adhesive penetrates deeply into cell cavities, but also when an adhesive diffuses into cell walls to make molecular-level contact with the hemicellulosics and cellulosics of wood. If an adhesive penetrates deeply enough into sound wood and becomes rigid enough upon curing, the strength of the bond can be expected to exceed the strength of the wood.

Physical forces of attraction composed of three intermolecular attraction forces are believed to be important to the formation of bonds between adhesive polymers and molecular structures of wood. Generally called van der Waal's forces, these include dipole–dipole forces, which are positively and negatively charged polar molecules that have strong attractions for other polar molecules; London forces, which include the weaker forces of attraction that nonpolar molecules have for each other; and hydrogen bonding, a special type of dipole–dipole force that accounts for strong attractions between positively charged hydrogen atoms of one polar molecule and the electronegative atom of another molecule. Hydrogen bonding forces are important in the interfacial attraction of polar adhesive polymers for the hemicellulosics and cellulosics, which are rich with polar hydroxyl groups. These physical forces of attraction, sometimes referred to as specific adhesion, are particularly important in wetting of water carriers and adsorption of adhesive polymers onto the molecular structures of wood.

Covalent chemical bonds form when atoms of nonmetals interact by sharing electrons to form molecules. The simplest example of a purely covalent bond is the sharing of electrons by two hydrogen atoms to form hydrogen. These covalent bonds are the strongest of chemical bonds; they are more than 11 times the strength of the hydrogen bond. Even though covalent chemical bonds between adhesive polymer and the molecular structure of wood seem a possibility, there is no clear evidence that such bonds constitute an important mechanism in adhesive bonding to wood.

For two wood adherends to be held together with maximum strength, a liquid adhesive must wet and spread freely to make intimate contact with both surfaces. Molecules of the adhesive must diffuse over and into each surface to make contact with the molecular structure of wood so that

intermolecular forces of attraction between adhesive and wood can become effective. As will be discussed later, wood adherends, as well as other materials, differ widely in their attractive energies, bulk properties, surface roughness, and surface chemistry. Wood surfaces may appear to be smooth and flat, but on microscopic examination, they become peaks, valleys, and crevices, littered with loose fibers and other debris. Such surface conditions cause gas pockets and blockages that prevent complete wetting by the adhesive and introduce stress concentrations when the adhesive has cured. Thus, the liquid adhesive must have high wettability, coupled with a viscosity that will produce good capillary flow to penetrate sound wood structure, while displacing and absorbing air, water, and contaminants at the surface. Pressure is normally used to enhance wetting by forcing liquid adhesive to flow over the surfaces, displace air blockages, and penetrate to sound wood.

Wetting of a surface occurs when the contact angle (the angle between the edge of a drop of adhesive and the surface of wood) approaches zero. The contact angle approaches zero when the surface has high attractive energy, the adhesive has an affinity for the adherend, and the surface tension of the adhesive is low. If a drop of adhesive spreads to a thin film approaching zero contact angle, the adhesive has spread well and made intimate contact with the surface. The differences in wettabilities of various wood surfaces are illustrated by a simple water drop test in Figure 9–1.

The process of adhesion is essentially completed after transition of the adhesive from liquid to solid form. After the viscosity of a liquid adhesive has increased and the adhesive has solidified to the point where the film effectively resists shear and tensile forces tending to separate the surfaces, the surfaces are effectively bonded. An adhesive film changes from liquid to solid form by one of three mechanisms, although two may be involved in some curing mechanisms. This transition can be a physical change as in thermoplastic adhesives or it can be a chemical change as in thermosetting adhesives. In thermoplastics, the physical change to solid form may occur by either (a) loss of solvent from the adhesive through evaporation and diffusion into the wood, or (b) cooling of molten adhesive on a cooler surface. In thermosets, the solid form occurs through chemical polymerization into cross-linked structures that resist softening on heating. Most thermosetting wood adhesives contain water as a carrier; therefore, water also must be evaporated and absorbed by the wood so that the adhesive can cure completely.

Surface Properties of Wood Adherends

Because adhesives bond by surface attachment, the physical and chemical conditions of the adherend's surface is extremely important to satisfactory joint performance. Wood surfaces should be smooth, flat, and free of machine marks and other surface irregularities, including planer skips and crushed, torn, and chipped grain. The surface should be free of burnishes, exudates, oils, dirt, and other debris.

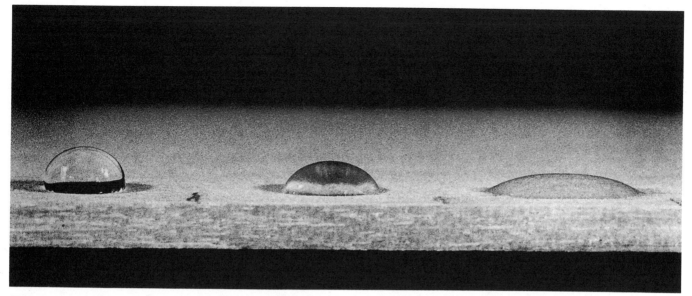

Figure 9–1. A simple water drop test shows differences in the wettability of a yellow birch veneer surface. Three drops were applied to the surface at the same time, then photographed after 30 s. The drop on the left retains a large contact angle on the aged, unsanded surface; the drop in the center has a smaller contact angle and improved wettability after the surface is renewed by two passes with 320-grit sandpaper; the drop on the right shows a small contact angle and good wettability after four passes with the sandpaper.

Overdrying and overheating deteriorates the physical condition of the wood surfaces by forcing extractives to diffuse to the surface, by reorienting surface molecules, and by irreversibly closing the larger micropores of cell walls. Wood surfaces can be chemically inactivated with respect to adhesion by airborne chemical contaminants, hydrophobic and chemically active extractives from the wood, oxidation and pyrolysis of wood bonding sites from overdrying, and impregnation with preservatives, fire retardants, and other chemicals. Unfortunately, some of these surface conditions are difficult to detect. Physical deterioration and chemical contamination interfere with essential wetting, flow, and penetration of adhesive but can also interfere with the cure and resulting cohesive strength of the adhesive.

Extractives on Surfaces

Extensive research indicates that extractives on wood surfaces are the principal physical and chemical contributors to surface inactivation, hence to poor wettability by adhesives. This is particularly true for resinous species, such as the southern pines and Douglas-fir. When subjected to high temperatures during processing, extractives diffuse to the surface where they concentrate and physically block adhesive contact with wood. Furthermore, resinous and oily exudates are hydrophobic; that is, they repel water. Most wood adhesives contain water as a carrier; therefore, they do not properly wet, flow, and penetrate extractive-covered surfaces. The acidity of extractives of some Southeast Asian hardwoods and oak species can interfere with the chemical cure of adhesives. The acid may accelerate the cure of an alkaline phenolic adhesive, causing the adhesive to gel prematurely and reducing its

ability to wet, flow, and penetrate. In contrast, normal polymerization of an acidic adhesive, such as urea-formaldehyde, can be retarded by an alkaline wood surface, which would compromise the integrity of the adhesive film and bond.

A simple water test can reveal much about the state of inactivation of a wood surface and how difficult it may be to wet and bond with adhesive. As a first test, place a small drop of water on the surface and observe how it spreads and absorbs. If the drop remains a bead and does not begin to spread within 30 s, the surface is resistant to adhesive wetting (Fig. 9–1). Another water drop test can be used to estimate the degree of surface inactivation of veneer. Place a drop of water in an area on the earlywood of a flat-grain surface that does not have checks or splits in the area of the drop. Good wettability is indicated if the drop is absorbed within 20 min. If the drop has spread out but some water still remains on the surface after 40 min, then bonding problems are likely to occur. If after 40 min the water drop still retains much of its original shape with little spreading, then bonding problems from surface inactivation is a certainty.

Knife- and Abrasive-Planed Surfaces

Wood should be surfaced or resurfaced within 24 h before bonding to remove extractives and other physical and chemical contaminants that interfere with bonding. Surfacing also removes any unevenness that may have occurred from changes in moisture content. Parallel and flat surfaces allow the adhesive to flow freely and form a uniformly thin layer of adhesive that is essential to the best performance of water-based wood adhesives.

Experience and testing have proven that a smooth, knife-cut surface is best for bonding. Surfaces made by saws usually are rougher than those made by planers and jointers. However, surfaces sawn with special blades on properly set straight-line ripsaws are satisfactory for both structural and nonstructural joints. Precision sawing of wood joints rather than two-step sawing and jointing is commonplace in furniture manufacture for purposes of reducing costs for labor, equipment, and material. Unless the saws and feed works are well maintained, however, joints made with sawed surfaces will be weaker and less uniform in strength than those made with sharp planer or jointer knives. Dull cutting edges of planer or jointer knives crush and burnish the wood surface. The crushed and burnished surface inhibits adhesive wetting and penetration. If the adhesive does not completely penetrate crushed cells to restore their original strength, a weak joint results. Another simple water test can be used to detect a surface that has been damaged during machining. Wipe a very wet rag over a portion of the surface. After waiting for a minute, remove any remaining water by blotting with a paper towel. Then compare the roughness of the wet and dry surfaces. If the wetted area is much rougher than the dry area, then the surface has been damaged in machining. This damage will significantly reduce the strength of adhesive-bonded joints.

Abrasive planing with grit sizes from 24 to 80 causes surface and subsurface crushing of wood cells. Figure 9–2 shows cross sections of bondlines between undamaged, knife-planed Douglas-fir lumber compared with surfaces damaged by abrasive planing. Such damaged surfaces are inherently weak and result in poor bond strength. Similar damage can be caused by dull planer knives or saws. There is some evidence that sanding with grits finer than 100 may improve an abrasive-planed surface. However, abrasive-planing is not recommended for structural joints that will be subjected to high swelling and shrinkage stresses from water soaking and drying. If abrasive-planing is to be used before bonding, then belts must be kept clean and sharp, and sanding dust must be removed completely from the sanded surface.

Veneer Surfaces

The wood properties of veneer are essentially no different from those of lumber; however, manufacturing processes, including cutting, drying, and laminating into plywood, can drastically change physical and chemical surface properties of veneer. Special knowledge and attention to these characteristics are required to ensure good wetting, flow, and penetration of adhesive.

Rotary cutting produces continuous sheets of flat-grain veneer by rotating a log by its ends against a knife. As the knife peels veneer from the log, the knife forces the veneer away from the log at a sharp angle, thereby breaking or checking the veneer on the knife side. The checked side is commonly called the loose side, and the opposite side without checking is called the tight side. When rotary-cut veneer is used for faces in plywood, the loose side should be bonded with the tight side presented to view. Otherwise, open checks in the faces produce imperfections in any finish that may be applied.

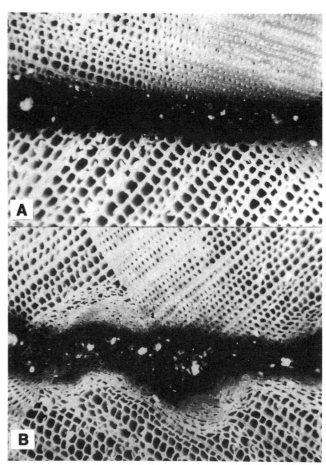

Figure 9–2. (A) Cross section of a bonded joint between two undamaged Douglas-fir surfaces that were planed with a sharp knife (120X). The wood cells are open, and their walls are distinct. The dark area at the center of micrograph is the adhesive bondline. (B) Cross section of a bonded joint between two damaged Douglas-fir surfaces abrasively planed with 36-grit sandpaper. The cells in and adjacent to the bondline are crushed, and their walls are indistinct.

Adhesive overpenetration into lathe checks usually is not a problem if the adhesive spread rate is adjusted correctly.

Sliced veneer is produced in long strips by moving a squared log, called a flitch, against a knife. As in rotary cutting, the veneer is forced by the knife away from the flitch at a sharp angle, causing fine checking of the veneer on the knife side. This checked surface will show imperfections in a finished surface, so the loose side should be bonded and the tight side finished. For book-matched face veneers, where grain patterns of adjacent veneers are near mirror images, half the veneers will be loosely cut and must be finished, so the veneer must be cut as tightly as possible. Generally, hardwood face veneers are sliced to reveal the most attractive grain patterns.

Sawn veneer is produced in long narrow strips from flitches that have been selected and sawn for attractive grain patterns. The two sides of sawn veneer are free from knife checks, so either surface may be bonded or exposed to view with satisfactory results.

Veneer is dried promptly after cutting, using continuous, high temperature dryers that are heated either with steam or hot gases from wood-residue or gas-fired burners. Drying temperatures range from 170°C to 230°C (330°F to 446°F) for short periods. Drying veneer to very low moisture content levels at very high temperatures and drying at moderate temperatures for prolonged periods inactivates surfaces, causing poor wetting of veneer, hence poor bonding of the plywood. Residues deposited on veneer surfaces from incomplete combustion of gases and fuel oils can cause serious adhesion problems in plywood production.

Veneer selected for its attractive appearance, or for use in sanded grades of plywood, should be uniform in thickness, smooth, flat, free from deep checks, knots, holes, and decay, and have face grain suitable for the intended face grade. For plywood of the lower grades, defect requirements are not as restricted. For example, loosely cut veneer with frequent deep checks and large defects is suitable for structural plywood, but more adhesive is required than for tightly cut veneer. Higher spread rates compensate for overpenetration of adhesive into loosely cut veneer. When rotary-cut veneer is bonded into plywood, the tight side is usually bonded to the loose side, except that in one bondline, the loose side must be bonded to the loose side. This orientation permits the face veneer to be presented with its tight side facing outward for sanding and appearance.

Surfaces of Wood and Nonwood Composite Products

The surfaces of wood products such as plywood, structural flakeboard, particleboard, fiberboard, and hardboard generally have poor wettability relative to that of freshly cut, polar wood surfaces. Surfaces of these materials may have a glazed appearance indicating they have been inactivated by pressing at high temperatures. During hot pressing, resinous extractives migrate to the surface, adhesives on the outer surfaces of particles and fibers cure, and caul release agents remain on product surfaces—all of which inactivate or block surfaces from being wetted by water-based wood adhesives. Furthermore, the strength of bonds to the surfaces of these products is limited by the strength with which surface flakes, particles, and fibers are bound to the inner flakes, particles, and fibers of the product. A much lower bond strength can be expected to the surfaces of products of particulate structure than to products of natural wood structure. Adhesion to composite panel products having poor wettability (Fig. 9–1) can be improved by lightly sanding with 320-grit sandpaper. However, too much sanding can change a flat surface to an uneven surface and perhaps produce too much loose-fiber debris that would interfere with adhesion.

Metal foils and plastic films are commonly laminated to wood panels usually by product manufacturers. Although high cohesive strength is not required of adhesives to support these materials in an indoor environment, adhesives still must be reasonably compatible with both the wood and nonwood surfaces. If a bond of greater structural integrity is required to bond wood to heavier, rigid metals and plastics, then only epoxy, polyurethane, and other isocyanate-based adhesives may be sufficiently compatible with metals and plastics. Even then, cleaning or special preparation of the nonwood surfaces may be required to remove contaminants and chemically activate the surfaces. Composite materials are becoming more common as manufacturers learn to bond dissimilar materials to gain extraordinary composite properties or cost advantages not available from a single component. Composite materials in which nonpolar thermoplastics are successfully bonded to polar wood materials with the aid of coupling agents are becoming commonplace.

Metals are stronger and stiffer than wood and if bonded well enough to effectively transfer stresses between metal and wood, the mechanical properties of wood can be enhanced by the metal so that the resultant composite performs as a single material. Metal has a much higher energy surface than does wood. On exposure to air, oxides of the metal quickly form, and with moisture, gases, and debris adsorbed from the air, the surfaces quickly develop a low energy, weak boundary layer. To restore the high energy surfaces, a series of cleaning procedures are required to prepare the surfaces for structural bonding. Steps in surface preparation include cleaning with liquid or vapor organic solvents, abrading by sandblasting, alkaline washing, chemical etching, and priming with adhesive solutions or coupling agents.

Plastics are organic polymers that may be either thermoplastic (soften on heating) or thermosetting (cross-linked and resist softening on heating). Thermoplastics generally are not as strong and stiff as wood, but thermoset materials approximate and even exceed the mechanical properties of wood. When plastics contain fibrous reinforcing materials, such as fiberglass, strength and stiffness of the composite materials greatly exceed some of the mechanical properties of wood. In so doing, reinforced plastics that are effectively bonded to wood offer stronger and more cost-effective structural composites. The surfaces of plastics generally are low energy, nonpolar, and hydrophobic. Traditional aqueous-based wood adhesives are polar and hydrophilic, so they do not bond well to plastics. Epoxies, polyurethanes, and isocyanate-based adhesives are capable of bonding many plastics to wood. Adhesion to plastic surfaces occurs primarily by physical intermolecular attraction forces and, in some cases, hydrogen bonding. Abrading and chemical etching of plastic surfaces provide some mechanical interlocking, thereby increasing adhesion. Coupling agents are particularly useful for chemically bridging dissimilar materials. They have molecules that are of either unlike or like functionalities that are capable of reacting with both the adhesive and the surface of the adherend. Treatment of plastic surfaces with an inert gas, including oxygen plasma activated by radio-frequency energy, cleans and activates surfaces for enhanced adhesion. Grafting of monomers onto cleaned plastic surfaces by means of plasma polymerization creates a polar surface that is more compatible with adhesives.

Chemical treatment of wood with preservatives, fire retardants, and dimensional stabilizers interferes with adhesion to the treated wood. Types of chemical treatment and adhesives, conditions of joint assembly and adhesive cure, and pre-bonding chemical surface treatments have varied, interacting, and even strong effects on the strength and durability of bonds. Certain combinations of these factors can lead to excellent bonds, despite the interference from chemical treatments.

Lumber treated with chromated copper arsenate (CCA) preservatives dominates the treated wood market; however, very little of the CCA-treated wood is used in adhesively bonded lumber products. Commercial adhesives do not adhere to CCA-treated wood well enough to consistently meet rigorous industrial standards for resistance to delamination in accelerated exterior service tests. Analytical studies have shown that cellular surfaces of CCA-treated wood are thoroughly covered with microscopic-size deposits of mixtures of chromium, copper, and arsenic oxides that are physicochemically fixed to cell walls. The presence of these insoluble metallic deposits is so pervasive that intermolecular forces of attraction that normally act between polar wood and adhesive are physically blocked (Fig. 9–3). A new hydroxymethylated resorcinol (HMR) coupling agent greatly improves adhesion to CCA-treated wood when HMR is applied as a dilute aqueous primer on lumber surfaces before bonding. The HMR physicochemically couples phenol-resorcinol, epoxy, emulsion polymer–isocyanate, polymeric methylene diphenyl disocyanate, and melamine-urea adhesives to treated wood so that bonds can meet rigorous industrial standards for strength and durability.

Wood preservatives other than CCA, even nonacidic waterborne preservatives including emulsion types, interfere with adhesion of hot-pressed phenolic plywood adhesives, particularly as levels of chemical retention in the wood increase. Generally, preservatives containing boron, copper, and zinc interfere with the cure of phenolic resins, although assembly conditions can be optimized to improve bonding. Certain alkyl ammonium and fluoride-based salt preservatives have demonstrated limited interference with adhesion.

The most common fire-retarding chemicals used for wood are inorganic salts based on phosphorous, nitrogen, and boron. These acid salts release acid at elevated temperatures to decrease flammable volatiles and increase char in wood, thereby effectively reducing flame spread. A few salts release acid at temperatures lower than fire conditions, and in the presence of elevated temperature and moisture service conditions, increasing acidity leads to destructive hydrolysis of the wood. The acidity of the fire-retardant-treated wood, particularly at the elevated temperature and moisture conditions of hot-press curing, also inhibits the cure and bond formation of alkaline phenolic adhesive. By priming treated-wood surfaces with certain alkaline aqueous solutions before bonding and selecting resins of appropriate molecular-size distribution, strong and durable bonds can be made to certain fire-retardant-treated woods.

Acetylation is a chemical modification of wood that drastically reduces moisture-related dimensional changes and rate of biodeterioration. Acetic anhydride is reacted with the

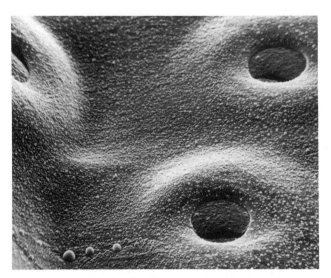

Figure 9–3. Surface of cell lumen of CCA-treated Southern Pine covered with chemically fixed deposits of insoluble mixture of chromium, copper, and arsenic oxides.

hydroxyl groups of hemicelluloses and lignin of wood. For every acetyl group reacted, one hydroxyl group is blocked from hydrogen bonding with a water molecule, and the result is lower affinity of acetylated wood for water. Reduced wettability from fewer available hydroxyl groups means poorer adhesion of aqueous-based wood adhesives. Adhesion is reduced to varying degrees among thermoplastic and thermosetting adhesives in proportion to their compatibility with the amount of nonpolar, hydrophobic acetate groups formed in the acetylated wood. Only room-temperature-curing resorcinolic adhesives and an acid-catalyzed phenolic hot-press adhesive have been found to develop durable bonds to acetylated wood. All other wood adhesives develop poorer bonds to acetylated wood than to untreated wood.

Physical Properties of Wood Adherends

Density and Porosity

The bondability of wood is not only affected by the surface properties of wood adherends but also by wood's physical properties, particularly density, porosity, moisture content, and dimensional movement.

Wood substance without void volume has a density approximating 1.5 g/cm^3 (93.6 lb/ft^3), regardless of the wood species. But density varies greatly between wood species, and even within a species, because species vary in void volume and thickness of cell walls. High density woods have thick walls and small lumen volumes, whereas low density woods have thin walls with large lumen volumes. The strength of wood is directly related to its density because thick-walled cells are capable of withstanding much greater stress than are thin-walled cells. Wood cells are an integral part of the wood–adhesive interphasing region; therefore, the adhesive bond must be at least as strong as the wood if the strength capability of the wood adherend is to be fully utilized.

The strength of adhesive bonds to wood increases with wood density up to a range of 0.7 to 0.8 g/cm^3 (43.7 to 49.9 lb/ft^3) (moisture content 12%). Above this level, joint strength decreases. Although strength increases with wood density, wood failure decreases gradually up to a density range of 0.7 to 0.8 g/cm^3 (43.7 to 49.9 lb/ft^3), then decreases more rapidly above 0.8 g/cm^3 (49.9 lb/ft^3). As wood density increases, high strength joints with high wood failure are more difficult to achieve consistently. (Wood failure means rupture of wood fibers during strength tests of adhesive bonds to wood. It is usually expressed as a percentage of the total bonded area of the joint.)

High density woods are difficult to bond for several reasons. Because of thicker cell walls and less lumen volume, adhesives do not penetrate easily, so important mechanical interlocking of adhesives is limited to one or two cells deep. Much greater pressure is required to compress stronger, stiffer, high density wood to bring contact between wood surface and adhesive. Higher concentrations of extractives that may interfere with the cure of adhesives are common in high density species, particularly domestic oaks and imported tropical hardwoods. The severe stresses produced by high density species as they change dimensions with changes in moisture content also contribute heavily to bonding difficulties.

Density is perhaps a crude indicator, but as previously noted, it is useful for estimating the bondability of a great variety of wood species. Table 9–1 categorizes commonly used domestic and imported species according to their relative ease of bonding. The categories for domestic woods are based on the average strength of side-grain joints of lumber as determined in laboratory tests and industrial experience. The laboratory tests included animal, casein, starch, urea-formaldehyde, and resorcinol-formaldehyde adhesives. The categories for imported woods are based on information found in the literature on bond strength, species properties, extractives content, and industrial experience. In most cases, the amount of data available for categorizing imported woods is not equivalent to that for domestic woods. However, a species that bonds poorly with one adhesive may develop much better bonds with another adhesive. A similar type of adhesive but with somewhat different working, penetration, curing, and even strength properties can often dramatically improve bondability of a given species. Adhesive suppliers will quite often adjust adhesive formulations to solve specific adhesion problems.

The void volume of wood, which can range from 46% to 80% of total volume, strongly affects the depth and direction that an adhesive flows. To attain the highest joint strength, the adhesive must penetrate and mechanically interlock several cells deep into sound, undamaged cell structure. In wood, porosity varies according to the grain direction. It is most porous on end-grain surfaces, being many times greater than on radial or tangential surfaces. Adhesives penetrate deeply into open fibers and vessels along the grain, so deeply that overpenetration occurs when pressure is applied to end-grain surfaces. This is a primary reason why it is so difficult to form strong, load-bearing bondlines in butt joints. Across the grain, porosity is limited because of fewer pathways in which adhesive can flow, so overpenetration under pressure generally is not a problem with a properly formulated adhesive.

The porosity of hardwoods and softwoods, both as species groups and as species within a group, varies greatly, which dramatically affects the amount and direction of adhesive flow. Highly porous softwoods, such as the southern pines, have fiber lumens that are interconnected by open pits. Pits are the small openings between fibers that permit lateral transfer of fluids in living trees. They form a complex capillary system that also allows adhesives to penetrate deeply, even in tangential and radial directions. The relatively large vessels in hardwoods have no end walls, so adhesive can penetrate indefinitely along the end grain. The remaining fibers have relatively few pits for lateral transfer of adhesive, except that hardwoods, such as the red oaks, have radially oriented rays that can allow excessive flow and overpenetration. Although adhesives for hardwoods and softwoods generally differ by chemical type according to product markets, adhesives must be specifically formulated for hardwoods or softwoods, including specific species within the groups, or have adjustable working properties for specific manufacturing situations.

Moisture Content and Dimensional Changes

Water occurs naturally in living trees—as free water in cell lumens and as adsorbed water within cell walls. Total water content of wood can range well above 200% (based on oven-dry weight), but when the free water is removed from cell lumens by drying, approximately 30% remains bound within cell walls. Water has strong molecular attraction to wood, primarily through hydrogen bonding with hydroxyl groups of wood cellulosics. Therefore, cell walls remain saturated with moisture (called the fiber saturation point) until the moisture content of the surrounding air falls below that of saturated cell walls. Actual moisture content at fiber saturation (roughly 30%) varies, depending on species, tree, temperature, and pressure. This is the critical point at which wood begins to shrink. If wood has dried below the fiber saturation point, then regains moisture, the wood will swell. These dimensional changes differ with the three principal directions, or grain directions in wood, that is, longitudinal, radial, and tangential, with intermediate changes varying with the angle between the principal directions. Longitudinal dimensional change along the grain is least and amounts to less than 1% in drying from fiber saturation point to oven-dry. Dimensional change is greatest across the grain, but the

Table 9–1. Categories of selected wood species according to ease of bonding

U.S. hardwoods	U.S. softwoods	Imported woods	

Bond easily[a]

U.S. hardwoods	U.S. softwoods	Imported woods	
Alder	Fir	Balsa	Hura
Aspen	White	Cativo	Purpleheart
Basswood	Grand	Courbaril	Roble
Cottonwood	Noble	Determa[b]	
Chestnut, American	Pacific		
Magnolia	Pine		
Willow, black	Eastern white		
	Western white		
	Redcedar, western		
	Redwood		
	Spruce, Sitka		

Bond well[c]

U.S. hardwoods	U.S. softwoods	Imported woods	
Butternut	Douglas-fir	Afromosia	Meranti (lauan)
Elm	Larch, western[d]	Andiroba	Light red
American	Pine	Angelique	White
Rock	Sugar	Avodire	Yellow
Hackberry	Ponderosa	Banak	Obeche
Maple, soft	Redcedar, eastern	Iroko	Okoume
Sweetgum		Jarrah	Opepe
Sycamore		Limba	Peroba rosa
Tupelo		Mahogany	Sapele
Walnut, black		African	Spanish-cedar
Yellow-poplar		American	Sucupira
			Wallaba

Bond satisfactorily[e]

U.S. hardwoods	U.S. softwoods	Imported woods	
Ash, white	Yellow-cedar	Angelin	Meranti (lauan), dark red
Beech, American	Port-Orford-cedar	Azobe	Pau marfim
Birch	Pines, southern	Benge	Parana-pine
Sweet		Bubinga	Pine
Yellow		Karri	Caribbean
Cherry			Radiata
Hickory			Ramin
Pecan			
True			
Madrone			
Maple, hard			
Oak			
Red[b]			
White[b]			

Bond with difficulty[f]

U.S. hardwoods	U.S. softwoods	Imported woods	
Osage-orange		Balata	Keruing
Persimmon		Balau	Lapacho
		Greenheart	Lignumvitae
		Kaneelhart	Rosewood
		Kapur	Teak

[a]Bond very easily with adhesives of a wide range of properties and under a wide range of bonding conditions.
[b]Difficult to bond with phenol-formaldehyde adhesive.
[c]Bond well with a fairly wide range of adhesives under a moderately wide range of bonding conditions.
[d]Wood from butt logs with high extractive content is difficult to bond.
[e]Bond satisfactorily with good-quality adhesives under well-controlled bonding conditions.
[f]Satisfactory results require careful selection of adhesives and very close control of bonding conditions; may require special surface treatment.

amounts differ with the direction; dimensional change varies with and within species. As a rule of thumb, tangential dimensional change is about twice that of the radial direction; but again, there are variations by species. (See Ch. 3 for a detailed discussion of wood moisture relations.)

Dimensional changes that accompany changes in moisture content have broad-ranging and significant consequences on performance of bonded joints. As wood in bonded assemblies swells and shrinks, stresses develop that can be great enough to rupture adhesive bond and wood. Ruptures may develop when adjacent pieces of wood in a bonded joint differ in grain direction and shrinkage coefficients, for example, radial grain bonded to tangential grain, or in the worst case, longitudinal grain bonded to either tangential or radial grain. Even if moisture content levels in adjacent pieces are equal, but changing, stresses could be severe. Moreover, if moisture content in one piece is at equilibrium with surrounding air, that is, stable, but the other piece with differing grain direction is shrinking as it approaches equilibrium moisture content (EMC), then resultant stresses would be compounded and almost sure to rupture either the adhesive bond or the wood, whichever is weaker. Some wood adhesives are elastic enough to yield to stresses so that fracture does not occur. Structural wood adhesives have greater moduli of elasticity than wood and can effectively transfer stresses from one adherend to the other without failure. However, if stresses are great enough from extraordinary moisture content changes within adjacent pieces of wood of differing shrinkage coefficients, then fracture in either wood or a poor bond is almost inevitable. Severe stresses on bondlines can be minimized by bonding pieces of wood with compatible grain directions of low shrinkage coefficients at a uniform moisture content equivalent to that which the bonded assembly will encounter in service.

The amount of moisture in wood combined with water in adhesive will greatly influence the wetting, flow, penetration, and even cure of aqueous wood adhesives. In general, these adhesives bond satisfactorily across moisture content levels ranging from 6% to 14% and even below and above this range when adhesives are formulated for specialized processing. The optimum moisture content range for bonding a specific product with a specific adhesive is determined from practical experience and product performance. Aqueous adhesives tend to dry out when applied to wood below 6% moisture content. Wood absorbs water from the adhesive so quickly that adhesive flow and penetration into the wood is drastically inhibited, even under high pressure. Wood may become so dry below 3% moisture content that it temporarily resists wetting by the adhesive because insufficient water remains bound to the wood to establish intermolecular attraction forces with water in the adhesive.

When wood contains excess amounts of moisture, then less water and adhesive can be absorbed by the wood. This leads to excessive adhesive mobility, followed by squeeze-out when pressure is applied. Control of moisture content is particularly critical to bonding in hot presses because excess moisture increases adhesive mobility, followed by overpenetration of the adhesive. Furthermore, high vapor pressure builds internally as water boils, and on release of platen pressure, sudden release of internal pressure actually separates laminates along the bondlines, called blows. Even if blows do not occur, excess moisture within thermosetting adhesives can prevent complete cross-linking with accompanying weakened adhesive film and bond. Appropriate moisture content levels of wood for bonding by hot-press methods are well known, as are target moisture content levels for satisfactory service of wood products throughout the United States. However, control of moisture content in bonding wood materials is not easily achieved. This is discussed in the Moisture Content Control section.

Adhesives

Composition

Organic polymers of either natural or synthetic origin are the major chemical ingredients in all formulations of wood adhesives. According to ASTM, a polymer is a compound formed by the reaction of simple molecules having functional groups that permit their combination to proceed to higher molecular weights under suitable conditions. Polysaccharides and proteins are high molecular weight natural polymers derived from plants and animals. Animal, blood, hide, casein, starch, soybean, dextrin, and cellulosic adhesives are all derived from the natural polymers found in these indicated sources. They have been used as adhesives for centuries and are still in use today, although they have been replaced mostly by adhesives made with synthetic polymers. The first wood adhesives based on synthetic polymers were produced commercially during the 1930s. This marked the beginning of fundamental changes in composition of adhesives from natural to synthesized polymers. These adhesives could not only be stronger, more rigid, and more durable than wood, but also have much greater resistance to water than adhesives from natural polymers.

Synthetic polymers are chemically designed and formulated into adhesives to perform a great variety of bonding functions. Whether the base polymer is thermoplastic or thermosetting has a major influence on how an adhesive will perform in service. Thermoplastics are long-chain polymers that soften and flow on heating, then harden again by cooling. They generally have less resistance to heat, moisture, and long-term static loading than do thermosetting polymers. Common wood adhesives that are based on thermoplastic polymers include polyvinyl acetate emulsions, elastomerics, contacts, and hot-melts. Thermosetting polymers make excellent structural adhesives because they undergo irreversible chemical change, and on reheating, they do not soften and flow again. They form cross-linked polymers that have high strength, have resistance to moisture and other chemicals, and are rigid enough to support high, long-term static loads without deforming. Phenolic, resorcinolic, melamine, isocyanate, urea, and epoxy are examples of types of wood adhesives that are based on thermosetting polymers.

A formulation of wood adhesive consists of a mixture of several chemically active and inert materials that vary in proportion with the basic adhesive polymer, which enhances performance, whether it be working characteristics, strength properties, shelf life, or durability. Solvents disperse or dissolve adhesive polymers, act as carriers of polymer and additives, aid wetting, and control flow and penetration of the adhesive. Water is used as the carrier for most wood adhesives, primarily because water readily absorbs into wood, is inexpensive, and is free of toxicity problems. Adhesive polymers can be brought into intimate, even molecular, contact with wood by water as the carrier. Organic solvents are used with elastomeric and contact adhesives, although water-based adhesive systems have lower toxicity and flammability. Fillers of both organic and inorganic origins contribute to rheological control of the fluid system, particularly in reducing the spreading and penetrating of the adhesive into wood. Reinforcing fibers, mostly inert and of organic origins, can enhance an adhesive film's mechanical properties, especially toughness, impact resistance, and shrinkage. Extenders are filler-like organic materials that may have sufficient chemical activity to improve adhesion to a small degree, but they are used primarily to control flow and other working characteristics, without excess sacrifice of adhesion capability, as is the case with most fillers.

Certain chemicals and polymeric systems plasticize adhesive polymers, and others are used to enhance tackiness. Plasticizers, such as dibutyl phthalate, are used to soften brittle vinyl acetate homopolymer in polyvinyl acetate emulsion adhesives, which facilitates diffusion of adhesive and formation of a flexible adhesive film from the emulsion at and below room temperature. Phenolic polymers are used as tackifiers and adhesion promoters in neoprene and nitrile rubber contact adhesives. Reactive polymeric fortifiers, such as melamine-formaldehyde, can be substituted in limited proportions in urea-formaldehyde adhesives to improve resistance to moisture and heat. Phenol-formaldehyde may be substituted for resorcinol-formaldehyde to reduce adhesive costs, without sacrificing adhesive strength and durability.

Catalysts are chemicals used to accelerate the rate of chemical reaction of polymeric components. Acids, bases, salts, peroxides, and sulfur compounds are a few examples of catalysts. Catalysts do not become a part of the reacted compound; they simply increase the rate of reaction. Hardeners are added to base polymers as reactive components, and they do become a part of the reacted compound. Examples are an amine hardener added to epoxy and formaldehyde added to resorcinol—all produce cross-linking reactions to solidify the adhesive. Other chemicals, such as antioxidants, acid scavengers, preservatives, wetting agents, defoamers, even colorants, may be added to control or eliminate some of the less desirable characteristics of certain adhesive formulations.

Health and Safety

Wood adhesives contain chemicals that are toxic to people if they are exposed to sufficient concentrations for prolonged periods. Generally, it is accepted that wood adhesives in a cured state do not present toxicity problems. A notable exception is urea-formaldehyde adhesive, which can release low concentrations of formaldehyde from bonded wood products under certain service conditions. Formaldehyde is a toxic gas that can react with proteins of the body to cause irritation and, in some cases, inflammation of membranes of eyes, nose, and throat. It is a suspected carcinogen, based on laboratory experiments with rats. Considerable research has led to new adhesive formulations with significantly reduced levels of formaldehyde emissions in both manufacturing operations and bonded wood products. Phenol-formaldehyde adhesives, which are used to manufacture plywood, flakeboard, and fiberglass insulation, also contain formaldehyde. However, formaldehyde is efficiently consumed in the curing reaction, and the highly durable phenol-formaldehyde, resorcinol-formaldehyde, and phenol-resorcinol-formaldehyde polymers do not chemically break down in service to release toxic gas.

Diisocyanates are highly reactive chemicals that polymerize rapidly on contact with strong alkali, mineral acids, and water. Polymeric methylene diphenyl diisocyanate (PMDI) adhesives develop strong and durable bonds to wood, so they are now widely used to manufacture composite wood products. They are potentially hazardous if mishandled, but the low vapor pressure of PMDI adhesives coupled with adequate ventilation to remove airborne PMDI on dust particles, permits manufacturing plants to operate safely. Properly cured PMDI adhesives are not considered hazardous in bonded wood products.

Construction and contact adhesives contain organic solvents that have low flash points. If these adhesives are used in unventilated areas where concentrations build to dangerously high levels, explosions can occur with an ignition source. Some adhesive producers now offer less flammable formulations based on chlorinated solvents. Organic solvents in these adhesives are toxic, but by following the manufacturer's handling and use instructions, coupled with adequate ventilation, harmful effects can be avoided.

Health and safety regulations require that toxic and hazardous chemicals be identified and visibly labeled to warn of their dangers. Material safety data sheets (MSDS) or instructions are provided with adhesive products to advise of proper handling procedures, protective gear and clothing, and procedures for dealing with spills and fire, as well as to offer guidance for first-aid and professional treatment of injuries. The statements made in this section concerning safety of adhesives and effects on the health of the user are general and not meant to be all inclusive. The user should consult the MSDS and follow the manufacturer's instructions and precautions before using any adhesive.

Strength and Durability

The ability of an adhesive to transfer load from one member of an assembly to another and to maintain integrity of the assembly under the expected conditions of service will govern the choice of adhesive for a given application.

In building construction, adhesives that contribute strength and stiffness during the life of the structure are considered structural. They generally are stronger and stiffer than the wood members. Structural bonds are critical because bond failure could result in serious damage to the structure, even loss of life. Examples of structural applications include glued-laminated beams, prefabricated I-joists, and stressed-skin panels. Adhesives that are strongest, most rigid, and most resistant to deterioration in service, unfortunately, are those least tolerant of wide variations in wood surface condition, wood moisture content, and assembly conditions including pressures, temperatures, and curing conditions. Examples of rigid structural adhesives include phenolic, resorcinol, melamine, urea, and casein (Table 9–2).

Adhesives are further categorized in Table 9–2 as to how well they transfer load relative to wood as the service environment becomes more severe. Structural adhesives that maintain their strength and rigidity under the most severe cyclic water-saturation and drying are considered fully exterior adhesives. Rigid adhesives that lose their ability to transfer load faster than does wood as service conditions worsen, particularly with regard to moisture, are considered interior adhesives. Between exterior and interior adhesives are the intermediate adhesives that maintain strength and rigidity in short-term water soaking but deteriorate faster than wood during long-term exposure to water and heat. Adhesives that are the weakest, least rigid, and least resistant to severe service conditions are those most tolerant of wide variations in wood surface, assembly, and curing conditions.

Semistructural adhesives impart strength and stiffness to an adhesive-bonded assembly, and in some instances, they may be as strong and rigid as wood. However, semistructural adhesives generally do not withstand long-term static loading without deformation. They are capable of short-term exposure to water but not long-term saturation, hence their limited exterior classification. Examples are cross-linking polyvinyl acetate and polyurethane adhesives. Another example of the semistructural adhesive application is the nailed–glued assembly where failure of the bond would not cause serious loss of structural integrity because the load would be carried by mechanical fasteners.

Table 9–2. Wood adhesives categorized according to their expected structural performance at varying levels of environmental exposure [a,b]

Structural integrity	Service environment	Adhesive type
Structural	Fully exterior (withstands long-term water soaking and drying)	Phenol-formaldehyde
		Resorcinol-formaldehyde
		Phenol-resorcinol-formaldehyde
		Emulsion polymer/isocyanate
		Melamine-formaldehyde
	Limited exterior (withstands short-term water soaking)	Melamine-urea-formaldehyde
		Isocyanate
		Epoxy
	Interior (withstands short-term high humidity)	Urea-formaldehyde
		Casein
Semistructural	Limited exterior	Cross-linked polyvinyl acetate
		Polyurethane
Nonstructural	Interior	Polyvinyl acetate
		Animal
		Soybean
		Elastomeric construction
		Elastomeric contact
		Hot-melt
		Starch

[a]Assignment of an adhesive type to only one structural/service environment category does not exclude certain adhesive formulations from falling into the next higher or lower category.
[b]Priming wood surfaces with hydroxymethylated resorcinol coupling agent improves resistance to delamination of epoxy, isocyanate, emulsion polymer/isocyanate, melamine and urea, phenolic, and resorcinolic adhesives in exterior service environment, particularly bonds to CCA-treated lumber.

Nonstructural adhesives typically support the dead weight of the material being bonded and can equal the strength and rigidity of wood in the dry condition. However, on exposure to water or high humidity, nonstructural adhesives quickly lose their load transfer ability. Examples are adhesives used for bonding wall tiles and fixtures.

Elastomeric construction adhesives are categorized as nonstructural. However, they are used normally for field assembly of panelized floor and wall systems in the light-frame construction industry. Nails are used in the assembly so that if failure did occur in the adhesive bond, the structural load would be carried by nails. The adhesive enables the nailed assembly to act as a composite with increased stiffness. With nails providing structural safety in this application, elastomeric adhesives could be included in the semistructural category.

Some adhesives listed in Table 9–2 could be included easily in more than one category because they can be formulated for a broad range of applications. Isocyanate and polyurethane adhesives are examples. Polymeric methylene diphenyl diisocyanates of low molecular weight develop highly durable bonds in structural flakeboards, although flakeboard products deteriorate from swelling and shrinkage stresses. One-part polyurethane adhesives have highly durable adhesive films, but as molecular weight increases, adhesion to porous wood generally decreases and bonds become increasingly susceptible to deterioration from swelling and shrinkage stresses. Polyurethane adhesives liberate carbon dioxide on reaction with water. As a result, they foam, and in thick bondlines, polyurethane bonds become more deformable under static loading. Two-part polyurethanes can be formulated for rigidity, depending on the degree of structural loading required.

Adhesive Selection

Adhesive selection begins by considering the types of wood adhesives, along with their strength and durability, preparation and use characteristics, and typical applications, as shown in abbreviated form in Table 9–3. Their relative strength and durability are categorized into levels of structural integrity (Table 9–2) and were discussed previously. Adhesive selection for a wood product manufacturer may begin as a cooperative effort between the manufacturer and an adhesive supplier. Together, they completely review the product, its intended service environment, and all production processes and equipment before choosing an appropriate adhesive. Whatever the approach to adhesive selection might be, the following general discussion should be helpful.

A broad array of adhesive types, with significant variations within each type, are available for bonding wood materials, even for bonding wood to nonwood materials. The selection process begins with determining which adhesives are compatible with the physical and chemical properties of the adherends, particularly their surface properties. The polar, aqueous wood adhesive must be capable of wetting the usually polar wood surface, within its normal variations in hydrophilicity. As the adhesive wets, it must have flow properties that enable it to spread over surfaces of variable roughness and to penetrate wood structures that differ in porosity, with respect to grain orientation at the bondline. The adhesive must make molecular contact with the lignocellulosics of wood and penetrate deeply enough to mechanically interlock with the wood's cell structure. Metals and plastics cannot be penetrated, so these materials generally cannot be bonded with aqueous wood adhesives. However, nonaqueous, 100% solids adhesives, including epoxy, isocyanate, and polyurethane, are capable of sound bonds to nonwood and wood materials.

The structural integrity expected of the adhesive bond under anticipated service loads in the presence of expected environmental exposure conditions should be one of the foremost considerations. To intelligently select an adhesive for a given bonded assembly, it is necessary to have an approximation of the nature, direction, level, and duration of loading that the assembly and bondlines must withstand. Furthermore, it is essential to know the range and duration of temperature and moisture content levels to which bondlines will be subjected. For example, prolonged exposure to high moisture content levels will significantly reduce the load-carrying ability of any adhesive in a wood joint. Failure to give full consideration to these factors could risk structural failure of the bonded assembly, even severe personal injury.

There may be need for tradeoffs between bonding requirements of adhesives and their resistance to stress, duration of load, and service environment. Adhesives that are the strongest, most rigid, and durable are generally those least tolerant of bonding conditions, including wood moisture content, surface roughness, cleanliness, inactivation, grain orientation, bondline thickness, and pressure and temperature of cure. Adhesives that are the weakest, least rigid, and least resistant to service conditions are those most tolerant of bonding conditions. Many adhesives are positioned between these extremes of bonding requirements and performance (Tables 9–2 and 9–3).

When a group of adhesives with suitable performance capabilities for a particular bonded assembly has been determined, the user also must choose within that group an adhesive that can be mixed, applied, and cured with available equipment or consider the cost of purchasing equipment to meet specific working properties of another adhesive. Important working properties must be considered when making cost decisions. The working life of an adhesive is the time between mixing and the end of its useful life when it becomes too viscous to properly wet and flow over a surface.

If an adhesive requires mixing with a hardener or catalyst, then mixing and application equipment appropriate for the working life must be considered. Given the consistency of an adhesive, specific types of application equipment are required. Depending on the size of the spreading operation, the equipment can range from brush to roll-spreader to extruder to spray to meter-mixed extrusion. Wood adhesives, including phenolic, melamine, urea, and isocyanate adhesives,

Table 9–3. Working and strength properties of adhesives, with typical uses

Type	Form and color	Preparation and application	Strength properties	Typical uses
Natural origin				
Animal, protein	Solid and liquid; brown to white bondline	Solid form added to water, soaked, and melted; adhesive kept warm during application; liquid form applied directly; both pressed at room temperature; bonding process must be adjusted for small changes in temperature	High dry strength; low resistance to water and damp atmosphere	Assembly of furniture and stringed instruments; repairs of antique furniture
Blood, protein	Solid and partially dried whole blood; dark red to black bondline	Mixed with cold water, lime, caustic soda, and other chemicals; applied at room temperature; pressed either at room temperature or 120°C (250°F) and higher	High dry strength; moderate resistance to water and damp atmosphere and to microorganisms	Interior-type softwood plywood, some times in combination with soybean adhesive; mostly replaced by phenolic adhesive
Casein, protein	Powder with added chemicals; white to tan bondline	Mixed with water; applied and pressed at room temperature	High dry strength; moderate resistance to water, damp atmospheres, and intermediate temperatures; not suitable for exterior uses	Interior doors; discontinued use in laminated timbers
Soybean, protein	Powder with added chemicals; white to tan, similar color in bondline	Mixed with cold water, lime, caustic soda, and other chemicals; applied and pressed at room temperatures, but more frequently hot pressed when blended with blood adhesive	Moderate to low dry strength; moderate to low resistance to water and damp atmospheres; moderate resistance to intermediate temperatures	Softwood plywood for interior use, now replaced by phenolic adhesive. New fast-setting resorcinol-soybean adhesives for fingerjointing of lumber being developed
Lignocellulosic residues and extracts	Powder or liquid; may be blended with phenolic adhesive; dark brown bondline	Blended with extender and filler by user; adhesive cured in hot-press 130°C to 150°C (266°F to 300 °F) similar to phenolic adhesive	Good dry strength; moderate to good wet strength; durability improved by blending with phenolic adhesive	Partial replacement for phenolic adhesive in composite and plywood panel products
Synthetic origin				
Cross-linkable polyvinyl acetate emulsion	Liquid, similar to polyvinyl acetate emulsions but includes copolymers capable of cross-linking with a separate catalyst; white to tan with colorless bondline	Liquid emulsion mixed with catalyst; cure at room temperature or at elevated temperature in hot press and radio-frequency press	High dry strength; improved resistance to moisture and elevated temperatures, particularly long-term performance in moist environment	Interior and exterior doors; moulding and architectural woodwork; cellulosic overlays
Elastomeric contact	Viscous liquid, typically neoprene or styrene-butadiene elastomers in organic solvent or water emulsion; tan to yellow	Liquid applied directly to both surfaces, partially dried after spreading and before pressing; roller-pressing at room temperature produces instant bonding	Strength develops immediately upon pressing, increases slowly over a period of weeks; dry strengths much lower than those of conventional wood adhesives; low resistance to water and damp atmospheres; adhesive film readily yields under static load	On-the-job bonding of decorative tops to kitchen counters; factory lamination of wood, paper, metal, and plastic sheet materials
Elastomeric mastic (construction adhesive)	Putty like consistency, synthetic or natural elastomers in organic solvent or latex emulsions; tan, yellow, gray	Mastic extruded in bead to framing members by caulking gun or like pressure equipment; nailing required to hold materials in place during setting and service	Strength develops slowly over several weeks; dry strength lower than conventional wood adhesives; resistant to water and moist atmospheres; tolerant of out door assembly conditions; gap-filling; nailing required to ensure structural integrity	Lumber to plywood in floor and wall systems; laminating gypsum board and rigid foam insulating; assembly of panel system in manufactured homes
Emulsion polymer/isocyanate	Liquid emulsion and separate isocyanate hardener; white with hardener; colorless bondline	Emulsion and hardener mixed by user; reactive on mixing with controllable pot-life and curing time; cured at room and elevated temperatures; radio-frequency curable; high pressure required	High dry and wet strength; very resistant to water and damp atmosphere; very resistant to prolonged and repeated wetting and drying; adheres to metals and plastics	Laminated beams for interior and exterior use; lamination of plywood to steel metals and plastics; doors and architectural materials

Table 9–3. Working and strength properties of adhesives, with typical uses—con.

Type	Form and color	Preparation and application	Strength properties	Typical uses
Epoxy	Liquid resin and hardener supplied as two parts; completely reactive leaving no free solvent; clear to amber; colorless bondline	Resin and hardener mixed by user; reactive with limited pot-life; cured at room or elevated temperatures; only low pressure required for bond development	High dry and wet strength to wood, metal, glass, and plastic; formulations for wood resist water and damp atmospheres; delaminate with repeated wetting and drying; gap-filling	Laminating veneer and lumber in cold-molded wood boat hulls; assembly of wood components in aircraft; lamination of architectural railings and posts; repair of laminated wood beams and architectural building components; laminating sports equipment; general purpose home and shop
Hot melt	Solid blocks, pellets, ribbons, rods, or films; solvent-free; white to tan; near colorless bondline	Solid form melted for spreading; bond formed on solidification; requires special application equipment for controlling melt and flow	Develops strength quickly on cooling; lower strength than conventional wood adhesives; moderate resistance to moisture; gap-filling with minimal penetration	Edge-banding of panels; plastic lamination; patching; film and paper overlays; furniture assembly; general purpose home and shop
Isocyanate	Liquid containing isomers and oligomers of methylene diphenyl diisocyanate; light brown liquid and clear bondline	Adhesive applied directly by spray; reactive with water; requires high temperature and high pressure for best bond development in flake boards	High dry and wet strength; very resistant to water and damp atmosphere; adheres to metals and plastics	Flakeboards; strand-wood products
Melamine and melamine-urea	Powder with blended catalyst; may be blended up to 40% with urea; white to tan; colorless bondline	Mixed with water; cured in hot press at 120°C to 150°C (250°F to 300°F); particularly suited for fast curing in high-frequency presses	High dry and wet strength; very resistant to water and damp atmospheres	Melamine-urea primary adhesive for durable bonds in hardwood plywood; end-jointing and edge-gluing of lumber; and scarf joining softwood plywood
Phenolic	Liquid, powder, and dry film; dark red bondline	Liquid blended with extenders and fillers by user; film inserted directly between laminates; powder applied directly to flakes in composites; all formulations cured in hot press at 120°C to 150°C (250°F to 300°F) up to 200°C (392°F) in flakeboards	High dry and wet strength; very resistant to water and damp atmospheres; more resistant than wood to high temperatures and chemical aging	Primary adhesive for exterior softwood plywood, flakeboard, and hardboard
Polyvinyl acetate emulsion	Liquid ready to use; often polymerized with other polymers; white to tan to yellow; colorless bondline	Liquid applied directly; pressed at room temperatures and in high-frequency press	High dry strength; low resistance to moisture and elevated temperatures; joints yield under continued stress	Furniture; flush doors; plastic laminates; panelized floor and wall systems in manufactured housing; general purpose in home and shop
Polyurethane	Low viscosity liquid to high viscosity mastic; supplied as one part; two-part systems completely reactive; color varies from clear to brown; colorless bondline	Adhesive applied directly to one surface, preferably to water-misted surface; reactive with moisture on surface and in air; cures at room temperature; high pressure required, but mastic required only pressure from nailing	High dry and wet strength; resistant to water and damp atmosphere; limited resistance to prolonged and repeated wetting and drying; gap-filling	General purpose home and shop; construction adhesive for panelized floor and wall systems; laminating plywood to metal and plastic sheet materials; specialty laminates; installation of gypsum board
Resorcinol and phenol-resorcinol	Liquid resin and powdered hardener supplied as two parts; phenol may be copolymerized with resorcinol; dark red bondline	Liquid mixed with powdered or liquid hardener; resorcinol adhesives cure at room temperatures; phenol-resorcinols cure at temperatures from 21°C to 66°C (70°F to 150°F)	High dry and wet strength; very resistant to moisture and damp atmospheres; more resistant than wood to high temperature and chemical aging.	Primary adhesives for laminated timbers and assembly joints that must withstand severe service conditions.
Urea	Powder and liquid forms; may be blended with melamine or other more durable resins; white to tan resin with colorless bondline	Powder mixed with water, hardener, filler, and extender by user; some formulations cure at room temperatures, others require hot pressing at 120°C (250°F); curable with high-frequency heating	High dry and wet strength; moderately durable under damp atmospheres; moderate to low resistance to temperatures in excess of 50°C (122°F)	Hardwood plywood; furniture; fiberboard; particleboard; underlayment; flush doors; furniture cores

must be cured at high temperatures and require expensive, heated presses. Some of these can be cured within minutes in expensive high frequency heated presses. Cold presses or clamps are satisfactory for room-temperature-curing adhesives, although the long curing time in production can be a constraint. Even after hot or cold pressing, adhesive bonds must remain undisturbed until most of the curing has occurred.

There are other important considerations, particularly in furniture and interior millwork, where appearance is all-important. Adhesive color, ability to absorb stains and finishes, and freedom from bleeding and staining are critical factors. The urea-formaldehyde and polyvinyl acetate adhesives used in the furniture industry are formulated to give a tan or colorless joint with good acceptance of stain.

Ease and simplicity of use can also be important factors. One-part adhesives, like liquid animal, polyvinyl acetate, hot-melt, and phenol-formaldehyde film, are the simplest to use because there is no chance for error in weighing and mixing components. Water-dispersed and film adhesives are easy to clean up, whereas films are the least messy. Two-, three-, or multiple-part adhesives require careful measuring and mixing of components. They often require special solvents for cleanup after bonding. Frequently, adhesives are toxic to the skin or give off toxic fumes. Formaldehyde hardener for resorcinol, phenol, melamine, and urea adhesives is an irritant to many people. Amine hardeners in some epoxy adhesives are strong skin sensitizers.

The cost of an adhesive and related application equipment must be balanced against comparable cost factors for substituted adhesives. In recent years, the cost of organic solvents and the cost of recovering volatiles to prevent air pollution have increased. Substituted water-based systems can be cheaper due to low cost of the solvent; however, grain raising of the wood and slower drying must be considered because of their effects on performance and overall cost.

Bonding Process

The bonding process involves a great number of factors that determine how successfully an adhesive bond will ultimately perform in service. The better these factors are understood and controlled, the fewer bonding problems will be encountered, along with their attendant expense. It is not necessary to be an adhesive expert to manufacture acceptable bonds, although more knowledge is always helpful. However, it is essential that the user follow the instructions of the adhesive supplier during the entire bonding process. The supplier has extensive technical knowledge of an adhesive's composition, working characteristics, and performance properties, which is reinforced by the experience of customers.

Moisture Content Control

After adhesive selection, the next most important factor contributing to trouble-free service of adhesive bonds is control of wood moisture content before and during the bonding process. Moisture content strongly affects the final strength and durability of joints, development of surface checks in the wood, and dimensional stability of the bonded assembly. Large changes in the moisture content compared with that at the time of bonding will cause shrinking or swelling stresses that can seriously weaken both wood and joints and can cause warping, twisting, and surface irregularities. Wood should not be bonded at high moisture content, particularly high density hardwoods that have large coefficients of shrinkage, unless the in-service moisture content is also expected to be high. The wood should be dry enough so that even if moisture is added during bonding, the moisture content is at about the level expected for the assembly in service.

Determining the proper moisture content for bonding depends primarily on the amount of moisture that is contained in the wood and adhesive and whether or not the adhesive curing process involves heating. For example, if boards are bonded at room temperature, the final moisture content is controlled mainly by the moisture content of the wood. In a lumber laminate, the number of bondlines are so few that a waterborne adhesive adds only 1% to 2% to the total moisture content of the laminate. However, if several pieces of veneer are bonded at room temperature, the moisture added by the adhesive in many bondlines can significantly increase the moisture content of the wood well above the target in-service level. Thus, thickness of the laminates, number of laminates, density of the wood, water content of the adhesive, quantity of adhesive spread, and hot or cold pressing all have a cumulative effect on the moisture content of the wood. During hot pressing, a moderate amount of water evaporates from the laminate as it is removed from the press. However, to minimize plastic flow of the hot and moist wood and prevent steam blisters or blows, the total moisture content of the assembly should not exceed 10% during hot pressing. A lumber moisture content of 6% to 7%, assuming 1% to 2% will be added by aqueous adhesives, is satisfactory for cold pressing of furniture and interior millwork. Lumber being laminated for exterior use should contain 10% to 12% moisture before bonding. A moisture content of 3% to 5% in veneer at the time of hot pressing is satisfactory for hardwood plywood intended for furniture and interior millwork and for softwood plywood intended for construction and industrial uses.

Lumber that has been kiln dried to the approximate average moisture content intended for bonding may still be at different moisture content levels between boards and within individual boards. Large differences in the moisture content between adjacent boards bonded together result in considerable stress on the common joint as the boards equalize toward a common moisture content. Best results are achieved when differences are not greater than about 5% for lower density species and 2% for high density species.

The moisture content of wood in bonded products should be targeted to the EMC that the product will experience in

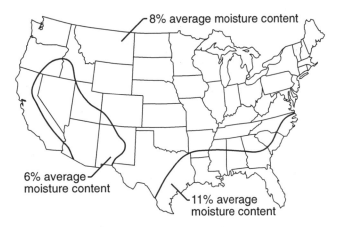

Figure 9–4. Average equilibrium moisture content for wood in building interiors in regions of the United States.

service. These conditions vary in the United States; regional average EMC values of wood in building interiors are shown in Figure 9–4. The average moisture content for most of the United States is 8%. The average increases to 11% along the Atlantic and Gulf coastal regions; in the arid southwest, the EMC is relatively low at 6%. The moisture content of wood exposed to outdoor air generally is higher and more variable and averages near 12% and ranges from 7% to 14% in most of the United States. During winter in the northern states, heating of indoor air that is normally dry lowers wood EMC to 4% to 5%. Furniture manufactured in the southeast at 11% EMC, then sold or moved to northern states where EMC drops to 4%, usually will experience some splitting, delamination of joints, or other noticeable appearance defects. Manufacturers of bonded wood products must be aware of these regional and seasonal variations, then condition the wood and bond it at moisture content levels that are consistent with regional service conditions.

Surface Preparation

The physical and chemical condition of wood and nonwood surfaces was described in a previous section where emphasis was placed on understanding the relationships between surface condition and adhesive bond performance. Wood surfaces are best prepared for maximum adhesive wetting, flow, and penetration by removing all materials that might interfere with bond formation to sound wood. Ideally, wood should be knife-planed within 24 h of adhesive spreading. However, other surfacing methods have been used successfully for certain types of bonded joints, including sawing for furniture and millwork, knife-cutting for veneer, and abrasive-planing for panels. All must produce smooth, flat, parallel surfaces, free from machining irregularities, such as burnishes, skips, and crushed, torn, and chipped grain. Properly planed flat surfaces help ensure that a layer of adhesive of uniform thickness can be uniformly spread over the adherend.

Adhesive Spreading

Regardless of method, the purpose in spreading adhesive is to distribute an adequate amount of adhesive of uniform thickness over the bonding area, so that under pressure, the adhesive will flow into a uniformly thin layer. Assuming that the spreader is capable of applying adhesive uniformly and that surfaces are smooth, flat, and parallel, then adhesive will flow ideally if uniform pressure is applied. The amount of adhesive needed will depend on the wood species, moisture content, type of adhesive, temperature and humidity of the air, assembly time, and whether adhesive will be applied to one or both surfaces. Adhesives can be spread by hand with brush, roller, or bead-extruder, but in manufacturing, adhesives are applied by machines, such as roll-spreader, extruder, curtain-coater, or spray. Instead of applying a uniform film, extruders apply continuous, uniformly spaced beads of discreet diameter and flow rate. When pressure is applied to both adherends, the adhesive is squeezed into a uniformly thin layer. An extruder of this type is used to apply adhesive to veneer in the manufacture of laminated veneer lumber (LVL) (Fig. 9–5). A pressurized extruder is used in the field to apply a single bead of elastomeric construction adhesive to joists for a plywood floor system (Fig. 9–6).

Assembly and Pressing

Control of consistency after the adhesive has been spread and until pressure is applied is a balancing act of a variety of factors. The relationships between adhesive consistency and bonding pressure as they affect formation of strong bonds are illustrated in Figure 9–7. Adhesive consistency strongly affects adhesive wetting, flow, and penetration, particularly the transfer of adhesive to an unspread wood surface, when pressure is applied to the assembly. Adhesive consistency depends upon type of adhesive, type of solvent, and proportion of solvent in the mixture, age of adhesive mixture, amount of adhesive spread, species of wood, moisture content of wood, temperature of wood, temperature and humidity of surrounding air, and the critically important evaporation and absorption of solvent during the assembly time. Assembly time is the time between spreading adhesive on wood surfaces and applying pressure to the assembly. When the adhesive-spread surfaces remain open before assembly (open assembly), then consistency is most affected by evaporative capacity of the surrounding air and absorbency of the wood's surface. When the assembly is closed and before applying pressure (closed assembly), consistency is most influenced by absorbency factors and least affected by evaporation. Cold-setting waterborne wood adhesives lose water by absorption and evaporation so that consistency steadily increases until they eventually set. Thermosetting waterborne adhesives also dry out, but despite water loss, they flow to some extent in the presence of heat, then harden with additional heating.

Pressure serves several useful purposes: it forces entrapped air from the joint; it brings adhesive into molecular contact with the wood surfaces; it forces adhesive to penetrate into the wood structure for more effective mechanical interlocking;

Figure 9–5. An extruder applies continuous and uniformly sized and spaced beads of adhesive to veneer for laminating into LVL.

Figure 9–6. A pressurized extruder applies a single bead of elastomeric construction adhesive to floor joists for assembly of a plywood floor system.

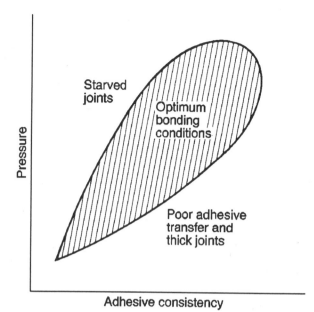

Figure 9–7. An illustration of the relationships between adhesive consistency and bonding pressure as they affect bond formation by a thermosetting adhesive.

it squeezes the adhesive into a thin continuous film; and it holds the assembly in position while the adhesive cures. But if pressure is too high, the adhesive can overpenetrate porous woods and cause starved joints that are inferior in bond strength (Fig. 9–7). The strongest joints result when the consistency of the adhesive permits the use of moderately high pressures that are consistent with the recommended pressures for the density of the wood.

Low pressures near 700 kPa (100 lb/in²) are suitable for low density wood because the surfaces easily conform to each other, thus ensuring intimate contact between adhesive and wood. High pressures up to 1,700 kPa (247 lb/in²) are required for the highest density woods that are difficult to compress. Flat, well-planed surfaces of small area can be bonded satisfactorily at lower pressures; however, because high pressure tends to squeeze adhesive into the wood or out of the joint, adhesives of greater consistency are required for denser woods (Fig. 9–7). Greater consistency can be achieved with longer assembly time, which allows increased absorption of liquid solvent by the wood and evaporation into the air. Care is required, regardless of wood density, to ensure that the assembly time is not excessive, lest the adhesive dry out or even precure before pressure is applied. Predried or precured adhesive will result in inadequate transfer of adhesive to an opposite unspread surface, and the bondline will be thick and weak (Fig. 9–7).

Lumber joints should be kept under pressure until they have enough strength to withstand handling stresses that tend to separate the pieces of wood. When cold-pressing lumber under normal bonding conditions, this stage can be reached in as little as 15 min or as long as 24 h, depending on the temperature of the room and the wood, the curing characteristics of the adhesive, and the thickness, density, and absorptive characteristics of the wood. When hot pressing, the time under pressure varies with temperature of platens, thickness and species of wood, and adhesive formulation. In actual practice, hot-pressing times vary from 2 to 15 min and up to 30 min for very thick laminates. The time under pressure can be reduced to less than 3 min with high frequency heating. High frequency concentrates energy in the conductive bondline to rapidly cure the adhesive. It is commonly used for bonding lumber, forming end- and edge-grain joints, patching, scarfing, fingerjointing plywood, and in manufacturing various panel products. Careful control of power and press time is essential to prevent formation of steam that could lead to steam blows and even arcing.

It has been observed that bondlines of structural adhesives that withstand the highest of stresses from mechanical loading and dimensional changes generally have bondline thicknesses within the range of 0.076 to 0.152 mm (0.003 to 0.006 in.). Below this range, the bondlines are too thin to effectively transfer stresses from one adherend to the other, particularly stresses from moisture-induced dimensional changes. Above this range, bond strength becomes progressively weaker as bondline thickness increases. Structural wood adhesives are brittle, so they fracture more in thicker bondlines than in thinner ones. These adhesives also contain solvents, and because solvent is lost while curing, the thicker adhesive film shrinks and fractures more than the thinner and may contain more voids from entrapped solvent gases. Thick bondlines result from inadequate pressure, either from low applied pressure or from rough, uneven, poorly mated surfaces. When uneven surfaces are joined, pressure will not be uniform along the bondline. As a result, the adhesive will be squeezed out from the areas of very high pressure, and the areas of little to no pressure will have very thick bondlines. Both starved and thick bondlines produce weak joints.

Post-Cure Conditioning

In the process of bonding edge-grain joints, the wood in the joint absorbs moisture from the adhesive, then swells. If the bonded assembly is surfaced before this excess moisture is evaporated or absorbed uniformly, more wood is removed along the swollen joint than elsewhere. Later, when the added moisture evaporates, the wood in the joint shrinks beneath the surface. These sunken bondlines become very conspicuous under a high-gloss finish. This is a particularly important consideration when using adhesives that contain relatively large amounts of water. Redistribution of moisture added by the adhesive can be accomplished by conditioning the bonded assembly for 24 h at 70°C (158°F), 4 days at 50°C (122°F), or at least 7 days at room temperature before surfacing. In each case, the relative humidity must be adjusted to prevent drying the wood below the target moisture content.

After bonding, plywood-type constructions should be conditioned to the average moisture content expected in service. The best conditioning is accomplished by controlling humidity on time schedules. If bonded products cured at room temperature are exposed to excessively low moisture content, warping, checking, and opening of joints will increase significantly. Softwood plywood is very dry after hot pressing, so panels may be sprayed with water and tightly stacked to allow moisture to diffuse uniformly. This practice restores some of the panel thickness lost by compression during hot pressing and apparently minimizes warping in service.

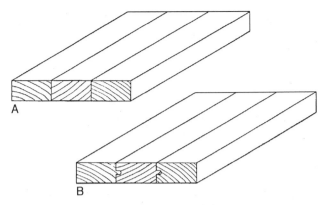

Figure 9–8. Edge-grain joints: A, plain; B, tongue-and-groove.

Bonded Joints

Edge-Grain Joints

Face-grain joints (wide surface of a board) are commonly seen in structural laminated lumber products, where adhesive bonds are stronger than the wood. Edge-grain joints (narrow surface of a board) (Fig. 9–8) can be almost as strong as the wood in shear parallel to the grain, tension across the grain, and cleavage. The tongue-and-groove joint (Fig. 9–8) and other shaped edge-grain joints have a theoretical strength advantage because of greater surface area than the straight, edge-grain joints, but they do not produce higher strength. The theoretical advantage is lost, wholly or partly, because the shaped sides of the two mating surfaces cannot be machined precisely enough to produce the perfect fit that will distribute pressure uniformly over the entire joint area. Because of poor contact, the effective bonding area and strength can actually be less in a shaped joint than on a flat surface. The advantage of the tongue-and-groove and other shaped joints is that the parts can be more quickly aligned in clamps or presses. A shallow-cut tongue-and-groove is just as useful in this respect as a deeper cut, and less wood is wasted.

End-Grain Joints

It is practically impossible to make end-grain butt joints (Fig. 9–9) sufficiently strong to meet the requirements of ordinary service with conventional bonding techniques. Even with special techniques, not more than about 25% of the tensile strength of the wood parallel-to-grain can be obtained in a butt joint. To approximate the tensile strength of clear solid wood, a scarf joint or fingerjoint must closely approach the parallel-to-grain direction of the edge-grain joint (Fig. 9–8). The surface area of this edge-grain joint should be at least 10 times greater than the cross-sectional area of the piece, because wood is approximately 10 times stronger in tension than in shear. In plywood scarfs and fingerjoints, a slope of 1 in 8 is typical for structural products. For nonstructural, low-strength joints, these requirements need not be met.

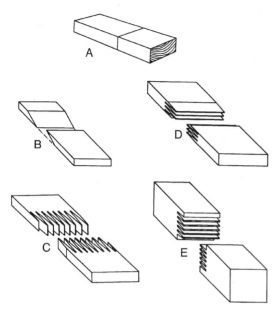

Figure 9–9. End-grain joints: A, butt; B, plain scarf; C, vertical structural fingerjoint; D, horizontal structural fingerjoint; E, nonstructural fingerjoint.

Fingerjoints can be cut with the profile showing either on the wide face (vertical joint) or on the edge (horizontal joint) (Fig. 9–9). There is greater area for designing shapes of fingers in the vertical joint, but a longer cutting head with more knives is needed. When the adhesive is cured by high frequency heating, the cure is more rapid with the vertical than with the horizontal joint. A nonstructural fingerjoint, with fingers much shorter than in the two structural finger-joints, is shown in Figure 9–9.

A scarf joint is shown in Figure 9–9. Slopes of 1 in 12 or flatter produce the highest strength. This is also true in fingerjoints, but the tip thickness must be small and no greater than 0.8 mm (0.031 in.). A thickness of 0.4 to 0.8 mm (0.016 to 0.031 in.) is about the practical minimum for machined tips. Sharper tips can be created with dies, which are forced into the end grain of the board.

A well-manufactured end joint of either scarf, finger, or lap type can have up to 90% of the tensile strength of clear wood and exhibit behavior much like that of clear wood. However, test results indicate that the cycles-to-failure for a well-manufactured end joint are somewhat lower compared with the results of similar tests for clear wood.

End-to-Edge-Grain Joints

Plain end-to-edge-grain joints (Fig. 9–10) are difficult to design to carry appreciable loading. Furthermore, internal stresses develop in the members in service from unequal dimensional changes with moisture content changes. Such stresses can be great enough to cause failure. As a result, it is necessary to design these joints with interlocking

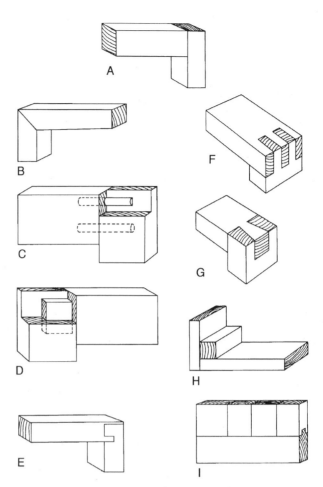

Figure 9–10. End-to-edge-grain joints: A, plain; B, miter; C, dowel; D, mortise and tenon; E, dado tongue and rabbet; F, slip or lock corner; G, dovetail; H, blocked; I, tongue-and-groove.

surfaces, for example, dowels, mortise and tenons, rabbets (Figs. 9–10), so that edge grain of the interlocking piece is bonded to the edge grain of the adjoining piece. The joint area is enlarged as well. All end-to-edge-grain joints should be protected from appreciable changes in moisture content in service.

Construction Joints

Elastomeric construction adhesives are commonly used in the light-frame construction industry for field assembly of panelized floor and wall systems. Structural panels are bonded to floor joists and wall studs with mastic adhesives that have the unique capability of bridging gaps up to 6.5 mm (0.25 in.) between rough and poorly fitting surfaces (Fig. 9–11). Without any premixing, the adhesive is extruded in a bead along framing members with a hand-held caulking gun or a pressurized dispenser similar to that shown in Figure 9–6. Nails or screws provide the only pressure for bonding, and they hold materials in position while the adhesive sets. Elastomerics are also uniquely tolerant of the

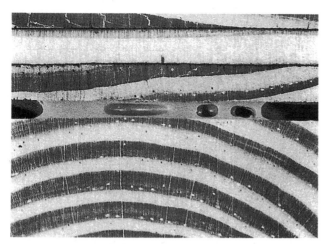

Figure 9–11. Gap-filling construction adhesive in field-assembled plywood floor system.

temperature and moisture content variations at field construction sites. Although they do not deliver the strength and durability of conventional structural adhesives, elastomerics are strong and flexible enough to give long-term performance under most conditions of installation and service.

Construction adhesives enable a nailed floor system to act to some degree as a composite assembly with increased stiffness. Greater stiffness permits joists to be longer and spaced more widely, with one layer of plywood subflooring replacing two. Floors are less bouncy with fewer squeaks and nail pops. However, structural design of the composite assembly is based only on the increased stiffness of nailed panel and framing materials. Structural credit for strength is not allowed for the adhesive in the engineering design.

Testing and Performance

An adhesive is expected to hold materials together and transfer design loads from one adherend to the other within a given service environment for the life of the structure. The purpose of testing performance is to ensure that adhesive bonds will not deteriorate before they can meet these expectations. A variety of methods are available to test bonding performance, particularly for bonded assemblies. Generally, these testing methods attempt to predict how bonded joints are likely to perform in a specific loading mode (shear, tensile, creep) in an assembly at specific temperature and moisture conditions for a specific time.

Most performance tests are short term. They are based on chemical, mechanical, and rheological laboratory tests of adhesive polymers and their adhesives and bonds. Intermediate-term tests of products that are conducted in pilot operations and field experiments are integrated with short-term laboratory tests in an effort to extrapolate these data into long-term performance. Long-term tests of bonded assemblies under actual environmental exposures are conducted, but these supporting data may not be available for 10 to

30 years. Therefore, heavy reliance must be placed on short-term tests to predict long-term performance. As the relationships between chemical structure and mechanical performance, particularly long-term performance, are better understood, the greater the reliance will be on short-term testing.

Analytic Chemical and Mechanical Testing of Polymers

The molecular structures of adhesive polymers are chemically characterized spectroscopically by nuclear magnetic resonance, either in the liquid or solid state. Molecular-size distributions of polymers are determined by gel permeation chromatography. Rates of chemical reaction are studied by differential scanning calorimetry. The rheological properties of curing and cured adhesives are characterized by dynamic mechanical analysis and torsional-braid analysis. Sophisticated fracture mechanics techniques are used to measure toughness of adhesive bonds as they fail in a cleavage mode. High magnification microscopes, including scanning electron microscope, transmission electron microscope, and atomic force microscope, enable scientists to visually analyze surfaces of adhesives and adherends before, during, and after fracture. Much can be learned from measurements of chemical, mechanical, and rheological properties of polymers and adhesives as they exist apart from adherends. Until such data can be correlated with performance, there is no substitute for testing performance in bonded assemblies prepared with specific adhesives and materials, and tested under specific loading modes, environmental conditions, and duration of loading. When adhesives are formulated through a blend of scientific analysis and art of formulation, they are tested for strength and durability in the laboratory and field, usually by industry- and government-accepted standard methods of test and product specifications.

Mechanical Testing of Bonded Assemblies

Responses of adhesive-bonded assemblies to mechanical loading are defined in terms of several commonly used modes of applying stress to joints. In all test modes, specific materials, conditions of materials and test, and testing procedures are completely specified to ensure repeatability to enable valid comparisons of data. Most test methods, specifications, and practices for adhesives and bonded assemblies are consensus standards published each year in the *Annual Book of ASTM Standards* by the American Society for Testing and Materials (ASTM). Several trade associations have their own specifications and performance standards that apply to their specific wood products. The Federal government also has specifications that are used by the General Services Administration to purchase products.

Four basic stressing modes—shear, tensile, cleavage, and peel—are commonly used to test bonded wood assemblies with variations of these to determine strength levels during impact, flexure, fatigue, and creep under long-term stress.

The following describes the basic stress modes in adhesive-bonded joints:

- Shear, resulting from forces applied parallel to the bondline

- Tensile, resulting from forces applied perpendicular to the bondline

- Cleavage, resulting from separation along a bondline by a wedge or other crack-opening type of force

- Peel, resulting from forces applied to a bondline that tend to progressively separate a flexible member from a rigid member or another flexible member

As the names imply, impact, fatigue, and creep are tests that have more to do with the rate at which basic modes and variations are applied. Impact loads are sudden, much faster relative to the controlled slow rates of shear or tensile stressing. Fatigue is the loss in strength from repeated loading and reflects deterioration of bonds from mechanical rather than environmental stresses, although the latter may be imposed during fatigue testing. Creep loads are statically applied but are of prolonged duration that can last from a few days to years, usually at extreme conditions of environmental exposure. The flexure test applies a bending force to a simple beam at midspan, perpendicular to the bondline. In a laminated beam, the test directs a large proportion of the shear forces to bondlines between the laminates.

The common measures used to estimate potential performance of bonded wood joints are strength, wood failure, and delamination. Best performance produces a bond strength that is greater than that of the wood, wood failure that is more than 75% over the bonded area, and delamination of the joint that is less than 5% for softwoods and 8% for hardwoods, under severe service conditions. These performance values reflect how wood adherend, adhesive bond, and environmental exposure have interacted in response to loading.

Bond strength is tested most commonly in shear parallel to the grain. Because most wood adhesives exceed the shear strength of wood in this direction, the maximum potential strength of the adhesive may not be realized, particularly for moderate to lower density species. Bonds in structural assemblies are expected to exceed the strength of the wood, so in traditional design of joints, adhesive strength has been ignored. Adhesives not as strong as wood simply have not been used in design because methods for determining allowable mechanical properties of adhesives for engineering design had not been developed. One such method now exists as a consensus standard—ASTM D5574–97 (ASTM 1997). Exceeding the strength of wood is an essential performance criterion; therefore, the amount of wood that fails in a joint is estimated as a percentage of the area of the bonded joint. This is an important indicator of bond strength, often more important than the measured shear strength of the bond. The higher the wood failure and the deeper the fracture into the grain of the wood, the stronger and more durable the bond, particularly with durable types of adhesives. If wood failure is shallow with only wood fibers remaining attached to the adhesive film, then bond strength and probably durability is lacking in the bond. Thus, a consistently high level of wood failure, above 75% in some standards and above 85% in others, means that shear strength associated with these average wood failures are good estimates of the load-carrying capability of the joint. High levels of wood failure and shear strength in a wet and hot environment might indicate that the adhesive bond is as strong as the wood. If cycles of alternate drying were included with cycles of wet and hot conditions, then high wood failure would indicate even more durable bonds. High wood failure in shear tests of water-saturated bonds is also a strong indicator of bond durability, particularly with durable types of adhesives. Wood failure is considered a valid measure of bond strength only to solid wood, not to reconstituted products made of bonded wood particles.

High shear strength and wood failure in themselves are not sufficient indicators of the durability of a structural bond. Delamination is an indicator of how well the bonded joint withstands severe swelling and shrinking stresses in the presence of high moisture and heat. Delamination is the separation between laminates because of adhesive failure, either in the adhesive or at the interface between adhesive and adherend. If strength of adhesion is not as strong as the wood in resisting forces tending to separate laminates, then delamination occurs. If adhesion does resist delaminating forces, then the wood will fail adjacent to the bondline, but not within the adhesive. The stressing modes induced by stresses from moisture-related dimensional changes are combinations of tensile and shear forces with cleavage acting at joint edges. Delamination of adhesives in structural laminated wood products exposed to the cyclic delamination test in ASTM D2559–97 (ASTM 1997) cannot exceed 5% in softwoods and 8% in hardwoods.

Short- and Long-Term Performance

In the short term, the mechanical properties of wood, adhesives, and bonded products vary with the specific environmental exposure. In most cases, all properties decrease as the temperature and moisture levels increase. Strength and stiffness may return to their original levels if the yield points of the materials have not been exceeded while under load. The properties of rigid thermosetting adhesives like resorcinol-formaldehyde, phenol-formaldehyde, melamine-formaldehyde, and urea-formaldehyde change less than do wood properties under equivalent temperature and moisture changes. Therefore, evaluating short-term performance of products made with these adhesives is simply a matter of testing bonds at room temperature in dry and wet conditions. Thermoplastic adhesives like casein, polyvinyl acetate, and elastomerics, whose properties change more rapidly than those of wood with changes in moisture and heat, are tested dry, dry after water soaking, and after prolonged exposure to high humidity environments. In addition, some specifications require testing of bonded structural and nonstructural products at elevated temperatures such as occur in roofs or enclosed shipping containers. A short-term dead-load test at elevated temperatures may also be required. Specifications for adhesives for structural products like laminated beams and plywood require conformance to high minimum strength and wood failure values after several different water exposure tests. Adhesive bonds in laminated beams must also withstand severe cyclic moisture content and temperature changes, with only low levels of delamination allowable.

In the long term, wood, adhesives, and bonded products deteriorate at a rate determined by the levels of temperature, moisture, stress and, in some instances, by concentrations of certain chemicals and presence of microorganisms. Long-term performance is equated with the ability of a product to resist loss of a measured mechanical property over the time of exposure. A durable product is one that shows no greater loss of properties during its life in service than wood of the same species and quality.

Many adhesives in bonded products have decades of documented performance in many environments. Thus, it is possible to predict with a high degree of certainty the long-term performance of similar products. Well-designed and well-made joints with any of the commonly used woodworking adhesives will retain their strength indefinitely if the moisture content of the wood does not exceed approximately 15% and if the temperature remains within the range of human comfort. However, some adhesives deteriorate when exposed either intermittently or continuously to temperatures greater than 38°C (100°F) for long periods. Low temperatures seem to have no significant effect on strength of bonded joints.

Products made with phenol-formaldehyde, resorcinol-formaldehyde, and phenol-resorcinol-formaldehyde adhesives have proven to be more durable than wood when exposed to warm and humid environments, water, alternate wetting and drying, and even temperatures sufficiently high to char wood. These adhesives are entirely adequate for use in products that are exposed indefinitely to the weather (Fig. 9–12).

Products well-made with melamine-formaldehyde, melamine-urea-formaldehyde, and urea-formaldehyde resin adhesives have proven to be less durable than wood. Melamine-formaldehyde is only slightly less durable than phenol-formaldehyde or resorcinol-formaldehyde, but it is still considered acceptable for structural products. Although considered less durable, melamine-urea-formaldehyde is also accepted in structural products at a melamine-to-urea ratio of 60:40. Urea-formaldehyde resin is susceptible to deterioration by heat and moisture (Fig. 9–12).

Products bonded with polyvinyl acetate and protein-based adhesives will not withstand prolonged exposure to water or repeated high–low moisture content cycling in bonds of high density woods. However, if they are properly formulated, these adhesives are durable in a normal interior environment.

Some isocyanate, epoxy, polyurethane, and cross-linked polyvinyl acetate adhesives are durable enough to use on lower density species even under exterior conditions, but exterior exposure must be limited for most of these. Some elastomer-based adhesives may be durable enough for limited exposure to moisture with lower density species in

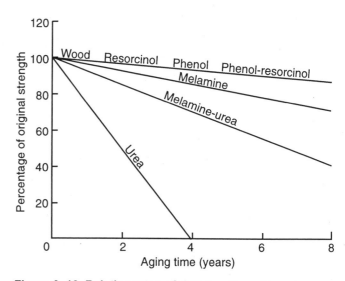

Figure 9–12. Relative rates of deterioration of bond strength of small specimens exposed directly to weather.

nonstructural applications or in structural applications when used in conjunction with approved nailing schedules. Polyurethane adhesives that chemically cure and still remain flexible are among the most durable construction adhesives.

New adhesives do not have a history of long-term performance in service environments, so accelerated laboratory exposures that include cycles of heat, moisture, and stress are used to estimate long-term performance. However, laboratory exposures cannot duplicate the actual conditions of a service environment. Estimates of long-term performance can be obtained by exposing specimens outdoors for up to 30 years. Outdoor exposures may be intensified by facing specimens south at an angle perpendicular to the noonday sun and by establishing exposure sites in regions with the most extreme of service environments, for example, southern coastal and arid southwestern regions. Only four long-term laboratory aging methods have been standardized, and none specifies minimum performance levels. Therefore, performance of any new adhesive or bonded product must be compared with the performance of established adhesives or products tested in the same laboratory exposure.

Product Quality Assurance

After the short- and long-term performance of a product has been established, then maintenance of the manufacturing process to ensure that the product will be made and perform at that level is the major concern of a quality-assurance program that consists of three parts:

1. Establishing limits on bonding process factors that will ensure acceptable joints and product.

2. Monitoring the production processes and quality of bond in joints and product.

3. Detecting unacceptable joints and product, determining the cause, and correcting the problem.

The structural panel, laminated-beam, particleboard, millwork, and other industrial trade associations have established quality-assurance programs that effectively monitor the joint and product performance at the time of manufacture for compliance with voluntary product standards. Usually, product performance is evaluated immediately after manufacture by subjecting specimens from the product to a series of swell–shrink cycles. The treatments are more rigorous for products intended for exterior exposure. For example, exterior softwood plywood is subjected to two boil–dry cycles, while interior plywood is subjected to a single soak–dry cycle at room temperature. After exposure, the specimens are examined for delamination or evaluated for percentage wood failure. The test results are compared with the minimum requirement in the trade association's standards. Lengthy experience and correlations between exterior performance and accelerated laboratory tests have shown that products with at least the minimum values will probably perform satisfactorily in service. If the product meets the requirement, it is certified by the association as meeting the standard for satisfactory performance.

References

AITC. 1992. Inspection manual for structural glued laminated timber, AITC 200–92. Englewood, CO: American Institute of Timber Construction.

AITC. 1992. American national standard for wood products–structural glued laminated timber ANSI/AITC A190.1–1992. New York, NY: American National Standards Institute, Inc.

APA. 1983. U.S. product standard PS1–83 for construction and industrial plywood with typical APA trademarks. Washington, DC: U.S. Department of Commerce, National Bureau of Standards.

APA. 1988. Performance standards and policies for structural-use panels, APA PRP–108. Tacoma, WA: American Plywood Association.

ASTM. 1997. Annual book of ASTM standards, Vol. 15.06 Adhesives. West Conshohocken, PA: American Society for Testing and Materials.

ASTM D2559. Standard specification for adhesives for structural laminated wood products for use under exterior (wet use) exposure conditions.

ASTM D5574. Standard methods for establishing allowable mechanical properties of wood bonding adhesives for design of structural joints.

Blomquist, R.F.; Christiansen, A.W.; Gillespie, R.H.; Myers, G.E. eds. 1984. Adhesive bonding of wood and other structural materials. Clark C. Heritage memorial series on wood, Vol. 3. Educational modules for material science and engineering (EMMSE). University Park, PA: Pennsylvania State University.

Blomquist, R.F.; Vick, C.B. 1977. Adhesives for building construction. In: Skeist, I., ed. Handbook of adhesives, 2d edition. New York, NY: Van Nostrand Reinhold Company.

Bryant, B.S. 1977. Wood adhesion. In: Skeist, I., ed. Handbook of adhesives, 2d edition. New York, NY: Van Nostrand Reinhold Company.

Caster, R.W. 1980. Correlation between exterior exposure and automatic boil test results. In: John, W.E.; Gillespie, R.H., eds. Proceedings of a symposium, Wood adhesives—research, application, needs. 1980 September 23–25; Madison, WI: Madison, WI: U.S. Department of Agriculture, Forest Service, Forest Products Laboratory.

Christiansen, A.W. 1990. How overdrying wood reduces its bonding to phenol-formaldehyde adhesives: a critical review of the literature. Part I. Physical responses. Wood and Fiber Science. 22(4): 441–459.

Christiansen, A.W. 1991. How overdrying wood reduces its bonding to phenol-formaldehyde adhesives: a critical review of the literature. Part II. Chemical reactions. Wood and Fiber Science. 23(1): 69–84.

Collett, B.M. 1972. A review of surface and interfacial adhesion in wood science and related fields. Wood Science and Technology. 6(1): 1–42.

Gillespie, R.H. 1965. Accelerated aging of adhesives in plywood-type joints. Forest Products Journal. 15(9): 369–378.

Gillespie, R.H. 1981. Wood composites. In: Oliver, J.F., ed. Adhesion in cellulose and wood-based composites. New York: Plenum Press.

Gillespie, R.H., ed. 1984. Adhesives for wood–research, applications, and needs. Park Ridge, NJ: Noyes Publications.

Gillespie, R.H.; River, B.H. 1975. Durability of adhesives in plywood: dry-heat effects by rate-process analysis. Forest Products Journal. 25(7): 26–32.

Gillespie, R.H.; River, B.H. 1976. Durability of adhesives in plywood. Forest Products Journal. 26(10): 21–25.

Gillespie, R.H.; Countryman, D.; Blomquist, R.F. 1978. Adhesives in building construction. Agric. Handb. 516. Washington, DC: U.S. Department of Agriculture, Forest Service.

Gollob, L.; Wellons, J.D. 1990. Wood adhesion. In: Skeist, I., ed. Handbook of adhesives, 3d ed. New York, NY: Van Nostrand Reinhold Company.

Hardwood Plywood & Veneer Association. 1995. American national standard for hardwood and decorative plywood. ANSI/HPVA HP–1–1994. New York, NY: American National Standards Institute, Inc.

Hoyle, R.J. 1976. Designing wood structures bonded with elastomeric adhesives. Forest Products Journal. 26(3): 28–34.

Jarvi, R.A. 1967. Exterior glues for plywood. Forest Products Journal. 17(1): 37–42.

Jokerst, R.W. 1981. Finger-jointed wood products. Res. Pap. FPL–RP–382. Madison, WI: U.S. Department of Agriculture, Forest Service, Forest Products Laboratory.

Lambuth, A.L. 1977. Bonding tropical hardwoods with phenolic adhesives. In: Proceedings, IUFRO meeting on processing of tropical hardwoods. 1977 October; Merida, Venezuela: Laboratorio Nacional de Productos Forestales.

Landrock, A.H. 1985. Adhesives technology handbook. Park Ridge, NJ: Noyes Publications.

Marra, A.A. 1992. Technology of wood bonding-principals in practice. New York, NY: Van Nostrand Reinhold.

McGee, W.D.; Hoyle, R.J. 1974. Design method for elastomeric adhesive bonded wood joist-deck systems. Wood and Fiber Science. 6(2): 144–155.

Miller, R.S. 1990. Adhesives for building construction. In: Skeist, I., ed. Handbook of adhesives, 3d ed. New York, NY: Van Nostrand Reinhold Company.

Murmanis, L.; River, B.H.; Stewart, H.A. 1986. Surface and subsurface characteristics related to abrasive-planing conditions. Wood and Fiber Science. 18(1): 107–117.

National Particleboard Association. 1993. Particleboard. ANSI A208.1–1993 New York, NY: American National Standards Institute.

Pizzi, A., ed. 1983. Wood adhesives chemistry and technology. New York, NY: Marcel Dekker, Inc.

Pizzi, A., ed. 1989. Wood adhesives chemistry and technology, Vol. 2. New York, NY: Marcel Dekker, Inc.

Pizzi, A. 1994. Advanced wood adhesives technology. New York, NY: Marcel Dekker, Inc.

Pizzi, A.; Mittal, K.L. 1994. Handbook of adhesive technology. New York, NY: Marcel Dekker, Inc.

River, B.H. 1973. Mastic construction adhesives in fire exposure. Res. Pap. FPL–RP–198. Madison, WI: U.S. Department of Agriculture, Forest Service, Forest Products Laboratory.

River, B.H. 1981. Behavior of construction adhesives under long-term load. Res. Pap. FPL–RP–400. Madison, WI: U.S. Department of Agriculture, Forest Service, Forest Products Laboratory.

River, B.H. 1984. Accelerated, real-time aging for 4 construction adhesives. Adhesives Age. (2) 16–21.

River, B.H. 1994. Fracture of adhesive-bonded wood joints. In: Pizzi, A; Mittal, K.L., eds. Handbook of adhesive technology. New York, NY: Marcel Dekker, Inc.

River, B.H.; Okkonen, E.A. 1991. Delamination of edge-glued wood panels–moisture effects. Res. Note FPL–RN–0259. Madison, WI: U.S. Department of Agriculture, Forest Service, Forest Products Laboratory.

River, B.H.; Gillespie, R.H.; Vick, C.B. 1991. Wood as an adherend. In: Minford, J.D., ed. Treatise on adhesion and adhesives. New York, NY: Marcel Dekker, Inc. Vol. 7.

Selbo, M.L. 1975. Adhesive bonding of wood. Tech. Bull. 1512. Washington, DC: U.S. Department of Agriculture, Forest Service.

Sellers, T., Jr. 1985. Plywood and adhesive technology. New York, NY: Marcel Dekker, Inc.

Skeist, I., ed. 1977. Handbook of adhesives. 2d ed. New York, NY: Van Nostrand Reinhold.

Skeist, I., ed. 1990. Handbook of adhesives. 3d ed.. New York: Van Nostrand Reinhold.

Snogren, R.C. 1974. Handbook of surface preparation. New York, NY: Palmerton Publishing.

Vick, C.B. 1971. Elastomeric adhesives for field-gluing plywood floors. Forest Products Journal. 21(8): 34–42.

Vick, C.B.; Rowell, R.M. 1990. Adhesive bonding of acetylated wood. Gildford, Surry, England: International Journal of Adhesion and Adhesives. 10(4): 263–272.

Vick, C.B.; DeGroot, R.C.; Youngquist, J. 1990. Compatibility of nonacidic waterborne preservatives with phenol-formaldehyde adhesive. Forest Products Journal. 40(2): 16–22.

Vick, C.B. 1994. Phenolic adhesive bonds to aspen veneers treated with amino-resin fire retardants. Forest Products Journal. 44(1): 33–40.

Vick, C.B. 1995. Coupling agent improves durability of PRF bonds to CCA-treated Southern Pine. Forest Products Journal. 45(3): 78–84.

Vick, C.B. 1996. Hydroxymethylated resorcinol coupling agent for enhanced adhesion of epoxy and other thermosetting adhesives to wood. In: Christiansen, A.W.; Conner, A.H., eds. Wood adhesives 1995. Proceedings of a symposium; 1995, June 29–30; Portland, OR. Proc. 7296. Madison, WI: Forest Products Society.

Chapter 10

Wood-Based Composites and Panel Products

John A. Youngquist

Contents

 ecause wood properties vary among species, between trees of the same species, and between pieces from the same tree, solid wood cannot match reconstituted wood in the range of properties that can be controlled in processing. When processing variables are properly selected, the end result can sometimes surpass nature's best effort. With solid wood, changes in properties are studied at the cellular level. With reconstituted wood materials, changes in properties are studied at the fiber, particle, flake, or veneer level. Properties of such materials can be changed by combining, reorganizing, or stratifying these elements.

The basic element for composite wood products may be the fiber, as it is in paper, but it can also be larger wood particles composed of many fibers and varying in size and geometry. These characteristics, along with control of their variations, provide the chief means by which materials can be fabricated with predetermined properties.

In any discussion of the strength properties of wood-based panels and other adhesive-bonded wood composites, the first consideration is the constituents from which these products are made (O'Halloran and Youngquist 1984; Youngquist 1987, 1988). The basic wood elements that can be used in the production of wood-based panels are shown in Figure 10–1. The elements can be made in a great variety of sizes and shapes and can be used alone or in combination. The choice is almost unlimited.

Currently, the term composite is being used to describe any wood material adhesive-bonded together. This product mix ranges from fiberboard to laminated beams and components. Table 10–1 shows a logical basis for classifying wood composites proposed by Maloney (1986). For the purposes of this chapter, these classifications were slightly modified from those in the original version to reflect the latest product developments. Composites are used for a number of structural and nonstructural applications in product lines ranging from panels for interior covering purposes to panels for exterior uses and in furniture and support structures in many different types of buildings.

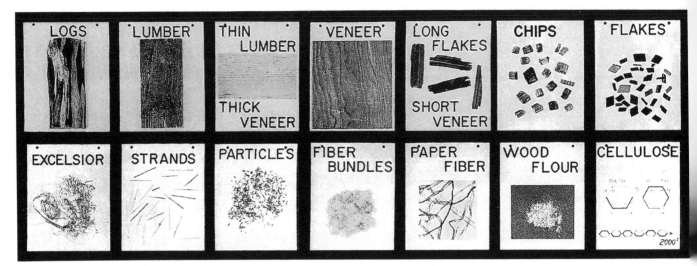

Figure 10–1. Basic wood elements, from largest to smallest (Marra 1979).

Table 10–1. Classification of wood-based composites[a]

Veneer-based material

Plywood
Laminated veneer lumber (LVL)
Parallel-laminated veneer (PLV)

Laminates

Laminated beams
Overlayed materials
Wood–nonwood composites[b]

Composite material

Cellulosic fiberboard
Hardboard
Particleboard
Waferboard
Flakeboard
Oriented strandboard (OSB)
COM-PLY[c]

Edge-adhesive-bonded material

Lumber panels

Components

I-beams
T-beam panels
Stress-skin panels

Wood–nonwood composites

Wood fiber–plastic composites
Inorganic-bonded composites
Wood fiber–agricultural fiber composites

[a]Maloney 1986.
[b]Panels or shaped materials combined with nonwood materials such as metal, plastic, and fiberglass.
[c]Registered trademark of APA–The Engineered Wood Association.

Figure 10–2 provides a useful way to further classify wood-based composite materials. This figure presents an overview of the most common types of products discussed in this chapter as well as a quick reference to how these composite materials compare to solid wood from the standpoint of density and general processing considerations. The raw material classifications of fibers, particles, and veneers are shown on the left y axis. Specific gravity and density are shown on the top and bottom horizontal axes (x axes). The right y axis, wet and dry processes, describes in general terms the processing method used to produce a particular product. Note that both roundwood and chips can serve as sources of fiber for wet-process hardboard. Roundwood or wood in the form of a waste product from a lumber or planing operation can be used for dry-processed products. For medium-density fiberboard (MDF), resin is usually applied to the fiber after the fiber is released from the pressurized refiner. The fiber is then dried, formed into a mat, and pressed into the final product. For other dry-processed products, the material is fiberized and dried and then adhesive is added in a separate operation prior to hot pressing into the final composite product. Figure 10–3 shows examples of some composite materials that are represented in schematic form in Figure 10–2.

Scope

Although there is a broad range of wood composites and many applications for such products, for the purposes of this chapter, wood composites are grouped into three general categories: plywood, particle and fiber composites, and wood–nonwood composites. Books have been written about each of these categories, and the constraints of this chapter necessitate that the discussion be general and brief. References are provided for more detailed information. Information on adhesive-bonded-laminated (glulam, timbers, and structural composite lumber, including laminated veneer lumber) and adhesive-bonded members for lumber and panel products

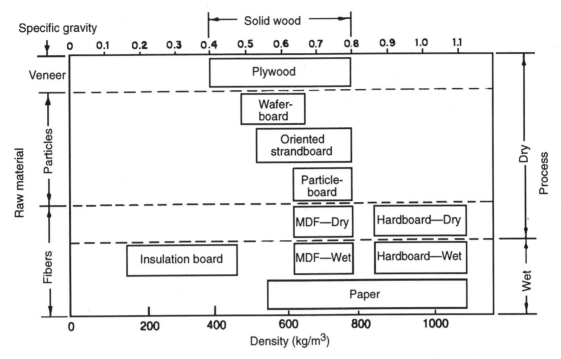

Figure 10–2. Classification of wood composite boards by particle size, density, and process type (Suchsland and Woodson 1986).

is presented in Chapter 11 of this handbook. Many composite materials, like fiberboard, MDF, and particleboard, can be made from wood alone or in combination with agricultural fibers (Youngquist and others 1993a, 1994; Rowell and others 1997).

The first category, plywood, is covered in some detail because the process for manufacturing this kind of material is quite different from that used for other composite materials and because there are many different classes and grades of plywood in the marketplace. The second category, composite materials, includes oriented strandboard (OSB),

Figure 10–3. Examples of various composite products. From left to right: plywood, OSB, particleboard, MDF, and hardboard.

particleboard, and fiberboard. These types of composites undergo similar processing steps, which are discussed in general terms for all the products in the Particle and Fiber Composites section. The first and second categories of composite materials are further generally classified as conventional composite materials. The third category, wood–nonwood composites, includes products made from combining wood fibers with agricultural fibers, with thermoplastics, and with inorganic materials.

Types of Conventional Composite Materials

Conventional wood composite materials fall into five main categories based on the physical configuration of the wood used to make the products: plywood, oriented strandboard, particleboard, hardboard, and cellulosic fiberboard. Within limits, the performance of a conventional type of composite can be tailored to the end-use application of the product. Varying the physical configuration of the wood and adjusting the density of the composites are just two ways to accomplish this. Other ways include varying the resin type and amount and incorporating additives to increase water or fire resistance or to resist specific environmental conditions.

Adhesive Considerations

The conventional wood-based composite products discussed in this chapter are typically made with a thermosetting or heat-curing resin or adhesive that holds the lignocellulosic

209

(wood) fiber together. The physical and mechanical properties of wood-based veneer, fiber, and particle panel materials are determined by standard American Society for Testing and Materials (ASTM) test methods. Commonly used resin–binder systems include phenol-formaldehyde, urea-formaldehyde, melamine-formaldehyde, and isocyanate.

Phenol-formaldehyde (PF) resins are typically used in the manufacture of products requiring some degree of exterior exposure durability, for example, OSB, softwood plywood, and siding. These resins require longer press times and higher press temperatures than do urea-formaldehyde resins, which results in higher energy consumption and lower line speeds (productivity). Products using PF resins (often referred to as phenolics) may have lowered dimensional stability because of lower moisture contents in the finished products. The inherently dark color of PF resins may render them unsuitable for decorative product applications such as paneling and furniture.

Urea-formaldehyde (UF) resins are typically used in the manufacture of products where dimensional uniformity and surface smoothness are of primary concern, for example, particleboard and MDF. Products manufactured with UF resins are designed for interior applications. They can be formulated to cure anywhere from room temperature to 150°C (300°F); press times and temperatures can be moderated accordingly. Urea-formaldehyde resins (often referred to as urea resins) are more economical than PF resins and are the most widely used adhesive for composite wood products. The inherently light color of UF resins make them quite suitable for the manufacture of decorative products.

Melamine-formaldehyde (MF) resins are used primarily for decorative laminates, paper treating, and paper coating. They are typically more expensive than PF resins. MF resins may be blended with UF resins for certain applications (melamine urea).

Isocyanate as diphenylmethane di-isocyanate (MDI) is commonly used in the manufacture of composite wood products; MDI is used primarily in the manufacture of OSB. Facilities that use MDI are required to take special precautionary protective measures.

These adhesives have been chosen based upon their suitability for the particular product under consideration. Factors taken into account include the materials to be bonded together, moisture content at time of bonding, mechanical property and durability requirements of the resultant composite products, and of course, resin system costs.

Some natural options may someday replace or supplement these synthetic resins. Tannins, which are natural phenols, can be modified and reacted with formaldehyde to produce a satisfactory resin. Resins have also been developed by acidifying spent sulfite liquor, which is generated when wood is pulped for paper. In the manufacture of wet-process fiberboard, lignin, which is inherent in lignocellulosic material, is frequently used as the resin (Suchsland and Woodson 1986).

Except for two major uncertainties, UF and PF systems are expected to continue to be the dominant wood adhesives for lignocellulosic composites. The two uncertainties are the possibility of much more stringent regulation of formaldehyde-containing products and the possibility of limitations to or interruptions in the supply of petrochemicals. One result of these uncertainties is that considerable research has been conducted in developing new adhesive systems from renewable resources.

Additives

A number of additives are used in the production of conventional composite products. One of the most notable additives is wax, which is used to provide finished products with resistance to aqueous penetration. In particle- and fiberboard products, wax emulsion provides excellent water resistance and dimensional stability when the board is wetted. Even small amounts (0.5% to 1%) act to retard the rate of liquid water pickup. These improved water penetration properties are important for ensuring the success of subsequent secondary gluing operations and for providing protection upon accidental wetting to the product during and after construction. The water repellency provided by the wax has practically no effect upon dimensional changes or water adsorption of composites exposed to equilibrium conditions. Other additives used for specialty products, fire retardants, and impregnating.

General Manufacture

Successful manufacture of any composite wood product requires control over raw materials. Ideally, raw materials are uniform, consistent, and predictable. Wood does not offer these qualities but instead varies widely between species. For the purpose of producing a composite product, uniformity, consistency, and predictability are accomplished by reducing separated portions of the wood into small, relatively uniform and consistent particles, flakes, or fibers where effects of differences will average out. Size reduction is sometimes augmented by chemical treatments designed to weaken the bonds between the components. The degree of size reduction and the shape of individual lignocellulosic components will depend on the application. Different composites tolerate or demand different sizes and shapes. Generally speaking, all the conventional composite products discussed in this chapter are made to conform to product or performance standards (English and others 1997).

Standards for Wood–Based Panels

The general types of standards for panel products are product standards and performance standards. Table 10–2 lists standards for common conventional composite products. The term adhesive, as used in the following descriptions of product and performance standards, is synonymous with glue.

Table 10–2. Standards for frequently used panel products

Product category	Applicable standard	Name of standard	Source
Plywood	PS 1–95	Voluntary product standard PS 1–95 Construction and industrial plywood	NIST 1995
	PS 2–92	Voluntary product standard PS 2–92 Performance standard for wood-based structural-use panels	NIST 1992
Oriented strandboard	PS 2–92	Voluntary product standard PS 2–92 Performance standard for wood-based structural-use panels	NIST 1992
Particleboard	ANSI A208.1–1993	Particleboard	NPA 1993
Hardboard	ANSI/AHA A135.4–1995	Basic hardboard	AHA 1995a
	ANSI/AHA A135.5–1995	Prefinished hardboard paneling	AHA 1995b
	ANSI/AHA A135.6–1990	Hardboard siding	AHA 1990
Insulation board	ASTM C208–94	Standard specification for cellulosic fiber insulating board	ASTM current edition
	ANSI/AHA A194.1–1985	Cellulosic fiberboard	AHA 1985
Medium-density fiberboard	ANSI A208.2–1994	Medium-density fiberboard (MDF)	NPA 1994

Product Standards

Product standards may be further classified as manufacturing method standards and laboratory test standards. Probably the best example of a manufacturing method standard is Voluntary Product Standard PS 1–95 for construction and industrial plywood (NIST 1995). This standard specifies such matters as what wood species and grades of veneer may be used, what repairs are permissible, and how repairs must be made. For panels produced according to prescriptive manufacturing requirements, a comparison of wood failure to adhesive failure in small test specimens of plywood is the performance test specified.

A good example of a laboratory test product standard is the American National Standard for mat-formed particleboard, ANSI A208.1 (NPA 1993). The American National Standards Institute (ANSI) product standards for both particleboard and MDF are sponsored by the Composite Panel Association (CPA) in Gaithersburg, Maryland. The CPA is the association resulting from the 1997 consolidation of the U.S.-based National Particleboard Association and the Canadian Particleboard Association. This standard states that in laboratory tests, specimens show certain minimally acceptable physical and mechanical properties, identified by numeric values. The test values give some indication of product quality, but the tests on small specimens were not specifically developed to correlate with performance of whole panels in specific end-uses.

Performance Standards

Performance standards are written for panels in specific end-uses. These standards focus on panel performance in laboratory tests developed to indicate panel performance for particular end-uses. Federal legislation (Abourezk 1977)

encourages the development of performance standards in preference to commodity-type standards. The Voluntary Standards and Accreditation Act of 1977 states that "a performance standard does not limit the manufacturer's freedom to choose any method of design or any form of construction that achieves the desired level of performance" (Abourezk 1977)

The APA–The Engineered Wood Association (formerly American Plywood Association) was the leading proponent of performance-type standards for panel products, and their early work formed the basis for the performance standards in existence today (O'Halloran 1979, 1980; APA 1981). Wood-based panels manufactured in conformance with performance standards (APA–The Engineered Wood Association 1995a, TECO 1991) are approved by the three major model codes by virtue of approval by the Council of American Building Officials through the issuance of a national evaluation report. These wood-based panels can be used for construction applications such as sheathing for roofs, subflooring, and walls.

Similarly, wood-based panels may be used in light-frame construction for many single-layer floor applications. Plywood, OSB, and COM-PLY, a proprietary product, are all span-rated for particular end-uses.

Under PS 1–95 (NIST 1995), plywood panels intended for structural uses may be certified or rated using either prescriptive or performance-based criteria. Standard PS 2–92 (NIST 1992) is strictly performance based because it applies to all structural-use wood-based panels, including plywood, waferboard, and OSB; OSB is a second generation panel, with aligned fibers, that evolved from the original product called waferboard. The PS 2–92 standard is not a replacement for PS 1–95, which contains necessary veneer-grade and

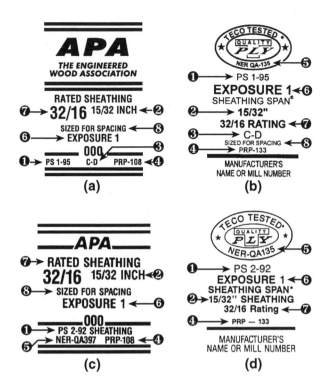

① Product Standard that governs specifics of production for construction and industrial plywood

② Nominal panel thickness subject to acceptable tolerances

③ Panel grade designation indicating minimum veneer grade used for panel face and back, or grade name based on panel use

④ Performance-rated panel standard indicating structural-use panel test procedure recognized by National Evaluation Service (NES)

⑤ NES report number from Council of American Building Officials (CABO)

⑥ Exposure durability classification: Exposure 1 indicates interior panel bonded with exterior glue suitable for uses not permanently exposed to weather

⑦ Span rating indicating maximum spacing of roof and floor supports for ordinary residential construction applications; 32/16 rating identifies a panel rated for use on roof supports spaced up to 813 mm (32 in.) o.c., or floor supports spaced up to 406 mm (16 in.) o.c.

⑧ Sized for spacing denotes panels that have been sized to allow for spacing of panel edges during installation to reduce the possibility of buckling

Figure 10–4. Typical grade stamps for plywood and OSB.

adhesive-bond requirements as well as prescriptive lay-up provisions and includes many plywood grades not covered under PS 2–92.

A significant portion of the market for construction and industrial plywood is in residential construction. This situation has resulted in the development of performance standards for sheathing and single-layer subflooring or underlayment for residential construction. Plywood panels conforming to these

performance standards for sheathing are marked with grade stamps such as those shown in Figure 10–4a,b. Structural flakeboards are usually marketed as conforming to a product standard for sheathing or single-layer subflooring or underlayment and are graded as a performance-rated product (PRP–108) similar to the grading for construction plywood. Voluntary Product Standard PS 2–92 is the performance standard for wood-based structural-use panels, which include such products as plywood, OSB, and waferboard. Panels conforming to these performance standards for sheathing are marked with grade stamps such as those shown in Figure 10–4c,d. As seen in Figure 10–4a,b, the grade stamps must show (1) conformance to plywood product standards, (2) nominal panel thickness, (3) grades of face and back veneers or grade name based on panel use, (4) performance-rated panel standard, (5) recognition as a quality assurance agency by the National Evaluation Service (NES), which is affiliated with the Council of American Building Officials, (6) exposure durability classification, (7) span rating, which refers to maximum allowable roof support spacing and maximum floor joist spacing, and (8) panel sizing for spacing.

Plywood

General Description

Plywood is a flat panel built up of sheets of veneer called plies, united under pressure by a bonding agent to create a panel with an adhesive bond between plies. Plywood can be made from either softwoods or hardwoods. It is always constructed with an odd number of layers with the grain direction of adjacent layers oriented perpendicular to one another. Since layers can consist of a single ply or of two or more plies laminated such that their grain is parallel, a panel can contain an odd or even number of plies but always an odd number of layers. The outside plies are called faces or face and back plies; the inner plies are called cores or centers; and the plies with grain perpendicular to that of the face and back are called crossbands. The core may be veneer, lumber, or particleboard, with the total panel thickness typically not less than 1.6 mm (1/16 in.) or more than 76 mm (3 in.). The plies may vary in number, thickness, species, and grade of wood. To distinguish the number of plies (individual sheets of veneer in a panel) from the number of layers (number of times the grain orientation changes), panels are sometimes described as three-ply, three-layer or four-ply, three-layer. The outer layers (face and back) and all odd-numbered layers (centers) generally have their grain direction oriented parallel to the length or long dimension of the panel. The grain of even-numbered layers (cores) is perpendicular to the length of the panel.

The alternation of grain direction in adjacent plies provides plywood panels with dimensional stability across their width. It also results in fairly similar axial strength and stiffness properties in perpendicular directions within the panel plane. The laminated construction distributes defects, markedly reduces splitting when the plywood is penetrated by fasteners (compared with splitting of solid wood), and improves resistance to checking.

Compared with solid wood, the chief advantages of plywood are that the properties along the length of the panel are more nearly equal to properties along the width, there is greater resistance to splitting, and the form permits many applications where large sheets are desirable. The use of plywood may result in improved utilization of wood. Plywood can cover large areas with a minimum amount of wood fiber because plywood that is thinner than sawn lumber can be used in some applications. The properties of plywood depend on the quality of the different layers of veneer, order of layer placement, adhesive used, and control of bonding conditions. The grade of the panel depends upon the quality of the veneers used, particularly of the face and back. The type of panel refers to the durability of the adhesive-to-wood bond and depends upon the adhesive-bonded joint, particularly its water resistance, and upon veneer grades used. Generally, face veneers with figured grain that are used in panels where appearance is important have numerous short, or otherwise deformed, wood fibers. These may significantly reduce strength and stiffness of the panels. On the other hand, face veneers and other plies may contain certain sizes and distributions of knots, splits, or growth characteristics that have no undesirable effects on strength properties for specific uses, such as sheathing for walls, roofs, or floors.

The plywood industry continues to develop new products. Hence, the reader should always refer directly to current specifications on plywood and its use for specific details.

Types of Plywood

Broadly speaking, two classes of plywood are available, covered by separate standards: (a) construction and industrial, and (b) hardwood and decorative. Construction and industrial plywood has traditionally been made from softwoods such as Douglas-fir, Southern Pine, white fir, larch, western hemlock, and redwood. However, the current standard lists a large number of hardwoods as qualifying for use. At the same time, the standard for hardwood and decorative plywood covers certain decorative softwood species for nonconstruction use.

Most construction and industrial plywood used in the United States is produced domestically, and U.S. manufacturers export some material. Generally speaking, the bulk of construction and industrial plywood is used where strength, stiffness, and construction convenience are more important than appearance. However, some grades of construction and industrial plywood are made with faces selected primarily for appearance and are used either with clear natural finishes or pigmented finishes.

Hardwood and decorative plywood is made of many different species, both in the United States and overseas. Well over half of all such panels used in the United States are imported. Hardwood plywood is normally used in such applications as decorative wall panels and for furniture and cabinet panels where appearance is more important than strength. Most of the production is intended for interior or protected uses, although a very small proportion is made with adhesives suitable for exterior service, such as in marine applications. A significant portion of all hardwood plywood is available completely finished.

The adhesives used in the manufacture of the two classes of plywood are quite different, but each type is selected to provide the necessary performance required by the appropriate specifications.

Construction and industrial plywood covered by Product Standard PS 1 is classified by exposure capability (type) and grade. The two exposure capabilities are exterior and interior. Exterior plywood is bonded with exterior adhesive, and veneers used in manufacture cannot be less than "C" grade as defined in PS 1. Interior-type plywood may be bonded with interior, intermediate, or exterior (waterproof) adhesive. "D" grade veneer is allowed as inner and back plies of certain interior-type plywoods. Adhesive bond performance requirements are specified in PS 1.

The four types of hardwood and decorative plywood in decreasing order of resistance to water are Technical (Exterior), Type I (Exterior), Type II (Interior), and Type III (Interior); adhesive bond requirements for these are specified in ANSI/HPVA–1–1994 (HPVA 1994).

Processing Considerations

After trees are felled and bucked to length, the logs are graded and sorted to make the most appropriate and efficient use of the wood fiber. For softwood plywood, in the past, logs graded as "peelers" were sent to veneer mills or plywood plants and "sawlogs" were shipped to lumber mills. Because of the dwindling availability of the clear, large-diameter peeler logs on which the plywood industry was founded, this practice has changed. Today, the higher grades of softwood peeler logs are sent to sawmills, and with few exceptions, plywood is made from low-grade sawlogs or peeler logs. This change came about because of the increasing demand for clear sawn lumber, and it has been made possible by innovations in veneer and plywood manufacturing and testing practices that ensure that panels are suitable for their intended use (McKay 1997).

Logs delivered to a veneer mill are sorted by grade and species, then debarked and crosscut into peeler blocks. Peeler blocks are often heated or conditioned by steaming or immersion in hot water prior to peeling, which makes them easier to peel, reduces veneer breakage, and results in smoother, higher quality veneer. The heated blocks are then conveyed to a veneer lathe. To maximize veneer yield, each block is gripped on the ends at the block's geometric center. While rotating at high speed, the block is fed against a stationary knife parallel to its length. Veneer is peeled from the block in a continuous, uniformly thin sheet, much like unwinding a roll of paper towels, but at a speed of up to 4.1 m/s (13.3 linear ft/s).

Depending on its intended use, veneer may range in thickness from 1.6 to 4.8 mm (1/16 to 3/16 in.) for softwood plywood and much thinner for hardwood and decorative plywood. After being peeled to a diameter from 127 to 51 mm (5 to 2 in.), the peeler core is ejected from the lathe. Peeler cores may be sawn into standard 38- by 89-mm (nominal 2- by 4-in.) lumber, used for fence posts, and landscape timbers, or chipped for use as pulp chips or fuel.

The continuous sheet of veneer is then transported by conveyor to a clipping station where it is clipped into usable widths and defects are removed. The wet veneer is then dried to an average moisture content that is compatible with the adhesive system being used to bond the panels. Since it is critical that veneer moisture content be low at the time adhesive is applied, each sheet is metered as it exits the dryer. Pieces that are too wet or dry are rerouted to be redried or reconditioned, respectively. Properly dried veneer is then sorted into one of as many as 15 to 20 different grades according to the size and number of knots and other natural and processing defects. Each grade has a specific use; some veneer requires special processing before it is assembled into plywood. After grading and/or processing, the veneer is taken to the lay-up area.

Adhesive is applied to veneers in the lay-up area by spray, curtain coating, roller coating, extrusion, and recently, foaming. Veneer is laid up into plywood by hand, machine, or a combination of both. Hand lay-up is the oldest method, and it is still the only practical way of making plywood for some applications. With this method, the face, back, and center veneers are hand-placed by workers called sheet turners. After being coated on both sides with adhesive, the alternating core plies are placed by hand or machine. The lay-up process is almost completely automated in newer plywood plants, although the narrow strips used for cores may still be placed manually. Before veneers are laid up, narrow strips are sometimes joined into full-width sheets with hot-melt adhesive-coated fiberglass thread so that they can be handled by machine. Also, veneers may be upgraded by punching out knots and other defects and replacing them with wood plugs or synthetic patches.

Once assembled, panels are conveyed from the lay-up area to the pressing area. Panels are first subjected to cold prepressing to flatten the veneers and transfer the adhesive to uncoated sheets; panels are then hot pressed. After hot pressing, panels are solid-piled or hot-stacked to ensure complete curing of the adhesive, then sawn to size. Panels are then graded with regard to the product standard under which they were manufactured. Knotholes and splits on the faces and backs of some panels may be repaired with wood plugs or with synthetic patches (by filling the holes and splits with what is essentially liquid plastic that quickly hardens). Those panels that do not meet the specification are downgraded or rejected. Panels needing further processing are sent to the finishing area where, depending on their intended use, they may be sanded to thickness, profiled with tongue and groove edges, surface textured, scarf- or finger-jointed, oiled and edge-sealed, or given other treatments. The panels are then ready for shipping (McKay 1997).

Specifications

The two general classes of plywood—(a) construction and industrial plywood and (b) hardwood and decorative plywood—are covered by separate standards. Construction and industrial plywood are covered by Product Standard PS 1–95 (NIST 1995), and hardwood and decorative plywood by American National Standard ANSI/HPVA–1–1994 (HPVA 1994). Each standard recognizes different exposure durability classifications, which are primarily based on moisture resistance of the adhesive and the grade of veneer used.

Model building codes in the United States stipulate that plywood used for structural applications like subflooring and sheathing must meet the requirements of certain U.S. Department of Commerce standards. Voluntary Product Standard PS 1–95 for construction and industrial plywood (NIST 1995) and Performance Standard PS 2–92 for wood-based structural-use panels (NIST 1992) spell out the ground rules for manufacturing plywood and establishing plywood or OSB properties, respectively. These standards have evolved over time from earlier documents (O'Halloran 1979, 1980; APA 1981) and represent a consensus opinion of the makers, sellers, and users of plywood products as well as other concerned parties. In addition, model building codes require that plywood manufacturers be inspected and their products certified for conformance to PS 1–95, PS 2–92, APA PRP–108, or TECO PRP–133 by qualified independent third-party agencies on a periodic unannounced basis.

With PS 1–95, as long as a plywood panel is manufactured using the veneer grades, adhesive, and construction established in the standard's prescriptive requirements, the panel is by definition acceptable. When plywood is assembled so that the proportion of wood with the grain perpendicular to the panel's face grain is greater than 33% or more than 70% of the panel's thickness, the plywood automatically meets the span rating. In panels with four or more plies, the combined thickness of the inner layers must equal 45% or more of the panel's thickness. Generally speaking, for panels of the same thickness and made with the face and back veneer of the same species, stiffness and strength increase as the thickness of the face and back veneers increases. All other things being equal, the stiffness and strength of plywood also increase as panel thickness increases.

All hardwood plywood represented as conforming to American National Standard ANSI/HPVA–1–1994 (HPVA 1994) is identified by one of two methods: by marking each panel with the Hardwood Plywood & Veneer Association (HPVA) plywood grade stamp (Fig. 10–5) or by including a written statement with this information with the order or shipment. The HPVA grade stamp shows (1) HPVA trademark, (2) standard that governs manufacture, (3) HPVA mill number, (4) plywood adhesive bond type, (5) flame spread index class, (6) description of lay-up, (7) formaldehyde emission characteristics, (8) face species, and (9) veneer grade of face.

HARDWOOD PLYWOOD & VENEER ASSOCIATION		
FORMALDEHYDE EMISSION 0.2 PPM CONFORMS TO HUD REQUIREMENTS ❼	RED OAK ❽ PLYWOOD ⬤ hpva ❶	FLAME SPREAD 200 OR LESS ASTM E84 ❺
LAY UP 6 1/4 INCH THICK HP-SG-86 ❻	MILL 000 ❸ SPECIALTY GRADE ❾	BOND LINE TYPE II ❹ ANSI/HPVA HP-1-1994 ❷

Explanation of numbering

❶ HPVA trademark

❷ Standard governing manufacture

❸ HPVA mill number

❹ Plywood bondline type

❺ Flame spread index class as determined by testing in accordance with ASTM E84, standard test method for surface burning characteristics of building materials

❻ Lay-up description references structural attributes of wall panels as described in HPMA design guide HP-SG-86, Structural design Guide for Hardwood Plywood Wall Panels as published by the Hardwood Plywood & Veneer Association

❼ Formaldehyde emission characteristics to determine compliance with U.S. Department of Housing and Urban Development requirements for building product use in manufactured homes by testing in accordance with ASTM E1333, Standard Test Method for Determining Formaldehyde Levels From Wood Products Under Defined Test Conditions Using a Large Chamber

❽ Face species (face species designation is not required for wall panels when the surface is a decorative simulation such as that of a wood grain of another species or of a pattern)

❾ Veneer grade of face (grade of veneer of back is shown following grade of face for industrial panels)

Figure 10–5. Grade stamp for hardwood plywood conforming to ANSI/HPVA–1–1994.

The span-rating system for plywood was established to simplify plywood specification without resorting to specific structural engineering design. This system indicates performance without the need to refer to species group or panel thickness. It gives the allowable span when the face grain is placed across supports with a minimum of three supports.

If design calculations are desired, a design guide is provided by the APA–The Engineered Wood Association in *Plywood Design Specification* (PDS) and APA Technical Note N375B (APA–The Engineered Wood Association 1995a,b). The design guide contains tables of grade stamp references, section properties, and allowable stresses for plywood used in construction of buildings and similar structures.

Grades and Classification

Plywood is classified by both exposure durability class and grade. Exposure durability class refers to the ability of a panel to resist the damaging effects of exposure to the weather or moisture. Panel grades are either names that describe the intended use of the panel, such as underlayment or concrete form, or letters that identify the grades of the face and back veneers, such as A–B.

Veneers for plywood are visually graded according to the size, number, and location of natural and processing defects that affect their strength and appearance. Knots, decay, splits, insect holes, surface roughness, number of surface repairs, and other defects are considered. More surface repairs, such as elliptical (boat-shaped) wood patches and bigger knots are allowed in the lower veneer grades. Veneers are graded as N, A, B, C, C-Plugged, and D. N-grade or natural finish veneers are virtually blemish-free, and they contain only a few minor surface repairs. A and B veneers have solid surfaces with neatly made repairs and small, tight knots. Knotholes up to 25 mm (1 in.) in diameter are allowed in C veneers, whereas D veneers may have knotholes as large as 51 mm (2 in.) across. Because their appearance is usually of secondary importance, panels meant for sheathing and other structural uses are made mostly from C and D veneers. The N, A, and B veneers are reserved for panels where appearance is the primary consideration in such uses as exterior trim and soffits, interior paneling, doors, and cabinets.

Construction Plywood Exposure Durability Class

The exposure durability classifications for construction and industrial plywood specified in PS–1 are as follows: exterior, exposure 1, intermediate adhesive, exposure 2, and interior. Exterior plywood is bonded with exterior (waterproof) adhesive and is composed of C-grade or better veneers throughout. Exposure 1 plywood is bonded with exterior adhesives, but it may include D-grade veneers. Exposure 2 plywood is made with adhesive of intermediate resistance to moisture. Interior-type plywood may be bonded with interior, intermediate, or exterior (waterproof) adhesive. D-grade veneer is allowed on inner and back plies of certain interior-type grades.

The exposure durability classifications for hardwood and decorative plywood specified in ANSI/HPVA HP–1–1994 are as follow, in decreasing order of moisture resistance: technical (exterior), type I (exterior), type II (interior), and type III (interior). Hardwood and decorative plywood are not typically used in applications where structural performance is a prominent concern. Therefore, most of the remaining discussion of plywood performance will concern construction and industrial plywood.

Plywood Grades

There are many plywood grade names (Tables 10–3 and 10–4). In addition to the 30 or so generic names listed in PS 1–95, each agency that inspects plywood mills and certifies their products has coined its own trademarked grade names. For example, panels intended for use as single-layer

Table 10–3. Grade names for interior plywood grades[a]

Panel grade designation	Minimum face	Veneer back	Quality inner plies	Surface
N–N	N	N	C	S2S[b]
N–A	N	A	C	S2S
N–B	N	B	C	S2S
N–D	N	D	D	S2S
A–A	A	A	D	S2S
A–B	A	B	D	S2S
A–D	A	D	D	S2S
B–B	B	B	D	S2S
B–D	B	D	D	S2S
Underlayment	C plugged	D	C & D	Touch sanded
C–D plugged	C plugged	D	D	Touch sanded
Structural I C–D				Unsanded
Structural I C–D plugged, underlayment				Touch sanded
C–D	C	D	D	Unsanded
C–D with exterior adhesive	C	D	D	Unsanded

[a]NIST 1995.
[b]Sanded on two sides.

Table 10–4. Grade names for exterior plywood grades[a]

Panel grade designation	Minimum face	Veneer back	Quality inner plies	Surface
Marine, A–A, A–B. B–B, HDO, MDO				See regular grades
Special exterior, A–A, A–B, B–B, HDO, MDO				See regular grades
A–A	A	A	C	S2S[b]
A–B	A	B	C	S2S
A–C	A	C	C	S2S
B–B (concrete form)				
B–B	B	B	C	S2S
B–C	B	C	C	S2S
C–C plugged	C plugged	C	C	Touch sanded
C–C	C	C	C	Unsanded
A–A high-density overlay	A	A	C plugged	—
B–B high-density overlay	B	B	C plugged	—
B–B high-density concrete form overlay	B	B	C plugged	—
B–B medium-density overlay	B	B	C	—
Special overlays	C	C	C	—

[a]NIST 1995.
[b]Sanded on two sides.

flooring (combined subfloor and underlayment) made by TECO-certified manufacturers are called Floorspan, while those made by mills certified by the APA–The Engineered Wood Association are named Sturd-I-Floor. Although the trade names may be different, the minimum stiffness and strength properties of the panels are not. With the exception of custom-order panels, plywood is strictly a commodity product; panels of the same grade and thickness conforming to either PS 1–95 or PS 2–92 are interchangeable among manufacturers.

Span Rating and General Property Values

The more than 70 species of wood used for making softwood plywood (including some hardwoods) are classified into five groups according to their stiffness and strength (Table 10–5). The strongest woods are in Group 1; the weakest, in Group 5. Today, almost all plywood intended for structural use is marked with a two-number span rating (for example, 32/16) instead of a species group number (Fig. 10–4). As with softwood lumber allowable design values, plywood span ratings were developed by breaking thousands of full-size panels of varying construction and thickness. The left-hand number of the rating represents the maximum

Table 10–5. Softwood plywood species groups by stiffness and strength[a]

Group 1	Group 2	Group 3	Group 4	Group 5
Apitong	Cedar, Port Orford	Alder, red	Aspen	Basswood
Beech, American	Cypress	Birch, paper	Bigtooth	Poplar
Birch	Douglas-fir[b]	Cedar, yellow	Quaking	Balsam
Sweet	Fir	Fir, subalpine	Cativo	
Yellow	Balsam	Hemlock, eastern	Cedar	
Douglas-fir[c]	California red	Maple, bigleaf	Incense	
Kapur	Grand	Pine	Western	
Keruing	Noble	Jack	Red	
Larch, western	Pacific silver	Lodgepole	Cottonwood	
Maple, sugar	White	Ponderosa	Eastern	
Pine	Hemlock, western	Spruce	Black	
Caribbean	Lauan	Redwood	(Western Poplar)	
Ocote	Almon	Spruce	Pine, eastern	
Pine, Southern	Bagtikan	Engelman	White, sugar	
Loblolly	Mayapis	White		
Longleaf	Red lauan			
Shortleaf	Tangile			
Slash	White lauan			
Tanoak	Maple, black			
	Mengkulang			
	Meranti, red			
	Mersawa			
	Pine			
	Pond			
	Red			
	Virginia			
	Western white			
	Spruce			
	Black			
	Red			
	Sitka			
	Sweetgum			
	Tamarack			
	Yellow poplar			

[a]From NIST 1995. Strongest species in Group 1; weakest in Group 5.
[b]Trees grown in Nevada, Utah, Colorado, Arizona, and New Mexico.
[c]Trees grown in Washington, Oregon, California, Idaho, Montana, Wyoming, and Canadian provinces of Alberta and British Columbia.

recommended on-center (OC) spacing for framing when the panel is used as roof sheathing; the right-hand number is the maximum recommended OC spacing for framing when the panel is used as subflooring. Panels intended for single-layer flooring (combined subfloor and underlayment) have only one span-rating number; for example, 24 OC. In all cases, the panels are meant to be installed with their length perpendicular to framing and across three or more supports. Again, panels of the same grade and span rating can be substituted for one another regardless of who made or certified them.

Table 10–6 provides approximate properties of sheathing-grade plywood. Plywood may be used under loading conditions that require the addition of stiffeners to prevent it from buckling. It may also be used in the form of cylinders or curved plates, which are beyond the scope of this handbook but are discussed in U.S. Department of Defense Bulletin ANC–18.

It is obvious from its construction that a strip of plywood cannot be as strong in tension, compression, or bending as a strip of solid wood of the same size. Those layers having

Table 10–6. General property values for sheathing-grade plywood[a]

Property	Value	ASTM test method[b] (where applicable)
Linear hygroscopic expansion (30%–90% RH)	0.15%	
Linear thermal expansion	6.1×10^{-6} cm/cm/°C (3.4×10^{-6} in/in/°F)	
Flexure		
Modulus of rupture	20.7–48.3 MPa (3,000–7,000 lb/in^2)	D3043
Modulus of elasticity	6.89–13.1 GPa ($1–1.9 \times 10^6$ lb/in^2)	
Tensile strength	10.3–27.6 MPa (1,500–4,000 lb/in^2)	D3500
Compressive strength	20.7–34.5 MPa (3,000–5,000 lb/in^2)	D3501
Shear through thickness (edgewise shear)		
Shear strength	4.1–7.6 MPa (600–1,100 lb/in^2)	D2719
Shear modulus	0.47–0.761 GPa ($68–110 \times 10^3$ lb/in^2)	D3044
Shear in plane of plies (rolling shear)		D2718
Shear strength	1.7–2.1 MPa (250–300 lb/in^2)	
Shear modulus	0.14–0.21 GPa ($20–30 \times 10^3$ lb/in^2)	

[a]All mechanical properties are based on gross section properties of plywood panels, with stress applied parallel to grain direction of face plies where applicable. Note: Data are not to be used in developing allowable design values. Information on engineering design methods for plywood courtesy of APA–The Engineered Wood Association, Tacoma, WA.

[b]Standard methods of testing strength and elastic properties of structural panels are given in ASTM standards (see References).

their grain direction oriented at 90° to the direction of stress can contribute only a fraction of the strength contributed by the corresponding areas of a solid strip because they are stressed perpendicular to the grain. Strength properties in the length and width directions tend to be equalized in plywood because adjacent layers are oriented at an angle of 90° to each other.

Characteristics

Although plywood is an engineered wood product, it is also used as a component in other engineered wood products and systems in applications such as prefabricated I-joists, box beams, stressed-skin panels, and panelized roofs. Plywood has high strength-to-weight and strength-to-thickness ratios, and its stiffness and strength are more equal in width and length than are stiffness and strength of solid wood. Plywood also has excellent dimensional stability along its length and across its width. Minimal edge-swelling makes plywood perhaps the best choice for adhesive-bonded tongue-and-groove joints, even where some wetting is expected. Because the alternating grain direction of its layers significantly reduces splitting, plywood is an excellent choice for uses that call for fasteners to be placed very near the edges of a panel. In uses where internal knotholes and voids may pose a

problem, such as in small pieces, plywood can be ordered with a solid core and face veneers.

Other Considerations

Plywood of thin, cross-laminated layers is very resistant to splitting. Therefore, nails and screws can be placed close together and close to the edges of panels. Of course, highly efficient, rigid joints can be obtained by bonding plywood to itself or to heavier wood members, such as those needed in prefabricated wood I-joists, box beams, and stressed-skin panels. Adhesive-bonded joints should not be designed to transmit load in tension primarily normal to the plane of the plywood sheet because of the rather low tensile strength of wood perpendicular to grain. Adhesive-bonded joints should be arranged to transmit loads through shear. It must be recognized that shear strength across the grain of wood (often called rolling shear strength because of the tendency to roll the wood fibers) is only 20% to 30% of that parallel to the grain. Thus, sufficient area must be provided between plywood and flange members of box beams and between plywood and stringers of stressed-skin panels to avoid perpendicular-to-grain shearing failure in the face veneer, in the crossband veneer next to the face veneer, or in the wood member. Various details of design are given in Chapter 11.

Specialty Panels

Some plywood panels are designed for special uses, including marine decorative underlayment and concrete form and special exterior applications. The treating of plywood with preservatives and fire retardants is done by manufacturers outside of the plywood industry. Plywood is easily pressure-treated with waterborne preservatives and fire retardants, and treated plywood is readily available for use where such protection is needed.

Particle and Fiber Composites

Many wood-based composite materials have become popular. These composites are usually available in panel form and are widely used in housing and furniture. Conventional composites are typically made with a heat-curing adhesive that holds the wood fiber components together. The physical and mechanical properties of wood-based fiber and particle panel materials are determined by standard ASTM test methods.

General Processing Considerations

All the products in the family of particle and fiber composite materials are processed in similar ways. Raw material for OSB, waferboard, and fiberboard is obtained by flaking or chipping roundwood. For fiberboard, chips are reduced to wood fiber using refiners that usually use steam to soften the wood. The comminuted wood is then dried, adhesive is applied, and a mat of wood particles, fibers, or strands is formed; the mat is then pressed in a platen-type press under heat and pressure until the adhesive is cured. The bonded product is allowed to cool and is further processed into specified width, length, and surface qualities.

Oriented Strandboard

Oriented strandboard is an engineered structural-use panel manufactured from thin wood strands bonded together with waterproof resin under heat and pressure, and it is used extensively for roof, wall, and floor sheathing in residential and commercial construction. Orientation of wood strands with a typical aspect ratio (that is, strand length divided by width) of at least 3 can produce a panel product with greater bending strength and stiffness in the oriented or aligned direction.

Raw Materials

The raw material for the original waferboard product, which was made from square wafers, was aspen. As this industry expanded and OSB became the predominant product manufactured, other species such as Southern Pine, white birch, red maple, sweetgum, and yellow-poplar were found to be suitable raw materials as well. Small amounts of some other hardwoods can also be used for OSB.

Manufacturing Process

In the general manufacturing process for OSB, debarked logs are often heated in soaking ponds, then sliced into thin wood elements. The strands are dried, blended with resin and wax, and formed into thick, loosely consolidated mats that are pressed under heat and pressure into large panels.

Figure 10–6 shows an OSB manufacturing process. Oriented strandboard is made from long, narrow strands, with the strands of each layer aligned parallel to one another but perpendicular to strands in adjacent layers, like the cross-laminated veneers of plywood. It is this perpendicular orientation of different layers of aligned strands that gives OSB its unique characteristics and allows it to be engineered to suit different uses.

Stranding Process

Typically, logs are debarked and then sent to a soaking pond or directly to the stranding process. Long log disk or ring stranders are commonly used to produce wood strands typically measuring 114 to 152 mm (4.5 to 6 in.) long, 12.7 mm (0.5 in.) wide, and 0.6 to 0.7 mm (0.023 to 0.027 in.) thick.

Drying Process

Green strands are stored in wet bins and then dried in a traditional triple-pass dryer, a single-pass dryer, a combination triple-pass/single-pass dryer, or a three-section conveyor dryer. A relatively recent development is a continuous chain dryer, in which the strands are laid on a chain mat that is mated with an upper chain mat and the strands are held in place as they move through the dryer. The introduction of new drying techniques allows the use of longer strands, reduces surface inactivation of strands, and lowers dryer outfeed temperatures. Dried strands are screened and sent to dry bins.

Adhesive Application or Blending

The blending of strands with adhesive and wax is a highly controlled operation, with separate rotating blenders used for face and core strands. Typically, different resin formulations are used for face and core layers. Face resins may be liquid or powdered phenolics, whereas core resins may be phenolics or isocyanates. Several different resin application systems are used; spinning disk resin applicators are frequently used.

Mat Formation

Mat formers take on a number of configurations, ranging from electrostatic equipment to mechanical devices containing spinning disks to align strands along the panel's length and star-type cross-orienters to position strands across the panel's width. All formers use the long and narrow characteristic of the strand to place it between the spinning disks or troughs before it is ejected onto a moving screen or conveyor belt below the forming heads. Oriented layers of strands within the mat—face, core, face, for example—are dropped sequentially, each by a different forming head. Modern mat formers either use wire screens laid over a moving conveyor belt to carry the mat into the press or screenless systems in which the mat lies directly on the conveyor belt.

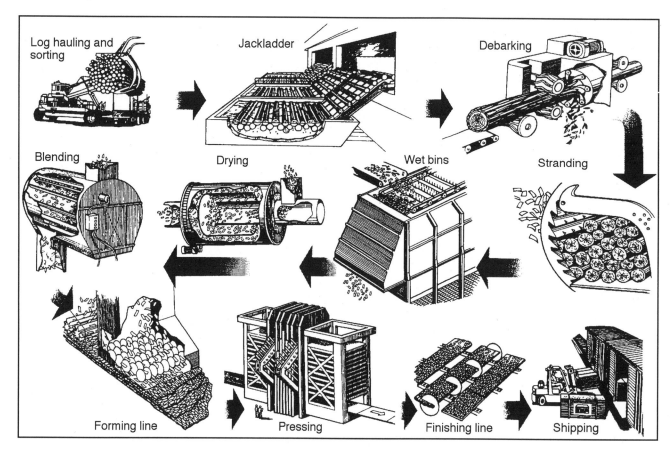

Figure 10–6. Schematic of OSB manufacturing process. (Courtesy of Structural Board Association, Willowdale, Ontario, Canada.)

Hot Pressing

In hot pressing, the loose layered mat of oriented strands is compressed under heat and pressure to cure the resin. As many as sixteen 3.7- by 7.3-m (12- by 24-ft) panels may be formed simultaneously in a multiple-opening press. A more recent development is the continuous press for OSB. The press compacts and consolidates the oriented and layered mat of strands and heats it to 177°C to 204°C (350°F to 400°F) to cure the resin in 3 to 5 min.

Design Capacities and Panel Certification

Design capacities of performance-rated products, which include OSB and waferboard, can be determined by using procedures outlined in Technical Note N375B (APA–The Engineered Wood Association 1995a). In this reference, allowable design strength and stiffness properties, as well as nominal thickness and section properties, are specified based on the span rating of the panel. Additional adjustment factors based on panel grade and construction are also provided. Table 10–7 provides general property values for sheathing-grade OSB.

Under PS 2–92, a manufacturer is required to enter into an agreement with an accredited testing agency to demonstrate that its panels conform with the requirements of the chosen standard. The manufacturer must also maintain an in-plant quality control program in which panel properties are regularly checked, backed by an independent third-party-administered quality assurance program. The third-party agency must visit the mill on a regular unannounced basis. The agency must confirm that the in-plant quality control program is being maintained and that panels meet the minimum requirements of the standard. Today, OSB manufactured to standard PS 2–92 is quality-certified by the following organizations: APA–The Engineered Wood Association, Professional Services and Industries, Inc., Pittsburgh Testing Laboratories, and PFS/TECO Corporations. Examples of grade stamps for performance-rated panels are shown in Figure 10–4c,d.

Particleboard

The wood particleboard industry grew out of a need to dispose of large quantities of sawdust, planer shavings, and to a lesser extent, the use of mill residues and other relatively homogeneous waste materials produced by other wood industries. Simply put, particleboard is produced by mechanically reducing the material into small particles, applying adhesive to the particles, and consolidating a loose mat of

Table 10–7. General property values for sheathing-grade OSB[a]

Property	Value	ASTM test method[b] (where applicable)
Linear hygroscopic expansion (30%–90% RH)	0.15%	
Linear thermal expansion	6.1×10^{-6} cm/cm/°C (3.4×10^{-6} in/in/°F)	
Flexure		
Modulus of rupture	20.7–27.6 MPa (3,000–4,000 lb/in^2)	D3043
Modulus of elasticity	4.83–8.27 GPa (700–1,200 × 10^3 lb/in^2)	
Tensile strength	6.9–10.3 MPa (1,000–1,500 lb/in^2)	D3500
Compressive strength	10.3–17.2 MPa (1,500–2,500 lb/in^2)	D3501
Shear through thickness (edgewise shear)		
Shear strength	6.9–10.3 MPa (1,000–1,500 lb/in^2)	D2719
Shear modulus	1.24–2.00 GPa (180–290 × 10^3 lb/in^2)	D3044
Shear in plane of plies (rolling shear)		D2718
Shear strength	1.38–2.1 MPa (200–300 lb/in^2)	
Shear modulus	0.14–0.34 GPa (20–50 × 10^3 lb/in^2)	

[a]All mechanical properties are based on gross section properties of OSB panels, with stress applied parallel to panel major axis where applicable. Note: Data are not to be used in developing allowable design values. Information courtesy of APA–The Engineered Wood Association, Tacoma, WA.
[b]Standard methods of testing strength and elastic properties of structural panels are given in ASTM standards (see References).

the particles with heat and pressure into a panel product (Fig. 10–7). All particleboard is currently made using a dry process, where air or mechanical formers are used to distribute the particles prior to pressing.

Particleboard is typically made in three layers. The faces of the board consists of fine wood particles, and the core is made of the coarser material. Producing a panel this way improves utilization of the material and the smooth face presents a better surface for laminating, overlaying, painting, or veneering. Particleboard is also readily made from a variety of agricultural residues. Low-density insulating or sound-absorbing particleboard can be made from kenaf core or jute stick. Low-, medium-, and high-density panels can be produced with cereal straw, which has begun to be used in North America. Rice husks are commercially manufactured into medium- and high-density products in the Middle East.

All other things being equal, reducing lignocellulosic materials to particles requires less energy than reducing the same material into fibers. However, particleboard is generally not as strong as fiberboard because the fibrous nature of lignocellulosics is not exploited as well. Particleboard is used for furniture cores, where it is typically overlaid with other materials for decorative purposes. Particleboard can be used in flooring systems, in manufactured houses, for stair treads, and as underlayment. Thin panels can be used as a paneling substrate. Since most applications are interior,

Figure 10–7. Particles, which are sometimes produced by hammermilling, are used to produce composites such as particleboard.

particleboard is usually bonded with a UF resin, although PF and MF resins are sometimes used for applications requiring more moisture resistance. The various steps involved in particleboard manufacturing are described in the following text.

Particle Preparation

Standard particleboard plants based on particulate material use combinations of hogs, chippers, hammermills, ring flakers, ring mills, and attrition mills. To obtain particleboards with good strength, smooth surfaces, and equal swelling, manufacturers ideally use a homogeneous material with a high degree of slenderness (long, thin particles), no oversize particles, no splinters, and no dust. Depending on the manufacturing process, the specifications for the ideal particle size are different. For a graduated board, wider tolerances are acceptable. For a three-layer board, the core particles should be longer and surface particles shorter, thinner, and smaller. For a five-layer or multi-layer board, the furnish for the intermediate layer between surface and core should have long and thin particles for building a good carrier for the fine surface and to give the boards high bending strength and stiffness.

Particle Classification and Conveying

Very small particles increase furnish surface area and thus increase resin requirements. Oversized particles can adversely affect the quality of the final product because of internal flaws in the particles. While some particles are classified through the use of air streams, screen classification methods are the most common. In screen classification, the particles are fed over a vibrating flat screen or a series of screens. The screens may be wire cloth, plates with holes or slots, or plates set on edge.

The two basic methods of conveying particles are by mechanical means and by air. The choice of conveying method depends upon the size of the particles. In air conveying, care should be taken that the material does not pass through many fans, which reduces the size of the particles. In some types of flakes, damp conditions are maintained to reduce break-up of particles during conveying.

Particle Drying

The furnish drying operation is a critical step in the processing of composite products. The raw materials for these products do not usually arrive at the plant at a low enough moisture content for immediate use. Furnish that arrives at the plant can range from 10% to 200% moisture content. For use with liquid resins, for example, the furnish must be reduced to about 2% to 7% moisture content.

The moisture content of particles is critical during hot-pressing operations. Thus, it is essential to carefully select proper dryers and control equipment. The moisture content of the material depends on whether resin is to be added dry or in the form of a solution or emulsion. The moisture content of materials leaving the dryers is usually in the range of 4% to 8%. The main methods used to dry particles are rotary, disk, and suspension drying.

A triple-pass rotary dryer consists of a large horizontal rotating drum that is heated by either steam or direct heat. Operating temperatures depend on the moisture content of the incoming furnish. The drum is set at a slight angle, and material is fed into the high end and discharged at the low end. A series of flights forces the furnish to flow from one end to the other three times before being discharged. The rotary movement of the drum moves the material from input to output.

Addition of Resins and Wax

Frequently used resins for particleboard include urea-formaldehyde and, to a much lesser extent, phenol-formaldehyde, melamine-formaldehyde, and isocyanates. The type and amount of resin used for particleboard depend on the type of product desired. Based on the weight of dry resin solids and ovendry weight of the particles, the resin content can range between 4% and 10%, but usually ranges between 6% and 9% for UF resins. The resin content of the outer face layers is usually slightly higher than that of the core layer. Urea-formaldehyde resin is usually introduced in water solutions containing about 50% to 65% solids. Besides resin, paraffin or microcrystalline wax emulsion is added to improve short-term moisture resistance. The amount of wax ranges from 0.3% to 1% based on the ovendry weight of the particles.

Mat Formation

After the particles have been prepared, they must be laid into an even and consistent mat to be pressed into a panel. This is typically accomplished in a batch mode or by continuous formation. The batch system employs a caul or tray on which a deckle frame is placed. The mat is formed by the back-and-forth movement of the tray or hopper feeder. The mat is usually cold pressed to reduce mat thickness prior to hot pressing. The production of three-layer boards requires three or more forming stations. The two outer layers consist of particles that differ in geometry from those in the core. The resin content of the outer layers is usually higher (about 8% to 15%) than that of the core (about 4% to 8%).

In continuous mat-forming systems, the particles are distributed in one or several layers on traveling cauls or on a moving belt. Mat thickness is controlled volumetrically. The two outer face layers usually consist of particles that differ in geometry from those in the core. Continuous-formed mats are often pre-pressed, with either a single-opening platen or a continuous press. Pre-pressing reduces mat height and helps to consolidate the mat for pressing.

Hot Pressing

After pre-pressing, the mats are hot-pressed into panels. Presses can be divided into platen and continuous types. Further development in the industry has made possible the construction of presses for producing increasingly larger panel sizes in both single- and multi-opening presses. Both of these types of presses can be as wide as 3.7 m (12 ft). Multi-opening presses can be as long as 10 m (33 ft) and single-opening presses, up to 30.5 m (100 ft) long. Hot-press temperatures for UF resins usually range from 140°C to 165°C (284°F to 325°F). Pressure depends on a number of factors, but it is usually in the range of 1.37 to 3.43 MPa (199 to 498 lb/in^2) for medium-density boards. Upon entering the hot press, mats usually have a moisture content of 8% to 12%, but this is reduced to about 5% to 9% during pressing.

Alternatively, some particleboards are made by the extrusion process. In this system, formation and pressing occur in one operation. The particles are forced into a long, heated die (made of two sets of platens) by means of reciprocating pistons. The board is extruded between the platens. The particles are oriented in a plane perpendicular to the plane of the board, resulting in properties that differ from those obtained with flat pressing.

Finishing

After pressing, the board is trimmed to obtain the desired length and width and to square the edges. Trim losses usually amount to 0.5% to 8%, depending on the size of the board, the process employed, and the control exercised. Trimmers usually consist of saws with tungsten carbide tips. After trimming, the boards are sanded or planed prior to packaging and shipping. Particleboards may also be veneered or overlaid with other materials to provide a decorative surface, or they may be finished with lacquer or paint. Treatments with fire-resistant chemicals are also available.

Properties

Tables 10–8 and 10–9 show requirements for grades of particleboard and particleboard flooring products, as specified by the American National Standard for Particleboard A208.1 (NPA 1993). This standard is typically updated at least every 5 years. Today, approximately 85% of interior-type particleboard is used as core stock for a wide variety of furniture and cabinet applications. Floor underlayment and manufactured home decking represent particleboard construction products and approximately 10% of the market. Low-density panels produced in thicknesses >27 mm (>1-1/16 in.) are used for solid-core doors.

Particleboard Grade Marks and Product Certification

Particleboard that has been grade marked ensures that the product has been periodically tested for compliance with voluntary industry product performance standards. These inspection or certification programs also generally require that the quality control system of a production plant meets strict criteria. Particleboard panels conforming to these product performance standards are marked with grade stamps such as those shown in Figure 10–8.

Fiberboard

The term fiberboard includes hardboard, medium-density fiberboard (MDF), and insulation board. Several things differentiate fiberboard from particleboard, most notably the physical configuration of the comminuted material (Fig. 10–9). Because wood is fibrous by nature, fiberboard exploits the inherent strength of wood to a greater extent than does particleboard.

To make fibers for composites, bonds between the wood fibers must be broken. In its simplest form, this is

Table 10–8. Particleboard grade requirements[a,b,c]

Grade[d]	MOR (MPa)	MOE (MPa)	Internal bond (MPa)	Hardness (N)	Linear expansion max avg (%)	Screw-holding (N) Face	Screw-holding (N) Edge	Formaldehyde maximum emission (ppm)
H–1	16.5	2,400	0.90	2,225	NS	1,800	1,325	0.30
H–2	20.5	2,400	0.90	4,450	NS	1,900	1,550	0.30
H–3	23.5	2,750	1.00	6,675	NS	2,000	1,550	0.30
M–1	11.0	1,725	0.40	2,225	0.35	NS	NS	0.30
M–S	12.5	1,900	0.40	2,225	0.35	900	800	0.30
M–2	14.5	2,225	0.45	2,225	0.35	1,000	900	0.30
M–3	16.5	2,750	0.55	2,225	0.35	1,100	1,000	0.30
LD–1	3.0	550	0.10	NS	0.35	400	NS	0.30
LD–2	5.0	1,025	0.15	NS	0.35	550	NS	0.30

[a]From NPA (1993). Particleboard made with phenol-formaldehyde-based resins does not emit significant quantities of formaldehyde. Therefore, such products and other particleboard products made with resin without formaldehyde are not subject to formaldehyde emission conformance testing.
[b]Panels designated as "exterior adhesive" must maintain 50% MOR after ASTM D1037 accelerated aging.
[c]MOR = modulus of rupture; MOE = modulus of elasticity. NS = not specified. 1 MPa = 145 lb/in^2; 1 N = 0.22 lb.
[d]H = density > 800 kg/m^3 (> 50 lb/ft^3), M = density 640 to 800 kg/m^3 (40 to 50 lb/ft^3). LD = density < 640 kg/m^3 (< 40 lb/ft^3). Grade M–S refers to medium density; "special" grade added to standard after grades M–1, M–2, and M–3. Grade M–S falls between M–1 and M–2 in physical properties.

Table 10–9. Particleboard flooring product grade requirements[a]

Grade[b]	MOR (MPa)	MOE (MPa)	Internal bond (MPa)	Hardness (N)	Linear expansion max avg (%)	Formaldehyde maximum emission (ppm)
PBU	11.0	1,725	0.40	2,225	0.35	0.20
D–2	16.5	2,750	0.55	2,225	0.30	0.20
D–3	19.5	3,100	0.55	2,225	0.30	0.20

[a]From NPA (1993). Particleboard made with phenol-formaldehyde-based resins does not emit significant quantities of formaldehyde. Therefore, such products and other particleboard products made with resin without formaldehyde are not subject to formaldehyde emission conformance testing. Grades listed here shall also comply with appropriate requirements listed in section 3. Panels designated as "exterior adhesive" must maintain 50% MOR after ASTM D1037 accelerated aging (3.3.3).
[b]PBU = underlayment; D = manufactured home decking.

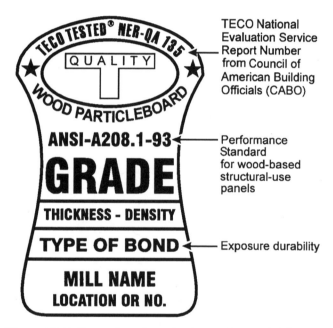

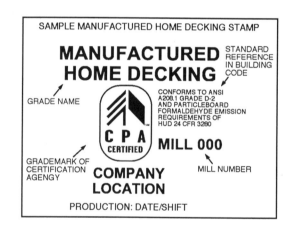

Figure 10–8. Examples of grade stamps for particleboard.

accomplished by attrition milling. Attrition milling is an age-old concept whereby material is fed between two disks, one rotating and the other stationary. As the material is forced through the preset gap between the disks, it is sheared, cut, and abraded into fibers and fiber bundles. Grain has been ground in this way for centuries.

Attrition milling, or refining as it is commonly called, can be augmented by water soaking, steam cooking, or chemical treatments. Steaming the lignocellulosic weakens the lignin bonds between the cellulosic fibers. As a result, the fibers are more readily separated and usually are less damaged than fibers processed by dry processing methods. Chemical treatments, usually alkali, are also used to weaken the lignin bonds. All of these treatments help increase fiber quality and

reduce energy requirements, but they may reduce yield as well. Refiners are available with single- or double-rotating disks, as well as steam-pressurized and unpressurized configurations. For MDF, steam-pressurized refining is typical.

Fiberboard is normally classified by density and can be made by either dry or wet processes (Fig. 10–2). Dry processes are applicable to boards with high density (hardboard) and medium density (MDF). Wet processes are applicable to both high-density hardboard and low-density insulation board. The following subsections briefly describe the manufacturing of high- and medium-density dry-process fiberboard, wet-process hardboard, and wet-process low-density insulation board. Suchsland and Woodson (1986) and Maloney (1993) provide more detailed information.

Figure 10–9. Fibers can be made from many lignocellulosics and form the raw materials for many composites, most notably fiberboard. Fibers are typically produced by the refining process.

Figure 10–11. Air-laid mat about to enter a laboratory press.

Figure 10–10. Laboratory-produced air-laid mat before pressing. Approximate dimensions are 686 by 686 by 152 mm (27 by 27 by 6 in.) thick. Resin was applied to fibers before mat production. This mat will be made into a high-density fiberboard approximately 3 mm (0.12 in.) thick.

SAMPLE BUNDLE TAG FOR MDF CERTIFICATION

CONFORMS TO MDF
FORMALDEHYDE EMISSION REQUIREMENTS
OF ANSI A208.2-1994

STANDARD REFERENCE IN BUILDING CODE

GRADEMARK OF CERTIFICATION AGENCY

C P A
CERTIFIED

MILL 000

MILL NUMBER

COMPANY LOCATION

PRODUCTION DATE/SHIFT

Figure 10–12. Example of MDF formaldehyde emissions certification tag.

Dry-Process Fiberboard

Dry-process fiberboard is made in a similar fashion to particleboard. Resin (UF, PF) and other additives may be applied to the fibers by spraying in short-retention blenders or introduced as the wet fibers are fed from the refiner into a blowline dryer. Alternatively, some fiberboard plants add the resin in the refiner. The adhesive-coated fibers are then air-laid into a mat for subsequent pressing, much the same as mat formation for particleboard.

Pressing procedures for dry-process fiberboard differ somewhat from particleboard procedures. After the fiber mat is formed (Fig. 10–10), it is typically pre-pressed in a band press. The densified mat is then trimmed by disk cutters and transferred to caul plates for the hardboard pressing operation; for MDF, the trimmed mat is transferred directly to the press

(Fig. 10–11). All dry-formed boards are pressed in multiopening presses at approximately 140°C to 165°C (284°F to 329°F) for UF-bonded products and 190°C (410°F) for PF-bonded products. Continuous pressing using large, high-pressure band presses is also gaining in popularity. Board density is a basic property and an indicator of board quality. Since density is greatly influenced by moisture content, this is constantly monitored by moisture sensors using infrared light. An example of an MDF formaldehyde emissions certification tag is shown in Figure 10–12.

Wet-Process Hardboard

Wet-process hardboards differ from dry-process fiberboards in several significant ways. First, water is used as the distribution medium for forming the fibers into a mat. As such, this technology is really an extension of paper manufacturing

225

technology. Secondly, some wet-process boards are made without additional binders. If the lignocellulosic contains sufficient lignin and if lignin is retained during the refining operation, lignin can serve as the binder. Under heat and pressure, lignin will flow and act as a thermosetting adhesive, enhancing the naturally occurring hydrogen bonds.

Refining is an important step for developing strength in wet-process hardboards. The refining operation must also yield a fiber of high "freeness;" that is, it must be easy to remove water from the fibrous mat. The mat is typically formed on a Fourdrinier wire, like papermaking, or on cylinder formers. The wet process employs a continuously traveling mesh screen, onto which the soupy pulp flows rapidly and smoothly. Water is drawn off through the screen and then through a series of press rolls, which use a wringing action to remove additional water.

Wet-process hardboards are pressed in multi-opening presses heated by steam. The press cycle consists of three phases and lasts 6 to 15 min. The first phase is conducted at high pressure, and it removes most of the water while bringing the board to the desired thickness. The primary purpose of the second phase is to remove water vapor. The final phase is relatively short and results in the final cure. A maximum pressure of about 5 MPa (725 lb/in^2) is used. Heat is essential during pressing to induce fiber-to-fiber bond. A high temperature of up to 210°C (410°F) is used to increase production by causing faster evaporation of the water. Lack of sufficient moisture removal during pressing adversely affects strength and may result in "springback" or blistering.

Post-Treatment of Wet- and Dry-Process Hardboard

Several treatments are used to increase the dimensional stability and mechanical performance of hardboard. Heat treatment, tempering, and humidification may be done singularly or in conjunction with one another.

Heat treatment—exposure of pressed fiberboard to dry heat—improves dimensional stability and mechanical properties, reduces water adsorption, and improves interfiber bonding.

Tempering is the heat treatment of pressed boards, preceded by the addition of oil. Tempering improves board surface hardness and is sometimes done on various types of wet-formed hardboards. It also improves resistance to abrasion, scratching, scarring, and water. The most common oils used include linseed oil, tung oil, and tall oil.

Humidification is the addition of water to bring the board moisture content into equilibrium with the air. Initially, a pressed board has almost no moisture content. When the board is exposed to air, it expands linearly by taking on 3% to 7% moisture. Continuous or progressive humidifiers are commonly used for this purpose. Air of high humidity is forced through the stacks where it provides water vapor to the boards. The entire process is controlled by a dry-bulb-wet-bulb controller. Another method involves spraying water on the back side of the board.

Insulation Board

Insulation boards are low-density, wet-laid panel products used for insulation, sound deadening, carpet underlayment, and similar applications. In the manufacture of insulation board, the need for refining and screening is a function of the raw material available, the equipment used, and the desired end-product. Insulation boards typically do not use a binder, and they rely on hydrogen bonds to hold the board components together. Sizing agents are usually added to the furnish (about 1%) to provide the finished board with a modest degree of water resistance and dimensional stability. Sizing agents include rosin, starch, paraffin, cumarone, resin, asphalt, and asphalt emulsions.

Like the manufacture of wet-process hardboard, insulation board manufacture is a modification of papermaking. A thick fibrous sheet is made from a low-consistency pulp suspension in a process known as wet felting. Felting can be accomplished through use of a deckle box, Fourdrinier screen, or cylinder screen. A deckle box is a bottomless frame that is placed over a screen. A measured amount of stock is put in the box to form one sheet; vacuum is then applied to remove most of the water. The use of Fourdrinier screen for felting is similar to that for papermaking, except that line speeds are reduced to 1.5 to 15 m/min (5 to 49 ft/min).

Insulation board is usually cold-pressed to remove most of the free water after the mat is formed. The wet mats are then dried to the final moisture content. Dryers may be a continuous tunnel or a multi-deck arrangement. The board is generally dried in stages at temperatures ranging from 120°C to 190°C (248°F to 374°F). Typically, about 2 to 4 h are required to reduce moisture content to about 1% to 3%.

After drying, some boards are treated for various applications. Boards may be given tongue-and-groove or shiplap edges or can be grooved to produce a plank effect. Other boards are laminated by means of asphalt to produce roof insulation.

Properties and Applications

Medium-Density Fiberboard—Minimum property requirements, as specified by the American National Standard for MDF, A208.2 (NPA 1994) are given in Table 10–10. This standard is typically updated every 5 years or less. The furniture industry is by far the dominant MDF market. Medium-density fiberboard is frequently used in place of solid wood, plywood, and particleboard in many furniture applications. It is also used for interior door skins, mouldings, and interior trim components (Youngquist and others 1997).

Hardboard—Table 10–11 provides basic hardboard physical properties (ANSI/AHA A135.4–1995 (AHA 1995a)) for selected products. The uses for hardboard can generally be grouped as construction, furniture and furnishings, cabinet and store work, appliances, and automotive and rolling stock. Typical hardboard products are prefinished paneling (ANSI/AHA A135.5–1995 (AHA 1995b)), house siding (ANSI/AHA A135.6–1990 (AHA 1990)), floor underlayment, and concrete form board. Table 10–12 shows physical

Table 10–10. Medium-density fiberboard (MDF) property requirements[a]

Product class[b]	Nominal thickness (mm)	MOR (MPa)	MOE (MPa)	Internal bond (MPa)	Screw-holding (N) Face	Screw-holding (N) Edge	Formaldehyde emission[c] (ppm)
Interior MDF							
HD		34.5	3,450	0.75	1,555	1,335	0.30
MD	≤21	24.0	2,400	0.60	1,445	1,110	0.30
	>21	24.0	2,400	0.55	1,335	1,000	0.30
LD		14.0	1,400	0.30	780	670	0.30
Exterior MDF							
MD–Exterior	≤21	34.5	3,450	0.90	1,445	1,110	0.30
adhesive	>21	31.0	3,100	0.70	1,335	1,000	0.30

[a]From NPA (1994). Metric property values shall be primary in determining product performance requirements.
[b]MD–Exterior adhesive panels shall maintain at least 50% of listed MOR after ASTM D1037–1991, accelerated aging (3.3.4). HD = density > 800 kg/m^3 (> 50 lb/ft^3), MD = density 640 to 800 kg/m^3 (40 to 50 lb/ft^3), LD = density < 640 kg/m^3 (< 40 lb/ft^3).
[c]Maximum emission when tested in accordance with ASTM E1333–1990, Standard test method for determining formaldehyde levels from wood products under defined test conditions using a larger chamber (ASTM).

Table 10–11. Hardboard physical property requirements[a]

Product class	Normal thickness (mm)	Water resistance (max avg/panel) Water absorption based on weight (%)	Water resistance (max avg/panel) Thickness swelling (%)	MOR (min avg/panel) (MPa)	Tensile strength (min avg/panel) (MPa) Parallel to surface	Tensile strength (min avg/panel) (MPa) Perpendicular to surface
Tempered	2.1	30	25	41.4	20.7	0.90
	2.5	25	20	41.4	20.7	0.90
	3.2	25	20	41.4	20.7	0.90
	4.8	25	20	41.4	20.7	0.90
	6.4	20	15	41.4	20.7	0.90
	7.9	15	10	41.4	20.7	0.90
	9.5	10	9	41.4	20.7	0.90
Standard	2.1	40	30	31.0	15.2	0.62
	2.5	35	25	31.0	15.2	0.62
	3.2	35	25	31.0	15.2	0.62
	4.8	35	25	31.0	15.2	0.62
	6.4	25	20	31.0	15.2	0.62
	7.9	20	15	31.0	15.2	0.62
	9.5	15	10	31.0	15.2	0.62
Service-tempered	3.2	35	30	31.0	3.8	0.52
	4.8	30	30	31.0	3.8	0.52
	6.4	30	25	31.0	3.8	0.52
	9.5	20	15	31.0	3.8	0.52

[a]AHA 1995a.

Table 10–12. Physical and mechanical properties of hardboard siding[a]

Property[b]	Requirement	
Water absorption (based on weight)	12% (max avg/panel)	
Thickness swelling	8% (max avg/panel)	
Weatherability of substrate (max residual swell)	20%	
Weatherability of primed substrate	No checking, erosion, flaking, or objectionable fiber raising; adhesion, less than 3.2 mm (0.125 in.) of coating picked up	
Linear expansion 30% to 90% RH (max)	Thickness range (cm)	Maximum linear expansion (%)
	0.220–0.324	0.36
	0.325–0.375	0.38
	0.376–0.450	0.40
	>0.451	0.40
Nail-head pull-through	667 N (150 lb) (min avg/panel)	
Lateral nail resistance	667 N (150 lb) (min avg/panel)	
Modulus of rupture	12.4 MPa (1,800 lb/in^2) for 9.5, 11, and 12.7 mm (3/8, 7/16, and 1/2 in.) thick (min avg/panel)	
	20.7 MPa (3,000 lb/in^2) for 6.4 mm (1/4 in.) thick (min avg/panel)	
Hardness	2002 N (450 lb) (min avg/panel)	
Impact	229 mm (9 in.) (min avg/panel)	
Moisture content[c]	4% to 9% included, and not more than 3% variance between any two boards in any one shipment or order	

[a]From Youngquist and others 1992.
[b]Refer to ANSI/AHA A135.6 I–1990 for test method for determining information on properties.
[c]Since hardboard is a wood-based material, its moisture content varies with environmental humidity conditions. When the environmental humidity conditions in the area of intended use are a critical factor, the purchaser should specify a moisture content range more restrictive than 4% to 9% so that fluctuation in the moisture content of the siding will be kept to a minimum.

properties of hardboard siding. Hardboard siding products come in a great variety of finishes and textures (smooth or embossed) and in different sizes. For application purposes, the AHA siding classifies into three basic types:

Lap siding—boards applied horizontally, with each board overlapping the board below it

Square edge panels—siding intended for vertical application in full sheets

Shiplap edge panel siding—siding intended for vertical application, with the long edges incorporating shiplap joints

The type of panel dictates the application method. The AHA administers a quality conformance program for hardboard for both panel and lap siding. Participation in this program is voluntary and is open to all (not restricted to AHA members). Under this program, hardboard siding products are tested by an independent laboratory in accordance with product standard ANSI/AHA A135.6. Figure 10–13a provides an example of a grade stamp for a siding product meeting this standard.

Insulation Board—Physical and mechanical properties of insulation board are published in the ASTM C208 standard specification for cellulosic fiber insulation board. Physical

(a)

(b)

Figure 10–13. Examples of grade stamps: (a) grade stamp for siding conforming to ANSI/AHA A135.6 standard, and (b) grade mark stamp for cellulosic fiberboard products conforming to ANSI/AHA A194.1 standard.

properties are also included in the ANSI standard for cellulosic fiberboard, ANSI/AHA A194.1 (AHA 1985). Insulation board products can be divided into three categories (Suchsland and Woodson 1986): exterior, interior, and industrial.

Exterior products

- Sheathing—board used in exterior construction because of its insulation and noise control qualities, bracing strength, and low price

- Roof decking—three-in-one component that provides roof deck, insulation, and a finished interior ceiling surface; insulation board sheets are laminated together with waterproof adhesive Roof insulation—insulation board designed for use on flat roof decks

- Aluminum siding backer board—fabricated insulation board for improving insulation of aluminum-sided houses

Interior products

- Building board—general purpose product for interior construction

- Ceiling tile—insulation board embossed and decorated for interior use; valued for acoustical qualities; also decorative, nonacoustical tiles

- Sound-deadening board—special product designed to control noise levels in buildings

Industrial products

- Mobile home board

- Expansion joint strips

- Boards for automotive and furniture industries

The AHA administers a quality conformance program for cellulosic fiberboard products including sound-deadening board, roof insulation boards, structural and nonstructural sheathings, backer board, and roof decking in various thicknesses. These products are tested by an independent laboratory in accordance with product standard ANSI/AHA A194.1. An example of the grade mark stamp for these products is shown in Figure 10–13b.

Finishing Techniques

Several techniques are used to finish fiberboard: trimming, sanding, surface treatment, punching, and embossing.

Trimming—Trimming consists of reducing products into standard sizes and shapes. Generally, double-saw trimmers are used to saw the boards. Trimmers consist of overhead-mounted saws or multiple saw drives. Trimmed boards are stacked in piles for future processing.

Sanding—If thickness tolerance is critical, hardboard is sanded prior to finishing. S1S (smooth on one side) boards require this process. Sanding reduces thickness variation and improves surface paintability. Single-head, wide-belt sanders are used with 24- to 36-grit abrasive.

Surface treatment—Surface treatments improve the appearance and performance of boards. Boards are cleaned by spraying with water and then dried at about 240°C (464°F) for 30 seconds. Board surfaces are then modified with paper overlay, paint, or stain or are printed directly on the panel.

Punching—Punching changes boards into the perforated sheets used as peg board. Most punching machines punch three rows of holes simultaneously while the board advances.

Embossing—Embossing consists of pressing the unconsolidated mat of fibers with a textured form. This process results in a slightly contoured board surface that can enhance the resemblance of the board to that of sawn or weathered wood, brick, and other materials.

Specialty Composites

Special-purpose composites are produced to obtain desirable properties like water resistance, mechanical strength, acidity control, and decay and insect resistance. Overlays and veneers can also be added to enhance both structural properties and appearance (Fig. 10–14).

Moisture-Resistant Composites

Sizing agents, wax, and asphalt can be used to make composites resistant to moisture. Sizing agents cover the surface of fibers, reduce surface energy, and render the fibers relatively hydrophobic. Sizing agents can be applied in two ways. In the first method, water is used as a medium to ensure thorough mixing of sizing and fiber. The sizing is forced to precipitate from the water and is fixed to the fiber surface. In the second method, the sizing is applied directly to the fibers. Rosin is a common sizing agent that is obtained from living pine trees, from pine stumps, and as a by-product of kraft pulping of pines. Rosin sizing is added in amounts of less than 3% solids based on dry fiber weight.

Waxes are high molecular weight hydrocarbons derived from crude oil. Wax sizing is used in dry-process fiberboard production; for wet processes, wax is added in solid form or as

Figure 10–14. Medium-density fiberboard with veneer overlay. Edges can be shaped and finished as required by end product.

an emulsion. Wax sizing tends to lower strength properties to a greater extent than does rosin.

Asphalt is also used to increase water resistance, especially in low-density wet-process insulation board. Asphalt is a black–brown solid or semi-solid material that liquefies when heated. The predominant component of asphalt is bitumen. Asphalt is precipitated onto fiber by the addition of alum.

Flame-Retardant Composites

Two general application methods are available for improving the fire performance of composites with fire-retardant chemicals. One method consists of pressure impregnating the wood with waterborne or organic solventborne chemicals. The second method consists of applying fire-retardant chemical coatings to the wood surface. The impregnation method is usually more effective and longer lasting; however, this technique sometimes causes damage to the wood–adhesive bonds in the composite and results in the degradation of some physical and mechanical properties of the composite. For wood in existing constructions, surface application of fire-retardant paints or other finishes offers a practical method to reduce flame spread.

Preservative-Treated Composites

Wood is highly susceptible to attack by fungi and insects; thus, treatment is essential for maximum durability in adverse conditions.

Composites can be protected from the attack of decay fungi and harmful insects by applying selected chemicals as wood preservatives. The degree of protection obtained depends on the kind of preservative used and the ability to achieve proper penetration and retention of the chemicals. Wood preservative chemicals can be applied using pressure or nonpressure processes. As in the application of fire-retardant chemicals, the application of wood preservatives can sometimes cause damage to wood–adhesive bonds, thus reducing physical and mechanical properties of the composite. Common preservative treatments include chromated copper arsenate (CCA) and boron compounds.

Wood–Nonwood Composites

Interest has burgeoned in combining wood and other raw materials, such as plastics, gypsum, and concrete, into composite products with unique properties and cost benefits (Youngquist and others 1993a, 1993b, 1994; Rowell and others 1997). The primary impetus for developing such products has come from one or more of the following research and development goals:

- Reduce material costs by combining a lower cost material (acting as a filler or extender) with an expensive material

- Develop products that can utilize recycled materials and be recyclable in themselves

- Produce composite products that exhibit specific properties that are superior to those of the component materials

Figure 10–15. Laboratory-produced low-density, cement-bonded composite panel. Full-scale panels such as these are used in construction.

alone (for example, increased strength-to-weight ratio, improved abrasion resistance)

Composites made from wood and other materials create enormous opportunities to match product performance to end-use requirements (Youngquist 1995).

Inorganic–Bonded Composites

Inorganic-bonded wood composites have a long and varied history that started with commercial production in Austria in 1914. A plethora of building materials can be made using inorganic binders and lignocellulosics, and they run the normal gamut of panel products, siding, roofing tiles, and precast building members (Fig. 10–15).

Inorganic-bonded wood composites are molded products or boards that contain between 10% and 70% by weight wood particles or fibers and conversely 90% to 30% inorganic binder. Acceptable properties of an inorganic-bonded wood composite can be obtained only when the wood particles are fully encased with the binder to make a coherent material. This differs considerably from the technique used to manufacture thermosetting-resin-bonded boards where flakes or particles are "spot welded" by a binder applied as a finely distributed spray or powder. Because of this difference and because hardened inorganic binders have a higher density than that of most thermosetting resins, the required amount of inorganic binder per unit volume of composite material is much higher than that of resin-bonded wood composites. The properties of inorganic-bonded wood composites are significantly influenced by the amount and nature of the inorganic binder and the woody material as well as the density of the composites.

Inorganic binders fall into three main categories: gypsum, magnesia cement, and Portland cement. Gypsum and magnesia cement are sensitive to moisture, and their use is

230

generally restricted to interior applications. Composites bonded with Portland cement are more durable than those bonded with gypsum or magnesia cement and are used in both interior and exterior applications. Inorganic-bonded composites are made by blending proportionate amounts of lignocellulosic fiber with inorganic materials in the presence of water and allowing the inorganic material to cure or "set up" to make a rigid composite. All inorganic-bonded composites are very resistant to deterioration, particularly by insects, vermin, and fire.

A unique feature of inorganic-bonded composites is that their manufacture is adaptable to either end of the cost and technology spectrum. This is facilitated by the fact that no heat is required to cure the inorganic material. For example, in the Philippines, Portland cement-bonded composites are mostly fabricated using manual labor and are used in low-cost housing. In Japan, the fabrication of these composites is automated, and they are used in very expensive modular housing.

The versatility of manufacture makes inorganic-bonded composites ideally suited to a variety of lignocellulosic materials. With a very small capital investment and the most rudimentary of tools, satisfactory inorganic-bonded lignocellulosic composite building materials can be produced on a small scale using mostly unskilled labor. If the market for such composites increases, technology can be introduced to increase manufacturing throughput. The labor force can be trained concurrently with the gradual introduction of more sophisticated technology.

Gypsum-Bonded Composites

Gypsum can be derived by mining from natural sources or obtained as a byproduct of flue gas neutralization. Flue gas gypsum, now being produced in very large quantities in the United States because of Clean Air Act regulations, is the result of introducing lime into the combustion process to reduce sulfur dioxide emissions. In 1995, more than 100 power plants throughout the United States were producing gypsum. Flue gas gypsum can be used in lieu of mined gypsum.

Gypsum panels are frequently used to finish interior wall and ceiling surfaces. In the United States, these products are generically called "dry wall" because they replace wet plaster systems. To increase the bending strength and stiffness, gypsum panels are frequently wrapped in paper, which provides a tension surface. An alternative to wrapping gypsum with fiber is to place the fiber within the panel, as several U.S. and European firms are doing with recycled paper fiber. There is no technical reason that other lignocellulosics cannot be used in this way. Gypsum is widely available and does not have the highly alkaline environment of cement.

Gypsum panels are normally made from a slurry of gypsum, water, and lignocellulosic fiber. In large-scale production, the slurry is extruded onto a belt, which carries the slurry through a drying oven to evaporate water and facilitate cure of the gypsum. The panel is then cut to length and trimmed if necessary.

Magnesia-Cement-Bonded Composites

Fewer boards bonded with magnesia cement have been produced than cement- or gypsum-bonded panels, mainly because of price. However, magnesia cement does offer some manufacturing advantages over Portland cement. First, the various sugars in lignocellulosics apparently do not have as much effect on the curing and bonding of the binder. Second, magnesia cement is reported to be more tolerant of high water content during production. This opens up possibilities to use lignocellulosics not amenable to Portland cement composites, without leaching or other modification, and to use alternative manufacturing processes and products. Although composites bonded with magnesia cement are considered water-sensitive, they are much less so than gypsum-bonded composites.

One successful application of magnesia cement is a low-density panel made for interior ceiling and wall applications. In the production of this panel product, wood wool (excelsior) is laid out in a low-density mat. The mat is then sprayed with an aqueous solution of magnesia cement, pressed, and cut into panels.

In Finland, magnesia-cement-bonded particleboard is manufactured using a converted conventional particleboard plant. Magnesia oxide is applied to the lignocellulosic particles in a batch blender along with other chemicals and water. Depending on application and other factors, boards may be cold- or hot-pressed.

Other processes have been suggested for manufacturing magnesia-cement-bonded composites. One application may be to spray a slurry of magnesia cement, water, and lignocellulosic fiber onto existing structures as fireproofing. Extrusion into a pipe-type profile or other profiles is also possible.

Portland-Cement-Bonded Composites

The most apparent and widely used inorganic-bonded composites are those bonded with Portland cement. Portland cement, when combined with water, immediately reacts in a process called hydration to eventually solidify into a solid stone-like mass. Successfully marketed Portland-cement-bonded composites consist of both low-density products made with excelsior and high-density products made with particles and fibers. General mechanical property values for a low density cement–wood excelsior product are given in Table 10–13.

The low-density products may be used as interior ceiling and wall panels in commercial buildings. In addition to the advantages described for low-density magnesia-bonded composites, low-density composites bonded with Portland cement offer sound control and can be quite decorative. In some parts of the world, these panels function as complete wall and roof decking systems. The exterior of the panels is stuccoed, and the interior is plastered. High-density panels can be used as flooring, roof sheathing, fire doors, load-bearing walls, and cement forms. Fairly complex molded shapes can be molded or extruded, such as decorative roofing tiles or non-pressure pipes.

Table 10–13. General properties of low-density cement–wood composites fabricated using an excelsior-type particle[a,b]

Property	From	To
Bending strength	1.7 MPa (250 lb/in^2)	5.5 MPa (800 lb/in^2)
Modulus of elasticity	621 MPa (0.9 × 10^5 lb/in^2)	1,241 MPa (1.8 × 10^5 lb/in^2)
Tensile strength	0.69 MPa (100 lb/in^2)	4.1 MPa (600 lb/in^2)
Compression strength	0.69 MPa (100 lb/in^2)	5.5 MPa (800 lb/in^2)
Shear[c]	0.69 MPa (100 lb/in^2)	1.4 MPa (200 lb/in^2)
E/G[d]	40	100

[a]Data represent compilation of raw data from variety of sources for range of board properties. Variables include cement–wood mix, particle configuration, board density, and the forming and curing methods.
[b]Specific gravity range, 0.5 to 1.0.
[c]Shear strength data are limited to a small sample of excelsior boards having a specific gravity of 0.5 to 0.65.
[d]E/G is ratio of bending modulus of elasticity to modulus of rigidity or shear modulus. For wood, this ratio is often assumed to be around 16.

Problems and Solutions

Although the entire sphere of inorganic-bonded lignocellulosic composites is attractive, and cement-bonded composites are especially so, the use of cement involves limitations and tradeoffs. Marked embrittlement of the lignocellulosic component is known to occur and is caused by the alkaline environment provided by the cement matrix. In addition, hemicellulose, starch, sugar, tannins, and lignin, all to a varying degree, affect the cure rate and ultimate strength of these composites. To make strong and durable composites, measures must be taken to ensure long-term stability of the lignocellulosic in the cement matrix. To overcome these problems, various schemes have been developed. The most common is leaching, whereby the lignocellulosic is soaked in water for 1 or 2 days to extract some of the detrimental components. However, in some parts of the world, the water containing the leachate is difficult to dispose of. Low water–cement ratios are helpful, as is the use of curing accelerators like calcium carbonate. Conversely, low alkali cements have been developed, but they are not readily available throughout the world. Two other strategies are natural pozzolans and carbon dioxide treatment.

Natural Pozzolans—Pozzolans are defined as siliceous or siliceous and aluminous materials that can react chemically with calcium hydroxide (lime) at normal temperatures in the presence of water to form cement compounds (ASTM 1988). Some common pozzolanic materials include volcanic ash, fly ash, rice husk ash, and condensed silica fume. All these materials can react with lime at normal temperatures to make a natural water-resistant cement.

In general, when pozzolans are blended with Portland cement, they increase the strength of the cement but slow the cure time. More important, pozzolans decrease the alkalinity of Portland cement, which indicates that adding lignocellulosic-based material (rice husk ash) to cement-bonded lignocellulosic composites may be advantageous.

Carbon Dioxide Treatment—In the manufacture of a cement-bonded lignocellulosic composite, the cement hydration process normally requires from 8 to 24 h to develop sufficient board strength and cohesiveness to permit the release of consolidation pressure. By exposing the cement to carbon dioxide, the initial hardening stage can be reduced to less than 5 min. This phenomenon results from the chemical reaction of carbon dioxide with calcium hydroxide to form calcium carbonate and water.

Reduction of initial cure time of the cement-bonded lignocellulosic composite is not the only advantage of using carbon dioxide injection. Certain species of wood have varying amounts of sugars and tannins that interfere with the hydration or setting of Portland cement. Research has shown that the use of carbon dioxide injection reduces the likelihood of these compounds to inhibit the hydration process, thus allowing the use of a wider range of species in these composites. In addition, research has demonstrated that composites treated with carbon dioxide can be twice as stiff and strong as untreated composites (Geimer and others 1992). Finally, carbon-dioxide-treated composites do not experience efflorescence (migration of calcium hydroxide to surface of material), so the appearance of the surface of the final product is not changed over time.

Wood Fiber–Thermoplastic Composites

As described elsewhere in this chapter, the use of lignocellulosic materials with thermosetting polymeric materials, like phenol- or urea-formaldehyde, in the production of composites has a long history. The use of lignocellulosics with thermoplastics, however, is a more recent innovation. Broadly defined, a thermoplastic softens when heated and hardens when cooled. Thermoplastics selected for use with lignocellulosics must melt or soften at or below the degradation point of the lignocellulosic component, normally 200°C to 220°C (392°F to 428°F). These thermoplastics include polypropylene, polystyrene, vinyls, and low- and high-density polyethylenes.

Wood flour is a readily available resource that can be used as a filler in thermoplastic composites. Wood flour is processed commercially, often from post-industrial materials such as planer shavings, chips, and sawdust. Several grades are available depending upon wood species and particle size. Wood fibers, although more difficult to process compared with wood flour, can lead to superior composite properties and act more as a reinforcement than as a filler. A wide variety of wood fibers are available from both virgin and recycled resources.

Other materials can be added to affect processing and product performance of wood–thermoplastic composites. These additives can improve bonding between the thermoplastic and wood component (for example, coupling agents), product performance (impact modifiers, UV stabilizers, flame retardants), and processability (lubricants).

Several considerations must be kept in mind when processing wood with thermoplastics. Moisture can disrupt many thermoplastic processes, resulting in poor surface quality, voids, and unacceptable parts. Materials must either be predried or vented equipment must be used to remove moisture. The low degradation temperature of wood must also be considered. As a general rule, melt temperatures should be kept below 200°C (392°F), except for short periods. Higher temperatures can result in the release of volatiles, discoloration, odor, and embrittlement of the wood component.

There are two main strategies for processing thermoplastics in lignocellulosic composites (Youngquist and others 1993b). In the first, the lignocellulosic component serves as a reinforcing agent or filler in a continuous thermoplastic matrix. In the second, the thermoplastic serves as a binder to the majority lignocellulosic component. The presence or absence of a continuous thermoplastic matrix may also determine the processability of the composite material. In general, if the matrix is continuous, conventional thermoplastic processing equipment may be used to process composites; however, if the matrix is not continuous, other processes may be required. For the purpose of discussion, we present these two scenarios for composites with high and low thermoplastic content.

Composites With High Thermoplastic Content

In composites with high thermoplastic content, the thermoplastic component is in a continuous matrix and the lignocellulosic component serves as a reinforcement or filler (Fig. 10–16). In the great majority of reinforced thermoplastic composites available commercially, inorganic materials (for example, glass, clays, and minerals) are used as reinforcements or fillers. Lignocellulosic materials offer some advantages over inorganic materials; they are lighter, much less abrasive, and renewable. As a reinforcement, lignocellulosics can stiffen and strengthen the thermoplastic and can improve thermal stability of the product compared with that of unfilled material.

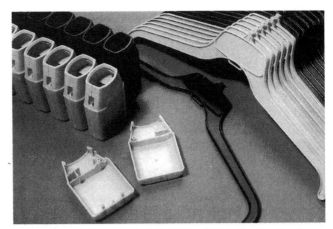

Figure 10–16. The use of lignocelulosics as reinforcing fillers allows thermoplastics to be molded into a wide variety of shapes and forms.

Thermoplastics in pellet form have bulk density in the range of 500 to 600 kg/m^3 (31 to 37 lb/ft^3). Lignocellulosics typically have an uncompacted bulk density of 25 to 250 kg/m^3 (1.6 to 16 lb/ft^3). Wood fibers are at the low end of the lignocellulosic bulk density continuum and wood flours at the high end. Although processing of wood flour in thermoplastics is relatively easy, the low bulk density and difficulty of dispersing fibrous materials make thermoplastics more difficult to compound. More intensive mixing and the use of special feeding equipment may be necessary to handle longer fibers.

The manufacture of thermoplastic composites is usually a two-step process. The raw materials are first mixed together, and the composite blend is then formed into a product. The combination of these steps is called in-line processing, and the result is a single processing step that converts raw materials to end products. In-line processing can be very difficult because of control demands and processing trade-offs. As a result, it is often easier and more economical to separate the processing steps.

Compounding is the feeding and dispersing of the lignocellulosic component in a molten thermoplastic to produce a homogeneous material. Various additives are added and moisture is removed during compounding. Compounding may be accomplished using either batch mixers (for example, internal and thermokinetic mixers) or continuous mixers (for example, extruders and kneaders). Batch systems allow closer control of residence time, shear, and temperature than do continuous systems. Batch systems are also more appropriate for operations consisting of short runs and frequent change of materials. On the other hand, continuous systems are less operator-dependent than are batch systems and have less batch-to-batch differences (Anon. 1997).

The compounded material can be immediately pressed or shaped into an end product while still in its molten state or pelletized into small, regular pellets for future reheating and forming. The most common types of product-forming methods for wood–thermoplastic composites involve forcing molten material through a die (sheet or profile extrusion) into a cold mold (injection molding) or pressing in calenders (calendering) or between mold halves (thermoforming and compression molding).

Properties of wood–plastic composites can vary greatly depending upon such variables as type, form, and weight fractions of constituents, types of additives, and processing history. Table 10–14 shows some of the properties for several unfilled polypropylene and wood–polypropylene composites.

Composites with high thermoplastic content are not without tradeoffs. Impact resistance of such composites decreases compared with that of unfilled thermoplastics, and these composites are also more sensitive to moisture than unfilled material or composites filled with inorganic material. From a practical standpoint, however, the thermoplastic component usually makes the temperature sensitivity of the composite more significant than any change in properties brought about by moisture absorption.

Composites With Low Thermoplastic Content

Composites with low thermoplastic content can be made in a variety of ways. In the simplest form, the thermoplastic component acts much the same way as a thermosetting resin; that is, as a binder to the lignocellulosic component. An alternative is to use the thermoplastic in the form of a textile fiber. The thermoplastic textile fiber enables a variety of lignocellulosics to be incorporated into a low-density, non-woven, textile-like mat. The mat may be a product in itself, or it may be consolidated into a high-density product.

Experimentally, low-thermoplastic-content composites have been made that are very similar to conventional lignocellulosic composites in many performance characteristics (Youngquist and others 1993b). In their simplest form, lignocellulosic particles or fibers can be dry-blended with thermoplastic granules, flakes, or fibers and pressed into panel products.

Because the thermoplastic component remains molten when hot, different pressing strategies must be used than when thermosetting binders are used. Two options have been developed to accommodate these types of composites. In the first, the material is placed in the hot press at ambient temperature. The press then closes and consolidates the material, and heat is transferred through conduction to melt the thermoplastic component, which flows around the lignocellulosic component. The press is then cooled, "freezing" the thermoplastic so that the composite can be removed from the press. Alternatively, the material can be first heated in an oven or hot press. The hot material is then transferred to a cool press where it is quickly consolidated and cooled to make a rigid panel. Some commercial nonstructural lignocellulosic–thermoplastic composites are made in this way.

Nonwoven Textile-Type Composites

In contrast to high-thermoplastic-content and conventional low-thermoplastic-content composites, nonwoven textile-type composites typically require long fibrous materials for their manufacture. These fibers might be treated jute or kenaf, but more typically they are synthetic thermoplastic materials. Nonwoven processes allow and tolerate a wider range of lignocellulosic materials and synthetic fibers, depending on product applications. After fibers are dry-blended, they are air-laid into a continuous, loosely consolidated mat. The mat is then passed through a secondary operation in which the fibers are mechanically entangled or otherwise bonded together. This low-density mat may be a product in itself, or the mat may be shaped and densified in a thermoforming step (Youngquist and others 1993b).

If left as low density and used without significant modification by post-processing, the mats have a bulk density of

Table 10–14. Mechanical properties of wood–polypropylene composites[a,b]

| Composite[c] | Density (g/cm³ (lb/ft³)) | Tensile | | | Flexural | | Izod impact energy | | Heat deflection temperature (°C (°F)) |
		Strength (MPa (lb/in²))	Modulus (GPa (lb/in²))	Elongation (%)	Strength (MPa (lb/in²))	Modulus (GPa (lb/in²))	Notched (J/m (ft-lbf/in))	Unnotched (J/m (ft-lbf/in))	
Polypropylene	0.9 (56.2)	28.5 (4,130)	1.53 (221,000)	5.9	38.3 (5,550)	1.19 (173,000)	20.9 (0.39)	656 (12.3)	57 (135)
PP + 40% wood flour	1.05 (65.5)	25.4 (3,680)	3.87 (561,000)	1.9	44.2 (6,410)	3.03 (439,000)	22.2 (0.42)	73 (1.4)	89 (192)
PP + 40% hardwood fiber	1.03 (64.3)	28.2 (4,090)	4.20 (609,000)	2.0	47.9 (6,950)	3.25 (471,000)	26.2 (0.49)	91 (1.7)	100 (212)
PP + 40% hardwood fiber + 3% coupling agent	1.03 (64.3)	52.3 (7,580)	4.23 (613,000)	3.2	72.4 (10,500)	3.22 (467,000)	21.6 (0.41)	162 (3.0)	105 (221)

[a]Unpublished data.
[b]Properties measured according to ASTM standards for plastics.
[c]PP is polypropylene; percentages based on weight.

50 to 250 kg/m³ (3 to 16 lb/ft³). These products are particularly well known in the consumer products industry, where nonwoven technology is used to make a variety of absorbent personal care products, wipes, and other disposable items. The products are made from high-quality pulps in conjunction with additives to increase absorptive properties. A much wider variety of lignocellulosics can be used for other applications, as described in the following text.

One interesting application for low-density nonwoven mats is for mulch around newly planted seedlings. The mats provide the benefits of natural mulch; in addition, controlled-release fertilizers, repellents, insecticides, and herbicides can be added to the mats. The addition of such chemicals could be based on silvicultural prescriptions to ensure seedling survival and early development on planting sites where severe nutritional deficiencies, animal damage, insect attack, and weeds are anticipated.

Low-density nonwoven mats can also be used to replace dirt or sod for grass seeding around new home sites or along highway embankments. Grass seed can be incorporated directly into the mat. These mats promote seed germination and good moisture retention. Low-density mats can also be used for filters. The density can be varied, depending on the material being filtered and the volume of material that passes through the mat per unit of time.

High-density fiber mats can be defined as composites that are made using the nonwoven mat process and then formed into rigid shapes by heat and pressure. To ensure good bonding, the lignocellulosic can be precoated with a thermosetting resin such as phenol–formaldehyde, or it can be blended with synthetic fibers, thermoplastic granules, or any combination of these materials. High-density fiber mats can typically be pressed into products having a specific gravity of 0.60 to 1.40. Table 10–15 presents mechanical and physical property

Table 10–15. Properties of nonwoven web composite panels with specific gravity of 1.0[a]

Property	Formulation[b]		
	90H/10PE	90H/10PP	80H/10PE/PR
Static bending MOR, MPa (lb/in²)	23.3 (3,380)	25.5 (3,700)	49.3 (7,150)
Cantilever bending MOR, MPa (lb/in²)	21.1 (3,060)	27.1 (3,930)	45.6 (6,610)
Static bending MOE, GPa (×10³ lb/in²)	2.82 (409)	2.99 (434)	3.57 (518)
Dynamic MOE, GPa (×10³ lb/in²)	4.75 (689)	5.27 (764)	5.52 (800)
Tensile strength, MPa (lb/in²)	13.5 (1,960)	12.5 (1,810)	27.7 (4,020)
Tensile MOE, GPa (×10³ lb/in²)	3.87 (561)	420 (609)	5.07 (735)
Internal bond, MPa (lb/in²)	0.14 (20)	0.28 (41)	0.81 (120)
Impact energy, J (ft·lbf)	26.7 (19.7)	21.5 (15.9)	34.3 (25.3)
Water-soak, 24 h			
Thickness swell, %	60.8	40.3	21.8
Water absorption, %	85.0	54.7	45.1
Water boil, 2 h			
Thickness swell, %	260.1	77.5	28.2
Water absorption, %	301.6	99.5	55.7
Linear expansion[c]			
Ovendry to			
30% RH, %	0.13	0.00	0.55
65% RH, %	0.38	0.25	0.76
90% RH, %	0.81	0.78	0.93
Equilibrium MC at			
30% RH, %	3.4	3.4	3.4
65% RH, %	6.4	6.2	6.3
90% RH, %	15.6	14.9	14.1

[a]From Youngquist and others 1992.
[b]Values connected by solid line are not statistically different at 0.05 significance level. 90H/10PE, 90% hemlock and 10% polyester; 90H/10PP, 90% hemlock and 10% polypropylene; 80H/10PE/10PR, 80% hemlock, 10% polyester, and 10% phenolic resin.
[c]RH = relative humidity.

data for nonwoven web composite panels with a specific gravity of 1.0 for three different formulations of wood, synthetic fibers, and phenolic resin. After thermoforming, the products possess good temperature resistance. Because longer fibers are used, these products exhibit better mechanical properties than those obtained with high-thermoplastic-content composites; however, the high lignocellulosic content leads to increased moisture sensitivity.

References

Abourezk, J. 1977. Statements on introduced bills and joint resolutions. Congressional Record–U.S. Senate Mar. 1 S3156-S3179.

AHA. 1985. Cellulosic fiberboard, ANSI/AHA A194.1–1985. Palatine, IL: American Hardboard Association.

AHA. 1990. Hardboard siding, ANSI/AHA A135.6–1990. Palatine, IL: American Hardboard Association.

AHA. 1995a. Basic hardboard, ANSI/AHA A135.4–1995. Palatine, IL: American Hardboard Association.

AHA. 1995b. Prefinished hardboard paneling, ANSI/AHA A135.5–1995. Palatine, IL: American Hardboard Association.

Anon. 1997. Machinery and equipment. Plastics Compounding: 1996/97 Redbook. Advanstar Communications, Inc. 19: 58–70.

APA. 1981. Performance standards and policies for APA structural use panels. Tacoma, WA: American Plywood Association.

APA–The Engineered Wood Association. 1991. Performance standards and policies for structural use panels. APA PRP–108. Tacoma, WA: APA–The Engineered Wood Association.

APA–The Engineered Wood Association. 1995a. Design capacities of APA performance-rated structural-use panels. Technical Note N375 B. Tacoma, WA: APA–The Engineered Wood Association.

APA–The Engineered Wood Association. 1995b. Plywood design specification. Tacoma, WA: APA–The Engineered Wood Association.

ASTM. 1988. Concrete and mineral aggregates. 1988. Annual Book of ASTM Standards, Sec. 4, Vol. 4.02, 4.03. Philadelphia, PA: American Society for Testing and Materials.

ASTM. (Current edition). Annual Book of ASTM Standards. Philadelphia, PA: American Society for Testing and Materials.

ASTM C208–94. Standard specification for cellulosic fiber insulating board.

ASTM D1037–94. Standard test methods for evaluating the properties of wood-based fiber and particle panel materials.

ASTM D2718–90. Standard test method for structural panels in planar shear (rolling shear).

ASTM D2719–89. Standard test methods for structural panels in shear through-the-thickness.

ASTM D3043–87. Standard methods of testing structural panels in flexure.

ASTM D3044–76. Standard test method for shear modulus of plywood.

ASTM D3500–90. Standard test methods for structural panels in tension.

ASTM D3501–76. Standard methods of testing plywood in compression.

ASTM E1333–90. Standard test method for determining formaldehyde levels from wood products under defined test conditions using a large chamber.

English, B.; Chow, P.; Bajwa, D.S. 1997. Processing into composites. In: Rowell, Roger M.; Young, Raymond A.; Rowell, Judith K., eds. Paper and composites from agro-based resources. Boca Raton, FL: CRC Lewis Publishers: 269–299. Chapter 8.

Geimer, R.L.; Souza, M.R.; Moslemi, A.A.; Simatupang, M.H. 1992. Carbon dioxide application for rapid production of cement particleboard. In: Proceedings, inorganic bonded wood and fiber composite materials conference; 1992 September 27–30; Spokane, WA.

HPVA. 1994. American national standard for hardwood and decorative plywood, ANSI/HPVA–1–1994. Reston, VA: Hardwood Plywood & Veneer Association.

Maloney, T.M. 1986. Terminology and products definitions—A suggested approach to uniformity worldwide. In: Proceedings, 18th international union of forest research organization world congress; 1986 September; Ljubljana, Yugoslavia. IUFRO World Congress Organizing Committee.

Maloney, T.M. 1993. Modern particleboard and dry-process fiberboard manufacturing. San Francisco, CA: Miller Freeman Publications.

Marra, G. 1979. Overview of wood as material. Journal of Educational Modules for Materials Science and Engineering. 1(4): 699–710.

McKay, M. 1997. Plywood. In: Smulski, S., ed.. Engineered wood products—A guide for specifiers, designers and users. Madison, WI: PFS Research Foundation.

NIST. 1992. Voluntary product standard PS 2–92. Performance standard for wood-base structural-use panels. National Institute of Standards and Technology. Gaithersburg, MD: United States Department of Commerce.

NIST. 1995. Voluntary product standard PS 1–95 Construction and industrial plywood. National Institute of Standards and Technology. Gaithersburg, MD: United States Department of Commerce.

NPA. 1993. Particleboard, ANSI A208.1–1993. Gaithersburg, MD: National Particleboard Association.

NPA. 1994. Medium density fiberboard (MDF), ANSI A208.2–1994. Gaithersburg, MD: National Particleboard Association.

O'Halloran, M.R. 1979. Development of performance specifications for structural panels in residential markets. Forest Products Journal. 29(12): 21–26.

O'Halloran, M.R. 1980. The performance approach to acceptance of building products. In: Proceedings, 14th Washington State University international symposium on particleboard. Pullman, WA: 77–84.

O'Halloran, M.R.; Youngquist, J.A. 1984. An overview of structural panels and structural composite products. In: Rafik, Y. Itani; Faherty, Keith F., eds. Structural wood research. State-of-the-art and research needs. Proceedings, American Society of Civil Engineers; 1983 October 5–6; Milwaukee, WI. New York, NY: American Society of Civil Engineers: 133–147.

Rowell, R.M.; Young, R.A.; Rowell, J.K. eds. 1997. Paper and composites from agro-based resources. Boca Raton, FL: CRC Lewis Publishers.

Suchsland, O.; Woodson, G.E. 1986. Fiberboard manufacturing practices in the United States, Agric. Handb. 640. Washington, DC: U. S. Department of Agriculture.

TECO. 1991. TECO PRP–133 Performance standards and policies for structural-use panels. Madison, WI: TECO.

U.S. Department of Defense. 1951. Design of wood aircraft structures. ANC–18 Bull. (Issued by Subcommittee on Air Force–Navy–Civil Aircraft Design Criteria. Aircraft Comm.) 2d ed. Washington, DC: Munitions Board.

Youngquist, J.A. 1987. Wood-based panels, their properties and uses—A review. In: Proceedings, Technical consultation on wood-based panel. Expert Consultation, Food and Agriculture Organization of the United Nations; 1987 September 28–October 1; Rome, Italy: 116–124.

Youngquist, J.A. 1988. Wood-based composites: The panel and building components of the future. In: Proceedings, IUFRO Division 5, Forest Products subject group 5.03: Wood protection; 1987 May 16–17; Honey Harbour, Canada: 5–22.

Youngquist, J,A. 1995. Unlikely partners? The marriage of wood and nonwood materials. Forest Products Journal. 45(10): 25–30.

Youngquist, J.A.; Krzysik, A.M.; Muehl, J.H.; Carll, C. 1992. Mechanical and physical properties of air-formed wood-fiber/polymer–fiber composites. Forest Products Journal. 42(6): 42–48.

Youngquist, J.A.; English, B.E.; Spelter, H.; Chow, P. 1993a. Agriculture fibers in composition panels, In: Maloney, Thomas M., ed. Proceedings, 27th international particleboard/composite materials symposium; 1993 March 30–April 1; Pullman, WA. Pullman, WA: Washington State University: 133–152.

Youngquist, J.A.; Myers, G.E.; Muehl, J.M. [and others]. 1993b. Composites from recycled wood and plastics. Final Rep., U.S. Environmental Protection Agency, Project IAG DW12934608–2. Madison, WI: U.S. Department of Agriculture, Forest Service, Forest Products Laboratory.

Youngquist, J.A.; English, B.E.; Scharmer, R.C. [and others]. 1994. Literature review on use of non-wood plants fibers for building materials and panels. Gen. Tech. Rep. FPL–GTR–80. Madison, WI: U.S. Department of Agriculture, Forest Service, Forest Products Laboratory.

Youngquist, J.A.; Krzysik, A.M.; Chow, P.; Meimban, R. 1997. Properties of composite panels. In: Rowell, Roger M., Young, Raymond A.; Rowell, Judith K., eds. Paper and composites from agro-based resources. Boca Raton, FL: CRC Lewis Publishers.

Chapter 11

Glued Structural Members

Russell C. Moody, Roland Hernandez, and Jen Y. Liu

Contents

 lued structural members are manufactured in a variety of configurations. Structural composite lumber (SCL) products consist of small pieces of wood glued together into sizes common for solid-sawn lumber. Glued-laminated timber (glulam) is an engineered stress-rated product that consists of two or more layers of lumber in which the grain of all layers is oriented parallel to the length of the lumber. Glued structural members also include lumber that is glued to panel products, such as box beams and I-beams, and structural sandwich construction.

Structural Composite Lumber

Structural composite lumber was developed in response to the increasing demand for high quality lumber at a time when it was becoming difficult to obtain this type of lumber from the forest resource. Structural composite lumber products are characterized by smaller pieces of wood glued together into sizes common for solid-sawn lumber.

One type of SCL product is manufactured by laminating veneer with all plies parallel to the length. This product is called laminated veneer lumber (LVL) and consists of specially graded veneer. Another type of SCL product consists of strands of wood or strips of veneer glued together under high pressures and temperatures. Depending upon the component material, this product is called laminated strand lumber (LSL), parallel strand lumber (PSL), or oriented strand lumber (OSL) (Fig. 11–1). These types of SCL products can be manufactured from raw materials, such as aspen or other underutilized species, that are not commonly used for structural applications. Different widths of lumber can be ripped from SCL for various uses.

Structural composite lumber is a growing segment of the engineered wood products industry. It is used as a replacement for lumber in various applications and in the manufacture of other engineered wood products, such as prefabricated wood I-joists, which take advantage of engineering design values that can be greater than those commonly assigned to sawn lumber.

Figure 11–1. Examples of three types of SCL (top to bottom): laminated veneer lumber (LVL), parallel strand lumber (PSL), and oriented strand lumber (OSL).

Types

Laminated Veneer Lumber

Work in the 1940s on LVL targeted the production of high strength parts for aircraft structures using Sitka spruce veneer. Research on LVL in the 1970s was aimed at defining the effects of processing variables for veneer up to 12.7 mm (1/2 in.) thick. In the 1990s, production of LVL uses veneers 3.2 to 2.5 mm (1/8 to 1/10 in.) thick, which are hot pressed with phenol-formaldehyde adhesive into lengths from 2.4 to 18.3 m (8 to 60 ft) or more.

The veneer for the manufacture of LVL must be carefully selected for the product to achieve the desired engineering properties. The visual grading criteria of PS 1–95 (NIST 1995) are sometimes used but are generally not adequate without additional grading. Veneers are often sorted using ultrasonic testing to ensure that the finished product will have the desired engineering properties.

End joints between individual veneers may be staggered along the product to minimize their effect on strength. These end joints may be butt joints, or the veneer ends may overlap for some distance to provide load transfer. Some producers provide structural end joints in the veneers using either scarf or fingerjoints. Laminated veneer lumber may also be made in 2.4-m (8-ft) lengths, having no end joints in the veneer; longer pieces are then formed by end jointing these pieces to create the desired length.

Sheets of LVL are commonly produced in 0.6- to 1.2-m (2- to 4-ft) widths in a thickness of 38 mm (1.5 in.). Continuous presses can be used to form a potentially endless sheet, which is cut to the desired length. Various widths of lumber can be manufactured at the plant or the retail facility.

Parallel Strand Lumber

Parallel strand lumber (PSL) is defined as a composite of wood strand elements with wood fibers primarily oriented along the length of the member. The least dimension of the strands must not exceed 6.4 mm (0.25 in.), and the average length of the strands must be a minimum of 150 times the least dimension. In 1997, one commercial product in the United States was classified as PSL.

Parallel strand lumber is manufactured using veneer about 3 mm (1/8 in.) thick, which is then clipped into strands about 19 mm (3/4 in.) wide. These strands are commonly at least 0.6 m (24 in.) long. The manufacturing process was designed to use the material from roundup of the log in the veneer cutting operation as well as other less than full-width veneer. Thus, the process can utilize waste material from a plywood or LVL operation. Species commonly used for PSL include Douglas-fir, southern pines, western hemlock, and yellow-poplar, but there are no restrictions on using other species.

The strands are coated with a waterproof structural adhesive, commonly phenol-resorcinol formaldehyde, and oriented in a press using special equipment to ensure proper orientation and distribution. The pressing operation results in densification of the material, and the adhesive is cured using microwave technology. Billets larger than those of LVL are commonly produced; a typical size is 0.28 by 0.48 m (11 by 19 in.). This product can then be sawn into smaller pieces, if desired. As with LVL, a continuous press is used so that the length of the product is limited by handling restrictions.

Laminated Strand Lumber and Oriented Strand Lumber

Laminated strand lumber (LSL) and oriented strand lumber (OSL) products are an extension of the technology used to produce oriented strandboard (OSB) structural panels. One type of LSL uses strands that are about 0.3 m (12 in.) long, which is somewhat longer than the strands commonly used for OSB. Waterproof adhesives are used in the manufacture of LSL. One type of product uses an isocyanate type of adhesive that is sprayed on the strands and cured by steam injection. This product needs a greater degree of alignment of the strands than does OSB and higher pressures, which result in increased densification.

Advantages and Uses

In contrast with sawn lumber, the strength-reducing characteristics of SCL are dispersed within the veneer or strands and have much less of an effect on strength properties. Thus, relatively high design values can be assigned to strength properties for both LVL and PSL. Whereas both LSL and OSL have somewhat lower design values, they have the advantage of being produced from a raw material that need not be in a log size large enough for peeling into veneer. All SCL products are made with structural adhesives and are dependent upon a minimum level of strength in these bonds. All SCL products are made from veneers or strands that are dried to a moisture content that is slightly less than that for most service conditions. Thus, little change in moisture content will occur in many protected service conditions.

When used indoors, this results in a product that is less likely to warp or shrink in service. However, the porous nature of both LVL and PSL means that these products can quickly absorb water unless they are provided with some protection.

All types of SCL products can be substituted for sawn lumber products in many applications. Laminated veneer lumber is used extensively for scaffold planks and in the flanges of prefabricated I-joists, which takes advantage of the relatively high design properties. Both LVL and PSL beams are used as headers and major load-carrying elements in construction. The LSL and OSL products are used for band joists in floor construction and as substitutes for studs and rafters in wall and roof construction. Various types of SCL are also used in a number of nonstructural applications, such as the manufacture of windows and doors.

Standards and Specifications

The ASTM D5456 (ASTM 1997a) standard provides methods to develop design properties for SCL products as well as requirements for quality assurance during production. Each manufacturer of SCL products is responsible for developing the required information on properties and ensuring that the minimum levels of quality are maintained during production. An independent inspection agency is required to monitor the quality assurance program.

Unlike lumber, no standard grades or design stresses have been established for SCL. Each manufacturer may have unique design properties and procedures. Thus, the designer should consult information provided by the manufacturer.

Glulam

Structural glued-laminated timber (glulam) is one of the oldest glued engineered wood products. Glulam is an engineered, stress-rated product that consists of two or more layers of lumber that are glued together with the grain of all layers, which are referred to as laminations, parallel to the length. Glulam is defined as a material that is made from suitably selected and prepared pieces of wood either in a straight or curved form, with the grain of all pieces essentially parallel to the longitudinal axis of the member. The maximum lamination thickness permitted is 50 mm (2 in.), and the laminations are typically made of standard 25- or 50-mm- (nominal 1- or 2-in.-) thick lumber. North American standards require that glulam be manufactured in an approved manufacturing plant. Because the lumber is joined end to end, edge to edge, and face to face, the size of glulam is limited only by the capabilities of the manufacturing plant and the transportation system.

Douglas Fir–Larch, Southern Pine, Hem–Fir, and Spruce–Pine–Fir (SPF) are commonly used for glulam in the United States. Nearly any species can be used for glulam timber, provided its mechanical and physical properties are suitable and it can be properly glued. Industry standards cover many softwoods and hardwoods, and procedures are in place for including other species.

Advantages

Compared with sawn timbers as well as other structural materials, glulam has several distinct advantages in size capability, architectural effects, seasoning, variation of cross sections, grades, and effect on the environment.

Size Capabilities—Glulam offers the advantage of the manufacture of structural timbers that are much larger than the trees from which the component lumber was sawn. In the past, the United States had access to large trees that could produce relatively large sawn timbers. However, the present trend is to harvest smaller diameter trees on much shorter rotations, and nearly all new sawmills are built to accommodate relatively small logs. By combining the lumber in glulam, the production of large structural elements is possible. Straight members up to 30 m (100 ft) long are not uncommon and some span up to 43 m (140 ft). Sections deeper than 2 m (7 ft) have been used. Thus, glulam offers the potential to produce large timbers from small trees.

Architectural Effects—By curving the lumber during the manufacturing process, a variety of architectural effects can be obtained that are impossible or very difficult with other materials. The degree of curvature is controlled by the thickness of the laminations. Thus, glulam with moderate curvature is generally manufactured with standard 19-mm- (nominal 1-in.-) thick lumber. Low curvatures are possible with standard 38-mm (nominal 2-in.) lumber, whereas 13 mm (1/2 in.) or thinner material may be required for very sharp curves. As noted later in this chapter, the radius of curvature is limited to between 100 and 125 times the lamination thickness.

Seasoning Advantages—The lumber used in the manufacture of glulam must be seasoned or dried prior to use, so the effects of checking and other drying defects are minimized. In addition, design can be on the basis of seasoned wood, which permits greater design values than can be assigned to unseasoned timber.

Varying Cross Sections—Structural elements can be designed with varying cross sections along their length as determined by strength and stiffness requirements. The beams in Figure 11–2 show how the central section of the beam can be made deeper to account for increased structural requirements in this region of the beam. Similarly, arches often have varying cross sections as determined by design requirements.

Varying Grades—One major advantage of glulam is that a large quantity of lower grade lumber can be used within the less highly stressed laminations of the beams. Grades are often varied within the beams so that the highest grades are used in the highly stressed laminations near the top and bottom and the lower grade for the inner half or more of the beams. Species can also be varied to match the structural requirements of the laminations.

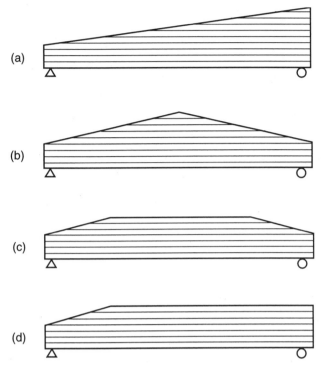

Figure 11–2. Glulam timbers may be (a) single tapered, (b) double tapered, (c) tapered at both ends, or (d) tapered at one end.

Environmentally Friendly—Much is being written and discussed regarding the relative environmental effects of various materials. Several analyses have shown that the renewability of wood, its relatively low requirement for energy during manufacture, its carbon storage capabilities, and its recyclability offer potential long-term environmental advantages over other materials. Although aesthetics and economic considerations usually are the major factors influencing material selection, these environmental advantages may increasingly influence material selection.

The advantages of glulam are tempered by certain factors that are not encountered in the production of sawn timber. In instances where solid timbers are available in the required size, the extra processing in making glulam timber usually increases its cost above that of sawn timbers. The manufacture of glulam requires special equipment, adhesives, plant facilities, and manufacturing skills, which are not needed to produce sawn timbers. All steps in the manufacturing process require care to ensure the high quality of the finished product. One factor that must be considered early in the design of large straight or curved timbers is handling and shipping.

History

Glulam was first used in Europe in the construction of an auditorium in Basel, Switzerland, in 1893, which is often cited as the first known significant use of this product. It was patented as the "Hertzer System" and used adhesives that, by today's standards, are not waterproof. Thus, applications were limited to dry-use conditions. Improvements in

adhesives during and following World War I stimulated additional interest in Europe in regard to using glulam in aircraft and building frames.

In the United States, one of the first examples of glulam arches designed and built using engineering principles is in a building erected in 1934 at the USDA Forest Service, Forest Products Laboratory, Madison, Wisconsin (Fig. 11–3). The founder of a company that produced many of these initial buildings in the United States was a German immigrant who transferred the technology to his manufacturing facility in Peshtigo, Wisconsin. Applications included gymnasiums, churches, halls, factories, and barns. Several other companies based on the same technology were soon established.

World War II stimulated additional interest and the development of synthetic resin adhesives that were waterproof. This permitted the use of glulam timber in bridges and other exterior applications that required preservative treatment. By the early 1950s, there were at least a dozen manufacturers of glulam timber in the United States, who joined together to form the American Institute of Timber Construction (AITC). In 1963, this association produced the first national manufacturing standard. The AITC continues to prepare, update, and distribute industry standards for manufacture and design of glulam. By the mid-1990s, about 30 manufacturing plants across the United States and Canada were qualified to produce glulam, according to the requirements of the AITC standard.

From the mid-1930s through the 1980s, nearly all glulam production was used domestically. During the 1990s, the export market was developed and significant quantities of material were shipped to Pacific Rim countries, mainly Japan.

Types of Glulam Combinations

Bending Members

The configuring of various grades of lumber to form a glulam cross section is commonly referred to as a glulam combination. Glulam combinations subjected to flexural loads, called bending combinations, were developed to provide the most efficient and economical section for resisting bending stress caused by loads applied perpendicular to the wide faces of the laminations. This type of glulam is commonly referred to as a horizontally laminated member. Lower grades of laminating lumber are commonly used for the center portion of the combination, or core, where bending stress is low, while a higher grade of material is placed on the outside faces where bending stress is relatively high. To optimize the bending stiffness of this type of glulam member, equal amounts of high quality laminations on the outside faces should be included to produce a "balanced" combination. To optimize bending strength, the combination can be "unbalanced" with more high quality laminations placed on the tension side of the member compared with the quality used on the compression side. For high quality lumber placed on the tension side of the glulam combination, stringent requirements are

Figure 11–3. Erected in 1934 at the Forest Products Laboratory in Madison, Wisconsin, this building is one of the first constructed with glued-laminated timbers arched, designed, and built using engineering principles.

placed on knot size, slope of grain, and lumber stiffness. For compression-side laminations, however, knot size and slope-of-grain requirements are less stringent and only lumber stiffness is given high priority. In the case where the glulam member is used over continuous supports, the combination would need to be designed as a balanced member for strength and stiffness because of the exposure of both the top and bottom of the beam to tensile stresses. The knot and slope-of-grain requirements for this type of combination are generally applied equally to both the top and bottom laminations.

Axial Members

Glulam axial combinations were developed to provide the most efficient and economical section for resisting axial forces and flexural loads applied parallel to the wide faces of the laminations. Members having loads applied parallel to the wide faces of the laminations are commonly referred to as vertically laminated members. Unlike the practice for bending combinations, the same grade of lamination is used throughout the axial combination. Axial combinations may also be loaded perpendicular to the wide face of the lamina-

tions, but the nonselective placement of material often results in a less efficient and less economical member than does the bending combination. As with bending combinations, knot and slope-of-grain requirements apply based on the intended use of the axial member as a tension or compression member.

Curved Members

Efficient use of lumber in cross sections of curved glulam combinations is similar to that in cross sections of straight, horizontally-laminated combinations. Tension and compression stresses are analyzed as tangential stresses in the curved portion of the member. A unique behavior in these curved members is the formation of radial stresses perpendicular to the wide faces of the laminations. As the radius of curvature of the glulam member decreases, the radial stresses formed in the curved portion of the beam increase. Because of the relatively low strength of lumber in tension perpendicular-to-the-grain compared with tension parallel-to-the-grain, these radial stresses become a critical factor in designing curved glulam combinations. Curved members are commonly manufactured with standard 19- and 38-mm- (nominal 1- and 2-in.-) thick lumber. Naturally, the curvature that is obtainable with the

243

standard 19-mm- (nominal 1-in.-) thick lumber will be sharper than that for the standard 38-mm- (nominal 2-in.-) thick lumber. Recommended practice specifies that the ratio of lamination thickness t to the radius of curvature R should not exceed 1/100 for hardwoods and Southern Pine and 1/125 for other softwoods (AF&PA 1997). For example, a curved Southern Pine beam ($t/R \leq 1/100$) manufactured with standard 38-mm- (nominal 2-in.-) thick lumber ($t = 1.5$ in.) should have a radius of curvature greater than or equal to 3.81 m (150 in.)

Tapered Straight Members

Glulam beams are often tapered to meet architectural requirements, provide pitched roofs, facilitate drainage, and lower wall height requirements at the end supports. The taper is achieved by sawing the member across one or more laminations at the desired slope. It is recommended that the taper cut be made only on the compression side of the glulam member, because violating the continuity of the tension-side laminations would decrease the overall strength of the member. Common forms of straight, tapered glulam combinations include (a) single tapered, a member having a continuous slope from end to end on the compression side; (b) double tapered, a member having two separate slopes sawn on the compression side; (c) tapered at both ends, a member with slopes sawn on the ends, but the middle portion remains straight; and (d) tapered at one end, similar to (c) with only one end having a slope. These four examples are illustrated in Figure 11–2.

Standards and Specifications

Manufacture

The ANSI/AITC A190.1 standard of the American National Standards Institute (ANSI 1992) contains requirements for the production, testing, and certification of structural glulam timber in the United States. Additional details and commentary on the requirements specified in ANSI A190.1 are provided in AITC 200 (AITC 1993a), which is part of ANSI A190.1 by reference. A standard for glulam poles, ANSI O5.2 (ANSI 1996), addresses special requirements for utility uses. Requirements for the manufacture of structural glulam in Canada are given in CAN/CSA O122 (CSA 1989).

Derivation of Design Values

ASTM D3737 (ASTM 1997b) covers the procedures to establish design values for structural glulam timber. Properties considered include bending, tension, compression parallel to grain, modulus of elasticity, horizontal shear, radial tension, and compression perpendicular to grain.

Design Values and Procedures

Manufacturers of glulam timber have standardized the target design values in bending for beams. For softwoods, these design values are given in AITC 117, "Standard Specifications for Structural Glued-Laminated Timber of Softwood Species" (AITC 1993b). This specification contains design values and recommended modification of stresses for the

design of glulam timber members in the United States. A comparable specification for hardwoods is AITC 119, "Standard Specifications for Structural Glued-Laminated Timber of Hardwood Species" (AITC 1996). The *National Design Specification for Wood Construction* (NDS) summarizes the design information in AITC 117 and 119 and defines the practice to be followed in structural design of glulam timbers (AF&PA 1997). For additional design information, see the *Timber Construction Manual* (AITC 1994). APA—The Engineered Wood Association has also developed design values for glulam under National Evaluation Report 486, which is recognized by all the model building codes.

In Canada, CAN/CSA O86, the code for engineering design in wood, provides design criteria for structural glulam timbers (CSA 1994).

Manufacture

The manufacture of glulam timber must follow recognized national standards to justify the specified engineering design values. When glulam is properly manufactured, both the quality of the wood and the adhesive bonds should demonstrate a balance in structural performance.

The ANSI A190.1 standard (ANSI 1992) has a two-phase approach to all phases of manufacturing. First is the qualification phase in which all equipment and personnel critical to the production of a quality product are thoroughly examined by a third-party agency and the strength of samples of glued joints is determined. In the second phase, after successful qualification, daily quality assurance procedures and criteria are established, which are targeted to keep each of the critical phases of the process under control. An employee is assigned responsibility for supervising the daily testing and inspection. The third-party agency makes unannounced visits to the plants to monitor the manufacturing process and the finished product and to examine the daily records of the quality assurance testing.

The manufacturing process can be divided into four major parts: (a) drying and grading the lumber, (b) end jointing the lumber, (c) face bonding, and (d) finishing and fabrication.

In instances where the glulam will be used in high moisture content conditions, it is also necessary to pressure treat the member with preservative. A final critical step in ensuring the quality of glulam is protection of the glulam timber during transit and storage.

Lumber Drying and Grading

To minimize dimensional changes following manufacture and to take advantage of the increased structural properties assigned to lumber compared with large sawn timbers, it is critical that the lumber be properly dried. This generally means kiln drying. For most applications, the maximum moisture content permitted in the ANSI standard is 16% (ANSI 1992). Also, the maximum range in moisture content is 5% among laminations to minimize differential changes in dimension following manufacture. Many plants use lumber at or slightly below 12% moisture content for two reasons. One reason is that the material is more easily end jointed at 12% moisture content than at higher levels. The other reason is that 12% is an overall average equilibrium moisture content for many interior applications in the United States (see Ch. 12, Tables 12–1 and 12–2). Exceptions are some areas in the southwest United States. Matching the moisture content of the glulam timber at the time of manufacture to that which it will attain in application minimizes shrinkage and swelling, which are the causes of checking.

The moisture content of lumber can be determined by sampling from the lumber supply and using a moisture meter. Alternatively, most manufacturers use a continuous in-line moisture meter to check the moisture content of each piece of lumber as it enters the manufacturing process. Pieces with greater than a given moisture level are removed and redried.

Grading standards published by the regional lumber grading associations describe the characteristics that are permitted in various grades of lumber. Manufacturing standards for glulam timber describe the combination of lumber grades necessary for specific design values (AITC 117) (AITC 1993b). Two types of lumber grading are used for laminating: visual grading and E-rating.

The rules for visually graded lumber are based entirely upon the characteristics that are readily apparent. The lumber grade description consists of limiting characteristics for knot sizes, slope of grain, wane, and several other characteristics. An example of the knot size limitation for visually graded western species is as follows:

Laminating grade	Maximum knot size
L1	1/4 of width
L2	1/3 of width
L3	1/2 of width

E-rated lumber is graded by a combination of lumber stiffness determination and visual characteristics. Each piece of lumber is evaluated for stiffness by one of several acceptable procedures, and those pieces that qualify for a specific grade are then visually inspected to ensure that they meet the requirement for maximum allowable edge knot size. The grades are expressed in terms of their modulus of elasticity followed by their limiting edge knot size. Thus, a 2.0E–1/6 grade has a modulus of elasticity of 13.8 GPa (2×10^6 lb/in^2) and a maximum edge knot size of 1/6 the width.

Manufacturers generally purchase graded lumber and verify the grades through visual inspection of each piece and, if E-rated, testing of a sample. To qualify the material for some of the higher design stresses for glulam timber, manufacturers must also conduct additional grading for material to be used in the tension zone of certain beams. High quality material is required for the outer 5% of the beam on the tension size, and the grading criteria for these "tension laminations" are given in AITC 117 (AITC 1993b). Special criteria are applied to provide material of high tensile strength. Another option is

Figure 11–4. Typical fingerjoint used in the manufacture of glulam.

to purchase special lumber that is manufactured under a quality assurance system to provide the required tensile strength. Another option practiced by at least one manufacturer has been to use LVL to provide the required tensile strength.

End Jointing

To manufacture glulam timber in lengths beyond those commonly available for lumber, laminations must be made by end jointing lumber to the proper length. The most common end joint, a fingerjoint, is about 28 mm (1.1 in.) long (Fig. 11–4). Other configurations are also acceptable, provided they meet specific strength and durability requirements. The advantages of fingerjoints are that they require only a short length of lumber to manufacture (thus reducing waste) and continuous production equipment is readily available. Well-made joints are critical to ensure adequate performance of glulam timber. Careful control at each stage of the process—determining lumber quality, cutting the joint, applying the adhesive, mating, applying end pressure, and curing—is necessary to produce consistent high strength joints.

Just prior to manufacture, the ends of the lumber are inspected to ensure that there are no knots or other features that would impair joint strength. Then, joints are cut on both ends of the lumber with special knives. Adhesive is applied. The joints in adjacent pieces of lumber are mated, and the adhesive is cured under end pressure. Most manufacturing equipment features a continuous radio-frequency curing system that provides heat to partially set the adhesive in a matter of a few seconds. Fingerjoints obtain most of their strength during this process, and residual heat permits the joint to reach its full strength within a few hours.

Fingerjoints have the potential to reach at least 75% of the strength of clear wood in many species if properly manufactured. These joints are adequate for most applications because most lumber grades used in the manufacture of glulam timber permit natural characteristics that result in strength reductions of at least 25% less than that of clear wood.

The ANSI standard requires that manufacturers qualify their production joints to meet the required strength level of the highest grade glulam timber they wish to produce. This requires that the results of tensile tests of end-jointed lumber meet certain strength criteria and that durability meets certain criteria. When these criteria are met, daily quality control testing in tension is required to ensure that the strength level is being maintained. Durability tests are also required.

A continuing challenge in the glulam production process is to eliminate the occurrence of an occasional low-strength end joint. Visual inspection and other nondestructive techniques have been shown to be only partially effective in detecting low-strength joints. An approach used by many manufacturers to ensure end joint quality is the use of a proof loading system for critical end joints. This equipment applies a specified bending or tension load to check the joint strength for critical laminations on the tension side of beams. By applying loads that are related to the strength desired, low-strength joints can be detected and eliminated. The qualification procedures for this equipment must prove that the applied loads do not cause damage to laminations that are accepted.

Face Bonding

The assembly of laminations into full-depth members is another critical stage in manufacture. To obtain clear, parallel, and gluable surfaces, laminations must be planed to strict tolerances. The best procedure is to plane the two wide faces of the laminations just prior to the gluing process. This ensures that the final assembly will be rectangular and that the pressure will be applied evenly. Adhesives that have been prequalified are then spread, usually with a glue extruder. Phenol resorcinol is the most commonly used adhesive for face gluing, but other adhesives that have been adequately evaluated and proven to meet performance and durability requirements may also be used.

The laminations are then assembled into the required layup; after the adhesive is given the proper open assembly time, pressure is applied. The most common method for applying pressure is with clamping beds; the pressure is applied with either a mechanical or hydraulic system (Fig. 11–5). This results in a batch-type process, and the adhesive is allowed to cure at room temperature from 6 to 24 h. Some newer automated clamping systems include continuous hydraulic presses and radio-frequency curing to shorten the face gluing process from hours to minutes. Upon completion of the face bonding process, the adhesive is expected to have attained 90% or more of its bond strength. During the next few days, curing continues, but at a much slower rate.

The face bonding process is monitored by controls in the lumber planing, adhesive mixing, and adhesive spreading

Figure 11–5. After being placed in the clamping bed, the laminations of these arches are forced together with an air-driven screw clamp.

and clamping processes. Performance is evaluated by conducting shear tests on samples cut off as end trim from the finished glulam timber. The target shear strength of small specimens is prescribed in ANSI A190.1 (ANSI 1992) and equals about 90% of the average shear strength for the species. Thus, the adhesive bonds are expected to develop nearly the full strength of the wood soon after manufacture.

Finishing and Fabrication

After the glulam timber is removed from the clamping system, the wide faces are planed to remove the adhesive that has squeezed out between adjacent laminations and to smooth out any slight irregularities between the edges of adjacent laminations. As a result, the finished glulam timber is slightly narrower than nominal dimension lumber. The remaining two faces of the member can be lightly planed or sanded using portable equipment.

The appearance requirements of the beam dictate the additional finishing necessary at this point. Historically, three classifications of finishing have been included in the industry standard, AITC 110: Industrial, Architectural, and Premium (AITC 1984). Industrial appearance is generally applicable when appearance is not a primary concern, such as industrial plants and warehouses. Architectural appearance is suitable for most applications where appearance is an important requirement. Premium appearance is the highest classification. The primary difference among these classifications is the

246

amount of knot holes and occasional planer skips that are permitted. A recently introduced classification, called Framing, consists of hit-and-miss planing and permits a significant amount of adhesive to remain on the surface. This finishing is intended for uses that require one member to have the same width as the lumber used in manufacture for framing into walls. These members are often covered in the finished structure.

The next step in the manufacturing process is fabrication, where the final cuts are made, holes are drilled, connectors are added, and a finish or sealer is applied, if specified. For various members, different degrees of prefabrication are done at this point. Trusses may be partially or fully assembled. Moment splices can be fully fabricated, then disconnected for transportation and erection. End sealers, surface sealers, primer coats, and wrapping with waterproof paper or plastic all help to stabilize the moisture content of the glulam timber between the time it is manufactured and installed. The extent of protection necessary depends upon the end use and must be specified.

Preservative Treatment

In instances where the moisture content of the finished glulam timber will approach or exceed 20% (in most exterior and some interior uses), the glulam timber should be preservative treated following AITC (1990) and AWPA (1997b). Three main types of preservatives are available: creosote, oilborne, and waterborne. Creosote and oilborne preservatives are applied to the finished glulam timbers. Some light oil solvent treatments can be applied to the lumber prior to gluing, but the suitability must be verified with the manufacturer. Waterborne preservatives are best applied to the lumber prior to the laminating and manufacturing process because they can lead to excessive checking if applied to large finished glulam timbers.

Creosote Solutions—Treatment with creosote solutions is suitable for the most severe outdoor exposure. It results in a dark, oily surface appearance that is difficult to alter. This, coupled with a distinct odor, restricts creosote solutions to structures, such as bridges, that do not come in direct contact with humans. Creosote solutions are an extremely effective preservative as proven by their continued use for railway structures. Another advantage is that the creosote treatment renders the timbers much less susceptible to moisture content changes than are untreated timbers. Creosote solutions are often used as a preservative treatment on bridge stringers.

Oilborne Treatments—Pentachlorophenol and copper napthanate are the most common oilborne preservatives. The solvents are classified in AWPA Standard P9 as Type A, Type C, and Type D (AWPA 1997a). Type A results in an oily finish and should not be used when a plain table surface is needed. Type B or C can be stained or painted. More details are given in AITC (1990) and AWPA (1997a).

Waterborne Treatments—Waterborne preservative treatments conform to AWPA P5 (AWPA 1997b) and use water-soluble preservative chemicals that become fixed in the wood. The effectiveness of this treatment depends upon the depth to which the chemicals penetrate into the lumber. Different processes are quite effective for some species but not for others. In addition, the treated lumber is generally more difficult to bond effectively and requires special manufacturing procedures. Thus, it is recommended that the manufacturer be contacted to determine the capabilities of waterborne-preservative-treated products.

The major advantage of a waterborne treatment is that the surface of the timber appears little changed by the treatment. Different chemicals can leave a green, gray, or brown color; all result in a surface that is easily finished with stains or paints. To avoid the potential of corrosive interactions with the chemical treatments, special care must be given when selecting the connection hardware. In addition, waterborne-preservative-treated glulam timber is much more subject to moisture content cycling than is creosote-treated or oilborne-preservative-treated glulam timber.

A major consideration in selecting a preservative treatment is the local regulations dealing with the use and disposal of waste from preservative-treated timber. Recommended retention levels for applications of various preservatives are given in AITC 109 (AITC 1990) along with appropriate quality assurance procedures.

Development of Design Values

The basic approach to determine the engineered design values of glulam members is through the use of stress index values and stress modification factors.

Stress Index Values

Stress index values are related to the properties clear of wood that is free of defects and other strength-reducing characteristics. Stress index values for several commonly used species and E-rated grades of lumber are given in ASTM D3737 (ASTM 1997b). Procedures are also given for developing these values for visual grades of other species.

Stress Modification Factors

Stress modification factors are related to strength-reducing characteristics and are multiplied by the stress index values to obtain allowable design properties. Detailed information on determination of these factors for bending, tension, compression, and modulus of elasticity are given in ASTM D3737 (1997b).

Other Considerations

Effect of End Joints on Strength—Both fingerjoints and scarf joints can be manufactured with adequate strength for use in structural glulam. Adequacy is determined by physical testing procedures and requirements in ANSI A190.1 (ANSI 1992).

Joints should be well scattered in portions of structural glulam that is highly stressed in tension. Required spacings of end joints are given in ANSI A190.1. End joints of two qualities can be used in a glulam member, depending upon strength requirements at various depths of the cross section.

However, laminators usually use the same joint throughout the members for ease in manufacture.

The highest strength values are obtained with well-made plain scarf joints; the lowest values are obtained with butt joints. This is because scarf joints with flat slopes have essentially side-grain surfaces that can be well bonded to develop high strength, and butt joints have end-grain surfaces that cannot be bonded effectively. Structural fingerjoints (either vertical or horizontal) are a compromise between scarf and butt joints; the strength of structural fingerjoints varies with joint design.

No statement can be made regarding the specific joint strength factor of fingerjoints, because fingerjoint strength depends on the type and configuration of the joint and the manufacturing process. However, the joint factor of commonly used fingerjoints in high-quality lumber used for laminating can be about 75%. High-strength fingerjoints can be made when the design is such that the fingers have relatively flat slopes and sharp tips. Tips are essentially a series of butt joints that reduce the effectiveness of fingerjoints as well as creating sources of stress concentration.

Generally, butt joints cannot transmit tensile stress and can transmit compressive stress only after considerable deformation or if a metal bearing plate is tightly fitted between the abutting ends. In normal assembly operations, such fitting would not be done. Therefore, it is necessary to assume that butt joints are ineffective in transmitting both tensile and compressive stresses. Because of this ineffectiveness and because butt joints cause concentration of both shear stress and longitudinal stress, butt joints are not permitted for use in structural glued-laminated timbers.

Effect of Edge Joints on Strength—It is sometimes necessary to place laminations edge-to-edge to provide glulam members of sufficient width. Because of difficulties in fabrication, structural edge joint bonding may not be readily available, and the designer should investigate the availability of such bonding prior to specifying.

For tension, compression, and horizontally laminated bending members, the strength of edge joints is of little importance to the overall strength of the member. Therefore, from the standpoint of strength, it is unnecessary that edge joints be glued if they are not in the same location in adjacent laminations. However, for maximum strength, edge joints should be glued where torsional loading is involved. Other considerations, such as the appearance of face laminations or the possibility that water will enter the unglued joints and promote decay, should also dictate if edge joints are glued.

If edge joints in vertically laminated beams are not glued, shear strength could be reduced. The amount of reduction can be determined by engineering analysis. Using standard laminating procedures with edge joints staggered in adjacent laminations by at least one lamination thickness, shear strength of vertically laminated beams with unglued edge joints is approximately half that of beams with adhesive-bonded edge joints.

Effect of Shake, Checks, and Splits on Shear Strength—In general, checks and splits have little effect on the shear strength of glulam. Shake occurs infrequently and should be excluded from material for laminations. Most laminated timbers are made from laminations that are thin enough to season readily without developing significant checks and splits.

Designs for Glued-Laminated Timber

Most basic engineering equations used for sawn lumber also apply to glulam beams and columns. The design of glulam in this chapter is only applicable to glulam combinations that conform to AITC 117 (AITC 1993b) for softwood species and AITC 119 (AITC 1996) for hardwood species and are manufactured in accordance with ANSI/AITC A190.1 (ANSI 1992). The AITC 117 standard is made up of two parts: (a) manufacturing, which provides details for the many configurations of glulam made from visually graded and E-rated softwood lumber; and (b) design, which provides tabular design values of strength and stiffness for these glulam combinations. The AITC 119 standard provides similar information for glulam made from hardwood species of lumber. These standards are based on laterally-braced straight members with an average moisture content of 12%. For bending members, the design values are based on an assumed reference size of 305 mm deep, 130 mm wide, and 6.4 m long (12 in. deep, 5.125 in. wide, and 21 ft long).

Tabular Design Values

Tabular design values given in AITC 117 and AITC 119 include the following:

F_b allowable bending design value,

F_t allowable tension design value parallel to grain,

F_v allowable shear design value parallel to grain,

$F_{c\text{-perp}}$ allowable compression design value perpendicular to grain,

F_c allowable compression design value parallel to grain,

E allowable modulus of elasticity, and

F_{rt} allowable radial tension design value perpendicular to grain.

Because glulam members can have different properties when loaded perpendicular or parallel to the wide faces of the laminations, a common naming convention is used to specify the design values that correspond to a particular type of orientation. For glulam members loaded perpendicular to the wide faces of the laminations, design values are commonly denoted with a subscript x. For glulam members loaded parallel to the wide faces of the laminations, design values are commonly denoted with a subscript y. Some examples include F_{bx} and E_x for design bending stress and design modulus of elasticity, respectively.

End-Use Adjustment Factors

When glulam members are exposed to conditions other than the described reference condition, the published allowable design values require adjustment. The following text describes each of the adjustment factors that account for the end-use condition of glulam members.

Volume—The volume factor C_v accounts for an observed reduction in strength when length, width, and depth of structural glulam members increase. This strength reduction is due to the higher probability of occurrence of strength-reducing characteristics, such as knots and slope of grain, in higher volume beams. This volume factor adjustment is given in the *National Design Specification for Wood Construction* (AF&PA 1997) in the form

$$C_v = \left(\frac{305}{d}\right)^{0.10}\left(\frac{130}{w}\right)^{0.10}\left(\frac{6.4}{L}\right)^{0.10} \quad \text{(metric)} \quad (11\text{--}1a)$$

$$C_v = \left(\frac{12}{d}\right)^{0.10}\left(\frac{5.125}{w}\right)^{0.10}\left(\frac{21}{L}\right)^{0.10} \quad \text{(inch--pound)} \quad (11\text{--}1b)$$

for Douglas-fir and other species, and

$$C_v = \left(\frac{305}{d}\right)^{0.05}\left(\frac{130}{w}\right)^{0.05}\left(\frac{6.4}{L}\right)^{0.05} \quad \text{(metric)} \quad (11\text{--}2a)$$

$$C_v = \left(\frac{12}{d}\right)^{0.05}\left(\frac{5.125}{w}\right)^{0.05}\left(\frac{21}{L}\right)^{0.05} \quad \text{(inch--pound)} \quad (11\text{--}2b)$$

for southern pines, where d is depth (mm, in.), w width (mm, in.), and L length (m, ft). (Eqs. (11–1a) and (11–2a) in metric, Eqs. (11–1b) and (11–2b) in inch–pound system.)

Moisture Content—The moisture content factor C_M accounts for the reduction in strength as moisture content increases. A moisture content adjustment is listed in both ASTM D3737 (ASTM 1997b) and AITC 117–Design (AITC 1993b).

$$C_M = 1.0 \text{ for moisture content} \leq 16\%$$

For moisture content >16%, as in ground contact and many other exterior conditions, use the following C_M values:

	F_b	F_t	F_v	$F_{c\text{-perp}}$	F_c	E
C_M	0.8	0.8	0.875	0.53	0.73	0.833

Loading—An adjustment for the type of loading on the member is also necessary because the volume factors are derived assuming a uniform load. This method of loading factor C_L is recommended in the *National Design Specification for Wood Construction* (AF&PA 1997).

$$C_L = 1.00 \text{ for uniform loading on a simple span}$$
$$= 1.08 \text{ for center point loading on a simple span}$$
$$= 0.92 \text{ for constant stress over the full length}$$

For other loading conditions, values of C_L can be estimated using the proportion of the beam length subjected to 80% or more of the maximum stress L_0 and

$$C_L = \left(\frac{0.45}{L_0}\right)^{0.1} \quad (11\text{--}3)$$

Tension Lamination—Past research has shown that special provisions are required for the tension lamination of a glulam beam to achieve the specified design bending strength levels. Properties listed in AITC 117 and 119 are applicable to beams with these special tension laminations. If a special tension lamination is not included in the beam combination, strength reduction factors must be applied. Tension lamination factors C_T, which can be found in ASTM D3737 (ASTM 1997b), have the following values:

$$C_T = 1.00 \text{ for special tension laminations per AITC 117}$$
$$= 0.85 \text{ without tension laminations and for depth} \leq 380 \text{ mm} (\leq 15 \text{ in.})$$
$$= 0.75 \text{ without tension laminations and for depth} > 380 \text{ mm} (>15 \text{ in.}).$$

Curvature—The curvature factor accounts for the increased stresses in the curved portion of curved glulam beams. This factor does not apply to design values in the straight portion of a member, regardless of the curvature elsewhere. The curvature factor C_c, which can be found in the *National Design Specification* (AF&PA 1997), has the following relation:

$$C_c = 1 - 2000\left(\frac{t}{R}\right)^2 \quad (11\text{--}4)$$

where t is thickness of lamination and R is radius of curvature on inside face of lamination. The value $t/R \leq 1/100$ for hardwoods and southern pines; $t/R \leq 1/125$ for other softwoods.

Flat Use—The flat use factor is applied to bending design values when members are loaded parallel to wide faces of laminations and are less than 305 mm (12 in.) in depth. Flat use factors C_{fu}, which can be found in the *National Design Specification* (AF&PA 1997), have the following values:

Member dimension parallel to wide faces of laminations	C_{fu}
273 or 267 mm (10-3/4 or 10-1/2 in.)	1.01
222 or 216 mm (8-3/4 or 8-1/2 in.)	1.04
171 mm (6-3/4 in.)	1.07
130 or 127 mm (5-1/8 or 5 in.)	1.10
79 or 76 mm (3-1/8 or 3 in.)	1.16
64 mm (2-1/2 in.)	1.19

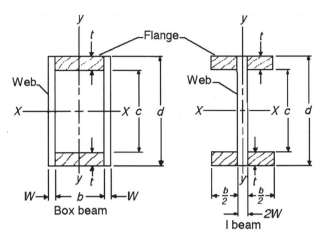

Figure 11–6. Beams with structural panel webs.

Lateral Stability—The lateral stability factor is applied to bending design values to account for the amount of lateral support applied to bending members. Deep bending members that are unsupported along the top surface are subject to lateral torsional buckling and would have lower bending design values. Members that are fully supported would have no adjustments ($C_L = 1.0$).

Glued Members With Lumber and Panels

Highly efficient structural components can be produced by combining lumber with panel products through gluing. These components, including box beams, I-beams, "stressed-skin" panels, and folded plate roofs, are discussed in detail in technical publications of the APA—The Engineered Wood Association (APA 1980). One type of member, prefabricated wood I-joists, is discussed in detail. Details on structural design are given in the following portion of this chapter for beams with webs of structural panel products and stressed-skin panels wherein the parts are glued together with a rigid, durable adhesive.

These highly efficient designs, although adequate structurally, can suffer from lack of resistance to fire and decay unless treatment or protection is provided. The rather thin portions of the cross section (the panel materials) are more vulnerable to fire damage than are the larger, solid cross sections.

Box Beams and I-Beams

Box beams and I-beams with lumber or laminated flanges and structural panel webs can be designed to provide the desired stiffness, bending, moment resistance, and shear resistance. The flanges resist bending moment, and the webs provide primary shear resistance. Proper design requires that the webs must not buckle under design loads. If lateral stability is a problem, the box beam design should be chosen because it is stiffer in lateral bending and torsion than is the I-beam. In contrast, the I-beam should be chosen if buckling of the web is of concern because its single web, double the thickness of that of a box beam, will offer greater buckling resistance.

Design details for beam cross sections (including definitions of terms in the following equations) are presented in Figure 11–6. Both flanges in these beams are the same thickness because a construction symmetrical about the neutral plane provides the greatest moment of inertia for the amount of material used. The following equations were derived by basic principles of engineering mechanics. These methods can be extended to derive designs for unsymmetrical constructions, if necessary.

Beam Deflections

Beam deflections can be computed using Equation (8–2) in Chapter 8. The following equations for bending stiffness $(EI)_x$ and shear stiffness GA' apply to the box and I-beam shown in Figure 11–6. The bending stiffness is given by

$$(EI)_x = \frac{1}{12}[E(d^3 - c^3)b + 2E_wWd^3] \qquad (11\text{–}5)$$

where E is flange modulus of elasticity and E_w is web modulus of elasticity. For plywood, values of E_w for the appropriate structural panel construction and grain direction can be computed from Equations (11–1), (11–2), and (11–3).

An approximate expression for the shear stiffness is

$$GA' = 2WcG \qquad (11\text{–}6)$$

where G is shear modulus for the structural panel for appropriate direction and A' is the effective area of the web. An improvement in shear stiffness can be made by properly orienting the web, depending upon its directional properties. Equation (11–6) is conservative because it ignores the shear stiffness of the flange. This contribution can be included by use of APA design methods that are based on Orosz (1970). (For further information on APA design methods, contact APA—The Engineered Wood Association in Tacoma, Washington.)

Flange Stresses

Flange compressive and tensile stresses at outer beam fibers are given by

$$f_x = \frac{6M}{(d^3 - c^3)\dfrac{b}{d} + \dfrac{2E_w W d^2}{E}} \qquad (11\text{–}7)$$

where M is bending moment.

Web Shear Stress

Web shear stress at the beam neutral plane is given by

$$f_{xy} = \frac{3V}{4W}\left[\frac{E(d^2 - c^2)b + 2E_w W d^2}{E(d^3 - c^3)b + 2E_w W d^3}\right] \qquad (11\text{–}8)$$

where V is shear load. The shear stress must not exceed allowable values. To avoid web buckling, either the web should be increased in thickness or the clear length of the web should be broken by stiffeners glued to the web.

Web edgewise bending stresses at the inside of the flanges can be computed by

$$f_{xw} = \frac{6M}{\dfrac{E}{E_w}(d^3 - c^3)\dfrac{b}{c} + 2\dfrac{d^3}{c}W} \qquad (11\text{–}9)$$

Although it is not likely, the web can buckle as a result of bending stresses. Should buckling as a result of edgewise bending appear possible, the interaction of shear and edgewise bending buckling can be examined using the principles of Timoshenko (1961).

Lateral Buckling

Possible lateral buckling of the entire beam should be checked by calculating the critical bending stress (Ch. 8, Lateral–Torsional Buckling section). The slenderness factor p, required to calculate this stress, includes terms for lateral flexural rigidity EI_y and torsional rigidity GK that are defined as follows:

For box beams,

$$EI_y = \frac{1}{12} E(d - c)b^3 \qquad (11\text{–}10)$$
$$+ E_w[(b + 2W)^3 - b^3]d$$

$$GK = \left[\frac{(d + c)(d^2 - c^2)(b + W)^2 W}{(d^2 - c^2) + 4(b + W)W}\right]G \qquad (11\text{–}11)$$

For I-beams,

$$EI_y = \frac{1}{12}\Big\{E[(b + 2W)^3 - (2W)^3](d - c) \qquad (11\text{–}12)$$
$$+ E_{fw}(2W)^3 d\Big\}$$

$$GK = \frac{1}{3}\left[\frac{1}{4}(d - c)^3 b + d(2W)^3\right]G \qquad (11\text{–}13)$$

where E_{fw} is flexural elastic modulus of the web.

In Equations (11–11) and (11–13), the shear modulus G can be assumed without great error to be about 1/16 of the flange modulus of elasticity E_L. The resultant torsional stiffness GK will be slightly low if beam webs have plywood grain at 45° to the neutral axis. The lateral buckling of I-beams will also be slightly conservative because bending rigidity of the flange has been neglected in writing the equations given here. If buckling of the I-beam seems possible at design loads, the more accurate analysis of Forest Products Laboratory Report 1318B (Lewis and others 1943) should be used before redesigning.

Stiffeners and Load Blocks

Determination of the number and sizes of stiffeners and load blocks needed in a particular construction does not lend itself to a rational procedure, but certain general rules can be given that will help the designer of a structure obtain a satisfactory structural member. Stiffeners serve a dual purpose in a structural member of this type. One function is to limit the size of the unsupported panel in the web, and the other is to restrain the flanges from moving toward each other as the beam is stressed.

Stiffeners should be glued to the webs and in contact with both flanges. A rational way of determining how thick the stiffener should be is not available, but tests of box beams made at the Forest Products Laboratory indicate that a thickness of at least six times the thickness of the web is sufficient. Because stiffeners must also resist the tendency of the flanges to move toward each other, the stiffeners should be as wide as (extend to the edge of) the flanges.

For plywood webs containing plies with the grain of the wood oriented both parallel and perpendicular to the axis of the member, the spacing of the stiffeners is relatively unimportant for the web shear stresses that are allowed. Maximum allowable stresses are less than those that will produce buckling. A clear distance between stiffeners equal to or less than two times the clear distance between flanges is adequate. Load blocks are special stiffeners placed along the member at points of concentrated load. Load blocks should be designed so that stresses caused by a load that bears against the side-grain material in the flanges do not exceed the allowable design for the flange material in compression perpendicular to grain.

Prefabricated Wood I-Joists

In recent years, the development of improved adhesives and manufacturing techniques has led to the development of the prefabricated I-joist industry. This product is a unique type of I-beam that is replacing wider lumber sizes in floor and roof applications for both residential and commercial buildings (Fig. 11–7).

Significant savings in materials are possible with prefabricated I-joists that use either plywood or oriented strandboard (OSB) for the web material and small dimension lumber or structural composite lumber (SCL) for the flanges. The high quality lumber needed for these flanges has been difficult to obtain using visual grading methods, and both mechanically

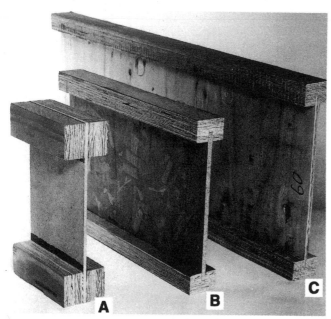

Figure 11–7. Prefabricated I-joists with laminated veneer lumber flanges and structural panel webs. (A) One experimental product has a hardboard web. The other two commercial products have (B) oriented strandboard and (C) plywood webs.

graded lumber and SCL are being used by several manufacturers. The details of fastening the flanges to the webs vary between manufacturers; all must be glued with a waterproof adhesive. Prefabricated I-joists are becoming popular with builders because of their light weight, dimensional stability and ease of construction. Their accurate and consistent dimensions, as well as uniform depth, allow the rapid creation of a level floor. Utility lines pass easily through openings in the webs.

The ASTM standard D5055 (ASTM 1997d) gives procedures for establishing, monitoring, and reevaluating structural capacities of prefabricated I-joists. Each manufacturer of prefabricated I-joists is responsible for developing the required property information and ensuring that the minimum levels of quality are maintained during production. An independent inspection agency is required to monitor the quality assurance program.

Standard grades, sizes, and span tables have not been established for all prefabricated I-joists. The production of each manufacturer may have unique design properties and procedures. Thus, the designer must consult information provided by the manufacturer. Many engineering equations presented in the previous section also apply to prefabricated I-joists.

During the 1980s, the prefabricated wood I-joists industry was one of the fastest growing segments of the wood products industry. Prefabricated I-joists are manufactured by about 15 companies in the United States and Canada and are often distributed through building material suppliers. Each manufacturer has developed its building code acceptance and provides catalogs with span tables and design information.

Recently, a performance standard for prefabricted I-joists has been promulgated for products used in residential floor construction (APA 1997).

Stressed-Skin Panels

Constructions consisting of structural panel "skins" glued to wood stringers are often called stressed-skin panels. These panels offer efficient structural constructions for floor, wall, and roof components. They can be designed to provide desired stiffness, bending moment resistance, and shear resistance. The skins resist bending moment, and the wood stringers provide shear resistance.

The details of design for a panel cross section are given in Figure 11–8. The following equations were derived by basic principles of engineering mechanics. A more rigorous design procedure that includes the effects of shear lag is available in Kuenzi and Zahn (1975).

Panel deflections can be computed using Equation (8–2) in Chapter 8. The bending stiffness EI and shear stiffness GA' are given by the following equations for the stressed-skin panel shown in Figure 11–8.

$$
EI = \left[\frac{b}{\left(E_1 t_1 + E_2 t_2 + E t_c (s/b) \right)} \right]
$$
$$
\times \Big\{ E_1 t_1 E_2 t_2 [(t_1 + t_c) + (t_2 + t_c)]^2
$$
$$
+ E_1 t_1 E t_c (s/b)(t_1 + t_c)^2 + E_2 t_2 E t_c (s/b)(t_2 + t_c)^2 \Big\}
$$
$$
+ \frac{b}{12} \left(E_{f1} t_1^3 + E_{f2} t_2^3 + E t_c^3 \frac{s}{b} \right)
$$

$$(11–14)$$

where E_1 and E_2 are modulus of elasticity values for skins 1 and 2, E_{f1} and E_{f2} flexural modulus of elasticity values for skins 1 and 2, E stringer modulus of elasticity, and s total width of all stringers in a panel.

An approximate expression for shear stiffness is

$$
GA' = Gst_c \qquad (11–15)
$$

where G is stringer shear modulus.

Skin Stresses

Skin tensile and compressive stresses are given by

$$
f_{x1} = \frac{ME_1 y_1}{EI}
$$
$$
f_{x2} = \frac{ME_2 y_2}{EI}
$$

$$(11–16)$$

where EI is given by Equation (11–14), M is bending moment, and

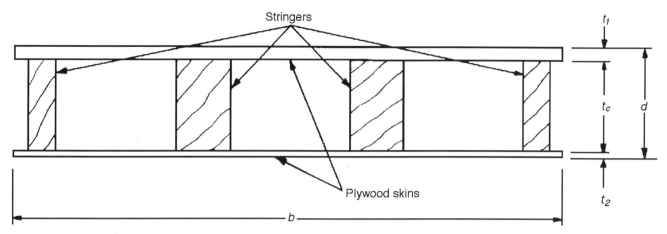

Figure 11–8. Stressed-skin panel cross section.

$$y_1 = \frac{E_2 t_2 [(t_1 + t_c) + (t_2 + t_c)] + E t_c \frac{s}{b}(t_1 + t_c)}{2\left(E_1 t_1 + E_2 t_2 + E t_c \frac{s}{b}\right)}$$

$$y_2 = \frac{E_1 t_1 [(t_1 + t_c) + (t_2 + t_c)] + E t_c \frac{s}{b}(t_2 + t_c)}{2\left(E_1 t_1 + E_2 t_2 + E t_c \frac{s}{b}\right)}$$

Either the skins should be thick enough or the stringers spaced closely enough so that buckling does not occur in the compression skin. Buckling stress can be analyzed by the principles in Ding and Hou (1995). The design stress for the structural panel in tension and compression strength should not be exceeded.

Stringer Bending Stress

The stringer bending stress is the larger value given by

$$f_{sx1} = \frac{ME(y_1 - t_1/2)}{EI}$$

$$f_{sx2} = \frac{ME(y_2 - t_2/2)}{EI} \qquad (11\text{--}17)$$

and these should not exceed appropriate values for the species.

The stringer shear stress is given by

$$f_{sxy} = \frac{V(EQ)}{sEI} \qquad (11\text{--}18)$$

where $EQ = (E_1 t_1 b + E s\, y_1/2)\, y_1$. This also should not exceed appropriate values for the species.

Glue Shear Stress

Glue shear stress in the joint between the skins and stringers is given by

$$f_{gl} = \frac{V(EQ)}{sEI} \qquad (11\text{--}19)$$

where $EQ = E_1 t_1 b y_1$. This stress should not exceed values for the glue and species. It should also not exceed the wood stress f_{TR} ("rolling" shear) for solid wood because, for plywood, the thin plies allow the glue shear stresses to be transmitted to adjacent plies and could cause rolling shear failure in the wood.

Buckling

Buckling of the stressed-skin panel of unsupported length under end load applied in a direction parallel to the length of the stringers can be computed by

$$P_{cr} = \frac{\pi^2 EI}{L^2} \qquad (11\text{--}20)$$

where L is unsupported panel length and EI is bending stiffness given by Equation (11–14).

Compressive stress in the skins is given by

$$f_{xc1} = \frac{PE_1}{EA}$$

$$f_{xc2} = \frac{PE_2}{EA} \qquad (11\text{--}21)$$

and in the stringers by

$$f_{sxc} = \frac{PE}{EA} \qquad (11\text{--}22)$$

253

Figure 11–9. Cutaway section of sandwich construction with plywood facings and a paper honeycomb core.

where $EA = E_1t_1b + E_2t_2b + Et_os$. These compressive stresses should not exceed stress values for the structural panel or stringer material. For plywood, compressive stress should also be less than the critical buckling stress.

Structural Sandwich Construction

Structural sandwich construction is a layered construction formed by bonding two thin facings to a thick core (Fig. 11–9). The thin facings are usually made of a strong and dense material because they resist nearly all the applied edgewise loads and flatwise bending moments. The core, which is made of a weak and low density material, separates and stabilizes the thin facings and provides most of the shear rigidity of the sandwich construction. By proper choice of materials for facings and core, constructions with high ratios of stiffness to weight can be achieved. As a crude guide to the material proportions, an efficient sandwich is obtained when the weight of the core is roughly equal to the total weight of the facings. Sandwich construction is also economical because the relatively expensive facing materials are used in much smaller quantities than are the usually inexpensive core materials. The materials are positioned so that each is used to its best advantage.

Specific nonstructural advantages can be incorporated in a sandwich construction by proper selection of facing and core materials. An impermeable facing can act as a moisture barrier for a wall or roof panel in a house; an abrasion-

resistant facing can be used for the top facing of a floor panel; and decorative effects can be obtained by using panels with plastic facings for walls, doors, tables, and other furnishings. Core material can be chosen to provide thermal insulation, fire resistance, and decay resistance. Because of the light weight of structural sandwich construction, sound transmission problems must also be considered in choosing sandwich component parts.

Methods of joining sandwich panels to each other and other structures must be planned so that the joints function properly and allow for possible dimensional change as a result of temperature and moisture variations. Both structural and nonstructural advantages need to be analyzed in light of the strength and service requirements for the sandwich construction. Moisture-resistant facings, cores, and adhesives should be used if the construction is to be exposed to adverse moisture conditions. Similarly, heat-resistant or decay-resistant facings, cores, and adhesives should be used if exposure to elevated temperatures or decay organisms is expected.

Fabrication

Facing Materials

One advantage of sandwich construction is the great latitude it provides in choice of facings and the opportunity to use thin sheet materials because of the nearly continuous support by the core. The stiffness, stability, and to a large extent, the strength of the sandwich are determined by the characteristics of the facings. Facing materials include plywood, single veneers, or plywood overlaid with a resin-treated paper, oriented strandboard, hardboard, particleboard, glass–fiber-reinforced polymers or laminates, veneer bonded to metal, and metals, such as aluminum, enameled steel, stainless steel, magnesium, and titanium.

Core Materials

Many lightweight materials, such as balsa wood, rubber foam, resin-impregnated paper, reinforced plastics, perforated chipboard, expanded plastics, foamed glass, lightweight concrete and clay products, and formed sheets of cloth, metal, or paper have been used as a core for sandwich construction. New materials and new combinations of old materials are constantly being proposed and used. Cores of formed sheet materials are often called honeycomb cores. By varying the sheet material, sheet thickness, cell size, and cell shape, cores of a wide range in density can be produced. Various core configurations are shown in Figures 11–10 and 11–11. The core cell configurations shown in Figure 11–10 can be formed to moderate amounts of single curvature, but cores shown in Figure 11–11 as configurations A, B, and C can be formed to severe single curvature and mild compound curvature (spherical).

Four types of readily formable cores are shown as configurations D, E, F, and G in Figure 11–11. The type D and F cores form to a cylindrical shape, the type D and E cores to a spherical shape, and the type D and G cores to various compound curvatures.

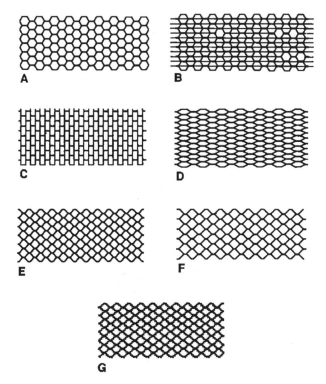

Figure 11–10. Honeycomb core cell configurations.

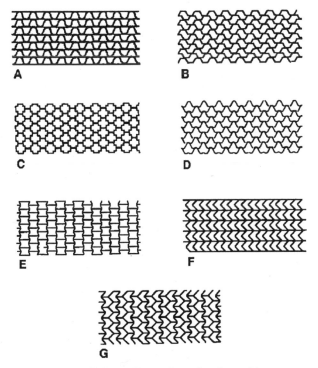

Figure 11–11. Cell configurations for formable paper honeycomb cores.

If the sandwich panels are likely to be subjected to damp or wet conditions, a core of paper honeycomb should contain a synthetic resin. When wet, paper with 15% phenolic resin provides good strength, decay resistance, and desirable handling characteristics during fabrication. Resin amounts in excess of about 15% do not seem to produce a gain in strength commensurate with the increased quantity of resin required. Smaller amounts of resin may be combined with fungicides to offer primary protection against decay.

Manufacturing Operations

The principal operation in the manufacture of sandwich panels is bonding the facings to the core. Special presses are needed for sandwich panel manufacture to avoid crushing lightweight cores, because the pressures required are usually lower than can be obtained in the range of good pressure control on presses ordinarily used for structural panels or plastic products. Because pressure requirements are low, simple and perhaps less costly presses could be used. Continuous roller presses or hydraulic pressure equipment may also be suitable. In the pressing of sandwich panels, special problems can occur, but the manufacturing process is basically not complicated.

Adhesives must be selected and applied to provide the necessary joint strength and permanence. The facing materials, especially if metallic, may need special surface treatment before the adhesive is applied.

In certain sandwich panels, loading rails or edgings are placed between the facings at the time of assembly. Special fittings or equipment, such as heating coils, plumbing, or electrical wiring conduit, can easily be installed in the panel before its components are fitted together.

Some of the most persistent difficulties in the use of sandwich panels are caused by the necessity of introducing edges, inserts, and connectors. In some cases, the problem involves tying together thin facing materials without causing severe stress concentrations. In other cases, such as furniture manufacture, the problem is "show through" of core or inserts through decorative facings. These difficulties are minimized by a choice of materials in which the rate and degree of differential dimensional movement between core and insert are at a minimum.

Structural Design

The structural design of sandwich construction can be compared with the design of an I-beam. The facings and core of the sandwich are analogous to the flanges and web of the I-beam, respectively. The two thin and stiff facings, separated by a thick and light core, carry the bending loads. The functions of the core are to support the facings against lateral wrinkling caused by in-plane compressive loads and to carry, through the bonding adhesive, shear loads. When the strength requirements for the facings and core in a particular design are met, the construction should also be checked for possible buckling, as for a column or panel in compression, and for possible wrinkling of the facings.

The contribution of the core material to the stiffness of the sandwich construction can generally be neglected because of the core's low modulus of elasticity; when that is the case, the shear stress can be assumed constant over the depth of the core. The facing moduli of elasticity are usually more than 100 times as great as the core modulus of elasticity. The core material may also have a small shear modulus. This small shear modulus causes increased deflections of sandwich construction subjected to bending and decreased buckling loads of columns and edge-loaded panels, compared with constructions in which the core shear modulus is high. The effect of this low shear modulus is greater for short beams and columns and small panels than it is for long beams and columns and large panels.

Without considering the contribution of core material, the bending stiffness of sandwich beams having facings of equal or unequal thickness is given by

$$D = \frac{h^2 t_1 t_2 (E_1 t_2 + E_2 t_1)}{(t_1 + t_2)^2} + \frac{1}{12}(E_1 t_1^3 + E_2 t_2^3) \qquad (11\text{–}23)$$

where D is the stiffness per unit width of sandwich construction (product of modulus of elasticity and moment of inertia of the cross section), E_1 and E_2 moduli of elasticity of facings 1 and 2, t_1 and t_2 facing thickness, and h distance between facing centroids.

The shear stiffness per unit width is given by

$$U = \frac{h^2}{t_c} G_c \qquad (11\text{–}24)$$

where G_c is the core shear modulus associated with distortion of the plane perpendicular to the facings and parallel to the sandwich length and t_c is the thickness of the core.

The bending stiffness D and shear stiffness U are used to compute deflections and buckling loads of sandwich beams. The general expression for the deflection of flat sandwich beams is given by

$$\frac{d^2 y}{dx^2} = -\frac{M_x}{D} + \frac{1}{U}\left(\frac{dS_x}{dx}\right) \qquad (11\text{–}25)$$

where y is deflection, x distance along the beam, M_x bending moment per unit width at point x, and S_x shear force per unit width at point x.

Integration of Equation (11–25) leads to the following general expression for deflection of a sandwich beam:

$$y = \frac{k_b P a^3}{D} + \frac{k_s P a}{U} \qquad (11\text{–}26)$$

where P is total load per unit width of beam, a is span, and k_b and k_s are constants dependent upon the loading condition. The first term in the right side of Equation (11–26) gives the bending deflection and the second term the shear deflection. Values of k_b and k_s for several loadings are given in Table 11–1.

For sandwich panels supported on all edges, the theory of plates must be applied to obtain analytical solutions. A comprehensive treatment of sandwich plates under various loading and boundary conditions can be found in the books by Allen (1969), Whitney (1987), and Vinson and Sierak-owski (1986). Many extensive studies of sandwich construction performed at the Forest Products Laboratory are referenced in those books. In addition, some high-order analyses of sandwich construction that consider general material properties for component parts in specified applications can be found in the references at the end of this chapter.

The buckling load per unit width of a sandwich panel with no edge members and loaded as a simply supported column is given by

$$N = \frac{N_E}{1 + N_E/U} \qquad (11\text{–}27)$$

where critical load

$$N_E = \frac{\pi^2 n^2 D}{a^2} \qquad (11\text{–}28)$$

in which n is the number of half-waves into which the column buckles and a is the panel length. The minimum value of N_E is obtained for $n = 1$ and is called the Euler load.

Table 11–1. Values of k_b and k_s for several beam loadings

Loading	Beam ends	Deflection at	k_b	k_s
Uniformly distributed	Both simply supported	Midspan	5/384	1/8
	Both clamped	Midspan	1/384	1/8
Concentrated at midspan	Both simply supported	Midspan	1/48	1/4
	Both clamped	Midspan	1/192	1/4
Concentrated at outer quarter points	Both simply supported	Midspan	11/76	1/8
	Both simply supported	Load point	1/96	1/8
Uniformly distributed	Cantilever, 1 free, 1 clamped	Free end	1/8	1/2
Concentrated at free end	Cantilever, 1 free, 1 clamped	Free end	1/3	1

At this load, the buckling form is often called "general buckling," as illustrated in Figure 11–12A.

The buckling load N is often expressed in the equivalent form

$$\frac{1}{N} = \frac{1}{N_E} + \frac{1}{U} \qquad (11\text{–}29)$$

When U is finite, $N < N_E$; when U is infinite, $N = N_E$; and when N_E is infinite (that is, $n \to \infty$ in Eq. (11–28)), $N = U$, which is often called the "shear instability" limit. The appearance of this buckling failure resembles a crimp (Fig. 11–12B). Shear instability or crimping failure is always possible for edge-loaded sandwich construction and is a limit for general instability and not a localized failure.

For a sandwich panel under edge load and with edge members, the edge members will carry a load proportional to their transformed area (area multiplied by ratio of edge member modulus of elasticity to facing modulus of elasticity). Edge members will also increase the overall panel buckling load because of restraints at edges. Estimates of the effects of edge members can be obtained from Zahn and Cheng (1964).

Buckling criteria for flat rectangular sandwich panels under edgewise shear, bending, and combined loads and those for sandwich walls of cylinders under torsion, axial compression or bending, and external pressure have all been investigated by various researchers at the Forest Products Laboratory. Details can be found in *Military Handbook 23A* by the U.S.

Department of Defense (1968) and some publications listed in the References.

Buckling of sandwich components has been emphasized because it causes complete failure, usually producing severe shear crimping at the edges of the buckles. Another important factor is the necessity that the facing stress be no more than its allowable value at the design load. The facing stress is obtained by dividing the load by the facing area under load. For an edgewise compressive load per unit width N, the facing stress is given by

$$f = \frac{N}{t_1 + t_2} \qquad (11\text{–}30)$$

In a strip of sandwich construction subjected to bending moments, the mean facing stresses are given by

$$f_i = \frac{M}{t_i h} \qquad i = 1, 2 \qquad (11\text{–}31)$$

where f_i is mean compressive or tensile stress per unit width in facing i and M is bending moment per unit width of sandwich. If the strip is subjected to shear loads, the shear stress in the core is given by

$$f_{cs} = \frac{S}{h} \qquad (11\text{–}32)$$

where S is the applied shear load per unit width of sandwich.

Localized failure of sandwich construction must be avoided. Such failure is shown as dimpling and wrinkling of the facings in Figure 11–12C and D, respectively. The stress at which dimpling of the facing into a honeycomb core begins is given by the empirical equation

$$f_d = 2E\left(\frac{t_f}{s}\right)^2 \qquad (11\text{–}33)$$

where f_d is facing stress at dimpling, E facing modulus of elasticity at stress f_d, t_f facing thickness, and s cell size of honeycomb core (diameter of inscribed circle).

Increase in dimpling stress can be attained by decreasing the cell size. Wrinkling of the sandwich facings can occur because they are thin and supported by a lightweight core that functions as their elastic foundation. Wrinkling can also occur because of a poor facing-to-core bond, resulting in separation of facing from the core (Fig. 11–12D). Increase in bond strength should produce wrinkling by core crushing. Thus, a convenient rule of thumb is to require that the sandwich flatwise tensile strength (bond strength) is no less than flatwise compressive core strength. Approximate wrinkling stress for a fairly flat facing (precluding bond failure) is given by

$$f_w = \frac{3}{4}(EE_cG_c)^{1/3} \qquad (11\text{–}34)$$

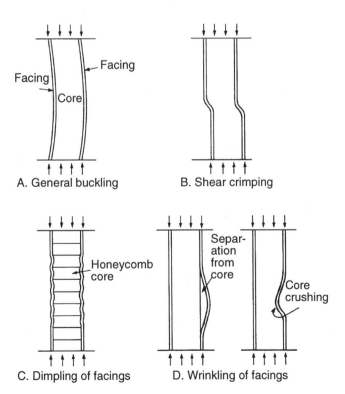

A. General buckling

B. Shear crimping

C. Dimpling of facings

D. Wrinkling of facings

Figure 11–12. Modes of failure of sandwich construction under edgewise loads.

where f_w is facing wrinkling stress, E facing modulus of elasticity, E_c core modulus of elasticity in a direction perpendicular to facing, and G_c core shear modulus.

Wrinkling and other forms of local instability are described in detail in *Military Handbook 23A* (U.S. Department of Defense 1968) and in a book by Allen (1969). Localized failure is not accurately predictable, and designs should be checked by ASTM tests of laboratory specimens.

Because sandwich constructions are composed of several materials, it is often of interest to attempt to design a construction of minimum weight for a particular component. One introduction to the problem of optimum design is presented by Kuenzi (1970). For a sandwich with similar facings having a required bending stiffness D, the dimensions for the minimum weight design are given by

$$h = 2\left(\frac{Dw}{Ew_c}\right)^{1/3} \qquad (11\text{--}35)$$

$$t = \frac{w_c}{4w}h$$

where h is distance between facing centroids, t facing thickness, E facing modulus of elasticity, w facing density, and w_c core density.

The resulting construction will have very thin facings on a very thick core and will be proportioned so that the total core weight is two-thirds the total sandwich weight minus the bond weight. However, such a construction may be impracticable because the required facings may be too thin.

Many detailed design procedures necessary for rapid design of sandwich components for aircraft are summarized in *Military Handbook 23A* (U.S. Department of Defense 1968). The principles contained therein and in some publications listed in the References are broad and can be applied to sandwich components of all structures.

Dimensional Stability, Durability, and Bowing

In a sandwich panel, any dimensional movement of one facing with respect to the other as a result of changes in moisture content and temperature causes bowing of an unrestrained panel. Thus, although the use of dissimilar facings is often desirable from an economic or decorative standpoint, the dimensional instability of the facings during panel manufacture or exposure may rule out possible benefits. If dimensional change of both facings is equal, the length and width of the panel will increase or decrease but bowing will not result.

The problem of dimensional stability is chiefly related to the facings because the core is not stiff enough either to cause bowing of the panel or to cause the panel to remain flat. However, the magnitude of the bowing effect depends on the thickness of the core.

It is possible to calculate mathematically the bowing of a sandwich construction if the percentage of expansion of each facing is known. The maximum deflection is given approximately by

$$\Delta = \frac{ka^2}{800h}$$

where k is the percentage of expansion of one facing compared with the opposite facing, a the length of the panel, and h the distance between facing centroids.

In conventional construction, vapor barriers are often installed to block migration of vapor to the cold side of a wall. Various methods have been tried or suggested for reducing vapor movement through sandwich panels, which causes a moisture differential with resultant bowing of the panels. These methods include bonding metal foil within the sandwich construction, blending aluminum flakes with the resin bonding adhesives, and using plastic vapor barriers between veneers, overlay papers, special finishes, or metal or plastic facings. Because added cost is likely, some methods should not be used unless their need has been demonstrated.

A large test unit simulating the use of sandwich panels in houses was constructed at the Forest Products Laboratory. The panels consisted of a variety of facing materials, including plywood, aluminum, particleboard, hardboard, paperboard, and cement asbestos, with cores of paper honeycomb, polyurethane, or extruded polystyrene. These panels were evaluated for bowing and general performance after various lengths of service between 1947 and 1978. The experimental assembly shown in Figure 11–13 represents the type of construction used in the test unit. The major conclusions were that (a) bowing was least for aluminum-faced panels, (b) bowing was greater for plywood-faced panels with polyurethane or polystyrene cores than for plywood-faced panels with paper cores, and (c) with proper combinations of facings, core, and adhesives, satisfactory sandwich panels can be ensured by careful fabrication techniques.

Thermal Insulation

Satisfactory thermal insulation can best be obtained with sandwich panels by using cores having low thermal conductivity, although the use of reflective layers on the facings is of some value. Paper honeycomb cores have thermal conductivity values (k values), ranging from 0.04 to 0.09 W/m·K (0.30 to 0.65 Btu·in/h·ft^2·°F), depending on the particular core construction. The k value does not vary linearly with core thickness for a true honeycomb core because of direct radiation through the core cell opening from one facing to the other. Honeycomb with open cells can also have greater conductivity if the cells are large enough (greater than about 9 mm (3/8 in.)) to allow convection currents to develop.

An improvement in the insulation value can be realized by filling the honeycomb core with insulation or a foamed-in-place resin.

Figure 11–13. Cutaway to show details of sandwich construction in an experimental structure.

Fire Resistance

In tests at the Forest Products Laboratory, the fire resistance of wood-faced sandwich panels was appreciably greater than that of hollow panels faced with the same thickness of plywood. Fire resistance was greatly increased when coatings that intumesce on exposure to heat were applied to the core material. The spread of fire through the honeycomb core depended to a large extent on the alignment of the flutes in the core. In panels with flutes perpendicular to the facings, only slight spread of flame occurred. In cores in which flutes were parallel to the length of the panel, the spread of flame occurred in the vertical direction along open channels.

Resistance to flame spread could be improved by placing a barrier sheet at the top of the panel or at intervals in the panel height, or if strength requirements permit, by simply turning the length of the core blocks at 90° angles in the vertical direction.

References

General

Smulski, S., ed. 1997. Engineered wood products, a guide to specifiers, designers and users. PFS Research Foundation.

Structural Composite Lumber

ASTM. 1997a. Standard specification for evaluation of structural composite lumber products. ASTM D5456. West Conshohocken, PA: American Society for Testing and Materials.

Bohlen, J.C. 1972. Laminated veneer lumber—development and economics. Forest Products Journal. 22(1): 18–26.

Jung, J. 1982. Properties of parallel-laminated veneer from stress-wave-tested veneers. Forest Products Journal. 32(7): 30–35.

Kunesh, R.H. 1978. MICRO=LAM: Structural laminated veneer lumber. Forest Products Journal. 28(7): 41–44.

Laufenberg, T. 1983. Parallel laminated veneer: processing and performance research review. Forest Products Journal. 33(9):21–28.

Moody, R.C. 1972. Tensile strength of lumber laminated from 1/8 in. thick veneers. Res. Pap. FPL–RP–181. Madison, WI: U.S. Department of Agriculture, Forest Service, Forest Products Laboratory.

NIST. 1995. Voluntary product standard PS 1–95. Construction and industrial plywood. Gaithersburg, MD: U.S. Department of Commerce, National Institute of Standards and Technology.

Press–Lam Team. 1972. Feasibility of producing a high-yield laminated structural product. Res. Pap. FPL–RP–175. Madison, WI: U.S. Department of Agriculture, Forest Service, Forest Products Laboratory.

Glulam

AF&PA. 1997. National design specification for wood construction. Washington, DC: American Forest & Paper Association.

AITC. 1979. Recommended practice for protection of structural glued-laminated timber during transit, storage, and erection. AITC 111. Englewood, CO: American Institute of Timber Construction.

AITC. 1984. Standard appearance grades for structural glued-laminated timber. AITC 110. Englewood, CO: American Institute of Timber Construction.

AITC. 1990. Standard for preservative treatment of structural glued-laminated timber. AITC 109. Englewood, CO: American Institute of Timber Construction.

AITC. 1993a. Inspection manual. AITC 200. Englewood, CO: American Institute of Timber Construction.

AITC. 1993b. Standard specifications for structural glued-laminated timber of softwood species. AITC 117. Englewood, CO: American Institute of Timber Construction.

AITC. 1994. Timber construction manual. American Institute of Timber Construction. 4th ed. New York: John Wiley & Sons.

AITC. 1996. Standard specifications for structural glued-laminated timber of hardwood species. AITC 119. Englewood, CO: American Institute of Timber Construction.

ANSI. 1992. Structural glued laminated timber. ANSI/AITC A190.1. New York: American National Standards Institute.

ANSI. 1996. Structural glued laminated timber for utility structures. ANSI O5.2. New York: American National Standards Institute.

ASCE. 1975. Wood structures, a design guide and commentary. New York: American Society of Civil Engineers.

ASCE. 1982. Evaluation, maintenance and upgrading of wood structures. New York: American Society of Civil Engineers.

ASTM. 1997b. Standard practice for establishing stresses for structural glued-laminated timber (glulam). ASTM D3737. Philadelphia, PA: American Society for Testing and Materials.

ASTM. 1997c. Standard practice for establishing structural grades and related allowable properties for visually graded lumber. ASTM D245. Philadelphia, PA: American Society for Testing and Materials.

AWPA. 1997a. Standards for solvents and formulations for organic preservative system. P9. Woodstock, MD: American Wood Preservers' Association.

AWPA. 1997b. Standards for waterborne preservatives. P5. Woodstock, MD: American Wood Preservers' Association.

CSA. 1989. Structural glued-laminated timbers. CAN/CSA O122. Rexdale, ON: Canadian Standards Association.

CSA. 1994. Engineering design of wood (limit state design). CAN/CSA O86. Rexdale, ON: Canadian Standards Association.

Freas, A.D.; Selbo, M.L. 1954. Fabrication and design of glued laminated wood structural members. U.S. Department of Agriculture Tech. Bull. 1069. Available from: Englewood, CO: American Institute of Timber Construction.

Jokerst, R.W. 1981. Finger-jointed wood products. Res. Pap. FPL–RP–382. Madison, WI: U.S. Department of Agriculture, Forest Service, Forest Products Laboratory.

Moody, R.C. 1977. Improved utilization of lumber in glued laminated beams. Res. Pap. FPL–RP–292. Madison, WI: U.S. Department of Agriculture, Forest Service, Forest Products Laboratory.

Peterson, J.; Madson, G.; Moody, R.C. 1981. Tensile strength of one-, two-, and three-ply glulam members of 2 by 6 Douglas-fir. Forest Products Journal. 31(1): 42–48.

Selbo, M.L.; Knauss, A.C.; Worth, H.E. 1965. After two decades of service, glulam timbers show good performance. Forest Products Journal. 15(11): 466–472.

Wolfe, R.W.; Moody, R.C. 1979. Bending strength of vertically glued laminated beams with one to five plies. Res. Pap. FPL–RP–333. Madison, WI: U.S. Department of Agriculture, Forest Service, Forest Products Laboratory.

Glued Members With Lumber and Panels

APA. 1980. Plywood Design Specification. Tacoma, WA: APA—The Engineered Wood Association.

　Supp. 1. Design and fabrication of plywood curved panels

　Supp. 2. Design and fabrication of plywood-lumber beams

　Supp. 3. Design and fabrication of plywood stressed-skin panels

　Supp. 4. Design and fabrication of plywood sandwich panels

APA. 1997. Performance standard for I-joists used in residential floor construction. PRI–400. Tacoma, WA: APA—The Engineered Wood Association.

ASTM. 1997d. Standard specification for establishing and monitoring structural capacities of prefabricated wood I-joists. ASTM D5055. West Conshohocken, PA: American Society for Testing and Materials.

ASTM. 1997e. Standard methods for testing veneer, plywood, and other glued veneer constructions. ASTM D805. West Conshohocken, PA: American Society for Testing and Materials.

Ding, Y.; Hou, J. 1995. General buckling analysis of sandwich constructions. Computers & Structures. 55(3): 485–493.

Forest Products Laboratory. 1943. Design of plywood webs for box beams. FPL Rep. 1318. Madison, WI: U.S. Department of Agriculture, Forest Service, Forest Products Laboratory.

Kuenzi, E.W.; Zahn, J.J. 1975. Stressed-skin panel deflection and stresses. Res. Pap. FPL–RP–251. Madison, WI: U.S. Department of Agriculture, Forest Service, Forest Products Laboratory.

Lewis, W.C.; Heebink, T.B.; Cottingham, W.S.; Dawley, E.R. 1943. Buckling in shear webs of box and I-beams and their effect upon design criteria. FPL Rep. 1318B. Madison, WI: U.S. Department of Agriculture, Forest Service, Forest Products Laboratory.

Lewis, W.C.; Heebink, T.B.; Cottingham, W.S. 1944. Effects of certain defects and stress concentrating factors on the strength of tension flanges of box beams. FPL Rep. 1513. Madison, WI: U.S. Department of Agriculture, Forest Service, Forest Products Laboratory.

Lewis, W.C.; Heebink, T.B.; Cottingham, W. S. 1945. Effect of increased moisture on the shear strength at glue lines of box beams and on the glue–shear and glue–tension strengths of small specimens. FPL Rep. 1551. Madison, WI: U.S. Department of Agriculture, Forest Service, Forest Products Laboratory.

McNatt, J.D. 1980. Hardboard-webbed beams: Research and application. Forest Products Journal. 30(10): 57–64.

Orosz, I. 1970. Simplified method for calculating shear deflections of beams. Res. Note FPL–RN–0210. Madison, WI: U.S. Department of Agriculture, Forest Service, Forest Products Laboratory.

Superfesky, M.J.; Ramaker, T.J. 1976. Hardboard-webbed I-beams subjected to short-term loading. Res. Pap. FPL–RP–264. Madison, WI: U.S. Department of Agriculture, Forest Service, Forest Products Laboratory.

Superfesky, M.J.; Ramaker, T.J. 1978. Hardboard-webbed I-beams: Effects of long-term loading and loading environment. Res. Pap. FPL–RP–306. Madison, WI: U.S. Department of Agriculture, Forest Service, Forest Products Laboratory.

Timoshenko, S. 1961. Theory of elastic stability. 2d ed. New York: McGraw–Hill.

Structural Sandwich Construction

Allen, H.G. 1969. Analysis and design of structural sandwich panels. Oxford, England: Pergamon.

ASTM. 1997f. Annual book of ASTM standards. ASTM Section 15, Vol. 03. Philadelphia, PA: American Society for Testing and Materials.

C271–88. Density of core materials for structural sandwich constructions

C273–88. Shear properties in flatwise plane of flat sandwich constructions or sandwich core

C297–88. Tensile strength of flat sandwich constructions in flatwise plane

C363–88. Delamination strength of honeycomb type core material

C364–88. Compressive strength, edgewise, of flat sandwich constructions

C365–88. Compressive strength, flatwise, of sandwich cores

C366–88. Thickness of sandwich cores, measurement of

C393–88. Flexural properties of flat sandwich constructions

C394–88. Shear fatigue of sandwich core materials

C480–88. Flexure-creep of sandwich constructions

C481–88. Laboratory aging of sandwich constructions

Cheng, S. 1961. Torsion of sandwich plates of trapezoidal cross section. Journal of Applied Mechanics, American Society of Mechanical Engineers Transactions. 28(3): 363–366.

Hall, R.B. 1996. Performance limits for stiffness-critical graphitic foam structures. Pt. II. Comparisons of foams, foam-core and honeycomb-core sandwiches in bending/shear. Journal of Composite Materials. 30(17): 1938–1956.

Holmes, C.A. 1978. Room corner-wall fire tests of some structural sandwich panels and components. Journal of Fire and Flammability. 9: 467–488.

Holmes, C.A.; Eickner, H.W.; Brenden, J.J. [and others]. 1980. Fire development and wall endurance in sandwich and wood-frame structures. Res. Pap. FPL–RP–364. Madison, WI: U.S. Department of Agriculture, Forest Service, Forest Products Laboratory.

Karlsson, K.F.; Astrom, B.T. 1997. Manufacturing and applications of structural sandwich components. Composites, Part A: Applied Science and Manufacturing. 28(2): 88–97.

Kimel, W.R. 1956. Elastic buckling of a simply supported rectangular sandwich panel subjected to combined edgewise bending and compression- results for panels with facings of either equal or unequal thickness and with orthotropic cores. FPL Rep. 1857-A. Madison, WI: U.S. Department of Agriculture, Forest Service, Forest Products Laboratory.

Krajcinovic, D. 1972. Sandwich beam analysis. Journal of Applied Mechanics, American Society of Mechanical Engineers Transactions. 39(3): 773–778.

Kuenzi, E.W. 1970. Minimum weight structural sandwich. Res. Note FPL–086. Madison, WI: U.S. Department of Agriculture, Forest Service, Forest Products Laboratory.

Kuenzi, E.W.; Ericksen, W.S.; Zahn, J.J. 1962. Shear stability of flat panels of sandwich construction. FPL Rep. 1560. (Rev.) Madison, WI: U.S. Department of Agriculture, Forest Service, Forest Products Laboratory.

Kuenzi, E.W.; Bohannan, B.; Stevens, G.H. 1965. Buckling coefficients for sandwich cylinders of finite length under uniform external later pressure. Res. Note FPL–RN–0104. Madison, WI: U.S. Department of Agriculture, Forest Service, Forest Products Laboratory.

Noor, A.K.; Burton, W.S.; Bert, C.W. 1996. Computational models for sandwich panels and shells. Applied Mechanics Reviews. 49(3): 155–199.

Palms, J.; Sherwood, G.E. 1979. Structural sandwich performance after 31 years of service. Res. Pap. FPL–RP–342. Madison, WI: U.S. Department of Agriculture, Forest Service, Forest Products Laboratory.

Plantema, F.J. 1966. Sandwich construction. New York, NY: John Wiley.

Reddy, J.N.; Miravete, A. 1995. Practical analysis of composite laminates. Boca Raton, FL: CRC Press, Inc.

Seidl, R.J. 1952. Paper honeycomb cores for structural sandwich panels. FPL Rep. R1918. Madison, WI: U.S. Department of Agriculture, Forest Service, Forest Products Laboratory.

Sherwood, G.E. 1970. Longtime performance of sandwich panels in Forest Products Laboratory experimental unit. Res. Pap. FPL–RP–144. Madison, WI: U.S. Department of Agriculture, Forest Service, Forest Products Laboratory.

U.S. Department of Defense. 1968. Structural sandwich composites. Military Handbook 23A. Washington, DC: Superintendent of Documents.

Vinson, J.R.; Sierakowski, R.L. 1986. The behavior of structures composed of composite materials. Martinus Nijhoff.

Whitney, J.M. 1987. Structural analysis of laminated anisotropic plates. Lancaster, PA: Technomic Publishing Co., Inc.

Zahn, J.J.; Cheng, S. 1964. Edgewise compressive buckling of flat sandwich panels: Loaded ends simply supported and sides supported by beams. Res. Note FPL–RN–019. Madison, WI: U.S. Department of Agriculture, Forest Service, Forest Products Laboratory.

Zheng, Shiying; Yao, J. 1995. Exact solution of sandwich beams. Applied Mathematics and Mechanics. 16(6): 539–548.

Chapter 12

Drying and Control of Moisture Content and Dimensional Changes

William T. Simpson

Contents

n the living tree, wood contains large quantities of water. As green wood dries, most of the water is removed. The moisture remaining in the wood tends to come to equilibrium with the relative humidity of the surrounding air. Correct drying, handling, and storage of wood will minimize moisture content changes that might occur after drying when the wood is in service and such changes are undesirable. If moisture content is controlled within reasonable limits by such methods, major problems from dimensional changes can usually be avoided.

The discussion in this chapter is concerned with moisture content determination, recommended moisture content values, drying methods, methods of calculating dimensional changes, design factors affecting such changes in structures, and moisture content control during transit, storage, and construction. Data on green moisture content, fiber saturation point, shrinkage, and equilibrium moisture content are given with information on other physical properties in Chapter 3.

Wood in service is virtually always undergoing at least slight changes in moisture content. Changes in response to daily humidity changes are small and usually of no consequence. Changes that occur as a result of seasonal variation, although gradual, tend to be of more concern. Protective coatings can retard dimensional changes in wood but do not prevent them. In general, no significant dimensional changes will occur if wood is fabricated or installed at a moisture content corresponding to the average atmospheric conditions to which it will be exposed. When incompletely dried material is used in construction, some minor dimensional changes can be tolerated if the proper design is used.

Determination of Moisture Content

The amount of moisture in wood is ordinarily expressed as a percentage of the weight of the wood when ovendry. Four methods of determining moisture content are covered in ASTM D4442. Two of these—the oven-drying and the electrical methods—are described in this chapter.

The oven-drying method has been the most universally accepted method for determining moisture content, but it is slow and necessitates cutting the wood. In addition, the oven-drying method may give values slightly greater than true moisture content with woods containing volatile extractives. The electrical method is rapid, does not require cutting the wood, and can be used on wood in place in a structure. However, considerable care must be taken to use and interpret the results correctly. Use of the electrical method is generally limited to moisture content values less than 30%.

Oven-Drying Method

In the oven-drying method, specimens are taken from representative boards or pieces of a quantity of lumber. With lumber, the specimens should be obtained at least 500 mm (20 in.) from the end of the pieces. They should be free from knots and other irregularities, such as bark and pitch pockets. Specimens from lumber should be full cross sections and 25 mm (1 in.) long. Specimens from larger items may be representative sectors of such sections or subdivided increment borer or auger chip samples. Convenient amounts of chips and particles can be selected at random from larger batches, with care taken to ensure that the sample is representative of the batch. Veneer samples should be selected from four or five locations in a sheet to ensure that the sample average will accurately indicate the average of the sheet.

Each specimen should be weighed immediately, before any drying or reabsorption of moisture has taken place. If the specimen cannot be weighed immediately, it should be placed in a plastic bag or tightly wrapped in metal foil to protect it from moisture change until it can be weighed. After weighing, the specimen is placed in an oven heated to 101°C to 105°C (214°F to 221°F) and kept there until no appreciable weight change occurs in 4-h weighing intervals. A lumber section 25 mm (1 in.) along the grain will reach a constant weight in 12 to 48 h. Smaller specimens will take less time. The constant or ovendry weight and the weight of the specimen when cut are used to determine the percentage of moisture content using the formula

Moisture content (%)

$$= \frac{\text{Weight when cut} - \text{Ovendry weight}}{\text{Ovendry weight}} \times 100 \quad (12\text{–}1)$$

Electrical Method

The electrical method of determining the moisture content of wood uses the relationships between moisture content and measurable electrical properties of wood, such as conductivity (or its inverse, resistivity), dielectric constant, or power-loss factor. These properties vary in a definite and predictable way with changing moisture content, but correlations are not perfect. Therefore, moisture determinations using electrical methods are always subject to some uncertainty.

Electric moisture meters are available commercially and are based on each of these properties and identified by the property measured. Conductance-type (or resistance) meters measure moisture content in terms of the direct current conductance of the specimen. Dielectric-type meters are of two types. Those based principally on dielectric constant are called capacitance or capacitive admittance meters; those based on loss factor are called power-loss meters.

The principal advantages of the electrical method compared with the oven-drying method are speed and convenience. Only a few seconds are required for the determination, and the piece of wood being tested is not cut or damaged, except for driving electrode needle points into the wood when using conductance-type meters. Thus, the electrical method is adaptable to rapid sorting of lumber on the basis of moisture content, measuring the moisture content of wood installed in a building, or establishing the moisture content of a quantity of lumber or other wood items, when used in accordance with ASTM D4442.

For conductance meters, needle electrodes of various lengths are driven into the wood. There are two general types of electrodes: insulated and uninsulated. Uninsulated electrodes will sense the highest moisture content along their length (highest conductance). Moisture gradients between the surface and the interior can lead to confusion. If the wood is wetter near the center than the surface, which is typical for drying wood, the reading will correspond to the depth of the tip of the insulated electrodes. If a meter reading increases as the electrodes are being driven in, then the moisture gradient is typical. In this case, the pins should be driven in about one-fifth to one-fourth the thickness of the wood to reflect the average moisture content of the entire piece. Dried or partially dried wood sometimes regains moisture in the surface fibers, and the surface moisture content is greater than the interior. In this case, the meter with the uninsulated pins will read the higher moisture content surface, possibly causing a significant deviation from the average moisture content. To guard against this problem, electrodes with insulated shanks have been developed. They measure moisture content of only the wood at the tips of the electrodes.

Dielectric-type meters are fitted with surface contact electrodes designed for the type of specimen material being tested. The electric field from these electrodes penetrates well into the specimen, but with a strength that decreases rapidly with depth of penetration. For this reason, the readings of dielectric meters are influenced predominantly by the surface layers of the specimen, and the material near midthickness may not be adequately represented in the meter reading if there is a moisture content gradient.

To obtain accurate moisture content values, each instrument should be used in accordance with its manufacturer's instructions. The electrodes should be appropriate for the material being tested and properly oriented according to meter manufacturer's instructions. The readings should be carefully taken as soon as possible after inserting the electrode. A species correction supplied with the instrument should be applied when appropriate. Temperature corrections should then be made if the temperature of the wood differs considerably from the temperature of calibration used by the manufacturer.

Approximate corrections for conductance-type (resistance) meters are made by adding or subtracting about 0.5% for each 5.6°C (10°F) the wood temperature differs from the calibration temperature. The correction factors are added to the readings for temperatures less than the calibration temperature and subtracted from the readings for temperatures greater than the calibration temperature. Temperature corrections for dielectric meters are rather complex and are best made from published charts (James 1988).

Although some meters have scales that go up to 120%, the range of moisture content that can be measured reliably is 4% to about 30% for commercial dielectric meters and about 6% to 30% for resistance meters. The precision of the individual meter readings decreases near the limits of these ranges. Readings greater than 30% must be considered only qualitative. When the meter is properly used on a quantity of lumber dried to a reasonably constant moisture content below fiber saturation, the average moisture content from the corrected meter readings should be within 1% of the true average.

Recommended Moisture Content

Wood should be installed at moisture content levels as close as possible to the average moisture content it will experience in service. This minimizes the seasonal variation in moisture content and dimension after installation, avoiding problems such as floor buckling or cracks in furniture. The in-service moisture content of exterior wood (siding, wood trim) primarily depends on the outdoor relative humidity and exposure to rain or sun. The in-service moisture content of interior wood primarily depends on indoor relative humidity, which in turn is a complex function of moisture sources, ventilation rate, dehumidification (for example, air conditioning), and outdoor humidity conditions.

The recommended values for interior wood presented in this chapter are based on measurements in well-ventilated buildings without unusual moisture sources and without air conditioning. In air-conditioned buildings, moisture conditions depend to a great extent on the proper sizing of the air-conditioning equipment. Wood installed in basements or over a crawl space may experience a moisture content greater than the range provided, and wood in insulated walls or roofs and attics may experience a moisture content greater or less than the range. Nevertheless, the recommended values for installation provide a useful guideline.

Timbers

Ideally, solid timbers should be dried to the average moisture content they will reach in service. Although this optimum is possible with lumber less than 76 mm (3 in.) thick, it is seldom practical to obtain fully dried timbers, thick joists, and planks. When thick solid members are used, some shrinkage of the assembly should be expected. In the case of built-up assemblies, such as roof trusses, it may be necessary to tighten bolts or other fastenings occasionally to maintain full bearing of the connectors as the members shrink.

Lumber

The recommended moisture content of wood should be matched as closely as is practical to the equilibrium moisture content (EMC) conditions in service. Table 12–1 shows the EMC conditions in outdoor exposure in various U.S. cities for each month. The EMC data are based on the average relative humidity and temperature data (30 or more years) available from the National Climatic Data Center of the National Oceanic and Atmospheric Administration. The relative humidity data were the average of the morning and afternoon values, and in most cases would be representative of the EMC attained by the wood. However, in some locations, early morning relative humidity may occasionally reach 100%. Under these conditions, condensation may occur and the surface fibers of wood will exceed the EMC. The moisture content requirements are more exacting for finished lumber and wood products used inside heated and air-conditioned buildings than those for lumber used outdoors or in unheated buildings. For general areas of the United States, the recommended moisture content values for wood used inside heated buildings are shown in Figure 12–1. Values and tolerances for both interior and exterior uses of wood in various forms are given in Table 12–2. If the average moisture content is within 1% of that recommended and all pieces fall within the individual limits, the entire lot is probably satisfactory.

General commercial practice is to kiln dry wood for some products, such as flooring and furniture, to a slightly lower moisture content than service conditions demand, anticipating a moderate increase in moisture content during processing and construction. This practice is intended to ensure uniform distribution of moisture among the individual pieces. Common grades of softwood lumber and softwood dimension lumber are not normally dried to the moisture content values indicated in Table 12–2. Dry lumber, as defined in the American Softwood Lumber Standard, has a maximum moisture content of 19%. Some industry grading rules provide for an even lower maximum. For example, to be grade marked KD 15, the maximum moisture content permitted is generally 15%.

Glued Wood Products

When veneers are bonded with cold-setting adhesives to make plywood, they absorb comparatively large quantities of moisture. To keep the final moisture content low and to minimize redrying of the plywood, the initial moisture content of the veneer should be as low as practical. However, very dry veneer is brittle and difficult to handle without damage, so the minimum practical moisture content is about 4%. Freshly glued plywood intended for interior service should be dried to the moisture content values given in Table 12–2.

Table 12–1. Equilibrium moisture content of wood, exposed to outdoor atmosphere, in several U.S. locations in 1997

State	City	Equilibrium moisture content[a] (%)											
		Jan.	Feb.	Mar.	Apr.	May	June	July	Aug.	Sept.	Oct.	Nov.	Dec.
AK	Juneau	16.5	16.0	15.1	13.9	13.6	13.9	15.1	16.5	18.1	18.0	17.7	18.1
AL	Mobile	13.8	13.1	13.3	13.3	13.4	13.3	14.2	14.4	13.9	13.0	13.7	14.0
AZ	Flagstaff	11.8	11.4	10.8	9.3	8.8	7.5	9.7	11.1	10.3	10.1	10.8	11.8
AZ	Phoenix	9.4	8.4	7.9	6.1	5.1	4.6	6.2	6.9	6.9	7.0	8.2	9.5
AR	Little Rock	13.8	13.2	12.8	13.1	13.7	13.1	13.3	13.5	13.9	13.1	13.5	13.9
CA	Fresno	16.4	14.1	12.6	10.6	9.1	8.2	7.8	8.4	9.2	10.3	13.4	16.6
CA	Los Angeles	12.2	13.0	13.8	13.8	14.4	14.8	15.0	15.1	14.5	13.8	12.4	12.1
CO	Denver	10.7	10.5	10.2	9.6	10.2	9.6	9.4	9.6	9.5	9.5	11.0	11.0
DC	Washington	11.8	11.5	11.3	11.1	11.6	11.7	11.7	12.3	12.6	12.5	12.2	12.2
FL	Miami	13.5	13.1	12.8	12.3	12.7	14.0	13.7	14.1	14.5	13.5	13.9	13.4
GA	Atlanta	13.3	12.3	12.0	11.8	12.5	13.0	13.8	14.2	13.9	13.0	12.9	13.2
HI	Honolulu	13.3	12.8	11.9	11.3	10.8	10.6	10.6	10.7	10.8	11.3	12.1	12.9
ID	Boise	15.2	13.5	11.1	10.0	9.7	9.0	7.3	7.3	8.4	10.0	13.3	15.2
IL	Chicago	14.2	13.7	13.4	12.5	12.2	12.4	12.8	13.3	13.3	12.9	14.0	14.9
IN	Indianapolis	15.1	14.6	13.8	12.8	13.0	12.8	13.9	14.5	14.2	13.7	14.8	15.7
IA	Des Moines	14.0	13.9	13.3	12.6	12.4	12.6	13.1	13.4	13.7	12.7	13.9	14.9
KS	Wichita	13.8	13.4	12.4	12.4	13.2	12.5	11.5	11.8	12.6	12.4	13.2	13.9
KY	Louisville	13.7	13.3	12.6	12.0	12.8	13.0	13.3	13.7	14.1	13.3	13.5	13.9
LA	New Orleans	14.9	14.3	14.0	14.2	14.1	14.6	15.2	15.3	14.8	14.0	14.2	15.0
ME	Portland	13.1	12.7	12.7	12.1	12.6	13.0	13.0	13.4	13.9	13.8	14.0	13.5
MA	Boston	11.8	11.6	11.9	11.7	12.2	12.1	11.9	12.5	13.1	12.8	12.6	12.2
MI	Detroit	14.7	14.1	13.5	12.6	12.3	12.3	12.6	13.3	13.7	13.5	14.4	15.1
MN	Minneapolis–St.Paul	13.7	13.6	13.3	12.0	11.9	12.3	12.5	13.2	13.8	13.3	14.3	14.6
MS	Jackson	15.1	14.4	13.7	13.8	14.1	13.9	14.6	14.6	14.6	14.1	14.3	14.9
MO	St. Louis	14.5	14.1	13.2	12.4	12.8	12.6	12.9	13.3	13.7	13.1	14.0	14.9
MT	Missoula	16.7	15.1	12.8	11.4	11.6	11.7	10.1	9.8	11.3	12.9	16.2	17.6
NE	Omaha	14.0	13.8	13.0	12.1	12.6	12.9	13.3	13.8	14.0	13.0	13.9	14.8
NV	Las Vegas	8.5	7.7	7.0	5.5	5.0	4.0	4.5	5.2	5.3	5.9	7.2	8.4
NV	Reno	12.3	10.7	9.7	8.8	8.8	8.2	7.7	7.9	8.4	9.4	10.9	12.3
NM	Albuquerque	10.4	9.3	8.0	6.9	6.8	6.4	8.0	8.9	8.7	8.6	9.6	10.7
NY	New York	12.2	11.9	11.5	11.0	11.5	11.8	11.8	12.4	12.6	12.3	12.5	12.3
NC	Raleigh	12.8	12.1	12.2	11.7	13.1	13.4	13.8	14.5	14.5	13.7	12.9	12.8
ND	Fargo	14.2	14.6	15.2	12.9	11.9	12.9	13.2	13.2	13.7	13.5	15.2	15.2
OH	Cleveland	14.6	14.2	13.7	12.6	12.7	12.7	12.8	13.7	13.8	13.3	13.8	14.6
OK	Oklahoma City	13.2	12.9	12.2	12.1	13.4	13.1	11.7	11.8	12.9	12.3	12.8	13.2
OR	Pendleton	15.8	14.0	11.6	10.6	9.9	9.1	7.4	7.7	8.8	11.0	14.6	16.5
OR	Portland	16.5	15.3	14.2	13.5	13.1	12.4	11.7	11.9	12.6	15.0	16.8	17.4
PA	Philadelphia	12.6	11.9	11.7	11.2	11.8	11.9	12.1	12.4	13.0	13.0	12.7	12.7
SC	Charleston	13.3	12.6	12.5	12.4	12.8	13.5	14.1	14.6	14.5	13.7	13.2	13.2
SD	Sioux Falls	14.2	14.6	14.2	12.9	12.6	12.8	12.6	13.3	13.6	13.0	14.6	15.3
TN	Memphis	13.8	13.1	12.4	12.2	12.7	12.8	13.0	13.1	13.2	12.5	12.9	13.6
TX	Dallas–Ft.Worth	13.6	13.1	12.9	13.2	13.9	13.0	11.6	11.7	12.9	12.8	13.1	13.5
TX	El Paso	9.6	8.2	7.0	5.8	6.1	6.3	8.3	9.1	9.3	8.8	9.0	9.8
UT	Salt Lake City	14.6	13.2	11.1	10.0	9.4	8.2	7.1	7.4	8.5	10.3	12.8	14.9
VA	Richmond	13.2	12.5	12.0	11.3	12.1	12.4	13.0	13.7	13.8	13.5	12.8	13.0
WA	Seattle–Tacoma	15.6	14.6	15.4	13.7	13.0	12.7	12.2	12.5	13.5	15.3	16.3	16.5
WI	Madison	14.5	14.3	14.1	12.8	12.5	12.8	13.4	14.4	14.9	14.1	15.2	15.7
WV	Charleston	13.7	13.0	12.1	11.4	12.5	13.3	14.1	14.3	14.0	13.6	13.0	13.5
WY	Cheyenne	10.2	10.4	10.7	10.4	10.8	10.5	9.9	9.9	9.7	9.7	10.6	10.6

[a]EMC values were determined from the average of 30 or more years of relative humidity and temperature data available from the National Climatic Data Center of the National Oceanic and Atmospheric Administration.

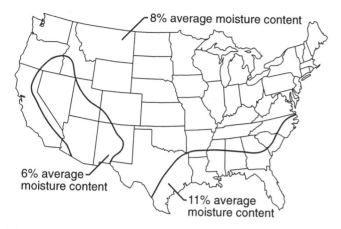

Figure 12–1. Recommended average moisture content for interior use of wood products in various areas of the United States.

Hot-pressed plywood and other board products, such as particleboard and hardboard, usually do not have the same moisture content as lumber. The high temperatures used in hot presses cause these products to assume a lower moisture content for a given relative humidity. Because this lower equilibrium moisture content varies widely, depending on the specific type of hot-pressed product, it is recommended that such products be conditioned at 30% to 40% relative humidity for interior use and 65% for exterior use.

Lumber used in the manufacture of large laminated members should be dried to a moisture content slightly less than the moisture content expected in service so that moisture absorbed from the adhesive will not cause the moisture content of the product to exceed the service value. The range of moisture content between laminations assembled into a single member should not exceed 5 percentage points. Although laminated members are often massive and respond rather slowly to changes in environmental conditions, it is desirable to follow the recommendations in Table 12–2 for moisture content at time of installation.

Drying of Wood

Drying is required for wood to be used in most products. Dried lumber has many advantages over green lumber for producers and consumers. Removal of excess water reduces weight, thus shipping and handling costs. Proper drying confines shrinking and swelling of wood in use to manageable amounts under all but extreme conditions of relative humidity or flooding. As wood dries, most of its strength properties increase, as well as its electrical and thermal insulating properties. Properly dried lumber can be cut to precise dimensions and machined more easily and efficiently; wood parts can be more securely fitted and fastened together with nails, screws, bolts, and adhesives; warping, splitting, checking, and other harmful effects of uncontrolled drying are largely eliminated; and paint, varnish, and other finishes are more effectively applied and maintained. Wood must be relatively dry before it can be glued or treated with decay-preventing and fire-retardant chemicals.

The key to successful and efficient drying is control of the drying process. Timely application of optimum or at least adequate temperature, relative humidity, and air circulation conditions is critical. Uncontrolled drying leads to drying defects that can adversely affect the serviceability and economics of the product. The usual strategy is to dry as fast as the particular species, thickness, and end-product requirements allow without damaging the wood. Slower drying can be uneconomical as well as introduce the risk of stain.

Softwood lumber intended for framing in construction is usually targeted for drying to an average moisture content of 15%, not to exceed 19%. Softwood lumber for many other uses is dried to a low moisture content, 10% to 12% for many appearance grades to as low as 7% to 9% for furniture, cabinets, and millwork. Hardwood lumber for framing in construction, although not in common use, should also be dried to an average moisture content of 15%, not to exceed 19%. Hardwood lumber for furniture, cabinets, and millwork is usually dried to 6% to 8% moisture content.

Table 12–2. Recommended moisture content values for various wood items at time of installation

| | Recommended moisture content (%) in various climatological regions | | | | | |
| | Most areas of the United States | | Dry southwestern area[a] | | Damp, warm coastal area[a] | |
Use of wood	Average[b]	Individual pieces	Average[b]	Individual pieces	Average[b]	Individual pieces
Interior: woodwork, flooring, furniture, wood trim	8	6–10	6	4–9	11	8–13
Exterior: siding, wood trim, sheathing, laminated timbers	12	9–14	9	7–12	12	9–14

[a]Major areas are indicated in Figure 12–1.
[b]To obtain a realistic average, test at least 10% of each item. If the quantity of a given item is small, make several tests. For example, in an ordinary dwelling having about 60 floor joists, at least 10 tests should be made on joists selected at random.

Lumber drying is usually accomplished by some combination of air drying, accelerated air drying or pre-drying, and kiln drying. Wood species, lumber thickness, economics, and end use are often the main factors in determining the details of the drying process.

Air Drying

The main purpose of air drying lumber is to evaporate as much of the water as possible before end use or transfer to a dry kiln. Air drying usually extends until wood moisture content is as low as 20% to 25%, at which time the lumber is transferred to a dry kiln if final drying to a lower moisture content is required. Sometimes, depending on a mill's scheduling, air drying may be cut short at a higher moisture content before the wood is sent to the dry kiln. Air drying saves energy costs and reduces required dry kiln capacity. Limitations of air drying are generally associated with uncontrolled drying. The drying rate is very slow during the cold winter months. At other times, hot, dry winds may increase degrade and volume losses as a result of severe surface checking and end splitting. Warm, humid periods with little air movement may encourage the growth of fungal stains, as well as aggravate chemical stains. Another limitation of air drying is the high cost of carrying a large inventory of high value lumber for extended periods. Air drying time to 20% to 25% moisture content varies widely, depending on species, thickness, location, and the time of year the lumber is stacked. Some examples of extremes for 25-mm- (1-in.-) thick lumber are 15 to 30 days for some of the low density species, such as pine, spruce, red alder, and soft maple, stacked in favorable locations and favorable times of the year, to 200 to 300 days for slow drying species, such as sinker hemlock and pine, oak, and birch, in northern locations and stacked at unfavorable times of the year. Details of important air drying considerations, such as lumber stacking and air drying yard layout, are covered in *Air Drying of Lumber: A Guide to Industry Practices* (Rietz and Page 1971).

Accelerated Air Drying and Pre-Drying

The limitations of air drying have led to increased use of technology that reduces drying time and introduces some control into drying from green to 20% to 25% moisture content. Accelerated air drying involves the use of fans to force air through lumber piles in a shed. This protects the lumber from the elements and improves air circulation compared with air drying. Small amounts of heat are sometimes used to reduce relative humidity and slightly increase temperature. Pre-dryers take this acceleration and control a step further by providing control of both temperature and relative humidity and providing forced air circulation in a completely enclosed compartment. Typical conditions in a pre-dryer are 27°C to 38°C (80°F to 100°F) and 65% to 85% relative humidity.

Kiln Drying

In kiln drying, higher temperatures and faster air circulation are used to increase drying rate considerably. Specific kiln schedules have been developed to control temperature and relative humidity in accordance with the moisture content and stress situation within the wood, thus minimizing shrinkage-caused defects.

Drying Mechanism

Water in wood normally moves from high to low zones of moisture content, which means that the surface of the wood must be drier than the interior if moisture is to be removed. Drying can be broken down into two phases: movement of water from the interior to the surface of the wood and evaporation of water from the surface. The surface fibers of most species reach moisture equilibrium with the surrounding air soon after drying begins. This is the beginning of the development of a typical moisture gradient (Fig. 12–2), that is, the difference in moisture content between the inner and outer portions of a board. If air circulation is too slow, a longer time is required for the surfaces of the wood to reach moisture equilibrium. This is one reason why air circulation is so important in kiln drying. If air circulation is too slow, drying is also slower than necessary and mold could develop on the surface of lumber. If drying is too fast, electrical energy in running the fans is wasted, and in certain species,

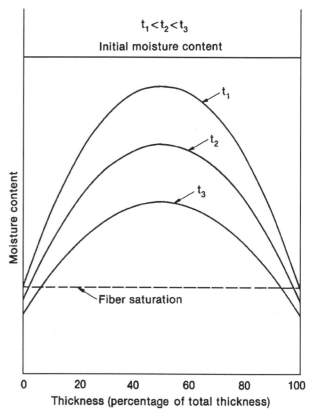

Figure 12–2. Typical moisture gradient in lumber during drying at time increasing from t_1 to t_3.

surface checking and other drying defects can develop if relative humidity and air velocity are not coordinated.

Water moves through the interior of wood as a liquid or vapor through various air passageways in the cellular structure of the wood, as well as through the wood cell walls. Moisture moves in these passageways in all directions, both across and with the grain. In general, lighter species dry faster than heavier species because the structure of lighter wood contains more openings per unit volume and moisture moves through air faster than through wood cell walls. Water moves by two main mechanisms: capillary action (liquid) and diffusion of bound water (vapor). Capillary action causes free water to flow through cell cavities and the small passageways that connect adjacent cell cavities. Diffusion of bound water moves moisture from areas of high concentration to areas of low concentration. Diffusion in the longitudinal direction is about 10 to 15 times faster than radial or tangential diffusion, and radial diffusion is somewhat faster than tangential diffusion. This explains why flatsawn lumber generally dries faster than quartersawn lumber. Although longitudinal diffusion is much faster than diffusion across the grain, it generally is not of practical importance in lumber that is many times longer than it is thick.

Because chemical extractives in heartwood plug up passageways, moisture generally moves more freely in sapwood than in heartwood; thus, sapwood generally dries faster than heartwood. However, the heartwood of many species is lower in moisture content than is the sapwood and can reach final moisture content as fast.

The rate at which moisture moves in wood depends on the relative humidity of the surrounding air, the steepness of the moisture gradient, and the temperature of the wood. The lower the relative humidity, the greater the capillary flow. Low relative humidity also stimulates diffusion by lowering the moisture content at the surface, thereby steepening the moisture gradient and increasing the diffusion rate. The greater the temperature of the wood, the faster moisture will move from the wetter interior to the drier surface. If relative humidity is too low in the early stages of drying, excessive shrinkage may occur, resulting in surface and end checking. If the temperature is too high, collapse, honeycomb, or strength reduction can occur.

Drying Stresses

Drying stresses are the main cause of nonstain-related drying defects. Understanding these stresses provides a means for minimizing and recognizing the damage they can cause. The cause of drying stresses in the differential shrinkage between the outer part of a board (the shell) and the interior part (the core) can also cause drying defects. Early in drying, the fibers in the shell dry first and begin to shrink. However, the core has not yet begun to dry and shrink; consequently, the core prevents the shell from shrinking. Thus, the shell goes into tension and the core into compression (Fig. 12–3). If the shell dries too rapidly, it is stressed beyond the elastic limit and dries in a permanently stretched (set) condition without attaining full shrinkage. Sometimes surface cracks,

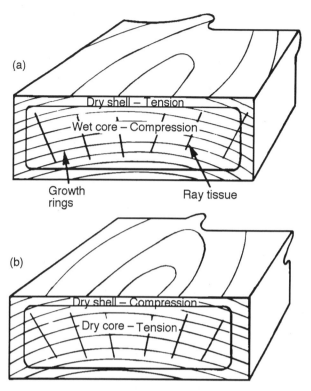

Figure 12–3. End view of board showing development of drying stresses (a) early and (b) later in drying.

or checks, occur during this initial stage of drying, and they can be a serious defect for many uses. As drying progresses, the core begins to dry and attempts to shrink. However, the shell is set in a permanently expanded condition and prevents normal shrinkage of the core. This causes the stresses to reverse; the core goes into tension and the shell into compression. The change in the shell and core stresses and in the moisture content level during drying is shown in Figure 12–4. These internal tension stresses may be severe enough to cause internal cracks (honeycomb).

Differential shrinkage caused by differences in radial, tangential, and longitudinal shrinkage is a major cause of warp. The distortions shown in Figure 3–3 in Chapter 3 are due to differential shrinkage. When juvenile or reaction wood is present on one edge or face of a board and normal wood is present on the opposite side, the difference in their longitudinal shrinkage can also cause warp.

Dry Kilns

Most dry kilns are thermally insulated compartments designed for a batch process in which the kiln is completely loaded with lumber in one operation and the lumber remains stationary during the entire drying cycle. Temperature and relative humidity are kept as uniform as possible throughout the kiln and can be controlled over a wide range. Temperature and relative humidity are changed as the wood dries based on a schedule that takes into account the moisture content and/or the drying rate of the lumber. All dry kilns

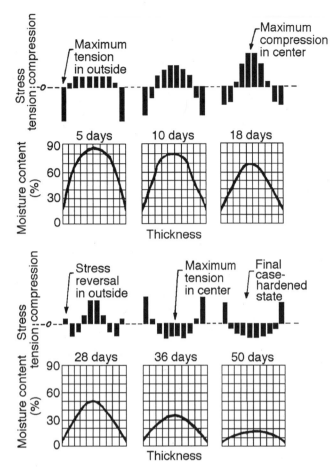

Figure 12–4. Moisture–stress relationship during six stages of kiln drying 50-mm- (2-in.-) thick red oak.

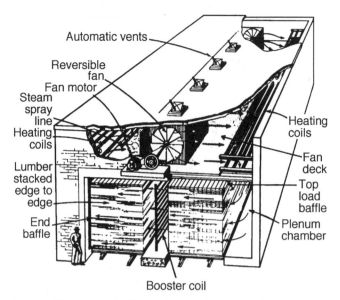

Figure 12–5. Lineshaft, double-track, compartment kiln with alternately opposing fans. Vents are over fan shaft between fans. Vent on high pressure side of fans becomes fresh air inlet when direction of circulation is reversed.

use some type of forced-air circulation, with air moving through the lumber perpendicular to the length of the lumber and parallel to the spacers (stickers) that separate each layer of lumber in a stack.

Three general types of kilns are in common use. One is the track-loaded type (Fig. 12–5), where lumber is stacked on kiln trucks that are rolled in and out of the kiln on tracks. The majority of softwood lumber in the United States is dried in this kiln type. Another major type is the package-loaded kiln (Fig 12–6), where individual stacks of lumber are fork-lifted into place in the kiln. This type of kiln is commonly used for drying hardwood lumber. These kilns are most commonly heated with steam, although softwood lumber kilns are sometimes directly heated. A third common type of kiln, usually package loaded, is the dehumidification kiln. Instead of venting humid air to remove water, as the other two types of kilns do, water is removed by condensation on cold dehumidifier coils (Fig. 12–7).

Kiln Schedules

A kiln schedule is a carefully developed compromise between the need to dry lumber as fast as possible for economic

efficiency and the need to avoid severe drying conditions that will lead to drying defects. A kiln schedule is a series of temperatures and relative humidities that are applied at various stages of drying. In most schedules, the temperature is gradually increased and the relative humidity decreased. The schedule for Southern Pine structural lumber is an exception to this general rule. This is lumber usually dried at a constant temperature and relative humidity. Temperatures are chosen to strike this compromise of a satisfactory drying rate and avoidance of objectionable drying defects. The stresses that develop during drying are the limiting factor in determining the kiln schedule. The schedule must be developed so that the drying stresses do not exceed the strength of the wood at any given temperature and moisture content. Otherwise, the wood will crack either on the surface or internally or be crushed by forces that collapse the wood cells. Wood generally becomes stronger as the moisture content decreases, and to a lesser extent, it becomes weaker as temperature increases. The net result is that as wood dries it becomes stronger because of the decreasing moisture content and can tolerate higher drying temperatures and lower relative humidities without cracking. This is a fortunate circumstance because as wood dries, its drying rate decreases at any given temperature, and the ability to increase drying temperature helps maintain a reasonably fast drying rate. Thus, rapid drying is achieved in kilns by the use of temperatures as high as possible and relative humidities as low as possible.

Drying schedules vary by species, thickness, grade, and end use of lumber. There are two general types of kiln schedules: moisture content schedules and time-based schedules. Most hardwood lumber is dried by moisture content schedules. This means that the temperature and relative humidity conditions are changed according to various moisture content

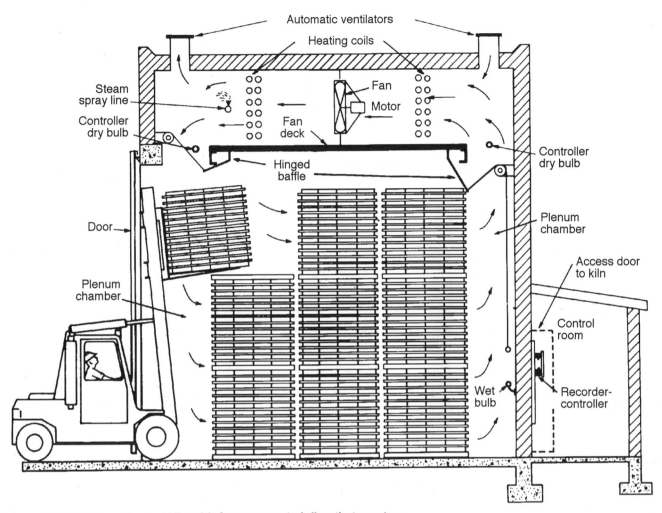

Figure 12–6. Package-loaded kiln with fans connected directly to motors.

evels attained by the lumber during drying. A typical hard-wood schedule might begin at 49°C (120°F) and 80% rela-ive humidity when the lumber is green. By the time the umber has reached 15% moisture content, the temperature is s high as 82°C (180°F). A typical hardwood drying sched-le is shown in Table 12–3. Some method of monitoring moisture content during drying is required for schedules based on moisture content. One common method is the use of short kiln samples that are periodically weighed, usually manually but potentially remotely with load cells. Alterna-ively, electrodes are imbedded in sample boards to sense the change in electrical conductivity with moisture content. This system is limited to moisture content values less than 30%.

Softwood kiln schedules generally differ from hardwood schedules in that changes in kiln temperature and relative humidity are made at predetermined times rather than mois-ure content levels. Examples of time-based schedules, both conventional temperature (<100°C (<212°F)) and high temperature (>110°C (>230°F)), are given in Table 12–3.

Drying Defects

Most drying defects or problems that develop in wood prod-ucts during drying can be classified as fracture or distortion, warp, or discoloration. Defects in any one of these categories are caused by an interaction of wood properties with process-ing factors. Wood shrinkage is mainly responsible for wood ruptures and distortion of shape. Cell structure and chemical extractives in wood contribute to defects associated with uneven moisture content, undesirable color, and undesirable surface texture. Drying temperature is the most important processing factor because it can be responsible for defects in each category.

Fracture or Distortion

Surface checks occur early in drying when the shell of a board is stressed in tension enough to fracture the wood. These checks occur most often on the face of flatsawn boards and are illustrated in Figure 12–8. End checks (Fig. 12–9) are simi-lar to surface checks but appear on the ends of boards. End checks occur because the rapid longitudinal movement of moisture causes the board end to dry very quickly and

271

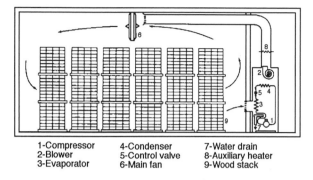

1-Compressor	4-Condenser	7-Water drain
2-Blower	5-Control valve	8-Auxiliary heater
3-Evaporator	6-Main fan	9-Wood stack

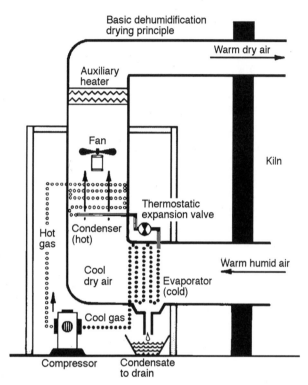

Fig. 12–7. A typical dehumidification kiln (top) and dehumidification drying system (bottom).

develop high stresses, therefore fracturing. End coatings, either on the log or freshly sawn lumber, are an effective preventative measure. Collapse is a distortion, flattening, or crushing of wood cells. In severe cases (Fig. 12–10), collapse usually shows up as grooves or corrugations, a washboarding effect. Less severe collapse shows up as excessive thickness shrinkage and may not be a serious problem. Honeycomb (Fig. 12–11) is an internal crack that occurs in the later stages of kiln drying when the core of a board is in tension. It is caused when the core is still at a relatively high moisture content and drying temperatures are too high for too long during this critical drying period. Nondestructive testing methods, using speed of sound, have been found to be effective in detecting the presence of these cracks in dried lumber. Knots may loosen during drying because of the unequal shrinkage between the knot and the surrounding wood (Fig. 12–12).

Warp

Warp in lumber is any deviation of the face or edge of a board from flatness or any edge that is not at right angles to the adjacent face or edge. Warp can be traced to two causes: (a) differences between radial, tangential, and longitudinal shrinkage in the piece as it dries or (b) growth stresses. Warp is aggravated by irregular or distorted grain and the presence of abnormal types of wood, such as juvenile and reaction wood. The six major types of warp are bow, crook, twist, oval, diamond, and cup (Fig. 12–13).

Discoloration

The use of dried wood products can be impaired by discoloration, particularly when the end use requires a clear, natural finish. Unwanted discoloration can develop in the tree, during storage of logs and green lumber, or during drying. There are two general types of discoloration: chemical and fungal.

Chemical discoloration is the result of oxidative and enzymatic reactions with chemical constituents in wood. Discolorations range from pinkish, bluish, and yellowish hues through gray and reddish brown to dark brown shades. Brown stain in pines and darkening in many hardwoods is a common problem when drying temperatures are too high (Fig. 12–14). A deep grayish-brown chemical discoloration can occur in many hardwood species if initial drying is too slow (Fig. 12–15).

Fungal stains, often referred to as blue or sap stain, are caused by fungi that grow in the sapwood (Fig. 12–16). Blue-stain fungi do not cause decay of the sapwood, and fungi generally do not grow in heartwood. Blue stain can develop if initial drying is too slow.

Another common type of stain develops under stickers (Fig. 12–17). This stain results from contact of the sticker with the board. Sticker stains (sometimes called shadow) are imprints of the sticker that are darker or lighter than the wood between the stickers and can be caused by either chemical or fungal action, or both.

Moisture Content of Dried Lumber

Although widely used, the trade terms "shipping dry," "air dry," and "kiln dry" may not have identical meanings as to moisture content in the different producing regions. Despite the wide variations in the use of these terms, they are sometimes used to describe dried lumber. The following statements, which are not exact definitions, outline these categories.

Shipping Dry

Shipping dry means lumber that has been partially dried to prevent stain or mold during brief periods of transit; ideally the outer 3.2 mm (1/8 in.) is dried to 25% or less moisture content.

Table 12–3. Typical dry kiln schedules for lumber

Moisture content-based schedule for 25-mm (1-in.) (4/4) black walnut, dried to 7% moisture content

Moisture content (%)	Temperature (°C(°F))		Relative humidity (%)	Equilibrium moisture content (%)
	Dry-bulb	Wet-bulb		
Above 50	49.0 (120)	45.0 (113)	80	14.4
50 to 40	49.0 (120)	43.5 (110)	72	12.1
40 to 35	49.0 (120)	40.5 (105)	60	9.6
35 to 30	49.0 (120)	35.0 (95)	40	6.5
30 to 25	54.5 (130)	32.0 (90)	22	4.0
25 to 20	60.0 (140)	32.0 (90)	15	2.9
20 to 15	65.5 (150)	37.5 (100)	18	3.2
15 to 7	82.2 (180)	54.5 (130)	26	3.5
Equalize	82.2 (180)	58.3 (137)	30	3.8
Condition	82.2 (180)	76.7 (170)	79	11.1

Time-based schedule for 25- to 50-mm (1- to 2-in.) (4/4 to 8/4) Douglas Fir, upper grades, dried to 12% moisture content

Time (h)	Temperature (°C(°F))		Relative humidity (%)	Equilibrium moisture content (%)
	Dry-bulb	Wet-bulb		
0 to 12	76.5 (170)	73.5 (164)	86	14.1
12 to 24	76.5 (170)	71.0 (160)	78	11.4
24 to 48	79.5 (175)	71.0 (160)	69	9.1
48 to 72	82.2 (180)	71.0 (160)	62	7.7
72 to 96 or until dry	82.2 (180)	60.0 (140)	36	4.5

High temperature schedule for 50- by 100-mm to 50- by 250-mm (2- by 4-in. to 2- by 10-in.) Southern Pine, dried to 15% moisture content

Time (h)	Temperature (°C(°F))		Relative humidity (%)	Equilibrium moisture content (%)
	Dry-bulb	Wet-bulb		
0 until dry	116 (240)	82.2 (180)	29	2.5

Air Dry

Air dry means lumber that has been dried by exposure to the air outdoors or in a shed or by forced circulation of air that has not been heated above 49°C (120°F). Commercial air-dry stock generally has an average moisture content low enough for rapid kiln drying or rough construction use. Moisture content is generally in the range of 20% to 25% for dense hardwoods and 15% to 20% for softwoods and low-density hardwoods. Extended exposure can bring standard 19- and 38-mm (nominal 1- and 2-in.) lumber within one or two percentage points of the average exterior equilibrium moisture content of the region. For much of the United States, the minimum moisture content of thoroughly air-dried lumber is 12% to 15%.

Figure 12–8. Surface checking on Douglas Fir dimension lumber.

Figure 12–9. End checking in oak lumber.

Figure 12–10. Severe collapse in western redcedar.

Figure 12–11. Board machined into millwork shows honeycomb (top). Surface of planed red oak board shows no honeycomb (bottom).

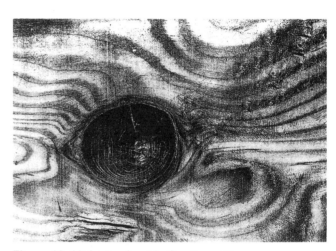

Figure 12–12. Loose knot in Southern Pine.

Kiln Dry

Kiln dry means lumber that has been dried in a kiln or by some special drying method to an average moisture content specified or understood to be suitable for a certain use. The average moisture content should have upper and lower tolerance limits, and all values should fall within these limits. Kiln-dried softwood dimension lumber generally has an average moisture content of 19% or less; the average moisture content for many other softwood uses is 10% to 20%. Hardwood and softwood lumber for furniture, cabinetry, and millwork usually has a final moisture content of 6% to 8% and can be specified to be free of drying stresses. The importance of suitable moisture content values is recognized, and provisions covering them are now incorporated in some softwood standards as grading rules. Moisture content values in the general grading rules may or may not be suitable for a specific use; if not, a special moisture content specification should be made.

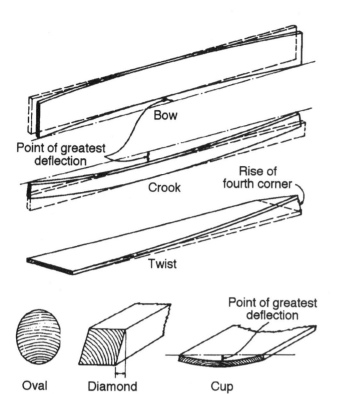

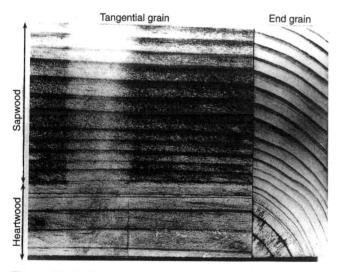

Figure 12–13. Various types of warp that can develop in boards during drying.

Oval

Diamond

Cup

Point of greatest deflection

Bow

Point of greatest deflection

Crook

Rise of fourth corner

Twist

Figure 12–14. Brown sapwood stain in Southern Pine lumber.

Tangential grain

End grain

Sapwood

Heartwood

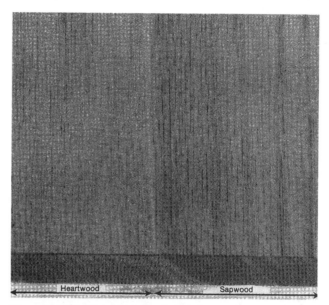

Heartwood

Sapwood

Figure 12–15. Gray sapwood stain in southern red oak that was dried green with humid, low temperature conditions and poor air circulation.

Figure 12–16. Sap stain in Southern Pine. Color ranges from bluish gray to black.

Figure 12–17. Sticker stain in sapwood of sugar maple after planing.

Moisture Control During Transit and Storage

Lumber and other wood items may change in moisture content and dimension while awaiting shipment, during fabrication, in transit, and in storage.

When standard 19-mm (nominal 1-in.) dry softwood lumber is shipped in tightly closed boxcars, shipping containers, or trucks or in packages with complete and intact wrappers, average moisture content changes for a package can generally be held to 0.2% or less per month. In holds or between decks of ships, dry material usually adsorbs about 1.5% moisture during normal shipping periods. If green material is included in the cargo, the moisture regain of the dry lumber may be doubled. On the top deck, if unprotected from the elements, the moisture regain can be as much as 7%.

When standard 19-mm (nominal 1-in.) softwood lumber, kiln dried to 8% or less, is piled solid under a good pile roof in a yard in humid weather, average moisture content of a pile can increase at the rate of about 2% per month during the first 45 days. An absorption rate of about 1% per month can then be sustained throughout a humid season. Comparable initial and sustaining absorption rates are about 1% per month in open (roofed) sheds and 0.3% per month in closed sheds. Stock that was piled for a year in an open shed in a western location increased 2.7% on the inside of solid piles and 3.5% on the outside of the piles. All stock that has been manufactured in any way should be protected from precipitation and spray, because water that gets into a solid pile tends to be absorbed by the wood instead of evaporating. The extent to which additional control of the storage environment is required depends upon the use to which the wood will be put and the corresponding moisture content recommendations. The moisture content of all stock should be determined when it is received. If moisture content is not as specified or required, stickered storage in an appropriate condition could ultimately bring the stock within the desired moisture content range. If a large degree of moisture change is required, the stock must be redried.

Plywood and Structural Items

Green or partially dried lumber and timbers should be open piled on stickers and protected from sunshine and precipitation by a tight roof. Framing lumber and plywood with 20% or less moisture content can be solid piled in a shed that provides good protection against sunshine and direct or wind-driven precipitation. However, a better practice for stock with greater than 12% moisture content is the use of stickered piling to bring moisture content more in line with the moisture content in use. Dry lumber can be piled solid in the open for relatively short periods, but at least a minimum pile cover of waterproofed paper should be used whenever possible. Because it is difficult to keep rain out completely, storing solid-piled lumber in the open for long periods is not recommended. If framing lumber must be stored in the open for a long time, it should be piled on stickers over good supports and the piles should be roofed. Solid-piled material that has become wet again should also be re-piled on stickers.

Table 12–4. Amount by which temperature of storage area must be increased above outside temperature to maintain equilibrium moisture content

Outside relative humidity (%)	Temperature differential (°C (°F)) for desired equilibrium moisture content						
	6%	7%	8%	9%	10%	11%	12%
90	18.3 (33)	16.1 (29)	12.8 (23)	10.0 (18)	8.3 (15)	6.1 (11)	5.0 (9)
80	16.7 (30)	13.9 (25)	10.5 (19)	7.8 (14)	6.1 (11)	4.4 (8)	3.3 (6)
70	13.9 (25)	11.1 (20)	8.3 (15)	5.6 (10)	3.9 (7)	2.2 (4)	1.7 (3)
60	11.1 (20)	8.3 (15)	5.0 (9)	3.3 (6)	1.7 (3)	—	—
50	8.3 (15)	5.6 (10)	2.8 (5)	0.6 (1)	—	—	—

Finish and Factory Lumber

Such kiln-dried items as exterior finish, siding, and exterior millwork should be stored in a closed but unheated shed. They should be placed on supports raised above the floor, at least 150 mm (6 in.) high if the floor is paved or 300 mm (12 in.) if not paved. Interior trim, flooring, cabinet work, and lumber for processing into furniture should be stored in a room or closed shed where relative humidity is controlled. Kiln-dried and machined hardwood dimension or softwood cut stock should also be stored under controlled humidity conditions.

Dried and machined hardwood dimension or softwood lumber intended for remanufacture should also be stored under controlled humidity conditions. Under uncontrolled conditions, the ends of such stock may attain a greater moisture content than the balance of the length. Then, when the stock is straight-line ripped or jointed before edge gluing, subsequent shrinkage will cause splitting or open glue joints at the ends of panels. The simplest way to reduce relative humidity in storage areas of all sizes is to heat the space to a temperature slightly greater than that of the outside air. Dehumidifiers can be used in small, well-enclosed spaces.

If the heating method is used, and there is no source of moisture except that contained in the air, the equilibrium moisture content can be maintained by increasing the temperature of the storage area greater than the outside temperature by the amounts shown in Table 12–4. When a dehumidifier is used, the average temperature in the storage space should be known or controlled. Table 3–4 in Chapter 3 should be used to select the proper relative humidity to give the desired average moisture content. Wood in a factory awaiting or following manufacture can become too dry if the area is heated to 21°C (70°F) or greater when the outdoor temperature is low. This often occurs in the northern United States during the winter. Under such circumstances, exposed ends and surfaces of boards or cut pieces will tend to dry to the low equilibrium moisture content condition, causing shrinkage and warp. In addition, an equilibrium moisture content of 4% or more below the moisture content of the core of freshly crosscut boards can cause end checking. Simple remedies are to cover piles of partially manufactured items with plastic film and lower the shop temperature during nonwork hours. Increased control can be obtained in critical shop and storage areas by humidification. In warm weather, cooling can increase relative humidity and dehumidification may be necessary.

Dimensional Changes in Wood

Dry wood undergoes small changes in dimension with normal changes in relative humidity. More humid air will cause slight swelling, and drier air will cause slight shrinkage. These changes are considerably smaller than those involved with shrinkage from the green condition. Equation (12–2) can be used to approximate dimensional changes caused by shrinking and swelling by using the total shrinkage coefficient from green to ovendry. However, the equation assumes that the shrinkage–moisture content relationship is linear. Figure 3–4 (Ch. 3) shows that this is not the case, so some error is introduced. The error is in the direction of underestimating dimensional change, by about 5% of the true change. Many changes of moisture content in use are over the small moisture content range of 6% to 14%, where the shrinkage–moisture content relationship is linear (Ch. 3, Fig. 3–4). Therefore, a set of shrinkage coefficients based on the linear portion of the shrinkage–moisture content curve has been developed (Table 12–5). Approximate changes in dimension can be estimated by a simple formula that involves a dimensional change coefficient, from Table 12–5, when moisture content remains within the range of normal use. (Dimensional changes are further discussed in Chs. 3 and 6.)

Estimation Using Dimensional Change Coefficient

The change in dimension within the moisture content limits of 6% to 14% can be estimated satisfactorily by using a dimensional change coefficient based on the dimension at 10% moisture content:

$$\Delta D = D_I\big[C_T(M_F - M_I)\big] \tag{12–2}$$

where ΔD is change in dimension, D_I dimension in units of length at start of change, C_T dimensional change coefficient tangential direction (for radial direction, use C_R), M_F moisture content (%) at end of change, and M_I moisture content (%) at start of change.

Values for C_T and C_R, derived from total shrinkage values, are given in Table 12–5. When $M_F < M_I$, the quantity $(M_F - M_I)$ will be negative, indicating a decrease in dimension; when greater, it will be positive, indicating an increase in dimension.

As an example, assuming the width of a flat-grained white fir board is 232 mm (9.15 in.) at 8% moisture content, its change in width at 11% moisture content is estimated as

$$\Delta D = 232[0.00245(11 - 8)]$$
$$= 232(0.00735)$$
$$= 1.705 \text{ mm}$$
$$\Delta D = 9.15[0.00245(11 - 8)]$$
$$= 9.15[0.00735]$$
$$= 0.06725 \text{ or } 0.067 \text{ in.}$$

Then, dimension at end of change

$$D_I + \Delta D = 232 + 1.7 \qquad (= 9.15 + 0.067)$$
$$= 233.7 \text{ mm} \qquad (= 9.217 \text{ in.})$$

The thickness of the same board at 11% moisture content can be estimated by using the coefficient $C_R = 0.00112$.

Table 12–5. Coefficients for dimensional change as a result of shrinking or swelling within moisture content limits of 6% to 14% (C_T = dimensional change coefficient for tangential direction; C_R = radial direction)

Species	Dimensional change coefficient[a]		Species	Dimensional change coefficient[a]	
	C_R	C_T		C_R	C_T
Hardwoods					
Alder, red	0.00151	0.00256	Honeylocust	0.00144	0.00230
Apple	0.00205	0.00376	Locust, black	0.00158	0.00252
Ash, black	0.00172	0.00274	Madrone, Pacific	0.00194	0.00451
Ash, Oregon	0.00141	0.00285	Magnolia, cucumbertree	0.00180	0.00312
Ash, pumpkin	0.00126	0.00219	Magnolia, southern	0.00187	0.00230
Ash, white	0.00169	0.00274	Magnolia, sweetbay	0.00162	0.00293
Ash, green	0.00169	0.00274	Maple, bigleaf	0.00126	0.00248
Aspen, quaking	0.00119	0.00234	Maple, red	0.00137	0.00289
Basswood, American	0.00230	0.00330	Maple, silver	0.00102	0.00252
Beech, American	0.00190	0.00431	Maple, black	0.00165	0.00353
Birch, paper	0.00219	0.00304	Maple, sugar	0.00165	0.00353
Birch, river	0.00162	0.00327	Oak, black	0.00123	0.00230
Birch, yellow	0.00256	0.00338	Red Oak, commercial	0.00158	0.00369
Birch, sweet	0.00256	0.00338	Red oak, California	0.00123	0.00230
Buckeye, yellow	0.00123	0.00285	Red oak: water, laurel, willow	0.00151	0.00350
Butternut	0.00116	0.00223	White Oak, commercial	0.00180	0.00365
Catalpa, northern	0.00085	0.00169	White oak, live	0.00230	0.00338
Cherry, black	0.00126	0.00248	White oak, Oregon white	0.00144	0.00327
Chestnut, American	0.00116	0.00234	White oak, overcup	0.00183	0.00462
Cottonwood, black	0.00123	0.00304	Persimmon, common	0.00278	0.00403
Cottonwood, eastern	0.00133	0.00327	Sassafras	0.00137	0.00216
Elm, American	0.00144	0.00338	Sweet gum	0.00183	0.00365
Elm, rock	0.00165	0.00285	Sycamore, American	0.00172	0.00296
Elm, slippery	0.00169	0.00315	Tanoak	0.00169	0.00423
Elm, winged	0.00183	0.00419	Tupelo, black	0.00176	0.00308
Elm, cedar	0.00183	0.00419	Tupelo, water	0.00144	0.00267
Hackberry	0.00165	0.00315	Walnut, black	0.00190	0.00274
Hickory, pecan	0.00169	0.00315	Willow, black	0.00112	0.00308
Hickory, true	0.00259	0.00411	Willow, Pacific	0.00099	0.00319
Holly, American	0.00165	0.00353	Yellow-poplar	0.00158	0.00289
Softwoods					
Baldcypress	0.00130	0.00216	Pine, eastern white	0.00071	0.00212
Cedar, yellow	0.00095	0.00208	Pine, jack	0.00126	0.00230
Cedar, Atlantic white	0.00099	0.00187	Pine, loblolly	0.00165	0.00259
Cedar, eastern red	0.00106	0.00162	Pine, pond	0.00165	0.00259
Cedar, Incense	0.00112	0.00180	Pine, lodgepole	0.00148	0.00234
Cedar, Northern white[b]	0.00101	0.00229	Pine, Jeffrey	0.00148	0.00234
Cedar, Port-Orford	0.00158	0.00241	Pine, longleaf	0.00176	0.00263
Cedar, western red[b]	0.00111	0.00234	Pine, ponderosa	0.00133	0.00216
Douglas-fir, Coast-type	0.00165	0.00267	Pine, red	0.00130	0.00252
Douglas-fir, Interior north	0.00130	0.00241	Pine, shortleaf	0.00158	0.00271
Douglas-fir, Interior west	0.00165	0.00263	Pine, slash	0.00187	0.00267
Fir, balsam	0.00099	0.00241	Pine, sugar	0.00099	0.00194
Fir, California red	0.00155	0.00278	Pine, Virginia	0.00144	0.00252
Fir, noble	0.00148	0.00293	Pine, western white	0.00141	0.00259

Table 12–5. Coefficients for dimensional change as a result of shrinkage or swelling within moisture content limits of 6% to 14% (C_T = dimensional change coefficient for tangential direction; C_R = radial direction)—con.

Species	Dimensional change coefficient[a]		Species	Dimensional change coefficient[a]	
	C_R	C_T		C_R	C_T
Softwoods—con.					
Fir, Pacific silver	0.00151	0.00327	Redwood, old-growth[b]	0.00120	0.00205
Fir, subalpine	0.00088	0.00259	Redwood, second-growth[b]	0.00101	0.00229
Fir, grand	0.00112	0.00245	Spruce, black	0.00141	0.00237
Fir, white	0.00112	0.00245	Spruce, Engelmann	0.00130	0.00248
Hemlock, eastern	0.00102	0.00237	Spruce, red	0.00130	0.00274
Hemlock, western	0.00144	0.00274	Spruce, white	0.00130	0.00274
Larch, western	0.00155	0.00323	Spruce, Sitka	0.00148	0.00263
			Tamarack	0.00126	0.00259
Imported Woods					
Andiroba, crabwood	0.00137	0.00274	Light red "Philippine mahogany"	0.00126	0.00241
Angelique	0.00180	0.00312	Limba	0.00151	0.00187
Apitong, keruing[b] (all *Dipterocarpus* spp.)	0.00243	0.00527	Mahogany[b]	0.00172	0.00238
			Meranti	0.00126	0.00289
Avodire	0.00126	0.00226	Obeche	0.00106	0.00183
Balsa	0.00102	0.00267	Okoume	0.00194	0.00212
Banak	0.00158	0.00312	Parana, pine	0.00137	0.00278
Cativo	0.00078	0.00183	Paumarfim	0.00158	0.00312
Cuangare	0.00183	0.00342	Primavera	0.00106	0.00180
Greenheart[b]	0.00390	0.00430	Ramin	0.00133	0.00308
Iroko[b]	0.00153	0.00205	Santa Maria	0.00187	0.00278
Khaya	0.00141	0.00201	Spanish-cedar	0.00141	0.00219
Kokrodua[b]	0.00148	0.00297	Teak[b]	0.00101	0.00186
Lauans: dark red "Philippine mahogany"	0.00133	0.00267			

[a]Per 1% change in moisture content, based on dimension at 10% moisture content and a straight-line relationship between moisture content at which shrinkage starts and total shrinkage. (Shrinkage assumed to start at 30% for all species except those indicated by footnote b.)
[b]Shrinkage assumed to start at 22% moisture content.

Because commercial lumber is often not perfectly flatsawn or quartersawn, this procedure will probably overestimate width shrinkage and underestimate thickness shrinkage. Note also that if both a size change and the percentage of moisture content are known, Equation (12–2) can be used to calculate the original moisture content.

Calculation Based on Green Dimensions

Approximate dimensional changes associated with moisture content changes greater than 6% to 14% , or when one moisture value is outside of those limits, can be calculated by

$$\Delta D = \frac{D_I(M_F - M_I)}{30(100)/S_T - 30 + M_I} \tag{12–3}$$

where S_T is tangential shrinkage (%) from green to ovendry (Ch. 3, Tables 3–5 and 3–6) (use radial shrinkage S_R when appropriate).

Neither M_I nor M_F should exceed 30%, the assumed moisture content value when shrinkage starts for most species.

Design Factors Affecting Dimensional Change

Framing Lumber in House Construction

Ideally, house framing lumber should be dried to the moisture content it will reach in use, thus minimizing future dimensional changes as a result of frame shrinkage. This ideal condition is difficult to achieve, but some drying and shrinkage of the frame may take place without being visible or causing serious defects after the house is completed. If, at the time the wall and ceiling finish is applied, the moisture content of the framing lumber is not more than about 5% above that which it will reach in service, there will be little or no evidence of defects caused by shrinkage of the frame. In heated houses in cold climates, joists over heated basements, studs, and ceiling joists may reach a moisture content as low as 6% to 7% (Table 12–2). In mild climates, the minimum moisture content will be greater.

The most common signs of excessive shrinkage are cracks in plastered walls, truss rise, open joints, and nail pops in drywall construction; distortion of door openings; uneven floors; and loosening of joints and fastenings. The extent of vertical shrinkage after the house is completed is proportional to the depth of wood used as supports in a horizontal position, such as girders, floor joists, and plates. After all, shrinkage occurs primarily in the width of members, not the length.

Thorough consideration should be given to the type of framing best suited to the whole building structure. Methods should be chosen that will minimize or balance the use of wood across the grain in vertical supports. These involve variations in floor, wall, and ceiling framing. The factors involved and details of construction are covered extensively in *Wood-Frame House Construction* (Sherwood and Stroh 1991).

Heavy Timber Construction

In heavy timber construction, a certain amount of shrinkage is to be expected. A column that bears directly on a wood girder can result in a structure settling as a result of the perpendicular-to-grain shrinkage of the girder. If not provided for in the design, shrinkage may cause weakening of the joints or uneven floors or both. One means of eliminating part of the shrinkage in mill buildings and similar structures is to use metal post caps; the metal in the post cap separates the upper column from the lower column. The same thing is accomplished by bolting wood corbels to the side of the lower column to support the girders.

When joist hangers are installed, the top of the joist should be above the top of the girder; otherwise, when the joist shrinks in the stirrup, the floor over the girder will be higher than that bearing upon the joist. Heavy planking used for flooring should be near 12% moisture content to minimize openings between boards as they approach moisture

equilibrium. When standard 38- or 64-mm (nominal 2- or 3-in.) joists are nailed together to provide a laminated floor of greater depth for heavy design loads, the joist material should be somewhat less than 12% moisture content if the building is to be heated.

Interior Finish

The normal seasonal changes in the moisture content of interior finish are not enough to cause serious dimensional change if the woodwork is carefully designed. Large members, such as ornamental beams, cornices, newel posts, stair stringers, and handrails, should be built up from comparatively small pieces. Wide door and window trim and base should be hollow-backed. Backband trim, if mitered at the corners, should be glued and splined before erection; otherwise butt joints should be used for the wide faces. Large, solid pieces, such as wood paneling, should be designed and installed so that the panels are free to move across the grain. Narrow widths are preferable.

Flooring

Flooring is usually dried to the moisture content expected in service so that shrinking and swelling are minimized and buckling or large gaps between boards do not occur. For basement, large hall, or gymnasium floors, however, enough space should be left around the edges to allow for some expansion.

Wood Care and Installation During Construction

Lumber and Trusses

Although it should be, lumber is often not protected from the weather at construction sites. Lumber is commonly placed on the ground in open areas near the building site as bulked and strapped packages. Supports under such packages are useful to prevent wetting from mud and ground water and should elevate the packages at least 150 mm (6 in.) off the ground. The packages should also be covered with plastic tarpaulins for protection from rain.

Lumber that is green or nearly green should be piled in stickers under a roof for additional drying before it is built into the structure. The same procedure is required for lumber that has been treated with a waterborne preservative but not fully redried. Prefabricated building parts, such as roof trusses, sometimes lie unprotected on the ground at the building site. In warm, rainy weather, moisture regain can result in fungal staining. Wetting of the lumber also results in swelling, and subsequent shrinkage of the framing may contribute to structural distortions. Extended storage of lumber at moisture contents greater than 20% without drying can allow decay to develop.

If framing lumber has a greater moisture content when installed than that recommended in Table 12–2, shrinkage can be expected. Framing lumber, even thoroughly air-dried stock, will generally have a moisture content greater than that recommended when it is delivered to the building site. If carelessly handled in storage at the site, the lumber can take up more moisture. Builders can schedule their work so an appreciable amount of drying can take place during the early stages of construction. This minimizes the effects of additional drying and shrinkage after completion. When the house has been framed, sheathed, and roofed, the framing is so exposed that in time it can dry to a lower moisture content than would ordinarily be expected in yard-dried lumber. The application of the wall and ceiling finish is delayed while wiring and plumbing are installed. If this delay is about 30 days in warm, dry weather, framing lumber should lose enough moisture so that any additional drying in place will be relatively unimportant. In cool, damp weather, or if wet lumber is used, the period of exposure should be extended. Checking moisture content of door and window headers and floor and ceiling joists at this time with an electric moisture meter is good practice. When these members approach an average of 12% moisture content, interior finish and trim can normally be installed. Closing the house and using the heating system will hasten the rate of drying.

Before wall finish is applied, the frame should be examined and defects that may have developed during drying, such as warped or distorted studs, shrinkage of lintels over openings, or loosened joints, should be corrected.

Exterior Trim and Millwork

Exterior trim, such as cornice and rake mouldings, fascia boards, and soffit material, is normally installed before the shingles are laid. Trim, siding, and window and door frames should be protected on the site by storing in the house or garage until time of installation. Although items such as window frames and sashes are usually treated with some type of water-repellent preservative to resist absorption of water, they should be stored in a protected area if they cannot be installed soon after delivery. Wood siding is often received in packaged form and can ordinarily remain in the package until installation.

Finished Flooring

Cracks develop in flooring if it absorbs moisture either before or after it is laid, then shrinks when the building is heated. Such cracks can be greatly reduced by observing the following practices:

- Specify flooring manufactured according to association rules and sold by dealers that protect it properly during storage and delivery.

- Do not allow flooring to be delivered before masonry and plastering are completed and fully dry, unless a dry storage space is available.

- Install the heating plant before flooring is delivered.

- Break open flooring bundles and expose all sides of flooring to the atmosphere inside the structure.

- Close up the house at night and increase the temperature about 8°C (15°F) greater than the outdoor temperature for about 3 days before laying the floor.

- If the house is not occupied immediately after the floor is laid, keep the house closed at night or during damp weather and supply some heat if necessary.

Better and smoother sanding and finishing can be done when the house is warm and the wood has been kept dry.

Interior Finish

In a building under construction, average relative humidity will be greater than that in an occupied house because of the moisture that evaporates from wet concrete, brickwork, plaster, and even the structural wood members. The average temperature will be lower because workers prefer a lower temperature than is common in an occupied house. Under such conditions, the finish tends to have greater moisture content during construction than it will have during occupancy.

Before the interior finish is delivered, the outside doors and windows should be hung in place so that they can be kept closed at night. In this way, conditions of the interior can be held as close as possible to the higher temperature and lower humidity that ordinarily prevail during the day. Such protection may be sufficient during dry warm weather, but during damp or cool weather, it is highly desirable that some heat be maintained in the house, particularly at night. Whenever possible, the heating plant should be placed in the house before the interior trim is installed, to be available for supplying the necessary heat. Portable heaters can also be used. The temperature during the night should be maintained about 8°C (15°F) greater than the outside temperature but should not be allowed to drop below about 21°C (70°F) during the summer or 17°C (62°F) when the outside temperature is below freezing.

After buildings have thoroughly dried, less heat is needed, but unoccupied houses, new or old, should not be allowed to stand without some heat during the winter. A temperature of about 8°C (15°F) greater than the outside temperature and above freezing at all times will keep the woodwork, finish, and other parts of the house from being affected by dampness or frost.

Plastering

During a plastering operation in a moderate-sized, six-room house, approximately 450 kg (1,000 lb) of water are used, all of which must be dissipated before the house is ready for the interior finish. Adequate ventilation to remove the evaporated moisture will keep it from being absorbed by the framework. In houses plastered in cold weather, the excess moisture can also cause paint to blister on exterior finish and siding.

During warm, dry weather, with the windows wide open, the moisture will be gone within a week after the final coat of plaster is applied. During damp, cold weather, the heating system or portable heaters are used to prevent freezing of plaster and to hasten its drying. Adequate ventilation should be provided at all times of the year because a large volume of air is required to carry away the amount of water involved. Even in the coldest weather, the windows on the side of the house away from the prevailing winds should be opened 50 to 75 mm (2 to 3 in.), preferably from the top.

References

ASTM. [current edition]. Direct moisture content measurement of wood and wood-based materials. ASTM D4442–92. West Conshohocken, PA: American Society for Testing and Materials.

Forest Products Laboratory. 1961. Wood floors for dwellings. Agric. Handb. 204. Washington, DC: U.S. Department of Agriculture.

Forest Products Laboratory. 1972. Methods of controlling humidity in woodworking plants. Res. Note FPL–RN–0218. Madison, WI: U.S. Department of Agriculture, Forest Service, Forest Products Laboratory.

James, W.L. 1988. Electric moisture meters for wood. Gen. Tech. Rep. FPL–GTR–6. Madison, WI: U.S. Department of Agriculture, Forest Service, Forest Products Laboratory.

McMillen, J.M.; Wengert, E.M. 1978. Drying eastern hardwood lumber. Agric. Handb. 528. Washington, DC: U.S. Department of Agriculture.

Rietz, R.C. 1978. Storage of lumber. Agric. Handb. 531. Washington, DC: U.S. Department of Agriculture.

Rietz, R.C.; Page, R.H. 1971. Air drying of lumber: A guide to industry practices. Agric. Handb. 402. Washington, DC: U.S. Department of Agriculture.

Sherwood, G.E.; Stroh, R.C. 1991. Wood-Frame House Construction. USDA Agric. Handb. 73. Washington, DC: U.S. Department of Agriculture.

Simpson, W.T. 1989. Drying wood: a review. Drying Technology. An International Journal, Pt. 1. 2(2): 235–265, Pt. 2, 2(3): 353–368.

Simpson, W.T., ed. 1991. Dry kiln operator's manual. Agric. Handb. 188. Washington, DC: U.S. Department of Agriculture.

USDC. 1970. American softwood lumber standard. NBS Voluntary Prod. Stand. PS 20–70; Washington, DC: U.S. Department of Commerce.

Chapter 13

Biodeterioration of Wood

Terry L. Highley

Contents

Under proper conditions, wood will give centuries of service. However, if conditions exist that permit the development of wood-degrading organisms, protection must be provided during processing, merchandising, and use.

The principal organisms that can degrade wood are fungi, insects, bacteria, and marine borers.

Molds, most sapwood stains, and decay are caused by fungi, which are microscopic, thread-like microorganisms that must have organic material to live. For some of them, wood offers the required food supply. The growth of fungi depends on suitably mild temperatures, moisture, and air (oxygen). Chemical stains, although they are not caused by organisms, are mentioned in this chapter because they resemble stains caused by fungi.

Insects also may damage wood, and in many situations must be considered in protective measures. Termites are the major insect enemy of wood, but on a national scale, they are a less serious threat than fungi.

Bacteria in wood ordinarily are of little consequence, but some may make the wood excessively absorptive. In addition, some may cause strength losses over long periods of exposure, particularly in forest soils.

Marine borers are a fourth general type of wood-degrading organism. They can attack susceptible wood rapidly in salt water harbors where they are the principal cause of damage to piles and other wood marine structures.

Wood degradation by organisms has been studied extensively, and many preventive measures are well known and widely practiced. By taking ordinary precautions with the finished product, the user can contribute substantially to ensuring a long service life.

Fungus Damage and Control

Fungus damage to wood may be traced to three general causes: (a) lack of suitable protective measures when storing

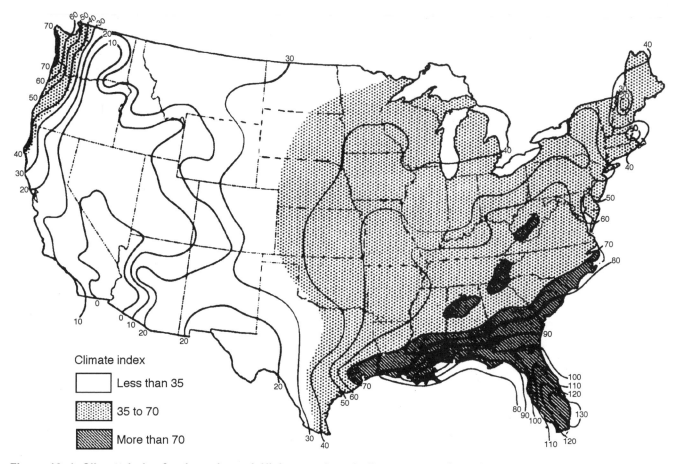

Figure 13–1. Climate index for decay hazard. Higher numbers indicate greater decay hazard.

Climate index

☐ Less than 35

▨ 35 to 70

▨ More than 70

logs or bolts; (b) improper seasoning, storing, or handling of the raw material produced from the log; and (c) failure to take ordinary simple precautions in using the final product. The incidence and development of molds, decay, and stains caused by fungi depend heavily on temperature and moisture conditions (Fig. 13–1).

Molds and Fungus Stains

Molds and fungus stains are confined to a great extent to sapwood and are of various colors. The principal fungus stains are usually referred to as sap stain or blue stain. The distinction between molding and staining is made primarily on the basis of the depth of discoloration. With some molds and the lesser fungus stains, there is no clear-cut differentia-tion. Typical sap stain or blue stain penetrates into the sapwood and cannot be removed by surfacing. Also, the discoloration as seen on a cross section of the wood often appears as pie-shaped wedges oriented radially, correspond-ing to the direction of the wood rays (Fig. 13–2). The dis-coloration may completely cover the sapwood or may occur as specks, spots, streaks, or patches of various intensities of color. The so-called blue stains, which vary from bluish to bluish black and gray to brown, are the most common, although various shades of yellow, orange, purple, and red are sometimes encountered. The exact color of the stain

depends on the infecting organisms and the species and moisture condition of the wood. The fungal brown stain mentioned here should not be confused with chemical brown stain.

Mold discolorations usually become noticeable as fuzzy or powdery surface growths, with colors ranging from light shades to black. Among the brighter colors, green and yel-lowish hues are common. On softwoods, though the fungus may penetrate deeply, the discoloring surface growth often can easily be brushed or surfaced off. However, on large-pored hardwoods (for example, oaks), the wood beneath the surface growth is commonly stained too deeply to be surfaced off. The staining tends to occur in spots of varying concentration and size, depending on the kind and pattern of the superficial growth.

Under favorable moisture and temperature conditions, stain-ing and molding fungi may become established and develop rapidly in the sapwood of logs shortly after they are cut. In addition, lumber and such products as veneer, furniture stock, and millwork may become infected at any stage of manufacture or use if they become sufficiently moist. Freshly cut or unseasoned stock that is piled during warm, humid weather may be noticeably discolored within 5 or 6 days. Recommended moisture control measures are given in Chapter 12.

Figure 13–2. Typical radial penetration of log by stain. The pattern is a result of more rapid penetration by the fungus radially (through the ray) than tangentially.

Ordinarily, stain and mold fungi affect the strength of the wood only slightly; their greatest effect is usually confined to strength properties that determine shock resistance or toughness (Ch. 4). They increase the absorbency of wood, and this can cause over-absorption of glue, paint, or wood preservative during subsequent processing. Increased porosity also makes wood more wettable, which can lead to colonization by typical wood-decay fungi.

Stain- and mold-infected stock is practically unimpaired for many uses in which appearance is not a limiting factor, and a small amount of stain may be permitted by standard grading rules. Stock with stain and mold may not be entirely satisfactory for siding, trim, and other exterior millwork because of its greater water absorbency. Also, incipient decay may be present, though inconspicuous, in the discolored areas. Both of these factors increase the possibility of decay in wood that is rain-wetted unless the wood has been treated with a suitable preservative.

Chemical Stains

Nonmicrobial or chemical stains are difficult to control and represent substantial loss in wood quality. These stains include a variety of discolorations in wood that are often promoted by slow drying of lumber and warm to hot temperatures. Such conditions allow naturally occurring chemicals in wood to react with air (enzymatic oxidation) to form a new chemical that is typically dark in color. Common chemical stains include (a) interior sapwood graying, prevalent in oak, hackberry, ash, and maple; (b) brown stain in softwoods; and (c) pinking and browning in the interior of light-colored woods such as maple. Another common

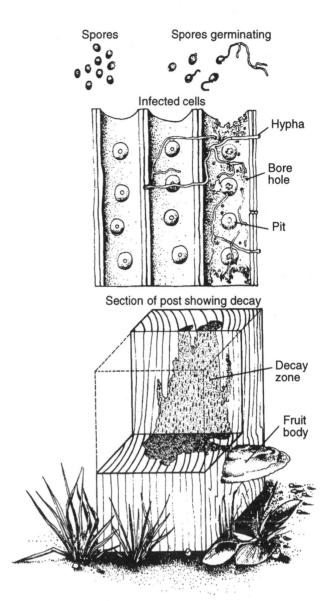

Figure 13–3. The decay cycle (top to bottom). Thousands of spores produced in a fruiting body are distributed by wind or insects. On contacting moist, susceptible wood, they germinate to create new infections in the wood cells. In time, serious decay develops that may be accompanied by formation of new fruiting bodies.

discoloration is caused by the interaction of iron with tannins in wood. Iron stain is more prevalent in hardwoods (for example, oak and many tropical hardwoods) and in some softwoods such as Douglas-fir. Control is achieved by eliminating the source of iron.

Decay

Decay-producing fungi may, under conditions that favor their growth, attack either heartwood or sapwood in most wood species (Fig. 13–3). The result is a condition designated as decay, rot, dote, or doze. Fresh surface growths of decay

285

Figure 13–4. Mycelial fans on a wood door.

fungi may appear as fan-shaped patches (Fig. 13–4), strands, or root-like structures, usually white or brown. Sometimes fruiting bodies are produced that take the form of mushrooms, brackets, or crusts. The fungus, in the form of microscopic, threadlike strands, permeates the wood and uses parts of it as food. Some fungi live largely on the cellulose; others use the lignin as well as the cellulose.

Certain decay fungi colonize the heartwood (causing heart rot) and rarely the sapwood of living trees, whereas others confine their activities to logs or manufactured products, such as sawn lumber, structural timbers, poles, and ties. Most fungi that attack trees cease their activities after the trees have been cut, as do the fungi causing brown pocket (peck) in baldcypress or white pocket in Douglas-fir and other conifers. Relatively few fungi continue their destruction after the trees have been cut and worked into products and then only if conditions remain favorable for their growth. Although heartwood is more susceptible to decay than is sapwood in living trees, for many species the sapwood of wood products is more susceptible to decay than is the heartwood.

Most decay can progress rapidly at temperatures that favor growth of plant life in general. For the most part, decay is relatively slow at temperatures below 10°C (50°F) and above 35°C (95°F). Decay essentially ceases when the temperature drops as low as 2°C (35°F) or rises as high as 38°C (100°F).

Serious decay occurs only when the moisture content of the wood is above the fiber saturation point (average 30%). Only when previously dried wood is contacted by water, such as provided by rain, condensation, or contact with wet ground, will the fiber saturation point be reached. By itself, the water vapor in humid air will not wet wood sufficiently to support significant decay, but it will permit development of some mold fungi. Fully air-dried wood usually will have a moisture content not exceeding 20% and should provide a reasonable margin of safety against fungus damage. Thus, wood will not decay if it is kept air dry, and decay already present from prior infection will not progress.

Wood can be too wet for decay as well as too dry. If the wood is water-soaked, the supply of air to the interior of a piece may not be adequate to support development of typical decay fungi. For this reason, foundation piles buried beneath the water table and logs stored in a pond or under a suitable system of water sprays are not subject to decay by typical wood-decay fungi.

The early or incipient stages of decay are often accompanied by a discoloration of the wood, which is more evident on freshly exposed surfaces of unseasoned wood than on dry wood. Abnormal mottling of the wood color, with either unnatural brown or bleached areas, is often evidence of decay infection. Many fungi that cause heart rot in the standing tree produce incipient decay that differs only slightly from the normal color of the wood or gives a somewhat water-soaked appearance to the wood.

Typical or late stages of decay are easily recognized, because the wood has undergone definite changes in color and properties, the character of the changes depending on the organism and the substances it removes.

Two kinds of major decay fungi are recognized: brown rot and white rot. With brown-rot fungi, only the cellulose is extensively removed, the wood takes on a browner color, and it can crack across the grain, shrink, collapse, and be crushed into powder (Fig. 13–5). With white-rot fungi, both lignin and cellulose usually are removed, the wood may lose color and appear "whiter" than normal, it does not crack across the grain, and until severely degraded, it retains its outward dimensions, does not shrink or collapse, and often feels spongy. Brown-rot fungi commonly colonize softwoods, and white-rot fungi commonly occur on hardwoods, but both brown- and white-rot fungi occasionally colonize both types of wood.

Brown, crumbly rot, in the dry condition, is sometimes called dry rot, but the term is incorrect because wood must be damp to decay, although it may become dry later.

A few fungi, however, have water-conducting strands; such fungi are capable of carrying water (usually from the soil) into buildings or lumber piles, where they moisten and rot wood that would otherwise be dry. They are sometimes referred to technically as dry-rot fungi or water-conducting fungi. The latter term better describes the true situation because these fungi, like the others, must have water.

A third and generally less important kind of decay is known as soft rot. Soft rot is caused by fungi related to the molds rather than those responsible for brown and white rot. Soft rot typically is relatively shallow; the affected wood is greatly degraded and often soft when wet, but immediately beneath the zone of rot, the wood may be firm (Fig. 13–6). Because soft rot usually is rather shallow, it is most likely to damage relatively thin pieces of wood such as slats in cooling towers. It is favored by wet situations but is also prevalent on surfaces that have been alternately wet and dry over a substantial period. Heavily fissured surfaces, familiar to many as weathered wood, generally have been quite degraded by soft-rot fungi.

Decay Resistance of Wood

Chapter 3 discusses the natural resistance of wood to fungi and ranks a grouping of species according to decay resistance. In decay-resistant domestic species, only the heartwood has significant resistance because the natural preservative chemicals in wood that retard the growth of fungi are essentially restricted to the heartwood. Natural resistance of species to fungi is important only where conditions conducive to decay exist or may develop. If wood is subjected to severe decay conditions, pressure-treated wood, rather than resistant heartwood, is generally recommended.

Effect of Decay on Strength of Wood

Decay initially affects toughness, or the ability of wood to withstand impacts. This is generally followed by reductions in strength values related to static bending. Eventually, all strength properties are seriously reduced.

Figure 13–5. Brown rot in Southern Pine railroad tie. Note the darker color and the cubical checking in the wood.

Figure 13–6. Soft-rotted preservative-treated pine utility pole. Note the shallow depth of decay.

Strength losses during early stages of decay can be considerable, depending to a great extent upon the fungi involved and, to a lesser extent, upon the type of wood undergoing decay. In laboratory tests, losses in toughness ranged from 6% to >50% by the time a 1% weight loss had occurred in the wood as a result of fungal attack. By the time weight losses resulting from decay have reached 10%, most strength losses may be expected to exceed 50%. At such weight losses, decay is detectable only microscopically. It may be assumed that wood with visually discernible decay has been greatly reduced in all strength values.

Prevention of Mold, Stain, and Decay

Logs, Poles, Piles, and Ties

The wood species, geographic region, and time of the year determine what precautions must be taken to avoid serious damage from fungi in logs, poles, piles, ties, and similar thick products during seasoning or storage. In dry climates, rapid surface seasoning of poles and piles will retard development of mold, stain, and decay. The bark is peeled from the pole and the peeled product is decked on high skids or piled on high, well-drained ground in the open to dry. In humid regions, such as the Gulf States, these products often do not air-dry fast enough to avoid losses from fungi. Preseasoning treatments with approved preservative solutions can be helpful in these circumstances.

For logs, rapid conversion into lumber or storage in water or under a water spray (Fig. 13–7) is the surest way to avoid fungal damage. Preservative sprays promptly applied to the wood will protect most timber species during storage for 2 to 3 months, except in severe decay hazard climates, such as in Mississippi (Fig. 13–1). For longer storage, an end coating is needed to prevent seasoning checks, through which infection can enter the log.

Lumber

Growth of decay fungi can be prevented in lumber and other wood products by rapidly drying them to a moisture content of 20% or less and keeping them dry. Standard air-drying practices will usually dry the wood fast enough to protect it, particularly if the protection afforded by drying is supplemented by dip or spray treatment of the stock with an EPA-approved fungicidal solution. Successful control by this method depends not only upon immediate and adequate treatment but also upon proper handling of the lumber after treatment. However, kiln drying is the most reliable method of rapidly reducing moisture content.

Figure 13–7. Spraying logs with water protects them against fungal stain and decay.

Figure 13–8. A sanitary, well-drained air-drying yard.

Air-drying yards should be kept as sanitary and as open as possible to air circulation (Fig. 13–8). Recommended practices include locating yards and sheds on well-drained ground; removing debris (which serves as a source of infection) and weeds (which reduce air circulation); and employing piling methods that permit rapid drying of the lumber and protect against wetting. Storage sheds should be constructed and maintained to prevent significant wetting of the stock. Ample roof overhang on open sheds is desirable. In areas where termites or water-conducting fungi may be troublesome, stock to be held for long periods should be set on foundations high enough so that the wood can be inspected from beneath.

The user's best assurance of receiving lumber free from decay other than light stain is to buy stock marked by a lumber association in a grade that eliminates or limits such quality-reducing features. Surface treatment for protection at the drying yard is only temporarily effective. Except for temporary structures, lumber to be used under conditions conducive to decay should be all heartwood of a naturally durable species or should be adequately treated with a wood preservative (Ch. 14).

Buildings

The lasting qualities of properly constructed wood buildings are apparent in all parts of the country. Serious decay problems are almost always a sign of faulty design or construction, lack of reasonable care in the handling of the wood, or improper maintenance of the structure.

Construction principles that ensure long service and avoid decay in buildings include (a) building with dry lumber, free of incipient decay and not exceeding the amounts of mold and blue stain permitted by standard grading rules; (b) using construction details and building designs that will keep exterior wood dry and accelerate runoff; (c) using wood treated with a preservative or heartwood of a decay-resistant species for parts exposed to aboveground decay hazards; and (d) using pressure-treated wood for the high hazard situation associated with ground contact.

A building site that is dry or for which drainage is provided will reduce the possibility of decay. Stumps, wood debris, stakes, or wood concrete forms are frequently subject to decay if left under or near a building.

Unseasoned or infected wood should not be enclosed until it is thoroughly dried. Unseasoned wood includes green lumber. Wood can become infected because of improper handling at the sawmill or retail yard or after delivery on the job.

Untreated wood parts of substructures should not be permitted to contact the soil. A minimum of 200 mm (8 in.) clearance between soil and framing and 150 mm (6 in.) between soil and siding is recommended. Where frequent hard rains occur, a foundation height above grade of 300 to 460 mm (12 to 18 in.) is advocated. An exception may be made for certain temporary constructions. If contact with soil is unavoidable, the wood should be pressure treated (Ch. 14).

Sill plates and other wood resting on a concrete slab foundation generally should be pressure treated and protected by installing a moisture-resistant membrane such as polyethylene beneath the slab. Girder and joist openings in masonry walls should be big enough to ensure an air space around the ends of these wood members. If the members are below the outside soil level, moisture proofing of the outer face of the wall is essential.

In buildings without basements but with crawl spaces, wetting of the wood by condensation during cold weather or by air-conditioning may result in serious decay damage. However, serious condensation leading to decay may be prevented by laying a barrier such as polyethylene on the soil. To facilitate inspection of the crawl space, a minimum 460-mm (18-in.) clearance should be left under wood joists.

Wood should also be protected from rain during construction. Protection from rainwater or condensation in walls and roofs will prevent the development of decay. A fairly wide roof overhang (0.6 m (2 ft)) with gutters and downspouts that are kept free of debris is desirable. Roofs must be kept tight, and cross ventilation in attics is recommended in cold climates. The use of sound, dry lumber is important in all parts of buildings.

Where service conditions in a building are such that the wood cannot be kept dry, the use of preservative-treated wood (Ch. 14) or heartwood of a durable species is advised. Examples include porches, exterior steps, and platforms and such places as textile mills, pulp and paper mills, and cold storage plants.

In making repairs necessitated by decay, every effort should be made to correct the moisture condition that led to the damage. If the condition cannot be corrected, all infected parts should be replaced with preservative-treated wood or with all-heartwood lumber of a naturally decay-resistant wood species. If the sources of moisture that caused the decay are entirely eliminated, it is necessary only to replace the weakened wood with dry lumber.

Other Structures and Products

In general, the principles underlying the prevention of mold, stain, or decay damage to veneer, plywood containers, boats, and other wood products and structures are similar to those

289

described for buildings—dry the wood rapidly and keep it dry or treat it with approved protective and preservative solutions. Interior grades of plywood should not be used where the plywood will be exposed to moisture; the adhesives, as well as the wood, may be damaged by fungi and bacteria as well as degraded by moisture. With exterior-type panels, joint construction should be carefully designed to prevent the entrance of rainwater.

In treated bridge or wharf timbers, checking may occur and may expose untreated wood to fungal attack. Annual in-place treatment of these checks will provide protection from decay. Similarly, pile tops may be protected by treatment with a wood preservative followed by application of a suitable capping compound.

Wood boats present certain problems that are not encountered in other uses of wood. The parts especially subject to decay are the stem, knighthead, transom, and frameheads, which can be reached by rainwater from above or condensation from below. Frayed surfaces are more likely to decay than are exposed surfaces, and in salt water service, hull members just below the weather deck are more vulnerable than those below the waterline. Recommendations for avoiding decay include (a) using only heartwood of durable species, free of infection, and preferably below 20% moisture content; (b) providing and maintaining ventilation in the hull and all compartments; (c) keeping water out as much as is practicable, especially fresh water; and (d) where it is necessary to use sapwood or nondurable heartwood, impregnating the wood with an approved preservative and treating the fully cut, shaped, and bored wood before installation by soaking it for a short time in preservative solution. Where such mild soaking treatment is used, the wood most subject to decay should also be flooded with an approved preservative at intervals of 2 or 3 years. During this treatment, the wood should be dry so that joints are relatively loose.

Remedial Treatment of Internally Decayed Wood

Four fumigants, 32% sodium N-methyldithiocarbamate in water, methylisocyanate, Basamid (tetrahydro-3, 5-dimethyl-2-H-1,3,5, thiodazine-6-thione), and chloropicrin (trichloronitromethane), are registered for use to arrest internal decay in wood. All these fumigants produce volatile toxic gases when applied to wood and move several meters from the point of application. These chemicals are restricted-use preservatives, and applicators must be trained and pass a test on pesticide handling and safety before using the chemicals. Fumigant treating poses risks, and thus the chemicals cannot be used safely in some situations.

Water diffusible boron- and fluoride-based rods, pastes, or solutions can be applied to wood by flooding or as external coatings (for example, bandage wraps containing borate or fluoride paste applied to the groundline of poles).

Bacteria

Most wood that has been wet for a considerable length of time probably will contain bacteria. The sour smell of logs that have been held under water for several months, or of lumber cut from them, manifests bacterial action. Usually, bacteria have little effect on wood properties, except over long periods, but some may make the wood excessively absorptive. This can result in excessive pickup of moisture, adhesive, paint, or preservative during treatment or use. This effect has been a problem in the sapwood of millwork cut from pine logs that have been stored in ponds. There also is evidence that bacteria developing in pine veneer bolts held under water or sprayed with water may cause noticeable changes in the physical character of the veneer, including some strength loss. Additionally, a mixture of different bacteria, as well as fungi, was found capable of accelerating decay of treated cooling tower slats and mine timbers.

Insect Damage and Control

The more common types of damage caused by wood-attacking insects are shown in Table 13–1 and Figure 13–9. Methods of controlling and preventing insect attack of wood are described in the following paragraphs.

Beetles

Bark beetles may damage the surface of the components of logs and other rustic structures from which the bark has not been removed. These beetles are reddish brown to black and vary in length from approximately 1.5 to 6.5 mm (1/16 to 1/4 in.) They bore through the outer bark to the soft inner part, where they make tunnels in which they lay their eggs. In making tunnels, bark beetles push out fine brownish-white sawdust-like particles. If many beetles are present, their extensive tunneling will loosen the bark and permit it to fall off in large patches, making the structure unsightly.

To avoid bark beetle damage, logs may be debarked rapidly, sprayed with an approved insecticidal solution, stored in water or under a water spray, or cut during the dormant season (October or November, for instance). If cut during this period, logs should immediately be piled off the ground and arranged for good air movement, to promote rapid drying of the inner bark. This should occur before the beetles begin to fly in the spring. Drying the bark will almost always prevent damage by insects that prefer freshly cut wood.

Ambrosia beetles, roundheaded and flatheaded borers, and some powder-post beetles that get into freshly cut timber can cause considerable damage to wood in rustic structures and some manufactured products. Certain beetles may complete development and emerge several years after the wood is dry, often raising a question as to the origin of the infestation.

Table 13–1. Types of damage caused by wood-attacking insects

Type of damage	Description	Causal agent	Damage Begins	Damage Ends
Pin holes	0.25 to 6.4 mm (1/100 to 1/4 in.) in diameter, usually circular			
	Tunnels open:			
	Holes 0.5 to 3 mm (1/50 to 1/8 in.) in diameter, usually centered in dark streak or ring in surrounding wood	Ambrosia beetles	In living trees and unseasoned logs and lumber	During seasoning
	Holes variable sizes; surrounding wood rarely dark stained; tunnels lined with wood-colored substance	Timber worms	In living trees and unseasoned logs and lumber	Before seasoning
	Tunnels packed with usually fine sawdust:			
	Exit holes 0.8 to 1.6 mm (1/32 to 1/16 in.) in diameter; in sapwood of large-pored hardwoods; loose floury sawdust in tunnels	Lyctid powder-post beetles	During or after seasoning	Reinfestation continues until sapwood destroyed
	Exit holes 1.6 to 3 mm (1/16 to 1/8 in.) in diameter; primarily in sapwood, rarely in heartwood; tunnels loosely packed with fine sawdust and elongate pellets	Anobiid powder-post beetles	Usually after wood in use (in buildings)	Reinfestation continues; progress of damage very slow
	Exit holes 2.5 to 7 mm (3/32 to 9/32 in.) in diameter; primarily sapwood of hard woods, minor in softwoods; sawdust in tunnels fine to coarse and tightly packed	Bostrichid powder-post beetles	Before seasoning or if wood is rewetted	During seasoning or redrying
	Exit holes 1.6 to 2 mm (1/16 to 1/12 in.) in diameter; in slightly damp or decayed wood; very fine sawdust or pellets tightly packed in tunnels	Wood-boring weevils	In slightly damp wood in use	Reinfestation continues while wood is damp
Grub holes	3 to 13 mm (1/8 to 1/2 in.) in diameter, circular or oval			
	Exit holes 3 to 13 mm (1/8 to 1/2 in.) in diameter; circular; mostly in sapwood; tunnels with coarse to fibrous sawdust or it may be absent	Roundheaded borers (beetles)	In living trees and unseasoned logs and lumber	When adults emerge from seasoned wood or when wood is dried
	Exit holes 3 to 13 mm (1/8 to 1/2 in.) in diameter; mostly oval; in sapwood and heartwood; sawdust tightly packed in tunnels	Flatheaded borers (beetles)	In living trees and unseasoned logs and lumber	When adults emerge from seasoned wood or when wood is dried
	Exit holes ~6 mm (~1/4 in.) in diameter; circular; in sapwood of softwoods, primarily pine; tunnels packed with very fine sawdust	Old house borers (a roundheaded borer)	During or after seasoning	Reinfestation continues in seasoned wood in use
	Exit holes perfectly circular, 4 to 6 mm (1/6 to 1/4 in.) in diameter; primarily in softwoods; tunnels tightly packed with coarse sawdust, often in decay softened wood	Woodwasps	In dying trees or fresh logs	When adults emerge from seasoned wood, usually in use, or when kiln dried
	Nest entry hole and tunnel perfectly circular ~13 mm (~1/2 in.) in diameter; in soft softwoods in structures	Carpenter bees	In structural timbers, siding	Nesting reoccurs annually in spring at same and nearby locations
Network of galleries	Systems of interconnected tunnels and chambers	Social insects with colonies		
	Walls look polished; spaces completely clean of debris	Carpenter ants	Usually in damp partly decayed, or soft-textured wood in use	Colony persists unless prolonged drying of wood occurs
	Walls usually speckled with mud spots; some chambers may be filled with "clay"	Subterranean termites	In wood structures	Colony persists
	Chambers contain pellets; areas may be walled-off by dark membrane	Dry-wood termites (occasionally damp wood termites)	In wood structures	Colony persists
Pitch pocket	Openings between growth rings containing pitch	Various insects	In living trees	In tree
Black check	Small packets in outer layer of wood	Grubs of various insects	In living trees	In tree
Pith fleck	Narrow, brownish streaks	Fly maggots or adult weevils	In living trees	In tree
Gum spot	Small patches or streaks of gum-like substances	Grubs of various insects	In living trees	In tree
Ring distortion	Double growth rings or incomplete annual layers of growth	Larvae of defoliating insects or flatheaded cambium borers	In living trees	In tree
	Stained area more than 25.4 mm (1 in.) long introduced by insects in trees or recently felled logs	Staining fungi	With insect wounds	With seasoning

291

Figure 13–9. Types of insect damage most likely to occur in a building. Upper left—Termite attack; feeding galleries (often parallel to the grain) contain excrement and soil. Upper right—Powder-post beetle attack; exit holes usually filled with wood flour and not associated with discolored wood. Lower left—Carpenter ant attack; nesting galleries usually cut across grain and are free of residue. Lower right—Beetle attack; feeding galleries (made in the wood while green) free of residue and surrounding wood darkly stained.

Proper cutting practices, rapid debarking, storing under water, and spraying the material with an approved chemical solution, as recommended for bark beetles, will control these insects. Damage by ambrosia beetles can be prevented in freshly sawn lumber by dipping the product in a chemical solution. The addition of one of the sap-stain preventives approved for controlling molds, stains, and decay will keep the lumber bright. Powder-post beetles attack both hardwoods and softwoods and both freshly cut and seasoned lumber and timber. Powder-post damage is indicated by holes made in the surface of the wood by the winged adults as they emerge and by the fine powder that may fall from the wood. The powder-post beetles that cause most of the damage to dry hardwood lumber belong to the genus *Lyctus*. They attack the sapwood of ash, hickory, oak, and other large-pored hardwoods as it begins to season. Eggs are laid in pores of the wood, and the larvae burrow through the wood, making tunnels from 1.5 to 2 mm (1/16 to 1/12 in.)

in diameter, which they leave packed with a fine powder. Species of anobiid beetles colonize coniferous materials.

Susceptible hardwood lumber used for manufacturing purposes should be protected from powder-post beetle attack as soon as it is sawn and when it arrives at the plant. An approved insecticide applied in water emulsion to the green lumber will provide protection. Such treatment may be effective even after the lumber is kiln dried, until it is surfaced.

Good plant sanitation is extremely important in alleviating the problem of infestation. Proper sanitation measures can often eliminate the necessity for other preventative steps. Damage to manufactured items frequently is traceable to infestation that occurred before the products were placed on the market, particularly if a finish is not applied to the surface of the items until they are sold. Once wood is infested, the larvae will continue to develop, even though the surface is subsequently painted, oiled, waxed, or varnished.

When selecting hardwood lumber for building or manufacturing purposes, any evidence of powder-post infestation should not be overlooked, because the beetles may continue to be active long after the wood is put to use. For standard 19-mm (nominal 1-in.) lumber, sterilization of green wood with steam at 54°C (130°F) or sterilization of wood with a lower moisture content at 82°C (180°F) under controlled conditions of relative humidity for about 2 h is effective for checking infestation or preventing attack. Thicker material requires a longer time. A 3-min soaking in a petroleum oil solution containing an insecticide is also effective for checking infestation or preventing attack on lumber up to standard 19 mm (nominal 1 in.) thick. Small dimension stock also can be protected by brushing or spraying with approved chemicals. For infested furniture or finished woodwork in a building, the same insecticides may be used, but they should be dissolved in a refined petroleum oil, like mineral spirits. Because the *Lyctus* beetles lay their eggs in the open pores of wood, infestation can be prevented by covering the entire surface of each piece of wood with a suitable finish.

Powder-post beetles in the family Anobiidae, depending on the species, infest hardwoods and softwoods. Their life cycle takes 2 to 3 years and they require a wood moisture content around 15% or greater for viable infestation. Therefore, in most modern buildings, the wood moisture content is generally too low for anobiids. When ventilation is inadequate or in more humid regions of the United States, wood components of a building can reach the favorable moisture conditions for anobiids. This is especially a problem in airconditioned buildings where water condenses on cooled exterior surfaces. Susceptibility to anobiid infestation can be alleviated by lowering the moisture content of wood through improved ventilation and the judicious use of insulation and vapor barriers. Insecticides registered for use against these beetles are generally restricted for exterior applications to avoid potential safety hazards indoors. Wood being reused or recycled from older structures often has lyctid or anobiid larvae in it. Such wood should be fumigated or kiln dried before use in another structure.

Beetles in the family Bostrichidae and weevils in the family Curculionidae are associated with wood moisture contents favorable for wood-infesting fungi because they may benefit nutritionally from the fungi. Thus, protection against these insects consists of the same procedures as for protection against wood-decay fungi.

A roundheaded beetle, commonly known as the old house borer, causes damage to seasoned coniferous building materials. The larvae reduce the sapwood to a powdery or granular consistency and make a ticking sound while at work. When mature, the beetles make an oval hole approximately 6.5 mm (1/4 in.) in diameter in the surface of the wood and emerge. Anobiid powder-post beetles, which make holes 1.6 to 3.2 mm (1/16 to 1/8 in.) in diameter, also cause damage to pine joists. Infested wood should be drenched with a solution of one of the currently recommended insecticides in a highly penetrating solvent. Beetles nesting in wood behind plastered or paneled walls can be eliminated through fumigation of the building by a licensed operator.

Termites

Termites superficially resemble ants in size, general appearance, and habit of living in colonies. About 56 species are known in the United States. From the standpoint of their methods of attack on wood, termites can be grouped into two main classes: (a) ground-inhabiting or subterranean termites and (b) wood-inhabiting or nonsubterranean termites.

Subterranean Termites

Subterranean termites are responsible for most of the termite damage done to wood structures in the United States. This damage can be prevented. Subterranean termites are more prevalent in the southern than in the northern states, where low temperatures do not favor their development (Fig. 13–10). The hazard of infestation is greatest (a) beneath buildings without basements that were erected on a concrete slab foundation or were built over a crawl space that is poorly drained and ventilated and (b) in any substructure wood component close to the ground or an earth fill (for example, an earth-filled porch).

The subterranean termites develop their colonies and maintain their headquarters in the ground. They build their tunnels through earth and around obstructions to reach the wood they need for food. They also must have a constant source of moisture, whether from the wood on which they are feeding or the soil where they nest. The worker members of the colony cause destruction of wood. At certain seasons of the year, usually spring, male and female winged forms swarm from the colony, fly a short time, lose their wings, mate, and if successful in locating a suitable home, start new colonies. The appearance of "flying ants" or their shed wings is an indication that a termite colony may be near and causing serious damage. Not all "flying ants" are termites; therefore, suspicious insects should be identified before investing in eradication (Fig. 13–11).

Figure 13–10. A, the northern limit of recorded damage done by subterranean termites in the United States; B, the northern limit of damage done by dry-wood termites.

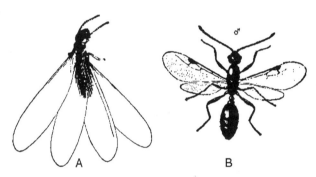

Figure 13–11. A, winged termite; B, winged ant (both greatly enlarged). The wasp waist of the ant and the long wings of the termite are distinguishing characteristics.

Subterranean termites normally do not establish themselves in buildings by being carried there in lumber; they primarily enter from ground nests after the building has been constructed. An introduced species, the Formosan termite, is adept at initiating aboveground infestations and nests in structures where wood remains wet for prolonged periods, such as from roof leaks. Telltale signs of subterranean termite presence are the earthen tubes or runways built by these insects over the surfaces of the foundation or other exposed areas to reach the wood above. Another sign is the swarming of winged adults early in the spring or fall. In the wood itself, the termites make galleries that generally follow the grain, leaving a shell of sound wood to conceal their activities. Because the galleries seldom show on the wood surfaces, probing with a pick or knife is advisable if the presence of termites is suspected.

The best protection for wood in areas where subterranean termites are prevalent is to prevent the termites from gaining hidden access to a building. The foundations should be of concrete, pressure-treated wood, or other material through which the termites cannot penetrate. With brick, stone, or concrete block, cement mortar should be used because

293

termites can work through some other kinds of mortar. Also, it is a good precaution to cap the foundation with 100 mm (4 in.) of reinforced concrete. Posts supporting floor girders should, if they bear directly on the ground, be of concrete. If there is a basement, it should be floored with concrete. Untreated posts in such a basement should rest on concrete piers extending a few inches above the basement floor. However, pressure-treated posts can rest directly on the basement floor. With the crawl-space type of foundation, wood floor joists should be kept at least 460 mm (18 in.) and girders 300 mm (12 in.) from the earth and good ventilation should be provided beneath the floor. A rule of thumb is to have a minimum of 1 unit area of ventilation for every 150 units of crawlspace (for example, 1 ft^2 of ventilated area for 150 ft^2 of crawlspace).

Moisture condensation on the floor joists and subflooring, which may cause conditions favorable to decay and contribute to infestation by termites, can be avoided by covering the soil below with a moisture barrier, maintaining adequate ventilation, and assuming proper drainage of rainwater away from all sides of a structure. All concrete forms, stakes, stumps, and wastewood should be removed from the building site because they are possible sources of infestation. Generally, the precautions effective against subterranean termites are also helpful against decay.

The principal method of protecting buildings in high termite areas is to thoroughly treat the soil adjacent to the foundation walls and piers beneath the building with a soil insecticide. When concrete slab floors are laid directly on the ground, all soil under the slab should be treated with an approved insecticide before the concrete is poured. Furthermore, insulation containing cellulose that is used as a filler in expansion joints should be impregnated with an approved chemical toxic to termites. Sealing the top 13 mm (1/2 in.) of the expansion joint with roofing-grade coal-tar pitch also provides effective protection from ground-nesting termites. New modifications in soil treatment and an insecticidal bait control method are currently under investigation and appear promising. Current references (available from national pest control operator associations) should be consulted to take advantage of the new developments in termite control.

To control termites already in a building, contact between the termite colony in the soil and the woodwork must be broken. This can be done by blocking the runways from soil to wood, treating the soil, repairing leaks that keep wood within the structure wet (for example, plumbing leaks), or some combination of these techniques. Possible reinfestations can be guarded against by frequent inspections for signs of termites.

Nonsubterranean Termites

In the United States, nonsubterranean termites have been found only in a narrow strip of territory extending from central California around the southern edge of the continental United States to Virginia (Fig. 13–10) and in the West Indies and Hawaii. Their principal damage is confined to an area in southern California, to parts of southern Florida,

notably Key West, and to the islands of Hawaii. They also are a localized problem in Arizona and New Mexico.

The nonsubterranean termites, especially the dry-wood type, do not multiply as rapidly as the subterranean termites and have somewhat different colony life and habits. The total amount of destruction they cause in the United States is much less than that caused by the subterranean termites. The ability of dry-wood termites to live in dry wood without outside moisture or contact with the ground, however, makes them a definite menace in the regions where they occur. Their depredations are not rapid, but they can thoroughly riddle timbers with their tunnelings if allowed to work undisturbed for many years. Nonsubterranean termites are often moved from structure to structure in infested items such as furniture.

In constructing a building in localities where the dry-wood type of nonsubterranean termite is prevalent, it is good practice to inspect the lumber carefully to see that it was not infested before arrival at the building site. If the building is constructed during the swarming season, the lumber should be watched during the course of construction, because infestation by colonizing pairs can easily take place. Because paint is a good protection against the entrance of dry-wood termites, exposed wood (except that which is preservative treated) should be kept covered with a paint film. Fine screen should be placed over any openings to the interior unpainted parts of the building. As in the case of ground-nesting termites, dead trees, old stumps, posts, or wood debris of any kind that could serve as sources of infestation should be removed from the premises.

If a building is infested with dry-wood termites, badly damaged wood should be replaced. If the wood is only slightly damaged or is difficult to replace, further termite activity can be arrested by injecting a small amount of an approved pesticidal dust or liquid formulation into each nest. Current recommendations for such formulations can be found from state pest control associations. Buildings heavily infested with nonsubterranean termites can be successfully fumigated. This method is quicker than the use of poisonous liquids and dusts and does not require finding all of the colonies. However, it does not prevent the termites from returning because no poisonous residue is left in the tunnels. Fumigation is very dangerous and should be conducted only by licensed professional fumigators. Infested pieces of furniture, picture frames, and other small pieces can be individually fumigated, heated, or placed in a freezer for a short time. In localities where dry-wood termites do serious damage to posts and poles, the best protection for these and similar forms of outdoor timbers is full-length pressure treatment with a preservative.

Naturally Termite-Resistant Woods

Only a limited number of woods grown in the United States offer any marked degree of natural resistance to termite attack. The close-grained heartwood of California redwood has some resistance, especially when used above ground. Very resinous heartwood of Southern Pine is practically immune to attack, but it is not available in large quantities and is seldom used.

Carpenter Ants

Carpenter ants are black or brown. They usually occur in stumps, trees, or logs but sometimes damage poles, structural timbers, or buildings. One form is easily recognized by its giant size relative to other ants. Carpenter ants use wood for shelter rather than for food, usually preferring wood that is naturally soft or has been made soft by decay. They may enter a building directly by crawling or may be carried there in fuelwood. If left undisturbed, they can, in a few years, enlarge their tunnels to the point where replacement or extensive repairs are necessary. The parts of dwellings they frequent most often are porch columns, porch roofs, window sills, and sometimes the wood plates in foundation walls. They often nest in hollow-core doors. The logs of rustic cabins are also attacked.

Precautions that prevent attack by decay and termites are usually effective against carpenter ants. Decaying or infested wood, such as logs, stumps, or retaining walls, should be removed from the premises, and crevices present in the foundation or woodwork of the building should be sealed. Particularly, leaks in porch roofs should be repaired because the decay that may result makes the wood more desirable to the ants.

When carpenter ants are found in a structure, any badly damaged timbers should be replaced. Because the carpenter ant needs high humidity in its immature stages, alterations in the construction may also be required to eliminate moisture from rain or condensation. In wood not sufficiently damaged to require replacement, the ants can be killed by injection of approved insecticide into the nest galleries. Carpenter ant nests are relatively easy to find because they keep their internal nest sites very clean and free of debris. As particles of wood are removed to create galleries or as pieces of insects that have been fed upon accumulate, the debris is removed from the nest and then accumulates below the nest opening.

Carpenter Bees

Carpenter bees resemble large bumblebees, but the top of their abdomen is hairless, causing their abdomens to shine, unlike bumblebees. The females make large (13-mm- (1/2-in.-) diameter) tunnels into unfinished soft wood for nests. They partition the hole into cells; each cell is provided with pollen and nectar for a single egg. Because carpenter bees reuse nesting sites for many years, a nesting tunnel into a structural timber may be extended several feet and have multiple branches. In thin wood, such as siding, the holes may extend the full thickness of the wood. They nest in stained wood and wood with thin paint films or light preservative salt treatments as well as in bare wood. A favorite nesting site is in unfinished exterior wood not directly exposed to sunlight (for example, the undersides of porch roofs, and grape arbors).

Control is aimed at discouraging the use of nesting sites in and near buildings. The tunnel may be injected with an insecticide labeled for bee control and plugged with caulk. Treating the surface around the entry hole will discourage reuse of the tunnel during the spring nesting period. A good paint film or pressure preservative treatment protects exterior wood surfaces from nesting damage. Bare interior wood surfaces, such as in garages, can be protected by screens and tight-fitting doors.

Marine Borer Damage and Control

Damage by marine-boring organisms to wood structures in salt or brackish waters is practically a worldwide problem. Evidence of attack is sometimes found in rivers even above the region of brackishness. The rapidity of attack depends upon local conditions and the kinds of borers present. Along the Pacific, Gulf, and South Atlantic Coasts of the United States, attack is rapid, and untreated pilings may be completely destroyed in a year or less. Along the coast of the New England States, the rate of attack is slower because of cold water temperatures but is still sufficiently rapid to require protection of wood where long life is desired. The principal marine borers from the standpoint of wood damage in the United States are described in this section. Control measures discussed in this section are those in use at the time this handbook was revised. Regulations should be reviewed at the time control treatments are being considered so that approved practices will be followed.

Shipworms

Shipworms are the most destructive of the marine borers. They are mollusks of various species that superficially are worm-like in form. The group includes several species of *Teredo* and several species of *Bankia*, which are especially damaging. These mollusks are readily distinguishable on close observation but are all very similar in several respects. In the early stages of their life, they are minute, free-swimming organisms. Upon finding suitable lodgment on wood, they quickly develop into a new form and bury themselves in the wood. A pair of boring shells on the head grows rapidly in size as the boring progresses, while the tail part or siphon remains at the original entrance. Thus, the animal grows in length and diameter within the wood but remains a prisoner in its burrow, which it lines with a shell-like deposit. It lives on the wood borings and the organic matter extracted from the sea water that is continuously being pumped through its system. The entrance holes never grow large, and the interior of wood may be completely honeycombed and ruined while the surface shows only slight perforations. When present in great numbers, shipworms grow only a few centimeters before the wood is so completely occupied that growth is stopped. However, when not crowded, they can grow to lengths of 0.3 to 1.2 m (1 to 4 ft) depending on the species.

Pholads

Another group of wood-boring mollusks is the pholads, which clearly resemble clams and therefore are not included with the shipworms. They are entirely encased in their double shells. The *Martesia* are the best-known species, but another well-known group is the *Xylophaga*. Like the shipworms, the *Martesia* enter the wood when they are very small, leaving a small entrance hole, and grow larger as they burrow into the wood. They generally do not exceed 64 mm (2-1/2 in.) long and 25 mm (1 in.) in diameter but are capable of doing considerable damage. Their activities in the United States appear to be confined to the Gulf Coast, San Diego, and Hawaii.

Limnoria and *Sphaeroma*

Another distinct group of marine borers are crustaceans, which are related to lobsters and shrimp. The principal borers in this group are species of *Limnoria* and *Sphaeroma*. Their attack differs from that of the shipworms and the *Martesia* in that the bore hole is quite shallow; the result is that the wood gradually is thinned from the surface inward through erosion by the combined action of the borers and water erosion. Also, the *Limnoria* and *Sphaeroma* do not become imprisoned in the wood but may move freely from place to place.

Limnoria are small, 3 to 4 mm (1/8 to 1/6 in.) long, and bore small burrows in the surface of wood. Although they can change their location, they usually continue to bore in one place. When great numbers of *Limnoria* are present, their burrows are separated by very thin walls of wood that are easily eroded by the motion of the water or damaged by objects floating upon it. This erosion causes the *Limnoria* to burrow continually deeper; otherwise, the burrows would probably not become greater than 51 mm (2 in.) long or 13 mm (1/2 in.) deep. Because erosion is greatest between tide levels, piles heavily attacked by *Limnoria* characteristically wear within this zone to an hourglass shape. In heavily infested harbors, untreated piling can be destroyed by *Limnoria* within a year.

Sphaeroma are somewhat larger, sometimes reaching a length of 13 mm (1/2 in.) and a width of 6 mm (1/4 in.). In general appearance and size, they resemble the common sow bug or pill bug that inhabits damp places. *Sphaeroma* are widely distributed but are not as plentiful as *Limnoria* and cause much less damage. Nevertheless, piles in some structures have been ruined by them. Occasionally, they have been found working in fresh water. In types of damage, *Sphaeroma* action resembles that of *Limnoria*. It has been reported that *Sphaeroma* attack salt-treated wood in Florida.

The average life of well-creosoted structures is many times the average life obtained from untreated structures. However, even thorough creosote treatment will not always stop *Martesia*, *Sphaeroma*, and especially *Limnoria*; shallow or erratic creosote penetration affords only slight protection. The spots with poor protection are attacked first, and from there,

the borers spread inward and destroy the untreated interior of the pile.

When wood is to be used in salt water, avoidance of cutting or injuring the surface after treatment is even more important than when wood is to be used on land. No cutting or injury of any kind for any purpose should be permitted in the underwater part of the pile. Where piles are cut to grade above the waterline, the exposed surfaces should be protected from decay. This may be accomplished by in-place application of a wood preservative followed by a suitable capping compound.

Natural Resistance to Marine Borers

No wood is immune to marine-borer attack, and no commercially important wood of the United States has sufficient marine-borer resistance to justify its use untreated in any important structure in areas where borers are active. The heartwood of several foreign species, such as greenheart, jarrah, azobe, and manbarklak, has shown resistance to marine-borer attack. Service records on these woods, however, do not always show uniform results and are affected by local conditions.

Protection of Permanent Structures

The best practical protection for piles in sea water with shipworms and moderate *Limnoria* hazard is heavy treatment with coal-tar creosote or creosote coal-tar solution. Where severe *Limnoria* hazard exists, dual treatment (copper-arsenate-containing waterborne preservatives followed by coal-tar creosote) is recommended. The treatment must be thorough, the penetration as deep as possible, and the retention high to give satisfactory results in heavily infested waters. It is best to treat such piles by the full-cell process to refusal; that is, to force in all the preservative the piles can hold without using treatments that cause serious damage to the wood. For highest retentions, it is necessary to air- or kiln-dry the piling before treatment. Details of treatments are discussed in Chapter 14.

The life of treated piles is influenced by the thoroughness of the treatment, the care and diligence used in avoiding damage to the treated shell during handling and installation, and the severity of borer attack. Differences in exposure conditions, such as water temperature, salinity, dissolved oxygen, water depth, and currents, tend to cause wide variations in the severity of borer attack even within limited areas. Service records show average-life figures of 22 to 48 years on well-treated Douglas-fir piles in San Francisco Bay waters. In South Atlantic and Gulf of Mexico waters, creosoted piles are estimated to last 10 to 12 years and frequently much longer. On the North Atlantic Coast, where exposure conditions are less severe, piles can last even longer than the 22- to 48-year life recorded in the San Francisco Bay.

Metal armor and concrete or plastic jacketing have been used with varying degrees of success for the protection of marine piles. The metal armor may be in the form of sheets, wire, or nails. Sheathing of piles with copper or muntz metal has been only partially successful, owing to difficulty in maintaining a continuous armor. Theft, damage in driving, damage by storm or driftwood, and corrosion of sheathing have sooner or later let in the borers, and in only a few cases has long pile life been reported. Attempts during World War II to electroplate wood piles with copper were not successful. Concrete casings are now in greater use than is metal armor, and they appear to provide better protection when high-quality materials are used and carefully applied. Unfortunately, they are readily damaged by ship impact. For this reason, concrete casings are less practical for fender piles than for foundation piles that are protected from mechanical damage.

Jacketing piles by wrapping them with heavy polyvinyl plastic is one recent form of supplementary protection. If properly applied, the jacketing will kill any borers that may have already become established by creating stagnant water, thereby decreasing oxygen levels in the water that is in contact with the piles. Like other materials, the plastic jacket is subject to mechanical damage.

Protection of Boats

Wood barges have been constructed with planking or sheathing pressure-treated with creosote to protect the hull from marine borers, and the results have been favorable. Although coal-tar creosote is an effective preservative for protecting wood against marine borers in areas of moderate borer hazard, it has disadvantages in many types of boats. Creosote adds considerably to the weight of the boat hull, and its odor is objectionable to boat crews. In addition, antifouling paints are difficult to apply over creosoted wood.

Some copper bottom paints protect boat hulls against marine-borer attack, but the protection continues only while the coating remains unbroken. Because it is difficult to maintain an unbroken coating of antifouling paint, the U.S. Navy has found it desirable to impregnate the hull planking of some wood boats with certain copper-containing preservatives. Such preservatives, when applied with high retentions (24 to 32 kg/m^3 (1.5 to 2.0 lb/ft^3)), have some effectiveness against marine borers and should help to protect the hull of a boat during intervals between renewals of the antifouling coating. These copper preservatives do not provide protection equivalent to that furnished by coal-tar creosote; their effectiveness in protecting boats is therefore best assured if the boats are dry docked at regular and frequent intervals and the antifouling coating maintained. However, the leach-resistant wood preservatives containing copper arsenates have shown superior performance (at a retention of 40 kg/m^3 (2.5 lb/ft^3)) to creosote in tests conducted in areas of severe borer hazard.

Plywood as well as plank hulls can be protected against marine borers by preservative treatment. The plywood hull presents a surface that can be covered successfully with a protective membrane of reinforced plastic laminate. Such coverings should not be attempted on wood that has been treated with a preservative carried in oil, because the bond will be unsatisfactory.

References

Beal, R.H. 1967. Formosan invader. Pest Control. 35(2): 13–17.

Beal, R.H.; Maulderi, J.K.; Jones, S.C. 1983. Subterranean termites, their prevention and control in buildings. Home & Garden Bull. 64 (rev.). Washington, DC: U.S. Department of Agriculture.

Cassens, D.L.; Eslyn, W.E. 1981. Fungicides to prevent sapstain and mold on hardwood lumber. Forest Products Journal. 31: 39–42.

Ebeling, W. 1975. Wood destroying insects and fungi. In: Urban entomology. Berkeley, CA: University of California, Division of Agriculture Science: 128–216.

Esenther, G.R.; Beal, R.H. 1979. Termite control: decayed wood bait. Sociobiology. 4(2): 215–222.

Eslyn, W.E.; Clark, J.W. 1976. Appraising deterioration in submerged piling. Materials und Organismen. Supplement 3: 43–52.

Eslyn, W.E.; Clark, J.W. 1979. Wood bridges—decay inspection and control. Agric. Handb. 557. Washington, DC: U.S. Department of Agriculture.

Forest Products Society. 1997. Prevention of discolorations in hardwood and softwood logs and lumber. FPS Proceedings 7283. Madison, WI: Forest Products Society.

Greaves, H. 1969. Wood-inhabiting bacteria: general considerations. Commonwealth Scientific and Industrial Research Organization, Forest Products Newsletter 359.

Hartley, C.; May, C. ; 1943. Decay of wood in boats. U.S. Department of Agriculture, Forest Path. Spec. Release 8; U.S. Department of Agriculture, Forest Service.

Highley, T.L.; Eslyn, W.E. 1982. Using fumigants to control interior decay in waterfront timbers. Forest Products Journal. 32: 32–34.

Highley, T.L.; Scheffer, T.C. 1978. Controlling decay in above-water parts of waterfront structures. Forest Products Journal. 28: 40–43.

Hunt, G.M.; Garratt, G.A. 1967. Wood preservation, 3d ed. The American forestry series. New York: McGraw–Hill Book Company.

Jones, E.B.G.; Eltringham, S.K., eds. 1971. Marine borers, fungi and fouling organisms of wood. In: Proceedings of Organization for Economic Cooperation and Development; 1968 March 27–April 3; Paris, France. OECD.

Krishna, K.; Weesner, F.M., eds. 1969. Biology of termites. New York: Academic Press. Vol. I.

Krishna, K.; Weesner, F.M., eds. 1970. Biology of termites. New York: Academic Press. Vol. II.

Lee, K.E.; Wood, T.G. 1971. Termites and soils. New York: Academic Press.

Moore, H.B. 1979. Wood-inhabiting insects in houses: their identification, biology, prevention, and control. Prepared as part of interagency agreement IAA–25–75 between the U.S. Department of Agriculture, Forest Service, and the Department of Housing and Urban Development. Washington, DC: U.S. Department of Agriculture, Forest Service, and the Department of Housing and Urban Development.

Morrell, J.J. 1996. Wood pole maintenance manual. Corvallis, OR: Forest Research Laboratory, Oregon State University.

Morrell, J.J.; Corden, M.E. 1982. Controlling wood deterioration with fumigants: a review. Forest Products Journal. 36(10): 26–34.

NPCA. 1976. Carpenter ants. Tech. Release ESPC 052101. Dunn Loring, VA: National Pest Control Association.

NPCA. 1963. Carpenter bees. Tech. Release 3–63. Dunn Loring, VA: National Pest Control Association.

NPCA. 1964. The horntails. Tech. Release 14–64. Dunn Loring, VA: National Pest Control Association.

Rietz, R.C. 1978. Storage of lumber. Agric. Handb. 531. Washington, DC: U.S. Department of Agriculture.

Roff, J.W.; Cserjesi, A.J.; Swan, G.W. 1980. Prevention of sap stain and mold in packaged lumber. FORINTEK Canada Corp. Tech. Rep. 14 Ottawa, ON: FORINTEK.

Scheffer, T.C. 1972. A climate index for estimating potential decay in wood structures above ground. Forest Products Journal. 21(10): 25–31.

Scheffer, T.C.; Eslyn, W.E. 1976. Winter treatments protect birch roundwood during storage. Forest Products Journal. 26: 27–31.

Scheffer, T.C.; Verrall, A.F. 1973. Principles of protecting wood buildings from decay. Res. Pap. FPL 190. Madison, WI: U.S. Department of Agriculture, Forest Service, Forest Products Laboratory.

Schmidt, E. 1990. Remedial decay treatment with fused borate rods: Recent developments and opportunities. In: Proceedings, First international conference on wood protection with diffusible preservatives: 1989 November; Nashville, TN. Madison, WI: Forest Products Society: 91–92.

Sherwood, G.E.; TenWolde, A. 1982. Moisture movement and control in light frame structures. Forest Products Journal. 32: 69–73.

Weesner, F.M. 1965. The termites of the United States, a handbook. Elizabeth, NJ: National Pest Control Association.

Wilcox, W.W. 1978. Review of literature on the effect of early stages of decay on wood strength. Wood and Fiber. 9: 252–257.

Williams, L.H. 1973. Anobiid beetles should be controlled. Pest Control. 41(6): 18,20,22,38,40,42,44.

Zabel, R.A.; Morrell, J.J. 1992. Wood microbiology: Decay and its prevention. San Diego, CA: Academic Press.

Wood Preservation

Rebecca E. Ibach

Contents

When left untreated in many outdoor applications, wood becomes subject to degradation by a variety of natural causes. Although some trees possess naturally occurring resistance to decay (Ch. 3, Decay Resistance), many are in short supply or are not grown in ready proximity to markets. Because most commonly used wood species, such as Southern Pine, ponderosa pine, and Douglas-fir, possess little decay resistance, extra protection is needed when they are exposed to adverse environments. Wood can be protected from the attack of decay fungi, harmful insects, or marine borers by applying chemical preservatives. The degree of protection achieved depends on the preservative used and the proper penetration and retention of the chemicals. Some preservatives are more effective than others, and some are more adaptable to certain use requirements. Not only are different methods of treating wood available, but treatability varies among wood species—particularly their heartwood, which generally resists preservative treatment more than does sapwood. To obtain long-term effectiveness, adequate penetration and retention are needed for each wood species, chemical preservative, and treatment method.

Wood preservatives that are applied at recommended retention levels and achieve satisfactory penetration can greatly increase the life of wood structures. Thus, the annual replacement cost of treated wood in service is much less than that of wood without treatment. In considering preservative treatment processes and wood species, the combination must provide the required protection for the conditions of exposure and life of the structure. All these factors are considered by the consensus technical committees in setting reference levels required by the American Wood-Preservers' Association (AWPA), the American Society for Testing and Materials (ASTM), and the Federal Specification Standards. Details are discussed later in this chapter.

Note that mention of a chemical in this chapter does not constitute a recommendation; only those chemicals registered by the U.S. Environmental Protection Agency (EPA) may be recommended. Registration of preservatives is under constant review by EPA and the U.S. Department of Agriculture. Use only preservatives that bear an EPA registration number and carry directions for home and farm use. Preservatives, such as creosote and pentachlorophenol, should not be applied to the interior of dwellings that are occupied by humans.

Because all preservatives are under constant review by EPA, a responsible State or Federal agency should be consulted as to the current status of any preservative.

Wood Preservatives

The EPA regulates pesticides, and wood preservatives are one type of pesticide. Preservatives that are not restricted by EPA are available to the general consumer for nonpressure treatments, and the sale of others is restricted to certified pesticide applicators. These preservatives can be used only in certain applications and are referred to as "restricted use." Restricted use refers to the chemical preservative and not to the treated wood product. The general consumer may buy and use wood products treated with restricted-use pesticides; EPA does not consider treated wood a toxic substance nor is it regulated as a pesticide.

Consumer Information Sheets (EPA-approved) are available from retailers of treated-wood products. The sheets provide information about the preservative and the use and disposal of treated-wood products. Consumer information sheets are available for three major groups of wood preservatives (Table 14–1):

- Creosote pressure-treated wood
- Pentachlorophenol pressure-treated wood
- Inorganic arsenical pressure-treated wood

Wood preservatives can be divided into two general classes: (1) oilborne preservatives, such as creosote and petroleum solutions of pentachlorophenol and (2) waterborne preservatives that are applied as water solutions. Many different chemicals are in each of these classes, and each has differing effectiveness in various exposure conditions. The three exposure categories for preservatives are (1) ground contact (high decay hazard that needs a heavy-duty preservative), (2) aboveground contact (low decay hazard that does not usually require pressure treatment), and (3) marine exposure (high decay hazard that needs a heavy-duty preservative or possibly dual treatment). In this chapter, both oilborne and waterborne preservative chemicals are described as to their potential and uses. See Table 14–2 for a summary of preservatives and their retention levels for various wood products. Some active ingredients can be used in both oilborne and waterborne preservatives.

Oilborne Preservatives

Wood does not swell from treatment with preservative oils, but it may shrink if it loses moisture during the treating process. Creosote and solutions with heavy, less volatile petroleum oils often help protect wood from weathering, but may adversely influence its cleanliness, odor, color, paintability, and fire performance. Volatile oils or solvents with oilborne preservatives, if removed after treatment, leave the wood cleaner than do the heavy oils but may not provide as much protection. Wood treated with some preservative oils can be glued satisfactorily, although special processing or

cleaning may be required to remove surplus oils from surfaces before spreading the adhesive.

Coal-Tar Creosote

Coal-tar creosote (creosote) is a black or brownish oil made by distilling coal tar that is obtained after high temperature carbonization of coal. Advantages of creosote are (a) high toxicity to wood-destroying organisms; (b) relative insolubility in water and low volatility, which impart to it a great degree of permanence under the most varied use conditions; (c) ease of application; (d) ease with which its depth of penetration can be determined; (e) relative low cost (when purchased in wholesale quantities); and (f) lengthy record of satisfactory use.

The character of the tar used, the method of distillation, and the temperature range in which the creosote fraction is collected all influence the composition of the creosote. Therefore, the composition of the various coal-tar creosotes available may vary considerably. However, small differences in composition do not prevent creosotes from giving good service. Satisfactory results in preventing decay may generally be expected from any coal-tar creosote that complies with the requirements of standard specifications.

Several standards prepared by different organizations are available for creosote oils of different kinds. Although the oil obtained under most of these standards will probably be effective in preventing decay, the requirements of some organizations are more exacting than others. The American Society for Testing and Materials Standard D390 for coal-tar creosote has been approved for use by U.S. Department of Defense agencies. This standard covers new coal-tar creosote and creosote in use for the preservative treatment of piles, poles, and timber for marine, land, and fresh water use. Under normal conditions, requirements of this standard can be met without difficulty by most creosote producers. The requirements of this specification are similar to those of the AWPA standard P1/P13 for creosote, which is equally acceptable to the user.

Although coal-tar creosote (AWPA P1/P13) or creosote solutions (AWPA P2) are well-suited for general outdoor service in structural timbers, this creosote has properties that are undesirable for some purposes. The color of creosote and the fact that creosote-treated wood usually cannot be painted satisfactorily make this preservative unsuitable where appearance and paintability are important. Creosote is commonly used for heavy timbers, poles, piles, and railroad ties.

The odor of creosote-treated wood is unpleasant to some people. Also, creosote vapors are harmful to growing plants, and foodstuffs that are sensitive to odors should not be stored where creosote odors are present. Workers sometimes object to creosote-treated wood because it soils their clothes, and creosote vapor photosensitizes exposed skin. With normal precautions to avoid direct skin contact with creosote, there appears to be no danger to the health of workers handling or working near the treated wood. The EPA or the treater should be contacted for specific information on this subject.

Table 14–1. EPA-approved consumer information sheets for three major groups of preservative pressure-treated wood

Preservative treatment	Inorganic arsenicals	Pentachlorophenol	Creosote
Consumer information	This wood has been preserved by pressure-treatment with an EPA-registered pesticide containing inorganic arsenic to protect it from insect attack and decay. Wood treated with inorganic arsenic should be used only where such protection is important. Inorganic arsenic penetrates deeply into and remains in the pressure-treated wood for a long time. Exposure to inorganic arsenic may present certain hazards. Therefore, the following precautions should be taken both when handling the treated wood and in determining where to use or dispose of the treated wood.	This wood has been preserved by pressure-treatment with an EPA-registered pesticide containing pentachlorophenol to protect it from insect attack and decay. Wood treated with pentachlorophenol should be used only where such protection is important. Pentachlorophenol penetrates deeply into and remains in the pressure-treated wood for a long time. Exposure to pentachlorophenol may present certain hazards. Therefore, the following precautions should be taken both when handling the treated wood and in determining where to use and dispose of the treated wood.	This wood has been preserved by pressure treatment with an EPA-registered pesticide containing creosote to protect it from insect attack and decay. Wood treated with creosote should be used only where such protection is important. Creosote penetrates deeply into and remains in the pressure-treated wood for a long time. Exposure to creosote may present certain hazards. Therefore, the following precautions should be taken both when handling the treated wood and in determining where to use the treated wood.
Handling precautions	Dispose of treated wood by ordinary trash collection or burial. Treated wood should not be burned in open fires or in stoves, fireplaces, or residential boilers because toxic chemicals may be produced as part of the smoke and ashes. Treated wood from commercial or industrial use (e.g., construction sites) may be burned only in commercial or industrial incinerators or boilers in accordance with state and Federal regulations. Avoid frequent or prolonged inhalation of sawdust from treated wood. When sawing and machining treated wood, wear a dust mask. Whenever possible, these operations should be performed outdoors to avoid indoor accumulations of airborne sawdust from treated wood. When power-sawing and machining, wear goggles to protect eyes from flying particles. After working with the wood, and before eating, drinking, and using tobacco products, wash exposed areas thoroughly. If preservatives or sawdust accumulate on clothes, launder before reuse. Wash work clothes separately from other household clothing.	Dispose of treated wood by ordinary trash collection or burial. Treated wood should not be burned in open fires or in stoves, fireplaces, or residential boilers because toxic chemicals may be produced as part of the smoke and ashes. Treated wood from commercial or industrial use (e.g., construction sites) may be burned only in commercial or industrial incinerators or boilers rated at 20 million BTU/hour or greater heat input or its equivalent in accordance with state and Federal regulations. Avoid frequent or prolonged inhalation of sawdust from treated wood. When sawing and machining treated wood, wear a dust mask. Whenever possible, these operations should be performed outdoors to avoid indoor accumulations of airborne sawdust from treated wood. Avoid frequent or prolonged skin contact with pentachlorophenol-treated wood. When handling the treated wood, wear long-sleeved shirts and long pants and use gloves impervious to the chemicals (for example, gloves that are vinyl-coated). When power-sawing and machining, wear goggles to protect eyes from flying particles. After working with the wood, and before eating, drinking, and using tobacco products, wash exposed areas thoroughly. If oily preservatives or sawdust accumulate on clothes, launder before reuse. Wash work clothes separately from other household clothing.	Dispose of treated wood by ordinary trash collection or burial. Treated wood should not be burned in open fires or in stoves, fireplaces, or residential boilers, because toxic chemicals may be produced as part of the smoke and ashes. Treated wood from commercial or industrial use (e.g., construction sites) may be burned only in commercial or industrial incinerators or boilers in accordance with state and Federal regulations. Avoid frequent or prolonged inhalations of sawdust from treated wood. When sawing and machining treated wood, wear a dust mask. Whenever possible these operations should be performed outdoors to avoid indoor accumulations of airborne sawdust from treated wood. Avoid frequent or prolonged skin contact with creosote-treated wood; when handling the treated wood, wear long-sleeved shirts and long pants and use gloves impervious to the chemicals (for example, gloves that are vinyl-coated). When power-sawing and machining, wear goggles to protect eyes from flying particles. After working with the wood and before eating, drinking, and using tobacco products, wash exposed areas thoroughly. If oily preservative or sawdust accumulate on clothes, launder before reuse. Wash work clothes separately from other household clothing.

Table 14–1. EPA-approved consumer information sheets for three major groups of preservative pressure-treated wood—con.

Preservative treatment	Inorganic arsenicals	Pentachlorophenol	Creosote
Use site precautions	Wood pressure-treated with waterborne arsenical preservatives may be used inside residences as long as all sawdust and construction debris are cleaned up and disposed of after construction. Do not use treated wood under circumstances where the preservative may become a component of food or animal feed. Examples of such sites would be structures or containers for storing silage or food. Do not use treated wood for cutting boards or countertops. Only treated wood that is visibly clean and free of surface residue should be used for patios, decks, and walkways. Do not use treated wood for construction of those portions of beehives that may come into contact with the honey. Treated wood should not be used where it may come into direct or indirect contact with public drinking water, except for uses involving incidental contact such as docks and bridges.	Logs treated with pentachlorophenol should not be used for log homes. Wood treated with pentachlorophenol should not be used where it will be in frequent or prolonged contact with bare skin (for example, chairs and other outdoor furniture), unless an effective sealer has been applied. Pentachlorophenol-treated wood should not be used in residential, industrial, or commercial interiors except for laminated beams or building components that are in ground contact and are subject to decay or insect infestation and where two coats of an appropriate sealer are applied. Sealers may be applied at the installation site. Urethane, shellac, latex epoxy enamel, and varnish are acceptable sealers for pentachlorophenol-treated wood. Wood treated with pentachlorophenol should not be used in the interiors of farm buildings where there may be direct contact with domestic animals or livestock that may crib (bite) or lick the wood. In interiors of farm buildings where domestic animals or livestock are unlikely to crib (bite) or lick the wood, pentachlorophenol-treated wood may be used for building components which are in ground contact and are subject to decay or insect infestation and where two coats of an appropriate sealer are applied. Sealers may be applied at the installation site. Do not use pentachlorophenol-treated wood for farrowing or brooding facilities. Do not use treated wood under circumstances where the preservative may become a component of food or animal feed. Examples of such sites would be structures or containers for storing silage or food. Do not use treated wood for cutting boards or countertops. Only treated wood that is visibly clean and free of surface residue should be used for patios, decks, and walkways. Do not use treated wood for construction of those portions of beehives that may come into contact with the honey. Pentachlorophenol-treated wood should not be used where it may come into direct or indirect contact with public drinking water, except for uses involving incidental contact such as docks and bridges. Do not use pentachlorophenol-treated wood where it may come into direct or indirect contact with drinking water for domestic animals or livestock, except for uses involving incidental contact such as docks and bridges.	Wood treated with creosote should not be used where it will be in frequent or prolonged contact with bare skin (for example, chairs and other outdoor furniture) unless an effective sealer has been applied. Creosote-treated wood should not be used in residential interiors. Creosote-treated wood in interiors of industrial buildings should be used only for industrial building components that are in ground contact and are subject to decay or insect infestation and for wood-block flooring. For such uses, two coats of an appropriate sealer must be applied. Sealers may be applied at the installation site. Wood treated with creosote should not be used in the interiors of farm buildings where there may be direct contact with domestic animals or livestock that may crib (bite) or lick the wood. In interiors of farm buildings where domestic animals or livestock are unlikely to crib (bite) or lick the wood, creosote-treated wood may be used for building components that are in ground contact and are subject to decay or insect infestation if two coats of an effective sealer are applied. Sealers may be applied at the installation site. Coal-tar pitch and coal-tar pitch emulsion are effective sealers for creosote-treated wood-block flooring. Urethane, epoxy, and shellac are acceptable sealers for all creosote-treated wood. Do not use creosote-treated wood for farrowing or brooding facilities. Do not use treated wood under circumstances where the preservative may become a component of food or animal feed. Examples of such use would be structures or containers for storing silage or food. Do not use treated wood for cutting boards or countertops. Only treated wood that is visibly clean and free of surface residues should be used for patios, decks, and walkways. Do not use treated wood for construction of those portions of beehives that may come into contact with the honey. Creosote-treated wood should not be used where it may come into direct or indirect contact with public drinking water, except for uses involving incidental contact such as docks and bridges. Do not use creosote-treated wood where it may come into direct or indirect contact with drinking water for domestic animals or livestock, except for uses involving incidental contact such as docks and bridges.

Table 14–2. Creosote, oilborne, and waterborne preservatives and retention levels for various wood products[a]

Form of product and service condition	Creosote and oilborne preservative retention (kg/m³ (lb/ft³))							AWPA standard
	Creosote	Creosote solutions	Creosote-petroleum	Pentachloro-phenol, P9, Type A	Pentachloro-phenol, P9, Type E	Copper naphthenate	Oxine copper	
A. Ties (crossties and switch ties)	96–128 (6–8)	112–128 (7–8)	112–128 (7–8)	5.6–6.4 (0.35–0.4)	NR	NR	NR	C2/C6
B. Lumber, timber, ply-wood; bridge and mine ties								
(1) Salt water[b]	400 (25)	400 (25)	NR	NR	NR	NR	NR	C2/C9
(2) Soil and fresh water	160 (10)	160 (10)	160 (10)	8 (0.50)	NR	0.96 (0.06)	NR	C2/C9
(3) Above ground	128 (8)	128 (8)	128 (8)	6.41 (0.40)	6.4 (0.40)	0.64 (0.04)	0.32 (0.02)	C2/C9
C. Piles								
(1) Salt water[b]								C3/C14/C18
Borer hazard, moderate	320 (20)	320 (20)	NR	NR	NR	NR	NR	
Borer hazard, severe	NR	NR	NR	NR	NR	NR	NR	
Dual treatment	320 (20)	320 (20)	NR	NR	NR	NR	NR	
(2) Soil, fresh water, or foundation	96–272 (6–17)	96–272 (6–17)	96–272 (6–17)	4.8–13.6 (0.30–0.85)	NR	1.60 (0.10)	NR	C3/C14/C24
D. Poles (length >5 m (>16 ft))								
(1) Utility	120–256 (7.5–16)	120–256 (7.5–16)	120–256 (7.5–16)	4.8–12.8 (0.30–0.80)	NR	1.2–2.4 (0.075–0.15)	NR	C4
(2) Building, round and sawn	144–216 (9–13.5)	NR	NR	7.2–10.9 (0.45–0.68)	NR	NR	NR	C4/C23/C24
(3) Agricultural, round and sawn	120–256 (7.5–16)	120–256 (7.5–16)	NR, round (sawn, 192 (12))	6.1–9.6 (0.38–0.60)	NR	NR, round (sawn, 1.2 (0.075))	NR	C4/C16
E. Posts (length <5 m (<16 ft))								
(1) Agricultural, round and sawn, fence	128–160 (8–10)	128–160 (8–10)	128–160 (8–10)	6.4–8.0 (0.40–0.50)	NR	sawn, 0.96 (0.060)	round, 0.88 (0.055)	C2/C5/C16
(2) Commercial–residential construction, round and sawn	128–192 (8–12)	128–192 (8–12)	128–192 (8–12)	8–9.6 (0.50–0.60)	NR	NR	NR	C2/C5/C15/C23
(3) Highway construction								
Fence, guide, sign, and sight	128–160 (8–10)	128–160 (8–10)	128–160 (8–10)	6.4–8.1 (0.40–0.50)	NR	sawn four sides, 0.96 (0.06)	NR	C2/C5/C14
Guardrail and spacer blocks	160–192 (10–12)	160–192 (10–12)	160–192 (10–12)	8–9.6 (0.50–0.60)	NR	sawn four sides, 1.2 (0.075)	NR	C2/C5/C14
F. Glued-laminated timbers/laminates								
(1) Soil and fresh water	160 (10)	160 (10)	160 (10)	9.6 (0.60)	NR	9.6 (0.60)	NR	C28
(2) Above ground	128 (8)	128 (8)	128 (8)	4.8 (0.30)	NR	6.4 (0.40)	3.2 (0.20)	C28

303

Table 14–2. Creosote, oilborne, and waterborne preservatives and retention levels for various wood products[a]—con.

Form of product and service condition	Waterborne preservative retention (kg/m³ (lb/ft³))								AWPA standard
	ACC	ACZA or ACA	CCA Types I, II, or III	ACQ Type B	ACQ Type D	CDDC as Cu	CC	CBA Type A	
A. Ties (crossties and switch ties)	NR	NR	NR	NR	NR	NR	NR	NR	C2/C6
B. Lumber, timber, plywood; bridge and mine ties									
(1) Salt water[b]	NR	40 (2.50)	40 (2.50)	NR	NR	NR	40 (2.50)	NR	C2/C9
(2) Soil and fresh water	6.4 (0.40)	6.4 (0.40)	6.4 (0.40)	6.4 (0.40)	6.4 (0.40)	3.2 (0.20)	6.4 (0.40)	NR	C2/C9
(3) Above ground[c]	4.0 (0.25)	4.0 (0.25)	4.0 (0.25)	4.0 (0.25)	4.0 (0.25)	1.6 (0.10)	4.0 (0.25)	3.27 (0.20)	C2/C9
C. Piles									
(1) Salt water[b]									C3/C14/ C18
Borer hazard, moderate	NR	24 (1.5)	24.1 (1.5)	NR	NR	NR	NR	NR	
Borer hazard, severe	NR	40 (2.50)	40 (2.50)	NR	NR	NR	NR	NR	
Dual treatment	NR	16 (1.00)	16 (1.00)	NR	NR	NR	NR	NR	
(2) Soil, fresh water or foundation	NR	12–16 (0.80–1.0)	12–16 (0.80–1.0)	NR	NR	NR	NR	NR	C3/C14/ C24
D. Poles (length >5 m (>16 ft))									
(1) Utility	NR	9.6 (0.60)	9.6 (0.60)	9.6 (0.60)	NR	NR	NR	NR	C4
(2) Building, round and sawn timber	NR	9.6–12.8 (0.60–0.80)	9.6–12.8 (0.60–0.80)	9.6 (0.60)	9.6 (0.60)	3.2 (0.2)	NR	NR	C4/C23/ C24
(3) Agricultural, round and sawn	NR	9.6 (0.60)	9.6 (0.60)	9.6 (0.60)	NR	NR	NR	NR	C4/C16
E. Posts (length < 5 m (<16 ft))									
(1) Agricultural, round and sawn, fence	NR	6.4 (0.40)	6.4 (0.40)	6.4 (0.40)	NR	NR	NR	NR	C2/C5/ C16
(2) Commercial– residential construction, round and sawn	8 (0.50), (NR, sawn structural members)	6.4–9.6 (0.40–0.60)	6.4–9.6 (0.40–0.60)	6.4–9.6 (0.40– 0.60)	6.4–9.6 (0.40– 0.6)	3.2 (0.20)	6.4 (0.4), (NR, sawn structural members)	NR	C2/C5/ C15/ C23
(3) Highway construction									
Fence, guide, sign, and sight	8–9.9 (0.50–0.62)	6.4 (0.40)	6.4 (0.40)	6.4 (0.40)	NR	NR	NR	NR	C2/C5/ C14
Guardrail and spacer blocks	NR	8 (0.50)	8 (0.50)	8 (0.50)	NR	NR	NR	NR	C2/C5/ C14
F. Glued- laminated timbers/laminates									
(1) Soil and fresh water	8 (0.50)[d]	6.4 (0.40)[d]	6.4 (0.40)[d]	NR	NR	NR	NR	NR	C28
(2) Above ground	3.2 (0.20)	4 (0.25)	4 (0.25)	NR	NR	NR	NR	NR	C28

[a]Retention levels are those included in Federal Specification TT–W–571 and Commodity Standards of the American Wood Preservers' Association. Refer to the current issues of these specifications for up-to-date recommendations and other details. In many cases, the retention is different depending on species and assay zone. Retentions for lumber, timber, plywood, piles, poles, and fence posts are determined by assay of borings of a number and location as specified in Federal Specification TT–W–571 or in the Standards of the American Wood Preservers' Association referenced in last column. Unless noted, all waterborne preservative retention levels are specified on an oxide basis. NR is not recommended.
[b]Dual treatments are recommended when marine borer activity is known to be high (see AWPA C2, C3, C14, and C18 for details).
[c]For use when laminations are treated prior to bonding.

In 1986, creosote became a restricted-use pesticide and is available only to certified pesticide applicators. For use and handling of creosote-treated wood, refer to the EPA-approved Consumer Information Sheet (Table 14–1).

Freshly creosoted timber can be ignited and burns readily, producing a dense smoke. However, after the timber has seasoned for some months, the more volatile parts of the oil disappear from near the surface and the creosoted wood usually is little, if any, easier to ignite than untreated wood. Until this volatile oil has evaporated, ordinary precautions should be taken to prevent fires. Creosote adds fuel value, but it does not sustain ignition.

Coal-Tar Creosotes for Nonpressure Treatments

Special coal-tar creosotes are available for nonpressure treatments, although these creosotes can only be purchased by licensed pesticide applicators. Special coal-tar creosotes differ somewhat from regular commercial coal-tar creosote in (a) being crystal-free to flow freely at ordinary temperatures and (b) having low-boiling distillation fractions removed to reduce evaporation in thermal (hot and cold) treatments in open tanks. Consensus standards do not exist for coal-tar creosote applied by brush, spray, or open-tank treatments.

Other Creosotes

Creosotes distilled from tars other than coal tar are used to some extent for wood preservation, although they are not included in current Federal or AWPA specifications. These include wood-tar creosote, oil-tar creosote, and water–gas-tar creosote. These creosotes protect wood from decay and insect attack but are generally less effective than coal-tar creosote.

Creosote Solution

For many years, either coal tar or petroleum oil has been mixed with coal-tar creosote, in various proportions, to lower preservative costs. These creosote solutions have a satisfactory record of performance, particularly for railroad ties and posts where surface appearance of the treated wood is of minor importance.

The ASTM D391 "Creosote–Coal-Tar Solution" standard covers creosote–coal-tar solution for use in the preservative treatment of wood. This standard has been approved for use by agencies of the U.S. Department of Defense. This specification contains four grades of creosote solutions:

- A (land and fresh water), contains no less than 80% coal-tar distillate (creosote) by volume

- B (land and fresh water), contains no less than 70% coal-tar distillate (creosote) by volume

- C (land and fresh water), contains no less than 60% coal-tar distillate (creosote) by volume

- Marine

The AWPA standard P2 similarly describes the requirements for creosote solutions. The AWPA standard P3 (for creosote–petroleum oil solution) stipulates that creosote–petroleum oil

solution shall consist solely of specified proportions of 50% coal-tar creosote by volume (which meets AWPA standard P1/P13) and 50% petroleum oil by volume (which meets AWPA standard P4). However, because no analytical standards exist to verify the compliance of P3 solutions after they have been mixed, the consumer assumes the risk of using these solutions.

Compared with straight creosote, creosote solutions tend to reduce weathering and checking of the treated wood. These solutions have a greater tendency to accumulate on the surface of the treated wood (bleed) and penetrate the wood with greater difficulty because they are generally more viscous than is straight creosote. High temperatures and pressures during treatment, when they can be safely used, will often improve penetration of high viscosity solutions.

Even though petroleum oil and coal tar are less toxic to wood-destroying organisms and mixtures of the two are also less toxic in laboratory tests than is straight creosote, a reduction in toxicity does not necessarily imply less preservative protection. Creosote–petroleum and creosote–coal-tar solutions help reduce checking and weathering of the treated wood. Posts and ties treated with standard formulations of these solutions have frequently shown better service than those similarly treated with straight coal-tar creosote.

Pentachlorophenol Solutions

Water-repellent solutions containing chlorinated phenols, principally pentachlorophenol (penta), in solvents of the mineral spirits type, were first used in commercial dip treatments of wood by the millwork industry about 1931. Commercial pressure treatment with pentachlorophenol in heavy petroleum oils on poles started about 1941, and considerable quantities of various products soon were pressure treated. The standard AWPA P8 defines the properties of pentachlorophenol preservative. Pentachlorophenol solutions for wood preservation shall contain not less than 95% chlorinated phenols, as determined by titration of hydroxyl and calculated as pentachlorophenol. The performance of pentachlorophenol and the properties of the treated wood are influenced by the properties of the solvent used.

The AWPA P9 standard defines solvents and formulations for organic preservative systems. A commercial process using pentachlorophenol dissolved in liquid petroleum gas (LPG) was introduced in 1961, but later research showed that field performance of penta/LPG systems was inferior to penta/P9 systems. Thus, penta/LPG systems are no longer used.

The heavy petroleum solvent included in AWPA P9 Type A is preferable for maximum protection, particularly when wood treated with pentachlorophenol is used in contact with the ground. The heavy oils remain in the wood for a long time and do not usually provide a clean or paintable surface.

Pentachlorophenol in AWPA P9, Type E solvent (dispersion in water), is only approved for aboveground use in lumber, timber, bridge ties, mine ties, and plywood for southern pines, coastal Douglas-fir, and redwood (Table 14–2; AWPA C2 and C9).

Because of the toxicity of pentachlorophenol, care is necessary when handling and using it to avoid excessive personal contact with the solution or vapor. Do not use indoors or where human, plant, or animal contact is likely. Pentachlorophenol became a restricted-use pesticide in November 1986 and is only available to certified applicators. For use and handling precautions, refer to the EPA-approved Consumer Information Sheet (Table 14–1).

The results of pole service and field tests on wood treated with 5% pentachlorophenol in a heavy petroleum oil are similar to those with coal-tar creosote. This similarity has been recognized in the preservative retention requirements of treatment specifications. Pentachlorophenol is effective against many organisms, such as decay fungi, molds, stains, and insects. Because pentachlorophenol is ineffective against marine borers, it is not recommended for the treatment of marine piles or timbers used in coastal waters.

Copper Naphthenate

Copper naphthenate is an organometalic compound that is a dark-green liquid and imparts this color to the wood. Weathering turns the color of the treated wood to light brown after several months of exposure. The wood may vary from light brown to chocolate-brown if heat is used in the treating process. The AWPA P8 standard defines the properties of copper naphthenate, and AWPA P9 covers the solvents and formulations for organic preservative systems.

Copper naphthenate is effective against wood-destroying fungi and insects. It has been used commercially since the 1940s for many wood products (Table 14–2). It is a reaction product of copper salts and naphthenic acids that are usually obtained as byproducts in petroleum refining. Copper naphthenate is not a restricted-use pesticide but should be handled as an industrial pesticide. It may be used for superficial treatment, such as by brushing with solutions with a copper content of 1% to 2% (approximately 10% to 20% copper naphthenate).

Chlorothalonil

Chlorothalonil (CTL) [tetrachloroisophthalonitrile] is an organic biocide that is used to a limited extent for mold control in CCA-treated wood (AWPA P8). It is effective against wood decay fungi and wood-destroying insects. The CTL has limited solubility in organic solvents and very low solubility in water, but it exhibits good stability and leach resistance in wood. This preservative is being evaluated for both aboveground and ground contact applications. The solvent used in the formulation of the preservative is AWPA P9 Type A.

Chlorothalonil/Chlorpyrifos

Chlorothalonil/chlorpyrifos (CTL/CPF) is a preservative system composed of two active ingredients (AWPA P8). The ratio of the two components depends upon the retention specified. CTL is an effective fungicide, and CPF is very effective against insect attack. The solvent used for formulation of this preservative is specified in AWPA P9.

Oxine Copper (copper-8-quinolinolate)

Oxine copper (copper-8-quinolinolate) is an organometalic compound, and the formulation consists of at least 10% copper-8-quinolinolate, 10% nickel-2-ethylhexanoate, and 80% inert ingredients (AWPA P8). It is accepted as a stand-alone preservative for aboveground use for sapstain and mold control and is also used for pressure treating (Table 14–2). A water-soluble form can be made with dodecylbenzene sulfonic acid, but the solution is corrosive to metals.

Oxine copper solutions are greenish brown, odorless, toxic to both wood decay fungi and insects, and have a low toxicity to humans and animals. Because of its low toxicity to humans and animals, oxine copper is the only EPA-registered preservative permitted by the U.S. Food and Drug Administration for treatment of wood used in direct contact with food. Some examples of its uses in wood are commercial refrigeration units, fruit and vegetable baskets and boxes, and water tanks. Oxine copper solutions have also been used on nonwood materials, such as webbing, cordage, cloth, leather, and plastics.

Zinc Naphthenate

Zinc naphthenate is similar to copper naphthenate but is less effective in preventing decay from wood-destroying fungi and mildew. It is light colored and does not impart the characteristic greenish color of copper naphthenate, but it does impart an odor. Waterborne and solventborne formulations are available. Zinc naphthenate is not used for pressure treating and is not intended as a stand-alone preservative.

Bis(tri-n-butyltin) Oxide

Bis(tri-n-butyltin) oxide, commonly called TBTO, is a colorless to slightly yellow organotin compound that is soluble in many organic solvents but insoluble in water. It is not used for pressure treating or as a stand-alone preservative for in-ground use. TBTO concentrate contains at least 95% bis(tri-n-butyltin) oxide by weight and from 38.2% to 40.1% tin (AWPA P8). This preservative has lower mammalian toxicity, causes less skin irritation, and has better paintability than does pentachlorophenol, but it is not effective against decay when used in ground contact. Therefore, TBTO is recommended only for aboveground use, such as millwork. It has been used as a marine antifoulant, but this use has been almost eliminated because of the environmental impact of tin on shellfish.

3-Iodo-2-Propynyl Butyl Carbamate

3-Iodo-2-propynyl butyl carbamate (IPBC) is a preservative that is intended for nonstructural, aboveground use only (for example, millwork). It is not used for pressure treating applications such as decks. The IPBC preservative is included as the primary fungicide in several water-repellent-preservative formulations under the trade name Polyphase and marketed by retail stores. However, it is not an effective insecticide. Waterborne and solventborne formulations are available. Some formulations yield an odorless, treated product that can be painted if dried after treatment. IPBC is also being used in combination with didecyldimethylammonium chloride in a sapstain–mold formulation (NP–1). IPBC contains 97% 3-iodo-2-propynyl butyl carbamate, with a minimum of 43.4% iodine (AWPA P8).

Alkyl Ammonium Compound

Alkyl ammonium compound (AAC) or didecyldimethylammonium chloride (DDAC) is a compound that is effective against wood decay fungi and insects. It is soluble in both organic solvents and water and is stable in wood as a result of chemical fixation reactions. It is currently being used as a component of ammoniacal copper quat (ACQ) (see section on Waterborne Preservatives) for aboveground and ground contact and is a component of NP–1 for sapstain and mold control.

Propiconazole

Propiconazole is an organic triazole biocide that is effective against wood decay fungi but not against insects (AWPA P8). It is soluble in some organic solvents, but it has low solubility in water and is stable and leach resistant in wood. It is currently being used commercially for aboveground and sapstain control application in Europe and Canada. Solvents used in the formulation of the preservative are specified in either AWPA P9 Type C or Type F.

4,5-Dichloro-2-N-Octyl-4-Isothiazolin-3-One

4,5-dichloro-2-N-octyl-4-isothiazolin-3-one is a biocide that is effective against wood decay fungi and insects. It is soluble in organic solvents, but not in water, and is stable and leach resistant in wood. This biocide is not currently being used as a wood preservative. The solvent used in the formulation of the preservative is specified in AWPA P9 Type C.

Tebuconazole

Tebuconazole (TEB) is an organic triazole biocide that is effective against wood decay fungi, but its efficacy against insects has not yet been evaluated. It is soluble in organic solvents but not in water, and it is stable and leach resistant in wood. Currently, TEB has no commercial application. The solvents used in the formulation of this preservative are specified in either AWPA P9 Type C or Type F.

Chlorpyrifos

Chlorpyrifos (CPF) is a preservative recently put into standard (AWPA P8). It is very effective against insect attack but not fungal attack. If fungal attack is a concern, then CPF should be combined with an appropriate fungicide, such as chlorothalonil/chlorpyrifos or IPBC/chlorpyrifos.

Water-Repellent and Nonpressure Treatments

Effective water-repellent preservatives will retard the ingress of water when wood is exposed above ground. Therefore, these preservatives help reduce dimensional changes in the wood as a result of moisture changes when the wood is exposed to rainwater or dampness for short periods. As with any wood preservative, the effectiveness in protecting wood

against decay and insects depends upon the retention and penetration obtained in application. These preservatives are most often applied using nonpressure treatments like brushing, soaking, or dipping.

Preservative systems containing water-repellent components are sold under various trade names, principally for the dip or equivalent treatment of window sash and other millwork. Many are sold to consumers for household and farm use. Federal specification TT–W–572 stipulates that such preservatives (a) be dissolved in volatile solvents, such as mineral spirits, (b) do not cause appreciable swelling of the wood, and (c) produce a treated wood product that meets a performance test on water repellency.

The preservative chemicals in Federal specification TT–W–572 may be one of the following:

- Not less than 5% pentachlorophenol

- Not less than 1% copper in the form of copper naphthenate

- Not less than 2% copper in the form of copper naphthenate for tropical conditions

- Not less than 0.045% copper in the form of oxine copper for uses when foodstuffs will be in contact with the treated wood

The National Wood Window and Door Association (NWWDA) standard for water-repellent preservative nonpressure treatment for millwork, IS 4–94, permits other preservatives, provided the wood preservative is registered for use by the EPA under the latest revision of the Federal Insecticide, Fungicide, and Rodenticide Act (FIFRA) and that all water-repellent preservative formulations are tested for effectiveness against decay according to the soil block test (NWWDA TM1).

The AWPA Standard N1 for nonpressure treatment of millwork components also states that any water-repellent preservative formulation must be registered for use by the EPA under the latest revision of FIFRA. The preservative must also meet the *Guidelines for Evaluating New Wood Preservatives for Consideration by the AWPA* for nonpressure treatment.

Water-repellent preservatives containing oxine copper are used in nonpressure treatment of wood containers, pallets, and other products for use in contact with foods. When combined with volatile solvents, oxine copper is used to pressure-treat lumber intended for use in decking of trucks and cars or related uses involving harvesting, storage, and transportation of foods (AWPA P8).

Waterborne Preservatives

Waterborne preservatives are often used when cleanliness and paintability of the treated wood are required. Several formulations involving combinations of copper, chromium, and arsenic have shown high resistance to leaching and very good performance in service. Waterborne preservatives are included in specifications for items such as lumber, timber, posts, building foundations, poles, and piling.

Test results based on sea water exposure have shown that dual treatment (waterborne copper-containing salt preservatives followed by creosote) is possibly the most effective method of protecting wood against all types of marine borers. The AWPA standards have recognized this process as well as the treatment of marine piles with high retention levels of ammoniacal copper arsenate (ACA), ammoniacal copper zinc arsenate (ACZA), or chromated copper arsenate (CCA). The recommended treatment and retention in kilograms per cubic meter (pounds per cubic foot) for round timber piles exposed to severe marine borer hazard are given in Table 14–3. Poorly treated or untreated heartwood faces of wood species containing "high sapwood" that do not require heartwood penetration (for example, southern pines, ponderosa pine, and red pine) have been found to perform inadequately in marine exposure. In marine applications, only sapwood faces should be allowed for waterborne-preservative-treated pine in direct sea water exposure.

Waterborne preservatives leave the wood surface comparatively clean, paintable, and free from objectionable odor. CCA and acid copper chromate (ACC) must be used at low treating temperatures (38°C to 66°C (100°F to 150°F)) because they are unstable at higher temperatures. This restriction may involve some difficulty when higher temperatures are needed to obtain good treating results in woods such as Douglas-fir. Because water is added to the wood in the treatment process, the wood must be dried after treatment to the moisture content required for the end use intended.

Inorganic arsenicals are a restricted-use pesticide. For use and handling precautions of pressure-treated wood containing inorganic arsenicals, refer to the EPA-approved Consumer Information Sheet (Table 14–1).

Standard wood preservatives used in water solution include ACC, ACZA, and CCA (Types A and C). Other preservatives in AWPA P5 include alkyl ammonium compound (AAC) and inorganic boron. Waterborne wood preservatives, without arsenic or chromium, include ammoniacal copper quat (ACQ) (Types B and D), copper bis(dimethyldithiocarbamate) (CDDC), ammoniacal copper citrate (CC), and copper azole–Type A (CBA–A), for aboveground use only.

Acid Copper Chromate

Acid copper chromate (ACC) contains 31.8% copper oxide and 68.2% chromium trioxide (AWPA P5). The solid, paste, liquid concentrate, or treating solution can be made of copper sulfate, potassium dichromate, or sodium dichromate. Tests on stakes and posts exposed to decay and termite attack indicate that wood well-impregnated with ACC gives acceptable service, but it is more prone to leaching than are most other waterborne preservatives. Use of ACC is generally limited to cooling towers that cannot allow arsenic leachate in cooling water.

Ammoniacal Copper Zinc Arsenate

Ammoniacal copper zinc arsenate (ACZA) is used in the United States but not in Canada. It is commonly used on the West Coast for the treatment of Douglas-fir. The penetration

Table 14–3. Preservative treatment and retention necessary to protect round timber piles from severe marine borer attack

Treatment	Retention (kg/m^3 (lb/ft^3))		
	Southern Pine, red pine	Coastal Douglas-fir	AWPA standard
Limnoria tripunctata only			
Ammoniacal copper arsenate	40 (2.50), (24 (1.5))[a]	40 (2.50)	C3, C18
Ammoniacal copper zinc arsenate	40 (2.50), (24 (1.5))[a]	40 (2.50)	C3, C18
Chromated copper arsenate	40 (2.50), (24 (1.5))[a]	Not recommended	C3, C18
Creosote	320 (20), (256 (16))[a]	320 (20)	C3, C18
Limnoria tripunctata and Pholads (dual treatment)			
First treatment			
Ammoniacal copper arsenate	16 (1.0)	16 (1.0)	C3, C18
Ammoniacal copper zinc arsenate	16 (1.0)	16 (1.0)	C3, C18
Chromated copper arsenate	16 (1.0)	16 (1.0)	C3, C18
Second treatment			
Creosote	320 (20.0)	320 (20.0)	C3, C18
Creosote solution	320 (20.0)	Not recommended	C3, C18

[a]Lower retention levels are for marine piling used in areas from New Jersey northward on the East Coast and north of San Francisco on the West Coast in the United States.

of Douglas-fir heartwood is improved with ACZA because of the chemical composition and stability of treating at elevated temperatures. Wood treated with ACZA performs and has characteristics similar to those of wood treated with CCA (Table 14–2).

ACZA should contain approximately 50% copper oxide, 25% zinc oxide, and 25% arsenic pentoxide dissolved in a solution of ammonia in water (AWPA P5). The weight of ammonia is at least 1.38 times the weight of copper oxide. To aid in solution, ammonium bicarbonate is added (at least equal to 0.92 times the weight of copper oxide).

A similar formulation, ammoniacal copper arsenate (ACA), is used in Canada. This preservative is used most commonly to treat refractory species, such as Douglas-fir. Service records on structures treated with ACA show that this preservative provides protection against decay and termites. High retention levels of preservative will provide extended service life to wood exposed to the marine environment, provided pholad-type borers are not present. ACZA replaced ACA in the United States because ACZA has less arsenic and is less expensive than ACA.

Chromated Copper Arsenate

Three types of chromated copper arsenate (CCA)—Types A, B, C—are covered in AWPA P5, but Type C is by far the most commonly used formulation. The compositions of the three types are given in Table 14–4. Standard P5 permits substitution of potassium or sodium dichromate for chromium trioxide; copper sulfate, basic copper carbonate, or copper hydroxide for copper oxide; and arsenic acid, sodium arsenate, or pyroarsenate for arsenic pentoxide.

1. CCA Type A (Greensalt)—Currently, CCA Type A is only being used by a few treaters in California. CCA Type A is high in chromium. Service data on treated poles, posts, and stakes installed in the United States since 1938 have shown that CCA Type A provides excellent protection against decay fungi and termites.

2. CCA Type B (K–33) —Commercial use of this preservative in the United States started in 1964, but it is no longer used in significant quantities. CCA Type B is high in

arsenic and has been commercially used in Sweden since 1950. It was included in stake tests in the United States in 1949 and has been providing excellent protection.

3. CCA Type C (Wolman)—Currently, Type C is by far the most common formulation of CCA being used because it has the best leach resistance and field efficacy of the three CCA formulations. CCA Type C composition was selected by AWPA technical committees to encourage a single standard for CCA preservatives. Commercial preservatives of similar composition have been tested and used in England since 1954, then in Australia, New Zealand, Malaysia, and in various countries of Africa and Central Europe; they are performing very well.

High retention levels (40 kg/m^3 (2.5 lb/ft^3)) of the three types of CCA preservative will provide good resistance to *Limnoria* and *Teredo* marine borer attack. In general, Douglas-fir heartwood is very resistant to treatment with CCA.

Ammoniacal Copper Quat

There are basically two types of ammoniacal copper quat (ACQ) preservatives (AWPA P5):

- Type B (ACQ–B) [ammoniacal]

- Type D (ACQ–D) [amine-based]

The compositions of these two types are given in Table 14–5. ACQ is used for many of the same applications as are ACZA and CCA, but it is not recommended for use in salt water. ACQ–B, the ammoniacal formulation, is better able to penetrate difficult to treat species such as Douglas-fir; ACQ–D provides a more uniform surface appearance. Wood products treated with ACQ Type B and D are included in the AWPA Commodity Standards (Table 14–2).

Copper bis(dimethyldithiocarbamate)

Copper bis(dimethyldithiocarbamate) (CDDC) is a reaction product formed in wood as a result of the dual treatment of two separate treating solutions. The first treating solution contains a maximum of 5% bivalent copper–ethanolamine (2-aminoethanol), and the second treating solution contains a minimum of 2.5% sodium dimethyldithiocarbamate

Table 14–4. Composition of the three types of chromated copper arsenate[a]

Component	Chromated copper arsenate (parts by weight)		
	Type A	Type B	Type C
Chromium trioxide	65.5	35.3	47.5
Copper oxide	18.1	19.6	18.5
Arsenic pentoxide	16.4	45.1	34.0

[a]As covered in AWPA P5.

Table 14–5. Composition of two types of ammoniacal copper quat[a]

Component	Ammoniacal cooper quat (parts by weight)	
	Type B	Type D
Copper oxide	66.7	66.7
Quat as DDAC[b]	33.3	33.3
Formulation	ammoniacal	amine

[a]As covered in AWPA P5.
[b]DDAC is didecyldimethylammonium chloride.

(AWPA P5). CDDC-treated wood products are included in the AWPA Commodity Standards (Table 14–2) for uses such as residential construction. Like CCA and ACQ–D, CDDC is not recommended for treatment of refractory species such as Douglas-fir.

Ammoniacal Copper Citrate

Ammoniacal copper citrate (CC) has 62.3% copper as copper oxide and 35.8% citric acid dissolved in a solution of ammonia in water (AWPA P5). CC-treated wood products are included in the AWPA Commodity Standards (Table 14–2). Like other ammonia-based preservatives, CC can be used to treat refractory species such as Douglas-fir.

Copper Azole–Type A

Copper azole–Type A (CBA–A) has 49% copper as Cu, 49% boron as boric acid, and 2% azole as tebuconazole dissolved in a solution of ethanolamine in water (AWPA P5). Wood products treated with CBA–A are included in the AWPA Commodity Standards for aboveground use only (Table 14–2).

Inorganic Boron (Borax/Boric Acid)

Borate preservatives are readily soluble in water, are highly leachable, and should only be used above ground where the wood is protected from wetting. When used above ground and protected from wetting, this preservative is very effective against decay, termites, beetles, and carpenter ants. Borates are odorless and can be sprayed, brushed, or injected. They will diffuse into wood that is wet; therefore, these preservatives are often used as a remedial treatment. Borates are widely used for log homes, natural wood finishes, and hardwood pallets.

The solid or treating solution for borate preservatives (borates) should be greater than 98% pure, on an anhydrous basis (AWPA P5). Acceptable borate compounds are sodium octaborate, sodium tetraborate, sodium pentaborate, and boric acid. These compounds are derived from the mineral sodium borate, which is the same material used in laundry additives.

Preservative Effectiveness

Preservative effectiveness is influenced not only by the protective value of the preservative chemical, but also by the method of application and extent of penetration and retention of the preservative in the treated wood. Even with an effective preservative, good protection cannot be expected with poor penetration or substandard retention levels. The species of wood, proportion of heartwood and sapwood, heartwood penetrability, and moisture content are among the important variables that influence the results of treatment. For various wood products, the preservatives and retention levels listed in Federal Specification TT–W–571 and the AWPA Commodity Standards are given in Table 14–2.

Few service tests include a variety of preservatives under comparable conditions of exposure. Furthermore, service tests may not show a good comparison between different preservatives as a result of the difficulty in controlling the previously mentioned variables. Such comparative data under similar exposure conditions, with various preservatives and retention levels, are included in the USDA Forest Service, Forest Products Laboratory, stake test study on Southern Pine sapwood (Gutzmer and Crawford 1995). A summary of these test results is included in Table 14–6.

In the same manner, a comparison of preservative treatments in marine exposure (Key West, Florida) of small wood panels is included in Johnson and Gutzmer (1990). These preservatives and treatments include creosotes with and without supplements, waterborne preservatives, waterborne preservative and creosote dual treatments, chemical modifications of wood, and various chemically modified polymers. In this study, untreated panels were badly damaged by marine borers after 6 to 18 months of exposure while some treated panels have remained free of attack after 19 years in the sea.

Effect of Species on Penetration

The effectiveness of preservative treatment is influenced by the penetration and distribution of the preservative in the wood. For maximum protection, it is desirable to select species for which good penetration is best assured.

The heartwood of some species is difficult to treat. There may be variations in the resistance to preservative penetration of different wood species. Table 14–7 gives the relative resistance of the heartwood to treatment of various softwood and hardwood species (MacLean 1952).

In general, the sapwood of most softwood species is not difficult to treat under pressure. Examples of species with sapwood that is easily penetrated when it is well dried and pressure treated are the pines, coastal Douglas-fir, western larch, Sitka spruce, western hemlock, western redcedar, northern white-cedar, and white fir (*A. concolor*). Examples of species with sapwood and heartwood somewhat resistant to penetration are the red and white spruces and Rocky Mountain Douglas-fir. Cedar poles are commonly incised to obtain satisfactory preservative penetration. With round members, such as poles, posts, and piles, the penetration of the sapwood is important in achieving a protective outer zone around the heartwood.

The heartwood of most species resists penetration of preservatives, but well-dried white fir, western hemlock, northern red oak, the ashes, and tupelo are examples of species with heartwood that is reasonably easy to penetrate. The southern pines, ponderosa pine, redwood, Sitka spruce, coastal Douglas-fir, beech, maples, and birches are examples of species with heartwood that is moderately resistant to penetration.

Table 14–6. Results of Forest Products Laboratory studies on 5- by 10- by 46-cm (2- by 4- by 18-in.) Southern Pine sapwood stakes, pressure-treated with commonly used wood preservatives, installed at Harrison Experimental Forest, Mississippi

Preservative	Average retention (kg/m³ (lb/ft³))[a]		Average life (year) or condition at last inspection
Control (untreated stakes)			1.8 to 3.6 years
Acid copper chromate	2.08	(0.13)	11.6 years
	2.24	(0.14)	6.1 years
	4.01	(0.25)	70% failed after 24 years
	4.17	(0.26)	60% failed after 46 years
	4.65	(0.29)	4.6 years
	5.93	(0.37)	50% failed after 46 years
	8.01	(0.50)	40% failed after 24 years
	12.18	(0.76)	20% failed after 24 years
Ammoniacal copper borate	2.72	(0.17)	65% failed after 16 years
	3.52	(0.22)	30% failed after 16 years
	5.29	(0.33)	10% failed after 16 years
	7.21	(0.45)	5% failed after 16 years
	.41	(0.65)	5% failed after 16 years
	21.31	(1.33)	No failures after 16 years
Ammoniacal copper arsenate	2.56	(0.16)	60% failed after 16 years
	3.52	(0.22)	10% failed after 16 years
	3.84	(0.24)	67% failed after 47 years
	4.01	(0.25)	20% failed after 24 years
	7.37	(0.46)	10% failed after 24 years
	8.17	(0.51)	10% failed after 47 years
	15.54	(0.97)	No failures after 47 years
	20.02	(1.25)	No failures after 47 years
Chromated copper arsenate Type I	2.40	(0.15)	70% failed after 46 years
	3.52	(0.22)	30% failed after 24 years
	4.65	(0.29)	30% failed after 46 years
	7.05	(0.44)	10% failed after 24 years
	7.05	(0.44)	10% failed after 46 years
Type II	3.68	(0.23)	30% failed after 24 years
	4.17	(0.26)	10% failed after 42 years
	5.93	(0.37)	No failures after 42 years
	8.33	(0.52)	No failures after 42 years
	12.66	(0.79)	No failures after 42 years
	16.66	(1.04)	No failures after 42 years
Type III	2.24	(0.14)	No failures after 12-1/2 years
	3.20	(0.20)	No failures after 20 years
	4.01	(0.25)	No failures after 14 years
	4.33	(0.27)	No failures after 12-1/2 years
	6.41	(0.40)	No failures after 20 years
	6.41	(0.40)	No failures after 14 years
	6.41	(0.40)	No failures after 12-1/2 years
	9.61	(0.60)	No failures after 20 years
	9.93	(0.62)	No failures after 12-1/2 years
	12.34	(0.77)	No failures after 14 years
	12.66	(0.79)	No failures after 12-1/2 years
Chromated zinc arsenate	1.76	(0.11)	22.1 years
	3.52	(0.22)	33.0 years
	4.65	(0.29)	89% failed after 51-1/2 years
	3.20	(0.20)	10% failed after 40 years
	6.41	(0.40)	No failures after 40 years
	8.49	(0.53)	No failures after 40 years
	6.09	(0.38)	40% failed after 51-1/2 years
	8.33	(0.52)	10% failed after 51-1/2 years
	11.21	(0.70)	No failures after 51-1/2 years

Table 14–6. Results of Forest Products Laboratory studies on 5- by 10- by 46-cm (2- by 4- by 18-in.) Southern Pine sapwood stakes, pressure-treated with commonly used wood preservatives, installed at Harrison Experimental Forest, Mississippi—con.

Preservative	Average retention (kg/m³ (lb/ft³))[a]	Average life (year) or condition at last inspection
Chromated zinc chloride	4.81 (0.30)	14.2 years
	7.53 (0.47)	20.2 years
	7.37 (0.46)	13.7 years
	10.09 (0.63)	20.1 years
	9.93 (0.62)	14.9 years
	14.74 (0.92)	23.4 years
	15.38 (0.96	90% failed after 24 years
	28.52 (1.78)	32.7 years
		90% failed after 38 years
	58.79 (3.67)	No failures after 38 years
Oxine copper	0.16 (0.01)	5.3 years
(Copper-8-quinolinoate)	0.32 (0.02)	4.2 years
Stoddard solvent	0.96 (0.06)	5.6 years
	1.92 (0.12)	7.8 years
Oxine copper	0.22 (0.014)	80% failed after 28 years
(Copper-8-quinolinolate)	0.48 (0.03)	70% failed after 28 years
AWPA P9 heavy petroleum	0.95 (0.059)	20% failed after 28 years
	1.99 (0.124)	No failures after 28 years
Copper naphthenate		
0.11% copper in No. 2 fuel oil	0.19 (0.012)	15.9 years
0.29% copper in No. 2 fuel oil	0.46 (0.029)	21.8 years
0.57% copper in No. 2 fuel oil	0.98 (0.061)	27.2 years
0.86% copper in No. 2 fuel oil	1.31 (0.082)	29.6 years
Creosote, coal-tar	52.87 (3.3)	24.9 years
	65.68 (4.1)	14.2 years
	67.28 (4.2)	17.8 years
	73.69 (4.6)	21.3 years
	124.96 (7.8)	70% failed after 49-1/2 years
	128.24 (8.0)	80% failed after 51-1/2 years
	132.97 (8.3)	40% failed after 42 years
	160.2 (10.0)	90% failed after 51 years
	189.04 (11.8)	30% failed after 51-1/2 years
	211.46 (13.2)	20% failed after 49-1/2 years
	232.29 (14.5)	No failures after 51 years
	264.33 (16.5)	No failures after 51-1/2 years
Low residue, straight run	128.16 (8.0)	17.8 years
Medium residue, straight run	128.16 (8.0)	18.8 years
High residue, straight run	124.96 (7.8)	20.3 years
Medium residue, low in tar acids	129.76 (8.1)	19.4 years
Low in naphthalene	131.36 (8.2)	21.3 years
Low in tar acids and naphthalene	128.16 (8.0)	18.9 years
Low residue, low in tar acids and naphthalene	128.16 (8.0)	19.2 years
High residue, low in tar acids and naphthalene	131.36 (8.2)	20.0 years
English vertical retort	84.91 (5.3)	80% failed after 44 years
	128.16 (8.0)	18.9 years
	161.80 (10.1)	80% failed after 44 years
	240.30 (15.0)	No failures after 44 years
English coke oven	75.29 (4.7)	16.3 years
	126.56 (7.9)	13.6 years
	161.80 (10.1)	70% failed after 44 years
	237.10 (14.8)	70% failed after 44 years

Table 14–6. Results of Forest Products Laboratory studies on 5- by 10- by 46-cm (2- by 4- by 18-in.) Southern Pine sapwood stakes, pressure-treated with commonly used wood preservatives, installed at Harrison Experimental Forest, Mississippi—con.

Preservative	Average retention $(kg/m^3 \ (lb/ft^3))^a$	Average life (year) or condition at last inspection
Fluor chrome arsenate phenol	1.92 (0.12)	10.2 years
type A	3.04 (0.19)	18.0 years
	3.52 (0.22)	18.3 years
	4.97 (0.31)	18.5 years
	6.09 (0.38)	24.1 years
Pentachlorophenol (various solvents)		
Liquefied petroleum gas	2.24 (0.14)	90% failed after 30-1/2 years
	3.04 (0.19)	15.9 years
	5.45 (0.34)	No failures after 30-1/2 years
	5.45 (0.34)	70% failed after 28 years
	7.85 (0.49)	No failures after 28 years
	9.29 (0.58)	No failures after 30-1/2 years
	10.41 (0.65)	No failures after 28 years
Stoddard solvent	2.24 (0.14)	13.7 years
(mineral spirits)	2.88 (0.18)	15.9 years
	3.20 (0.20)	9.5 years
	3.20 (0.20)	13.7 years
	6.09 (0.38)	40% failed after 30-1/2 years
	6.41 (0.40)	15.5 years
	10.73 (0.67)	No failures after 30-1/2 years
Heavy gas oil	3.20 (0.20)	67% failed after 44-1/2 years
(Mid-United States)	6.41 (0.40)	60% failed after 44-1/2 years
	9.61 (0.60)	10% failed after 44-1/2 years
No. 4 aromatic oil	3.36 (0.21)	21.0 years
(West Coast)	6.57 (0.41)	50% failed after 42 years
AWPA P9 (heavy petroleum)	1.76 (0.11)	80% failed after 30-1/2 years
	3.04 (0.19)	No failures after 30-1/2 years
	4.65 (0.29)	No failures after 30-1/2 years
	8.49 (0.53)	No failures after 28 years
	10.73 (0.67)	No failures after 30-1/2 years
Tributyltin oxide		
Stoddard solvent	0.24 (0.015)	6.3 years
	0.40 (0.025)	4.5 years
	0.48 (0.030)	7.2 years
	0.72 (0.045)	7.4 years
	0.75 (0.047)	7.0 years
AWPA P9 (heavy petroleum)	0.38 (0.024)	20.8 years
	0.77 (0.048)	24.0 years
Petroleum solvent controls	64.08 (4.0)	7.6 years
	65.68 (4.1)	4.4 years
	75.29 (4.7)	12.9 years
	123.35 (7.7)	14.6 years
	126.56 (7.9)	90% failed after 44-1/2 years
	128.16 (8.0)	19.7 years
	128.16 (8.0)	23.3 years
	128.16 (8.0)	14.6 years
	129.76 (8.1)	3.4 years
	136.17 (8.5)	90% failed after 28 years
	157.00 (9.8)	6.3 years
	192.24 (12.0)	17.1 years
	193.84 (12.1)	20% failed after 44-1/2 years
	310.79 (19.4)	9.1 years

[a]Retention values are based on preservative oxides or copper metal.

Table 14–7. Penetration of the heartwood of various softwood and hardwood species[a]

Ease of treatment	Softwoods	Hardwoods
Least difficult	Bristlecone pine (*Pinus aristata*) Pinyon (*P. edulis*) Pondersosa pine (*P. pondersosa*) Redwood (*Sequoia sempervirens*)	American basswood (*Tilia americana*) Beech (white heartwood) (*Fagus grandifolia*) Black tupelo (blackgum) (*Nyssa sylvatica*) Green ash (*Fraxinus pennsylvanica* var. *lanceolata*) Pin cherry (*Prunus pensylvanica*) River birch (*Betula nigra*) Red oaks (*Quercus* spp.) Slippery elm (*Ulmus fulva*) Sweet birch (*Betula lenia*) Water tupelo (*Nyssa aquatica*) White ash (*Fraxinus americana*)
Moderately difficult	Baldcypress (*Taxodium distichum*) California red fir (*Abies magnifica*) Douglas-fir (coast) (*Pseudotsuga taxifolia*)) Eastern white pine (*Pinus strobus*) Jack pine (*P. banksiana*) Loblolly pine (*P. taeda*) Longleaf pine (*P. palustris*) Red pine (*P. resinosa*) Shortleaf pine (*P. echinata*) Sugar pine (*P. lambertiana*) Western hemlock (*Tsuga heterophylla*)	Black willow (*Salix nigra*) Chestnut oak (*Quercus montana*) Cottonwood (*Populus* sp.) Bigtooth aspen (*P. grandidentata*) Mockernut hickory (*Carya tomentosa*) Silver maple (*Acer saccharinum*) Sugar maple (*A. saccharum*) Yellow birch (*Betula lutea*)
Difficult	Eastern hemlock (*Tsuga canadensis*) Engelmann spruce (*Picea engelmanni*) Grand fir (*Abies grandis*) Lodgepole pine (*Pinus contorta* var. *latifolia*) Noble fir (*Abies procera*) Sitka spruce (*Picea sitchensis*) Western larch (*Larix occidentalis*) White fir (*Abies concolor*) White spruce (*Picea glauca*)	American sycamore (*Platanus occidentalis*) Hackberry (*Celtis occidentalis*) Rock elm (*Ulmus thomoasi*) Yellow-poplar (*Liriodendron tulipifera*)
Very difficult	Alpine fir (*Abies lasiocarpa*) Corkbark fir (*A. lasiocarpa* var. *arizonica*) Douglas-fir (Rocky Mountain) (*Pseudotsuga taxifolia*) Northern white-cedar (*Thuja occidentalis*) Tamarack (*Larix laricina*) Western redcedar (*Thuja plicata*)	American beech (red heartwood) (*Fagus grandifolia*) American chestnut (*Castanea dentata*) Black locust (*Robinia pseudoacacia*) Blackjack oak (*Quercus marilandica*) Sweetgum (redgum) (*Liquidambar styraciflua*) White oaks (*Quercus* spp.)

[a]As covered in MacLean (1952).

Preparation of Timber for Treatment

For satisfactory treatment and good performance, the timber must be sound and suitably prepared. Except in specialized treating methods involving unpeeled or green material, the wood should be well peeled and either seasoned or conditioned in the cylinder before treatment. It is also highly desirable that all machining be completed before treatment. Machining may include incising to improve the preservative penetration in woods that are resistant to treatment, as well as the operations of cutting or boring of holes.

Peeling

Peeling round or slabbed products is necessary to enable the wood to dry quickly enough to avoid decay and insect damage and to permit the preservative to penetrate satisfactorily. Even strips of the thin inner bark may prevent penetration. Patches of bark left on during treatment usually fall off in time and expose untreated wood, thus permitting decay to reach the interior of the member.

Careful peeling is especially important for wood that is to be treated by a nonpressure method. In the more thorough processes, some penetration may take place both longitudinally and tangentially in the wood; consequently, small strips of bark are tolerated in some specifications. Processes in which a preservative is forced or permitted to diffuse through green wood lengthwise do not require peeling of

the timber. Machines of various types have been developed for peeling round timbers, such as poles, piles, and posts (Fig. 14–1).

Drying

Drying of wood before treatment is necessary to prevent decay and stain and to obtain preservative penetration. However, for treatment with waterborne preservatives by certain diffusion methods, high moisture content levels may be permitted. For treatment by other methods, however, drying before treatment is essential. Drying before treatment opens up the checks before the preservative is applied, thus increasing penetration, and reduces the risk of checks opening after treatment and exposing unpenetrated wood. Good penetration of heated organic-based preservatives may be possible in wood with a moisture content as high as 40% to 60%, but severe checking while drying after treatment can expose untreated wood.

For large timbers and railroad ties, air drying is a widely used method of conditioning. Despite the increased time, labor, and storage space required, air drying is generally the most inexpensive and effective method, even for pressure treatment. However, wet, warm climatic conditions make it difficult to air dry wood adequately without objectionable infection by stain, mold, and decay fungi. Such infected wood is often highly permeable; in rainy weather, infected wood can absorb a large quantity of water, which prevents satisfactory treatment.

Figure 14–1. Machine peeling of poles. The outer bark has been removed by hand, and the inner bark is being peeled by machine. Frequently, all the bark is removed by machine.

How long the timber must be air dried before treatment depends on the climate, location, and condition of the seasoning yard, methods of piling, season of the year, timber size, and species. The most satisfactory seasoning practice for any specific case will depend on the individual drying conditions and the preservative treatment to be used. Therefore, treating specifications are not always specific as to moisture content requirements.

To prevent decay and other forms of fungal infection during air drying, the wood should be cut and dried when conditions are less favorable for fungus development (Ch. 13). If this is impossible, chances for infection can be minimized by prompt conditioning of the green material, careful piling and roofing during air drying, and pretreating the green wood with preservatives to protect it during air drying.

Lumber of all species, including Southern Pine poles, is often kiln dried before treatment, particularly in the southern United States where proper air seasoning is difficult. Kiln drying has the important added advantage of quickly reducing moisture content, thereby reducing transportation charges on poles.

Conditioning of Green Products

Plants that treat wood by pressure processes can condition green material by means other than air and kiln drying. Thus, they avoid a long delay and possible deterioration of the timber before treatment.

When green wood is to be treated under pressure, one of several methods for conditioning may be selected. The steaming-and-vacuum process is used mainly for southern pines, and the Boulton or boiling-under-vacuum process is used for Douglas-fir and sometimes hardwoods.

In the steaming process, the green wood is steamed in the treating cylinder for several hours, usually at a maximum of 118°C (245°F). When steaming is completed, a vacuum is immediately applied. During the steaming period, the outer part of the wood is heated to a temperature approaching that of the steam; the subsequent vacuum lowers the boiling point so that part of the water is evaporated or forced out of the wood by the steam produced when the vacuum is applied. The steaming and vacuum periods used depend upon the wood size, species, and moisture content. Steaming and vacuum usually reduce the moisture content of green wood slightly, and the heating assists greatly in getting the preservative to penetrate. A sufficiently long steaming period will also sterilize the wood.

In the Boulton or boiling-under-vacuum method of partial seasoning, the wood is heated in the oil preservative under vacuum, usually at about 82°C to 104°C (180°F to 220°F). This temperature range, lower than that of the steaming process, is a considerable advantage in treating woods that are especially susceptible to injury from high temperatures. The Boulton method removes much less moisture from heartwood than from sapwood.

Incising

Wood that is resistant to penetration by preservatives may be incised before treatment to permit deeper and more uniform penetration. To incise, lumber and timbers are passed through rollers equipped with teeth that sink into the wood to a predetermined depth, usually 13 to 19 mm (1/2 to 3/4 in.). The teeth are spaced to give the desired distribution of preservative with the minimum number of incisions. A machine of different design is required for deeply incising the butts of poles, usually to a depth of 64 mm (2.5 in.) (Fig. 14–2).

The effectiveness of incising depends on the fact that preservatives usually penetrate into wood much farther in the longitudinal direction than in a direction perpendicular to the faces of the timber. The incisions open cell lumens along the grain, which greatly enhances penetration. Incising is especially effective in improving penetration in the heartwood areas of sawn surfaces.

Incising is practiced primarily on Douglas-fir, western hemlock, and western larch ties and timbers for pressure treatment and on cedar and Douglas-fir poles. Incising can result in significant reductions in strength (Ch. 4).

Cutting and Framing

All cutting and boring of holes should be done prior to preservative treatment. Cutting into the wood in any way after treatment will frequently expose the untreated interior of the timber and permit ready access to decay fungi or insects.

Figure 14–2. Deep incising permits better penetration of preservative.

316

In some cases, wood structures can be designed so that all cutting and framing is done before treatment. Railroad companies have followed this practice and have found it not only practical but economical. Many wood-preserving plants are equipped to carry on such operations as the adzing and boring of crossties; gaining, roofing, and boring of poles; and framing of material for bridges and specialized structures, such as water tanks and barges.

Treatment of the wood with preservative oils results in little or no dimensional change. With waterborne preservatives, however, some change in the size and shape of the wood may occur even though the wood is redried to the moisture content it had before treatment. If precision fitting is necessary, the wood is cut and framed before treatment to its approximate final dimensions to allow for slight surfacing, trimming, and reaming of bolt holes. Grooves and bolt holes for timber connectors are cut before treatment and can be reamed out if necessary after treatment.

Application of Preservatives

Wood-preserving methods are of two general types: (a) pressure processes, in which the wood is impregnated in closed vessels under pressures considerably above atmospheric, and (b) nonpressure processes, which vary widely in the procedures and equipment used.

Pressure Processes

In commercial practice, wood is most often treated by immersing it in a preservative in a high pressure apparatus and applying pressure to drive the preservative into the wood. Pressure processes differ in details, but the general principle is the same. The wood, on cars or trams, is run into a long steel cylinder (Fig. 14–3), which is then closed and filled with preservative. Pressure forces the preservative into the wood until the desired amount has been absorbed. Considerable preservative is absorbed, with relatively deep penetration. Three pressure processes are commonly used: full-cell, modified full-cell, and empty-cell.

Full-Cell

The full-cell (Bethel) process is used when the retention of a maximum quantity of preservative is desired. It is a standard procedure for timbers to be treated full-cell with creosote when protection against marine borers is required. Waterborne preservatives are generally applied by the full-cell process, and control over preservative retention is obtained by regulating the concentration of the treating solution. Steps in the full-cell process are essentially the following:

1. The charge of wood is sealed in the treating cylinder, and a preliminary vacuum is applied for a half-hour or more to remove the air from the cylinder and as much as possible from the wood.

2. The preservative, at ambient or elevated temperature depending on the system, is admitted to the cylinder without breaking the vacuum.

3. After the cylinder is filled, pressure is applied until the wood will take no more preservative or until the required retention of preservative is obtained.

4. When the pressure period is completed, the preservative is withdrawn from the cylinder.

5. A short final vacuum may be applied to free the charge from dripping preservative.

When the wood is steamed before treatment, the preservative is admitted at the end of the vacuum period that follows steaming. When the timber has received preliminary conditioning by the Boulton or boiling-under-vacuum process, the cylinder can be filled and the pressure applied as soon as the conditioning period is completed.

Modified Full-Cell

The modified full-cell process is basically the same as the full-cell process except for the amount of initial vacuum and the occasional use of an extended final vacuum. The modified full-cell process uses lower levels of initial vacuum; the actual amount is determined by the wood species, material size, and final retention desired.

Empty-Cell

The objective of the empty-cell process is to obtain deep penetration with a relatively low net retention of preservative. For treatment with oil preservatives, the empty-cell process should always be used if it will provide the desired retention. Two empty-cell processes, the Rueping and the Lowry, are commonly employed; both use the expansive force of compressed air to drive out part of the preservative absorbed during the pressure period.

The Rueping empty-cell process, often called the empty-cell process with initial air, has been widely used for many years in Europe and the United States. The following general procedure is employed:

1. Air under pressure is forced into the treating cylinder, which contains the charge of wood. The air penetrates some species easily, requiring but a few minutes application of pressure. In treating the more resistant species, common practice is to maintain air pressure from 1/2 to 1 h before admitting the preservative, but the necessity for lengthy air-pressure periods does not seem fully established. The air pressures employed generally range between 172 to 689 kPa (25 to 100 lb/in^2), depending on the net retention of preservative desired and the resistance of the wood.

2. After the period of preliminary air pressure, preservative is forced into the cylinder. As the preservative is pumped in, the air escapes from the treating cylinder into an equalizing or Rueping tank, at a rate that keeps the pressure constant within the cylinder. When the treating cylinder is filled with preservative, the treating pressure is increased above that of the initial air and is maintained until the wood will absorb no more preservative, or until enough has been absorbed to leave the required retention of preservative in the wood after the treatment.

Figure 14–3. Interior view of treating cylinder at wood-preserving plant, with a load about to come in.

3. At the end of the pressure period, the preservative is drained from the cylinder, and surplus preservative is removed from the wood with a final vacuum. The amount of preservative recovered can be from 20% to 60% of the gross amount injected.

The Lowry is often called the empty-cell process without initial air pressure. Preservative is admitted to the cylinder without either an initial air pressure or a vacuum, and the air originally in the wood at atmospheric pressure is imprisoned during the filling period. After the cylinder is filled with the preservative, pressure is applied, and the remainder of the treatment is the same as described for the Rueping treatment.

The Lowry process has the advantage that equipment for the full-cell process can be used without other accessories that the Rueping process usually requires, such as an air compressor, an extra cylinder or Rueping tank for the preservative, or a suitable pump to force the preservative into the cylinder against the air pressure. However, both processes have advantages and are widely and successfully used.

With poles and other products where bleeding of preservative oil is objectionable, the empty-cell process is followed by either heating in the preservative (expansion bath) at a maximum of 104°C (220°F) or a final steaming for a specified time limit at a maximum of 116°C (240°F) prior to the final vacuum.

318

Treating Pressures and Preservative Temperatures

The pressures used in treatments vary from about 345 to 1,723 kPa (50 to 250 lb/in²), depending on the species and the ease with which the wood takes the treatment; most commonly, pressures range from about 862 to 1,207 kPa (125 to 175 lb/in²). Many woods are sensitive to high treating pressures, especially when hot. For example, AWPA standards permit a maximum pressure of 1,034 kPa (150 lb/in²) in the treatment of Douglas-fir, 862 kPa (125 lb/in²) for redwood, and 1,723 kPa (250 lb/in²) for oak. In commercial practice, even lower pressures are frequently used on such woods.

The AWPA C1 standard requires that the temperature of creosote and creosote solutions, as well as that of the oil-borne preservatives, during the pressure period shall not be greater than 93°C (200°F) for Western redcedar and 99°C (210°F) for all other species. With a number of waterborne preservatives, especially those containing chromium salts, maximum temperatures are limited to avoid premature precipitation of the preservative. The AWPA specifications require that the temperature of the preservative during the entire pressure period not exceed the maximum of 49°C (120°F) for ACC and CCA and 60°C (150°F) for ACA, CC, ACQ Type B, ACQ Type D, ACZA, CBA–A, and CDDC. The limit for inorganic boron is 93°C (200°F).

Penetration and Retention

Penetration and retention requirements are equally important in determining the quality of preservative treatment. Penetration levels vary widely, even in pressure-treated material. In most species, heartwood is more difficult to penetrate than sapwood. In addition, species differ greatly in the degree to which their heartwood may be penetrated. Incising tends to improve penetration of preservative in many refractory species, but those highly resistant to penetration will not have deep or uniform penetration even when incised. Penetration in unincised heart faces of these species may occasionally be as deep as 6 mm (1/4 in.) but is often not more than 1.6 mm (1/16 in.).

Experience has shown that even slight penetration has some value, although deeper penetration is highly desirable to avoid exposing untreated wood when checks occur, particularly for important members that are costly to replace. The heartwood of coastal Douglas-fir, southern pines, and various hardwoods, although resistant, will frequently show transverse penetrations of 6 to 12 mm (1/4 to 1/2 in.) and sometimes considerably more.

Complete penetration of the sapwood should be the ideal in all pressure treatments. It can often be accomplished in small-size timbers of various commercial woods, and with skillful treatment, it may often be obtained in piles, ties, and structural timbers. Practically, however, the operator cannot always ensure complete penetration of sapwood in every piece when treating large pieces of round material with thick sapwood, for example, poles and piles. Therefore, specifications permit some tolerance. For instance, AWPA C4 for

Southern Pine poles requires that 63 mm (2-1/2 in.) or 85% of the sapwood thickness be penetrated for 96 kg/m³ (6 lb/ft³) retention of creosote. This applies only to the smaller class of poles. The requirements vary, depending on the species, size, class, and specified retention levels.

At one time, all preservative retention levels were specified in terms of the weight of preservative per cubic foot (0.028 m³) of wood treated, based on total weight of preservative retained and the total volume of wood treated in a charge. This is commonly called gauge retention. However, specifications for most products now stipulate a minimum retention of preservative as determined from chemical analysis of borings from specified zones of the treated wood, known as a "assay-retention" or results-type specification.

The preservatives and retention levels listed in Federal Specification TT–W–571 and the AWPA Commodity Standards are shown in Table 14–2. The retention levels are often a range. The current issues of these specifications should be referenced for up-to-date recommendations and other details. In many cases, the retention level is different depending on species and assay zone. Higher preservative retention levels are justified in products to be installed under severe climatic or exposure conditions. Heavy-duty transmission poles and items with a high replacement cost, such as structural timbers and house foundations, are required to be treated to higher retention levels. Correspondingly, deeper penetration or heartwood limitations are also necessary for the same reasons.

It may be necessary to increase retention levels to ensure satisfactory penetration, particularly when the sapwood is either unusually thick or is somewhat resistant to treatment. To reduce bleeding of the preservative, however, it may be desirable to use preservative-oil retention levels less than the stipulated minimum. Treatment to refusal is usually specified for woods that are resistant to treatment and will not absorb sufficient preservative to meet the minimum retention requirements. However, such a requirement does not ensure adequate penetration of preservative, should be avoided, and must not be considered as a substitute for results-type specification in treatment.

Nonpressure Processes

The numerous nonpressure processes differ widely in the penetration and retention levels of preservative attained, and consequently in the degree of protection they provide to the treated wood. When similar retention and penetration levels are achieved, wood treated by a nonpressure method should have a service life comparable to that of wood treated by pressure. Nevertheless, results of nonpressure treatments, particularly those involving surface applications, are not generally as satisfactory as those of pressure treatment. The superficial processes do serve a useful purpose when more thorough treatments are impractical or exposure conditions are such that little preservative protection is required.

Nonpressure methods, in general, consist of (a) surface application of preservatives by brushing or brief dipping,

319

(b) soaking in preservative oils or steeping in solutions of waterborne preservatives, (c) diffusion processes with waterborne preservatives, (d) vacuum treatment, and (e) a variety of miscellaneous processes.

Surface Applications

The simplest treatment is to apply the preservative to the wood with a brush or by dipping. Preservatives that are thoroughly liquid when cold should be selected, unless it is possible to heat the preservative. The preservative should be flooded over the wood rather than merely painted. Every check and depression in the wood should be thoroughly filled with the preservative, because any untreated wood left exposed provides ready access for fungi. Rough lumber may require as much as 40 L of oil per 100 m^2 (10 gallons of oil per 1,000 ft^2) of surface, but surfaced lumber requires considerably less. The transverse penetration obtained will usually be less than 2.5 mm (1/10 in.), although in easily penetrated species, end-grain (longitudinal) penetration is considerably greater. The additional life obtained by such treatments over that of untreated wood will be affected greatly by the conditions of service. For wood in contact with the ground, service life may be from 1 to 5 years.

Compared with brushing, dipping for a few seconds to several minutes in a preservative gives greater assurance that all surfaces and checks are thoroughly coated with the preservative; it usually results in slightly greater penetration. It is a common practice to treat window sash, frames, and other millwork, either before or after assembly, by dipping the item in a water-repellent preservative. Such treatment is covered by NWWDA IS 4–94, which also provides for equivalent treatment by the vacuum process. AWPA also has a new nonpressure standard, N1, that includes preservative treatments by nonpressure processes for all millwork products.

In some cases, preservative oil penetrates the end surfaces of ponderosa pine sapwood as much as 25 to 76 mm (1 to 3 in.). However, end penetration in such woods as the heartwood of Southern Pines and Douglas-fir is much less. Transverse penetration of the preservative applied by brief dipping is very shallow, usually only less than a millimeter (a few hundredths of an inch). The exposed end surfaces at joints are the most vulnerable to decay in millwork products; therefore, good end penetration is especially advantageous. Dip applications provide very limited protection to wood used in contact with the ground or under very moist conditions, and they provide very limited protection against attack by termites. However, they do have value for exterior woodwork and millwork that is painted, not in contact with the ground, and exposed to moisture only for brief periods.

Cold Soaking and Steeping

Cold soaking well-seasoned wood for several hours or days in low viscosity preservative oils or steeping green or seasoned wood for several days in waterborne preservatives has provided varying success on fence posts, lumber, and timbers.

Pine posts treated by cold soaking for 24 to 48 h or longer in a solution containing 5% of pentachlorophenol in No. 2 fuel oil have shown an average life of 16 to 20 years or longer. The sapwood in these posts was well penetrated, and preservative solution retention levels ranged from 32 to 96 kg/m^3 (2 to 6 lb/ft^3). Most species do not treat as satisfactorily as do the pines by cold soaking, and test posts of such woods as birch, aspen, and sweetgum treated by this method have failed in much shorter times.

Preservative penetration and retention levels obtained by cold soaking lumber for several hours are considerably better than those obtained by brief dipping of similar species. However, preservative retention levels seldom equal those obtained in pressure treatment except in cases such as sapwood of pines that has become highly absorptive through mold and stain infection.

Steeping with waterborne preservatives has very limited use in the United States but it has been used for many years in Europe. In treating seasoned wood, both the water and the preservative salt in the solution soak into the wood. With green wood, the preservative enters the water-saturated wood by diffusion. Preservative retention and penetration levels vary over a wide range, and the process is not generally recommended when more reliable treatments are practical.

Diffusion Processes

In addition to the steeping process, diffusion processes are used with green or wet wood. These processes employ waterborne preservatives that will diffuse out of the water of the treating solution or paste into the water of the wood.

The double-diffusion process developed by the Forest Products Laboratory has shown very good results in fence post tests and standard 38- by 89-mm (nominal 2- by 4-in.) stake tests, particularly for full-length immersion treatments. This process consists of steeping green or partially seasoned wood first in one chemical solution, then in another (Fig. 14–4). The two chemicals diffuse into the wood, then react to precipitate an effective preservative with high resistance to leaching. The process has had commercial application in cooling towers and fence posts where preservative protection is needed to avoid early replacement of the wood.

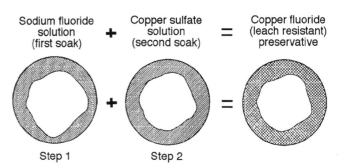

Figure 14–4. Double-diffusion steps for applying preservatives.

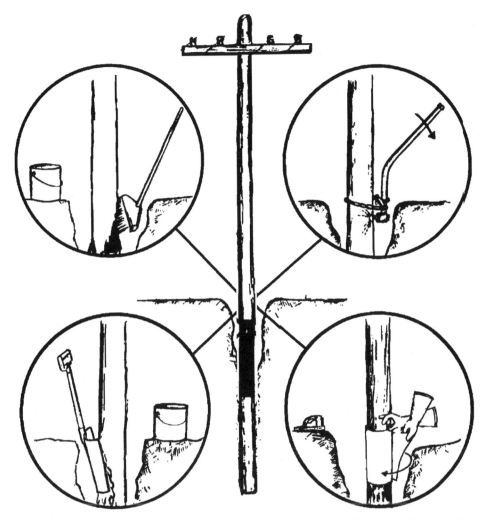

Figure 14–5. Methods of applying groundline treatment to utility poles. Preservative is injected into the pole at the groundline with a special tool or applied on the pole surface as a paste or bandage.

Other diffusion processes involve applying preservatives to the butt or around the groundline of posts or poles. In treatments of standing poles, the preservative can be injected into the pole at groundline with a special tool, applied on the pole surface as a paste or bandage (Fig. 14–5), or poured into holes bored in the pole at the groundline. These treatments have recognized value for application to untreated standing poles and treated poles where preservative retention levels are determined to be inadequate.

Vacuum Process

The vacuum process, or "VAC–VAC" as referred to in Europe, has been used to treat millwork with water-repellent preservatives and construction lumber with waterborne and water-repellent preservatives.

In treating millwork, the objective is to use a limited quantity of water-repellent preservative and obtain retention and penetration levels similar to those obtained by dipping for 3 min. The vacuum process treatment is included in NWWDA IS–94 for "Water-Repellent Preservative Nonpressure Treatment for Millwork." In this treatment, a quick, low initial vacuum is followed by filling the cylinder under vacuum, releasing the vacuum and soaking, followed by a final vacuum. The treatment is better than the 3-min dip treatment because of better penetration and retention, and the surface of the wood is quickly dried, thus expediting glazing, priming, and painting. The vacuum treatment is also reported to be less likely than dip treatment to leave objectionably high retention levels in bacteria-infected wood referred to as "sinker stock."

Lumber intended for buildings has been treated by the vacuum process, either with a waterborne preservative or a water-repellent pentachlorophenol solution, with preservative retention levels usually less than those required for pressure treatment. The process differs from that used in treating millwork in employing a higher initial vacuum and a longer immersion or soaking period.

In a study by the Forest Products Laboratory, an initial vacuum of –93 kPa (27.5 inHg) was applied for 30 min, followed by a soaking for 8 h, and a final or recovery vacuum of –93 kPa (27.5 inHg) for 2 h. Results of the study showed good penetration of preservative in the sapwood of dry lumber of easily penetrated species such as the pines. However, in heartwood and unseasoned sapwood of pine and heartwood of seasoned and unseasoned coastal Douglas-fir, penetration was much less than that obtained by pressure treatment. Preservative retention was less controllable in vacuum than in empty-cell pressure treatment. Good control over retention levels is possible in vacuum treatment with a waterborne preservative by adjusting concentration of the treating solution.

Miscellaneous Nonpressure Processes

Several other nonpressure methods of various types have been used to a limited extent. Many of these involve the application of waterborne preservatives to living trees. The Boucherie process for the treatment of green, unpeeled poles has been used for many years in Europe. This process involves attaching liquid-tight caps to the butt ends of the poles. Then, through a pipeline or hose leading to the cap, a waterborne preservative is forced under hydrostatic pressure into the pole.

A tire-tube process is a simple adaptation of the Boucherie process used for treating green, unpeeled fence posts. In this treatment, a section of used inner tube is fastened tight around the butt end of the post to make a bag that holds a solution of waterborne preservative. There are limitations for application of this process in the United States because of the loss of preservative to the soil around the treatment site.

Effect on Mechanical Properties

Coal-tar creosote, creosote solutions, and pentachlorophenol dissolved in petroleum oils are practically inert to wood and have no chemical influence that would affect its strength. Chemicals commonly used in waterborne salt preservatives, including chromium, copper, arsenic, and ammonia, are reactive with wood. Thus, these chemicals are potentially damaging to mechanical properties and may also promote corrosion of mechanical fasteners.

Significant reductions in mechanical properties may be observed if the treating and subsequent drying processes are not controlled within acceptable limits. Factors that influence the effect of the treating process on strength include (a) species of wood, (b) size and moisture content of the timbers treated, (c) type and temperature of heating medium, (d) length of the heating period in conditioning the wood for treatment and time the wood is in the hot preservative, (e) post-treatment drying temperatures, and (f) amount of pressure used. Most important of those factors are the severity and duration of the in-retort heating or post-treatment redrying conditions used. The effect of wood preservatives on the mechanical properties of wood is covered in Chapter 4.

Handling and Seasoning of Timber After Treatment

Treated timber should be handled with sufficient care to avoid breaking through the treated areas. The use of pikes, cant hooks, picks, tongs, or other pointed tools that dig deeply into the wood should be prohibited. Handling heavy loads of lumber or sawn timber in rope or cable slings can crush the corners or edges of the outside pieces. Breakage or deep abrasions can also result from throwing or dropping the lumber. If damage results, the exposed places should be retreated, if possible.

Wood treated with preservative oils should generally be installed as soon as practicable after treatment to minimize lateral movement of the preservative, but sometimes cleanliness of the surface can be improved by exposing the treated wood to the weather for a limited time before installation. Waterborne preservatives or pentachlorophenol in a volatile solvent are best suited to uses where cleanliness or paintability is of great importance.

Lengthy, unsheltered exterior storage of treated wood before installation should be avoided because such storage encourages deep and detrimental checking and can also result in significant loss of some preservatives. Treated wood that must be stored before use should be covered for protection from the sun and weather.

Although cutting wood after treatment is highly undesirable, it cannot always be avoided. When cutting is necessary, the damage can be partly overcome in timber for land or freshwater use by a thorough application of copper naphthenate (2% copper) to the cut surface. This provides a protective coating of preservative on the surface that may slowly migrate into the end grain of the wood. A special device is available for pressure treating bolt holes that are bored after treatment. For wood treated with waterborne preservatives, a 2% (as copper) solution of copper naphthenate should be used. Thoroughly brushing cut surfaces with two coats of hot creosote (applicator license required) is also helpful, although brush coating of cut surfaces provides little protection against marine borers.

For treating the end surfaces of piles where they are cut off after driving, at least two generous coats of creosote should be applied. A coat of asphalt or similar material may be thoroughly applied over the creosote, followed by some protective sheet material, such as metal, roofing felt, or saturated fabric, fitted over the pile head and brought down the sides far enough to protect against damage to the treatment and against the entrance of storm water. AWPA M4 contains instructions for the care of pressure-treated wood after treatment.

With waterborne preservatives, seasoning after treatment is important for wood that will be used in buildings or other places where shrinkage after placement in the structure would be undesirable. Injecting waterborne preservatives puts large amounts of water into the wood, and considerable shrinkage is to be expected as subsequent seasoning takes place. For best results, the wood should be dried to approximately the moisture content it will ultimately reach in service. During drying, the wood should be carefully piled and, whenever possible, restrained by sufficient weight on the top of the pile to prevent warping.

With some waterborne preservatives, seasoning after treatment is recommended. During this seasoning period, volatile chemicals can escape and chemical reactions are completed within the wood. Thus, the resistance of the preservative to leaching by water is increased. This physical or chemical process whereby a wood preservative system is rendered leach resistant in both water and soil application is called "fixation." In this process, the active ingredient or ingredients maintain fungal or insecticidal efficacy.

The Western Wood Preservers' Institute and the Canadian Institute of Treated Wood (1996) have developed a publication to address best management practices (BMPs) for the use of treated wood in aquatic environments. Their purpose is to protect the quality of the water and diversity of the various life forms found in the lakes, streams, estuaries, bays, and wetlands of North America. The document is continually updated as better methods for risk assessment and research are developed.

Quality Assurance for Treated Wood

Treating Conditions and Specifications

Specifications on the treatment of various wood products by pressure processes have been developed by AWPA. These specifications limit pressures, temperatures, and time of conditioning and treatment to avoid conditions that will cause serious injury to the wood. The specifications also contain minimum requirements for preservative penetration and retention levels and recommendations for handling wood after treatment to provide a quality product.

Specifications are broad in some respects, allowing the purchaser some latitude in specifying the details of individual requirements. However, the purchaser should exercise great care so as not to hinder the treating plant operator from doing a good treating job and not to require treating conditions so severe that they will damage the wood. Federal Specification TT–W–571 lists treatment practices for use on U.S. Government orders for treated wood products; other purchasers have specifications similar to those of AWPA.

The AWPA is working on the development of a Use Category System (UCS), which is a new way to organize the Commodity Standards. The system utilizes seven different exposure categories for treated-wood products, with each exposure category representing a different degree of biodeterioration hazard and/or product expectation. Product users will be able to specify treated-wood products based on the

biodeterioration risk to which the product will be exposed. The UCS is expected to appear in the 1998 AWPA Book of Standards for information only and with standardization parallel to the current C-Standards in 1999.

Inspection

There are two important factors to consider depending upon the intended end use of preservative-treated wood: (a) the grade or appearance of the lumber and (b) the quality of the preservative treatment in the lumber. The U.S. Department of Commerce American Lumber Standard Committee (ALSC), an accrediting agency for treatment quality assurance, has an ink stamp or end tag for each grade stamp (Fig. 14–6) and quality mark (Fig. 14–7). These marks indicate that the producer of the treated-wood product subscribes to an independent inspection agency. However, there are non-ALSC end tags or ink stamps that are similar to ALSC tags. Only end tags or ink stamps with the logo of an accredited ALSC–QA agency are acceptable. (A current list is available from ALSC.)

Quality control overview by ALSC is preferable to simple treating plant certificates or other claims of conformance made by the producer without inspection by an independent agency. These third-party agencies verify for customers that the wood was properly treated in accordance with AWPA standards. Thus, the purchaser may either accept the stamps as their quality assurance or have an independent inspector inspect and analyze the treated products to ensure compliance with the specifications. The latter is recommended for treated-wood products used for critical structures. Railroad companies and other corporations that purchase large quantities of treated timber usually maintain their own inspection services.

Purchase of Treated Wood

To obtain a treated-wood product of high quality, the purchaser should use the appropriate specifications. Specifications and standards of importance here are Federal Specification TT–W–571, "Wood Preservation—Treating Practices;" Federal Specification TT–W–572, "Fungicide: Pentachlorophenol;" and the *AWPA Book of Standards*. The inspection of material for conformity to the minimum requirements listed in these specifications should be in accordance with the American Wood Preservers' M2, "Standard for Inspection of Treated Timber Products."

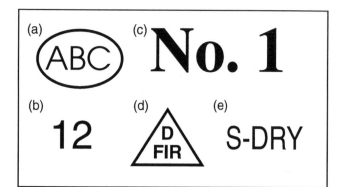

a Trademark indicates agency quality supervision.
b Mill Identification—firm name, brand, or assigned mill number
c Grade Designation—grade name, number, or abbreviation
d Species Identification—indicates species individually or in combination
e Condition of Seasoning at time of surfacing
   S-DRY — 19% max. moisture content
   MC 15 — 15% max. moisture content
   S-GRN — over 19% moisture content (unseasoned)

Figure 14–6. Typical lumber grade stamp as approved by ALSC and its interpretation for Douglas Fir lumber.

ABC (a)

XXX (g)

19_-19_ (c)
GROUND CONTACT (f)

.40 (e)

AWPA ____ STDS (b)

PRESERVATIVE (d)
KDAT (h)
X-XX (i)

a Identifying symbol, logo, or name of the accredited agency.
b Applicable American Wood Preservers' Association (AWPA) commodity standard.
c Year of treatment, if required by AWPA standard.
d Preservative used, which may be abbreviated.
e Preservative retention.
f Exposure category (e.g. Above Ground, Ground Contact, etc.).
g Plant name and location, plant name and number, or plant number.
h If applicable, moisture content after treatment.
i If applicable, length, and/or class.

Figure 14–7. Typical quality mark for preservative-treated lumber to conform to the ALSC accreditation program.

References

AWPA. Annual proceedings. (Reports of Preservations and Treatment Committees contain information on new wood preservatives considered in the development of standards.) Granbury, TX: American Wood Preservers' Association.

AWPA. 1995. Answers to often-asked question about treated wood. Vienna, VA: American Wood Preservers' Institute.

AWPA. 1997. Book of Standards. (Includes standards on preservatives, treatments, methods of analysis, and inspection.) Granbury, TX: American Wood Preservers' Association.

ASTM. 1992. Standard specification for coal-tar creosote for the preservative treatment of piles, poles, and timbers for marine, land, and freshwater use. ASTM D390. Philadelphia, PA: American Society for Testing and Materials.

ASTM. 1994. Standard specification for creosote-coal tar solution. ASTM D391. Philadelphia, PA: American Society for Testing and Materials.

Baechler, R.H.; Roth, H.G. 1964. The double-diffusion method of treating wood: a review of studies. Forest Products Journal. 14(4): 171–178.

Baechler, R.H.; Blew, J.O.; Roth, H.G. 1962. Studies on the assay of pressure-treated lumber. Proceedings of American Wood Preservers' Association. 58: 21–34.

Baechler, R.H.; Gjovik, L.R.; Roth, H.G. 1969. Assay zones for specifying preservative-treated Douglas-fir and Southern Pine timbers. Proceedings of American Wood Preservers' Association. 65: 114–123.

Baechler, R.H.; Gjovik, L.R.; Roth, H.G. 1970. Marine tests on combination-treated round and sawed specimens. Proceedings of American Wood Preservers' Association. 66: 249–257.

Blew, J.O.; Davidson, H.L. 1971. Preservative retentions and penetration in the treatment of white fir. Proceedings of American Wood Preservers' Association. 67: 204–221.

Boone, R.S.; Gjovik, L.R.; Davidson, H.L. 1976. Treatment of sawn hardwood stock with double-diffusion and modified double-diffusion methods. Res. Pap. FPL–RP–265. Madison, WI: U.S. Department of Agriculture, Forest Service, Forest Products Laboratory.

Cassens, D.L.; Johnson, B.R.; Feist, W.C.; De Groot, R.C. 1995. Selection and use of preservative-treated wood. Publication N. 7299. Madison, WI: Forest Products Society.

Eaton, R.A.; Hale, M.D.C. 1993. Wood: decay, pests and protection. New York, NY: Chapman & Hall.

Gaby, L.I.; Gjovik, L.R. 1984. Treating and drying composite lumber with waterborne preservatives: Part I. Short specimen testing. Forest Products Journal. 34(2): 23–26.

Gjovik, L.R.; Baechler, R.H. 1970. Treated wood foundations for buildings. Forest Products Journal. 20(5): 45–48.

Gjovik, L.R.; Baechler, R.H. 1977. Selection, production, procurement and use of preservative treated wood. Gen. Tech. Rep. FPL–15. Supplementing Federal Specification TT–W–571. Madison, WI: U.S. Department of Agriculture, Forest Service, Forest Products Laboratory.

Gjovik, L.R.; Davidson, H.L. 1975. Service records on treated and untreated posts. Res. Note FPL–068. Madison, WI: U.S. Department of Agriculture, Forest Service, Forest Products Laboratory.

Gjovik, L.R.; Roth, H.G.; Davidson, H.L. 1972. Treatment of Alaskan species by double-diffusion and modified double-diffusion methods. Res. Pap. FPL–182. Madison, WI: U.S. Department of Agriculture, Forest Service, Forest Products Laboratory.

Gjovik, L.R.; Johnson, D.B.; Kozak, V.; [and others]. 1980. Biologic and economic assessment of pentachlorophenol, inorganic arsenicals, and creosote. Vol. I: Wood preservatives. Tech. Bull 1658–1. Washington, DC: U.S. Department of Agriculture, in cooperation with State Agricultural Experimental Stations, Cooperative Extension Service, other state agencies and the Environmental Protection Agency.

Gutzmer, D.I.; Crawford, D.M. 1995. Comparison of wood preservative in stake tests. 1995 Progress Report. Res. Note FPL–RN–02. Madison, WI: U.S. Department of Agriculture, Forest Service, Forest Products Laboratory.

Hunt, G.M.; Garratt, G.A. 1967. Wood preservation. 3d ed. The American Forestry Series. New York, NY: McGraw–Hill.

Johnson, B.R.; Gutzmer, D.I. 1990. Comparison of preservative treatments in marine exposure of small wood panels. Res. Note. FPL–RN–0258. Madison, WI: U.S. Department of Agriculture, Forest Service, Forest Products Laboratory.

Lebow, S. 1996. Leaching of wood preservative components and their mobility in the environment—summary of pertinent literature. Gen. Tech. Rep. FPL–GTR–93. Madison, WI: U.S. Department of Agriculture, Forest Service, Forest Products Laboratory.

Mac Lean, J.D. 1952. Preservation of wood by pressure methods. Agric. Handb. 40. Washington, DC: U. S. Department of Agriculture, Forest Service.

Micklewright, J.T.; Gjovik, L.R. 1981. Wood preserving statistics: update. Proceedings of American Wood Preservers' Association. 77: 143–147.

NFPA. 1982. The all-weather wood foundation. NFPA Tech. Rep. 7. Washington, DC: National Forest Products Association.

NFPA. 1982. All-weather wood foundation system, design fabrication installation manual. NFPA report; Washington DC: National Forest Products Association.

NWWDA. 1994. Industry standard for water-repellent preservative non-pressure treatment for millwork. IS–4–94. Des Plaines, IL: National Wood Window and Door Association.

Naval Facilities Engineering Command. 1990. Wood Protection. NAVFAC MO–312, Philadelphia, PA: Naval Facilities Engineering Command. Wood Protection. May.

Naval Facilities Engineering Command. 1992. Wood Protection Training Manual. NAVFAC MO–312.4, Philadelphia, PA: Naval Facilities Engineering Command. Wood Protection. March.

Nicholas, D.D.; Schultz, T.P. 1994 Biocides that have potential as wood preservatives—an overview. In: Wood preservatives in the '90s and beyond. Proceedings, conference sponsored by the Forest Products Society; 1994 September 26–28; Savannah, GA.

USFSS. 1968. Wood preservation treating practices. Federal Specification TT–W–571. Washington, DC: U.S. Federal Supply Service.

USFSS. 1969. Fungicide: Pentachlorophenol. Federal Specification TT–W–572. Washington, DC: U.S. Federal Supply Service.

Western Wood Preservers Institute and Canadian Institute of Treated Wood. 1996. Best management practices for the use of treated wood in aquatic environments. Vancouver, WA: Western Wood Preservers Institute and Canadian Institute of Treated Wood. (USA Version). July rev.

Finishing of Wood

R. Sam Williams

Contents

The primary function of any wood finish (paint, varnish, and stain, for example) is to protect the wood surface, help maintain a certain appearance, and provide a cleanable surface. Although wood can be used both outdoors and indoors without finishing, unfinished wood surfaces exposed to the weather change color, are roughened by photodegradation and surface checking, and erode slowly. Unfinished wood surfaces exposed indoors may also change color; moreover, unfinished wood is more difficult to clean than is finished wood.

Wood and wood-based products in a variety of species, grain patterns, textures, and colors can be finished effectively by many different methods. Selection of a finish will depend on the appearance and degree of protection desired and on the substrates used. Because different finishes give varying degrees of protection, the type of finish, its quality and quantity, and the method used to apply the finish must be considered when finishing or refinishing wood and wood products.

Factors Affecting Finish Performance

Satisfactory performance of wood finishes is achieved when the many factors that affect these finishes are given full consideration. These factors include the effect of the wood substrate, properties of the finishing material, details of application, and severity of exposure. Some important considerations are reviewed in this chapter. Sources of more detailed information are provided in a list of references at the end of this chapter.

Wood Properties

Wood surfaces that have the least tendency to shrink and swell are best for painting. For this reason, vertical- or edge-grain surfaces are far better than flat-grain surfaces (Fig. 15–1), especially when the wood is used outside where wide ranges of relative humidity and periodic wetting can produce wide ranges of swelling and shrinking. In addition, because the swelling of wood is directly proportional to specific gravity, species with low specific gravity are preferred to those with high specific gravity. Vertical-grain heartwood

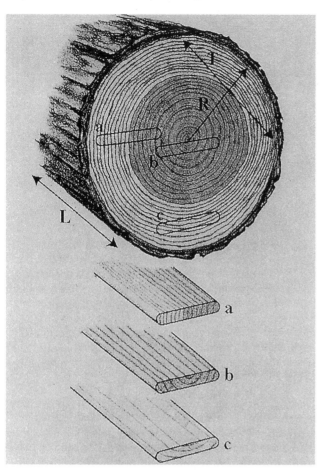

Figure 15–1. Lumber grain affects finish performance: (a) edge-grain (vertical-grain or quartersawn) board; (b) edge-grain board containing pith; (c) flat-grain (slash-grain or plainsawn) board. Arrows show radial (R), tangential (T), and longitudinal (L) orientation of wood grain.

of western redcedar and redwood are the species usually recommended for use as exterior siding and trim when painting is desired. These species are classified in Group I, woods with the best paint-holding characteristics (Table 15–1). Although vertical-grain surfaces of most species are considered excellent for painting, most species are generally available only as flat-grain lumber.

Very few wood species are graded according to vertical- or flat-grain specifications. Without a grade for marketing the lumber, there is no incentive for a mill to either cut to maximize the yield of vertical-grain lumber or to select vertical-grain lumber from the mill run. Exceptions are redwood and western redcedar, which are marketed in a range of grades, including vertical grain. The premium grade is all-heartwood and vertical-grain. This grade is usually sold as resawn bevel siding and it demands a high price; it is worthwhile for a mill to cut to maximize the yield of this grade. Most often, cutting is only practical with fairly large-diameter logs. For those species that are primarily available

in small-diameter logs, the yield of vertical-grain lumber is small. It is not practical to cut the log to maximize the vertical grain because such cutting would substantially decrease overall yield from the log.

Species normally cut as flat-grain lumber that are high in specific gravity and swelling, or have defects such as knots or pitch, are classified in Groups II through V, depending upon their general paint-holding characteristics. Many species in Groups II through IV are commonly painted, particularly the pines, Douglas-fir, and spruce; however, these species generally require more careful surface preparation than do the vertical-grain (also called edge-grain) surfaces of Group I. Exterior paint will be more durable on vertical-grain boards than on flat-grain boards for any species with marked differences in specific gravity between earlywood and latewood, even if the species are rated in Group I (Fig. 15–2). Flat-grain lumber will hold paint reasonably well if it is used in areas protected from rain and sun, particularly if the wood is rough sawn or scuff sanded.

Other wood properties that affect wood finishing are defects such as knots and colored materials (extractives) in the wood. These colored materials include a wide range of chemicals with different solubilities in water, organic solvents, and paint polymers. Their effects on wood finishing are covered in detail later in this chapter. See Chapters 1 to 3 for more detailed information on wood properties.

Wood Extractives

Water-soluble colored extractives occur naturally in the heartwood of such species as western redcedar, cypress, and redwood. These substances give the heartwood of some species their attractive color, water repellency, and natural decay resistance. However, discoloration of paint may occur when the extractives are dissolved and leached from the wood by water. The water carries the extractives to the painted surface, then evaporates, leaving the extractives as a yellow to reddish brown stain on the paint. The water that gets behind the paint and causes moisture blisters also causes migration of extractives.

Wood also contains resins and oils that are insoluble in water. The type and amount of these compounds in lumber depend on the wood species. For example, many pines contain pitch and the knots of almost all wood species contain sufficient oils and resins to cause discoloration of light-colored paint. Since these oils and resins are organic in nature, they are similar chemically to oil-based and/or alkyd paints; therefore, they cannot be blocked by typical oilborne stain-blocking primers as can the water-soluble extractives. Latex-based formulations are also ineffective. Knots can be sealed prior to priming with shellac or similar finishes specifically formulated to block oils and resins. Because shellac is sensitive to moisture, it is essential to use it only over the knots and to seal it into the knots with a good paint system. In many species, bleeding of oils and resins from knots is a difficult problem. At present, there is no easy fix other than the extra step of sealing knots before priming.

Table 15–1. Characteristics of selected woods for painting

Wood species	Specific gravity[a] green/dry	Shrinkage (%)[b] Flat grain	Shrinkage (%)[b] Vertical grain	Paint-holding characteristic (I, best; V, worst)[c] Oil-based paint	Latex paint	Weathering Resistance to cupping (1, most; 4, least)	Conspicuousness of checking (1, least; 2, most)	Color of heartwood
Softwoods								
Baldcypress	0.42/0.46	6.2	3.8	I	I	1	1	Light brown
Cedars								
Incense	0.35/0.37	5.2	3.3	I	I	—	—	Brown
Northern white	0.29/0.31	4.9	2.2	I	I	—	—	Light brown
Port-Orford	0.39/0.43	6.9	4.6	I	I	—	1	Cream
Western red	0.31/0.32	5	2.4	I	I	1	1	Brown
Yellow	0.42/0.44	6	2.8	I	I	1	1	Yellow
Douglas-fir[d]	0.45/0.48[e]	7.6	4.8	IV	II	2	2	Pale red
Larch, western	0.48/0.52	9.1	4.5	IV	II	2	2	Brown
Pine								
Eastern white	0.34/0.35	6.1	2.1	II	II	2	2	Cream
Ponderosa	0.38/0.42	6.2	3.9	III	II	2	2	Cream
Southern[d]	0.47/0.51[f]	8	5	IV	III	2	2	Light brown
Sugar	0.34/0.36	5.6	2.9	II	II	2	2	Cream
Western white	0.36/0.38	7.4	4.1	II	II	2	2	Cream
Redwood, old growth	0.38/0.40	4.4	2.6	I	I	1	1	Dark brown
Spruce, Engelmann	0.33/0.35	7.1	3.8	III	II	2	2	White
Tamarack	0.49/0.53	7.4	3.7	IV	—	2	2	Brown
White fir	0.37/0.39	7.0	3.3	III	—	2	2	White
Western hemlock	0.42/0.45	7.8	4.2	III	II	2	2	Pale brown
Hardwoods								
Alder	0.37/0.41	7.3	4.4	III	—	—	—	Pale brown
Ash, white	0.55/0.60	8	5	V or III	—	4	2	Light brown
Aspen, bigtooth	0.36/0.39	7	3.5	III	II	2	1	Pale brown
Basswood	0.32/0.37	9.3	6.6	III	—	2	2	Cream
Beech	0.56/0.64	11.9	5.5	IV	—	4	2	Pale brown
Birch, yellow	0.55/0.62	9.5	7.3	IV	—	4	2	Light brown
Butternut	0.36/0.38	6.4	3.4	V or III	—	—	—	Light brown
Cherry	0.47/0.50	7.1	3.7	IV	—	—	—	Brown
Chestnut	0.40/0.43	6.7	3.4	V or III	—	3	2	Light brown
Cottonwood, eastern	0.37/0.40	9.2	3.9	III	II	4	2	White
Elm, American	0.46/0.50	9.5	4.2	V or III	—	4	2	Brown
Hickory, shagbark	0.64/0.72	11	7	V or IV	—	4	2	Light brown
Lauan plywood	—[g]	8	4	IV	—	2	2	Brown
Magnolia, southern	0.46/0.50	6.6	5.4	III	—	2	—	Pale brown
Maple, sugar	0.56/0.63	9.9	4.8	IV	—	4	2	Light brown
Oak								
White	0.60/0.68	8.8	4.4	V or IV	—	4	2	Brown
Northern red	0.56/0.63	8.6	4.0	V or IV	—	4	2	Brown
Sweetgum	0.46/0.52	10.2	5.3	IV	III	4	2	Brown
Sycamore	0.46/0.49	8.4	5	IV	—	—	—	Pale brown
Walnut	0.51/0.55	7.8	5.5	V or III	—	3	2	Dark brown
Yellow-poplar	0.40/0.42	8.2	4.6	III	II	2	1	Pale brown

[a]Specific gravity based on weight ovendry and volume at green or 12% moisture content.
[b]Value obtained by drying from green to ovendry.
[c]Woods ranked in Group V have large pores that require wood filler for durable painting. When pores are properly filled before painting, Group II applies. Vertical-grain lumber was used for cedars and redwood. Other species were primarily flat-grain. Decrease in paintability is caused by a combination of species characteristics, grain orientation, and greater dimensional change of flat-grain lumber. Flat-grain lumber causes at least 1 unit decrease in paintability.
[d]Lumber and plywood.
[e]Coastal Douglas-fir.
[f]Loblolly, shortleaf, specific gravity of 0.54/0.59 for longleaf and slash.
[g]Specific gravity of different species varies from 0.33 to 0.55.

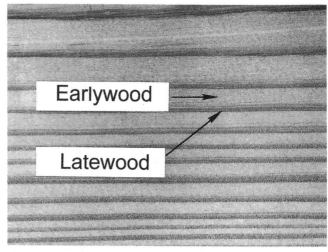

Figure 15–3. Earlywood and latewood bands in Southern Pine.

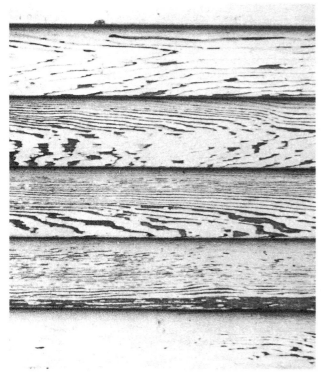

Figure 15–2. Paint applied over edge-grain boards (top and bottom) performs better than that applied to flat-grain boards (middle).

Wood Product Characteristics

Five general categories of wood products are commonly used in exterior construction: (a) lumber, (b) plywood, (c) finger-jointed wood, (d) reconstituted wood products (such as hardboard, oriented strandboard (OSB), and particleboard), and (e) preservative–fire-retardant-treated wood. Each product has unique characteristics that affect the application and performance of finishes.

Lumber

Although several alternative materials are being used for siding (such as vinyl, aluminum, OSB, and hardboard), lumber is still the preferred choice for siding in many areas of the country and for a variety of architectural designs. Many older homes have wood siding. The ability of lumber to retain and hold a finish is affected by species, grain orientation, and surface texture.

The specific gravity of wood varies tremendously among wood species (Table 15–1). The specific gravity of wood is important because denser woods generally shrink and swell more than less dense woods. In lumber, this dimensional change occurs as the wood gains or loses moisture. Excessive dimensional change in wood constantly stresses a paint film and may cause early paint failure. If two species have the same specific gravity but shrink and swell differently, their paintability will be greatly affected by dimensional changes. For example, redwood and western white pine have about the

same specific gravity (0.38), but their shrinkage values for flat- and vertical-grain wood are different (4.4% and 2.6% for redwood and 7.4% and 4.1% for western white pine, respectively) (Table 15–1). Redwood has a paintability rating of I and western white pine, a rating of II. The greater dimensional instability of the flat-grain western white pine results in lower paintability compared with that of the vertical-grain redwood.

The shrinkage values given in Table 15–1 were obtained from drying wood from its green state to ovendry. The swelling rates would be about the same. The paintability values for western redcedar and redwood were obtained from vertical-grain lumber; other species were primarily flat-grain. Note that the shrinkage values for vertical-grain lumber are about half that of flat-grain lumber. The paintability rating for flat-grain lumber is probably at least one unit lower than that for vertical-grain lumber. The values given in Table 15–1 for oil-based paints were obtained from research conducted in the 1930s and 1940s using lumber from large-diameter logs. It is not known how the properties of lumber from small-diameter logs and new paint formulations would affect these ratings. Therefore, the ratings given in Table 15–1 should be used to rank paintability rather than obtain absolute paintability values.

Some species have wide bands of earlywood and latewood (Fig. 15–3). These distinct bands often lead to early paint failure. Wide, prominent bands of latewood are characteristic of the southern pines and Douglas-fir, and paint will not hold well on these species. In contrast, redwood and cedar do not have wide latewood bands, and these species are preferred for painting.

Grain orientation also affects paint-holding characteristics and is determined by the way lumber is cut from a log (Fig. 15–1). Most standard grades of lumber contain a high percentage of flat-grain lumber. Lumber used for board and batten, drop, or shiplap siding is frequently flat-grain. Bevel siding is commonly produced in several grades. The highest grade of redwood and western redcedar bevel siding is vertical-grain all-heartwood. Other grades of redwood and western redcedar may be flat, vertical, or mixed grain and may not be required to be all-heartwood.

The texture (roughness or smoothness) of the wood surface has an important effect on the selection, application, and service life of finishes. Until recently, a general rule of thumb for matching substrates to finishes was to paint smooth wood and stain rough-sawn wood. This easy rule of thumb no longer applies. Although it is true that penetrating finishes such as semitransparent stains give much better service life on rough-sawn wood compared with smooth wood, many film-forming finishes such as opaque stains and paints also give much better service life on rough-sawn wood. The paint adheres better, the film buildup is better, and the service life is longer on a roughened than a smooth (planed) surface, particularly when flat-grain lumber or siding is used. Surface texture is discussed in more detail in later sections of this chapter.

Plywood

As with lumber, species, grain orientation, and surface texture are important variables that affect the finishing of plywood. In addition, plywood contains small checks (face checks) that are caused by the lathe when the veneer is cut during plywood manufacture. Cycles of wetting and drying with subsequent swelling and shrinking tend to worsen face-checking of plywood veneer. Face checking sometimes extends through paint coatings to detract from the appearance and durability of the paint. Face checks can lead to early paint failure, particularly with oil or alkyd paint systems (Fig. 15–4). Latex primer and top coat paint systems generally perform better than oil or alkyd systems. For use as exterior siding, plywood is often overlaid with resin-treated paper (medium-density overlay (MDO)); MDO eliminates cracks caused by lathe checking and provides plywood with excellent paintability (equal to or better than that of Group I vertical-grain lumber).

Plywood for exterior use nearly always has a flat-grain surface, and if it is used for exterior wood siding, the surface is rough sawn. Smooth-sanded plywood is not recommended for siding, although it is often used for soffits. The flat-grain pattern in nearly all plywood can contribute to early paint failure. Therefore, if plywood is to be painted, take special care to prepare the surface and use high quality latex paint. Rough-sawn plywood holds paint much better than does smooth plywood. Smooth plywood should be scuff-sanded with 50-grit sandpaper prior to priming, and both smooth and rough plywood should be edge-treated with a water-repellent preservative. Penetrating stains are often more appropriate for rough-sawn than smooth-sawn exterior plywood surfaces.

Fingerjointed Lumber

In recent years, many mills have been producing lumber that consists of many small pieces of wood that are glued together and have fingerjoints to improve strength (Chs. 9 and 11). This process is done to eliminate knots and other defects from the lumber. The lumber is commonly used for fascia boards, interior and exterior trim, windows and doors, and siding. Although fingerjointed lumber contains no knots or other defects, the wood pieces are generally not sorted in regard to heartwood or sapwood or to grain orientation prior to gluing. However, with some suppliers, care is taken to decrease variability in fingerjointed lumber. For example, fingerjointed redwood siding is available in Clear All Heart vertical grain and Clear flat grain. Fingerjointed lumber is usually sold as a particular species, although this is not always the case. Because a particular board may contain pieces from many trees and in many grain orientations, the finishing requirements are determined by the worst piece of wood in a single board. It is quite common for paint failure to occur in a "patchwork" manner according to the paintability of the particular piece of wood in the board (Fig. 15–5). The finishing of fingerjointed lumber requires special care to ensure that the finish will adhere to the whole board. Rough-sawn lumber should hold paint better than will planed lumber. Planed wood should be scuff-sanded with 50-grit sandpaper prior to priming.

Figure 15–4. Early paint failure on plywood caused by penetration of moisture into surface face-checks.

Figure 15–5. Differences in stain from extractives on fingerjointed yellow pine (probably ponderosa pine) painted with acrylic solid-color stain.

Particleboard and Similar Reconstituted Wood Products

Reconstituted wood products are those made by forming small pieces of wood into large sheets, usually 1.2 by 2.4 m (4 by 8 ft) or as required for a specialized use such as clapboard siding. These products may be classified as fiberboard or particleboard, depending upon the nature of the basic wood component (see Ch. 10).

Although wood characteristics such as grain orientation, specific gravity of earlywood and latewood, warping, and splitting are not considerations with reconstituted wood products, other characteristics must be addressed when finishing these products. The surface of fiberboard accepts and holds paint very well, and it can be improved with the addition of a resin-treated paper overlay. Film-forming finishes such as paints and solid-color stains will provide the most protection to reconstituted wood products. Some reconstituted wood products may be factory primed with paint, and factory-applied top-coats are becoming more common. The edges of these products are sensitive to moisture, and extra care should be used to assure that edges get a good coat of paint. Better yet, edges can be sealed with a paintable water-repellent preservative. Reconstituted wood products should not be finished with semitransparent stain or other penetrating finishes.

Fiberboard is produced from wood that is pulped by mechanical means. Hardboard is a relatively heavy type of fiberboard. The tempered or treated form of hardboard is designed for outdoor exposure and is used for exterior siding. Hardboard is often sold in 1.2- by 2.4-m (4- by 8-ft) sheets and in 152- to 203-mm (6- to 8-in.) widths as a substitute for solid-wood beveled siding.

Particleboard is manufactured from whole wood in the form of splinters, chips, flakes, strands, or shavings. Flakeboard is a type of particleboard made from relatively large flakes or shavings. Oriented strandboard (OSB) is a refinement of flakeboard in that the flakes have a large length-to-width aspect ratio and are laid down in layers, with the flakes in each layer oriented 90° to each other as are veneers in plywood (Ch. 10). Particleboard that is to be used outdoors must be overlaid with either wood veneer or resin-treated paper; exterior particleboard can be finished in the same way as are other paper over-laid products. As with fiberboard, special care must taken to assure a good paint film on the edges of particleboard.

Treated Wood

Wood used in severe outdoor exposures requires special treatment for proper protection and best service. The most common hazard in such exposures is decay (rot) and insect attack, particularly by termites. Marine exposure also requires wood to be protected with special treatment. Many building codes require fire-retardant treatment of wood for some uses.

When wood is used in situations with high decay and termite hazards, it is usually treated with a wood preservative.

The three main types of preservatives are (a) preservative oils (such as coal–tar creosote), (b) organic solvent solution (such as pentachlorophenol), and (c) waterborne salts (such as chromated copper arsenate (CCA)) (Ch. 14). These preservatives can be applied in several ways, but pressure treatment generally provides the greatest protection against decay. Wood preservatives may also improve the wood's resistance to weathering, particularly if the preservative contains chromium salts. Chromium-containing preservatives protect wood against ultraviolet degradation, an important factor in the weathering process.

Wood treated with waterborne preservatives, such as CCA, can be painted or stained if the wood is clean and dry. Wood treated with a water-repellent preservative, by vacuum-pressure or dipping, is paintable. Wood treated with coal–tar creosote or other dark oily preservatives is not paintable; even if the paint adheres to the treated wood, the dark oils tend to discolor the paint, especially light-colored paint.

Fire-retardant treatment of wood does not generally interfere with adhesion of paint coatings, unless the treated wood has extremely high moisture content because of its increased hygroscopicity. Fire-retardant-treated wood is generally painted according to the manufacturer's recommendations rather than left unfinished because the treatment and subsequent drying often darken and discolor the wood. It is critical that wood to be used outside be treated with only those fire-retardant treatments that are specifically recommended for outdoor exposure.

Weathering

Weathering is the general term used to describe the degradation of materials exposed outdoors. This degradation occurs on the surface of all organic materials, including wood and finishes used on wood such as paints and stains. The process occurs through photo-oxidation of the surface catalyzed by ultraviolet (UV) radiation in sunlight, and it is augmented by other processes such as washing by rain, changes in temperature, changes in moisture content, and abrasion by windblown particles. The weathering process can take many forms depending on the exposed material; in general, the process begins with a color change, followed by slow erosion (loss of material) from the surface. The surface initially develops slight checking; with some materials, deep cracks may ultimately develop. Weathering is dependent on the chemical makeup of the affected material. Because the surface of a material may be composed of many different chemicals, not all materials on the surface may erode at the same rate.

Effect on Wood

The surface of wood consists of four types of organic materials: cellulose, hemicellulose, lignin, and extractives. Each of these materials is affected by the weathering process in a different way. The extractives (that is, the material in the wood that gives each species its distinctive color) undergo changes upon exposure to sunlight and lighten or darken in color. With some wood species, this color change can take place within minutes of exposure. Changes in the color of the surface are accompanied by other changes that affect the wettability and surface chemistry of the wood. The mechanism of these early changes is not very well understood, but these changes can have a drastic effect on the surface chemistry of wood and thus the interaction of the wood with other chemicals, such as paint and other finishes.

From 20% to 30% of the wood surface is composed of lignin, a polymeric substance that is the adhesive that holds wood celluloses together. Because lignin is affected by photodegradation more than are celluloses, lignin degrades and cellulose fibers remain loosely attached to the wood surface. Further weathering causes fibers to be lost from the surface (a process called erosion); but this process is so slow that on the average only about 6 mm (1/4 in.) of wood is lost in a century (Fig. 15–6). This erosion rate is slower for most

hardwoods and faster for certain softwoods. Other factors like growth rate, degree of exposure, grain orientation, temperature, and wetting and drying cycles are important in determining the rate of erosion. Table 15–2 shows erosion rates for several wood species that were measured over a 16-year period.

Water and the swelling and shrinking stresses set up by fluctuations in moisture content accelerate erosion. Cyclic wetting and drying roughen the surface, raise the grain, cause differential swelling of earlywood and latewood bands, and result in many small, parallel checks and cracks. Larger and deeper cracks may also develop. Fewer checks develop in woods with moderate to low specific gravity than in those with high specific gravity, and vertical-grain boards have fewer checks than do flat-grain boards. Flat-grain lumber frequently warps as well.

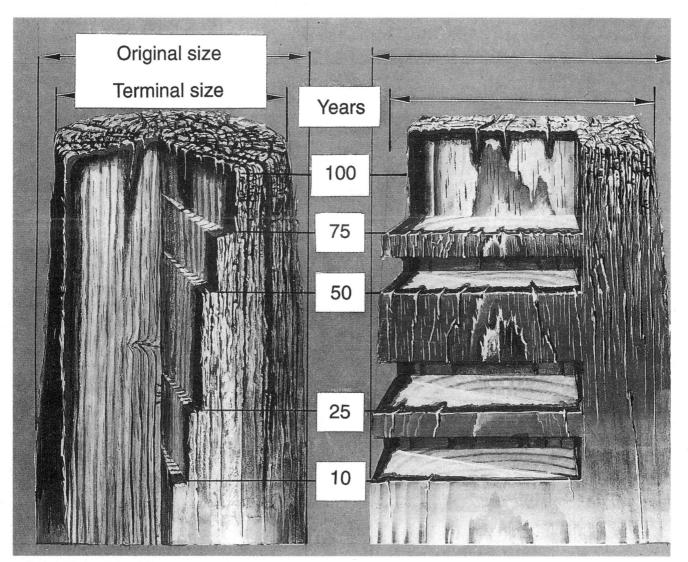

Figure 15–6. Artist's rendition of weathering process of round and square timbers. As cutaway shows, interior wood below surface is relatively unchanged.

333

Table 15–2. Erosion of earlywood and latewood on smooth planed surfaces of various wood species after outdoor exposure[a]

Wood species	Avg SG[b]	Erosion (μm) after various exposure times[c]											
		4 years		8 years		10 years		12 years		14 years		16 years	
		LW	EW	LW	EW	LW	EW	LW	EW	LW	EW	LW	EW
Western redcedar plywood	—	170	580	290	920	455	1,095	615	1,165	805	1,355	910	1,475
Redwood plywood	—	125	440	295	670	475	800	575	965	695	1,070	845	1,250
Douglas-fir plywood	—	110	270	190	390	255	500	345	555	425	770	515	905
Douglas-fir	0.46	105	270	210	720	285	905	380	.980	520	1,300	500	1,405
Southern Pine	0.45	135	320	275	605	315	710	335	710	445	1,180	525	1,355
Western redcedar	0.31	200	500	595	1,090	765	1,325	970	1,565	1,160	1,800	1,380	1,945
Redwood	0.36	165	405	315	650	440	835	555	965	670	1,180	835	1,385
Loblolly pine	0.66	80	205	160	345	220	490	—	—	—	—	—	—
Western redcedar	0.35	115	495	240	1,010	370	1,225	—	—	—	—	—	—
Southern Pine	0.57	95	330	180	640	195	670	—	—	—	—	—	—
Yellow-poplar	0.47	—	220	—	530	—	640	—	—	—	—	—	—
Douglas-fir	0.48	75	255	175	605	225	590	—	—	—	—	—	—
Red oak	0.57	180	245	340	555	440	750	—	—	—	—	—	—
Ponderosa pine	0.35	130	270	315	445	430	570	Decay	Decay	Decay	Decay	—	—
Lodgepole pine	0.38	105	255	265	465	320	580	475	745	560	810	—	—
Engelmann spruce	0.36	125	320	310	545	390	650	505	795	590	950	—	—
Western hemlock	0.34	145	320	310	575	415	680	515	1,255	600	1,470	—	—
Red alder	0.39	—	295	—	545	—	620	—	920	—	955	—	—

[a]Data from three studies are shown. Specimens were exposed vertically facing south. Radial surfaces were exposed with the grain vertical.
[b]SG is specific gravity.
[c]All erosion values are averages of nine observations (three measurements of three specimens). EW denotes earlywood; LW, latewood.

The time required for wood to become fully weathered depends on the severity of the exposure. Once weathered, and in the absence of decay, stain, and mildew, wood remains nearly unaltered in appearance (Fig. 15–7). As a result of weathering, boards tend to warp (particularly cup) and fasteners are loosened. The tendency to cup varies with the specific gravity, width, and thickness of the board. The greater the specific gravity and the greater the width in proportion to thickness, the greater the tendency to cup. For best resistance to cup, the width of a board should not exceed eight times its thickness. Warping also is more pronounced in flat-grain boards than in vertical-grain boards.

Biological attack of a wood surface by microorganisms is recognized as a contributing factor to color change or graying of wood. This biological attack, commonly called mildew, does not cause erosion of the surface, but it may cause initial graying or an unsightly dark gray and blotchy appearance. These color changes are caused by dark-colored fungal spores and mycelia on the wood surface. In advanced stages of weathering, when the surface has been enriched by cellulose,

it may develop a silvery-gray sheen. This formation of a bright, light gray, silvery sheen on weathered wood occurs most frequently where micro-organism growth is inhibited by a hot, arid climate or a salty atmosphere in coastal regions. The microorganisms primarily responsible for gray discoloration of wood are commonly found on weathered wood (see subsection on mildew under Finish Failure or Discoloration).

Effect on Paint Adhesion

Although the erosion of the wood surface through weathering is a slow process, the chemical changes that occur within a few weeks of outdoor exposure can drastically decrease the adhesion of paints subsequently applied to the weathered surface. It is fairly obvious that a badly weathered, powdery wood surface cannot hold paint very well. This fact is not so obvious for wood that has weathered for only 2 to 3 weeks. The wood appears sound and much the same as when it was installed. The extent of damage to the wood surface after such a short exposure has yet to be determined. However,

Figure 15–7. Weathered surfaces of softwood after 15 years of exposure in Madison, Wisconsin.

long-term outdoor exposure of panels that had been pre-weathered for 1, 2, 4, 8, or 16 weeks before being painted showed a direct relationship between preweathering time and the time when the paint started to peel. For panels that had been preweathered for 16 weeks, the paint peeled within 3 years; for panels preweathered for only 1 week, the paint peeled after 13 years. Panels that were not preweathered showed no sign of peeling after 13 years. The paint system was a commercial oil–alkyd primer with two acrylic latex top-coats over planed all-heartwood vertical-grain western redcedar.

Several other wood species were tested in addition to western redcedar. In general, there was a direct relationship between wood specific gravity and amount of time the wood could be exposed without a deleterious effect on paint performance. More dense wood species such as Douglas-fir and the southern pines showed no preweathering effect until they had been preweathered for 3 to 4 weeks. For species with low specific gravity, it is essential to finish the wood as soon as possible after installation, or better yet, to preprime it before installation. The wood could be back-primed at the same time (see section on back-priming).

The best remedy for restoring a weathered wood surface is to sand it with 50- to 80-grit sandpaper. Sanding can easily be done by hand using a sheet rock sander. This tool consists of a sanding pad attached to a pole with a swivel connection. Large areas of siding can be quickly scuff-sanded to remove the weathered surface. Even if wood has not been weathered, scuff sanding provides a much better surface for painting, increases the service life of the paint, and improves the paint bond.

Effect on Wood Finishes

Finishes used on wood also undergo surface photodegradation because the primary ingredient that holds a paint film together or seals the wood surface is an organic polymer and thus is susceptible to photo-oxidative degradation. The UV radiation in sunlight breaks down the polymer in paint, causing a slow erosion similar to that which occurs on wood. The pigments in paint are not usually affected by UV radiation. Therefore, as film-forming finishes such as paints or solid-color stains weather, they do so by the slow break-down of the polymer, which loosens the pigments. The surface becomes chalky because of the loose pigments. Eventually, these pigments and the degraded polymer erode from the surface. The rate of weathering primarily depends on the resistance of the polymer to UV radiation. Paints and stains based on acrylic polymers are more UV-resistant than those based on oil and oil–alkyds. Weathering is strictly a surface phenomenon on the finish, and as with wood, a painted surface can be attacked by mildew.

Control of Water or Moisture in Wood

Moisture Content

The moisture content of wood is the amount of water contained in the wood (see Ch. 3). Moisture content includes both water absorbed into the wood cell wall and free water within the hollow center of the cell, and it is expressed as a weight percentage. The amount of water that wood can absorb (that is, that can be bound in the cell wall) depends on the wood species; most species can absorb about 30% water. This limit to the amount of water that can be bound in the wood cell wall is called the fiber saturation point. Wood can reach the fiber saturation point by absorbing either liquid water or water vapor.

The amount of water vapor that can be absorbed primarily depends on the relative humidity (RH) of the surrounding air. If wood is stored at zero RH, the moisture content will eventually reach 0%. If wood is stored at 100% RH, it will eventually reach fiber saturation (about 30% water). Of course, if kept at a constant RH between these two extremes, the wood will reach a moisture content between 0 and 30%. The moisture content is controlled by the RH, and when the moisture content is in balance with the RH, the wood is at its equilibrium moisture content. This rarely happens because as the RH changes so does the moisture content of the wood, and atmospheric RH is almost always changing. It varies through daily and seasonal cycles, thus driving the moisture content of wood through daily and seasonal cycles. See Chapter 3 for a more detailed discussion of moisture content and equilibrium moisture content.

Equilibrium moisture content cannot be changed through the application of finishes. The only way that finishes can affect absorption of water or water vapor is to affect the rate at which absorption occurs. Finishes can decrease daily and seasonal moisture absorption and desorption, but they do not change the equilibrium moisture content. See the section on moisture-excluding effectiveness of finishes for discussion of this topic.

Wood exposed outdoors cycles around a moisture content of about 12% in most areas of the United States. In the Southeast, average moisture content can be slightly higher and in the Southwest, the average can be lower (9%) (Ch. 12, Table 12–1). Daily and annual moisture content will vary from these average values. In general, for wood exposed outdoors, moisture content decreases during the summer and increases during the winter. (For wood in interior use in northern climates, moisture content increases during the summer and decreases during the winter.) Even in very humid areas, the RH is rarely high enough for long enough to bring the moisture content of wood above 20%. Wood that is warmed by the sun experiences a virtual RH far below the ambient RH. Wood will dry faster and become drier than expected given the ambient RH. This is why checking often occurs on decking boards; the surface is much drier than the rest of the board. Shrinkage of the top portion of the board commensurate with this dryness goes beyond the elastic limit of the wood at the surface and checks form parallel to the grain.

As mentioned, fiber saturation is the greatest amount of water that can be absorbed by wood via water vapor absorption. This absorption is rather slow compared with the moisture changes that can occur through absorption of liquid water. Liquid water can quickly cause the wood to reach fiber saturation, and it is the only way to bring the moisture content of wood above fiber saturation. Liquid water must be present. Liquid water can reach wood through windblown rain, leaks, condensation, dew, melting ice and snow, and other ways. As wood continues to absorb water above its fiber saturation point, the water is stored in the hollow center of the wood cell; when all the air in the hollow center has been replaced by water, the wood is waterlogged and moisture content can be as high as 200%. The sources and ways by which wood can get wet sometimes seem endless. The result is always the same—poor performance, both of the wood and of the finish.

Wood decay (rot) cannot occur unless the moisture content of the wood is near fiber saturation. This requires water. Water also causes peeling of paint. Even if other factors are involved, water accelerates paint degradation. Fortunately, the moisture content of lumber can be controlled. But all too often, this critical factor is neglected during the construction and finishing processes. It is best to paint wood when its average moisture content is about that expected to prevail during its service life. Painting at this time can prevent a drastic change in wood dimension, which occurs as wood equilibrates to ambient conditions. The moisture content and thus the dimensions of the piece will still fluctuate somewhat, depending on the cyclic changes in atmospheric RH, but the dimensional change will not be excessive. Therefore, film-forming finishes (such as paints) will not be stressed unnecessarily, and service life should be better.

The recommended moisture content for wood used in exterior applications varies somewhat depending on climatic conditions. These conditions include, but are not limited to, coastal exposure, rainfall, elevation, and wind. However, problems associated with changes in moisture content should be minimized if the moisture content is between 9% and 14%. Most lumber is kiln dried to less than 20% moisture content before shipment. Material that has been kept dry during shipment and storage at the construction site should be close to the desired moisture content.

Lumber is often marketed for construction purposes in the kiln-dried condition, but it is sometimes exposed to moisture later during shipping, storage, and/or at the construction site. Wood that is obviously wet and sometimes discolored may not give optimum performance. If wet wood is used, it will dry in service, but shrinkage and accompanying warping, twisting, and checking can occur. If the moisture content of the wood exceeds 20% when the wood is painted, the risk of blistering and peeling is increased. Moreover, dark water-soluble extractives in woods like redwood and western redcedar may discolor the paint shortly after it is applied.

Plywood, particleboard, hardboard, and other wood composites undergo a significant change in moisture content during manufacture. Frequently, the moisture content of these materials is not known and may vary depending on the manufacturing process. To improve the service life of the finish, wood composites should be conditioned prior to finishing, as are other wood products.

Water Repellents

The control of water and/or water vapor requires different types of finishes. Water repellent is a generic name for a wide variety of sealers and wood treatments that change the surface properties of wood so that the wood sheds liquid water. Water repellents have almost no effect on the transmission of water vapor; that is, they have little effect on the change in wood moisture content caused by changes in RH. Water repellents work exceptionally well to retard the absorption of water into the end grain of wood, the most absorptive of the wood surfaces. Although water repellents do not stop all water absorption, they are an excellent treatment for wood used outdoors because they inhibit the absorption of liquid water during rain, yet allow the wood to dry after rain. Water-repellent formulations usually include a mildewcide or a wood preservative and are then referred to as water-repellent preservatives. These finishes are discussed in greater detail in later sections of this chapter.

Finish Moisture-Excluding Effectiveness

The moisture-excluding effectiveness of a finish is a measure of its resistance to the transmission of water vapor to the finished wood. It is basically a measure of the permeability of a coating to water vapor. It is not a measure of water repellency. Moisture-excluding effectiveness is determined by comparing the moisture pickup of a coated specimen with that of a matched uncoated control. A coating that blocks all moisture would be 100% effective; however, no coating is entirely moisture proof. There is as yet no way of completely keeping moisture out of wood that is exposed to prolonged periods of high RH. As wood is exposed to varying RH conditions, it absorbs or desorbs moisture depending on the RH. A coating that is effective at excluding moisture merely slows absorption or desorption of moisture; it cannot change the equilibrium moisture content (Ch. 3).

To achieve a high degree of moisture-excluding effectiveness, it is necessary to form a moisture barrier on the wood surface. In addition to repelling liquid water, this film will slow the diffusion of water vapor into or out of the wood. Water-repellent treatments differ from moisture-excluding coatings in that they do not slow the absorption–desorption of water vapor. They repel liquid water only. For example, a water-repellent treatment, which may have no moisture-excluding effectiveness against water vapor, might have more than 60% water repellency when tested using standard immersion tests. The high degree of protection provided by water repellents and water-repellent preservatives to short periods of wetting by liquid water is the major reason they are recommended for exterior finishing.

The protection afforded by coatings in excluding moisture from wood depends on a great number of variables. Among them are coating film thickness, defects and voids in the film, type of pigment, chemical composition of the oil or polymer, volume ratio of pigment to vehicle (pigment volume concentration), vapor-pressure gradient across the film, and length of exposure. Values in Table 15–3 indicate the range in protection against moisture in vapor form for some conventional finish systems when exposed to continuous high humidity. The degree of protection provided also depends on the kind of exposure.

Porous paints, such as latex paints and low-luster (flat) or breather-type oil-based paints formulated at a pigment volume concentration usually above 40%, afford little protection against moisture. These paints permit rapid entry of water vapor and water from dew and rain unless applied over a nonporous primer or pretreated with a paintable water-repellent preservative. In addition to being porous, latex finishes contain surfactants that can encourage absorption of water into the coating and wood, particularly just after the coating has been applied. It is thought that these surfactants wash out of the coating after a short time, but detailed information on this is not available.

The moisture-excluding effectiveness of coatings changes only slightly with age. As long as the original appearance and integrity of the coatings are retained, most effectiveness remains. Paint that is slowly fading or chalking will remain effective at excluding moisture; the paint is still effective if there is a glossy film underneath the chalk (which can be removed by rubbing). Deep chalking, checking, or cracking indicates serious impairment of moisture-excluding effectiveness.

The numerical values for percentage of effectiveness in Table 15–3 should be considered relative rather than absolute because the percentage of effectiveness varies substantially with exposure to moisture conditions. The values for effective coatings ($\geq$60%) are reliable in the sense that they can be reproduced closely on repeating the test; values for ineffective coatings (<20%) must be regarded as rough approximations only. These percentages are based on average amounts of moisture absorbed per unit surface area by newly coated and uncoated wood panels. In addition, the values were determined from specimens coated on all sides. Since wood used in normal construction is seldom coated on all sides, the actual absorption–desorption will differ from the values listed in Table 15–3.

Effect of Finish on Liquid Water and Water Vapor Absorption

The various dimensions of wood and wood-based building materials are constantly changing because of changes in moisture content, which in turn are caused by fluctuations in atmospheric RH as well as the periodic presence of free moisture such as rain or dew. Water repellents provide protection against liquid water but are ineffective against water vapor (humidity). Film-forming finishes such as paint and varnish shed liquid water and retard the absorption of water vapor, provided the films are thick enough. Because film-forming wood finishes like paint will last longer on stable wood, it is desirable to stabilize the wood by finishing it with a water-repellent preservative as the first step in the finish system. As mentioned previously, there is no way to completely eliminate the changing moisture content of wood in response to changing RH. The coating simply slows down the rate at which the wood changes moisture content.

Film-forming finishes slow both the absorption of water vapor and drying of wood (Fig. 15–8). Aluminum flake paint is a laboratory formulation designed to block water vapor movement into wood. It is about 80% effective at blocking water vapor absorption compared with water vapor absorption in an unpainted control. Almost all common wood finishes, both oil and latex, are less effective than aluminum flake paint at blocking water vapor absorption. However, oil-based formulations are more effective than latex formulations. The coating slows the rate of drying. In cyclic high and low RH, the moisture content of the wood increases with time (Fig. 15–9).

The moisture-excluding effectiveness described in the previous section was obtained from specimens consisting of single pieces of wood that were painted on all sides. In normal construction, wood is seldom coated on all sides. In addition to absorbing water vapor, paint coatings usually crack at the joint between two pieces of wood, particularly if they have different grain orientations (and thus different dimensional stability). Water enters the wood through these cracks and is trapped by the coating, thus causing an increase in moisture content much higher than that shown in Figure 15–9.

Table 15–3. Moisture-excluding effectiveness of various finishes on ponderosa pine[a]

Finish	No. of coats	Moisture-excluding effectiveness (%)			Finish	No. of coats	Moisture-excluding effectiveness (%)		
		1 day	7 days	14 days			1 day	7 days	14 days
Linseed oil sealer (50%)	1	7	0	0	Alkyd house primer paint	1	85	46	24
	2	15	1	0	(tall maleic alkyd resin)	2	93	70	49
	3	18	2	0		3	95	78	60
Linseed oil	1	12	0	0	Enamel paint, satin	1	93	69	50
	2	22	0	0	(soya/tung/alkyd;	2	96	83	70
	3	33	2	0	interior/exterior)	3	97	86	80
Tung oil	1	34	0	0		4	98	92	85
	2	46	2	0		5	98	93	88
	3	52	6	2		6	98	94	89
Paste furniture wax	1	6	0	0	Floor and deck enamel	1	80	31	18
	2	11	0	0	(phenolic alkyd)	2	89	53	35
	3	17	0	0		3	92	63	46
Water repellent	1	12	0	0	Shellac	1	65	10	3
	2	46	2	0		2	84	43	20
	3	78	27	11		3	91	64	42
Latex flat wall paint	1	5	0	0		4	93	75	58
(vinyl acrylic resin)	2	11	0	0		5	94	81	67
	3	22	0	0		6	95	85	73
Latex primer wall paint	1	78	37	20	Nitrocellulose lacquer	1	40	4	1
(butadiene–styrene resin)	2	86	47	27		2	70	22	8
	3	88	55	33		3	79	37	19
Alkyd flat wall paint	1	9	1	0	Floor seal	1	31	1	0
(soya alkyd)	2	21	2	0	(phenolic resin/tung oil)	2	80	37	18
	3	37	5	0		3	88	56	35
Acrylic latex house	1	43	6	1	Spar varnish	1	48	6	0
primer paint	2	66	14	2	(soya alkyd)	2	80	36	15
	3	72	20	4		3	87	53	30
Acrylic latex flat	1	52	12	5	Urethane varnish	1	55	10	2
house paint	2	77	28	11	(oil-modified)	2	83	43	23
	3	84	39	16		3	90	64	44
Solid-color latex stain	1	5	0	0		4	91	68	51
(acrylic resin)	2	38	4	0		5	93	72	57
	3	50	6	0		6	93	76	62
Solid-color oil-based stain	1	45	7	1	Aluminum flake pigmented	1	90	61	41
(linseed oil)	2	84	48	26	urethane varnish	2	97	87	77
	3	90	64	42	(oil-modified)	3	98	91	84
FPL natural finish (linseed-	1	62	14	3		4	98	93	87
oil-based semitransparent	2	70	21	6		5	98	94	89
stain)	3	76	30	11		6	99	95	90
Semitransparent oil-based	1	7	0	0	Polyurethane finish, clear	1	48	6	0
stain (commercial)	2	13	0	0	(two components)	2	90	66	46
	3	21	1	0		3	94	81	66
Marine enamel, gloss (soya	1	79	38	18	Polyurethane paint, gloss (two	1	91	66	44
alkyd)	2	91	66	46	components)	2	94	79	62
	3	93	74	57		3	96	86	74
					Paraffin wax, brushed	1	97	82	69
					Paraffin wax, dipped	1	100	97	95

[a]Sapwood was initially finished and conditioned to 26°C (80°F) and 30% RH, then exposed to the same temperature and 90% RH.

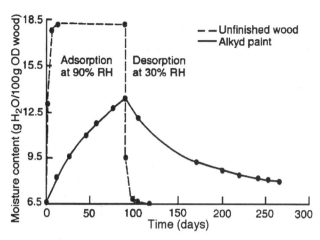

Figure 15–8. Change in moisture content of ponderosa pine sapwood finished with three coats of aluminum pigmented alkyd paint and exposed to 90% and 30% RH at 26°C (80°F), compared with moisture content of unfinished wood.

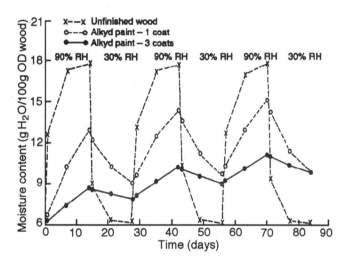

Figure 15–9. Change in moisture content of ponderosa pine sapwood finished with three coats of aluminum pigmented alkyd paint and exposed to alternating cycles of 90% and 30% RH at 26°C (80°F), compared with moisture content of unfinished wood.

The paint film inhibits drying, as shown. This retardation of drying can have a drastic effect on the durability of painted wood fully exposed to the weather. The moisture content of the wood can approach the range where decay fungi can become active. This type of wood paint failure usually occurs on painted fences and porch railings that are fully exposed to the weather (Fig. 15–10). Applying a water-repellent preservative or priming the end grain of wood used in these applications inhibits the absorption of water at the end grain and thus works in concert with the coating to keep the wood dry.

For a coating to be effective in minimizing moisture content changes in the wood, it must be applied to all surfaces,

Figure 15–10. Decay in wood railing fully exposed to weather.

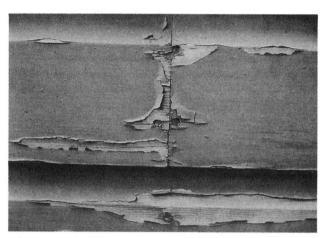

Figure 15–11. Paint failure at ends of boards.

particularly the end grain. The end grain of wood absorbs moisture much faster than does the face grain, and finishes generally fail in the end grain first (Fig. 15–11). Coatings with good moisture-excluding effectiveness that are applied to only one side of the wood will cause unequal sorption of moisture, increasing the likelihood that the wood will cup (warp). When finishing siding, it is important to allow the back side of the wood to dry, particularly if it is finished with paint with high moisture-excluding effectiveness. Applying a water-repellent preservative or primer to the end grain and back of siding (see section on back-priming) prior to installing the siding improves resistance to water yet allows the siding to dry. Cupping can be minimized by using vertical-grain lumber and by minimizing the aspect ratio.

In those houses where moisture moves from the living quarters to the outside wall because of the lack of a vapor barrier (or a poor vapor barrier), the application of moisture-excluding finishes to the outside will not prevent paint peeling. In fact, finishes with higher moisture-excluding effectiveness are more prone to fail by peeling because they trap moisture.

Types of Exterior Wood Finishes

The types of exterior finishes for wood are separated into two groups, those that penetrate wood and those that form a film. As a general rule, penetrating finishes tend to give a more "natural" look to the wood. That is, they allow some of the character of the wood to show through the finish. Also, in general, the more natural a finish, the less durable it is. Natural finishes may be penetrating finishes such as semi-transparent stains or film-forming finishes such as varnish. The penetrating natural finishes generally give better performance and are easier to refinish. This section also addresses weathered wood as a "finish."

The properties, treatment, and maintenance of exterior finishes are summarized in Table 15–4. The suitability and expected life of the most commonly used exterior finishes on several wood and wood-based products are summarized in Table 15–5. The information in these tables should be considered as a general guideline only. Many factors affect the performance and lifetime of wood finishes.

Table 15–4. Initial application and maintenance of exterior wood finishes[a]

| Finish | Initial application | | | Maintenance | | |
	Process	Cost	Appearance of wood	Process	Cost	Service life[b]
Water-repellent preservative	Brushing	Low	Grain visible; wood brown to black, fades slightly with age	Brush to remove surface dirt; remove mildew	Low	1–3 years
Waterborne preservative[c]	Pressure (factory applied)	Medium	Grain visible; wood greenish or brownish, fades with age	Brush to remove surface dirt; remove mildew	Nil, unless stained or painted	None, unless stained, or painted
Organic solvent preservative[d]	Pressure, steeping, dipping, and brushing	Low to medium	Grain visible; color as desired	Brush and reapply	Medium	2–3 years or when preferred
Water repellent[e]	One or two brush coats of clear material or, preferably, dip application	Low	Grain and natural color visible, becoming darker and rougher textured with age	Clean and reapply	Low to medium	1–3 years or when preferred
Semitransparent stain	One or two brush coats	Low to medium	Grain visible; color as desired	Clean and reapply	Low to medium	3–6 years or when preferred
Clear varnish	Three coats (minimum)	High	Grain and natural color unchanged if adequately maintained	Clean, sand, and stain bleached areas; apply two more coats	High	2 years or at breakdown
Paint and solid-color stain	Brushing: water repellent, prime, and two top-coats	Medium to high	Grain and natural color obscured	Clean and apply top coat, or re-move and repeat initial treatment if damaged	Medium	7–10 years for paint;[f] 3–7 years for solid-color stain

[a]Compilation of data from observations of many researchers.
[b]For vertical exposure.
[c]Although wood treated with waterborne preservative may be left unfinished, it is best to finish it with water-repellent preservative or semitransparent stain. See maintenance of water repellent and semitransparent stain.
[d]Pentachlorophenol, bis(tri-n-butyltin oxide), copper naphthenate, copper-8-quinolinolate, and similar materials.
[e]With or without added preservatives. Addition of preservative helps control mildew growth.
[f]If top-quality acrylic latex top-coats are used.

Table 15–5. Suitability and expected service life of finishes for exterior wood surfaces[a]

| Type of exterior wood surface | Water-repellent preservative and oil | | Semitransparent stain | | Paint and solid-color stain | | |
| | Suit-ability | Expected life[b] (years) | Suitability | Expected life[c] (years) | Suitability | Expected life[d] (years) | |
						Paint	Solid-color stain
Siding							
Cedar and redwood							
Smooth (vertical grain)	High	1–2	Moderate	2–4	High	4–6	3–5
Rough-sawn	High	2–3	High	5–8	Moderate	5–7	4–6
Pine, fir, spruce							
Smooth (flat grain)	High	1–2	Low	2–3	Moderate	3–5	3–4
Rough (flat grain)	High	2–3	High	4–7	Moderate	4–6	4–5
Shingles							
Sawn	High	2–3	High	4–8	Moderate	3–5	3–4
Split	High	1–2	High	4–8	—	3–5	3–4
Plywood (Douglas-fir and Southern Pine)							
Sanded	Low	1–2	Moderate	2–4	Moderate	2–4	2–3
Textured (smooth-sawn)	Low	1–2	Moderate	2–4	Moderate	3–4	2–3
Textured (rough-sawn)	Low	2–3	High	4–8	Moderate	4–6	3–5
MDO plywood, cedar and redwood[e]	—	—	—	—	Excellent	6–8	5–7
Sanded	Low	1–2	Moderate	2–4	Moderate	2–4	2–3
Textured (smooth-sawn)	Low	1–2	Moderate	2–4	Moderate	3–4	2–3
Textured (rough-sawn)	Low	2–3	High	5–8	Moderate	4–6	3–5
Hardboard, medium density[f]							
Smooth-sawn							
Unfinished	—	—	—	—	High	4–6	3–5
Preprimed	—	—	—	—	High	4–6	3–5
Textured							
Unfinished	—	—	—	—	High	4–6	3–5
Preprimed	—	—	—	—	High	4–6	3–5
Millwork (usually pine)[g]	High[h]	—	Moderate	2–3	High	3–6	3–4
Decking							
New (smooth-sawn)	High	1–2	Moderate	2–3	Low	2–3	1–2
Weathered (rough-sawn)	High	2–3	High	3–6	Low	2–3	1–2
Glued-laminated members							
Smooth-sawn	High	1–2	Moderate	3–4	Moderate	3–4	2–3
Rough-sawn	High	2–3	High	6–8	Moderate	3–5	3–4
Oriented strandboard	—	—	Low	1–3	Moderate	2–4	2–3

[a]Data were compiled from observations of many researchers. Expected life predictions are for average location in continental United States; expected life will vary in extreme climates or exposure (such as desert, seashore, and deep woods).

[b]Development of mildew on surface indicates need for refinishing.

[c]Smooth, unweathered surfaces are generally finished with only one coat of stain. Rough-sawn or weathered surfaces, which are more adsorptive, can be finished with two coats; second coat is applied while first coat is still wet.

[d]Expected life of two coats, one primer and one top-coat. Applying second top-coat (three-coat job) will approximately double the life. Top-quality acrylic latex paints have the best durability.

[e]Medium-density overlay (MDO) is generally painted.

[f]Semitransparent stains are not suitable for hardboard. Solid-color stains (acrylic latex) will perform like paints. Paints are preferred.

[g]Windows, shutters, doors, exterior trim.

[h]Exterior millwork, such as windows, should be factory treated according to Industry Standard IS4–99 of the Window and Door Manufacturer's Association. Other trim should be liberally treated by brushing before painting.

Figure 15–12. Front view of exterior grade of plywood siding after 10 years of exposure.

Weathered Wood as Natural Finish

The simplest finish for wood is that created by the weathering process. Without paint or treatment of any kind, wood surfaces gradually change in color and texture, and they may stay almost unaltered for a long time if the wood does not decay. Generally, dark-colored woods become lighter and light-colored woods become darker. As weathering continues, all woods become gray because of the loss of colored components from the wood surface and the growth of mildew. As the surface erodes, it becomes uneven because of the different erosion rates of earlywood and latewood. (Fig. 15–6).

Although leaving wood to weather to a natural finish may seem like an inexpensive low-maintenance alternative to finishing, there are many problems to this approach. To avoid decay, wood must be all heartwood from a decay-resistant species such as redwood or western redcedar. Wood should have vertical grain to decrease the potential for splitting, grain raising, and cupping. Composite wood products, such as plywood, must never be left unprotected to weather. The surface veneer of plywood can be completely destroyed within 10 years if not protected from weathering. Figure 15–12 shows weathering of unfinished plywood; the intact portion of the plywood (left) had been covered with a board to give a board-and-batten appearance.

To allow a wood structure to weather to a natural finish, the structure must be designed to keep the wood from getting wet from wind-driven rain (for example, wide roof overhangs). In most climates in the United States, exterior wood develops blotchy mildew growth and there is no protection against surface erosion or decay. It is very difficult to obtain the silvery-gray weathered patina that weathering can give. The climate along the coastal regions of New England and in some high mountains seems to encourage the development of this finish. Even when the climatic conditions favor the development of a weathered finish, it takes several years to achieve an even silvery-gray appearance.

Penetrating Wood Finishes

Penetrating finishes constitute a broad classification of natural wood finishes that do not form a film on the wood surface. Penetrating finishes are classified as (a) transparent or clear systems, (b) lightly colored systems, (c) pigmented or semitransparent systems, and (d) oils.

Transparent or Clear Finishes

Penetrating transparent or clear finishes are generally a type of water repellent or water-repellent preservative. Water-repellent preservatives may be used as a natural finish. They differ from water repellents in that they contain a fungicide such as 3-iodo-2-propynyl butyl carbamate. As with water repellents, water-repellent preservatives contain a small amount of wax, a resin, or a drying oil. They were traditionally formulated using a solvent such as turpentine or mineral spirits, but they are presently available in a wide range of other solvent systems, including waterborne formulations.

Penetrating finishes that use paraffin oil as the solvent system are also available. These formulations penetrate wood like solventborne formulations do and the oil helps improve water repellency. Since penetrating finishes with paraffin oil are usually formulated without any volatile solvents, they meet air quality requirements. (See section on VOC-compliant finishes.) They are usually a good value because virtually all of what comes in the can ends up in the wood.

Water-repellent preservatives maintain the original appearance of the wood, but they are not very durable. Treating wood surfaces with a water-repellent preservative will protect wood exposed outdoors with little initial change in appearance. A bright, golden-tan color can be achieved with most wood species. The treatment decreases warping and cracking, prevents water staining at edges and ends of wood siding, and helps control mildew growth. The first application of a water-repellent preservative may protect exposed wood surfaces for only 1 to 2 years, but subsequent reapplications may last 2 to 4 years because the weathered boards absorb more finish. When a surface starts to show blotchy discoloration caused by extractives or mildew, it should be cleaned with a commercial cleaner or liquid household bleach and detergent solution, allowed to dry, and retreated.

> **Caution**: Because of the toxicity of some fungicides in water-repellent preservative solutions and some semitransparent stains, care should be exercised to avoid excessive contact with the solution or its vapor. Shrubs and plants should also be protected from accidental contamination.

Paintable water-repellent preservatives may also be used as a treatment for bare wood before priming and painting or in areas where old paint has peeled and the bare wood is exposed, particularly around butt joints or in corners. This treatment keeps rain or dew from penetrating into the wood, especially at joints and end grain, and thus decreases shrinking and swelling of the wood. As a result, less stress is placed on the paint film and its service life is extended

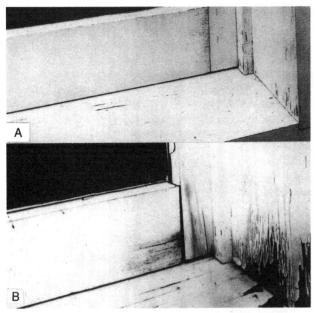

Figure 15–13. Effect of water-repellent preservative treatment. A, Window sash and frame treated with a water-repellent preservative and then painted; B, window sash and frame not treated before painting. Both window sash–frame sets were weathered for 5 years.

(Fig. 15–13). This stability is achieved by the small amount of wax present in water-repellent preservatives. The wax decreases the capillary movement or wicking of water up the back side of lap or drop siding. The fungicide inhibits decay.

A large number and variety of waterborne penetrating clear finishes are available for use on wood. The formulations of these finishes are generally proprietary, and it is difficult to determine the nature of these finishes. These formulations are usually water emulsions of synthetic polymers. The polymers do not penetrate the lateral surface of the wood very well, but they can change the surface properties. The polymer helps seal the surface and provides some water repellency. The formulations may include additional additives such as UV stabilizers, additional water repellents, mildewcides, and colorants.

Lightly Colored Finishes

Traditional solventborne formulations of water-repellent preservatives did not contain any coloring pigments. Therefore, the resulting finish varied little from the original color of the wood. Many of the newer formulations are slightly colored and have other additives such as UV stabilizers. As with traditional formulations, the preservative also prevents wood from darkening (graying) through mildew growth.

These lightly colored finishes may be water- or solventborne formulations. The color may be obtained from dyes or finely ground pigment. Although they are still classified as a penetrating finish or sealer for wood, many of the newer

formulations form a slight film on the wood surface. This is particularly true for the waterborne formulations. As with the uncolored clear finishes, the durability of lightly colored finishes is somewhat limited. Although their durability is improved by the inclusion of UV stabilizers and finely ground pigment, lightly colored finishes still lack sufficient pigment to stop UV degradation of the wood.

Semitransparent Stains

Inorganic pigments can also be added to water-repellent preservative solutions to provide special color effects, and the mixture is then classified as a semitransparent stain. A semitransparent stain is a pigmented penetrating stain. Colors that match the natural color of the wood and extractives are usually preferred. The addition of pigment to the finish helps stabilize the color and increase the durability of the finish, but they give a less natural appearance because the pigment partially hides the original grain and color of the wood. Semitransparent stains are generally much more durable than are water-repellent preservatives and provide more protection against weathering. These stains slow weathering by retarding the alternate wetting and drying of wood, and the pigment particles on the wood surface minimize the degrading effects of sunlight. The amount of pigment in semitransparent stains can vary considerably, thus providing different degrees of protection against UV degradation and masking of the original wood surface. Higher pigment concentration yields greater protection against weathering, but it also hides the natural color of the wood.

Solventborne oil-based semitransparent penetrating stains penetrate the wood surface, are porous, and do not form a surface film like paints. As a result, they will not blister or peel even if moisture moves through the wood. Semitransparent penetrating stains are only moderately pigmented and do not totally hide the wood grain. Penetrating stains are alkyd or oil based, and some may contain a fungicide as well as a water repellent. Moderately pigmented latex-based (waterborne) stains are also available, but they do not penetrate the wood surface as well as the oil-based stains. Some latex-based formulations are oil modified. These formulations give better penetration than do the unmodified formulations.

Semitransparent stains are most effective on rough lumber or rough-sawn plywood surfaces. They may be used on smooth surfaces but have less than half the service life compared with that on rough surfaces. Stains are available in a variety of colors and are especially popular in the brown or red earth tones because these give a natural or rustic appearance to the wood. They are an excellent finish for weathered wood. Semitransparent stains are not effective when applied over a solid-color stain or old paint.

Many resin and paint manufacturers have tried to achieve the properties of solventborne semitransparent stains using waterborne formulations. Some of these finishes achieved a semitransparent appearance by the formation of a rather thin coating on the wood surface. The resins used in these formulations did not penetrate the wood surface. Therefore, these finishes were prone to fail within a few years through flaking of the thin coating from the surface. When the surfaces were refinished, the subsequent finish increased the film thickness and obscured the original appearance of the wood. Because the film buildup is not sufficient to give the good performance provided by a film-forming finish, waterborne semi-transparent stains generally continue to fail by flaking. Many new formulations are modified with oil–alkyds. The oil penetrates the surface, thus improving the performance of the finish. Efforts are continuing to improve these formulations; it is advisable to check with a local paint supplier for the latest developments in this area.

Oils

Drying oils, such as linseed and tung, are sometimes used by themselves as natural finishes. Such oils are not recommended for exterior use unless they are formulated with a mildewcide. These oils are natural products and therefore provide food for mildew. When drying oils are used on highly colored woods such as redwood or the cedars, they tend to increase problems with mildew.

Film-Forming Finishes

Clear Varnish

Clear varnish is the primary transparent film-forming material used for a natural wood finish, and it greatly enhances the natural beauty and figure of wood. However, varnish lacks exterior permanence unless protected from direct exposure to sunlight, and varnish finishes on wood exposed outdoors without protection will generally require refinishing every 1 to 2 years. Thus, varnish is not generally recommended for exterior use on wood. Varnish coatings embrittle by exposure to sunlight and develop severe cracking and peeling. Varnish used in areas that are protected from direct sunlight by an overhang or used on the north side of the structure will last considerably longer. However, even in protected areas, a minimum of three coats of varnish is recommended, and the wood should be treated with a paintable water-repellent preservative before finishing. The use of pigmented stains and sealers as undercoats will also contribute to greater life of the clear finish. In marine exposures, up to six coats of varnish should be used for best performance.

Pigmented Varnish

Several finish manufacturers have formulated varnish with finely ground inorganic pigments that partially block UV radiation yet allow much of the visible light to pass through the finish. These products give much better performance than do traditional clear varnishes, and if a clear film is desired for exterior use, they may be a better choice. Pigmented varnish gives excellent performance on structures that are protected from sunlight by wide overhangs and wooded surroundings. The degradation of pigmented varnish initially occurs on the film surface as crazing and checking. These surface checks can be repaired by refinishing in a timely manner. Eventually, however, the buildup of coats will block much of the visible light and the wood will appear dark.

Solid-Color Stains

Solid-color stains are opaque finishes (also called hiding, heavy-bodied, or blocking) that come in a wide range of colors and are made with a much higher concentration of pigment than are semitransparent penetrating stains. As a result, solid-color stains totally obscure the natural color and grain of the wood. Solid-color stains (both oil- and latex-based) tend to form a film much like paint, and as a result they can also peel from the substrate. Both oil and latex solid-color stains are similar to paints and can usually be applied over old paint or to unfinished wood if adequately primed. As with any film-forming finish, good service life requires 4- to 5-mil dry film thickness.

Paint

Paints are highly pigmented film-forming coatings that give the most protection to wood. Paints are used for esthetic purposes, to protect the wood surface from weathering, and to conceal certain defects. They also provide a cleanable surface. Of all the finishes, paints provide the most protection for wood against surface erosion and offer the widest selection of colors. Paints are the only way to achieve a bright white finish. A nonporous paint film retards penetration of moisture and decreases discoloration by wood extractives as well as checking and warping of the wood. Paint is *not* a preservative. It will not prevent decay if conditions are favorable for fungal growth.

Paints do not penetrate the surface of the wood except to fill cut cells and vessels. They do not penetrate the cell wall of the wood as do some penetrating finishes. The wood grain is completely obscured as the surface film is formed. Paints perform best on vertical-grain lumber of species with low specific gravity. As with other film-forming finishes, paints can blister or peel if the wood is wetted or if inside water vapor moves through the house wall to the wood.

Latex paints are generally easier to use because water is used in cleanup. They are also porous and thus allow some moisture movement. In comparison, oil-based paints require organic solvents for cleanup, and some oil-based paints are resistant to moisture movement. Latex paints mainly formulated with acrylic resins are extremely resistant to weathering and maintain their gloss better than do oil-based paints. Such latex paints remain flexible throughout their service life. Oil-based paints tend to lose gloss within a year or two and are prone to embrittle over time.

The cost of finishes varies widely depending on the type of finish and quality (Table 15–4). Within a particular type of finish (for example, oil-based paint, all-acrylic latex paint, oil-based solid-color stain), cost usually correlates with quality. Better quality paints usually contain higher amounts of solids by weight. Paints with a lower percentage of solids may cost less by the unit but be more expensive per unit of solids, and more or heavier coats will have to be applied to achieve equal coverage. Comparing solids content and price can be the first criterion for selecting the better value because only the solids are left on the surface after the solvent evaporates. For example, if one paint is 50% solids and costs $20 and a second paint is 40% solids and costs $18, all other things being equal the $20 paint is a better value (25% more solids for about 11% more money). Another criterion is the amount and type of pigment because these determine the hiding power of the finish. Paint that contains primarily titanium dioxide pigment will have better hiding power than that with calcium carbonate filler. A paint with poor hiding power may require the application of more coats. Finally, the type and amount of binder affect the quality of the paint. For latex paints, all acrylic binders are more weather-resistant than are vinyl and vinyl–acrylic binders.

Fire-Retardant Coatings

Many commercial fire-retardant coating products are available to provide varying degrees of protection of wood against fire. These paint coatings generally have low surface flammability characteristics and "intumesce" to form an expanded low-density film upon exposure to fire, thus insulating the wood surface from heat and retarding pyrolysis reactions. The paints have added ingredients to restrict the flaming of any released combustible vapors. Chemicals may also be present in these paints to promote decomposition of the wood surface to charcoal and water rather than the formation of volatile flammable products. Most fire-retardant coatings are intended for interior use, but some are available for exterior application. Wood shakes and shingles are often impregnated with a fire retardant.

Compliance of VOC Finishes With Pollution Regulations

Volatile organic compounds (VOCs) are those organic materials in finishes that evaporate as the finish dries and/or cures. These materials are regarded as air pollutants, and the amount that can be released for a given amount of solids (for example, binder, pigments) in the paints is now regulated in many areas. Regulations that restrict the amount of VOCs in paints have been enacted in many states, including California, New York, Texas, Massachusetts, New Jersey, and Arizona, and legislation is pending in many others.

The result of such legislation is that all major paint companies have had to either change their paint formulation or market additional low-VOC formulations. Some smaller companies have been unaffected by VOC regulations because they market their products in limited geographic areas outside those affected by existing State and local legislation. This situation is slated to change soon. Under the 1990 New Clean Air Act, the U.S. Environmental Protection Agency (EPA) has been charged to enact a regulation that affects all of the United States. This regulation will take effect in 1999 and will regulate the amount of VOC in all types of architectural finishes, including paints, solid-color stains, and penetrating finishes, such as semitransparent stains and water-repellent preservatives.

Existing and pending regulations are a serious concern throughout the U.S. paint industry, particularly with regard to a national rule that will affect areas of the country that have not previously had to comply with VOC regulations. Many traditional wood finishes may no longer be acceptable, including oil-based semi-transparent stains, oil- and alkyd-based primers and top coats, solventborne water-repellents, and solventborne water-repellent preservatives. Many current wood finishes, including some latex-based materials, may be reformulated. These changes affect the properties of the finish, application, interaction with the wood (for example, adhesion, penetration, moisture-excluding effectiveness), and possibly durability.

Many penetrating finishes, such as semitransparent stains, have low solids content (pigment, oils, polymers) levels and are being reformulated to meet low-VOC regulations. To meet the VOC requirements, these reformulated finishes may contain higher solids content, reactive diluents, new types of solvents and/or cosolvents, or other nontraditional substituents. These low-VOC formulations are prone to form films rather than penetrate the wood surface. There is little information about the way these new penetrating finishes interact with the substrate to protect the wood or about the degradation mechanisms of these finishes when exposed to various outdoor conditions. Because such formulations may not interact with the wood in the same way as do traditional finishes, the effect of moisture may be different.

Application of Wood Finishes
Type of Finish
Water-Repellent Preservatives

The most effective method of applying a water repellent or water-repellent preservative is to dip the entire board into the solution. However, other application methods can be used if they are followed by back brushing. It is advantageous to treat the back side of the siding, particularly with highly colored wood species. (See section on back-priming.) When wood is treated in place, liberal amounts of the solution should be applied to all lap and butt joints, edges and ends of boards, and edges of panels with end grain. Other areas especially vulnerable to moisture, such as the bottoms of doors and window frames, should also be treated. Coverage is about 6.1 m²/L (250 ft²/gal) on a smooth surface or 3.7 m²/L (150 ft²/gal) on a rough surface. Smooth wood will usually accept only a single coat; a second coat will not penetrate the wood. Water-repellent preservative treatment generally lasts longer on rough surfaces than on smooth surfaces because more finish penetrates the wood. As a natural finish, the life expectancy of a water-repellent preservative is only 1 to 2 years, depending upon the wood and exposure. However, reapplication is easy, particularly on decks and fences. Multiple coats brush-applied to the point of refusal (failure to penetrate) will enhance durability and performance of the wood.

Water-repellent-preservative-treated wood that is painted will not need retreatment unless the protective paint layer has peeled or weathered away. The water-repellent preservative should be applied only to the areas where the paint has peeled. The water-repellent preservative should be allowed

Figure 15–14. Lap marks on wood finished with semitransparent stain.

to dry for 3 days, and the peeled area should be reprimed before it is repainted.

Semitransparent Penetrating Stains

Semitransparent penetrating stains may be brushed, sprayed, or rolled on, but they must be back-brushed. Brushing works the finish into the wood and evens out the application so that there is less chance for lap marks. Semitransparent penetrating stains are generally thin and runny, so application can be messy. Lap marks may form if stains are improperly applied, but such marks can be prevented by staining only a small number of boards or one panel at a time (Fig. 15–14). This method prevents the front edge of the stained area from drying out before a logical stopping place is reached. Working in the shade is desirable because the drying rate is slower. Coverage is usually about 4.9 to 9.8 m²/L (200 to 400 ft²/gal) on a smooth wood surface and from 2.4 to 4.9 m²/L (100 to 200 ft²/gal) on a rough or weathered surface. Stains perform much better on rough-sawn wood.

To give penetrating oil-based semitransparent stains a long life on rough-sawn or weathered lumber, use two coats and apply the second coat before the first is dry (wet on wet application). Apply the first coat to a panel or area in a manner to prevent lap marks. Then, work on another area so that the first coat can soak into the wood for 20 to 60 min. Apply the second coat before the first coat has dried. If the first coat dries completely, it may seal the wood surface so that the second coat cannot penetrate the wood. About an hour after applying the second coat, use a cloth, sponge, or dry brush lightly wetted with stain to wipe off excess stain that has not penetrated into the wood. Otherwise, areas of stain that did not penetrate may form an unsightly shiny surface film. Avoid intermixing different brands or batches of stain. Stir the stain occasionally and thoroughly during application to prevent settling and color change.

A two-coat system of semitransparent penetrating stain may last as long as 10 years on rough wood in certain exposures as a result of the large amount of stain absorbed. By comparison, the life expectancy of one coat of stain on new smooth wood is only 2 to 4 years; successive recoats last longer (Table 15–5).

> **Caution**: Sponges or cloths that are wet with oil-based stain are particularly susceptible to spontaneous combustion. To prevent fires, immerse such materials in water and seal in a water-filled air-tight metal container immediately after use.

Waterborne Semitransparent Stains

Waterborne semitransparent stains do not penetrate the wood surface as well as oilborne semitransparent stains, but they are easy to apply and less likely to form lap marks. These stains form a thin film, and a second coat will improve their durability. Apply the second coat any time after the first has dried.

Solid-Color Stains

Solid-color stains may be applied to a smooth wood surface by brush, spray, or roller; if the finish is applied by spray or roller, it is necessary to "back-brush" immediately after application. Solid-color stains act much like paint. One coat of solid-color stain is **not** considered adequate for siding. Some manufacturers recommend using the first coat as a primer, but a primer paint might be better, particularly if there is a possibility for extractives bleed. Two coats of solid-color stain applied over a quality latex or oil primer should give service life similar to that of a good paint system. Solid-color stains are not generally recommended for horizontal wood surfaces such as decks, roofs, and window sills.

Unlike paint, solid-color stain is subject to lap marks during application. Latex-based stains are particularly fast-drying and are more likely to show lap marks than are oil-based stains. To prevent lap marks, follow the procedures suggested in the section on application of semitransparent penetrating stains.

Paint

Wood and wood-based products should be protected from sunlight and water while stored prior to delivery to a construction site and while stored on the construction site. The finish should be applied as soon as possible after the wood is installed. Surface contamination from dirt, oil, and other foreign substances must be eliminated. The paint bond with the wood is greatly increased if the wood is painted within 1 week, weather permitting, after installation (see Weathering—Effect of weathering on paint adhesion). To achieve maximum paint life, do the following:

1. Treat wood siding and trim with a paintable water-repellent preservative or water repellent. Water repellents protect the wood against the absorption of rain and dew and thus help to minimize swelling and shrinking. Water repellents can be applied by brushing or dipping. Lap and butt joints and the edges of panel products such as plywood, hardboard, and particleboard should be especially well treated because these areas are prone to absorb

moisture, which leads to paint failure. Allow at least three warm, sunny days for adequate drying before painting the treated surface. If the wood has been dip treated, allow at least 1 week of favorable weather before painting.

2. Prime the bare wood after the water-repellent preservative has dried (see section on back-priming). The primer coat forms a base for all succeeding paint coats. For woods with water-soluble extractives, such as redwood and cedar, primers block the bleed of extractives into the top coat. Use a primer that is labeled to "block extractives bleed," usually a quality alkyd-based paint. Many manufacturers are also formulating stain-blocking acrylic-latex-based paints. Allow a latex stain-blocking primer to dry for at least 24 to 48 h before applying the top coat. If the primer has not fully cured, extractives may bleed into the top coat. Apply a primer regardless of whether the top coat is an oil-based or latex-based paint. For species that are predominantly sapwood and free of extractives, such as pine, using a quality primer is still necessary to give a good base for the top coat. Apply enough primer to obscure the wood grain. Follow the application rates recommended by the manufacturer. Do not spread the primer too thinly. A primer coat that is uniform and of the proper thickness will distribute the swelling stresses that develop in wood and thus help to prevent premature paint failure.

3. Apply two coats of a good-quality acrylic latex house paint over the primer. Oil-based, alkyd-based, and vinyl–acrylic paints can also be used. If it is not practical to apply two top-coats to the entire house, consider two top-coats for fully exposed areas on the south and west sides as a minimum for good protection. Areas fully exposed to sunshine and rain are the first to deteriorate and therefore should receive two top-coats. On those wood surfaces best suited for painting, one coat of a good house paint over a properly applied primer (a conventional two-coat paint system) should last 4 to 5 years, but two top-coats can last 10 years (Table 15–5).

Primer will cover about 6.1 to 7.4 m^2/L (250 to 300 ft^2/gal) on smooth bare wood; for repainting, coverage will be about 9.8 m^2/L (400 ft^2/gal). However, coverage can vary with different paints, surface characteristics, and application procedures. Research has indicated that the optimal thickness for the total dry paint coat (primer and two top-coats) is 0.10 to 0.13 mm (4 to 5 mils) (or about the thickness of a sheet of newspaper). The quality of paint is usually, but not always, related to price. Brush application is always superior to roller or spray application, especially for the first coat.

4. To avoid peeling between paint coats, apply the first top-coat within 2 weeks after the primer and the second coat within 2 weeks of the first. As certain paints weather, they can form a soaplike substance on their surface that may prevent proper adhesion of new paint coats. If more than 2 weeks elapse before applying another paint coat, scrub the old surface with water using a bristle brush or sponge. If necessary, use a mild detergent to remove all dirt and

deteriorated paint. Then rinse the cleaned wood with water and allow all surfaces to dry before painting.

5. To avoid temperature blistering, do not apply oil-based paint on a cool surface that will be heated by the sun within a few hours. Temperature blistering is most common with thick coats of dark-colored paint applied in cool weather. The blisters usually show up in the last coat of paint and occur within a few hours or up to 1 or 2 days after painting. They do not contain water.

6. Apply latex-based waterborne paints when the temperature is at least 10°C (50°F); oil-based paint may be applied when the temperature is at least 4°C (40°F). For proper curing of latex paint films, the temperature should not drop below 10°C (50°F) for at least 24 h after paint application. Low temperatures will result in poor coalescence of the paint film and early paint failure. Some new latex formulations are being developed for application at lower temperatures. Refer to application instructions on the label of the paint can.

7. To avoid wrinkling, fading, or loss of gloss of oil-based paints and streaking of latex paints, do not apply the paint during autumn days or cool spring evenings when heavy dews form during the night. Serious water absorption problems and major finish failure can occur with some paints when applied under these conditions.

Porches, Decks, and Fences

Exposed flooring on porches is usually painted. Since porches often get wet from windblown rain, it is particularly important to pretreat the wood surface with a water-repellent preservative prior to painting. Use primers and paints specially formulated for porches. These paints are formulated to resist abrasion and wear.

Many fully exposed decks are more effectively finished with only a water-repellent preservative or a penetrating-type semitransparent pigmented stain. Decks finished with these finishes will need more frequent refinishing than do painted surfaces, but refinishing is easy because there is no need for the laborious surface preparation required for painted surfaces that have peeled. It is essential to limit the application of semitransparent stain to what the surface can absorb. Roller and spray application may put too much stain on the horizontal surfaces of decks. The best application method for such smooth surfaces is by brush. Unless specially formulated for use on decks, solid-color stains should not be used on any horizontal surface because they lack abrasion resistance, and because they form a film, they tend to fail by flaking.

Like decks, fences are fully exposed to the weather and at least some parts (such as posts) are in contact with the soil. As a result, wood decay and termite attack are potential problems. Often in the design of fences, little consideration is given to protecting exposed end-grain of various fence components or to avoiding trapped moisture. If a film-forming finish is to be used on a fence, it is extremely important to seal the end grain and protect exposed end-grain wherever possible. Use lumber pressure-treated with preservatives or naturally durable wood species for all posts and other fence components that are in ground contact.

In regard to the service life of naturally durable wood species compared with wood pressure-treated with preservatives, there are no absolute "rules." In ground contact uses, pressure-treated wood species often outperform naturally durable species in warm wet climates, but less difference in service life often occurs in dry climates. The service life of naturally durable and preservative-treated woods is quite comparable in aboveground exposures, such as decking boards, railing, and fence boards. In selecting wood for porches, decks, and fences, whether preservative treated or a naturally durable species, consideration must be given to the exposure conditions, design of the structure, and properties of the wood, including its variability.

In aboveground uses, the weathering of wood can be as much a factor in long-term service life as is decay resistance. Whether naturally durable wood species or preservative-treated wood is used in full exposures to weather, it is necessary to protect the wood with a finish. Periodic treatment with a penetrating sealer, such as a water-repellent preservative, will decrease checking and splitting, and pigmented finishes will retard weathering.

Treated Wood

Treated wood is often used to construct porches, decks, and fences, particularly wood treated with chromated copper arsenate (CCA). Woods that have been pressure treated for decay sometimes have special finishing requirements. Wood pressure treated with waterborne chemicals, such as copper, chromium, and arsenic salts (CCA), that react with the wood or form an insoluble residue presents no major problem in finishing if the wood is properly redried and thoroughly cleaned after treating. The finishing characteristics are more controlled by species and grain orientation than by preservative treatment. Wood treated with solvent- or oilborne preservative chemicals, such as creosote or pentachlorophenol, is not considered paintable.

None of the common pressure preservative treatments (creosote, pentachlorophenol, water-repellent preservatives, and waterborne preservatives) will significantly change the weathering characteristics of woods. All preservative-treated wood will weather when exposed above ground and may develop severe checking and cracking. Finishing generally retards this weathering. However, there is one exception: waterborne treatments containing chromium decrease the degrading effects of weathering.

Creosote and pentachlorophenol are generally used only for industrial and commercial applications where applying a finish is not considered practical. Creosote is oily and therefore does not accept a finish very well. Pentachlorophenol is often formulated in heavy oil. In general, preservatives formulated in oil will not accept a finish. In some cases, oil-based

semitransparent penetrating stains can be used on these products, but only after the preservative-treated wood has weathered for 1 to 2 years, depending on exposure.

The only preservative-treated woods that should be painted or stained immediately after treatment and without further exposure are the waterborne preservative treatments (such as CCA-treated wood). Since wood treated with these preservatives is often used for residential structures, it needs to be finished not only for esthetic reasons, but also to protect it from weathering. Many manufacturers of chemicals for treating wood with waterborne preservatives include a water-repellent treatment to give the treated wood better resistance to weathering, particularly checking and splitting. Even if the wood was treated with water repellent by the manufacturer, it should be maintained with a finish to extend its service life. Wood used in aboveground applications that has been properly treated with preservative is usually replaced because of weathering, not decay.

Marine Uses

The marine environment is particularly harsh on wood. As discussed, the natural surface deterioration process occurs slowly. Marine environments speed up the natural weathering process to some extent, and wood for marine uses is often finished with paint or varnish for protection. Certain antifouling paints are also used to protect piers and ship hulls against marine organisms.

For best protection, wood exposed to marine environments above water and above ground should be treated with a paintable water-repellent preservative, painted with a suitable paint primer, and top coated (at least two coats) with quality exterior marine products.

> **Note:** Any wood in contact with water or the ground should be pressure treated to specifications recommended for in-ground or marine use. Such treated woods are not always paintable. As indicated previously, CCA-treated woods are paintable when dry and clean.

Wood trim on boats is often varnished. When applied to boats, varnish is subjected to greater exposure to sunlight and water than when used on structures; therefore, it needs regular and frequent care and refinishing. Varnishes should be specially formulated for harsh exposure; three to six coats should be applied for best performance. The durability of the varnish can be extended by finishing the wood with a semitransparent stain prior to varnishing, but this obscures many natural characteristics of the wood. Keeping the appearance of varnished wood trim bright and new is labor intensive but often well worth the effort.

Refinishing

Exterior wood surfaces need to be refinished only when the old finish has worn thin and no longer protects the wood. In repainting, one coat may be adequate if the old paint surface is in good condition. Dirty paint can often be renewed and cleaned by washing with detergent. Too-frequent repainting with an oil-based system produces an excessively thick film that is likely to crack abnormally across the grain of the wood. Complete removal of the paint and repainting are the only cure for cross-grain cracking (see subsection on cross-grain cracking under Finish Failure or Discoloration). Latex paints seldom develop cross-grain cracking because they are more flexible than are oil-based paints. Since latex paints have replaced oil-based paints for most exterior application on residential structures, cross-grain cracking is rather rare unless the latex paint has been applied over many coats of oil-based paint. However, even with latex paints, excessive paint buildup should be avoided. Additional top-coats should be applied only when the primer begins to show.

Water-Repellent Preservatives

Water-repellent preservatives used as natural finishes can be renewed by simply brushing the old surface with a dry stiff-bristle brush to remove dirt and applying a new coat of finish. To determine if a water-repellent preservative has lost its effectiveness, splash a small quantity of water against the wood surface. If the water beads up and runs off the surface, the treatment is still effective. If the water soaks in, the wood needs to be refinished. Refinishing is also required when the wood surface shows signs of graying. Gray discoloration can be removed by washing the wood with a commercial mildew cleaner or liquid household bleach (see subsection on mildew under Finish Failure or Discoloration).

Semitransparent Penetrating Stains

Surfaces finished with semitransparent penetrating stains are relatively easy to refinish; heavy scraping and sanding are generally not required. Simply use a dry stiff-bristle brush to remove all surface dirt, dust, and loose wood fibers, and then apply a new coat of stain. The second coat of penetrating stain often lasts longer than the first because it penetrates into small surface checks that open as the wood weathers.

In refinishing surfaces originally finished with semitransparent stains, it is extremely important that the wood accept the stain. That is, the stain must penetrate the wood. Since the weathering rate of a stain varies with exposure, the stain may not penetrate well in some areas. For example, an area under the eaves, even on the south side of a structure, may be relatively unweathered. When applying stain to such an area, feather the new stain into the old. If the stain does not penetrate the wood within an hour, remove the excess. If the excess stain is not removed it will form shiny spots, which will flake from the surface as it weathers. The north side of a structure may not need to be restained nearly as often as the south side (northern hemisphere).

Note: Steel wool and wire brushes should not be used to clean surfaces to be finished with semitransparent stain or water-repellent preservatives because small iron deposits may be left behind. These small iron deposits can react with certain water-soluble extractives in woods like western redcedar, redwood, Douglas-fir, and the oaks, to yield dark blue–black stains on the surface (see subsection on iron stain under Finish Failure or Discoloration).

Paint and Solid-Color Stains

In refinishing painted (or solid-color stained) surfaces, proper surface preparation is essential if the new coat is to have a long service life. First, scrape away all loose paint. Sand areas of exposed wood with 50- to 80-grit sandpaper to remove the weathered surface and to feather the abrupt paint edge. Then scrub any remaining old paint with a brush or sponge and water. Rinse the scrubbed surface with clean water, then wipe the surface with your hand or cloth (see subsection on chalking under Finish Failure or Discoloration). If the surface is still dirty or chalky, scrub it again using a detergent. Use a commercial cleaner or a dilute household bleach solution to remove mildew (see subsection on mildew under Finish Failure or Discoloration). Rinse the cleaned surface thoroughly with fresh water and allow it to dry before repainting. Treat bare wood with a water-repellent preservative and allow it to dry for at least 3 days before priming. Top coats can then be applied.

Note: Special precautions are necessary if the old paint contains lead. See section on lead-based paint.

It is particularly important to clean areas that are protected from sun and rain, such as porches, soffits, and side walls protected by overhangs. These areas tend to collect dirt and water-soluble materials that interfere with the adhesion of new paint. It is probably adequate to repaint these protected areas every other time the house is painted.

Latex paint or solid-color stain can be applied over freshly primed surfaces and on weathered paint surfaces if the old paint is clean and sound (chalk-free). Before repainting surfaces with latex paint, conduct a simple test. After cleaning the surface, repaint a small, inconspicuous area with latex paint and allow it to dry at least overnight. Then, to test for adhesion, firmly press one end of an adhesive bandage onto the repainted surface. Remove the bandage with a snapping action. If the tape is free of paint, the fresh latex paint is well-bonded and the old surface does not need priming or additional cleaning. If the fresh latex paint adheres to the tape, the old surface is too chalky and needs more cleaning or priming with an oil-based primer. If both the fresh latex paint and the old paint coat adhere to the tape, the old paint is not well-bonded to the wood and must be removed before repainting.

Back-Priming

Back-priming simply means the application of a primer or water-repellent preservative to the back side of wood (usually wood siding) before the wood is installed. Back-priming retards absorption of water, thus improving dimensional stability and extending the service life of the paint. It improves the appearance of the wood by decreasing extractives staining, particularly run-down extractives bleed. Treating the back side of siding with a water-repellent preservative is probably more effective than back-priming for improving dimensional stability and retarding extractives bleed. Water-repellent preservatives are particularly effective if used as a pretreatment before back-priming. However, back-priming with a stain-blocking primer alone has some benefit.

By slowing the absorption of water, the primer or water-repellent preservative improves dimensional stability of siding. Siding is less likely to cup, an important consideration for flat-grain wood. By decreasing shrinking and swelling, less stress is placed on the finish, thereby extending its service life. At the same time that the siding is back-primed, the end grain should be sealed with primer. This process has an even greater effect in stopping water absorption. Most paint failure near the end grain of siding can be eliminated by including end-grain priming along with the back-priming. When boards are cut during installation, the cut ends should be spot-primed.

Run-down extractives bleed occurs because water from wind-blown rain, leaks, and/or condensation of moisture wets the back of siding and absorbs extractives from the wood. If water from one course of siding runs down the front face of the course below it, the water may deposit the extractives on this surface, causing unsightly streaks (see subsection on extractives bleed under Finish Failure or Discoloration). Back-priming stops extractives bleed by forming a barrier between the water and the extractives. The primer should be stain-blocking, just as the primer used for the front (outside) surface of the siding. When finish is applied to siding in the factory, the back surface of the siding is routinely finished at the same time as the front surface.

Factory Finishing

Many siding, trim, and decking products are now available prefinished. Although it has been standard industry practice to preprime hardboard siding, factory finishing of solid wood products has rapidly grown during the last several years. The industry is currently growing at about 60% per year, and this growth is anticipated to continue into the early part of the next century. Coating suppliers for this industry predict that more than half of all wood siding materials will be factory finished by that time. In addition to siding, other wood products like interior trim and paneling are being prefinished. Much of this factory finishing has been made possible by the development of rapid-cure finish systems and the availability of efficient equipment to apply the finish.

Prefinishing wood at the factory rather than after installation results in overall cost savings as well as several other advantages. Weather and climate conditions during construction do not affect prefinished wood. This is a crucial consideration in northern climates where acceptable exterior finishing is impossible during the winter. In factory finishing, coverage can be controlled to give a consistent 100 to 127 μm (4 to 5 mil) dry film. The controlled conditions enable many factory finishers to guarantee their products against cracking, peeling, and blistering for 15 years. Another advantage of factory finishing is that siding is finished on all sides, including the end grain. When prefinished siding is installed, the end grain is sealed after any cross-cuts are made. This end-grain sealing is seldom done during installation of unfin-

ished siding. The end-grain seal greatly increases resistance of siding to end-grain absorption of water, thus decreasing extractives bleed and other problems related to moisture.

Finish Failure or Discoloration

Paint is probably the most common exterior finish in use on wood today. It appears somewhere on practically every residential structure and on most commercial buildings. Even brick and aluminum-sided structures usually have some painted wood trim. When properly applied to the appropriate type of wood substrate, paint should have a service life of at least 10 years. If it does not, the selection of the paint, application, type of substrate, type of structure, and construction practices were not done properly or were not compatible.

Modern paint formulations based on acrylic polymers are extremely resistant to degradation by ultraviolet (UV) radiation. These paints degrade by a slow erosion process, which eventually exposes the primer. The erosion process depends on the exposure to the weather. Areas that deteriorate rapidly are those exposed to the greatest amount of sunshine and rain, usually on the west and south sides of a building (in the northern hemisphere). The normal deterioration process begins with soiling or a slight accumulation of dirt and then leads to gradual change and erosion of the coating. When the primer begins to show, that side of the structure should be repainted. It may not be necessary to paint all sides of the structure, since the erosion rate varies depending on exposure. This is particularly true for structures finished with white paint.

> **Note:** The most common cause of premature paint failure on wood is moisture.

Early paint failure may develop under certain conditions of service. Excessive moisture, flat grain, high coating porosity, and application of a new paint coat without proper preparation of the old surface can all contribute to early paint failure. Paint on the outside walls of residential structures is subject to wetting from rain, dew, and frost. Equally serious is "unseen" moisture that moves from inside the structure to the outside. This is particularly true for buildings in cold northern climates that do not have effective air and vapor barriers. Many moisture-related problems can be prevented by furring out the siding 9 to 19 mm (3/8 to 3/4 in.) prior to installation. For siding placed directly on insulation board or a wind barrier, placing wedges between the siding courses can reduce problems with moisture.

The next most common cause of paint failure is a poor bond between the substrate and the coating. Even in the absence of moisture, paint can peel if it does not bond well to the wood. If moisture is also present, paint failure is accelerated. The wide bands of latewood on flat-grain surfaces hold paint very poorly. If possible, flat-grain boards should be exposed "bark-side" out to minimize raising and separation of grain, and the boards should either be rough-sawn or scuff-sanded with 50-grit sandpaper prior to priming. Wood must be protected from the weather prior to installation and painted as soon as possible afterwards. Exposure to the weather for as little as 2 weeks will reduce the paint-holding properties of smooth wood. Scuff sanding prior to painting is necessary if the wood is exposed to the weather for more than 2 weeks. In fact, scuff sanding is always a good idea on planed lumber.

Moisture Blisters

Moisture blisters are bubble-like swellings of the paint film on the wood surface. As the name implies, these blisters usually contain moisture when they are formed. Moisture blisters may occur where outside moisture, such as rain, enters through joints and other end-grain areas of boards and siding. Moisture may also enter as a result of poor construction and maintenance practices. The blisters appear after spring rains and throughout the summer. Paint failure is most severe on the sides of buildings that face the prevailing winds and rain. Blisters may occur in both heated and unheated buildings.

Moisture blisters may also result from the movement of water from the inside of a structure to the outside. Plumbing leaks, humidifiers, overflow (sinks, bathtubs), and shower spray are sources of inside water, and improperly sealed walls can contribute to the problem. Such blisters are not seasonal and occur when the faulty condition develops.

Moisture blisters form between the wood substrate and the first coat of paint. After the blisters appear, they may dry out and collapse. Small blisters may disappear completely and fairly large ones may leave rough spots; in severe cases, the paint peels (Fig. 15–15). Thin coatings of new oil-based paint are the most likely to blister. Old, thick coats are usually too rigid to swell and form blisters; cracking and peeling usually result. Elimination of the moisture problem is the only practical way to prevent moisture blisters in paint. In addition, elimination of moisture problems can help prevent more serious problems such as decay (rot), warp, and splitting of the wood substrate.

To prevent moisture-related paint problems, follow good construction and painting practices. First, do whatever is possible to keep the wood dry. Provide an adequate roof overhang and properly maintain shingles, gutters, and downspouts. Window and door casings should slope away from the house, allowing water to drain away rapidly. Vent clothes dryers, showers, and cooking areas to the outside, not to the crawl space or attic. Avoid the use of humidifiers. If the house contains a crawl space, cover the soil with a vapor-retarding material to prevent migration of water vapor into the living quarters. In northern climates, use a vapor retarder on the interior side of all exterior walls and an air barrier to prevent condensation in the wall. In buildings in southern climates that are air conditioned a substantial part of the year, place the vapor retarder directly under the sheathing.

Mill Glaze

Since the mid-1980s, a condition known as "mill glaze" (also called planer's glaze) has occasionally occurred on smooth flat-grain western redcedar siding as well as other species. There is controversy over the exact cause of this

Figure 15–15. Paint can peel from wood when excessive moisture moves through house wall. Some cross-grain cracking is also evident on this older home.

condition, but it seems to occur as a result of planing and/or drying of the lumber. The condition seems to be caused by dull planer blades and is exacerbated on flat-grain surfaces, which are more difficult to plane. The problem is most severe on flat-grain boards because of the orientation of latewood to earlywood. Dull blades tend to burnish the surface and crush the less dense earlywood bands that lie directly beneath the more dense latewood bands at the surface. Later, when these boards are exposed to weather, particularly cyclic moisture conditions, the crushed earlywood absorbs moisture and rebounds, which causes the surface latewood bands to raise. In vertical-grain wood, the earlywood–latewood bands are perpendicular to the surface and the lumber is easier to plane, even with dull tooling.

During the planing or milling process, overheating may bring more water-soluble extractives to the surface, creating a hard, varnish-like glaze. Excess water-soluble extractives can also form (bleed) on the surface during kiln drying. As these extractives age, particularly in direct sunlight, they become insoluble and are difficult to remove. If extractives bleed to the surface prior to final planing or sanding of the lumber, this final surface preparation usually removes them.

Sanding may remove some extractives buildup, but it is not likely to remove all the crushed wood. Subsequent wetting may still cause the surface to deform. One or more wetting and drying cycles are necessary to remove these planer-induced stresses in the wood, but the wood should not be exposed to sunlight for more than 2 weeks before application of a film-forming finish because exposure decreases the adhesion of the coating (see Weathering, Effects on Paint Adhesion).

Mill glaze can cause failure of the finish. Failure is most common on flat-grain siding finished with one or two thin coats of oil-based solid-color stain (also called opaque or full-bodied stain). These low-solids coatings provide only 25 to 50 µm (1 to 2 mil) of dry-film thickness, whereas a brush-applied three-coat paint system (primer and two top-coats) provides 100 to 127 µm (4 to 5 mil) of dry-film thickness. Thin coatings of solid-color stain do not build up enough film to withstand the stresses caused by raised grain, particularly if the coating–wood bond is weakened by extractives buildup on the wood surface.

When using flat-grain bevel siding, the simplest and best solution to the problem of mill glaze and finish failure is to install the siding rough-side out. The rough side is the side of choice for application of penetrating semi-transparent stains, and although solid-color stains form films, they also will provide much better service life when applied to the rough-sawn side. In addition to the lack of mill glaze, the rough side gives two additional advantages. The film buildup on the rough side will be greater and the film will have greater mechanical adhesion or "bite." The best film buildup is obtained by brush application. If the finish is applied by roller or spray, it is advisable to back-brush immediately after application to even out the finish and to work it into the wood surface, thus avoiding bridging, gaps, and lap marks.

If the flat-grain siding must be installed smooth-side out, remove the planing stresses by wetting the surface, then allow 2 to 3 days for the surface to dry before applying the finish. Scratch-sanding the surface with 50- to 80-grit sandpaper also improves paint adhesion. Use either a top quality three-coat paint system or apply a stain-blocking primer prior to applying solid-color stain. In selecting finishes for highly colored wood such as western redcedar or redwood, choose a primer that is impervious to bleed of water-soluble extractives. Although many waterborne primers are being marketed for use on western redcedar and redwood, many paint manufacturers still recommend an oil-based, stain-blocking primer followed by two coats of high quality, acrylic latex top coat. Solid-color stains, particularly the latex formulations, do not block water-soluble extractives very well, especially when only one coat is applied.

Mill glaze has not been common in recent years because paint companies are recommending the use of a primer prior to the application of a solid-color stain, and painting contractors are generally following these recommendations.

Intercoat Peeling

Intercoat peeling is the separation of the new paint film from the old paint coat, which indicates a weak bond between the two (Fig. 15–16). Intercoat peeling usually results from inadequate cleaning of weathered paint and usually occurs within 1 year of repainting. This type of paint peeling can be prevented by following good painting practices. Intercoat peeling can also result from allowing too much time between

Figure 15–16. Intercoat peeling of paint, usually caused by poor preparation of old paint surface.

applying the primer coat and top coat in a new paint job. If more than 2 weeks elapse between applying an oil-based primer and a top coat, soap-like materials may form on the surface and interfere with bonding of the next coat of paint. When the period between applications exceeds 2 weeks, scrub the surface before applying the second coat. Do not apply a primer coat in the fall and wait until spring to finish with the top coat.

Cross-Grain Cracking

Cross-grain cracking occurs when oil-based or alkyd paint coatings become too thick (Fig. 15–17). This problem often occurs on older homes that have been painted many times. Paint usually cracks parallel to the wood grain; cross-grain cracks run across the grain. Once cross-grain cracking has occurred, the only solution is to completely remove the old paint and apply a new finishing system to the bare wood. To prevent cross-grain cracking, follow the paint manufacturer's recommendations for spreading rates. Do not repaint unweathered, protected areas such as porch ceilings and roof overhangs as often as the rest of the house. If possible, repaint these areas only as they weather and require new paint.

Chalking

Chalking results from weathering of the paint's surface, which releases pigment and degraded resin particles. These particles form a fine powder on the paint surface. Most paints chalk to some extent. This phenomenon is desirable because it allows the paint surface to self-clean, and it is the most desirable mechanism for removing degraded paint. However, chalking is objectionable when the paint pigment washes down a surface with a different color or when it causes premature paint failure through excessive erosion.

The paint formulation determines how fast the paint chalks; discoloration from chalking can be decreased by selecting a paint with a slow chalking rate. Therefore, if chalking is likely to be a problem, select a paint that the manufacturer has indicated will chalk slowly. Latex paints, particularly those based on acrylic polymers, chalk very slowly.

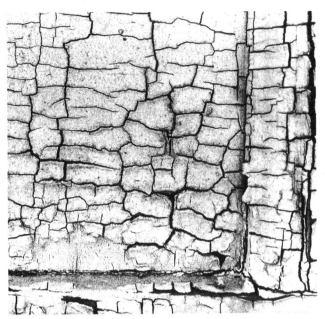

Figure 15–17. Cross-grain cracking from excessive buildup of paint.

When repainting surfaces that have chalked excessively, proper preparation of the old surface is essential to prevent premature paint peeling. Scrub the old surface thoroughly with a detergent solution to remove all old deposits and dirt. Rinse thoroughly with clean water before repainting. To check for excessive chalking, lightly rub the paint surface with a dark (for light-colored paint) or white (for dark-colored paint) cloth. The amount of pigment removed by the cloth is a good indication of the chalking. If the surface is still chalky after cleaning, it may need to be primed prior to repainting. Otherwise, the new paint coat may peel. Discoloration or chalk that has run down a lower surface may be removed by vigorous scrubbing with a good detergent. This discoloration will gradually weather away if chalking on the painted surface above the discolored surface is corrected.

Mildew

Mildew is probably the most common cause of house paint discoloration and gray discoloration of unfinished wood (Fig. 15–18). Mildew is a form of microscopic stain fungi. The most common fungal species are black, but some are red, green, or other colors. Mildew grows most extensively in warm, humid climates, but it is also found in cold northern climates. Mildew may be found anywhere on a building, although it is most common on walls behind trees or shrubs where air movement is restricted. Mildew may also be associated with the dew pattern of the house. Dew will form on those parts of the house that are not heated and tend to cool rapidly, such as eaves and ceilings of carports and porches. The dew then provides a source of moisture for mildew fungi.

Mildew fungi can be distinguished from dirt by examination under a high-power magnifying glass. In the growing stage,

Figure 15–18. Mildew is most common in shaded, moist, or protected areas.

when the surface is damp or wet, the fungus is characterized by its threadlike growth. In the dormant stage, when the surface is dry, the fungus has numerous egg-shaped spores; by contrast, granular particles of dirt appear irregular in size and shape. A simple test for the presence of mildew on wood or paint is to apply a drop or two of liquid household bleach solution (5% sodium hypochlorite) to the discolored surface. The dark color of mildew will usually bleach out in 1 or 2 min. A surface discoloration that does not bleach is probably dirt. It is important to use fresh bleach solution because bleach deteriorates upon aging and loses its potency.

In warm, damp climates where mildew occurs frequently, use a paint containing zinc oxide and a mildewcide for both the primer and top coats. Before repainting mildew-infected wood or painted wood, the mildew must be killed or it will grow through the new paint coat. To kill mildew on wood or on paint, and to clean an area for general appearance or for repainting, use a bristle brush or sponge to scrub the painted surface with a commercial cleaner formulated for mildew removal. Mildew can also be removed using a dilute solution of household bleach with detergent:

- 1 part household detergent
- 10 parts (5%) sodium hypochlorite (household bleach)
- 30 parts warm water

Warning: Do not mix bleach with ammonia or with any detergents or cleansers that contain ammonia. Mixed together, bleach and ammonia form a lethal combination, similar to mustard gas. Many household cleaners contain ammonia, so be extremely careful in selecting the type of cleaner to mix with bleach. Avoid splashing the cleaning solution on yourself or on shrubbery or grass.

Rinse the cleaned surface thoroughly with fresh water. Before the cleaned surface can become contaminated, repaint it with a paint containing a mildewcide. When finishing new wood or refinishing areas that have peeled, pretreatment of wood surfaces with a water-repellent preservative prior to priming can also help deter mildew growth, even after the wood has been painted. Oil-based paints are somewhat more prone to mildew than are latex paints because the oils may be a food source for mildew.

Discoloration From Water-Soluble Extractives

In some wood species, the heartwood contains water-soluble extractives. (Sapwood does not contain extractives.) These extractives can occur in both hardwoods and softwoods. Western redcedar and redwood are two common softwood species that contain large quantities of extractives. The extractives give these species their attractive color, good stability, and natural decay resistance, but they can also discolor paint. Extractive staining problems can occur occasionally with such woods as Douglas-fir and southern yellow pine.

When extractives discolor paint, moisture is usually the culprit. The extractives are dissolved and leached from the wood by water. The water then moves to the paint surface, evaporates, and leaves the extractives behind as a reddish brown stain (Fig. 15–19). Diffused discoloration from wood extractives is caused by water from rain and dew that penetrates a porous or thin paint coat. It may also be caused by rain and dew that penetrates joints in the siding or by water from faulty roof drainage and gutters.

Diffused discoloration is best prevented by following good painting practices. Apply a water-repellent preservative or water repellent to the bare wood before priming. Use an oil-based, stain-resistant primer or a latex primer especially formulated for use over woods likely to discolor from extractives. Do not use porous paints such as flat alkyds and latex directly over these extractive-rich woods. If the wood is already painted, clean the surface, apply an oil-based or latex stain-resistant primer and then the top coat. Be sure to allow sufficient time for the primer to cure so that it blocks the extractives stain. Before priming and repainting, apply a water-repellent preservative or water repellent to any wood exposed by peeled paint.

Water-soluble extractives can also cause a run-down or streaked type of discoloration. This discoloration results when the back of siding is wetted, the extractives are dissolved, and the colored water then runs down the face of the adjacent painted board below the lap joint.

Figure 15–19. Water-soluble extractive discoloration can result from water wetting the back of the siding and then running down the front (top). Water causing discoloration also leads to paint failure (bottom).

Water that produces a run-down discoloration can result from the movement of water vapor within the house to the exterior walls and condensation during cold weather. Major sources of water vapor are humidifiers, unvented clothes dryers, showers, and moisture from cooking and dishwashing. Run-down discoloration may also be caused by draining of water into exterior walls from roof leaks, faulty gutters, ice dams, and wind-driven rain blown beneath the siding.

Run-down discoloration can be prevented by decreasing condensation or the accumulation of moisture in the wall. The same precautions to avoid moisture buildup in walls as described in the section on moisture blisters will also prevent extractives bleed. Water from rain and snow can be prevented from entering the walls by proper maintenance of the gutters and roof. The formation of ice dams can be prevented by installing adequate insulation in the attic and by providing adequate ventilation. If discoloration is to be stopped, moisture problems must be eliminated.

Extractives discoloration will usually weather away in a few months once the cause of the extractives bleed is eliminated. However, discoloration in protected areas can become darker and more difficult to remove with time. In these cases, wash the discolored areas with a mild detergent soon after the problem develops. Paint cleaners are effective on darker stains.

Highly colored woods such as redwood and the cedars benefit from back-priming or treatment with a water-repellent preservative. Although such methods will not completely eliminate extractives staining, they will help reduce staining, particularly from wind-driven rain blown underneath siding (see subsection on back-priming in Application of Wood Finishes).

Blue Stain

Blue stain is caused by microscopic fungi that commonly infect only the sapwood of trees. In some species, these fungi are prone to develop a blue–black discoloration of the wood. Blue stain does not weaken wood structurally, but conditions that favor blue stain are also ideal for wood decay and paint failure.

Wood in service may contain blue stain, and no detrimental effects will result as long as the moisture content is kept below 20%. (Wood in properly designed and well-maintained structures usually has a moisture content of 8% to 13%.) However, if the wood is exposed to moisture from sources such as rain, condensation, or leaky plumbing, the moisture content will increase and the blue-stain fungi may develop and become visible.

A commercial mildew cleaner or a 5% sodium hypochlorite solution (ordinary liquid household bleach) with detergent may remove some blue discoloration, but it is not a permanent cure. The bleach removes the stain from the surface only. To prevent blue stain, the lumber must be cut and dried as soon as possible after harvesting the logs. The lumber must then be kept dry until used and while it is in service. With some wood species that are prone to develop blue stain, the logs are often treated with a fungicide while in storage before the lumber is cut.

Iron Stain

Iron stains on wood can occur through rusting of fasteners or by the reaction of iron with tannins in the wood. When standard steel nails are used on exterior siding and then painted, a reddish brown discoloration may occur through the paint in the immediate vicinity of the nailhead. This reddish brown discoloration is rust, and it can be prevented by using corrosion-resistant nails, which include high-quality galvanized, stainless steel, and aluminum nails. Poor

quality galvanized nails can corrode easily and, like steel nails, can cause unsightly staining of the wood and paint. The galvanizing on nailheads should not "chip loose" as the nails are driven into the wood.

Unsightly rust stains may also occur when standard steel nails are used in association with finishing systems such as solid-color or opaque stains, semitransparent penetrating stains, and water-repellent preservatives. Rust stains can also result from screens and other steel objects or fasteners, which corrode and/or release iron compounds.

A chemical reaction of iron with tannins in wood results in an unsightly blue–black discoloration of wood. In this case, discoloration results from the reaction of iron with certain wood extractives. Steel nails are the most common source of iron for such discoloration, but problems have also been associated with traces of iron left from cleaning the wood surface with steel wool or wire brushes. The discoloration can sometimes become sealed beneath a new finishing system. When this happens, the problem is extremely difficult to fix. The coating must be stripped before the iron stain can be removed.

Oxalic acid will remove the blue–black discoloration from iron. Apply a saturated solution containing about 0.5 kg (1 lb) of oxalic acid per 4 L (1 gal) of hot water to the stained surface. Many commercial brighteners contain oxalic acid, and these are usually effective for removing iron stains. A saturated solution of sodium bifluoride ($NaHF_2$) works as well but it may be more difficult to obtain than oxalic acid. After removing the stain, wash the surface thoroughly with warm fresh water to remove the oxalic acid. If all sources of iron are not removed or the wood is not protected from corrosion, the discoloration will recur.

> **Caution**: Use extreme care when using oxalic acid, which is toxic.

If iron stain is a serious problem on a painted surface, the nails can be countersunk and caulked, and the area spot primed and top coated. This is a costly and time-consuming process that is only possible with opaque finishes. Little can be done to give a permanent fix to iron stains on natural finishes other than removing the fasteners, cleaning the affected areas with oxalic acid solution, and replacing the fasteners. It is best to use corrosion-resistant fasteners such as stainless steel rather than risk iron stain, particularly when using natural finishes on wood containing high amounts of tannin, such as western redcedar, redwood, and oak.

Brown Stain Over Knots

The knots in many softwood species, particularly pine, contain an abundance of resins and other highly colored compounds. These compounds can sometimes cause paint to peel or turn brown. The resins that compose pitch can be "set" or hardened by the high temperatures used in kiln drying construction lumber if the proper kiln schedule is used. Some of the other compounds are not affected by kiln drying.

The elimination of staining of paint by colored resins and water-soluble extractives in knots is often difficult because the resins are soluble in oil-based primers and diffuse through them. Latex-based formulations are also not very effective in this regard. It is generally necessary to treat the knot with a specially formulated knot sealer or shellac. Do not use ordinary shellac or varnish to seal knots because such finishes are not formulated for this use; they can cause early paint failure in outdoor exposure. After sealing the knots, apply primer, followed by two top-coats.

Finishing of Interior Wood

Interior finishing differs from exterior finishing primarily in that interior woodwork usually requires much less protection against moisture but more exacting standards of appearance and cleanability. A much wider range of finishes and finish methods are possible indoors because weathering does not occur. Good finishes used indoors should last much longer than paint or other coatings on exterior surfaces. The finishing of veneered panels and plywood may still require extra care because of the tendency of these wood composites to surface check.

Much of the variation in finishing methods for wood used indoors is caused by the wide latitude in the uses of wood—from wood floors to cutting boards. There is a wide range of finishing methods for just furniture. Factory finishing of furniture is often proprietary and may involve more than a dozen steps. Methods for furniture finishing will not be included in this publication; however, most public libraries contain books on furniture finishing. In addition, product literature often contains recommendations for application methods. This section will include general information on wood properties, some products for use in interior finishing, and brief subsections on finishing of wood floors and kitchen utensils.

Color change of wood can sometimes cause concern when using wood in interiors, particularly if the wood is finished to enhance its natural appearance. This color change is a natural aging of the newly cut wood, and nothing can be done to prevent it, except, of course, to keep the wood in the dark. The color change is caused by visible light, not the UV radiation associated with weathering. It is best to keep all paintings and other wall coverings off paneling until most of the color change has occurred. Most of this change occurs within 2 to 3 months, depending on the light intensity. If a picture is removed from paneling and there is a color difference caused by shadowing by the picture, it can be corrected by leaving the wood exposed to light. The color will even out within several months.

To avoid knots, the use of fingerjointed lumber has become common for interior trim. As with exterior wood, the quality of the lumber is determined by the poorest board. Pieces of wood for fingerjointed lumber often come from many different trees that have different amounts of extractives and resins. These extractives and resins can discolor the finish, particularly in humid environments such as bathrooms and kitchens. When finishing fingerjointed lumber, it is prudent to use a high-quality stain-blocking primer to minimize discoloration.

Types of Finish and Wood Fillers

Opaque Finishes

The procedures used to paint interior wood surfaces are similar to those used for exterior surfaces. However, interior woodwork, especially wood trim, requires smoother surfaces, better color, and a more lasting sheen. Therefore, enamels or semigloss enamels are preferable to flat paints. Imperfections such as planer marks, hammer marks, and raised grain are accentuated by high-gloss finishes. Raised grain is especially troublesome on flat-grain surfaces of the denser softwoods because the hard bands of latewood are sometimes crushed into the soft earlywood in planing, and later expand when the wood moisture content changes. To obtain the smoothest wood surface, it is helpful to sponge it with water, allow to dry thoroughly, and sand before finishing. Remove surface dust with a tack cloth. In new buildings, allow woodwork adequate time to come to equilibrium moisture content in the completed building before finishing the woodwork.

To effectively paint hardwoods with large pores, such as oak and ash, the pores must be filled with wood filler (see subsection on wood fillers). The pores are first filled and sanded, then interior primer/sealer, undercoat, and top coat are applied. Knots, particularly in the pines, should be sealed with shellac or a special knot-sealer before priming to retard discoloration of light-colored finishes by colored resins in the heartwood of these species. One or two coats of undercoat are next applied, which should completely hide the wood and also provide a surface that can be easily sanded smooth. For best results, the surface should be sanded just before applying the coats of finish. After the final coat has been applied, the finish may be left as is, with its natural gloss, or rubbed to a soft sheen.

Transparent Finishes

Transparent finishes are often used on hardwoods and some softwood trim and paneling. Most finish processes consist of some combination of the fundamental operations of sanding, staining, filling, sealing, surface coating, and sometimes waxing. Before finishing, planer marks and other blemishes on the wood surface that would be accentuated by the finish must be removed.

Stains

Some softwoods and hardwoods are often finished without staining, especially if the wood has an attractive color. When stain is used, however, it often accentuates color differences in the wood surface because of unequal absorption into different parts of the grain pattern. With hardwoods, such emphasis of the grain is usually desirable; the best stains for this purpose are dyes dissolved in either water or solvent. The water-soluble stains give the most pleasing results, but they raise the grain of the wood and require extra sanding after they dry.

The most commonly used stains are those that do not raise grain and are dissolved in solvents that dry quickly. These stains often approach the water-soluble stains in clearness and uniformity of color. Stains on softwoods color the earlywood more strongly than the latewood, reversing the natural gradation in color unless the wood has been initially sealed. To give more nearly uniform color, softwoods may be coated with penetrating clear sealer before applying any type of stain. This sealer is often called a "wash coat."

If stain absorbs into wood unevenly causing a blotchy appearance, the tree was probably infected with bacteria and/or blue-stain fungi prior to being cut for lumber. Once the log is cut into lumber, the infection occurs across grain boundaries and makes infected areas more porous than normal wood. When such areas are stained, they absorb excessive amounts of stain very quickly, giving the wood an uneven blotchy appearance. Although this problem is not very common, should it occur it can be difficult to fix. Blue stain on lumber can easily be seen; the infected pieces can either be discarded or sealed before staining. However, bacteria-infected areas cannot be detected prior to staining. If the wood is to be used for furniture or fine woodwork, it might be a good idea to check the lumber, before planing, by applying a stain. Pieces on which the stain appears blotchy should not be used. Sealing the lumber with varnish diluted 50/50 with mineral spirits prior to staining may help; commercial sealers are also available. Bacteria or blue-stain infection may occur in the sapwood of any species, but it seems to be more problematic with the hardwoods because these species tend to be used for furniture, cabinets, and fine woodwork.

Fillers

In hardwoods with large pores, the pores must be filled, usually after staining and before varnish or lacquer is applied, if a smooth coating is desired. The filler may be transparent and not affect the color of the finish, or it may be colored to either match or contrast with the surrounding wood. For finishing purposes, hardwoods may be classified as shown in Table 15–6. Hardwoods with small pores may be finished with paints, enamels, and varnishes in exactly the same manner as softwoods. A filler may be a paste or liquid, natural or colored. Apply the filler by brushing it first across and then with the grain. Remove surplus filler immediately after the glossy wet appearance disappears. First, wipe across the grain of the wood to pack the filler into the pores; then, wipe with a few light strokes along the grain. Allow the filler to dry thoroughly and lightly sand it before finishing the wood.

Sealers

Sealers are thinned varnish, shellac, or lacquer that are used to prevent absorption of surface coatings and to prevent the bleeding of some stains and fillers into surface coatings, especially lacquer coatings. Lacquer and shellac sealers have the advantage of drying very quickly.

Table 15–6. Classification of hardwoods by size of pores[a]

Large pores	Small pores
Ash	Aspen
Butternut	Basswood
Chestnut	Beech
Elm	Cherry
Hackberry	Cottonwood
Hickory	Gum
Lauan	Magnolia
Mahogany	Maple
Mahogany, African	Red alder
Oak	Sycamore
Sugarberry	Yellow-poplar
Walnut	

[a]Birch has pores large enough to take wood filler effectively, but small enough to be finished satisfactorily without filling.

Surface Coats

Transparent surface coatings over the sealer may be gloss varnish, semigloss varnish, shellac, nitrocellulose lacquer, or wax. Wax provides protection without forming a thick coating and without greatly enhancing the natural luster of the wood. Other coatings are more resinous, especially lacquer and varnish; they accentuate the natural luster of some hardwoods and seem to give the surface more "depth." Shellac applied by the laborious process of French polishing probably achieves this impression of depth most fully, but the coating is expensive and easily marred by water. Rubbing varnishes made with resins of high refractive index for light (ability to bend light rays) are nearly as effective as shellac. Lacquers have the advantages of drying rapidly and forming a hard surface, but more applications of lacquer than varnish are required to build up a lustrous coating. If sufficient film buildup is not obtained and the surface is cleaned often, such as the surface of kitchen cabinets, these thin films can fail.

Varnish and lacquer usually dry to a high gloss. To decrease the gloss, surfaces may be rubbed with pumice stone and water or polishing oil. Waterproof sandpaper and water may be used instead of pumice stone. The final sheen varies with the fineness of the powdered pumice stone; coarse powders make a dull surface and fine powders produce a bright sheen. For very smooth surfaces with high polish, the final rubbing is done with rottenstone and oil. Varnish and lacquer made to produce a semigloss or satin finish are also available.

Flat oil finishes commonly called Danish oils are also very popular. This type of finish penetrates the wood and does not form a noticeable film on the surface. Two or more coats of oil are usually applied; the oil may be followed by a paste wax. Such finishes are easily applied and maintained but they are more subject to soiling than is a film-forming type of finish. Simple boiled linseed oil or tung oil are also used extensively as wood finishes.

357

Finishes for Floors

Wood possesses a variety of properties that make it a highly desirable flooring material for homes, factories, and public buildings. A variety of wood flooring products are available, both unfinished and prefinished, in many wood species, grain characteristics, flooring types, and flooring patterns.

The natural color and grain of wood floors accentuate many architectural styles. Floor finishes enhance the natural beauty of wood, protect it from excessive wear and abrasion, and make the floor easier to clean. The finishing process consists of four steps: sanding the surface, applying a filler (for open-grain woods), staining to achieve a desired color effect, and finishing. Detailed procedures and specified materials depend to a great extent on the species of wood used and finish preference.

Careful sanding to provide a smooth surface is essential for a good finish because any irregularities or roughness in the surface will be accentuated by the finish. Development of a top-quality surface requires sanding in several steps with progressively finer sandpaper, usually with a machine unless the area is small. When sanding is complete, all dust must be removed with a vacuum cleaner and then a tack cloth. Steel wool should not be used on floors unprotected by finish because minute steel particles left in the wood later cause iron stains. A filler is required for wood with large pores, such as oak and walnut, if a smooth, glossy varnish finish is desired (Table 15–6).

Stains are sometimes used to obtain a more nearly uniform color when individual boards vary too much in their natural color. However, stains may also be used to accent the grain pattern. The stain should be an oil-based or non-grain-raising type. Stains penetrate wood only slightly; therefore, the finish should be carefully maintained to prevent wearing through to the wood surface; the clear top-coats must be replaced as they wear. It is difficult to renew the stain at worn spots in a way that will match the color of the surrounding area.

Finishes commonly used for wood floors are classified as sealers or varnishes. Sealers, which are usually thinned varnishes, are widely used for residential flooring. They penetrate the wood just enough to avoid formation of a surface coating of appreciable thickness. Wax is usually applied over the sealer; however, if greater gloss is desired, the sealed floor makes an excellent base for varnish. The thin surface coat of sealer and wax needs more frequent attention than do varnished surfaces. However, rewaxing or resealing and waxing of high traffic areas is a relatively simple maintenance procedure, as long as the stained surface of the wood hasn't been worn.

Varnish may be based on phenolic, alkyd, epoxy, or polyurethane resins. Varnish forms a distinct coating over the wood and gives a lustrous finish. The kind of service expected usually determines the type of varnish. Varnishes especially designed for homes, schools, gymnasiums, or other public buildings are available. Information on types of floor finishes can be obtained from flooring associations or individual flooring manufacturers.

The durability of floor finishes can be improved by keeping them waxed. Paste waxes generally provide the best appearance and durability. Two coats are recommended, and if a liquid wax is used, additional coats may be necessary to get an adequate film for good performance.

Finishes for Items Used for Food

The durability and beauty of wood make it an attractive material for bowls, butcher blocks, and other items used to serve or prepare food. A finish also helps keep the wood dry, which makes it less prone to harbor bacteria and less likely to crack. When wood soaks up water, it swells; when it dries out, it shrinks. If the wood dries out rapidly, its surface dries faster than the inside, resulting in cracks and checks. Finishes that repel water will decrease the effects of brief periods of moisture (washing), making the wood easier to clean.

Finishes that form a film on wood, such as varnish or lacquer, may be used but they may eventually chip, crack, and peel. Penetrating finishes, either drying or nondrying, are often a better choice for some products.

Types of Finish

Sealers and Drying Oils

Sealers and drying oils penetrate the wood surface, then solidify to form a barrier to liquid water. Many commercial sealers are similar to thinned varnish. These finishes can include a wide range of formulations including polyurethane, alkyds, and modified oils. Unmodified oils such as tung, linseed, and walnut oil can also be used as sealers if they are thinned to penetrate the wood.

Nondrying Oils

Nondrying oils simply penetrate the wood. They include both vegetable and mineral oils. Vegetable oils (such as olive, corn, peanut, and safflower) are edible and are sometimes used to finish wood utensils. Mineral (or paraffin) oil is a nondrying oil from petroleum. Since it is not a natural product, it is not prone to mildew or to harbor bacteria.

Paraffin Wax

Paraffin wax is similar to paraffin oil but is solid at room temperature. Paraffin wax is one of the simplest ways to finish wood utensils, especially countertops, butcher blocks, and cutting boards.

Eating Utensils

Wood salad bowls, spoons, and forks used for food service need a finish that is resistant to abrasion, water, acids, and stains and a surface that is easy to clean when soiled.

Appropriate finishes are varnishes and lacquers, penetrating wood sealers and drying oils, and nondrying vegetable oils.

Many varnishes and lacquers are available, and some of these are specifically formulated for use on wood utensils, bowls, and/or cutting boards. These film-forming finishes resist staining and provide a surface that is easy to keep clean; however, they may eventually chip, peel, alligator, or crack. These film-forming finishes should perform well if care is taken to minimize their exposure to water. Utensils finished with such finishes should never be placed in a dishwasher.

Penetrating wood sealers and drying oils may also be used for eating utensils. Some of these may be formulated for use on utensils. Wood sealers and oils absorb into the pores of the wood and fill the cavities of the wood cells. This decreases the absorption of water and makes the surface easy to clean and more resistant to scratching compared with unfinished wood. Penetrating wood sealers are easy to apply and dry quickly. Worn places in the finish may be easily refinished. Some of these finishes, particularly drying oils, should be allowed to dry thoroughly for several weeks before use.

Nondrying vegetable oils are edible and are sometimes used to finish wood utensils. They penetrate the wood surface, improve its resistance to water, and can be refurbished easily. However, such finishes can become rancid and can sometimes impart undesirable odors and/or flavors to food.

Of these finish types, the impermeable varnishes and lacquers may be the best option for bowls and eating utensils; this kind of finish is easiest to keep clean and most resistant to absorption of stains.

> **Note**: Whatever finish is chosen for wood utensils used to store, handle, or eat food, it is important to be sure that the finish is safe and not toxic (poisonous). Also be sure that the finish you select is recommended for use with food or is described as food grade. For information on the safety and toxicity of any finish, check the label, contact the manufacturer and/or the Food and Drug Administration, or check with your local extension home economics expert or county agent.

Butcher Blocks and Cutting Boards

One of the simplest treatments for wood butcher blocks and cutting boards is the application of melted paraffin wax (the type used for home canning). The wax is melted in a double-boiler over hot water and liberally brushed on the wood surface. Excess wax, which has solidified on the surface, can be melted with an iron to absorb it into the wood, or it may be scraped off. Refinishing is simple and easy. Other penetrating finishes (sealers, drying and nondrying oils) may also be used for butcher blocks and cutting boards. As mentioned in the subsection on eating utensils, vegetable oils may become rancid. If a nondrying oil is desired, mineral oil may be used. Film-forming finishes are not recommended for butcher blocks or cutting boards.

Wood Cleaners and Brighteners

The popularity of wood decks and the desire to keep them looking bright and new has led to a proliferation of commercial cleaners and brighteners. The removal of mildew from wood was discussed in an earlier section of this chapter (see Finish Failure or Discoloration). Mildew growth on unpainted and painted wood continues to be the primary cause of discoloration. Although it can be removed with a dilute solution of household bleach and detergent, many commercial products are available that can both remove mildew and brighten the wood surface.

The active ingredient in many of these products is sodium percarbonate (disodium peroxypercarbonate). This chemical is an oxidizing agent as is bleach, and it is an effective mildew cleaner. It also helps brighten the wood surface. Some cleaners and brighteners are reported to restore color to wood. It is not possible to add color to wood by cleaning it. Removing the discoloration reveals the original color. Brightening the wood may make it appear as if it has more color. Once all the colored components of the wood surface have been removed through the weathering process, the surface will be a silvery gray. If color is desired after weathering occurs, it must be added to the wood by staining.

In addition to sodium percarbonate, other oxidizing products may contain hydrogen peroxide by itself or in combination with sodium hydroxide. If sodium hydroxide is used without a brightener, it will darken the wood. Commercial products are also formulated with sodium hypochlorite and/or calcium hypochlorite (household bleach is a solution of sodium hypochlorite). These products usually contain a surfactant or detergent to enhance the cleansing action of the oxidizing agent. Other types of brighteners contain oxalic acid. This chemical removes stains caused by extractives bleed and iron stains and also brightens the wood, but it is not very effective for removing mildew.

Paint Strippers

Removing paint and other film-forming finishes from wood is a time-consuming and often difficult process. It is generally not done unless absolutely necessary to refinish the wood. Removing the finish is necessary if the old finish has extensive cross-grain cracking caused by buildup of many layers of paint, particularly oil-based paint. If cracking and peeling are extensive, it is usually best to remove all the paint from the affected area. Total removal of paint is also necessary if the paint has failed by intercoat peeling. It may be necessary to remove paint containing lead; however, if the paint is still sound and it is not illegal to leave it on the structure, it is best to repaint the surface without removing the old paint (see Lead-Based Paint).

This discussion of paint strippers is limited to film-forming finishes on wood used in structures. Removing paint from furniture can be done using the same methods as described here. Companies that specialize in stripping furniture usually immerse the furniture in a vat of paint stripper and then clean and brighten the wood. This procedure removes the paint very efficiently.

Some of the same methods can be used for the removal of interior and exterior paint. Because of the dust caused by mechanical methods or the fumes given off by chemical strippers, it is extremely important to use effective safety equipment, particularly when working indoors. A good respirator is essential, even if the paint does not contain lead (see Lead-Based Paint).

Note: The dust masks sold in hardware stores do not block chemical fumes and are not very effective against dust.

Two general types of stripping methods are discussed here: mechanical and chemical. The processes are discussed in general terms primarily in regard to their effect on wood; some attention is given to their ease of use and safety requirements. Consult product literature for additional information on appropriate uses and safety precautions.

Mechanical Methods

Finishes can be removed by scraping, sanding, wet or dry sandblasting, spraying with pressurized water (power washing), and using electrically heated pads, hot air guns, and blow torches. Scraping is effective only in removing loosely bonded paint or paint that has already partially peeled from the wood. It is generally used when paint needs to be removed only from small areas of the structure, and it is generally combined with sanding to feather the edge of the paint still bonded to the wood (see Lead-Based Paint).

When the paint is peeling and partially debonded on large areas of a structure, the finish is usually removed by power washing or wet sandblasting. These methods work well for paint that is loosely bonded to the wood. If the paint is well bonded, complete removal can be difficult without severely damaging the wood surface. The pressure necessary to debond paint from the wood can easily cause deep erosion of the wood. The less dense earlywood erodes more than the dense latewood, leaving behind a surface consisting of latewood, which is more difficult to repaint. Power washing is less damaging to the wood than is wet or dry sandblasting, particularly if low pressure is used. If high pressure is necessary to remove the paint, it is probably bonded well enough that it does not need to be removed for normal refinishing. If more aggressive mechanical methods are required, wet sandblasting can remove even well-bonded paint, but it causes more damage to the wood than does water blasting. Dry sandblasting is not very suitable for removing paint from wood because it can quickly erode the wood surface along with the paint, and it tends to glaze the surface.

A number of power sanders and similar devices are available for complete paint removal. Many of these devices are suitable for removing paint that contains lead; they have attachments for containing the dust. Equipment that has a series of blades similar to a power hand-planer is less likely to "gum up" with paint than equipment that merely sands the surface. Some of this equipment is advertised in the *Old House Journal* and the *Journal of Light Construction*. Please consult the manufacturers' technical data sheets for detailed information to determine the suitability of their equipment for your needs and to meet government regulations on lead-containing paint.

Paint can be removed by heating then scraping it from the wood, but this method must not be used for paint that contains lead. Paint can be softened by using electrically heated pads, hot air guns, or blow torches. Heated pads and hot air guns are slow methods, but they cause little damage to the wood. Sanding is still necessary, but the wood should be sound after the paint is removed. Blow torches have been used to remove paint and, if carefully used, do not damage the wood. Blow torches are extremely hazardous; the flames can easily ignite flammable materials beneath the siding through gaps in the siding. These materials may smolder, undetected, for hours before bursting into flame and causing loss of the structure.

Note: Removing paint with a blow torch is not recommended.

Chemical Methods

If all the paint needs to be removed, then mechanical methods should be used in concert with other methods, such as chemical paint strippers. For all chemical paint strippers, the process involves applying paint stripper, waiting, scraping off the softened paint, washing the wood (and possibly neutralizing the stripper), and sanding the surface to remove the wood damaged by the stripper and/or the raised grain caused by washing. Chemical paint strippers, although tedious to use, are sometimes the most reasonable choice. A range of paint strippers are available. Some are extremely strong chemicals that quickly remove paint but are dangerous to use. Others remove the paint slowly but are safer. With the exception of alkali paint stripper (discussed below), there appears to be an inverse correlation between how safe a product is and how fast it removes the paint.

Solvent-Based Strippers

Fast-working paint strippers usually contain methylene chloride, a possible carcinogen that can burn eyes and skin. Eye and skin protection and a supplied-air respirator are essential when using this paint stripper. Paint strippers having methylene chloride can remove paint in as little as 10 min. Because of concerns with methylene chloride, some paint strippers are being formulated using other strong solvents; the same safety precautions should be used with these formulations as with those containing methylene chloride. To remain effective in removing paint, a paint stripper must remain liquid or semiliquid; slow-acting paint stripers are often covered to keep them active. Solvent-type strippers contain a wax that floats to the surface to slow the evaporation of the solvent. Covering the paint stripper with plastic wrap also helps to contain the solvent.

Alkali-Based Strippers

As an alternative to strong solvents, some paint strippers contain strong bases (alkali). Like solvent-based paint strippers, alkali-based strippers require eye and skin protection. Follow the manufacturer's recommendations about whether a respirator is necessary as well. Although alkali-based paint strippers soften the paint rather slowly, they are strong chemicals and can severely damage the wood substrate. Because they degrade the paint slowly, these strippers are often left on the painted wood a full day or overnight. They are usually covered with a cloth, which helps in peeling the weakened paint from the surface.

These cloth-covered types of products have the advantage of containing the paint stripper and paint extremely well, an important consideration when removing paint containing lead. They have the disadvantage of severely degrading the wood substrate. Strong alkali actually pulps the wood surface. Once the paint is removed, it is essential to neutralize the surface with acid. Oxalic acid is frequently used for this process. Unfortunately, it is extremely difficult to balance the acid and base concentrations. If excess alkali is left in the wood, it will continue to degrade it and to degrade the subsequent paint coating. Excess oxalic acid can also damage the wood. The neutralization procedure leaves behind reaction products of the acid and base (water and a salt). Often, the salt is hygroscopic (absorbs moisture from the air) and causes the wood to get wet. Wet wood does not hold paint very well.

> **Note:** Alkali-based strippers require extra care to ensure that the wood is neutralized and that residual salts are washed from the wood. The surface must be sanded before repainting.

Since the surface must be sanded before repainting, paint performance might be improved by letting the wood weather for an extended period (possibly as long as a year) before repainting to let rain leach unwanted chemicals from the wood. In addition, rinse the siding periodically using a hose, particularly areas that rain does not reach, such as siding under eaves and porches. Once all the residue has been removed, the surface can be sanded (50-grit sandpaper) and painted.

Although alkali paint strippers can cause burns on unprotected skin, the fumes are not nearly as toxic as those in solvent-type strippers. Alkali paint strippers are an excellent choice for indoor use such as door and window trim and fireplace mantles. Indoors, the weakened wood surface may not be as much of a concern because less stress is placed on the wood–paint interface; the wood is not exposed to weather extremes.

"Safe" Paint Strippers

Several paint strippers are being marketed under the "safe" caveat. These strippers work much slower than those having strong chemical solvents. The active ingredient in such paint strippers is usually proprietary. In regard to safety, follow the manufacturer's recommendations.

Avoidance of Problems

Failure of the finish on wood that has been stripped can be avoided by using methods that do not damage the wood surface. The best way to remove paint may involve a combination of methods. For example, use power washing to remove as much paint as possible. Then, use a solvent-based chemical paint stripper on paint that could not be removed by power washing. Avoid using excessive amounts of chemical stripper. Applying too much stripper or leaving it on the painted wood for too long can damage the wood. It is better to use less stripper and reapply it, if necessary, than to try to remove all the paint with one application, leaving the stripper on the paint for an extended period.

The problem of paint removal is complicated by the wide range of paint types and wood species. Companies that make paint strippers may optimize the formulations without considering their effects on the wood. Removing the paint from the wood is only half the task. Getting a paintable surface is the other half. Companies that formulate paint strippers must consider this other half. Those who use paint strippers need to understand the added burden of surface preparation.

Disposal of Old Paint

No matter what method you use to remove paint, be careful in disposing of the old paint, particularly paint that contains lead. Lead is considered hazardous waste, and there are regulations that restrict the handling and disposal of this material. Be sure to follow all regulations, both national and local, during the removal, storage, and disposal of paint, especially paint containing lead (see Lead-Based Paint).

Lead-Based Paint

The information in this section is taken from material prepared by the National Association of Home Builders (NAHB) and is contained in *Rehabilitation of Wood-Frame Houses* (USDA 1998). Lead-based paint was widely used in residential applications in the United States until the early 1940s, and its use was continued to some extent, particularly for the exterior of dwellings, until 1976. In 1971, Congress passed the Lead-Based Paint Poisoning Prevention Act, and in 1976, the Consumer Product Safety Commission (CPSC) issued a ruling under this Act that limited the lead content of paint used in residential dwellings, toys, and furniture to 0.06%.

Lead-based paint is still manufactured today for applications not covered by the CPSC ruling, such as paint for metal products, particularly those made of steel. Occasionally, such lead-based paint (for example, surplus paint from a shipyard) inadvertently gets into retail stores and the hands of consumers. A study conducted for the Environmental Protection Agency in 1986 indicated that about 42 million U.S. homes still contain interior and/or exterior lead-based paint. As rehabilitation of these homes increases, how to abate the toxicity of lead-based paint has become the subject of increased public and official concern.

Studies have shown that ingestion of even minute amounts of lead can have serious effects on health, including hypertension, fetal injury, and damage to the brain, kidneys, and red blood cells. Low levels of ingestion can also cause partial loss of hearing, impairment of mental development and IQ, growth retardation, inhibited metabolism of vitamin D, and disturbances in blood formation. The American Academy of Pediatrics regards lead as one of the foremost toxicological dangers to children.

Lead-based paint applied to the exterior of homes disintegrates into chalk and powder as a result of the effects of moisture and ultraviolet radiation. This extremely fine lead dust can accumulate in the soil near the house and can ultimately enter the house. Poor quality lead-based paint used on interior surfaces can also produce dust. Lead dust can be generated when coatings on surfaces are broken through aging or as a result of rehabilitation. The dust cannot be completely removed by conventional house-cleaning methods.

Methods used to abate the toxicity of lead-based paint or to remove the paint can themselves generate lead dust. This is particularly true when unacceptable methods and work practices are used. Poorly performed abatement can be worse than no abatement. The micron-sized lead dust particles can remain airborne for substantial periods and cannot be fully removed by standard cleaning methods from the surfaces on which they have settled. When working on old painted surfaces, the worker should assume that one or more of the paint coats contain lead. Proper precautions should be taken accordingly.

Paint coats may be checked for lead content. A portable x-ray fluorescence (XRF) analyzer is commonly used to determine the level of lead in paint. Because this device has the potential for giving very inaccurate results if used by an inexperienced person, the analysis should be done by a qualified professional. Chemical spot testing, using a solution of 6% to 8% sodium sulfide in water, is sometimes used to screen painted surfaces for the presence of lead. Be certain to check all paint coats, because the older ones are more likely to be lead based. Test kits for detecting lead-based paint are available in most paint and hardware stores.

Removal of lead-based paints can present some serious health problems. The U.S. Department of Health and Urban Development (HUD) has taken a leading role in developing guidelines for the removal of lead-based paints. At this time, HUD has approved three approaches to abating the toxicity of lead-based paint:

1. Covering the painted surface with wallboard, a fiberglass cloth barrier, or permanently attached wallpaper

2. Removing the paint

3. Replacing the entire surface to which lead-based paint has been applied

Certain practices are prohibited in residential structures owned and operated by HUD: machine sanding without an attached high-efficiency particulate air (HEPA) vacuum filtration apparatus, use of propane torches, contained water blasting, washing, and repainting.

Removal of lead-based paint by scraping or application of heat does not solve the problem of lead-particulate dust. Scraping should be accompanied by misting. Dry scraping is prohibited by Maryland abatement regulations. Sanding without a HEPA-filtered vacuum should not be used as a finishing method after scraping or any other method of toxicity abatement. The HEPA sanders are recommended for limited surface areas only; they are most appropriate for flat surfaces such as door jambs and stair risers. Open abrasive blasting is also prohibited by some regulations.

High levels of airborne lead can be produced by heat guns, and the use of a respirator is essential. Some lead is likely to be volatilized at the operating temperatures of most heat guns. Lead fumes are released at about 371°C (700°F). Heat guns capable of reaching or exceeding this temperature should not be operated in that range.

Chemical methods for removing lead-based paint may require multiple applications, depending on the number of paint coats. Caustic and solvent-based chemicals should not be allowed to dry on the lead-painted surface. If drying occurs, paint removal will not be satisfactory and the potential for creating lead dust will be increased.

Chemical substances used for paint removal are usually hazardous and should be used with great care. Some solvent-based chemical strippers are flammable and require ventilation. They may contain methylene chloride, which is a central nervous system depressant that at high concentrations can cause kidney and liver damage and is a possible carcinogen. Supplied-air respirators should be used when working with strippers containing this substance. If the solvent-based strippers do not contain methylene chloride, organic vapor filters must be added to respirators. Caustic chemical strippers also have a very high pH (alkaline content), which can cause severe skin and eye injuries.

> **Caution:** Remodeling or refinishing projects that require disturbing, removing, or demolishing portions of the structure that are coated with lead-based paint pose serious problems. The consumer should seek information, advice, and perhaps professional assistance for addressing these problems. Contact HUD for the latest information on the removal of lead-based paints. Debris coated with lead-based paint is regarded as hazardous waste.

References

APA. 1979. Stains and paints on plywood. Pamphlet B407B. Tacoma, WA: American Plywood Association.

Black, J.M.; Mraz, E.A. 1974. Inorganic surface treatments for weather-resistant natural finishes. Res. Pap. FPL–232. Madison, WI: U.S. Department of Agriculture, Forest Service, Forest Products Laboratory.

Cassens, D.L.; Feist, W.C. 1980. Wood finishing: Finishing exterior plywood, hardboard and particle board. North Central Region Extension Pub. 132. West Lafayette, IN: Purdue University, Cooperative Extension Service.

Cassens, D.L.; Feist, W.C. 1980. Wood finishing: paint failure problems and their cure. North Central Region Extension Publ. 133. West Lafayette, IN: Purdue University, Cooperative Extension Service.

Cassens, D.L.; Feist, W.C. 1980. Wood finishing: discoloration of house paint—causes and cures. North Central Region Extension Publ. 134. West Lafayette, IN: Purdue University, Cooperative Extension Service.

Cassens, D.L.; Feist, W.C. 1980. Wood finishing: selection and application of exterior finishes for wood. North Central Region Extension Publ. 135. West Lafayette, IN: Purdue University, Cooperative Extension Service.

Cassens, D.L.; Feist, W.C. 1980. Wood finishing: finishing and maintaining wood floors. North Central Region Extension Publ. 136. West Lafayette, IN: Purdue University, Cooperative Extension Service.

Feist, W.C. 1979. Protection of wood surfaces with chromium trioxide. Res. Pap. FPL–339. Madison, WI: U.S. Department of Agriculture, Forest Service, Forest Products Laboratory.

Feist, W.C. 1982. Weathering of wood in structural uses. In: Meyer, R.W.; Kellogg, R.M., eds. Structural use of wood in adverse environments. New York: Van Nostrand Reinhold Company: 156–178.

Feist, W.C. 1982. Weathering characteristics of finished wood-based panel products. Journal of Coating Technology. 54(686): 43–50.

Feist, W.C. 1990. Outdoor wood weathering and protection. In: Rowell, R., ed. Archaeological wood, properties, chemistry, and preservation. Advanced in Chemistry Series No. 225. Washington, DC: American Chemical Society. 263–298. Chapter 11.

Feist, W.C. 1996. Finishing exterior wood. Federation Series on Coatings Technology. Blue Bell, PA: Federation of Societies for Coatings Technology.

Feist, W.C.; Hon, D.N.–S. 1984. Chemistry of weathering and protection. In: Rowell, R.M., ed. The chemistry of solid wood. Advances in Chemistry Series No. 207. Washington DC: American Chemical Society: 401–451. Chapter 11.

Feist, W.C.; Mraz, E.A. 1980. Performance of mildewcides in a semitransparent stain wood finish. Forest Products Journal. 30(5): 43–46.

Feist, W.C.; Ross, A.S. 1995. Performance and durability of finishes on previously coated CCA-treated wood. Forest Products Journal. 45(9): 29–36.

Gorman, T.M.; Feist, W.C. 1989. Chronicle of 65 years of wood finishing research of the Forest Products Laboratory. Gen. Tech. Rep. FPL–GTR–60. Madison, WI: U.S. Department of Agriculture, Forest Service, Forest Products Laboratory.

Kalnins, M.A.; Feist, W.C. 1993. Increase in wettability of wood with weathering. Forest Products Journal. 43(2): 55–57.

McDonald, K.A.; Falk, R.H.; Williams, R.S.; Winandy, J.E. 1996. Wood decks: materials, construction, and finishing. Madison, WI: Forest Products Society.

Niemiec, S.S.; Brown, T.D. 1988. Care and maintenance of wood shingle and shake roofs. Corvallis, OR: Oregon State University Extension Service. EC 1271, September.

Richter, K.; Feist, W.C.; Knaebe, M.T. 1995. The effect of surface roughness on the performance of finishes. Part 1. Roughness characterization and stain performance. Forest Products Journal. 45(7/8): 91–97.

Ross, A.S.; Feist, W.C. 1993. The effects of CCA-treated wood on the performance of surface finishes. American Paint and Coatings Journal. 78(9): 41–54.

Ross, A.S.; Bussjaeger, R.C.; Feist, W.C. 1992. Professional finishing of CCA pressure-treated wood. American painting Contractor. 69(7): 107–114.

Sell, J.; Feist, W.C. 1986. Role of density in the erosion of wood during weathering. Forest Products Journal. 36(3): 57–60.

Tichy, R.J. 1997. Interior wood finishing: industrial use guide. Madison, WI: Forest Products Society.

USDA. 1998. Rehabilitation of wood-frame houses. Agric. Handb. 804. Washington, DC: U.S. Department of Agriculture, Forest Service.

WDMA. 1999. Industry standard for water-repellent preservative treatment for millwork. IS4–99. Des Plaines, IL: Window and Door Manufacturer's Association.

Williams, R.S. 1986. Effects of acid rain on painted wood surfaces: importance of the substrate. In: Baboian, R., ed. Materials degradation caused by acid rain. ACS Symposium Series 318. Washington DC: American Chemical Society: 310–331.

Williams, R.S. 1990. Effects of acidic deposition on painted wood. In: Effects of acidic deposition on materials. State of Science and State of Technology, Report 19. National Acid Precipitation Assessment Program: 19/165–19/202. Vol. 3.

Williams, R.S.; Feist, W.C. 1993. Durability of paint or solid-color stain applied to preweathered wood. Forest Products Journal. 43(1): 8–14.

Williams, R.S.; Feist, W.C. 1994. Effect of preweathering, surface roughness, and wood species on the performance of paint and stains. Journal of Coatings Technology. 66(828): 109–121.

Williams, R.S.; Winandy, J.E.; Feist, W.C. 1987. Adhesion of paint to weathered wood. Forest Products Journal. 37(11/12): 29–31.

Williams, R.S.; Winandy, J.E.; Feist, W.C. 1987. Paint adhesion to weathered wood. Journal of Coatings Technology. 59(749): 43–49.

Williams, R.S.; Knaebe, M.T.; Feist, W.C. 1996. Finishes for exterior wood. Madison, WI: Forest Products Society.

Chapter 16

Use of Wood in Buildings and Bridges

Russell C. Moody and Anton TenWolde

Contents

In North America, most housing and commercial structures built prior to the 20th century used wood as the major structural material. The abundant wood resource formed the basic structure for most houses, commercial buildings, bridges, and utility poles. Today, houses and many light commercial and industrial buildings are made using modern wood structural materials. Recently, there has been increased interest in using wood for various types of transportation structures, including bridges.

In this chapter, the features of various types of building systems are described. Emphasis is placed on how these systems have adapted to the use of modern materials and techniques. For example, where floor, wall, and roof sheathing for light-frame construction were once commonly made from wood boards, sheathing is now commonly made from structural panel products, such as plywood and structural flakeboard. Compared with boards, these panel products are quicker to install and provide improved structural resistance to wind and earthquake loadings. Furthermore, prefabricated floor and wall panels along with prefabricated roof and floor trusses or I-joists are replacing piece-by-piece on-site construction with dimension lumber. A structure can be enclosed within a short time on site using factory-made panelized systems.

Glulam and other panelized wood systems are being used increasingly for both highway and railroad bridges. A brief description of the uses of wood in these types of structures is included.

Light-Frame Buildings

Historically, two general types of light-frame construction have been used—balloon and platform framing. Balloon framing, which was used in the early part of the 20th century, consists of full-height wall framing members for two-story construction. Additional information on balloon framing is available from older construction manuals. In the latter part of the 20th century, platform framing has dominated the housing market and is widely used in commercial and light industrial applications. Platform framing features the construction of each floor on top of the one beneath. Platform framing construction differs from that of 50 years ago in the use of new and innovative materials, panel products for floor and roof sheathing, and prefabricated components and modules as opposed to "stick built" or on-site construction. A detailed description of the platform-type of construction is given in *Wood Frame House Construction* (Sherwood and Stroh 1989); additional information is given in the *Wood Frame Construction Manual for One- and Two-Family Dwellings, 1995 SBC High Wind Edition* (AF&PA 1995).

Foundations

Light-frame buildings with basements are typically supported on cast-in-place concrete walls or concrete block walls supported by footings. This type of construction with a basement is common in northern climates. Another practice is to have concrete block foundations extend a short distance above ground to support a floor system over a "crawl space." In southern and western climates, some buildings have no foundation; the walls are supported by a concrete slab, thus having no basement or crawl space.

Treated wood is also used for basement foundation walls. Basically, such foundations consist of wood-frame wall sections with studs and plywood sheathing supported on treated wood plates, all of which are preservatively treated to a specified level of protection. To distribute the load, the plates are laid on a layer of crushed stone or gravel. Walls, which must be designed to resist the lateral loads of the backfill, are built using the same techniques as conventional walls. The exterior surface of the foundation wall below grade is draped with a continuous moisture barrier to prevent direct water contact with the wall panels. The backfill must be

designed to permit easy drainage and provide drainage from the lowest level of the foundation.

Because a foundation wall needs to be permanent, the preservative treatment of the plywood and framing as well as the fasteners used for connections are very important. A special foundation (FDN) treatment has been established for the plywood and framing, with strict requirements for depth of chemical penetration and amount of chemical retention. Corrosion-resistant fasteners (for example, stainless steel) are recommended for all preservatively treated wood. Additional information and materials and construction procedures are given in *Permanent Wood Foundation Basic Requirements* (AF&PA 1987).

Floors

For houses with basements, the central supporting structure may consist of wood posts on suitable footings that carry a built-up girder, which is frequently composed of planks the same width as the joists (standard 38 by 184 mm to 38 by 286 mm (nominal 2 by 8 in. to 2 by 12 in.)), face-nailed together, and set on edge. Because planks are seldom sufficiently long enough to span the full length of the beam, butt joints are required in the layers. The joints are staggered in the individual layers near the column supports. The girder may also be a glulam beam or steel I-beam, often supported on adjustable steel pipe columns. Similar details may be applied to a house over a crawl space. The floor framing in residential structures typically consists of wood joists on 400- or 600-mm (16- or 24-in.) centers supported by the foundation walls and the center girder (Fig. 16–1).

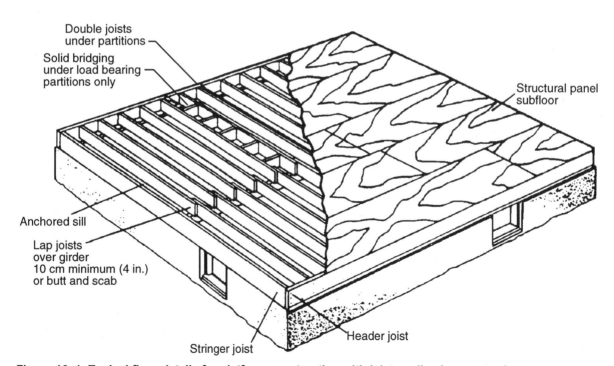

Figure 16–1. Typical floor details for platform construction with joists spliced on center beam.

Joist size depends on the anticipated loading, spacing between joists, distance between supports (span), species, and grade of lumber. Commonly used joists are standard 38- by 184-mm or 38- by 235-mm (nominal 2- by 8-in. or 2- by 10-in.) lumber, prefabricated wood I-joists, or parallel chord trusses. Lumber joists typically span from 3.6 to 4.8 m (12 to 16 ft). Span tables are available from the American Forest & Paper Association (AF&PA 1993). Span capabilities of the prefabricated wood I-joists or parallel chord trusses are recommended by the manufacturer.

Floor openings for stairways, fireplaces, and chimneys may interrupt one or more joists. Preferably, such openings are parallel to the length of the joists to reduce the number of joists that will be interrupted. At the interruption, a support (header) is placed between the uninterrupted joists and attached to them. A single header is usually adequate for openings up to about 1.2 m (4 ft) in width, but double headers are required for wider openings. Special care must be taken to provide adequate support at headers (using joist hangers, for example).

Cutting of framing members to install items such as plumbing lines and heating ducts should be minimized. Cut members may require a reinforcing scab, or a supplementary member may be needed. Areas of highly concentrated loads, such as under bathtubs, require doubling of joists or other measures to provide adequate support. One advantage of framing floors with parallel-chord trusses or prefabricated I-joists is that their longer span capabilities may eliminate the need for interior supports. An additional advantage is that the web areas of these components are designed for easy passing of plumbing, electrical, and heating ducts.

Floor sheathing, or subflooring, is used over the floor framing to provide a working platform and a base for the finish flooring. Older homes have board sheathing but newer homes generally use panel products. Common sheathing materials include plywood and structural flakeboard, which are available in a number of types to meet various sheathing requirements. Exterior-type panels with water-resistant adhesive are desirable in locations where moisture may be a problem, such as floors near plumbing fixtures or situations where the subfloor may be exposed to the weather for some time during construction.

Plywood should be installed with the grain direction of the face plies at right angles to the joists. Structural flakeboard also has a preferred direction of installation. Nailing patterns are either prescribed by code or recommended by the manufacturer. About 3 mm (1/8 in.) of space should be left between the edges and ends of abutting panels to provide for dimensional changes associated with moisture content.

Literature from APA–The Engineered Wood Association includes information on the selection and installation of the types of structural panels suitable for subfloors (APA 1996).

Exterior Walls

Exterior walls of light-frame structures are generally load bearing; they support upper floors and the roof. An exception is the gable ends of a one- or two-story building. Basically, wall framing consists of vertical studs and horizontal members, including top and bottom plates and headers (or lintels) over window and door openings. The studs are generally standard 38- by 89 mm, 38- by 114-mm, or 38- by 140-mm (nominal 2- by 4-in., 2- by 5-in., or 2- by 6-in.) members spaced between 300 and 600 mm (12 and 24 in.) on center. Selection of the stud size depends on the load the wall will carry, the need for support of wall-covering materials, and the need for insulation thickness in the walls. Headers over openings up to 1.2 m (4 ft) are often 38 by 140 mm (2 by 6 in.), nailed together face to face with spacers to bring the headers flush with the faces of the studs. Special headers that match the wall thickness are also available in the form of either prefabricated I-joists or structural composite lumber. Wall framing is erected over the platform formed by the first-floor joists and subfloor. In most cases, an entire wall is framed in a horizontal position on the subfloor, then tilted into place. If a wall is too long to make this procedure practical, sections of the wall can be formed horizontally and tilted up, then joined to adjacent sections.

Corner studs are usually prefabricated in such a configuration as to provide a nailing edge for the interior finish (Fig. 16–2). Studs are sometimes doubled at the points of intersection with an interior partition to provide backup support for the interior wall finish. Alternatively, a horizontal block is placed midheight between exterior studs to support the partition wall. In such a case, backup clips on the partition stud are needed to accommodate the interior finish.

Upper plates are usually doubled, especially when rafters or floor joists will bear on the top plate between studs. The second top plate is added in such a way that it overlaps the first plate at corners and interior wall intersections. This provides a tie and additional rigidity to the walls. In areas subject to high winds or earthquakes, ties should be provided between the wall, floor framing, and sill plate that should be anchored to the foundation. If a second story is added to the structure, the edge floor joist is nailed to the top wall plate, and subfloor and wall framing are added in the same way as the first floor.

Sheathing for exterior walls is commonly some type of panel product. Here again, plywood or structural flakeboard may be used. Fiberboard that has been treated to impart some degree of water resistance is another option. Several types of fiberboard are available. Regular-density board sometimes requires additional bracing to provide necessary resistance to lateral loads. Intermediate-density board is used where structural support is needed. Numerous foam-type panels can also be used to impart greater thermal resistance to the walls.

In cases where the sheathing cannot provide the required racking resistance, diagonal bracing must be used. Many foam sheathings cannot provide adequate racking resistance,

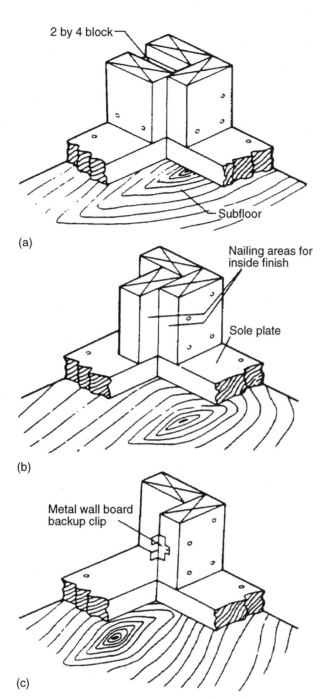

(a)

2 by 4 block

Subfloor

(b)

Nailing areas for inside finish

Sole plate

(c)

Metal wall board backup clip

Figure 16–2. Corner details for wood stud walls that provide support for interior sheathing: (a) traditional three-stud corner with blocking; (b) three-stud corner without blocking; (c) two-stud corner with wallboard backup clips.

so either diagonal braces must be placed at the corners or structural panels must be applied over the first 1.2 m (4 ft) of the wall from the corner. When light-weight insulating foam sheathings are used, bracing is commonly provided by standard 19- by 89-mm (nominal 1- by 4-in.) lumber or steel strapping.

Ceiling and Roof

Roof systems are generally made of either the joists-and-rafter systems or with trusses. Engineered trusses reduce on-site labor and can span greater distances without intermediate support, thus eliminating the need for interior load-carrying partitions. This provides greater flexibility in the layout of interior walls. Prefabricated roof trusses are used to form the ceiling and sloped roof of more than two-thirds of current light-frame buildings. For residential buildings, the trusses are generally made using standard 38- by 89-mm (nominal 2- by 4-in.) lumber and metal plate connectors with teeth that are pressed into the pieces that form the joints (TPI 1995).

Joists and rafter systems are found in most buildings constructed prior to 1950. Rafters are generally supported on the top plate of the wall and attached to a ridge board at the roof peak. However, because the rafters slope, they tend to push out the tops of the walls. This is prevented by nailing the rafters to the ceiling joists and nailing the ceiling joists to the top wall plates (Fig. 16–3a).

A valley or hip is formed where two roof sections meet perpendicular to each other. A valley rafter is used to support short-length jack rafters that are nailed to the valley rafter and the ridge board (Fig. 16–3b). In some cases, the roof does not extend to a gable end but is sloped from some point down to the end wall to form a "hip" roof. A hip rafter supports the jack rafters, and the other ends of the jack rafters are attached to the top plates (Fig. 16–3c). In general, the same materials used for wall sheathing and subflooring are used for roof sheathing.

Wood Decks

A popular method of expanding the living area of a home is to build a wood deck adjacent to one of the exterior walls. Decks are made of preservatively treated lumber, which is generally available from the local building supply dealer and, depending upon the complexity, may be built by the "do-it-yourselfer." To ensure long life, acceptable appearance, and structural safety, several important guidelines should be followed. Proper material selection is the first step. Then, proper construction techniques are necessary. Finally, proper maintenance practices are necessary. Detailed recommendations for all these areas are included in *Wood Decks: Materials, Construction, and Finishing* (McDonald and others 1996).

Post-Frame and Pole Buildings

In post-frame and pole buildings, round poles or rectangular posts serve both as the foundation and the principal vertical framing element. This type of construction was known as "pole buildings" but today, with the extensive use of posts, is commonly referred to as "post-frame" construction. For relatively low structures, light wall and roof framing are nailed to poles or posts set at fairly frequent centers, commonly 2.4 to 3.6 m (8 to 12 ft). This type of construction

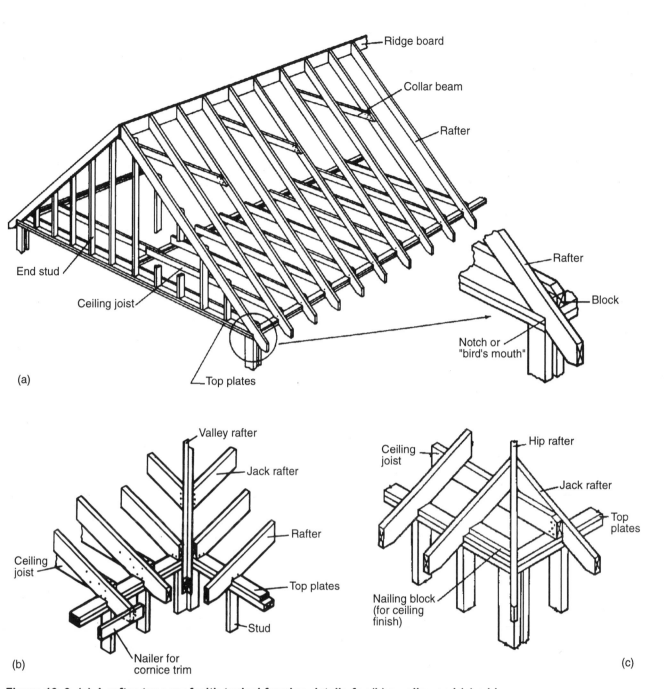

Figure 16–3. (a) A rafter-type roof with typical framing details for (b) a valley and (c) a hip corner.

was originally used with round poles for agricultural buildings, but the structural principle has been extended to commercial and residential buildings (Fig. 16–4).

Round poles present some problems for connecting framing members; these problems can be eased by slabbing the outer face of the pole. For corner poles, two faces may be slabbed at right angles. This permits better attachment of both light and heavy framing by nails or timber connectors. When the pole is left round, the outer face may be notched to provide seats for beams.

Rectangular posts are the most commonly used and may be solid sawn, glulam, or built-up by nail laminating. Built-up posts are advantageous because only the base of the post must be preservatively treated. The treated portion in the ground may have laminations of varying lengths that are matched with the lengths of untreated laminations in the upper part of the post. The design of these types of posts must consider the integrity of the splice between the treated and untreated lumber. The wall system consists of horizontal girts often covered by light-gauge metal that provides some degree of racking resistance.

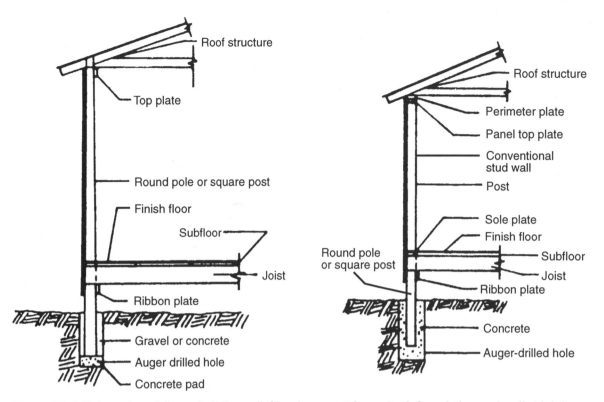

Figure 16–4. Pole and post-frame buildings: (left) pole or post forms both foundation and wall; (right) pole or post forms only the foundation for conventional platform-framed structure.

Roof trusses made with metal plate connectors are attached to each pole, or posts, and roof purlins are installed perpendicular to the trusses at spacings from 1.2 to 3.7 m (4 to 12 ft), with 2.4 m (8 ft) as a common spacing. For 2.4-m (8-ft) truss spacing, these purlins are often standard 38 by 89 mm (nominal 2 by 4 in.) spaced on 0.6-m (2-ft) centers and attached to either the top of the trusses or between the trusses using joists hangers. The roofing is often light-gauge metal that provides some diaphragm stiffness to the roof and transmits a portion of the lateral loading to the walls parallel to the direction of the load. Detailed information on the design of post-frame buildings is given in the *National Frame Builders Association* ([n.d.]) or Walker and Woeste (1992).

Log Buildings

Interest is growing in log houses—from small, simple houses for vacation use to large, permanent residences (Fig. 16–5). Many U.S. firms specialize in the design and material for log houses. Log homes nearly always feature wall systems built from natural or manufactured logs rather than from dimension lumber. Roof and floor systems may be also be built with logs or conventional framing. Log home companies tend to categorize log types into two systems: round and shaped. In the round log system, the logs are machined to a smooth, fully rounded surface, and they are generally all the same diameter. In the shaped system, the logs are machined to specific shapes, generally not fully round. The exterior surfaces of the logs are generally rounded, but the interior surfaces may be either flat or round. The interface between logs is machined to form an interlocking joint.

Consensus standards have been developed for log grading and the assignment of allowable properties, and these standards are being adopted by building codes (ASTM 1996). Builders and designers need to realize that logs can reach the building site at moisture content levels greater than ideal. The effects of seasoning and the consequences of associated shrinkage and checking must be considered. Additional information on log homes is available from The Log Home Council, National Association of Home Builders, Washington, DC.

Heavy Timber Buildings

Timber Frame

Timber frame houses were common in early America and are enjoying some renewed popularity today. Most barns and factory buildings dating prior to the middle of the 20th century were heavy timber frame. The traditional timber frame is made of large sawn timbers (larger than 114 by 114 mm (5 by 5 in.)) connected to one another by hand-fabricated joints, such as mortise and tenon. Construction of such a frame involves rather sophisticated joinery, as illustrated in Figure 16–6.

Figure 16–5. Modern log homes are available in a variety of designs.

In today's timber frame home, a prefabricated, composite sheathing panel (1.2 by 2.4 m (4 by 8 ft)) is frequently applied directly to the frame. This panel may consist of an inside layer of 13-mm (1/2-in.) gypsum, a core layer of rigid foam insulation, and an outside layer of exterior plywood or structural flakeboard. Finish siding is applied over the composite panel. In some cases, a layer of standard 19-mm (nominal 1-in.) tongue-and-groove, solid-wood boards is applied to the frame, and a rigid, foam-exterior, plywood composite panel is then applied over the boards to form the building exterior. Local fire regulations should be consulted about the acceptance of various foam insulations.

Framing members are cut in large cross sections; therefore, seasoning them before installation is difficult, if not impossible. Thus, the builder (and the owner) should recognize the dimensional changes that may occur as the members dry in place. The structure must be designed to accommodate these dimensional changes as well as seasoning checks, which are almost inevitable.

Mill Type

Mill-type construction has been widely used for warehouse and manufacturing structures, particularly in the eastern United States. This type of construction uses timbers of large cross sections with columns spaced in a grid according to the available lengths of beam and girder timbers. The size of the timbers makes this type of construction resistant to fire. The good insulating qualities of wood as well as the char that develops during fire result in slow penetration of fire into the large members. Thus, the members retain a large proportion of their original load-carrying capacity and stiffness for a relatively lengthy period after the onset of fire. Mill-type construction is recognized by some building codes as a 1-h fire-resistant construction, with some limitations.

To be recognized as mill-type construction, the structural elements must meet specific sizes—columns cannot be less than standard 184 mm (nominal 8 in.) in dimension and beams and girders cannot be less than standard 140 by 235 mm (nominal 6 by 10 in.) in cross section. Other limitations must be observed as well. For example, walls must be made of masonry, and concealed spaces must be avoided. The structural frame has typically been constructed of solid-sawn timbers, which should be stress graded. These timbers can now be supplanted with glulam timbers, and longer spans are permitted.

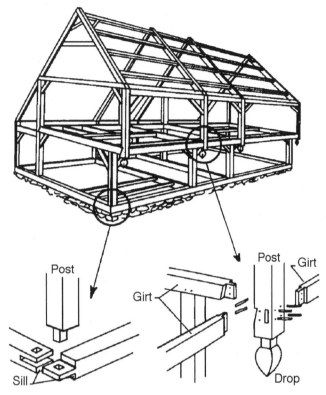

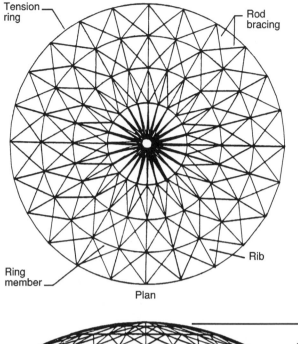

Figure 16–6. Timber frame structure with typical joint details.

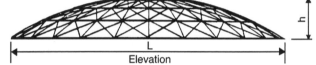

Figure 16–7. Member layout for a radial-rib dome.

Glulam Beam

A panelized roof system using glulam roof framing is widely used for single-story commercial buildings in the southwestern United States. This system is based on supporting columns located at the corners of pre-established grids. The main glulam beams support purlins, which may be sawn timbers, glulam, parallel chord trusses, or prefabricated wood I-joists. These purlins, which are normally on 2.4-m (8-ft) centers, support preframed structural panels. The basic unit of the preframed system is a 1.2- by 2.4-m (4- by 8-ft) structural panel nailed to standard 38- by 89-mm or 38- by 140-mm (nominal 2- by 4-in. or 2- by 6-in.) stiffeners (subpurlins). The stiffeners run parallel to the 2.4-m (8-ft) dimension of the structural panel. One stiffener is located at the centerline of the panel; the other is located at an edge, with the plywood edge at the stiffener centerline. The stiffeners are precut to a length equal to the long dimension of the plywood less the thickness of the purlin, with a small allowance for the hanger.

In some cases, the purlins are erected with the hangers in place. The prefabricated panels are lifted and set into place in the hangers, and the adjoining basic panels are then attached to each other. In other cases, the basic panels are attached to one purlin on the ground. An entire panel is lifted into place to support the loose ends of the stiffeners. This system is fully described in the *Laminated Timber Design Guide* (AITC 1994a).

Arch Structure

Arch structures are particularly suited to applications in which large, unobstructed areas are needed, such as churches, recreational buildings, and aircraft hangars. Many arch forms are possible with the variety limited only by the imagination of the architect. Churches have used arches from the beginning of glulam manufacture in the United States. Additional information on the use and design of arches is given in *The Timber Construction Manual* (AITC 1994b).

Dome

Radial-rib domes consist of curved members extending from the base ring (tension ring) to a compression ring at the top of the dome along with other ring members at various elevations between the tension and compression rings (Fig. 16–7). The ring members may be curved or straight. If they are curved to the same radius as the rib and have their centers at the center of the sphere, the dome will have a spherical surface. If the ring members are straight, the dome will have an umbrella look. Connections between the ribs and the ring members are critical because of the high compressive loads in the ring members. During construction, care must be taken to stabilize the structure because the dome has a tendency to rotate about the central vertical axis.

Other dome patterns called Varax and Triax are also used. Their geometries are quite complex and specialized computer

Figure 16–8. This 161.5-m- (530-ft-) diameter Tacoma dome (Tacoma, Washington), built in 1982–1983, is one of the longest clear roof spans in the world. (Photo courtesy of Western Wood Structures, Inc., Tualatin, Oregon.)

programs are used in their design. Steel hubs used at the joints and supports are critical. An example of a Triax dome is shown in Figure 16–8.

Timber Bridges

Prior to the 20th century, timber was the major material used for both highway and railroad bridges. The development of steel and reinforced concrete provided other options, and these have become major bridge building materials. However, the U.S. inventory does contain a significant number of timber bridges, many of which continue to carry loads beyond their design life. A recent initiative in the United States has focused research and technology transfer efforts on improving the design and performance of timber bridges. As a result, hundreds of timber highway bridges were built across the United States during the 1990s; many using innovative designs and materials.

Bridges consist of a substructure and a superstructure. The substructure consists of abutments, piers, or piling, and it supports the superstructure that consists of stringers and/or a deck. The deck is often covered with a wearing surface of asphalt. Timber may be combined with other materials to form the superstructure, for example, timber deck over steel stringers. Covered bridges, although once popular, are usually not economically feasible. The various types of timber bridge superstructures are described in the following sections. Detailed information on modern timber bridges is given in *Timber Bridges: Design, Construction, Inspection, and Maintenance* (Ritter 1990).

Log Stringer

A simple bridge type that has been used for centuries consists of one or more logs used to span the opening. Several logs may be laid side-by-side and fastened together. The log stringer bridge has been used to access logging areas and is advantageous when adequate-sized logs are available and the bridge is only needed for a short time. Unless built with a durable species, the life span of log stringer bridges is usually limited to less than 10 years.

Sawn Lumber

Several types of bridges can be built with sawn lumber. Even though the span is usually limited to about 9 m (30 ft) because of the limited size of lumber available, this span length entails the majority of bridges in the United States.

Several timbers can be used to span the opening, and a transverse lumber deck can be placed over them to form a stringer and deck bridge. Lumber can be placed side-by-side and used to span the entire opening, forming a longitudinal deck bridge. The lumber can be fastened together with large spikes or held together with tensioned rods to form a "stress-laminated" deck.

Figure 16–9. Glulam beam bridge over the Dangerous River, near Yukatat, Alaska, consists of three 43.5-m (143-ft) spans. Each span is supported by four 2.3-m- (91.5-in.-) deep glulam beams.

Glulam

Structural glued-laminated (glulam) timber greatly extends the span capabilities of the same types of bridges described in the previous paragraph. Glulam stringers placed 0.6 to 1.8 m (2 to 6 ft) on center can support a glulam deck system and result in spans of 12 to 30 m (40 to 100 ft) or more (Fig. 16–9). Using glulam panels to span the opening results in a longitudinal deck system, but this is usually limited to about 9-m (30-ft) spans. These panels are either interconnected or supported at one or more locations with transverse distributor beams. Glulam beams can be used to form a solid deck and are held together with tensioned rods to form a stress-laminated deck. Curved glulam members can be used to produce various aesthetic effects and special types of bridges (Fig. 16–10).

Structural Composite Lumber

Two types of structural composite lumber (SCL)—laminated veneer and oriented strand—are beginning to be used to build timber bridges. Most of the same type of bridges built with either solid sawn or glulam timber can be built with SCL (Ch. 11).

Considerations for Wood Buildings

Many factors must be considered when designing and constructing wood buildings, including structural, insulation, moisture, and sound control. The following sections provide a brief description of the design considerations for these factors. Fire safety, another important consideration, is addressed in Chapter 17.

Structural

The structural design of any building consists of combining the prescribed performance requirements with the anticipated loading. One major performance requirement is that there be an adequate margin of safety between the structures ultimate capacity and the maximum anticipated loading. The probability that the building will ever collapse is minimized using material property information recommended by the material manufacturers along with code-recommended design loads.

Another structural performance requirement relates to serviceability. These requirements are directed at ensuring that the structure is functional, and the most notable one is that

Figure 16–10. Three-hinge glulam deck arch bridge at the Keystone Wye interchange off U.S. Highway 16, near Mount Rushmore, South Dakota. The arch spans 47 m (155 ft) and supports an 8-m- (26-ft-) wide roadway.

deformations are limited. It is important to limit deformations so that floors are not too "bouncy" or that doors do not bind under certain loadings. Building codes often include recommended limits on deformation, but the designer may be provided some latitude in selecting the limits. The basic reference for structural design of wood in all building systems is the *National Design Specification for Wood Construction* (AF&PA 1991).

Thermal Insulation and Air Infiltration Control

For most U.S. climates, the exterior envelope of a building needs to be insulated either to keep heat in the building or prevent heat from entering. Wood frame construction is well-suited to application of both cavity insulation and surface-applied insulation. The most common materials used for cavity insulation are glass fiber, mineral fiber, cellulose insulation, and spray-applied foams. For surface applications, a wide variety of sheathing insulations exist, such as rigid foam panels. Insulating sheathing placed on exterior walls may also have sufficient structural properties to provide required lateral bracing. Prefinished insulating paneling can be used as an inside finish on exterior walls or one or both

sides of the interior partitions. In addition, prefinished insulation can underlay other finishes.

Attic construction with conventional rafters and ceiling joists or roof trusses can be insulated between framing members with batt, blanket, or loose-fill insulation. In some warm climates, radiant barriers and reflective insulations can provide an additional reduction in cooling loads. The "Radiant Barrier Attic Fact Sheet" from the U.S. Department of Energy (1991) provides information on climatic areas that are best suited for radiant barrier applications. This document also provides comparative information on the relative performance of these products and conventional fibrous insulations.

Existing frame construction can be insulated pneumatically using suitable loose-fill insulating material. When loose-fill materials are used in wall retrofit applications, extra care must be taken during the installation to eliminate the existence of voids within the wall cavity. All cavities should be checked prior to installation for obstructions, such as fire stop headers and wiring, that would prevent the cavity from being completely filled. Care must also be taken to install the material at the manufacturer's recommended density to ensure that the desired thermal performance is obtained.

Accessible space can be insulated by manual placement of batt, blanket, or loose-fill material.

In addition to being properly insulated, the exterior envelope of all buildings should be constructed to minimize air flow into or through the building envelope. Air flow can degrade the thermal performance of insulation and cause excessive moisture accumulation in the building envelope.

More information on insulation and air flow retarders can be found in the ASHRAE *Handbook of Fundamentals*, chapters 22 to 24 (ASHRAE 1997).

Moisture Control

Moisture control is necessary to avoid moisture-related problems with building energy performance, building maintenance and durability, and human comfort and health. Moisture degradation is the largest factor limiting the useful life of a building and can be visible or invisible. Invisible degradation includes the degradation of thermal resistance of building materials and the decrease in strength and stiffness of some materials. Visible degradation may be in the form of (a) mold and mildew, (b) decay of wood-based materials, (c) spalling caused by freeze–thaw cycles, (d) hydration of plastic materials, (e) corrosion of metals, (f) damage caused by expansion of materials from moisture (for example, buckling of wood floors), and (g) decline in visual appearance (for example, buckling of wood siding or efflorescence of masonry materials). In addition, high moisture levels can lead to mold spores in indoor air and odors, seriously affecting the occupant's health and comfort. Detailed discussions on the effects of moisture can be found in the ASHRAE *Handbook of Fundamentals,* chapters 22 and 23, (ASHRAE 1997) and Lstiburek and Carmody (1991).

Mold, Mildew, Dust Mites, and Human Health

Mold and mildew in buildings are offensive, and the spores can cause respiratory problems and allergic reactions in humans. Mold and mildew will grow on most surfaces if the relative humidity at the surface is above a critical value and the surface temperatures are conducive to growth. The longer the surface remains above this critical relative humidity level, the more likely mold will appear; the higher the humidity or temperature, the shorter the time needed for germination. The surface relative humidity is a complex function of material moisture content, material properties, local temperature, and humidity conditions. In addition, mold growth depends on the type of surface. Mildew and mold can usually be avoided by limiting surface relative humidity conditions >80% to short periods. Only for nonporous surfaces that are regularly cleaned should this criterion be relaxed. Most molds grow at temperatures approximately above 4°C (40°F). Moisture accumulation at temperatures below 4°C (40°F) may not cause mold and mildew if the material is allowed to dry out below the critical moisture content before the temperature increases above 4°C (40°F).

Dust mites can trigger allergies and are an important cause of asthma. They thrive at high relative humidity levels (>70%)

at room temperature, but will not survive at sustained relative humidity levels less than 50%. However, these relative humidity levels relate to local conditions in the typical places that mites tend to inhabit (for example, mattresses, carpets, soft furniture).

Paint Failure and Other Appearance Problems

Moisture trapped behind paint films may cause failure of the paint (Ch. 15). Water or condensation may also cause streaking or staining. Excessive swings in moisture content of wood-based panels or boards may cause buckling or warp. Excessive moisture in masonry and concrete can produce efflorescence, a white powdery area or lines. When combined with low temperatures, excessive moisture can cause freeze–thaw damage and spalling (chipping).

Structural Failures

Structural failures caused by decay of wood are rare but have occurred. Decay generally requires a wood moisture content equal to or greater than fiber saturation (usually about 30%) and between 10°C (50°F) and 43°C (100°F). Wood moisture content levels above fiber saturation are only possible in green lumber or by absorption of liquid water from condensation, leaks, ground water, or other saturated materials in contact with the wood. To maintain a safety margin, a 20% moisture content is sometimes used during field inspections as the maximum allowable level. Once established, decay fungi produce water that enables them to maintain moisture conditions conducive to their growth. See Chapter 13 for more information on wood decay.

Rusting or corrosion of nails, nail plates, or other metal building products is also a potential cause of structural failure. Corrosion may occur at high relative humidity levels near the metal surface or as a result of liquid water from elsewhere. Wood moisture content levels >20% encourage corrosion of steel fasteners in wood, especially if the wood is treated with preservatives. In buildings, metal fasteners are often the coldest surfaces, which encourages condensation and corrosion of fasteners.

Effect on Heat Flow

Moisture in the building envelope can significantly degrade the thermal performance of most insulation materials but especially the thermal resistance of fibrous insulations and open cell foams. The degradation is most pronounced when daily temperature reversals across the insulation drive moisture back and forth through the insulation.

Moisture Control Strategies

Strategies to control moisture accumulation fall into two general categories: (1) minimize moisture entry into the building envelope and (2) remove moisture from the building envelope. When basic moisture transport mechanisms and specific moisture control practices are understood, roof, wall, and foundation constructions for various climates can be reviewed in a systematic fashion to determine if every potentially significant moisture transport mechanism is explicitly controlled. It is not possible to prevent moisture migration completely; therefore, construction should include drainage, ventilation, and removal by capillary suction, or other provisions to carry away unwanted water.

The major moisture transport mechanisms, in order of importance, are (a) liquid water movement, including capillary movement; (b) water vapor transport by air movement; and (c) water vapor diffusion. In the past, much attention has focused on limiting movement by diffusion with vapor retarders (sometimes called vapor barriers), even though vapor diffusion is the least important of all transport mechanisms. Control of moisture entry should be accomplished in accordance with the importance of the transport mechanism: (a) control of liquid entry by proper site grading and installing gutters and downspouts and appropriate flashing around windows, doors, and chimneys; (b) control of air leakage by installing air flow retarders or careful sealing by taping and caulking; and (c) control of vapor diffusion by placing vapor retarders on the "warm" side of the insulation.

Options for moisture control under heating conditions often differ from those under cooling conditions, even though the physical principles of moisture movement are the same. Which moisture control options apply depends on whether the local climate is predominantly a heating or cooling climate. In heating climates, ventilation with outdoor air and limiting indoor sources of moisture (wet fire wood, unvented dryers, humidifiers) can be effective strategies. In cooling climates, proper dehumidification can provide moisture control. More information on the definition of heating and cooling climates and specific moisture control strategies can be found in the ASHRAE *Handbook of Fundamentals,* chapter 23 (ASHRAE 1997).

Sound Control

An important design consideration for residential and office buildings is the control of sound that either enters the structure from outside or is transmitted from one room to another. Wood frame construction can achieve the levels of sound control equal to or greater than more massive construction, such as concrete. However, to do so requires designing for both airborne and impact noise insulation.

Airborne noise insulation is the resistance to transmission of airborne noises, such as traffic or speech, either through or around an assembly such as a wall. Noises create vibrations on the structural surfaces that they contact, and the design challenge is to prevent this vibration from reaching and leaving the opposite side of the structural surface. Sound transmission class (STC) is the rating used to characterize airborne noise insulation. A wall system with a high STC rating is effective in preventing the transmission of sound. Table 16–1 lists the STC ratings for several types of wall systems; detailed information for both wall and floor are given in FPL–GTR–43 (Rudder 1985).

Impact noise insulation is the resistance to noise generated by footsteps or dropping objects, generally addressed at floor–ceiling assemblies in multi-family dwellings. Impact insulation class (IIC) is the rating used to characterize the impact noise insulation of an assembly. Both the character of the flooring material and the structural details of the floor influence the IIC rating. Additional information on IIC ratings for wood construction is given in FPL–GTR–59 (Sherwood and Moody 1989).

Table 16–1. Sound transmission class (STC) ratings for typical wood-frame walls

STC rating	Privacy afforded	Wall structure
25	Normal speech easily understood	6-mm (1/4-in.) wood panels nailed on each side of standard 38- by 89-mm (nominal 2- by 4-in.) studs.
30	Normal speech audible but not intelligible	9.5-mm (3/8-in.) gypsum wallboard nailed to one side of standard 38- by 89-mm (nominal 2- by 4-in.) studs.
35	Loud speech audible and fairly understandable	20-mm (5/8-in.) gypsum wallboard nailed to both sides of standard 38- by 89-mm (nominal 2- by 4-in.) studs.
40	Loud speech audible but not intelligible	Two layers of 20-mm (5/8-in.) gypsum wallboard nailed to both sides of standard 38- by 89-mm (nominal 2- by 4-in.) studs.
45	Loud speech barely audible	Two sets of standard 38- by 64-mm (nominal 2- by 3-in.) studs staggered 0.2 m (8 in.) on centers fastened by standard 38- by 89-mm (nominal 2- by 4-in.) base and head plates with two layers of 20-mm (5/8-in.) gypsum wallboard nailed on the outer edge of each set of studs.
50	Shouting barely audible	Standard 38- by 89-mm (nominal 2- by 4-in.) wood studs with resilient channels nailed horizontally to both sides with 20-mm (5/8-in.) gypsum wallboard screwed to channels on each side.
55	Shouting not audible	Double row of standard 38- by 89-mm (nominal 2- by 4-in.) studs 0.4 m (16 in.) on centers fastened to separate plates spaced 25 mm (1 in.) apart. Two layers of 20-mm (5/8-in.) gypsum wallboard screwed 0.3 m (12 in.) on center to the studs. An 89-mm- (3.5-in.-) thick sound-attenuation blanket is installed in one stud cavity.

References

AF&PA. 1987. Permanent wood foundation basic requirements. Tech. Rep. 7. Washington, DC: American Forest & Paper Association.

AF&PA. 1991. National design specification for wood construction. Washington, DC: American Forest & Paper Association.

AF&PA. 1993. Span tables for joists and rafters. Washington, DC: American Forest & Paper Association.

AF&PA. 1995. Wood frame construction manual for one- and two-family dwellings, 1995 SBC high wind edition. Washington, DC: American Forest & Paper Association.

AITC. 1994a. Laminated timber design guide. Englewood, CO: American Institute of Timber Construction.

AITC. 1994b. Timber construction manual. American Institute of Timber Construction. New York: John Wiley & Sons, Inc.

APA. 1996. Residential and commercial design/construction guide. E30P, April. Tacoma, WA: APA–The Engineered Wood Association, Tacoma, WA.

ASHRAE. 1997. Handbook of fundamentals. Atlanta, GA: American Society of Heating, Refrigerating and Air-Conditioning Engineers.

ASTM. 1996. Standard methods for establishing stress grades for structural members used in log buildings. ASTM D3957-80. Philadelphia, PA: American Society for Testing and Materials.

Lstiburek, J.; Carmody, J. 1991. The moisture control handbook—new low-rise, residential construction. ORNL/Sub/89-SD350/1. Oak Ridge, TN: Martin Marietta Energy Systems, Inc., Oak Ridge National Laboratory.

McDonald, K.A.; Falk, R.H.; Williams, R.S.; Winandy, J.E. 1996. Wood decks: materials, construction, and finishing. Madison, WI: Forest Products Society.

National Frame Builders Association. [n.d.] Recommended practices for the design and construction of agricultural and commercial post-frame buildings. Lawrence, KS: National Frame Builders Association.

Ritter, M.A. 1990. Timber bridges—design, construction, inspection and maintenance. EM 7700-8. Washington, DC: U.S. Department of Agriculture, Forest Service, Engineering Staff.

Rudder, F.F. Jr. 1985. Airborne sound transmission loss characteristics of wood-frame construction. Gen. Tech. Rep. FPL–GTR–43. Madison, WI: U.S. Department of Agriculture, Forest Service, Forest Products Laboratory.

Sherwood, G.E.; Moody, R.C. 1989. Light-frame wall and floor systems—analysis and performance. Gen. Tech. Rep. FPL–GTR–59. Madison, WI: U.S. Department of Agriculture, Forest Service, Forest Products Laboratory.

Sherwood, G.E.; Stroh, R.C. 1989. Wood frame house construction. Agric. Handb. 73. Washington, DC: U.S. Government Printing Office. (also available from Armonk Press, Armonk, NY).

TPI. 1995. National design standards for metal plate connected wood truss construction. ANSI/TPI–1995. Madison, WI: Truss Plate Institute.

U.S. Department of Energy. 1991. Radiant barrier attic fact sheet. Oak Ridge, TN: Oak Ridge National Laboratory.

Walker, J.N.; Woeste, F.E. 1992. Post-frame building design. ASAE Monograph No. 11, St. Joseph, MI.

Chapter 17

Fire Safety

Robert H. White and Mark A. Dietenberger

Contents

ire safety is an important concern in all types of construction. The high level of national concern for fire safety is reflected in limitations and design requirements in building codes. These code requirements are discussed in the context of fire safety design and evaluation in the initial section of this chapter. Since basic data on fire behavior of wood products are needed to evaluate fire safety for wood construction, the second major section of this chapter covers fire performance characteristics of wood products. The chapter concludes with a discussion of flame-retardant treatments that can be used to reduce the combustibility of wood.

Fire Safety Design and Evaluation

Fire safety involves prevention, containment, detection, and evacuation. Fire prevention basically means preventing the ignition of combustible materials by controlling either the source of heat or the combustible materials. This involves proper design, installation or construction, and maintenance of the building and its contents. Proper fire safety measures depend upon the occupancy or processes taking place in the building. Design deficiencies are often responsible for spread of heat and smoke in a fire. Spread of a fire can be prevented with design methods that limit fire growth and spread within a compartment and with methods that contain fire to the compartment of origin. Egress, or the ability to escape from a fire, often is a critical factor in life safety. Early detection is essential for ensuring adequate time for egress.

Statutory requirements pertaining to fire safety are specified in the building codes or fire codes. These requirements fall into two broad categories: material requirements and building requirements. Material requirements include such things as combustibility, flame spread, and fire endurance. Building requirements include area and height limitations, firestops and draftstops, doors and other exits, automatic sprinklers, and fire detectors.

Adherence to codes will result in improved fire safety. Code officials should be consulted early in the design of a building because the codes offer alternatives. For example, floor areas can be increased if automatic sprinkler systems are added. Code officials have the option to approve alternative materials and methods of construction and to modify provisions of the codes when equivalent fire protection and structural integrity is documented.

Most building codes in the United States are based on model building codes produced by the three building code organizations (Building Officials and Code Administrators International, Inc.; International Conference of Building Officials; and the Southern Building Code Congress International, Inc.). These three organizations are developing a single international building code that will replace the existing three model building codes. In addition to the building codes and the fire codes, the National Fire Protection Association's Life Safety Code provides guidelines for life safety from fire in buildings and structures. As with the model building codes, provisions of the life safety code are statutory requirements when adopted by local or State authorities.

In the following sections, various aspects of the building code provisions pertaining to fire safety of building materials are discussed under the broad categories of (a) types of construction, (b) fire growth within compartment, and (c) containment to compartment of origin. These are largely requirements for materials. Information on prevention and building requirements not related to materials (for example, detection) can be found in publications such as those listed at the end of this chapter. Central aspects of the fire safety provisions of the building codes are the classification of buildings by types of construction and the use or occupancy.

Types of Construction

Based on classifications of building type and occupancy, the codes set limits on the areas and heights of buildings. Major building codes generally recognize five classifications of construction based on types of materials and required fire resistance ratings. The two classifications known as fire-resistant construction (Type I) and noncombustible construction (Type II) basically restrict the construction to noncombustible materials. Wood is permitted to be used more liberally in the other three classifications, which are ordinary (Type III), heavy timber (Type IV), and light-frame (Type V). Heavy timber construction has wood columns, beams, floors, and roofs of certain minimum dimensions. Ordinary construction has smaller wood members used for walls, floors, and roofs including wood studs, wood joists, wood trusses, and wood I-joists. In both heavy timber and ordinary construction, the exterior walls must be of noncombustible materials. In light-frame construction, the walls, floors, and roofs may be of any dimension lumber and the exterior walls may be of combustible materials. Type II, III, and IV constructions are further subdivided based on fire-resistance requirements. Light-frame construction, or Type V, is subdivided into two parts, protected (1-hour) and unprotected.

In protected light-frame construction, most of the structural elements have a 1-hour fire resistance rating. There are no general requirements for fire resistance for buildings of unprotected light-frame construction.

Based on their performance in the American Society for Testing and Materials (ASTM) E136 test, both untreated and fire-retardant-treated wood are combustible materials. However, the building codes permit substitution of fire-retardant-treated wood for noncombustible materials in some specific applications otherwise limited to noncombustible materials.

In addition to the type of construction, the height and area limitations also depend on the use or occupancy of a structure. Fire safety is improved by automatic sprinklers, property line setbacks, or more fire-resistant construction. Building codes recognize the improved fire safety resulting from application of these factors by increasing the allowable areas and heights beyond that designated for a particular type of construction and occupancy. Thus, proper site planning and building design may result in a desired building area classification being achieved with wood construction.

Fire Growth Within Compartment

A second major set of provisions in the building codes are those that regulate the exposed interior surface of walls and ceilings (that is, the interior finish). Codes typically exclude trim and incidental finish, as well as decorations and furnishings that are not affixed to the structure, from the more rigid requirements for walls and ceilings. For regulatory purposes, interior finish materials are classified according to their flame spread index. Thus, flame spread is one of the most tested fire performance properties of a material. Numerous flame spread tests are used, but the one cited by building codes is ASTM E84, the "25-ft tunnel" test. In this test method, the 508-mm-wide, 7.32-m-long specimen completes the top of the tunnel furnace. Flames from a burner at one end of the tunnel provide the fire exposure, which includes forced draft conditions. The furnace operator records the flame front position as a function of time and the time of maximum flame front travel during a 10-min period. The standard prescribes a formula to convert these data to a flame spread index (FSI), which is a measure of the overall rate of flame spreading in the direction of air flow. In the codes, the classes for flame spread index are I (FSI of 0 to 25), II (FSI of 26 to 75), and III (FSI of 76 to 200). Some codes use A, B, and C instead of I, II, and III. Generally, codes specify FSI for interior finish based on building occupancy, location within the building, and availability of automatic sprinkler protection. The more restrictive classes, Classes I and II, are generally prescribed for stairways and corridors that provide access to exits. In general, the more flammable classification (Class III) is permitted for the interior finish of other areas of the building that are not considered exit ways or where the area in question is protected by automatic sprinklers. In other areas, there are no flammability restrictions on the interior finish and unclassified materials (that is, more than 200 FSI) can be used.

Table 17–1. ASTM E84 flame spread indexes for 19-mm-thick solid lumber of various wood species as reported in the literature

Species[a]	Flame spread index[b]	Smoke developed index[b]	Source[c]
Softwoods			
Yellow-cedar (Pacific Coast yellow cedar)	78	90	CWC
Baldcypress (cypress)	145–150	—	UL
Douglas-fir	70–100	—	UL
Fir, Pacific silver	69	58	CWC
Hemlock, western (West Coast)	60–75	—	UL
Pine, eastern white (eastern white, northern white)	85, 120–215[d]	122, —	CWC, UL
Pine, lodgepole	93	210	CWC
Pine, ponderosa	105–230[d]	—	UL
Pine, red	142	229	CWC
Pine, Southern (southern)	130–195	—	UL
Pine, western white	75[e]	—	UL
Redcedar, western	70	213	HPVA
Redwood	70	—	UL
Spruce, eastern (northern, white)	65	—	UL, CWC
Spruce, Sitka (western, Sitka)	100, 74	—, 74	UL, CWC
Hardwoods			
Birch, yellow	105–110	—	UL
Cottonwood	115	—	UL
Maple (maple flooring)	104	—	CWC
Oak (red, white)	100	100	UL
Sweetgum (gum, red)	140–155	—	UL
Walnut	130–140	—	UL
Yellow-poplar (poplar)	170–185	—	UL

[a]In cases where the name given in the source did not conform to the official nomenclature of the Forest Service, the probable official nomenclature name is given and the name given by the source is given in parentheses.

[b]Data are as reported in the literature (dash where data do not exist). Changes in the ASTM E84 test method have occurred over the years. However, data indicate that the changes have not significantly changed earlier data reported in this table. The change in the calculation procedure has usually resulted in slightly lower flame spread results for untreated wood. Smoke developed index is not known to exceed 450, the limiting value often cited in the building codes.

[c]CWC, Canadian Wood Council (CWC 1996); HPVA, Hardwood Plywood Manufacturers Association (Tests) (now Hardwood Plywood & Veneer Assoc.); UL, Underwriters Laboratories, Inc. (Wood-fire hazard classification. Card Data Service, Serial No. UL 527, 1971).

[d]Footnote of UL: In 18 tests of ponderosa pine, three had values over 200 and the average of all tests is 154.

[e]Footnote of UL: Due to wide variations in the different species of the pine family and local connotations of their popular names, exact identification of the types of pine tested was not possible. The effects of differing climatic and soil conditions on the burning characteristics of given species have not been determined.

The FSI for most domestic wood species is between 90 and 160 (Table 17–1). Thus, unfinished lumber, 10 mm or thicker, is generally acceptable for interior finish applications requiring a Class III rating. Flame-retardant treatments are usually necessary when a Class I or II flame spread index is required for a wood product. A few domestic softwood species can meet the Class II flame spread index and only require flame-retardant treatments to meet a Class I rating. A few imported species have reported FSIs of less than 25.

Additional FSI for many solid-sawn and panel products are provided in the American Forest and Paper Association's (AF&PA) design for code acceptance (DCA) No. 1, "Flame Spread Performance of Wood Products" (AWC 1999).

There are many other test methods for flame spread or flammability. Most are used only for research and development or quality control, but some are used in product specifications and regulations of materials in a variety of applications.

Since the fire exposure is on the underside of a horizontal specimen in the ASTM E84 test, it is not suitable for materials that melt and drip or are not self-supporting. Code provisions pertaining to floors and floor coverings may be based on another test criterion, the critical radiant flux test (ASTM E648, Critical Radiant Flux of Floor-Covering Systems Using a Radiant Heat Energy Source). The critical radiant flux apparatus is also used to test the flammability of cellulosic insulation (ASTM E970, Critical Radiant Flux of Exposed Attic Floor Insulation Using a Radiant Heat Energy Source). In the critical radiant flux test, the placement of the radiant panel is such that the radiant heat being imposed on the surface has a gradient in intensity down the length of the horizontal specimen. Flames spread from the ignition source at the end of high heat flux (or intensity) to the other end until they reach a location where the heat flux is not sufficient for further propagation. This is reported as the critical radiant flux. Thus, low critical radiant flux reflects materials with high flammability. Typical requirements are for a minimum critical radiant flux level of 2.2 or 4.5 kW/m^2 depending on location and occupancy. Data in the literature indicate that oak flooring has a critical radiant flux of 3.5 kW/m^2 (Benjamin and Adams 1976).

There is also a smoldering combustion test for cellulosic insulation. Cellulosic insulation is regulated by a product safety standard of the U.S. Consumer Product Safety Commission (Interim Safety Standard for Cellulosic Insulation: Cellulosic Insulation Labeling and Requirements, 44FR 39938, 16CFR Part 1209, 1979; also Gen. Serv. Admin. Spec. HH–I–515d). Proper chemical treatments of cellulosic insulation are required to reduce its tendency for smoldering combustion and to reduce flame spread. Proper installation around recessed light fixtures and other electrical devices is necessary.

Other tests for flammability include those that measure heat release. Other flammability tests and fire growth modeling are discussed in the Fire Performance Characteristics of Wood section.

Rated roof covering materials are designated either Class A, B, or C according to their performance in the tests described in ASTM E108, Fire Tests of Roof Coverings. This test standard includes intermittent flame exposure, spread of flame, burning brand, flying brand, and rain tests. There is a different version of the pass/fail test for each of the three classes. Class A test is the most severe and Class C the least. In the case of the burning brand tests, the brand for the Class B test is larger than that for the Class C test. Leach-resistant fire-retardant-treated shingles are available that carry a Class B or C fire rating.

Information on ratings for different products can be obtained from industry literature, evaluation reports issued by the model code organizations, and listings published by testing laboratories or quality assurance agencies. Products listed by Underwriters Laboratories, Inc., and other such organizations are stamped with the rating information.

Flashover

With sufficient heat generation, the initial growth of a fire in a compartment leads to the condition known as flashover. The visual criteria for flashover are full involvement of the compartment and flames out the door or window. The intensity over time of a fire starting in one room or compartment of a building depends on the amount and distribution of combustible contents in the room and the amount of ventilation.

The standard full-scale test for pre-flashover fire growth is the room/corner test (International Organization for Standardization (ISO) 9705, Fire Tests—Full-Scale Room Test for Surface Products). In this test, a gas burner is placed in the corner of the room, which has a single door for ventilation. Three of the walls are lined with the test material, and the ceiling may also be lined with the test material. Other room/corner tests use a wood crib or similar item as the ignition source. Such a room/corner test is used to regulate foam plastic insulation, a material that is not properly evaluated in the ASTM E84 test.

Observations are made of the growth of the fire and the duration of the test until flashover occurs. Instruments record the heat generation, temperature development within the room, and the heat flux to the floor. Results of full-scale room/corner tests are used to validate fire growth models and bench-scale test results. Fire endurance tests evaluate the relative performance of the assemblies during a post-flashover fire.

Containment to Compartment of Origin

The growth, intensity, and duration of the fire is the "load" that determines whether a fire is confined to the room of origin. Whether a given fire will be contained to the compartment depends on the fire resistance of the walls, doors, ceilings, and floors of the compartment. Requirements for fire resistance or fire endurance ratings of structural members and assemblies are another major component of the building code provisions. Fire resistance is the ability of materials or their assemblies to prevent or retard the passage of excessive heat, hot gases, or flames while continuing to support their structural loads. Fire-resistance ratings are usually obtained by conducting standard fire tests. In the standard fire-resistance test (ASTM E119), there are three failure criteria: element collapse, passage of flames, or excessive temperature rise on the non-fire-exposed surface (average increase of several locations exceeding 139°C or 181°C at a single location).

The self-insulating qualities of wood, particularly in the large wood sections of heavy timber construction, are an important factor in providing a degree of fire resistance. In Type IV or heavy timber construction, the need for fire-resistance requirements is achieved in the codes by specifying minimum sizes for the various members or portions of a building and other prescriptive requirements. In this type of construction, the wood members are not required to have specific fire-resistance ratings. The acceptance of heavy timber construction is based on historical experience with its performance in actual fires. Proper heavy timber construction includes using approved fastenings, avoiding concealed spaces under floors or roofs, and providing required fire resistance in the interior and exterior walls.

In recent years, the availability and code acceptance of a procedure to calculate the fire-resistance ratings for large timber beams and columns have allowed their use in fire-rated buildings not classified as heavy timber construction (Type IV). In the other types of construction, the structural members and assemblies are required to have specified fire-resistance ratings. Details on the procedure for large timbers can be found in American Institute of Timber Construction (AITC) Technical Note 7 and the AF&PA DCA #2 "Design of Fire-Resistive Exposed Wood Members" (AWC 1985).

The fire resistance of glued-laminated structural members, such as arches, beams, and columns, is approximately equivalent to the fire resistance of solid members of similar size. Available information indicates that laminated members glued with phenol, resorcinol, or melamine adhesives are at least equal in their fire resistance to a one-piece member of the same size. Laminated members glued with casein have only slightly less fire resistance.

Light-frame wood construction can provide a high degree of fire containment through use of gypsum board as the interior finish. This effective protective membrane provides the initial fire resistance rating. Many recognized assemblies involving wood-frame walls, floors, and roofs provide a 1- or 2-hour fire resistance rating. Fire-rated gypsum board (Type X or C) is used in rated assemblies. Type X and the higher grade Type C gypsum boards have textile glass filaments and other ingredients that help to keep the gypsum core intact during a fire. Fire-resistance ratings of various assemblies are listed in the model codes and other publications such as the *Fire Resistance Design Manual* (Gypsum Association). Traditional constructions of regular gypsum wallboard (that is, not fire rated) or lath and plaster over wood joists and studs have fire-resistance ratings of 15 to 30 min.

While fire-resistance ratings are for the entire wall, floor, or roof assembly, the fire resistance of a wall or floor can be viewed as the sum of the resistance of the interior finish and the resistance of the framing members. In a code-accepted procedure, the fire rating of a light-frame assembly is calculated by adding the tabulated times for the fire-exposed membrane to the tabulated times for the framing. For example, the fire-resistance rating of a wood stud wall with 16-mm-thick Type X gypsum board and rock wool insulation is computed by adding the 20 min listed for the stud wall, the 40 min listed for the gypsum board, and the 15 min listed for the rock wool insulation to obtain a rating for the assembly of 75 min. Additional information on this component additive method (CAM) can be found in the AF&PA DCA No. 4 "Component Additive Method (CAM) for Calculating and Demonstrating Assembly Fire Endurance" (AWC 1991). More sophisticated mechanistic models are being developed.

The relatively good structural behavior of a traditional wood member in a fire test results from the fact that its strength is generally uniform through the mass of the piece. Thus, the unburned fraction of the member retains high strength, and its load-carrying capacity is diminished only in proportion to its loss of cross section. Innovative designs for structural wood members may reduce the mass of the member and locate the principal load-carrying components at the outer edges where they are most vulnerable to fire, as in structural sandwich panels. With high strength facings attached to a low-strength core, unprotected load-bearing sandwich panels have failed to support their load in less than 6 min when tested in the standard test. If a sandwich panel is to be used as a load-bearing assembly, it should be protected with gypsum wallboard or some other thermal barrier. In any protected assembly, the performance of the protective membrane is the critical factor in the performance of the assembly.

Unprotected light-frame wood buildings do not have the natural fire resistance achieved with heavier wood members. In these, as in all buildings, attention to good construction details is important to minimize fire hazards. Quality of workmanship is important in achieving adequate fire resistance. Inadequate nailing and less than required thickness of the interior finish can reduce the fire resistance of an assembly. The method of fastening the interior finish to the framing members and the treatment of the joints are significant factors in the fire resistance of an assembly. The type and quantity of any insulation installed within the assembly may also affect the fire resistance of an assembly. Electrical receptacle outlets, pipe chases, and other through openings that are not adequately firestopped can affect the fire resistance. In addition to the design of walls, ceilings, floors, and roofs for fire resistance, stairways, doors, and firestops are of particular importance.

Fires in buildings can spread by the movement of hot fire gases through open channels in concealed spaces. Codes specify where firestops and draftstops are required in concealed spaces, and they must be designed to interfere with the passage of flames up or across a building. In addition to going along halls, stairways, and other large spaces, heated gases also follow the concealed spaces between floor joists and between studs in partitions and walls of frame construction. Obstruction of these hidden channels provides an effective means of restricting fire from spreading to other parts of the structure. Firestops are materials used to block off relatively small openings passing through building components such as floors and walls. Draftstops are barriers in larger concealed spaces such as those found within wood joist floor assemblies with suspended dropped ceilings or within an attic space with pitched chord trusses.

Doors can be critical in preventing the spread of fires. Doors left open or doors with little fire resistance can easily defeat the purpose of a fire-rated wall or partition. Listings of fire-rated doors, frames, and accessories are provided by various fire testing agencies. When a fire-rated door is selected, details about which type of door, mounting, hardware, and closing mechanism need to be considered.

Fire Safety Engineering

The field of fire safety engineering is undergoing rapid changes because of the development of more engineering and scientific approaches to fire safety. This development is evidenced by the publication of *The Society of Fire Protection Engineers Handbook of Fire Protection Engineering* and formation of fire safety engineering subcommittees in ISO and ASTM. Steady advances are being made in the fields of fire dynamics, fire hazard calculations, fire design calculations, and fire risk analysis. Such efforts support the worldwide trend to develop alternative building codes based on performance criteria rather than prescriptive requirements. Additional information on fire protection can be found in the various publications of the National Fire Protection Association (NFPA).

Fire Performance Characteristics of Wood

Wood will burn when exposed to heat and air. Thermal degradation of wood occurs in stages. The degradation process and the exact products of thermal degradation depend upon the rate of heating as well as the temperatures. The sequence of events for wood combustion is as follows:

- The wood, responding to heating, decomposes or pyrolyzes into volatiles and char. Char is the dominant product at internal temperatures less than 300°C, whereas volatiles become much more pronounced above 300°C.

- The volatiles, some of which are flammable, can be ignited if the volatile–air mixture is of the right composition in a temperature range of about 400°C to 500°C within the mixture. This gas-phase combustion appears as flames.

- With air ventilation, the char oxidation becomes significant around 200°C with two peaks in intensity reported at 360°C and 520°C. This char oxidation is seen as glowing or smoldering combustion until only ash residue remains. This solid-phase combustion will not proceed if flaming combustion prevents a supply of fresh air to the char surfaces.

Several characteristics are used to quantify this burning behavior of wood, including ignition from heat sources, growing rate of heat release leading to room flashover, flame spread in heated environments, smoke and toxic gases, flashover, and charring rates in a contained room.

Ignition

Ignition of wood takes place when wood is subject to sufficient heat and in atmospheres that have sufficient oxygen. Ignition can be of two types: piloted or unpiloted. Piloted ignition occurs in the presence of an ignition source (such as a spark or a flame). Unpiloted ignition is ignition that occurs where no pilot source is available. The wood surface is ignited by the flow of energy or heat flux from a fire or other heated objects. This flow of energy or heat flux can have both convective and radiative components.

Piloted ignition above a single flat surface has recently been studied in some depth because of the advent of fire growth research. The surface temperature of wood materials has been measured somewhere between 300°C to 400°C prior to piloted ignition. Surface temperature at ignition is an illusive quantity that is experimentally difficult to obtain. Equipment such as the Ohio State University (OSU) apparatus (ASTM E906), the cone calorimeter (ASTM 1354), and the lateral ignition and flame spread test (LIFT) apparatus (ASTM 1321) are used to obtain data on time to piloted ignition as a function of heater irradiance. Table 17–2 indicates the decrease in time to ignition with the increase in imposed heat flux for different species of wood measured with the OSU apparatus. Similar, perhaps identical, materials have been tested recently in cone calorimeter and LIFT apparatuses with somewhat similar results. From such tests, values of ignition temperature, critical ignition flux (heat flux below which ignition would not occur), and thermophysical properties have been derived using a transient heat conduction theory. These properties are also material dependent; they depend heavily on density of the material and moisture content. A range of wood products tested have ignition surface temperatures of 300°C to 400°C and a critical ignition flux of between 10 and 13 kW/m^2 in the cone calorimeter. The ignition surface temperature is lower for low density woods. Estimates of piloted ignition in various scenarios can be obtained using the derived thermal properties and an applicable heat conduction model.

Some, typically old, apparatuses for testing piloted ignition measured the temperature of the air flow rather than the imposed heat flux with the time to ignition measurement. These results were often reported as the ignition temperature and as varying with time to ignition, which is misleading. When the imposed heat flux is due to a radiant source, such reported air flow ignition temperature can be as much as 100°C lower than the ignition surface temperature. For a proper heat conduction analysis in deriving thermal properties, measurements of the radiant source flux and air flow rate are also required. Since imposed heat flux to the surface and the surface ignition temperature are the factors that directly determine ignition, some data of piloted ignition are inadequate or misleading.

Unpiloted ignition depends on special circumstances that result in different ranges of ignition temperatures. At this time, it is not possible to give specific ignition data that apply to a broad range of cases. For radiant heating of cellulosic solids, unpiloted transient ignition has been reported at 600°C. With convective heating of wood, unpiloted ignition has been reported as low as 270°C and as high as 470°C.

Unpiloted spontaneous ignition can occur when a heat source within the wood product is located such that the heat is not readily dissipated. This kind of ignition involves smoldering and generally occurs over a longer period of time. Smoldering is thermal degradation that proceeds without flames or

Table 17–2. Flammability data for selected wood species

Species	Density[a] (kg/m³)	Ignition time[b] (s)		Higher heating value[c] (MJ/kg)	Effective heat of combustion[d] (MJ/kg)		Average heat release rate[b] (kW/m²)	
		18-kW/m² heat flux	55-kW/m² heat flux		18-kW/m² heat flux	55-kW/m² heat flux	18-kW/m² heat flux	55-kW/m² heat flux
Softwoods								
Pine, Southern	508	740	5	20.5	9.1	13.9	40.4	119.6
Redwood	312	741	3	21.1	10.7	14.2	39.0	85.9
Hardwoods								
Basswood	312	183	5	20.0	10.9	12.2	52.8	113.0
Oak, red	660	930	13	19.8	9.0	11.7	48.7	113.3

[a]Based on weight and volume of ovendried wood.
[b]Ignition times, effective heat of combustion, and average rate of heat release (HRR) obtained using an ASTM E906 heat release apparatus modified to measured heat release using oxygen consumption method. Test durations were 50 to 98 min for 18-kW/m² heat flux and 30 to 53 min for 55-kW/m² heat flux. Test was terminated prior to the usual increase in HRR to a second peak as the specimen is consumed.
[c]From oxygen bomb calorimeter test.
[d]Apparent effective heat of combustion based on average HRR and mass loss rate, which includes the moisture driven from the wood. See footnote b.

visible glowing. Examples of such fires are (a) panels or paper removed from the press or dryer and stacked in large piles without adequate cooling and (b) very large piles of chips or sawdust with internal exothermic reactions such as biological activities. Potential mechanisms of internal heat generation include respiration, metabolism of microorganisms, heat of pyrolysis, abiotic oxidation, and adsorptive heat. These mechanisms, often in combination, may proceed to smoldering or flaming ignition through a thermal runaway effect within the pile if sufficient heat is generated and is not dissipated. The minimum environmental temperature to achieve ignition is called the self-accelerating decomposition temperature and includes the effects of specimen mass and air ventilation.

Unpiloted ignitions that involve wood exposed to low level external heat sources over very long periods is an area of dispute. This kind of ignition, which involves considerable charring, does appear to occur, based on fire investigations. However, these circumstances do not lend themselves easily to experimentation and observation. There is some evidence that the char produced under low heating temperatures can have a different chemical composition, which results in a somewhat lower ignition temperature than normally recorded. Thus, a major issue is the question of safe working temperature for wood exposed for long periods. Temperatures between 80°C to 100°C have been recommended as safe surface temperatures for wood. Since thermal degradation is a prerequisite for ignition of the char layer, conservative criteria for determining safe working temperatures can be the temperature and duration needed for thermal degradation. Schaffer (1980) used a residual weight criterion of 40% of the initial weight to suggest that wood can safely be heated to 150°C for a year or more before satisfying this conservative predictor of heating time to reach an incipient smoldering state.

Building codes do not generally regulate building materials on the basis of ignition or ignitability. As a result, general fire safety design criteria have not been developed. Rather, this subject is considered in conjunction with limits on combustibility and flame spread.

Heat Release

Heat release rates are important because they indicate the potential fire hazard of a material and also the combustibility of a material. Materials that release their potential chemical energy (and also the smoke and toxic gases) relatively quickly are more hazardous than those that release it more slowly. There are materials that will not pass the current definition of noncombustible in the model codes but will release only limited amounts of heat during the initial and critical periods of fire exposure. There is also some criticism of using limited flammability to partially define noncombustibility. One early attempt was to define combustibility in terms of heat release in a potential heat method (NFPA 259), with the low levels used to define low combustibility or noncombustibility. This test method is being used to regulate materials under some codes. The ground-up wood sample in this method is completely consumed during the exposure to 750°C for 2 h, which makes the potential heat for wood identical to the gross heat of combustion from the oxygen bomb calorimeter (the higher heating value in Table 17–2). The typical gross heat of combustion averaged around 20 MJ/kg for ovendried wood, depending on the lignin and extractive content of the wood.

A better or a supplementary measure of degrees of combustibility is a determination of the rate of heat release (RHR) or heat release rate (HRR). This measurement efficiently assesses the relative heat contribution of materials—thick, thin, untreated, or treated—under fire exposure. The cone calorimeter (ASTM E1354) is the most commonly used bench-scale HRR apparatus and is based on the oxygen consumption method. An average value of 13.1 kJ/g of oxygen consumed was the constant found for organic solids and is accurate with very few exceptions to within 5%. Thus, it is sufficient to measure the mass flow rate of oxygen consumed in a combustion system to determine the net HRR. The procedure known as ASTM E906 (the OSU apparatus) is a well-known and widely used calorimeter based on measurements of heat content of incoming and exiting air flow through the apparatus. Because of the errors caused by the heat losses and the fact that the mass flow rate is controlled in the OSU apparatus, several researchers have modified it to the oxygen consumption method. These bench-scale apparatuses use a radiant source to provide the external heat exposure to the test specimen. The imposed heat flux is kept constant at a specified heat flux level. The intermediate-scale apparatus (ASTM E1623) for testing 1- by 1-m assemblies or composites and the room full-scale test (ISO 9705) also use the oxygen consumption technique to measure the HRR of fires at larger scales.

The cone calorimeter is ideal for product development with its small specimen size of 100 by 100 mm. The specimen is continuously weighed by use of a load cell. In conjunction with HRR measurements, the effective heat of combustion as a function of time is calculated by the ASTM E1354 method. Basically, the effective heat of combustion is the HRR divided by the mass loss rate as determined from the cone calorimeter test as a function of time. A typical HRR profile as shown in Figure 17–1 for plywood begins with a sharp peak upon ignition, and as the surface chars, the HRR drops to some minimum value. After the thermal wave travels completely through the wood thickness, the back side of a wood sample reaches pyrolysis temperature, thus giving rise to a second, broader, and even higher HRR peak. For fire-retardant-treated wood products, the first HRR peak may be reduced or eliminated. Table 17–3 provides the peak and

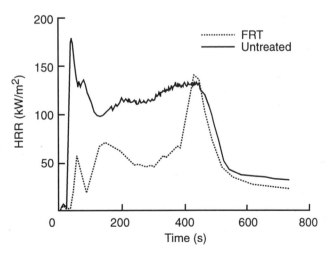

Figure 17–1. Heat release curves for untreated and FRT plywood exposed to 50-kW/m² radiance.

averaged HRR at 1-, 3-, and 5-min periods for various wood species.

Heat release rate depends upon the intensity of the imposed heat flux. Table 17–2 provides the average effective heat of combustion and average HRR for four wood species and two levels of heat flux (18 and 55 kW/m²). These results were obtained in an OSU apparatus modified by the Forest Products Laboratory (FPL). Similar values were also obtained in the cone calorimeter (Table 17–3). Generally, the averaged effective heat of combustion is about 65% of the oxygen bomb heat of combustion (higher heating value) with a small linear increase with irradiance. The HRR itself has a large linear increase with the heat flux. Data indicate that HRRs decrease with increasing moisture content of the sample and are markedly reduced by fire-retardant treatment (Fig. 17–1).

Flame Spread

The spread of flames over solids is a very important phenomenon in the growth of compartment fires. Indeed, in fires where large fuel surfaces are involved, the increase in HRR with time is primarily due to the increase in burning area. Many data have been acquired with the flame spread tests used in building codes. Table 17–1 lists the FSI and smoke index of ASTM E84 for solid wood. Some consistencies in the FSI behavior of the hardwood species can be related to their density. Considerable variations are found for wood-based composites; for example, the FSI of four structural flakeboards ranged from 71 to 189.

As a prescriptive regulation, the ASTM E84 tunnel test is a success in the reduction of fire hazards but is impractical in providing scientific data for fire modeling or in useful bench-scale tests for product development. Other full-scale tests (such as the ISO 9705 room/corner test) also use both an ignition burner and the ensuing flame spread to assist flow but can produce quite different results because of the size of the ignition burner or the test geometry. This is the case with foam plastic panels that melt and drip during a fire test. In the tunnel test, with the test material on top, a material that melts can have low flammability since the specimen does not stay in place. With an adequate burner in the room/corner test, the same material will exhibit very high flammability.

A flame spreads over a solid material when part of the fuel, ahead of the pyrolysis front, is heated to the critical condition of ignition. The rate of flame spread is controlled by how rapidly the fuel reaches the ignition temperature in response to heating by the flame front and external sources. The material's thermal conductivity, heat capacitance, thickness, and blackbody surface reflectivity influence the material's thermal response, and an increase in the values of these properties corresponds to a decrease in flame spread rate. On the other hand, an increase in values of the flame features, such as the imposed surface fluxes and spatial lengths, corresponds to a increase in the flame spread rate.

Table 17–3. Heat release data for selected wood species[a]

Species	Density[b] (kg/m³)	Heat release rate (kW/m²)				Average effective heat of combustion[c] (MJ/kg)	Ignition time (s)
		Peak	60-s avg	180-s avg	300-s avg		
Softwoods							
Pine, red	525	209	163	143	132	12.9	24
Pine, white	359	209	150	117	103	13.6	17
Redcedar, eastern	—	175	92	95	85	11.7	25
Redwood	408	227	118	105	95	13.2	17
Hardwoods							
Birch	618	218	117	150	141	12.2	29
Maple, hard	626	218	128	146	137	11.7	31
Oak, red	593	214	115	140	129	11.4	28

[a]Data for 50-kW/m² heat flux in cone calorimeter. Tested in specimen holder without retaining frame. Specimens conditioned to 23°C, 50% relative humidity.
[b]Ovendry mass and volume.
[c]Tests terminated when average mass loss rate dropped below 1.5 g/s m² during 1-min period.

Flame spread occurs in different configurations, which are organized by orientation of the fuel and direction of the main flow of gases relative to that of flame spread. Downward and lateral creeping flame spread involves a fuel orientation with buoyantly heated air flowing opposite of the flame spread direction. Related bench-scale test methods are ASTM E162 for downward flame spread, ASTM E648 for horizontal flame spread to the critical flux level, and ASTM E1321 (LIFT apparatus) for lateral flame spread on vertical specimen to the critical flux level. The heat transfer from the flame to the virgin fuel is primarily conductive within a spatial extent of a few millimeters and is affected by ambient conditions such as oxygen, pressure, buoyancy, and external irradiance. For most wood materials, this heat transfer from the flame is less than or equal to surface radiant heat loss in normal ambient conditions, so that excess heat is not available to further raise the virgin fuel temperature; flame spread is prevented as a result. Therefore, to achieve creeping flame spread, an external heat source is required in the vicinity of the pyrolysis front.

Upward or ceiling flame spread involves a fuel orientation with the main air flowing in the same direction as the flame spread (assisting flow). At present, there are no small-scale tests for upward flame spread potential. Thus, testing of flame spread in assisting flow exists mostly in both the tunnel tests and the room/corner burn tests. The heat transfer from the flame is both conductive and radiative, has a large spatial feature, and is relatively unaffected by ambient conditions. Rapid acceleration in flame spread can develop because of a large, increasing magnitude of flame heat transfer as a result of increasing total HRR in assisting flows. These complexities and the importance of the flame spread processes explain the many and often incompatible flame spread tests and models in existence worldwide.

Smoke and Toxic Gases

One of the most important problems associated with fires is the smoke they produce. The term smoke is frequently used in an all-inclusive sense to mean the mixture of pyrolysis products and air that is present near the fire site. In this context, smoke contains gases, solid particles, and droplets of liquid. Smoke presents potential hazards because it interacts with light to obscure vision and because it contains noxious and toxic substances.

Generally, two approaches are used to deal with the smoke problem: limit smoke production and control the smoke that has been produced. The control of smoke flow is most often a factor in the design and construction of large or tall buildings. In these buildings, combustion products may have serious effects in areas remote from the actual fire site.

Currently, several bench-scale test methods provide comparative smoke yield information on materials and assemblies. Each method has entirely different exposure conditions; none is generally correlated to full-scale fire conditions or experience. Until the middle 1970s, smoke yield restrictions in building codes were almost always based on data from ASTM E84. The smoke measurement is based on a percentage attenuation of white light passing through the tunnel exhaust stream and detected by a photocell. This is converted to the smoke development index (SDI), with red oak flooring set at 100. The flame spread requirements for interior finish generally are linked to an added requirement that the SDI be less than 450.

In the 1970s, the apparatus known as the NBS smoke chamber was developed and approved as an ASTM standard for research and development (ASTM E662). This test is a static smoke test because the specimen is tested in a closed chamber of fixed volume and the light attenuation is recorded over a known optical path length. The corresponding light transmission is reported as specific optical density as a function of time. Samples are normally tested in both flaming (pilot flame) and nonflaming conditions using a radiant flux of 25 kW/m^2.

The dynamic measurement of smoke in the heat release calorimeter (ASTM E906 and E1354) has recently gained increasing recognition and use. The E906 and E1354 tests are dynamic in that the smoke continuously flows out the exhaust pipe where the optical density is measured continuously. The appropriate smoke parameter is the smoke release rate (SRR), which is the optical density multiplied by the volume flow rate of air into the exhaust pipe and divided by the product of exposed surface area of the specimen and the light path length. Often the smoke extinction area, which is the product of SRR and the specimen area, is preferred because it can be correlated linearly with HRR in many cases. This also permits comparison with the smoke measured in the room/corner fire test because HRR is a readily available test result. Although SRR can be integrated with time to get the same units as the specific optical density, they are not equivalent because static tests involve the direct accumulation of smoke in a volume, whereas SRR involves accumulation of freshly entrained air volume flow for each unit of smoke. Methods investigated to correlate smoke between different tests included alternative parameters such as particulate mass emitted per area of exposed sample.

Toxicity of combustion products is an area of concern. About 75% to 80% of fire victims are not touched by flame but die as a result of exposure to smoke, exposure to toxic gases, or oxygen depletion. These life-threatening conditions can result from burning contents, such as furnishings, as well as from the structural materials involved. The toxicity resulting from the thermal decomposition of wood and cellulosic substances is complex because of the wide variety of types of wood smoke. The composition and the concentration of the individual constituents depend on such factors as the fire exposure, the oxygen and moisture present, the species of wood, any treatments or finishes that may have been applied, and other considerations. Toxicity data may be more widely available in the future with the recent adoption of a standard test method (ASTM E1678).

Carbon monoxide is a particularly insidious toxic gas. Small amounts of carbon monoxide are particularly toxic because the hemoglobin in the blood is much more likely to combine with carbon monoxide than with oxygen, even with plenty of breathable oxygen. This poisoning is called carboxyhemoglobin. Recent research has shown that the kind of fires that kill people by toxicity are principally those that reach flashover in a compartment or room some distance from the people. The vast majority of fires that attain flashover generate dangerous levels of carbon monoxide, independent of what is burning. The supertoxicants, such as hydrogen cyanide and neurotoxin, have been proven to be extremely rare, even in the laboratory. These factors impact the choice

of test furnace and the adjustment methods used in a standardized toxicity test.

Charring and Fire Resistance

As noted earlier in this chapter, wood exposed to high temperatures will decompose to provide an insulating layer of char that retards further degradation of the wood. The load-carrying capacity of a structural wood member depends upon its cross-sectional dimensions. Thus, the amount of charring of the cross section is the major factor in the fire endurance of structural wood members.

When wood is first exposed to fire, the wood chars and eventually flames. Ignition occurs in about 2 min under the standard ASTM E119 fire-test exposures. Charring into the depth of the wood then proceeds at a rate of approximately 0.8 mm/min for the next 8 min (or 1.25 min/mm). Thereafter, the char layer has an insulating effect, and the rate decreases to 0.6 mm/min (1.6 min/mm). Considering the initial ignition delay, the fast initial charring, and then the slowing down to a constant rate, the average constant charring rate is about 0.6 mm/min (or 1.5 in/h) (Douglas-fir, 7% moisture content). In the standard fire-resistance test, this linear charring rate is generally assumed for solid wood directly exposed to fire.

There are differences among species associated with their density, anatomy, chemical composition, and permeability. Moisture content is a major factor affecting charring rate. Density relates to the mass needed to be degraded and the thermal properties, which are affected by anatomical features. Charring in the longitudinal grain direction is reportedly double that in the transverse direction, and chemical composition affects the relative thickness of the char layer. Permeability affects the movement of moisture being driven from the wood or that being driven into the wood beneath the char layer. Normally, a simple linear model for charring where t is time (min), C is char rate (min/mm), and x_c is char depth (mm) is assumed:

$$t = Cx_c \qquad (17–1)$$

The temperature at the base of the char layer is generally taken to be 300°C or 550°F (288°C). With this temperature criterion, empirical equations for charring rate have been developed. Equations relating charring rate under ASTM E119 fire exposure to density and moisture content are available for Douglas-Fir, Southern Pine, and White Oak. These equations for rates transverse to the grain are

$C = (0.002269 + 0.00457\mu)\rho + 0.331$ for Douglas Fir
$$\qquad (17–2a)$$

$C = (0.000461 + 0.00095\mu)\rho + 1.016$ for Southern Pine
$$\qquad (17–2b)$$

$C = (0.001583 + 0.00318\mu)\rho + 0.594$ for White Oak
$$\qquad (17–2c)$$

where μ is moisture content (fraction of ovendry mass) and ρ is density, dry mass volume at moisture content μ (kg/m^3).

Table 17–4. Charring rate data for selected wood species

| | | | Wood exposed to ASTM E119 exposure[a] | | | | Wood exposed to a constant heat flux[b] | | | | | |
| | | | | | | | Linear charring rate[e] (min/mm) | | Thermal penetra-tion depth d [g] (mm) | | Average mass loss rate (g/m² s) | |
Species	Den-sity[c] (kg/m³)	Char contrac-tion factor[d]	Linear charring rate[e] (min/mm)	Non-linear charring rate[f] (min/mm$^{1.23}$)	Thermal penetra-tion depth [g] (mm)		18- kW/m² heat flux	55- kW/m² heat flux	18- kW/m² heat flux	55- kW/m² heat flux	18- kW/m² heat flux	55- kW/m² heat flux
Softwoods												
Southern Pine	509	0.60	1.24	0.56	33		2.27	1.17	38	26.5	3.8	8.6
Western redcedar	310	0.83	1.22	0.56	33		—	—	—	—	—	—
Redwood	343	0.86	1.28	0.58	35		1.68	0.98	36.5	24.9	2.9	6.0
Engelmann spruce	425	0.82	1.56	0.70	34		—	—	—	—	—	—
Hardwoods												
Basswood	399	0.52	1.06	0.48	32		1.32	0.76	38.2	22.1	4.5	9.3
Maple, hard	691	0.59	1.46	0.66	31		—	—	—	—	—	—
Oak, red	664	0.70	1.59	0.72	32		2.56	1.38	27.7	27.0	4.1	9.6
Yellow-poplar	504	0.67	1.36	0.61	32		—	—	—	—	—	—

[a]Moisture contents of 8% to 9%.
[b]Charring rate and average mass loss rate obtained using ASTM E906 heat release apparatus. Test durations were 50 to 98 min for 18-kW/m² heat flux and 30 to 53 min for 55-kW/m² heat flux. Charring rate based on temperature criterion of 300°C and linear model. Mass loss rate based on initial and final weight of sample, which includes moisture driven from the wood. Initial average moisture content of 8% to 9%.
[c]Based on weight and volume of ovendried wood.
[d]Thickness of char layer at end of fire exposure divided by original thickness of charred wood layer (char depth).
[e]Based on temperature criterion of 288°C and linear model.
[f]Based on temperature criterion of 288°C and nonlinear model of Equation (17–3).
[g]As defined in Equation (17–6). Not sensitive to moisture content.

A nonlinear char rate model has been found useful. This alternative model is

$$t = mx_c^{1.23} \qquad (17\text{–}3)$$

where m is char rate coefficient (min/mm$^{1.23}$).

Based on data from eight species (Table 17–4), the following equation was developed for the char rate coefficient:

$$m = -0.147 + 0.000564\rho + 1.21\mu + 0.532\,f_c \qquad (17\text{–}4)$$

where ρ is density, ovendry mass and volume, and f_c is char contraction factor (dimensionless).

The char contraction factor is the thickness of the residual char layer divided by the original thickness of the wood layer that was charred (char depth). Average values for the eight species tested in the development of the equation are listed in Table 17–4.

These equations and data are valid when the member is thick enough to be a semi-infinite slab. For smaller dimensions, the charring rate increases once the temperature has risen above the initial temperature at the center of the member or at the unexposed surface of the panel. As a beam or column chars, the corners become rounded.

Charring rate is also affected by the severity of the fire expo-sure. Data on charring rates for fire exposures other than ASTM E119 have been limited. Data for exposure to con-stant temperatures of 538°C, 815°C, and 927°C are available in Schaffer (1967). Data for a constant heat flux are given in Table 17–4.

The temperature at the innermost zone of the char layer is assumed to be 300°C. Because of the low thermal conductiv-ity of wood, the temperature 6 mm inward from the base of the char layer is about 180°C. This steep temperature gradi-ent means the remaining uncharred cross-sectional area of a large wood member remains at a low temperature and can continue to carry a load. Moisture is driven into the wood as charring progresses. A moisture content peak is created inward from the char base. The peak moisture content occurs where the temperature of the wood is about 100°C, which is at about 13 mm from the char base.

Once a quasi-steady-state charring rate has been obtained, the temperature profile beneath the char layer can be expressed as an exponential term or a power term. An equation based on a power term is

$$T = T_i + \left(300 - T_i\right)\left(1 - x/d\right)^2 \qquad (17\text{–}5)$$

where T is temperature (°C), T_i initial temperature (°C),

x distance from the char front (mm), and d thermal penetration depth (mm).

In Table 17–4, values for the thermal penetration depth parameter are listed for both the standard fire exposure and the constant heat flux exposure. As with the charring rate, these temperature profiles assume a semi-infinite slab. The equation does not provide for the plateau in temperatures that often occurs at 100°C in moist wood. In addition to these empirical data, there are mechanistic models for estimating the charring rate and temperature profiles. The temperature profile within the remaining wood cross-section can be used with other data to estimate the remaining load-carrying capacity of the uncharred wood during a fire and the residual capacity after a fire.

Flame-Retardant Treatments

To meet building code and standards specifications, lumber and plywood are treated with flame retardants to improve their fire performance. The two general application methods are pressure treating and surface coating.

Fire-Retardant-Treated Wood

To meet the specifications in the building codes and various standards, fire-retardant-treated lumber and plywood is wood that has been pressure treated with chemicals to reduce its flame spread characteristics. Flame-retardant treatment of wood generally improves the fire performance by reducing the amount of flammable volatiles released during fire exposure or by reducing the effective heat of combustion, or both. Both results have the effect of reducing the HRR, particularly during the initial stages of fire, and thus consequently reducing the rate of flame spread over the surface. The wood may then self-extinguish when the primary heat source is removed.

The performance requirement for fire-retardant-treated wood is that its FSI is 25 or less when tested according to the ASTM E84 flame spread test and that it shows no evidence of significant progressive combustion when this 10-min test is continued for an additional 20 min. In addition, it is required that the flame front in the test shall not progress more than 3.2 m beyond the centerline of the burner at any given time during the test. Underwriters Laboratories, Inc., assigns the designation FR–S to products that satisfy these requirements. In applications where the requirement is not for fire-retardant-treated wood but only for Class I or II flame spread, the flame-retardant treatments only need to reduce the FSI to the required level in the ASTM E84 flame spread test (25 for Class I, 75 for Class II). Various laboratories perform fire-performance rating tests on these treated materials and maintain lists of products that meet certain standards.

Fire-retardant-treated wood and plywood are often used for interior finish and trim in rooms, auditoriums, and corridors where codes require materials with low surface flammability.

While fire-retardant-treated wood is not considered a non-combustible material, many codes have accepted the use of fire-retardant-treated wood and plywood in fire-resistive and noncombustible construction for the framing of nonload-bearing walls, roof assemblies, and decking. Fire-retardant-treated wood is also used for such special purposes as wood scaffolding and for the frame, rails, and stiles of wood fire doors.

In addition to specifications for flame spread performance, fire-retardant-treated wood for use in certain applications is specified to meet other performance requirements. Wood treated with inorganic flame-retardant salts is usually more hygroscopic than is untreated wood, particularly at high relative humidities. Increases in equilibrium moisture content of this treated wood will depend upon the type of chemical, level of chemical retention, and size and species of wood involved. Applications that involve high humidity will likely require wood with low hygroscopicity. The American Wood Preservers' Association (AWPA) Standards C20 and C27 requirements for low hygroscopicity (Interior Type A treatment) stipulate that the material shall have an equilibrium moisture content of not more than 28% when tested in accordance with ASTM D3201 procedures at 92% relative humidity.

Exterior flame-retardant treatments should be specified whenever the wood is exposed to exterior weathering conditions. The AWPA Standards C20 and C27 also mandate that an exterior type treatment is one that has shown no increase in fire hazard classification after being subjected to the rain test specified in ASTM D2898 as Method A.

For structural applications, information on the fire-retardant-treated wood product needs to be obtained from the treater or chemical supplier. This includes the design modification factors for initial strength properties of the fire-retardant-treated wood, including values for the fasteners. Flame-retardant treatment generally results in reductions in the mechanical properties of wood. Fire-retardant-treated wood is often more brash than untreated wood.

In field applications with elevated temperatures, such as roof sheathings, there is the potential for further losses in strength with time. For such applications in elevated temperatures and high humidity, appropriate design modification factors need to be obtained from the treater or chemical supplier. The AWPA Standards C20 and C27 mandate that fire-retardant-treated wood that will be used in high-temperature applications (Interior Type A High Temperature), such as roof framing and roof sheathing, be strength tested in accordance with ASTM D5664 (lumber) or ASTM D5516 (plywood) or by an equivalent methodology. Some flame-retardant treatments are not acceptable because of thermal degradation of the wood that will occur with time at high temperatures. Screw-withdrawal tests to predict residual in-place strength of fire-retardant-treated plywood roof sheathing have been developed (Winandy and others 1998).

Corrosion of fasteners can be accelerated under conditions of high humidity and in the presence of flame-retardant salts.

For flame-retardant treatments containing inorganic salts, the type of metal and chemical in contact with each other greatly affects the rate of corrosion. Thus, information on proper fasteners also needs to be obtained from the treater or chemical supplier. Other issues that may require contacting the treater or chemical supplier include machinability, gluing characteristics, and paintability.

Flame-retardant treatment of wood does not prevent the wood from decomposing and charring under fire exposure (the rate of fire penetration through treated wood approximates the rate through untreated wood). Fire-retardant-treated wood used in doors and walls can slightly improve fire endurance of these doors and walls. Most of this improvement is associated with the reduction in surface flammability rather than any changes in charring rates.

Flame-Retardant Pressure Treatments

In the impregnation treatments, wood is pressure impregnated with chemical solutions using pressure processes similar to those used for chemical preservative treatments. However, considerably heavier absorptions of chemicals are necessary for flame-retardant protection. Standards C20 and C27 of the AWPA recommend the treating conditions for lumber and plywood. The penetration of the chemicals into the wood depends on the species, wood structure, and moisture content. Since some species are difficult to treat, the degree of impregnation needed to meet the performance requirements for fire-retardant-treated wood may not be possible. One option is to incise the wood prior to treatment to improve the depth of penetration.

Inorganic salts are the most commonly used flame retardants for interior wood products, and their characteristics have been known for more than 50 years. These salts include monoammonium and diammonium phosphate, ammonium sulfate, zinc chloride, sodium tetraborate, and boric acid. Guanylurea phosphate is also used. These chemicals are combined in formulations to develop optimum fire performance yet still retain acceptable hygroscopicity, strength, corrosivity, machinability, surface appearance, glueability, and paintability. Cost is also a factor in these formulations. Many commercial formulations are available. The AWPA Standard P17 provides information on formulations of some current proprietary waterborne treatments. The fire-retardant salts are water soluble and are leached out in exterior applications or with repeated washings. Water-insoluble organic flame retardants have been developed to meet the need for leach-resistant systems. Such treatments are also an alternative when a low hygroscopic treatment is needed. These water-insoluble systems include (a) resins polymerized after impregnation into wood and (b) graft polymer flame retardants attached directly to cellulose. An amino resin system based on urea, melamine, dicyandiamide, and related compounds is of the first type.

Flame-Retardant Coatings

For some applications, the alternative method of applying the flame-retardant chemical as a coating to the wood surface may be acceptable. Such commercial coating products are available to reduce the surface flammability characteristics of wood. The two types of coatings are intumescent and nonintumescent. The widely used intumescent coatings "intumesce" to form an expanded low-density film upon exposure to fire. This multicellular carbonaceous film insulates the wood surface below from the high temperatures. Intumescent formulations include a dehydrating agent, a char former, and a blowing agent. Potential dehydrating agents include polyammonium phosphate. Ingredients for the char former include starch, glucose, and dipentaerythritol. Potential blowing agents for the intumescent coatings include urea, melamine, and chlorinate parafins. Nonintumescent coating products include formulations of the water-soluble salts such as diammonium phosphate, ammonium sulfate, and borax.

References

General

APA—The Engineered Wood Association. [Current edition]. Fire-rated systems. Tacoma, WA: APA—The Engineered Wood Association.

Browne, F.L. 1958. Theories of the combustion of wood and its control—a survey of the literature. Rep. No. 2136. Madison, WI: U.S. Department of Agriculture, Forest Service, Forest Products Laboratory.

CWC. 1996. Fire safety design in buildings. Ottawa, ON, Canada: Canadian Wood Council.

NFPA. 1995. Guide for fire and explosion investigations. NFPA 921. Quincy, MA: National Fire Protection Association.

NFPA. [Current edition]. Fire protection handbook. Quincy, MA: National Fire Protection Association.

Schaffer, E.L.; White, R.H.; Brenden, J. 1989. Part II. Fire safety. In: Light-frame wall and floor systems—analysis and performance. Gen. Tech. Rep. FPL–GTR–59. Madison, WI: U.S. Department of Agriculture, Forest Service, Forest Products Laboratory: 51–86.

Society of Fire Protection Engineers. [Current edition]. The Society of Fire Protection Engineers handbook of fire protection engineering. Quincy, MA: National Fire Protection Association.

Fire Test Standards

ASTM. [Current edition]. West Conshohocken, PA: American Society for Testing and Materials.

ASTM E84. Surface burning characteristics of building materials.

ASTM E108. Fire tests of roof coverings.

ASTM E119. Fire tests of building construction and materials.

ASTM E136. Behavior of materials in a vertical tube furnace at 750°C.

ASTM E162. Surface flammability of materials using a radiant heat energy source.

ASTM E648. Critical radiant flux of floor-covering systems using a radiant heat energy source.

ASTM E662. Specific optical density of smoke generated by solid materials.

ASTM E906. Heat and visible smoke release rates from materials and products.

ASTM E970. Critical radiant flux of exposed attic floor insulation using a radiant heat energy source.

ASTM E1321. Determining material ignition and flame spread properties.

ASTM E1354. Heat and visible smoke release rates for materials and products using an oxygen consumption calorimeter.

ASTM E1623. Determination of fire and thermal parameters of materials, products, and systems using an intermediate scale calorimeter (ICAL).

ASTM E1678. Measuring smoke toxicity for use in fire hazard analysis.

ICBO. [Current edition]. Fire tests of door assemblies. Uniform Building Code Standard 7-2. Whittier, CA: International Conference of Building Officials.

ISO. Fire tests—full-scale room test for surface products. ISO 9705. International Organization for Standardization, Geneva, Switzerland.

NFPA. [Current edition]. Potential heat of building materials. NFPA 259. Quincy, MA: National Fire Protection Association.

Fire-Rated Products and Assemblies

American Insurance Association. [Current edition]. Fire resistance ratings. New York: American Insurance Association.

Gypsum Association. [Current edition]. Fire resistance design manual. Washington, DC: Gypsum Association.

Technomic Publishing Co., Inc. 1994. Handbook of fire-retardant coatings and fire testing services. Lancaster, PA: Technomic Publishing Co., Inc.

Underwriters Laboratories, Inc. [Current edition]. Building materials directory. Northbrook, IL: Underwriters Laboratories, Inc.

Underwriters Laboratories, Inc. [Current edition]. Fire resistance directory. Northbrook, IL: Underwriters Laboratories, Inc.

U.S. Department of Housing and Urban Development. 1980. Guideline on fire ratings of archaic materials and assemblies. Rehabilitation Guidelines. Part 8. Washington, DC: Superintendent of Documents.

Ignition

Brenden, J.J.; Schaffer, E. 1980. Smoldering wave-front velocity in fiberboard. Res. Pap. FPL 367. Madison, WI: U.S. Department of Agriculture, Forest Service, Forest Products Laboratory.

Dietenberger, M.A. Ignitability analysis of siding materials using modified protocol for LIFT apparatus. In: Proceedings, 3d Fire and Materials Conference; 1994 October 27–28; Crystal City, VA. London: Interscience Communications Limited: 259–268.

Kubler, H. 1990. Self-heating of lignocellulosic materials. In: Nelson, G.L., ed. Fire and polymers—hazards identification and prevention. ACS Symposium Series 425. Washington DC: American Chemical Society: 429–449.

LeVan, S.; Schaffer, E. 1982. Predicting weight loss from smoldering combustion in cellulosic insulation. Journal of Thermal Insulation. 5: 229–244.

Matson, A.F.; Dufour, R.E.; Breen, J.F. 1959. Part II. Survey of available information on ignition of wood exposed to moderately elevated temperatures. In: Performance of type B gas vents for gas-fired appliances. Bull. of Res. 51. Chicago, IL: Underwriters Laboratories: 269–295.

Shafizadeh, F.; Sekiguchi, Y. 1984. Oxidation of chars during smoldering combustion of cellulosic materials. Combustion and Flame. 55: 171–179.

Schaffer, E.L. 1980. Smoldering in cellulosics under prolonged low-level heating. Fire Technology. 16(1): 22–28.

Flame Spread

AWC. 1999. Flame spread performance of wood products (1998). Design for code acceptance No. 1. http://www.forestprod.org/awcpubs.html (11 Feb. 1999).

Benjamin, I.A.; Adams, C.H. 1976. The flooring radiant panel test and proposed criteria. Fire Journal. 70(2): 63–70. March.

Holmes, C.A.; Eickner, H.W.; Brenden, J.J.; White, R.H. 1979. Fire performance of structural flakeboard from forest residue. Res. Pap. FPL–RP–315. Madison, WI: U.S. Department of Agriculture, Forest Service, Forest Products Laboratory.

Underwriters Laboratories, Inc. 1971. Wood-fire hazard classification. Card Data Service, Serial No. UL527, Chicago, IL: Underwriters Laboratories, Inc.

Yarbrough, D.W.; Wilkes, K.E. 1997. Thermal properties and use of cellulosic insulation produced from recycled paper. In: The use of recycled wood and paper in building applications. Proc. 7286. Madison, WI: Forest Products Society: 108–114.

Flashover and Room/Corner Tests

Bruce, H.D. 1959. Experimental dwelling—room fires. Rep. 1941. Madison, WI: U.S. Department of Agriculture, Forest Service, Forest Products Laboratory.

Dietenberger, M.A.; Grexa, O.; White, R.H. [and others]. 1995. Room/corner test of wall linings with 100/300 kW burner. In: Proceedings, 4th international fire and materials conference; 1995 November 15–16; Crystal City, MD. London: InterScience Communications Limited: 53–62.

Holmes, C. 1978. Room corner-wall fire tests of some structural sandwich panels and components. Journal of Fire & Flammability. 9: 467–488.

Holmes, C.; Eickner, H.; Brenden, J.J. [and others]. 1980. Fire development and wall endurance in sandwich and wood-frame structures. Res. Pap. FPL 364. Madison, WI: U.S. Department of Agriculture, Forest Service, Forest Products Laboratory.

Schaffer, E.L.; Eickner, H.W. 1965. Effect of wall linings on fire performance within a partially ventilated corridor. Res. Pap. FPL 49. Madison, WI: U.S. Department of Agriculture, Forest Service, Forest Products Laboratory.

Tran, H.C. 1991. Wall and corner fire tests on selected wood products. Journal of Fire Sciences. 9: 106–124. March/April.

Heat Release and Heat of Combustion

Babrauskas, V.; Grayson, S.J. eds. 1992. Heat release in fires. New York: Elsevier Applied Science.

Chamberlain, D.L. 1983. Heat release rates of lumber and wood products. In: Schaffer, E.L., ed., Behavior of polymeric materials in fire. ASTM STP 816. Philadelphia, PA: American Society for Testing and Materials: 21–41.

Tran, H.C. 1990. Modifications to an Ohio State University apparatus and comparison with cone calorimeter results. In: Quintiere, J.G.; Cooper, L.Y. eds. Heat and mass transfer in fires. Proceedings, AIAA/ASME thermophysics and heat transfer conference; 1990 June 18–20; Seattle, WA. New York: The American Society of Mechanical Engineers: 141: 131–139.

Tran, H.C. 1992. (B) Experimental data on wood materials. In: Babrauskas, V.; Grayson, S.J. eds. Heat release in fires. Chapter 11 Part. B. New York: Elsevier Applied Science: 357–372.

White, R.H. 1987. Effect of lignin content and extractives on the higher heating value of wood. Wood and Fiber Science. 19(4): 446–452.

Smoke and Other Combustion Products

Brenden, J.J. 1970. Determining the utility of a new optical test procedure for measuring smoke from various wood products. Res. Pap. FPL 137. Madison, WI: U.S. Department of Agriculture, Forest Service, Forest Products Laboratory.

Brenden, J.J. 1975. How nine inorganics salts affected smoke yield from Douglas-fir plywood. Res. Pap. FPL 249. Madison, WI: U.S. Department of Agriculture, Forest Service, Forest Products Laboratory.

Hall, J.R., Jr. 1996. Whatever happened to combustion toxicity. Fire Technology. 32(4): 351–371.

Tran, H.C. 1990. Correlation of wood smoke produced from NBS smoke chamber and OSU heat release apparatus. In: Hasegawa, H.K. ed., Characterization and toxicity of smoke. ASTM STP 1082. Philadelphia, PA: American Society for Testing and Materials: 135–146.

Charring and Fire Resistance

AITC. [Current edition]. Calculation of fire resistance of glued laminated timbers. Tech. Note 7. Englewood, CO: American Institute of Timber Construction.

ASCE. 1982. Evaluation, maintenance and upgrading of wood structures—a guide and commentary. New York: American Society of Civil Engineers. 428 p.

AWC. 1985. Design of fire-resistive exposed wood members (1985). Design for code acceptance No. 2. Pub. T18 Washington, DC: American Wood Council.

AWC. 1991. Component additive method (CAM) for calculating and demonstrating assembly fire endurance. DCA No. 4, Design for code acceptance. Pub. T20. Washington, DC: American Forest & Paper Association.

Janssens, M. 1994. Thermo-physical properties for wood pyrolysis models. In: Proceedings, Pacific Timber Engineering conference; 1994 July 11–15; Gold Coast, Australia. Fortitude Valley MAC, Queensland, Australia: Timber Research and Development Advisory Council: 607–618.

Janssens, M.L.; White, R.H. 1994. Short communication: temperature profiles in wood members exposed to fire. Fire and Materials. 18: 263–265.

Schaffer, E.L. 1966. Review of information related to the charring rate of wood. Res. Note FPL–145. Madison, WI: U.S. Department of Agriculture, Forest Service, Forest Products Laboratory.

Schaffer, E.L. 1967. Charring rate of selected woods-transverse to grain. Res. Pap. FPL 69. Madison, WI: U.S. Department of Agriculture, Forest Service, Forest Products Laboratory.

Schaffer, E.L. 1977. State of structural timber fire endurance. Wood and Fiber. 9(2): 145–170.

Schaffer, E.L. 1984. Structural fire design: Wood. Res. Pap. FPL 450. Madison, WI: U.S. Department of Agriculture, Forest Service, Forest Products Laboratory.

Tran, H.C.; White, R.H. 1992. Burning rate of solid wood measured in a heat release calorimeter. Fire and Materials. 16: 197–206.

White, R.H. 1995. Analytical methods for determining fire resistance of timber members. In: The SFPE handbook of fire protection engineering. 2d ed. Quincy, MA: National Fire Protection Association.

White, R.H.; Nordheim, E.V. 1992. Charring rate of wood for ASTM E119 exposure. Fire Technology. 28: 5–30.

White, R.H.; Tran, H.C. 1996. Charring rate of wood exposed to a constant heat flux. In: Proceedings, Wood & Fire Safety, third international conference. The High Tatras; 1996 May 6–9; Zvolen, Slovakia. Zvolen, Slovakia: Faculty of Wood Technology, Technical University: 175–183.

Woeste, F.E.; Schaffer, E.L. 1981. Reliability analysis of fire-exposed light-frame wood floor assemblies. Res. Pap. FPL 386. Madison, WI: U.S. Department of Agriculture, Forest Service, Forest Products Laboratory.

Fire-Retardant-Treated Wood

Treated Wood Standards

ASTM. [Current edition]. West Conshohocken, PA: American Society for Testing and Materials.

ASTM E69. Combustible properties of treated wood by fire-tube apparatus.

ASTM D2898. Accelerated weathering of fire-retardant treated wood for fire testing.

ASTM D3201. Hygroscopic properties of fire-retardant wood and wood-base products.

ASTM D5516. Standard method for evaluating the mechanical properties of fire-retardant treated softwood plywood exposed to elevated temperatures.

ASTM D5664. Standard method for evaluating the effects of fire-retardant treatments and elevated temperatures on strength properties of fire-retardant treated lumber.

AWPA. [Current edition]. Gransbury, TX: American Wood-Preservers' Association.

Standard A2. Analysis of waterborne preservatives and fire-retardant formulations.

Standard A3. Determining penetration of preservative and fire retardants.

Standard A9. Analysis of treated wood and treating solutions by x-ray spectroscopy.

Standard C20. Structural lumber—Fire-retardant pressure treatment by pressure processes.

Standard C27. Plywood—Fire-retardant treatment by pressure processes.

Standard P17. Fire-retardant formulations.

Treated Wood Literature

Holmes, C.A. 1977. Effect of fire-retardant treatments on performance properties of wood. In: Goldstein, I.S., ed. Wood technology: Chemical aspects. Proceedings, ACS symposium Series 43. Washington, DC: American Chemical Society.

LeVan, S.L. 1984. Chemistry of fire retardancy. In: Rowell, Roger M., ed. The chemistry of solid wood. Advances in Chemistry Series 207. Washington, DC: American Chemical Society.

LeVan, S.L.; Holmes, C.A. 1986. Effectiveness of fire-retardant treatments for shingles after 10 years of outdoor weathering. Res. Pap. RP–FPL–474. Madison, WI: U.S. Department of Agriculture, Forest Service, Forest Products Laboratory.

LeVan, S.L.; Tran, H.C. 1990. The role of boron in flame-retardant treatments. In: Hamel, Margaret, ed. 1st International conference on wood protection with diffusible preservatives: Proceedings 47355; 1990 November 28–30; Nashville, TN. Madison, WI: Forest Products Research Society: 39–41.

LeVan, S.L.; Winandy, J.E. 1990. Effects of fire-retardant treatments on wood strength: a review. Wood and Fiber Science. 22(1): 113–131.

LeVan, S.L.; Ross, R.J.; Winandy, J.E. 1990. Effects of fire retardant chemicals on the bending properties of wood at elevated temperatures. Res. Pap. FPL–RP–498. Madison, WI: U.S. Department of Agriculture, Forest Service, Forest Products Laboratory.

NAHB National Research Center. 1990. Home builders guide to fire retardant treated plywood. Evaluation, testing, and replacement. Upper Marlboro, MD: National Association of Home Builders, National Research Center.

Winandy, J.E. 1995. Effects of fire retardant treatments after 18 months of exposure at 150°F (66°C). Res. Note FPL–RN–0264. Madison, WI: U.S. Department of Agriculture, Forest Service, Forest Products Laboratory.

Winandy, J.E. 1997. Effects of fire retardant retention, borate buffers, and redrying temperature after treatment on thermal-induced degradation. Forest Products Journal. 47(6): 79–86.

Winandy, J.E.; LeVan, S.L.; Ross, R.J.; Hoffman, S.P.; McIntyre, C.R. 1991. Thermal degradation of fire-retardant-treated plywood—development and evaluation of a test protocol. Res. Pap. FPL–RP–501. Madison, WI: U.S. Department of Agriculture, Forest Service, Forest Products Laboratory.

Winandy, J.E.; Lebow, P. K.; Nelson, W. 1998. Predicting bending strength of fire-retardant-treated plywood from screw-withdrawal tests. Res. Pap. FPL–RP–568. Madison, WI: U.S. Department of Agriculture, Forest Service, Forest Products Laboratory.

Round Timbers and Ties

Ronald W. Wolfe

Contents

ound timbers and ties represent some of the most efficient uses of our forest resources. They require a minimum of processing between harvesting the tree and marketing the structural commodity. Poles and piles are debarked or peeled, seasoned, and often treated with preservative prior to use as structural members. Construction logs are usually shaped to facilitate construction. Ties, used for railroads, landscaping, and mining, are slab-cut to provide flat surfaces. Because these products are relatively economical to produce, compared with glulam, steel, and concrete products, they are commonly used throughout the United States.

Standards and Specifications

Material standards and specifications listed in Table 18–1 were created through the joint efforts of producers and users to ensure compatibility between product quality and end use. These guidelines include recommendations for production, treatment, and engineering design. They are updated periodically to conform to changes in material and design technology.

Material Requirements

Round timber and tie material requirements vary with intended use. The majority of uses involve exposure to harsh environments. Thus, in addition to availability, form, and weight, durability is also an important consideration for the use of round timbers and ties. Availability reflects the economic feasibility of procuring members of the required size and grade. Form or physical appearance refers to visual characteristics, such as straightness and occurrence of knots and spiral grain. Weight affects shipping and handling costs and is a function of volume, moisture content, and wood density. Durability is directly related to expected service life and is a function of treatability and natural decay resistance. Finally, regardless of the application, any structural member must be strong enough to resist imposed loads with a reasonable factor of safety. Material specifications available for most applications of round timbers and ties contain guidelines for evaluating these factors.

Table 18–1. Standards and specifications for round timbers and ties[a]

Product	Material requirements	Preservative treatment	Engineering design stresses	
			Procedures	Design values
Utility poles	ANSI O5.1	TT-W-571 AWPA C1,C4,C35	—	ANSI O5.1
Construction poles	ANSI O5.1	TT-W-571 AWPA C23	ASTM D3200	ASAE EP 388
Piles	ASTM D25	TT-W-571 AWPA CI,C3	ASTM D2899	NDS
Construction logs	(See material supplier)	—	ASTM D3957	(See material supplier)
Ties	AREA	TT-W-571 AWPA C2,C6 AREA	—	AREA

[a]ANSI, American National Standards Institute; ASTM, American Society for Testing and Materials; ASAE, American Society of Agricultural Engineers; AREA, American Railway Engineers Association; NDS, National Design Specification (for Wood Construction); AWPA, American Wood-Preservers' Association.

Availability

Material evaluation begins with an assessment of availability. For some applications, local species of timber may be readily available in an acceptable form and quality. However, this is not normally the case. Pole producers and tie mills are scattered throughout heavily forested regions. Their products are shipped to users throughout North America.

Poles

Most structural applications of poles require timbers that are relatively straight and free of large knots. Poles used to support electric utility distribution and transmission lines (Fig. 18–1) range in length from 6 to 38 m (20 to 125 ft) and from 0.13 to 0.76 m (5 to 30 in.) in diameter, 1.8 m (6 ft) from the butt. Poles used to support local area distribution lines are normally <15 m (<50 ft) long and are predominately Southern Pine.

Hardwood species can be used for poles when the trees are of suitable size and form; their use is limited, however, by their weight, by their excessive checking, and because of the lack of experience in preservative treatment of hardwoods. Thus, most poles are softwoods.

The Southern Pine lumber group (principally loblolly, longleaf, shortleaf, and slash) accounts for roughly 80% of poles treated in the United States. Three traits of these pines account for their extensive use: thick and easily treated sapwood, favorable strength properties and form, and availability in popular pole sizes. In longer lengths, Southern Pine poles are in limited supply, so Douglas-fir, and to some extent western redcedar, Ponderosa pine, and western larch, are used to meet requirements for 15-m (50-ft) and longer transmission poles.

Douglas-fir is used throughout the United States for transmission poles and is used in the Pacific Coast region for distribution and building poles. Because the heartwood of Douglas-fir is resistant to preservative penetration and has limited decay and termite resistance, serviceable poles need a well-treated shell of sapwood that is free of checking. To minimize checking after treatment, poles should be adequately seasoned or conditioned before treatment. With these precautions, the poles should compare favorably with treated Southern Pine poles in serviceability.

A small percentage of the poles treated in the United States are of western redcedar, produced mostly in British Columbia. The number of poles of this species used without treatment is not known but is considered to be small. Used primarily for utility lines in northern and western United States, well-treated redcedar poles have a service life that compares favorably with poles made from other species and could be used effectively in pole-type buildings.

Lodgepole pine is also used in small quantities for treated poles. This species is used both for utility lines and for pole-type buildings. It has a good service record when well treated. Special attention is necessary, however, to obtain poles with sufficient sapwood thickness to ensure adequate penetration of preservative, because the heartwood is not usually penetrated and is not decay resistant. The poles must also be well seasoned prior to treatment to avoid checking and exposure of unpenetrated heartwood to attack by decay fungi.

Western larch poles produced in Montana and Idaho came into use after World War II because of their favorable size, shape, and strength properties. Western larch requires preservative treatment full length for use in most areas and, as in the case of lodgepole pine poles, must be selected for adequate sapwood thickness and must be well seasoned prior to treatment. Other species occasionally used for poles are listed in the American National Standards Institute (ANSI) O5.1 standard. These minor species make up a very small portion of pole production and are used locally.

Figure 18–1. Round timber poles form the major structural element in these transmission structures. (Photo courtesy of Koppers Co.)

Glued-laminated, or glulam, poles are also available for use where special sizes or shapes are required. The ANSI Standard O5.2 provides guidelines for specifying these poles.

Piles

Material available for timber piles is more restricted than that for poles. Most timber piles used in the eastern half of the United States are Southern Pine, while those used in western United States are coast Douglas-fir. Oak, red pine, and cedar piles are also referenced in timber pile literature but are not as widely used as Southern Pine and Douglas-fir.

Construction Logs

Round timbers have been used in a variety of structures, including bridges, log cabins, and pole buildings. Log stringer bridges (Fig. 18–2) are generally designed for a limited life on logging roads intended to provide access to remote areas. In Alaska where logs may exceed 1 m (3 ft) in diameter, bridge spans may exceed 9 m (30 ft). Building poles, on the other hand, are preservative-treated logs in the

0.15- to 0.25-m- (6- to 10-in.-) diameter range. These poles rarely exceed 9 m (30 ft) in length. Although poles sold for this application are predominately Southern Pine, there is potential for competition from local species in this category. Finally, log cabin logs normally range from 0.2 to 0.25 m (8 to 10 in.) in diameter, and the availability of logs in this size range is not often a problem. However, because logs are not normally preservative treated for this application, those species that offer moderate to high natural decay resistance, such as western redcedar, are preferred. Pole buildings, which incorporate round timbers as vertical columns and cantilever supports, require preservative-treated wood. Preservative-treated poles for this use may not be readily available.

Ties

The most important availability consideration for railroad cross ties is quantity. Ties are produced from most native species of timber that yield log lengths >2.4 m (8 ft) with diameters >0.18 m (7 in.). The American Railway Engineering Association (AREA) lists 26 U.S. species that may be used for ties. Thus, the tie market provides a use for many low-grade hardwood and softwood logs.

Form

Natural growth properties of trees play an important role in their use as structural round timbers. Three important form considerations are cross-sectional dimensions, straightness, and the presence of surface characteristics such as knots.

Poles and Piles

Standards for poles and piles have been written with the assumption that trees have a round cross section with a circumference that decreases linearly with height. Thus, the shape of a pole or pile is often assumed to be that of the frustum of a cone. Actual measurements of tree shape indicate that taper is rarely linear and often varies with location along the height of the tree. Average taper values from the ANSI O5.1 standard are shown in Table 18–2 for the more popular pole species. Guidelines to account for the effect of taper on the location of the critical section above the groundline are given in ANSI O5.1. The standard also tabulates pole dimensions for up to 15 size classes of 11 major pole species.

Taper also affects construction detailing of pole buildings. Where siding or other exterior covering is applied, poles are generally set with the taper to the interior side of the structures to provide a vertical exterior surface (Fig. 18–3). Another common practice is to modify the round poles by slabbing to provide a continuous flat face. The slabbed face permits more secure attachment of sheathing and framing members and facilitates the alignment and setting of intermediate wall and corner poles. The slabbing consists of a minimum cut to provide a single continuous flat face from the groundline to the top of intermediate wall poles and two continuous flat faces at right angles to one another from the groundline to the top of corner poles. However, preservative

Figure 18–2. Logs are used to construct logging bridges in remote forest areas.

Table 18–2. Circumference taper

Species	Centimeter change in circumference per meter	Inch change in circumference per foot[a]
Western redcedar	3.7	0.38
Ponderosa pine	2.4	0.29
Jack, lodgepole, and red pine	2.5	0.30
Southern Pine	2.1	0.25
Douglas-fir, larch	1.7	0.21
Western hemlock	1.7	0.20

[a]Taken from ANSI O5.1.

penetration is generally limited to the sapwood of most species; therefore slabbing, particularly in the groundline area of poles with thin sapwood, may result in somewhat less protection than that of an unslabbed pole. All cutting and sawing should be confined to that portion of the pole above the groundline and should be performed before treatment.

The American Standards for Testing and Materials (ASTM) D25 standard provides tables of pile sizes for either friction piles or end-bearing piles. Friction piles rely on skin friction rather than tip area for support, whereas end-bearing piles resist compressive force at the tip. For this reason, a friction pile is specified by butt circumference and may have a smaller tip than an end-bearing pile. Conversely, end-bearing piles are specified by tip area and butt circumference is minimized.

Straightness of poles or piles is determined by two form properties: sweep and crook. Sweep is a measure of bow or gradual deviation from a straight line joining the ends of the pole or pile. Crook is an abrupt change in direction of the centroidal axis. Limits on these two properties are specified in both ANSI O5.1 and ASTM D25.

Construction Logs

Logs used in construction are generally specified to meet the same criteria for straightness and knots as poles and piles (ASTM D25). For log stringer bridges, the log selection criteria may vary with the experience of the person doing the selection but straightness, spiral grain, wind shake, and knots are limiting criteria. Although no consensus standard

398

Figure 18–3. Poles provide economical foundation and wall systems for agricultural and storage buildings.

Figure 18–4. Construction logs can be formed in a variety of shapes for log homes. Vertical surfaces may be varied for aesthetic purposes, while the horizontal surfaces generally reflect structural and thermal considerations.

is available for specifying and designing log stringers, the *Design Guide for Native Log Stringer Bridges* was prepared by the USDA Forest Service.

Logs used for log cabins come in a wide variety of cross-sectional shapes (Fig. 18–4). Commercial cabin logs are usually milled so that their shape is uniform along their length. The ASTM D3957 standard, a guide for establishing stress grades for building logs, recommends stress grading on the basis of the largest rectangular section that can be inscribed totally within the log section. The standard also provides commentary on the effects of knots and slope of grain.

Ties

Railroad ties are commonly shaped to a fairly uniform section along their length. The AREA publishes specifications for the sizes, which include seven size classes ranging from 0.13 by 0.13 m (5 by 5 in.) to 0.18 by 0.25 m (7 by 10 in.). These tie classes may be ordered in any of three standard lengths: 2.4 m (8 ft), 2.6 m (8.5 ft), or 2.7 m (9 ft).

Weight and Volume

The weight of any wood product is a function of its volume, density, moisture content, and any retained treatment substance. An accurate estimate of volume of a round pole would require numerous measurements of the circumference and shape along the length, because poles commonly exhibit neither a uniform linear taper nor a perfectly round shape. The American Wood Preservers' Association (AWPA) Standard F3 therefore recommends volume estimates be based on the assumption that the pole is shaped as the frustum of a cone (that is, a cone with the top cut perpendicular to the axis), with adjustments dependent on species. The volume in this case is determined as the average cross-sectional area A times the length. Estimates of average cross-sectional area may be obtained either by measuring the circumference at mid-length ($A = C_m^2/4\pi$) or taking the average of the butt and tip diameters ($A = \pi(D + d)^2/16$) to estimate the area of a circle. The AWPA recommends that these estimates then be adjusted by the following correction factors for the given species and application:

Oak piles	0.82
Southern Pine piles	0.93
Southern Pine and red pine poles	0.95

Tables for round timber volume are given in AWPA Standard F3. The volume of a round timber differs little whether it is green or dry. Drying of round timbers causes checks to open, but there is little reduction of the gross diameter of the pole.

Wood density also differs with species, age, and growing conditions. It will even vary along the height of a single tree. Average values, tabulated by species, are normally expressed as specific gravity (SG), which is density expressed as a ratio of the density of water (see Ch. 4). For commercial species grown in the United States, SG varies from 0.32 to 0.65. If you know the green volume of a round timber and its SG, its dry weight is a product of its SG, its volume, and the unit weight of water (1000 kg/m^3 (62.4 lb/ft^3)). Wood moisture content can also be highly variable. A pole cut in the spring when sap is flowing may have a moisture content exceeding 100% (the weight of the water it contains may exceed the weight of the dry wood substance). If you know the moisture content (MC) of the timber, multiply the dry weight by (1 + MC/100) to get the wet weight.

Finally, in estimating the weight of a treated wood product such as a pole, pile, or tie, you must take into account the weight of the preservative. Recommended preservative retentions are listed in Table 14–3 in Chapter 14. By knowing the volume, the preservative weight can be approximated by multiplying volume by the recommended preservative retention.

Durability

For most applications of round timbers and ties, durability is primarily a question of decay resistance. Some species are noted for their natural decay resistance; however, even these may require preservative treatment, depending upon the environmental conditions under which the material is used and the required service life. For some applications, natural decay resistance is sufficient. This is the case for temporary piles, marine piles in fresh water entirely below the permanent water level, and construction logs used in building construction. Any wood members used in ground contact should be pressure treated, and the first two or three logs above a concrete foundation should be brush treated with a preservative–sealer.

Preservative Treatment

Federal Specification TT–W–571 (U.S. Federal Supply Service (USFSS)) covers the inspection and treatment requirements for various wood products including poles, piles, and ties. This specification refers to the AWPA Standards C1 and C3 for pressure treatment, C2 and C6 for treatment of ties, C8 for full-length thermal (hot and cold) treatment of western redcedar poles, C10 for full-length thermal (hot and cold) treatment of lodgepole pine poles, and C23 for pressure treatment of construction poles. The AREA specifications for cross ties and switch ties also cover preservative treatment. Retention and types of various preservatives recommended for various applications are given in Table 14–3.

Inspection and treatment of poles in service has been effective in prolonging the useful life of untreated poles and those with inadequate preservative penetration or retention. The Forest Research Laboratory at Oregon State University has published guidelines for developing an in-service pole maintenance program.

Service Life

Service conditions for round timbers and ties vary from mild for construction logs to severe for cross ties. Construction logs used in log homes may last indefinitely if kept dry and properly protected from insects. Most railroad ties, on the other hand, are continually in ground contact and are subject to mechanical damage.

Poles

The life of poles can vary within wide limits, depending upon properties of the pole, preservative treatments, service conditions, and maintenance practices. In distribution or transmission line supports, however, service life is often limited by obsolescence of the line rather than the physical life of the pole.

It is common to report the average life of untreated or treated poles based on observations over a period of years. These average life values are useful as a rough guide to the service life to be expected from a group of poles, but it should be kept in mind that, within a given group, 60% of the poles will have failed before reaching an age equal to the average life.

Early or premature failure of treated poles can generally be attributed to one or more of three factors: (a) poor penetration and distribution of preservative, (b) an inadequate retention of preservative, or (c) use of a substandard preservative. Properly treated poles can last 35 years or longer.

Western redcedar is one species with a naturally decay-resistant heartwood. If used without treatment, however, the average life is somewhat less than 20 years.

Piles

The expected life of a pile is also determined by treatment and use. Wood that remains completely submerged in water does not decay although bacteria may cause some degradation; therefore, decay resistance is not necessary in all piles, but it is necessary in any part of the pile that may extend above the permanent water level. When piles that support the foundations of bridges or buildings are to be cut off above the permanent water level, they should be treated to conform to recognized specifications such as Federal Specification TT–W–571 and AWPA Standards C1 and C3. The untreated surfaces exposed at the cutoffs should also be given protection by thoroughly brushing the cut surface with coal-tar creosote. A coat of pitch, asphalt, or similar material may then be applied over the creosote and a protective sheet material, such as metal, roofing felt, or saturated fabric, should be fitted over the pile cut-off in accordance with AWPA Standard M4. Correct application and maintenance of these materials are critical in maintaining the integrity of piles.

Piles driven into earth that is not constantly wet are subject to about the same service conditions as apply to poles but are generally required to last longer. Preservative retention requirements for piles are therefore greater than for poles (Table 14–3). Piles used in salt water are subject to destruction by marine borers even though they do not decay below the waterline. The most effective practical protection against marine borers has been a treatment first with a waterborne preservative, followed by seasoning with a creosote treatment. Other preservative treatments of marine piles are covered in Federal Specification TT–W–571 and AWPA Standard C3 (Table 14–3).

Ties

The life of ties in service depends on their ability to resist decay and mechanical destruction. Under sufficiently light traffic, heartwood ties of naturally durable wood, even if of low strength, may give 10 or 15 years of average service without preservative treatment; under heavy traffic without adequate mechanical protection, the same ties might fail in 2 or 3 years. Advances in preservatives and treatment processes, coupled with increasing loads, are shifting the primary cause of tie failure from decay to mechanical damage. Well-treated ties, properly designed to carry intended loads, should last from 25 to 40 years on average. Records on life of treated and untreated ties are occasionally published in the annual proceedings of the American Railway Engineering Association (AREA) and AWPA.

Strength Properties

Allowable strength properties of round timbers have been developed and published in several standards. In most cases, published values are based on strength of small clear test samples. Allowable stresses are derived by adjusting small clear values for effects of growth characteristics, conditioning, shape, and load conditions as discussed in applicable standards. In addition, published values for some species of poles and piles reflect results of full-sized tests.

Poles

Most poles are used as structural members in support structures for distribution and transmission lines. For this application, poles may be designed as single-member or guyed cantilevers or as structural members of a more complex structure. Specifications for wood poles used in single pole structures have been published by ANSI in Standard O5.1. Guidelines for the design of pole structures are given in the ANSI National Electric Safety Code (NESC) (ANSI C2).

The ANSI O5.1 standard gives values for fiber stress in bending for species commonly used as transmission or distribution poles. These values represent the near-ultimate fiber stress for poles used as cantilever beams. For most species, these values are based partly on full-sized pole tests and include adjustments for moisture content and pretreatment conditioning. The values in ANSI O5.1 are compatible with the ultimate strength design philosophy of the NESC, but they are not compatible with the working stress design philosophy of the *National Design Specification* (NDS).

Reliability-based design techniques have been developed for the design of distribution–transmission line systems. This approach requires a strong database on the performance of pole structures. Supporting information for these design procedures is available in a series of reports published by the Electric Power Research Institute (EPRI).

Piles

Bearing loads on piles are sustained by earth friction along their surface (skin friction), by bearing of the tip on a solid stratum, or by a combination of these two methods. Wood piles, because of their tapered form, are particularly efficient in supporting loads by skin friction. Bearing values that depend upon friction are related to the stability of the soil and generally do not approach the ultimate strength of the pile. Where wood piles sustain foundation loads by bearing of the tip on a solid stratum, loads may be limited by the compressive strength of the wood parallel to the grain. If a large proportion of the length of a pile extends above ground, its bearing value may be limited by its strength as a long column. Side loads may also be applied to piles extending above ground. In such instances, however, bracing is often used to reduce the unsupported column length or to resist the side loads.

The most critical loads on piles often occur during driving. Under hard driving conditions, piles that are too dry (<18% moisture content at a 51-mm (2-in.) depth) have literally exploded under the force of the driving hammers. Steel banding is recommended to increase resistance to splitting, and driving the piles into predrilled holes reduces driving stresses.

The reduction in strength of a wood column resulting from crooks, eccentric loading, or any other condition that will result in combined bending and compression is not as great as would be predicted with the NDS interaction equations. This does not imply that crooks and eccentricity should be without restriction, but it should relieve anxiety as to the influence of crooks, such as those found in piles. Design procedures for eccentrically loaded columns are given in Chapter 8.

There are several ways to determine bearing capacity of piles. Engineering formulas can estimate bearing values from the penetration under blows of known energy from the driving hammer. Some engineers prefer to estimate bearing capacity from experience or observation of the behavior of pile foundations under similar conditions or from the results of static-load tests.

Working stresses for piles are governed by building code requirements and by recommendations of ASTM D2899. This standard gives recommendations for adjusting small clear strength values listed in ASTM D2555 for use in the design of full-sized piles. In addition to adjustments for properties inherent to the full-sized pile, the ASTM D2899 standard also provides recommendations for adjusting allowable stresses for the effects of pretreatment conditioning.

Design stresses for timber piles are tabulated in the NDS for wood construction. The NDS values include adjustments for the effects of moisture content, load duration, and preservative treatment. Recommendations are also given to adjust for lateral support conditions and factors of safety.

Construction Logs

Design values for round timbers used as structural members in pole or log buildings may be determined following standards published by ASTM and ASAE. The ASTM standard refers pole designers to the same standard used to derive design stresses for timber piles (D2899). The ASAE standard (EP388), which governed the derivation of construction poles for agricultural building applications, is being revised. The future revision will be designated EP560 and will deal only with round wood poles. Derivation of design stresses for construction logs used in log homes is covered in ASTM D3957, which provides a method of establishing stress grades for structural members of any of the more common log configurations. Manufacturers can use this standard to develop grading specifications and derive engineering design stresses for their construction logs.

Ties

Railroad cross and switch ties have historically been over-designed from the standpoint of rail loads. Tie service life was limited largely by deterioration rather than mechanical damage. However, because of advances in decay-inhibiting treatment and increased axle loads, adequate structural design is becoming more important in increasing railroad tie service life.

Rail loads induce stresses in bending and shear as well as in compression perpendicular to the grain in railroad ties. The AREA manual gives recommended limits on ballast bearing pressure and allowable stresses for cross ties. This information may be used by the designer to determine adequate tie size and spacing to avoid premature failure due to mechanical damage.

Specific gravity and compressive strength parallel to the grain are also important properties to consider in evaluating cross tie material. These properties indicate the resistance of the wood to both pull out and lateral thrust of spikes.

References

General

ASTM. [Current edition]. Standard test methods for establishing clear wood strength values. ASTM D2555. West Conshohocken, PA: American Society for Testing and Materials.

AWPA. [Current edition]. Book of standards (includes standards on pressure and thermal treatment of poles, piles, and ties). (American Wood-Preserver's Bureau official quality control standards.) Bethesda, MD: American Wood-Preservers' Association.

Engineering Data Management and Colorado State University. 1989–1998. International conference—Wood poles and piles. Conference proceedings. Fort Collins, CO: Engineering Data Management and Colorado State University.

USFSS. [Current edition]. Poles and piles, wood. Federal specification MM–P–371c—ties, railroad (cross and switch); Federal Specification MM–T–371d—wood preservation: treating practice; Federal Specification TT–W–571. Washington, DC: U.S. Federal Supply Service.

Poles

ANSI. [Current edition]. New York, NY: American National Standards Institute.

ANSI O5.1. Specifications and dimensions for wood poles.

ANSI C2. National electrical safety code.

ANSI O5.2. Structural glued laminated timber for utility structures.

ASTM. [Current edition]. West Conshohocken, PA: American Society for Testing and Materials.

ASTM D3200. Standard specification and methods for establishing recommended design stresses for round timber construction poles.

ANSI/ASTM D1036–58. Standard methods of static tests of wood poles.

Carson, J.M.; Dougherty, M., eds. 1997. Post-frame building handbook: Materials, design considerations, construction procedures. Ithaca, NY: Northeast Regional Agricultural Engineering Service.

EPRI. 1981. Probability-based design of wood transmission structures. (a) Vol. 1: Strength and stiffness of wood utility poles. (b) Vol. 2: Analysis and probability-based design of wood utility structures. (c) Vol. 3: Users manual. POLEDA–80. Pole design and analysis. Prepared by Research Institute of Colorado for Electric Power Research Institute. Palo Alto, CA: Electric Power Research Institute. EL1–2040. Vols. 1–3, Proj. 1352-1. September.

EPRI. 1985. Wood pole properties. Vol. 1: Background and Southern Pine data. Prepared by Research Institute of Colorado for Electric Power Research Institute. Palo Alto, CA: Electric Power Research Institute. EL–4109, Proj. 1352–2, July.

EPRI. 1986. Wood pole properties. (a) Vol. 2: Douglas Fir data. (b) Vol. 3: Western redcedar. Prepared by Research Institute of Colorado for Electric Power Research Institute. Palo Alto, CA: Electric Power Research Institute. EL–4109, Proj. 1352–2, January.

Morrell, J.J. 1996. Wood pole maintenance manual. Corvallis, OR: College of Forestry, Forest Research Laboratory, Oregon State University.

NRAES. 1997. Post-frame building construction. Ithaca, NY: Northeast Regional Agricultural Engineering Service.

Thompson, W.S. 1969. Effect of steaming and kiln drying on properties of Southern Pine poles. Part I—mechanical properties. Forest Products Journal. 19(1): 21–28.

Wood, L.W.; Erickson, E.C.O.; Dohr, A.W. 1960. Strength and related properties of wood poles. Philadelphia, PA: American Society for Testing and Materials.

Wood, L.W.; Markwardt, L.J. 1965. Derivation of fiber stresses from strength values of wood poles. Res. Pap. FPL 39. Madison, WI: U.S. Department of Agriculture, Forest Service, Forest Products Laboratory.

Piles

AREA. 1982. Timber structures. In: Manual for railway engineering. Washington, DC: American Railway Engineering Association. Chapter 7.

ASTM. [Current edition]. West Conshohocken, PA: American Society for Testing and Materials.

ASTM D25. Standard specification for round timber piles.

ASTM D2899. Establishing design stresses for round timber piles.

Armstrong, R.M. 1979. Structural properties of timber piles. In: Behavior of deep foundations. ASTM STP670. Philadelphia, PA: American Society for Testing and Materials: 118–152.

AWPI. 1969. Pile foundations know-how. Washington, DC: American Wood Preservers Institute.

NFPA. [Current edition]. National design specification for wood construction. Washington, DC: National Forest Products Association.

Thompson, W.S. 1969. Factors affecting the variation in compressive strength of Southern Pine piling. Washington, DC: American Wood-Preservers' Association.

Construction Logs

ASTM. [Current edition]. Standard methods for establishing stress grades for structural members used in log buildings. ASTM D3957. West Conshohocken, PA: American Society for Testing and Materials.

Muchmore, F.W. 1977. Design guide for native log stringer bridges. Juneau, AK: U.S. Department of Agriculture, Forest Service, Region 10.

Rowell, R.M.; Black, J.M.; Gjovik, L.R.; Feist, W.C. 1977. Protecting log cabins from decay. Gen. Tech. Rep. FPL–11. Madison, WI: U.S. Department of Agriculture, Forest Service, Forest Products Laboratory.

Ties

AREA. 1982. Ties and wood preservation. In: Manual for railway engineering. Washington, DC: American Railway Engineering Association. Chapter 3.

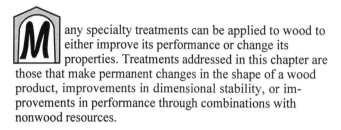

Chapter 19

Specialty Treatments

Roger M. Rowell

Contents

Many specialty treatments can be applied to wood to either improve its performance or change its properties. Treatments addressed in this chapter are those that make permanent changes in the shape of a wood product, improvements in dimensional stability, or improvements in performance through combinations with nonwood resources.

Plasticizing Wood

Principles of Plasticizing and Bending

In simple terms, the wood cell wall is a composite made of a rigid cellulose polymer in a matrix of lignin and the hemicelluloses. The lignin polymer in the middle lamella and S2 layer is thermoplastic; that is, it softens upon heating. The glass transition temperature T_g of the lignin in the matrix is approximately 170°C (338°F). Above the matrix T_g, it is possible to cause the lignin to undergo thermoplastic flow and, upon cooling, reset in the same or modified configuration. This is the principal behind bending of wood.

The matrix can be thermoplasticized by heat alone, but the T_g of the unmodified matrix is so high that some fiber decomposition can occur if high temperatures are maintained for a lengthy period. The T_g of the matrix can be decreased with the addition of moisture or through the use of plasticizers or softeners.

Heat and moisture make certain species of wood sufficiently plastic for bending operations. Steaming at atmospheric or a low gage pressure, soaking in boiling or nearly boiling water, or microwave heating moist wood are satisfactory methods of plasticizing wood. Wood at 20% to 25% moisture content needs to be heated without losing moisture; at a lower moisture content, heat and moisture must be added. As a consequence, the recommended plasticizing processes are steaming or boiling for about 15 min/cm (38 min/in) of thickness for wood at 20% to 25% moisture content and steaming or boiling for about 30 min/cm (75 min/in) of thickness for wood at lower moisture content levels. Steaming at high pressures causes wood to become plastic, but wood treated with high pressure steam generally does not bend as successfully as does wood treated at atmospheric or low pressure. Microwave heating requires much shorter times.

Wood can be plasticized by a variety of chemicals. Common chemicals that plasticize wood include water, urea, dimethylol urea, low molecular weight phenol-formaldehyde resin, dimethyl sulfoxide, and liquid ammonia. Urea and dimethylol urea have received limited commercial attention, and a bending process using liquid ammonia has been patented. Wood members can be readily molded or shaped after immersion in liquid ammonia or treatment under pressure with ammonia in the gas phase. As the ammonia evaporates, the lignin resets, the wood stiffens and retains its new shape. Plasticization of the matrix alone can be done using chemical modification technologies, which are covered later in this chapter.

It is also possible to bend wood without softening or plasticizing treatments. However, the stability of the final product may not be as permanent as from treatments in which softening and plasticizing methods are used.

Bent Wood Members

Bending can provide a variety of functional and esthetically pleasing wood members, ranging from large curved arches to small furniture components. The curvature of the bend, size of the member, and intended use of the product determine the production method.

Laminated Members

At one time in the United States, curved pieces of wood were laminated chiefly to produce small items such as parts for furniture and pianos. However, the principle was extended to the manufacture of arches for roof supports in farm, industrial, and public buildings and other types of structural members (see Ch. 11). The laminations are bent without end pressure against a form and adhesively bonded together. Both softwoods and hardwoods are suitable for laminated bent structural members, and thin material of any species can be bent satisfactorily for such purposes. The choice of species and adhesive depends primarily on the cost, required strength, and demands of the application.

Laminated curved members are produced from dry stock in a single bending and adhesive bond formation operation. This process has the following advantages compared with bending single-piece members:

- Bending thin laminations to the required radius involves only moderate stress and deformation of the wood fibers, eliminating the need for treatment with steam or hot water and associated drying and conditioning of the finished product. In addition, the moderate stresses involved in curving laminated members result in stronger members when compared with curved single-piece members.

- The tendency of laminated members to change shape with changes in moisture content is less than that of single-piece bent members.

- Ratios of thickness of member to radius of curvature that are impossible to obtain by bending single pieces can be attained readily by laminating.

- Curved members of any desired length can be produced.

Design criteria for glued-laminated timber are discussed in Chapter 11. Straight-laminated members can be steamed and bent after they are bonded together. However, this type of procedure requires an adhesive that will not be affected by the steaming or boiling treatment and complicates conditioning of the finished product.

Curved Plywood

Curved plywood is produced either by bending and adhesive bonding the plies in one operation or by bending previously bonded flat plywood. Plywood curved by bending and bonding simultaneously is more stable in curvature than plywood curved by bending previously bonded material.

Plywood Bent and Adhesively Bonded Simultaneously

In bending and bonding plywood in a single operation, adhesive-coated pieces of veneer are assembled and pressed over or between curved forms. Pressure and sometimes heat are applied through steam or electrically heated forms until the adhesive sets and holds the assembly to the desired curvature. Some laminations are at an angle, usually 90°, to other laminations, as in the manufacture of flat plywood. The grain direction of the thicker laminations is normally parallel to the axis of the bend to facilitate bending.

A high degree of compound curvature can be obtained in an assembly comprising a considerable number of thin veneers. First, for both the face and back of the assembly, the two outer plies are bonded at 90° to each other in a flat press. The remaining veneers are then adhesive-coated and assembled at any desired angle to each other. The entire assembly is hot-pressed to the desired curvature.

Bonding the two outer plies before molding allows a higher degree of compound curvature without cracking the face plies than could otherwise be obtained. Where a high degree of compound curvature is required, the veneer should be relatively thin (under 3 mm (1/8 in.)) with a moisture content of about 12%.

The molding of plywood with fluid pressure applied by flexible bags of some impermeable material produces plywood parts of various degrees of compound curvature. In "bag molding," fluid pressure is applied through a rubber bag by air, steam, or water. The veneer is wrapped around a form, and the whole assembly is enclosed in a bag and subjected to pressure in an autoclave, the pressure in the bag being "bled." Or, the veneer may be inserted inside a metal form and, after the ends have been attached and sealed, pressure is applied by inflating a rubber bag. The form may be heated electrically or by steam.

The advantages of bending and bonding plywood simultaneously to form a curved shape are similar to those for curved-laminated members. In addition, the cross plies give the curved members properties that are characteristic of cross-banded plywood. Curved plywood shells for furniture manufacture are examples of these bent veneer and adhesive-bonded products.

Plywood Bent After Bonding

After the plies are bonded together, flat plywood is often bent by methods that are somewhat similar to those used in bending solid wood. To bend plywood properly to shape, it must be plasticized by some means, usually moisture or heat, or a combination of both. The amount of curvature that can be introduced into a flat piece of plywood depends on numerous variables, such as moisture content, direction of grain, thickness and number of plies, species and quality of veneer, and the technique applied in producing the bend. Plywood is normally bent over a form or a bending mandrel.

Flat plywood bonded with a waterproof adhesive can be bent to compound curvatures after bonding. However, no simple criterion is available for predetermining whether a specific compound curvature can be imparted to flat plywood. Soaking the plywood prior to bending and using heat during forming are aids in manipulation. Usually, the plywood to be postformed is first thoroughly soaked in hot water, then dried between heated forming dies attached to a hydraulic press. If the use of postforming for bending flat plywood to compound curvatures is contemplated, exploratory trials to determine the practicability and the best procedure are recommended. Remember that in postforming plywood to compound curvatures, all the deformation must be by compression or shear because plywood cannot be stretched. Hardwood species, such as birch, poplar, and gum, are usually used in plywood that is to be postformed.

Veneered Curved Members

Veneered curved members are usually produced by bonding veneer to one or both faces of a curved solid-wood base. The bases are ordinarily sawn to the desired shape or bent from a piece grooved with saw kerfs on the concave side at right angles to the direction of bend. Pieces bent by making saw kerfs on the concave side are commonly reinforced and kept to the required curvature by bonding splines, veneer, or other pieces to the curved base. Veneering over curved solid wood is used mainly in furniture. The grain of the veneer is commonly laid in the same general direction as the grain of the curved wood base. The use of crossband veneers, that is, veneers laid with the grain at right angles to the grain of the back and face veneer, reduces the tendency of the member to split.

Bending of Solid Members

Wood of certain species that is steamed, microwaved, or soaked in boiling water can be compressed as much as 25% to 30% parallel to the grain. The same wood can be stretched only 1% to 2%. Because of the relation between attainable tensile and compressive deformations, if bending involves severe deformation, then most of the deformation must be compression. The inner or concave side must assume the maximum amount of compression, and the outer or convex side must experience zero strain or a slight tension. To accomplish this, a metal strap equipped with end fittings is customarily used. The strap makes contact with the outer or convex side and, acting through the end fittings, places the whole piece of wood in compression. The tensile stress that would normally develop in the outer side of the piece of wood during bending is borne by the metal strap. A bending form is shown in Figure 19–1.

Selection of Stock

In general, hardwoods possess better bending quality than softwoods, and certain hardwoods surpass others in this quality. This is interesting from a theoretical point of view because hardwoods contain less lignin than softwoods. Hardwoods also contain much more hemicelluloses in the matrix than do softwoods. The species commonly used to produce bent members are white oak, red oak, elm, hickory, ash, beech, birch, maple, walnut, sweetgum, and mahogany. As stated, most softwoods have a poor bending quality and are not often used in bending operations. However, Pacific yew and yellow-cedar are exceptions to this rule. In addition, Douglas-fir, southern yellow pine, northern and Atlantic white-cedar, and redwood are used for ship and boat planking for which purpose they are often bent to moderate curvature after being steamed or soaked.

Bending stock should be free from serious cross grain and distorted grain, such as may occur near knots. The slope of cross grain should not be steeper than about 1 to 15. Decay, knots, shake, pith, surface checks, and exceptionally light or brashy wood should be avoided.

Moisture Content of Bending Stock

Although green wood can be bent to produce many curved members, difficulties are encountered in drying and fixing the bend. Another disadvantage with green stock is that hydrostatic pressure may be developed during bending. Hydrostatic pressure can cause compression failures on the concave side if the wood is compressed by an amount greater than the air space in the cells of the green wood. Bending stock that has been dried to a low moisture content level requires a lengthy steaming or soaking process to increase its moisture content to the point where it can be made sufficiently plastic for successful bending. For most chair and furniture parts, the moisture content of the bending stock should be 12% to 20% before it is steamed or microwave heated. The preferred moisture content level varies with the severity of the curvature to which the wood is bent and the method used in drying and fixing the bent member. For example, chair-back slats, which have a slight curvature and are subjected to severe drying conditions between steam-heated platens, can be produced successfully from stock at 12% moisture content. For furniture parts that need a more severe bend where the part must be bent over a form, 15% to 20% moisture content is recommended.

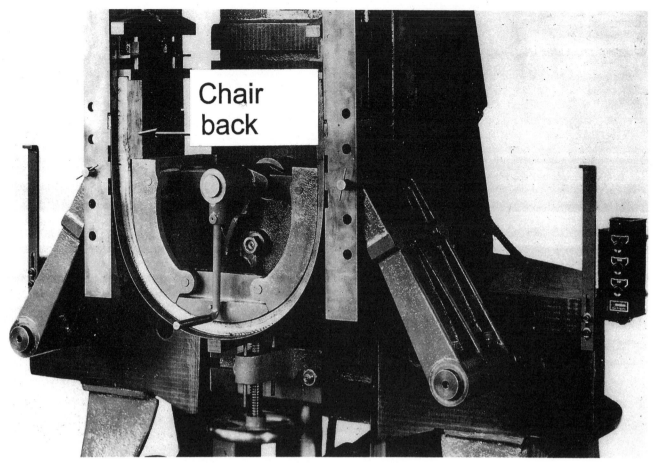

Figure 19–1. Chair back being bent through an arc of 180° in a bending machine.

Bending Operation and Apparatus

After being plasticized, the stock should be quickly placed in the bending apparatus and bent to shape. The bending apparatus consists essentially of a form (or forms) and a means of forcing the piece of steamed wood against the form. If the curvature to be obtained demands a difference of much more than 3% between lengths of the outer and inner surfaces of the pieces, then the apparatus should include a device for applying end pressure. This generally takes the form of a metal strap or pan provided with end blocks, end bars, or clamps.

Fixing the Bend

After being bent, the piece should be cooled and dried while held in its curved shape. One method is to dry the piece in the bending machine between the plates of a hot-plate press. Another method is to secure the bent piece to the form and place both the piece and the form in a drying room. Still another is to keep the bent piece in a minor strap with tie rods or stays so that it can be removed from the form and placed in a drying room. When the bent member has cooled and dried to a moisture content suitable for its intended use, the restraining devices can be removed and the piece will hold its curved shape.

Characteristics of Bent Wood

After a bent piece of wood is cooled and dried, the curvature will be maintained. An increase in moisture content may cause the piece to lose some of its curvature. A decrease in moisture content may cause the curve to become sharper, although repeated changes in moisture content bring about a gradual straightening. These changes are caused primarily by lengthwise swelling or shrinking of the inner (concave) face, the fibers of which were wrinkled or folded during the bending operation.

A bent piece of wood has less strength than a similar unbent piece. However, the reduction in strength brought about by bending is seldom serious enough to affect the utility value of the member.

Modified Woods

Wood can be chemically modified to improve water repellency, dimensional stability, resistance to acids or bases, ultraviolet radiation, biodeterioration, and thermal degradation. Wood can also be chemically treated, then compressed to improve dimensional stability and increase hardness.

Sheets of paper treated with resins or polymers can be laminated and hot pressed into thick panels that have the appearance of plastic rather than paper. These sheets are used in special applications because of their structural properties and in items requiring hard, impervious, and decorative surfaces.

Modified woods, modified wood-based materials, and paper-based laminates are usually more expensive than wood because of the cost of the chemicals and the special processing required to produce them. Thus, modified wood use is generally limited to special applications where the increased cost is justified by the special properties needed.

Wood is treated with chemicals to increase hardness and other mechanical properties, as well as its resistance to decay, fire, weathering, and moisture. The rate and extent of swelling and shrinking of the wood when in contact with water is reduced by application of water-resistant chemicals to the surface of wood, impregnation of the wood with such chemicals dissolved in water or volatile solvents, or bonding chemicals to the cell wall polymer. Such treatments may also reduce the rate at which wood changes dimension as a result of humidity, even though these treatments do not affect the final dimensional changes caused by lengthy duration exposures. Paints, varnishes, lacquers, wood-penetrating water repellents, and plastic and metallic films retard the rate of moisture absorption but have little effect on total dimensional change if exposure to moisture is extensive and prolonged.

Resin-Treated Wood (Impreg)

Permanent stabilization of the dimensions of wood is needed for certain specialty uses. This can be accomplished by depositing a bulking agent within the swollen structure of the wood fibers. The most successful bulking agents that have been commercially applied are highly water-soluble, thermosetting, phenol-formaldehyde resin-forming systems, with initially low molecular weights. No thermoplastic resins have been found that effectively stabilize the dimensions of wood.

Wood treated with a thermosetting, fiber-penetrating resin and cured without compression is known as impreg. The wood (preferably green veneer to facilitate resin pickup) is soaked in the aqueous resin-forming solution or, if air dry, is impregnated with the solution under pressure until the resin content equals 25% to 35% of the weight of dry wood. The treated wood is allowed to stand under nondrying conditions for 1 to 2 days to permit uniform distribution of the solution throughout the wood. The resin-containing wood is dried at moderate temperatures to remove the water, then heated to higher temperatures to cure the resin.

Uniform distribution of the resin has been effectively accomplished with thick wood specimens only in sapwood of readily penetrated species. Although thicker material can be treated, the process is usually applied to veneers up to about 8 mm (0.3 in.) thick, because treating time increases rapidly with increases in thickness. Drying thick, resin-treated wood may result in checking and honeycombing. For these

reasons, treatments should be confined to veneer and the treated-cured veneer used to build the desired products. Any species can be used for the veneer except the resinous pines. The stronger the original wood, the stronger the end product.

Impreg has a number of properties differing from those of normal wood and ordinary plywood. These properties are given in Table 19–1, with similar generalized findings for other modified woods. Data for the strength properties of yellow birch impreg are given in Table 19–2. Information on thermal expansion properties of ovendry impreg is given in Table 19–3.

The good dimensional stability of impreg is the basis of one use where its cost is not a deterrent. Wood dies of automobile body parts serve as the master from which the metal-forming dies are made for actual manufacture of parts. Small changes in moisture content, even with the most dimensionally stable wood, produce changes in dimension and curvature of an unmodified wood die. Such changes create major problems in making the metal-forming dies where close final tolerances are required. The substitution of impreg, with its high antishrink efficiency (ASE) (Table 19–4), almost entirely eliminated the problem of dimensional change during the entire period that the wood master dies were needed. Despite the tendency of the resins to dull cutting tools, pattern makers accepted the impreg readily because it machines with less splitting than unmodified wood.

Patterns made from impreg are also superior to unmodified wood in resisting heat when used with shell-molding techniques where temperatures as high as 205°C (400°F) are required to cure the resin in the molding sand.

Resin-Treated Compressed Wood (Compreg)

Compreg is similar to impreg except that it is compressed before the resin is cured within the wood. The resin-forming chemicals (usually phenol-formaldehyde) act as plasticizers for the wood so that it can be compressed under modest pressure (6.9 MPa; 1,000 lb/in^2) to a specific gravity of 1.35. Some properties of compreg are similar to those of impreg, and others vary considerably (Tables 19–1 and 19–2). Compared with impreg, the advantages of compreg are its natural lustrous finish that can be developed on any cut surface by sanding with fine-grit paper and buffing, its greater strength properties, and its ability to mold (Tables 19–1 and 19–2). However, thermal expansion coefficients of ovendry compreg are also increased (Table 19–3).

Compreg can be molded by (a) gluing blocks of resin-treated (but still uncured) wood with a phenolic glue so that the gluelines and resin within the plies are only partially set; (b) cutting to the desired length and width but two to three times the desired thickness; and (c) compressing in a split mold at about 150°C (300°F). Only a small flash squeeze out at the parting line between the two halves of the mold needs to be machined off. This technique was used for motor-test propellers and airplane antenna masts during World War II.

Table 19–1. Properties of modified woods

Property	Impreg	Compreg	Staypak
Specific gravity	15% to 20% greater than normal wood	Usually 1.0 to 1.4	1.25 to 1.40
Equilibrium swelling and shrinking	1/4 to 1/3 that of normal wood	1/4 to 1/3 that of normal wood at right angle to direction of compression, greater in direction of compression but very slow to attain	Same as normal wood at right angle to compression, greater in direction of compression but very slow to attain
Springback	None	Very small when properly made	Moderate when properly made
Face checking	Practically eliminated	Practically eliminated for specific gravities less than 1.3	About the same as in normal wood
Grain raising	Greatly reduced	Greatly reduced for uniform-texture woods, considerable for contrasting grain woods	About the same as in normal wood
Surface finish	Similar to normal wood	Varnished-like appearance for specific gravities greater than about 1.0. Cut surfaces can be given this surface by sanding and buffing	Varnished-like appearance. Cut surfaces can be given this surface by sanding and buffing
Permeability to water vapor	About 1/10 that of normal wood	No data but presumably much less than impreg	No data but presumably lower than impreg
Decay and termite resistance	Considerably better than normal wood	Considerably better than normal wood	Normal but decay occurs somewhat more slowly
Acid resistance	Considerably better than normal wood	Better than impreg because of impermeability	Better than normal wood because of impermeability but not as good as compreg
Alkali resistance	Same as normal wood	Somewhat better than normal wood because of impermeability	Somewhat better than normal wood because of impermeability
Fire resistance	Same as normal wood	Same as normal wood for long exposures somewhat better for short exposures	Same as normal wood for long exposures somewhat better for short exposures
Heat resistance	Greatly increased	Greatly increased	No data
Electrical conductivity	1/10 that of normal wood at 30% RH; 1/1,000 that of normal wood at 90% RH	Slightly more than impreg at low relative humidity values due to entrapped water	No data
Heat conductivity	Slightly increased	Increased about in proportion to specific gravity increase	No data but should increase about in proportion to specific gravity increase
Compressive strength	Increased more than proportional to specific gravity increase	Increased considerably more than proportional to specific gravity increase	Increased about in proportion to specific gravity increase parallel to grain, increased more perpendicular to grain
Tensile strength	Decreased significantly	Increased less than proportional to specific gravity increase	Increased about in proportion to specific gravity increase
Flexural strength	Increased less than proportional to specific gravity increase	Increased less than proportional to specific gravity increase parallel to grain, increased more perpendicular to grain	Increased proportional to specific gravity increase parallel to grain, increased more perpendicular to grain
Hardness	Increased considerably more than proportional to specific gravity increase	10 to 20 times that of normal wood	10 to 18 times that of normal wood
Impact strength Toughness	About 1/2 of value for normal wood but very susceptible to the variables of manufacture	1/2 to 3/4 of value for normal wood but very susceptible to the variables of manufacture	Same to somewhat greater than normal wood
Izod	About 1/5 of value for normal wood	1/3 to 3/4 of value for normal wood	Same to somewhat greater than normal wood
Abrasion resistance (tangential)	About 1/2 of value for normal wood	Increased about in proportion to specific gravity increase	Increased about in proportion to specific gravity increase
Machinability	Cuts cleaner than normal wood but dulls tools more	Requires metalworking tools and metal-working tool speeds	Requires metalworking tools and metalworking tool speeds
Moldability	Cannot be molded but can be formed to single curvatures at time of assembly	Can be molded by compression and expansion molding methods	Cannot be molded
Gluabilily	Same as normal wood	Same as normal wood after light sanding or in the case of thick stock, machining surfaces plane	Same as normal wood after light sanding, or in the case of thick stock, machining surfaces plane

Table 19–2. Strength properties of normal and modified laminates[a] of yellow birch and a laminated paper plastic

Property	Normal laminated wood[b]	Impreg (impregnated, uncompressed)[c]	Compreg (impregnated, highly compressed)[c]	Staypak (unimpregnated, highly compressed)[b]	Paper laminate (impregnated, highly compressed)[d]
Thickness of laminate (mm (in.))	23.9 (0.94)	26.2 (1.03)	16.0 (0.63)	12.2 (0.48)	3.2 (0.126) 13.0 (0.512)
Moisture content at time of test (%)	9.2	5.0	5.0	4.0	—
Specific gravity (based on weight and volume at test)	0.7	0.8	1.3	1.4	1.4
Parallel laminates					
Flexure—grain parallel to span (flatwise)[e]					
Proportional limit stress (MPa (lb/in^2))	79.3 (11,500)	109.6 (15,900)	184.1 (26,700)	138.6 (20,100)	109.6 (15,900)
Modulus of rupture (MPa (lb/in^2))	140.6 (20,400)	129.6 (18,800)	250.3 (36,300)	271.6 (39,400)	252.3 (36,600)
Modulus of elasticity (GPa (1,000 lb/in^2))	16.0 (2,320)	16.4 (2,380)	25.4 (3,690)	30.7 (4,450)	20.8 (3,010)
Flexure—grain perpendicular to span (flatwise)[e]					
Proportional limit stress (MPa (lb/in^2))	6.9 (1,000)	9.0 (1,300)	29.0 (4,200)	22.1 (3,200)	72.4 (10,500)
Modulus of rupture (MPa (lb/in^2))	13.1 (1,900)	11.7 (1,700)	31.7 (4,600)	34.5 (5,000)	167.5 (24,300)
Modulus of elasticity (GPa (1,000 lb/in^2))	1.0 (153)	1.5 (220)	4.3 (626)	4.2 (602)	10.2 (1,480)
Compression parallel to grain (edgewise)[e]					
Proportional limit stress (MPa (lb/in^2))	44.1 (6,400)	70.3 (10,200)	113.1 (16,400)	66.9 (9,700)	49.6 (7,200)
Ultimate strength (MPa (lb/in^2))	65.5 (9,500)	106.2 (15,400)	180.0 (26,100)	131.7 (19,100)	144.1 (20,900)
Modulus of elasticity (GPa (1,000 lb/in^2))	15.8 (2,300)	17.0 (2,470)	26.1 (3,790)	32.2 (4,670)	21.5 (3,120)
Compression perpendicular to grain (edgewise)[f]					
Proportional limit stress (MPa (lb/in^2))	4.6 (670)	6.9 (1,000)	33.1 (4,800)	17.9 (2,600)	29.0 (4,200)
Ultimate strength (MPa (lb/in^2))	14.5 (2,100)	24.8 (3,600)	96.5 (14,000)	64.8 (9,400)	125.5 (18,200)
Modulus of elasticity (GPa (1,000 lb/in^2))	1.1 (162)	1.7 (243)	3.9 (571)	4.0 (583)	11.0 (1,600)
Compression perpendicular to grain (flatwise)[e]					
Maximum crushing strength (MPa (lb/in^2))	—	29.5 (4,280)	115.1 (16,700)	91.0 (13,200)	291.0 (42,200)
Tension parallel to grain (lengthwise)					
Ultimate strength (MPa (lb/in^2))	153.1 (22,200)	108.9 (15,800)	255.1 (37,000)	310.3 (45,000)	245.4 (35,600)
Modulus of elasticity (GPa (1,000 lb/in^2))	15.8 (2,300)	17.3 (2,510)	27.2 (3,950)	31.8 (4,610)	25.1 (3,640)
Tension perpendicular to grain (edgewise)					
Ultimate strength (MPa (lb/in^2))	9.6 (1,400)	9.6 (1,400)	22.1 (3,200)	22.8 (3,300)	137.9 (20,000)
Modulus of elasticity (GPa (1,000 lb/in^2))	1.1 (166)	1.6 (227)	4.3 (622)	4.0 (575)	11.8 (1,710)
Shear strength parallel to grain (edgewise)[f]					
Johnson double shear across laminations (MPa (lb/in^2))	20.5 (2,980)	23.8 (3,460)	50.8 (7,370)	43.9 (6,370)	122.7 (17,800)
Cylindrical double shear parallel to laminations (MPa (lb/in^2))	20.8 (3,020)	24.5 (3,560)	39.2 (5,690)	21.2 (3,080)	20.7 (3,000)
Shear modulus					
Tension method (GPa (1,000 lb/in^2))	1.2 (182)	1.8 (255)	3.1 (454)	—	—
Plate shear method (FPL test) (GPa (1,000 lb/in^2))	—	—	—	2.6 (385)	6.3 (909)
Toughness (FPL test edgewise)[f] (J (in-lb))	26.6 (235)	14.1 (125)	16.4 (145)	28.2 (250)	—
Toughness (FPL test edgewise)[f] (J/mm of width (in-lb/in of width))	1.1 (250)	0.53 (120)	1.0 (230)	2.3 (515)	—
Impact strength (Izod)—grain lengthwise					
Flatwise (notch in face) (J/mm of notch (ft–lb/in of notch))	0.75 (14.0)	0.12 (2.3)	0.23 (4.3)	0.68 (12.7)	0.25 (4.7)
Edgewise (notch in face) (J/mm of notch (ft-lb/in of notch))	0.60 (11.3)	0.10 (1.9)	0.17 (3.2)[g]	—	0.036 (0.67)

411

Table 19–2. Strength properties of normal and modified laminates[a] of yellow birch and a laminated paper plastic—con.

Property	Normal laminated wood[b]	Impreg (impregnated, uncompressed)[c]	Compreg (impregnated, highly compressed)[c]	Staypak (unimpregnated, highly compressed)[b]	Paper laminate (impregnated, highly compressed)[d]
Hardness:					
Rockwell flatwise[e] (M–numbers)	—	22	84	—	110
Load to embed 11.3-mm (0.444-in.) steel ball to 1/2 its diameter (kN (lb))	7.1 (1,600)	10.7 (2,400)	—	—	—
Hardness modulus (H_M)[h] (MPa (lb/in^2))	37.2 (5,400)	63.4 (9,200)	284.8 (41,300)	302.0 (43,800)	245.4 (35,600)
Abrasion—Navy wear-test machine (flatwise)[e] wear per 1,000 revolutions (mm (in.))	0.76 (0.030)	1.45 (0.057)	0.46 (0.018)	0.38 (0.015)	0.46 (0.018)
Water absorption (24-h immersion) increase in weight (%)	43.6	13.7	2.7	4.3	2.2
Dimensional stability in thickness direction					
Equilibrium swelling (%)	9.9	2.8	8.0	29	—
Recovery from compression (%)	—	0	0	4	—
Crossband laminates					
Flexure—face grain parallel to span (flatwise)[e]					
Proportional limit stress (MPa (lb/in^2))	47.6 (6,900)	55.8 (8,100)	99.3 (14,400)	78.6 (11,400)	86.9 (12,600)
Modulus of rupture (MPa (lb/in^2))	90.3 (13,100)	78.6 (11,400)	157.2 (22,800)	173.0 (25,100)	215.8 (31,300)
Modulus of elasticity (GPa (1,000 lb/in^2))	9.0 (1,310)	11.5 (1,670)	17.1 (2,480)	20.0 (2,900)	15.4 (2,240)
Compression parallel to face grain (edgewise)[f]					
Proportional limit stress (MPa (lb/in^2))	22.8 (3,300)	35.8 (5,200)	60.0 (8,700)	35.8 (5,200)	34.5 (5,000)
Ultimate strength (MPa (lb/in^2))	40.0 (5,800)	78.6 (11,400)	164.8 (23,900)	96.5 (14,000)	130.3 (18,900)
Modulus of elasticity (GPa (1,000 lb/in^2))	9.4 (1,360)	10.3 (1,500)	15.8 (2,300)	18.6 (2,700)	16.3 (2,370)
Tension parallel to face grain (lengthwise)					
Ultimate strength (MPa (lb/in^2))	84.8 (12,300)	54.5 (7,900)	113.8 (16,500)	168.9 (24,500)	187.5 (27,200)
Modulus of elasticity (GPa (1,000 lb/in^2))	8.9 (1,290)	10.1 (1,460)	15.1 (2,190)	17.7 (2,570)	18.6 (2,700)
Toughness (FPL test edgewise)[f] (J/mm of width (in-lb/in of width))	0.47 (105)	0.18 (40)	0.51 (115)	1.4 (320)	—

[a]Laminates made from 17 plies of 1.6-mm (1/16-in.) rotary-cut yellow birch veneer.
[b]Veneer conditioned at 27°C (80°F) and 65% relative humidity before assembly with phenol resin film adhesive.
[c]Impregnation, 25% to 30% of water-soluble phenol-formaldehyde resin based on the dry weight of untreated veneer.
[d]High-strength paper (0.076-mm (0.003-in. thickness)) made from commercial unbleached black spruce pulp (*Mitscherlich subtile*), phenol resin content 36.3% based on weight of treated paper, Izod impact abrasion, flatwise compression, and shear specimens, all on 12.7-mm - (1/2-in.-) thick laminate.
[e]Load applied to the surface of the original material (parallel to laminating pressure direction).
[f]Forest Products Laboratory (FPL) test procedure: load applied to edge of laminations (perpendicular to laminating pressure direction).
[g]Values as high as 0.53 J/mm (10.0 ft-lb/in.) of notch have been reported for compreg made with alcohol-soluble resins and 0.37 J/mm (7.0 ft-lb/in) with water-soluble resins.
[h]Values based on the average slope of load–penetration plots where H_M is an expression for load per unit of spherical area of penetration of the 11.3-mm (0.444-in.) steel ball expressed in MPa (lb/in^2).

A more satisfactory molding technique, known as expansion molding, has been developed. The method consists of rapidly precompressing dry but uncured single sheets of resin-treated veneer in a cold press after preheating the sheets at 90°C to 120°C (195°F to 250°F). The heat-plasticized wood responds to compression before cooling. The heat is insufficient to cure the resin, but the subsequent cooling sets the resin temporarily. These compressed sheets are cut to the desired size, and the assembly of plies is placed in a split mold of the final desired dimensions. Because the wood was precompressed, the filled mold can be closed and locked. When the mold is heated, the wood is again plasticized and tends to recover its uncompressed dimensions. This exerts an internal pressure in all directions against the mold equal to about half the original compressing pressure. On continued heating, the resin is set. After cooling, the object may be removed from the mold in finished form. Metal inserts or metal surfaces can be molded to compreg or its handles are molded onto tools by this means. Compreg bands have been molded to the outside of turned wood cylinders without compressing the core. Compreg tubes and small airplane propellers have been molded in this way.

Past uses of compreg were related largely to aircraft; however, it is a suitable material where bolt-bearing strength is

Table 19–3. Coefficients of linear thermal expansion per degree Celsius of wood, hydrolyzed wood, and paper products[a]

| Material[b] | Specific gravity of product | Resin content[c] (%) | Linear expansion per °C (values multiplied by 10^6) | | | Cubical expansion per °C (values multiplied by 10^6) |
			Fiber or machine direction	Perpendicular to fiber or machine direction in plane of laminations	Pressing direction	
Yellow birch laminate	0.72	3.1	3.254	40.29	36.64	80.18
Yellow birch staypak laminate	1.30	4.7	3.406	37.88	65.34	106.63
Yellow birch impreg laminate	0.86	33.2	4.648	35.11	37.05	76.81
Yellow birch compreg laminate	1.30	24.8	4.251	39.47	59.14	102.86
	1.31	34.3	4.931	39.32	54.83	99.08
Sitka spruce laminate	0.53	6.0[d]	3.887	37.14	27.67	68.65
Parallel-laminated paper laminate	1.40	36.5	5.73	15.14	65.10	85.97
Crossbanded paper laminate	1.40	36.5	10.89	11.0[e]	62.2	84.09
Molded hydrolyzed-wood plastic	1.33	25	42.69	42.69	42.69	128.07
Hydrolyzed-wood sheet laminate	1.39	18	13.49	224.68	77.41	115.58

[a]These coefficients refer to bone-dry material. Generally, air-dry material has a negative thermal coefficient, because the shrinkage resulting from the loss in moisture is greater than the normal thermal expansion.
[b]All wood laminates made from rotary-cut veneer, annual rings in plane of sheet.
[c]On basis of dry weight of product.
[d]Approximate.
[e]Calculated value.

Table 19–4. Comparison of wood treatments and the degree of dimensional stability achieved

Treatment	Antishrink efficiency (%)
Simple wax dip	2 to 5
Wood–plastic combination	10 to 15
Staypak/staybwood	30 to 40
Impreg	65 to 70
Chemical modification	65 to 75
Polyethylene glycol	80 to 85
Formaldehyde	82 to 87
Compreg	90 to 95

required, as in connector plates, because of its good specific strength (strength per unit of weight). Layers of veneer making up the compreg for such uses are often cross laminated (alternate plies at right angles to each other, as in plywood) to give nearly equal properties in all directions.

As a result of its excellent strength properties, dimensional stability, low thermal conductivity, and ease of fabrication, compreg is extremely useful for aluminum drawing and forming dies, drilling jigs, and jigs for holding parts in place while welding.

Compreg has also been used in silent gears, pulleys, water-lubricated bearings, fan blades, shuttles, bobbins, and picker sticks for looms, nuts and bolts, instrument bases and cases, musical instruments, electrical insulators, tool handles, and various novelties. At present, compreg finds considerable use in handles for knives and other cutlery. The expansion-molding techniques of forming and curing of the compreg around the metal parts of the handle as well as attaching previously made compreg with rivets are two methods used.

Veneer of any nonresinous species can be used for making compreg. Most properties depend upon the specific gravity to which the wood is compressed rather than the species used. Up to the present, however, compreg has been made almost exclusively from yellow birch or sugar maple.

Untreated Compressed Wood (Staypak)

Resin-treated wood in both the uncompressed (impreg) and compressed (compreg) forms is more brittle than the original wood. To meet the demand for a tougher compressed product than compreg, a compressed wood containing no resin (staypak) was developed. It will not lose its compression under swelling conditions as will untreated compressed wood. In making staypak, the compressing conditions are modified so that the lignin-cementing material between the cellulose fibers flows sufficiently to eliminate internal stresses.

Staypak is not as water resistant as compreg, but it is about twice as tough and has higher tensile and flexural strength properties (Tables 19–1 and 19–2). The natural finish of staypak is almost equal to that of compreg. Under weathering conditions, however, it is definitely inferior to compreg. For outdoor use, a good synthetic resin varnish or paint finish should be applied to staypak.

Staypak can be used in the same way as compreg where extremely high water resistance is not needed. It shows promise in tool handles, forming dies, connector plates, propellers, and picker sticks and shuttles for weaving, where high impact strength is needed. Staypak is not impregnated; therefore, it can be made from solid wood as well as from veneer. The cost of staypak is less than compreg.

A material similar to staypak was produced in Germany prior to World War II. It was a compressed solid wood with much less dimensional stability than staypak and was known as lignostone. Another similar German product was a laminated compressed wood known as lignofol.

Untreated Heated Wood (Staybwood)

Heating wood under drying conditions at higher temperatures (95°C to 320°C (200°F to 600°F)) than those normally used in kiln drying produces a product known as staybwood that reduces the hygroscopicity and subsequent swelling and shrinking of the wood appreciably. However, the stabilization is always accompanied by loss of mechanical properties. Toughness and resistance to abrasion are most seriously affected.

Under conditions that cause a reduction of 40% in shrinking and swelling, the toughness is reduced to less than half that of the original wood. Extensive research to minimize this loss was not successful. Because of the reduction in strength properties from heating at such high temperatures, wood that is dimensionally stabilized in this manner is not used commercially.

Wood Treated With Polyethylene Glycol (PEG)

The dimensional stabilization of wood with polyethylene glycol-1000 (PEG), also known as Carbowax, is accomplished by bulking the fiber to keep the wood in a partially swollen condition. PEG acts in the same manner as does the previously described phenolic resin. It cannot be further cured. The only reason for heating the wood after treatment is to drive off water. PEG remains water soluble in the wood. Above 60% relative humidity, it is a strong humectant and, unless used with care and properly protected, PEG-treated wood can become sticky at high levels of relative humidity. Because of this, PEG-treated wood is usually finished with a polyurethane varnish.

Treatment with PEG is facilitated by using green wood. Here, pressure is not applied because the treatment is based on diffusion. Treating times are such that uniform uptakes of 25% to 30% of chemical are achieved (based on dry weight of wood). The time necessary for this uptake depends on the thickness of the wood and may require weeks. The PEG treatment is being effectively used for cross-sectional wood plaques and other decorative items. Table tops of high quality furniture stay remarkably flat and dimensionally stable when made from PEG-treated wood.

Another application of this chemical is to reduce the checking of green wood during drying. For this application, a high degree of PEG penetration is not required. This method of treatment has been used to reduce checking during drying of small wood blanks or turnings.

Cracking and distortion that old, waterlogged wood undergoes when it is dried can be substantially reduced by treating the wood with PEG. The process was used to dry 200-year-old waterlogged wooden boats raised from Lake George, New York. The "Vasa," a Swedish ship that sank on its initial trial voyage in 1628, was also treated after it was raised. There have been many applications of PEG treatment for the restoration of waterlogged wood from archeological sites.

Wood–Polymer Composites

In the modified wood products previously discussed, most of the chemical resides in cell walls; the lumens are essentially empty. If wood is vacuum impregnated with certain liquid vinyl monomers that do not swell wood and are later polymerized *in situ* by gamma radiation or chemical catalyst-heat systems, the resulting polymer resides almost exclusively in the lumens. Methyl methacrylate is a common monomer used for a wood–polymer composites. It is converted to polymethyl methacrylate. The hygroscopic characteristics of the wood substance are not altered because little, if any, polymer penetrates the cell walls. However, because of the high polymer content (70% to 100% based on the dry weight of wood), the normally high void volume of wood is greatly reduced. With the elimination of this very important pathway for vapor or liquid water diffusion, the response of the wood substance to changes in relative humidity or water is very slow, and moisture resistance or water repellent effectiveness (WRE) is greatly improved. Water repellent effectiveness is measured as follows:

WRE = [(Swelling or moisture uptake of control specimen during exposure to water for *t* minutes)
÷ (Swelling or moisture uptake of treated specimen during exposure to water also for *t* minutes)]
× 100

Hardness is increased appreciably. Wood–polymer composite materials offer desirable aesthetic appearance, high compression strength, and abrasion resistance and are much stronger than untreated wood (Table 19–5), and commercial application of these products is largely based on increased strength and hardness properties. Improvements in physical properties

Table 19–5. Strength properties of wood–polymer composites[a]

Strength property	Unit	Untreated[b]		Treated[b]	
Static bending					
Modulus of elasticity	MPa (10^3 lb/in²)	9.3	(1.356)	11.6	(1.691)
Fiber stress at proportional limit	MPa (lb/in²)	44.0	(6,387)	79.8	(11,582)
Modulus of rupture	MPa (lb/in²)	73.4	(10,649)	130.6	(18,944)
Work to proportional limit	μJ/mm³ (in-lb/in³)	11.4	(1.66)	29.1	(4.22)
Work to maximum load	μJ/mm³ (in-lb/in³)	69.4	(10.06)	122.8	(17.81)
Compression parallel to grain					
Modulus of elasticity	GPa (10^6 lb/in²)	7.7	(1.113)	11.4	(1.650)
Fiber stress at proportional limit	MPa (lb/in²)	29.6	(4,295)	52.0	(7,543)
Maximum crushing strength	MPa (lb/in²)	44.8	(6,505)	68.0	(9,864)
Work to proportional limit	μJ/mm³ (in-lb/in³)	77.8	(11.28)	147.6	(21.41)
Toughness	μJ/mm³ (in-lb/in³)	288.2	(41.8)	431.6	(62.6)

[a]Menthyl methacrylate impregnated basswood.
[b]Moisture content 7.2%.

of wood–polymer composites are related to polymer loading. This, in turn, depends not only on the permeability of the wood species but also on the particular piece of wood being treated. Sapwood is filled to a much greater extent than heartwood for most species. The most commonly used monomers include styrene, methyl methacrylate, vinyl acetate, and acrylonitrile. Industrial applications include certain sporting equipment, musical instruments, decorative objects, and high performance flooring.

At present, the main commercial use of wood polymer composites is hardwood flooring. Comparative tests with conventional wood flooring indicate that wood–polymer materials resisted indentation from rolling, concentrated, and impact loads better than did white oak. This is largely attributed to improved hardness. Abrasion resistance is also increased. A finish is usually used on these products to increase hardness and wear resistance even more.

Wood–polymer composites are also being used for sporting goods, musical instruments, and novelty items.

Chemical Modification

Through chemical reactions, it is possible to add an organic chemical to the hydroxyl groups on wood cell wall components. This type of treatment bulks the cell wall with a permanently bonded chemical. Many reactive chemicals have been used experimentally to chemically modify wood. For best results, chemicals used should be capable of reacting with wood hydroxyls under neutral or mildly alkaline conditions at temperatures less than 120°C. The chemical system should be simple and must be capable of swelling the wood structure to facilitate penetration. The complete molecule should react quickly with wood components to yield stable

chemical bonds while the treated wood retains the desirable properties of untreated wood. Reaction of wood with chemicals such as anhydrides, epoxides, isocyanates, acid chlorides, carboxylic acids, lactones, alkyl chlorides, and nitriles result in antishrink efficiency (ASE) values (Table 19–4) of 65% to 75% at chemical weight gains of 20% to 30%. Antishrink efficiency is determined as follows:

$$S = \frac{V_2 - V_1}{V_1} \times 100$$

where S is volumetric swelling coefficient, V_2 is wood volume after humidity conditioning or wetting with water, and V_1 is wood volume of ovendried sample before conditioning or wetting.

Then,

$$\text{ASE} = \frac{S_2 - S_1}{S_1} \times 100$$

where ASE is reduction in swelling or antishrink efficiency resulting from a treatment, S_2 is treated volumetric swelling coefficient, and S_1 is untreated volumetric swelling coefficient.

Reaction of these chemicals with wood yields a modified wood with increased dimensional stability and improved resistance to termites, decay, and marine organisms.

Mechanical properties of chemically modified wood are essentially unchanged compared with untreated wood.

The reaction of formaldehyde with wood hydroxyl groups is an interesting variation of chemical modification. At weight gains as low as 2%, formaldehyde-treated wood is not attacked by wood-destroying fungi. An antishrink efficiency

(Table 19–4) of 47% is achieved at a weight gain of 3.1%, 55% at 4.1, 60% at 5.5, and 90% at 7. The mechanical properties of formaldehyde-treated wood are all reduced from those of untreated wood. A definite embrittlement is observed, toughness and abrasion resistance are greatly reduced, crushing strength and bending strength are reduced about 20%, and impact bending strength is reduced up to 50%.

Paper-Based Plastic Laminates

Commercially, paper-based plastic laminates are of two types: industrial and decorative. Total annual production is equally divided between the two types. They are made by superimposing layers of paper that have been impregnated with a resinous binder and curing the assembly under heat and pressure.

Industrial Laminates

Industrial laminates are produced to perform specific functions requiring materials with predetermined balances of mechanical, electrical, and chemical properties. The most common use of such laminates is electrical insulation. The paper reinforcements used in the laminates are kraft pulp, alpha pulp, cotton linters, or blends of these. Kraft paper emphasizes mechanical strength and dielectric strength perpendicular to laminations. Alpha paper is used for its electric and electronic properties, machineability, and dimensional stability. Cotton linter paper combines greater strength than alpha paper with excellent moisture resistance.

Phenolic resins are the most suitable resins for impregnating the paper from the standpoint of high water resistance, low swelling and shrinking, and high strength properties (except for impact). Phenolics also cost less than do other resins that give comparable properties. Water-soluble resins of the type used for impreg impart the highest water resistance and compressive strength properties to the product, but they make the product brittle (low impact strength). Alcohol-soluble phenolic resins produce a considerably tougher product, but the resins fail to penetrate the fibers as well as water-soluble resins, thus imparting less water resistance and dimensional stability to the product. In practice, alcohol-soluble phenolic resins are generally used.

Paper-based plastic laminates inherit their final properties from the paper from which they are made. High strength papers yield higher strength plastic laminates than do low strength papers. Papers with definite directional properties result in plastic laminates with definite directional properties unless they are cross laminated (alternate sheets oriented with the machine direction at 90° to each other).

Improving the paper used has helped develop paper-based laminates suitable for structural use. Pulping under milder conditions and operating the paper machines to give optimum orientation of the fibers in one direction, together with the desired absorbency, contribute markedly to improvements in strength.

Strength and other properties of a paper plastic laminate are shown in Table 19–2. The National Electric Manufacturers Association L1–1 specification has additional information on industrial laminates. Paper is considerably less expensive than glass fabric or other woven fabric mats and can be molded at considerably lower pressures; therefore, the paper-based laminates generally have an appreciable price advantage over fabric laminates. However, some fabric laminates give superior electrical properties and higher impact properties. Glass fabric laminates can be molded to greater double curvatures than can paper laminates.

During World War II, a high strength paper plastic known as papreg was used for molding nonstructural and semistructural airplane parts such as gunner's seats and turrets, ammunition boxes, wing tabs, and the surfaces of cargo aircraft flooring and catwalks. Papreg was tried to a limited extent for the skin surface of airplane structural parts, such as wing tips. One major objection to its use for such parts is that it is more brittle than aluminum and requires special fittings. Papreg has been used to some extent for heavy-duty truck floors and industrial processing trays for nonedible materials. Because it can be molded at low pressures and is made from thin paper, papreg is advantageous for use where accurate control of panel thickness is required.

Decorative Laminates

Although made by the same process as industrial laminates, decorative laminates are used for different purposes and bear little outward resemblance to industrial laminate. They are used as facings for doors and walls and tops of counters, flooring, tables, desks, and other furniture.

These decorative laminates are usually composed of a combination of phenolic- and melamine-impregnated sheets of paper. Phenolic-impregnated sheets are brown because of the impregnating resins and comprise most of the built-up thickness of the laminate. Phenolic sheets are overlaid with paper impregnated with melamine resin. One sheet of the overlay is usually a relatively thick one of high opacity and has the color or design printed on it. Then, one or more tissue-thin sheets, which become transparent after the resin is cured, are overlaid on the printed sheet to protect it in service. The thin sheets generally contain more melamine resin than do the printed sheets, providing stain and abrasion resistance as well as resistance to cigarette burns, boiling water, and common household solvents.

The resin-impregnated sheets of paper are hot pressed, cured, then bonded to a wood-based core, usually plywood, hardboard, or particleboard. The thin transparent (when cured) papers impregnated with melamine resin can be used alone as a covering for decorative veneers in furniture to provide a permanent finish. In this use, the impregnated sheet is bonded to the wood surface in hot presses at the same time the resin is cured. The heat and stain resistance and the strength of this kind of film make it a superior finish.

The overall thickness of a laminate may obviously be varied by the number of sheets of kraft-phenolic used in the core assembly. Some years ago, a 2-mm (0.08-in.) thickness was used with little exception because of its high impact strength and resistance to substrate show through. Recently, a 1-mm (0.04-in.) thickness has become popular on vertical surfaces such as walls, cabinet doors, and vertical furniture faces. This results in better economy, because the greater strength of the heavier laminate is not necessary. As applications have proliferated, a whole series of thicknesses have been offered from about 20 to 60 mm (0.8 to 2.4 in.), even up to 150 mm (6 in.) when self-supportive types are needed. These laminates may have decorative faces on both sides if desired, especially in the heavier thicknesses. Replacement bowling lanes made from high-density fiberboard core and phenolic-melamine, high-pressure laminated paper on the face and back are commercially used.

The phenolic sheets may also contain special postforming-type phenolic resins or extensible papers that make it possible to postform the laminate. By heating to 160°C (320°F) for a short time, the structure can readily undergo simple bending to a radius of 10 mm (0.4 in.) and 5 to 6 mm (0.20 to 0.24 in.) with careful control. Rolled furniture edges, decorative moldings, curved counter tops, shower enclosures, and many other applications are served by this technique. Finally, the core composition may be modified to yield a fire-retardant, low smoking laminate to comply with fire codes. These high-pressure decorative laminates are covered by the National Electrical Manufacturers Association Specification LD3.

Paper will absorb or give off moisture, depending upon conditions of exposure. This moisture change causes paper to shrink and swell, usually more across the machine direction than along it. In the same manner, the laminated paper plastics shrink and swell, although at a much slower rate. Cross laminating minimizes the amount of this shrinking and swelling. In many furniture uses where laminates are bonded to cores, the changes in dimension, as a result of moisture fluctuating with the seasons, are different than those of the core material. To balance the construction, a paper plastic with similar properties may be glued to the opposite face of the core to prevent bowing or cupping caused by the moisture variation.

Lignin-Filled Laminates

The cost of phenolic resins at one time resulted in considerable effort to find impregnating and bonding agents that were less expensive and yet readily available. Lignin-filled laminates made with lignin recovered from the spent liquor of the soda pulping process have been produced as a result of this search. Lignin is precipitated from solution within the pulp or added in a pre-precipitated form before the paper is made. The lignin-filled sheets of paper can be laminated without the addition of other resins, but their water resistance is considerably enhanced when some phenolic resin is applied to the paper in a second operation. The water resistance can also be improved by impregnating only the surface sheet with phenolic resin. It is also possible to introduce lignin, together with phenolic resin, into untreated paper sheets.

The lignin-filled laminates are always dark brown or black. They have better toughness than phenolic laminates; in most other strength properties, they are comparable or lower.

Reduction in cost of phenolic resins has virtually eliminated the lignin-filled laminates from American commerce. These laminates have several potential applications, however, where a cheaper laminate with less critical properties than phenolic laminates can be used.

Paper-Face Overlays

Paper has found considerable use as an overlay material for veneer or plywood. Overlays can be classified into three different types according to their use—masking, structural, and decorative. Masking overlays are used to cover minor defects in plywood, such as face checks and patches, minimize grain raising, and provide a more uniform paintable surface, thus making possible the use of lower grade veneer. Paper for this purpose need not be of high strength, because the overlays do not need to add strength to the product. For adequate masking, a single surface sheet with a thickness of 0.5 to 1 mm (0.02 to 0.04 in.) is desirable. Paper impregnated with phenolic resins at 17% to 25% of the weight of the paper gives the best all-around product. Higher resin content makes the product too costly and tends to make the overlay more transparent. Appreciably lower resin content gives a product with low scratch and abrasion resistance, especially when the panels are wet or exposed to high relative humidities.

The paper faces can be applied at the same time that the veneer is assembled into plywood in a hot press. Thermal stresses that might result in checking are not set up if the machine direction of the paper overlays is at right angles to the grain direction of the face plies of the plywood.

The masking-paper-based overlays or vulcanized fiber sheets have been used for such applications as wood house siding that is to be painted. These overlays mask defects in the wood, prevent bleed through of resins and extractives in the wood, and provide a better substrate for paint. The paper-based overlays improve the across-the-board stability from changes in dimension as a result of changes in moisture content.

The structural overlay, also known as the high-density overlay, contains no less than 45% thermosetting resin, generally phenolic. It consists of one or more plies of paper similar to that used in the industrial laminates described previously. The resin-impregnated papers can be bonded directly to the surface of a wood substrate during cure of the sheet, thus requiring only a single pressing operation.

The decorative-type overlay is described in the Decorative Laminates section.

References

Clark, W.M. 1965. Veneering and wood bending in the furniture industry. New York, NY: Pergamon Press.

Forest Products Laboratory. 1962. Physical and mechanical properties of lignin-filled laminated paper plastic. FPL Rep. 1579. Madison, WI: U.S. Department of Agriculture, Forest Service, Forest Products Laboratory.

Heebink, B.G. 1959. Fluid-pressure molding of plywood. FPL Rep. 1624. Madison, WI: U.S. Department of Agriculture, Forest Service, Forest Products Laboratory.

Heebink, B.G. 1963. Importance of balanced construction in plastic-faced wood panels. Res. Note FPL–021. Madison, WI: U.S. Department of Agriculture, Forest Service, Forest Products Laboratory.

Heebink, B.G.; Haskell, H.H. 1962. Effect of heat and humidity on the properties of high-pressure laminates. Forest Products Journal. 12(11): 542–548.

Hoadley, R.B. 1980. Understanding wood: a craftsman's guide to wood technology. Newtown, CT: The Taunton Press.

Hurst, K. 1962. Plywood bending. Australian Timber Journal. June.

Inoue, M.; Norimoto, M.; Tanahashi, M.; Rowell, R.M. 1993. Steam and heat fixation of compressed wood. Wood and Fiber Science. 25(3): 224–235.

Jorgensen, R.N. 1965. Furniture wood bending, Part I. Furniture Design and Manufacturing. Dec.

Jorgensen, R.N. 1966. Furniture wood bending, Part II. Furniture Design and Manufacturing. Jan.

Langwig, J.E.; Meyer, J.A.; Davidson, R.W. 1968. Influence of polymer impregnation on mechanical properties of basswood. Forest Products Journal. 18(7): 33–36.

McKean, H.B.; Blumenstein, R.R.; Finnorn, W.F. 1952. Laminating and steam bending of treated and untreated oak for ship timbers. Southern Lumberman. 185: 2321.

Meyer, J.A. 1965. Treatment of wood–polymer systems using catalyst-heat techniques. Forest Products Journal. 15(9): 362–364.

Meyer, J.A.; Loos, W.E. 1969. Treating Southern Pine wood for modification of properties. Forest Products Journal. 19(12): 32–38.

National Electrical Manufacturers Association. (Current edition). Standard specification for industrial laminated thermosetting products. Designation L1-1 and Standard specification for high-pressure decorative laminates. Designation LD–3. Washington, DC: NEMA.

Peck, E.C. 1957. Bending solid wood to form. Agric. Handb. 125. Washington, DC: U.S. Department of Agriculture.

Perry, T.D. 1951. Curves from flat plywood. Wood Products. 56(4).

Rowell, R.M. 1975. Chemical modification of wood: advantages and disadvantages. American Wood-Preservers Association Proceedings. 71: 41–51.

Rowell, R.M., ed. 1984. The chemistry of solid wood. Advances in Chemistry Series No. 207. American Chemical Society.

Schuerch, C. 1964. Principles and potential of wood plasticization. Forest Products Journal. 14(9): 377–381.

Seborg, R.M.; Inverarity, R.B. 1962. Preservation of old, waterlogged wood by treatment with polyethylene glycol. Science. 136(3516): 649–650.

Seborg, R.M.; Vallier, A.E. 1954. Application of impreg for patterns and die models. Forest Products Journal. 4(5): 305–312.

Seborg, R.M.; Millett, M.A.; Stamm, A.J. 1945. Heat-stabilized compressed wood (staypak). Mechanical Engineering. 67(1): 25–31.

Seidl, R.J. 1947. Paper and plastic overlays for veneer and plywood. Madison, WI: Forest Products Research Society Proceedings. 1: 23–32.

Spielman, F. 1980. Working green wood with PEG. New York, NY: Sterling Publishing Company.

Stamm, A.J. 1959. Effect of polyethylene glycol on dimensional stability of wood. Forest Products Journal. 9(10): 375–381.

Stamm, A.J. 1964. Wood and cellulose science. New York, NY: Ronald Press.

Stamm, A.J.; Seborg, R.M. 1951. Forest Products Laboratory resin-treated laminated, compressed wood (compreg). FPL Rep. 1381. Madison, WI: U.S. Department of Agriculture, Forest Service, Forest Products Laboratory.

Stamm, A.J.; Seborg, R.M. 1962. Forest Products Laboratory resin-treated wood (impreg). FPL Rep. 1380. (rev.) Madison, WI: U.S. Department of Agriculture, Forest Service, Forest Products Laboratory.

Stevens, W.C.; Turner, N. 1970. Wood bending handbook. London, England: Her Majesty's Stationery Office.

Weatherwax, R.C.; Stamm, A.J. 1945. Electrical resistivity of resin-treated wood (impreg and compreg), hydrolyzed-wood sheet (hydroxylin), and laminated resin-treated paper (papreg). FPL Rep. 1385. Madison, WI: U.S. Department Agriculture, Forest Service, Forest Products Laboratory.

Weatherwax, R.C.; Stamm, A.J. 1946. The coefficients of thermal expansion of wood and wood products. Transactions of American Society of Mechanical Engineering. 69(44): 421–432.

Glossary

Adherend. A body that is held to another body by an adhesive.

Adhesion. The state in which two surfaces are held together by interfacial forces which may consist of valence forces or interlocking action or both.

Adhesive. A substance capable of holding materials together by surface attachment. It is a general term and includes cements, mucilage, and paste, as well as glue.

Assembly Adhesive—An adhesive that can be used for bonding parts together, such as in the manufacture of a boat, airplane, furniture, and the like.

Cold-Setting Adhesive—An adhesive that sets at temperatures below 20°C (68°F).

Construction Adhesive—Any adhesive used to assemble primary building materials into components during building construction—most commonly applied to elastomer-based mastic-type adhesives.

Contact Adhesive—An adhesive that is apparently dry to the touch and, which will adhere to itself instantaneously upon contact; also called contact bond adhesive or dry bond adhesive.

Gap-Filling Adhesive—An adhesive capable of forming and maintaining a bond between surfaces that are not close fitting.

Hot-Melt Adhesive—An adhesive that is applied in a molten state and forms a bond on cooling to a solid state.

Hot-Setting Adhesive—An adhesive that requires a temperature at or above 100°C (212°F) to set it.

Room-Temperature-Curing Adhesive—An adhesive that sets in the temperature range of 20°C to 30°C (68°F to 86°F), in accordance with the limits for Standard Room Temperature specified in the Standard Methods of Conditioning Plastics and Electrical Insulating Materials for Testing (ASTM D618).

Solvent Adhesive—An adhesive having a volatile organic liquid as a vehicle. (This term excludes water-based adhesives.)

Structural Adhesive—A bonding agent used for transferring required loads between adherends exposed to service environments typical for the structure involved.

Air-Dried. (See **Seasoning**.)

Allowable Property. The value of a property normally published for design use. Allowable properties are identified with grade descriptions and standards, reflect the orthotropic structure of wood, and anticipate certain end uses.

Allowable Stress. (See **Allowable Property**.)

American Lumber Standard. The American Softwood Lumber Standard, Voluntary Product Standard PS–20 (National Institute of Standards and Technology), establishes standard sizes and requirements for the development and coordination of lumber grades of various species, the assignment of design values when called for, and the preparation of grading rules applicable to each species. It provides for implementation of the standard through an accreditation and certification program to assure uniform industry-wide marking and inspection. A purchaser must, however, make use of grading association rules because the basic standards are not in themselves commercial rules.

Anisotropic. Exhibiting different properties when measured along different axes. In general, fibrous materials such as wood are anisotropic.

Assembly Joint. (See **Joint**.)

Assembly Time. (See **Time, Assembly**.)

Balanced Construction. A construction such that the forces induced by uniformly distributed changes in moisture content will not cause warping. Symmetrical construction of plywood in which the grain direction of each ply is perpendicular to that of adjacent plies is balanced construction.

Bark Pocket. An opening between annual growth rings that contains bark. Bark pockets appear as dark streaks on radial surfaces and as rounded areas on tangential surfaces.

Bastard Sawn. Lumber (primarily hardwoods) in which the annual rings make angles of 30° to 60° with the surface of the piece.

Beam. A structural member supporting a load applied transversely to it.

Bending, Steam. The process of forming curved wood members by steaming or boiling the wood and bending it to a form.

Bent Wood. (See **Bending, Steam**.)

Bird Peck. A small hole or patch of distorted grain resulting from birds pecking through the growing cells in the tree. The shape of bird peck usually resembles a carpet tack with the point towards the bark; bird peck is usually accompanied by discoloration extending for considerable distance along the grain and to a much lesser extent across the grain.

Birdseye. Small localized areas in wood with the fibers indented and otherwise contorted to form few to many small circular or elliptical figures remotely resembling birds' eyes on the tangential surface. Sometimes found in sugar maple and used for decorative purposes; rare in other hardwood species.

Blister. An elevation of the surface of an adherend, somewhat resembling in shape a blister on human skin; its boundaries may be indefinitely outlined, and it may have burst and become flattened. (A blister may be caused by insufficient adhesive; inadequate curing time, temperature, or pressure; or trapped air, water, or solvent vapor.)

Bloom. Crystals formed on the surface of treated wood by exudation and evaporation of the solvent in preservative solutions.

Blow. In plywood and particleboard especially, the development of steam pockets during hot pressing of the panel, resulting in an internal separation or rupture when pressure is released, sometimes with an audible report.

Blue Stain. (See **Stain**.)

Board. (See **Lumber**.)

Board Foot. A unit of measurement of lumber represented by a board 12 in. long, 12 in. wide, and 1 in. thick or its cubic equivalent. In practice, the board foot calculation for lumber 1 in. or more in thickness is based on its nominal thickness and width and the actual length. Lumber with a nominal thickness of less than 1 in. is calculated as 1 in.

Bole. The main stem of a tree of substantial diameter—roughly, capable of yielding sawtimber, veneer logs, or large poles. Seedlings, saplings, and small-diameter trees have stems, not boles.

419

Bolt. (1) A short section of a tree trunk. (2) In veneer production, a short log of a length suitable for peeling in a lathe.

Bond. (1) The union of materials by adhesives. (2) To unite materials by means of an adhesive.

Bondability. Term indicating ease or difficulty in bonding a material with adhesive.

Bond Failure. Rupture of adhesive bond.

Bondline. The layer of adhesive that attaches two adherends.

Bondline Slip. Movement within and parallel to the bondline during shear.

Bond Strength. The unit load applied in tension, compression, flexure, peel impact, cleavage, or shear required to break an adhesive assembly, with failure occurring in or near the plane of the bond.

Bow. The distortion of lumber in which there is a deviation, in a direction perpendicular to the flat face, from a straight line from end-to-end of the piece.

Box Beam. A built-up beam with solid wood flanges and plywood or wood-based panel product webs.

Boxed Heart. The term used when the pith falls entirely within the four faces of a piece of wood anywhere in its length. Also called boxed pith.

Brashness. A condition that causes some pieces of wood to be relatively low in shock resistance for the species and, when broken in bending, to fail abruptly without splintering at comparatively small deflections.

Breaking Radius. The limiting radius of curvature to which wood or plywood can be bent without breaking.

Bright. Free from discoloration.

Broad-Leaved Trees. (See **Hardwoods.**)

Brown Rot. (See **Decay.**)

Brown Stain. (See **Stain.**)

Built-Up Timbers. An assembly made by joining layers of lumber together with mechanical fastenings so that the grain of all laminations is essentially parallel.

Burl. (1) A hard, woody outgrowth on a tree, more or less rounded in form, usually resulting from the entwined growth of a cluster of adventitious buds. Such burls are the source of the highly figured burl veneers used for purely ornamental purposes. (2) In lumber or veneer, a localized severe distortion of the grain generally rounded in outline, usually resulting from overgrowth of dead branch stubs, varying from one to several centimeters (one-half to several inches) in diameter; frequently includes one or more clusters of several small contiguous conical protuberances, each usually having a core or pith but no appreciable amount of end grain (in tangential view) surrounding it.

Butt Joint. (See **Joint.**)

Buttress. A ridge of wood developed in the angle between a lateral root and the butt of a tree, which may extend up the stem to a considerable height.

Cambium. A thin layer of tissue between the bark and wood that repeatedly subdivides to form new wood and bark cells.

Cant. A log that has been slabbed on one or more sides. Ordinarily, cants are intended for resawing at right angles to their widest sawn face. The term is loosely used. (See **Flitch.**)

Casehardening. A condition of stress and set in dry lumber characterized by compressive stress in the outer layers and tensile stress in the center or core.

Catalyst. A substance that initiates or changes the rate of chemical reaction but is not consumed or changed by the reaction.

Cell. A general term for the anatomical units of plant tissue, including wood fibers, vessel members, and other elements of diverse structure and function.

Cellulose. The carbohydrate that is the principal constituent of wood and forms the framework of the wood cells.

Check. A lengthwise separation of the wood that usually extends across the rings of annual growth and commonly results from stresses set up in wood during seasoning.

Chemical Brown Stain. (See **Stain.**)

Chipboard. A paperboard used for many purposes that may or may not have specifications for strength, color, or other characteristics. It is normally made from paper stock with a relatively low density in the thickness of 0.1524 mm (0.006 in.) and up.

Cleavage. In an adhesively bonded joint, a separation in the joint caused by a wedge or other crack-opening-type action.

Close Grained. (See **Grain.**)

Coarse Grained. (See **Grain.**)

Cohesion. The state in which the constituents of a mass of material are held together by chemical and physical forces.

Cold Pressing. A bonding operation in which an assembly is subjected to pressure without the application of heat.

Cold-Press Plywood. (See **Wood-Based Composite Panel.**)

Collapse. The flattening of single cells or rows of cells in heartwood during the drying or pressure treatment of wood. Often characterized by a caved-in or corrugated appearance of the wood surface.

Compartment Kiln. (See **Kiln.**)

Composite Assembly. A combination of two or more materials bonded together that perform as a single unit.

Composite Panel. (See **Wood-Based Composite Panel.**)

Compound Curvature. Wood bent to a compound curvature, no element of which is a straight line.

Compreg. Wood in which the cell walls have been impregnated with synthetic resin and compressed to give it reduced swelling and shrinking characteristics and increased density and strength properties.

Compression Failure. Deformation of the wood fibers resulting from excessive compression along the grain either in direct end compression or in bending. It may develop in standing trees due to bending by wind or snow or to internal longitudinal stresses developed in growth, or it may result from stresses imposed after the tree is cut. In surfaced lumber, compression failures may appear as fine wrinkles across the face of the piece.

Compression Wood. Abnormal wood formed on the lower side of branches and inclined trunks of softwood trees. Compression wood is identified by its relatively wide annual rings (usually eccentric when viewed on cross section of branch or trunk), relatively large amount of latewood (sometimes more than 50% of the width of the annual rings in which it occurs), and its lack of demarcation between earlywood and latewood in the same annual rings. Compression wood shrinks excessively longitudinally, compared with normal wood.

Conditioning (pre and post). The exposure of a material to the influence of a prescribed atmosphere for a stipulated period of time or until a stipulated relation is reached between material and atmosphere.

Conifer. (See **Softwoods.**)

Connector, Timber. Metal rings, plates, or grids that are embedded in the wood of adjacent members, as at the bolted points of a truss, to increase the strength of the joint.

Consistency. That property of a liquid adhesive by virtue of which it tends to resist deformation. (Consistency is not a fundamental property but is composed of rheological properties such as viscosity, plasticity, and other phenomena.)

Construction Adhesive. (See **Adhesive.**)

Contact Angle. The angle between a substrate plane and the free surface of a liquid droplet at the line of contact with the substrate.

Cooperage. Containers consisting of two round heads and a body composed of staves held together with hoops, such as barrels and kegs.

> **Slack Cooperage**—Cooperage used as containers for dry, semidry, or solid products. The staves are usually not closely fitted and are held together with beaded steel, wire, or wood hoops.

> **Tight Cooperage**—Cooperage used as containers for liquids, semisolids, or heavy solids. Staves are well fitted and held tightly with cooperage-grade steel hoops.

Copolymer. Substance obtained when two or more types of monomers polymerize.

Corbel. A projection from the face of a wall or column supporting a weight.

Core Stock. A solid or discontinuous center ply used in panel-type glued structures (such as furniture panels and solid or hollowcore doors).

Coupling Agent. A molecule with different or like functional groups that is capable of reacting with surface molecules of two different substances, thereby chemically bridging the substances.

Covalent Bond. A chemical bond that results when electrons are shared by two atomic nuclei.

Creep. (1) Time dependent deformation of a wood member under sustained wood. (2) In an adhesive, the time-dependent increase in strain resulting from a sustained stress.

Crook. The distortion of lumber in which there is a deviation, in a direction perpendicular to the edge, from a straight line from end-to-end of the piece.

Crossband. To place the grain of layers of wood at right angles in order to minimize shrinking and swelling; also, in plywood of three or more plies, a layer of veneer whose grain direction is at right angles to that of the face plies.

Cross Break. A separation of the wood cells across the grain. Such breaks may be due to internal stress resulting from unequal longitudinal shrinkage or to external forces.

Cross Grained. (See **Grain.**)

Cross-Link. An atom or group connecting adjacent molecules in a complex molecular structure.

Cup. A distortion of a board in which there is a deviation flatwise from a straight line across the width of the board.

Cure. To change the properties of an adhesive by chemical reaction (which may be condensation, polymerization, or vulcanization) and thereby develop maximum strength. Generally accomplished by the action of heat or a catalyst, with or without pressure.

Curing Agent. (See **Hardener.**)

Curing Temperature. (See **Temperature, Curing.**)

Curing Time. (See **Time, Curing.**)

Curly Grained. (See **Grain.**)

Curtain Coating. Applying liquid adhesive to an adherend by passing the adherend under a thin curtain of liquid falling by gravity or pressure.

Cut Stock. (See **Lumber for Dimension.**)

Cuttings. In hardwoods, portions of a board or plank having the quality required by a specific grade or for a particular use. Obtained from a board by crosscutting or ripping.

Decay. The decomposition of wood substance by fungi.

> **Advanced (Typical) Decay**—The older stage of decay in which the destruction is readily recognized because the wood has become punky, soft and spongy, stringy, ringshaked, pitted, or crumbly. Decided discoloration or bleaching of the rotted wood is often apparent.

> **Brown Rot**—In wood, any decay in which the attack concentrates on the cellulose and associated carbohydrates rather than on the lignin, producing a light to dark brown friable residue—hence loosely termed "dry rot." An advanced stage where the wood splits along rectangular planes, in shrinking, is termed "cubical rot."

> **Dry Rot**—A term loosely applied to any dry, crumbly rot but especially to that which, when in an advanced stage, permits the wood to be crushed easily to a dry powder. The term is actually a misnomer for any decay, since all fungi require considerable moisture for growth.

> **Incipient Decay**—The early stage of decay that has not proceeded far enough to soften or otherwise perceptibly impair the hardness of the wood. It is usually accompanied by a slight discoloration or bleaching of the wood.

> **Heart Rot**—Any rot characteristically confined to the heartwood. It generally originates in the living tree.

> **Pocket Rot**—Advanced decay that appears in the form of a hole or pocket, usually surrounded by apparently sound wood.

Soft Rot—A special type of decay developing under very wet conditions (as in cooling towers and boat timbers) in the outer wood layers, caused by cellulose-destroying microfungi that attack the secondary cell walls and not the intercellular layer.

White-Rot—In wood, any decay or rot attacking both the cellulose and the lignin, producing a generally whitish residue that may be spongy or stringy rot, or occur as pocket rot.

Delamination. The separation of layers in laminated wood or plywood because of failure of the adhesive, either within the adhesive itself or at the interface between the adhesive and the adherend.

Delignification. Removal of part or all of the lignin from wood by chemical treatment.

Density. As usually applied to wood of normal cellular form, density is the mass per unit volume of wood substance enclosed within the boundary surfaces of a wood–plus–voids complex. It is variously expressed as pounds per cubic foot, kilograms per cubic meter, or grams per cubic centimeter at a specified moisture content.

Density Rules. A procedure for segregating wood according to density, based on percentage of latewood and number of growth rings per inch of radius.

Dew Point. The temperature at which a vapor begins to deposit as a liquid. Applies especially to water in the atmosphere.

Diagonal Grained. (See **Grain.**)

Diffuse-Porous Wood. Certain hardwoods in which the pores tend to be uniform in size and distribution throughout each annual ring or to decrease in size slightly and gradually toward the outer border of the ring.

Dimension. (See **Lumber for Dimension.**)

Dipole–Dipole Forces. Intermolecular attraction forces between polar molecules that result when positive and negative poles of molecules are attracted to one another.

Dote. "Dote," "doze," and "rot" are synonymous with "decay" and are any form of decay that may be evident as either a discoloration or a softening of the wood.

Double Spread. (See **Spread.**)

Dry-Bulb Temperature. The temperature of air as indicated by a standard thermometer. (See **Psychrometer.**)

Dry Kiln. (See **Kiln.**)

Dry Rot. (See **Decay.**)

Dry Strength. The strength of an adhesive joint determined immediately after drying under specified conditions or after a period of conditioning in a standard laboratory atmosphere.

Dry Wall. Interior covering material, such as gypsum board, hardboard, or plywood, which is applied in large sheets or panels.

Durability. A general term for permanence or resistance to deterioration. Frequently used to refer to the degree of resistance of a species of wood to attack by wood-destroying fungi under conditions that favor such attack. In this connection, the term "decay resistance" is more specific. As applied to bondlines, the life expectancy of the structural qualities of the adhesive under the anticipated service conditions of the structure.

Earlywood. The portion of the growth ring that is formed during the early part of the growing season. It is usually less dense and weaker mechanically than latewood.

Edge Grained. (See **Grain.**)

Edge Joint. (See **Joint.**)

Elastomer. A macromolecular material that, at room temperature, is deformed by application of a relatively low force and is capable of recovering substantially in size and shape after removal of the force.

Embrittlement. A loss in strength or energy absorption without a corresponding loss in stiffness. Clear, straight-grained wood is generally considered a ductile material; chemical treatments and elevated temperatures can alter the original chemical composition of wood, thereby embrittling the wood.

Encased Knot. (See **Knot.**)

End Grained. (See **Grain.**)

End Joint. (See **Joint.**)

Equilibrium Moisture Content. The moisture content at which wood neither gains nor loses moisture when surrounded by air at a given relative humidity and temperature.

Excelsior. (See **Wood Wool.**)

Extender. A substance, generally having some adhesive action, added to an adhesive to reduce the amount of the primary binder required per unit area.

Exterior Plywood. (See **Wood-Based Composite Panel.**)

Extractive. Substances in wood, not an integral part of the cellular structure, that can be removed by solution in hot or cold water, ether, benzene, or other solvents that do not react chemically with wood components.

Extrusion Spreading. A method of adhesive application in which adhesive is forced through small openings in the spreader head.

Factory and Shop Lumber. (See **Lumber.**)

Failure, Adherend. Rupture of an adhesive joint, such that the separation appears to be within the adherend.

Failure, Adhesive. Rupture of an adhesive joint, such that the plane of separation appears to be at the adhesive–adherend interface.

Failure, Cohesive. Rupture of an adhesive joint, such that the separation appears to be within the adhesive.

Feed Rate. The distance that the stock being processed moves during a given interval of time or operational cycle.

Fiber, Wood. A wood cell comparatively long (≤ 40 to 300 mm, ≤ 1.5 to 12 in.), narrow, tapering, and closed at both ends.

Fiberboard. (See **Wood-Based Composite Panel.**)

Fiber Saturation Point. The stage in the drying or wetting of wood at which the cell walls are saturated and the cell cavities free from water. It applies to an individual cell or group of cells, not to whole boards. It is usually taken as approximately 30% moisture content, based on ovendry weight.

Fibril. A threadlike component of cell walls, invisible under a light microscope.

Figure. The pattern produced in a wood surface by annual growth rings, rays, knots, deviations from regular grain such as interlocked and wavy grain, and irregular coloration.

Filler. In woodworking, any substance used to fill the holes and irregularities in planed or sanded surfaces to decrease the porosity of the surface before applying finish coatings. As applied to adhesives, a relatively nonadhesive substance added to an adhesive to improve its working properties, strength, or other qualities.

Fine Grained. (See **Grain**.)

Fingerjoint. (See **Joint**.)

Finish (Finishing). (1) Wood products such as doors, stairs, and other fine work required to complete a building, especially the interior. (2) Coatings of paint, varnish, lacquer, wax, or other similar materials applied to wood surfaces to protect and enhance their durability or appearance.

Fire Endurance. A measure of the time during which a material or assembly continues to exhibit fire resistance under specified conditions of test and performance.

Fire Resistance. The property of a material or assembly to withstand fire or give protection from it. As applied to elements of buildings, it is characterized by the ability to confine a fire or to continue to perform a given structural function, or both.

Fire Retardant. (See **Flame Retardant**.)

Fire-Retardant-Treated Wood. As specified in building codes, a wood product that has been treated with chemicals by a pressure process or treated during the manufacturing process for the purpose of reducing its flame spread performance in an ASTM E84 test conducted for 30 min to performance levels specified in the codes.

Flake. A small flat wood particle of predetermined dimensions, uniform thickness, with fiber direction essentially in the plane of the flake; in overall character resembling a small piece of veneer. Produced by special equipment for use in the manufacture of flakeboard.

Flakeboard. (See **Wood-Based Composite Panel**.)

Flame Retardant. A treatment, coating, or chemicals that when applied to wood products delays ignition and reduces the flame spread of the product.

Flame Spread. The propagation of a flame away from the source of ignition across the surface of a liquid or a solid, or through the volume of a gaseous mixture.

Flat Grained. (See **Grain**.)

Flat Sawn. (See **Grain**.)

Flecks. (See **Rays, Wood**.)

Flitch. A portion of a log sawn on two or more faces—commonly on opposite faces leaving two waney edges. When intended for resawing into lumber, it is resawn parallel to its original wide faces. Or, it may be sliced or sawn into veneer, in which case the resulting sheets of veneer laid together in the sequence of cutting are called a flitch. The term is loosely used. (See **Cant**.)

Framing. Lumber used for the structural member of a building, such as studs and joists.

Full-Cell Process. Any process for impregnating wood with preservatives or chemicals in which a vacuum is drawn to re-move air from the wood before admitting the preservative. This favors heavy adsorption and retention of preservative in the treated portions.

Furnish. Wood material that has been reduced for incorporation into wood-based fiber or particle panel products.

Gelatinous Fibers. Modified fibers that are associated with tension wood in hardwoods.

Girder. A large or principal beam used to support concentrated loads at isolated points along its length.

Gluability. (See **Bondability**.)

Glue. Originally, a hard gelatin obtained from hides, tendons, cartilage, bones, etc., of animals. Also, an adhesive prepared from this substance by heating with water. Through general use the term is now synonymous with the term "adhesive."

Glue Laminating. Production of structural or nonstructural wood members by bonding two or more layers of wood together with adhesive.

Glueline. (See **Bondline**.)

Grade. The designation of the quality of a manufactured piece of wood or of logs.

Grain. The direction, size, arrangement, appearance, or quality of the fibers in wood or lumber. To have a specific meaning the term must be qualified.

Close-Grained (Fine-Grained) Wood—Wood with narrow, inconspicuous annual rings. The term is sometimes used to designate wood having small and closely spaced pores, but in this sense the term "fine textured" is more often used.

Coarse-Grained Wood—Wood with wide conspicuous annual rings in which there is considerable difference between earlywood and latewood. The term is sometimes used to designate wood with large pores, such as oak, keruing, meranti, and walnut, but in this sense, the term "open-grained" is more often used.

Cross-Grained Wood—Wood in which the fibers deviate from a line parallel to the sides of the piece. Cross grain may be either diagonal or spiral grain or a combination of the two.

Curly-Grained Wood—Wood in which the fibers are distorted so that they have a curled appearance, as in "birdseye" wood. The areas showing curly grain may vary up to several inches in diameter.

Diagonal-Grained Wood—Wood in which the annual rings are at an angle with the axis of a piece as a result of sawing at an angle with the bark of the tree or log. A form of cross-grain.

Edge-Grained Lumber—Lumber that has been sawed so that the wide surfaces extend approximately at right angles to the annual growth rings. Lumber is considered edge grained when the rings form an angle of 45° to 90° with the wide surface of the piece.

End-Grained Wood—The grain as seen on a cut made at a right angle to the direction of the fibers (such as on a cross section of a tree).

Fiddleback-Grained Wood—Figure produced by a type of fine wavy grain found, for example, in species of maple; such wood being traditionally used for the backs of violins.

Flat-Grained (Flat-Sawn) Lumber—Lumber that has been sawn parallel to the pith and approximately tangent to the growth rings. Lumber is considered flat grained when the annual growth rings make an angle of less than 45° with the surface of the piece.

Interlocked-Grained Wood—Grain in which the fibers put on for several years may slope in a right-handed direction, and then for a number of years the slope reverses to a left-handed direction, and later changes back to a right-handed pitch, and so on. Such wood is exceedingly difficult to split radially, though tangentially it may split fairly easily.

Open-Grained Wood—Common classification for woods with large pores such as oak, keruing, meranti, and walnut. Also known as "coarse textured."

Plainsawn Lumber—Another term for flat-grained lumber.

Quartersawn Lumber—Another term for edge-grained lumber.

Side-Grained Wood—Another term for flat-grained lumber.

Slash-Grained Wood—Another term for flat-grained lumber.

Spiral-Grained Wood—Wood in which the fibers take a spiral course about the trunk of a tree instead of the normal vertical course. The spiral may extend in a right-handed or left-handed direction around the tree trunk. Spiral grain is a form of cross grain.

Straight-Grained Wood—Wood in which the fibers run parallel to the axis of a piece.

Vertical-Grained Lumber—Another term for edge-grained lumber.

Wavy-Grained Wood—Wood in which the fibers collectively take the form of waves or undulations.

Green. Freshly sawed or undried wood. Wood that has become completely wet after immersion in water would not be considered green but may be said to be in the "green condition."

Growth Ring. The layer of wood growth put on a tree during a single growing season. In the temperate zone, the annual growth rings of many species (for example, oaks and pines) are readily distinguished because of differences in the cells formed during the early and late parts of the season. In some temperate zone species (black gum and sweetgum) and many tropical species, annual growth rings are not easily recognized.

Gum. A comprehensive term for nonvolatile viscous plant exudates, which either dissolve or swell up in contact with water. Many substances referred to as gums such as pine and spruce gum are actually oleoresins.

Hardboard. (See **Wood-Based Composite Panel.**)

Hardener. A substance or mixture of substances that is part of an adhesive and is used to promote curing by taking part in the reaction.

Hardness. A property of wood that enables it to resist indentation.

Hardwoods. Generally one of the botanical groups of trees that have vessels or pores and broad leaves, in contrast to the conifers or softwoods. The term has no reference to the actual hardness of the wood.

Heart Rot. (See **Decay.**)

Heartwood. The wood extending from the pith to the sapwood, the cells of which no longer participate in the life processes of the tree. Heartwood may contain phenolic compounds, gums, resins, and other materials that usually make it darker and more decay resistant than sapwood.

Hemicellulose. A celluloselike material (in wood) that is easily decomposable as by dilute acid, yielding several different simple sugars.

Hertz. A unit of frequency equal to one cycle per second.

High Frequency Curing. (See **Radiofrequency Curing.**)

Hollow-Core Construction. A panel construction with faces of plywood, hardboard, or similar material bonded to a framed-core assembly of wood lattice, paperboard rings, or the like, which support the facing at spaced intervals.

Honeycomb Core. A sandwich core material constructed of thin sheet materials or ribbons formed to honeycomb-like configurations.

Honeycombing. Checks, often not visible at the surface, that occur in the interior of a piece of wood, usually along the wood rays.

Horizontally Laminated Timber. (See **Laminated Timbers.**)

Hot-Setting Adhesive. (See **Adhesive.**)

Hydrogen Bond. An intermolecular attraction force that results when the hydrogen of one molecule and a pair of unshared electrons on an electronegative atom of another molecule are attracted to one another.

Hydrophilic. Having a strong tendency to bind or absorb water.

Hydrophobic. Having a strong tendency to repel water.

Impreg. Wood in which the cell walls have been impregnated with synthetic resin so as to reduce materially its swelling and shrinking. Impreg is not compressed.

Incising. A pretreatment process in which incisions, slits, or perforations are made in the wood surface to increase penetration of preservative treatments. Incising is often required to enhance durability of some difficult-to-treat species, but incising reduces strength.

Increment Borer. An augerlike instrument with a hollow bit and an extractor, used to extract thin radial cylinders of wood from trees to determine age and growth rate. Also used in wood preservation to determine the depth of penetration of a preservative.

Insulating Board. (See **Wood-Based Composite Panel.**)

Intergrown Knot. (See **Knot.**)

Interlocked Grained. (See **Grain.**)

Interlocking Action. (See **Mechanical Adhesion.**)

Internal Stresses. Stresses that exist within an adhesive joint even in the absence of applied external forces.

Interphase. In wood bonding, a region of finite thickness as a gradient between the bulk adherend and bulk adhesive in which the adhesive penetrates and alters the adherend's properties and in which the presence of the adherend influences the chemical and/or physical properties of the adhesive.

Intumesce. To expand with heat to provide a low-density film; used in reference to certain fire-retardant coatings.

Isotropic. Exhibiting the same properties in all directions.

Joint. The junction of two pieces of wood or veneer.

    Adhesive Joint—The location at which two adherends are held together with a layer of adhesive.

    Assembly Joint—Joints between variously shaped parts or subassemblies such as in wood furniture (as opposed to joints in plywood and laminates that are all quite similar).

    Butt Joint—An end joint formed by abutting the squared ends of two pieces.

    Edge Joint—A joint made by bonding two pieces of wood together edge to edge, commonly by gluing. The joints may be made by gluing two squared edges as in a plain edge joint or by using machined joints of various kinds, such as tongued-and-grooved joints.

    End Joint—A joint made by bonding two pieces of wood together end to end, commonly by finger or scarf joint.

    Fingerjoint—An end joint made up of several meshing wedges or fingers of wood bonded together with an adhesive. Fingers are sloped and may be cut parallel to either the wide or narrow face of the piece.

    Lap Joint—A joint made by placing one member partly over another and bonding the overlapped portions.

    Scarf Joint—An end joint formed by joining with adhesive the ends of two pieces that have been tapered or beveled to form sloping plane surfaces, usually to a featheredge, and with the same slope of the plane with respect to the length in both pieces. In some cases, a step or hook may be machined into the scarf to facilitate alignment of the two ends, in which case the plane is discontinuous and the joint is known as a stepped or hooked scarf joint.

    Starved Joint—A glue joint that is poorly bonded because an insufficient quantity of adhesive remained in the joint.

    Sunken Joint—Depression in wood surface at a joint (usually an edge joint) caused by surfacing material too soon after bonding. (Inadequate time was allowed for moisture added with the adhesive to diffuse away from the joint.)

Joint Efficiency or Factor. The strength of a joint expressed as a percentage of the strength of clear straight-grained material.

Joist. One of a series of parallel beams used to support floor and ceiling loads and supported in turn by larger beams, girders, or bearing walls.

Kiln. A chamber having controlled air-flow, temperature, and relative humidity for drying lumber. The temperature is increased as drying progresses, and the relative humidity is decreased.

Kiln Dried. (See **Seasoning**.)

Knot. That portion of a branch or limb that has been surrounded by subsequent growth of the stem. The shape of the knot as it appears on a cut surface depends on the angle of the cut relative to the long axis of the knot.

    Encased Knot—A knot whose rings of annual growth are not intergrown with those of the surrounding wood.

    Intergrown Knot—A knot whose rings of annual growth are completely intergrown with those of the surrounding wood.

    Loose Knot—A knot that is not held firmly in place by growth or position and that cannot be relied upon to remain in place.

    Pin Knot—A knot that is not more than 12 mm (1/2 in.) in diameter.

    Sound Knot—A knot that is solid across its face, at least as hard as the surrounding wood, and shows no indication of decay.

    Spike Knot—A knot cut approximately parallel to its long axis so that the exposed section is definitely elongated.

Laminate. A product made by bonding together two or more layers (laminations) of material or materials.

Laminate, Paper-Based. A multilayered panel made by compressing sheets of resin-impregnated paper together into a coherent solid mass.

Laminated Timbers. An assembly made by bonding layers of veneer or lumber with an adhesive so that the grain of all laminations is essentially parallel. (See **Built-Up Timbers**.)

    Horizontally Laminated Timbers—Laminated timbers designed to resist bending loads applied perpendicular to the wide faces of the laminations.

    Vertically Laminated Timbers—Laminated timbers designed to resist bending loads applied parallel to the wide faces of the laminations.

Laminated Veneer Lumber (LVL). (See **Wood-Based Composite Panel**.)

Lap Joint. (See **Joint**.)

Latewood. The portion of the growth ring that is formed after the earlywood formation has ceased. It is usually denser and stronger mechanically than earlywood.

Latex Paint. A paint containing pigments and a stable water suspension of synthetic resins (produced by emulsion polymerization) that forms an opaque film through coalescence of the resin during water evaporation and subsequent curing.

Lathe Checks. In rotary-cut and sliced veneer, the fractures or checks that develop along the grain of the veneer as the knife peels veneer from the log. The knife side of the veneer where checks occur is called the loose side. The opposite and log side of the veneer where checking usually does not occur is called the tight side.

Layup. The process of loosely assembling the adhesive-coated components of a unit, particularly a panel, to be pressed or clamped.

Lbs/MSGL. Abbreviation for rate of adhesive application in pounds of adhesive per 1,000 ft^2 of single glueline (bondline). (See **Spread**.) When both faces of an adherend are spread as in some plywood manufacturing processes, the total weight of adhesive applied may be expressed as Lbs/MDGL (pounds per 1,000 ft^2 double glueline).

Lignin. The second most abundant constituent of wood, located principally in the secondary wall and the middle lamella, which is the thin cementing layer between wood cells. Chemically, it is an irregular polymer of substituted propylphenol groups, and thus, no simple chemical formula can be written for it.

London Dispersion Forces. Intermolecular attraction forces between nonpolar molecules that result when instantaneous (nonpermanent) dipoles induce matching dipoles in neighboring molecules. London forces also exist between polar molecules.

Longitudinal. Generally, parallel to the direction of the wood fibers.

Loose Knot. (See **Knot**.)

Lumber. The product of the saw and planing mill for which manufacturing is limited to sawing, resawing, passing lengthwise through a standard planing machine, crosscutting to length, and matching. Lumber may be made from either softwood or hardwood (See also **Lumber for Dimension**.)

  Board—Lumber that is less than 38 mm standard (2 in. nominal) thickness and greater than 38 mm standard (2 in nominal) width. Boards less than 140 mm standard (6 in. nominal) width are sometimes called strips.

  Dimension—Lumber with a thickness from 38 mm standard (2 in. nominal) up to but not including 114 mm standard (5 in. nominal) and a width of greater than 38 mm standard (2 in. nominal).

  Dressed Size—The dimensions of lumber after being surfaced with a planing machine. The dressed size is usually 1/2 to 3/4 in. less than the nominal or rough size. A 2- by 4-in. stud, for example, actually measures about 1-1/2 by 3-1/2 in. (standard 38 by 89 mm).

  Factory and Shop Lumber—Lumber intended to be cut up for use in further manufacture. It is graded on the percentage of the area that will produce a limited number of cuttings of a specified minimum size and quality.

  Matched Lumber—Lumber that is edge dressed and shaped to make a close tongued-and-grooved joint at the edges or ends when laid edge to edge or end to end.

  Nominal Size—As applied to timber or lumber, the size by which it is known and sold in the market (often differs from the actual size).

  Patterned Lumber—Lumber that is shaped to a pattern or to a molded form in addition to being dressed, matched, or shiplapped, or any combination of these workings.

  Rough Lumber—Lumber that has not been dressed (surfaced) but has been sawed, edged, and trimmed.

  Shiplapped Lumber—Lumber that is edge dressed to make a lapped joint.

  Shipping-Dry Lumber—Lumber that is partially dried to prevent stain and mold in transit.

  Shop Lumber—(See **Factory and Shop Lumber**.)

  Side Lumber—A board from the outer portion of the log—ordinarily one produced when squaring off a log for a tie or timber.

  Structural Lumber—Lumber that is intended for use where allowable properties are required. The grading of structural lumber is based on the strength or stiffness of the piece as related to anticipated uses.

  Surfaced Lumber—Lumber that is dressed by running it through a planer.

  Timbers—Lumber that is standard 114 mm (nominal 5 in.) or more in least dimension. Timbers may be used as beams, stringers, posts, caps, sills, girders, or purlins.

  Yard Lumber—A little-used term for lumber of all sizes and patterns that is intended for general building purposes having no design property requirements.

Lumber for Dimension. The National Dimension Manufacturers Association defines both hardwood and softwood dimension components as being cut to a specific size from kiln-dried rough lumber, bolts, cants, or logs. Dimension components include Flat Stock (solid and laminated) for furniture, cabinet, and specialty manufactures. This term has largely superceded the terms "hardwood dimension" and "dimension parts." (See also **Lumber**).

Lumen. In wood anatomy, the cell cavity.

Manufacturing Defects. Includes all defects or blemishes that are produced in manufacturing, such as chipped grain, loosened grain, raised grain, torn grain, skips in dressing, hit and miss (series of surfaced areas with skips between them), variation in sawing, miscut lumber, machine burn, machine gouge, mismatching, and insufficient tongue or groove.

Mastic. A material with adhesive properties, usually used in relatively thick sections, that can be readily applied by extrusion, trowel, or spatula. (See **Adhesive**.)

Matched Lumber. (See **Lumber**.)

Mechanical Adhesion. Adhesion between surfaces in which the adhesive holds the parts together by interlocking action.

Medium-Density Fiberboard. (See **Wood-Based Composite Panel**.)

Millwork. Planed and patterned lumber for finish work in buildings, including items such as sash, doors, cornices, panelwork, and other items of interior or exterior trim. Does not include flooring, ceiling, or siding.

Mineral Streak. An olive to greenish-black or brown discoloration of undetermined cause in hardwoods.

Modified Wood. Wood processed by chemical treatment, compression, or other means (with or without heat) to impart properties quite different from those of the original wood.

Moisture Content. The amount of water contained in the wood, usually expressed as a percentage of the weight of the ovendry wood.

Molecular Weight. The sum of the atomic weights of the atoms in a molecule.

Moulded Plywood. (See **Wood-Based Composite Panel**.)

Moulding. A wood strip having a curved or projecting surface, used for decorative purposes.

Monomer. A relatively simple molecular compound that can react at more than one site to form a polymer.

Mortise. A slot cut into a board, plank, or timber, usually edgewise, to receive the tenon of another board, plank, or timber to form a joint.

Naval Stores. A term applied to the oils, resins, tars, and pitches derived from oleoresin contained in, exuded by, or extracted from trees, chiefly species of pines (genus *Pinus*). Historically, these were important items in the stores of wood sailing vessels.

Nominal-Size Lumber. (See **Lumber for Dimension.**)

Nonpolar. (See **Polar.**)

Nonpressure Process. Any process of treating wood with a preservative or fire retardant where pressure is not applied. Some examples are surface applications by brushing or brief dipping, soaking in preservative oils, or steeping in solutions of waterborne preservatives; diffusion processes with waterborne preservatives; and vacuum treatments.

Oil Paint. A paint containing a suspension of pigments in an organic solvent and a drying oil, modified drying oil, or synthetic polymer that forms an opaque film through a combination of solvent evaporation and curing of the oil or polymer.

Old Growth. Timber in or from a mature, naturally established forest. When the trees have grown during most if not all of their individual lives in active competition with their companions for sunlight and moisture, this timber is usually straight and relatively free of knots.

Oleoresin. A solution of resin in an essential oil that occurs in or exudes from many plants, especially softwoods. The oleoresin from pine is a solution of pine resin (rosin) in turpentine.

Open Assembly Time. (See **Time, Assembly.**)

Open Grain. (See **Grain.**)

Orthotropic. Having unique and independent properties in three mutually orthogonal (perpendicular) planes of symmetry. A special case of anisotropy.

Ovendry Wood. Wood dried to a relatively constant weight in a ventilated oven at 102°C to 105°C (215°F to 220°F).

Overlay. A thin layer of paper, plastic, film, metal foil, or other material bonded to one or both faces of panel products or to lumber to provide a protective or decorative face or a base for painting.

Paint. Any pigmented liquid, liquifiable, or mastic composition designed for application to a substrate in a thin layer that converts to an opaque solid film after application.

Pallet. A low wood or metal platform on which material can be stacked to facilitate mechanical handling, moving, and storage.

Paperboard. The distinction between paper and paperboard is not sharp, but broadly speaking, the thicker (greater than 0.3 mm (0.012 in.)), heavier, and more rigid grades of paper are called paperboard.

Papreg. Any of various paper products made by impregnating sheets of specially manufactured high-strength paper with synthetic resin and laminating the sheets to form a dense, moisture-resistant product.

Parallel Strand Lumber. A structural composite lumber made from wood strand elements with the wood fiber oriented primarily along the length of the member.

Parenchyma. Short cells having simple pits and functioning primarily in the metabolism and storage of plant food materials. They remain alive longer than the tracheids, fibers, and vessel elements, sometimes for many years. Two kinds of parenchyma cells are recognized—those in vertical strands, known more specifically as axial parenchyma, and those in horizontal series in the rays, known as ray parenchyma.

Particles. The aggregate component of particleboard manufactured by mechanical means from wood. These include all small subdivisions of wood such as chips, curls, flakes, sawdust, shavings, slivers, strands, wafers, wood flour, and wood wool.

Peck. Pockets or areas of disintegrated wood caused by advanced stages of localized decay in the living tree. It is usually associated with cypress and incense-cedar. There is no further development of peck once the lumber is seasoned.

Peel. To convert a log into veneer by rotary cutting. In an adhesively bonded joint, the progressive separation of a flexible member from either a rigid member or another flexible member.

Phloem. The tissues of the inner bark, characterized by the presence of sieve tubes and serving for the transport of elaborate foodstuffs.

Pile. A long, heavy timber, round or square, that is driven deep into the ground to provide a secure foundation for structures built on soft, wet, or submerged sites (for example, landing stages, bridge abutments).

Pin Knot. (See **Knot.**)

Pitch Pocket. An opening extending parallel to the annual growth rings and containing, or that has contained, pitch, either solid or liquid.

Pitch Streaks. A well-defined accumulation of pitch in a more or less regular streak in the wood of certain conifers.

Pith. The small, soft core occurring near the center of a tree trunk, branch, twig, or log.

Pith Fleck. A narrow streak, resembling pith on the surface of a piece; usually brownish, up to several centimeters long; results from burrowing of larvae in the growing tissues of the tree.

Plainsawn. (See **Grain.**)

Planing Mill Products. Products worked to pattern, such as flooring, ceiling, and siding.

Plank. A broad, thick board laid with its wide dimension horizontal and used as a bearing surface.

Plasticizing Wood. Softening wood by hot water, steam, or chemical treatment to increase its moldability.

Pocket Rot. (See **Decay.**)

Polar. Characteristic of a molecule in which the positive and negative electrical charges are permanently separated, as opposed to nonpolar molecules in which the charges coincide. Water, alcohol, and wood are polar in nature; most hydrocarbon liquids are not.

Polymer. A compound formed by the reaction of simple molecules having functional groups that permit their combination to proceed to high molecular weights under suitable conditions. Polymers may be formed by polymerization (addition polymer) or polycondensation (condensation polymer). When two or more different monomers are involved, the product is called a copolymer.

Polymerization. A chemical reaction in which the molecules of a monomer are linked together to form large molecules whose molecular weight is a multiple of that of the original substance. When two or more different monomers are involved, the process is called copolymerization.

Pore. (See **Vessel Elements.**)

Postformed Plywood. (See **Wood-Based Composite Panel.**)

Post Cure. (1) A treatment (normally involving heat) applied to an adhesive assembly following the initial cure, to complete cure, or to modify specific properties. (2) To expose an adhesive assembly to an additional cure, following the initial cure; to complete cure; or to modify specific properties.

Pot Life. (See **Working Life.**)

Precure. Condition of too much cure, set, or solvent loss of the adhesive before pressure is applied, resulting in inadequate flow, transfer, and bonding.

Preservative. Any substance that, for a reasonable length of time, is effective in preventing the development and action of wood-rotting fungi, borers of various kinds, and harmful insects that deteriorate wood.

Pressure Process. Any process of treating wood in a closed container whereby the preservative or fire retardant is forced into the wood under pressures greater than one atmosphere. Pressure is generally preceded or followed by vacuum, as in the vacuum-pressure and empty-cell processes respectively; or they may alternate, as in the full-cell and alternating-pressure processes.

Progressive Kiln. (See **Kiln.**)

Psychrometer. An instrument for measuring the amount of water vapor in the atmosphere. It has both a dry-bulb and wet-bulb thermometer. The bulb of the wet-bulb thermometer is kept moistened and is, therefore, cooled by evaporation to a temperature lower than that shown by the dry-bulb thermometer. Because evaporation is greater in dry air, the difference between the two thermometer readings will be greater when the air is dry than when it is moist.

Quartersawn. (See **Grain.**)

Radial. Coincident with a radius from the axis of the tree or log to the circumference. A radial section is a lengthwise section in a plane that passes through the centerline of the tree trunk.

Radiofrequency (RF) Curing. Curing of bondlines by the application of radiofrequency energy. (Sometimes called high-frequency curing.)

Rafter. One of a series of structural members of a roof designed to support roof loads. The rafters of a flat roof are sometimes called roof joists.

Raised Grain. A roughened condition of the surface of dressed lumber in which the hard latewood is raised above the softer earlywood but not torn loose from it.

Rays, Wood. Strips of cells extending radially within a tree and varying in height from a few cells in some species to 4 or more inches in oak. The rays serve primarily to store food and transport it horizontally in the tree. On quartersawn oak, the rays form a conspicuous figure, sometimes referred to as flecks.

Reaction Wood. Wood with more or less distinctive anatomical characters, formed typically in parts of leaning or crooked stems and in branches. In hardwoods, this consists of tension wood, and in softwoods, compression wood.

Relative Humidity. Ratio of the amount of water vapor present in the air to that which the air would hold at saturation at the same temperature. It is usually considered on the basis of the weight of the vapor but, for accuracy, should be considered on the basis of vapor pressures.

Resilience. The property whereby a strained body gives up its stored energy on the removal of the deforming force.

Resin. (1) Solid, semisolid, or pseudosolid resin—An organic material that has an indefinite and often high molecular weight, exhibits a tendency to flow when subjected to stress, usually has a softening or melting range, and usually fractures conchoidally. (2) Liquid resin—an organic polymeric liquid that, when converted to its final state for use, becomes a resin.

Resin Ducts. Intercellular passages that contain and transmit resinous materials. On a cut surface, they are usually inconspicuous. They may extend vertically parallel to the axis of the tree or at right angles to the axis and parallel to the rays.

Retention by Assay. The determination of preservative retention in a specific zone of treated wood by extraction or analysis of specified samples.

Rheology. The study of the deformation and flow of matter.

Ring Failure. A separation of the wood during seasoning, occurring along the grain and parallel to the growth rings. (See **Shake.**)

Ring-Porous Woods. A group of hardwoods in which the pores are comparatively large at the beginning of each annual ring and decrease in size more or less abruptly toward the outer portion of the ring, thus forming a distinct inner zone of pores, known as the earlywood, and an outer zone with smaller pores, known as the latewood.

Ring Shake. (See **Shake.**)

Rip. To cut lengthwise, parallel to the grain.

Roll Spreading. Application of a film of a liquid material to a surface by means of rollers.

Room-Temperature-Setting Adhesive. (See **Adhesive.**)

Rot. (See **Decay.**)

Rotary-Cut Veneer. (See **Veneer.**)

Rough Lumber. (See **Lumber.**)

Sandwich Construction. (See **Structural Sandwich Construction.**)

Sap Stain. (See **Stain.**)

Sapwood. The wood of pale color near the outside of the log. Under most conditions, the sapwood is more susceptible to decay than heartwood.

Sash. A frame structure, normally glazed (such as a window), that is hung or fixed in a frame set in an opening.

Sawn Veneer. (See **Veneer.**)

Saw Kerf. (1) Grooves or notches made in cutting with a saw. (2) That portion of a log, timber, or other piece of wood removed by the saw in parting the material into two pieces.

Scarf Joint. (See **Joint.**)

Schedule, Kiln Drying. A prescribed series of dry- and wet-bulb temperatures and air velocities used in drying a kiln charge of lumber or other wood products.

Seasoning. Removing moisture from green wood to improve its serviceability.

Air Dried—Dried by exposure to air in a yard or shed, without artificial heat.

Kiln Dried—Dried in a kiln with the use of artificial heat.

Second Growth. Timber that has grown after the removal, whether by cutting, fire, wind, or other agency, of all or a large part of the previous stand.

Semitransparent Stain. A suspension of pigments in either a drying oil–organic solvent mixture or a water–polymer emulsion, designed to color and protect wood surfaces by penetration without forming a surface film and without hiding wood grain.

Set. A permanent or semipermanent deformation. In reference to adhesives, to convert an adhesive into a fixed or hardened state by chemical or physical action, such as condensation, polymerization, oxidation, vulcanization, gelation, hydration, or evaporation of volatile constituents.

Shake. A separation along the grain, the greater part of which occurs between the rings of annual growth. Usually considered to have occurred in the standing tree or during felling.

Shakes. In construction, shakes are a type of shingle usually hand cleft from a bolt and used for roofing or weatherboarding.

Shaving. A small wood particle of indefinite dimensions developed incidental to certain woodworking operations involving rotary cutterheads usually turning in the direction of the grain. This cutting action produces a thin chip of varying thickness, usually feathered along at least one edge and thick at another and generally curled.

Shear. In an adhesively bonded joint, stress, strain, or failure resulting from applied forces that tends to cause adjacent planes of a body to slide parallel in opposite directions.

Sheathing. The structural covering, usually of boards, building fiberboards, or plywood, placed over exterior studding or rafters of a structure.

Shelf Life. (See **Storage Life.**)

Shiplapped Lumber. (See **Lumber.**)

Shipping-Dry Lumber. (See **Lumber.**)

Shop Lumber. (See **Lumber.**)

Side Grained. (See **Grain.**)

Side Lumber. (See **Lumber.**)

Siding. The finish covering of the outside wall of a frame building, whether made of horizontal weatherboards, vertical boards with battens, shingles, or other material.

Slash Grained. (See **Grain.**)

Sliced Veneer. (See **Veneer.**)

Soft Rot. (See **Decay.**)

Softwoods. Generally, one of the botanical groups of trees that have no vessels and in most cases, have needlelike or scalelike leaves, the conifers, also the wood produced by such trees. The term has no reference to the actual hardness of the wood.

Solid Color Stains (Opaque Stains). A suspension of pigments in either a drying oil–organic solvent mixture or a water–polymer emulsion designed to color and protect a wood surface by forming a film. Solid color stains are similar to paints in application techniques and in performance.

Solids Content. The percentage of weight of the nonvolatile matter in an adhesive.

Solvent Adhesive. (See **Adhesive.**)

Sound Knot. (See **Knot.**)

Specific Adhesion. Adhesion between surfaces that are held together by valence forces of the same type as those that give rise to cohesion.

Specific Gravity. As applied to wood, the ratio of the ovendry weight of a sample to the weight of a volume of water equal to the volume of the sample at a specified moisture content (green, air dry, or ovendry).

Spike Knot. (See **Knot.**)

Spiral Grained. (See **Grain.**)

Spread. The quantity of adhesive per unit joint area applied to an adherend. (See **Lbs/MSGL.**)

Single spread—Refers to application of adhesive to only one adherend of a joint.

Double spread—Refers to application of adhesive to both adherends of a joint.

Springwood. (See **Earlywood.**)

Squeezeout. Bead of adhesive squeezed out of a joint when pressure is applied.

Stain. A discoloration in wood that may be caused by such diverse agencies as micro-organisms, metal, or chemicals. The term also applies to materials used to impart color to wood.

Blue Stain—A bluish or grayish discoloration of the sapwood caused by the growth of certain dark-colored fungi on the surface and in the interior of the wood; made possible by the same conditions that favor the growth of other fungi.

Brown Stain—A rich brown to deep chocolate-brown discoloration of the sapwood of some pines caused by a fungus that acts much like the blue-stain fungi.

Chemical Brown Stain—A chemical discoloration of wood, which sometimes occurs during the air drying or kiln drying of several species, apparently caused by the concentration and modification of extractives.

Sap Stain—A discoloration of the sapwood caused by the growth of certain fungi on the surface and in the interior of the wood; made possible by the same conditions that favor the growth of other fungi.

Sticker Stain—A brown or blue stain that develops in seasoning lumber where it has been in contact with the stickers.

Starved Joint. (See **Joint.**)

Static Bending. Bending under a constant or slowly applied load; flexure.

Staypak. Wood that is compressed in its natural state (that is, without resin or other chemical treatment) under controlled conditions of moisture, temperature, and pressure that practically eliminate springback or recovery from compression. The product has increased density and strength characteristics.

Stickers. Strips or boards used to separate the layers of lumber in a pile and thus improve air circulation.

Sticker Stain. (See **Stain.**)

Storage Life. The period of time during which a packaged adhesive can be stored under specific temperature conditions and remain suitable for use. Sometimes called shelf life.

Straight Grained. (See **Grain.**)

Strength. (1) The ability of a member to sustain stress without failure. (2) In a specific mode of test, the maximum stress sustained by a member loaded to failure.

Strength Ratio. The hypothetical ratio of the strength of a structural member to that which it would have if it contained no strength-reducing characteristics (such as knots, slope-of-grain, shake).

Stress-Wave Timing. A method of measuring the apparent stiffness of a material by measuring the speed of an induced compression stress as it propagates through the material.

Stressed-Skin Construction. A construction in which panels are separated from one another by a central partition of spaced strips with the whole assembly bonded so that it acts as a unit when loaded.

Stringer. A timber or other support for cross members in floors or ceilings. In stairs, the support on which the stair treads rest.

Structural Insulating Board. (See **Wood-Based Composite Panel.**)

Structural Lumber. (See **Lumber.**)

Structural Sandwich Construction. A layered construction consisting of a combination of relatively high-strength facing materials intimately bonded to and acting integrally with a low-density core material.

Structural Timbers. Pieces of wood of relatively large size, the strength or stiffness of which is the controlling element in their selection and use. Examples of structural timbers are trestle timbers (stringers, caps, posts, sills, bracing, bridge ties, guardrails); car timbers (car framing, including upper framing, car sills); framing for building (posts, sills, girders); ship timber (ship timbers, ship decking); and crossarms for poles.

Stud. One of a series of slender wood structural members used as supporting elements in walls and partitions.

Substrate. A material upon the surface of which an adhesive-containing substance is spread for any purpose, such as bonding or coating. A broader term than adherend. (See **Adherend.**)

Summerwood. (See **Latewood.**)

Surface Inactivation. In adhesive bonding to wood, physical and chemical modifications of the wood surface that result in reduced ability of an adhesive to properly wet, flow, penetrate, and cure.

Surface Tension. The force per unit length acting in the surface of a liquid that opposes the increase in area of the liquid (spreading).

Surfaced Lumber. (See **Lumber.**)

Symmetrical Construction. Plywood panels in which the plies on one side of a center ply or core are essentially equal in thickness, grain direction, properties, and arrangement to those on the other side of the core.

Tack. The property of an adhesive that enables it to form a bond of measurable strength immediately after adhesive and adherend are brought into contact under low pressure.

Tangential. Strictly, coincident with a tangent at the circumference of a tree or log, or parallel to such a tangent. In practice, however, it often means roughly coincident with a growth ring. A tangential section is a longitudinal section through a tree or limb perpendicular to a radius. Flat-grained lumber is sawed tangentially.

Temperature, Curing. The temperature to which an adhesive or an assembly is subjected to cure the adhesive. The temperature attained by the adhesive in the process of curing (adhesive curing temperature) may differ from the temperature of the atmosphere surrounding the assembly (assembly curing temperature).

Temperature, Setting. (See **Temperature, Curing.**)

Tenon. A projecting member left by cutting away the wood around it for insertion into a mortise to make a joint.

Tension. In an adhesively bonded joint, a uniaxial force tending to cause extension of the assembly, or the counteracting force within the assembly that resists extension.

Tension Wood. Abnormal wood found in leaning trees of some hardwood species and characterized by the presence of gelatinous fibers and excessive longitudinal shrinkage. Tension wood fibers hold together tenaciously, so that sawed surfaces usually have projecting fibers and planed surfaces often are torn or have raised grain. Tension wood may cause warping.

Texture. A term often used interchangeably with grain. Sometimes used to combine the concepts of density and degree of contrast between earlywood and latewood. In this handbook, texture refers to the finer structure of the wood (See **Grain.**) rather than the annual rings.

Thermoplastic. (1) Capable of being repeatedly softened by heat and hardened by cooling. (2) A material that will repeatedly soften when heated and harden when cooled.

Thermoset. A cross-linked polymeric material.

Thermosetting. Having the property of undergoing a chemical reaction by the action of heat, catalyst, ultraviolet light, and hardener, leading to a relatively infusible state.

Timbers, Round. Timbers used in the original round form, such as poles, piling, posts, and mine timbers.

Timber, Standing. Timber still on the stump.

Timbers. (See **Lumber.**)

Time, Assembly. The time interval between the spreading of the adhesive on the adherend and the application of pressure or heat, or both, to the assembly. (For assemblies involving multiple layers or parts, the assembly time begins with the spreading of the adhesive on the first adherend.)

   Open Assembly Time—The time interval between the spreading of the adhesive on the adherend and the completion of assembly of the parts for bonding.

Closed Assembly Time—The time interval between completion of assembly of the parts for bonding and the application of pressure or heat, or both, to the assembly.

Time, Curing. The period during which an assembly is subjected to heat or pressure, or both, to cure the adhesive.

Time, Setting. (See **Time, Curing.**)

Toughness. A quality of wood that permits the material to absorb a relatively large amount of energy, to withstand repeated shocks, and to undergo considerable deformation before breaking.

Tracheid. The elongated cells that constitute the greater part of the structure of the softwoods (frequently referred to as fibers). Also present in some hardwoods.

Transfer. In wood bonding, the sharing of adhesive between a spread and an unspread surface when the two adherends are brought into contact.

Transverse. Directions in wood at right angles to the wood fibers. Includes radial and tangential directions. A transverse section is a section through tree or timber at right angles to the pith.

Treenail. A wooden pin, peg, or spike used chiefly for fastening planking and ceiling to a framework.

Trim. The finish materials in a building, such as moldings, applied around openings (window trim, door trim) or at the floor and ceiling of rooms (baseboard, cornice, and other moldings).

Truss. An assembly of members, such as beams, bars, rods, and the like, so combined as to form a rigid framework. All members are interconnected to form triangles.

Twist. A distortion caused by the turning or winding of the edges of a board so that the four corners of any face are no longer in the same plane.

Tyloses. Masses of parenchyma cells appearing somewhat like froth in the pores of some hardwoods, notably the white oaks and black locust. Tyloses are formed by the extension of the cell wall of the living cells surrounding vessels of hardwood.

Ultrasonics. (See **Stress-Wave Timing.**)

van der Waal Forces. Physical forces of attraction between molecules, which include permanent dipole, induced dipole, hydrogen bond, and London dispersion forces.

Vapor Retarder. A material with a high resistance to vapor movement, such as foil, plastic film, or specially coated paper, that is used in combination with insulation to control condensation.

Veneer. A thin layer or sheet of wood.

    Rotary-Cut Veneer—Veneer cut in a lathe that rotates a log or bolt, chucked in the center, against a knife.

    Sawn Veneer—Veneer produced by sawing.

    Sliced Veneer—Veneer that is sliced off a log, bolt, or flitch with a knife.

Vertical Grained. (See **Grain.**)

Vertically Laminated Timbers. (See **Laminated Timbers.**)

Vessel Elements. Wood cells in hardwoods of comparatively large diameter that have open ends and are set one above the other to form continuous tubes called vessels. The openings of the vessels on the surface of a piece of wood are usually referred to as pores.

Virgin Growth. The growth of mature trees in the original forests.

Viscoelasticity. The ability of a material to simultaneously exhibit viscous and elastic responses to deformation.

Viscosity. The ratio of the shear stress existing between laminae of moving fluid and the rate of shear between these laminae.

Waferboard. (See **Wood-Based Composite Panel.**)

Wane. Bark or lack of wood from any cause on edge or corner of a piece except for eased edges.

Warp. Any variation from a true or plane surface. Warp includes bow, crook, cup, and twist, or any combination thereof.

Water Repellent. A liquid that penetrates wood that materially retards changes in moisture content and dimensions of the dried wood without adversely altering its desirable properties.

Water-Repellent Preservative. A water repellent that contains a preservative that, after application to wood and drying, accomplishes the dual purpose of imparting resistance to attack by fungi or insects and also retards changes in moisture content.

Weathering. The mechanical or chemical disintegration and discoloration of the surface of wood caused by exposure to light, the action of dust and sand carried by winds, and the alternate shrinking and swelling of the surface fibers with the continual variation in moisture content brought by changes in the weather. Weathering does not include decay.

Wet Strength. The strength of an adhesive joint determined immediately after removal from water in which it has been immersed under specified conditions of time, temperature, and pressure.

Wet-Bulb Temperature. The temperature indicated by the wet-bulb thermometer of a psychrometer.

Wettability. A condition of a surface that determines how fast a liquid will wet and spread on the surface or if it will be repelled and not spread on the surface.

Wetting. The process in which a liquid spontaneously adheres to and spreads on a solid surface.

White-Rot. (See **Decay.**)

Wood-Based Composite Panel. A generic term for a material manufactured from wood veneer, strands, flakes, particles, or fibers or other lignocellulosic material and a synthetic resin or other binder.

    Cold-Pressed Plywood—Refers to interior-type plywood manufactured in a press without external applications of heat.

    Composite Panel—A veneer-faced panel with a reconstituted wood core. The flakeboard core may be random or have alignment in the direction 90° from the grain direction of the veneer faces.

    Exterior Plywood—A general term for plywood bonded with a type of adhesive that by systematic tests and service records has proved highly resistant to weather; micro-organisms; cold, hot, and boiling water; steam; and dry heat.

Extruded Particleboard—A particleboard made by ramming bindercoated particles into a heated die, which subsequently cures the binder and forms a rigid mass as the material is moved through the die.

Fiberboard—A broad generic term inclusive of sheet materials of widely varying densities manufactured of refined or partially refined wood (or other vegetable) fibers. Bonding agents and other materials may be added to increase strength, resistance to moisture, fire, or decay, or to improve some other property. (See **Medium-Density Fiberboard**.)

Flakeboard—A particle panel product composed of flakes.

Hardboard—A generic term for a panel manufactured primarily from interfelted lignocellulosic fibers (usually wood), consolidated under heat and pressure in a hot press to a density of 496 kg/m^3 (31 lb/ft^3) or greater and to which other materials may have been added during manufacture to improve certain properties.

Interior Plywood—A general term for plywood manufactured for indoor use or in construction subjected to only temporary moisture. The adhesive used may be interior, intermediate, or exterior.

Laminated Veneer Lumber (LVL)—A structural lumber manufactured from veneers laminated into a panel with the grain of all veneer running parallel to each other. The resulting panel is normally manufactured in 19- to 38-mm (3/4- to 1-1/2-in.) thicknesses and ripped to common lumber widths of 38 to 290 mm (1-1/2 to 11-1/2 in.) or wider.

Marine Plywood—Plywood panels manufactured with the same glueline durability requirements as other exterior-type panels but with more restrictive veneer quality requirements.

Mat-Formed Particleboard—A particleboard in which the particles (being previously coated with the binding agent) are formed into a mat having substantially the same length and width as the finished panel. This mat is then duly pressed in a heated flat-platen press to cure the binding agent.

Medium-Density Fiberboard—A panel product manufactured from lignocellulosic fibers combined with a synthetic resin or other suitable binder. The panels are manufactured to a density of 496 kg/m^3 (31 lb/ft^3) (0.50 specific gravity) to 880 kg/m^3 (55 lb/ft^3) (0.88 specific gravity) by the application of heat and pressure by a process in which the interfiber bond is substantially created by the added binder. Other materials may have been added during manufacturing to improve certain properties.

Mende-Process Board—A particleboard made in a continuous ribbon from wood particles with thermosetting resins used to bond the particles. Thickness ranges from 0.8 to 6.3 mm (1/32 to 1/4 in.).

Moulded Plywood—Plywood that is glued to the desired shape either between curved forms or more commonly by fluid pressure applied with flexible bags or blankets (bag moulding) or other means.

Multilayer Particleboard—A type of construction in which the wood particles are made or classified into different sizes and placed into the preprocessed panel configuration to produce a panel with specific properties. Panels that are destined for primarily nonstructural uses requiring smooth faces are configured with small particles on the outside and coarser particles on the interior (core). Panels designed for structural application may have flakes aligned in orthogonal directions in various layers that mimic the structure of plywood. Three- and five-layer constructions are most common.

Oriented Strandboard—A type of particle panel product composed of strand-type flakes that are purposefully aligned in directions that make a panel stronger, stiffer, and with improved dimensional properties in the alignment directions than a panel with random flake orientation.

Plywood. A glued wood panel made up of relatively thin layers of veneer with the grain of adjacent layers at right angles or of veneer in combination with a core of lumber or of reconstituted wood. The usual constructions have an odd number of layers.

Postformed Plywood—The product formed when flat plywood is reshaped into a curved configuration by steaming or plasticizing agents.

Structural Insulating Board—A generic term for a homogeneous panel made from lignocellulosic fibers (usually wood or cane) characterized by an integral bond produced by interfelting of the fibers, to which other materials may have been added during manufacture to improve certain properties, but which has not been consolidated under heat and pressure as a separate stage in manufacture; has a density of less than 496 kg/m^3 (31 lb/ft^3) (specific gravity 0.50) but more than 160 kg/m^3 (10 lb/ft^3) (specific gravity 0.16).

Waferboard—A particle panel product made of wafer-type flakes. Usually manufactured to possess equal properties in all directions parallel to the plane of the panel.

Wood Failure. The rupturing of wood fibers in strength tests of bonded joints usually expressed as the percentage of the total area involved that shows such failure. (See **Failure, Adherend**.)

Wood Flour. Wood reduced to finely divided particles, approximately the same as those of cereal flours in size, appearance, and texture, and passing a 40 to 100 mesh screen.

Wood Substance. The solid material of which wood is composed. It usually refers to the extractive-free solid substance of which the cell walls are composed, but this is not always true. There is not a wide variation in chemical composition or specific gravity between the wood substance of various species. (The characteristic differences of species are largely due to differences in extractives and variations in relative amounts of cell walls and cell cavities.)

Wood Wool. Long, curly, slender strands of wood used as an aggregate component for some particleboards.

Workability. The degree of ease and smoothness of cut obtainable with hand or machine tools.

Working Life. The period of time during which an adhesive, after mixing with catalyst, solvent, or other compounding ingredients, remains suitable for use. Also called pot life.

Working Properties. The properties of an adhesive that affect or dictate the manner of application to the adherends to be bonded and the assembly of the joint before pressure application (such as viscosity, pot life, assembly time, setting time).

Xylem. The portion of the tree trunk, branches, and roots that lies between the pith and the cambium (that is the wood).

Yard Lumber. (See **Lumber**.)

Index

452

flame spread index, 381t
interlocked grain, 8
locality of growth, 8
machining and related properties, 54t
moisture content, 44t
penetration, 314t
plywood stiffness and strength, 217t
shock resistance, 8
shrinkage values, 47t
strength properties, 68t, 73t
thermal conductivity, 57t
toughness values, 86t
uses, 8
Swelling, coefficient for changing moisture content, by species, 278t to 279t
Sycamore:
characteristics for painting, 329t
color and figure, 41t
decay resistance, 56t
ease of bonding, 190t
machining and related properties, 54t
nomenclature, 113t
size of pores, 357t
Sycamore, American:
characteristics, 8
connector joint strength, 163t
dimensional change coefficient, 278t
locality of growth, 8
moisture content, 44t
penetration, 314t
shock resistance, 8
shrinkage values, 47t
strength properties, 68t, 73t
thermal conductivity, 57t
uses, 8

Tamarack:
characteristics, 16
characteristics for painting, 329t
color and figure, 42t
decay resistance, 56t
dimensional change coefficient, 279t
locality of growth, 16
mechanical properties, 76t, 77t
moisture content, 44t, 96t
nomenclature, 121t
penetration, 314t
plywood stiffness and strength, 217t
shrinkage values, 47t
strength properties, 70t, 75t
uses, 16, 17
Tangare. See Andiroba
Tanoak:
characteristics, 32
decay resistance, 56t
dimensional change coefficient, 278t
locality of growth, 8
machineability, 9

machining and related properties, 54t
nomenclature, 113t
plywood stiffness and strength, 217t
shrinkage values, 47t
strength properties, 9, 68t, 73t
uses, 9
Teak:
characteristics, 32
characteristics affecting machining, 55t
decay resistance, 56t
dimensional change coefficient, 279t
ease of bonding, 190t
locality of growth, 32
machinability, 32
mechanical properties, 81t, 85t
shrinkage values, 48t
uses, 32
Tebuconazole:
effectiveness, 307
solubility, 307
Temperature blisters, avoiding while painting, 347
Temperature, effect on:
fatigue strength, 102 to 103
mechanical properties:
irreversible effects, 98 to 99, 100fig
reversible effects, 97 to 98, 98fig
properties, 142, 142t
relative humidity and moisture content, 45t
Tensile strength, end-grain bonded joints, 200 to 201
Tensile strength parallel to grain:
average values, 86
coefficient of variation, 85t
defined, 65
Tensile strength perpendicular to grain, 65
Tension wood:
definition, 93
density increase, 93
description, 93
effect on strength, 93
machining, 53
shrinkage, 94
Texture of wood, 39 to 40
Texture, effect on paintability, 331
Termites:
damage caused by, 291t, 292fig
nonsubterranean, 294
subterranean, 293 to 294
termite-resistant wood, 294 to 295
Thermal, conductivity of wood:
definition, 53
determination, 55
factors affecting, 55
selected species, 57t to 58t
Thermal diffusivity of wood, 55
Thermal expansion, 59

Thermal properties of wood, 53
Thermoplastics and adhesion, 191 to 192
Ties:
availability, 397
preservative penetration levels, 303t to 304t
service life, 400 to 401
sizes, 399
standards and specifications, 396t
strength properties, 402
weight and volume, 399
Timber:
inventory, 2
resources, 2
Timber bridges:
glulam, 374, 374fig
log stringer, 373
sawn lumber, 373
structural composite lumber, 374
Timber buildings:
arch structure, 372
dome, 372 to 373, 372fig
glulam beam, 372
mill-type construction:
fire resistance, 371
specifications, 371
timber frame houses, 370 to 371, 372fig
Timbers, recommended moisture content, 265
Timber from dead trees, properties of, 95 to 96
Time, effect on strength:
creep, 99 to 101
duration of load, 101 to 102
Tornillo:
characteristics, 32
decay resistance, 56t
locality of growth, 32
mechanical properties, 81t, 85t
uses, 32
workability, 32
Torsion, strength, 86
Toughness:
average values, 86t, 87
coefficient of variation, 85t
defined, 86
Tracheids, description and function, 37
Transverse and volumetric shrinkage of wood, 45 to 46
Trebol. See Macawood
Trim, exterior:
care during construction, 281
recommended moisture content, 267t
Trusses:
care during construction, 270 to 281
in light-frame construction, 368
in pole and post-frame construction, 370
Truss plates, 167, 168fig
Tupelo:
characteristics, 9

Page Number Equivalency Table

Page	Original	Page	Original	Page	Original	Page	Original	Page	Original	Page	Original	Page	Original	Page	Original	Page	Original
1	1-1	53	3-15	105	4-43	157	7-15	209	10-3	261	11-23	313	14-15	365	16-1	417	19-13
2	1-2	54	3-16	106	4-44	158	7-16	210	10-4	262	11-24	314	14-16	366	16-2	418	19-14
3	1-3	55	3-17	107	4-45	159	7-17	211	10-5	263	12-1	315	14-17	367	16-3	419	G-1
4	1-4	56	3-18	108	Blank	160	7-18	212	10-6	264	12-2	316	14-18	368	16-4	420	G-2
5	1-5	57	3-19	109	5-1	161	7-19	213	10-7	265	12-3	317	14-19	369	16-5	421	G-3
6	1-6	58	3-20	110	5-2	162	7-20	214	10-8	266	12-4	318	14-20	370	16-6	422	G-4
7	1-7	59	3-21	111	5-3	163	7-21	215	10-9	267	12-5	319	14-21	371	16-7	423	G-5
8	1-8	60	3-22	112	5-4	164	7-22	216	10-10	268	12-6	320	14-22	372	16-8	424	G-6
9	1-9	61	3-23	113	5-5	165	7-23	217	10-11	269	12-7	321	14-23	373	16-9	425	G-7
10	1-10	62	3-24	114	5-6	166	7-24	218	10-12	270	12-8	322	14-24	374	16-10	426	G-8
11	1-11	63	4-1	115	5-7	167	7-25	219	10-13	271	12-9	323	14-25	375	16-11	427	G-9
12	1-12	64	4-2	116	5-8	168	7-26	220	10-14	272	12-10	324	14-26	376	16-12	428	G-10
13	1-13	65	4-3	117	5-9	169	7-27	221	10-15	273	12-11	325	14-27	377	16-13	429	G-11
14	1-14	66	4-4	118	5-10	170	7-28	222	10-16	274	12-12	326	Blank	378	16-14	430	G-12
15	1-15	67	4-5	119	5-11	171	8-1	223	10-17	275	12-13	327	15-1	379	17-1	431	G-13
16	1-16	68	4-6	120	5-12	172	8-2	224	10-18	276	12-14	328	15-2	380	17-2	432	G-14
17	1-17	69	4-7	121	5-13	173	8-3	225	10-19	277	12-15	329	15-3	381	17-3	433	I-1
18	1-18	70	4-8	122	5-14	174	8-4	226	10-20	278	12-16	330	15-4	382	17-4	434	I-2
19	1-19	71	4-9	123	5-15	175	8-5	227	10-21	279	12-17	331	15-5	383	17-5	435	I-3
20	1-20	72	4-10	124	5-16	176	8-6	228	10-22	280	12-18	332	15-6	384	17-6	436	I-4
21	1-21	73	4-11	125	5-17	177	8-7	229	10-23	281	12-19	333	15-7	385	17-7	437	I-5
22	1-22	74	4-12	126	5-18	178	8-8	230	10-24	282	12-20	334	15-8	386	17-8	438	I-6
23	1-23	75	4-13	127	5-19	179	8-9	231	10-25	283	13-1	335	15-9	387	17-9	439	I-7
24	1-24	76	4-14	128	5-20	180	8-10	232	10-26	284	13-2	336	15-10	388	17-10	440	I-8
25	1-25	77	4-15	129	6-1	181	8-11	233	10-27	285	13-3	337	15-11	389	17-11	441	I-9
26	1-26	78	4-16	130	6-2	182	Blank	234	10-28	286	13-4	338	15-12	390	17-12	442	I-10
27	1-27	79	4-17	131	6-3	183	9-1	235	10-29	287	13-5	339	15-13	391	17-13	443	I-11
28	1-28	80	4-18	132	6-4	184	9-2	236	10-30	288	13-6	340	15-14	392	17-14	444	I-12
29	1-29	81	4-19	133	6-5	185	9-3	237	10-31	289	13-7	341	15-15	393	17-15	445	I-13
30	1-30	82	4-20	134	6-6	186	9-4	238	Blank	290	13-8	342	15-16	394	17-16	446	I-14
31	1-31	83	4-21	135	6-7	187	9-5	239	11-1	291	13-9	343	15-17	395	18-1	447	I-15
32	1-32	84	4-22	136	6-8	188	9-6	240	11-2	292	13-10	344	15-18	396	18-2	448	I-16
33	1-33	85	4-23	137	6-9	189	9-7	241	11-3	293	13-11	345	15-19	397	18-3	449	I-17
34	1-34	86	4-24	138	6-10	190	9-8	242	11-4	294	13-12	346	15-20	398	18-4	450	I-18
35	2-1	87	4-25	139	6-11	191	9-9	243	11-5	295	13-13	347	15-21	399	18-5	451	I-19
36	2-2	88	4-26	140	6-12	192	9-10	244	11-6	296	13-14	348	15-22	400	18-6	452	I-20
37	2-3	89	4-27	141	6-13	193	9-11	245	11-7	297	13-15	349	15-23	401	18-7	453	I-21
38	2-4	90	4-28	142	6-14	194	9-12	246	11-8	298	13-16	350	15-24	402	18-8	454	I-22
39	3-1	91	4-29	143	7-1	195	9-13	247	11-9	299	14-1	351	15-25	403	18-9	455	I-23
40	3-2	92	4-30	144	7-2	196	9-14	248	11-10	300	14-2	352	15-26	404	Blank	456	I-24
41	3-3	93	4-31	145	7-3	197	9-15	249	11-11	301	14-3	353	15-27	405	19-1	457	I-25
42	3-4	94	4-32	146	7-4	198	9-16	250	11-12	302	14-4	354	15-28	406	19-2	458	I-26
43	3-5	95	4-33	147	7-5	199	9-17	251	11-13	303	14-5	355	15-29	407	19-3	459	I-27
44	3-6	96	4-34	148	7-6	200	9-18	252	11-14	304	14-6	356	15-30	408	19-4	460	I-28
45	3-7	97	4-35	149	7-7	201	9-19	253	11-15	305	14-7	357	15-31	409	19-5	461	I-29
46	3-8	98	4-36	150	7-8	202	9-20	254	11-16	306	14-8	358	15-32	410	19-6	462	I-30
47	3-9	99	4-37	151	7-9	203	9-21	255	11-17	307	14-9	359	15-33	411	19-7	463	I-31
48	3-10	100	4-38	152	7-10	204	9-22	256	11-18	308	14-10	360	15-34	412	19-8		
49	3-11	101	4-39	153	7-11	205	9-23	257	11-19	309	14-11	361	15-35	413	19-9		
50	3-12	102	4-40	154	7-12	206	9-24	258	11-20	310	14-12	362	15-36	414	19-10		
51	3-13	103	4-41	155	7-13	207	10-1	259	11-21	311	14-13	363	15-37	415	19-11		
52	3-14	104	4-42	156	7-14	208	10-2	260	11-22	312	14-14	364	Blank	416	19-12		